1998 SONGWRITER'S MARKET

The cover illustration is a detail of a painting by Berge Missakian. Missakian is a Canadian artist from Montreal. He has studied art at the American University of Beruit; Cornell University, Ithaca, NY; and Concordia University, Montreal, Canada. Illusion, imagination and fantasy appear in his paintings and set as elements which unify his compositions with explosively brilliant shapes of color. Missakian, who is listed in several books on art, including *Who's Who in American Art* (22nd edition), exhibits internationally. He celebrates passion over passivity, movement over inertia and joy over melancholic outlook. His internet URL is http://www.generation.net/studiom1

Take Five with Luna
24″ × 20″
acrylic on canvas

Managing Editor, Annuals Department: Constance J. Achabal
Supervising Editor: Mark Garvey
Production Editor: Anne Bowling

International Standard Serial Number 0161-5971
International Standard Book Number 0-89879-795-0

Attention Booksellers: This is an annual directory of F&W Publications. Return deadline for this edition is December 31, 1998.

1998
SONG WRITER'S MARKET

2,000 PLACES TO MARKET YOUR SONGS

EDITED BY
CINDY LAUFENBERG

WRITER'S DIGEST BOOKS
CINCINNATI, OHIO

Contents

The Markets

Resources

Resources

From the Editor

Each year, as the deadline for the next edition of *Songwriter's Market* approaches, as the phone rings off the hook, faxes start pouring in and paperwork threatens to crowd me out of my office, the fundamental reason for this book's existence—the music—can nearly get lost in the shuffle. All I can think about are market listings, last minute additions, editing copy and writing articles. A few weeks ago, in the middle of all this mayhem, I was able to take a couple of days off and head down to Nashville for the Nashville Songwriters Association International's annual Spring Symposium. On the last night of the seminar, I attended the Legendary Songwriters Concert at the Ryman Auditorium. As I sat in that renowned music hall, listening to songs written by Jimmy Webb, Stephen Bishop, Hank Cochran, J.D. Souther, Barry Mann and Cynthia Weil (all sung by the writers themselves), I was reminded of just what was getting lost in the craziness of approaching deadlines—the importance and power of songwriters and their songs. The haunting first lines of Jimmy Webb's "Wichita Lineman" took me back to my parents' living room, lying in front of the big RCA stereo console listening to the crackle of AM radio. When J.D. Souther sang "Best of My Love," memories of schoolbooks, lockers and high school friends came crashing back. Each song sung by these talented writers conjured up a specific period in my life, evoking long-lost memories. From the responses of the audience to each and every song, I knew I wasn't the only one feeling that way at the Ryman that night.

Most of you aren't at the level of a Jimmy Webb or a Hank Cochran, but in picking up this book you've made it clear that's where you'd like to be someday. And you've chosen a great place to start learning about the business of songwriting. This year's edition features **Music, Money and Success: Where the Money Comes From**, written by **Jeffrey Brabec**, vice president of business affairs at Chrysalis Music in Los Angeles and his brother **Todd Brabec**, senior vice president and director of membership at ASCAP. They discuss the various ways a songwriter makes money, as well as the sources of that income. Another article, **Demo FAQs**, addresses the most frequently-asked questions about making demos. We interviewed several industry professionals from record labels and music publishers and asked them what they look for in the demos they receive, and they've passed their advice and expertise on to you.

In the Markets section, every listing has been updated to include the most current information possible. We've added over 400 companies new to this edition, as well as expanded listings for most major record labels and music publishers. Many companies have added website information this year, making it easier for you to research a company before contacting them. Be sure not to overlook the Resources section, listing organizations, workshops, conferences and contests that can help you make valuable contacts in the music industry.

The list of Insider Reports in this edition is diverse, offering the observations of long, successful careers in songwriting from calypso writer/artist **Irving Burgie**, writer of "Day-O," and Songwriters Guild of America President **George David Weiss**, who just happens to be the writer of standards such as "What A Wonderful World" and "The Lion Sleeps Tonight." You'll also get practical, inside advice from Warner/Chappell Music's Vice President of Creative Services **Judy Stakee**, Arista A&R Representative **John Rader**, hit producer **Rob Chiarelli** and manager **Rick Levy**. Learn about the new electronic frontier of the music business from **Jay Barbieri**, president of J-Bird Records, the first Internet-only record label. And gain insight into the classical and theater fields, with profiles of **D. Lynn Meyers**, producing artistic director at Cincinnati's Ensemble Theater and **Stephen Rosenthal**, director of the Amherst Saxophone Quartet. No matter what your songwriting style, there's valuable information here for you.

If you've purchased *Songwriter's Market* before, you'll notice that the format of the book has changed. The book has grown to a bigger size, to make room for even more information. Plus we've changed from hardcover to paper, making the book easier to handle when you're marking listings.

With all this talk of songwriting as a business, it's easy to lose sight of the reason you chose this profession in the first place—to write songs that mean something to you and to those who hear them. When the business side of songwriting starts getting confusing and overwhelming, take some time like I did that night at the Ryman and listen to songs that stir your memories, songs that inspired you to be a songwriter. Remind yourself how powerful songs can be, and how important they are in your life. One day perhaps your songs will be ones that evoke memories and emotions in the people who hear them and will become a valuable part of their lives as well. I wish you luck; be sure to keep in touch and let me know how you're doing!

Cindy Laufenberg
songmarket@fwpubs.com

How to Use *Songwriter's Market* to Get Your Songs Heard

The hardest task for you, the aspiring songwriter, is deciding where and to whom to submit your music. You're reading this book in the hope of finding information on good potential markets for your work. You may be seeking a publisher who will pitch your music, a record company that will offer you a recording contract, or a chamber music group or theater company to produce and perform your music live. *Songwriter's Market* is designed to help you make those submission decisions. Read the articles, Insider Report interviews and section introductions for an overview of the industry. With careful research you can target your submissions and move toward achieving your goals.

WHERE DO YOU START?

It's easiest to move from the very general to the very specific. The book is divided into Markets and Resources. The Resources section contains listings and information on organizations, workshops, contests and publications to help you learn more about the music industry and the craft of songwriting. The Markets section contains all the markets seeking new material and is the part of the book you will need to concentrate on for submissions.

Markets is further divided into sections corresponding to specific segments of the industry. This is of particular help to composers of music for the theater and concert hall, who can find prospective markets in the Play Producers & Publishers and Classical Performing Arts sections, respectively. Composers of audiovisual (film and TV) and commercial music will also find a section of the book, Advertising, AV and Commercial Music Firms, devoted to these possibilities.

THE GENERAL MARKETS

If you don't fall into these specific areas, you will need to do a little more work to target markets. Questions you need to ask are: Who am I writing this music for? Are these songs that I have written for an act I now belong to? Am I a songwriter hoping to have my music accepted and recorded by an artist?

If you fall into the first category, writing songs for an existing group or for yourself as a solo artist, you're probably trying to advance the career of your act. If you're seeking a recording contract, the Record Companies section will be the place to start. Look also at the Record Producers section. Independent record producers are constantly on the lookout for up-and-coming artists. They may also have strong connections with record companies looking for acts, and will pass your demo on or recommend the act to a record company. And if your act doesn't yet have representation, your demo submission may be included as part of a promotional kit sent to a prospective manager listed in the Managers and Booking Agents section.

If you are a songwriter seeking to have your songs recorded by other artists, you may submit to some of these same markets, but for different reasons. The Record Producers section contains mostly independent producers who work regularly with particular artists, rather than working fulltime for one record company. Because they work closely with a limited number of clients, they may be the place to send songs written with a specific act in mind. The independent producer is often responsible for picking cuts for a recording project. The Managers and Booking Agents section may be useful for the same reason. Many personal managers are constantly seeking new song material for the acts they represent, and a good song sent at the right time can mean a valuable cut for the songwriter.

The primary market for songwriters not writing with particular artists in mind will be found in the Music Publishers section. Music publishers are the jacks-of-all-trade in the industry, having knowledge about and keeping abreast of developments in all other segments of the music business. They act as the first line of contact between the songwriter and the music industry.

If you're uncertain about which markets will have the most interest in your material, review the introductory explanations at the beginning of each section. They will aid in explaining the various functions of each segment of the music industry, and will help you narrow your list of possible submissions.

NOW WHAT?

You've identified the market categories you're thinking about sending demos to. The next step is to research each section to find the individual markets that will be most interested in your work.

Most users of *Songwriter's Market* should check three items in the listings: location of the company, the type of music they're interested in hearing, and their submission policy. Each of these items should be considered carefully when deciding which markets to submit to.

If it's important to send your work to a company close to your home for more opportunities for face-to-face contact, location should be checked first. Each section contains listings from all over the U.S. as well as the rest of the world. Check the Geographic Index at the back of the book for listings of companies by state.

Your music isn't going to be appropriate for submission to all companies. Most music industry firms have specific music interests and needs, and you want to be sure your submissions are being seen and heard by companies who have a genuine interest in them. To find this information turn to the Category Indexes located at the end of the Music Publishers, Record Companies, Record Producers and Managers and Booking Agents sections. Locate the category of music that best describes the material you write, and refer to the companies listed under those categories. (Keep in mind that these are general categories. Some companies may not be listed in the Category Index because they either accept all types of music or the music they are looking for doesn't fit into any of the general categories.) When you've located a listing, go to the Music subheading. It will contain, in **bold** type, a more detailed list of the styles of music a company is seeking. Here is an example from a listing in the Record Companies section:

> **Music:** Mostly **heavy metal/hard rock** and **alternative guitar-based rock;** also **dance** and **pop**.

Pay close attention to the types of music described. For instance, if the music you write fits the category of "rock," there can be many variations on that style. Our sample above is interested in hard rock, another listing may be looking for country rock, and another, soft rock. These are three very different styles of music, but they all fall under the same general category. The Category Index is there to help you narrow down the listings within a certain music genre; it is up to you to narrow them down even further to fit the type of music you write. The music styles in each listing are in descending order of importance; if your particular specialty is country music, you may want to search out those listings that list country as their first priority as your primary targets for submissions. Going back to our sample Music subhead again, see the emphasis on rock, but also the interest in dance/pop.

You will also want to check and see if a listing has an editorial comment, see the sample below, which will be marked by a bullet (●).

> ● Note that Canyon Records is a very specialized label, and only wants to receive submissions by Native American artists.

Editorial comments give you additional information such as special submission requirements, any awards a company may have won, and other details that will help you narrow down which companies to submit to. They will also let you know if a company is listed in other sections of the book.

Finally, when you've placed the listings geographically and identified their music preferences, read the How to Contact subheading. As shown in the example below, it will give you pertinent information about what to send as part of a demo submission, how to go about sending it and when you can expect to hear back from them.

> **How to Contact:** Submit demo tape by mail. Unsolicited submissions are OK. "Telephoning A&R Director prior to submission is recommended." Prefers cassette, DAT or VHS videocassette with 3 songs and lyric sheet. SASE. Reports in 3-4 weeks.

This market accepts unsolicited submissions, but not all of the markets listed in *Songwriter's Market* do, so it's important to read this information carefully. Most companies have carefully considered their submission policy, and packages that do not follow their directions are returned or discarded without evaluation. Follow the instructions: it will impress upon the market your seriousness about getting your work heard.

You've now identified markets you feel will have the most interest in your work. Read the complete listing carefully before proceeding. Many of the listings have individualized information important for the submitting songwriter. Then, it's time for you to begin preparing your demo submission package to get your work before the people in the industry. For further information on that process, turn to Getting Started on page 6 and Demo FAQs on page 12.

Getting Started

To exist and thrive in the competitive music industry without being overwhelmed is perhaps the biggest challenge facing songwriters. Those who not only survive but also succeed have taken the time before entering the market to learn as much as they can about the inner workings of the music industry.

Newcomers to the music business can educate themselves about the industry through experience or education. Experience, while valuable, can be time-consuming and costly. Education can be just as effective, and less painful. Many sources exist to help you educate yourself about the intricacies of the industry *before* you jump in. Reading, studying and learning to use the information contained in sourcebooks such as *Songwriter's Market* expand your knowledge of the music industry and how it works, and help you market yourself and your work professionally and effectively.

IMPROVING YOUR CRAFT

Unfortunately, no magic formula can guarantee success in the music business. If you want to make it in this competitive business, you must begin by believing in yourself and your talent. As a songwriter, you must develop your own personal vision and stick with it. Why do you write songs? Is it because you want to make a lot of money, or because you love the process? Is every song you write an attempt to become famous, or a labor of love? Successful songwriters believe they have a talent that deserves to be heard, whether by two or two thousand people. Songwriting is a craft, like woodworking or painting. A lot of talent is involved, of course, but with time and practice the craft can be improved and eventually mastered.

While working on songs, learn all you can about the writing process. Look for support and feedback wherever you can. A great place to start is a local songwriting organization, which can offer friendly advice, support from other writers, and a place to meet collaborators. (For more information on songwriting organizations in your area, see the Organizations section on page 416.) Many organizations offer song critique sessions, which will help you identify strengths and weaknesses in your material and give you guidance to help improve your craft. Take any criticism you receive in a constructive manner, and use it to improve your writing style. The feedback you receive will help you write better songs, create connections within the industry and continue your education not only in the craft of songwriting but in the business as well.

Books and magazines pertaining to the music industry can also help you educate yourself about not only your songwriting technique but also the inner workings of the business. There are books to help you refine your songwriting skills, such as how to write better melodies, stronger lyrics and songs that sell. Many books cover the business side of music, explaining the various components of the music industry and how they work, including how to network with people in the business and how to get their attention. Music catalogs such as the Mix Bookshelf (call 1-800-233-9604 to receive their catalog) and Music Books Plus (call 1-800-265-8481 to receive their catalog) carry hundreds of books pertaining to the music industry, and can guide you to publications that can answer your questions about songwriting and the industry.

Music magazines can keep you up-to-date on the latest trends and happenings in today's ever-changing music business. From industry trade magazines like *Billboard* and *Variety* to more specific magazines such as *Performing Songwriter* and *Jazztimes*, there is a magazine that caters to just about every segment of the industry and type of music you can imagine. Since this is such a trend-oriented business, weekly and monthly magazines can help you stay abreast of what's hot and what's not. For some suggestions, see Publications of Interest on page 462.

If you own a computer, the Internet can be another valuable source of information. Not only are many record companies, publishers and magazines online, but an abundance of music sites exist where artists can showcase their songs for an unlimited audience, chat with other songwriters and musicians from all over the world, and even sell their product online. See Websites of Interest on page 466 for a listing of some of the music-oriented sites that are currently online. New ones are popping up every day, so surfing the Web frequently will help you find out what's available.

THE STRUCTURE OF THE MUSIC BUSINESS

The music business in the United States revolves around three major hubs: New York, Nashville and Los Angeles. Power is concentrated in those areas because that's where most record companies, publishers, songwriters and performers are. A lot of people trying to break into the music business, in whatever capacity, move to one of those three cities to be close to the people and companies they want to contact. From time to time a regional music scene will heat up in a non-hub city such as Austin, Chicago or Seattle. When this happens, songwriters and performers in that city experience a kind of musical Renaissance complete with better-paying gigs, a creatively charged atmosphere and intensified interest from major labels.

All this is not to say that a successful career cannot be nurtured from any city in the country, however. It can be, especially if you are a songwriter. By moving to a major music hub, you may be closer physically to the major companies, but you'll also encounter more competition than you would back home. Stay where you're comfortable; it's probably easier (and more cost-effective) to conquer the music scene where you are than it is in Los Angeles or Nashville. There are many smaller, independent companies located in cities across the country. Most international careers are started on a local level, and some may find a local career more satisfying, in its own way, than the constant striving to gain the attention of the major companies.

Any company, whether major or independent, relies on the buying public. Their support, in the form of money spent on records, concert tickets and other kinds of musical entertainment, keeps the music industry in business. Because of that, record companies, publishers and producers are eager to give the public what they want. To stay one step ahead of public tastes, record companies hire people who have a knack for spotting musical talent and anticipating trends, and put them in charge of finding and developing new talent. These talent scouts are called A&R representatives. "A&R" stands for "artist and repertoire," which simply means they are responsible for discovering new talent and matching songs to particular artists. The person responsible for the recording artist's product—the record—is called the producer. The producer's job is to develop the artist's work and come out of the studio with a good-sounding, saleable product that represents the artist in the best possible manner. His duties sometimes include choosing songs for a particular project, so record producers are also great contacts for songwriters.

Producers and A&R reps are aided in their search for talent by the music publisher. A publisher works as a songwriter's advocate who, for a percentage of the profits (typically 50% of all earnings from a particular song), attempts to find commercially profitable uses for the songs he represents. A successful publisher stays in contact with several A&R reps, trying to find out what upcoming projects are looking for new material, and whether any songs he represents will be appropriate.

When a song is recorded and subsequently released to the public, the recording artist, songwriter, record company, producer and publisher all stand to profit. Recording artists earn a negotiated royalty from a record company based on the number of records sold. Producers are usually paid either a negotiated royalty based on sales or a flat fee at the time of recording. Publishers and songwriters earn mechanical royalties (money a record company pays a publisher based on record sales) and performance royalties, which are based on radio airplay and live performances.

As you can see, the people you need to make contact with are publishers, A&R reps and producers. Managers can also be added to that list—many are looking for material for the acts they represent. Getting your material to these professionals and establishing relationships with as many people in the industry as you can should be your main goal as a songwriter. The more people who hear your songs, the better your chances of getting them recorded.

Any method of getting your songs heard, published, recorded and released is the best way if it works for you. *Songwriter's Market* lists music publishers, record companies, producers and managers (as well as advertising firms, play producers and classical performing arts organizations) along with specifications on how to submit your material to each. If you can't find a certain person or company you're interested in, there are other sources of information you can try. The *Recording Industry Sourcebook*, an annual directory published by Cardinal Business Media, lists record companies, music publishers, producers and managers, as well as attorneys, publicity firms, media, manufacturers, distributors and recording studios around the United States. Trade publications such as *Billboard* or *Variety*, available at most local libraries and bookstores, are great sources for up-to-date information. These periodicals list new companies as well as the artists, labels, producers and publishers for each song on the charts. Album covers, CD booklets and cassette j-cards can be valuable sources of information, providing the name of the record company, publisher, producer and usually the manager of an artist or group. Use your imagination in your research and be creative—any contacts you make in the industry can only help your career as a songwriter.

SUBMITTING YOUR SONGS

When it comes to presenting your material, the tool of the music industry is a demonstration recording—a demo. Cassette tapes have been the standard in the music industry for decades because they're so convenient. Songwriters use demos to present their songs, and musicians use them to showcase their performance skills. Demos are submitted to various professionals in the industry, either by mail or in person.

Demo quality

The production quality of demos can vary widely, but even simple guitar/vocal or piano/vocal demos must sound clean, with the instrument in tune and lyrics sung clearly. Many songwriters are investing in home recording equipment such as four- or eight-track recorders, keyboards and drum machines, so they can record their demos themselves. Other writers prefer to book studio time, hire musicians, and get professional input from an engineer or producer. Demo services are also available to record your demo for a fee. It's up to you to decide what you can afford and feel most comfortable with, and what you think best represents your song. Once a master recording is made of your song, you're ready to make cassette copies and start pitching your song to the contacts you've researched. (For a more in-depth discussion of demos, see Demo FAQs on page 12.)

Some markets indicate that you may send a videocassette of your act in performance or a group performing your songs, instead of the standard cassette demo. Most of the companies listed in *Songwriter's Market* have indicated that a videocassette is not required, but have indicated the format of their VCR should you decide to send one. Be aware that television systems vary widely from country to country, so if you're sending a video to a foreign listing check with them for the system they're using. For example, a VHS format tape recorded using the U.S. system (called NTSC) will not play back on a standard British VCR (using the PAL system), even if the recording formats are the same. It is possible to transfer a video from one system to another, but the expense in both time and money may outweigh its usefulness. Systems for some countries include: NTSC—U.S., Canada and Japan; PAL—United Kingdom, Australia and Germany; and SECAM—France.

Submitting by mail

When submitting material to companies listed in this book:

- Read the listing carefully and submit exactly what a company asks for and exactly how it asks that it be submitted. It's always a good idea to call first, just in case a company has changed its submission policy.
- Listen to each demo before sending to make sure the quality is satisfactory.
- Enclose a brief, typed cover letter to introduce yourself. Indicate what songs you are sending and why you are sending them. If you're a songwriter pitching songs to a particular artist, state that in the letter. If you're an artist/songwriter looking for a recording deal, you should say so. Have specific goals.
- Include typed lyric sheets or lead sheets if requested. Make sure your name, address and phone number appear on each sheet.
- Neatly label each tape with your name, address and phone number along with the names of the songs in the sequence in which they appear on the tape.
- If the company returns material (many do not; be sure to read each listing carefully), include a SASE for the return. Your return envelope to countries other than your own should contain a self-addressed envelope (SAE) and International Reply Coupon (IRC), available at your local post office. Be sure the return envelope is large enough to accommodate your material, and include sufficient postage for the weight of the package.
- Wrap the package neatly and write (or type on a shipping label) the company's address and your return address so they are clearly visible. Your package is the first impression a company has of you and your songs, so neatness is important.
- Mail first class. Stamp or write "First Class Mail" on the package and on the SASE you enclose. Don't send by registered or certified mail unless the company specifically requests it.
- Keep records of the dates, songs, and companies you submit to.

SAMPLE REPLY POSTCARD

I would like to hear:
____ "Name of Song" ____ "Name of Song" ____ "Name of Song"
I prefer:
____ cassette ____ DAT ____ videocassette

With:
____ lyric sheet ____ lead sheet ____ either ____ both
____ I am not looking for material at this time, try me later.
____ I am not interested.

____
Name Title

If you are writing to inquire about a company's needs or to request permission to submit (many companies ask you to do this first), your query letter should be typed, brief and pleasant.

Explain the type of material you have and ask for their needs and submission policy.

To expedite a reply, enclose a self-addressed, stamped postcard requesting the information you are seeking. Your typed questions (see the Sample Reply Postcard) should be direct and easy to answer. Place the company's name and address in the upper left hand space on the front of the postcard so you'll know which company you queried. Keep a record of the queries you send for future reference.

It's acceptable to submit your songs to more than one person at a time (this is called simultaneous submission). The one exception to this is when a publisher, artist or other industry professional asks if he may put a song of yours "on hold." This means he intends to record it, and doesn't want you to give the song to anyone else. Your song may be returned to you without ever having been recorded, even if it's been on hold for months. Or, your song may be recorded but the artist or producer decides to leave it off the album. If either of these things happens, you're free to pitch your song to other people again. (You can protect yourself from having a song on hold indefinitely. Establish a deadline for the person who asks for the hold, i.e., "You can put my song on hold for *X* number of months." Or modify the hold to specify that you will pitch the song to other people, but you will not sign a deal without allowing the person who has the song on hold to make you an offer.) When someone publishes your song and you sign a contract, you grant that publisher exclusive rights to your song and you may not pitch it to other publishers. You can, however, pitch it to any artists or producers interested in recording the song without publishing it themselves.

If a market doesn't respond within several weeks after you've sent your demo, don't despair. As long as your demo is in the possession of a market, there is a chance someone is reviewing it. That opportunity ends when your demo is returned to you. If after a reasonable amount of time you still haven't received word on your submission (check the reporting time each company states in its listing), following up with a friendly letter or phone call giving detailed information about your submission is a good idea. Many companies do not return submissions, so don't expect a company that states "Does not return material" to send your materials back to you.

Submitting in person

Planning a trip to one of the major music hubs will give you insight into how the music industry functions. Whether you decide to visit New York, Nashville or Los Angeles, have some specific goals in mind and set up appointments to make the most of your time there. It will be difficult to get in to see some industry professionals as many of them are extremely busy and may not feel meeting out-of-town writers is a high priority. Other people are more open to, and even encourage, face-to-face meetings. They may feel that if you take the time to travel to where they are, and you're organized enough to schedule meetings beforehand, you're more professional than many aspiring songwriters who blindly submit inappropriate songs through the mail. (For listings of companies by state, see the Geographic Index at the back of the book.)

Take several cassette copies and lyric sheets of each of your songs. More than one of the companies you visit may ask that you leave a copy to review and perhaps play for other professionals in the company. There's also a good chance that the person you have an appointment with will have to cancel (expect that occasionally) but wants you to leave a copy of the songs so he can listen and contact you later. Never give someone the last or only copy of your material—if it is not returned to you, all the hard work and money that went into making that demo will be lost.

Another good place to meet industry professionals face-to-face is at seminars such as the yearly South by Southwest Music and Media Conference in Austin, the National Academy of Songwriters' annual Songwriters Expo, or the Nashville Songwriters Association's Spring Symposium, to name a few (see the Workshops and Conferences section of this book for further ideas). Many of these conferences feature demo listening sessions, where industry professionals sit down and listen to demos submitted by songwriters attending the seminars.

Many good songs have been rejected simply because they just weren't what the particular publisher or record company was looking for at the time, so don't take rejection personally. Realize that if a few people don't like your songs, it doesn't mean they're not good. However, if there seems to be a consensus about your work—for instance, the feel of a song isn't right or the lyrics need work—give the advice serious thought. Listen attentively to what the reviewers say and use their criticism constructively to improve your songs.

Demo FAQs: Answers to the most frequently asked questions about demos

BY CINDY LAUFENBERG

In today's music business, the demonstration tape, or demo, is the accepted way of getting your songs heard by industry professionals. Unless you already have established contacts at major publishing and record companies in the industry, you're going to need a demo to display your talents as a songwriter or performer. Demos can range from a simple, two-track guitar/vocal arrangement to a fully-produced, 24-track recording by an 8-piece band. How do you know what type of demo will best represent your songs? What will make your demo stand out? What do music business professionals look for in a demo? We've compiled some of the most frequently-asked questions (FAQs) songwriters ask about submitting demos and asked several A&R reps and publishing professionals their opinions on the subject. They gave us tips on what they look for in the demos they receive, and offered advice on how to make your demos stand out and attract attention.

How elaborate does a demo have to be? Do I need a full arrangement, or is a simple guitar or piano/vocal sufficient?

The answer to this question lies in the type of music you write, and what an individual at a company is looking for. Usually, up-tempo pop, rock and dance demos need to be more fully produced than pop ballads and country demos. "The type of demo depends on the type of song," says Carla Berkowitz, director of creative affairs at EMI Music Publishing in Los Angeles. "A great ballad is best presented by a simple piano/vocal (with a good vocal) to show off the lyric and melody. A great pop/rock song may be served well by a 'fully-realized' demo." Julie Gordon, A&R representative at The Enclave in New York, agrees: "I think the type of demo depends to some extent on the type of artist that is submitting the demo. Certainly a techno artist needs quite a sophisticated/produced demo, whereas for a singer/songwriter type, a basic demo will suffice." Many of the companies listed in *Songwriter's Market* tell you what type of demo they prefer to receive, and if you're not sure you can always call and ask what their preference is. Either way, make sure your demo is clean and clear, and the vocals are up front.

If you are an artist looking for a record deal, obviously your demo needs to be as fully produced as possible to convey your talent as an artist. Many singer/songwriters record their demos as if they were going to be released as an album. That way, if they have already recorded 3 or 4 CD-quality demo tapes but haven't heard anything from the labels they've been submitting to, they can put those demos together and release a CD or cassette on their own. They end up with a professional-looking product, complete with album cover graphics and liner notes, to sell at shows and through mail order without spending a lot of money to re-record the songs.

Whether your demo is produced with a full band or just a solo piano, it is the quality of the writing that will get your songs noticed. "If a song is great you can tell even without production, and if the song is not there, all the production in the world won't help," says Julie Gordon.

How many songs should there be on a demo? Should they be in any particular order? Should the demo have complete songs, or just portions of songs?

The consensus throughout the industry is that three songs is sufficient. Most music business professionals don't have time to listen to more than three, and they figure if you can't catch their attention in three songs, your songs probably don't have hit potential. "A common mistake [many songwriters make] is sending too many songs," says Julie Gordon. "I think three songs is a good amount to start with to introduce yourself. Even if you have recorded an entire CD, you can send that later if you get a request for more material."

Put three complete songs on the tape, not just snippets of your favorites, and remember to put your best, most commercial song first on the tape. If it's an up-tempo number, that makes it even easier to catch someone's attention. "I prefer complete songs," says Lonn Friend, vice president of A&R at Arista Records in Los Angeles. "Always put your strongest track first on the tape. Most A&R people don't have the patience or time to get past the first couple of tracks if an impression isn't made early." Some individuals don't even need to hear three songs; for Carla Berkowitz at EMI, "one or two is enough." Whether two or three songs, all songs should be on the same side of the tape, and none of them should be longer than five minutes. Most professional managers and A&R reps are looking for hit songs, and hit songs are usually between three and four minutes long. David McPherson, senior director of A&R at Jive Records in New York, advises, "Don't talk on the tape—just music! Don't make the songs longer than five minutes each unless it's really necessary. And don't have long introductions for your songs."

What's the most preferable format: cassette, DAT or CD?

The cassette is still the preferable format for demos. David McPherson prefers cassettes because "I can listen to it in my car/house/office or almost anywhere. CDs and DATs are only more convenient because you can skip to the next song faster and the sound is better, but hits are hits on whatever configuration. A fully-produced full-length CD only impresses me if it is full of hit records, which does not usually happen." Carla Berkowitz also prefers the ease of cassettes over other formats. "I prefer a traditional cassette, so I can toss it in my bag and listen to it in my car. CDs do not impress me as far as if I will listen quicker or like the music more. Also, if I do like what I hear, I can always request a DAT or better recording." Cassettes are also cheaper to duplicate than CDs or DATs, and are cheaper and easier to mail.

Do I have to record my demo in a studio? What are my options if I can't afford to record at a studio?

With the advances in home recording technology, it's very acceptable—as well as affordable—to record your demos at home. Lonn Friend has received home-recorded demos, and finds them to be "very acceptable. When I received demos from (alternative rock band) the Eels, they were home recordings and, still to this day, the best demos I've ever heard."

It's up to you to decide how many tracks you think you need to record your songs. If you're recording a simple guitar/vocal demo, a four-track recording made in your living room would work just fine. The more instruments, vocals and effects you want to add, the more tracks you need. Home recording equipment has become quite affordable in recent years, and for the same amount of money it would cost you to have a few demos recorded at a studio you could invest in a good home studio setup in 4-, 8- and 16-track formats. You might even want to get together with other songwriters or performers in your area and pool your resources, buying equipment together you all can use to record demos.

Renting home recording equipment is also an option, as is finding alternate venues to record your songs. Look around your neighborhood for ideas; do you know any musician friends who have equipment you could borrow or rent for a few hours? Do you know of a local church or synagogue that has a good sound system? If they have recording equipment, ask the music director if you could use their facilities during off hours to record your demos.

If you decide you can't do it at home and want to go into the studio to record, be sure to find the right studio for your music and your budget. Shop around for studios (you can find them listed in the Yellow Pages or in your local newspaper), and remember that not only will you have to pay for recording time but also for any additional musicians, a producer or engineer, and the tapes you are recording on. Base your decision on what studio will work best for the type of music you write, and be sure to hear samples of work that have been recorded at that studio.

Yet another option is to consider using a demo service—see the next question for more information.

I'm a songwriter, not a performer. Where do I find someone to sing and/or perform on my demo? What about demo services?

Finding a good vocalist who can adequately convey the meaning of your songs is important, so if you can't sing that well you may want to find someone who can. Pat Finch, senior creative director at Famous Music in Nashville, says "For me, [a demo] has to be performed by competent singers and players. I don't have time to struggle through poorly recorded demos." Carla Berkowitz finds "bad vocalists to be really distracting from the song itself." Julie Gordon agrees. "Obviously the performance and the material are what make a good demo stand out. If I can't remember anything about a song after I have heard it, can't find a hook, can't hear the vocals or am presented with sub-par material, it stands out as bad." It pays to find a good vocalist and good musicians to record your demos, and there are many places to find musicians and singers willing to work with you. Check out local songwriting organizations, music stores and newspapers to find musicians in your area you can hire to play on your demo. Many singers who don't write their own songs will sing on demos in exchange for a copy of the tape that they can use as their own demo to help further their performing careers.

If you can't find local musicians, or don't want to go through the trouble of putting together a band just for the purposes of recording your demo, you may want to try a demo service. For a fee, a demo service will produce your songs in their studio using their own singers and musicians. Many of these services advertise in music magazines, songwriting newsletters and bulletin boards at local music stores. If you decide to deal with a demo service, make sure you can hear samples of work they've done in the past. Many demo services are mail-order businesses—you send them either a rough tape of your song or the sheet music and they'll produce and record a demo within a month or two. Be sure you find a service that will let you have creative control over how your demo is to be produced, and make sure you tell them exactly how you want your song to sound. As with studios, shop around and find the demo service that best suits your needs and budget.

What's the most effective way to package my demo? Does it need graphics, or should it be just a cassette with my name, address and telephone number on it?

"The simpler the better!," says Pat Finch, and most agree. A demo package doesn't have to be elaborate—most professionals aren't looking for slick graphics but a simple tape with the appropriate contact information. Brian Malouf, A&R representative and producer at RCA Records in New York, looks for a "simple package, no graphics necessary. Three songs, picture and a short bio/press release" are sufficient. According to Julie Gordon, "Presentation should be neat and professional but an expensive press kit is not necessary. Remember, it's not the package that matters, it's the material. A cassette is fine, as long as it has a label on it—all unlabeled cassettes go straight to the trash." Since your tape may become separated from the box it came in, it's imperative to have your name, address and telephone number on the cassette box as well as the cassette itself. The cassette label should provide your name and phone number, the titles of the songs, the name of your publisher (if you have one), and copyright information. Cue your tape to the beginning of the first song, and keep about 6 seconds between songs. A neat, professionally done package may be just enough to make your tape stand out from the hundreds of others that arrive on the desks of publishers and A&R reps.

What information should go with the demo when I send it out?

Your package should be as complete as possible, without overwhelming the listener with unnecessary information. A cover letter and lyric sheets along with the demo tape are fine if you're a songwriter looking for a publisher. If you're an artist looking for a record deal, a biography, photo and press clippings should be included in the package as well. Lonn Friend advises, "Prepare a good package with photo, lyrics, bio, etc., like a press kit. If it's impressive, it sets itself aside from the rest—and getting attention is the hardest part."

Include a short, to-the-point cover letter addressed to a specific person in the company, and briefly state why you're sending the tape. Are you a writer looking for a publishing deal, an artist looking for a record deal, or a writer wanting to have a song recorded by a particular artist? Add any important professional credits you may have, and ask for feedback if you want it. Be sure to thank the individual for their time and consideration, and don't forget to include your name, address and phone number. If you have professionally-printed letterhead, use it. It makes you look as though you take your career seriously.

Your lyric sheets should be neatly typed and inserted in the package in the order they appear on the tape. Include the names of all the writers of each song, as well as a copyright notice on the first page of the lyric sheet. It is not necessary to send lead sheets with your demo tape, unless they are specifically requested.

The outside of your package should be as neat as everything on the inside. Make sure you have adequate postage, and don't send your tape in a regular business envelope. Use an envelope that's large enough to accommodate your tape and your lyric sheets/press kit, one that's padded or insulated so your tape does not get damaged in mailing. Have a specific contact name to mail your tape to, and type your mailing label. Extra tape is not necessary to seal your envelope; the harder it is to open, the less likely it is to be listened to. The idea is to make your package as friendly and accessible as possible.

Many songwriters include SASEs in their packages so they can have their materials returned to them. Even if you include return postage, there is no guarantee that your tape will actually be returned, so it's up to you to decide if you want to risk spending the extra money. If you think the price of return postage is worth the price of the returned tape (if it is returned at all), include the SASE. If you do, make sure it's big enough and has sufficient postage for the materials you want returned.

When asked the question "What makes a good demo stand out?", all of the professionals interviewed for this article said the same thing: "Great songs!" No matter how professional your demo package is, and no matter how closely you follow submission guidelines, it's important that the songs you are sending are able to compete with the songs and artists that are currently on the radio. Ray McKenzie, president of indie label Zero Hour Records in New York, notes that he sees "too much time spent on production and packaging, and not enough on songcraft" in many of the submissions he receives. If you can combine well-crafted songs with an attractive, professional demo package, you and your songs stand a good chance of being noticed and listened to.

The Business of Songwriting

The more you know about how the music industry functions, the less likely you'll be to make a mistake dealing with contracts and agreements. Signing a contract without knowing exactly what you're agreeing to can ruin a career you've worked years to build. Becoming familiar with standard industry practices will help you learn what to look for and what to avoid.

COPYRIGHT

When you create a song and put it down in fixed form, it becomes a property you own and is automatically protected by copyright. This protection lasts for your lifetime (or the lifetime of the last surviving author, if you co-wrote the song) plus 50 years. When you prepare demos, place notification of copyright on all copies of your song—the lyric sheets, lead sheets and cassette labels. The notice is simply the word "copyright" or the symbol © followed by the year the song was created (or published) and your name: © 1998 by John L. Public.

For the best protection, you may want to consider registering your copyright with the Library of Congress. Although a song is copyrighted whether or not it is registered, registering a song establishes a public record of your copyright and could prove useful in any future litigation involving the song. Registration also entitles you to a potentially greater settlement in a copyright infringement suit. To register your song, request government form PA from the Copyright Office. Call the 24-hour hotline at (202)707-9100 and leave your name and address on the recorder. Once you receive a form, you can photocopy it if you want to register more than one song. It is possible to register groups of songs for one fee, but you cannot add future songs to that particular collection.

Once you receive the PA form, you will be required to return it, along with a registration fee and a tape or lead sheet of your song, to the Register of Copyrights, Copyright Office, Library of Congress, Washington DC 20559. It may take as long as four months to receive your certificate of registration from the Copyright Office, but your songs are protected from the date of creation, and the date of registration will reflect the date you applied for registration. If you need additional information about registering your songs, call the Copyright Office's Public Information Office at (202)707-3000 or visit their website at http://lcweb.loc.gov/copyright.

Don't be afraid to play your songs for people or worry about creating a song that might be similar to someone else's. True copyright infringement is rarer than most people think. First of all, a title cannot be copyrighted, nor can an idea or a chord progression. Only specific, fixed melodies and lyrics can be copyrighted. Second, a successful infringement suit would have to prove that another songwriter had access to the completed song and that he deliberately copied it, which is difficult to do and not really worthwhile unless the song is a huge hit. Song theft sometimes does happen, but not often enough for you to become paranoid. If you ever feel that one of your songs has been stolen—that someone has unlawfully infringed on your copyright—you must prove that you created the work. Copyright registration is the best proof of a date of creation. You *must* have your copyright registered in order to file a copyright infringement lawsuit. One way writers prove a work is original is to keep their rough drafts and revisions of songs, either on paper or on tape, if they record different versions of the song as they go along.

CONTRACTS

You will encounter several types of contracts as you deal with the business end of songwriting. You may sign a legal agreement between you and a co-writer establishing percentages of the writer's royalties each of you will receive, what you will do if a third party (e.g., a recording artist) wishes to change your song and receive credit as a co-writer, and other things. As long as the issues at stake are simple, and co-writers respect each other and discuss their business philosophy in advance of writing a song, they can write up an agreement without the aid of a lawyer. In other situations—when a publisher, producer or record company wants to do business with you—you should always have any contract reviewed by a knowledgeable entertainment attorney.

Single song contracts

The most common type of contract you may encounter at first will be the single song contract. A music publisher offers this type of contract when he wants to sign one or more of your songs, but he doesn't want to hire you as a staff writer. You assign your rights to a particular song to the publisher for an agreed-upon number of years (usually the life of the copyright).

Every single song contract should contain this basic information: the publisher's name, the writer's name, the song's title, the date and the purpose of the agreement. The songwriter also declares that the song is an original work and he is the creator of the work. The contract must specify the royalties the songwriter will earn from various uses of the song. These include performance, mechanical, print and synchronization royalties, as well as an agreement as to what will be paid for any uses of the song not specifically set forth in the contract.

The songwriter should receive no less than 50% of the income his song generates. That means that whatever the song earns in royalties, the publisher and songwriter should split 50/50. The songwriter's half is called the "writer's share" and the publisher's half is called the "publisher's share." If there is more than one songwriter, the songwriters split the writer's share. Sometimes songwriters will negotiate for a percentage of the publisher's share; that is, a co-publishing agreement. This usually happens only if the songwriter already has a successful track record.

Other issues a contract should address include whether or not an advance will be paid to the songwriter and how much it will be; when royalties will be paid (quarterly or semiannually); who will pay for demos—the publisher, songwriter or both; how lawsuits against copyright infringement will be handled, including the cost of such lawsuits; whether the publisher has the right to sell the song to another publisher without the songwriter's consent; and whether the publisher has the right to make changes in a song, or approve of changes written by someone else, without the songwriter's consent. In addition, the songwriter should have the right to audit the publisher's books if the songwriter deems it necessary and gives the publisher reasonable notice.

Songwriters should also negotiate for a reversion clause. This calls for the rights to the song to revert to the songwriter if some provision of the contract is not met. The most common type of reversion clause covers the failure to secure a commercial release of a song within a specified period of time (usually one or two years). If nothing happens with the song, the rights will revert back to the songwriter, who can then give the song to a more active publisher if he so chooses. Some publishers will agree to this, figuring that if they don't get some action on the song in the first year, they're not likely to ever get any action on it. Other publishers are reluctant to agree to this clause. They may invest a lot of time and money in a song, re-demoing it and pitching it to a number of artists; they may be actively looking for ways to exploit the song. If a producer puts a song on hold for a while and goes into a lengthy recording project, by the time the record company (or artist or producer) decides which songs to release as singles, a year can easily go by. That's why it's so important to have a good working relationship with your publisher. You need to trust that he has your best interests in mind. If a song really is on hold you can give him more time and/or know that if your song is recorded but ultimately not released by the artist, it's not your publisher's fault and he'll work just as hard to get another artist to record the song. (For more information on music publishers, see the Music Publishers section introduction on page 31.)

While there is no such thing as a "standard" contract, The Songwriters Guild of America (SGA) has drawn up a Popular Songwriter's Contract which it believes to be the best minimum songwriter contract available. The Guild will send a copy of the contract at no charge to any interested songwriter upon request (include a self-addressed stamped envelope). SGA will also review free of charge any contract offered to its members, checking it for fairness and completeness. For a thorough discussion of the somewhat complicated subject of contracts, see these two books published by Writer's Digest Books: *The Craft and Business of Songwriting*, by John Braheny and *Music Publishing: A Songwriter's Guide*, by Randy Poe.

The following list, taken from a Songwriters Guild of America publication entitled "10 Basic Points Your Contract Should Include," enumerates the basic features of an acceptable songwriting contract:

1. **Work for Hire.** When you receive a contract covering just one composition, you should make sure the phrases "employment for hire" and "exclusive writer agreement" are not included. Also, there should be no options for future songs.
2. **Performing Rights Affiliation.** If you previously signed publishing contracts, you should be affiliated with either ASCAP, BMI or SESAC. All performance royalties must be received directly by you from your performing rights organization and this should be written into your contract.
3. **Reversion Clause.** The contract should include a provision that if the publisher does not secure a release of a commercial sound recording within a specified time (one year, two years, etc.), the contract can be terminated by you.
4. **Changes in the Composition.** If the contract includes a provision that the publisher can change the title, lyrics or music, this should be amended so that only with your consent can such changes be made.
5. **Royalty Provisions.** You should receive fifty percent (50%) of all publisher's income on all licenses issued. If the publisher prints and sells his own sheet music, your royalty should be ten percent (10%) of the wholesale selling price. The royalty should not be stated in the contract as a flat rate ($.05, $.07, etc.).
6. **Negotiable Deductions.** Ideally, demos and all other expenses of publication should be paid 100% by the publisher. The only allowable fee is for the Harry Fox Agency collection fee, whereby the writer pays one half of the amount charged to the publisher for mechanical rights. The current rate charged by the Harry Fox Agency is 3.5%.
7. **Royalty Statements and Audit Provision.** Once the song is recorded, you are entitled to receive royalty statements at least once every six months. In addition, an audit provision with no time restriction should be included in every contract.
8. **Writer's Credit.** The publisher should make sure that you receive proper credit on all uses of the composition.
9. **Arbitration.** In order to avoid large legal fees in case of a dispute with your publisher, the contract should include an arbitration clause.
10. **Future Uses.** Any use not specifically covered by the contract should be retained by the writer to be negotiated as it comes up.

THE RIPOFFS

As in any business, the music industry has its share of dishonest, greedy people who try to unfairly exploit the talents and aspirations of others. Most of them use similar methods of attack which you can learn to identify and avoid. "Song sharks," as they're called, prey on beginners—

those writers who are unfamiliar with ethical industry standards. Song sharks will take any songs—quality doesn't count. They're not concerned with future royalties, since they get their money upfront from songwriters who think they're getting a great deal.

Here are some guidelines to help you recognize these "song sharks":

- Never pay to have your music "reviewed" by a company that may be interested in publishing, producing or recording it. Reviewing material—free of charge—is the practice of reputable companies looking for hits for their artists or recording projects.
- Never pay to have your songs published. A reputable company interested in your songs assumes the responsibility and cost of promoting them. That company invests in your material because it expects a profit once the songs are recorded and released.
- Never pay a fee to have a publisher make a demo of your songs. Some publishers may take demo expenses out of your future royalties, but you should never pay upfront for demo costs for a song that is signed to a publisher.
- Never pay to have your lyrics or poems set to music. "Music mills"—for a price—may use the same melody for hundreds of lyrics and poems, whether it sounds good or not. Publishers recognize one of these melodies as soon as they hear it.
- Avoid CD compilation deals where a record company asks you to pay a fee to be included on a CD. They ask you to supply a master recording (along with a check for an amount of $500 or more), and they include your song on a CD to be sent to radio stations, producers, etc. First of all, the company is making a lot of money on this. The cost of mastering, pressing and mailing the CD is going to be a lot less than the amount of money they take in from the artists they solicit. Second, radio stations and other industry professionals just don't listen to these things to find new artists. It would be better to spend the money making a quality demo or putting out a CD on your own. It's one thing if a record company puts out a compilation of the artists they've signed as a promotional item—it's another when they ask you to pay to be included.
- Read all contracts carefully before signing and don't sign any contract you're unsure about or that you don't fully understand. Don't assume any contract is better than no contract at all. It is well worth paying an attorney for the time it takes him to review a contract if you can avoid a bad situation that may cost you thousands of dollars in royalties if your song becomes a hit.
- Don't pay a company to pair you with a collaborator. A better way is to contact songwriting organizations that offer collaboration services to their members.
- Don't sell your songs outright. It's unethical for anyone to offer such a proposition.
- If you are asked by a record company or some other type of company to pay expenses upfront, be careful. A record producer may charge you a fee upfront to produce your record, or a small indie label may ask you to pay recording costs and they will finance mastering, pressing and promotional costs. Each situation is different, and it's up to you to decide whether or not it will be beneficial. Talk to other artists who have signed similar contracts before signing one yourself. Research the company and its track record by finding out what types of product they have released, and what kind of distribution they have. Visit their website on the Internet, if they have one. Beware of any company that won't let you know what it has done in the past. If it has had successes and good working relationships with other writers and artists, it should be happy to brag about them.
- Before participating in a songwriting contest, read the rules carefully. Be sure that what you're giving up in the way of entry fees, etc., is not greater than what you stand to gain by winning the contest. See the Contests and Awards section introduction on page 448 for more advice on this.
- There is a version of the age-old chain letter scheme with a special twist just for songwriters. The letter names five songwriters whose tapes you are supposed to buy. You then add your name to the letter and mail it to five more songwriters who, in turn, are supposed

to purchase your tape. Besides the fact that such chain letters or "pyramid" schemes generally fail, the five "amateur" songwriters named in the letter are known song sharks. Don't fall for it.

- Verify any situation about an individual or company if you have any doubts at all. Contact the performing rights society with which it is affiliated. Check with the Better Business Bureau in the town where it is located or the state's attorney general's office. Contact professional organizations you're a member of and inquire about the reputation of the company.

RECORD KEEPING

As your songwriting career continues to grow, you should keep a ledger or notebook containing all financial transactions relating to your songwriting. It should include a list of income from royalty checks as well as expenses incurred as a result of your songwriting business: cost of tapes, demo sessions, office supplies, postage, traveling expenses, dues to organizations, class and workshop fees and any publications you purchase pertaining to songwriting. It's also advisable to open a checking account exclusively for your songwriting activities, not only to make record keeping easier, but to establish your identity as a business for tax purposes.

Any royalties you receive will not reflect taxes or any other mandatory deductions. It is the songwriter's responsibility to keep track of income and file the appropriate tax forms. Contact the IRS or an accountant who serves music industry clients for specific information.

INTERNATIONAL MARKETS

Everyone talks about the world getting smaller, and it's true. Modern communication technology has brought us to the point where information can be transmitted around the globe instantly. No business has enjoyed the fruits of this progress more than the music industry. American music is heard in virtually every country in the world, and having a hit song in other countries as well as in the United States can greatly increase a songwriter's royalty earnings.

Each year there has been a steady increase in the number of international companies listed in *Songwriter's Market*. While these listings may be a bit more challenging to deal with than domestic companies, they offer additional avenues for songwriters looking for places to place their songs. To find international listings, see the Geographical Index at the back of the book.

Music, Money and Success: Where the Money Comes From

BY JEFFREY BRABEC AND TODD BRABEC

As you can see by the chart below, there are many different ways a songwriter can generate income. A songwriter makes money every time a CD or cassette containing one of his songs is sold, each time one of those songs is played on the radio, in a TV show, or even performed in a concert hall or broadcast in a public place. He can also generate income from the sale of sheet music or from the use of his song in a commercial or a motion picture. Since each source of income has its own distinct payment structure, figuring out exactly how a songwriter makes money and where that money comes from can be a challenge. Some of the major areas that generate income for songwriters are outlined here.

Songwriter/Publisher/Recording Artist Income Chart

$ 139,000	U.S. singles sales (1 million copies)
2,085,000	U.S. album sales (3 million copies)
600,000	U.S. radio and TV performances
57,000	Foreign single sales
140,000	Foreign album sales
400,000	Foreign radio and TV performances
25,000	Sheet music and folios
175,000	Advertising commercial
11,000	Song in a television series
25,000	Song in a motion picture
4,000	Foreign theatrical performances
221,000	Broadway show use
1,000	Lyric reprint in a novel
10,000	CD-ROM
1,250	Karaoke/video jukebox
115,000	Background music score fee
200,000	Foreign score royalties
35,000	U.S. background score TV royalties
25,000	Miscellaneous royalties
$4,269,250	Total writer and publisher royalties
+ 6,120,000	Recording artist royalties
$10,389,250	TOTAL GROSS INCOME

JEFFREY BRABEC, *an entertainment attorney and former recording artist, is vice president of business affairs for the Chrysalis Music Group. He is also an adjunct professor at USC School of Music, contributing editor to the* Entertainment Law & Finance Magazine *and has written numerous articles on the music industry.* **TODD BRABEC** *is senior vice president and director of membership for ASCAP. A former recording artist as well as entertainment attorney, he lectures extensively on all aspects of the entertainment industry and is an adjunct professor at USC School of Music. He is also a winner of the ASCAP-Deems Taylor Award for excellence in music journalism.*

CD, RECORD AND TAPE SALES (MECHANICAL ROYALTIES)

CERTIFICATION AWARD	ALBUMS SOLD
Triple Platinum	3,000,000
Platinum	1,000,000
Gold	500,000

One of the largest sources of income for the songwriter and music publisher is the mechanical royalties due from the sale of records, tapes and CDs. Under the U.S. mechanical rate in effect in 1997 (the "statutory mechanical rate"), a million-selling single would be worth a total of $69,500 per song in combined royalties to the publisher and writer. For album, tape and CD sales, the above royalties would be multiplied by the number of songs on the album, tape or CD. For example, if ten songs were included on a CD and each received a 6.95 cent statutory royalty, a total of 69.5 cents in mechanical royalties would be generated from the sale of each album. If the album, tape and CD sell between 1,000,000 and 10,000,000 copies, the total writer and publisher royalties for the album would range from $695,000 to $6,950,000. Beginning January 1, 1998, a new statutory mechanical rate will be in effect and will replace 1997's 6.95 cent rate.

It should be mentioned that the per-song statutory mechanical royalty can be reduced under certain circumstances (e.g., if the writer is the recording artist or if the record is sold as a mid-line, record club, television only, special products' compilation or budget album) so royalty figures can be less than those mentioned above. However, such "reduced rates" are voluntary and occur only if the publisher agrees or if the songwriter is a recording artist and has to accept such lower royalties in the record company agreement.

For example, the majority of recording artist and producer agreements contain language stating that if the recording artist or producer has written or co-written a song, has ownership or control of a song or has any interest in any composition on the album, tape, CD or single, the mechanical royalty rate payable by the record company is reduced. Such compositions are referred to as "controlled compositions." Many contracts attempt to establish a 75% rate for all controlled compositions computed at the mechanical rate in effect at either the time the recording is produced, the date of the recording contract with the artist, the date a particular album commences recording or the date the recording is originally released (regardless of whether the same recording is released again at a later date in another album).

Other times, the record company will establish a cap on the total amount of mechanical royalties it will pay for an album and the artist or producer guarantees that he or she will secure reduced mechanical rates on all songs on the album so the cap demanded by the record company to music publishers and songwriters is not exceeded. If this maximum aggregate album royalty rate is surpassed, the difference is normally deducted from the artist's or producer's record, songwriter and publishing royalties (or the per song royalty rates for the writer-artist or writer-producer will be reduced proportionately).

For example, if a writer-performer has a ten song×5.21 cent maximum royalty rate on his or her album, instead of writing all ten songs, writes only eight and records two songs written by outside writers who demand the 6.95 cent statutory rate per song in effect in 1997, mechanical royalties would look as follows:

52.1¢	Album Royalty Maximum
− 13.9¢	(2 Outside Songs at 6.95 cents each)
38.2¢	
÷ 8	Number of Artist-Written Songs
4.77¢	Per Song Royalty to Artist-Writer and Publisher

As you can see, the writer-artist's mechanical royalty has been reduced to 4.77 cents per song from 5.21 cents per song due to the inclusion of two outside written songs on the album. As the writer-artist records more outside written songs, the artist's per song royalties will be further reduced. In fact, in some cases, where the writer-artist has recorded a substantial number of songs written by other writers, the writer-artist may receive no royalties for his or her own songs since the aggregate album royalty maximum has been paid to outside songwriters and publishers. There have also been instances where the writer-artist's mechanical royalties have been in the minus column for every album sold because of these controlled composition clauses. Many of these clauses also provide that the writer-artist will only receive a mechanical royalty for one use of his or her song regardless of the number of versions contained on the album, CD or single. Even though there will be a new statutory mechanical rate established for 1998, the same principles and calculation procedures will apply; simply plug the new rate into the calculations.

ASCAP/BMI/SESAC (PERFORMANCE RIGHT PAYMENTS)

#1 Worldwide Song of the Year	$ 1,600,000
One Television Performance	$ 4,000
Standard Song Lifetime Earnings	$11,000,000

One of the most lucrative rights guaranteed by the Copyright Law of the United States and other countries is the performance right—the right which recognizes that a songwriter's creation (song, background score, symphony, etc.) is a property right and a license must be acquired to use a copyrighted musical work. In the multi-billion dollar music industry, close to one billion dollars is collected by the U.S. performing right organizations ASCAP, BMI and SESAC, with ASCAP and BMI responsible for about 98% of that amount. These organizations negotiate license fee agreements with the users of music (radio and television stations, cable stations, restaurants, concert halls, wired music services, airlines, etc.) and give the user the right to perform the music and lyrics of any writer belonging to one of these organizations. The license fees collected are then distributed to the writers and publishers whose works are performed.

In the United States, the primary types of music use which generate performance royalties are feature performances (a visual vocal or visual instrumental on television shows, a radio performance of a song, etc.); background music on television series, specials, movies of the week and feature films; theme songs to television series; advertising jingles; production company and network logos; promos; and copyrighted arrangements of public domain compositions. Each type of music use (background music, a theme song, etc.) has a different value relative to all other types of music (features are worth more than themes; themes are paid higher than background music, etc.).

In addition, ASCAP, BMI and SESAC have very different payment formula schedules, producing different payments for the same type of music use. These organizations may change their payment rules without notice to the writers and publishers, making knowledge of each performing rights society's rules essential for any writer, representative or publisher. The financial importance of this area cannot be overemphasized as literally fortunes can be made from one composition alone. For example, the #1 song of the year can generate in a few short years a 2 million dollar writer and publisher payout; a successful television series theme song can generate over 1.5 million dollars over a 10-year period; and a top box office film background can generate well over a million dollars in performance income over its copyright life.

MOTION PICTURES

FILM	SONG USED
Space Jam	"Fly Like an Eagle"
The Bodyguard	"I Will Always Love You"
Apollo 13	"Purple Haze"
Interview with the Vampire	"Sympathy for the Devil"
Mrs. Doubtfire	"Dude (Looks Like a Lady)"
Dangerous Minds	"Gangsta's Paradise"
Forrest Gump	"Running on Empty"

When a motion picture producer wants to use an existing song in a theatrically released film, the producer must negotiate with the music publisher for use of the composition. Once an agreement is reached, the producer will sign a synchronization license, giving him the right to distribute the film to motion picture theaters, sell it to television and use the song in "in context" television promos and theatrical previews. The amount of the motion picture synchronization fee depends upon a number of factors including: how the song is used (e.g., sung by a character in the film, background instrumental); the overall budget for the film and the music budget; the stature of the song being used; the actual timing of the song as used in the film (e.g., 32 seconds, 2 minutes); whether there are multiple uses of the song in different scenes; whether the use is over the opening or closing credits; if there is a lyric change; the term of the license (normally life of copyright); the territory of the license (the world or only certain countries); and whether there is a guarantee that the song will be used on a soundtrack album or released as a single.

The synchronization fees charged by music publishers are usually between $12,000 and $45,000 (with the majority between $15,000 and $40,000). On occasion, a music publisher will reduce the synchronization fee for a song if the producer guarantees that there is a soundtrack album commitment by a major label and that the song being licensed for the film will be on the album.

TELEVISION SERIES

SERIES	SONG USED
The Simpsons	"The X-Files Theme"
Married with Children	"Love and Marriage"
Grace Under Fire	"Lady Madonna"
Seinfeld	"The Way We Were"
NYPD Blue	"My Sharona"
Friends	"Someone to Watch Over Me"

When a producer wants to use an existing song in a television program, weekly series, special, miniseries or made-for-TV movie, permission must, with few exceptions, be secured from the music publisher of the song. The producer of the show will decide on how the song is to be used (e.g., background vocal or instrumental, sung by a character on camera, over the opening or ending credits) and the type of media over which the program will be broadcast (e.g., free television, pay television, basic cable). The producer or its music clearance representative will then contact the publisher of the composition, describe how the song will be used, ask for a specified period of time to use the song in the program (usually from three years to life of copyright), define the territory in which the program may be broadcast (usually the world but may be limited to only specified countries), negotiate a fee and then sign a synchronization license.

Since home video is an important ancillary market for TV programming, negotiations will take place for home use as well. Considering that some TV programs (normally miniseries and made-for-TV movies) are also released in motion picture theaters in countries outside the United States, the producer may also request such rights and negotiate additional fees for non-television uses. And since many television programs are eventually broadcast in media other than that on which they were initially aired (e.g., a pay-television program being broadcast on free over-the-air stations), a producer may also request prices for a wide range of additional options. Synchronization fees usually range from $900 to over $1,500 for a five-year worldwide "free television" license for the use of one song in a series and from $6,000 to over $10,000 for life of copyright licenses and "all television" licenses.

In most countries outside the United States, motion picture theaters are required to pay performance royalties for music used in theatrically distributed films. These fees are collected by the local performance rights society in each country which, in turn, distributes royalties to the writers and publishers of music contained in the films distributed in their territories. Because of the worldwide appeal of many motion pictures, it is not unusual for successful films to generate between $50,000 and $200,000 in theater performance royalties.

ADVERTISING AND COMMERCIALS

PRODUCT	SONG USED
American Express	"Imagine"
Microsoft	"Start Me Up"
Budweiser	"Stayin' Alive"
United Airlines	"Rhapsody in Blue"
Mercedes Benz	"(Oh Lord Won't You Buy Me A) Mercedes Benz"

One of the more lucrative sources of income for the songwriter and music publisher is the use of songs in radio and television commercials. The fees paid by advertising agencies and their clients for commercials can be substantial (from $75,000 to over $500,000 per year for successful songs), depending upon whether it is a radio or TV commercial, a national or limited territory campaign (e.g., the United States vs. only New York and New Jersey) and whether there are options for other countries of the world (e.g., an option to extend the commercial campaign into Canada, Europe, etc.).

On occasion, an advertising agency will ask for a non-broadcast test period during which it will test the commercial in shopping malls, inter-agency screenings, etc. to see if the pairing of the song and the product is effective. Fees for this off-air testing range from $3,000 to over $10,000 and the term is normally from a few weeks to four months. Other times, an agency will request a limited broadcast test period (during which a commercial will actually be aired) for a specified regional market (e.g., television in Florida only for two months or a three-month test in cities which contain not more than 10% of the total U.S. population). Fees for these types of regional broadcast test periods normally range from $5,000 to over $30,000 depending on, among other things, the duration of the test period, the importance of the song, the product being advertised and whether there has been a lyric change.

Certain major advertisers may request total exclusivity (all products as opposed to just similar or competing products) from a publisher, and the fees for this type of grant can be substantial for a recent hit song or well-known standard (from $125,000 to $500,000). However, most commercial licensing agreements restrict the music publisher from licensing the song to commercials featuring only competing, incompatible or similar products. For example, a beer commercial may restrict the writer or publisher from licensing the same song for another alcoholic beverage commercial but will allow licensing for use in a computer or automobile advertising campaign.

HOME VIDEO

The sale of videos represents a significant source of revenue for the music publisher and songwriter. Home video licensing is normally handled in one of three ways: (a) A Per Video Royalty: The royalty paid is based on a set rate (usually from 10 cents to 15 cents per song) for each video sold. For example, if 100,000 cassettes are sold and a particular song has a 10 cent royalty, the payment will be $10,000; (b) One Time Buy-Out: Many video distributors demand that publishers accept a one time buy-out fee for all video rights regardless of how many videos might be sold; and (c) Roll-Over Advance: The producer or video distributor pays a certain advance for a specified number of videos with additional pre-determined sums paid as additional sales plateaus are achieved (e.g, $10,000 for the first 100,000 units and an additional $10,000 for each additional 100,000 units sold).

BROADWAY MUSICALS

The Phantom of the Opera
Cats
A Chorus Line
Les Miserables
My Fair Lady
Rent

A very lucrative market for a song can be its use in a Broadway show. If the play is a hit, the income from live theatrical performances, soundtrack albums, singles, motion picture rights, touring productions, home videocassettes, sheet music and stock and amateur production rights can mean hundreds of thousands of dollars to the songwriter and music publisher. However, considering that the vast majority of musicals presented on Broadway lose all if not most of the money invested and that getting a song into a Broadway play is extremely difficult, this is an area with which most songwriters and publishers, unless they are involved with songs actually created for the play, will have very little or no contact.

Music and lyric royalties for Broadway and first-class national touring productions are 3% of the weekly gross box office receipts until all the costs of producing the Broadway musical have been recovered by the investors and 4% thereafter if a percentage royalty is negotiated (which can mean from $200,000 to over $10,000,000 per year for all songs in a hit show) or a fixed dollar amount per week (from $250 to $750 regardless of the success of the play) if a non-percentage royalty is agreed to.

INSTRUMENTAL RECORDINGS OF POPULAR SONGS/SING-ALONGS/KARAOKE

Certain companies specialize in selling instrumental versions of hit songs (accompanied by printed lyrics or lead sheets) so amateur singers can add their own voices to such tapes. Royalties payable to writers and publishers in this area are: (i) The statutory mechanical record royalty rate per song for each tape distributed; and (ii) a negotiated penny rate for each lyric sheet of the song included with a tape. A number of firms also market video versions of the sing-along (or "record your own version of a hit song") concept with the lyrics and music contained on either a laser disc, video disc or videocassette. Royalties paid for such uses are sometimes calculated on the wholesale price of each disc with all songs sharing the aggregate royalty on a pro-rata basis. It is more common, however, for a writer and publisher to charge a set penny royalty (e.g., from 12 cents to 14 cents per song for each sing-a-long disc or tape distributed).

In addition, there is usually a one-time fee given to each publisher of between $250 and $300 for the right to include the song in the video (sometimes referred to as a "fixation fee"). The licenses in this area normally last for ten years but can be longer and are usually for the world (or the world excluding Japan). It is also common to receive an upfront advance for the initial 5,000 to 7,500 copies distributed (e.g., $600 to $900 if you are licensing at a 12 cent rate or $700 to $1,050 at a 14 cent rate).

LYRIC REPRINTS IN NOVELS OR NONFICTION BOOKS

Another source of income for the songwriter and music publisher is the use of song lyrics in scenes contained in nonfiction books or novels. All fees are dependent on the number of lines being used (e.g., two lines, ten lines, whole song, etc.), the context in which the song is being used, the importance of the song, the number of other song lyrics being used in the book, the total budget for said clearances, the territory in which the book will be distributed and whether both English and foreign translation versions are being requested. Normal fees for hardcover books are between $250 to over $1,000 with additional fees required for paperback and book club editions. In addition, information on the plot of the book, the publisher and the context in which a lyric is to be used is normally requested by the music publisher prior to approval being given.

SHEET MUSIC AND FOLIOS

At one time, the sale of sheet music was a major source of income for the music publisher. With the increasing monies that can be earned from the sale of records, cassettes and CDs, the use of songs in commercials, synchronization fees from motion picture and television uses and the performance royalties received from ASCAP, BMI and their foreign affiliates, this area has become a less important source of income. Yet it remains a valuable area as it can provide a steady stream of income and a substantial infusion of royalties. For example, successful songs may be distributed in a multitude of configurations for piano solo, piano duet, guitar, regular concert band, jazz ensemble, vocal solo, choral arrangement, electronic piano, organ solo and as part of a "Best Of," "Songs by a Particular Writer," "Songs of a Particular Era" or "Songs From a Motion Picture" series.

MUSIC BOXES

There are a number of music box manufacturers throughout the world who, in addition to using public domain compositions, also utilize copyrighted songs in their product lines. These uses usually concentrate on songs whose melodies are very well-known or have a seasonal message such as a "White Christmas" or "I'll Be Home for Christmas." These uses are treated as a mechanical license with the fees per box being either a full statutory rate or, if the music box manufacturer can negotiate such, a lesser penny rate. Even though the retail price of music boxes can be somewhat substantial, hundreds of thousands are sold each year and, for the hit song with a strong melody, the royalties can be significant.

CD-ROM/MULTIMEDIA AUDIOVISUAL CONFIGURATIONS

Most licenses for multimedia use are either on a buy-out basis (e.g., a certain amount of money upfront regardless of the number of units that might be sold) or on a per unit or roll-over advance basis much like the arrangements in the videocassette and laser disc area (e.g., 10 cents to 14 cents per song per unit or $1,000 to $1,400 for each 10,000 units sold).

RECORDING ARTIST ROYALTIES

Artist royalties usually range from 10% to 25% of the suggested retail price for top line albums with deductions being made for album packaging costs. For example, if a songwriter/artist has a 16% royalty, a 25% packaging deduction and sells 3,000,000 CDs in the United States of a $17 suggested retail priced album, the basic calculations would look like this:

$17.00	CD retail price
× 25%	Packaging deduction
$ 4.25	Dollar deduction
$17.00	CD retail price
−4.25	Packaging deduction
$12.75	Royalty base
× 16%	Artist royalty %
$2.04	Artist royalty
×3,000,000	Album sales
$6,120,000	Artist royalties

Recording artist royalties are extremely complex, but the above illustration presents the basic principles involved. You need to be aware that there exist a number of issues, including but not limited to free or promotional goods, reserve accounts, return privileges, midline, budget line, record club and foreign reductions, 90% sale provisions, new technology rate reductions (which can reduce CD royalties), cut-out and surplus copy provisions, video costs, tour support and promotion expenses, album recording costs, advances and controlled composition clauses which affect the monies a songwriter/recording artist receives.

The world of songwriting and music publishing may be complex, but it's far from mysterious. Just as every other business has its particular rules, special ways of conducting business and unique income-generating areas, so too does the business of songwriting. It's important to know where your income comes from and how it's generated in order to get the best deal when signing a contract. Even though the music business is based on creativity, it's still a business, and knowledge of its inner workings is one of the keys to a lasting, productive and financially rewarding career.

This article is based on information contained in the book *Music, Money, and Success: The Insider's Guide to the Music Industry*, written by Jeffrey Brabec and Todd Brabec (published by Schirmer Books, an imprint of Simon & Schuster Macmillan).

IMPORTANT INFORMATION ON MARKET LISTINGS

- Although every listing in *Songwriter's Market* is updated, verified or researched prior to publication, some changes are bound to occur between publication and the time you contact any listing.
- Listings are based on interviews and questionnaires. They are not advertisements, nor are markets reported here necessarily endorsed by the editor.
- Companies that appeared in the 1997 edition of *Songwriter's Market*, but do not appear this year, are listed in the General Index at the back of the book along with a code explaining why they do not appear in this edition.
- A word of warning. Don't pay to have your song published and/or recorded or to have your lyrics—or a poem—set to music. Read "Ripoffs" in The Business of Songwriting section to learn how to recognize and protect yourself from the "song shark."
- Songwriter's Market *reserves the right to exclude any listing which does not meet its requirements.*

KEY TO SYMBOLS AND ABBREVIATIONS

‡ new listing in all sections and indexes
SASE—self-addressed, stamped envelope
SAE—self-addressed envelope
IRC—International Reply Coupon, for use in countries other than your own.

(For definitions of terms and abbreviations relating specifically to the music industry, see the Glossary in the back of the book.)

COMPLAINT PROCEDURE

If you feel you have not been treated fairly by a listing in *Songwriter's Market*, we advise you to take the following steps:

- First try to contact the listing. Sometimes one phone call or a letter can quickly clear up the matter.
- Document all your correspondence with the listing. When you write to us with a complaint, provide the details of your submission, the date of your first contact with the listing and the nature of your subsequent correspondence.
- We will enter your letter into our files and attempt to contact the listing.
- The number and severity of complaints will be considered in our decision whether or not to delete the listing from the next edition.

The Markets

Music Publishers

Finding songs and getting them recorded—that's the main function of a music publisher. Working as an advocate for you and your songs, a music publisher serves as a song plugger, administrator, networking resource and more. The knowledge and personal contacts a music publisher can provide may be the most valuable resources available for a songwriter just starting in the music business.

Music publishers attempt to derive income from a song through recordings, use in TV and film soundtracks and other areas. While this is their primary function, music publishers also handle administrative tasks such as copyrighting songs, collecting royalties for the songwriter, negotiating and issuing synchronization licenses for use of music in films, arranging and administering foreign rights, and producing new demos of the music submitted to them. In a small, independent publishing company, one or two people may provide all of these services. Larger publishing companies are more likely to be divided into the following departments: creative (or professional), copyright, licensing, legal affairs, royalty, accounting and foreign.

The creative department is responsible for finding talented writers and signing them to the company. Once a writer is signed, it is up to the creative department to develop and nurture the writer so he will write songs that will create income for the company. Staff members help put writers together to form collaborative teams. And, perhaps most important, the creative department is responsible for getting songs recorded by other artists and used in film and other media that will expose the song to the public. The head of the creative department, usually called the professional manager, is charged with locating talented writers for the company. Once a writer is signed, the professional manager arranges for a demo to be made of the writer's songs. Even though a writer may already have recorded his own demo, the publisher will often re-demo the songs using established studio musicians in an effort to produce the highest-quality demo possible.

Once a demo is produced, the professional manager begins shopping the song to various outlets. He may try to get the song recorded by a top artist on his or her next album or get the song used in an upcoming film. The professional manager uses all the contacts and leads he has to get the writer's songs recorded by as many artists as possible. Therefore, he must be able to deal efficiently and effectively with people in other segments of the music industry, including A&R personnel, producers, distributors, managers and lawyers. Through these contacts, he can find out what artists are looking for new material, and who may be interested in recording one of the writer's songs. The professional manager and those working with him must have extensive knowledge of all segments of the music industry.

After a writer's songs are recorded, the other departments at the publishing company come into play. The licensing and copyright departments are responsible for issuing any licenses for use of the writer's songs in film or TV, and for filing various forms with the copyright office. The legal affairs department works with the professional department in negotiating contracts with its writers. The royalty and accounting departments are responsible for ensuring the writer is receiving the proper royalty rate as specified in the contract, and that statements are mailed to the writer promptly. Finally, the foreign department's role is to oversee any publishing activities outside of the United States, and to make sure a writer is being paid for any uses of his material in foreign countries.

LOCATING A MUSIC PUBLISHER

How do you go about finding a music publisher that will work well for you? First, you must find out what kind of music a publisher handles. If a particular publisher works mostly with alternative music and you're a country songwriter, the contacts he has within the industry will hardly be beneficial to you. You must find a publisher suited to the type of music you write. Each listing in this section details the type of music that publisher is most interested in; the music types appear in boldface to make them easier to locate. You will also want to refer to the Category Index at the end of this section, which lists companies by the type of music they work with.

Do your research!

It's important to study the market and do research to identify which companies to submit to. Are you targeting a specific artist to sing your songs? If so, find out if that artist even considers outside material. Get a copy of the artist's latest album, and see who wrote most of the songs. If they were all written by the artist, he's probably not interested in hearing material from outside writers. If the songs were written by a variety of different writers, however, he may be open to hearing new songs. Check the album liner notes, which will list the name of the publishers of each writer. These publishers obviously have had luck pitching songs to the artist, and they may be able to get your songs to that artist as well. If the artist you're interested in has a recent hit on the *Billboard* charts, the publisher of that song will be listed in the "Hot 100 A-Z" index. Carefully choosing which publishers will work best for the material you write may take time, but it will only increase your chances of getting your songs heard. "Shotgunning" your demo packages (sending out many packages without regard for music preference or submission policy) not only is a waste of time and money, but it may also label you as an unprofessional songwriter with no regard for the workings and policies of the music business.

Once you've found some companies that may be interested in your work, find out what songs have been successfully handled by those publishers. Most publishers are happy to provide you with this information in order to attract high-quality material. Ask the publisher for the names of some of their staff writers, and give them a call. Ask them their opinion of how the publisher works. Keep in mind as you're researching music publishers how you get along with them personally. If you can't work with a publisher on a personal level, chances are your material won't be represented as you would like it to be. A publisher can become your most valuable contact to all other segments of the music industry, so it's important to find someone you can trust and feel comfortable with.

Also consider the size of the publishing company. The publishing affiliates of the major music conglomerates are huge, handling catalogs of thousands of songs by hundreds of songwriters. Unless you are an established songwriter, your songs probably won't receive enough attention from such large companies. Smaller, independent publishers offer several advantages. First, independent music publishers are located all over the country, making it easier for you to work face-to-face rather than by mail or phone. Smaller companies usually aren't affiliated with a particular record company, and are therefore able to pitch your songs to many different labels and acts. Independent music publishers are usually interested in a smaller range of music, allowing you to target your submissions more accurately. The most obvious advantage to working with a smaller publisher is the personal attention they can bring to you and your songs. With a smaller roster of artists to work with, the independent music publisher is able to concentrate more time and effort on each particular project.

SUBMITTING MATERIAL TO A PUBLISHER

When submitting material to a publisher, always keep in mind that a professional, courteous manner goes a long way in making a good impression. When you submit a demo through the mail, make sure your package is neat and meets the particular needs of the publisher. Review each publisher's submission policy carefully, and follow it to the letter. Disregarding this information will only make you look like an amateur in the eyes of the company you're submitting to. (For more detailed information on submitting your material, see Demo FAQs on page 12 and Getting Started on page 6.)

Listings of companies in countries other than the U.S. feature the name of the country in bold type. You will find an alphabetical list of these companies at the back of the book, along with an index of publishers by state.

PUBLISHING CONTRACTS

Once you've located a publisher you like and he's interested in shopping your work, it's time to consider the publishing contract—an agreement in which a songwriter grants certain rights to a publisher for one or more songs. The contract specifies any advances offered to the writer, the rights that will be transferred to the publisher, the royalties a songwriter is to receive and the length of time the contract is valid. When a contract is signed, a publisher will ask for a 50-50 split with the writer. This is standard industry practice; the publisher is taking that 50% to cover the overhead costs of running his business and for the work he's doing to get your songs recorded. It is always a good idea to have a publishing contract (or any music business contract) reviewed by a competent entertainment lawyer. There is no "standard" publishing contract, and each company offers different provisions for their writers. Make sure you ask questions about anything you don't understand, especially if you're new in the business. Songwriter organizations such as the Songwriters Guild of America provide contract review services, and can help you learn about music business language and what constitutes a fair music publishing contract

When signing a contract, it's important to be aware of the music industry's unethical practitioners. The "song shark," as he's called, makes his living by asking a songwriter to pay to have a song published. The shark will ask for money to demo a song and promote it to radio stations; he may also ask for more than the standard 50% publisher's share or ask you to give up all rights to a song in order to have it published. Although none of these practices is illegal, it's certainly not ethical, and no successful publisher uses these methods. *Songwriter's Market* works to list only honest companies interested in hearing new material. (For more on "song sharks," see The Business of Songwriting on page 16.)

ABALONE PUBLISHING, 26257 Regency Club Dr., Suite 6, Warren MI 48089-4125. Music Director: Jack Timmons. Music publisher and record company (L.A. Records). Estab. 1984. Publishes 20-30 songs/year; publishes 20-30 new songwriters/year. Hires staff songwriters. Pays standard royalty.
Affiliate(s): BGM Publishing, AL-KY Music, Bubba Music (BMI).
• Abalone's record label, L.A. Records, is listed in the Record Companies section.
How to Contact: Submit demo tape by mail. Unsolicited submissions are OK. Prefers cassette with 1-5 songs and lyric sheet. "Include cover letter describing your goals." SASE for postage up to 32¢. All others, please include $1 to cover fluctuating postal rates. Reports in 1 month.
Music: Mostly **rock**, **pop** and **alternative**; also **dance**, **pop/rock** and **country**. Published "Shive" (by Al Long), recorded by The Lords (rock); *Taboo* (by S. Stevens), recorded by Harry Carrike (pop); and *Love Junkie* (by K. Simmons), recorded by Slut (alternative), all on L.A. Records.
Tips: "Write what you feel, however, don't stray too far from the trends that are currently popular. Lyrical content should depict a definite story line and paint an accurate picture in the listener's mind."

AIM HIGH MUSIC COMPANY (ASCAP), 1300 Division St., Suite #200, Nashville TN 37203. (615)242-4722. (800)767-4984. Fax: (615)242-1177. E-mail: www.platinumr@aol.com. Producer: Robert Metzgar. Music publisher and record company (Platinum Plus Records). Estab. 1971. Publishes 250 songs/year; publishes 5-6 new songwriters/year. Hires staff writers. "Our company pays 100% to all songwriters."
Affiliate(s): Bobby & Billy Music (BMI), Billy Ray Music (BMI), Club Platinum Music (BMI).

• See the listings for Platinum Plus Records in the Record Companies section, Capitol Management and Talent in the Managers and Booking Agents section and Capitol Ad, Management and Talent Group in the Record Producers section.

How to Contact: Submit demo tape by mail. Unsolicited submissions are OK. Prefers cassette or VHS videocassette with 5-10 songs and lyric sheet. "I like to get to know songwriters personally prior to recording their songs." Does not return material. Reports in 3-4 weeks.

Music: Mostly **country, traditional country** and **pop country**; also **gospel, southern gospel** and **contemporary Christian**. Published *Honky Tonk Christmas* (by Bob Douglass), recorded by George Jones on MCA Records; *My Miss America* (by Bob Douglass), recorded by Carters on Curb Records; and "There By Now" (by T. Tucker), recorded by Le Clerc on Capitol Records.

Tips: "Please let us determine which songs you've written are commercial first and then get them formally recorded as demos."

ALADDIN MUSIC GROUP (BMI), P.O. Box 121738, Nashville TN 37212. (615)726-3556. Contact: A&R Dept. Music publisher. Estab. 1996. Publishes 20 songs/year; publishes 5 new songwriters/year. Hires staff writers. Pays standard royalty.

How to Contact: Submit demo tape by mail. Unsolicited submissions are OK. Prefers cassette with 2 songs and lyric sheet. SASE. Reports in 2-6 weeks.

Music: Mostly **country, rock** and **alternative**; also **blues, gospel** and **contemporary**. Published "If It Takes All Night" (by Ramsey C.), recorded by Ramsey on Kottage Records (country); "Reach Out," written and recorded by Allusion on Aladdin Records (alternative); and "Forever Jerry Lee" (by Neal James), recorded by William Rodel on Alternative Records (rockabilly).

Tips: "Listen and study current trends and try to write advanced versions of those trends. Screen your material very carefully and only submit what you feel is honestly your best. We are looking for quality A-side material with something said in a unique way; for songs and writers with a different edge or approach. Not only do we hope to supply even more material to the major record companies, but we are also looking for songs for possible placement in movies, soundtracks and television programming."

‡MARCUS ALAN MUSIC (BMI), P.O. Box 128132, Nashville TN 37212. (615)826-4146. Fax: (615)826-4141. Contact: Marcus Alan. Music publisher, record company (Music City Sound) and record producer. Estab. 1990. Publishes 20 songs/year; publishes 3-6 new songwriters/year. Hires staff songwriters. Pays standard royalty.

• See the listing for Music City Sound Records in the Record Companies section.

How to Contact: Submit demo tape by mail. Unsolicited submissions are OK. Prefers cassette with 5 songs and lyric sheet. SASE. Reports in 4-6 weeks.

Music: Mostly **country, rock** and **gospel**; also **jazz, pop** and **R&B.** Published *I Know You Hear Me* (by Mark Dreyer/Mark Gray/Beverley Ross), recorded by Englebert Humperdink on Core Music Records (country/R&B); *Me Lovin' You* (by Mark Gray/Randy Carter), recorded by Mark Gray (country); and *Thin Walls* (by Randy Carter/Woody Cochran), recorded by C.J. Riley on Wild Horse Records (country).

ALEXANDER SR. MUSIC (BMI), P.O. Box 8684, Youngstown OH 44507. (330)782-5031. Fax: (330)782-6954. A&R: LaVerne Chambers. Music publisher, record company (LRG Records), music consulting, distribution and promotional services and record producer. Estab. 1992. Publishes 12-22 songs/year; publishes 2-4 new songwriters/year. Pays standard royalty.

How to Contact: Write first and obtain permission to submit. Prefers cassette with 4 songs and lyric sheet. "We will accept finished masters (cassette or CD) for review." SASE. Reports in 2 months. "No phone calls or faxes please."

Music: Mostly **contemporary jazz, urban Christian** and **black gospel**; also **R&B**. Published *Phoenix, It Will Be Alright* and *No Greater Love*, all written and recorded by Darryl Alexander on LRG Records (jazz).

Tips: "Submit your best songs and follow submission guidelines. Finished masters open up additional possibilities. Lead sheets may be requested for material we are interested in. Must have SASE if you wish to have cassette returned. No phone calls, please."

ALEXIS (ASCAP), P.O. Box 532, Malibu CA 90265. (213)463-5998. President: Lee Magid. Music publisher, record company, personal management firm, and record and video producer. Member AIMP. Estab. 1950. Publishes 50 songs/year; publishes 20-50 new songwriters/year. Pays standard royalty.

Affiliate(s): Marvelle (BMI), Lou-Lee (BMI), D.R. Music (ASCAP) and Gabal (SESAC).
How to Contact: Submit a demo tape by mail. Unsolicited submissions are OK. Prefers cassette or VHS videocassette with 1-3 songs and lyric sheet. "Try to make demo as clear as possible—guitar or piano should be sufficient. A full rhythm and vocal demo is always better." Does not return material. Reports in 6-8 weeks "if interested."
Music: Mostly **R&B**, **jazz**, **MOR**, **pop** and **gospel**; also **blues**, **church/religious**, **country**, **dance-oriented**, **folk** and **Latin**. Published "Jesus Is Just Alright" (by Reynolds), recorded by D.C. Talk on Forefront Records (pop); "Blues For the Weepers" (by Rich/Magid), recorded by Lou Rawls on Capitol Records (pop/blues); and "What Shall I Do" (by Q. Fielding), recorded by Tramaine Hawkins on EMI/Sparrow Records (ballad).
Tips: "Try to create a good demo, vocally and musically. A good home-recorded tape will do."

AL-KY MUSIC (BMI), 6472 Seven Mile, South Lyon MI 48178. Phone/fax: (810)486-0505. Producer: J.D. Dudick. Music publisher, record company (Ruffcut Productions) and record producer. Estab. 1994. Publishes 10-15 songs/year; publishes 3-5 new songwriters/year. Pays standard royalty.

- See the listings for Ruffcut Productions in the Record Companies section and J.D. Dudick in the Record Producers section.

How to Contact: Submit demo tape by mail. Unsolicited submissions are OK. Prefers cassette with 3 songs and lyric sheet. Does not return material. Reports in 2 months.
Music: Mostly **modern rock**, **young country** and **alternative**; also **dance**, **pop** and **blues**. Published *Changes* (by Chris Pierce), recorded by "Q" (rock); *Itchin*, written and recorded by Laya, both on Ruffcut Records; and *Dreams Die Hard* (by Bil-Tol), recorded by Cidyzoo on Vehicle Garage Records.

ALL ROCK MUSIC, P.O. Box 2296, Rotterdam 3000 CG **Holland**. Phone: (31) 186-604266. Fax: (32) 1862-604366. President: Cees Klop. Music publisher, record company (Collector Records) and record producer. Estab. 1967. Publishes 50-60 songs/year; publishes several new songwriters/year. Pays standard royalty.
Affiliate(s): All Rock Music (England) and All Rock Music (Belgium).

- See the listings for Collector Records in the Record Companies and Record Producers sections.

How to Contact: Submit demo tape by mail. Unsolicited submissions are OK. Prefers cassette. SAE and IRC. Reports in 1-2 months.
Music: Mostly **'50s rock**, **rockabilly** and **country rock**; also **piano boogie woogie**. Published *Henpecked Daddy*, written and recorded by Ralph Johnson on Collector Records; *Pianorepairmen*, written and recorded by EricJan Oberbeek; and *Grand Hotel*, written and recorded by Rockin' Vincent, both on Down South Records.

ALLEGHENY MUSIC WORKS, 306 Cypress Ave., Johnstown PA 15902. (814)535-3373. Managing Director: Al Rita. Music publisher and record company (Allegheny Records). Estab. 1991. Pays standard royalty.
Affiliate(s): Allegheny Music Works Publishing (ASCAP) and Tuned on Music (BMI).

- See their listing in the Record Companies section.

How to Contact: Submit demo tape by mail. Unsolicited submissions are OK. Prefers cassette with 3 songs and lyric or lead sheet. SASE. Reports in 2-4 weeks.
Music: Mostly **country**; also **pop**, **A/C**, **R&B** and **inspirational**. Published "Sleeping Back to Back" (by Tony Rast/Bobby Rush), recorded by Tom Woodard on Pharoah Int'l. Records (country); "Angel on Fire" (by William Wilkinson), recorded by Lisa Whitney; and "Tommy's Tattoos" (by Richard Dale Johnson), recorded by James Grandy on WIR Records.
Tips: "We would like to receive more material written for female artists. Currently, we are getting in on average ten 'male' songs to one 'female' song."

ALLISONGS INC. (BMI, ASCAP), 1603 Horton Ave., Nashville TN 37212. (615)292-9899. President: Jim Allison. Music publisher, record company (ARIA Records) and record producer (Jim Allison). Estab. 1985. Publishes 50 songs/year. Pays standard royalty.

‡ **THE DOUBLE DAGGER** before a listing indicates that the listing is new in this edition.

Affiliate(s): Jim's Allisongs (BMI) and Annie Green Eyes Music (BMI).

- Reba McEntire's "What Am I Gonna Do About You," published by AlliSongs, Inc., was included on her triple-platinum album, *Greatest Hits*.

How to Contact: Submit demo tape by mail. Unsolicited submissions are OK. Send chrome cassette and lyric sheet. Does not return material. Reports in 1 month only if interested.
Music: Mostly **country**. Published "Fade To Blue" (by Reeves/Scott/Allison), recorded by LeAnn Rimes on Curb Records (country); "Preservation of the Wild Life" (by Allison/Young), recorded by Earl Thomas Conley on RCA Records (country); and "Against My Will" (by Hogan), recorded by Brenda Lee on Warner Bros. Records (pop).
Tips: "Send your best—we will contact you if interested."

‡ALMO MUSIC CORP., 360 N. LaCienega Blvd., Los Angeles CA 90048. (310)289-3500. (310)289-4000. Attn: A&R. Music publisher and record company.

- See the listing for Almo Sounds in the Record Companies section.

How to Contact: Submit demo tape by mail. Unsolicited submissions are OK. Prefers cassette with 3 songs maximum and lyric sheet.
Music: Published "Don't Let Go (Love)" (by Organized Noize/A. Martin/I. Matias/M. Etheridge), recorded by En Vogue on Eastwest Records (from the soundtrack *Set It Off*); and "It's All About U" (by Allstar/A. Martin/A. Burroughs), recorded by SWV on RCA Records. Other artists include Craig Wiseman.

ALPHA MUSIC INC. (BMI), 747 Chestnut Ridge Rd., Chestnut Ridge NY 10977. (914)356-0800. Fax: (914)356-0895. E-mail: trfemail@aol.com. Contact: Michael Nurko. Music publisher. Estab. 1931. Pays standard royalty.
Affiliate(s): Dorian Music Corp. (ASCAP), TRF Music Inc.
How to Contact: Submit demo tape by mail. Unsolicited submissions are OK. Prefers audio cassette. Does not return material. Reports in 2-4 months.
Music: All categories, mainly **instrumental** and **acoustic**; also **theme music** for television and film. "Have published over 50,000 titles since 1931."

AMEN, INC., (formerly Manny Music), 2035 Pleasanton Rd., San Antonio TX 78221-1306. (210)932-AMEN. Fax: (210)932-1888. E-mail: amen-inc.@postoffice.worldnet.att.net. Music publisher, record company (AMC Records). Estab. 1963. Pays standard royalty.
Affiliate(s): CITA Music (BMI).
How to Contact: Submit demo tape by mail. Unsolicited submissions are OK. Prefers cassette and lyric sheet. "Allow three to four weeks before calling to inquire about submission." SASE. Reports in 12-16 weeks.
Music: Evangelical Christian gospel regardless of presentation, whether Spanish, English or bilingual. Published "Imponme Tus Manos" (by Jesus Yorba Garcia), recorded by Rudy Guerra; "Jesucristo" (by Enrique Alvarez), recorded by Kiko Alvarez; and "Hey, Hey, Hey" (by Manny R. Guerra), all on AMC Records.

‡AMERICATONE INTERNATIONAL, 1817 Loch Lomond Way, Las Vegas NV 89102-4437. (702)384-0030. Fax: (702) 382-1926. President: Joe Jan Jaros. Estab. 1975. Publishes 25 songs/year. Pays variable royalty.
Affiliate(s): Americatone Records International, Christy Records International USA, Rambolt Music International (ASCAP).

- See the listing for Americatone Records International in the Record Companies section.

How to Contact: Submit demo tape by mail. Unsolicited submissions OK. Prefers cassettes, "studio production with top sound recordings." SASE. Reports in 1 month.
Music: Mostly **country**, **R&B**, **Spanish** and **classic ballads**. Published "Romantic Music," written and recorded by Chuck Mymit; "Explosion" (by Ray Sykora), recorded by Sam Trippe; and "From Las Vegas" (by Ladd Staide), recorded by Robert Martin, all on Americatone International Records.

AMIRON MUSIC (ASCAP), Dept. SM, 20531 Plummer St., Chatsworth CA 91311. (818)998-0443. Manager: A. Sullivan. Music publisher, record company, record producer and manager. Estab. 1970. Publishes 2-4 songs/year; publishes 1-2 new songwriters/year. Pays standard royalty.
Affiliate(s): Aztex Productions and Copan Music (BMI).

- See the listing for AKO Production in the Record Producers section.

How to Contact: Prefers cassette or videocassette with any number songs and lyric sheet. SASE. Reports in 10 weeks.
Music: Easy listening, **MOR**, **progressive**, **R&B**, **rock** and **top 40/pop**. Published "Let's Work It Out"

(by F. Cruz), recorded by Gangs Back; and "Try Me," written and recorded by Sana Christian, both on AKO Records (pop); and "Boys Take Your Mind Off Things" (by G. Litvak), recorded by Staunton on Les Disques Records (pop).

‡ANCY MUSIC GROUP (BMI), 1023 17th Ave., Suite 101, Nashville TN 37212. (615)321-5707. Fax: (615)320-3930. E-mail: ancymusic@earthlink.net. President: Jessie Renfroe, Sr. Director of A&R: Mitzi Mason. Music publisher and record company (Ancy Records). Estab. 1985. Hires staff songwriters. Pays standard royalty.

- See the listing for Ancy Records in the Record Companies section.

How to Contact: Submit demo tape by mail. Unsolicited submissions are OK. Prefers cassette, VHS videocassette, CD and/or lyric sheet. Does not return material. Reports in 3-4 weeks if interested.
Music: Mostly **country**, **R&B/blues**, **Christian/gospel** and **pop/rock/rap**. Published "The Voice on the Jukebox" (by Tommy Green/Rick Cogle), recorded by Jack Ferrell; and "Through Michael's Eyes" (by Gammeter/Christensen), recorded by Phyllis Christensen, both on Ancy Records (country).

ANDYLAND MUSIC (ASCAP), (formerly Baylor-Eselby Music), 106½ S. Urbana Ave., Urbana IL 61801. (217)384-0015. Fax: (217)355-9057. E-mail: hammerhd@prairienet.org. President: Andy Baylor. Music publisher and music producer (commercial music, jingles, etc.). Estab. 1995. Publishes 25 songs/year; publishes 2 new songwriters/year. Pays standard royalty.
How to Contact: Submit demo tape by mail. Unsolicited submissions are OK. Prefers cassette. Does not return material.
Music: Mostly **contemporary** and **rock**. Published "Achieving the Summit" (by Andy Baylor) (commercial); "Surf's Up" (by Andy Baylor/Buzzy Eselby) (commercial); and "Lou Henson Show" (by Andy Baylor) (theme show music).

ANTELOPE PUBLISHING INC., P.O. Box 55, Rowayton CT 06853. President: Tony LaVorgna. Music publisher. Estab. 1982. Publishes 5-10 new songs/year; publishes 3-5 new songwriters/year. Pays standard royalty.
How to Contact: Submit demo tape by mail. Unsolicited submissions are OK. Prefers cassette with lead sheet and résumé. Does not return material. Reports in 1 month "only if interested."
Music: Only **bebop** and **MOR**. Published "Somewhere Near" (by S. Lavorgina), recorded by Jeri Brown on Just N Time Records; "Dance Samba" (by Dan Wall), recorded by T. LaVorgna on Antelope Records (MOR); and *The Train* (by Alice Schweitzer), recorded by Swing Fever on Alto Sound Records.

AQUARIUS PUBLISHING, Servitengasse 24, Vienna A-1090 **Austria**. (+43)1-707-37-10. Fax:(+43)1-707-84-22. Owner: Peter Jordan. Music publisher and record company (World Int'l Records). Estab. 1987. Publishes 100-200 songs/year; publishes 10 new songwriters/year.
How to Contact: Submit demo tape by mail. Unsolicited submissions are OK. Prefers cassette with up to 10 songs. "Lyric sheets not important; send photo of artist." Does not return material. Reports in 2-4 weeks.
Music: Mostly **country, pop** and **rock/ballads**; also **folk, instrumental** and **commercial**. Published *If God Don't Like Country Music* (by T. Lenartz/W. Dewberry), recorded by Tom Woodward; *Gone, Gone, Gone Travellin' Man*, written and recorded by Carroll Baker; and *Don't Do The Crime* (by F.B. Whitley), recorded by Toni Whitley, all on WIR Records.

‡ARAS MUSIC (ASCAP), P.O. Box 320942, Cocoa Beach FL 32932-0942. (888)257-3401. E-mail: melodyco@aol.com. Website: http://members.aol.com/MelodyCo/index.html. A&R Director: Amy L. Young. Music publisher. Estab. 1996. Pays standard royalty.
Affiliate(s): SAV Music (BMI) and Pardo Music (SESAC).
How to Contact: Submit demo tape by mail. Unsolicited submissions are OK. Prefers cassette with 3 songs and lyric sheet. SASE. "Make sure enough postage is included to return tape." Reports in 2-3 months.
Music: Mostly **country**, **contemporary Christian** and **gospel**.

‡ARTISTIC NOISE PUBLISHING (BMI), P.O. Box 230914, Grand Rapids MI 49523-0914. (616)281-0617. Owner: Darryl Shanon Holt. Music publisher, record company (Artistic Noise) and record producer. Estab. 1996. Publishes 12-20 songs/year; publishes 0-1 new songwriters/year. Pays standard royalty.

- See the listings for Artistic Noise in the Record Companies and Record Producers sections.

How to Contact: Write or submit demo tape by mail. Unsolicited submissions are OK. Prefers cassette with 3-10 songs and lyric sheet. Does not return material. Reports in 2 months.
Music: Mostly **pop**, **dance** and **R&B**; also **alternative, ballads** and **techno**. Published *This Is Love* (pop

alternative); *Why* (ballad); and *My Car*, all written and recorded by Darryl Shanon Holt on Artistic Noise.

AUDIO IMAGES TWO THOUSAND MUSIC PUBLISHING (BMI), P.O. Box 250806, Holly Hill FL 32125-0806. (904)238-3820. Contact: D.L. Carter, submissions department. Music publisher. Estab. 1995. Pays standard royalty.
Affiliate(s): Sun Queen Publishing (ASCAP).
How to Contact: Write first and obtain permission to submit. "No phone calls, please." Does not return material. Reports in 4-6 weeks.
Music: Mostly **MOR**, **country** and **contemporary Christian**; also **gospel**. Published "Santa Claus Can't Get Down My Chimney" (by Bill Barber), recorded by Ana Cristina Randolph; "Don't Let The Christmas Lights Go Out Tonight" (by Robert L. Speegle), recorded by Tom Walker; and "Speak Lord" (by James D. Barnett), recorded by The Sunshine Singers, all on BJ's Records.

AUDIO MUSIC PUBLISHERS (ASCAP), 449 N. Vista St., Los Angeles CA 90036. (213)653-0693. E-mail: unclelenny@aol.com. Contact: Ben Weisman. Music publisher, record company and record producer (The Weisman Production Group). Estab. 1962. Publishes 25 songs/year; publishes 10-15 new songwriters/year. Pays standard royalty.
- See the listing for The Weisman Production Group in the Record Producers section.

How to Contact: Submit a demo tape by mail. Unsolicited submissions are OK. "No permission needed." Prefers cassette with 3-10 songs and lyric sheet. "We do not return unsolicited material without SASE. Don't query first; just send tape." Reports in 4-6 weeks. "We listen; we don't write back. If we like your material we will telephone you."
Music: Mostly **pop**, **R&B**, **rap**, **dance**, **funk**, **soul** and **rock** (all types).

BAD HABITS MUSIC PUBLISHING, P.O. Box 111, London W13 0ZH **England**. Phone: +44 7000 243243. Fax: +44 7000 740 223. Managing Director: John S. Rushton. Music publisher, record company (Bad Habits) and record producer. Estab. 1991. Hires staff songwriters. Royalty varies depending upon type of contract.
Affiliate(s): Great Life Music Publishing (ASCAP) and BHMP (America) (BMI).
How to Contact: Write or call first and obtain permission to submit. Prefers cassette or videocassette with 3 songs. "Include what the writer lyricist wants to do, brief details/aspirations." SAE and IRC. Reports in 2 months.
Music: Mostly **pop/rock/dance**, **soul** and **jazz**; also **classical/opera**, **soundtracks/shows** and **New Age**. Published "Before" (by various) and "Like Me" (by M. Smith), both recorded by EMW on Bad Habits Records; and "Tarzan" (by Van Rhijn), recorded by various artists on Musica Eclectica Records (techno opera).
Tips: "Know your market, and make sure you have created for that market."

BAGATELLE MUSIC PUBLISHING CO. (BMI), P.O. Box 925929, Houston TX 77292. (713)680-2160 or (800)845-6865. President: Byron Benton. Music publisher, record company and record producer. Publishes 40 songs/year; publishes 2 new songwriters/year. Pays standard royalty.
Affiliate(s): Floyd Tillman Publishing Co.
- See the listing for Bagatelle Record Co. in the Record Companies section.

How to Contact: Submit demo tape by mail. Unsolicited submissions are OK. Prefers cassette or videocassette with any number of songs and lyric sheet. SASE.
Music: Mostly **country**; also **gospel** and **blues**. Published "Everything You Touch," written and recorded by Johnny Nelms; "This Is Real" and "Mona from Daytona," written and recorded by Floyd Tillman, all on Bagatelle Records.

BAL & BAL MUSIC PUBLISHING CO. (ASCAP), P.O. Box 369, LaCanada CA 91012-0369. (818)548-1116. President: Adrian P. Bal. Music publisher, record company (Bal Records) and record producer. Member AGAC and AIMP. Estab. 1965. Publishes 2-6 songs/year; publishes 2-4 new songwriters/year. Pays standard royalty.
Affiliate(s): Bal West Music Publishing Co. (BMI).
- See the listing for Bal Records in the Record Producers section.

How to Contact: Submit demo tape by mail. Unsolicited submissions are OK. Prefers cassette with 3 songs and lyric sheet. SASE. Reports in 3 months.
Music: Mostly **MOR**, **country**, **rock** and **gospel**; also **blues**, **church/religious**, **easy listening**, **jazz**, **R&B**, **soul** and **top 40/pop**. Published "Fragile" (by James Jackson), recorded by Kathy Simmons; "Circles of Time," written and recorded by Paul Richards (A/C); and "Special Day," written and recorded by Rhonda Johnson (gospel), all on Bal Records.

‡BARE MINIMUM MUSIC (BMI), P.O. Box 49092, Jacksonville FL 32240. (904)241-3692. Fax: (904)241-4454. E-mail: rimshotrec@aol.com. Creative Director: Michael R. Fitzgerald. Music publisher, record company (Rimshot Records) and recording studio. Estab. 1993. Pays standard royalty.
How to Contact: Submit demo tape by mail. Unsolicited submissions are OK. Prefers cassette, DAT or VHS videocassette with 3-5 songs and lyric sheet. Does not return material. Reports in 3-4 weeks.
Music: Mostly **rock**, **adult alternative** and **R&B**. Artists include Trinket (modern rock) and Chain of Fools (funk rock).

BARKIN' FOE THE MASTER'S BONE, 1111 Elm St. #520, Cincinnati OH 45210-2271. Office Manager: Kevin Curtis. Music publisher. Estab. 1989. Publishes 16 songs/year; publishes 2 new songwriters/year. Pays standard royalty.
Affiliate(s): Beat Box Music (ASCAP) and Feltstar (BMI).
How to Contact: Submit demo tape by mail. Unsolicited submissions are OK. Prefers cassette or VHS videocassette with 3 songs. SASE. Reports in 2 weeks.
Music: Mostly **country**, **soft rock** and **pop**; also **soul**, **gospel** and **rap**. Published "We Know Why the Caged Bird Sings" (by Kevin Curtis), recorded by Concept on God's Garden Records; "Come Away" and "Bed of Lies" (by Kevin Curtis), both recorded by Santarr on Warner Bros. Records.

BARREN WOOD PUBLISHING (BMI), Auburn Tower, 2426 Auburn Ave., Dayton OH 45406. Phone/fax: (937)275-4221. E-mail: chris.tanner@worldnet.att.net. Website: http://www.infochase.com/ent/dme/index.html. President: Jack Froschauer. Creative Director: Chris Tanner. Music publisher. Estab. 1992. Publishes 5-6 songs/year; publishes 3-4 new songwriters/year. Pays standard royalty.
Affiliate(s): MerryGold Music Publishing (ASCAP).
- Barren Wood Publishing's record label, Emerald City Records, is listed in the Record Companies section.

How to Contact: Submit demo tape by mail. Unsolicited submissions are OK. Prefers cassette or DAT with 1-4 songs and lyric or lead sheet. "Studio quality demo cassette please." SASE. Reports in 4-6 weeks.
Music: Mostly **country**, **A/C** and **Christian**. Published *I've Got The Lord in Me*, written and recorded by David Schafer with Stephen Seifert (gospel) on Emerald City Records; "Whispers" (by Dale Walton), recorded by Dale Walton's Second Wind on Pork Records (rock); and "Ordinary People" (by Jack Froschauer), recorded by Baxter Road on Iron Gate Records (country).
Tips: "Recognize that songwriting is a business. Present yourself and your material in a professional, businesslike mannner."

BAY RIDGE PUBLISHING CO. (BMI), P.O. Box 5537, Kreole Station, Moss Point MS 39563. (601)475-2098. Estab. 1974. President/Owner: Joe Mitchell.
- See the listing for Missle Records in the Record Companies section.

How to Contact: Write first and obtain permission to submit. Include #10 SASE. "No collect calls; not reviewing unsolicited material."
Music: Mostly **country, hardcore, folk, contemporary, ballads, reggae, world, alternative, gospel, rap, heavy metal, jazz, bluegrass, R&B, soul, MOR, blues, rock** and **pop**. Published "Hirty Flirty Love" and "After The Rain," recorded by Jerry Piper; and "Have You Seen My Baby," written and recorded by Herbert Lacey on Missle Records.

BEARSONGS, Box 944, Birmingham, B16 8UT **England**. Phone: 44-021-454-7020. Managing Director: Jim Simpson. Professional Manager: Clare Jepson-Homer. Music publisher, record producer and record company (Big Bear Records). Member PRS, MCPS. Publishes 25 songs/year; publishes 15-20 new songwriters/year. Pays standard royalty.
- See the listings for Big Bear Records in the Record Companies section and Big Bear in the Record Producers section.

How to Contact: Submit demo tape by mail. Unsolicited submissions are OK. Prefers reel-to-reel or cassette. Does not return material. Reports in 3 months.
Music: **Blues** and **jazz**. Published *Blowing With Bruce* and *Cool Heights* (by Alan Barnes), recorded by Bruce Adams/Alan Barnes Quintet; and *Blues For My Baby* (by Charles Brown), recorded by King Pleasure & The Biscuit Boys, all on Big Bear Records.
Tips: "Have a real interest in jazz, blues, R&B."

BEAVERWOOD AUDIO-VIDEO (BMI), 133 Walton Ferry, Hendersonville TN 37075. (615)824-2820. Fax: (615)824-2833. Owner: Clyde Beavers. Music publisher, record company (Kash Records, JCL Records), record producer, audio-video duplication. Estab. 1976. Pays standard royalty.
Affiliate(s): Jackpot Music (BMI).

How to Contact: Submit demo tape by mail. Unsolicited submissions are OK. Prefers cassette, DAT or videocassette with 1-5 songs. Does not return material.
Music: Mostly **gospel** and **country**. Published "Mary Had a Little Lamb," *Listen to My Story* and *I Heard His Call*, all written and recorded by Lawrence Davis on JCL Records (gospel).

EARL BEECHER PUBLISHING (BMI, ASCAP), P.O. Box 2111, Huntington Beach CA 92647. (714)842-8635. E-mail: ebeecher@csulb.edu. Owner: Earl Beecher. Music publisher, record company (Outstanding and Morrhythm Records) and record producer (Earl Beecher). Estab. 1968. Publishes varying number of songs/year. Pays standard royalty.
How to Contact: Submit demo tape by mail. Unsolicited submissions are OK. "Please do not call in advance." Cassettes only. SASE. Reports in several months.
Music: Pop, **ballads**, **rock**, **gospel** and **country**. Published *Hero*, written and recorded by Ed Branson (country); *This Farm*, written and recorded by Nancy Learn (country); and *Help Me Elvis* (by Doug Koempel), recorded by Memory Bros. (country), all on Morrhythm Records.
Tips: "I am interested mainly in people who want to perform their songs and release albums on one of my labels rather than to submit material to my existing artists."

BERANDOL MUSIC LTD. (BMI), 2600 John St., Unit 220, Markham ON L3R 3W3 **Canada**. (905)475-1848. A&R Director: Ralph Cruickshank. Music publisher, record company (Berandol Records), music print publisher (Music Box Dancer Publications), record producer and distributor. Member CMPA, CIRPA, CRIA. Estab. 1969. Publishes 20-30 songs/year; publishes 5-10 new songwriters/year. Pays standard royalty.

- Berandol Music is also listed in the Record Companies section, and Music Box Dancer Publications is listed in the Music Print Publishers section.

How to Contact: Submit demo tape by mail. Unsolicited submissions are OK. Prefers cassette with 2-5 songs. Does not return material. Reports in 3 weeks.
Music: Mostly **instrumental**, **children**'s and **top 40**.
Tips: "Strong melodic choruses and original sounding music receive top consideration."

HAL BERNARD ENTERPRISES, INC., 2612 Erie Ave., P.O. Box 8385, Cincinnati OH 45208. (513)871-1500. Fax: (513)871-1510. President: Stan Hertzman. Professional Manager: Pepper Bonar. Music publisher, record company and management firm. Publishes 12-24 songs/year; 1-2 new songwriters/year. Pays standard royalty.

- Hal Bernard Enterprises is also listed in the Record Producers section, their management firm, Umbrella Artists Management, is in the Managers and Booking Agents section, and their record label, Strugglebaby Recording Co., can be found in the Record Companies section.

Affiliate(s): Sunnyslope Music (ASCAP), Bumpershoot Music (BMI), Apple Butter Music (ASCAP), Carb Music (ASCAP), Saiko Music (ASCAP), Smorgaschord Music (ASCAP), Clifton Rayburn Music (ASCAP) and Robert Stevens Music (ASCAP).
How to Contact: Submit demo tape by mail. Unsolicited submissions are OK. Prefers cassette with 3 songs and lyric sheet. SASE. Reports in 6 weeks.
Music: Rock, **R&B** and **top 40/pop**. Published "Here" and "Op Zop Too Wah," both written and recorded by Adrian Belew on Caroline Records (progressive pop); and "Mattress," "Joy and Madness" and "Moaner," all recorded by psychodots on Strugglebaby Records.
Tips: "Best material should appear first on demo. Cast your demos. If you as the songwriter can't sing it—don't. Get someone who can present your song properly, use a straight rhythm track and keep it as naked as possible. If you think it still needs something else, have a string arranger, etc. help you, but still keep the *voice up* and the *lyrics clear.*"

BEST BUDDIES, INC. (BMI), Dept. SM, 2100 Eighth Ave. S., Nashville TN 37204. (615)383-7664. Contact: Review Committee. Music publisher, record company (X-cuse Me) and record producer (Best Buddies Productions). Estab. 1981. Publishes 18 songs/year. Publishes 1-2 new songwriters/year. Pays standard royalty.
Affiliate(s): Swing Set Music (ASCAP), Best Buddies Music (BMI).

TO HELP YOU UNDERSTAND and use the information in these listings, see "How to Use *Songwriter's Market* to Get Your Songs Heard," on page 3.

How to Contact: Write first and obtain permission to submit. Must include SASE with permission letter. Prefers cassette or VHS videocassette with maximum 3 songs. Does not return material. Reports in 4-6 weeks. Do not call to see if tape received.
Music: Mostly **country**, **rock** and **pop**; also **gospel** and **R&B**. Published "Somebody Wrong is Looking Right" (by King/Burkholder), recorded by Bobby Helms; "Give Her Back Her Faith in Me" (by Ray Dean James), recorded by David Speegle (country); and "I Can't Get Over You Not Loving Me" (by Misty Efron/Bobbie Sallee), recorded by Sandy Garwood, all on Bitter Creek Records (country).

BETTY JANE/JOSIE JANE MUSIC PUBLISHERS (BMI, ASCAP), 7400 N. Adams Rd., North Adams MI 49262. Phone/fax: (517)287-4421. Website: http://cerrecordssimplenet.com. Professional Manager: Claude E. Reed. Music publisher, record company (C.E.R. Records) and record producer. Estab. 1980. Publishes 75-100 songs/year; 10 new songwriters/year. Pays standard royalty.
How to Contact: Submit demo tape by mail. Unsolicited submissions are OK. Prefers cassette or 7½ ips reel-to-reel with 1-5 songs and lyric or lead sheets. SASE. Reports in 2-3 weeks.
Music: Mostly **gospel** and **country western**; also **pop/R&B** and **MOR**. Published "Legend of the Longhorn" (by C.W. Warriner), recorded by Larry Beaird, and "Suddenly You're Gone," written and recorded by Keith Gibson, both on World International Records; and "Good Intentions" (by Jennie Shore Watkins), recorded by Toni Walker on C.E.R. Records (gospel).
Tips: "Try to be original, present your music in a professional way, submit only your very best songs with accurate lyric sheets and well made demo tape. Be patient! Send SASE with a sufficient amount of postage if you want your material returned."

BIG FISH MUSIC PUBLISHING GROUP, 11927 Magnolia Blvd. #3, N. Hollywood CA 91607. (818)984-0377. CEO: Chuck Tennin. Music publisher, record company (California Sun Records) and record producer. Estab. 1971. Publishes 10-20 songs/year; publishes 4 or 5 new songwriters/year. Pays standard royalty.
Affiliate(s): California Sun Music (ASCAP).
How to Contact: Write first and obtain permission to submit. "Please do not call." Prefers cassette with no more than 4 songs and lyric sheet. "Include a dated cover letter, with your source of referral (*Songwriter's Market*)." SASE. Reports in 2 weeks.
Music: Mostly **country**, including **country pop**, **country A/C** and **country crossover** with an edge; also **pop ballads**, **uplifting**, **inspirational contemporary gospel** with a message, **instrumental background music** for TV & films and **novelty type songs** for commercial use. Published "Espirit E," written and recorded by Don French on ABC-TV (background music for *General Hospital*); "Let Go and Let God" (by Corinne Porter), recorded by Molly Pasutti (gospel); and "Happy Landing," written and recorded by Brawley & Woodrich, all on California Sun Records.
Tips: "Demo should be professional, high quality, clean, simple and dynamic, and must get the song across on the first listen. Good clear vocals, a nice melody, a good musical feel, good musical arrangement and strong lyrics and chorus. Looking for unique country songs with a different edge for ongoing Nashville music projects and songs for a female country trio."

BIG SNOW MUSIC (BMI), P.O. Box 21323, St. Paul MN 55121. President: Mitch Viegut. Vice President and General Manager: Mark Alan. Music publisher and management firm. Estab. 1989. Publishes 30 new songs/year; publishes 2 new songwriters/year. Pays standard royalty.

- See the listing for Mark Alan Agency in the Managers and Booking Agents section.

How to Contact: Write first and obtain permission to submit. Prefers cassette with 3 songs and lyric sheet. Does not return material. Reports in 3 months.
Music: Mostly **rock**, **alternative**, **black**, **New Age** and **world music**. Published "Too Much Attitude" (by Eldon Fisher/Wayne Estrada/Mitch Viegut) and *Swag* (by Eldon Fisher/Wayne Estrada/Steve Kennedy), recorded by Crash Alley (rock); and *Somewhere* (by Mitch Viegut), recorded by Airkraft on Curb Records (rock).

‡BIXIO MUSIC GROUP/IDM PUBLISHING (ASCAP), 448 W. 37th St. #9G/10G, New York NY 10018. (212)695-3911. Fax: (212)967-6284. E-mail: tomo@mail.idt.net. Contact: Miriam Westercappel. Music publisher and artist management. Estab. 1985. Publishes a few hundred songs/year; publishes 2 new songwriters/year. Pays standard royalty.
How to Contact: Submit demo tape by mail. Unsolicited submissions are OK. Prefers cassette. SASE. Reports in 4-6 weeks.
Music: Mostly **soundtracks**, **rock** and **R&B**; also **country**. Published "Memnoch the Devil," written and recorded by Tomo on Commercial Records (pop); "Parlami d'Amen" and *La Mia Canzone* (by Bixio C.A.), recorded by Pavarotti on Polygram Records (evergreen).

INSIDER REPORT

Irving Burgie finds his niche in calypso music

Irving Burgie

©1996 Angel Records photo: Robin Visotsky

At 73, singer/songwriter Irving Burgie has decided it's time to reclaim his hits: the gentle, lilting Caribbean folk tunes that helped make Harry Belafonte a calypso star in the 1950s. With the release of his CD *Island in the Sun: The Songs of Irving Burgie* (Angel Records) and a return to club performance, Burgie can again call the standards "Day-O," "Jamaica Farewell" and "Yellow Bird" his own.

"I just felt the time was right," says Burgie. "When Belafonte sang the material, they didn't mention who the writer was, so I thought I'd go out and get my name attached to the work."

It could be argued that the work has eclipsed both songwriter and performer. "Day-O," with the lyric "Daylight come and me wan' go home," has become familiar to millions not just with Belafonte's recordings but its later use in film, television and commercials, selling everything from cookies to cars. It was one of eight Burgie songs that appeared on Belafonte's 1956 album *Calypso*, which became the first album in history to go platinum.

"When we were in rehearsal everybody liked it," Burgie recalls. "They predicted it would sell 200,000 albums, which was a big figure in those days. But the thing went way, way, way over that and nobody anticipated it because there was no precedent. Those songs are as big today as they were then—it's what I've lived on for the last 40 years."

Now in the enviable position of owning the copyrights to a catalog of standards, Burgie says, "It's great, but in a funny way my whole career is somewhat of a fluke. I never thought of myself as a writer until I had eight songs on Belafonte's *Calypso* album. So I started out with sales of eight million records. Which is like starting out at the very top of everything, so I've never had to go to a publisher."

Success was a happy accident for the New York native whose voice still carries a distinct patois inherited from his mother, born in Barbados. Burgie's first exposure to Caribbean music was during his childhood in a West Indian enclave of Brooklyn, where "we'd supply our own sort of music, and you'd begin to hear the strains of calypso—I just drank it all in."

Burgie began to explore his own musical ability during World War II. He befriended an alto sax player, "and he taught me my first music theory lessons. So by the time I came out of the Army, I was pretty well grounded in theory." Then Burgie entered Julliard as a voice major, where his studies included Italian art songs of the 16th and 17th centuries, French classics and the German lieder. "I was strictly classical," he recalls. "I was going to be another Caruso."

It was the likes of Leadbelly, Burl Ives, Pete Seeger and others who wrested Burgie's

INSIDER REPORT, *Burgie*

attention from the classics to folk music. "It was becoming the rage in the States at that time," he says. "I was studying folk music from all over the world, including the United States, and I started doing some things on the Caribbean, and out of that I organized a group."

That group was performing in New York when a TV scriptwriter for Belafonte discovered the rollicking rhythms and sun-splashed lyrics of Burgie's music. "I was writing material, but I never considered myself a songwriter," Burgie says. "I was just fleshing out material for the group."

Belafonte performed Burgie's tunes on the *Colgate Comedy Hour*, and "it was a smash," Burgie says. They went almost immediately to work on *Calypso*, which was released two years later and stayed at number one on the *Billboard* charts for 36 weeks. After *Calypso*—which earned him over $100,000 in royalties the first year—Burgie went on to supply songs for *Belafonte Sings Songs of the Caribbean* and *Jump Up Calypso*.

Critics have attributed the universal appeal of Burgie's music to its uplifting rhythms and sharp lyrical imagery ("I see a woman on bended knee/Cutting cane for her family/I see a man at the waterside/Casting nets at the surging tide"). But Burgie credits the music's appeal to its themes of liberation, nationalism, dignity and pride.

"When I started writing in the '50s, after World War II, countries around the world were talking about independence and freedom," Burgie says. "And in the United States, there was the beginnings of the civil rights movement. Independence and freedom aren't native to any particular ethnicity. It was sort of an issue that had come of age."

Burgie is also credited with making calypso music suitable for the mass market. "The Caribbean folk style was one that at that time was not exploited," he says. "One of the reasons for this was that many of the lyrics involved in calypso were pretty risque." Burgie points to the Andrews Sisters hit "Rum & Coca Cola," which was based on a Trinidadian folk song that referred to mothers and daughters working together in prostitution. Says Burgie: "My approach was totally different. These are images of people who are at work but who have developed a sense of dignity and aspiration."

As a songwriter, it wasn't hard to let his tunes become beloved as Belafonte signature songs, Burgie says. "Harry was building an image at that time, and the whole idea of me being tied to this kind of success was extremely appealing to me. Here I was, sitting on

Irving Burgie's debut album, *Island in the Sun: The Songs of Irving Burgie*, was released in 1997 on Angel Records. The album includes many of the calypso classics Burgie wrote for Harry Belafonte in the 1950s.

INSIDER REPORT, *continued*

top of the world, and making the equivalent of what would be today a million dollars a year—what am I fighting it for? I've got the greatest salesman that I could imagine to do my songs."

Burgie makes his major-label debut as a singer in a record industry much changed from the one he entered some 40 years ago. "It's an industry now—it was just a small business when I started out," he says. "The *Calypso* album was the first to sell a million records, but nowadays Bruce Springsteen comes out with an album and sells 15 million—there's a tremendous difference.

"And there are so many different musical areas," Burgie adds. "When you go to the Grammy Awards, it's so strange because they're giving out so many categories. It just shows the market is that big, that diversified.

"I think it makes it easier for new songwriters in the long run," he says. "Before it was so much of a closed market, but I think it's so big now people are looking for more material than they did before."

While the recording industry may have transformed since the 1950s, then as now the most important thing a songwriter can do is get exposure for his music, Burgie says: "A lot of songwriters, they're always talking about protecting or guarding their material, which is good. But I also feel the main thing to do is get it out there—get somebody to play it."

—Anne Bowling

BLACK ROSE PRODUCTIONS, (formerly One Hot Note Music Inc.), P.O. Box 216, Cold Spring Harbor NY 11724. (516)367-8544. Fax: (516)692-4709. New Jersey office: 15 Gloria Lane, Suite 201, Fairfield NJ 07004. (201)227-3884. Fax: (201)575-2749. President: Tito Batista. A&R: Barbara Bauer. Subpublished through BMG Music Publishing Japan Inc. Music publisher and record company (Reiter Records Ltd.). Estab. 1989. Publishes 200 songs/year; publishes 10 new songwriters/year. "We take 100% of publishing but can be negotiated based upon track history of composer."

Affiliate(s): One Hot Note Music Inc.

How to Contact: Submit demo tape by mail. Unsolicited submissions are OK. Prefers cassette. Does not return material.

Music: Mostly **pop**, **rock** and **jazz**; also **dance**, **country** and **rap**. Published "Be My Baby," written and recorded by T.C. Kross on Reiter Records; "Ready or Not" (by Lange/Bastianelli), recorded by Yolanda Yan on Cinepoly Records and by Camille Nivens on BMG Records.

Tips: "Make the song as well produced and recorded as you can."

BLACK STALLION COUNTRY PUBLISHING (BMI), P.O. Box 368, Tujunga CA 91043. (818)352-8142. Fax: (818)352-2122. President: Kenn Kingsbury. Music publisher, management firm and book publisher (*Who's Who in Country & Western Music*). Member CMA, CMF. Publishes 2 songs/year; publishes 1 new songwriter/year. Pays standard royalty.

- See the listing for Black Stallion Country Productions in the Managers and Booking Agents section.

How to Contact: Submit demo tape by mail. Unsolicited submissions are OK. Prefers 7½ ips reel-to-reel or cassette with 2-4 songs and lyric sheet. SASE. Reports in 1 month.

Music: Bluegrass and **country**.

‡BLACK STRAND MUSIC (ASCAP), P.O. Box 9273, Virginia Beach VA 23450. (757)408-0332. President: Pearl. Music publisher. Estab. 1987. Publishes 1-5 songs/year; publishes 2 new songwriters/year. Pays standard royalty.

Affiliate(s): Servindio Music (BMI).

How to Contact: Submit demo tape by mail. Unsolicited submissions are OK. Prefers cassette with 1-3 songs and lyric sheet. SASE. Reports in 1 month.

Music: Mostly **pop**, **A/C** and **rock**; also **R&B** and **gospel**. Published *This Morning* (by Pearl/Kennedy

Atkinson) and *I'm Not Going Out Like That* (by Pearl), both recorded by Pearl on Keiler Records (pop); and *Whatever It Is* (by Keith Butler), recorded by King's Crew on Refuge Records (gospel).

BLUE SPUR ENTERTAINMENT INC./GIT A ROPE PUBLISHING (BMI), 358 W. Hackamore, Gilbert AZ 85233-6425. (602)892-4451. Director of A&R: Esther Burch. President: Terry Olson. Music publisher. Estab. 1990. Royalty varies.
How to Contact: Write or call first and obtain permission to submit. Prefers cassette with 3-5 songs and lyric sheet. "Please send only songs protected by copyright. Please be sure submissions are cassette form and call for coded submission number to insure your material will be given our full attention." Does not return unsolicited material. Reports in 6-12 weeks.
Music: Mostly **traditional/contemporary country** and **gospel**.
Tips: "Study the market carefully, listen to the trends, attend a local songwriter's association; be committed to your craft and be persistent. Write, write and re-write!"

‡BMG MUSIC PUBLISHING, 810 Seventh Ave., 36th Floor, New York NY 10019. (212)830-2000. Fax: (212)930-4263. Website: http://www.bmgmusic.com. Nashville office: One Music Circle N., Suite 380, Nashville TN 37203. (615)780-5420. Fax: (615)780-5430. Music publisher.
How to Contact: BMG Music Publishing does not accept unsolicited submissions.
Music: Released "No More I Love You's" (by David Freeman/Joseph Hughes), recorded by Annie Lennox on Arista Records; and "Barely Breathing," written and recorded by Duncan Sheik on Atlantic Records. Other artists include Beck, John Hiatt, Carly Simon, Wu-Tang Clan, Peter Cetera, The Cure, Ace of Base, Stephen Bishop and Victoria Williams.

BOAM (ASCAP), P.O. Box 201, Smyrna GA 30081. (404)432-2454. A&R: Tom Hodges. Music publisher and record company (Trend Records and Stepping Stone Records). Estab. 1965. Publishes 20 songs/year; publishes 4 new songwriters/year. Pays standard royalty.
Affiliate(s): Mimic Music, Stepping Stone, Skip Jack (BMI).
- BOAM's record label, Trend Records, is listed in the Record Companies section.

How to Contact: Submit demo tape by mail. Unsolicited submissions are OK. Prefers cassette or VHS videocassette with 6 songs and lyric or lead sheet. SASE. Reports in 3 weeks.
Music: Mostly **country**, **R&B** and **MOR**; also **rock**, **gospel** and **folk**. Published "Hank's My Daddy Too," written and recorded by F. Brannon on Trend Records; "Young Years" (by Jonathan Carey), recorded by LaVey; and "Puro Tejano" (by Narz), recorded by Hilda Gonzalez, both on Stepping Stone Records.

BOURNE CO. MUSIC PUBLISHERS (ASCAP), 5 W. 37th St., New York NY 10018. (212)391-4300. Fax: (212)391-4306. Contact: Professional Manager. Music publisher. Estab. 1917. Publishes educational material and popular music.
Affiliate(s): ABC Music, Ben Bloom, Better Half, Bogat, Burke & Van Heusen, Goldmine, Harborn, Lady Mac and Murbo Music.
- See their listing in the Music Print Publishers section.

How to Contact: Write first and obtain permission to submit. SASE.
Music: **Piano/vocal**, **band pieces** and **choral pieces**. Published "Amen" and "Mary's Little Boy Child" (by Hairston); "When You Wish Upon a Star" (by Washington/Harline); and "Unforgettable" (by Irving Gordon), recorded by Natalie Cole with Nat 'King' Cole on Elektra Records (pop).

DAVID BOWMAN PRODUCTIONS & W. DAVID MUSIC, 28 Park Lane, Feasterville PA 19053. (215)942-9059 or (215)322-8078. President: David Bowman. Music publisher, music library producers/music production house. Estab. 1989. Publishes 10-20 songs/year; publishes 5-10 new songwriters/year. "Pays by the job."
- See their listing in the Advertising, AV and Commercial Music Firms section.

How to Contact: Write first and obtain permission to submit a demo. Prefers cassette. "We are looking for instrumental pieces of any length not exceeding 3 minutes for use in AV music library. Also looking for 30 and 60 second music spots for television, radio and all multimedia applications." Does not return material. Reports in 1-2 months.
Music: **All types**. Published "Techno," "The Streets of London" and *Looking Back*, all written and recorded by W. David Bowman on Warren Records.
Tips: "Network. Get your name and your work out there. Let everyone know what you are all about and what you are doing. Be patient, persistent and professional. What are you waiting for? Do it!"

ALLAN BRADLEY MUSIC (BMI), 484 S. Grand, Orange CA 92866. Owner: Allan Licht. Music publisher, record company (ABL Records) and record producer. Estab. 1993. Publishes 10 songs/year; publishes 5 new songwriters/year. Pays standard royalty.

How to Contact: Submit demo tape by mail. Unsolicited submissions are OK. Prefers cassette with 3 songs and lyric sheet. "Send only unpublished works." Does not return material. Reports in 2 weeks.
Music: Mostly **A/C, pop** and **R&B**; also **country** and **Christian contemporary**. Published "I Wanna Feel Your Body" (by Allan Licht), recorded by Debi Lewin; "This Christmas" (by Allan Licht), recorded by Kelly Rae, both on ABL Records; and "Cleveland's Got It All" (by Allan Licht), recorded by Alan Douglass and aired on the *Today In Cleveland* show (WKVC-TV3).
Tips: "Please send only songs that have Top 10 potential. Only serious writers are encouraged to submit."

BRANCH GROUP MUSIC (SOCAN), 1067 Sherwin Rd., Winnipeg MB R3H 0T8 **Canada**. (204)694-3101. E-mail: paquin@magic.mb.ca. President: Gilles Paquin. Music publisher, management firm (Paquin Entertainment), record company (Oak Street Music) and record producer (Oak Street Music). Estab. 1987. Publishes 10 songs/year; publishes 2 new songwriters/year. Pays negotiable royalty.
Affiliate(s): Forest Group Music (SOCAN).

- See the listing for Paquin Entertainment in the Managers and Booking Agents section.

How to Contact: Submit a demo tape by mail. Unsolicited submissions are OK. Prefers cassette or VHS videocassette with 2-3 songs and lyric and lead sheet. SAE and IRC.
Music: Mostly **children's** and **novelty**. Published *Moonlight Express*, written and recorded by Fred Penner; *Mosquito*, written and recorded by Al Simmons; and *Music Is Everywhere* (by F. Penner/V. Hennell), recorded by Fred Penner, all on Oak Street Music (children's/family).

KITTY BREWSTER SONGS, "Norden," 2 Hillhead Rd., Newtonhill Stonehaven AB39 3TS **Scotland**. Phone: 01569 730962. MD: Doug Stone. Music publisher, record company (KBS Records), record producer and production company (Brewster & Stone Productions). Estab. 1989. Pays standard royalty.
How to Contact: Submit demo tape by mail. Unsolicited submissions are OK. Prefers cassette or VHS videocassette with any amount of songs and lyric or lead sheet. Does not return material. Reports in 3-4 months.
Music: Mostly **AOR, pop, R&B** and **dance**; also **country, jazz, rock** and **contemporary**. Published *Sleepin' Alone* (by R. Donald); *I Still Feel the Same* (by R. Greig/K. Mundie); and *Your Love Will Pull Me Thru* (by R. Greig), all recorded by Kitty Brewster on KBS Records (AOR).

THE BROTHERS ORGANISATION, 74 The Archway, Station Approach, Ranelagh Gardens, London SW6 34H **England**. (0171)610-6183. Fax: (0171)610-6232. E-mail: bros@keepcalm.demon.co.uk. Director: Ian Titchener. Music publisher and record company. Estab. 1989. Publishes 20 songs/year. "Payment decided on a contract by contract basis."
How to Contact: Submit demo tape by mail. Unsolicited submissions are OK. Prefers cassette. Does not return material. Reports in 1 month if interested.
Music: Mostly **R&B/dance**, **rock (melodic)** and **pop**. Published "Brown Eyed One," written and recorded by Smart on Brothers Records (pop); "Groove" (by Titchener), recorded by McFly on Top Rhythm Records (dance); and "Klubbed Up" (by Peter/Ward), recorded by CNN on Hot Hands Records (dance).

BURIED TREASURE MUSIC (ASCAP), 524 Doral Country Dr., Nashville TN 37221. Executive Producer: Scott Turner. Music publisher and record producer (Aberdeen Productions). Estab. 1972. Publishes 30-50 songs/year; publishes 3-10 new songwriters/year. Pays standard royalty.
Affiliate(s): Captain Kidd Music (BMI).

- See the listing for Aberdeen Productions in the Record Producers section.

How to Contact: Submit demo tape by mail. Unsolicited submissions are OK. Prefers cassette or VHS videocassette with 1-4 songs and lyric sheet. Reports in 1 month. "Always enclose SASE if answer is expected."
Music: Country and **country/pop**; also **rock**, **MOR** and **contemporary**. Published *Stardust Again* (by Nanette Malher), recorded by Arden Gatlin (A/C); *Show Me the Way* (by Tony Graham), recorded by Roy Clark on Churchill Records (country); and *Your Dreams Will Be Safe* (by Tony Graham), recorded by Byron Whitman (country).
Tips: "*Don't* send songs in envelopes that are 15″x 20″, or by registered mail. The post office will not accept tapes in regular business-size envelopes."

CALIFORNIA COUNTRY MUSIC (BMI), 112 Widmar Pl., Clayton CA 94517. (510)672-8201. Owner: Edgar J. Brincat. Music publisher and record company (Roll On Records). Estab. 1985. Publishes 30 songs/year; publishes 2-4 new songwriters/year. Pays standard royalty.
Affiliate(s): Sweet Inspirations Music (ASCAP).

- California Country's record label, Roll On Records, can be found in the Record Companies section.

How to Contact: Submit demo tape by mail. Unsolicited submissions are OK. Do not call. Prefers

cassette with 3 songs and lyric sheet. Any calls will be returned collect to caller. SASE. Reports in 4-6 weeks.
Music: Mostly **MOR**, **contemporary country** and **pop**; also **R&B**, **gospel** and **light rock**. Published *For Realities Sake* (by F.L. Pittman/R. Barretta) and *Maddy* (by F.L. Pittman/M. Weeks), both recorded by Ron Banks & L.J. Reynolds on Life & Bellmark Records; and *Quarter Past Love* (by Irwin Rubinsky/Janet Fisher), recorded by Darcy Dawson on NNP Records.

CALINOH MUSIC GROUP, 608 W. Iris Dr., Nashville TN 37204. (615)292-3568. Contact: Ann Hofer or Tom Cornett. Music publisher. Estab. 1992. Publishes 50 songs/year; publishes 10 new songwriters/year. Pays standard royalty.
Affiliate(s): Little Liberty Town (ASCAP) and West Manchester Publishing (BMI).
How to Contact: Submit demo tape by mail. Unsolicited submissions are OK. Prefers cassette with 3 songs and lyric sheet. "Include SASE." Does not return material. "Writers are contacted only if we are interested in publishing their material."
Music: Mostly **country**, **gospel** and **pop**.

CAMEX MUSIC, 535 Fifth Ave., New York NY 10017. (212)682-8400. A&R Director: Alex Benedetto. Music publisher, record company and record producer. Estab. 1970. Publishes 100 songs/year; publishes 10 new songwriters/year. Query for royalty terms.
How to Contact: Submit demo tape by mail. Unsolicited submissions are OK. Prefers cassettes with 5-10 songs and lyric sheet or lead sheet. SASE. Reports in 3-6 months.
Music: Mostly **alternative rock**, **pop** and **hard rock**; also **R&B**, **MOR** and **movie themes**. Artists include Marmalade, SAM and Hallucination Station.

CASH PRODUCTIONS, INC. (BMI), 744 Joppa Farm Rd., Joppa MD 21085. (301)679-2262. President: Ernest W. Cash. Music publisher, record company (Continental Records, Inc.), national and international record distributor, artist management, record producer (Vision Music Group, Inc.) and video production. Estab. 1987. Publishes 30-60 songs/year; publishes 10-15 new songwriters/year. Pays standard royalty.
Affiliate(s): Big K Music, Inc. (BMI), Guerriero Music (BMI) and Deb Music (BMI).

- Cash Productions' record label, Continental Records, is listed in the Record Companies section and their management firm, Cash Productions, is listed in the Managers and Booking Agents section.

How to Contact: Call first and obtain permission to submit. Prefers cassette or VHS videocassette with 3 songs and lyric sheet. SASE. Reports in 2 weeks.
Music: Mostly **country**, **gospel** and **pop**; also **R&B** and **rock**. Published "The End of the Road" (by David Holiday); "Miracles" and "Better Place" (by Eunice Morris).
Tips: "Do the best job you can on your work—writing, arrangement and production. Demos are very important in placing material."

CASTLE MUSIC GROUP, 50 Music Square W., Suite 201, Nashville TN 37203. (615)320-7003. Fax: (615)320-7006. E-mail: castlerecord@earthlink.net. Website: http://www.earthlink.net/~cmg. Publishing Director: Petty Tresco. Music publisher, record company (Castle Records) and record producer. Estab. 1969. Publishes 50 songs/year; publishes 10 new songwriters/year. Pays standard royalty.
Affiliate(s): Cat's Alley Music (ASCAP) and Alley Roads Music (BMI).
How to Contact: Call first and obtain permission to submit or to arrange personal interview. Prefers cassette with 3 songs and lyric sheet. SASE. Reports in 2-3 months.
Music: Mostly **country** and **R&B**; also **pop** and **gospel**. Published *Little Bit of Love*, written and recorded by Chip Koehler and Clay Benson on Castle Records (country).

CHEAVORIA MUSIC CO. (BMI), 1219 Kerlin Ave., Brewton AL 36426. (205)867-2228. President: Roy Edwards. Music publisher, record company (Bolivia Records) and record producer (Known Artist Production). Estab. 1972. Publishes 20 new songwriters/year. Pays standard royalty.
Affiliate(s): Baitstring Music (ASCAP).

- Cheavoria Music's record label, Bolivia Records, is listed in the Record Companies section, and Known Artist Productions is listed in the Record Producers section.

How to Contact: Write first and obtain permission to submit. Prefers cassette with 3 songs and lyric sheet. Does not return material. Reports in 1 month.
Music: Mostly **R&B**, **pop** and **country**; also **ballads**. Published "Forever and Always," written and recorded by Jim Portwood on Bolivia Records (country).

‡CHERASNY ELIJAH ENTERTAINMENT PRODUCTION COMPANY (BMI), P.O. Box 10246, Parkville MD 21234. (410)254-1732. Music publisher: Rick Solimini. Music publisher. Estab. 1997. Pub-

lishes 4 songs/year; publishes 4 new songwriters/year. Hires staff writers. Pays standard royalty.
Affiliate(s): Trixie Leigh Music (BMI).
How to Contact: Call first and obtain permission to submit. Prefers cassette with 3 songs and lyric and lead sheets. SASE. Reports in 1 month.
Music: Mostly **contemporary Christian**, **country** and **dance**; also **easy listening** and **ballads**. Published "I Believe" (by John Solimini), recorded by Redemption on Toyz Records (contemporary Christian); "Who's Gonna Be the Fool?" (by Rick Solimini), recorded by Kay Weaver on Columbine Records (MOR); and "Just Awhile" (by Rick Solimini), recorded by Kay Weaver on Hollywood Gold Records (MOR).

CHERIE MUSIC (BMI), 3621 Heath Lane, Mesquite TX 75150. (214)279-5858. Contact: Jimmy Fields or Silvia Harra. Music publisher and record company. Estab. 1955. Publishes approximately 100 songs/year. Pays standard royalty.

- Cherie Music's record label, Jamaka Record Co., is listed in the Record Companies section.

How to Contact: Submit demo tape by mail. Unsolicited submissions are OK. Prefers cassette with up to 10 songs. SASE. Reports in approximately 2 months, "depending on how many new songs are received."
Music: Mostly **country** and **rock** (if not over produced—prefer 1950s type rock). Published "Cajun Baby Blues" and *Alive with Alan Dryman* (by Hank Williams/Jimmy Fields), recorded by Allen Dryman on Jamaka Records; and "Is The King Still Alive" (by Fields/McCoy/Kern), recorded by Johnny Harra on HIA Records.

CHRISTMAS & HOLIDAY MUSIC (BMI), 3517 Warner Blvd., Suite 4, Burbank CA 91505. (213)849-5381. President: Justin Wilde. Music publisher. Estab. 1980. Publishes 8-12 songs/year; publishes 8-12 new songwriters/year. "All submissions must be complete songs (i.e., music and lyrics)." Pays standard royalty.
Affiliate(s): Songcastle Music (ASCAP).
How to Contact: Submit demo tape by mail. Unsolicited submissions are OK. Do not call. "First class mail only. Registered or certified mail not accepted." Prefers cassette with 3 songs and lyric sheet. "Professional demos a must. Do not send lead sheets or promotional material, bios, etc." SASE. Reports in 1-2 weeks.
Music: Strictly **Christmas music** (and a little Hanukkah) in every style imaginable: easy listening, rock, R&B, pop, blues, jazz, country, reggae, rap, children's secular or religious. *Please do not send anything that isn't Christmas*. Published "What Made the Baby Cry?" (by William J. Golay), recorded by Toby Keith on Polydor Records (country); "First Day of The Son" (by Derrick Procell), recorded by the Brooklyn Tabernacle Choir on Warner/Alliance Records (gospel); and "It Must Have Been The Mistletoe" (by Justin Wilde/Doug Konecky), recorded by Kathie Lee Gifford on Warner Bros. Records (pop).
Tips: "If a stranger can hum your melody back to you after hearing it twice, it has 'standard' potential. Couple that with a lyric filled with unique, inventive imagery, that stands on its own, even without music. Combine the two elements, and workshop the finished result thoroughly to identify weak points. Only when the song is polished to perfection, then cut a master quality demo that sounds like a record or pretty close to it. Submit positive lyrics only. Avoid negative themes like 'Blue Christmas.' "

CIMIRRON MUSIC (BMI), 607 Piney Point Rd., Yorktown VA 23692. (804)898-8155. E-mail: lpuckett@lx.netcom.com. President: Lana Puckett. Music publisher, record company (Cimirron/Rainbird Records) and record producer. Estab. 1986. Publishes 10-20 songs/year. "Royalty depends on song and writer."

- Cimirron Music's record label, Cimirron/Rainbird Records, is listed in the Record Companies section.

How to Contact: Write or call first and obtain permission to submit. Prefers cassette with 1-3 songs and lyric sheet. Does not return material. Reports in 3 months.
Music: Mostly **country**, **acoustic**, **folk** and **bluegrass**. Published *Cornstalk Pony* (by Lana Puckett/K. Person), recorded by Lana Puckett; "This Box I'm Looking Through," written and recorded by Ron Fetner; and "Pictures," written and recorded by Stephen Bennett, all on Cimirron Records.

CISUM, 708 W. Euclid, Pittsburg KS 66762. (316)231-6443. Partner: Kevin Shawn. Music publisher, record company and record producer. Estab. 1985. Publishes 100 songs/year. Pays standard royalty.
How to Contact: Write first and obtain permission to submit a tape. Prefers cassette or VHS videocassette

and lyric sheet. "Unpublished, copyrighted, cassette with lyrics. Submit as many as you wish. We listen to everything, allow 3 months. When over 3 weeks please call."
Music: Mostly **novelty**, **country** and **rock**; also **pop**, **gospel** and **R&B**. Published "The World's Greatest Country Novelty Song" (by Jack Barlow); "Every Time I See a Pig I Think of You" (by Dave Talley) and "Shade Tree Mechanic," both recorded by Poison Ivy on Antique Records.

CLEAR POND MUSIC (BMI), P.O. Box 16555, Santa Fe NM 87506-6555. Fax: (505)474-7344. Publisher: Susan Pond. Music publisher and record producer (Crystal Clear Productions). Estab. 1992. Publishes 10-50 songs/year; publishes 1-5 new songwriters/year. Pays standard royalty.
How to Contact: "Demos must be submitted by a manager, attorney or paralegal." Prefers cassette with 1 song. "We are only interested in a singer/songwriter/artist, no exceptions!"
Music: Mostly **pop/rock**, **top 40**, **alternative** and **country** (all types). Published "Wish I Were In Love With You Again," written and recorded by Al Lancellotti (top 40); "Shaman's Song," written and recorded by MoonRage, both on Maxim Records (alternative); and "When All At Last" (by Steve Craig), recorded by Albert Hall on Metal Mind Records (pop/rock).
Tips: "We represent *Billboard* hit songwriters. We specialize in tracking and collecting royalties worldwide. Other areas of expertise are international music markets, encompassing publishing, distribution, licensing and radio markets."

‡CLEARWIND PUBLISHING (SESAC), P.O. Box 42381, Detroit MI 48242-0381. Contact: A&R Department Director. Music publisher and management company (Clearwind Management). Estab. 1983. Publishes 12-15 songs/year; publishes 2-4 new songwriters/year. Pays standard royalty.
How to Contact: Write first and obtain permission to submit. "Do NOT call! Unsolicited submissions will be returned unopened." Prefers cassette, CD or VHS videocassette with no more than 2 songs and lyric sheet. Does not return material. Reports in up to 12 weeks.
Music: Mostly **pop**, **highly commercial country** and **R&B**; also **highly commercial rock**. Published *Champion* and "What A Friend," written and recorded by Ron Moore on Morada Records.

R.D. CLEVÈRE MUSIKVERLAG (GEMA), Postfach 2145, D-63243 Neu-Isenburg, **Germany**. Phone: (6102)52696. Fax: (6102)52696. Professional Manager: Tony Hermonez. Music publisher and record company (Comma Records). Estab. 1967. Publishes 700-900 songs/year; publishes 40 new songwriters/year. Pays standard royalty.
Affiliate(s): Big Sound Music, Hot Night Music, Lizzy's Blues Music, Max Banana Music, R.D. Clevère-Cocabana-Music, R.D. Clevère-Far East & Orient-Music, and R.D. Clevère-America-Today-Music.
- R.D. Clevère's record label, Comma Records, is listed in the Record Companies section.

How to Contact: Submit demo tape by mail. Unsolicited submissions are OK. Prefers cassette with "no limit" on songs and lyric sheet. Does not return material. Reports in 3 weeks.
Music: Mostly **pop**, **disco**, **rock**, **R&B**, **country** and **folk**; also **musicals** and **classic/opera**.

COFFEE AND CREAM PUBLISHING COMPANY (ASCAP), Dept. SM, 1138 E. Price St., Philadelphia PA 19138. (215)842-3450. President: Bolden Abrams, Jr. Music publisher and record producer (Bolden Productions). Publishes 20 songs/year; publishes 4 new songwriters/year. Pays standard royalty.
How to Contact: Submit demo tape by mail. Unsolicited submissions are OK. Prefers cassette or VHS videocassette with 1-4 songs and lyric or lead sheets. SASE. Reports in 2 weeks "if we're interested."
Music: Mostly **dance**, **pop**, **R&B**, **gospel** and **country**. Published "I Can't Wait" (by Abrams/DeGrazio/Urbach), recorded by the Johnson Brothers on A&M Records (pop ballad); "Rhapsody In Groove" (by Brian Kierulf/Pablo Claudio), recorded by Pieces of a Dream on Capitol/Blue Note Records (smooth jazz); and "No Time For Tears" (by B. Abrams/K. Fairfax), recorded by Novella Sweetbriar on Stackhouse Records (R&B ballad).

COLSTAL MUSIC, P.O. Box 642, Robina, QLD 4226 **Australia**. Phone: (07)55722755. Fax: (07)55260322. Directors: Bernie Stahl and Suzanne Stahl. Music publisher and video distributor. Estab. 1985. Pays negotiable royalty.
How to Contact: Submit demo tape by mail. Prefers cassette or PAL videocassette. Does not return material.
Music: Mostly **country** and **comedy**. Published *What Have You Done for Australia* (by Colin Greatorix); *Gin Gin* (by Willy Hackett); and *Home Made Brew* (by Col Elliott), all recorded by Col Elliott on BMG Australia Records (country/comedy).

GLENN COLTON SHOWS, 256 Sunshine Dr., Amherst NY 14228. (716)691-7928. President: Glenn Colton. Music publisher. Estab. 1991. Publishes 10-15 songs/year; publishes 1-2 new songwriters/year. Pays variable royalty.

How to Contact: Submit demo tape by mail. Unsolicited submissions are OK. Prefers cassette with 3-7 songs and lead sheet. SASE. Reports in 3-4 weeks.
Music: Mostly **children's**, **folk** and **country**; also **rock**. Published *Let's Save The Planet*, written and recorded by Paul Swisher (children's); *Just A Cowboy*, written and recorded by Glenn Colton (country); and *The Power of the Mind* (by Paul Swisher/Glenn Colton), recorded by Glenn Colton, all on GCS Records (rock).
Tips: "Submit material with a positive message and a strong hook that will appeal to an elementary age audience in a live setting."

‡JERRY CONNELL PUBLISHING CO. (BMI), 130 Pilgrim Dr., San Antonio TX 78213. (210)979-0656. Fax: (210)979-7025. E-mail: jerryconnell@jerryconnell.com. Website: http://www.JerryConnell.com. Partner: Jerry Connell. Music publisher and record producer. Publishes 75 songs/year; publishes 50 new songwriters/year. Pays standard royalty.
Affiliate(s): Old Bob Music (ASCAP).
How to Contact: Submit demo tape by mail. Unsolicited submissions are OK. Prefers cassette with lyric or lead sheet (if possible). Does not return unsolicited material. Reports in 1 month.
Music: Mostly **country**, **gospel/religious** and **tejano**; also **jazz**, **easy listening** and **rock**. Published "December Song" and "Hard News" (by Steve Mallett), recorded by Johnny Bush; and "Drinking Will Kill Me," written and recorded by Richard Wolfe, all on Cherokee Records (country).
Tips: "If you have submitted work before, and were not accepted, don't stop now. Continue to submit. The business changes every day, and what was not acceptable yesterday may be acceptable today."

COPPERFIELD MUSIC GROUP (ASCAP, BMI), 54 Music Square E., Suite 304, Nashville TN 37203. (615)726-3100. Fax: (615)726-3172. President: Ken Biddy. Creative Director: Willis Jones. Music publisher and artist management. Estab. 1976. Pays standard royalty.
Affiliate(s): Top Brass Music (ASCAP) and Penny Annie Music (BMI).
How to Contact: Submit demo tape by mail. Unsolicited submissions are OK. Prefers cassette, DAT, VHS videotape or CD with 3 songs and lyric sheet. "3 song maximum." Does not return material. Reports in 2 weeks "only if considering a song for publishing."
Music: Mostly **country**, **R&B**, **Christian** and **pop**. Published "Good Lookin' Man" (by Joyce Harrison) and "Fade to Blue" (by Anne Reeves), both recorded by LeAnn Rimes on Curb Records (country); and "Montgomery to Memphis" (by Anne Reeves), recorded by LeAnn Wommack on Decca Records (country).

THE CORNELIUS COMPANIES (BMI, ASCAP), Dept. SM, 812 19th Ave. S., Suite 5, Nashville TN 37203. (615)321-5333. Owner/Manager: Ron Cornelius. A&R: David King. Music publisher and record producer (Ron Cornelius). Estab. 1987. Publishes 60-80 songs/year; publishes 2-3 new songwriters/year. Occasionally hires staff writers. Pays standard royalty.
Affiliate(s): RobinSparrow Music (BMI).
How to Contact: Write first and obtain permission to submit. Prefers cassette with 2-3 songs. SASE. Reports in 2 months.
Music: Mostly **country** and **pop**; also **positive country** and **gospel**. Published *Time Off for Bad Behavior* (by Bobby Keel/Larry Latimer), recorded by Confederate Railroad on Atlantic Records; "A Man's Home is His Castle," recorded by Faith Hill on Warner Bros. Records; and "Give Love Away," written and recorded by Dinah and the Desert Crusaders on Gateway Records.

COTTAGE BLUE MUSIC (BMI), P.O. Box 121626, Nashville TN 37212. (615)726-3556. Contact: Neal James. Music publisher, record company (Kottage Records), management firm (James Gang Management) and record producer (Neal James Productions). Estab. 1971. Publishes 30 songs/year; publishes 3 new songwriters/year. Pays standard royalty.
Affiliate(s): James & Lee (BMI), Neal James Music (BMI) and Hidden Cove Music (ASCAP).

- Cottage Blue's record label, Kottage Records, is listed in the Record Companies section, their management firm, James Gang Management, is listed in the Managers and Booking Agents section, and Neal James Productions is listed in the Record Producers section.

How to Contact: Submit demo tape by mail. Unsolicited submissions OK. Prefers cassette with 2 songs and lyric sheet. SASE. Reports in 1 month.
Music: Mostly **country**, **gospel** and **rock/pop**; also **R&B** and **alternative rock**. Published "All Over Me" (by Lance Wing/Bo Riddle), recorded by Joe Masesik on Kottage Records (country); "Generic People," written and recorded by Allusion (alternative rock); and "Lady Angel," written and recorded by Scott Dawson, both on Crosswind Records.
Tips: "Screen material carefully before submitting."

COUNTRY BREEZE MUSIC (BMI), 1715 Marty, Kansas City KS 66103. (913)384-1316. President: Ed Morgan Jr. Music publisher and record company (Country Breeze Records, Walkin' Hat Records). Estab. 1984. Publishes 100 songs/year; publishes 25-30 new songwriters/year. Pays standard royalty.
Affiliate(s): Walkin' Hat Music (ASCAP).

- You can find a listing for Country Breeze's record label, Country Breeze Records, in the Record Companies section.

How to Contact: Submit a demo tape by mail. Unsolicited submissions are OK. Prefers cassette or VHS videocassette with 4-5 songs and lyric sheet. SASE. "The songwriter/artist should perform on the video as though on stage giving a sold-out performance. In other words put heart and soul into the project. Submit in strong mailing envelopes." Reports in 2-3 weeks.
Music: Mostly **country (all types)**, **gospel (southern country and Christian country)** and **rock (no rap or metal)**. Published "I Bid the Blues Welcome," written and recorded by Tim Wave; "Burnin' Heart" (by J.D. Varacaue), recorded by Blue Mountain Express; and "Livin' on the Border Line," written and recorded by Jamie Mitchell, all on Country Breeze Records (country).

COUNTRY RAINBOW MUSIC (BMI), 9 Music Square S., Suite 225, Nashville TN 37203-3203. (513)489-8944. Owner: Samuel D. Rogers. Music publisher. Estab. 1995. Publishes 10-12 songs/year; publishes 4-6 new songwriters/year. Pays standard royalty.
Affiliate(s): Venture South Music (ASCAP).
How to Contact: Submit demo tape by mail. Unsolicited submissions are OK. Prefers cassette with 1-3 songs and lyric sheet. SASE. Reports in 2-3 weeks.
Music: Mostly **country**, **MOR** and **bluegrass**.
Tips: "Songs should be unique and well crafted (hit potential only). Professional, ready-to-plug full demos preferred on good quality tape. I like songs with clever concepts, good imagery, simple everyday words—a theme which may be cliché, but told from a different perspective."

COUNTRY SHOWCASE AMERICA (BMI), 14134 Brighton Dam Rd., Clarksville MD 21029. (301)854-2917. Contact: Francis Gosman. Music publisher, record company and record producer. Estab. 1971. Publishes 9 songs/year; publishes 1 new songwriter/year. Pays standard royalty.
How to Contact: Submit demo tape by mail. Unsolicited submissions are OK. Prefers cassette with 2 songs and lyric sheet. Does not return material. Reports only if interested.
Music: Country. Published "Take Me With You" and "Who's Gonna Tell My Heart" (by Cochran), both recorded by Johnny Anthony on CSA Records (country).

COUNTRY STAR MUSIC (ASCAP), 439 Wiley Ave., Franklin PA 16323. (814)432-4633. President: Norman Kelly. Music publisher, record company (Country Star, Process, Mersey and CSI) and record producer (Country Star Productions). Estab. 1970. Publishes 15-20 songs/year; publishes 4-6 new songwriters/year. Pays standard royalty.
Affiliate(s): Kelly Music Publications (BMI) and Process Music Publications (BMI).

- See the listings for Country Star International in the Record Companies section, Country Star Productions in the Record Producers section and Country Star Attractions in the Managers and Booking Agents section.

How to Contact: Submit demo tape by mail. Unsolicited submissions are OK. Prefers cassette with 1-4 songs and typed lyric or lead sheet. SASE. Reports in 1-2 weeks. "No SASE no return."
Music: Mostly **country** (80%); also **rock**, **gospel**, **MOR** and **R&B** (5% each). Published "Holiday Waltz" (by F. Stelzer), recorded by Debbie Sue on Star Records (country); "Climbing Mountains" (by Delamer-Gihara), recorded by Sugar Belle on Mersey Records; and "Teardrops Still Fall" (by Kelly/Barbaria), recorded by Larry Pieper on Star Records (country).
Tips: "Send only your best songs—ones you feel are equal to or better than current hits. Typed or printed lyrics, please. For return of demo, send mailing label and return postage."

COWBOY JUNCTION FLEA MARKET AND PUBLISHING CO. (BMI), Highway 44 West, Junction 490, Lecanto FL 34461. (904)746-4754. President: Elizabeth Thompson. Music publisher (Cowboy Junction Publishing Co.), record company (Cowboy Junction Records) and record producer. Estab. 1957. Publishes 5 songs/year. Pays standard royalty.
How to Contact: Submit demo tape by mail. Unsolicited submissions are OK. SASE. Reports as soon as possible.
Music: Country, **western**, **bluegrass** and **gospel**. Published "Lonesome George" (by Boris Max Pastuch), recorded by Buddy Max; "Feel The Power," written and recorded by Lenora Gray; and "Take Me Back To The West Virginia Hills," written and recorded by Wally Jones, all on Cowboy Junction Records.
Tips: "You could come to our flea market on Tuesday or Friday and present your material—or come to our Country and Western Bluegrass Music Show held any Saturday."

LOMAN CRAIG MUSIC, P.O. Box 111480, Nashville TN 37222-1480. (615)331-1219. President: Loman Craig. Vice President: Tommy Hendrick. Music publisher, record company (Bandit Records, HIS Records), record producer (Loman Craig Productions). Estab. 1979. Pays standard royalty.
Affiliate(s): Outlaw Music of Memphis (BMI), We Can Make It Music (BMI) and Doulikit Music (SESAC).
How to Contact: Submit a demo tape by mail. Unsolicited submissions are OK. Prefers cassette with 2-3 songs and lyric sheet. "Does not have to be a full production demo." SASE. Reports in 4-6 weeks.
Music: Mostly **country** and **pop**; also **bluegrass** and **gospel**.

‡CROAKY FROG MUSIC (BMI), 816 Hershberger Rd., Roanoke VA 24012. Phone/fax: (540)265-0321. E-mail: lhinchman@aol.com. Owner/president: Richard Hinchman Jr. Music publisher and recording studio. Estab. 1988. Publishes 30 songs/year; publishes 15 new songwriters/year. Pays standard royalty.
How to Contact: Submit demo tape by mail. Unsolicited submissions are OK. Prefers cassette or DAT with lyric sheet. "Would not hurt if I received a phone call after two weeks to follow up on submission." SASE. Reports in 3-4 weeks.
Music: Mostly **country**, **pop** and **rock**; also **bluegrass**, **commercial** and **rap (rarely)**. Published "I Believe American Way" (by G. Blankebeckler/L. Metz/J. Phillips), recorded by B. Courtney on Cameroon Records.

‡CROSSPOINT INTERNATIONAL, INC., 30 Monument Square #150B-2, Concord MA 01742. (508)731-2300. Fax: (508)287-5325. Product Development: Noah Tier. Music publisher and record company. Estab. 1995. Publishes 20 songs/year. Publishes 1 new songwriter/year. Hires staff songwriters. Pays negotiable royalty.

- See Crosspoint International's listing in the Record Companies section.

How to Contact: Submit demo tape by mail. Unsolicited submissions are OK. Prefers cassette or VHS videocassette. Does not return material. Reports in 3 months.
Music: Mostly **children's**. Published "Tricky Ricky," "To the Zooey," and "Frank the Freckled Froggie," all written by John Sara on Fun Tapes Records.
Tips: "Self-esteem building material is our theme."

CUNNINGHAM MUSIC (BMI), Dept. SM, P.O. Box 441124, Detroit MI 48244-1124. President: Jerome Cunningham. Music publisher. Estab. 1988. Publishes 8-9 songs/year; publishes 2 new songwriters/year. Pays standard royalty.
How to Contact: Submit a demo tape by mail. Unsolicited submissions are OK. Prefers cassette or VHS videocassette with 3 songs and lyric sheet. Does not return material. Reports in 1-2 months.
Music: Mostly **R&B**, **gospel** and **jazz**; also **pop** and **rock**. Published "Soul Desire" (by Julia M. Augusta).

D.S.M. PRODUCERS INC. (ASCAP), 161 W. 54th St., New York NY 10019. (212)245-0006. Producer: Suzan Bader. Music publisher, record producer and management firm (American Steel Management Co.). Estab. 1979. Publishes 25 songs/year; publishes 10 new songwriters/year. "Publishes and releases 10 CDs a year for TV, feature films and radio." Pays standard royalty.
Affiliate(s): Decidedly Superior Music (BMI).

- See D.S.M.'s other listings in the Record Producers and Advertising, AV and Commercial Music Firms sections.

How to Contact: Write first and obtain permission to submit. Prefers cassette or VHS videocassette and lyric or lead sheet. SASE. "Include SASE or we do not review nor respond to material." Reports in 3 months.
Music: Mostly **top 40**, **R&B/dance**, **CHR** and **rock**; also **jazz**, **country** and **instrumental tracks for background music**. Published *Dance America*, *Rock America* and *Horrific!*, all written and recorded by various artists on AACL Records.
Tips: "We can only publish finished masters for many uses which earn composers a steady income. We currently publish over 400 American composers. Their music is being licensed for network TV and feature films."

DAGENE MUSIC (ASCAP), P.O. Box 410851, San Francisco CA 94141. (415)822-1530. President: David Alston. Music publisher, record company (Cabletown Corp.) and record producer (Classic Disc Production). Estab. 1988. Hires staff songwriters. Pays standard royalty.
Affiliate(s): 1956 Music.
How to Contact: Call first and obtain permission to submit. Prefers cassette with 2 songs and lyric sheet. "Be sure to obtain permission before sending any material." SASE. Reports in 1 month.
Music: Mostly **R&B/rap**, **dance** and **pop**. Published "Maxin" (by Marcus Justice/Bernard Henderson), recorded by 2 Dominatorz on Dagene Records; "Love Don't Love Nobody" (by David Alston), recorded

by Rare Essence on Cabletown Records; and "Why Can't I Be Myself," written and recorded by David Alston on E-lect-ric Recordings.

‡DAPMOR PUBLISHING (ASCAP, BMI, SESAC), Box 121, Kenner LA 70065. (504)469-7500. President: Kelly Jones. Music publisher, record company and record producer. Estab. 1977. Publishes 10 songs/year. Publishes 3 new songwriters/year. Hires staff songwriters. Pays standard royalty.
How to Contact: Submit demo tape by mail. Unsolicited submissions are OK. Prefers 10-song CD. Does not return material. Reports in 1 month.
Music: Mostly **R&B**, **soul**, and **pop**; also **top 40**, **country** and **rap**. Published "Tell Me, Tell Me," and "Sisco," both written and recorded by Kelly Jones on Justice Recordings (R&B).

DARBONNE PUBLISHING CO. (BMI), Dept. SM, Route 3, Box 172, Haynesville LA 71038. (318)927-5253. President: Edward N. Dettenheim. Music publisher and record company (Wings Record Co.). Estab. 1987. Publishes 50 songs/year; publishes 8-10 new songwriters/year. Pays standard royalty.
How to Contact: Submit a demo tape by mail. Unsolicited submissions are OK. Prefers cassette or 7½ ips reel-to-reel with up to 12 songs and lyric sheet. Does not return material. Reports in 6 weeks.
Music: Mostly **country** and **gospel**. Published "Blanche" (by E. Dettenheim) and "It Don't Always Thunder" (by E. Dettenheim/T.J. Lynn), both recorded by T.J. Lynn on Wings Records (country); and "The Room" (by T.J. Lynn/E. Dettenheim), recorded by Kathy Shelby (country).
Tips: "The better the demo, the better your chances of interesting your listener."

DAVIS & DAVIS MUSIC (BMI), Rt. 1 Box 145A, Salem MO 65560-9721. (573)674-3299. President: Angel Davis. Music publisher, record company and producer. Estab. 1994. Pays standard royalty.
Affiliate(s): Late Dee Music Publishing (ASCAP), Music in the Right Key (BMI), High N' Low Note (ASCAP), Far Flung Music (BMI), Tuned On Music (BMI), Allegheny Music (ASCAP) and Believer's Choice (BMI).
How to Contact: Submit demo tape by mail. Unsolicited submissions are OK. Prefers cassette, DAT or VHS videocassette with up to 3 songs and lyric sheet. "Full studio demo and copyrighted material only!" SASE. Reports in 4-6 weeks.
Music: **Country**, **contemporary Christian**, **gospel**, **blues**, **R&B** and **ballads** in all genres. Published "Why" (by Jill Michaels), recorded by Tony Garron on Pharoah Records; "Stranger on the Street" and "Silence of Yours," written and recorded by Cody Blake on Sheheshe Records.
Tips: "We work with major artists, producers and labels. All demos should be on chrome II tape, full studio demo. Include SASE, no more than three songs per submission."

THE EDWARD DE MILES MUSIC COMPANY (BMI), 4475 Allisonville Rd., 8th Fl., Indianapolis IN 46205. (317)546-2912. Attn: Professional Manager. Music publisher, record company (Sahara Records), record producer, management, bookings and promotions. Estab. 1984. Publishes 50-75 songs/year; publishes 5 new songwriters/year. Hires staff songwriters. Pays standard royalty.

- See the listings for Edward De Miles in the Record Producers section, and Sahara Records and Filmworks Entertainment in the Record Companies section.

How to Contact: Write first and obtain permission to submit. Prefers cassette with 1-3 songs and lyric sheet. Does not return material. Reports in 1 month.
Music: Mostly **top 40 pop/rock**, **R&B/dance** and **C&W**; also **musical scores for TV, radio, films and jingles**. Published "Dance Wit Me" and "Moments," written and recorded by Steve Lynn on Sahara Records (R&B).
Tips: "Copyright all songs before submitting to us."

DEAN ENTERPRISES MUSIC GROUP, Dept. SM-8, P.O. Box 620, Redwood Estates CA 95044-0620. (408)353-1006. Attn: Executive Director. Music publisher, record company. Member: NARAS, Harry Fox Agency. Estab. 1989. Publishes 10-15 songs/year; publishes 6-8 new songwriters/year. Pays standard royalty.
Affiliate(s): Mikezel Music Co. (ASCAP), Teenie Deanie Music Co. (BMI) and Minotaur Records.
How to Contact: Submit demo tape by mail. Unsolicited submissions are OK. "Do not write or call for permission to submit." Prefers professional recording with a maximum of 4 songs on cassette or CD "with typed lyric sheets and brief letter of introduction as to why material is being submitted by songwriter. Material must be copyrighted and not assigned to a publisher. Will return tape only if SASE is included. A free evaluation is given with first-class SASE if evaluation form is provided by songwriter." Reports in 3 weeks. "Show name, address, phone number and © sign on tape and lyric sheets."
Music: Mostly **modern country**, **pop**, **MOR/easy listening**, **soft/easy rock**, **A/C** and **top 40**. No instrumentals. Published "Durango," written and recorded by Ronn Tomich; "Let It Go," written and recorded

by Bill Kirkpatrick; and "From the Pages of Time" (by Melba Blake), recorded by Chris Fertitta.
Tips: "Present a professional package with typed lyric sheets and do not send by anything other than First Class Mail, unless otherwise requested. Have a studio demo done with a good vocalist. Join songwriting organizations and read songwriting books; submit good quality tapes and always include a SASE if a response is requested. Do not send lyric sheets only."

DELEV MUSIC COMPANY, 7231 Mansfield Ave., Philadelphia PA 19138-1620. (215)276-8861. President: W. Lloyd Lucas. Music publisher, record company (Surprize Records, Inc.), record producer and management. Publishes 6-10 songs/year; publishes 6-10 new songwriters/year. Pays standard royalty.
Affiliate(s): Sign of the Ram Music (ASCAP), Gemini Lady Music (SESAC), and Delev Music (BMI).
• Delev Music Company's record label, Surprize Records, is listed in the Record Companies section.
How to Contact: Submit demo tape by mail. Unsolicited submissions OK. Prefers cassette or VHS videocassette with 1-3 songs and lyric sheet. "Video must be in VHS format and as professionally done as possible. It does not necessarily have to be done at a professional video studio, but should be a very good quality production showcasing artist's performance. We will not accept certified mail." Does not return material. Reports in 1-2 months.
Music: R&B ballads and **dance-oriented**, **pop ballads**, **crossover** and **country/western**. Published "Night Minds" and "When We're Alone" (by B. Heston/G. Fernandez), both recorded by Renee Francine on Transsonic Records (jazz); and "Good Things Come To Those Who Wait" (by Barbara Heston).
Tips: "Persevere regardless if it is sent to our company or any other company. Believe in yourself."

FRANK DELL MUSIC, P.O. Box 7171, Duluth MN 55807. (218)628-3003. President: Frank Dell. Music publisher, record company (Music Services and Marketing), record producer and management. Estab. 1980. Publishes 2 songs/year. Pays standard royalty.
Affiliate(s): Albindell Music (BMI).
• Frank Dell's record label, Music Services and Marketing, can be found in the Record Companies section.
How to Contact: Submit demo tape by mail. Unsolicited submissions are OK. Prefers cassette. Does not return material. Reports in 3 months.
Music: Mostly **country**, **gospel** and **pop**. Published *Memories*, written and recorded by Frank Dell on Country Legends Records.

DEMI MONDE RECORDS & PUBLISHING LTD., Foel Studio, Llanfair Caereinion, POWYS, **Wales**. Phone/fax: (01938)810758. Managing Director: Dave Anderson. Music publisher, record company (Demi Monde Records & Publishing Ltd.) and record producer (Dave Anderson). Member MCPS. Estab. 1983. Publishes 50-70 songs/year; publishes 10-15 new songwriters/year. Pays standard royalty.
• See Demi Monde's other listings in the Record Companies and Record Producers sections.
How to Contact: Submit demo tape by mail. Unsolicited submissions are OK. Prefers cassette or VHS videocassette with 3-4 songs. SAE and IRC. Reports in 6 weeks.
Music: Mostly **rock**, **R&B** and **pop**. Published "I Feel So Lazy" (by D. Allen), recorded by Gong (rock); "Phalarn Dawn" (by E. Wynne), recorded by Ozric Tentacles (rock); and "Pioneer" (by D. Anderson), recorded by Amon Dual (rock), all on Demi Monde Records.

DENNY MUSIC GROUP, Dept. SM, 3325 Fairmont Dr., Nashville TN 37203-1004. (615)269-4847. E-mail: pandora@aol.com. Contact: Pandora Denny. Estab. 1983. Music publisher, record company (Dollie Record Co., Jed Record Production) and record producer. Publishes 100 songs/year; 20 new songwriters/year. Pays standard royalty.
How to Contact: Submit demo tape by mail. Unsolicited submissions are OK. Prefers cassette with 3 songs and lyric sheet. SASE. Reports in 6 weeks.
Music: Mostly **country**, **bluegrass** and **gospel**. Published "Angel Band" and "On the Other Side" (by Wes Homner).

DINGO MUSIC, 4, Galleria Del Corso, Milan **Italy** 20122. Phone: (02)76021141. Fax: 0039/2/76021141. Website: http://www.staffre.interbusiness.it/md. Managing Director: Guido Palma. Music publisher and record company (Top Records). Estab. 1977. Publishes 30-35 songs/year; publishes 5 new songwriters/year. Hires staff writers. Pays standard royalty.
Affiliate(s): Top Records, Kiwi, Sap, Smoking.
• See the listing for Top Records in the Record Companies section.
How to Contact: Submit demo tape by mail. Unsolicited submissions are OK. Prefers cassette with 2 songs. Does not return material. Reports in 1 month.
Music: Mostly **rock**, **pop** and **R&B (pop)**; also **New Age** and **gospel**. Published "Mira El Macaron,"

written and recorded by Giangiacomino (pop/Latino); "To 'C' and 'A,' " written and recorded by Paul Mauriat (pop); and "Don't Give In" (by Penny Lea), recorded by Claudia Delon, all on Top Records.

DOC PUBLISHING, 10 Luanita Lane, Newport News VA 23606. (804)930-1814. A&R: Judith Guthro. Music publisher and management firm (Doc Holiday Productions). Estab. 1975. Publishes 30-40 songs/year; publishes 20 new songwriters/year. Pays standard royalty.
Affiliate(s): Dream Machine (SESAC), Doc Holiday Music (ASCAP).

- See the listing for Doc Holiday Productions in the Managers and Booking Agents section.

How to Contact: Submit demo tape by mail. Unsolicited submissions are OK. SASE. Reports in 2 weeks.
Music: Mostly **country** and **cajun**. Published *Sneaky Freaky People*, written and recorded by Big Al Downing on Tug Boat Records (country); *He Didn't Give Up on Me* (by Steven Johnson), recorded by The Johnson Family on Everlasting Records (gospel); and *D'Amore* (by Don Moore), recorded by D'Amore on Mega Records (R&B).

DON DEL MUSIC (BMI), P.O. Box 321, Port Washington WI 53074. (414)284-9777. Fax: (414)284-5242. Manager: Joseph C. DeLucia. Music publisher, record company (Cha Cha Records) and music promoter (Wisconsin Singer/Songwriter Series). Pays standard royalty.

- Don Del Music's record label, Cha Cha Records, is listed in the Record Companies section.

How to Contact: Write first and obtain permission to submit. Prefers cassette with 4-6 songs and lyric sheet. "A simple arrangement is much better than a major production—make sure the lyrics can be heard." Does not return material. Reports in 3 months.
Music: Mostly **acoustic folk**.

BUSTER DOSS MUSIC (BMI), 341 Billy Goat Hill Rd., Winchester TN 37398. (615)649-2577. Fax: (615)649-2732. E-mail: cbd@edge.net. President: Buster Doss. Music publisher, record producer, management firm and record company (Stardust). Estab. 1959. Publishes 500 songs/year; publishes 50 new songwriters/year. Pays standard royalty.

- See the listings for Stardust Records in the Record Companies section, and Col. Buster Doss Presents in the Record Producers and Managers and Booking Agents sections.

How to Contact: Write first and obtain permission to submit. Prefers cassette with 2 songs and lyric sheet. SASE. Reports ASAP.
Music: Mostly **country**; also **rock**. Published *I Only Sing The Blues* (by Buster Doss), recorded by Joey Welz on Caprice Records (country boogie); *I Don't Love You Anymore* (by Buster Doss), recorded by Jerri Arnold; and *Any Place in Texas* (by Buster Doss), recorded by Rooster Quantrell, both on Stardust Records.

DREAM SEEKERS PUBLISHING (BMI), 3199 Logan Dr., Newburgh IN 47630. (812)853-8980. President: Sally Sidman. Music publisher. Estab. 1993. Publishes 25-50 songs/year; publishes 15-20 new songwriters/year. Hires staff songwriters. Pays standard royalty.
Affiliate(s): Dream Builders Publishing (ASCAP).
How to Contact: Submit demo tape by mail. Unsolicited submissions are OK. Prefers cassette with 2-3 songs and lyric sheet. "If one of your songs is selected for publishing, we prefer to have it available on DAT for dubbing off copies to pitch to artist. Do not send your DAT until you have received a publishing contract." SASE. Reports in 4-6 weeks.
Music: Mostly **country** and **pop**. Published "Starting Tonight" (by Sam Storey), recorded by Wayne Horsburgh on Rotation Records (country); "Full Moon" (by Rebecca Dills), recorded by Karla Penner on Magna Records (country); and "An Elvis Night Before Christmas" (by Keith Collins), recorded by C.C. McCartney on Rotation Records (country).
Tips: "Try to make your demos sound as good as possible and always remember to cue the tape to the first song. We have a sister office in Hendersonville, TN and pitch directly to Nashville producers, labels and artists on a bi-weekly basis. We also pitch material to Los Angeles and New York. We only sign material that we feel is commercially competitive. We are extremely active in pitching our catalog. We never sign songs and then just leave them sitting on the shelf."

LISTINGS OF COMPANIES in countries other than the U.S. have the name of the country in boldface type.

DRIVE MUSIC, INC. (BMI), 10351 Santa Monica Blvd., Los Angeles CA 90025. (310)553-3490. Fax: (310)553-3373. E-mail: drive@earthlink.net. President: Don Grierson. CEO: Stephen Powers. Music publisher and record company (Drive Entertainment). Estab. 1993. Publishes 25 songs/year. Hires staff songwriters. Pays negotiated royalty. "Seeks single songs for representation. Acquires catalogs, large and small."
Affiliate(s): Donunda Music (ASCAP).
• Drive Music's record label, Drive Entertainment, is listed in the Record Companies section.
How to Contact: Submit demo tape by mail. Unsolicited submissions are OK. Prefers 3 songs and lyric sheet. "Send regular mail only." SASE. Reports in 4 weeks.
Music: Mostly **dance**, **pop** and **rock**; also **R&B**. Published all Sharon, Lois and Bram products (children's).

DUANE MUSIC, INC. (BMI), 382 Clarence Ave., Sunnyvale CA 94086. (408)739-6133. President: Garrie Thompson. Music publisher. Publishes 10-20 songs/year; publishes 1 new songwriter/year. Pays standard royalty.
Affiliate(s): Morhits Publishing (BMI).
• See their listing in the Record Producers section.
How to Contact: Submit demo tape by mail. Unsolicited submissions are OK. Prefers cassette with 1-2 songs. SASE. Reports in 4-8 weeks.
Music: Blues, **country**, **disco**, **easy listening**, **rock**, **soul** and **top 40/pop**. Published "Little Girl," recorded by The Syndicate of Sound & Ban (rock); "Warm Tender Love," recorded by Percy Sledge (soul); and "My Adorable One," recorded by Joe Simon (blues).

EARITATING MUSIC PUBLISHING (BMI), P.O. Box 1101, Gresham OR 97030. Music publisher. Estab. 1979. Publishes 40 songs/year; publishes 5 new songwriters/year. Pays individual per song contract, usually greater than 50% to writer.
How to Contact: Submit demo tape by mail. Unsolicited submissions are OK. Prefers cassette with lyric sheet. "Submissions should be copyrighted by the author. We will deal for rights if interested." Does not return material. No reply unless interested.
Music: Mostly **rock**, **contemporary Christian** and **country**; also **folk**.
Tips: "Melody is most important, lyrics second. Style and performance take a back seat to these. A good song will stand with just one voice and one instrument. Also, don't use staples on your mailers."

EARTHSCREAM MUSIC PUBLISHING CO. (BMI), 8377 Westview Dr., Houston TX 77055. (713)464-GOLD. Contact: Jeff Wells. Music publisher, record company and record producer. Estab. 1975. Publishes 12 songs/year; publishes 4 new songwriters/year. Pays standard royalty.
Affiliate(s): Reach For The Sky Music Publishing (ASCAP).
How to Contact: Submit demo tape by mail. Unsolicited submissions are OK. Prefers cassette or videocassette with 2-5 songs and lyric sheet. Does not return material. Reports in 2 months.
Music: New rock, **country**, **blues** and **top 40/pop**. Published "Baby Never Cries" (by Carlos DeLeon), recorded by Jinkies on Surface Records (pop); "Telephone Road," written and recorded by Mark May on Icehouse Records (blues); and "Do You Remember" (by Barbara Pennington), recorded by Perfect Strangers on Earth Records (rock).

‡EAST COAST MUSIC PUBLISHING (BMI), P.O. Box 12, Westport MA 02790-0012. (508)679-4272. Fax: (508)673-1235. President: Mary-Ann Thomas. Music publisher. Estab. 1996. Publishes 20 songs/year; publishes 10 new songwriters/year. Pays standard royalty.
Affiliate(s): Eastern Musicals (BMI).
How to Contact: Submit demo tape by mail. Unsolicited submissions are OK. Prefers cassette with 3-5 songs and lyric or lead sheet. "If you send a SASE I will get back to you within one month. If no SASE I will only respond if interested. We keep submissions in case we decide to publish the song at a future date." Does not return material. Reports in 1 month.
Music: Mostly **pop**, **country** and **rock**; also **R&B**, **alternative**, **dance** and **rap**. Published *My Desire* (by La Pointe/Davis), recorded by Freedom (pop); *Broken Promises* (by Ron Ettress), recorded by Separation Anxiety (rock); and *Battered Women* (by La Pointe/Davis), recorded by Friends & Relatives (R&B), all on Prolific Records.

EDITION ROSSORI, (formerly Musikverlag Rossori), Hietzinger Hptstr 94, Vienna A-1130 **Austria**. Phone: (01)8762400. Fax: (01)8762400. Manager: Mario Rossori. Music publisher and management agency. Estab. 1990. Publishes 150 songs/year; publishes 10 new songwriters/year. Pays standard royalty.
How to Contact: Submit demo tape by mail. Unsolicited submissions are OK. Does not return material. Reports in 1 month.

Music: Mostly **pop, dance** and **rock**. Published "Count on Me," recorded by Back Off! on BMG Records (pop); "Einsam," written and recorded by Heinz on MCA Records (pop); and "Make Your Dream Come True . . ." (by S. Silwester), recorded by Stand By on Music Research Records (dance).

ELECT MUSIC PUBLISHING (BMI), P.O. Box 22, Underhill VT 05489. (802)899-3787. Founder: Bobby Hackney. Music publisher, record producer and record company (LBI Records). Estab. 1980. Publishes 24 songs/year; publishes 3 new songwriters/year. Pays standard royalty.
How to Contact: Write first and obtain permission to submit. Prefers cassette and VHS videocassette with 3-4 songs and lyric sheet. SASE. Reports in 1 month.
Music: Mostly **reggae**, **R&B** and **rap**; also **rock**, some **jazz** and **poetry**. Published "Natural Woman" and "Sleeping With One Eye Open" (by B. Hackney), recorded by Lambsbread; and "African Princess," written and recorded by Mikey Dread, all on LBI Records.
Tips: "Send your best and remember, the amount of postage it took to get to the publisher is the same amount it will take to have your tape returned."

EMANDELL TUNES, 10220 Glade Ave., Chatsworth CA 91311. (818)341-2264. Fax: (818)341-1008. President/Administrator: Leroy C. Lovett, Jr. Estab. 1979. Publishes 6-12 songs/year; publishes 3-4 new songwriters/year. Pays standard royalty.
Affiliate(s): Ben-Lee Music (BMI), Birthright Music (ASCAP), Em-Jay Music (ASCAP), Northworth Songs, Chinwah Songs, Gertrude Music (all SESAC), Alvert Music (BMI) and Andrask Music, Australia (BMI).
How to Contact: Write first and obtain permission to submit. Prefers cassette or videocassette with 4-5 songs and lead or lyric sheet. Include bio of writer, singer or group. SASE. Reports in 4-6 weeks.
Music: Inspirational, **contemporary gospel** and **choral**; also **strong country** and **light top 40 gospel**. Published "Shake the Devil Off" (by Norwood/Thompson), recorded by Dorothy Norwood on Malaco Records (gospel); "Happy/You're Good to Me" (by Askey/Mayfield), recorded by Mary J. Blige on MCA Records; and *Get Busy With It* (by James Jernigan), recorded by The Jamz Gang on Faith Records (gospel).

EMF PRODUCTIONS, 1000 E. Prien Lake Rd., Suite D, Lake Charles LA 70601. (318)474-0435. President: Ed Fruge. Music publisher and record company. Estab. 1984. Pays standard royalty.

- See their listing in the Record Companies section.

How to Contact: Submit demo tape by mail. Unsolicited submissions are OK. Prefers cassette or VHS videocassette with 4 songs and lyric sheet. Does not return material. Reports in 6 weeks.
Music: Mostly **R&B**, **pop** and **rock**; also **country** and **gospel**.

EMI MUSIC PUBLISHING, 810 Seventh Ave., 36th Floor, New York NY 10019. (212)830-2000. Fax: (212)245-5868. Los Angeles office: 8730 Sunset Blvd., Penthouse East, Los Angeles CA 90069. (310)652-8078. Fax: (310)657-7485. Website: http://www.emimusic.com. Music publisher.
How to Contact: EMI does not accept unsolicited material.
Music: Published "If We Fall In Love Tonight" (by J. Harris III/T. Lewis), recorded by Rod Stewart on Warner Bros. Records; "Wonderwall" (by Noel Gallagher), recorded by Oasis on Epic Records; and "Back for Good" (by Gary Barlow), recorded by Take That on RCA Records.

ENID OKLAHOMA MUSIC PUBLISHING (BMI), P.O. Box 454, Enid OK 73702. (800)481-1866. Music Publisher: James O. Brown. Music publisher. Estab. 1995. Publishes 10-15 songs/year; publishes 4 new songwriters/year. Hires staff songwriters. Pays standard royalty.
How to Contact: Submit demo tape by mail. Unsolicited submissions are OK. Prefers cassette or CD with 1-3 songs, lyric and lead sheet. SASE. Reports in 2 weeks.
Music: Mostly **country, western swing** and **gospel**; also **ballads, country/crossover** and **cajun**. Published "Cajun Ways" (by Jim O. Brown), recorded by Shane Glover (cajun); "Jesus By My Side" (by Jim O. Brown), recorded by Jennifer Lowery (country gospel); and "Love You, Love Me" (by Jim O. Brown), recorded by Dave LaBrue (ballad), all on Oklahoma Records.

REMEMBER: Don't "shotgun" your demo tapes. Submit only to companies interested in the type of music you write. For more submission hints, refer to Getting Started on page 6.

ESI MUSIC GROUP (BMI), 9 Music Square S., Suite 118, Nashville TN 37203-9336. (615)297-9336. Administrator: Curt Conroy. Music publisher. Estab. 1990. Publishes 50-60 songs/year. Pays standard royalty.

How to Contact: Submit a demo tape by mail. Unsolicited submissions are OK. Prefers "good quality 3-4 song demo" and lyric sheet. "Guitar or piano-vocal OK. All envelopes must meet postal requirements for content." Does not return material. "To insure reply, include stamped, self-addressed envelope with adequate postage attached." Reports within 3-6 weeks.

Music: Mostly "**new**" **country**, **country rock** and **country pop**; also **country blues**. Published "Wine Over Matter," written and recorded by Pinto Bennett on MCM Records (country); "In the Wings," written and recorded by David Stewart on Wings Records; and "I've Been Branded," written and recorded by Hannah Onassis on Badger Records (country/rock).

Tips: "Research the artists you want to pitch to and match your songs to those artists. Listen carefully to current songs on the radio. This is your competition. Record the best demo that you can. Write for a list of available songwriter information that is available through our company."

EVER-OPEN-EYE MUSIC (PRS), Wern Fawr Farm, Pencoed, MID, Glam CF356NB **United Kingdom**. Phone: (0656)860041. Managing Director: M.R. Blanche. Music publisher and record company (Red-Eye Records). Member PPL and MCPS. Estab. 1980. Publishes 6 songs/year. Pays negotiable royalty.

- Ever-Open-Eye's record label, Red-Eye Records, is listed in the Record Companies section.

How to Contact: Submit demo tape by mail. Unsolicited submissions are OK. Prefers cassette or VHS videocassette. Does not return material. Reports in 2 months.

Music: Mostly **R&B**, **gospel** and **pop**; also **swing**. Published "Breakdown Song," "Shadow of the Sun" and "Outside Looking In," all written by Finn/Jones on Red Eye Records.

DOUG FAIELLA PUBLISHING (BMI), 19153 Paver Barnes Rd., Marysville OH 43040. (937)644-8295. President: Doug Faiella. Music publisher, record company (Studio 7 Records) and recording studio. Estab. 1984. Publishes 25 songs/year; publishes 5 new songwriters/year. Pays standard royalty.

How to Contact: Write to obtain permission to submit a tape. Prefers cassette with 3 songs and lyric sheets. Does not return material. Reports in 4 weeks.

Music: Mostly **country** and **gospel**.

FAMOUS MUSIC PUBLISHING COMPANIES, 10635 Santa Monica Blvd., Suite 300, Los Angeles CA 90025. (310)441-1300. Fax: (310)441-4722. President: Ira Jaffe. Senior Creative Director, Film and TV: Bob Knight. Creative Coordinator: Sarah Troy. Senior Creative Director: Bobby Carlton. Creative Director, Urban Music: Brian Postelle. New York office: 1633 Broadway, 11th Floor, New York NY 10019. Senior Creative Director: Ross Elliot. Senior Creative Director, Standard Catalogue: Mary Beth Roberts. Nashville office: 65 Music Square E., Nashville TN 37212. Senior Creative Director: Pat Finch. Creative Director: Curtis Green. Estab. 1929. Publishes 500 songs/year. Hires staff songwriters. Pays standard royalty.

Affiliate(s): Famous Music (ASCAP) and Ensign Music (BMI).

How to Contact: Query first. Does not accept unsolicited material. Prefers cassette with 3 songs and lyric sheet. Reports in 2-3 months.

Music: Mostly **rock, urban, R&B** and **country**. Published "Human Behaviour," recorded by Bjork (alternative); "One Sweet Day," recorded by Mariah Carey and Boyz II Men; and "100% Pure Love," recorded by Crystal Waters.

FARR-AWAY MUSIC, 701 N. Graycroft, Madison TN 37115. (615)865-2639. President: Tony Farr. Music publisher. Estab. 1970.

How to Contact: Submit demo tape by mail. Unsolicited submissions are OK. Prefers cassette or videocassette with 2-3 songs and lyric sheet. Does not return material.

Music: Mostly **country**.

FAT CITY PUBLISHING, 1906 Chet Atkins Place, Suite 502, Nashville TN 37212. (615)320-7678. Fax: (615)321-5382. President: Noel Michael. Music publisher, record producer, record company and booking agency (Fat City Artists). Estab. 1972. Pays standard royalty.

Affiliate(s): Fort Forever (BMI).

- See the listings for Fat City Artists in the Record Companies and Managers and Booking Agents sections.

How to Contact: Submit demo tape by mail. Unsolicited submissions are OK. Prefers cassette or VHS videocassette with 4-6 songs and lyric sheet. SASE. Reports in 2 weeks.

Music: Mostly **rock**, **country** and **blues**; also **alternative**, **rockabilly** and **jazz**.

FIRST RELEASE MUSIC PUBLISHING, 943 N. Madison Ave., Pasadena CA 91104. Phone/fax: (818)794-5545. President: Danny Howell. Operations Manager: Tony Jennaway. Music publisher. Publishes 30-50 songs/year. Hires staff songwriters. Pays standard royalty; co-publishing negotiable. "Very active in obtaining cover records and film and TV uses."
Affiliate(s): Fully Conscious Music, Cadillac Pink, Reggatta Music, Magnetic Publishing Ltd., Animal Logic Publishing and Blue Turtle Music.
How to Contact: "We *never* accept unsolicited tapes or phone calls—you must have referral or request." Returns all unsolicited material. Reports only if interested, but "retain personally written critique for every song I agree to accept."
Music: "We are interested in great songs and great writers. We are currently successful in all areas." Published "Power of Love" (by Tom Kimmel/Elizabeth Vidal), recorded by Sam Moore on Sony Records (R&B).
Tips: "Show up at one of my guest workshops and play me the last song you would ever play for a publisher; not the worst, the last! Educate yourself as to what writers we represent before pitching me (e.g., Sting, Lyle Lovett)."

FIRST TIME MUSIC (PUBLISHING) U.K. (PRS), Sovereign House, 12 Trewartha Road, Praa Sands, Penzance, Cornwall TR20 9ST **United Kingdom**. Phone: (01736)762826. Fax: (01736)763328. E-mail: panamus@aol.com. Website: http://www.lcn.co.uk/gisc.html. Managing Director: Roderick G. Jones. Music publisher, record company (First Time Records), record producer (Panama Music Library) and management firm (First Time Management and Production Co.). Member MCPS. Estab. 1986. Publishes 500-750 songs/year; 20-50 new songwriters/year. Hires staff writers. Pays standard royalty; "50-60% to established and up-and-coming writers with the right attitude."
Affiliate(s): Scamp Music Publishing.

- See the listings for First Time Records in the Record Companies section and First Time Management in the Managers and Booking Agents section.

How to Contact: Submit demo tape by mail. Unsolicited submissions are OK. Prefers cassette, 1⅞ ips cassette or VHS videocassette "of professional quality" with unlimited number of songs and lyric or lead sheets, but not necessary. Reports in 4-10 weeks. SAE and IRC. "Postal costs in the U.K. are much higher than the U.S.—one IRC doesn't even cover the cost of a letter to the U.S., let alone the return of cassettes. Enclose the correct amount for return and contact as stated." Reports in 4-10 weeks.
Music: Mostly **country**, **folk**, **pop/soul/top 20/rock** and **country with an Irish/Scottish crossover**; also **gospel/Christian**. Published "Lovers Chain" (by Charlie Landsborough), recorded by Daniel O'Donnell on Ritz Records (country); "I Remember Mary" (by Pete Arnold), recorded by The Fureys on EMI Records (folk); and "Love Song to You" (by Walt Young), recorded by P.J. Proby on J'Ace Records (pop).
Tips: "Have a professional approach—present well produced demos. First impressions are important and may be the only chance you get. Writers are advised to join the Guild of International Songwriters and Composers in the United Kingdom."

FLAMING STAR WEST MUSIC (BMI), P.O. Box 2400, Gardnerville NV 89410. (702)265-6825. Contact: Publishing Department. Music publisher, record company (Flaming Star Records) and record producer. Estab. 1988. Pays standard royalty.
How to Contact: Submit demo tape by mail. Unsolicited submissions are OK. Prefers cassette or DAT with 3 songs and lyric sheet. "Quality demos only. We prefer studio demos." SASE. Reports in 3-4 weeks.
Music: Mostly **country**, **rock** and **gospel**. Published *What Would You Give* (by Brian Williams); *'59 Caddy* (by N. LeDune); and *Adios Amigo* (by J. Johnson), all recorded by Ted Snyder on Flaming Star Records.

HAROLD FLAMMER MUSIC, 49 Waring Dr., Delaware Water Gap PA 18327. (717)476-0550. Fax: (717)476-5247. Editor: Lew Kirby. Music publisher. Estab. 1917. Publishes 50 songs/year. Pays negotiable royalty.
Affiliate(s): Glory Sound, Shawnee Press, Inc.
How to Contact: Write first and obtain permission to submit a demo. Prefers cassette with lyric and/or lead sheet. SASE. Reports in 6 months.
Music: Mostly **church/liturgical**.

FLEA CIRCUS MUSIC (ASCAP), 1820 Charles Yeargin Rd., Elberton GA 30635. Professional Manager: Dianna Kirk. Music publisher. Estab. 1991. Pays standard royalty.
How to Contact: Submit demo tape by mail. Unsolicited submissions are OK. Prefers cassette with 3 songs and lyric sheet. SASE. Reports in 1 month.
Music: Mostly **rock** and **alternative**. Published "Bug Bite," "LA LA" and "Little Love," all recorded by Cookieman.

FLYING RED HORSE PUBLISHING (BMI), 2932 Dyer St., Dallas TX 75205. (214)691-5318. E-mail: dashley@airmail.com. Website: http://web2.airmail/dashley/frhfin. Contact: Barbara McMillen. Music publisher, record company (Remarkable Records) and record producer (Texas Fantasy Music). Estab. 1993. Publishes 15-30 songs/year; publishes 6-10 new songwriters/year. Pays standard royalty.

• See the listing for Texas Fantasy Music in the Record Producers section.

How to Contact: Write or call first and obtain permission to submit. Prefers cassette with 3 songs and lyric sheet. SASE. Reports in 6 weeks.

Music: Mostly **children's songs** and **stories**. Published "The Little Last Note" (by Lauren Shapiro), recorded by Rollie Anderson and Richard Theisen; "My Friend Sam," written and recorded by Jeanie Perkins; and *Dinosaur Rag* (by Beverly Houston), recorded by Dixie Chicks, both on Remarkable Records.

Tips: "Even when a song is written for children, it should still meet the criteria for a well-written song—and be pleasing to adults as well."

FRESH ENTERTAINMENT (ASCAP), 1315 Simpson Rd., Atlanta GA 30314. (770)642-2645. Vice President of A&R: Willie W. Hunter. Music publisher and record company. Publishes 5 songs/year. Hires staff songwriters. Pays standard royalty.

Affiliate(s): !Hserf Music (ASCAP), Blair Vizzion Music (BMI), Santron Music (BMI).

• See their listing in the Record Companies section.

How to Contact: Submit demo tape by mail. Unsolicited submissions are OK. Prefers cassette or videocassette with 3 songs and lyric sheet. "Send photo if available." SASE. Reports in 3 weeks.

Music: Mostly **rap**, **R&B** and **pop/dance**. Published "Nasy Dancer" and "Animosity" (by Kilo/Taz), recorded by Kilo on Ichiban Records (rap); and "Good Thang" (by Cirocco), recorded by Diamond on Warlock Records (R&B).

FRETBOARD PUBLISHING (BMI), Box 40855, Nashville TN 37204. (615)269-5638. Contact: A&R Department. Music publisher, record company (Mosrite Records), record producer (Mark Moseley). Estab. 1963. Publishes 25 songs/year; publishes 3 new songwriters/year. Pays standard royalty.

Affiliate(s): Woodgrain Publishing Co. (ASCAP).

How to Contact: Submit a demo tape by mail. Prefers cassette with 2 songs and lyric sheets. Does not return unsolicited material. Reports in 6 weeks "only if we want to hear more."

Music: Mostly **country**, **rock** (not heavy) and **southern gospel**. Published "Even Now" (by Mark Moseley) and "Mommy's Playing Santa Claus" (by Maurice Brandon), both recorded by Marie Lester (Christmas); and "Queen For a Day" (by Billy Mize), recorded by Barbara Mandrell (country), all on Mosrite Records.

Tips: "Give us time to get to your songs before you make another contact."

FRICK MUSIC PUBLISHING CO. (BMI), 404 Bluegrass Ave., Madison TN 37115. (615)865-6380. Contact: Bob Frick. Music publisher, record company (R.E.F. Records), management firm (Bob Scott Frick Enterprises) and record producer (Bob Scott Frick). Publishes 50 songs/year; publishes 2 new songwriters/year. Pays standard royalty.

Affiliate(s): Sugarbakers Music (ASCAP).

• Frick Music's record label, R.E.F. Records, is listed in the Record Companies section; their booking agency, Bob Scott Frick Enterprises, is listed in the Managers and Booking Agents section; and producer Bob Scott Frick is listed in the Record Producers section.

How to Contact: Write or call first and obtain permission to submit. Prefers 7½ ips reel-to-reel, cassette or videocassette with 2-10 songs and lyric sheet. SASE. Reports in 2 weeks.

Music: Mostly **gospel**; also **country**, **rock** and **top 40/pop**. Published "I Found Jesus in Nashville" (by Lin Butler), recorded by Bob Scott Frick; and "Good Lovin'," written and recorded by Teresa Ford, both on R.E.F. Records.

‡FRICON MUSIC COMPANY (BMI), 11 Music Square E., Nashville TN 37203. (615)826-2288. Fax: (615)826-0500. President: Terri Fricon. Music publisher. Estab. 1981. Publishes 25 songs/year; publishes 1-2 new songwriters/year. Pays standard royalty.

Affiliate(s): Fricout Music Company (ASCAP) and Now and Forever Songs (SESAC).

How to Contact: Write first and obtain permission to submit. Prefers cassette with 1-2 songs and lyric

THE TYPES OF MUSIC each listing is interested in are printed in boldface.

or lead sheet. "Prior permission must be obtained or packages will be returned." SASE. Reports in 4-6 weeks.
Music: Mostly **country**.

‡FRO'S MUSIC PUBLISHING, 163 Tetreau St. #B, Thibodaux LA 70301. (504)446-8718. Fax: (504)455-7076. Owner: J. Roel Lungay. Music Editor: Vincent S. Tan. Music publisher, record company (Fro's Records) and record producer. Estab. 1992. Publishes 5-8 songs/year; publishes 2-3 new songwriters/year. "Pays negotiable royalty, but usually the standard."
Affiliate(s): Telldem Records (Philippines), Foreign Brain Music (Philippines) and PB Music.
How to Contact: Submit demo tape by mail. Unsolicited submissions are OK. Prefers cassette or DAT with 3-5 songs and lyric and lead sheet (optional but encourageable). "Submit good clear demo with typed lyric and/or lead sheet and cover letter. Make sure name, address, phone number are printed on the tape. SASE for reply only; no phone calls." Does not return material. Reports in 2-4 weeks.
Music: Mostly **Christian**, **inspirational** and **church/religious**; also **positive country**, **pop** and **Christmas**. Published *Dear Jesus* (by J. Roel Lungay), recorded by Sara Estes on Fro's Records (Christian); *One Heart, One Mind* (by T.Q. Solis, Jr.), recorded by various artists on PB Records (inspirational); and *Be My Santa Claus* (by Arnold Zamora), recorded by J. Roel Lungay on Fro's Records (ballad).

FROZEN INCA MUSIC, 1800 Peachtree St., Suite 333, Atlanta GA 30309. (404)355-5580. Fax: (404)351-2786. E-mail: mrland@mindspring.com. President: Michael Rothschild. Music publisher, record company (Landslide Records) and record producer. Estab. 1981. Publishes 12 songs/year; publishes 3 new songwriters/year. Pays standard royalty.
Affiliate(s): Landslide Records.

- Frozen Inca's record label, Landslide, is listed in the Record Companies section.

How to Contact: Submit demo tape by mail. Unsolicited submissions are OK. Prefers cassette with 6-12 songs and lyric sheet. SASE. Reports in 2 months.
Music: Mostly **R&B**, **blues** and **roots music**; also **rock**. Published "A Quitter Never Wins" (by T. Ellis/M. Sampson), recorded by Jonny Lang on A&M Records; *To The Devil For A Dime* (by T. Ellis/C. Long), recorded by Tinsley Ellis on Alligator Records (blues); and *Winning* (by R. Keller), recorded by Trammel Starks on InterSound Records (jazz).

‡FULL MOON MUSIC, INC. (BMI), P.O. Box 520195, Bronx NY 10452. (212)492-9202. Fax: (212)716-2963. Operations Officer: Leon G. Pinkston. Music publisher and record company (Crescent Recording Corporation). Estab. 1995. Publishes 2-5 songs/year; publishes 1-3 new songwriters/year. Hires staff writers. Pays standard royalty.

- See the listing for Crescent Recording Corporation in the Record Companies section.

How to Contact: Submit demo tape by mail. Unsolicited submissions are OK. Prefers cassette, DAT or CD with 2-5 songs and lyric sheet. "Submit demos that are professionally finished and well-produced. Songs should be complete with 2-5 songs." Does not return material. Reports in 2-3 months.
Music: Mostly **R&B/soul**, **rock/pop** and **rap**; also **dance/club**, **country** and **jazz/gospel**. Published "Something On My Mind" (by C. Watson/Q. Allen), recorded by Camille Watson (soul/R&B); and "Crazytown," written and recorded by Dodging Reality (rock), both on Crescent Records.

FUNZALO MUSIC (BMI), P.O. Box 35880, Tucson AZ 85740. (520)628-8655. Fax: (520)628-9072. E-mail: mikespoop@aol.com. President: Michael J. Lembo. Music publisher. Estab. 1976. Publishes 50-150 songs/year. Hires staff songwriters. Pays standard royalty.
Affiliate(s): Tomata-du-Plenti Music (ASCAP).
How to Contact: Submit demo tape by mail. Unsolicited submissions are OK. Prefers cassette with 3 songs and lyric sheet. Does not return material. Reports in 2 weeks.
Music: Mostly **hits**; also **rock**, **pop** and **alternative**.

FURROW MUSIC (BMI), P.O. Box 4121, Edmond OK 73083-4121. (405)348-6534. Owner/Publisher: G.H. Derrick. Music publisher, record company (Gusher Records) and record producer. Estab. 1984. Publishes 10-15 songs/year. Pays standard royalty.
How to Contact: Submit demo tape by mail. Unsolicited submissions are OK. (No phone calls prior to submission). Prefers cassette or VHS videocassette with 1 song and lyric sheet. "One instrument and vocal is OK for demo." SASE. Reports in 2 weeks.
Music: Mostly **country**, **R&B** and **novelty**; also **patriotic**, **cowboy** and **Christmas**. Published "Home For Christmas," "Way Out on the Prairie" and "Take Me Back Home For Christmas," all written and recorded by Harvey Derrick and published by Pelican Records (songs part of a two-book narration of children's Christmas stories).

Tips: "Have your song critiqued by other writers (or songwriter organizations) prior to making the demo. Only make and send demos of songs that have a universal appeal. Make sure the vocal is out front of the music. Never be so attached to a lyric or tune that you can't rewrite it. Don't forget to include your SASE."

‡FUTURE-1 MUSIC PUBLISHING (BMI), 914 Walters St., Bethlehem PA 18017-6024. Phone/fax: (610)865-2050. President/CEO: Chris Michaels. Music publisher, record company (Graylady Records) and record producer. Estab. 1993. Publishes 4 songs/year; publishes 1 new songwriter/year. Pays standard royalty.
Affiliate(s): Mic-Walk Music Publishing Co. (BMI).
How to Contact: Submit demo tape by mail. Unsolicited submissions are OK. Prefers cassette or VHS videocassette with lyric sheet. Does not return material. Reports in 2 months.
Music: Mostly **contemporary jazz**, **gospel** and **new tech**; also **jazz/country**, **contemporary ballads** and **songs with emotion**. Published "Loddidoddi," written and recorded by Clint Washington (rap); "Brighter Days" (by Eddie Hollman III/Richard Wallen III), recorded by Toni Chappelle (hip hop), both on RCP Records; and "Hot-N-Stickey," written and recorded by Chris Michaels (contemporary jazz) on GLR Records.

ALAN GARY MUSIC, P.O. Box 179, Palisades Park NJ 07650. President: Alan Gary. Creative Director: Fran Levine. Creative Assistant: Harold Green. Music publisher. Estab. 1987. Publishes a varying number of songs/year. Pays standard royalty.
How to Contact: Submit demo tape by mail. Unsolicited submissions are OK. Prefers cassette or VHS videocassette with lyric sheet. SASE.
Music: Mostly **pop**, **R&B** and **dance**; also **rock**, **A/C** and **country**. Published "Liberation" (by Gary/Julian), recorded by Les Julian on Music Tree Records (A/C); "Love Your Way Out of This One" (by Gary/Rosen), recorded by Deborah Steel on Bad Cat Records (contemporary country); and "Dueling Rappers" (by Gary/Free), recorded by Prophets of Boom on You Dirty Rap! Records (rap/R&B).

GENETIC MUSIC PUBLISHING (ASCAP), 10 Church Rd., Merchantville NJ 08109. (609)662-4428. E-mail: webcore@webcom.com or dedtrooper@aol.com. Website: http://thewebslinger.com/svengali/genetic.html. Contact: Vince Andrews. Music publisher, record company (Svengali) and record producer (Whey Cooler Production). Estab. 1982. Publishes 1-5 songs/year. Pays standard royalty.
Affiliate(s): Cooler By A Mile (ASCAP), BC Music (ASCAP) SIV Songs (ASCAP) and Baggy Music (BMI).
How to Contact: Write or call first and obtain permission to submit. Prefers cassette. SASE. Reports in 3-6 weeks.
Music: Mostly **dance**, **R&B** and **pop**; also **alternative rock** and **jazz**. Published *Sexual Playground*, written and recorded by Father MC on Spoiled Brat Records (rap); *Pretty Poison's Greatest Hits* (by Starling/Cooler), recorded by Pretty Poison on Svengali Records (pop/R&B); and "Crawl" (remix) (by Starling/Cooler), recorded by Sex in Violets on FTS Records (industrial).

GFI WEST MUSIC PUBLISHING, P.O. Box 641351, Los Angeles CA 90064. (310)281-7454. E-mail: jjjingle@aol.com. A&R: "J.C." Music publisher. Estab. 1991. Publishes 10 songs/year; 10 new songwriters/year. Pays standard royalty.
How to Contact: Write or call first for permission to submit. Prefers cassette with 1-5 songs and lyric sheet. "Submissions must be copyrighted." Does not return material. Reports in 2-3 months.
Music: Mostly **instrumentals** and **incidental music**; also **pop**, **rock** and **R&B**. Published "Crazy Motion" (by Paul McCarty/Janet Jeffrey), recorded by Janet Jeffrey for the soundtrack *Stranger in the City*; "Touch My Soul" (by Alex Varden/Kent Pearse), recorded by Alex Varden for the soundtrack *The Forest*; and "I Know" (by Janet Jeffrey), recorded by Janet J. on TBRC Records.
Tips: "Strong melodies attract my attention. I look for crossover appeal as well as songs that leave you humming the words in your head."

GIFTNESS ENTERPRISE (BMI, ASCAP), Dept. SM, 1315 Simpson Rd. NW, Suite #5, Atlanta GA 30314. (404)642-2645. Contact: New Song Department. Music publisher. Publishes 30 songs/year; publishes 15 new songwriters/year. Employs songwriters on a salary basis. Pays standard royalty.
Affiliate(s): Blair Vizzion Music (BMI) and Fresh Entertainment (ASCAP).
How to Contact: Submit demo tape by mail. Unsolicited submissions are OK. Prefers cassette with 4 songs and lyric or lead sheet. SASE. Reports in 3 weeks.
Music: Mostly **R&B**, **pop** and **rock**; also **country**, **gospel** and **jazz**. Published "Nasty Dancer" (by Taz/Kilo), recorded by Kilo on Ichiban Records (rap); "Good Thang" (by Cirocco/Mr. G.), recorded by Diamond on Wahock Records (R&B); and "That's Right" (by Raheem/Taz), recorded by D.J. Taz on Success Records (rap).

GLOBEART INC., % JPMC Music Inc., 80 Pine St., 2nd Floor, New York NY 10005-1702. (212)344-5588. Fax: (212)344-5566. E-mail: music@jpmc.com. Website: http://www.JPMC.com. President: Jane Peterer. Music publisher. Estab. 1989. Publishes 50 songs/year; publishes 5 new songwriters/year. Pays standard royalty.
Affiliate(s): GlobeSound Publishing (ASCAP).
How to Contact: Submit a demo tape by mail. Unsolicited submissions are OK. Prefers cassette or videocassette with 3-5 songs and lyric or lead sheet. SASE. Reports in 6-8 weeks.
Music: Mostly **pop/R&B**, **jazz** and **gospel**; also **country**. Published "Runnin' " (by Hank/Swan), recorded by Funky Bud on JPMC Records (funk); "Echoes," written and recorded by JoAnne Brackeen on DA Music Records (jazz); and "Woman Of the Sea" (by Antonio Breschi), recorded by Breschi/Cassidy on Pick Records (instrumental).

JAY GOLD MUSIC PUBLISHING (BMI), P.O. Box 409, East Meadow NY 11554-0409. Phone/fax: (516)486-8699. President: Jay Gold. Music publisher. Estab. 1981. Publishes 25 songs/year; publishes 6 new songwriters/year. Pays standard royalty.
How to Contact: Submit a demo tape by mail. Unsolicited submissions are OK. Prefers cassette with 2 songs and lyric sheets. Does not return material. Reports ASAP. "Use only high quality chrome cassettes for submissions."
Music: Mostly **pop**, **rock** and **country**. Published "A Touch of the Heart," recorded by Eric Burdon; "All the Wrong Reasons," written and recorded by Jay Gold on Turbo Records (pop); and "Long Time" (by Jay Gold), recorded by Joe-Joe Bentry on Cardinal Records.
Tips: "Make the best demo you can afford. It's better to have a small publisher pushing your songs than a large one keeping them on the shelf."

‡GOLDEN HARP MUSIC (BMI), P.O. Box 210982, Nashville TN 37221. (615)356-9691. Fax: (615)356-7274. Professional Manager: Glen Edwards. Music publisher. Estab. 1984. Publishes 15 songs/year; publishes 3 new songwriters/year. Pays standard royalty.
How to Contact: Submit demo tape by mail. Unsolicited submissions are OK. Prefers cassette with no more than 4 songs and lyric sheet. Does not return material. Reports back by mail in 1 month.
Music: Mostly **country**, **rock** and **folk**; also **blues**. Published *Life Is A Mystery*, *Unbreakable Heart* and *Wine & Memories*, written and recorded by Steve Haggard on Wild Oats Records (country).

THE GOODLAND MUSIC GROUP INC., P.O. Box 24454, Nashville TN 37202. (615)269-7074. Contact: Publishing Dept. Music publisher. Estab. 1988. Publishes 50 songs/year; 5-10 new songwriters/year. Pays standard royalty.
Affiliate(s): Goodland Publishing Company (ASCAP), Marc Isle Music (BMI) and Gulf Bay Publishing (SESAC).
How to Contact: Submit demo tape by mail. Unsolicited submissions are OK. SASE. "Request inclusion of 32¢ SASE for reply only." Reports in 2-4 weeks.
Music: Contemporary country. Published "Where Does Love Go When It's Gone?" (by Barton/Byram), recorded by Warren Johnson on MDL Records; "Swingin' for the Fences" (by Myers/Meier) and "The Best Mistake" (by Primamore), both recorded by Daniel Glidwell on Starborn Records.

‡GOODNIGHT KISS MUSIC (BMI), 10153½ Riverside Dr. #239, Toluca Lake CA 91602. (213)883-1518. Fax: (213)850-1964. E-mail: hlywdgrl@aol.com. Managing Director: Janet Fisher. Music publisher. Estab. 1986. Publishes 8-10 songs/year; publishes 5-7 new songwriters/year. Pays standard royalty.
How to Contact: Submit demo tape by mail. Unsolicited submissions are OK. Prefers cassette, DAT or CD with 1-3 songs and lyric sheet. Send SASE for reply. Does not return material. Reports in 3-6 months.
Music: Mostly **heavy metal**, **R&B** and **alternative rock**; also **rap**, **hip hop** and **rock**. Published "Heart-shaped Heartache" (by J. Fisher/B. Turner), recorded by Ricky Kershaw in the film *Good Luck*, with James Earl Jones and Gregory Hines; "King of Romance" (by J. Fisher), recorded by The More in the film *Quake*, starring Steve Railsback; and "Hard Love" (by T. Horrigan/J. Fisher), recorded by Tim Horrigan in the film *Final Judgment*, starring Sally Kirkland.
Tips: "We will call you when possible, if we are interested. We use a basic SGA contract, with a few paragraphs excepted."

GREEN ONE MUSIC (BMI), Rockin' Chair Center Suite 102, 1033 W. State Highway 76, Branson MO 65616. (417)334-2336. Fax: (417)334-2306. President: George J. Skupien. Music publisher, record label and recording studio. Estab. 1992. Publishes 6-12 songs/year. Pays standard royalty.

- Green One Music's record label, Green Bear Records, is listed in the Record Companies section.

How to Contact: Submit demo tape by mail. Unsolicited submissions are OK. Prefers cassette or DAT

with 2-4 songs. Does not return material. Reports in 3 months.
Music: Mostly **country**, **MOR** and **light rock**; also **American polka music**, **waltzes** and **comedy—fun songs**. Published "Don't Ever Let Your Young Love Grow Old" (by Marty Nevers/Carla Elliott); "Oh My Aching Back" and "Lotto Polka" (by George Skupien).
Tips: "Always put your best song first on your tapes submitted. If possible, submit a professional demo of your song. Be sure your vocal is clear!"

GREEN ZEBRA MUSIC (BMI), (formerly Tooth & Nail Music), P.O. Box 140136, Nashville TN 37214. Manager: Jenny Travis. Music publisher and record producer. Estab. 1993. Publishes 30 songs/year; publishes 3 new songwriters/year. Pays standard royalty.
Affiliate(s): 1st Page Music (BMI).
How to Contact: Submit demo tape by mail. Unsolicited submissions are OK. Prefers cassette or VHS videocassette with 1-10 songs and lyric sheet. "Artists send a picture with tape." SASE. Reports in 6 weeks.
Music: Mostly **pop**, **rock** and **R&B**. Published *Waiting For You* (by Darrell Yokochi/Anderson Page), recorded by Dream Street on Tooth & Nail Records; "Tell" (by Darrell Yokochi/Stephany Delray) and "Ophelia" (by Anderson Page/Billy Herzing), both recorded by Daryo on Green Zebra Records.

G-STRING PUBLISHING (BMI, SOCAN), P.O. Box 1096, Hudson, Quebec, J0P 1H0 **Canada**. (613)780-1163. Fax: (514)458-2819. E-mail: larecord@total.net. Music Coordinator: Ms. Tanya Hart. Music publisher, record company (L.A. Records), record producer. Estab. 1991. Publishes 20 songs; publishes 5-10 new songwriters/year. Pays standard royalty.

- G-String's record label, L.A. Records, is listed in the Record Companies section and their management firm, M.B.H. Music Management, is listed in the Managers and Booking Agents section.

How to Contact: Submit demo tape by mail. Unsolicited submissions are OK. Prefers cassette or DAT with 3 songs and lyric sheet. Reports in 4 months.
Music: Mostly **commercial rock**, **A/C** and **dance**; also **country**. Published *I Never Needed You*, written and recorded by Jessica Ehrenworth; "Love Can Make You" (by M. Lengies), recorded by Tommy Hayes; and *Desire* (by A. Jameson/M. Lengies), recorded by Jessica Ehrenworth, all on L.A. Records.
Tips: "Know your craft; songs must have great lyrics and good melody, and create a strong emotional reaction. They must be under 4 minutes and must be radio friendly."

HALO INTERNATIONAL (BMI), P.O. Box 101, Sutton MA 01590. E-mail: mass38m@aol.com. Owner/Publisher: John Gagne. Music publisher, record company (MSM Records, Hālo Records, Bronco Records) and record producer. Estab. 1979. Publishes 6-8 songs/year. Pays standard royalty.
Affiliate(s): Pick the Hits Music (ASCAP) and Mount Scott Music (BMI).
How to Contact: Write first and obtain permission to submit. Prefers cassette with 2 songs and lyric sheets. SASE. Reports in 1 month.
Music: Mostly **soundtracks** (theater and TV themes), **contemporary country**, **traditional country** and **folk**. Working with playwrights and composers for musical and theater works with incidental music. Published "Fog" (by John Scott), recorded by Boston Jazzazz Latina on Halo Records; and *Backyard Strut*, written and recorded by Backyard Strut (R&B).

R.L. HAMMEL ASSOCIATES, INC., P.O. Box 531, Alexandria IN 46001-0531. Phone/fax: (317)724-3900. E-mail: rlh@lquest.net. President: Randal Hammel. Music publisher, record producer and consultant. Estab. 1974. Pays standard royalty.
Affiliate(s): Ladnar Music (ASCAP) and Lemmah Music (BMI).
How to Contact: Write first and obtain permission to submit a demo. Prefers cassette, DAT or VHS/8mm videocassette with 3 songs and typed lyric sheet. SASE. Reports ASAP.
Music: Mostly **pop**, **Christian** and **R&B**; also **MOR**, **rock** and **country**. Published *Lessons For Life* (by Kelly Hubbell/Jim Boedicker) and *I Just Want Jesus* (by Mark Condon), both recorded by Kelly Connor on Impact Records.

HARBOR GOSPEL MUSIC PRODUCTION (BMI), P.O. Box 641, Findlay OH 45839. (419)422-4981. President: Paul Steinhour. Music publisher. Estab. 1990. Publishes 15-20 songs/year; publishes 2 new songwriters/year. Pays standard royalty.

REFER TO THE CATEGORY INDEX (at the end of this section) to find exactly which companies are interested in the type of music you write.

How to Contact: Submit demo tape by mail. Unsolicited submissions are OK. Prefers cassette or VHS videocassette with 1-10 songs and lyric sheet. SASE. Reports in 3 months.
Music: Mostly **country gospel**, **southern gospel** and **Christian contemporary**. Published "I'll Be Gone" (by Jeff Smith) and "He's Living Today" (by Rusty Vansicle), both recorded by The Fishermen on Clearwater Records; and "He Still Does Miracles" (by Paul Steinhour), recorded by The Majestics on Voice One Records.
Tips: "Make sure your message is consistent and your hook line is used throughout the song."

‡HAUTBOY MUSIC, Lawford House, Berrister Place, Raunds, Northants NN9 6JN **England**. Phone: (0933)460628. Proprietor: Peter Malski. Music publisher. Estab. 1988. Publishes 12 songs/year; publishes 5 new songwriters/year. Pays standard royalty.
How to Contact: Submit demo tape by mail. Unsolicited submissions are OK. Prefers cassette or VHS videocassette with 5 songs and lyric or lead sheet. SAE and IRC. Reports in 2 weeks.
Music: Mostly **dance/pop** and **rock/indie**. Published "Tell The DJ" (by Alan Coote/Pete Gibbs), recorded by Speedy Gonzales on Bubblegum Records (dance); "The Sweetest Dream" and "Let The Music Hypnotise" (by Chetcutti/McGuinness), both recorded by RM Project on ZYX Records (dance).
Tips: "Submit the material that I work with. On many occasions writers take little notice of required style and send in the wrong style which wastes everyone's time and resources!"

HAWKSBILL MUSIC (BMI), P.O. Box 1281, Orange VA 22960. (540)672-0122. President: Parke Stanley. Music publisher. Estab. 1991. Pays standard royalty.
How to Contact: Submit demo tape by mail. Unsolicited submissions are OK. Prefers cassette with 3 songs and lyric sheet. SASE. Reports in 2 weeks.
Music: Mostly **country rock**, **country** and **R&B**; also **crossover** and **pop**. Published "Talkin To The Walls" (by Mike Raley); "Bourbon Copy" (by Lou Sweigmon) and "Hello Greyhound" (by the Coreys), all recorded by Scott Ryan on White Oak Records.
Tips: "Strive to say the ordinary in a fresh way! Learn techniques such as alliteration, antonyms, inner rhymes, etc. which catch the ears of hit producers and artists. This is explained in my free report, '16 Ways to Make Your Songs More Commercial.' Write and request it, include SASE. I have connections at Nashville major labels, and strong U.S. independent labels. Positive, uptempo songs have the best chance of a cut, but make sure they have good melody, not just 12-bar blues. Constantly write down hit songs from the radio and observe their structure, rhyming pattern, length, etc. It's good to time your songs and write the minutes and seconds on lyric sheets. Study hard—you can make money from your music!"

‡HEADACHES & HEARTBURN MUSIC (BMI), 3637 Bellaire Ave., Suite #302, White Bear Lake MN 55110. President: James C. Burau. Music publisher. Estab. 1994. Publishes 10-20 songs/year; publishes 10-12 new songwriters/year. Pays standard royalty of 50%.
How to Contact: Submit demo tape by mail. Unsolicited submissions are OK. Prefers cassette and cover letter with 1-4 songs and lyric sheet. Does not return material. Reports in 1 month.
Music: Mostly **country**; also **Southern rock** and **Southern folk**. Published "Man In Cowboy's Clothes" (by James Burau) and "Strange Book Of Matches" (by Burau/McKoskey), both recorded by Jim Diamond on Metro Records (country); and *The Man He Has Become* (by Jim Diamond), recorded by Dale St. Cloud on A&K Records (country).
Tips: "You have to be better than the best you're hearing on the radio today. Be unique and honest with your songs. Be open to constructive criticism."

HENLY MUSIC ASSOCIATES (ASCAP), 45 Perham St., W. Roxbury MA 02132. President: Bill Nelson. Music publisher, record company (Woodpecker Records) and record producer. Estab. 1987. Publishes 5 songs/year; publishes 5 new songwriters/year. Pays standard royalty.

- Bill Nelson, Henly Music's president, is listed in the Record Producers section.

How to Contact: Submit demo tape by mail. Unsolicited submissions are OK. Prefers cassette with 4 songs and lyric sheet. SASE. Reports in 1 month.
Music: Mostly **country**, **pop** and **gospel**. Published "Kentucky Memory," by Michael Walsh and David Finnerty; "Seasons of Our Love," by Connie Makris, DJ Oklahoma and Jim Sweeney; and "All Is Well," by Pam Healy.

HEUPFERD MUSIKVERLAG GmbH, Ringwaldstr. 18, Dreieich 63303 **Germany**. Phone/fax: (06103)86970. E-mail: heupferd@t-online.de. General Manager: Christian Winkelmann. Music publisher. GEMA. Publishes 60 songs/year. Pays "royalties after GEMA distribution plan."
Affiliate(s): Song Bücherei (book series).
How to Contact: Write first and obtain permission to submit. Prefers cassette and lead sheet. SAE and

IRC. Reports in 1 month.
Music: Mostly **folk**, **jazz** and **fusion**; also **New Age**, **rock** and **ethnic music**. Published "Valse Mélancolique," written and recorded by Rüdiger Oppermann (New Age); and "Rainy Sundays" (by Andy Irvine), recorded by Andy Irvine and others, both on Wundertüte Records.

HICKORY LANE PUBLISHING AND RECORDING (SOCAN, ASCAP), P.O. Box 2275, Vancouver, British Columbia V6B 3W5 **Canada**. (604)987-3756. Fax: (604)987-0616. E-mail: waveshape@msn.com. President: Chris Urbanski. A&R Manager: Dave Rogers. Music publisher, record company and record producer. Estab. 1988. Hires staff writers. Pays standard royalty.

- See Hickory Lane's listing in the Record Producers section.

How to Contact: Write or call first and obtain permission to submit. Prefers cassette or VHS videocassette with 1-5 songs. SAE and IRC. Reports in 4-6 weeks.
Music: Country. Produced "Country Drives Me Wild," recorded by Chris Michaels on Hickory Lane Records; and *Until Now* (by Steve Mitchell/Chris Michaels), recorded by Chris Michaels.
Tips: "Send us a good quality sounding demo, with the vocals upfront. Be original and professional in your approach. We are looking for good songs, and so are the major record labels that we deal with."

HICKORY VALLEY MUSIC (ASCAP), 10303 Hickory Valley, Ft. Wayne IN 46835. E-mail: alstraten@aol.com. President: Allan Straten. Music publisher, record company (Yellow Jacket Records) and record producer (Al Straten Productions). Estab. 1988. Publishes 10 songs/year; publishes 5 new songwriters/year. Pays standard royalty.
Affiliate(s): Straten's Song (BMI).

- Hickory Valley's record label, Yellow Jacket Records, is listed in the Record Companies section.

How to Contact: Submit demo tape by mail. Unsolicited submissions are OK. Prefers cassette with 3-4 songs and lyric sheets. Use a 6×9 envelope with no staples. Does not return material. Reports in 3-4 weeks.
Music: Mostly **country** and **MOR**. Published "She's My Number One Fan" (by R. Hartman/S. Grogg/A. Straten); "She's My 'X' and I Know 'Y' " (by D. Crisman/S. Grogg/A. Straten); and "Kisa Marie" (by S. Grogg/A. Straten), all recorded by Tom Woodward on Pharoah Records (country).

HIGH-MINDED MOMA PUBLISHING & PRODUCTIONS (BMI), P.O. Box 959, Coos Bay OR 97420. Contact: Kai Moore Snyder. Music publisher and production company. Pays standard royalty.
How to Contact: Prefers 7½ ips reel-to-reel, CD or cassette with 4-8 songs and lyric sheet. SASE. Reports in 1 month.
Music: Country, **MOR**, **rock (country)**, **New Age** and **top 40/pop**.

HIT & RUN MUSIC PUBLISHING INC., 1325 Avenue of the Americas, 7th Floor, New York NY 10019. (212)956-2882. E-mail: hitrun@ix.netcom.com. President: Joey Gmerek. Creative & International Director: Susan Koc. Music publisher. Publishes 20-30 songs/year; publishes 2 new songwriters/year. Hires staff writers. Pays standard royalty.
Affiliate(s): Charisma Music Publishing USA Inc. and Hidden Pun Music Publishing Inc. (BMI).
How to Contact: Write or call first and obtain permission to submit. Prefers cassette or VHS videocassette with lyric sheet. Does not return material.
Music: Mostly **pop**, **rock** and **R&B**; also **dance**. Published "Falling Into You," recorded by Celine Dion on Epic Records; "One & One," recorded by Robert Miles on Arista Records; and "Bitch," recorded by Meredith Brooks on Capitol Records.

HIT-FABRIK MUSIKVERLAG, Mühlgasse 1, Obj. 20, Guntramsdorf A-2353 **Austria**. Phone: ++43-2236/53006. Fax: ++43-2236/53006-90. E-mail: hit.fabrik@magnet.at. Director: Franz Groihs. Music publisher, record company and record producer. Estab. 1985. Publishes 150-200 songs/year; publishes 12 new songwriters/year. Hires staff songwriters. Pays standard royalty.
How to Contact: Submit demo tape by mail. Unsolicited submissions are OK. Prefers cassette, DAT, VHS videocassette or CD with lyric sheet. Does not return material. Reports in 1 month.
Music: Mostly **jazz**, **rock** and **pop**; also **classical** and **instrumental**. Published "Jazzline," written and recorded by Jon Becher (jazz); "Girls," written and recorded by Rohan Sillip (piano ballad); and "Runner," written and recorded by Peter Paul (rock), all on Ear Records.

HITSBURGH MUSIC CO. (BMI), P.O. Box 1431, 233 N. Electra, Gallatin TN 37066. (615)452-0324. President/General Manager: Harold Gilbert. Music publisher. Estab. 1964. Publishes 12 songs/year. Pays standard royalty.
Affiliate(s): 7th Day Music (BMI).

How to Contact: Submit demo tape by mail. Unsolicited submissions are OK. Prefers cassette or quality videocassette with 2-4 songs and lead sheet. Prefers studio produced demos. SASE. Reports in 6-8 weeks.
Music: Country gospel and **MOR**. Published "Blue Tears" (by H. Gilbert), recorded by Damon Gilbert; "The Depth of His Love" (by Harold Gilbert), recorded by Kim Crutcher; and "Search for a New Love," written and recorded by K'leetha Gee, all on Southern City Records.

HOLTON MUSIC (BMI), P.O. Box 270262, Nashville TN 37227. (615)355-9694. Fax: (901)366-3669. President: Harvey Turner. Music publisher, record company and record producer. Estab. 1986. Publishes 50 songs/year; publishes 10 new songwriters/year. Hires staff songwriters. Pays standard royalty.
How to Contact: Submit demo tape by mail. Unsolicited submissions are OK. Prefers cassette with 3 songs and lyric sheet. Does not return material. Reports in 1 month.
Music: Mostly **country**, **Christian country** and **gospel**. Published *Rose In A Bible* (by P. Pritchett/T. Pritchett/H. Pruett/D. Anderson), recorded by Lewis Family on Daywind Records (gospel); "Golden Memories" (by P. Pritchett/D. Ingkeep/H. Turner), recorded by Dolly Dailey on Holton Records (country); and "Dancin' Fool" (by T. Pritchett/D. Dixon), recorded by T. Pritchett on ALH Records.

HOLY SPIRIT MUSIC (BMI), P.O. Box 31, Edmonton KY 42129. (502)432-3183. President: W. Junior Lawson. Music publisher. Member GMA, International Association of Gospel Music Publishers. Estab. 1973. Publishes 4 songs/year; publishes 2 new songwriters/year. Pays standard royalty.
How to Contact: Submit demo tape by mail. Unsolicited submissions are OK. Prefers cassette with 2 songs and lyric sheet. SASE. Reports in 3 weeks.
Music: Mostly **Southern gospel** and **country gospel**. Published "Raptured Away" and "God Still Provides," written and recorded by Julia P. Rautenberg; and "The Master of Happy Endings," written and recorded by Jimmy D. Clark, all on Sims Records (southern gospel).
Tips: Send "good clear cut tape with typed or printed copy of lyrics."

GREGG HUTCHINS MUSIC (BMI), 116 Roberta Dr., Hendersonville TN 37075. (615)264-1373. Owner: Gregg Hutchins. Music publisher and record company. Estab. 1993. Publishes 20 songs/year. Pays standard royalty.

- Gregg Hutchins's record label, Rejoice Records, is listed in the Record Companies section.

How to Contact: Write or call first and obtain permission to submit. Prefers cassette with 1 song and lyric sheet. Does not return material. Only replies if interested.
Music: Mostly **Christian country** and **bluegrass gospel**. Published "The Last Time I Fall" (by Jim Watters/Charlie Louvin), recorded by Charlie Louvin; "Adam's Side" (by Jesse Wilson), recorded by Billy Walker on Rejoice Records; and *Grand Ole Christmas* (by various), recorded by Bobby Bare, Jeannie C. Riley, Stu Phillips and others.
Tips: "Use creative lyrics to describe a familiar topic; i.e., say it in a different way."

INSIDE RECORDS/OK SONGS, Bisschopstraat 25, 2060 Antwerp 6 **Belgium**. Phone: (32)+3+226-77-19. Fax: (32)+3+226-78-05. MD: Jean Ney. Music publisher and record company. Estab. 1989. Publishes 50 songs/year; publishes 30-40 new songwriters/year. Hires staff writers. Royalty varies "depending on teamwork."
How to Contact: Submit demo tape by mail. Unsolicited submissions are OK. Prefers cassette with complete name, address, telephone and fax number. SAE and IRC. Reports in 2 months.
Music: Mostly **dance, pop** and **MOR contemporary**; also **country, reggae** and **Latin**. Published *Fiesta De Bautiza* (by Andres Manzana); *I'm Freaky* (by Maes-Predu'homme-Robinson); and *Heaven* (by KC One-King Naomi), all on Inside Records.

INTERPLANETARY MUSIC (BMI), 584 Roosevelt, Gary IN 46404. (219)886-2003. Fax: (219)886-1000. CEO: James R. Hall III. Music publisher, record company (Interplanetary Records) and record producer. Estab. 1972. Publishes 10 songs/year; publishes 4 new songwriters/year. Pays standard royalty.
How to Contact: Write first and obtain permission to submit. Prefers cassette. SASE. Reports in 5 weeks.
Music: R&B, **rap** and **Top 40/urban contemporary**. Published "Put It In Gear" (by J. Hall/M. Booker), recorded by Kyle Slack; and "Player Haters," recorded by Subliminal, both on Interplanetary Records.

● **A BULLET** introduces comments by the editor of *Songwriter's Market* indicating special information about the listing.

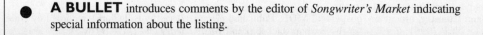

Tips: "Please submit a good quality cassette recording of your best work."

IRON SKILLET MUSIC, 229 Ward Circle, #A21, Brentwood TN 37027. (615)371-0646. Fax: (615)370-0353. President: Jack Schneider. Music publisher, record company (Rustic Records Inc.), record producer. Estab. 1984. Publishes 20 songs/year. Pays standard royalty.
Affiliate(s): Covered Bridge Music (BMI), Town Square Music (SESAC).
How to Contact: Submit demo tape by mail. Unsolicited submissions are OK. Prefers cassette with 3 songs and lyric sheet. SASE. Reports in 3 months.
Music: Mostly **country**. Published "Borderline Insane," "Rock-A-Bye My Baby," and "Are We Just Passing Time," all written and recorded by Holt Wilson on Rustic Records.
Tips: "Send three or four traditional country songs, story songs or novelty songs with strong hook. Enclose SASE (manila envelope)."

ISBA MUSIC PUBLISHING INC. (ASCAP), 2860 Blvd. De La Concorde, La Val Quebec H7E 2B4 **Canada**. (514)669-4088. Fax: (514)669-5838. E-mail: isba.music@citenet.net. Contact: Maurice Velenosi or Larry Mancini. Music publisher. Estab. 1983. Publishes 85 songs/year; publishes 20 new songwriters/year. Pays standard royalty.
Affiliate(s): Gabbro Music (BMI).
How to Contact: Write first and obtain permission to submit. Prefers cassette with 3 songs and lyric sheet. SAE and IRC. Reports in 4-6 weeks.
Music: Mostly **pop/rock**, **rap/hip hop** and **dance**; also **R&B, A/C** and **MOR**. Published *Secret Admirer* (by R. Geddes/A. Breault), recorded by DJ Ray (reggae); *Ole Ola* (by G. Diodati/F. Summer), recorded by Collage (dance); and *If You Treat My Body Right*, written and recorded by M. Dozier, all on ISBA Records.
Tips: "Send well-produced quality cassettes."

‡ISLAND CULTURE MUSIC PUBLISHERS (BMI), Chateau Bordeaux, St. John **U.S. Virgin Islands** 00830. Phone/fax: (809)693-5544. E-mail: 103444.2534cm@compuserve.com. President: Liston Monsanto, Jr. Music publisher and record company (Conscious Music). Estab. 1996. Publishes 10 songs/year; publishes 3 new songwriters/year. Hires staff songwriters. Pays standard royalty.
How to Contact: Submit demo tape by mail. Unsolicited submissions are OK. Prefers cassette with 8 songs and lyric sheet. Send bio and 8×10 glossy. Does not return material. Reports in 1 month.
Music: Mostly **reggae**, **calypso** and **zouk**; also **house**. Published "Love, Turn the World Around" "Dance Hall Lady" and "Love Comes Down" (by Gary Clendinen/Liston Monsanto), all recorded by Gary Clendinen on Conscious Music (reggae).

JACKSONG® MUSIC (ASCAP), P.O. Box 6771, Cleveland OH 44101. (216)942-6998. Fax: (216)341-1060. E-mail: 105347.1164@compuserve.com. Website: http://ourworld.compuserve.com/homepages/Jacksongs. Owner/President: Don Thomas Jackson. Music publisher and record company. Estab. 1995. Publishes 20-40 songs/year; publishes 5-10 new songwriters/year. Pays standard royalty.
How to Contact: Submit demo tape by mail. Unsolicited submissions are OK. Prefers cassette with 3 songs and lyric sheets. Does not return material. Reports in 1-2 months.
Music: Mostly **country**, **ballads**, **pop/Christian/rock** and **Christian/gospel**; also **pop**, **rock/light** and **Christmas**. Published "Over the Moon" and "True Love" (by D.T. Jackson), recorded by Lisa Gregg; and "Buyin' A Dream" (by D.T. Jackson), recorded by Ray & Jacksong Band, all on Sun Moon Stars Records.

JACLYN MUSIC (BMI), 306 Millwood Dr., Nashville TN 37217-1604. (615)366-9999. President: Jack Lynch. Music publisher, record producer, recording company (Jalyn, Nashville Bluegrass and Nashville Country) and distributor (Nashville Music Sales). Estab. 1963. Publishes 50-100 songs/year; 25-50 new songwriters/year. Pays standard royalty.
Affiliate(s): JLMG (ASCAP), Jack Lynch Music Group (parent company), Nashville Country Productions and Nashville Music Sales.

- Jaclyn Music's record label, Jalyn Recording Co., is listed in the Record Companies section, and their production company, Nashville Country Productions, is listed in the Record Producers section.

How to Contact: Submit a demo tape by mail, or write to arrange personal interview. Unsolicited submissions are OK. Send good quality cassette recording, neat lyric sheets and SASE. Prefers 1-2 selections per tape. Reports in 1 month.
Music: Country, **bluegrass**, **gospel** and **MOR**. Published *Forever Love* (by Bill Clark), recorded by Odie Gal on NCP-19961; *I'm Wanted* (by Barbara Jackson) and *Wasted Years and Dreams* (by Shirley P. Hickcox), both recorded by Don Hendrix on NCP-19964 Records.

JANA JAE MUSIC (BMI), P.O. Box 35726, Tulsa OK 74153. (918)786-8896. E-mail: janajae@aol.com. Website: http://members.aol.com/janajae/home.htm. Secretary: Kathleen Pixley. Music publisher, record company (Lark Records) and record producer (Lark Talent and Advertising). Estab. 1977. Publishes 5-10 songs/year; publishes 1-2 new songwriters/year. Pays standard royalty.

- See the listings for Lark Records in the Record Companies section, and Lark Talent and Advertising in the Record Producers section.

How to Contact: Submit demo tape by mail. Unsolicted submissions are OK. Prefers cassette or VHS videocassette with 4-5 songs and lyric and lead sheet if possible. Does not return material.
Music: Country, **pop** and **instrumentals** (**classical** or **country**). Published "Mayonnaise," "Bus 'n' Ditty" (by Steven Upfold) and "Let the Bible Be Your Roadmap" (by Irene Elliot), all recorded by Jana Jae on Lark Records.

JAELIUS ENTERPRISES (ASCAP, BMI), 325 FM2453, Royse City TX 75189. (972)636-2600. E-mail: jaelius@flash.net. Owner: James Cornelius. Music publisher. Publishes 3-5 songs/year; publishes 3 new songwriters/year. Pays standard royalty.
Affiliate(s): Jaelius Music (ASCAP), Hitzgalore Music (BMI), Air Rifle Music (ASCAP) and Bee Bee Gun Music (BMI).
How to Contact: Write first and obtain permission to submit. Prefers cassette. SASE. Reports in 3 weeks.
Music: Mostly **pop**, **country** and **gospel**; also **R&B**. Published "Dark Shadows of Night" (by Rich Wilbur/Penny Wigley), recorded by Nashville Bluegrass Band on Sugar Hill Records (bluegrass); "The Price Is Right," written and recorded by Joe Williams; and "Mama's Sunday Plates" (by Ann Cornelius/Wayne Ruff), recorded by Anne Hunter, both on Ascension Records (Christian).
Tips: "Today's market requires good demos. Strong lyrics are a must."

JAMMY MUSIC PUBLISHERS LTD., The Beeches, 244 Anniesland Rd., Glasgow G13 1XA, **Scotland**. Phone: (041)954-1873. E-mail: 100734.2674@compuserve.com. Managing Director: John D. R. MacCalman. Music publisher and record company. PRS. Estab. 1977. Publishes 45 songs/year; publishes 2 new songwriters/year. Pays royalty "in excess of 50%."
How to Contact: Contact by e-mail only and obtain permission to submit. Does not return material. Reports in 3 months.
Music: Mostly **rock**, **pop**, **country** and **instrumental**; also **Scottish**. Published "The Wedding Song," (by Bill Padley/Grant Mitchell), recorded by True Love Orchestra on BBC Records (pop); *The Old Button Box* (by D. McCrone), recorded by Foster & Allen on Stylus Records; and "Absent Friends" (by D. McCrone), recorded by Dominic Kirwan on Ritz Records.
Tips: "We will give faster responses by e-mail. We cannot accept music across the net, but if you convince us we should listen to your stuff we will ask for a tape by snail mail."

JASPER STONE MUSIC (ASCAP)/JSM SONGS (BMI), 10 Deepwell Farms Rd., South Salem NY 10590. President: Chris Jasper. Vice President/General Counsel: Margie Jasper. Music publisher. Estab. 1986. Publishes 20-25 songs/year. "Each contract is worked out individually and negotiated depending on terms." Pays standard royalty.
How to Contact: Submit demo tape by mail. Unsolicited submissions are OK. Prefers cassette with maximum of 3 songs and lyric sheets. SASE. Reports in 2-3 weeks.
Music: Mostly **R&B/pop**, **rap** and **rock**. Published *Deep Inside* and *Praise The Eternal*, written and recorded by Chris Jasper; and "Forever," recorded by Brothaz By Choice, all on Gold City Records.
Tips: "Keep writing. Keep submitting tapes. Be persistent. Don't give up. Send your best songs in the best form (best production possible)."

JERJOY MUSIC (BMI), P.O. Box 1264, Peoria IL 61654-1264. (309)673-5755. E-mail: uarltd@unitedcyber.com. Website: http://www.unitedcyber.com/~uarltd. Professional Manager: Jerry Hanlon. Music publisher and record company (Universal-Athena Records). Estab. 1978. Publishes 4 songs/year; publishes 2 new songwriters/year. Pays standard royalty.

- Jerjoy Music's record label, Universal-Athena Records, is listed in the Record Companies section.

How to Contact: Submit a demo tape by mail. Unsolicited submissions are OK. "We do not return phone calls." Prefers cassette with 4-8 songs and lyric sheet. SASE. Reports in 2 weeks.
Music: Country (modern or traditional), **gospel/Christian** and **Irish music**. Published *Livin' On Dreams* (by Eddie Crew), recorded by Jerry Hanlon; *When Autumn Leaves* (by Clint Miller) and *Look for Love Again* (by Steve Warner), both recorded by Clint Miller, all on UAR Records (country).
Tips: "Compare, study and evaluate your music to the hit songs you hear on the radio. Let your songs tell a story. Choose your lyrics carefully and make every word count. Long and drawn-out songs don't seem to make it in writing. Every word should be chosen to its best commercial value. Don't submit any song that you don't honestly feel is well constructed and strong in commercial value."

JODA MUSIC (BMI), P.O. Box 100, Spirit Lake IA 51360. (712)336-2859. President: John Senn. A&R Director: Wes Weller. Music publisher and record company. Estab. 1970. Publishes 10 songs/year. Pays standard royalty.
Affiliate(s): Okoboji Music (BMI).
How to Contact: Prefers cassette with no more than 4 songs and lyric sheet. "Keep demos short." SASE. Reports in 2-3 weeks.
Music: Mostly **light rock**, **country** and **gospel**. Published "Beer & Popcorn" (by Dave Peterson), recorded by Ralph Lundquist (country); "Change is Going to Come" (by Roger Hughes), recorded by Silver $ Band (pop); and *Time Keeps Taking You*, written and recorded by Wes Weller (country), all on IGL Records.

JOEY BOY PUBLISHING CO. (BMI), 3081 NW 24th St., Miami FL 33142. (305)633-7469. Contact: Dorita Rodriguez. Music publisher and record company. Estab. 1985. Publishes 100-150 songs/year; publishes 12-15 new songwriters/year. Pays standard royalty.
Affiliate(s): Beam of Light (ASCAP) and Too Soon To Tell (SESAC).
- Joey Boy's record label, Joey Boy Records, can be found in the Record Companies section.

How to Contact: Write first and obtain permission to submit. Prefers cassette with no more than 3 songs and lyric sheets. "Type or print lyric sheet legibly please!" SASE. Reports in 6 weeks.
Music: Mostly **R&B** and **rap**; also **dance**, **jazz**, **comedy** and **bass**. Published *Nothing But Bass* (by B. Graham), recorded by Bass Patrol; "Funky Y-2-C" and "Summer Delight," (both by C. Mills), recorded by The Puppies on Chaos Records.

LITTLE RICHIE JOHNSON MUSIC (BMI), 318 Horizon Vista Blvd., Belen NM 87002. (505)864-7441. Manager: Tony Palmer. Music publisher, record company (LRJ Records) and record producer (Little Richie Johnson). Estab. 1959. Publishes 50 songs/year; publishes 10 new songwriters/year. Pays standard royalty.
Affiliate(s): Little Cowboy Music (ASCAP).
- Little Richie Johnson is also listed in the Record Producers section, and LRJ Records is listed in the Record Companies section.

How to Contact: Write first and obtain permission to submit. SASE. Reports in 6 weeks.
Music: Country and **Spanish**. Published *Moonlight, Roses and the Wine* (by Jerry Jaramillo), recorded by Gabe Neoto; *Ship of Fools*, recorded by Reta Lee; and *Honky Tonk Cinderella*, written and recorded by Jerry Jaramillo, all on LRJ Records.

AL JOLSON BLACK & WHITE MUSIC (BMI), 116 17th Ave. S., Nashville TN 37203. (615)244-5656. President: Albert Jolson. Music publisher. Estab. 1981. Publishes 600 songs/year; publishes 50 new songwriters/year. Pays standard royalty.
Affiliate(s): Jolie House Music (ASCAP).
How to Contact: Submit a demo tape by mail. Unsolicited submissions are OK. Prefers cassette with 3 songs and lyric sheet. Send: Attn. Johnny Drake. SASE. Reports in 6 weeks.
Music: Mostly **country crossover**, **light rock** and **pop**. Published "Come Home to West Virginia" (by Scott Phelps), recorded by Kathy Mattea; "Ten Tiny Fingers, Ten Tiny Toes" (by David John Hanley), recorded by Kelly Dawn; and "Indiana Highway," recorded by Staggerlee, both on ASA Jolson Records (country).
Tips: "Make sure it has a strong hook. Ask yourself if it is something you would hear on the radio five times a day. Have good audible vocals on demo tape."

JON MUSIC (BMI), P.O. Box 233, Church Point LA 70525. (318)684-2176. Owner: Lee Lavergne. Music publisher, record company (Lanor Records), record producer and recording studio (Sound Center Recorders). Estab. 1960. Publishes 30-40 songs/year; publishes 3-4 new songwriters/year. Pays standard royalty.
- Jon Music's record label, Lanor Records, is listed in the Record Companies section.

How to Contact: Write or call first and obtain permission to submit. Prefers cassette with 4 songs and lyric sheet. "Use a good quality cassette and make sure the vocals are above the music." SASE. Reports in 2 weeks. ("Depends how busy we are and if I am undecided.")

REFER TO THE GEOGRAPHIC INDEX (at the back of this book) to find listings of companies by state, as well as foreign listings.

Music: Mostly **country**. Published *Pictures*, written and recorded by Tommy McLain (country); *Bridges* (by D. Jones/B. Cheshire), recorded by David Jones (country); and *Hey Jolie* (by R. Naquin/V. Bruce), recorded by Vin Bruce (country), all on Lanor Records.

JOSENA MUSIC (SESAC), P.O. Box 566, Los Altos CA 94022. President: Joe Vilchez-Nardone. Music publisher and producer. Estab. 1983. Pays standard royalty.
Affiliate(s): Reigninme Music (SESAC).
How to Contact: Write first and obtain permission to submit a tape. Prefers cassette with 3 songs and lyric sheet. Does not return material. Reports in 2 months if interested.
Music: Mostly **pop** and **gospel**; also **modern rock** and **Latin Music** as well—**flamenco**, **rumba style** (Spanish) and **Spanish ballads**. Published "Coming Home" (by Dino Veloz/Joe Vilchez-Nardone), recorded by Joe Vilchez-Nardone (modern Christian rock); "Make Us One" (by Lee Kalem/Joe Vilchez-Nardone), recorded by Lillie Knauls (gospel); and "Go God's Way" (by Mike Palos), recorded by Joe Vilchez-Nardone (jazz).
Tips: "Make sure it is a hot marketable tune—get unbiased opinions on your song—would it be playable on the radio?"

JUMP MUSIC, Langemunt 71, 9420 AAIGEM, **Belgium**. Phone: (053)62-73-77. General Manager: Eddy Van Mouffaert. Music publisher, record company (Jump Records) and record producer (Jump Productions). Member of SABAM S.V., Brussels. Publishes 100 songs/year; publishes 8 new songwriters/year. Pays royalty via SABAM S.V.

- See the listing for Jump Music in the Music Print Publishers section.

How to Contact: Submit demo tape by mail. Unsolicited submissions are OK. Prefers cassette. Does not return material. Reports in 2 weeks.
Music: Mostly **easy listening**, **disco** and **light pop**; also **instrumentals**. Published "Just A Friend" (by Eddy Govert), recorded by Sherly on Ideal Records (pop); "Go Go Go" (by H. Deschuyteneer), recorded by Rudy Silvester on Scorpion Records (Flemish); and *Won't You Stay With Me* (by Eddy Govert), recorded by Frank Valentino on Holy Hole Records (Flemish).
Tips: "Music wanted with easy, catchy melodies (very commercial songs)."

JUST A NOTE (ASCAP, BMI), 815 Ohio Ave., Jeffersonville KY 47130-3634. (503)637-2877. E-mail: lad@iglou.com. General Partner: John V. Heath. Music publisher, record companies (Hillview, Estate) and record producer (MVT Productions). Estab. 1979. Publishes 35 songs/year; publishes 10-15 new songwriters/year. Pays standard royalty.
Affiliate(s): Two John's Music (ASCAP).
How to Contact: Submit demo tape by mail. Unsolicited submissions are OK. Prefers cassette, 7½ ips reel-to-reel or VHS videocassette with 3 songs and lead sheet. SASE. Reports in 1 month.
Music: Mostly **pop**, **country**, **R&B** and **MOR**; also **gospel**. Published *Old Age* and *Rose*, written and recorded by Mark Gibbs on Hillview Records; and *Area Code 502*, written and recorded by Adonis on Estate Records.

JW ONE MUSIC PUBLISHING CO. (BMI), P.O. Box 218146, Nashville TN 37221-8146. (615)646-0506. Website: http://www.geocities.com/sunsetstrip/palms/3915. Executive Producer: Jimmy Walton. Project Director: S. Hardesty. Music publisher, record company (Walton Record Productions) and record producer. Estab. 1992. Publishes 50-100 songs/year; publishes 40 new songwriters/year. Pays standard royalty.
How to Contact: Submit demo tape by mail. Unsolicited submissions are OK. Prefers cassette or VHS videocassette with 1-4 songs and lyric sheet. "Lyric sheets must be clearly printed." SASE. Reports in 1-8 weeks.
Music: Mostly **country ballads**, **new country/uptempo**, **pop/MOR**, **comedy**, **R&B**, **lite rock** and **modern gospel**. Published "Barnyard Ho Down" (by Jimmy Walton); "How Many Heartaches" (by Herman House/Jimmy Walton); and "Writing on the Wall" (by Bob Bates/Paula St. Gelais), all recorded by Bob Bates.
Tips: "Submit a clear demo with typewritten lyric sheet. Keep your songs under three minutes."

KANSA RECORDS CORPORATION, P.O. Box 1878, Frisco TX 75034. (214)335-8004. Secretary and Treasurer/General Manager: Kit Johnson. Music publisher, record company and record producer. Estab. 1972. Publishes 50-60 songs/year; publishes 8-10 new songwriters/year. Pays standard royalty.
Affiliate(s): Great Leawood Music, Inc. (ASCAP) and Twinsong Music (BMI).
How to Contact: Submit demo tape by mail. Unsolicited submissions are OK. Prefers cassette with 4 songs and lyric sheet. SASE. Reports in 4-6 weeks.

Music: Mostly **country**, **MOR** and **country rock**; also **R&B** (leaning to country) and **Christian**. Published "Freight Liner Blues" (by Paul Hotchkiss) and "New York Times" (by Glenn Freed), both recorded by Jerry Piper on Kansa Records.

KAUPPS & ROBERT PUBLISHING CO. (BMI), P.O. Box 5474, Stockton CA 95205. (209)948-8186. Fax: (209)942-2163. E-mail: robnan7777@aol.com. President: Nancy L. Merrihew. Music publisher, record company (Kaupp Records), manager and booking agent (Merri-Webb Productions and Most Wanted Bookings). Estab. 1990. Publishes 15-20 songs/year; publishes 5 new songwriters/year. Pays standard royalty.

- Kaupps & Robert Publishing's record label, Kaupp Records, is listed in the Record Companies section and their management firm, Merri-Webb Productions, is in the Managers and Booking Agents section.

How to Contact: Write first and obtain permission to submit or set up personal interview. Prefers cassette or VHS videocassette with 3 songs maximum and lyric sheet. "If artist, send PR package." SASE. Reports in 3 months.
Music: Mostly **country**, **R&B** and **A/C rock**; also **pop**, **rock** and **gospel**. Published "Dodge City" and "Familiar Strangers" (by N. Merrihew/B. Bolin), recorded by by Nanci Lynn (country); and "Miss Fire" (by N. Merrihew/B. Bolin), recorded by Bruce Bolin, all on Kaupp Records.
Tips: "Know what you want, set a goal, focus in on your goals, be open to constructive criticism, polish tunes and keep polishing."

KAREN KAYLEE MUSIC GROUP (BMI), R.D. #11, Box 360, Greensburg PA 15601. (412)836-0966. President: Karen Kaylee. Music publisher. Estab. 1989. Publishes 15-20 songs/year; publishes 3 new songwriters/year. Pays standard royalty.
How to Contact: Submit demo tape by mail. Unsolicited submissions are OK. Prefers cassette or VHS videocassette with 3 songs and lyric sheet. "No phone calls please." SASE. Reports in 1 month.
Music: Mostly **country**, **gospel** and **traditional country**. Published "I Picked You Up Again," written and recorded by Carlene Haggerty; "The Pathway of God's Love," written and recorded by Matt Furin; and "Grandpa's Brew," written and recorded by Karen Kaylee, all on Ka-De Records.
Tips: "Only submit professional packages on clear tapes, recorded on one side only. Must include SASE."

KEL-CRES PUBLISHING (ASCAP), 2525 E. 12th St., Cheyenne WY 82001. (307)638-9894. E-mail: cheytown@worldnet.att.net. Website: http://www.chey-townrecords.com. A&R Manager: Gary J. Kelley. Music publisher, record company (Chey-Town Records) and record producer. Estab. 1989. Publishes 2 songs/year. Pays standard royalty.
Affiliate(s): Kelley-Kool Music (BMI).
How to Contact: Submit demo tape by mail. Unsolicited submissions are OK. Prefers cassette, CD, DAT or VHS videocassette with 3 songs and lyric sheets. Guitar/piano demo with "words up front" is sufficient. SASE. Reports in 3-4 weeks.
Music: Mostly **rock**, **'50s-'60s**, **blues** and **rockabilly**. Published "Hard Headed Lovin'," (by Jay D. Lansky); "Shadow" (by Binky Bumstead); and "Cryin' Won't Help" (by Tim Anderson), all recorded by Lug Nut and the Spare Tires on Chey-Town Records.
Tips: "Keep songs simple, very few lyrics with strong repeated 'hook-line.' Can a stranger hum your tune after hearing it?"

KENO PUBLISHING (BMI), P.O. Box 4429, Austin TX 78765-4429. (512)441-2422. Fax: (512)441-7072. Owner: Keith A. Ayres. Music publisher and record company (Glitch Records). Estab. 1984. Publishes 12 songs/year; publishes 10 new songwriters/year. Pays standard royalty.
How to Contact: Write first and obtain permission to submit a tape. Prefers cassette or VHS videocassette with 2-3 songs and lyric or lead sheets. Does not return material.
Music: Rock, **rap**, **reggae** and **pop**; also **metal**, **R&B** and **alternative** (all types). Published "I Wrote the Note" (by George Alistair Sanger), recorded by European Sex Machine (computerized); "Here It Is" (by John Patterson), recorded by Cooly Girls (rap); and "Kick'em in the Ass" (by Los Deflectors/Keith Ayres), recorded by Ron Rogers (rock), all on Glitch Records.

KIDSOURCE PUBLISHING (BMI), 1324 Oakton, Evanston IL 60202. (847)328-4203. Fax: (847)328-4236. E-mail: hitsrce@miso.wwa.com. Contact: Alan Goldberg. Music publisher. Estab. 1994. Publishes 12 songs/year; publishes 1-3 new songwriters/year. Pays standard royalty.
Affiliate(s): Grooveland Music (ASCAP), Hitsource Publishing (BMI).
How to Contact: Write or call first and obtain permission to submit a demo. Prefers cassette with 3 songs and lyric sheet. SASE. Reports in 1-3 months.

Music: Mostly **children's music**. Published *Songs for Safe And Secure Children* (by Bob Gibson/Rich Hudson), recorded by Bob Gibson.

KINGSPORT CREEK MUSIC PUBLISHING (BMI), P.O. Box 6085, Burbank CA 91510. Contact: Vice President. Music publisher, record producer and record company (Cowgirl Records). Estab. 1980. Pays standard royalty.

- Kingsport Creek's record label, Cowgirl Records, is listed in the Record Companies section and Kingsport Creek Music is listed in the Record Producers section.

How to Contact: Submit demo tape by mail. Unsolicited submissions are OK. Prefers cassette or VHS videocassette with any number of songs and lyric sheet. "Include photos and bio if possible." Does not return material.
Music: Mostly **country** and **gospel**; also **R&B** and **MOR**. Published "Who Am I," "Golden Wedding Ring" and "Let's Give Love," all written and recorded by Melvena Kaye on Cowgirl Records.

KIRCHSTEIN PUBLISHING CO. (BMI), 3830 Hwy. 78, Mt. Horeb WI 53572. (608)439-8970. Fax: (608)437-4362. President: Jim Kirchstein. Music publisher, record company (Cuca/AMC) and record producer. Estab. 1960. Publishes 10 songs/year; publishes 3 new songwriters/year. Pays standard royalty.
Affiliate(s): Seven Sounds Publishing (ASCAP).
How to Contact: Write first and obtain permission to submit a demo. Prefers cassette. Does not return material. Reports in 3 weeks.
Music: Mostly **R&B**, **ethnic** and **country**; also **folk** and **rock**. Published *Spring* (by Banks), recorded by Birdlegs (R&B); and *In So Many Ways* (by Banks), recorded by Pauline, both on Cuca Records.

KOZKEEOZKO MUSIC (ASCAP), 928 Broadway, Suite 602, New York NY 10010. (212)505-7332. Professional Managers: Ted Lehrman and Libby Bush. Music publisher, record producer and management firm (Landslide Management). Estab. 1978. Publishes 5 songs/year; publishes 3 new songwriters/year. Pays standard royalty.

- See the listing for Landslide Management in the Managers and Booking Agents section.

How to Contact: Write or call first and obtain permission to submit. Prefers cassette or VHS ½" videocassette with 2 songs maximum and typewritten lyric sheet for each song. SASE. Reports in 2 months.
Music: Mostly **soul/pop**, **dance**, **pop/rock** (no heavy metal), **A/C** and **country**. Published "Ain't No Cure For You" (by Ed Chalfin and Tedd Lawson), recorded by Roger Clinton on Pyramid Records; "River of Love" (by Frank Scozzari/Tedd Lawson); and "That One Love" (by Suzanne Stokes/Tedd Lawson).

KWAZ SONG MUSIC (SOCAN), 2305 Vista Court, Coquitlam British Columbia V3J 6W2 **Canada**. (604)202-3644. Fax: (604)469-9359. E-mail: ksmrecords@infomatch.com. Contact: David London. Music publisher and record company (KSM Records). Estab. 1991. Pays standard royalty.

- Kwaz Song's record label, KSM Records, is listed in the Record Companies section.

How to Contact: Submit demo tape by mail. Unsolicited submissions are OK. Prefers cassette, VHS videocassette or CD with 2 songs and lyric sheet. Include press material. Does not return material. Reports in 1 month.
Music: Mostly **Gothic rock**, **industrial** and **electronic**; **experimental** and **avante-garde**. Published "Angelic" (by Chad Bishop), recorded by Idiot Stare; and "Guilt" (by Andrew Amy/David Collings), recorded by Fourthman, all on KSM Records.

LARGO MUSIC PUBLISHING (ASCAP, BMI), 425 Park Ave., New York NY 10022. (212)756-5080. Fax: (212)207-8167. Creative Manager: Peter Oriol. Music publisher. Estab. 1980. Pays variable royalty.
Affiliate(s): Catharine Hiren Music, American Compass Music Corp., Diplomat Music Corp., Larry Shayne Enterprises (ASCAP) and Largo Cargo Music (BMI).
How to Contact: Submit demo tape by mail. Unsolicited submissions are OK. Prefers cassette or CD with 4 songs and lyric sheet. "Spend money on recording well, not packaging." Does not return material. Reports in 2-4 weeks.
Music: Mostly **alternative rock**, **AOR** and **adult alternative**; "good music that transcends categories." Published "Crazy Crazy Nights," "Little Caesar" and "I'll Fight Like Hell to Hold You" (by Adam Mitchell), all recorded by KISS on Polygram Records (hard rock).
Tips: "Good songs are not enough—you must be a complete artist and writer."

LARI-JON PUBLISHING (BMI), 325 W. Walnut, Rising City NE 68658. (402)542-2336. Owner: Larry Good. Music publisher, record company (Lari-Jon Records), management firm (Lari-Jon Promotions) and record producer (Lari Jon Productions). Estab. 1967. Publishes 20 songs/year; publishes 2-3 new songwriters/year. Pays standard royalty.

• See the listings for Lari-Jon Records in the Record Companies section, Lari-Jon Productions in the Record Producers section and Lari-Jon Promotions in the Managers and Booking Agents section.

How to Contact: Submit a demo tape by mail. Unsolicited submissions are OK. Prefers cassette with 5 songs and lyric sheet. "Be professional." SASE. Reports in 2 months.

Music: Mostly **country**, **Southern gospel** and **'50's rock**. Published "Glory Bound Train," written and recorded by Tom Campbell; "Nebraskaland," written and recorded by Larry Good; and *Her Favorite Song*, written and recorded by Johnny Nace, all on Lari-Jon Records.

LAST BRAIN CELL (BMI), P.O. Box 1750, Santa Rosa Beach FL 32459. (904)864-7835. Owner: Christine R. Puccia. Music publisher. Estab. 1993. Pays standard royalty.

How to Contact: Submit demo tape by mail. Unsolicited submissions are OK. Prefers cassette with 4 songs and lyric sheet. Include résumé and picture. SASE. Reports in 1-2 months.

Music: Mostly **alternative**, **R&B** and **rock**; also **blues**, **gospel** and **country**. Published "No Children Here," written and recorded by Christine R. Puccia.

LCS MUSIC GROUP, INC. (BMI, ASCAP, SESAC), 6301 N. O'Connor Blvd., The Studios of Las Colinas, Irving TX 75039. (972)869-0700. Fax: (972)869-7756. Contact: Publishing Assistant. Music publisher. Pays standard royalty.

Affiliate(s): Bug and Bear Music (ASCAP), Chris Christian Music (BMI), Court and Case Music (ASCAP), Home Sweet Home Music (ASCAP), Monk and Tid Music (SESAC), Preston Christian Music (BMI).

How to Contact: Submit demo tape by mail. Unsolicited submissions are OK. Prefers cassette (lyric sheet is only necessary if the words are difficult to understand). "Put all pertinent information on the tape itself, such as how to contact the writer. Do not send Express!" Does not return material. Reports in 4-6 months.

Music: Mostly **contemporary Christian** and **inspirational**. Published "Touch," written and recorded by Eric Champion on Myrrh Records; "You Were Always There" (by Joe Ninowski/Jeff Smith), recorded by Jeff Smith on Myrrh Records; and "The Me Nobody Knows" (by Vincent Grimes), recorded by Marilyn McCoo on Warner Alliance Records.

LILLY MUSIC PUBLISHING (SOCAN), 61 Euphrasia Dr., Toronto, Ontario M6B 3V8 **Canada**. (416)782-5768. Fax: (416)782-7170. President: Panfilo DiMatteo. Music publisher and record company (P. & N. Records). Estab. 1992. Publishes 20 songs/year; publishes 8 new songwriters/year. Pays standard royalty.

Affiliate(s): San Martino Music Publishing and Paglieta Music Publishing (CMRRA).

• Lilly Music's record label, P. & N. Records, is listed in the Record Companies section.

How to Contact: Submit demo tape by mail. Unsolicited submissions are OK. Prefers cassette or videocassette with 3 songs and lyric and lead sheets. "We will contact you only if we are interested in the material." SASE. Reports in 1 month.

Music: Mostly **dance**, **ballads** and **rock**; also **country**. Published "I Will Stand" (by Shanon Purvis/Tod Stewart); "Never Knew A Love Like This" (by Ken Wank); and "In Your Arms Tonight (by Tod Stewart), all recorded by A. Castro on P.&N. Records.

DORIS LINDSAY PUBLISHING (ASCAP), P.O. Box 35005, Greensboro NC 27425. (910)882-9990. President: Doris Lindsay. Music publisher and record company (Fountain Records). Estab. 1979. Publishes 20 songs/year; publishes 4 songwriters/year. Pays standard royalty.

Affiliate(s): Better Times Publishing (BMI) and Doris Lindsay Publishing (ASCAP).

• Doris Lindsay Publishing's record label, Fountain Records, is listed in the Record Companies section.

How to Contact: Submit demo tape by mail. Unsolicited submissions are OK. Prefers cassette with 2 songs. "Submit good quality demos." SASE. Reports in 2 months.

Music: Mostly **country**, **pop** and **contemporary gospel**. Published *Service Station Cowboy* (by Hoss Ryder), recorded by Ace Diamond on Sabre Records; "Amusin' Cruisin," by Susan and Frank Rosario; and "America's Song" (by Cathy Roeder), recorded by Terry Michaels, both on Fountain Records.

Tips: "Present a good quality demo (recorded in a studio). Positive clean lyrics and up-tempo music are easiest to place."

LINEAGE PUBLISHING CO. (BMI), P.O. Box 211, East Prairie MO 63845. (314)649-2211. Professional Manager: Tommy Loomas. Staff: Alan Carter and Joe Silver. Music publisher, record producer, management firm (Staircase Promotions) and record company (Capstan Record Production). Pays standard royalty.

- Lineage Publishing's record label, Capstan Record Production, is listed in the Record Companies section and Staircase Promotions is listed in the Managers and Booking Agents section.

How to Contact: Submit demo tape by mail. Unsolicited submissions are OK. Prefers cassette with 2-4 songs and lyric sheet; include bio and photo if possible. SASE. Reports in 1-2 months.
Music: Country, **easy listening**, **MOR**, **country rock** and **top 40/pop**. Published "Let It Rain" (by Roberta Boyle), recorded by Vicarie Arcoleo on Treasure Coast Records; "Country Boy," written and recorded by Roger Lambert; and "Boot Jack Shuffle" (by Zachary Taylor), recorded by Skid Row Joe, both on Capstan Records.

LIN'S LINES (ASCAP), 156 Fifth Ave. #434, New York NY 10010. (212)691-5631. E-mail: fifthavmed@aol.com. President: Linda K. Jacobson. Music publisher. Estab. 1978. Publishes 4 songs/year; publishes 4 new songwriters/year. Pays standard royalty.
How to Contact: Submit demo tape by mail. Unsolicited submissions are OK. Prefers cassette or VHS ¾" videocassette with 3-5 songs and lyric or lead sheet. SASE. Reports in 3 weeks.
Music: Mostly **rock**, **pop** and **rap**; also **world music**, **R&B** and **gospel**.

LION HILL MUSIC PUBLISHING CO. (BMI), P.O. Box 110983, Nashville TN 37222-0983. Phone/fax: (615)731-2935. Publisher: Wayne G. Leinsz. Music publisher and record company (Richway Records). Estab. 1988. Publishes 40-50 songs/year; publishes a few new songwriters/year. Pays standard royalty.

- See the listing for Richway Records in the Record Companies section.

How to Contact: Submit demo tape by mail. Unsolicited submissions are OK. Prefers cassette with 3 songs and lead sheets. SASE. Reports in 1 month.
Music: Mostly **country**; also **gospel** and **bluegrass**. Published "Date With A Memory" and "I Can't Get You Off My Mind," written and recorded by Linda Winner; and "Love Marks," written and recorded by Jack Batey, all on Richway Records.

LOUX MUSIC CO. & DOVEHOUSE EDITIONS (ASCAP), 2 Hawley Lane, Hannacroix NY 12087-0034. Phone/fax: (518)756-2273. Contact: Editorial Review Committee. Music publisher. Estab. 1984. Publishes 12 pieces/year; mostly individual songs, folios or educational material. Publishes 3 new songwriters/year. Pays 5% royalty.
How to Contact: Write or call first and obtain permission to submit a demo. Prefers manuscript and audio tape. "Write for manuscript preparation guidelines." SASE. Reports in 6 months.
Music: Mostly **music for recorder, viol, flute, violin, small chamber group**; also **pro musica** and **modern**. Published "How Sleeps This Little Child," written and recorded by Corie Bolick-Droppert on Loux Records (Christmas) and "In the Middle of the Night Now Here Comes St. Nicholas," written and recorded by Corie Bolick-Droppert on Dutch Music Box Records.

LOVEY MUSIC, INC. (BMI), P.O. Box 630755, Miami FL 33163. (305)935-4880. President: Jack Gale. Music publisher, record company (Playback Records) and record producer (Jack Gale). Estab. 1981. Publishes 25 songs/year; publishes 10 new songwriters/year. Pays standard royalty.
Affiliate(s): Cowabonga Music, Inc. (ASCAP).

- See the listings for Playback Records in the Record Companies section and Jack Gale in the Record Producers section.

How to Contact: Submit demo tape by mail. Unsolicited submissions are OK. Prefers cassette or VHS videocassette with 2 songs max and lyric sheets. Does not return material. Reports in 2 weeks if interested.
Music: Mostly **country crossover** and **country**. Published *Angel In Disguise* (by Scheder/Turney), recorded by Tommy Cash (country); *Second Time Around* (by Rocky Priola), recorded by Del Reeves (country); and "When They Ring Those Golden Bells," written and recorded by Charlie Louvin (country), all on Playback Records.

M & T WALDOCH PUBLISHING, INC. (BMI), 4803 S. Seventh St., Milwaukee WI 53221. (414)482-2194. VP, Creative Management: Timothy J. Waldoch. Music publisher. Estab. 1990. Publishes 2-3 songs/year; publishes 2-3 new songwriters/year. Pays standard royalty.

TO HELP YOU UNDERSTAND and use the information in these listings, see "How to Use *Songwriter's Market* to Get Your Songs Heard," on page 3.

How to Contact: Submit demo tape by mail. Unsolicited submissions are OK. Prefers cassette with 3-6 songs and lyric or lead sheet. "We prefer a studio produced demo tape." SASE. Reports in 2-3 months.
Music: Mostly **country/pop**, **rock** and **top 40 pop**; also **melodic metal**, **dance** and **R&B**. Published "It's Only Me" and "Let Peace Rule the World" (by Kenny LePrix), recorded by Brigade on SBD Records (rock).
Tips: "Study the classic pop songs from the 1950s through the present time. There is a reason why good songs stand the test of time. Today's hits will be tomorrow's classics. Send your *best* well-crafted, polished song material."

JIM McCOY MUSIC (BMI), Rt. 2, Box 114, Berkeley Springs WV 25411. Owners: Bertha and Jim McCoy. Music publisher, record company (Winchester Records) and record producer (Jim McCoy Productions). Estab. 1973. Publishes 20 songs/year; publishes 3-5 new songwriters/year. Pays standard royalty.
Affiliate(s): New Edition Music (BMI).

• See the listings for Winchester Records in the Record Companies section and Jim McCoy Productions in the Record Producers section.

How to Contact: Submit demo tape by mail. Unsolicited submissions are OK. Prefers cassette, 7½ or 15 ips reel-to-reel or VHS or Beta videocassette with 6 songs. SASE. Reports in 1 month.
Music: Mostly **country**, **country/rock** and **rock**; also **bluegrass** and **gospel**. Published "One Time" (by T. Miller), recorded by J.B. Miller on Hilton Records (country); and "Like Always" (by J. Alford), recorded by Al Hogan on Winchester Records (country).

McGIBONY PUBLISHING, 203 Mission Rdg. Rd., Rossville GA 30741. (706)861-2186. Fax: (706)866-2593. Music Publisher: Richard McGibony. Music publisher, record company (R.R. & R. Music) and record producer. Estab. 1986. Publishes 20 songs/year; publishes 10-15 new songwriters/year. Pays standard royalty.
Affiliate(s): Sounds of Aicram (BMI).
How to Contact: Write or call first and obtain permission to submit. Prefers cassette or VHS videocassette with 2 songs and lyric sheet. "Have a clear understandable tape with legible lyric sheets." SASE. Reports in 3 weeks.
Music: Mostly **country**, **gospel** and **R&B**. Published "Friday Nite Boogie" (by Terry Hogan), recorded by Billy James on J.P. Records; "Puro Tejano" (by Narz Hernandez Jr.), recorded by Hilda Gonzalez; and "August Rain," written and recorded by Carl Towns, both on Trend Records.
Tips: "Present a good demo. Don't just throw something together. The competition is fierce."

DANNY MACK MUSIC, 3484 Nicolette Dr., Crete IL 60417. (708)672-6457. General Manager: Col. Danny Mack. Music publisher, record company (Briarhill Records) and independent record producer. Estab. 1984. Publishes 1-8 songs/year. Pays standard royalty.
Affiliate(s): Syntony Publishing (BMI).

• Danny Mack's record label, Briarhill Records, is listed in the Record Companies section.

How to Contact: Submit demo tape by mail. Unsolicited submissions are OK. Prefers cassette or phono records with no more than 4 songs and typed lyric sheets. SASE. Reports in 4-5 weeks.
Music: Mostly **country**, **gospel** (**southern/country**) and **polka**. Published "Cold Wind" (by Ed Godleski), recorded by Rebecca Thompson; "Ordinary People" (by Tim Garrison), recorded by Danny Mack; and "Somewhere East of Eden" (by Ed Godleski), recorded by Helen Arbour, all on Briarhill Records.
Tips: "Patience is a virtue. Since we will return songs to writers after 24 months if we haven't got a commercial release, persistent phone calls as to the song's status are bothersome, annoying and expensive. You'll be the first to know if something is happening."

MAGIC MESSAGE MUSIC (ASCAP), P.O. Box 9117, Truckee CA 96162. (916)587-0111. E-mail: alanred@felis.org. Owner: Alan Redstone. Music publisher and record company (Sureshot Records). Estab. 1979. Publishes 6 songs/year; publishes 1 new songwriter/year. Pays standard royalty.
How to Contact: Write or call first and obtain permission to submit. SASE. Reports in 1 week.
Music: Mostly **country**, **ballads** and **rock**. Published "Emily," "Girls" and "For Yesterday," all written and recorded by Alan Redstone on Sureshot Records (country rock).
Tips: "We're looking for comedy/novelty/parody songs and blues."

MAJESTIC CONTROL (BMI), 250 W. 57th St., Suite 629, New York NY 10107. (212)489-1500. CEO: Matt "Half Pint" Davis. President: Tatiana. Music publisher, record company (Pirate Records), promotions and public relations. Estab. 1983.

• Majestic Control's record label, Pirate Records, is listed in the Record Companies section.

How to Contact: Submit demo tape by mail. Unsolicited submissions are OK. Prefers cassette with 3

songs. SASE. Reports in 2 months.
Music: Mostly **rap** and **R&B**. Artists include Stik-E and the Hoods, K.P. Capone, Big Daddy Kane and Kamakaze.

MAKERS MARK GOLD (ASCAP), 3033 W. Redner St., Philadelphia PA 19121. (215)236-4817. Producer: Paul Hopkins. Music publisher and record producer. Estab. 1991. Pays standard royalty.
How to Contact: Submit demo tape by mail. Unsolicited submissions are OK. Prefers cassette with 2-4 songs. Does not return material. Reports in 4-6 weeks if interested.
Music: Mostly **R&B**, **hip hop**, **gospel**, **pop**, **country** and **house**. Published "Last Kiss" and "Top of the World" (by C. Foreman/P. Hopkins), recorded by Rachel Scarborough; and "In the Still of the Night," recorded by Emerge, all on Prolific Records.

‡MASTER SOURCE (ASCAP, BMI), 13903 Sherman Way #14, Van Nuys CA 91405. Phone/fax: (818)994-3400. E-mail: marc127@aol.com. Owner: Marc Ferrari. Music publisher. Estab. 1993. Publishes 100 songs/year; publishes 20 new songwriters/year. Pays standard royalty.
Affiliate(s): Red Engine Music (ASCAP) and Revision West (BMI).
How to Contact: Call first and obtain permission to submit. Prefers cassette with up to 5 songs and lyric sheet. SASE. Reports in 3 weeks.
Music: Mostly **reggae/salsa**, **rap/urban** and **ethnic**; also **country**, **jazz** and **world beat**. Published "My Man" (by Maureen Bailey), recorded by Ron Keel; and "Bad Medicine" (by Bruce Wojich), recorded by The Children.
Tips: "We specialize in film and TV placements."

THE MATHES COMPANY, P.O. Box 22653, Nashville TN 37202. (615)252-6912. Owner: David W. Mathes. Music publisher, record company (Star Image, Heirborn, Kingdom), record producer and music industry consultant. Estab. 1962. Publishes 10-30 new songwriters/year. Pays standard royalty.
Affiliate(s): Sweet Singer Music (BMI), Sing Sweeter Music (ASCAP) and Star of David (SESAC).
• See the listing for David Mathes Productions in the Record Producers section.
How to Contact: Submit a demo tape by mail. Unsolicited submissions are OK. "Registered or certified mail refused." Prefers cassette with maximum of 3 songs and lyric sheet. "Only positive country songs (not controversial, political, demeaning or sex oriented). Only gospel songs that are not rock contemporary, and no New Age music." SASE. Reports in 1 month.
Music: Mostly **gospel** (**country**), **country** and **instrumental**; also **jingle ideas**. Published *My Love For You* (by DeAnna and David Mathes), recorded by Warner Mack on Sapphire Records (country); *My Ole Guitar*, written and recorded by Gene Taylor on Music of America Records (country); and *I Can't Wait To Get To Heaven* (by Cherie Mullins), recorded by The Mullins on Canaan Records.
Tips: "Have fresh ideas, current song structure, no outdated clichés. Good demos (not done by song mills)."

‡MAVERICK MUSIC COMPANY (ASCAP), 8000 Beverly Blvd., Los Angeles CA 90048. (213)852-1177. Fax: (213)852-1505. A&R Rep: Joe Belliotti. President: Lionel Conway. Music publisher. Estab. 1993.
Affiliate(s): Nomad-Noman Music (BMI), Edinburgh Songs (SESAC).
How to Contact: Write first and obtain permission to submit. Prefers cassette or DAT with 3 songs and photograph. Does not return material. Reports in 3-4 weeks.
Music: Mostly **pop/rock**, **country** and **R&B**. Published "This Is How We Do It," recorded by Montel Jordan on RAL Records (R&B); "Passionate Kisses" (by Lucinda Williams), recorded by Mary Chapin Carpenter on Columbia Records (rock); and *Candlebox*, written and recorded by Candlebox on Maverick Records (rock).

MCA MUSIC PUBLISHING (ASCAP), 2440 S. Sepulveda Blvd., Suite 100, Los Angeles CA 90064. (310)235-4700. Fax: (310)235-4901. Executive Vice President: John Alexander. New York office: 1755

‡ **THE DOUBLE DAGGER** before a listing indicates that the listing is new in this edition.

Broadway, New York NY 10019. (212)841-8000. Music publisher. Estab. 1964. "The MCA catalog contains over 100,000 copyrights." Hires staff songwriters.
Affiliate(s): Music Corporation of America (BMI) and Musicor (SESAC).
How to Contact: MCA does not accept unsolicited material.
Music: Published "Can't Really Be Gone" (by Gary Burr), recorded by Tim McGraw on Curb Records; "Don't Cry For Me, Argentina" (by T. Rice/A.L. Webber), recorded by Madonna on Warner Bros. Records (from the soundtrack *Evita*); and "Under the Water" (by M. Bainbridge/O. Bolwell/S. Paulzen), recorded by Merril Bainbridge on Universal Records.

‡MELLOW HOUSE MUSIC (BMI), P.O. Box 8234, Pittsburg CA 94565. (510)439-8904. President: Darren Brown. Music publisher, record company (Mellow House Recordings) and record producer. Estab. 1992. Publishes 10 songs/year; publishes 10 new songwriters/year. Hires staff writers. Pays standard royalty.
How to Contact: Submit demo tape by mail. Unsolicited submissions are OK. Prefers cassette, DAT or CD with 3 songs and lyric sheet. SASE. Reports in 2 months.
Music: Mostly **funk**, **R&B** and **hip hop**; also **pop/rock**, **alternative jazz** and **gospel**. Published *Witnis Tu Man* and "When U Come to Da Moe" (by Mel-O-D), both recorded by Witnis Tu Man (rap/R&B); and *Everyday People* (by Verry/Finlestein), recorded by Everyday People (funk), all on Mellow House Recordings.

MENTO MUSIC GROUP, Winterhuder Weg 142, D-22085, Hamburg **Germany**. Phone: (040)22716552 + -53. Fax: (040)22716554. General Manager: Arno H. Van Vught. Music publisher and record company. Estab. 1970. Pays standard royalty.
Affiliate(s): Auteursunie, Edition Lamplight, Edition Melodisc, Massimo Jauch Music Productions, Marathon Music.

- See the listing for Playbones Records in the Record Companies section.

How to Contact: Submit demo tape by mail. Unsolicited submissions are OK. Prefers cassette with 3 or 4 songs. "Put your strongest/best song first. Put your name and address on the inside sleeve of the tape. If you have a fax number, inform us. Tell us in a typed cover letter what you want/what you are looking for." SAE and IRC. Reports in 2 weeks.
Music: Mostly **instrumental, pop, MOR, country, background music** and **film music**. Published *Anytime and Anywhere* (by Massimo-Jauch/Raschner) and *Rodeo 93* (by Massimo-Jauch), both recorded by Stephan Massimo on EMI Records (pop); and *Fusión*, written and recorded by Jan Hengmith on Acoustic Music (flamenco).

MERRY MARILYN MUSIC PUBLISHING (BMI), 33717 View Crest Dr., Wildomar CA 92595. (909)245-2763. Fax: (909)245-4423. Owner: Marilyn Hendricks. Music publisher. Estab. 1980. Publishes 5-10 songs/year; publishes 1-2 new songwriters/year. Pays standard royalty.
How to Contact: Submit demo tape by mail. Unsolicited submissions are OK. No more than 2 songs per submission. "Submit complete songs only. No lyrics without music." SASE. Reports in 1-3 months (depending on volume of submissions). "Don't call. If we like what we hear, we'll call you."
Music: Country. Published "Pushing Up Daisies," "Talk About the Weather" and "Betting on Love" (by J. Hendricks).

MIGHTY TWINNS MUSIC (BMI), 6635 So. Campbell Ave., Chicago IL 60629. (312)737-4348. E-mail: rispiano@aol.com. General Manager: Ron Scott. Music publisher and record producer. Member NMPA, Midwest Inspirational Writers Association, NARAS. Estab. 1977. Publishes 4-10 songs/year; publishes 5 new songwriters/year. Pays standard royalty.
How to Contact: Submit demo tape by mail. Unsolicited submissions are OK. Prefers cassette with 2-4 songs and lyric sheet. Does not return material. Reports in 6-8 weeks.
Music: Mostly **top 40**, **R&B**, "**hot**" **inspirational** and **gospel**; also **children's**. Published "Steady" and "Reality" (by Chuck Chu), recorded by MTM (reggae); and "Finders Keepers" (by Betty Ober), recorded by Kookie Scott (country).
Tips: Looking for "good hot songs with hot hooks. Please have tapes cued up. *Do not write for permission!* Submit a cued up cassette and wait for our response. No materials returned without proper postage. Take the time to write and re-write to get the song in its best form; then make a good clear/audible demo."

MOON JUNE MUSIC (BMI), 4233 SW Marigold, Portland OR 97219. President: Bob Stoutenburg. Music publisher. Estab. 1971. Pays standard royalty.
How to Contact: Submit demo tape by mail. Unsolicited submissions are OK. Prefers cassette or VHS videocassette with 2-10 songs. Does not return material.
Music: Country, **Christmas** and **comedy**.

MORE BRAND MUSIC (BMI), (formerly Cactus Music and Winnebago Publishing), P.O. Box 1027, Neenah WI 54957-1027. E-mail: sowtoner@aol.com. President: Tony Ansems. Music publisher and record company (Fox Records). Estab. 1984. Publishes 5-8 songs/year; publishes 3-5 new songwriters/year. Pays standard royalty.
How to Contact: Submit demo tape by mail. Unsolicited submissions are OK. Prefers cassette with 3 songs maximum and lyric sheet. SASE. Reports in 2 months.
Music: Mostly **C&W** and **gospel**. Published *Funny* (by T.H. Pete/E. Wellman/T. Ansems), recorded by Jimmy Glass on Dynamite Records; *Waiting for the Telephone* (by Mike Kaiser/Allen Jahnke) and *Sealed With A Kiss* (by Mike Kaiser), both recorded by Sheridan's Ride on Bonzai Records.

MOTOR MUSIC CO. (ASCAP), 2717 Motor Ave., Los Angeles CA 90064. (310)559-5580. Fax: (310)559-5581. President: Don Sorkin. Music publisher, manager. Estab. 1976. Publishes 12-20 songs/year; publishes 2 new songwriters/year. Pays standard royalty.
Affiliate(s): Outgoing Music Co. (BMI).
How to Contact: Write or call first and obtain permission to submit a demo. Prefers cassette with 3 songs and lyric sheet. "If a group or single artist, send a photo." Does not return material. Reports in 1 week.
Music: Mostly **pop** and **R&B**.
Tips: "Have good strong hooks and chorus. Singles-oriented songs preferred."

MUSIC IN THE RIGHT KEYS PUBLISHING COMPANY (BMI), 9108 Arthur Ave., Crystal Lake IL 60014. (815)477-2072. President: Bert Swanson. Music publisher. Estab. 1985. Publishes 200-500 songs/year; publishes 50-100 new songwriters/year. Pays standard royalty.
Affiliate(s): High 'n Low Notes (ASCAP).
How to Contact: Submit a demo tape (professionally made) by mail. Unsolicited submissions are OK. Prefers cassette with 3-10 songs and lyric sheets. SASE. Reports in 5 weeks.
Music: Mostly **country**, **gospel**, **R&B**, **blues** and **MOR**. Published "Love Can Say Hello" (by Bert Swanson), recorded by Vivanco-Vargas on Goldband Records (country); "I Can't Tell My Heart" (by J. Cox/D. Davis), recorded by James Cox on Wingerter Records (country); and "Big Ruby" (by R. Wilcox/J. Bathon), recorded by C. Louvin on Walton Records (country).
Tips: "Always submit a good demo for presentation. The better the demo, the better your chances for placement. Remember, Music In The Right Keys will listen to your melodies; all that I ask of you is to send me good demos please."

THE MUSIC ROOM PUBLISHING GROUP, P.O. Box 219, Redondo Beach CA 90277. (310)316-4551. President/Owner: John Reed. Music publisher and record producer. Estab. 1982. Pays standard royalty.
Affiliate(s): MRP (BMI).
How to Contact: Write first and obtain permission to submit. Prefers cassette with 2 songs and lyric sheet. SASE. Reports in 2-4 weeks.
Music: Mostly **pop/rock/R&B** and **crossover**.

‡MUSIKUSER PUBLISHING (ASCAP), 15030 Ventura Blvd., Suite 425, Sherman Oaks CA 91403. (818)783-2182. Fax: (818)783-3204. E-mail: musikuser@aol.com. President: John Sloate. Music publisher. Estab. 1974. Publishes 20 songs/year; publishes 3 new songwriters/year. Pays standard royalty.
How to Contact: Write first and obtain permission to submit. Prefers DAT with lyric and lead sheet. Does not return material.
Music: All areas. Published *Thief of Hearts* (by Hattler/Kraus), recorded by Tina Turner on Virgin Records.

MUSIKVERLAG K. URBANEK, A-8982, Tauplitz 100 **Austria**. Phone: (+43)3688-2672. Contact: Mr. K. Urbanek. Music publisher. Estab. 1988. Pays standard royalty.
How to Contact: Write first to arrange personal interview. Prefers cassette with lead sheet. SAE and IRC. Reports in 2 months.
Music: Mostly **instrumental** and **choir music in middle grade difficulties**.

MYKO MUSIC (BMI), 1324 S. Avenida Polar, C208, Tucson AZ 85710. (602)885-5931. E-mail: tomdukes@concentric.net. President: James M. Gasper. Music publisher, record company (Ariana Records) and record producer (Future 1 Productions). Estab. 1980. Publishes 4 songs/year; publishes 2 new songwriters/year. Pays negotiable royalty.
How to Contact: Submit demo tape by mail. Unsolicited submissions are OK. Prefers cassette or ½" VHS videocassette with 3 songs and lyric sheet. SASE. Reports in 2 months.

Music: **Top 40**, **AOR**, **ambient** and **atmospheric electronic**. Published "Dancing Animals" (by J. Gasper), recorded by Scuba Tails (New Age); "Saturday Night" (by J. Gasper/T. Privett), recorded by Undercover (funk); and "Pretty As A Picture" (by J. Gasper/T. Privett), recorded by Rakeheads, all on Ariana Records.

CHUCK MYMIT MUSIC PRODUCTIONS (BMI), 9840 64th Ave., Flushing NY 11374. A&R: Chuck Mymit. Music publisher and record producer (Chuck Mymit Music Productions). Estab. 1978. Publishes 3-5 songs/year; publishes 2-4 new songwriters/year. Pays standard royalty.
Affiliate(s): Viz Music (BMI), Chargo Music (ASCAP) and Tore Music (BMI).
How to Contact: Submit demo tape by mail. Unsolicited submissions are OK. Prefers cassette or VHS videocassette with 3-5 songs and lyric and lead sheets. "Bio and picture would be helpful." Does not return material but will contact if interested.
Music: Mostly **pop**, **soft rock** and **A/C**. Published "It's Over Now" and "The Beginning of the End" (by Chuck Mymit), recorded by Robert Chase on CMR Records.

NAMAX MUSIC PUBLISHING (BMI), P.O. Box 24162, Richmond VA 23224. Music publisher. Estab. 1989. Publishes 2-4 songs/year; publishes 2 new songwriters/year. Pays standard royalty.
How to Contact: Submit demo tape by mail. Unsolicited submissions are OK. Prefers cassette with 2 songs and lyric sheet. SASE. Reports in 6-8 weeks.
Music: Mostly **R&B** and **pop/top 40**; also **contemporary gospel**. Published "Love Affair" (by D. Trebor/B. Tenan), recorded by Destiny on Xaman Records (R&B).
Tips: "Namax is looking for great songs with a strong hook. Our background is R&B music—do not send us country."

NASHVILLE SOUND MUSIC PUBLISHING CO. (SOCAN), P.O. Box 728, Peterborough, Ontario K9J 6Z8 **Canada**. (705)742-2381. President: Andrew Wilson Jr. Music publisher. Estab. 1985. Publishes 10 songs/year; publishes 5 new songwriters/year. Pays standard royalty.
Affiliate(s): Northern Sound Music Publishing Co. (SOCAN).
How to Contact: Submit demo tape by mail. Unsolicited submissions are OK. Prefers cassette with 2-4 songs and lyric sheets. "Will return material and/or reply to submissions if U.S. writers send $1 U.S. currency, no postage, please! Canadian writers: send SASE for tape return and/or reply." Reports in 3 weeks.
Music: Mostly **country**, **country/pop** and **crossover country**. Published "Slip Of The Heart" (by Steve Console), recorded by Bob Bates; "Let An Old Race Horse Run" (by Ron Simons), recorded by Tommy Cash; and "Fallin' Out of Love Can Break Your Heart" (by Andrew Wilson, Jr./Joseph Pickering, Jr.), recorded by Mark Poncy, all on Playback Records.

NAUTICAL MUSIC CO. (BMI), Box 120675, Nashville TN 37212. (615)883-9161. Owner: Ray McGinnis. Music publisher and record company (Orbit Records). Estab. 1965. Publishes 25 songs/year; 10 new songwriters/year. Pays standard royalty.

- Nautical Music's record label, Orbit Records, can be found in the Record Companies section.

How to Contact: Submit demo tape by mail. Unsolicited submissions are OK. Prefers cassette with 4 songs and lyric sheets. SASE. Reports in 4-6 weeks.
Music: Mostly **country ballads** and **country rock**. Published *Falling*, *Bad Reputation* and *Burning Love* (by Alan Warren), recorded by Bo Jest (rock), all on Orbit Records.

NEBO RIDGE PUBLISHING COMPANY (ASCAP), P.O. Box 194 or 457, New Hope AL 35760. President: Walker Ikard. Manager: Jim Lewis. Music publisher, promotions firm, record producer, record company (Nebo Record Company), management firm (Nebo Management) and booking agency (Nebo Booking Agency). Estab. 1985. Pays standard royalty.
How to Contact: Submit demo tape by mail. Unsolicited submissions are OK. Prefers cassette with 1 song and lyric sheet. Does not return material. Reports as soon as possible.
Music: Mostly **modern** and **traditional country**, **modern** and **traditional gospel**, **country/rock**, **rock**, **pop**, **MOR** and **bluegrass**. Published "Hold It Now, Babe (by Linda Carter), recorded by Joy Little (country); "I Need Your Love" (by Tammy Rose), recorded by Pat Jones (pop); and "On Top Again" (by Mary Dean), recorded by Bill Jack (gospel), all on Nebo Records.
Tips: "We need several female singers for our Nebo Record label. Female singers should send a personal bio, a few full-length photos, and a demo cassette tape for a review."

NERVOUS PUBLISHING, 7-11 Minerva Rd., London, NW10 6HJ **England**. Phone: +44(181)963-0352. E-mail: 100613.3456@compuserve.com. Website: http://www.nervous.co.uk. Managing Director: Roy Williams. Music publisher, record company (Nervous Records) and record producer. MCPS, PRS and

Phonographic Performance Ltd. Estab. 1979. Publishes 100 songs/year; publishes 25 new songwriters/year. Pays standard royalty; royalties paid directly to US songwriters.

- Nervous Publishing's record label, Nervous Records, is listed in the Record Companies section.

How to Contact: Submit demo tape by mail. Unsolicited submissions are OK. Prefers cassette with 3-10 songs and lyric sheet. "Include letter giving your age and mentioning any previously published material." SAE and IRC. Reports in 3 weeks.
Music: Mostly **psychobilly**, **rockabilly** and **rock** (impossibly fast music—ex.: Stray Cats but twice as fast); also **blues**, **country**, **R&B** and **rock** ('50s style). Published "Rockin' Till the Day I Die" (by McElroy), recorded by Bill McElroy; "Uh-Huh" (by Griffiths), recorded by The Backbeats; and "Lone Star" (by Eckhardt), recorded by King Memphis, all on Nervous Records.
Tips: "Submit *no* rap, soul, funk—we want *rockabilly.*"

‡NEW CLARION MUSIC GROUP (ASCAP, BMI, SESAC), P.O. Box 121081, Nashville TN 37212. Phone/fax: (615)269-4746. President: Sue K. Patton. Music publisher and record producer. Estab. 1984.
Affiliate(s): Golden Reed Music, Inc. (ASCAP), Little Admiral Music (ASCAP), Lac Grand Musique, Inc. (ASCAP), Triumvirate Music, Inc. (BMI), Lac de Charles Musique, Inc. (BMI), Little General Music (BMI), Grand Staff Music, Inc. (SESAC). All copyrights administered by Lagniappe Group, Inc.
How to Contact: Write or call first and obtain permission to submit. Prefers cassette, DAT or VHS videocassette with 3-5 songs and lyric sheet. "Submit what you consider your best work, regardless of when written. Demos not necessary, but preferred. Guitar/ or piano/vocals are fine." SASE. Reports in 1-6 months.
Music: Mostly **progressive country**, **A/C** and **AOR**; also **traditional country**, **pop** and **R&B**. Published "Is That A Tear" (by Kenny Beard/John Jarrard), recorded by Tracy Lawrence on Atlantic Records (country); "Does He Love You" (by Billy Stritch/Sandy Knox), recorded by Reba McEntire (duet with Linda Davis) on MCA Records (progressive country, A/C); and "Rebecca Lynn" (by Don Sampson/Skip Ewing), recorded by Bryan White on Curb Records (country).
Tips: "Live in Nashville. Hook up with a successful mentor. Learn the craft and persevere. Be nice and don't burn any bridges. Write a lot. Make it your daily 'go to work' routine."

A NEW RAP JAM PUBLISHING, P.O. Box 683, Lima OH 45802. (419)228-0691. President: James Milligan. Music publisher and record company (New Experience/Grand Slam Records). Estab. 1989. Publishes 30 songs/year; publishes 2-3 new songwriters/year. Hires staff songwriters. Pays standard royalty.
Affiliate(s): Party House Publishing (BMI), Creative Star Management.

- A New Rap Jam Publishing's record label, New Experience/Grand Slam Records, is listed in the Record Companies section.

How to Contact: Submit demo tape by mail. Unsolicited submissions are OK. Prefers cassette with 3-5 songs and lyric or lead sheet. SASE. Reports in 1 month.
Music: Mostly **R&B**, **pop** and **rock/rap**; also **contemporary**, **gospel**, **country** and **soul**. Published "Release Me" (by 419 Squad), recorded by William Roach; "Broadcast" (by Techno-3), recorded by Melquan K., both on Pump It Up Records; and "Still" (by L. Richie), recorded by James Junior on New Experience Records.
Tips: "Establish music industry contacts, write and keep writing and most of all believe in yourself. Use a good recording studio but be very professional. And if there is interest we will contact you."

NEWCREATURE MUSIC (BMI), P.O. Box 1444, Hendersonville TN 37077-1444. President: Bill Anderson, Jr. Professional Manager: G.L. Score. Music publisher, record company, record producer (Landmark Communications Group) and radio and TV syndicator. Publishes 25 songs/year; publishes 2 new songwriters/year. Pays standard royalty.
Affiliate(s): Mary Megan Music (ASCAP).

- See the listing for Landmark Communications Group in the Record Producers and Record Companies sections.

How to Contact: Submit demo tape by mail. Unsolicited submissions are OK. Prefers cassette or videocassette with 4-10 songs and lyric sheet. SASE. Reports in 4-6 weeks.
Music: Country, **gospel**, **jazz**, **R&B**, **rock** and **top 40/pop**. Published *Glory* and *Popcorn, Peanuts and Jesus* (by Harry Yates), both recorded by Joanne Cash Yates on Angel Too Records (gospel); and *Were You Thinkin' Of Me*, written and recorded by Jack Mosley on Landmark Records (country).

NON-STOP MUSIC PUBLISHING, 915 W. 100 South, Salt Lake City UT 84104. (801)531-0060. Fax: (801)531-0346. Vice President: Michael L. Dowdle. Music publisher. Estab. 1990. Publishes 50-100 songs/year; 3-4 new songwriters/year. Pays standard royalty.
Affiliate(s): Non-Stop Outrageous Publishing, Inc. (ASCAP), Non-Stop International Publishing, Inc. (BMI) and Airus International Publishing.

How to Contact: Write first and obtain permission to submit. SASE. Reports in 3 months.
Music: Mostly **pop**, **R&B** and **country**; also **jazz** and **New Age**. Published *Emerald Mist* and *Wishing Well*, written and recorded by Sam Cardon; and *A Brighter Day*, written and recorded by Mike Dondle, all on Airus Records.

NSP MUSIC PUBLISHING INC. (ASCAP), 345 Sprucewood Rd., Lake Mary FL 32746-5917. (407)321-3702. Fax: (407)321-2361. President, A&R: Vito Fera. Office Manager, A&R: Rhonda Fera. Music publisher, record company (S.P.I.N. Records), record producer (Vito Fera Productions). Estab. 1980. Publishes 10 songs/year; publishes 3 new songwriters/year. Hires staff writers "on agreement terms." Pays standard royalty.
Affiliate(s): Fera Music Publishing (BMI).
• See the listing for Vito Fera Productions in the Record Producers section.
How to Contact: Submit demo tape by mail. Unsolicited submissions are OK. Prefers cassette or VHS videocassette with 3 songs maximum and lyric sheet. "Package song material carefully. Always label (name, address and phone) both cassette and lyric sheet. Copyright songs. If you need assistance or advice on submission procedures or packaging, please contact us." SASE. Reports in 1-2 months.
Music: Mostly **modern jazz**, **instrumentals**, **R&B**, **kid's music** and **Christian music**. Published "The Magic Is Hot" for the Orlando Magic games on WESH TV Channel 2, recorded by Vito Fera and The Falcon Neighbors on S.P.I.N. Records; *Reindeer Rock*, kid's Christmas songs by various artists; and "Momenti Con Te Signore," performed by Salvatore Cristiano on S.P.I.N. Records.
Tips: "Carefully follow each music publisher's review instructions. Always include lyrics and a SASE for reply. A professional package and music production will help your songs stand out amongst the crowd. Use short intros and 'quality' vocalists to record your demo. Supply us with your best songs, commercial styling and catchy lyrics but not too personal. If you are submitting yourself or band as the 'Artist or Act,' please specify your intentions. Finally, read every available songwriting book, music business manual and publication on the subject and inquire about songwriting organizations."

‡N-THE WATER PUBLISHING, INC. (ASCAP), P.O. Box 924190, Houston TX 79292. (713)680-8588. Publishing Administrator: De Andrea Y. Canada. Music publisher, record company (Rap-A-Lot Records) and record producer. Estab. 1985. Pays standard royalty.
How to Contact: Submit demo tape by mail. Unsolicited submissions are OK. Prefers cassette with 4 songs. Does not return material. Reports in 2-3 months "if interested."
Music: Mostly **rap** and **R&B**. Published "Game Over" and "People Don't Believe" (by Brad Jordan), recorded by Scarface; and "Po Pimp," recorded by Do Or Die, all on Rap-A-Lot Records.
Tips: "Have patience. The music industry is a slow process and sometimes difficult to enter."

‡OBCB MUSIC PUBLISHING (BMI), P.O. Box 5580, New York NY 10027-8834. (212)662-5395. Owner: Carolyn E. Blanchard. Music publisher. Estab. 1992. Publishes 5 songs/year. Pays standard royalty.
How to Contact: Call first to arrange personal interview. Prefers VHS videocassette with 2 songs and lyric sheet. "Prospective songwriters should be members of BMI at least!" SASE. Reports in 1 month.
Music: Mostly **R&B**, **country** and **heavy metal**; also **rap (R&B)**, **rap (country)** and **rap (words only)**. Published "Please Love Me Forever" (by Ollie Blanchard/Johnny Malone), recorded by Bobby Vinton on Epic Records (easy listening).

OLD SLOWPOKE MUSIC (BMI), P.O. Box 52681, Tulsa OK 74152. (918)742-8087. E-mail: cherryst@msn.com. President: Rodney Young. Music publisher and record producer. Estab. 1977. Publishes 24-36 songs/year; publishes 2-3 new songwriters/year. Pays standard royalty.
How to Contact: Write first and obtain permission to submit. Prefers cassette with 4 songs and lyric sheet. SASE. Reports in 4 months.
Music: Mostly **rock**, **country** and **R&B**; also **jazz**. Published "Land of the Living," written and recorded by Richard Elkerton; "2 Crazy World," written and recorded by Steve Hardin; and "Find You Tonight," written and recorded by Brad Absher, all on CSR Records.
Tips: "SASE must be sent or demo will be destroyed after 30 days."

OMNI 2000, INC., 413 Cooper St., Camden NJ 08102. (609)963-6400. President: Michael Nise. Music publisher, record company (Power Up-Sutra), recording studio (Power House) and production company. Publishes 10 songs/year; publishes 5 new songwriters/year. Pays standard royalty.
• See their listing in the Record Producers section and the listing for Master-Trak Enterprises in the Record Companies section.
How to Contact: Write first and obtain permission to submit. Prefers cassette or videocassette with 3 songs. Send Attention: Michael Nise. SASE a must. Reports in 1-3 months.

Music: Dance, **R&B**, **country rock** and **pop**, all with pop crossover potential; also **children's**, **church/religious**, **easy listening**, **folk**, **gospel** and **jazz**.

ONTRAX COMPANIES (ASCAP), P.O. Box 769, Crown Point IN 46307. (219)736-5815. Contact: Professional Manager. Music publisher, record company (Lennistic Records) and record producer. Estab. 1991. Publishes 30 songs/year; publishes 7 new songwriters/year. Pays standard royalty.
How to Contact: Submit demo tape by mail. Unsolicited submissions are OK. Prefers cassette or DAT with 4-6 songs and lyric sheet. "Tapes should be mailed in as small a package as possible, preferrably in a 4×7 bubble mailer. Please include typed lyric sheet. All items must be labeled and bear the proper copyright notice. If you require a reply, please include a stamped, self-addressed card with your submissions. We listen to all submissions in the order they arrive. No phone calls please." Does not return material. Reports in 6 weeks.
Music: Mostly **pop/rock**, **country** and **crossover country**. Published *All Along*, written and recorded by Don Joseph on Lennistic Records; *Days and Nights*, written and recorded by D. Drasich on Canyonsongs Records; and "Better Be Good To Me" (by David Gulyas), recorded by 39th Avenue on Kinghead Records.

OPERATION PERFECTION (BMI), 6245 Bristol Pkwy., Suite 206, Culver City CA 90230. Contact: Larry McGee. Vice-President: Darryl McCorkle. Music publisher, record producer, record company and management firm. Estab. 1976. Publishes 15 songs/year; publishes 1-2 new songwriters/year. Pays standard royalty.

- See the listings for Intrigue Production in the Record Producers section, Boogie Band Records in the Record Companies section and LMP Management in the Managers and Booking Agents section.

How to Contact: Submit demo tape by mail. Unsolicited submissions are OK. Prefers cassette or VHS videocassette with 1-4 songs and lyric sheet. SASE. Reports in 2 months.
Music: Rock, **rap**, **pop**, **MOR/adult contemporary** and **R&B**. Published "Starflower (by Joe Caccamise), recorded by Star Flower (A/C); "Too Tough" (by Terrence Jones), recorded by En-Tux (pop); and "Got It Goin' On" (by Alan Walker), recorded by Executives, all on Mega-Star Records.

ORCHID PUBLISHING (BMI), Bouquet-Orchid Enterprises, P.O. Box 1335, Norcross GA 30091. (770)497-9086. President: Bill Bohannon. Music publisher, record company, record producer (Bouquet-Orchid Enterprises) and artist management. Member CMA, AFM. Publishes 10-12 songs/year; publishes 3 new songwriters/year. Pays standard royalty.

- Orchid Publishing's record label, Bouquet Records, is listed in the Record Companies section.

How to Contact: Submit demo tape by mail. Unsolicited submissions are OK. Prefers cassette with 3-5 songs and lyric sheet. "Send biographical information if possible—even a photo helps." SASE. Reports in 1 month.
Music: Religious ("Amy Grant, etc., contemporary gospel"); **country** ("Garth Brooks, Trisha Yearwood-type material"); and **top 100/pop** ("Bryan Adams, Whitney Houston-type material"). Published "Blue As Your Eyes," written and recorded by Adam Day; "Spare My Feelings" (by Clayton Russ), recorded by Terri Palmer; and "Trying to Get By" (by Tom Sparks), recorded by Bandoleers, all on Bouquet Records.

OTTO PUBLISHING CO. (ASCAP), P.O. Box 16540, Plantation FL 33318. (305)741-7766. President: Frank X. Loconto. Music publisher, record company (FXL Records) and record producer (Loconto Productions). Estab. 1978. Publishes 25 songs/year; publishes 1-5 new songwriters/year. Pays standard royalty.
Affiliate(s): Betty Brown Music Co. (BMI), Clara Church Music Co. (SESAC) and True Friends Music (BMI).

- See the listings for Loconto Productions in the Record Companies and Record Producers sections.

How to Contact: Submit demo tape by mail. Unsolicited submissions are OK. Prefers cassette with 1-4 songs and lyric sheet. SASE. Reports in 2-3 months.
Music: Mostly **country**, **MOR**, **religious** and **gospel**. Published "Don't Wake Me," written and recorded by Chris Risi (MOR); "It's Christmas Time," written and recorded by Bill Dillon (seasonal); and "Total Package," written and recorded by Joseph E. Ford (gospel), all on FXL Records.
Tips: "The more you write the better you get. If you are a good writer, it will happen."

PANCHATANTRA MUSIC ENTERPRISES, P.O. Box 91012, Nashville TN 37209-1012. President: Ben Reed Williams. Music publisher, record producer, promotion/public relations and personal management. Estab. 1968. Publishes 3-6 songs/year. Pays standard royalty.
Affiliates: Hickory Hollow Music, Steeple Music (BMI), Benrow Music (ASCAP) and Lancaster Music (SESAC).
How to Contact: Write first and obtain permission to submit. Prefers cassette or VHS videocassette with

3 songs and lyric or lead sheet. Does not return material. Reports in 1-3 months.
Music: Mostly **country**, **folk** and **blues**; also **bluegrass**, **A/C-pop** and **black gospel**. Published "A Bird With Broken Wings Can't Fly" (by Benny R. Williams), recorded by The Carter Family on Columbia Records (folk); "I've Got a Conscience (And You've Got a Wife)" (by Benny R. Williams/Paul Gasper), recorded by Lonnie Lynn Lacour on Rhinestone Rooster Records (country); and "Hey, Mr. Landlord" (by Benny R. Williams/Eugene "Texas" Ray), recorded by Eugene "Texas" Ray on Nashville Sound Records (blues).
Tips: "Give us something to listen to that doesn't sound like a repetition of the same old thing. What's needed is a lyric that has *meat* instead of *vanilla* and a melody that serves as a perfect vehicle to get the message delivered."

‡PARADIGM PUBLISHERS (BMI), 4419 Linden Ave., Suite 4, Long Beach CA 90807. (310)984-7841. Fax: (310)984-8241. President: Audre Shapiro. Music publisher, record company (Paradigm Productions), record producer and artist management. Estab. 1993. Publishes 30-60 songs/year; publishes 10-15 new songwriters/year. Pays standard royalty.
Affiliate(s): J&R Music, Maverick Man, Shapiro Publishing (BMI).

- See the listing for Paradigm Productions in the Record Companies section.

How to Contact: Submit demo tape by mail. Unsolicited submissions are OK. Prefers cassette with no more than 5 songs and lyric sheet. "Include photo and bio if you have one." SASE. "We do not report unless we're interested."
Music: Mostly **folk-rock**, **alternative** and **rock**; also **contemporary Christian** and **New Age**. Published "From the Heart," written and recorded by Jewel X on J&R Records (rock); "Running" and "Dancing In the Rain" (by R. Rossi), recorded by Full Circle on Maverick Man Records (alternative).
Tips: "Bare your soul. Bleed emotionally in what you write. Avoid trite expressions. Study Dylan and other great lyricists. Study the Beatles to learn how to write melody lines."

PARRAVANO MUSIC, 17 Woodbine St., Cranston RI 02910. (401)785-2677. Owner: Amy Parravano. Music publisher, record company (Peridot Records), record producer (Peridot Productions). Estab. 1986. Publishes 5 songs/year. Pays standard royalty.

- See the listings for Peridot Productions in the Record Producers section and Peridot Records in the Record Companies section.

How to Contact: Submit demo tape by mail. Unsolicited submissions are OK. Prefers cassette with 3-4 songs and lyric sheet. Lead sheets are optional. Does not return material. Reports in 6 months.
Music: Mostly **country**, **gospel** and **folk**; also **MOR**, **children's**, **country/blues** and **novelty**. Published "I'm A Survivor," (by Barbara-Jean Smith/Amy Parravano), recorded by Amy Beth on Caprice Records (country/blues); "Doctor of Romance" (by Amy Parravano), recorded by Amy Beth on Peridot Records (top 40 country); and "Steppin' Out Cafe" (by Ellen J. Allison/Amy Parravano), recorded by Joey Welz and Amy Beth on Caprice Records (country rock).
Tips: "Make sure lyrics tell a story to your listener."

PAS MAL PUBLISHING SARL, 283 FBG St. Antoine, Paris 75020 **France**. (33)1 43485151. Fax: (33)1 43485753 Managing Director: Jammes Patrick. Music publisher. Estab. 1990. Publishes 5-10 songs/year. Pays 60% royalty.
How to Contact: Submit demo tape by mail. Unsolicited submissions are OK. Prefers cassette or PAL videocassette. Does not return material. Reports in 6-12 months.
Music: Mostly **new industrial** and **metal**. Published "Skinflowers," "Only Heaven" and "Kissing the Sun" (by F. Treichler, A. Monod, U. Hiestand, R. Mosimann), all recorded by The Young Gods on Interscope Records (rock).

‡PASCARELLA MUSIC PUBLISHING (BMI), 233 E. Main St. #D, Branford CT 06405. (203)481-7558. Owner: Antonio Pascarella. Music publisher. Estab. 1997. Publishes 10-12 songs/year; publishes 1-2 new songwriters/year. Hires staff songwriters. Pays standard royalty.
How to Contact: Submit demo tape by mail. Unsolicited submissions are OK. Prefers cassette or CD with 1-5 songs and lyric sheet. "Make sure name and address are on CD or cassette. Typed lyrics are preferred; lead sheets optional. We prefer copyrighted material." SASE. Reports in 4-6 weeks.
Music: Mostly **pop/rock**, **instrumental** and **country**; also **MOR**, **R&B** and **children's songs**. Published "The Silence And I," written and recorded by A. Pascarella (instrumental); "The Boy Who Cried" and "Just Two" (by Pascarella-Nardella).
Tips: "Songs need not be elaborately produced (voice and piano/guitar are fine) but they should be clear. Songs must be well constructed, lyrically tight, good strong hook, interesting melody, easily remembered."

PECOS VALLEY MUSIC (BMI), 2709 W. Pine Lodge, Roswell NM 88201. (505)622-0244. E-mail: roswell@pvtnetworks.net. Website: http://www.pvtnetworks.net/roswell. President: Ray Willmon. Music publisher. Estab. 1989. Publishes 15-20 songs/year; publishes 4-5 new songwriters/year. Pays standard royalty.

• Pecos Valley's record label, SunCountry Records, is listed in the Record Companies section.

How to Contact: Submit demo tape by mail. Unsolicited submissions are OK. "No phone calls please." Prefers cassette, CD or VHS videocassette with 1-2 songs and lyric sheet. Does not return material.
Music: Country. Published "Wrong Man" and "Wrong Woman" (by Ray Willmon), both recorded by Jimmy Maples on SunCountry Records.
Tips: "Listen to what's playing on radio and TV and write with these in mind. Use proper song format (AAAA, ABAB, AABA, etc.) Also, please follow submission instructions. Do not phone. Learn proper song structure and proper meter."

PEERMUSIC (ASCAP, BMI), 8159 Hollywood Blvd., Los Angeles CA 90069. (213)656-0364. Fax: (213)656-3298. Assistant to the Head of Talent Acquisitions: Nicole Bahuchet. Music publisher and artist development promotional label. Estab. 1928. Publishes 600 songs/year (worldwide); publishes 1-2 new songwriters/year. Hires staff songwriters. Royalty standard, but negotiable.
Affiliate(s): Peer Southern Organization (ASCAP) and Peer International Corporation (BMI).
How to Contact: "We do NOT accept unsolicited submissions. We only accept material through agents, attorneys and managers." Prefers cassette and lyric sheet. Does not return material. Reports in 6 weeks.
Music: Mostly **pop**, **rock** and **R&B**. Published "Run to You" (by Jud Friedman/Allan Rich), recorded by Whitney Houston on Arista Records (pop); "Can't Cry Hard Enough" (by Williams/Williams/Etzioni), recorded by The Williams Brothers on Warner Bros. Records (rock); and "I'm Gonna Get You" (by A. Scott/Bizarre, Inc./Toni C.), recorded by Bizarre, Inc. on Columbia Records (pop).

PEGASUS MUSIC, P.O. Box 127, Otorohanga 2564, **New Zealand**. Professional Manager: Errol Peters. Music publisher and record company. Estab. 1981. Publishes 20-30 songs/year; publishes 5 new songwriters/year. Pays standard royalty.
How to Contact: Submit demo tape by mail. Unsolicited submissions are OK. Prefers cassette with 3-5 songs and lyric sheet. SAE and IRC. Reports in 1 month.
Music: Mostly **country**; also **bluegrass**, **easy listening** and **top 40/pop**. Published "If This Is Love" (by Ginny Peters), recorded by Dennis Marsh on BMG Records; "I Learnt A Thing or Two (by Ginny Peters), recorded by Quinton Horton on Spectrum/Polygram Records; and "Too Long Gone" (by Andrea Clarke), recorded by Anne Conway on Briubi Records.
Tips: "Get to the meat of the subject without too many words. Less is better."

PEN COB PUBLISHING INC. (BMI), 5660 E. Virginia Beach Blvd., Norfolk VA 23502. (804)455-8454. Fax: (804)461-4669. A&R: Tres Swann. Music publisher. Estab. 1991. Publishes 100 songs/year; publishes 6 new songwriters/year. Pays standard royalty.

• See the listings for Trumpeter Records in the Record Companies section and Sirocco Productions in the Managers and Booking Agents section.

How to Contact: Write first to obtain permission to submit. Prefers cassette or VHS videocassette. SASE. Reports in 6-8 weeks.
Music: Mostly **alternative/progressive** and **rock (heavy)**. Published "Froggy Style," recorded by Big Stoner Creek; "Everything," recorded by Everything; and *Flow*, recorded by Egypt, all on Trumpeter Records.

JUSTIN PETERS MUSIC (BMI), P.O. Box 271056, Nashville TN 37214. (615)331-6056. Fax: (615)831-0991. President: Justin Peters. Music publisher. Estab. 1981.
Affiliate(s): Lita Music, Abet International Music, Tourmaline Music Inc. and World House Publishing.
How to Contact: Prefers cassette with 3 songs and lyric sheet. Does not return material. "Place code 3005 on each envelope submission."
Music: Published "Saved By Love," recorded by Amy Grant on A&M Records; "Love Still Changing

Hearts," recorded by Imperials on Starsong Records; and "Wipe a Tear," recorded by Russ Taff and Olanda Daper on Word Records, all written by Justin Peters.

PLANET DALLAS RECORDING STUDIOS (BMI, ASCAP), P.O. Box 191447, Dallas TX 75219. (214)521-2216. Music publisher, record producer (Rick Rooney) and recording studio. Estab. 1985. Publishes 20 songs/year; 2-3 new songwriters/year. Pays standard royalty.
Affiliate(s): Stoli Music (BMI) and Planet Mothership Music (ASCAP).

- See their listing in the Record Producers section.

How to Contact: Call first and obtain permission to submit. Prefers cassette with 1-3 songs and lyric sheet. SASE for reply. Reports in 6-8 weeks.
Music: Mostly **modern rock**. Published "This Property is Condemned" (by P. Sugg), recorded by Maria McKee on Geffen Records (pop); *Ozone* (by various), recorded by MC 500 Ft. Jesus on Nettwerk/IRS Records; and *Scattered Remains/Poet*, written and recorded by the Blue Johnnies on Ganglion Records.

PLATINUM BOULEVARD PUBLISHING (BMI), 525 E. Moana Lane, Reno NV 89502. (702)827-4424. President: Lawrence Davis. Music publisher. Estab. 1984. Publishes 12 songs/year; publishes 1 new songwriter/year. Pays standard royalty.

- See Platinum Boulevard's listing in the Record Companies section.

How to Contact: Submit a demo tape by mail. Unsolicited submissions are OK. Prefers cassette or VHS videocassette with unlimited songs and lyric or lead sheets. Does not return material. "We report only if interested."
Music: Mostly **rock**, **country** and **R&B**; also **jazz** and **New Age**. Published *Crazy Thing*, *Take My Heart* and *Lonely Lovers*, all written and recorded by Lawrence Davis on Platinum Boulevard Records.

PLATINUM GOLD MUSIC (ASCAP), 18653 Ventura Blvd., Suite 292, Tarzana CA 91356. (310)275-7329. Fax: (818)757-7300. Managers: Steve Cohen and David Cook. Music publisher. Estab. 1981.
How to Contact: Write or call first and obtain permission to submit a demo. Prefers cassette with no more than 4 songs. Does not return material. Reports in 3 weeks.
Music: Mostly **R&B**, **pop** and **hip hop**; also **country** and **rock**. Published *Misunderstanding* (by Steven Russell), recorded by The Whispers on Capitol Records (R&B); *My Music* (by R. Warren/R. Benford/J. Harreld), recorded by Troop on Atlantic Records (R&B); and *Come To Me* (by L.A. McNeil), recorded by Michael Cooper on Warner Bros. Records (R&B).

POLLARD SOUND WORLD (BMI), 1615 Pine Tree Rd., Longview TX 75604. (903)297-2096. Owner: John Pollard. Music publisher, recording studio and music store. Estab. 1979. Publishes 2-20 songs/year; publishes 1-5 new songwriters/year. Pays standard royalty.
How to Contact: Write or call first and obtain permission to submit a demo. Prefers cassette with 1 or 2 songs and lead sheet or chord chart. Does not return material. Reports in 1-2 weeks.
Music: Mostly **Southern rock**, **blues** and **country**; also **gospel** and **easy rock**. Published "It Ain't Easy" (easy rock) and "I'm Your Man" (country), (by John Pollard/Mike Willbanks), recorded by Southern Pride; and *Dangerous* (by John Pollard/Alan Fox), recorded by J.A. Band (rock), all on Pollard Sound World Records.

POLLYBYRD PUBLICATIONS LIMITED (ASCAP, BMI, SESAC), P.O. Box 8442, Universal CA 91608. (818)505-0488. Fax: (818)506-8534. Branch office: 333 Proctor St., Carson City NV 89703. (818)884-1946. Fax: (818)882-6755. Professional Manager: Maxx Diamond. Music publisher. Estab. 1979. Publishes 100 songs/year; publishes 25-40 new songwriters/year. Hires staff writers. Pays standard royalty.
Affiliate(s): Kellijai Music (ASCAP), Pollyann Music (ASCAP), Ja'Nikki Songs (BMI), Velma Songs International (BMI), Lonnvanness Songs (SESAC), PPL Music (ASCAP), Zettitalia Music, Zett Two Music (ASCAP) and Zett One Songs (BMI).

- See the listings for PPL Entertainment Group in the Record Companies section and Sa'mall Management in the Managers and Booking Agents section.

How to Contact: Write or fax for permission to submit. Prefers cassette or VHS videocassette with 4 songs and lyric and lead sheet. SASE. Reports in 6 weeks.
Music: Published *A Song for Lillie* (by Suzutte Cuseo), recorded by Condottiere on Credence Records (classical/New Age); *Homeless* (by Jaeson St. James), recorded by Buddy Wright on Bouvier Sony Records (blues); and *Why Are You Here* (by Ken Allen), recorded by Big Daddy and the Blazers on Houston Blues Records (blues).
Tips: "Make those decisions—are you really a songwriter? Are you prepared to starve for your craft? Do you believe in delayed gratification? Are you commercial or do you write only for yourself? Can you take rejection? Do you want to be the best? If so, contact us—if not, keep your day job."

POLYGRAM MUSIC PUBLISHING, 825 Eighth Ave., 27th Floor, New York NY 10019. (212)333-8300. Fax: (212)333-1442. Hollywood office: 1416 N. LaBrea Ave., Hollywood CA 90028. (213)856-2776. Fax: (213)856-2664. Music publisher.
How to Contact: Polygram Music does not accept unsolicited submissions.

POWER VOLTAGE MUSIC (BMI), P.O. Box 808, Daytona Beach FL 32115-0808. Branch: P.O. Box 45 Church Street Station, New York NY 10008. (212)388-2767. E-mail: umapumdday@aol.com. Website: http://www.geocities.com/hollywood/set/3498. President: Russ Mate. Vice President: Mike Fass. Music publisher, record company (Power Voltage Records). Estab. 1984. Publishes 200 songs/year; 50 new songwriters/year. Pays standard royalty.
Affiliate(s): Digital Dawn Music (ASCAP).
How to Contact: Submit demo tape by mail. Unsolicited submissions are OK. Prefers cassette with 3-6 songs and lyric sheet. "Send only high quality tapes. Have songs listed on tape, in order of play. Include name and phone numbers of songwriter(s), as well as band contact or artist/songwriter representative." Does not return submissions. Reports in 2-8 weeks.
Music: Mostly **rock (all types)** and **dance (most types)**; also **instrumental (all types)**. Published "Never Again," by Joe Estrada (rock); "Our Nation," by Tommy West (rock); and "Change Your Attitude," by Gus Ferrari (dance).
Tips: "We primarily publish and work with songwriters who write material for bands that they perform with. We are an ambitious company and are signing a lot of new writers and songs. Keep aware of current trends, but stay away from formula writing and never try to purposely write a hit. Check out our website. Communicate with us by regular mail, e-mail, or fax. We do not have the spare time to talk on the phone. Remember, we're trying to get your music out there and we are busy on the phone trying to do just that."

PPI/PETER PAN INDUSTRIES, 88 St. Francis St., Newark NJ 07105. (201)344-4214. Director of A&R: Marianne Eggleston. Music publisher, record and video company (Compose Records, Parade Video, JA Records, Power Music, Peter Pan Music) and record producer (Dunn Pearson, Jr., Niney the Observer). Estab. 1928. Publishes over 100 songs/year. Hires staff songwriters. Pays standard royalty "based on negotiation."
Affiliate(s): Tifton Publishing, Compose Pubishing, Observer International, Discover International, Rego Irish-Colleen, Aurophon Classics.
- See PPI's listing in the Record Companies section.

How to Contact: Submit a demo tape by mail. Unsolicited submissions are OK. Prefers cassette with completed full length recording only."No longer accepting one or two songs because there are too many producers submitting material." Please include name, address and phone numbers on all materials, along with picture, bio and contact information." SASE. Reports in 6 months.
Music: Mostly **reggae**, **oldies**, **children's—audio**, **R&B** and **jazzy**; also **exercise—video**, **audio book on cassette** and **classical**. Published "Where Do Trolls Come From" (by Barry Hirschberg), recorded by various artists on Peter Pan Records; and "Johnny Clark," written by Niney the Observer on J.A. Records (reggae).
Tips: "Submit materials professionally packaged with typewritten correspondence."

PREJIPPIE MUSIC GROUP (BMI), Box 312897, Penobscot Station, Detroit MI 48231. Partner: Bruce Henderson. Music publisher, record company (PMG Records) and record producer (PMG Productions). Estab. 1990. Publishes 50-75 songs/year; publishes 2-3 new songwriters/year. Hires staff writers. Pays standard royalty.
- See the listings for PMG Records in the Record Companies section and Prejippie Music Group in the Record Producers section.

How to Contact: Submit demo tape by mail. Unsolicited submissions are OK. Prefers cassette with 3-4 songs and lyric sheet. "No phone calls please." SASE. Reports in 3 months.
Music: Mostly **alternative R&B**, **alternative rock**, **techno/house** and **experimental**. Published "Everything" and "Work Your Spell on Me," written and recorded by Bourgeoisie Paper Jam (funk/rock); and "Webbslinger," written and recorded by Tony Webb (jazz), all on PMG Records.
Tips: "We're always looking for new approaches to traditional genres. We want to hear vocals, lyrics and music that is passionate and takes a chance, but still keeps hooks that are solid."

PRESCRIPTION COMPANY (BMI), Box 222249, Great Neck NY 11021. (516)482-7697. E-mail: medmike525@aol.com. Website: www.cnms.com/prescription. President: David F. Gasman. Vice President of Finance: Robert Murphy. Music publisher and record producer. Pays standard royalty.
- See Prescription Company's listing in the Record Producers section.

How to Contact: Call or write first about your interest or submit demo tape by mail. Prefers cassette with any number of songs and lyric sheet. "Send all submissions with SASE (or no returns)." Reports in 1 month.

Music: Bluegrass, blues, children's and **country, dance-oriented**; also **easy listening, folk, jazz, MOR, progressive, R&B, rock, soul** and **top 40/pop**. Published "I Need You I Want You" (by D.F. Gasman); "Good Lookin' Thing" (by Giant, Baum and Ray) and "Let It Go" (by D.F. Gasman), all recorded by Medicine Mike on Prescription Records.

Tips: "Songs should be good and written to last. Forget fads—we want songs that'll sound as good in ten years as they do today. Organization, communication and exploration of form are as essential as message (and sincerity matters, too)."

PRETTY SHAYNA MUSIC (BMI), 2461 Santa Monica Blvd. #C331, Santa Monica CA 90404. (310)450-3677. Fax: (310)452-3268. Professional Manager: Stephanie Perom. Music publisher and management company (Perom International). Estab. 1994. Pays standard royalty.

Affiliate(s): Forever Shayna Music (ASCAP).

- See the listing for Perom International in the Managers and Booking Agents section.

How to Contact: Submit demo tape by mail. Unsolicited submissions are OK. Prefers cassette with 2 songs and lyric sheet. SASE. Reports in 12-18 weeks.

Music: Mostly **pop, dance** and **R&B**; also **pop-rock** and **Christmas**.

Tips: "Simple demos are OK, but be certain vocal presentation is the best it can be. Short intros to songs. Always have address and phone number on cassette. Please include lyric sheets."

PRITCHETT PUBLICATIONS (BMI), P.O. Box 725, Daytona Beach FL 32114-0725. (904)252-4848. Vice President: Charles Vickers. Music publisher and record company (King of Kings Record Co.). Estab. 1975. Publishes 21 songs/year; publishes 12 new songwriters/year.

Affiliate(s): Alison Music (ASCAP) and Charles H. Vickers (BMI).

- Pritchett's record label, Pickwick/Mecca/Internation Records, is listed in the Record Companies section.

How to Contact: Write first and obtain permission to submit. Prefers cassette with 6 songs and lyric or lead sheet. Does not return material.

Music: Gospel, rock-disco and **country**. Published "Have You Heard of the Holy City," "Christ is Mine" and "Every Feeling I Have Comes From God," all written and recorded by Charles Vickers on King of Kings Records (gospel).

PROMO, Avenue Massenet 16, 1190 Brussels **Belgium**. Phone/Fax: (32)2-3442559. President: Hascher Francois. Music publisher, record producer. Estab. 1986. Publishes 50 songs/year; publishes 2-3 new songwriters/year. Pays standard royalty.

How to Contact: Submit demo tape by mail. Unsolicited submissions are OK. Prefers cassette and lyric sheet. SAE and IRC. Reports in 2 months.

Music: Mostly **rock** and **blues**; also **French songs**. Published *Obsession* (by F. Sterckx), recorded by M.C. Michael (French); *Marylin's Busstop* (by J. Lauwers), recorded by John Lauwers Band (rock); and *Dreammaker* (by T. Frantzis), recorded by Tuner (rock), all on Krazy Kobra Rekords.

Tips: "Make real music—no sampling. Melodious, if possible."

PROSPECTOR THREE D PUBLISHING (BMI), 4003 Turnberry Cir., Houston TX 77025. (713)665-4676. Fax: (713)665-5576. Consultant-Owners: Dave or Peggy Davidson. Music publisher, record producer and management company. Estab. 1989. Publishes 2 or 3 new songwriters/year. Pays standard royalty.

How to Contact: Submit demo tape by mail. Unsolicited submissions are OK. (No replies unless interested in songs or singer.) Prefers cassette or VHS videocassette with 4 songs and lyric sheet. Does not return material. Reports in 3 months.

Music: Mostly **country, country/Christian** and **pop**; also **blues, pop rock** and **bluegrass**. Published "Gulf Coast Christmas," written and recorded by Dave Davidson on PRS (soul); "Wicker Rocker" (by Michael Hodges), recorded by Harry Fish on HMC (bluegrass); and "W Tx De Ja Vu" (by D. Davidson/Tadd Williams), recorded by Tadd on Triumph (country).

Tips: "Great songs to break the career of a new unknown artist are hard to find. Keep improving on your writing skills and let me hear them—if I can use them, I'll respond."

PURPLE HAZE MUSIC (BMI), P.O. Box 1243, Beckley WV 25802. President: Richard L. Petry. A&R: Carol Lee. Music publisher. Estab. 1968. Publishes 50 songs/year; publishes 5-10 new songwriters/year. Pays standard royalty.

How to Contact: Submit demo tape by mail. Unsolicited submissions are OK. Prefers cassette with 3-4 songs and lyric sheet. "Submit typed lyrics (in capital letters) and a separate lyric sheet for each song." SASE. Reports in 1-2 months.

Music: Country, rock and **R&B**. Published "My Old Friend," written and recorded by Chuck Paul on Rising Sun Records; and "Home Sweet W.V.," written and recorded by Dave Runyon on Country Bridge Records.

QUARK, INC., P.O. Box 7320, New York NY 10150-7320. (212)838-6775. E-mail: quarkent@aol.com. Manager: Curtis Urbina. Music publisher, record company (Quark Records), record producer (Curtis Urbina). Estab. 1986. Publishes 12 songs/year; 2 new songwriters/year. Pays standard royalty.
Affiliate(s): Quarkette Music (BMI) and Freedurb Music (ASCAP).
How to Contact: Write first and obtain permission to submit. Prefers cassette with 2 songs. SASE. Reports in 3 months.
Music: New Age (instrumentals) and **storytelling** (all kinds—spoken word).
Tips: "Research—know what style of music or stories we release. If you have no clue, give us a call and we will tell you."

R. J. MUSIC, 10A Margaret Rd., Barnet, Herts. EN4 9NP **United Kingdom**. Phone: (0181)440-9788. Managing Directors: Roger James and Susana Boyle. Music publisher and management firm (Roger James Management). PRS. Pays negotiable royalty (up to 50%).
- R.J. Music's management firm, Roger James Management, is listed in the Managers and Booking Agents section.

How to Contact: Submit demo tape by mail. Unsolicited submissions are OK. Prefers cassette with 1 song and lyric or lead sheet. "Will return cassettes, but only with correct *full* postage!"
Music: Mostly **MOR, blues, country** and **rock**; also **chart material**. "No disco or rap!"

R.T.L. MUSIC, White House Farm, Shropshire TF9 4HA **England**. Phone: (01630)647374. Fax: (01630)647612. Art Director: Ron Lee. Music publisher, record company (Le Matt Music) and record producer. Estab. 1971. Publishes approximately 30 songs/year. Pays standard royalty.
Affiliate(s): Lee Music, Ltd., Swoop Records, Grenouille Records, Check Records, Zarg Records, Pogo Records, Ltd., R.T.F.M., Value for Money Productions, Lee Sound Productions, Le Matt Distributors, Hoppy Productions.
- R.T.L.'s record label, Le Matt Music, can be found in the Record Companies section.

How to Contact: Submit demo tape or CD by mail. Unsolicited submissions are OK. Prefers CD, cassette or DAT (also VHS 625/PAL system videocassette) with 1-3 songs and lyric and lead sheets; include still photos and bios. "Make sure name and address are on CD or cassette." SAE and IRC. Reports in 6 weeks.
Music: All types. Published "Sacrifice," written and recorded by Suzy Jordan on Check Records (religious); "White Man Come" (by M.J. Lawson), recorded by Emmitt Till on Swoop Records (country/blues/rock); and "New Orleans" (by Ron Dickson), recorded by Nightmare on Zarg Records (shock/rock).

RAVING CLERIC MUSIC PUBLISHING/EUROEXPORT ENTERTAINMENT, P.O. Box 4735, Austin TX 78765-4735. (512)452-2701. Fax: (512)452-0815. E-mail: rcmrecords@aol.com. President: L.A. Evans. Music publisher, record company (RCM Productions), record producer, artist management and development. Estab. 1985. Publishes 5-10 songs/year; publishes 6-8 new songwriters/year. Pays standard royalty.
Affiliate(s): Tripoli Inferno Music Publishing (BMI).
How to Contact: Write first and obtain permission to submit. Prefers cassette with 3 songs maximum and lyric sheet. "Submissions of more than 3 songs will not be listened to." Does not return material. Reports in 4-6 weeks.
Music: Mostly **rock, pop** and **R&B**. Published *Is It Hot?* (by Bernard/Rose/St. George); *Blue Ballet* and *Faster Than the Speed of Love* (by Epp/Van Hofwegen), all recorded by Tracy Mitchell on RCM Records.
Tips: "Unsolicited material is not accepted."

RHYTHMS PRODUCTIONS (ASCAP), P.O. Box 34485, Los Angeles CA 90034. President: Ruth White. Music and multimedia publisher. Member NARAS. Publishes 4 titles/year. Pays negotiable royalty.
Affiliate(s): Tom Thumb Music.
How to Contact: Submit tape with letter outlining background in educational children's music. SASE. Reports in 2 months.
Music: "We're only interested in **children's songs** and interactive programs that have educational value. Our materials are sold in schools and homes, so artists/writers with an 'edutainment' background would be most likely to understand our requirements." Published "Professor Whatzit®" series including "Adventures of Professor Whatzit & Carmine Cat" (cassette series for children); "Musical Math," "Musical Reading" and "Theme Songs."

RIDGE MUSIC CORP. (BMI, ASCAP), 38 Laurel Ledge Court, Stamford CT 06903. President/General Manager: Paul Tannen. Music publisher and management firm. Estab. 1961. Member CMA. Publishes 12 songs/year. Pays standard royalty.
Affiliate(s): Tannen Music Inc. and Deshufflin, Inc.
How to Contact: Submit demo tape by mail. Unsolicited submissions OK. Prefers cassette with 3 songs and lyric sheet. SASE. Reports in 2 months.
Music: Country, rock, top 40/pop and **jazz.** Published "Forever," written and recorded by Mark Whitfield on Verve Records (jazz).

RIVERHAWK MUSIC (BMI), 417 N. Pine Dr., Surfside Beach SC 29575. (803)238-1633. President: Arthur W. Byman. Music publisher, record company (Peregrine Records) and record producer. Estab. 1994. Publishes 10 songs/year; publishes 3 new songwriters/year. Pays standard royalty.
How to Contact: Submit demo tape by mail. Unsolicited submissions are OK. Prefers cassette with 3 songs and lyric sheet. "Follow submission outlines exactly. Be neat." SASE. Reports in 1 month.
Music: Mostly **MOR, country** and **A/C**; also **cowboy-type western** and **comedy**. Published "Dark Hearted Woman" (by A. Byman/J. Carothers), and "Summer in Myrtle Beach" (by Charles Brewer), recorded by Art Byman on Magenta Records; and "Just One Time" (by A. Byman), recorded by Vivian Ulbrich on Riverhawk Records.

RNR PUBLISHING (ASCAP), 212 N. 12th St., Philadelphia PA 19107. (215)977-7779. Fax: (215)569-4939. E-mail: rage@netaxs.com. President: David Ivory. Music publisher and record producer. Estab. 1995. Publishes 5 new songwriters/year. Hires staff songwriters. Pays variable royalties.
How to Contact: Call first and obtain permission to submit. Prefers cassette or DAT and lyric sheet. SASE. Reports in 4-6 weeks.

- See the listings for Ikon Records in the Record Companies section and Ivory Productions in the Record Producers section.

Music: Mostly **commercial rock**, **AAA**, **A/C** and **R&B**; also **blues**. Published "Smack Dab" (by Ron Doroba/Mike Sanfosso/Bill Currier), recorded by Slideways; "Can't Love Yourself," written and recorded by Stevie LaRocca; and "Shelter," written and recorded by Billy Freeze, all on Ikon Records.

ROCKER MUSIC/HAPPY MAN MUSIC (BMI, ASCAP), 4696 Kahlua Lane, Bonita Springs, FL 34134. (813)947-6978. Executive Producer: Dick O'Bitts. Estab. 1960. Music publisher, record company (Happy Man Records, Condor Records and Air Corp Records), record producer (Rainbow Collections Ltd.) and management firm (Gemini Complex). Publishes 25-30 songs/year; publishes 8-10 new songwriters/year. Pays standard royalty.

- Rocker Music's record label, Happy Man Records, is listed in the Record Companies section.

How to Contact: Submit demo tape by mail. Unsolicited submissions are OK. Prefers cassette or VHS videocassette with 4 songs and lyric or lead sheet. SASE. Do not call. Reports in 1 month.
Music: Country, **rock**, **pop**, **gospel**, **Christian** and **off-the-wall**. Published *Take That Chance* and *Yours For the Takin'* (by Ken Cowden), recorded by Overdue (rock); and *A Prayer That Has Been Answered*, recorded by Challengers, all on Happy Man Records.

ROCKFORD MUSIC CO. (BMI, ASCAP), 150 West End Ave., Suite 6-D, New York NY 10023. Manager: Danny Darrow. Music publisher, record company (Mighty Records), record and video tape producer. Publishes 1-3 songs/year; publishes 1-3 new songwriters/year. Pays standard royalty.

- Rockford's record label, Mighty Records, is listed in the Record Companies section and Danny Darrow is listed in the Record Producers section.

Affiliate(s): Corporate Music Publishing Company (ASCAP) and Stateside Music Company (BMI).
How to Contact: Submit demo tape by mail. Unsolicited submissions are OK. Prefers cassette with 3 songs and lyric sheet. "SASE a must!" Reports in 1-2 weeks.
Music: Mostly **MOR** and **top 40/pop**; also **adult pop**, **country**, **adult rock**, **dance-oriented**, **easy listening**, **folk** and **jazz**. Published *Corporate Lady* (by Michael Greer), recorded by Danny Darrow (MOR); *Impulse* and *Let There Be Peace*, written and recorded by Danny Darrow, all on Mighty Records.
Tips: "Listen to top 40 and write current lyrics and music."

RONDOR MUSIC INTERNATIONAL, 360 N. La Cienega, Los Angeles CA 90048. (310)289-3500. Fax: (310)289-4000. Creative Staff Assistant: Barbara Vander Linde. Music publisher. Estab. 1965. Hires staff writers. Royalty amount depends on deal.
Affiliate(s): Almo Music Corp. (ASCAP) and Irving Music, Inc. (BMI).
How to Contact: Call first and obtain permission to submit. Unsolicited material is not accepted. Prefers cassette with 3 songs and lyric sheet. "Send DATs if possible, discography if applicable." SASE. Reports in 6-8 weeks.

Music: **A/C**, **alternative**, **R&B** and **rock**. Published "Before You Walk Out of My Life" (by Andrea Martin), recorded by Monica; "I Want to Come Over," written and recorded by Melissa Etheridge; and "Hook" (by John Popper), recorded by Blues Traveler.

ROOTS MUSIC (BMI), Box 282, 885 Broadway, Bayonne NJ 07002. President: Robert Bowden. Music publisher, record company (Nucleus Records) and record producer (Robert Bowden). Estab. 1979. Publishes 2 songs/year; publishes 1 new songwriter/year. Pays standard royalty.

- Robert Bowden, Roots Music's president, has a listing in the Record Producers section, and his record label, Nucleus Records, is listed in the Record Companies section.

How to Contact: Write first and obtain permission to submit or to arrange a personal interview. Prefers cassette or VHS videocassette with 3 songs and lyric sheet; include photo and bio. "I only want inspired songs written by talented writers." SASE. Reports in 1 month.
Music: Mostly **country** and **pop**; also **church/religious**, **classical**, **folk**, **MOR**, **progressive**, **rock (soft, mellow)** and **top 40**. Published "Henrey C" and "Selfish Heart," written and recorded by Robert Bowden; and "Always," written and recorded Marco Sission, all on Nucleus Records (country).

ROSE HILL GROUP, 1326 Midland Ave., Syracuse NY 13205. (315)475-2936. A&R Director: V. Taft. Music publisher. Estab. 1979. Publishes 1-15 songs/year; publishes 1-5 new songwriters/year. Pays standard royalty.
Affiliate(s): Katch Nazar Music (ASCAP) and Bleecker Street Music (BMI).
How to Contact: Submit demo tape by mail. Unsolicited submissions are OK. Prefers cassette. "Please include typed lyric sheet. No promotional material please." SASE. Reports in 2-4 weeks.
Music: Mostly **pop/rock**, **pop/dance** and **contemporary country**. Published "Love Cake" and "Take A Chance" (by R. Ajemian), recorded by A-Jay on Sunday Records; and *Paula Goodvibes* (by G. Davidson), recorded by Smitty on Cherry Records.
Tips: "Write a simple, memorable melody with a convincing, real story."

‡ROYAL KING MUSIC (BMI), P.O. Box 5368, Buena Park CA 90622. (714)522-2383. Executive Director: Jerry Smith. Music publisher, record company (Royal Records), record producer and management firm (Five-Star Management & Entertainment). Estab. 1959. Hires staff songwriters. Pays standard royalty.
Affiliates: Melodeer Music (BMI).

- See the listings for Royal Records in the Record Companies and Advertising sections, as well as Five-Star Management & Entertainment in the Managers and Booking Agents section.

How to Contact: Write first and obtain permission to submit. Enclose SASE for rapid reply. Prefers cassette, VHS videocassette or CD with any number of songs. "Good professional sounding recordings are preferred and easier for us to shop to motion picture producers, television, ad agencies, artists and agents. If you want material returned, include SASE. But we prefer to keep material on file." Reports in 1-3 weeks.
Music: **All styles.**

RUSTRON MUSIC PUBLISHERS (BMI), 1156 Park Lane, West Palm Beach FL 33417-5957. (561)686-1354. Professional Managers: Rusty Gordon, Ron Caruso and Davilyn Whims. Music publisher, record company, management firm and record producer (Rustron Music Productions). Estab. 1972. Publishes 100-150 songs/year; publishes 10-20 new songwriters/year. Pays standard royalty.
Affiliate(s): Whimsong Publishing (ASCAP).

- See the listing for Rustron Music Productions in the Record Companies, Record Producers and Managers and Booking Agents sections.

How to Contact: Submit demo tape by mail. Unsolicited submissions are OK. Prefers cassette with 1-3 songs and lyric or lead sheet. "Clearly label your tape and container. Include cover letter." SASE required for all correspondence. Reports in 4 months.
Music: Mostly **pop** (ballads, blues, theatrical, cabaret), **progressive country** and **folk/rock**; also **R&B** and **New Age** instrumental fusions with classical, jazz, pop themes and women's music. Published "I'm Still Leaving You Today," written and recorded by Cilla Smith (pop); "When I Look Into Your Eyes" (by Jayne Margo-Reby/Vic Bersok), recorded by Jayne Margo-Reby; and "Pass A Smile," written and recorded by Star Smiley, all on Rustron Records.
Tips: "Write strong hooks. Keep song length 3½ minutes or less. Avoid predictability—create original lyric themes. Tell a story. Compose definitive melody. Tune in to the trends and fusions indicative of the '90s."

S.M.C.L. PRODUCTIONS, INC., P.O. Box 84, Boucherville, Quebec J4B 5E6 **Canada**. (514)641-2266. President: Christian Lefort. Music publisher and record company. CAPAC. Estab. 1968. Publishes 25 songs/year. Pays standard royalty.

Affiliate(s): A.Q.E.M. Ltee, Bag Enrg., C.F. Music, Big Bazaar Music, Sunrise Music, Stage One Music, L.M.S. Ltee, ITT Music, Machine Music, Dynamite Music, Danava Music, Coincidence Music, Music and Music, Cinemusic Inc., Cinafilm, Editions La Fete Inc., Groupe Concept Musique, Editions Dorimen, C.C.H. Music (PRO/SDE) and Lavagot Music.
How to Contact: Write first and obtain permission to submit. Prefers cassette with 4-12 songs and lead sheet. SAE and IRC. Reports in 2-3 months.
Music: Dance, **easy listening** and **MOR**; also **top 40/pop** and **TV and movie soundtracks**. Published *Always and Forever* (by Maurice Jarre/Nathalie Carien), recorded by N. Carsen on BMG Records (ballad); *Au Noy De La Passion*, written and recorded by Alex Stanke on Select Records; and many soundtracks of French-Canadian TV series like: *Shadow of the Wolf* (Maurice Jarre); *The Breakthrough* (Oswaldo Montes); *Bethune* (Alan Reeves) and *The First Circle* (Gabriel Yared).

SABTECA MUSIC CO. (ASCAP), P.O. Box 10286, Oakland CA 94610. (415)465-2805. A&R: Sean Herring. President: Duane Herring. Music publisher and record company (Sabteca Record Co., Andre Romare). Estab. 1980. Publishes 8-10 songs/year; 1-2 new songwriters/year. Pays standard royalty.
• See the listing for Sabteca Record Co. in the Record Companies section.
Affiliate(s): Toyiabe Publishing (BMI).
How to Contact: Write first and obtain permission to submit a tape. Prefers cassette with 2 songs and lyric sheet. SASE. Reports in 2-4 weeks.
Music: Mostly **R&B**, **pop** and **country**. Published "Here She Comes," "Hanging on to Yesterday" and "Come Back ASAP" (by Duane Herring/Tom Roller), all recorded by Johnny B on Andre Romare Records.

SADDLESTONE PUBLISHING (SOCAN, BMI), 264 "H" St., Box 8110-21, Blaine WA 98230. Canada Address: 6260-130 St., Surrey British Columbia V3X 1R6 **Canada**. (604)572-4232. Fax: (604)572-4252. CEO: Candice James. Music publisher, record company (Saddlestone) and record producer (Silver Bow Productions). Estab. 1988. Publishes 100 songs/year; publishes 12-30 new songwriters/year. Pays standard royalty.
Affiliate(s): Silver Bow Publishing (SOCAN, ASCAP).
• See the listing for Silver Bow Productions in the Record Producers section and Silver Bow Management in the Managers and Booking Agents Section.
How to Contact: Submit demo tape by mail. Unsolicited submissions are OK. Prefers cassette with 3 songs and lyric sheet. "Make sure vocal is clear." SASE. Reports in 3 months.
Music: Mostly **country**, **rock** and **pop**; also **gospel** and **R&B**. Published "Page of a Poet" (by Billy O'Hara), recorded by Debbie Davis on Richway Records (country); *She's Something* (by James Earl Wilson), recorded Razzy Bailey on BMG Records (crossover); and *Read Between the Lies* (by Frank Turner), recorded by Debbie Davis on Sabre.
Tips: "Submit clear demos, good hooks and avoid long intros or instrumentals. Have a good singer do vocals."

SAMUEL THREE PRODUCTIONS (BMI), 73-4662 Mamalahoa Hwy. #A, Kailua Kona HI 96740. (808)325-1510. Fax: (808)325-3406. President: Samuel Egnot. Music publisher and record company (Alpha Recording Co.). Estab. 1992. Publishes 12 songs/year; publishes 7 new songwriters/year. Pays standard royalty.
• See the listing for Alpha Recording Co. in the Record Companies section.
How to Contact: Submit demo tape by mail. Unsolicited submissions are OK. Prefers cassette with lead sheet. SASE. Reports in 6 weeks.
Music: Mostly **country**, **country-gospel** and **gospel**; also **southern gospel**. Published "Now That You're Gone" (by Sam Egnot), recorded by Sam Younger; "Jesus Loves You and Me" (by Sam Egnot), recorded by Samuel Three; and "Head for the Roundhouse, Nellie" (by Robert Fogel), recorded by Sam Younger, all on Alpha Recording Co. Records.
Tips: "Be aggressive in getting your demos out. Don't stop at one turndown, send to another and another till you feel it's going to receive recognition. If it's good to you, ask for perhaps another musical group to consider redoing your material."

SCI-FI MUSIC (SOCAN), P.O. Box 941, N.D.G., Montreal Quebec H4A 3S3 **Canada**. (514)487-8953. President: Gary Moffet (formerly guitarist/composer with April Wine). Music publisher and record producer. Estab. 1984. Publishes 10 songs/year; publishes 2 new songwriters/year. Pays standard royalty.
• See the listing for Gary Moffet in the Record Producers section.
How to Contact: Submit demo tape by mail. Unsolicited submissions are OK. Submit cassette with 3-10 songs and lyric sheet. Does not return material.
Music: Mostly **rock** and **pop**.

TIM SCOTT MUSIC GROUP (BMI), 622 State St., Room 36, Springfield MA 01109. (413)746-4604. E-mail: tscottkiss@aol.com. President: Timothy Scott. Music publisher and record company (Keeping It Simple and Safe). Estab. 1993. Publishes 20-50 songs/year. Hires staff writers. Pays standard royalty.
Affiliates: Tim Scott Music (ASCAP).

- Tim Scott's record label, Keeping It Simple and Safe, is listed in the Record Companies section.

How to Contact: Submit demo tape by mail. Unsolicited submissions are OK. Prefers cassette with 3-5 songs and lyric sheet. SASE. Reports in 2 months.
Music: Mostly **R&B** and **pop**; also **country**, **rock** and **gospel**. Published "Just in Time," written and recorded by Willie Gray; "Everything You" (by Tim Scott), recorded by Loveworld; and "Sweet Music," written and recorded by Mike Johnson, all on Nightowl Records.

SCRUTCHINGS MUSIC (BMI), 429 Homestead St., Akron OH 44306. (330)773-8529. Owner/President: Walter E. L. Scrutchings. Music publisher. Estab. 1980. Publishes 35 songs/year; publishes 10-20 new songwriters/year. Hires staff songwriters. Pays standard royalty.
How to Contact: Submit demo tape by mail. Unsolicited submissions are OK. Prefers cassette or videocassette with 2 songs, lyric and lead sheet. Does not return material.
Music: Mostly **gospel**, **contemporary** and **traditional**. Published "God Can Fix It For You" (by R. Hinton), recorded by Raymond Hinton and the Voices of Praise Ensemble; "Everything Will Be Alright" (by W. Scrutchings), recorded by Rev. Clay Evans and the AARC Mass Choir; and "Follow Jesus" (by W. Scrutchings), recorded by Akron City Family Mass Choir.
Tips: "Music must be clear and uplifting in message."

SEGAL'S PUBLICATIONS (BMI), P.O. Box 507, Newton MA 02159. (617)969-6196. Contact: Charles Segal. Music publisher and record producer (Segal's Productions). Estab. 1963. Publishes 80 songs/year; publishes 6 new songwriters/year. Pays standard royalty.
Affilate(s): Charles Segal's Publications (BMI) and Charles Segal's Music (SESAC).

- See the listing for Segal's Productions in the Record Producers section.

How to Contact: Submit demo tape by mail. Unsolicited submissions are OK. Prefers cassette or VHS videocassette with 3 songs and lyric or lead sheet. Does not return material. Reports on accepted material only.
Music: Mostly **rock**, **pop** and **country**; also **R&B**, **MOR** and **children's songs**. Published "A Time to Care" (by Brilliant/Segal), recorded by Rosemary Wills (MOR); "Go to Bed" (by Colleen Segal), recorded Susan Stark (MOR); and "Only In Dreams" (by Chas. Segal), recorded by Rosemary Wills (MOR), all on Spin Records.
Tips: "Besides making a good demo cassette, include a lead sheet of music—words, melody line and chords."

SELLWOOD PUBLISHING (BMI), 170 N. Maple, Fresno CA 93702. (209)255-1717. Owner: Stan Anderson. Music publisher, record company (TRAC Record Co.) and record producer. Estab. 1972. Publishes 10 songs/year; publishes 3 new songwriters/year. Pays standard royalty.

- Sellwood Publishing's record label, TRAC Record Co., is listed in the Record Companies and Record Producers sections.

How to Contact: Submit demo tape by mail. Unsolicited submissions are OK. Prefers cassette or VHS videocassette with 2 songs and lyric sheet. SASE. Reports in 3 weeks. Submit clear studio demos.
Music: Mostly **traditional country** and **country**. Published *Grandpa's Old Piano* (by Ray Richmond), recorded by Jessica James; *Kick Me When I'm Down*; and *They Play Country Music in Heaven*, both written and recorded by Jimmy Walker, all on TRAC Records.
Tips: "We're looking for all styles of country, especially uptempo dance types."

SHAOLIN MUSIC (ASCAP), P.O. Box 58547, Salt Lake City UT 84158. (801)595-1123. President: Richard O'Connor. Vice President, A&R: Don Dela Vega. Music publisher, record company (Shaolin Film and Records) and record producer (Richard O'Connor). Estab. 1984. Pays standard royalty.

- Shaolin Music's record label, Shaolin Film and Records, is listed in the Record Companies section.

How to Contact: Submit demo tape by mail. Unsolicited submissions are OK. Prefers cassette with 3-

LISTINGS OF COMPANIES in countries other than the U.S. have the name of the country in boldface type.

4 songs and lyric sheet. Include bio and press kit. Does not return material. Reports in 6 weeks.
Music: Mostly **rock**, **hard rock** and **pop**; also **soundtracks**. Published *Peace of Mind* and *Black of Night* (by T. Coyote), recorded by American Zen (rock); and *Tai Chi Magic*, written and recorded by Zhen Shen-Lang, all on Shaolin Film and Records.

SHU'BABY MONTEZ MUSIC, 1447 N. 55th St., Philadelphia PA 19131. (215)473-5527. E-mail: schubaby@aol.com. President: Leroy Schuler. Music publisher. Estab. 1986. Publishes 25 songs/year; publishes 10 new songwriters/year. Pays standard royalty.
How to Contact: Write first and obtain permission to submit. Prefers cassette with 3 songs and lyric sheet. SASE. Reports in 1 month.
Music: Mostly **R&B**, **pop** and **hip-hop**. Published "I Want You" (K. Chaney/Shu'Baby); "If You Were Here With Me" (by Shu'Baby/Mike Washington/Clint Washington); and "Secret Love Affair" (by Clint Washington/Shu'Baby) all recorded by PK Lyle on Urban Logic Records (R&B).

SIEGEL MUSIC COMPANIES, Friedastr 22, 81479, Munich **Germany**. Phone: +49-89-7498070. Fax: +49-89-7498077. E-mail: meteormusik@t-online.de. Managing Director: Joachim Neubauer. Music publisher, record company (Jupiter Records and 69-Records) and record producer. Estab. 1948. GEMA. Publishes 1,500 songs/year; publishes 50 new songwriters/year. Hires staff songwriters. Pays 60% according to the rules of GEMA.
Affiliate(s): Sounds of Jupiter, Inc. (USA), Step Five (Brazil), Gobian Music (ASCAP), Symphonie House Music (ASCAP), Krok 12 (Čech Republic).
How to Contact: Submit demo tape by mail. Unsolicited submissions are OK. Prefers cassette (or VHS videocassette, but not necessary). SAE and IRC. Reports in 6 weeks.
Music: Mostly **pop**, **disco** and **MOR**; also **"hard and heavy" rock**, **country** and **soul**. Published "Forever" (by Siegel/O'Flynn), recorded by Bellamy Bros. on Jupiter Records (country); "Wake Up" (by Andy Knole), recorded by Farahy on Sony Records (dance); and "One Night Stand" (by Lederer/Wruss/Bischoff), recorded by King Of Paradise on Jupiter Records (dance).

SILICON MUSIC PUBLISHING CO. (BMI), Ridgewood Park Estates, 222 Tulane St., Garland TX 75043. President: Gene Summers. Vice President: Deanna L. Summers. Public Relations: Steve Summers. Music publisher and record company (Front Row Records). Estab. 1965. Publishes 10-20 songs/year; publishes 2-3 new songwriters/year. Pays standard royalty.
How to Contact: Submit demo tape by mail. Unsolicited submissions are OK. Prefers cassette with 1-2 songs. Does not return material. Reports ASAP.
Music: Mostly **rockabilly** and **'50s material**; also **old-time blues/country** and **MOR**. Published "Thanks For The Hanks" and "Run With the Big Dogs," written and recorded by Joe Hardin Brown (country); and "Domino" (by Dea Summers/Gene Summers/James McClung), recorded by Gene Summers on UK Pollytone Records (rockabilly).
Tips: "We are very interested in '50s rock and rockabilly *original masters* for release through overseas affiliates. If you are the owner of any '50s masters, contact us first! We have releases in Holland, Switzerland, England, Belgium, France, Sweden, Norway and Australia. We have the market if you have the tapes!"

SILVER BLUE MUSIC/OCEANS BLUE MUSIC, 5370 Vanalden Ave., Tarzana CA 91356. (818)345-2558. Music publisher. Estab. 1971. Publishes 25 songs/year. Pays standard royalty.
How to Contact: Submit demo tape by mail. Unsolicited submissions are OK. Prefers cassette with lead sheet. Does not return material.
Music: Mostly **pop** and **R&B**; also **rap**. Published "After the Lovin" (by Bernstead/Adams), recorded by Englebert Humperdinck.

SILVER THUNDER MUSIC GROUP, P.O. Box 41335, Nashville TN 37204. (615)391-5035. Fax: (615)902-0200. President: Rusty Budde. Music publisher and record producer (Rusty Budde Productions). Estab. 1985. Publishes 200 songs/year. Publishes 5-10 new songwriters/year. Hires staff songwriters. Pays standard royalty.
How to Contact: Write first and obtain permission to submit. Prefers cassette or VHS videocassette. Does not return material.
Music: Mostly **country**, **pop** and **R&B**. Published *Rock N Cowboys*, written and recorded by Jeff Samules on STR Records; *This Ain't the Real Thing* (by Rusty Budde), recorded by Les Taylor on CBS Records; and "Feel Again" (by Rusty Budde/Shara Johnson), recorded by Shara Johnson on Warner Bros. Records.
Tips: "Send clear, clean recording on cassette with lyric sheets."

SIMPLY GRAND MUSIC, INC. (ASCAP, BMI), P.O. Box 41981, Memphis TN 38174-1981. (901)272-7039. E-mail: wahani@aol.com. President: Linda Lucchesi. Music publisher. Estab. 1965. Pays standard royalty.
Affiliate(s): Memphis Town Music, Inc. (ASCAP) and Beckie Publishing Co. (BMI).
How to Contact: Submit demo tape by mail. Unsolicited submissions are OK. Prefers cassette with 1-3 songs and lyric sheet. SASE. Reports in 3-4 weeks. "Please do not send demos by certified or registered mail."
Music: **Pop**, **soul**, **country**, **soft rock**, **children's songs**, **jazz** and **R&B**.
Tips: "We are the publishing home of 'Wooly Bully'."

‡SINUS MUSIK PRODUKTION, ULLI WEIGEL, Geitnerweg 30a, D-12209, Berlin **Germany**. Phone: (0)30-715905-0. Fax: (0)30-715905-22. E-mail: ulli.weigel@t-online.de. Owner: Ulli Weigel. Music publisher, record producer and producer of radio advertising spots. GEMA, GVL. Estab. 1976. Publishes 20 songs/year; publishes 6 new songwriters/year. Pays according to GEMA conditions.
Affiliate(s): Sinus Musikverlag H.U. Weigel GmbH.
How to Contact: Submit a demo tape by mail. Unsolicited submissions are OK. Prefers cassette or CD-R with up to 10 songs and lyric sheets. SASE. Reports in 6 weeks.
Music: Mostly **rock**, **pop** and **New Age**; also **background music for movies/advertising**. Published "Simple Story," recorded by MAANAM on RCA (Polish rock); *Die Musik Maschine* (by Klaus Lage), recorded by CWN Productions on Hansa Records (pop/German); and "Maanam" (by Jakowskyl/Jakowska), recorded by CWN Productions on RCA Records (pop/English).
Tips: "Take more time working on the melody than on the instrumentation."

SISKATUNE MUSIC PUBLISHING CO., 285 Chestnut St., West Hempstead NY 11552. (516)489-0738. Fax: (516)565-9425. E-mail: platear1@aol.com. President: Mike Siskind. Music publisher and management firm. Estab. 1981. Publishes 20 songs/year; publishes 10 new songwriters/year. Pays standard royalty.

- Siskatune's management firm, Platinum Ears Ltd., is listed in the Managers and Booking Agents section.

How to Contact: Write first and obtain permission to submit. Prefers cassette with a maximum of 3 songs and lyric sheet. "Send any and all pertinent information." SASE. Reports in 2-3 months. "No phone calls."
Music: **R&B** and **country**; also **dance** and **ballads**. Published "Slice of Life" and "Caught in the Crosshairs," written and recorded by Michael Ellis on Storehouse Records; and "The Music Box" (by Larry Anderson), recorded by Off The Wall on Rubber Room Records.
Tips: "Send three songs maximum. Think songs that are coverable. Please don't check if we got the package unless it's been three months and you haven't heard from us. It is essential that demo is more than piano/vocal or guitar/vocal, as we send out those demos. Also include lyric sheets."

SIZEMORE MUSIC (BMI), P.O. Box 23275, Nashville TN 37202. (615)385-1662. Fax: (904)799-9958. Contact: Gary Sizemore. Music publisher, record company (The Gas Co.) and record producer (Gary Sizemore). Estab. 1960. Publishes 5 songs/year; 1 new songwriter/year. Pays standard royalty.
How to Contact: Submit a demo tape by mail. Unsolicited submissions are OK. Prefers cassette or VHS videocassette with lyric sheets. Does not return material. Reports in 2 weeks.
Music: Mostly **soul** and **R&B**; also **blues**, **pop** and **country**. Published "Liquor and Wine" and "The Wind," written and recorded by K. Shackleford on Heart Records (country); and "She's Tuff" (by Jerry McCain), recorded by The Fabulous Thunderbirds on Chrysalis Records (blues).

SLANTED CIRCLE MUSIC (BMI), 15114 Campbell Lane, Dale City VA 22193. (703)670-8092. A&R Dept.: Pete Lawrence. Music publisher and record producer. Estab. 1993. Publishes 15 songs/year; publishes 10 new songwriters/year. Pays standard royalty.
How to Contact: Submit demo tape by mail. Unsolicited submissions are OK. Prefers cassette or DAT with 2 songs and lyric sheet. "Only fully produced band demos." Does not return material. Reports in 6 weeks if interested.
Music: Mostly **go cat rockabilly**; also **Chicago blues**, **Christian pop** and **contemporary jazz**. *Absolutely no country!* Published "Full Size Woman," written and recorded by Larry LaVey; "If You Get to Know Him" (by LaVey/Voyles), recorded by Larry LaVey and Kim Clennan; and "Another Empty Table For Two" (by LaVey/Kingery), recorded by Teri Schaeffer, all on Trend Records.
Tips: "Have a good clear demo made and use the best tape when pitching material. A demo should sound authentic to the style the publisher wants. Research the style before sending."

SLEEPING GIANT MUSIC INTERNATIONAL LTD., 34 Great James St., London WCIN 3HB **United Kingdom**. (071)405-3786. Fax: (071)405-5245. A&R Director: Ian Taylor King. Music publisher, record company and record producer. Pays varying royalty.
How to Contact: Submit demo tape by mail. Unsolicited submissions are OK. Prefers cassette or VHS videocassette with 4 songs and lyric sheet. Does not return material. Reporting time varies.
Music: All types. Published "World Is So Small," recorded by Francesco Bruno and Richie Havens; "Till the Next Somewhere," recorded by Dee Dee Bridgewater and Ray Charles; and "Back At My Side," recorded by George Williams, all on Prestige Records Ltd.

‡SMOKIN' COWBOYS PUBLISHING CO. (ASCAP), 17329 Hawthorne St., Fontana CA 92335. (909)427-1792. A&R: Stevie Ray Hansen. Music publisher and record company (K.Y. Record Label). Estab. 1985. Publishes 75 songs/year; publishes 10 new songwriters/year. Hires staff songwriters. Pays standard royalty.
Affiliate(s): Stevie Ray Hansen Music Group (ASCAP).
How to Contact: Submit demo tape by mail. Unsolicited submissions are OK. Prefers cassette with 1-3 songs and lyric sheet. "We prefer typewritten numbered lyric sheets and good professional quality demo tapes. Put name and phone number on all material. We will call if interested." SASE. Reports in 2-4 weeks.
Music: Mostly **country**, **country rock**, **surf music**, **gospel**, **rockabilly** and **blues**; also **R&B**, **top 40** and **MOR**. No rap or metal. Published "Thirty Something" and "Storms" (by Stevie Ray Hansen); and "Love Those Girls" (by Johnny Fortune/Stevie Ray Hansen), all recorded by Johnny Fortune on Media Records (country).
Tips: "Our international division needs songs for Europe. We specialize in producing overseas singers. We are interested in C&W and rockabilly artists. We request a photo and bio with material."

SNOWCLIFF PUBLISHING (BMI), P.O. Box 82, De Ridder LA 70634. (318)462-3514. President: Cliff Shelder. Vice President: Gene Snow. Music publisher, record company (SME Records), record producer, music production company (SME Music). Estab. 1993. Publishes 10-15 songs/year; publishes 3-5 new songwriters/year. Pays standard royalty.
Affiliate(s): Snowcap Publishing (BMI).
How to Contact: Write or call first and obtain permission to submit a demo. Prefers cassette or DAT with no more than 3 songs and lyric sheet. Does not return material. Reports in 1 month.
Music: Contemporary Christian, **country gospel** and **country**; also **pop**, **jazz** and **blues**. Published "Out of the Darkness" and "I Stand Amazed" (by Cliff Shelder), recorded by Rebecca Yerg on SME Records (contemporary Christian); and "Heartaches and Roses" (by Cliff Shelder), recorded by Kim May on BJD Records (country).
Tips: "We prefer songs with a positive message—not beer drinkin' music. Submit good quality demos in a neat package. Have your music performed in public and gauge the audience response. If people keep asking to hear a particular song, we'd like to hear it too."

SOLID ENTERTAINMENT, 11328 Magnolia Blvd., Suite 3, N. Hollywood CA 91601. (818)508-1101. President: James Warsinske. Music publisher. Estab. 1988. Publishes 30-60 songs/year; publishes 10-20 new songwriters/year. Pays standard royalty.
Affiliate(s): Harmonious Music (BMI).
How to Contact: Submit demo tape by mail. Unsolicited submissions are OK. Prefers cassette or VHS videocassette with 2-5 songs and lyric sheet. "Clearly labelled tapes with phone numbers." SASE. Reports in 1 month.
Music: Mostly **R&B**, **hip hop**, **rock**, **A/C** and **AAA**. Published "Let It Be Right," written and recorded by Duncan Faure on AVC Records (pop/rock); "Melissa Mainframe" (by Hohl/Rocca), recorded by Rocca on Life Records (pop/rap); and "In Service" (by Michael Williams), recorded by Madrok on AVC Records (rap).

SONG FARM MUSIC (BMI), P.O. Box 24561, Nashville TN 37202. (615)742-1557. President: Tom Pallardy. Music publisher and record producer (T.P. Productions). Estab. 1980. Publishes 2-5 songs/year; publishes 1-2 new songwriters/year. Pays standard royalty.
How to Contact: Write first and obtain permission to submit. Prefers cassette with maximum 2 songs and lyric or lead sheet. SASE required with enough postage for return of all materials. Reports in 2-6 weeks.
Music: Mostly **country** and **R&B**. Published "Mississippi River Rat" (by J. Hall/R. Hall/E. Dickey), recorded by Tom Powers on Fountain Records (Cajun country); "Today's Just Not the Day" (by J. Bell, E. Bobbitt), recorded by Liz Draper (country); and "In Mama's Time" (by T. Crone), recorded by Pat Tucker on Radioactive Records (country/pop).
Tips: "Material should be submitted neatly and professionally with as good quality demo as possible.

Songs need not be elaborately produced (voice and guitar/piano are fine) but they should be clear."

‡SONGS FROM OUT OF THE BLUE (BMI), 2016 Douglas Ave., Clearwater FL 34615. (813)449-8814. President: Tony Blue. Vice President: James Dina. Music publisher. Estab. 1995. Pays standard royalty.
How to Contact: Submit demo tape by mail. Unsolicited submissions OK. Prefers cassette or CD with 3-4 songs and lyric sheet. "Writers who also perform should also include a photo and a bio." SASE. Reports in 2-3 months.
Music: Rock (acoustic), country and **pop, alternative, blues, gospel** and **dance.**

‡SONY MUSIC GROUP, 550 Madison Ave., 18th Floor, New York NY 10022. (212)833-4729. Fax: (212)833-5552. Santa Monica office: 2100 Colorado Ave., Santa Monica CA 90404. (310)449-2545. Fax: (310)449-2544. Music publisher.
How to Contact: Sony Music does not accept unsolicited submissions.
Music: Published "Missing" (by Tracey Thorn/Ben Watt), recorded by Everything But The Girl on Atlantic Records.

‡SOUND AND FURY MUSIC PUBLISHING (ASCAP), P.O. Box 332, Southbridge MA 01550. (508)248-1799. Contact: Submissions Department. Music publisher. Estab. 1996. Publishes 15 songs/year; publishes 1-5 new songwriters/year. Pays standard royalty.
How to Contact: Write first and obtain permission to submit. Prefers cassette with 3 songs, lyric and lead sheet. "We do not consider or return unsolicited material." SASE (only if solicited). Reports in 2-3 months.
Music: Mostly **rock**. Published *Enemy Glory* (by Karen Michalson/Bill Michalson/Kevin Dion), recorded by Point of Ares on Arula Records (rock).

SOUND CELLAR MUSIC, 116 N. Peoria, Dixon IL 61021. (815)288-2900. President: Todd Joos. Music publisher, record company, record producer and recording studio. Estab. 1987. Publishes 15-25 songs/year. Publishes 5 or 6 new songwriters/year. Pays standard royalty.
- Sound Cellar Music's record label, Cellar Records, is listed in the Record Companies section.

How to Contact: Submit demo tape by mail. Unsolicited submissions are OK. Prefers cassette with 3 or 4 songs and lyric sheet. Does not return material. "We contact by phone only if we want to work with the artist."
Music: Mostly **metal, country** and **rock**; also **pop, rap** and **blues**. Published *Collins*, written and recorded by Snap Judgment (alternative); "Soul Searchin," written and recorded by Justice 4 (rock); and "Spill A Tear," written and recorded by Impetus (metal), all on Cellar Records.

THE SPACEK CO., P.O. Box 741506, Dallas TX 75374. (903)882-1375. President: Ed Spacek. Music publisher. Estab. 1978. Pays standard royalty.
Affiliate(s): Woodcreek (ASCAP), Eagles Nest (BMI).
How to Contact: Submit demo tape by mail. Unsolicited submissions are OK. Prefers cassette. Does not return material. Reports in 1 month.
Music: All types.

‡SPINWILLY MUSIC PUBLISHING (BMI), 127 Grace St., Wilmington NC 28401. (910)343-0153. Director A&R: Rick Smith. Creative Manager: Julie Helgekhi. Creative Director: Sarah Swart. Music publisher, record company (Radio Records, Star Diner Records, Exchange Music). Estab. 1987. Publishes 15 songs/year. Pays standard royalty.
How to Contact: Submit demo tape by mail. Unsolicited submissions are OK. Prefers cassette with lyric sheet. Does not return material. Reports in 2 months.
Music: Published "You Complete Me" (by Michael Parker/Rick D'Anjolell), recorded by GE; "It Turns in Turn," written and recorded by Rick D'Anjolell, both on Exchange Music; and "Cool Groove" (by Kylet Lance), recorded by Self Spray on Star Diner Records.
Tips: "Bug the heck out of us because we're very busy. Be creative with your songs to bring them to our attention."

SPRADLIN/GLEICH PUBLISHING (BMI), 4234 N. 45th St., Phoenix AZ 85018-4307. Manager: Lee Gleich. Music publisher. Estab. 1988. Publishes 4-10 songs/year; 2-4 new songwriters. Pays standard royalty.
Affiliate(s): Paul Lee Publishing (ASCAP).
How to Contact: Write first and obtain permission to submit. Prefers cassette with 3 songs and lyric or

lead sheet. "It must be very good material, as I only have time for promoting songwriters who really care." SASE. Reports in 1 month.
Music: Mostly **country** geared to the US and European country markets. Published "I Gotta Learn to Dance" and "Love's Gone Crazy," both written and recorded by Bob Cesaro on Wild Sky Records (rock); and *Go Slow and Wait* (by Paul Spradlin), recorded by the Goose Creek Symphony on Goose Records (country).

STARBOUND PUBLISHING CO. (BMI), Dept. SM, 207 Winding Rd., Friendswood TX 77546. (713)482-2346. E-mail: bh207@msn.com. President: Buz Hart. Music publisher, record company (Juke Box Records, Quasar Records and Eden Records) and record producer (Lonnie Wright and Buz Hart). Estab. 1970. Publishes 35-100 songs/year; publishes 5-10 new songwriters/year. Pays standard royalty.
How to Contact: Write or call first and obtain permission to submit. Prefers cassette with 3 songs and lyric sheet. SASE. Reports in 2 months.
Music: Mostly **country**, **R&B** and **gospel**. Published "Butterfly" (by Pamela Parkins/Buz Hart), recorded by Frankie Laine on Score Records; "Let it Slide" (by James Watson/Buz Hart), recorded by Stan Steel on Gallery II Records; and "Country Boy's Dream" (by Gene Thomas/Buz Hart), recorded by Charlie Louvin, Waylon Jennings, and George Jones on Playback Records.

STEEL RAIN PUBLISHING (BMI), 437 Gilbert Ridge, Alexandria KY 41001. (606)635-1160. President/Manager: Sharon Karr. Estab. 1993. Publishes 10 songs/year; publishes 3 new songwriters/year. Pays standard royalty.
How to Contact: Submit demo tape by mail. Unsolicited submissions are OK. Prefers cassette or VHS videocassette with 3 songs and lyric sheet. "Please print clearly, if not typed." Does not return material. Reports in 4-8 weeks.
Music: Mostly **country**, **country rock** and **country gospel**. Published *Steel Rain* (by Bryan Karr); *Run-Away Stage* and *Cross Roads* (by Bryan Karr/Sharon Karr), all recorded by Bryan Karr/Steel Rain on Sagegrass Records (country).

JEB STUART MUSIC CO. (BMI), P.O. Box 6032, Station B, Miami FL 33101-6032. (305)547-1424. President: Jeb Stuart. Music publisher, record producer (Esquire International) and management firm. Estab. 1975. Publishes 4-6 songs/year. Pays standard royalty.

- See the listing for Esquire International in the Record Producers section.

How to Contact: Submit demo tape by mail. Unsolicited submissions are OK. Prefers cassette or CD with 2-4 songs and lead sheet. SASE. Reports in 1 month.
Music: Mostly **gospel**, **jazz/rock**, **pop**, **R&B** and **rap**; also **blues**, **church/religious**, **country**, **disco** and **soul**. Published "Love in the Rough," "Guns, Guns (No More Guns)" and "Come On Cafidia," all written and recorded by Jeb Stuart on Esquire Int'l Records.

SUCCES, Pijnderslaan 84, 9200 Dendermonde **Belgium**. (052)21 89 87. Fax: (052)22 52 60. Director: Deschuyteneer Hendrik. Music publisher, record company and record producer. Estab. 1978. Publishes 400 songs/year. Hires staff songwriters. Pays standard royalty.
How to Contact: Submit demo tape by mail. Unsolicited submissions are OK. Prefers cassette or VHS videocassette with 3 songs. SAE and IRC. Reports in 2 months.
Music: Mostly **pop**, **dance** and **variety**; also **instrumental** and **rock**. Published "Accordian Goes Classic," written and recorded by Le Grand Julot on Hit Plus Records (classic); "Romantic Dreams" (by Ricky Mondes), recorded by Romantic Dream Orchestra on Arcade Records (instrumental); and "Locomoslurf," written and recorded by Roy Payne on Style Records (pop).

‡SUGARFOOT PRODUCTIONS (ASCAP), P.O. Box 1065, Joshua Tree CA 92252. A&R Director: Sheila Dobson. Music publisher, record company (Sugarfoot, Babydoll, Durban) and record producer (Sugarfoot Records). Estab. 1987. Publishes 10-15 songs/year; publishes 4 new songwriters/year. Pays standard royalty.
How to Contact: Submit demo tape by mail. Unsolicited submissions are OK. Prefers cassette with 3 songs and lyric sheet. "Make sure tape and vocal are clear." Does not return material. Reports in 2-3 weeks.
Music: Mostly **jazz**, **blues**, **swing**, **country**, **R&B**, **salsa** and **dance**; also **bassas**, **conga**, **Cuban** and **easy listening**. Published "Not for Love" (by Elijah), recorded by Carolee on Westways Records (R&B); "You're Blue" (by Deke), recorded by Sheila on Sweet N Smooth (jazz); and "I'm Yours" (by Dewey), recorded by Sheila on Sugarfoot Records (jazz).
Tips: "Listen to Irving Berlin, Johnny Mercer, Cole Porter, George Gershwin for professional music and lyrics."

SUN STAR SONGS, P.O. Box 1387, Pigeon Forge TN 37868. (423)429-4121. Fax: (423)429-7090. President: Tony Glenn Rast. Music publisher. Estab. 1965, reactivated 1992. Pays standard royalty.
How to Contact: Submit demo tape by mail. Unsolicited submissions OK. Prefers cassette with 3 songs and lyric sheets. SASE. Reports in 2 weeks.
Music: Mostly **country**, **Christian country-gospel** and **bluegrass**; also **pop-rock**. Published *Let's Go Racing* (by Rast/Ruby/Rabbain), recorded by Nevada on SunStar Records (country); *If You Ain't Got Jesus* (by Jim Sales), recorded by Tommy Cash on Rejoice Records (gospel); and *You Are the Christ* (by Tony Glenn Rast/Betty Ross), recorded by Holly Robinson on Heartlight Records (gospel).
Tips: "Submit quality demos. Also interested in good lyrics for co-writing."

SUNSONGS MUSIC (BMI, ASCAP, SESAC), 52 N. Evarts Ave., Elmsford NY 10523. (914)592-2563. Professional Manager: Michael Berman. Music publisher, record producer and talent agency (Hollywood East Entertainment). Estab. 1981. Publishes 20 songs/year; publishes 10 new songwriters/year. Pays standard royalty; co-publishing deals available for established writers.
Affiliate(s): Media Concepts Music and Dark Sun Music (SESAC).
How to Contact: Submit demo tape by mail. Unsolicited submissions are OK. Prefers cassette with 3-4 songs and lyric sheet. SASE. Reports in 3 months.
Music: Dance-oriented, **techno-pop** and **R&B**; also **rock (all styles)** and **top 40/pop**. Published "Livin' For the Weekend" and "New Love Affair" (by Henderson/Rick), recorded by The Joneses on Karrousell Records (USA) and P-Vine Records (Japan and Far East); and "Christmas Rappin' " (arrangements by John Henderson), recorded by the Grand Rapmasters on BMG Records (R&B).
Tips: "Submit material with strong hook and know the market being targeted by your song."

SURESPIN SONGS (BMI), 1217 16th Ave. S., Nashville TN 37212. (615)327-8129. Fax: (615)327-0928. Music publisher. Estab. 1983. Publishes 25 songs/year; publishes 2 new songwriters/year.
Affiliate(s): Preston Sullivan Music (ASCAP).
How to Contact: Call first and obtain permission to submit. Prefers cassette with 3 songs. Does not return material. Reports in 2 months.
Music: Mostly **rock** and **country**.

SWEET GLENN MUSIC (BMI), P.O. Box 1067, Santa Monica CA 90406. (310)452-0116. Fax: (310)452-2585. E-mail: muzikbiz4u@aol.com. Vice President Talent: Mr. Friedwin. Music publisher and management company. Estab. 1980. Publishes 3-5 songs/year; publishes 1 new songwriter/year. Royalty rate varies.
Affiliate(s): Sweet Karol Music (ASCAP).
How to Contact: Write first and obtain permission to submit. "You must write before submitting." Reports in 2 months.
Music: Mostly **retro R&B** and **cutting edge country**. Published "Rhythm of Romance" (by Scott), recorded by Randy Crawford.
Tips: "Must be part of a performing act or established producer/arranger-writer only!"

SWEET JUNE MUSIC (BMI), P.O. Box 669, Fulton TX 78358. (512)729-4249. Fax: (512)729-5338. E-mail: tbsr@sat.net. Owner: Tom Thrasher. Music publisher, record company (TBS Records) and record producer. Estab. 1963. Publishes 4 songs/year; publishes 1-3 new songwriters/year. Pays standard royalty.
How to Contact: Submit demo tape by mail. Unsolicited submissions are OK. Prefers cassette or DAT with 3 songs and lyric and/or lead sheet. "Copyright all material *before* submitting!" Does not return material. Reports in 6 weeks.
Music: Mostly **Christian country**, **Southern gospel** and **traditional hymns**; also **bluegrass**, **folk** and **country**. Published "Fallen Angel" and "God Is Not Through With Me," written and recorded by Tom Thrasher (Christian country); and "Easy To Love" (by Thomas R. Thrasher), recorded by Donna Bryant (Southern gospel), all on TBS Records.

T.C. PRODUCTIONS/ETUDE PUBLISHING CO. (BMI), 121 Meadowbrook Dr., Somerville NJ 08876. (908)359-5110. Fax: (908)359-1962. President: Tony Camillo. Music publisher and record producer. Estab. 1992. Publishes 25-50 songs/year; publishes 3-6 new songwriters/year. Pays standard royalty.
Affiliate(s): We Iz It Music Publishing (ASCAP), Etude/Barcam (BMI).
How to Contact: Call first and obtain permission to submit a demo. Prefers cassette with 3-4 songs and lyric sheet. SASE. Reports in 2 weeks.
Music: Mostly **R&B** and **dance**; also **country** and **outstanding pop ballads**. Published "One of a Kind" (by Sandy Farina/Lisa Ratner), recorded by Vanessa Williams; "Waiting for Last Goodbye" and "I Feel a Song" (by Tony Camillo/Mary Sawyer), recorded by Gladys Knight, all on P.A.R. Records (R&B).

DALE TEDESCO MUSIC CO. (BMI), 16020 Lahey St., Granada Hills CA 91344. (818)360-7329. Fax: (818)886-1338. President: Dale T. Tedesco. General Manager: Betty Lou Tedesco. Music publisher. Estab. 1981. Publishes 20-40 songs/year; publishes 20-30 new songwriters/year. Pays standard royalty.
Affiliate(s): Tedesco Tunes (ASCAP).
How to Contact: Submit a demo tape by mail. Unsolicited submissions are OK. Prefers cassette with 1 song and lyric sheet. SASE or postcard for critique. "Dale Tedesco Music hand-critiques all material submitted. Only reviews 1 song. Free evaluation." Reports in 2-3 weeks.
Music: Mostly **pop**, **R&B** and **A/C**; also **dance-oriented**, **instrumentals** (for TV and film), **jazz**, **MOR**, **rock**, **soul** and **ethnic instrumentals**. Published *One Child* (by David Brisbin), recorded by Ernestine Anderson on Quest Records (jazz).

‡TEXAS TUFF MUSIC COMPANY (BMI), P.O. Box 630555, Irving TX 75063-0555. (972)831-1272. Fax: (972)831-8644. E-mail: ttuffmuz@aol.com. Owner: Janice Matson. Music publisher. Estab. 1996. Publishes 20 songs/year; publishes 3-5 new songwriters/year. Pays standard royalty.
Affiliate(s): Jan Matson Publishing (ASCAP).
How to Contact: Submit demo tape by mail. Unsolicited submissions are OK. Prefers cassette with 3-5 songs and lyric sheet. SASE. Reports in 6 weeks.
Music: Country only.

THIRD WAVE PRODUCTIONS LIMITED, P.O. Box 563, Gander Newfoundland A1V 2E1 **Canada**. (709)256-8009. Fax: (709)256-7411. President: Arch. Bonnell. Music publisher, record company (Third Wave/Street Legal), distribution and marketing company. Estab. 1986. Publishes 20 songs/year; publishes 2 new songwriters/year.

- See their listing in the Record Companies section.

How to Contact: Submit demo tape by mail. Unsolicited submissions are OK. Prefers cassette or DAT with lyric sheet. SASE. Reports in 2 months.
Music: Mostly **traditional Newfoundland**, **Celtic/Irish** and **folk**; also **bluegrass**, **country** and **pop/rock**. Published *Salt Beef Junkie* and *He's a Part of Me* (by Buddy Wosisname), recorded by The Other Fellers (traditional); and *Nobody Never Told Me*, written and recorded by The Psychobilly Cadillacs (country), all on Third Wave Productions.

THIS HERE MUSIC (ASCAP), P.O. Box 277, Arnolds Park IA 51331. (712)338-2663. Fax: (712)338-2614. E-mail: thisheremu@aol.com. President: Rikk Colligan. Music publisher, record company, record producer and songcrafting workshop. Estab. 1991. Publishes 5 songs/year; publishes 2 new songwriters/year. Pays standard royalty.
How to Contact: Write, call or e-mail first and obtain permission to submit. Prefers cassette, list of goals for your music and 3 songs. "Simply produced cassette is fine. Send SASE and we'll critique your work." Does not return material. Reports in 6 months.
Music: Mostly **folk influenced**, **pop** and **rock**; also **Lutheran worship music**, **Bible Camp sing alongs** and **children's songs**. Published "Where You Are" (by R. Colligan), recorded by Sojourn on Sojourn Records (CCM); "Gravity," written and recorded by R. Colligan on This Here Music Records (alternative); and "There's A Promise" (by R. Colligan), recorded by Hans Peterson on Dakota Road Records (worship).
Tips: "Prepare yourself for a complete lack of hype if you contact us. We're grass roots and would be happy to talk with you about your dreams and goals for your music. We can introduce you to a Midwest network of good people to help you make a living with your music."

TIKI ENTERPRISES, INC. (BMI, ASCAP), 195 S. 26th St., San Jose CA 95116. (408)286-9840. President: Gradie O'Neal. Music publisher, record company (Rowena Records) and record producer (Jeannine O'Neal and Gradie O'Neal). Estab. 1967. Publishes 40 songs/year; publishes 12 new songwriters/year. Pays standard royalty.
Affiliate(s): Tooter Scooter Music (BMI), Janell Music (BMI) and O'Neal & Friend (ASCAP).
How to Contact: Submit a demo tape by mail. Unsolicited submissions are OK. Prefers cassette with 3 songs and lyric or lead sheets. SASE. Reports in 3 weeks.
Music: Mostly **country**, **Mexican**, **rock/pop gospel**, **R&B** and **New Age**. Published "Yamor Indio," by Roy De Hoyos (Mexican Tex-Mex); "Palomita Triste," by Jaque Lynn (Mexican); and "I Know That I Know," by Jeannine O'Neal (contemporary Christian).

‡TIMBA YUMA, 529 W. 42nd St. #4V, New York NY 10036. E-mail: rumbaman@sprynet.com. President: Michel Vega. Music publisher. Estab. 1996.
How to Contact: Submit demo tape by mail. Unsolicited submissions are OK. Prefers cassette, DAT or VHS videocassette with 4 songs and lyric sheet. Does not return material. Reports in 2 months.

Music: Mostly **Latin music** and **jazz**.

TOPS AND BOTTOMS MUSIC (BMI), P.O. Box 1341, New York NY 10113. (212)366-6636. Fax: (212)366-4646. Director: Richard Dworkin. Music publisher. Estab. 1988. Publishes 5 songs/year; publishes 1 new songwriter/year. Pays standard royalty.
How to Contact: Submit demo tape by mail. Unsolicited submissions are OK. Prefers cassette or VHS videocassette with 3-5 songs and lyric sheet. Does not return material. Reports in 4 months.
Music: Music relating to gay/lesbian life. Published "Love Worth Fighting For" (by Michael Callen/Marsha Malamet), recorded by Lee Lessack on LML Records (ballad); "We've Had Enough" and *Crazy World*, both written and recorded by Michael Callen on Significant Other Records (rock/ballad).

‡TOULOUSE MUSIC PUBLISHING CO., INC. (BMI), Box 96, El Cerrito CA 94530. Executive Vice President: James Bronson, Jr. Music publisher, record company (Touché Records) and record producer (Mom and Pop Productions). Member AIMP. Publishes 1 new songwriter/year. Hires staff writers. Pays standard royalty.

- See the listings for Touché Records in the Record Companies section and Mom and Pop Productions in the Record Producers section.

How to Contact: Prefers cassette with 2-4 songs and lyric sheet. SASE. Reports in 1 month.
Music: Bluegrass, gospel, jazz, R&B and **soul**.

TRANSAMERIKA MUSIKVERLAG KG, Wilhelmstrasse 10, 23611 Bad Schwartan, **Germany**. Phone: (0451)21530. General Manager: Pia Kaminsky. GEMA, PRS, KODA, NCB, APRA. Music publisher and administrator. Estab. 1978. Publishes 2-4 songs/year; publishes 1 new songwriter/year. Pays 50% if releasing a record; 85% if only administrating.
Affiliate(s): Loosong Copyright Service Ltd. (London, United Kingdom) and Leosong Music Australia Pty. Ltd., Sydney.
How to Contact: Submit demo tape by mail. Unsolicited submissions are OK. Prefers cassette or VHS videocassette. Does not return material. Reports in 1-2 months.
Music: Mostly **pop**; also **rock, country, film music** and **reggae**. Published *Sandcastle* (by Dominic Suhle); *The City (Where You Live)* (by Dieter Hoffmann); and *Why Glorify* (by Dirk Latus), all recorded by Gary's Best Friend on Rockwerk Records.

‡TRANSITION MUSIC CORPORATION (ASCAP, BMI, SESAC), 11328 Magnolia, N. Hollywood CA 91601. (818)760-1001. Fax: (818)760-7625. E-mail: onestopmus@aol.com. Contact: Rich Dickerson. Music publisher. Estab. 1988. Publishes 250 songs/year; publishes 20 new songwriters/year. Variable royalty based on song placement and writer.
Affiliate(s): Pushy Publishing (ASCAP), Creative Entertainment Music (BMI) and One Stop Shop Music (SESAC).
How to Contact: Submit demo tape by mail. Unsolicited submissions are OK. Prefers cassette, DAT or CD with 3 songs. SASE. Reports in 3 weeks.
Music: Mostly **alternative, pop** and **hip hop**; also **urban** and **R&B**. "TMC provides music for television shows on a weekly basis. Credits include *Entertainment Tonight*, *Coach*, *Beverly Hills 90210* and *Melrose Place*."

TREASURE TROVE MUSIC (BMI), P.O. Box 48864, Los Angeles CA 90048. (213)739-4824. Contact: Larry Rosenblum. Music publisher, record company (L.S. Disc) and record producer. Estab. 1987. Publishes 3-15 songs/year; publishes 1-5 new songwriters/year. Pays standard royalty.
Affiliate(s): Lazy Rose Music (ASCAP), Laca Music (ASCAP) and Straight from the Hip Music (BMI).
How to Contact: Submit demo tape by mail. Unsolicited submissions are OK. Prefers cassette or CD with 1-10 songs and lyric sheet. SASE. Reports in 1 month.
Music: Mostly **rock, progressive rock** and **punk**; also **jazz, folk** and **psychedelic rock**. Published "Nobody for President" (by Fenson and Peri Traynor); "Your Love is Like a Pizza" and "Fair Trade" (by Fenson), all recorded by the Bob Dole Band on L.S. Disc.

REMEMBER: Don't "shotgun" your demo tapes. Submit only to companies interested in the type of music you write. For more submission hints, refer to Getting Started on page 6.

TRUSTY PUBLICATIONS (BMI), 8771 Rose Creek Rd., Nebo KY 42441. (502)249-3194. E-mail: trusty@wko.com. Website: http://www.wko.com/business/trusty/trusty.htm. President: Elsie Childers. Music publisher, record company (Trusty Records) and record producer. Member CMA. Estab. 1960. Publishes 2-3 songs/year; publishes 2 new songwriters/year. Pays standard royalty.

- Trusty's affiliated record label, Trusty Records, is listed in the Record Companies section.

How to Contact: Submit demo tape by mail. Unsolicited submissions are OK. "SASE for answer, please." Prefers cassette or VHS videocassette with 2-4 songs and lead sheet. Does not return material. Reports in 6 weeks.
Music: Country, **R&B**, **rock**, **contemporary Christian**, **Southern gospel**, **Christian country**, **jazz** and **line dancing**. Published "God's On My Side" (by Steve Holland), recorded by Still Water on Still Water Records (gospel); and "Good News From Home," written and recorded by Alishia Luckett (country).

‡TWIN BEARS PUBLISHING (BMI), P.O. Box 23362, Knoxville TN 37933-1362. (423)719-5636. E-mail: cncdad@aol.com. President: John Condrone. Music publisher and record company (Kare Bear Records). Estab. 1997. Publishes 30 songs/year; publishes 10-12 new songwriters/year. Pays standard royalty.
Affiliate(s): Condrone Music (ASCAP).
How to Contact: Submit demo tape by mail. Unsolicited submissions are OK. Prefers good clear demos with 3 songs with lyric sheet. SASE. Reports in 1 month.
Music: Mostly **country**, **rock** and **pop**; also **contemporary Christian**, **dance/hip hop** and **MOR**. Published "Through the Eyes of a Child" (by John Condrone), recorded by Paula Foust (pop); "Love Is The Cure"' (by John Condrone), recorded by T.J. Knox (country/pop); and "In the Middle of the Night" (by John Condrone), recorded by Johnny Meadows (pop), all on Kare Bear Records.

TWIN SPIN PUBLISHING (BMI), P.O. Box 2114, Valparaiso IN 46384. Phone/fax: (219)477-4075. President: Tony Nicoletto. Management firm, music publisher and record company (KNG Records). Estab. 1990. Publishes 50 songs/year; publishes 12 new songwriters/year. Pays standard royalty.

- Twin Spin's management company, Nic of Tyme Productions, can be found in the Managers and Booking Agents section.

How to Contact: Submit demo tape by mail. Unsolicited submissions are OK. Prefers cassette with 4-6 songs. "Send all important information: bio, song history, etc." Does not return material. Reports in 3-4 weeks.
Music: Mostly **rock**, **pop** and **alternative**; also **gospel** and **country**. Published "Little Man" (by Joseph Gaal), recorded by Rising Jes (alternative); "Rendezvous," written and recorded by Mary LaFleur (top 40); and "19 Days in Brazil" (by Revelle Smith), recorded by Kuul Hand, all on KNG Records (jazz).

TWIN TOWERS PUBLISHING CO., Dept. SM, 8833 Sunset Blvd., Penthouse West, Los Angeles CA 90069. (310)659-9644. President: Michael Dixon. Music publisher and booking agency (Harmony Artists, Inc.). Publishes 24 songs/year. Pays standard royalty.
How to Contact: Call first to get permission to submit a tape. Prefers cassette with 3 songs and lyric sheet. SASE. Will respond only if interested.
Music: Mostly **pop**, **rock** and **R&B**. Published "Magic," from *Ghostbusters* soundtrack on Arista Records; and "Kiss Me Deadly" (by Lita Ford) on RCA Records.

ULTIMATE PEAK MUSIC (BMI), P.O. Box 707, Nashville TN 37076. Manager: Danny Crader. Music publisher. Estab. 1992. Publishes 35 songs/year; publishes 4 new songwriters/year. Hires staff writers. Pays standard royalty.
How to Contact: Submit demo tape by mail. Unsolicited submissions are OK. Prefers cassette with 1-6 songs and lyric sheet. SASE. Reports in 6 weeks.
Music: Mostly **country** and **MTV pop/rock**. Published *Test of Time* and *Mathematics* (by Anderson Page/Billy Herzig); and *Colorful Romance* (by Daryl Girard), all recorded by Dream Street on Tooth & Nail Records (pop).
Tips: "Listen to the radio and compare your songs to the hits—not for recording quality, but for substance and content and structure—and be objective and realistic and honest with yourself."

UNIMUSICA INC. (ASCAP), 6303 Blue Lagoon Dr., Miami FL 33126. (305)264-0606. Fax: (305)265-2399. Manager: Maria Flores. Music publisher. Estab. 1981. Publishes 5,000 songs/year; publishes 500 new songwriters/year. Pays standard royalty.
Affiliate(s): Musica Unica Publishing (BMI).
How to Contact: Submit demo tape by mail. Unsolicited submissions are OK. Prefers cassette. Does not return material. Reports in 2 months.

Music: Mostly **salsa**, **baladas** and **merengues**. Published "Por Amarte" (by Robert Morales) and "Experiencia Religiosia" (by Chien Garcia Alonso), recorded by Enrique Iglesias on Fonovisa Records.
Tips: "Supply record companies with the best possible demo."

VAAM MUSIC GROUP (ASCAP, BMI), P.O. Box 29550, Hollywood CA 90029-0688. (213)664-7765. President: Pete Martin. Music publisher and record producer. Estab. 1967. Publishes 9-24 new songs/year. Pays standard royalty.
Affiliate(s): Pete Martin Music.

- See the listing for Pete Martin/Vaam Productions in the Record Producers section.

How to Contact: Prefers cassette with 2 songs maximum and lyric sheet. SASE. Reports in 1 month. "Small packages only."
Music: **Top 40/pop**, **country** and **R&B**. "Submitted material must have potential of reaching top 5 on charts." Published "The Greener Years," recorded by Frank Loren on Blue Gem Records (country/MOR); "Bar Stool Rider" (by Peggy Hackworth); and "I Love a Cowboy," written and performed by Sherry Weston in the feature film "Far Out Man," with Tommy Chong (of Cheech & Chong comedy team) and also co-starring Martin Mull.
Tips: "Study the top 10 charts in the style you write. Stay current and up-to-date with today's market."

VALET PUBLISHING CO. (BMI), 2442 N.W. Market St., Suite 273, Seattle WA 98107. Administrative offices: 5503 Roosevelt Way NE, Seattle WA 98105. (206)524-1020. Fax: (206)524-1102. Publishing Director: Buck Ormsby. Music publisher and record company (Etiquette/Suspicious Records). Estab. 1961. Publishes 5-10 songs/year. Pays standard royalty.

- See the listing for John "Buck" Ormsby in the Record Producers section.

How to Contact: Call first and obtain permission to submit a demo tape. Prefers cassette with 3-4 songs and lyric sheets. SASE. Reports in 6-8 weeks.
Music: Mostly **R&B**, **rock** and **pop**; also **dance** and **country**.
Tips: "Production of tape must be top quality and lyric sheets professional."

VELOCITY PRODUCTIONS, P.O. Box 518, Leander TX 78646-0518. E-mail: jbsters@inetport.com. Contact: Review Coordinator. Music publisher and record producer. Estab. 1986. Publishes 10-20 songs/year; publishes 2-3 new songwriters/year. Pays standard royalty.
Affiliate(s): Velocity Publishing (BMI).
How to Contact: Write and obtain permission to submit. Does not return material. Reports in 6 weeks.
Music: **All types.**

‡VICEROY MUSIC GROUP, INC., 547 W. 27th St., New York NY 10001. (212)465-2357. (212)279-6520. E-mail: vroy@aol.com. COO: Anthony Roger. Music publisher and record company. Estab. 1990. Publishes 30-45 songs/year; publishes 1-3 new songwriters/year. Pays standard royalty.
How to Contact: Write first and obtain permission to submit. Prefers cassette, DAT or VHS videocassette with 5 songs and lyric sheet. Does not return material. Reports in 2-4 weeks.
Music: Mostly **rock** and **blues**.

VOKES MUSIC PUBLISHING (BMI), Box 12, New Kensington PA 15068-0012. (412)335-2775. President: Howard Vokes. Music publisher, record company, booking agency and promotion company.

- Vokes Music's record label, Vokes Music Record Co., is listed in the Record Companies section and their booking agency, Vokes Booking Agency, is listed in the Managers and Booking Agents section.

How to Contact: Submit cassette (3 songs only), lyric or lead sheet. SASE. Reports within a week.
Music: **Traditional country-bluegrass** and **gospel**. Published "A Million Tears" (by Duke & Null), recorded by Johnny Eagle Feather on Vokes Records; "I Won't Be Your Honky Tonk Queen" (by Vokes/Wallace), recorded by Bunnie Mills on Pot-Of-Gold Records; and "Break The News" (by Vokes/Webb), recorded by Bill Beere on Oakhill Records.
Tips: "We're always looking for country songs that tell a story, and only interested in hard-traditional-bluegrass, country and country gospel songs. Please no 'copy-cat songwriters.' "

WARNER/CHAPPELL MUSIC CANADA LTD. (SOCAN), 85 Scarsdale Rd. #101, Don Mills Ontario M3B 2R2 **Canada**. (416)445-3131. Fax: (416)445-2473. E-mail: wcmca@inforamp.net. Creative Manager: Anne-Marie Smith. Music publisher.
How to Contact: Write first and obtain permission to submit a demo. Prefers cassette with 3 songs with bio and lyric sheet. SAE and IRC. Reports in 2 months.
Music: **All genres** with music and lyrics completed. Published "I Love You Always Forever," written

INSIDER REPORT

Music publishers provide a powerful support network

photo: Jeff Conroy

Judy Stakee

Judy Stakee says the best part about her job as Vice President of Creative Services at Warner/Chappell Music is she gets to work with "the most talented writers in the world." From Cole Porter and George Gershwin to Elton John and Sheryl Crow, Warner/Chappell publishes a wide variety of music. Stakee is in charge of the Pop Department at Warner/Chappell (covering pop rock, pop R&B and pop alternative) and currently manages 20 writers. The company has ten creative people in Los Angeles, where Stakee works, with others in New York, Nashville, Miami and almost every international territory. Each of her creative staff members is an expert in a different genre of music, and each develops and manages songwriters. They are the ones who sign and develop acts, get record deals, put collaborations together, and place songs in film and TV.

At Warner/Chappell, monthly writer meetings are held to bring writers together and share information about present and future projects. Stakee puts together writing teams and collaborators—anything she thinks will help make a great song. "Finding a good match is like being set up with a blind date," she says. "You get a feel for who would go well together not only musically, but also as people. The best collaborations are ones that go much deeper than just writing a song."

Stakee and her writers act as a team. "My writers tell me what they need and vice versa. It is not a one-sided deal. Together we map out goals of what we expect." When signing a contract with a publisher, Stakee recommends writers look for mutual respect and a common vision of the writer's career.

Warner/Chappell does not accept unsolicited tapes, but if a tape is referred to Stakee by someone who has given the demo an initial screening, she will listen to it. These initial screenings are done by members of organizations such as ASCAP, BMI and the National Academy of Songwriters, as well as managers and entertainment lawyers. Most of the beginning songwriters Stakee has signed have come to her via a recommendation. "If a manager called me and said, 'I came across a songwriter I think is really great, I want you to hear him,' I would listen to the demo. If someone from BMI called me and said 'I just had a meeting with this young songwriter. I think you'd like him,' then I would take a meeting. That is a solicited account."

To get an initial screening at a publishing company, Stakee says be persistent and do whatever it takes to get someone to listen: send tapes, take classes, sign up for workshops and go to lectures and functions. She emphasizes to "always, always, always treat the assistants like they're royalty! They're the ones who will sometimes go in and say, 'Look, I want to give this person a chance.' "

INSIDER REPORT, *Stakee*

On the average, Stakee personally signs one new writer and two new acts per year, depending on her needs. She's always looking for the next "brilliant writer," but she doesn't know who that's going to be. That's why if a manager calls her about someone, she's going to listen to his tape. "I have so many writers I develop and manage, I don't really need anybody else. But if you're telling me the next Sheryl Crow is going to come into my office and I get a chance to sign her, I'm probably going to take that chance! It's a balancing act."

Friday afternoons at Warner/Chappell are set aside to listen to demos. Stakee rejects songs that either don't move her in some way or can't be placed commercially. She listens for mood, clever lines and for an artist who could cover the song. Stakee says songwriters don't need a fully-produced demo; they need to decide how to best present their songs. For instance, if a writer wants to present a ballad to Celine Dion, a piano vocal might be enough to get the song across. "But if you're going to do a dance track," Stakee says, "and you're trying to get Madonna to do one of your songs, then you know what? You'd better go produce the hell out of it!" Stakee says it's about deciding where and when to spend the money and when to pull out all the stops. "Do you spend a thousand dollars on a ballad where you could have taken care of it with a great piano vocal? What is best for the song?"

Most of Stakee's time is spent developing and managing her writers, figuring out how she can increase their chances for success. She says a music publisher is very important in helping a performing songwriter get a record deal. "If you're a beginning singer/songwriter and you don't know anybody in town but you've got a publisher, you've got the size and the talent and experience of that company behind you. If I sign you, you don't just get me, you get everybody on this staff. That's a lot to have behind you instead of going out there and trying it on your own." The publishing industry has always done this, but more so in recent years. They will support and guide a songwriter until he or she is ready to get a record deal.

Stakee believes the pop writer will always be in demand. "Some years are better than others but the industry will always need great songs." To succeed, even though they hate doing it, songwriters must rewrite and rewrite some more. The hardest things to teach beginning songwriters, according to Stakee, are getting them to trust their gut instinct and face their emotions. "You have to learn to challenge yourself. Don't fall into patterns. Stand with your eyes open and your arms out at all times. Be willing to learn and explore."

—*Tara A. Horton*

and recorded by Donna Lewis on Warner Bros. Records (pop); "If It Makes You Happy," written and recorded by Sheryl Crow on A&M Records (rock); and "It's Alright It's OK," written and recorded by Leah Andreone on BMG Records (pop/rock).

WARNER/CHAPPELL MUSIC, INC., 10585 Santa Monica Blvd., Third Floor, Los Angeles CA 90025-4950. (310)441-8600. Fax: (310)470-3232. Vice President of Creative Services: Judy Stakee. New York office: 1290 Avenue of the Americas, 9th Floor, New York NY 10019. (212)399-6910. Fax: (212)644-1859. Music publisher.

- See the interview with Vice President of Creative Services Judy Stakee in this section.

How to Contact: Warner/Chappell does not accept unsolicited material.
Music: Published "Without Love" (by D. Lewis/D. Taylor), recorded by Donna Lewis on Atlantic Records; "Space Jam" (by J. McGowan/N. Orange/V. Bryant), recorded by Quad City DJs on Warner Sunset Records; and "Get It Together" (by D. Jones), recorded by 702 on BIV Records.

WATCHESGRO MUSIC (BMI), 9208 Spruce Mountain Way, Las Vegas NV 89134-6024. (702)363-8506. President: Eddie Carr. Music publisher. Estab. 1987. Publishes 100 songs/year; publishes 5 new songwriters/year. Pays standard royalty.
Affiliate(s): Watch Us Climb Music (ASCAP).

- Watchesgro Music's record label, Interstate 40 Records, is listed in the Record Companies section.

How to Contact: Write first and obtain permission to submit. Prefers cassette. SASE. Reports in 1 week.
Music: Published "7th & Sundance" (by Aileen/Dempsey), recorded by Rita Aileen (country); "Eatin' My Words" (by M. Jones), recorded by Michael Jones; and "Precious Memories" (by D. Horn), recorded by Cindy Jane, all on Interstate 40 Records (country).

WEAVER WORDS OF MUSIC (BMI), P.O. Box 803, Tazewell VA 24651. (703)988-6267. President: H. R. Cook. Music publisher and record company (Fireball Records). Estab. 1978. Publishes 12 songs/year. Pays standard royalty.
Affiliate(s): Weaver of Melodies Music (ASCAP).
How to Contact: Submit demo tape by mail. Unsolicited submissions are OK. Prefers cassette with 3 songs and lyric or lead sheets. SASE. Reports in 1 month.
Music: Mostly **country**. Published "Winds of Change," written and recorded by Cecil Surrett; "Texas Saturday Night" and "Old Flame Burning," written and recorded by H.R. Cook, all on Fireball Records (country).

‡WEMAR MUSIC CORP. (BMI), 12403 Ventura Court, Studio City CA 91604. (818)980-8887. Fax: (818)980-9111. President: Stuart Wiener. Music publisher. Estab. 1940. Publishes 30 songs/year; publishes 30 new songwriters/year. Pays standard royalty.
Affiliate(s): Grand Music Corp. (ASCAP).
How to Contact: Submit demo tape by mail. Unsolicited submissions are OK. SASE. Reports in 2 months.
Music: Mostly **pop**, **R&B** and **dance**. Published "Pearl" and "Heavy Hitter," written and recorded by Geri Verdi on Mills Records (blues); and "Meat Street," written and recorded by Neal Fox on Gravity Records (Broadway Show).

BERTHOLD WENGERT (MUSIKVERLAG), Waldstrasse 27, D-76327, Pfinztal-Sollingen, **Germany**. Contact: Berthold Wengert. Music publisher. Pays standard GEMA royalty.
How to Contact: Prefers cassette and complete score for piano. SAE and IRC. Reports in 4 weeks. "No cassette returns!"
Music: Mostly **light music** and **pop**.

WESTUNES MUSIC GROUP (ASCAP/BMI), 1115 Inman Ave., Suite 330, Edison NJ 08820-1132. (908)548-6700. Fax: (908)548-6748. President: Victor Kaply. A&R Coordinator: Steve Willoughby. Professional Manager: Elena Petillo. Music publisher and management firm (Westwood Entertainment Group). Publishes 15 songs/year; publishes 2 new songwriters/year. Pays standard royalty.

- Westunes Music's management firm, Westwood Entertainment, is listed in the Managers and Booking Agents section.

How to Contact: Write first and obtain permission to submit. Prefers cassette with 3 songs and lyric sheet. SASE. Reports in 2 months.
Music: Mostly **rock**; also **pop**. Published "Come out of The Past" (by Regine Urbach/Tanya Leah), recorded by Renee Grace; and "Lost in Carolina" (by Steve Willoughby), recorded by Timmy.
Tips: Submit a "neat promotional package with bio and lyrics."

WHITE CAT MUSIC, 10603 N. Hayden Rd., Suite 114, Scottsdale AZ 85260. (602)951-3115. Fax: (602)951-3074. E-mail: songs@comstock-records.com. Website: http://comstock-records.com. Professional Manager: Frank Fara. Producer: Patty Parker. Music publisher, record company and record producer. Member CMA, CCMA, BCCMA and BBB. Estab. 1978. Publishes 30 songs/year; publishes 20 new songwriters/year. "50% of our published songs are from non-charted and developing writers." Pays standard royalty.
Affiliate(s): Rocky Bell Music (BMI), How The West Was Sung Music (BMI) and Crystal Canyon Music (ASCAP).

- See the listings for Comstock Records in the Record Companies section and Patty Parker in the Record Producers section.

How to Contact: Submit demo tape by mail. Unsolicited submissions are OK. Prefers cassettes with 2-4 songs and include lyric sheet. SASE. Reports in 2 weeks.
Music: All styles of **country**—traditional to crossover. Published "The Ricochet" (by Michael Ray),

recorded by Rolf Raggenbass; "A Special Kind of Lady" (by Ed Le Clair), recorded by Colin Clark; and "Curse of the Honky Tonk Queen" (Ann Tygart/Bob Wilkins), recorded by Patti Mayo, all on Comstock Records (country).

Tips: "Stack the odds in your favor by sending fewer songs—two to four at most, medium to up-tempo songs are always in demand. Long instrumental intros and breaks detract, go for a clear out-front vocal presentation."

WHITEWING MUSIC (BMI), 413 N. Parkerson Ave., Crowley LA 70526. (318)788-0773. Fax: (318)788-0776. Owner: Georgia Miller. Music publisher and record company (Master-Trak, Showtime, Par T, MTE, Blues Unlimited, Kajun, Cajun Classics). Estab. 1946. Publishes 12-15 songs/year. Publishes 6 new songwriters/year. Pays standard royalty.

Affiliate(s): Jamil Music (BMI).

- Whitewing Music's record label, Master-Trak Enterprises, is listed in the Record Companies section.

How to Contact: Submit demo tape by mail. Unsolicited submissions are OK. Prefers cassette or videocassette with 6 songs and lyric or lead sheets. Reports in 5-6 weeks.

Music: Mostly **country**, **rock** and **MOR**; also **cajun**. Published *Avec Amis* (by Lee Benoit); and *Old Fashion Love* (by Kenne Wayne).

WILCOM PUBLISHING (ASCAP), Box 4456, West Hills CA 91308. (818)348-0940. Owner: William Clark. Music publisher. Estab. 1989. Publishes 10-15 songs/year; publishes 1-2 new songwriters/year. Pays standard royalty.

How to Contact: Write first and obtain permission to submit a tape. Prefers cassette with 1-2 songs and lyric sheet. SASE. Reports in 3 weeks.

Music: Mostly **R&B**, **pop** and **rock**; also **country**. Published "Girl Can't Help It" (by W. Clark/D. Walsh/P. Oland), recorded by Stage 1 on Rockit Records (top 40).

SHANE WILDER MUSIC (BMI), P.O. Box 3503, Hollywood CA 90078. (805)251-7526. President: Shane Wilder. Music publisher, record producer (Shane Wilder Productions) and management firm (Shane Wilder Artist Management). Estab. 1960. Publishes 25-50 songs/year; publishes 15-20 new songwriters/year. Pays standard royalty.

- Shane Wilder's management firm, Shane Wilder Artists Management, is listed in the Managers and Booking Agents section.

How to Contact: Submit demo tape by mail. Unsolicited submissions are OK. Prefers cassette or VHS videocassette with 3 songs and lyric sheet. "Include SASE if you wish tape returned. Photo and résumé should be sent if you're looking for a producer." Reports in 2 weeks.

Music: Mostly **traditional country**. Published "Give That Man A Medal" and "When Does Getting Over You Get Over" (by Kimber Cunningham), recorded by Teresa Lynn on High Dollar; and "A Good Shot of Whiskey" (by Billy O'Hara), recorded by Glenn Mayo on Sollie Sunshine Records.

Tips: "See what is comin' out of Nashville and submit the same type strong country material. We only publish highly commercial songs. Constantly looking for songs that have a good story line. We publish country only and are a BMI company. Do not send ASCAP material."

WINSTON & HOFFMAN HOUSE MUSIC PUBLISHERS (ASCAP/BMI), P.O. Box 1415, Burbank CA 91507-1415. President: Lynne Robin Green. Music publisher. Estab. 1958. Publishes 25 songs/year. Pays standard royalty.

Affiliate(s): Lansdowne Music Publishers (ASCAP), Bloor Music (BMI), Clemitco Publishing (BMI), Ben Ross Music (ASCAP), Triple Scale Music (BMI), Pietro Carlos Music and Vassars Music (ASCAP).

How to Contact: Submit demo tape by mail. Unsolicited submissions are OK. "Do not query first." Prefers cassette with 3 songs maximum and lyric sheet. "*Must* SASE, or *no* reply!" Reports in 1 month.

Music: Mostly **R&B dance**, **ballads**, **hip hop**, **vocal jazz**, **alternative rock** and **R&B**; also **country**, **Spanish pop** and **pop ballads**. Published "So Goes Love" (by Benny Ray), recorded by Charles Brown on Polygram Records; "I Can Do Bad By Myself" (by Scales/McClelland/Robinson/Kidd), recorded by Rufus Thomas on Castle Records; and "Peppermint Man" (by Alonzo Willis), recorded by Dick Dale on Beggars Banquet Records.

THE TYPES OF MUSIC each listing is interested in are printed in boldface.

Tips: "Be selective in what you send. Be realistic about which artist it suits! Be patient in allowing time to place songs. Be open to writing for films—be interesting lyrically and striking melodically."

WITHOUT PAPERS MUSIC PUBLISHING INC., 7450 A Industrial Park, Lorain OH 44053. (216)282-8008, ext. 204. Fax: (216)282-8822. President: Michele Norton. Music publisher. Estab. 1992. Publishes 4 songs/year; publishes 2 new songwriters/year. Pays standard royalty.
How to Contact: Write or call first and obtain permission to submit. Prefers cassette with lyric sheet. SASE. Reports in 1 month.
Music: Mostly **rock**, **R&B** and **country** (with R&B or rock base); also **children's**, **classical**, **different** and **commercial**. Published "Brown's Blues" (by Stutz Bearcat), recorded by Butch Armstrong on Doubleneck Records (blues).
Tips: "Be patient and be willing to work with us and the song."

WOODRICH PUBLISHING CO. (BMI), P.O. Box 38, Lexington AL 35648. (205)247-3983. President: Woody Richardson. Music publisher, record company (Woodrich Records) and record producer. Estab. 1959. Publishes 25 songs/year; publishes 12 new songwriters/year. Pays standard royalty.
- See the listing for Woodrich Records in the Record Companies section.

Affiliate(s): Mernee Music (ASCAP), Melstep Music (BMI) and Tennesse Valley Music (SESAC).
How to Contact: Submit demo tape by mail. Unsolicited submissions are OK. Prefers cassette with 2-4 songs. Prefers studio produced demos. SASE. Reports in 2 weeks.
Music: Mostly **country** and **gospel**; also **bluegrass**, **blues**, **choral**, **church/religious**, **easy listening**, **folk**, **jazz**, **MOR**, **progressive**, **rock**, **soul** and **top 40/pop**. Published *Somewhere Above Tennessee*, written and recorded by Jerry Piper on Missle Records; "He's With Me Wherever I Go" (by Lamar Mixon), recorded by Jerry Hanlon on VAR Records (gospel); and "Everything's Roses" (by Woody Richardson), recorded by Marty Whiddon on Woodrich Records.
Tips: "Use a studio demo if possible. If not, be sure the lyrics are extremely clear. Be sure to include a SASE with *sufficient* return postage. We will not respond otherwise."

WORLD FAMOUS MUSIC CO. (ASCAP), 1364 Sherwood Rd., Highland Park IL 60035. (847)831-3123. E-mail: getchip@interacess.com. President: Chip Altholz. Music publisher and record producer. Estab. 1986. Publishes 25 songs/year; 3-4 new songwriters/year. Pays standard royalty.
How to Contact: Submit demo tape by mail. Unsolicited submissions are OK. Prefers cassette with 3 songs and lyric sheet. SASE. Reports in 1 month.
Music: Mostly **pop**, **R&B** and **rock**. Published "Harmony," (by Altholz/Faldner), recorded by Barry Faldner on Amertel Records (ballad); "Running" and "Serious," both written and recorded by Nick Bak on Pink Street Records.
Tips: "Have a great melody, a lyric that is visual and tells a story and a commercial arrangement."

YORGO MUSIC (BMI), 615 Valley Rd., Upper Montclair NJ 07043. (201)746-2359. President: George Louvis. Affiliated with Warner/Chappell Music Publishing. Music publisher. Estab. 1987. Publishes 5-10 songs/year; publishes 3-5 new songwriters/year. Pays standard royalty.
How to Contact: Submit demo tape by mail. Unsolicited submissions are OK. Prefers cassette with 1-3 songs and lyric or lead sheets. "Specify if you are a writer/artist or just a writer." Does not return material. Reports in 2-3 months.
Music: Gospel, **contemporary Christian**, **R&B** and **pop ballads**.

YOUR BEST SONGS PUBLISHING, 1210 Auburn Way N., Suite P171, Auburn WA 98002. General Manager: Craig Markovich. Music publisher. Estab. 1988. Publishes 1-5 songs/year; publishes 1-3 new songwriters/year. Query for royalty terms.
How to Contact: Submit demo tape by mail. Unsolicited submissions are OK. Prefers cassette with 1-3 songs and lyric sheet. "Submit your 1-3 best songs per type of music. Use separate cassettes per music type and indicate music type on each cassette." SASE. Reports in 1-3 months.
Music: Mostly **country**, **rock/blues** and **pop/rock**; also **progressive**, **A/C** and some **heavy metal**.
Tips: "We just require good lyrics, good melodies and good rhythm in a song."

‡ZETTITALIA MUSIC INTERNATIONAL (ASCAP, BMI), P.O. Box 8221, Universal City CA 91618. (818)506-4866. Fax: (818)506-8534. Professional Manager: Cheyenne Phoenix. Music publisher. Estab. 1965. Publishes 40 songs/year; publishes 2 new songwriters/year. Hires staff songwriters. Pays standard royalty.
Affiliate(s): Zett One Songs (ASCAP) and Zett Two Music (BMI).
How to Contact: Write first and obtain permission to submit. Prefers cassette with 2 songs and lyric

sheet. SASE. Reports in 6 weeks.
Music: Mostly **pop**, **film music** and **country**; also **R&B**.

ZOMBA MUSIC PUBLISHING (ASCAP, BMI), 137-139 W. 25th St., New York NY 10001. (212)824-1744. Fax: (212)242-7462. Senior Director of Creative Services: Tse Williams. Creative Manager: Marvin Pert. Music publisher. Publishes 5,000 songs/year; publishes 25 new songwriters/year.
Affiliate(s): Zomba Enterprises, Inc. (ASCAP) and Zomba Songs, Inc. (BMI).
How to Contact: Call first and obtain permission to submit. Prefers cassette or DAT with no more than 4 songs and lyric sheet. SASE.
Music: Mostly **R&B**, **pop** and **rap**; also **rock** and **alternative**. Published "You Are Not Alone" (by R. Kelly), recorded by Michael Jackson on Epic Records (pop); *Any Man Of Mine* (by Mutt Lange), recorded by Shania Twain on Mercury Records (country/pop); and "Can I Touch You There" (by Mutt Lange), recorded by Michael Bolton on Sony Records (pop).

Category Index

The Category Index is a good place to begin searching for a market for your songs. Below is an alphabetical list of 20 general music categories. If you write country songs and are looking for a publisher to pitch them, check the Country section in this index. There you will find a list of music publishers interested in hearing country songs. Once you locate the listings for those publishers, read the music subheading *carefully* to determine which companies are most interested in the type of country music you write. Some of the markets in this section do not appear in the Category Index because they have not indicated a specific preference. Most of these said they are interested in "all types" of music. Listings that were very specific, or whose description of the music they're interested in doesn't quite fit into these categories, also do not appear here.

Adult Contemporary

Alexis; Allegheny Music Works; Amiron Music; Antelope Publishing Inc.; Audio Images Two Thousand Music Publishing; Bal & Bal Music Publishing Co.; Barren Wood Publishing; Bay Ridge Publishing Co.; Betty Jane/Josie Jane Music Publishers; Big Fish Music Publishing Group; ‡Black Strand Music; Boam; Bradley Music, Allan; Buried Treasure Music; California Country Music; Camex Music; ‡Cherasny Elijah Entertainment Production Company; ‡Connell Publishing Co., Jerry; Country Rainbow Music; Country Star Music; Dean Enterprises Music Group; Denny Music Group; Duane Music, Inc.; Gary Music, Alan; Green One Music; G-String Publishing; Hammel Associates, Inc., R.L.; Hickory Valley Music; High-Minded Moma Publishing & Productions; Hitsburgh Music Co.; Inside Records/OK Songs; ISBA Music Publishing Inc.; Jaclyn Music; Jump Music; Just a Note; JW One Music Publishing Co.; Kansa Records Corporation; Kaupps & Robert Publishing Co.; Kingsport Creek Music Publishing; Kozkeeozko Music; Largo Music Publishing; Lineage Publishing Co.; Mento Music Group; Music in the Right Keys Publishing Company; Nebo Ridge Publishing Company; ‡New Clarion Music Group; New Rap Jam Publishing, A; Omni 2000, Inc.; Operation Perfection; Otto Publishing Co.; Panchatantra Music Enterprises; Parravano Music; ‡Pascarella Music Publishing; Pegasus Music; Prescription Company; R. J. Music; Riverhawk Music; RNR Publishing; Rockford Music Co.; Rondor Music International; Roots Music; S.M.C.L. Productions, Inc.; Segal's Publications; Siegel Music Companies; Silicon Music Publishing Co.; ‡Smokin' Cowboys Publishing Co.; Solid Entertainment; ‡Sugarfoot Productions; Tedesco Music Co., Dale; Twin Bears Publishing; Whitewing Music; Woodrich Publishing Co.; Your Best Songs Publishing

Alternative

Abalone Publishing; Aladdin Music Group; Al-Ky Music; ‡Artistic Noise Publishing; ‡Bare Minimum Music; Bay Ridge Publishing Co.; Big Snow Music; Camex Music; Clear Pond Music; Cottage Blue Music; ‡East Coast Music Publishing; Fat City Publishing; Flea Circus Music; Funzalo Music; Genetic Music Publishing; ‡Goodnight Kiss Music; ‡Hautboy Music; Josena Music; Keno Publishing; Kwaz Song Music; Largo Music Publishing; Last Brain Cell; ‡Paradigm Publishers; Pas Mal Publishing; Pen Cob Publishing Inc.; Planet Dallas Recording Studios; Prejippie Music Group; Rondor Music International; ‡Songs From Out of the Blue; ‡Spinwilly Music Publishing; ‡Transition Music Corporation; Treasure Trove Music; Twin Spin Publishing; Winston & Hoffman House Music Publishers; Zomba Music Publishing

Blues

Aladdin Music Group; Alexis; Al-Ky Music; ‡Ancy Music Group; Bagatelle Music Publishing Co.; Bal & Bal Music Publishing Co.; Bay Ridge Publishing Co.; Bearsongs; Davis & Davis Music; Duane Music, Inc.; Earthscream Music Publishing Co.; ESI Music Group; Fat City Publishing; Frozen Inca Music; ‡Golden Harp Music; Kel-Cres Publishing; Last Brain Cell; Music in the Right Keys Publishing Company; Nervous Publishing; Panchatantra Music Enterprises; Parravano Music; Pollard Sound World; Prescription Company; Promo; Prospector Three D Publishing; R. J. Music; RNR Publishing; Silicon Music Publishing Co.; Sizemore Music;

Slanted Circle Music; ‡Smokin' Cowboys Publishing Co.; Snowcliff Publishing; ‡Songs From Out of the Blue; ‡Sugarfoot Productions; ‡Viceroy Music Group, Inc.; Woodrich Publishing Co.

Children's

Berandol Music Ltd.; Branch Group Music; Colton Shows, Glenn; ‡Crosspoint International, Inc.; Flying Red Horse Publishing; Kidsource Publishing; Mighty Twinns Music; NSP Music Publishing Inc.; Omni 2000, Inc.; Parravano Music; ‡Pascarella Music Publishing; PPI/Peter Pan Industries; Prescription Company; Rhythms Productions; Segal's Publications; Simply Grand Music, Inc.; This Here Music; Velocity Productions; Without Papers Music Publishing Inc.

Classical

Bad Habits Music Publishing; Clevère Musikverlag, R.D.; Hit-Fabrik Musikverlag; Jae Music, Jana; PPI/Peter Pan Industries; Roots Music; Without Papers Music Publishing Inc.

Country

Abalone Publishing; Aim High Music Company; Aladdin Music Group; ‡Alan Music, Marcus; Alexis; Al-Ky Music; Allegheny Music Works; AlliSongs Inc.; ‡Americatone International; ‡Ancy Music Group; Aquarius Publishing; ‡ARAS Music; Audio Images Two Thousand Music Publishing; Bagatelle Music Publishing Co.; Bal & Bal Music Publishing Co.; Barkin' Foe the Master's Bone; Barren Wood Publishing; Bay Ridge Publishing Co.; Beaverwood Audio-Video; Beecher Publishing, Earl; Best Buddies, Inc.; Betty Jane/Josie Jane Music Publishers; Big Fish Music Publishing Group; ‡Bixio Music Group/IDM Publishing; Black Rose Productions; Black Stallion Country Publishing; Blue Spur Entertainment, Inc./Git a Rope Publishing; Boam; Bradley Music, Allan; Brewster Songs, Kitty; Buried Treasure Music; California Country Music; Calinoh Music Group; Cash Productions, Inc.; Castle Music Group; Cheavoria Music Co.; ‡Cherasny Elijah Entertainment Production Company; Cherie Music; Cimirron Music; Cisum; Clear Pond Music; ‡Clearwind Publishing; Clevère Musikverlag, R.D.; Coffee and Cream Publishing Company; Colstal Music; Colton Shows, Glenn; ‡Connell Publishing Co., Jerry; Copperfield Music Group; Cornelius Companies, The; Cottage Blue Music; Country Breeze Music; Country Rainbow Music; Country Showcase America; Country Star Music; Cowboy Junction Flea Market and Publishing Co.; Craig Music, Loman; ‡Croaky Frog Music; D.S.M. Producers Inc.; ‡Dapmor Publishing; Darbonne Publishing Co.; Davis & Davis Music; De Miles Music Company, The Edward; Dean Enterprises Music Group; Delev Music Company; Dell Music, Frank; Denny Music Group; Doc Publishing; Doss Music, Buster; Dream Seekers Publishing; Duane Music, Inc.; Earitating Music Publishing; Earthscream Music Publishing Co.; ‡East Coast Music Publishing; Emandell Tunes; EMF Productions; Enid Oklahoma Music Publishing; ESI Music Group; Faiella Publishing, Doug; Famous Music Publishing Companies; Farr-Away Music; Fat City Publishing; First Time Music (Publishing) U.K.; Flaming Star West Music; Fretboard Publishing; Frick Music Publishing Co.; ‡Fricon Music Company; ‡Fro's Music Publishing; ‡Full Moon Music, Inc.; Furrow Music; ‡Future-1 Music Publishing; Gary Music, Alan; Giftness Enterprise; GlobeArt Inc.; Gold Music Publishing, Jay; ‡Golden Harp Music; Goodland Music Group Inc., The; Green One Music; G-String Publishing; Halo International; Hammel Associates, Inc., R.L.; Hawksbill Music; ‡Headaches & Heartburn Music; Henly Music Associates; Hickory Lane Publishing and Recording; Hickory Valley Music; High-Minded Moma Publishing & Productions; Hitsburgh Music Co.; Holton Music; Inside Records/OK Songs; Iron Skillet Music; Jacksong Music; Jaclyn Music; Jae Music, Jana; Jaelius Enterprises; Jammy Music Publishers Ltd.; Jerjoy Music; JoDa Music; Johnson Music, Little Richie; Jolson Black & White Music, Al; Jon Music; Just a Note; JW One Music Publishing Co.; Kansa Records Corporation; Kaupps & Robert Publishing Co.; Kaylee Music Group, Karen; Kingsport Creek Music Publishing; Kirchstein Publishing Co.; Kozkeeozko Music; Lari-Jon Publishing; Last Brain Cell; Lilly Music Publishing; Lindsay Publishing, Doris; Lineage Publishing Co.; Lion Hill Music Publishing Co.; Lovey Music, Inc.; M & T Waldoch Publishing, Inc.; McCoy Music, Jim; McGibony Publishing; Mack Music, Danny; Magic Message Music; Makers Mark Gold; ‡Master Source; Mathes Company, The; ‡Maverick Music Company; Mento Music Group; Merry Marilyn Music Publishing; Moon June Music; More Brand Music; Music in the Right

Keys Publishing Company; Nashville Sound Music Publishing Co.; Nautical Music Co.; Nebo Ridge Publishing Company; Nervous Publishing; ‡New Clarion Music Group; New Rap Jam Publishing, A; Newcreature Music; Non-Stop Music Publishing; ‡OBCB Music Publishing; Old Slowpoke Music; Omni 2000, Inc.; Ontrax Companies; Orchid Publishing; Otto Publishing Co.; Panchatantra Music Enterprises; Parravano Music; ‡Pascarella Music Publishing; Pecos Valley Music; Pegasus Music; Pen Cob Publishing Inc.; Platinum Boulevard Publishing; Platinum Gold Music; Pollard Sound World; Prescription Company; Pritchett Publications; Prospector Three D Publishing; Purple Haze Music; R. J. Music; Ridge Music Corp.; Riverhawk Music; Rocker Music/Happy Man Music; Rockford Music Co.; Roots Music; Rose Hill Group; Rustron Music Publishers; Sabteca Music Co.; Saddlestone Publishing; Samuel Three Productions; Scott Music Group, Tim; Segal's Publications; Sellwood Publishing; Siegel Music Companies; Silicon Music Publishing Co.; Silver Thunder Music Group; Simply Grand Music, Inc.; Siskatune Music Publishing Co.; Sizemore Music; ‡Smokin' Cowboys Publishing Co.; Snowcliff Publishing; Song Farm Music; ‡Songs From Out of the Blue; Sound Cellar Music; ‡Spinwilly Music Publishing; Spradlin/Gleich Publishing; Starbound Publishing Co.; Steel Rain Publishing; Stuart Music Co., Jeb; ‡Sugarfoot Productions; Sun Star Songs; Surespin Songs; Sweet Glenn Music; Sweet June Music; T.C. Productions/Etude Publishing Co.; ‡Texas Tuff Music Company; Third Wave Productions Limited; Tiki Enterprises, Inc.; ‡Toulouse Music Publishing Co., Inc.; Transamerika Musikverlag KG; Trusty Publications; Twin Bears Publishing; Twin Spin Publishing; Ultimate Peak Music; Vaam Music Group; Valet Publishing Co.; Vokes Music Publishing; Warner/Chappell Music Canada Ltd.; Weaver Words of Music; White Cat Music; Whitewing Music; Wilcom Publishing; Wilder Music, Shane; Winston & Hoffman House Music Publishers; Without Papers Music Publishing Inc.; Woodrich Publishing Co.; Your Best Songs Publishing; ‡Zettitalia Music International

Dance

Abalone Publishing; Alexis; Al-Ky Music; ‡Artistic Noise Publishing; Audio Music Publishers; Bad Habits Music Publishing; Black Rose Productions; Brewster Songs, Kitty; Brothers Organisation, The; ‡Cherasny Elijah Entertainment Production Company; Clevère Musikverlag, R.D.; Coffee and Cream Publishing Company; D.S.M. Producers Inc.; Dagene Music; De Miles Music Company, The Edward; Delev Music Company; Drive Music, Inc.; Duane Music, Inc.; ‡East Coast Music Publishing; Edition Rossori; Fresh Entertainment; ‡Full Moon Music, Inc.; Gary Music, Alan; Genetic Music Publishing; G-String Publishing; ‡Hautboy Music; Hit & Run Music Publishing Inc.; Inside Records/OK Songs; ISBA Music Publishing Inc.; ‡Island Culture Music Publishers; Joey Boy Publishing Co.; Jump Music; Kozkeeozko Music; Lilly Music Publishing; M & T Waldoch Publishing, Inc.; Makers Mark Gold; Omni 2000, Inc.; Power Voltage Music; Prejippie Music Group; Prescription Company; Pretty Shayna Music; Rockford Music Co.; Rose Hill Group; S.M.C.L. Productions, Inc.; Siegel Music Companies; Siskatune Music Publishing Co.; ‡Songs From Out of the Blue; Stuart Music Co., Jeb; Succes; ‡Sugarfoot Productions; Sunsongs Music; T.C. Productions/Etude Publishing Co.; Tedesco Music Co., Dale; Trusty Publications; Twin Bears Publishing; Valet Publishing Co.; ‡Wemar Music Corp.; Winston & Hoffman House Music Publishers

Folk

Alexis; Aquarius Publishing; Bay Ridge Publishing Co.; Boam; Cimirron Music; Clevère Musikverlag, R.D.; Colton Shows, Glenn; Don Del Music; Earitating Music Publishing; First Time Music (Publishing) U.K.; ‡Golden Harp Music; Halo International; ‡Headaches & Heartburn Music; Heupferd Musikverlag; Kirchstein Publishing Co.; Omni 2000, Inc.; Panchatantra Music Enterprises; ‡Paradigm Publishers; Parravano Music; Prescription Company; Rockford Music Co.; Roots Music; Rustron Music Publishers; Sweet June Music; Third Wave Productions Limited; This Here Music; Treasure Trove Music; Woodrich Publishing Co.

Instrumental

Alpha Music Inc.; D.S.M. Producers Inc.; Hit-Fabrik Musikverlag; Musikverlag K. Urbanek; ‡Pascarella Music Publishing

Jazz

‡Alan Music, Marcus; Alexander Sr. Music; Alexis; Antelope Publishing Inc.; Bad Habits Music Publishing; Bal & Bal Music Publishing Co.; Bay Ridge Publishing Co.; Bearsongs; Black Rose Productions; Brewster Songs, Kitty; ‡Connell Publishing Co., Jerry; Cunningham Music; D.S.M. Producers Inc.; Elect Music Publishing Company; Fat City Publishing; ‡Future-1 Music Publishing; Genetic Music Publishing; Giftness Enterprise; GlobeArt Inc.; Heupferd Musikverlag; Hit-Fabrik Musikverlag; Joey Boy Publishing Co.; ‡Master Source; ‡Mellow House Music; Newcreature Music; Non-Stop Music Publishing; NSP Music Publishing Inc.; Old Slowpoke Music; Omni 2000, Inc.; Platinum Boulevard Publishing; Prescription Company; Ridge Music Corp.; Rockford Music Co.; Simply Grand Music, Inc.; Slanted Circle Music; Snowcliff Publishing; Stuart Music Co., Jeb; ‡Sugarfoot Productions; Tedesco Music Co., Dale; ‡Timba Yuma; ‡Toulouse Music Publishing Co., Inc.; Treasure Trove Music; Trusty Publications; Winston & Hoffman House Music Publishers; Woodrich Publishing Co.

Latin

Alexis; Amen, Inc.; ‡Americatone International; Inside Records/OK Songs; Johnson Music, Little Richie; Josena Music; ‡Sugarfoot Productions; ‡Timba Yuma; Unimusica Inc.

Metal

Bay Ridge Publishing Co.; ‡Goodnight Kiss Music; Keno Publishing; M & T Waldoch Publishing, Inc.; ‡OBCB Music Publishing; Pas Mal Publishing; Sound Cellar Music; Your Best Songs Publishing

New Age

Bad Habits Music Publishing; Big Snow Music; Dingo Music; Heupferd Musikverlag; High-Minded Moma Publishing & Productions; Myko Music; Non-Stop Music Publishing; ‡Paradigm Publishers; Platinum Boulevard Publishing; Quark, Inc.; Rustron Music Publishers; ‡Sinus Musik Produktion, Ulli Weigel; Tiki Enterprises, Inc.

Novelty

Big Fish Music Publishing Group; Branch Group Music; Cisum; Colstal Music; Davis & Davis Music; Dean Enterprises Music Group; Furrow Music; Green One Music; Joey Boy Publishing Co.; JW One Music Publishing Co.; Moon June Music; Parravano Music; Riverhawk Music

Pop

Abalone Publishing; ‡Alan Music, Marcus; Alexis; Al-Ky Music; Allegheny Music Works; Amiron Music; ‡Ancy Music Group; Aquarius Publishing; ‡Artistic Noise Publishing; Audio Music Publishers; Bad Habits Music Publishing; Bal & Bal Music Publishing Co.; Barkin' Foe the Master's Bone; Bay Ridge Publishing Co.; Beecher Publishing, Earl; Berandol Music Ltd.; Bernard Enterprises, Inc., Hal; Best Buddies, Inc.; Betty Jane/Josie Jane Music Publishers; Big Fish Music Publishing Group; Black Rose Productions; ‡Black Strand Music; Bradley Music, Allan; Brewster Songs, Kitty; Brothers Organisation, The; Buried Treasure Music; California Country Music; Calinoh Music Group; Camex Music; Cash Productions, Inc.; Castle Music Group; Cheavoria Music Co.; Cisum; Clear Pond Music; ‡Clearwind Publishing; Clevère Musikverlag, R.D.; Coffee and Cream Publishing Company; Copperfield Music Group; Cornelius Companies, The; Cottage Blue Music; Craig Music, Loman; ‡Croaky Frog Music; Cunningham Music; D.S.M. Producers Inc.; Dagene Music; ‡Dapmor Publishing; De Miles Music Company, The Edward; Dean Enterprises Music Group; Delev Music Company; Dell Music, Frank; Demi Monde Records & Publishing Ltd.; Dingo Music; Dream Seekers Publishing; Drive Music, Inc.; Duane Music, Inc.; Earthscream Music Publishing Co.; ‡East Coast Music Publishing; Edition Rossori; EMF Productions; ESI Music Group; Ever-Open-Eye Music; First Time Music (Publishing) U.K.; Fresh Entertainment; Frick Music Publishing Co.; ‡Fro's Music Publishing; ‡Full Moon Music, Inc.; Funzalo Music; Gary Music, Alan; Genetic Music Publishing; GFI West Music Publishing; Giftness Enterprise; GlobeArt Inc.; Gold Music Publishing, Jay; Green Zebra Music; Hammel Associates, Inc., R.L.; ‡Hautboy Music; Hawksbill Music; Henly Music Associates; High-Minded Moma Publishing & Productions; Hit & Run Music Publishing Inc.; Hit-Fabrik Musikverlag; Inside Records/OK Songs; Interplanetary Music; ISBA Music Publishing Inc.; Jae Music, Jana; Jaelius Enterprises; Jammy Music Publishers Ltd.; Jasper Stone Music/JSM Songs; Jolson Black & White Music, Al; Josena Music; Jump Music; Just a Note; JW One Music Publishing Co.; Kaupps & Robert Publishing Co.; Keno Publishing; Kozkeeozko Music; Lindsay Publishing, Doris; Lineage Publishing Co.; Lin's Lines; M & T Waldoch Publishing, Inc.; Makers Mark Gold; ‡Maverick Music Company; ‡Mellow House Music; Mento Music Group; Mighty Twinns Music; Motor Music Co.; Music Room Publishing Group, The; Myko Music; Mymit Music Productions, Chuck; Namax Music Publishing; Nebo Ridge Publishing Company; ‡New Clarion Music Group; New Rap Jam Publishing, A; Newcreature Music; Non-Stop Music Publishing; Omni 2000, Inc.; Ontrax Companies; Operation Perfection; Orchid Publishing; ‡Pascarella Music Publishing; peermusic; Pegasus Music; Platinum Gold Music; Prescription Company; Pretty Shayna Music; Prospector Three D Publishing; Raving Cleric Music Publishing/Euroexport Entertainment; Ridge Music Corp.; Rocker Music/Happy Man Music; Rockford Music Co.; Roots Music; Rose Hill Group; Rustron Music Publishers; S.M.C.L. Productions, Inc.; Sabteca Music Co.; Saddlestone Publishing; Sci-Fi Music; Scott Music Group, Tim; Segal's Publications; Shaolin Music; Shu'Baby Montez Music; Siegel Music Companies; Silver Blue Music/Oceans Blue Music; Silver Thunder Music Group; Simply Grand Music, Inc.; ‡Sinus Musik Produktion, Ulli Weigel; Sizemore Music; ‡Smokin' Cowboys Publishing Co.; Snowcliff Publishing; ‡Songs From Out of the Blue; Sound Cellar Music; ‡Spinwilly Music Publishing; Stuart Music Co., Jeb; Succes; Sun Star Songs; Sunsongs Music; T.C. Productions/Etude Publishing Co.; Tedesco Music Co., Dale; Third Wave Productions Limited; This Here Music; Tiki Enterprises, Inc.; Transamerika Musikverlag KG; ‡Transition Music Corporation; Twin Bears Publishing; Twin Spin Publishing; Twin Towers Publishing Co.; Ultimate Peak Music; Vaam Music Group; Valet Publishing Co.; Warner/Chappell Music Canada Ltd.; ‡Wemar Music Corp.; Wengert, Berthold (Musikverlag); Westunes Music Group; Wilcom Publishing; Winston & Hoffman House Music Publishers; Woodrich Publishing Co.; World Famous Music Co.; Yorgo Music; Your Best Songs Publishing; ‡Zettitalia Music International; Zomba Music Publishing

R&B

‡Alan Music, Marcus; Alexander Sr. Music; Alexis; Allegheny Music Works; ‡Americatone International; Amiron Music; ‡Ancy Music Group; ‡Artistic Noise Publishing; Audio Music Publishers; Bad Habits Music Publishing; Bal & Bal Music Publishing Co.; ‡Bare Minimum Music; Barkin' Foe the Master's Bone; Bay Ridge Publishing Co.; Bernard Enterprises, Inc., Hal; Best Buddies, Inc.; Betty Jane/Josie Jane Music Publishers; ‡Bixio Music Group/IDM Publishing; ‡Black Strand Music; Boam; Bradley Music, Allan; Brewster Songs, Kitty; Brothers Organisation, The; California Country Music; Camex Music; Cash Productions, Inc.; Castle Music Group; Cheavoria Music Co.; Cisum; ‡Clearwind Publishing; Clevère Musikverlag, R.D.; Coffee and Cream Publishing Company; Copperfield Music Group; Cottage Blue Music; Country Star Music; Cunningham Music; D.S.M. Producers Inc.; Dagene Music; ‡Dapmor Publishing; Davis & Davis Music; De Miles Music Company, The Edward; Dean Enterprises Music Group; Delev Music Company; Demi Monde Records & Publishing Ltd.; Dingo Music; Drive Music, Inc.; Duane Music, Inc.; ‡East Coast Music Publishing; Elect Music Publishing Company; EMF Productions; Ever-Open-Eye Music; Famous Music Publishing Companies; First Time Music (Publishing) U.K.; Fresh Entertainment; Frozen Inca Music; ‡Full Moon Music, Inc.; Furrow Music; Gary Music, Alan; Genetic Music Publishing; GFI West Music Publishing; Giftness Enterprise; GlobeArt Inc.; ‡Goodnight Kiss Music; Green Zebra Music; Hammel Associates, Inc., R.L.; Hawksbill Music; Hit & Run Music Publishing Inc.; Interplanetary Music; ISBA Music Publishing Inc.; Jaelius Enterprises; Jasper Stone Music/JSM Songs; Joey Boy Publishing Co.; Just a Note; JW One Music Publishing Co.; Kansa Records Corporation; Kaupps & Robert Publishing Co.; Keno Publishing; Kingsport Creek Music Publishing; Kirchstein Publishing Co.; Kozkeeozko Music; Last Brain Cell; Lin's Lines; M & T Waldoch Publishing, Inc. (BMI); McGibony Publishing; Majestic Control; Makers Mark Gold; ‡Maverick Music Company; ‡Mellow House Music; Mighty Twinns Music; Motor Music Co.; Music in the Right Keys Publishing Company; Music Room Publishing Group, The; Mymit Music Productions, Chuck; Namax Music Publishing; Nervous Publishing; ‡New Clarion Music Group; New Rap Jam Publishing, A; Newcreature Music; Non-Stop Music Publishing; NSP Music Publishing

Inc.; N-The Water Publishing, Inc.; ‡OBCB Music Publishing; Old Slowpoke Music; Omni 2000, Inc.; Operation Perfection; ‡Pascarella Music Publishing; peermusic; Platinum Boulevard Publishing; Platinum Gold Music; Prescription Company; Pretty Shayna Music; Purple Haze Music; Raving Cleric Music Publishing/Euroexport Entertainment; RNR Publishing; Rondor Music International; Rustron Music Publishers; Sabteca Music Co.; Saddlestone Publishing; Scott Music Group, Tim; Segal's Publications; Shu'Baby Montez Music; Siegel Music Companies; Silver Blue Music/Oceans Blue Music; Silver Thunder Music Group; Simply Grand Music, Inc.; Siskatune Music Publishing Co.; Sizemore Music; ‡Smokin' Cowboys Publishing Co.; Solid Entertainment; Song Farm Music; Sound Cellar Music; ‡Spinwilly Music Publishing; Starbound Publishing Co.; Stuart Music Co., Jeb; ‡Sugarfoot Productions; Sunsongs Music; Sweet Glenn Music; T.C. Productions/Etude Publishing Co.; Tedesco Music Co., Dale; Tiki Enterprises, Inc.; ‡Toulouse Music Publishing Co., Inc.; ‡Transition Music Corporation; Trusty Publications; Twin Towers Publishing Co.; Vaam Music Group; Valet Publishing Co.; ‡Wemar Music Corp.; Wilcom Publishing; Winston & Hoffman House Music Publishers; Without Papers Music Publishing Inc.; Woodrich Publishing Co.; World Famous Music Co.; Yorgo Music; Your Best Songs Publishing; ‡Zettitalia Music International; Zomba Music Publishing

Rap

‡Ancy Music Group; Audio Music Publishers; Barkin' Foe the Master's Bone; Bay Ridge Publishing Co.; Black Rose Productions; ‡Croaky Frog Music; Dagene Music; ‡Dapmor Publishing; ‡East Coast Music Publishing; Elect Music Publishing Company; Fresh Entertainment; ‡Full Moon Music, Inc.; ‡Goodnight Kiss Music; Interplanetary Music; ISBA Music Publishing Inc.; Jasper Stone Music/JSM Songs; Joey Boy Publishing Co.; Keno Publishing; Lin's Lines; Majestic Control; Makers Mark Gold; ‡Master Source; ‡Mellow House Music; New Rap Jam Publishing, A; ‡N-The Water Publishing, Inc.; ‡OBCB Music Publishing; Operation Perfection; Platinum Gold Music; Shu'Baby Montez Music; Silver Blue Music/Oceans Blue Music; Solid Entertainment; Sound Cellar Music; Stuart Music Co., Jeb; ‡Transition Music Corporation; Treasure Trove Music; Twin Bears Publishing; Winston & Hoffman House Music Publishers; Zomba Music Publishing

Religious

Aim High Music Company; Aladdin Music Group; ‡Alan Music, Marcus; Alexander Sr. Music; Alexis; Allegheny Music Works; Amen, Inc.; ‡Ancy Music Group; ‡ARAS Music; Audio Images Two Thousand Music Publishing; Bagatelle Music Publishing Co.; Bal & Bal Music Publishing Co.; Barkin' Foe the Master's Bone; Barren Wood Publishing; Bay Ridge Publishing Co.; Beaverwood Audio-Video; Beecher Publishing, Earl; Best Buddies, Inc.; Betty Jane/Josie Jane Music Publishers; Big Fish Music Publishing Group; ‡Black Strand Music; Blue Spur Entertainment, Inc./Git a Rope Publishing; Boam; Bradley Music, Allan; California Country Music; Calinoh Music Group; Cash Productions, Inc.; Castle Music Group; ‡Cherasny Elijah Entertainment Production Company; Cisum; Coffee and Cream Publishing Company; ‡Connell Publishing Co., Jerry; Copperfield Music Group; Cornelius Companies, The; Cottage Blue Music; Country Breeze Music; Country Star Music; Cowboy Junction Flea Market and Publishing Co.; Craig Music, Loman; Cunningham Music; Darbonne Publishing Co.; Davis & Davis Music; Dell Music, Frank; Denny Music Group; Dingo Music; Earitating Music Publishing; Emandell Tunes; EMF Productions; Enid Oklahoma Music Publishing; Ever-Open-Eye Music; Faiella Publishing, Doug; First Time Music (Publishing) U.K.; Flaming Star West Music; Flammer Music, Harold; ‡Fretboard Publishing; Frick Music Publishing Co.; ‡Fro's Music Publishing; ‡Full Moon Music, Inc.; ‡Future-1 Music Publishing; Giftness Enterprise; GlobeArt Inc.; Hammel Associates, Inc., R.L.; Harbor Gospel Music Production; Henly Music Associates; Hitsburgh Music Co.; Holton Music; Holy Spirit Music; Hutchins Music, Gregg; Jacksong Music; Jaclyn Music; Jaelius Enterprises; Jerjoy Music; JoDa Music; Josena Music; Just a Note; JW One Music Publishing Co.; Kansa Records Corporation; Kaupps & Robert Publishing Co.; Kaylee Music Group, Karen; Kingsport Creek Music Publishing; Lari-Jon Publishing; Last Brain Cell; LCS Music Group, Inc.; Lindsay Publishing, Doris; Lin's Lines; Lion Hill Music Publishing Co.; McCoy Music, Jim; McGibony Publishing; Mack Music, Danny; Makers Mark Gold; Mathes Company, The; ‡Mellow House Music; Mighty Twinns Music; More Brand Music; Music in the Right Keys Publishing Company; Namax Music Publishing; Nebo Ridge Publishing Company; New Rap Jam Publishing, A; Newcreature Music; NSP Music Publishing Inc.; Omni

2000, Inc.; Orchid Publishing; Otto Publishing Co.; Panchatantra Music Enterprises; ‡Paradigm Publishers; Parravano Music; Pollard Sound World; Pritchett Publications; Prospector Three D Publishing; RNR Publishing; Rocker Music/Happy Man Music; Roots Music; Saddlestone Publishing; Samuel Three Productions; Scott Music Group, Tim; Scrutchings Music; ‡Smokin' Cowboys Publishing Co.; Snowcliff Publishing; ‡Songs From Out of the Blue; Starbound Publishing Co.; Steel Rain Publishing; Stuart Music Co., Jeb; Sun Star Songs; Sweet June Music; This Here Music; Tiki Enterprises, Inc.; ‡Toulouse Music Publishing Co., Inc.; Trusty Publications; Twin Bears Publishing; Twin Spin Publishing; Vokes Music Publishing; Woodrich Publishing Co.; Yorgo Music

Rock

Abalone Publishing; Aladdin Music Group; ‡Alan Music, Marcus; Al-Ky Music; All Rock Music; ‡Americatone International; Amiron Music; ‡Ancy Music Group; Andyland Music; Aquarius Publishing; Audio Music Publishers; Bad Habits Music Publishing; Bal & Bal Music Publishing Co.; ‡Bare Minimum Music; Bay Ridge Publishing Co.; Beecher Publishing, Earl; Bernard Enterprises, Inc., Hal; Best Buddies, Inc.; Big Snow Music; ‡Bixio Music Group/IDM Publishing; Black Rose Productions; ‡Black Strand Music; Boam; Brewster Songs, Kitty; Brothers Organisation, The; Buried Treasure Music; California Country Music; Camex Music; Cash Productions, Inc.; Cherie Music; Cisum; Clear Pond Music; ‡Clearwind Publishing; Clevère Musikverlag, R.D.; Colton Shows, Glenn; ‡Connell Publishing Co., Jerry; Cottage Blue Music; Country Breeze Music; Country Star Music; ‡Croaky Frog Music; Cunningham Music; D.S.M. Producers Inc.; Davis & Davis Music; De Miles Music Company, The Edward; Dean Enterprises Music Group; Demi Monde Records & Publishing Ltd.; Dingo Music; Doss Music, Buster; Drive Music, Inc.; Duane Music, Inc.; Earitating Music Publishing; Earthscream Music Publishing Co.; ‡East Coast Music Publishing; Edition Rossori; Elect Music Publishing Company; EMF Productions; ESI Music Group; Famous Music Publishing Companies; Fat City Publishing; First Time Music (Publishing) U.K.; Flaming Star West Music; Flea Circus Music; ‡Fretboard Publishing; Frick Music Publishing Co.; Frozen Inca Music; ‡Full Moon Music, Inc.; Funzalo Music; Gary Music, Alan; GFI West Music Publishing; Giftness Enterprise; Gold Music Publishing, Jay; ‡Golden Harp Music; ‡Goodnight Kiss Music; Green One Music; Green Zebra Music; G-String Publishing; Hammel Associates, Inc., R.L.; ‡Hautboy Music; Hawksbill Music; ‡Headaches & Heartburn Music; Heupferd Musikverlag; High-Minded Moma Publishing & Productions; Hit & Run Music Publishing Inc.; Hit-Fabrik Musikverlag; ISBA Music Publishing Inc.; Jacksong Music; Jammy Music Publishers Ltd.; Jasper Stone Music/JSM Songs; JoDa Music; Jolson Black & White Music, Al; JW One Music Publishing Co.; Kaupps & Robert Publishing Co.; Kel-Cres Publishing; Keno Publishing; Kirchstein Publishing Co.; Largo Music Publishing; Lari-Jon Publishing; Last Brain Cell; Lilly Music Publishing; Lin's Lines; M & T Waldoch Publishing, Inc.; McCoy Music, Jim; Magic Message Music; ‡Maverick Music Company; Music Room Publishing Group, The; Myko Music; Mymit Music Productions, Chuck; Nebo Ridge Publishing Company; Nervous Publishing; ‡New Clarion Music Group; New Rap Jam Publishing, A; Newcreature Music; Old Slowpoke Music; Omni 2000, Inc.; Ontrax Companies; Operation Perfection; ‡Paradigm Publishers; ‡Pascarella Music Publishing; peermusic; Pen Cob Publishing Inc.; Platinum Boulevard Publishing; Platinum Gold Music; Pollard Sound World; Power Voltage Music; Prejippie Music Group; Prescription Company; Pretty Shayna Music; Pritchett Publications; Promo; Prospector Three D Publishing; Purple Haze Music; R. J. Music; Raving Cleric Music Publishing/Euroexport Entertainment; Ridge Music Corp.; RNR Publishing; Rocker Music/Happy Man Music; Rockford Music Co.; Rondor Music International; Roots Music; Rose Hill Group; Saddlestone Publishing; Sci-Fi Music; Scott Music Group, Tim; Segal's Publications; Shaolin Music; Siegel Music Companies; Silicon Music Publishing Co.; Simply Grand Music, Inc.; ‡Sinus Musik Produktion, Ulli Weigel; ‡Smokin' Cowboys Publishing Co.; Solid Entertainment; ‡Songs From Out of the Blue; ‡Sound and Fury Music Publishing; Sound Cellar Music; ‡Spinwilly Music Publishing; Steel Rain Publishing; Stuart Music Co., Jeb; Succes; Sun Star Songs; Sunsongs Music; Surespin Songs; Tedesco Music Co., Dale; Third Wave Productions Limited; This Here Music; Tiki Enterprises, Inc.; Transamerika Musikverlag KG; Treasure Trove Music; Trusty Publications; Twin Bears Publishing; Twin Spin Publishing; Twin Towers Publishing Co.; Ultimate Peak Music; Valet Publishing Co.; ‡Viceroy Music

Group, Inc.; Warner/Chappell Music Canada Ltd.; Westunes Music Group; Whitewing Music; Wilcom Publishing; Without Papers Music Publishing Inc.; Woodrich Publishing Co.; World Famous Music Co.; Your Best Songs Publishing; Zomba Music Publishing

World Music

Bay Ridge Publishing Co.; Big Snow Music; ‡Connell Publishing Co., Jerry; Elect Music Publishing Company; ‡Hautboy Music; Heupferd Musikverlag; Inside Records/OK Songs; ‡Island Culture Music Publishers; Keno Publishing; Kirchstein Publishing Co.; Lin's Lines; ‡Master Source; PPI/Peter Pan Industries; Tedesco Music Co., Dale; Transamerika Musikverlag KG

‡ **THE DOUBLE DAGGER** before a listing indicates that the listing is new in this edition.

Music Print Publishers

The music print publisher's function is much more specific than that of the music publisher. Music publishers try to exploit a song in many different ways: on records, videos, movies and radio/TV commercials, to name a few. But, as the name implies, music print publishers deal in only one publishing medium: print.

Although the role of the music print publisher has virtually stayed the same over the years, demand for sheet music has declined substantially. Today there are only a few major sheet music publishers in operation, along with many smaller ones.

Most songs fall into one of two general categories: popular or educational music. Popular songs are pop, rock, adult contemporary, country and other hits heard on the radio. They are printed as sheet music (for single songs) and folios (collections of songs). Educational material includes pieces for chorus, band, orchestra, instrumental solos and instructional books. In addition to publishing original compositions, print publishers will sometimes print arrangements of popular songs.

Most major publishers of pop music won't print sheet music for a song until a popular recording of the song has become a hit single, or at least is on the *Billboard* Hot 100 chart. Some of the companies listed here indicate the lowest chart position of a song they've published, to give you a better idea of the market.

Chart action is obviously not a factor for original educational material. What print publishers look for is quality work that fits into their publishing program and is appropriate for the people who use their music, such as school and church choirs, school bands or orchestras.

When dealing with music print publishers, it is generally unacceptable to send out simultaneous submissions; that is, sending identical material to different publishers at the same time. Since most of the submissions they receive involve written music, whether single lead sheets or entire orchestrations, the time they invest in evaluating each submission is considerable—much greater than the few minutes it takes to listen to a tape. It would be discourteous and unprofessional to ask a music print publisher to invest a lot of time in evaluating your work and then possibly pull the deal out from under him before he has given you an answer.

Writers' royalties range from 10-15% of the retail selling price of music in print. For educational material that would be a percentage of the price of the whole set (score and parts). For a book of songs (called a folio), the 10-15% royalty would be pro-rated by the number of songs by that writer in the book. Royalties for sheet music are paid on a flat rate per sheet, which is usually about one-fifth of the retail price. If a music publisher licenses print publishing to a music print publisher, print royalties are usually split evenly between the music publisher and songwriter, but it may vary. You should read any publishing contract carefully to see how print deals fit in, and consult an entertainment attorney if you have any questions.

ABINGDON PRESS (ASCAP, BMI), Dept. SM, 201 Eighth Ave. S., Nashville TN 37203. (615)749-6158. Senior Music Editor: Gary Alan Smith. Music print publisher. Publishes approximately 50 songs/year; publishes as many new songwriters as possible. Pays 10% royalty.

How to Contact: Submit fully arranged manuscripts (demo tape optional) by mail. Unsolicited submissions are OK. "Unsolicited material must be addressed with Gary Alan Smith's name on the first line." Prefers no more than 4 songs per submission. "Please be sure name and address are on tapes and/or manuscripts." SASE. Reports in 6-8 weeks.

Music: Mostly **sacred choral** and **instrumental**. Published "We Believe You" (by Dan Adler); "Please Enter My Heart" (by Cathy Townly) and "Spirit-Child Jesus" (by John Horman).

Tips: "Focus material on small to mid-size, volunteer church choirs and musicians. Be flexible in your writing and be patient."

ALRY PUBLICATIONS, ETC., INC. (ASCAP), P.O. Box 36542, Charlotte NC 28236. (704)334-3413. Fax: (704)334-1143. President: Amy Rice Blumenthal. Music print publisher and music publisher. Estab. 1980. Publishes 20 pieces/year; mostly individual works or educational material. Publishes 3-5 new composers/year. Pays 10% print royalty.
How to Contact: Write or call first and obtain permission to submit. Prefers cassette and complete score or part(s). "Brief bio and any performance notes should be included." SASE. Reports in 1-3 months.
Music: Mostly **classical**, **educational** and **chamber music**; also **original**, **some popular** and **jazz**, all for wind instrumentation. Published "Serenade" (by David Uber) (chamber trio); "Flowers" (by Elizabeth Raum) (flute or oboe); and "Sacred Medley" (by Tommy Goff) (flute choir).
Tips: "Be aware of the market for sheet music/educational and classical."

BOSTON MUSIC CO. (ASCAP), 172 Tremont St., Boston MA 02111. (617)426-5100. E-mail: bmco@earthlink.net. Contact: Editorial Department. Music print publisher. Prints 100 pieces/year, both individual pieces and music books. Pays 10% royalty.
How to Contact: Write or call first and obtain permission to submit. SASE. Reports in 4-5 months.
Music: Choral pieces, educational material, instrumental solo pieces and **"piano instructional materials that piano teachers would be interested in."** Published "Torches" (by Frederick Koch) (SA/SATB choral); "Musical Imprints" (by William Catania) (piano collection); and "Adagio For Tuba and Piano" (by Mark Stupp) (tuba/piano).
Tips: "Please submit only music suitable to our catalog—no vocal music, no pop or rock."

BOURNE COMPANY, 5 W. 37th St., New York NY 10018. (212)391-4300. Contact: Professional Manager. Music print publisher. Estab. 1917. Publishes educational material and popular music.
Affiliate(s): ABC Music, Ben Bloom, Better Half, Bogat, Burke & Van Heusen, Goldmine, Harborn, Lady Mac, Murbo Music.

- See their listing in the Music Publishers section.

How to Contact: Write first and obtain permission to submit. SASE.
Music: Band pieces, choral pieces and **handbell pieces.** Published "When You Wish Upon A Star" (by Washington/Harline); "Unforgettable" (by Gordon), recorded by Natalie Cole on Elektra Records (vocal duet); and "The Songs of Charlie Chaplin."

ECS PUBLISHING, Dept. SM, 138 Ipswich St., Boston MA 02215. (617)236-1935. President: Robert Schuneman. Music print publisher. Prints 200 pieces/year, mostly individual pieces and music books. Pays 10% royalty on sales and 50% on performance/license.
Affiliate(s): Galaxy Music Corporation (ASCAP), E.C. Schirmer Music Co. Inc. (ASCAP), Ione Press, Inc. (BMI) and Highgate Press (BMI).
How to Contact: Query with complete score and tape of piece. Prefers cassette. "Submit a clean, readable score." SASE. Reports in 6-8 months.
Music: Choral pieces, orchestral pieces, instrumental solo pieces, instrumental ensemble pieces, methods books, books on music and **keyboard pieces**.

CARL FISCHER, INC. (ASCAP), 62 Cooper Square, New York NY 10003. (212)777-0900. Fax: (212)477-4129. Vice President, Publishing: Mr. Lauren Keiser. Music print publisher and music publisher. Estab. 1872. Publishes over 100 pieces/year; mostly individual songs, folios or educational material. Publishes 3-4 new composers/year. Lowest chart position held by a song published in sheet form is 40. Pays 10% royalty.
Affiliate(s): Pembroke (BMI).
How to Contact: Write first and obtain permission to submit. Prefers cassette with lead sheet and/or scores. SASE. Reports in 4-5 months.
Music: Mostly **sacred choral** and **band.** Published "Symphony #2" (by Howard Hanson), recorded by Seattle Symphony; "Waltzing Matilda" (traditional); and "Concerto for Left Hand" (by Lukas Foss).

MARK FOSTER MUSIC COMPANY, P.O. Box 4012, Champaign IL 61824-4012. (217)398-2760. Fax: (217)398-2791. E-mail: markfostermus@champ.il.aads.net. President: Jane C. Menkhaus. Music print publisher, music publisher and retail music division. Estab. 1962. Publishes 20-30 pieces/year; choral music and books. Publishes 3-4 new composers/year. Pays 5-10% over first 3,000 copies sold.
Affiliate(s): Fostco (ASCAP) and Marko (BMI).
How to Contact: Submit materials by mail. Send to the attention of Assistant Editor. "If new composer/arranger, submit bio. Submission guidelines available upon request by either electronic or standard mail."

Unsolicited submissions are OK. Prefers cassette with 1 composition and choral manuscript. SASE. Reports in 4-6 weeks.

Music: Mostly **sacred SATB**, **secular SATB** and **sacred** and **secular treble** and **male choir music**; also **conducting books** and **Kodaly materials**. Published "Crown Him with Many Crowns," arranged by J. Harold Moyer; "Chalet Girls Sunday" (by Bull/Shields); and "Alleluia" (by Noël Goemanne).

Tips: "Must be well-constructed composition, presented in a clear and legible manuscript, with a keyboard reduction of the voice parts if it is for unaccompanied chorus. We do not accept lyric sheets, lead sheets or demo tapes without a manuscript."

GENEVOX MUSIC GROUP (ASCAP, BMI, SESAC), 127 Ninth Ave. N., Nashville TN 37234. (615)251-3770. Music print publisher. Estab. 1986. Director: Mark Blankenship. Prints 75-100 songs/year; publishes 10 new songwriters/year. Pays 10% royalty.

How to Contact: Submit demo tape and choral arrangement, lead sheet or complete score. Unsolicited submissions are OK. Prefers cassette with 1-5 songs. SASE. Reports in 2 weeks acknowledging receipt, 3 months response.

Music: Choral, **orchestral**, **instrumental solo** and **instrumental ensemble pieces**. "We publish all forms of choral sacred music for all ages, and instrumental for handbell, organ, piano and orchestra." Published "Go, Go Jonah," by Kathie Hill (children's choral musical); "Bless the Lord," arranged by Dave Williamson (praise/worship); and "God So Loved the World," arranged by Camp Kirkland and Tom Fettke (musical).

Tips: "Most of what we publish is designed for use by church choirs and instrumentalists. Middle-of-the-road, traditional anthems, hymn arrangements, praise and worship, contemporary and inspirational songs in an SATB/keyboard choral format stand the best chance for serious consideration."

HINSHAW MUSIC, INC. (ASCAP), P.O. Box 470, Chapel Hill NC 27514-0470. (919)933-1691. Vice President: Roberta Van Ness. Music print publisher. Estab. 1975. Prints 100 pieces/year, both individual pieces and music books. Publishes educational material. Pays 10% royalty.

Affiliate(s): Hindon Publications (BMI) and Chapel Hill Music (SESAC).

How to Contact: Call first and obtain permission to submit. After receiving permission, "Send the complete score. Lyric sheets and/or tapes alone are not acceptable. We do not review lyrics alone. Cassette tapes may be sent in addition to the written manuscript. Send clear, legible photocopies, *not* the original. Submit only 2 or 3 manuscripts at a time that are representative of your work. An arrangement of a copyrighted work will not be considered unless copy of written permission from copyright owner(s) is attached. Once a manuscript has been submitted, do not telephone or write for a 'progress report.' Be patient." SASE. Reports in 6-8 months.

Music: Choral pieces and **organ**. Published "Joseph Haydn and the Choral Tradition" (by Lawrence Schenbeck); "Choral Warmups From A-Z: Singing Dr. Seuss's ABC" (by Karle Erickson); and "Group Vocal Technique—The Choral Warmups" (video) (by James Jordan).

Tips: "Submit your manuscript to only one publisher at a time. It requires considerable time and expense for us to thoroughly review a work, so we want the assurance that if accepted, the manuscript is available for publication. We are unable to 'critique' rejected works. A pamphlet, 'Submitting Music for Publication,' is available with SASE."

‡JACKMAN MUSIC CORP., P.O. Box 1900, Orem UT 84059-1900. (801)225-0859. Fax: (801)225-0851. President: Jerry Jackman. Music print publisher. Estab. 1937. Publishes 40-60 chorals, 1-2 folios/year; mostly individual songs or folios. Publishes 2-3 new songwriters/year. Pays standard royalty.

Affiliate(s): Sonos Music Resources, Jackman Universe (sold through Theodore Presser Co.), Pioneer Music Press, Praiseworthy and Choir Publishing.

How to Contact: Submit demo tape by mail. Unsolicited submissions are OK. "Complete copy of manuscript by mail is preferred. Demo tape OK, but not necessary. Please be sure the manuscript is readable." SASE. Reports in 1 month.

Music: Mostly **sacred choral**, **hymn-based anthems** and **Easter/Christmas sacred choral**. Published *Christmas with the Mormon Tabernacle Choir* (by J. Longhurst/C. Christiansen/R. Elliot/D. Ripplinger), recorded by Salt Lake Mormon Tabernacle Choir on LaserLight Records (Christmas); and *Noel* (by D. Ripplinger), recorded by Salt Lake Mormon Tabernacle Choir on Bonneville Records (Christmas).

Tips: "We cater mostly to small, English-speaking, congregational choirs (L.D.S. and other Christian denominations) with limited rehearsal time, so 'easy without being patronizing' is best. We will not, however, turn down a difficult piece if it fits into our yearly plan; pieces that are faithful to basic music theory principles have the best chance of being published."

JUMP MUSIC, Langemunt 71, 9420 Aaigem, **Belgium**. Phone: (053)62-73-77. Estab. 1976. General Manager: Eddy Van Mouffaert. Music print publisher. Publishes educational material and popular music. Prints 150 songs/year, mostly individual songs. Pays 5% royalty.

- See their listing in the Music Publishers section.

How to Contact: Submit demo tape by mail. Unsolicited submissions are OK. Prefers cassette and lead sheet or complete score. Does not return material. Reports in 2 weeks.
Music: Pop, ballads, band pieces and **instrumentals**. Published *Tot Ziens* (by Eddy Govert), recorded by Eigentijdse Jevgd on Youth Sound Records (Flemish); "Go Go Go" (by Henry Spider), recorded by Rudy Silvester on Scorpion Records (Flemish); and *Onze Vader* (by Paul Severs), recorded by P.P. Michiels on Youth Sound Records (Flemish).

KALLISTI MUSIC PRESS, 810 S. Saint Bernard St., Philadelphia PA 19143-3309. (215)724-6511. E-mail: kallisti@ix.netcom.com. Website: http://www.netcom.com/~kallisti/. Publisher: Andrew Stiller. Music print publisher. Estab. 1991. Publishes 12 pieces/year; mostly individual songs or folios. Publishes 1-2 new songwriters/year. Pays 30-50% royalty.
How to Contact: Write or call first and obtain permission to submit. Prefers cassette with résumé or bio, and complete list of works. "Cassette should include works covering the composer's full chronological and stylistic range. Résumé should indicate date of birth. Works list should indicate forces, duration, and date of each item. Do not send scores." SASE. Reports in 2 weeks.
Music: Mostly **"serious" music, new and old**; also **traditional/folk anthologies** and **jazz transcriptions**. Published *The Kairn of Koridwen* (by Charles Tomlinson Griffes) on Koch International Records (ballet); *Metaphors* (by Lejaren Hiller) on New World Records (guitar quartet); and *The Water is Wide, Daisy Bell* (by Andrew Stiller) on MMC Records (piano).
Tips: "Bear in mind that we want to publish music that will still be performed 200 years from now. All manuscripts accepted for publication must be submitted in Finale or other music-notation software format of comparable sophistication."

‡LAWSON GOULD MUSIC PUBLISHERS, INC. (ASCAP), 250 W. 57th St., New York NY 10107. (212)247-3920. Fax: (212)247-3991. President: Walter Gould. Music print publisher. Estab. 1954. Publishes 60-70 pieces/year; mostly educational material. Pays standard royalty.
How to Contact: Submit manuscript by mail. Unsolicited submissions are OK. Prefers choral arrangement. SASE. Reports in 1-2 months.
Music: Mostly **choral music**.

THE LORENZ CORPORATION (ASCAP, BMI, SESAC), Box 802, Dayton OH 45401-0802. (513)228-6118. Contact: Editorial Department. Music print publisher. Estab. 1890. Publishes 500 titles/year; 10 new composers/year. Hires staff writers. Pays standard royalty.
How to Contact: Submit manuscript (completely arranged, not songs or lead sheets); tape not necessary. "No demos—only full arrangement." SASE. Reports in 4-6 weeks.
Music: Interested in **religious/Christian choral, high school, junior high, elementary choral** and **organ/piano music**; also **sacred** and **educational band music** and **handbell music**.
Tips: "Send in a legible copy. We do not produce vocal solo collections or sheet music. We encourage new composers/arrangers but do not use lead sheets or vocal solos, only fully arranged pieces for chorus, keyboard or handbell."

HAROLD LUICK & ASSOCIATES (BMI), Box B, Carlisle IA 50047. (515)989-3748. President: Harold Luick. Music print publisher. Prints 4-5 songs/year, mostly individual songs. Lowest chart position held by a song published in sheet form is 98. Pays 4% royalty.

- See Harold Luick's listing in the Record Producers section.

How to Contact: Write first and obtain permission to submit or submit through publisher or attorney. Prefers cassette or reel-to-reel and lyric sheet. SASE. Reports in 3 weeks.
Music: Mostly **traditional country**; also **novelty songs**. Published "Mrs. Used To Be," written and recorded by Joe Harris on River City Records (country).

MUSIC BOX DANCER PUBLICATIONS LTD., 2600 John St. #220, Markham Ontario L3R 3W3 **Canada**. (905)475-1848. (905)474-9870. President: John Loweth. Music print publisher, record company (Berandol Records) and music publisher (Berandol Music). Estab. 1979. Publishes 20-30 pieces/year; mostly individual songs, folios and educational material. Publishes 2 new songwriters/year. Pays standard royalty.

- See the listing for Berandol Music in the Music Publishers section and Berandol Records in the Record Companies section.

How to Contact: Submit demo tape by mail. Unsolicited submissions are OK. Prefers cassette. Does not return material. Reports in 2 months.
Music: Mostly **instrumental, piano** and **other instrumentation**. Published *Shadows of the Dancer*, written and recorded by Frank Mills (piano); *Fields*, written and recorded by Brian Langill (pop instrumental), both on MBD Records; and *Flute Quartet No. 1*, written and recorded by Daniel Theaker (instrumental) on DTee Records.
Tips: "You must have a professional demo, and indicate your achievements to date."

PLYMOUTH MUSIC CO., INC., 170 NE 33rd St., Ft. Lauderdale FL 33334. (954)563-1844. General Manager: Bernard Fisher. Music print publisher. Estab. 1953. Prints 50 pieces/year: individual pieces, individual songs, music books and folios. Pays 10% of retail selling price.
Affiliate(s): Aberdeen Music (ASCAP), Galleria Press (ASCAP), Walton Music (ASCAP) and Music for Percussion (BMI).
How to Contact: Submit demo tape by mail. Unsolicited submissions are OK. Prefers cassette and lead sheet or complete score. SASE. Reports within 1 month.
Music: Choral pieces and **percussion music**.
Tips: "Send choral music for church and school with cassette tape if available. Manuscripts should be legible."

THEODORE PRESSER CO. (ASCAP, BMI, SESAC), Dept. SM, One Presser Place, Bryn Mawr PA 19010. (215)525-3636. Fax: (215)527-7841. E-mail: presser@presser.com. Contact: Editorial Committee. Music print publisher. Member MPA. Publishes 90 works/year. Pays varying royalty.
Affiliate(s): Merion Music (BMI), Elkan-Vogel, Inc. (ASCAP), and Mercury Music Corp. (SESAC).
How to Contact: Submit scores by mail. Unsolicited submissions are OK. Prefers cassette with 1-2 works and score. SASE. Reports in 1 month.
Music: Serious, **educational** and **choral music**. "We primarily publish serious music of emerging and established composers, and vocal/choral music which is likely to be accepted in the church and educational markets, as well as gospel chorals of high musical quality. We are *not* a publisher of song sheets or pop songs."
Tips: "Do not submit more than three works, unless requested. Do not send anything other than choral, educational or serious concert music. We do not do 'pop' music."

SHELLEY MUSIC, 1731 Red Bud Rd., Bolingbrook IL 60440. President: Guy Shelley. Music print publisher. Estab. 1992. Publishes 20-50 songs/year; publishes 4 new songwriters/year. Pays 10% standard sheet music royalty.
Affiliate(s): Guy Smilo Music (BMI).
How to Contact: Write first and obtain permission to submit. Prefers cassette with 1-3 songs and lyric sheet. SASE. Reports in 6 months. "No phone calls."
Music: Mostly **classical (educational)**. Published "Savannah," "Camel Caper" and "Barnyard Hoedown" all piano pieces written by Donna Shelley.
Tips: "Have a clear demo with a clear score of music to follow."

‡SONGWRITER'S MONTHLY, 332 Eastwood Ave., Feasterville PA 19053. Phone/fax: (215)953-0952. Publisher: Allen Foster. Music print publisher. Estab. 1991. Publishes 6 pieces/year; mostly folios. Publishes 6 new songwriters/year. Pays standard royalty, "but sometimes more."
How to Contact: Write to find out what the theme of the songbook is for that year. Prefers cassette with lead sheet and cover letter. SASE. Reports in 1-2 months.
Music: Published "Lost in the Shuffle," written by George Stock; "Winter," written by W. David Bowman; and "Boogie Woogie Christmas," written by Jim O'Grady.

WILLIAM GRANT STILL MUSIC (ASCAP), 4 S. San Francisco St., Suite 422, Flagstaff AZ 86001-5737. (520)526-9355. Estab. 1983. Manager: Judith Anne Still. Music print publisher. Publishes educational material and classical and popular music. Prints 2-3 arrangements/year; 2-3 new arrangers/year. Pays 10% royalty for arrangements sold. "We publish arrangements of works by William Grant Still. This year we are especially interested in developing a catalog of clarinet arrangements, though other sorts of arrangements may be considered."
How to Contact: Write or call first and obtain permission to submit. Does not return material. Reports in 2-6 weeks.
Music: Mostly **instrumental solo pieces**. Published "Songs of Separation" (by William Grant Still), recorded by Videmus on New World Records (vocal/instrumental); *Golden Days* (by William Grant Still), recorded by Manhattan Chamber Orchestra on Newport Classic Records (vocal/orchestra); and *Radiant*

Night (by William Grant Still), recorded by Darryl Taylor on WGSM Records (vocal/piano).
Tips: "Develop arrangements of the music of William Grant Still, sometime after 1998. We are booked up with publications for the next two years."

‡SUNHAWK CORPORATION, 7770 39th Ave., Seattle WA 98115. (206)528-0876. Fax: (206)528-0942. E-mail: judym@oz.net. Website: http://www.sunhawk.com. Director, Artist Relations: Judy McOstrich. Music print and digital (Internet) publisher. "We publish print and digital sheet music." Estab. 1992. Publishes 1,000 pages/month; mostly individual songs, folios and educational material. "We can offer artists better royalties than print publishers because we can deliver playable, printable scores electronically. We have encryption and electronic commerce software so we can sell scores over the Internet."
How to Contact: Submit demo tape by mail or send e-mail. Prefers cassette or DAT with lyric and lead sheet, manuscripts, computer data and score files. SASE. Reports in 3 weeks (e-mail within 7 days).
Music: Mostly **rock**, **classical** and **country**; also **New Age**, **jazz** and **pop**. Published *Total Joplin* (by Scott Joplin) (ragtime); *Handel's Messiah* (by George Handel) (classical); and *Mozart's Symphonies* (by Mozart) (classical), all on Sunhawk.
Tips: "Submit material in a digital format. Include all necessary information (i.e., background information and goals, etc.) Clear handwriting or typed submissions preferred."

TRANSCONTINENTAL MUSIC PUBLICATIONS (ASCAP), Dept. SM, 838 Fifth Ave., New York NY 10021. (212)650-4101. Fax: (212)650-4109. Website: http://www.shamash.org/reform/uahc/transmp/. Senior Editor: Dr. Judith B. Tischler. Music print publisher. Estab. 1941. Pays 10% royalty. "We publish serious solo and choral Jewish music. The standard royalty is 10% except for rentals—there is no cost to the songwriter. Distributes audio cassettes and CDs if 50% or more of the content is published by Transcontinental. Currently producing CDs of children's songs and synagogue choral Jewish music."
Affiliate(s): New Jewish Music Press (BMI).
How to Contact: Query first. Prefers cassette. "We usually do not accept lead sheets. Most all of our music is accompanied. Full and complete arrangements should accompany the melody." Does not return material. Reports in 10 months.
Music: Only **Jewish vocal** and **Jewish choral**. Published "Hand In Hand" (by Michael Isaacson) (pop-classical); "Jerusalem Is Mine" (by Kenny Korem) (pop-classical); and "Even When God Is Silent" (by Michael Horvit) (classical).
Tips: "Be sure the content is relevant (related to Judaism). Do not send unsolicited material."

TRILLENIUM MUSIC CO. (ASCAP), P.O. Box 88, Tunbridge VT 05077. (802)889-3354. President: Don Stewart. Music print publisher. Estab. 1986. Publishes 10-15 pieces/year; mostly educational material or serious music. Publishes 1 new songwriter/year. Pays 10% royalty.
How to Contact: Write or call first and obtain permission to submit. Prefers cassette with lead sheet and complete materials, if possible. SASE. Reports in 3 months.
Music: Mostly **serious, jazz-derived**. Published "Seven Little Etudes," "A Book of Sliding Things" and "Gesualdo Stanzas" (by Don Stewart).
Tips: "We don't publish 'songs' but rather compositions and arrangements of songs or musical theater."

VIVACE PRESS, NW 310 Wawawai Rd., Pullman WA 99163. (509)334-4660. Fax: (509)334-3551. E-mail: yordy@vivacepress.com. Website: http://www.vivacepress.com. Contact: Jonathan Yordy. Music print publisher. Estab. 1990. Publishes 40 pieces of music/year; publishes several new composers/year. Pays 10% royalty for sheet music sales.
How to Contact: Submit demo tape and sheet music. Unsolicited submissions OK. Prefers cassette. SASE. Reports in 1-2 weeks.
Music: Chamber music, with an emphasis on **historical classical** and **contemporary classical keyboard**. Published "Prelude For Organ," by Fanny Mendelssohn (organ); "Toccata For Harpsichord," by Emma Lou Diemer (harpsichord); and "Electric Church and The Walls of Jerusalem," by Robert Starer (piano).
Tips: "High-quality submissions in all categories considered."

FRANK E. WARREN MUSIC SERVICE (ASCAP), P.O. Box 650006, W. Newton MA 02165. (617)332-5394. Fax: (617)332-5394. E-mail: fewpub@juno.com. Owner/operator: Frank E. Warren. Music print publisher. Estab. 1994. Publishes 25-50 pieces/year (mostly chamber and choral music, including educational materials.) Publishes 5-25 new songwriters/year. Pays 12.5% royalty.
Affiliate(s): Earnestly Music (BMI).
How to Contact: Write or call first and obtain permission to submit a demo (and scores). "We will send guidelines to composers." Prefers clear manuscript or score, cassette optional (desirable). "Present everything (music, cassette, other supporting materials) in an orderly fashion that is explained well in a cover letter." SASE. Reports in 12-15 weeks.

Music: Mostly **chamber music**, **choral music** and **transcriptions/arrangements**; also **educational materials**, **string orchestra**. Published *Lucence* (by Frederick Koch).
Tips: "Provide camera-ready scores that meet industry standards in regard to notation and score layout. Be patient, and at the same time prepared to respond to publisher deadline dates in a timely manner. Don't be afraid to ask questions. Frank E. Warren Music Service is a composer-friendly organization, with flexible terms in helping to meet the needs of composers. Our primary concern is the distribution of music and the development of the composer's career. The compositions in our catalogue are from emerging, advanced, and professional composers. We welcome submissions from writers, and inquiries from dealers and libraries."

THE WILLIS MUSIC COMPANY, 7380 Industrial Rd., Florence KY 41022-0548. (606)283-2050. Estab. 1899. Editor: David B. Engle. Music print publisher. Publishes educational material. Prints 100 publications/year; "no charted songs in our catalog." Pays 5-10% of retail price or outright purchase.
Affiliate(s): Harry Fox Agency.
How to Contact: Prefers fully notated score. SASE. Reports in 3 months.
Music: Mostly **early level piano teaching material**; also **instrumental solo pieces**, **method books** and "supplementary materials—educational material only."

Record Companies

The role of the record company is to record and release records, cassettes and CDs—the mechanical products of the music industry. They sign artists to recording contracts, decide what songs those artists will record, and determine which songs to release. They are also responsible for providing recording facilities, securing producers and musicians, and overseeing the manufacture, distribution and promotion of new releases.

MAJOR LABELS AND INDEPENDENT LABELS

Major labels and independent labels—what's the difference between the two? Major labels are defined as those record companies distributed by one of the "Big 6" distribution companies: BMG Distribution, EMI Music Distribution (EMD), Polygram Distribution (PGD), Sony Music Distribution, Universal Music & Video Distribution (UNI) and Warner/Elektra/Atlantic Distribution (WEA). Distribution companies are wholesalers that sell records to retail outlets. If a label is distributed by one of these major distributors, you can be assured that any release coming out on that label has a large distribution network working behind it. It will most likely be distributed to most major retail stores in the United States. Independent labels go through smaller distribution companies to distribute their product. They usually don't have the ability to distribute records in massive quantities as the major distributors do. However, that doesn't mean independent labels aren't able to have hit records just like their major counterparts. For the first time in the history of the record business, independent distributors shipped more product in 1996 than the major distributors.

Many of the companies listed in this section are independent labels. They are usually the most receptive to receiving material from new artists. Major labels spend more money than most other segments of the music industry; the music publisher, for instance, pays only for items such as salaries and the costs of making demos. Record companies, at great financial risk, pay for many more services, including production, manufacturing and promotion. Therefore, they must be very selective when signing new talent. Also, the continuing fear of copyright infringement suits has closed avenues to getting new material heard by the majors. Most don't listen to unsolicited submissions, period. Only songs recommended by attorneys, managers and producers who record company employees trust and respect are being heard by A&R people at major labels. But that doesn't mean all major labels are closed to new artists. Several major labels listed in this year's *Songwriter's Market*, including Polydor Records, Interscope Records, Elektra Entertainment and Jive Records, accept unsolicited submissions. Following submission policies carefully and presenting a professional package could get you an attentive audience at a major label.

But the competition is fierce at the majors, so independent labels should not be overlooked. Since they're located all over the country, indie labels are easier to contact and can be important in building a local base of support for your music (consult the Geographic Index at the back of the book to find out which companies are located near you). Independent labels usually concentrate more on a specific type of music, which will help you target those companies your submissions should be sent to. And since the staff at an indie label is smaller, there are fewer channels to go through to get your music heard by the decision makers in the company.

If you're interested in getting a major label deal, it makes sense to look to independent record labels to get your start. Independent labels are seen by many as a stepping stone to a major recording contract. Very few artists are signed to a major label at the start of their careers;

usually, they've had a few independent releases that helped build their reputation in the industry. Major labels watch independent labels closely to locate up-and-coming bands and new trends. In the current economic atmosphere at major labels—with extremely high overhead costs for developing new bands and the fact that only 10% of acts on major labels actually make any profit—they're not willing to risk everything on an unknown act. Most major labels won't even consider signing a new act that hasn't had some indie success.

But independents aren't just farming grounds for future major label acts; many bands have long term relationships with indies, and prefer it that way. While they may not be able to provide the extensive distribution and promotion that a major label can (though there are exceptions), indie labels can help an artist become a regional success, and may even help the performer to see a profit as well. With the lower overhead and smaller production costs that an independent label operates on, it's much easier to be a "success" on an indie label than on a major.

Independent record labels can run on a small staff, with only a handful of people running the day-to-day business. Major record labels are more likely to be divided into the following departments: A&R, sales, marketing, promotion, product management, artist development, production, finance, business/legal and international.

The A&R department is staffed with A&R reps who search out new talent. They go out and see new bands, listen to demo tapes, and decide which artists to sign. They also look for new material for already signed acts, match producers with artists and oversee recording projects. Once an artist is signed by an A&R rep and a record is recorded, the rest of the departments at the company come into play.

The sales department is responsible for getting a record into stores. They make sure record stores and other outlets receive enough copies of a record to meet consumer demand. The marketing department is in charge of publicity, advertising in magazines and other media, promotional videos, album cover artwork, in-store displays, and any other means of getting the name and image of an artist to the public. The promotion department's main objective is to get songs from a new album played on the radio. They work with radio programmers to make sure a product gets airplay. The product management department is the ringmaster of the sales, marketing and promotion departments, assuring that they're all going in the same direction when promoting a new release. The artist development department is responsible for taking care of things while an artist is on tour, such as setting up promotional opportunities in cities where an act is performing. The production department works with the actual manufacture and printing of the record, making sure it gets shipped to distributors in a timely manner. People in the finance department compute and distribute royalties, as well as keep track of expenses and income at the company. The business/legal department takes care of contracts, not only between the record company and artists but with foreign distributors, record clubs, etc. And finally, the international department is responsible for working with international companies for the release of records in other countries.

LOCATING A RECORD LABEL

With the abundance of record labels out there, how do you go about finding one that's right for the music you create? First, it helps to know exactly what kind of music a record label releases. Become familiar with the records a company has released, and see if they fit in with what you're doing. Each listing in this section details the type of music a particular record company is interested in releasing. You will want to refer to the Category Index, located at the end of this section, to help you find those companies most receptive to the type of music you write. Visiting a company's website can also provide valuable information about a company's philosophy, the artists on the label and what types of music they work with.

Recommendations by key music industry people are an important part of making contacts with record companies. Songwriters must remember that talent alone does not guarantee success in the music business. You must be recognized through contacts, and the only way to make contacts is through networking. Networking is the process of building an interconnecting web of acquaintances within the music business. The more industry people you meet, the larger your contact base becomes, and the better are your chances of meeting someone with the clout to get your demo into the hands of the right people. If you want to get your music heard by key A&R representatives, networking is imperative.

Networking opportunities can be found anywhere industry people gather. A good place to meet key industry people is at regional and national music conferences and workshops. There are many held all over the country for all types of music (see the Workshops and Conferences section for more information). You should try to attend at least one or two of these events each year; it's a great way to increase the number and quality of your music industry contacts.

Another good way to attract A&R people is to make a name for yourself as an artist. By starting your career on a local level and building it from there, you can start to cultivate a following and prove to labels that you can be a success. A&R people figure if an act can be successful locally, there's a good chance they could be successful nationally. Start getting booked at local clubs, and start a mailing list of fans and local media. Once you gain some success on a local level, branch out. All this attention you're slowly gathering, this "buzz" you're generating, will not only get to your fans but to influential people in the music industry as well.

SUBMITTING TO RECORD COMPANIES

When submitting to a record company, major or independent, a professional attitude is imperative. Just because independent companies are small doesn't mean you should forget professionalism. When submitting material to a record company, be specific about what you are submitting and what your goals are. If you are strictly a songwriter and the label carries a band you believe would properly present your song, state that in your cover letter. If you are an artist looking for a contract, make sure you showcase your strong points as a performer. Whatever your goals are, follow submission guidelines closely, be as neat as possible and include a top-notch demo. If you need more information concerning a company's requirements, write or call for more details. (For more information on submitting your material, see Demo FAQs on page 12 and Getting Started on page 6.)

RECORD COMPANY CONTRACTS

Once you've found a record company that is interested in your work, either major or independent, the next step is signing a contract. Independent label contracts are usually not as long and complicated as major label ones, but they are still binding, legal contracts. Make sure the terms are in the best interest of both you and the label. Avoid anything in your contract that you feel is too restrictive. It's important to have your contract reviewed by a competent entertainment lawyer. A basic recording contract can run from 40-100 pages, and you need a lawyer to help you understand it. A lawyer will also be essential in helping you negotiate a deal that is in your best interest.

Recording contracts cover many areas, and just a few of the things you will be asked to consider will be: What royalty rate is the record label willing to pay you? What kind of advance are they offering? How many records will the company commit to? Will they offer tour support? Will they provide a budget for video? What sort of a recording budget are they offering? Are they asking you to give up any publishing rights? Are they offering you a publishing advance? These are only a few of the complex issues raised by a recording contract, so it's vital to have an entertainment lawyer on your side when discussing a recording contract, whether with a major label or an independent.

A&M RECORDS, 1416 N. LaBrea, Hollywood CA 90028. (213)469-2411. Fax: (213)856-7152. Website: http://www.amrecords.com. Director of A&R: Jr. Regisford. New York office: 825 Eighth Ave., New York NY 10019. (212)333-1328. Fax: (212)333-1301. Distributed by PGD; labels include Polydor Records. Record company.

How to Contact: Write first and obtain permission to submit. Prefers cassette with 4 songs and lyric

sheet. Does not return material. Reports in 2 months.
Music: Mostly **R&B**, **rap** and **pop**; also **gospel** and **jazz**. Released *Definition of a Band*, recorded by Mint Condition (R&B); *I'm Here For You*, recorded by Ann Nesby (R&B); and *Solo*, recorded by Solo, all on A&M Records. Other artists include Smooth, Sheryl Crow, Jonny Lang, Sting, Bryan Adams, Ashley MacIssac and Sounds of Blackness.

A&R RECORDS, 900 19th Ave. S., Suite 207, Nashville TN 37212. (615)329-9127. E-mail: ruanst@aol.com. Website: http://www.io.org/~mladent. Owner/President: R. Steele/David Steele. Distributed by Europromotions; labels include South Side of Heaven Records and Aarrow Records. Record company, record producer, music publisher and talent development/booking. Estab. 1986. Releases 10 CDs/year. Royalty varies, depending on individual agreement. Pays statutory rate to publisher per song on record.
How to Contact: Submit demo tape by mail. Unsolicited submissions are OK. Must be coded: "Songwriter's Market." Prefers cassette with 2 songs and lyric sheet. "We are currently working with writer/artists only. We are not currently soliciting songs from outside writers who are not singers." Does not return material. Reports only if interested.
Music: Mostly **country**, **gospel** and **alternative/folk/bluegrass**; also **Cajun**, **instrumental (fiddle)** and **children's**. Released *Ty Saunders Live*, written and recorded by Ty Saunders; *Stone Cold Country*, written and recorded by Sutton Taylor; and *Here's To Kitty*, written and recorded by Sharla McCoy, all on A&R Records (country). Other artists include David Steele, Bethany Reynolds, Jaison Allen Stiehl and Michael Fender.
Tips: "Only dedicated, business-minded artists can be considered. Identifiable, unique voice is a must."

‡AFM RECORDS INC., 1469 Third Ave., New Brighton PA 15066. (412)847-0111. A&R Director: Jeff Boller. Record company, production company and recording studio. Estab. 1995. Releases 6 CDs/year. Pays negotiable royalty to artists on contract; statutory royalty to publisher per song on record.
How to Contact: Submit demo tape by mail. Unsolicited submissions are OK. Prefers DAT with 3 songs and lyric sheet. Does not return material. Reports in 3 months.
Music: All styles. Recently released albums by Gram Vogel (rock), Wailin', Flailin, and Low Down (blues) and Puppetshow (alternative folk).

THE AFRICAN DIASPORA PROJECT, P.O. Box 470642, San Francisco CA 94147-0642. (415)398-8336. Fax: (415)835-9951. Executive Director: Pietro Giacomo Poggi. Independent record label co-op.
How to Contact: Call first and obtain permission to submit. Prefers cassette or VHS videocassette and lyric sheet. Does not return material. Reports in 2-3 weeks.
Music: Only interested in **music from the African Diaspora**, especially **African**, **Caribbean** and **Latin**. Current acts include Chuscales (contemporary flamenco instrumental), Sol Y Luna (flamenco, salsa, rumba), Jungular Grooves (International Soul), Cool Breeze (Musique Tropique) and Sonacay (rumba gitana).

ALADDIN RECORDINGS, P.O. Box 121738, Nashville TN 37212. (615)726-3556. Contact: A&R Department. Record company. Estab. 1996. Releases 6 singles, 3 LPs and 3 CDs/year. Pays standard royalty to artists on contract; statutory rate to publisher per song on record.
How to Contact: Submit demo tape by mail. Unsolicited submissions are OK. Prefers cassette with 3 songs and lyric sheet. "Send all pertinent information." SASE. Reports in 3-6 weeks.
Music: Mostly **country**, **rock** and **alternative**; also **blues**, **gospel** and **contemporary/R&B**. Released *The Ballad of Jack* (by Drey Hawkins), recorded by Allusion on Alternative Records (alternative); *Tangle James*, written and recorded by Tangle James on Aladdin Recordings (country); and *Only Room 4U* (by R. Cox/N. James), recorded by Terry Barbay on Kottage Records (contemporary).
Tips: "We are looking for songs and artists with a different approach. We need more artists and songs to possibly place with major record companies and also for possible placement in movies, soundtracks, commercials and television programs."

ALBATROSS RECORDS, 2405 Wentworth St., Houston TX 77004. (713)521-2616. Marketing/Sales: Craig Baham. Distributed by INDI; labels include R&D Productions and FW Records. Record company. Estab. 1990. Releases 20 singles, 10 LPs and 10 CDs/year. Pays negotiable royalty to artists on contract; statutory rate to publisher per song on record.
How to Contact: Submit demo tape by mail. Unsolicited submissions are OK. Prefers cassette with lyric and lead sheets. Does not return material. Reports in 4-5 weeks.
Music: Mostly **R&B**, **rap** and **Latino/TexMex**; also **jazz**, **country** and **blues**. Released *Bass Fantasy*, written and recorded by various artists; and *Jeffrey Liggins*, written and recorded by Jeffrey Liggins, both on Albatross Records. Other artists include D.G.I. Posse, Hollister Fraucus, Dead Poetts and 4-Deep.

ALL AMERICAN MUSIC GROUP, 808 Wilshire Blvd., 3rd Floor, Santa Monica CA 90401. (310)656-1100. Fax: (310)656-7430. A&R: Eric B. and Bruce Saidi. Distributed by WEA; labels include Scotti Bros. Records, Street Life Records and Backyard Records. Record company and music publisher (AllAm Songs/BMI and AACI Songs/ASCAP). Estab. 1978. Releases 25 singles and 25 CDs/year.
How to Contact: Submit demo tape by mail. Unsolicited submissions are OK. Prefers cassette, photo and major press. Does not return material.
Music: Mostly **R&B**, **rap**, **contemporary jazz**, **pop** and **dance**. Released *Bad Hair Day* (by various), recorded by "Weird Al" Yankovic on Scotti Bros. Records (pop); *Alfonzo Blackwell* (by various), recorded by Alfonzo Blackwell on Street Life Records (contemporary jazz); and *I Wish* (by various), recorded by Skee-Lo on Scotti Bros. Records (rap). Other artists include James Brown, Sweet Sable, Comrads, Craig Mack and Artie The One Man Party.

ALLEGHENY MUSIC WORKS, 306 Cypress Ave,. Johnstown PA 15902. (814)535-3373. Managing Director: Al Rita. Labels include Allegheny Records. Record company and music publisher (Allegheny Music Works Publishing/ASCAP and Tuned on Music/BMI). Estab. 1991. Pays 10-12% royalty to artists on contract; statutory rate to publisher per song on record.
• See their listing in the Music Publishers section.
How to Contact: Submit demo tape by mail. Unsolicited submissions are OK. Prefers cassette with 3 songs and lyric sheet or lead sheet. SASE. Reports in 2-4 weeks.
Music: Mostly **country (all styles)**; also **pop**, **A/C**, **R&B** and **inspirational**. Released "A Little Something I Ate," written and recorded by Susan Gulick (pop); "Hound Dog Riding In A Pick-up Truck" (by Tony G. Rast/Craig Reeder), recorded by Michael Holloman (country); and "All That I Need Is You" (by Dennis Legrande), recorded by Mark McLelland and Wanda Copier (country), all on Allegheny Records.

‡ALMO SOUNDS, 360 N. LaCienega Blvd., Los Angeles CA 90048. (310)289-3500. Fax: (310)389-4000. Website: http://www.geffen.com/almo. Contact: A&R. Distributed by UNI. Record company and music publisher.
• See the listing for Almo Music in the Music Publishers section.
How to Contact: Submit demo tape by mail. Unsolicited submissions are OK. Prefers cassette with 3 songs maximum and lyric sheet.
Music: Released *Garbage*, recorded by Garbage on Almo Sounds. Other artists include Herb Alpert, Victor DeLorenzo, Gus, Lazlo Bane and Gillian Welch.

ALPHA RECORDING CO., 73-4662 Mamalahoa Hwy. #A, Kailua Kona HI 96740. (808)325-1510. Fax: (808)325-3406. Owner: Samuel Egnot. Record company and music publisher (Samuel Three Productions). Estab. 1992. Releases 6 singles, 6 LPs and 2 CDs/year. Pays negotiable royalty to artists on contract.
• See the listing for Samuel Three Productions in the Music Publishers section.
How to Contact: Submit demo tape by mail. Unsolicited submissions are OK. SASE. Reports in 2 months.
Music: Mostly **country** and **gospel**. No rap or heavy metal. Released "You Didn't Tell Me" (by S. Egnot), recorded by Sam Younger; "I've Fallen Agein," written and recorded by Sami McLemorec; and "Lady From Muleshoe" (by Ted Disko), recorded by Sam Younger, all on Alpha Recording Co.

ALPHABEAT, Box 12 01, D-97862 Wertheim/Main, **Germany**. Phone/fax: (09342)841 55. Owner: Stephan Dehn. A&R Managers: Ottmar Simon and Wolfgang Weinmann. Record company and record producer. Payment to artists on contract "depends on product."
How to Contact: Submit demo tape by mail. Unsolicited submissions are OK. Prefers cassette or PAL videocassette with maximum of 3 songs and lyric sheet. "When sending us your demo tapes, please advise us of your ideas and conditions." SAE and IRC. Reports in 3-4 weeks.
Music: Mostly **dance/disco/pop**, **synth/pop** and **electronic**; also **R&B**, **hip hop/rap** and **ballads**. Artists include Red Sky, Fabian Harloff, Silent Degree, Mode Control, Skyline, Lost in the Dessert and Oriental Bazar.
Tips: "We are a distributor of foreign labels. If foreign labels have interest in distribution of their productions in Germany (also Switzerland and Austria) they can contact us. We distribute all styles of music of foreign labels. Please contact our 'Distribution Service' department."

ALYSSA RECORDS, P.O. Box 587, Farmingville NY 11738. President: Andy Marvel. Labels include Ricochet Records. Record company, music publisher (Andy Marvel Music/ASCAP, Bing Bing Bing Music/ASCAP and Andysongs/BMI) and record producer (Marvel Productions). Estab. 1981. Releases 12-15 singles, 1 12" single and 4 LPs/year. Pays standard royalty to artists on contract; statutory rate to publisher per song on record.

How to Contact: Write first and obtain permission to submit. Prefers cassette or CD with 3 songs and lyric sheet. SASE. "Do not call." Reports in 2 months.
Music: Mostly **pop**, **R&B** and **Top 40**; also **country**.

‡AMERICAN ARTIST RECORDS, P.O. Box 131, Erie PA 16512-0131. (814)455-4796. Artistic Director: Carl P. Austin. Distributed by Partners Distributing; labels include Lakeland Records. Record company, music publisher (Weigaltown Publishing Company) and audio book publisher. Estab. 1971. Releases 1-2 singles, 2-3 LPs and 1-2 CDs/year. Pays negotiable royalty to artists on contract; statutory rate to publisher per song on record.
How to Contact: Submit demo tape by mail. Unsolicited submissions are OK. Prefers cassette or DAT with 3 songs and lyric sheet. SASE. Reports in 1 month.
Music: Mostly **folk**, **country** and **blues**. Released "Ballad of Lake Erie" and "If You Want Me" (by S. Neibauer), both recorded by Lakeland Rangers on Lakeland and WIER Records (folk/rock); and *Younger Than Yesterday* (by D. Massello/S. Niebauer), recorded by ARKAY IV on Cicadelic Records (light rock). Other artists include CPA, Jason John Jarrett and the Holy Clones.

AMERICAN MUSIC NETWORK, INC., P.O. Box 7018, Warner Robins GA 31095. (912)953-2800. President: Robert R. Kovach. Labels include Scaramouche Recordings. Record company, record producer and music marketing corp. Estab. 1986. Releases 25 singles, 12 LPs and 12 CDs/year. Pays varying royalty to artists on contract; statutory rate to publisher per song on record.
How to Contact: Submit demo tape by mail. Unsolicited submissions are OK. Prefers cassette with 4 songs and lyric sheet. "We need name, address and telephone number." SASE. Reports in 4 months.
Music: Mostly **country**, **A/C** and **bluegrass**; also **rock**, **gospel** and **other forms**. Released "Easy On Your Feet," written and recorded by Theresa Justus (A/C); "Real Country Livin'," written and recorded by Little Rudy (country); and "What Happens To Love," written and recorded by Wayne Little (country), all on Scaramouche Recordings. Other artists include Napoleon Starke, Ron Sullivan and Dusty Shelton.
Tips: "We are looking for a whole new stable of artists."

‡AMERICAN RECORDINGS, 3500 W. Olive Ave., Suite 1550, Burbank CA 91505. (818)973-4545. Fax: (818)973-4571. Website: http://www.american.recordings.com. Contact: A&R. Distributed by WEA; labels include Too Pure, Infinite Zero, UBL, Venture and Onion. Record company.
How to Contact: Submit demo tape by mail. Unsolicited submissions are OK. Prefers CD, cassette or videocassette with lyric and lead sheet.
Music: Released *Unchained*, recorded by Johnny Cash on American Recordings.

AMERICATONE RECORDS INTERNATIONAL USA, 1817 Loch Lomond Way, Las Vegas NV 89102-4437. (702)384-0030. Fax: (702)382-1926. E-mail: krb@ix.netcam.com. Estab. 1975. President: Joe Jan Jaros. Distributed by Big Band, Otter, World, North County and General Wash. Record company, producer and music publisher. Releases 8 CDs and cassettes/year. Pays 10% royalty.
How to Contact: Submit demo tape by mail. Unsolicited submissions are OK. Prefers cassette or CD. SASE. Reports in 1 month.
Music: Mostly **country**, **jazz**, **rock**, **Spanish** and **classic ballads**. Released *I Must Be Crazy*, written and recorded by Peter Sobel (R&B); *Simon City*, written and recorded by Cimon City Band (rock), both on Americatone International Records; and *The Best of Christy and Bella* (by various), recorded by Jerry Colston on Christy Records (rock). Other artists include Ladd McIntosh, Mark Masters, Penelope, Dick Shearer and Robert Martin.

AMIRON MUSIC/AZTEC PRODUCTIONS, 20531 Plummer St., Chatsworth CA 91311. (818)998-0443. General Manager: A. Sullivan. Labels include Dorn Records and Aztec Records. Record company, booking agency and music publisher (Amiron Music). Releases 2 singles/year. Pays 10% maximum royalty to artists on contract; standard royalty to songwriters on contract. Pays statutory rate to publishers.

- Amiron Music's management firm, AKO Productions, is listed in the Managers and Booking Agents section.

How to Contact: Prefers cassette and lead sheet. SASE. Reports in 3 weeks.

REFER TO THE CATEGORY INDEX (at the end of this section) to find exactly which companies are interested in the type of music you write.

Music: **Dance**, **easy listening**, **folk**, **jazz**, **MOR**, **rock** ("no heavy metal") and **top 40/pop**. Released "Look In Your Eyes," recorded by Newstreet; and "Midnight Flight," recorded by Papillon.
Tips: "Be sure the material has a hook; it should make people want to make love or fight. Write something that will give a talented new artist that edge on current competition."

ANCY RECORDS, (formerly Breeden Music Group), 1023 17th Ave. S., Suite 101, Nashville TN 37212. (615)321-5707. Fax: (615)320-3937. E-mail: ancymusic@earthlink.net. President: Jessie Renfroe, Sr. Director of A&R: Mitzi Mason. Labels include Talk of the Town, Top Knotch, Street Beat and Norman. Record company and music publisher. Estab. 1985. Releases 10 CDs/year. Pays negotiable rate to artists on contract; statutory rate to publisher per song on record.

- See the listing for Ancy Music in the Music Publishers section.

How to Contact: Submit demo tape by mail. Unsolicited submissions are OK. Prefers cassette, CD or videocassette and lyric sheet. Also include photo and bio. Does not return material. Reports in 3-4 weeks.
Music: **Country**, **Christian/gospel**, **blues/R&B** and **rock/pop/rap**. Released *Comfort Zone*, recorded by Jack Ferrell; *Forever Bound by the Heart*, recorded by Chris Curtice; and *Heart for A Heart*, recorded by Beth Profitt, all on Ancy Records. Other artists include Scott Allen Smith, Kristen Sterling, Troy Sowell and Lisa Pirro.
Tips: "We're independent labels who believe that 'specialty marketing' for new artists is the solid foundation needed in achieving a successful career in the music business. We have an inhouse marketing team to work with any artist we decide to sign. Make sure you understand that music is a profession and you must be willing to invest time, effort and money just like any other new venture. We have the ability to recognize potential regardless of the quality of the demo so don't be afraid to send a home recording."

‡ANGEL/EMI RECORDS, 810 Seventh Ave., 4th Floor, New York NY 10019. (212)603-8600. Distributed by EMI. Record company.

- See the interview with Angel recording artist Irving Burgie on page 42.

How to Contact: Angel Records does not accept unsolicited submissions.
Music: Released *Island in the Sun*, written and recorded by Irving Burgie; *The Classical Album*, recorded by Vanessa Mae; and *Chant III*, recorded by The Benedictine Monks of Santo Domingo De Silos, all on Angel Records.

‡AQUARIUS RECORDS, 1445 Lambert Closse #220, Montreal P.Q. H3H 1Z5 **Canada**. (514)939-3775. Fax: (514)939-2778. E-mail: aquarec@cam.org. A&R Director: Rene LeBlanc. Distributed by EMI Music. Record company and music publisher (Slalom, Crescent, Tacca and Attac). Estab. 1970. Releases 10-20 singles, 3-7 cassettes and 3-7 CDs/year. Pays negotiable royalty to artists on contract; statutory rate to publisher per song on record.
How to Contact: Submit demo tape by mail. Unsolicited submissions are OK. Prefers cassette, CD, DAT or VHS videocassette with 3-5 songs and lyric sheet. Does not return material. Reports in 2 months.
Music: Mostly **contemporary rock**, **modern rock** and **R&B**; also **French rock**, **French contemporary** and **folk**. Released *Bif Naked*, written and recorded by Bif Naked (modern rock); *Greatest Hits*, written and recorded by Men Without Hats (pop), both on Aquarius Records; and *Pigeon D'Argile*, written and recorded by Kevin Parent on Tacca Records (folk/rock). Other artists include Sass Jordan, Jerry Jerry, D'Amour and Marie Chantale.

ARIAL RECORDS, Box 831, Black Diamond, Alberta T0L 0H0 **Canada**. Manager: Tim Auvigne. Record company, management firm, booking agent and music publisher (Ster N' Ster Publishing). Estab. 1989.
How to Contact: Submit demo tape by mail. Unsolicited submissions are OK. Prefers cassette or VHS videocassette with 3 songs and lyric sheet. SASE. Reports in 1 month.
Music: Mostly **country**; also **pop**. Current acts include Brent McAthey (country singer/songwriter) and Jessy Oakley (country singer/songwriter).

ARIANA RECORDS, 1336 S. Avenida Polar #C208, Tucson AZ 85710. (520)790-7324. E-mail: tomdukes@concentric.net. President: James M. Gasper. Distributed by Impact Music Distributors and Care Free Music; labels include Egg White Records. Record company, music publisher and record producer. Estab. 1980. Releases 2 singles, 4 LPs and 4 CDs/year. Pays negotiable royalty to artists on contract; negotiable rate to publisher per song on record.
How to Contact: Submit demo tape by mail. Unsolicited submissions are OK. Prefers cassette or ½" VHS videocassette. SASE. Reports in 1 month.
Music: Mostly **New Age/atmospheric**, **rock**, **folk rock** and **funk jazz**; also **completed projects**. Released "You Can Do It" (by J. Gasper/T. Privett), recorded by JTiom (pop funk); *22nd St. Boogie* (by J. Gasper/

INSIDER REPORT

Arista Records seeks artists with hit song potential

John Rader

"I personally look for a very strong hook, a melody that implants itself in your brain and is there for life—that's a hit song," says John Rader, R&B/pop A&R representative for Arista Records in Los Angeles. Arista knows a few things about hit songs—since the label began in 1975, it has launched the careers of acts such as Whitney Houston, Kenny G, Crash Test Dummies and Ace of Base.

Rader understands well the travails of a songwriter's life. He started out as a songwriter before he landed a job in television at ABC, which led to his current position in A&R at Arista. His interest in the label was fueled by his desire to work with Arista founder and president, Clive Davis. "He is a legend in the music business," Rader says, "and I wanted to learn from him." Currently, Rader is working with R&B/pop singer Greg Wood and R&B quartet One Voice.

Though an A&R rep has various responsibilities, Rader characterizes himself as a talent scout most of all. "My days are spent listening to hundreds of tapes and attending showcases, and at night I'm out in the clubs looking for talent, hoping to find artists that really stand out." What Rader is looking for in an artist is a unique quality he feels can break through in today's market.

For Rader, listening is also a key part of the "R" in "A&R." Finding songs to contribute to a signed artist's repertoire fits prominently into the A&R rep's workload. These can be found in "every imaginable way," says Rader. "Through publishers, managers, attorneys, word of mouth, friends of friends. I look for songs everywhere." Rader is particularly interested in strong lyrics, "an original way of saying the same old thing."

Rader believes publishers are the best way for songwriters to get their work heard by an A&R rep. "Creative personnel at publishing companies spend all day every day developing writers," he says. If a songwriter has not cultivated a relationship with a particular A&R rep, Rader suggests the publishing route. For those songwriters who are not performers, Rader stresses the importance of finding great demo singers to bring their songs to life.

So, your demo winds up in the hands of an A&R rep. What will make it appealing? A flashy cover? A million-dollar layout? Rader insists spending a lot of money on a demo's look won't guarantee success. "I have received packages on which I'm sure hundreds of dollars have been spent for the artwork alone, and then I get to the music and the production is lousy." The one thing that sets a good demo apart from the rest, according to Rader, is professionalism. Current technology makes it relatively inexpensive to produce a good quality demo. "Concentrate on the songs and the production. Focus on the music. This is what you are trying to sell."

If the rep likes the demo, Rader feels the next step is to develop a relationship with the

INSIDER REPORT, *Rader*

artist. While this involves many things, including seeing the artist live, a crucial part of the alliance is the creation of a "buzz" at the record company, a "buzz" that reaches the promotion, marketing and publicity departments. "Then when the artist is signed," Rader says, "everyone feels involved and wants to make it happen."

But once an artist is signed, the real work has just begun. The A&R rep can play a major role in the choice of a producer or a studio for subsequent recording, as well as the songs the artist will include on the album. "This is one of the most important decisions to be made," Rader says. "The producer helps create the overall sound of the band."

As an artist develops, so does the relationship between him and his A&R rep. The rep can help guide the artist through the ups and downs of his career. But Rader is quick to point out that the A&R rep is not the keeper of the artist's dream. "The artist is the sculptor of the dream and the rep is the facilitator."

Another component of Rader's job as A&R rep is staying on top of the ever-changing inclinations of the music business. While he cites techno and rap as developments to watch in the future, Rader prefers not to follow trends. "To me, it always comes down to a great song. Great songs transcend trends!"

While Rader emphasizes the importance of professionalism and the need to develop relationships with publishers and A&R reps, he also encourages songwriters to be persistent and learn as much as they can about the music business. Above all, he says, "Stay true to yourself."

—Tricia E. Suit

T. Privett/T. Dukes), recorded by Cub Scout (jazz); and *Open Your Eyes* (by J. Gasper), recorded by Scuba Tails (ambient), all on Ariana Records. Other artists include Undercover Band, The Rakeheads and Redfish.

ARION RECORDS/SOUND RESOURCES, P.O. Box 16046, Chattanooga TN 37416-0046. President/Owner: Steve Babb. Record company, music publisher (Sound Resources/BMI) and recording studio. E-mail: audio111@aol.com. Website: http://www.mindspring.com/~dgpow/music/soundresources.htm. Estab. 1992. Releases 3-5 CDs/year. Pays 10% royalty to artists on contract; statutory rate to publishers per song on record.

How to Contact: Submit demo tape by mail. Unsolicited submissions are OK. Prefers DAT, CD or cassette (metal if possible). Does not return material. Reports in 2 months "if interested."

Music: Mostly **progressive rock** and **art rock**. Released *Journey of the Dunadan* and *Perelandra*, written and recorded by Glass Hammer; and *Love Changes*, recorded by Tracy Cloud, all on Arion Records. Other artists include Somnambulist, Michelle Young, Wyzards and Privy Member.

Tips: "We define progressive rock as being reminiscent of ELP, Yes, Genesis, etc. If your music fits that definition, we are interested. If your music somehow redefines progressive rock, we would be interested in that as well."

ARISTA RECORDS, 6 W. 57th St., New York NY 10019. (212)489-7400. Fax: (212)977-9843. Website: http://www.aristarec.com. Beverly Hills office: 9975 Santa Monica Blvd., Beverly Hills CA 90212. (310)789-3900. Fax: (310)789-3945. Nashville office: One Music Circle N., Nashville TN 37203. (615)780-9100. Fax: (615)780-9191. Austin office: 7447 Bee Caves Rd., Suite 208, Austin TX 78746. (512)329-9910. Fax: (512)329-0411. Contact: A&R. Distributed by BMG; labels include LaFace Records, Bad Boy Records, Arista Nashville, Rowdy Records, Arista Texas Records, Dedicated Records and Time Bomb Recordings. Record company.

- See the interview with Arista A&R rep John Rader in this section.

How to Contact: Arista Records does not accept unsolicited material.

Music: Released *The Preacher's Wife* (soundtrack); *The Greatest Hits Collection*, recorded by Alan Jackson (country); and *The Bridge*, recorded by Ace of Base (pop), all on Arista Records. Other artists include Deborah Cox, No Mercy, BR5-49, Brooks and Dunn, Diamond Rio, Whitney Houston, Crash Test Dummies, Sarah McLachlan, Real McCoy and Kenny G.

ARKADIA ENTERTAINMENT CORP., 34 E. 23rd St., New York NY 10010. (212)674-5550. (212)979-0266. Contact: A&R Song Submissions. Labels include Arkadia Jazz, Arkadia Classical, Arkadia Now and Arkadia Allworld. Record company, music publisher (Arkadia Music), record producer (Arkadia Productions) and Arkadia Video. Estab. 1995. Releases 6 singles, 12 LPs and 22 CDs/year. Pays statutory rate to publisher per song on record.
How to Contact: Submit demo tape by mail. Unsolicited submissions are OK. Prefers cassette, DAT or VHS videocassette with 3-4 songs and lyric and lead sheets. SASE. Reports ASAP.
Music: Mostly **jazz, pop/R&B** and **rock**; also **world**. Released *Velvet Moon*, recorded by Velvet Moon; and *Michel Gallois*, recorded by Michel Gallois, both on Arkadia Records. Other artists include Billy Taylor, Benny Golson, David Liebman and Nova Bossa Nova.

‡ARTISTIC NOISE, P.O. Box 230914, Grand Rapids MI 49523-0914. (616)281-0617. Owner: Darryl Shanon Holt. Record company, music publisher (Artistic Noise Publishing/BMI) and record producer. Estab. 1996. Releases 2 singles and 1 CD/year. Pays standard royalty to artists on contract; statutory rate to publisher per song on record.

- See the listings for Artistic Noise in the Music Publishers and Record Producers sections.

How to Contact: Submit demo tape by mail. Unsolicited submissions are OK. Prefers cassette with 3-10 songs and lyric sheet. Does not return material. Reports in 2 months.
Music: Mostly **pop**, **dance** and **R&B**; also **alternative**, **ballads** and **techno**. Released "This is Love," "My Car" and "Why," written and recorded by Darryl Shanon Holt on Artistic Noise (pop alternative).

‡ARULA RECORDS, P.O. Box 332, Southbridge MA 01550. E-mail: arularec@aol.com. Contact: A&R Department. Record company. Estab. 1996. Releases 2 albums/year. Pays varying royalty to artists on contract.
How to Contact: Write first and obtain permission to submit. "No calls please. We do not accept or return unsolicited material." Prefers cassette with 5 songs and lyric sheets for music submissions. Prefers cassette with ten minutes of reading and printed text for spoken word submissions. SASE. Reports in 1-2 months.
Music: Mostly **rock** and **spoken word**. Released *Enemy Glory*, written and recorded by Point of Ares (rock); and *Of No Importance*, written and recorded by Karen Michalson (spoken word), both on Arula Records.

‡ASCENCION RECORDINGS, INC., P.O. Box 1406, Elizabeth City NC 27906. Phone/fax: (919)331-5898. E-mail: ascencion.recordings@internetmci.com. Producer: Cathy Pescevich. Distributed by Ave Maria Press, Bayside Distribution, Valley Record Distributors, Bassin Distributors, CD One Stop, Abbey Road and Spring Arbor Distributors. Record company and music publisher. Estab. 1995. Releases 2-4 CDs/year. Pays 18% royalty to artists on contract; statutory rate to publisher per song on record.
How to Contact: Write first and obtain permission to submit. Prefers cassette, CD or DAT with sheet music/manuscript. "Be prepared to provide background information on musical training, and on personal vision for composition." SASE. Reports in 2 months.
Music: Mostly **classical/solo**, **classical/ensemble** and **jazz**. Released *Bach in Brazil* and *Cathedral*, both recorded by Gordon Kreplin on Ascencion Records (classical guitar).
Tips: "We are most interested in presenting recordings of classical or jazz music for solo guitar, other solo instruments, or small ensemble (with and without voice). Of special interest to us is new music, as well as delightful new settings of existing works. We are particularly eager to see music inspired by sacred themes and places."

ASSOCIATED ARTISTS MUSIC INTERNATIONAL, Maarschalklaan 47, 3417 SE Montfoort, **The Netherlands**. Phone/fax: 31-3484-72860. Release Manager: Joop Gerrits. Labels include Associated Artists, Disco-Dance Records and Italo. Record company, music publisher (Hilversum Happy Music/BUMA-STEMRA, Intermedlodie/BUMA-STEMRA and Hollands Glorie Productions), record producer (Associated Artists Productions) and TV promotions. Estab. 1975. Releases 10 singles, 25 12" singles, 6 LPs and 6 CDs/year. Pays 14% royalty to artists on contract; variable amount to publishers.
How to Contact: Submit demo tape by mail. Unsolicited submissions OK. Prefers compact cassette, 19 cm/sec reel-to-reel or VHS videocassette with any number of songs and lyric or lead sheets. Records also accepted. SAE and IRC. Reports in 6 weeks.
Music: Mostly **dance**, **pop**, **house**, **hip hop** and **rock**. Released "La Luna" (by P. Prins), recorded by The

Ethics on Virgin Records (dance); *Freedom*, written and recorded by D.J. Bobo on ZYX Records (dance); and "Labia" (by P. Prins), recorded by Indica on M.M. Records (dance). Other artists include Clubhouse, Silvio Pozzoli, Eating Habits, D.S.K. and Mikko Mission.
Tips: "We invite producers and independent record labels to send us their material for their entry on the European market. Mark all parcels as 'no commercial value—for demonstration only.' We license productions to record companies in all countries of Europe and South Africa. Submit good demos or masters."

‡ASYLUM RECORDS NASHVILLE, 1906 Acklen Ave., Nashville TN 37212. (615)292-7990. Fax: (615)292-8219. Distributed by WEA; labels include 143 Records. Record company.
How to Contact: Asylum Records does not accept unsolicited material.
Music: Released *Between Now & Forever*, recorded by Bryan White; "Be Honest" (by A. Jordan/K. Shiver), recorded by Thrasher Shiver, both on Asylum Records; and *Measure of a Man*, recorded by Kevin Sharp on 143 Records.

‡ATLAN-DEC/GROOVELINE RECORDS, 2529 Green Forest Court, Snellville GA 30278. Phone/fax: (770)985-1686. E-mail: lyye71a@prodigy.com. Website: http://gemm.com/s.cgi/ATLANDEC. President: James Hatcher. Record company, music publisher and record producer. Estab. 1994. Releases 3-4 singles, 3-4 LPs and 3-4 CDs/year. Pays negotiable royalty to artists on contract; statutory rate to publisher per song on record.
How to Contact: Submit demo tape by mail. Unsolicited submissions are OK. Prefers cassette and lyric sheet. Does not return material. Reports in 2-3 months.
Music: Mostly **R&B/urban**, **hip hop/rap** and **contemporary jazz**; also **soft rock**, **gospel** and **dance**. Released *Ace On Top* (by D. Clark), recorded by BlackJack (jazz); and "Focus On You" (by P. Kirtley), recorded by Focus Minds (dance), both on Atlan-Dec Records.

ATLANTIC RECORDS, 75 Rockefeller Plaza, New York NY 10019. (212)707-2000. Fax: (212)275-2315. Los Angeles office: 9229 Sunset Blvd., Suite 900, Los Angeles CA 90069. (310)205-7450. Fax: (310)205-7475. E-mail: jillian_schwartz@wmg.com or chargzvisa@aol.com. Website: http://www.atlantic-records.com. Assistant to Senior Vice President Craig Kallman: Jillian Schwartz. Distributed by WEA; labels include Curb Records, Big Beat Records, Nonesuch Records, Atlantic Classics and Rhino Records. Record company. Pays negotiable royalty to artists on contract; negotiable rate to publisher per song on record.
How to Contact: Atlantic Records does not accept unsolicited material.
Music: Released *Pieces of You*, recorded by Jewel; *Now In A Minute*, recorded by Donna Lewis; and *Fairweather Johnson*, recorded by Hootie & the Blowfish, all on Atlantic Records. Other artists include 7 Mary 3, Everything But the Girl, Poe, Junior M.A.F.I.A., Quad City DJs, Lil' Kim, Stone Temple Pilots, Brandy, Tori Amos and John Michael Montgomery.

aUDIOFILE TAPES, 209-25 18th Ave., Bayside NY 11360. E-mail: litlgrey@ix.netcom.com. Website: http://www.cnct.com/~litlgrey. Sheriff, aT County: Carl Howard. Cassette-only label of alternative music. Estab. 1984. Produces about 25 cassettes/year. "Money is solely from sales. Some artists ask $1 per tape sold."
How to Contact: Write first and obtain permission to submit. Prefers cassette. "Relevant artist information is nice. Master copies accepted on hi-bias or metal analog tape, or DAT." SASE. Reports in 3-6 weeks.
Music: Mostly **psych/electronic rock**, **non-rock electronic music** and **progressive rock**; also **free jazz** and **world music**. Released *Pastry With A Half Life*, written and recorded by Pastry With A Half Life (improvisational); *The Echoing Grove*, written and recorded by Alphane Moon (electronic/psychedelic); and *One Day In Golden Week*, written and recorded by Emil Hagstrom and Brian Lavelle (improvised mail collaboration), all on audiofile Tapes. Other artists include The Conspiracy, The Venus Fly Trap, Sphinx, Luster, Dachise, Bruce Atchinson and Blowhole.
Tips: "Please, no industrial music, no deliberately shocking images of racism and sexual brutality. And no New Age sleeping pills. Unfortunately, we are not in a position to help the careers of aspirant pop idols. Only true devotees *really* need apply. I mean it—money does not exist here. No artist has ever been under contract; this is real underground informal stuff."

‡AVALANCHE RECORDS, 12000 W. Pico Blvd., Suite 201, Los Angeles CA 90064. (310)477-4645. (310)477-5756. E-mail: avalanche@bonaire.com. Website: http://www.bonaire.com. Contact: A&R Dept. Distributed by Navarre Corp. (USA) and Distribution Fusion III (Canada); labels include Bonaire Records. Estab. 1993. Releases 5-9 CDs/year. Pays negotiable royalty to artists on contract; negotiable rate to publisher per song on record.
How to Contact: Write or e-mail first and obtain permission to submit. Prefers cassette or CD with a

few songs and lyric sheet. "Send professional packages with bio and photo if possible." SASE. Response time depends upon release schedule.
Music: Mostly **rock**, **alternative** and **world**; also **dance**. Released *High Centered*, written and recorded by Doug Aldrich (instrumental rock); *Gasoline*, written and recorded by Noodle House (alternative); and *This Way Up*, written and recorded by Chris DeBurgh (adult alternative), all on Avalanche Records.

‡AVENUE COMMUNICATIONS, P.O. Box 1432, Menlo Park CA 94026-1432. (415)321-8291. Fax: (415)321-7491. Website: http://www.5avenue.com. Vice President: Erik Nielsen. Distributed by CRD, Valley, Bayside and CD One-Stop. Record company. Estab. 1989. Releases 5 singles and 3 CDs/year. Pays negotiable royalty to artists on contract; statutory rate to publisher per song on record.
How to Contact: Submit demo tape by mail. Unsolicited submissions are OK. Prefers cassette, CD, DAT or VHS videocassette. Does not return material. Reports "next day if we like it."
Music: Mostly **adult**, **rock**, **pop**, **roots** and **R&B**; also **zydeco**, **reggae** and **world**. Released "Got the Whole Night," recorded by Denny Brown.

AZRA INTERNATIONAL, P.O. Box 459, Maywood CA 90270. (213)560-4223. A&R: Jeff Simins. Distributed by Vintage and Abnormal Media; labels include World Metal, Metal Storm, Iron Works, Not So Famous David's Records and Masque Records. Record company. Estab. 1978. Releases 10 singles, 5 LPs, 5 EPs and 5 CDs/year. "Artists usually carry their own publishing." Pays 10% royalty to artists on contract; statutory rate to publisher per song on record.
How to Contact: Submit demo tape by mail. Unsolicited submissions are OK. Prefers cassette or VHS videocassette with 3-5 songs and lyric sheet. Include bio and photo. SASE. Reports in 2 weeks.
Music: Mostly **rock**, **heavy metal** and **New Age**; also **novelty**. Released "Hey Little Boy" (by Stan Demski), recorded by Stan the Man (novelty); *Breakfast Is Served*, written and recorded by various artists (novelty), both on NSFD Records; and *Behind Closed Doors* (by Curtis Connor), recorded by Bondage Dunkers (techno) on Masque Records. Other artists include J. Kurt Iverson, Fuzzy Logic, 3-B Assylum, Toe Suck and Gothic Swank.

BABY FAZE RECORDS & TAPES, 45 Pearl St., San Francisco CA 94103. (415)495-5312. Big Cheese: g. miller marlin. Distributed by MARS Distributors and Music Web; labels include Dog Bite Records (singles-only label) and Sound Waves (So Wave Back). Record company and record producer (g. miller marlin, David S. Willers). Estab. 1989. Releases 20 singles and 10 cassettes/year
How to Contact: Submit demo tape by mail. Unsolicited submissions are OK. Prefers cassette or VHS videocassette. "We encourage submissions of all types and genres of music." Does not return material. Reports in 3 months.
Music: Mostly **alternative**, **industrial** and **rock**; also **rap**, **pop** and **R&B funk**. Released *King Size Size Queen* (by g. miller marlin), recorded by Cat Howdy (industrial); *Over Eight Grams* (by S. Fievet), recorded by LMNOP; and *Choice Cuts* (by Kenyata Sullivan), recorded by Pandora's Lunch Box (alternative), all on Baby Faze Records. Other artists include Eric Mars, Secret Team, Everybody's Famous, Threnody, Into Decline, Broken Toys and God's Favorite.
Tips: "Submit anything with a short release, intent letter or note, and if used in the future, we'll be in touch—so don't forget to include a contact name and address with all submissions (photos and band bios are also helpful)."

babysue, P.O. Box 8989, Atlanta GA 30306. (404)875-8951. E-mail: babysue@babysue.com. Website: http://www.babysue.com. President/Owner: Don W. Seven. Distributed by Not Lame Distribution. Record company, management firm. Estab. 1983. Releases 2 singles, 5 LPs, 2 EPs and 7 CDs/year. Pays 5-20% royalty to artists on contract; varying royalty to publisher per song on record.

- babysue also has a listing in the Managers and Booking Agents section.

How to Contact: Submit demo tape by mail. Unsolicited submissions are OK. Prefers cassette with any number of songs. Does not return material. "We only report back if we are interested in the artist or act."
Music: Mostly **rock**, **pop** and **gospel**; also **heavy metal**, **punk** and **classical**. Released *Pound*, written and recorded by LMNOP (rock); and *Hairy and Bossy* (by M. Lake), recorded by The Daddy, all on babysue records. Other artists include the Mushcakes, The Shoestrings and The Mommy.
Tips: "Send us cash (just kidding). Actually, we're just into sincere, good stuff."

BAGATELLE RECORD COMPANY, P.O. Box 925929, Houston TX 77292. President: Byron Benton. Record company, record producer and music publisher (Bagatelle Music, Floyd Tillman Music Co.). Releases 20 singles and 10 LPs/year. Pays negotiable royalty to artists on contract.

- See the listing for Bagatelle Music in the Music Publishers section.

How to Contact: Submit demo tape by mail. Prefers cassette and lyric sheet. SASE. Reports in 2 weeks.

Music: Mostly **country**; also **gospel**. Released "This is Real," by Floyd Tillman (country); "Lucille," by Sherri Jerrico (country); and "Everything You Touch," by Johnny Nelms (country). Other artists include Jerry Irby, Bobby Beason, Bobby Burton, Donna Hazard, Danny Brown, Sonny Hall, Ben Gabus, Jimmy Copeland and Johnny B. Goode.

BANDIT RECORDS, P.O. Box 111480, Nashville TN 37222. (615)331-1219. President: Loman Craig. Vice President: Tommy Hendrick. Labels include HIS Records (gospel). Record company and record producer (Loman Craig Productions). Estab. 1979. Releases 5 singles and 2 LPs/year. Pays statutory rate to publisher per song on record. "There is a charge for demo and custom sessions."
How to Contact: Submit demo tape by mail. Unsolicited submissions are OK. Prefers cassette with 2-3 songs and lyric sheet. SASE. Reports in 4-6 weeks.
Music: Mostly **country**, **ballads** and **gospel**. Released *One and the Same* (by Loman Craig/Tommy Hendrick) and *Cross My Heart* (by Chad Allen), both recorded by Loman Craig on Bandit Records; and *Conviction* (by Justin Sullivan), recorded by Mt. Zion Singers on HIS Records.
Tips: "Send a clear sounding demo and readable lyric sheets. Since we are a small independent record label, we do have to charge for services rendered."

BASSET HOUND PRODUCTIONS, 527 N. Azuza Ave. #280, Covina CA 91722. (818)453-1825. Producer/A&R Rep: Sean Hutch. Distributed by Azra International. Record company, music publisher (Basset Hound Publishing), record producer (Sean Hutch) and booking agency. Estab. 1995. Pays standard royalty.
How to Contact: Submit demo tape by mail. Unsolicited submissions are OK. Prefers cassette or CD, bio, résumé and picture with lyric and lead sheets. SASE. Reports in 2-3 weeks.
Music: Mostly **alternative rock, techno** and **industrial**; also **hard rock, gothic** and **dance**. Released *Torso*, written and recorded by Torso on Ironworks Records (industrial/techno); *Erotic Neurotic*, written and recorded by Crystal Breeze; and *The Struggle*, written and recorded by Sean Hutch, both on Basset Records (techno).

‡**BELUGA RECORDS**, P.O. Box 146751, Chicago IL 60614-6751. Website: http://www.bomis.com/beluga. Mastermind: Scott Beluga. Distributed by Cargo, Carrot Top and Choke. Record company. Estab. 1994. Releases 1-3 singles, 1-2 EPs and 2-6 CDs/year. Pays negotiable royalty to artists on contract; statutory rate to publisher per song on record.
How to Contact: Submit demo tape by mail. Unsolicited submissions are OK. Prefers cassette or CD. "Please don't call. Send SASE if you want materials returned." Reports in 3-9 months.
Music: Mostly **indie pop**, **indie rock** and **derivatives thereof**. Released *Landscapes*, recorded by the Velmas (pop); "$28,000", recorded by Jaws of Life (garage rock); and *Beluga . . . On the Rocks* (by various), a double CD compilation (pop/rock), all on Beluga Records. Other artists include Zipperhead and Today's My Super Spaceout Day.

BERANDOL MUSIC, 2600 John St., Unit 220, Markham, Ontario L3R 3W3 **Canada**. (905)475-1848. A&R: Ralph Cruickshank. Record company, music publisher (Berandol Music/SOCAN). Estab. 1947. Pays 10% royalty to artists on contract; statutory rate to publisher per song on record.
- Berandol Music is also listed in the Music Publishers section.

How to Contact: Submit demo tape by mail. Unsolicited submissions are OK. Prefers cassette with 4 songs. Does not return material. Reports in 3 weeks.
Music: Mostly **instrumental**, **children's** and **CHR (top 40)**.

BIG BEAR RECORDS, Box 944, Birmingham, B16 8UT, **United Kingdom**. Phone: 44-021-454-7020. Fax: 44-021-454-9996. A&R Director: Jim Simpson. Labels include Truckers Delight and Grandstand Records. Record company, record producer and music publisher (Bearsongs). Releases 6 LPs/year. Pays 8-10% royalty to artists on contract; 8¼% to publishers for each record sold. Royalties paid directly to songwriters and artists or through US publishing or recording affiliate.
- Big Bear's publishing affiliate, Bearsongs, is listed in the Music Publishers section, and Big Bear is listed in the Record Producers section.

How to Contact: Submit demo tape by mail. Unsolicited submissions are OK. Prefers 7½ or 15 ips reel-to-reel, DAT, cassette or videocassette and lyric sheet. Does not return material. Reports in 3 weeks.
Music: Blues and **jazz**. Released *I've Finished with the Blues* and *Blues for Pleasure* (by Skirving/Nicholls), both recorded by King Pleasure and the Biscuit Boys (jazz); and *Side-Steppin'* (by Barnes), recorded by Alan Barnes/Bruce Adams Quintet (jazz), all on Big Bear Records. Other artists include Lady Sings the Blues, Bill Allred and Kenny Baker's Dozen.

‡BIG BEAT RECORDS, 9229 Sunset Blvd., Suite 401, Los Angeles CA 90069. (310)205-7450. Fax: (310)205-5721. Contact: Mike Caren. Distributed by WEA; labels include Undeas Records and Quadrasound Records.

How to Contact: Submit demo tape by mail. Unsolicited submissions are OK. Prefers cassette, CD or DAT with bio and photo.

Music: Released *Hard Core*, recorded by Lil' Kim on Undeas Records; and *Get On Up and Dance*, recorded by Quad City DJs on Quadrasound Records.

BIG ROCK PTY. LTD., P.O. Box 273, Dulwich Hill, NSW 2203 **Australia**. Phone: (02)5692152. A&R Manager: Chris Turner. Distributed by Shock Records. Record company, music publisher (A.P.R.A.), management firm (Phill Shute Management Pty. Ltd.) and record producer (Big Rock P/L). Estab. 1979. Releases 5 singles and 10 CDs/year. Pays 5% royalty to artists on contract.

- See the listing for Phill Shute Management Pty. Ltd. in the Managers and Booking Agents section.

How to Contact: Write first and obtain permission to submit. Prefers cassette with 6 songs and lyric sheet. SAE and IRC. Reports in 2 months.

Music: Mostly **rock**, **R&B** and **pop**. Released *The Sweetest Thing* (by various), recorded by Stacy Morris (country); *Skybrain Surfing*, written and recorded by Adam Carl Stephens (rock guitar); and *Live* (by various), recorded by The Zips, all on Big Rock Records (covers). Other artists include Collage, Chris Turner, Phill Simmons, Cora Brandjes, Rick Veneer and Alan Blackburn.

‡BIG WHIG PRODUCTIONS, 442 Mesquite, Boise ID 83713. (208)327-0758. A&R Representative: Bryan Lass. Record company. Estab. 1992. Releases 3 singles and 2 CDs/year. Pays negotiable royalty to artists on contract; statutory rate to publisher per song on record.

How to Contact: Call first and obtain permission to submit. Prefers cassette or CD with 4 songs and lyric sheet. "Enclose any information regarding recent radio airtime and album sales if available." Does not return material. Reports in 2-6 weeks.

Music: Mostly **pop/top 40**, **contemporary** and **country**; also **gospel**, **folk** and **rock**. Released *Aviator of Love* and *Bang Bang* (by Jim Cochelle), both recorded by Trans Atlantic Crush on Screamin Fez Records (pop); and "Digital Madness" (by Bryan Lass), recorded by Hyperdigits on Big Whig Records (alternative).

‡BIONIC RECORDS, INC., P.O. Box 464, Mt. Freedom NJ 07970. Phone/fax: (201)927-5097. A&R: Jack Steele. Record company. Estab. 1995. Releases 5 singles, 5 EPs and 3 CDs/year. Pays negotiable royalty to artists on contract.

How to Contact: Submit demo tape by mail. Unsolicited submissions are OK. Prefers cassette. "Put your name and number on everything!" Does not return material.

Music: Mostly **techno**, **house** and **break beat**. Released *Acid Reflux*, *Cybertronic Technomatic* and "Eye Master," all recorded by Mind Collide on Bionic Records (techno). Other artists include Nanu and Cerebral Cortex.

Tips: "Put your name and phone number on every item you send out. For example: cassette, j-card, photo, bio, lyric sheet, etc. Target your mailings. We specialize in club music, therefore, sending us heavy metal/alternative would only be throwing your money away."

BLACK DIAMOND RECORDS INC., P.O. Box 8073, Pittsburg CA 94565. (510)980-0893. Fax: (510)432-4342. President: Jerry "J." Vice President: Joe Brown. Distributed by Bellmark/Life Records and Sony Distribution; labels include "In The House" Records, Hittin' Hard Records, Flash Point Records, Stay Down Records and Jairus Records. Record company, music publisher, management firm (It's Happening Present Entertainment) and record producer (Bobelli Productions, In The House Productions). Estab. 1988. Pays 8-14% royalty to artists on contract; statutory rate to publisher per song on record.

- See the listing for Its Happening Present Entertainment in the Managers and Booking Agents section.

How to Contact: Write or call first and obtain permission to submit. Prefers cassette with 2-4 songs, photo and lyric sheet. Does not return material. Reports in 6 months.

Music: Mostly **R&B**, **hip hop**, **country/jazz** and **hip hop rap**; also **jazz**, **blues** and **rock**. Released *Just For Your Love* (by Kapp/Rachael), recorded by Family Unit; "April Fool" (by various), recorded by Special Request; and "So Some Love," written and recorded by World One & Only, all on Black Diamond Records.

‡BLUE DUCK!! RECORDS, P.O. Box 10247, Pittsburgh PA 15232. (412)261-9050. Fax: (412)261-4414. E-mail: breefree@earthlink.net. Marketing & Distribution: Bree Freeman. A&R: Meg Siegel. Publicity & Promotions: Lovinda Weaver. Distributed by Com-Four, Oar Fin, NRM, Camelot and Galaxy; labels include Anthem Records U.S.A. and Blue Swan Records. Record company. Estab. 1992. Releases 5 singles and 6 CDs/year. Pays 15-25% royalty to artists on contract; statutory rate to publisher per song on record (depends on deal).

● Blue Duck!! Records was recently voted Best Local Record Label by the *Pittsburgh City Paper.*

How to Contact: Submit demo tape by mail. Unsolicited submissions are OK. Prefers cassette with 2-3 songs. "Keep it short." Does not return material. Reports in 5 weeks.

Music: Mostly **alternative**, **rock** and **world beat**; also **reggae** and **progressive rock-pop**. Released *Cruel Sun*, written and recorded by Rusted Root (world rock); *Paddy's New Bag*, written and recorded by Ploughman's Lunch (ska); and *Swan Songs*, written and recorded by various artists (AAA), all on Blue Duck!! Records. Other artists include The Means, Rasta Rafiki, Slack Jaw, Rachel McCartney, Nixon Clocks and Kama Sutra.

Tips: "No metal, no hype. If you've been together two years, have sold a couple hundred units on your own, and can draw 150 to 300 people in two or three markets on your name . . . you're ready to contact us."

‡BLUE EYED KITTY PRODUCTIONS, P.O. Box 189, Olancha CA 93549. Contact: Marty Elliott. Record company and music publisher. Estab. 1985. Releases 12 singles, 6 LPs and 6 CDs/year. Pays negotiable royalty to artists on contract; statutory rate to publisher per song on record.

How to Contact: Submit demo tape by mail. Unsolicited submissions are OK. Prefers cassette, DAT, videocassette (VHS) or DCC with any number of songs and lyric sheet. SASE. Reports in 2 weeks.

Music: Mostly **eclectic rock**, **alternative rock** and **punk**; also **classical rock**, **instrumental** and **"space" music**. Released *Earth is Calling*, written and recorded by Carol Elliott (eclectic rock); "Gestapo!" (by Cranky Franky), recorded by Red Dog (eclectic punk); and *Days of Hard Life*, written and recorded by Carol Suzanne (eclectic rock), all on Blue Eyed Kitty Productions. Other artists include Raunchy Knuckles.

Tips: "Do not copy others. We are looking for fresh, new artists, capable of their own sound. We don't care about the 'current' sound or current ideas about what's 'correct.' There is no 'correct' music! Play how you feel inside—that's always the best way to produce and write a song. Try to express your feelings with your music. If it sounds good to you, then it's good! Record your demos to the best of your ability and equipment available to you. Good luck!"

BLUE GEM RECORDS, P.O. Box 29550, Hollywood CA 90029. (213)664-7765. Contact: Pete Martin. Record company, music publisher (Vaam Music Group) and record producer (Pete Martin/Vaam Productions). Estab. 1981. Pays 6-15% royalty to artists on contract; statutory rate to publisher per song on record.

● See the listings for Pete Martin/Vaam Productions in the Record Producers section and Vaam Music Group in the Music Publishers section.

How to Contact: Submit demo tape by mail. Unsolicited submissions are OK. Prefers cassette with 2 songs. SASE. Reports in 3 weeks.

Music: Mostly **country** and **R&B**; also **pop/top 40** and **rock**. Released "The Greener Years," written and recorded by Frank Loren (country); "It's a Matter of Loving You" (by Brian Smith), recorded by Brian Smith & The Renegades (country); and "Two Different Women" (by Frank Loren and Greg Connor), recorded by Frank Loren (country), all on Blue Gem Records. Other artists include Sherry Weston (country).

BLUE WAVE, 3221 Perryville Rd., Baldwinsville NY 13027. (315)638-4286. President/Producer: Greg Spencer. Distributed by MS Distribution, Select-O-Hits, United and Valley; labels include Blue Wave/Horizon. Record company, music publisher (G.W. Spencer Music/ASCAP) and record producer (Blue Wave Productions). Estab. 1985. Releases 3 LPs and 3 CDs/year. Royalty to artists on contract varies; pays statutory rate to publisher per song on record.

How to Contact: Submit demo tape by mail. Unsolicited submissions are OK. Prefers cassette or videocassette (live performance only) and as many songs as you like. SASE. "We contact only if we are interested." Reports in 6 weeks.

Music: Mostly **blues/blues rock**, **roots rock** and **roots R&B/soul**; also **roots country/rockabilly** or **anything with "soul."** Released *You Burned Me* (by Matt Tarbell), recorded by Built For Comfort; *A Fool No More* (by Peter Green), recorded by Kim Lembo; and *Bad Morning*, written and recorded by Kim Simmonds, all on Blue Wave Records. Other artists include Backbone Slip and Downchild Bluesband.

BMX ENTERTAINMENT, P.O. Box 10857, Stamford CT 06904. (203)969-1071. Fax: (203)357-1676. President: Mauris Gryphon. Labels include Red Tape Records. Record company. Estab. 1984. Releases 7 singles, 7 12″ singles, 7 LPs, 7 EPs and 7 CDs/year. Pays 10-12% royalty to artists on contract.

How to Contact: Submit demo tape by mail. Unsolicited submissions are OK. Prefers cassette or VHS videocassette with 4 songs. "Send résumé, photo, management arrangements, if any." SASE. Reports in 2 weeks.

Music: Mostly **country**, **R&B** and **rock**; also **rap**, **pop**, **jazz** and **salsa**. Released "You & I," written and recorded by Edwin Rivera (ballad); "Hot As Fire," written and recorded by Damm Samm (rock); and

"Tick Tica Tock," written and recorded by Tic Tock (reggae), all on BMX Entertainment. Other artists include K. Nice, Head Banger, Singles, Donald Murray and Tom Adams.

BNA RECORDS, 1 Music Circle N., Nashville TN 37203. (615)313-4300. Fax: (615)313-4303. A&R Director: Reese Faw. Record company. Estab. 1990. Pays standard royalty to artists on contract; statutory rate to publisher per song on record.
How to Contact: Call first and obtain permission to submit. Prefers cassette or videocassette with 2 songs and lyric sheet. "We prefer that writers submit via a publisher." Refuses unsolicited submissions. Reply time "depends on the project."
Music: Mostly **country**. Artists include Mindy McCready, Kentucky Headhunters, K.T. Oslin, Ray Vega, Jason Sellers, Kenny Chesney, Lonestar and Lorrie Morgan.
Tips: "Put together a presentable package and showcase."

BODARC PRODUCTIONS, 4225 N. Hall St., Dallas TX 75219. (214)526-1062. Fax: (214)526-0223. Producer: Robert Weigel. Record company. Estab. 1980. Releases 5-6 LPs and 5-6 CDs/year. Pays negotiable royalty to artist on contract; statutory rate to publisher per song on record.
How to Contact: Submit demo tape by mail. Unsolicited submissions are OK. Prefers cassette. Does not return material. Reports in 3 months.
Music: Mostly **modern/disco**, **aerobics jazz** and **ballroom dancing**; also **children's songs** and **non-lyric**. Released *Joy of Ballet*, recorded by Lynn Stanford; *Tap With a Talent* and *Critters and Countries*, both recorded by Steven Mitchell, all on Bodarc Productions.
Tips: "We need music for dance classes—ballet, tap, jazz, ballroom, without lyrics."

BOLD 1 RECORDS, 2124 Darby Dr., Massillon OH 44646. (330)833-2061. A&R Dept.: Nick Boldi. Record company, record producer and music publisher (Bolnik Music/BMI). Estab. 1986. Releases 2 CDs/year. Pays 6% royalty on net to artists on contract; statutory rate to publisher per song on record.
How to Contact: Submit demo tape by mail. Unsolicited submissions are OK. Prefers cassette with 4 songs and lyric sheet. Does not return material. Reports in 10 weeks.
Music: Mostly **new country**, **rockabilly** and **ballads**. "We are not interested in rap, jazz, blues or heavy metal." Released "Bucken Bull Inn" and "Needa Needa," recorded by Kody Stormn (country); and "Who Do You Want Me To Be" (by Joey Welz/Lou Mishiff), recorded by Joey Welz (rockabilly).

BOLIVIA RECORDS, 1219 Kerlin Ave., Brewton AL 36426. (205)867-2228. President: Roy Edwards. Labels include Known Artist Records. Record company, record producer (Known Artist Productions) and music publisher (Cheavoria Music Co.). Estab. 1972. Releases 10 singles and 3 LPs/year. Pays 5% royalty to artists on contract; statutory rate to publishers for each record sold.

- Bolivia Records' publishing company, Cheavoria Music, is listed in the Music Publishers section and Known Artist Productions is listed in the Record Producers section.

How to Contact: Submit demo tape by mail. Unsolicited submissions are OK. Prefers cassette with 3 songs and lyric sheet. SASE for reply. All tapes will be kept on file. Reports in 1 month.
Music: Mostly **R&B**, **country** and **pop**; also **easy listening**, **MOR** and **soul**. Released "If You Only Knew" (by Horace Linsky), recorded by Roy Edwards; "Make Me Forget" (by Horace Linsky), recorded by Bobbie Roberson, both on Bolivia Records; and "We Make Our Reality," written and recorded by Brad Smiley on Known Artist Records. Other artists include Jim Portwood.

BOOGIE BAND RECORDS, 6245 Bristol Pkwy., Suite 206, Culver City CA 90230. Contact: Larry McGee. Distributed by New World Distribution; labels include Classic Records and Mega-Star Records. Record company, music publisher (Operation Perfection Publishing), record producer (Intrigue Productions) and management firm (LMP Management). Estab. 1976. Releases 6 singles, 3 12" singles, 1 LP, 4 EPs and 2 CDs/year. Pays 10% royalty to artists on contract; statutory rate to publishers per song on record.

- Boogie Band's publishing company, Operation Perfection, is listed in the Music Publishers section; their management firm, LMP Management, is in the Managers and Booking Agents section; and Intrigue Productions is listed in the Record Producers section.

How to Contact: Submit demo tape by mail. Unsolicited submissions are OK. Prefers cassette with 1-

● **A BULLET** introduces comments by the editor of *Songwriter's Market* indicating special information about the listing.

4 songs and lyric sheet. SASE. Reports in 2 months. "Please only send professional quality material."
Music: Urban contemporary, dance, rock, MOR/A/C, pop, rap and **R&B**. Released *Starflower* (by Joe Caccamise), recorded by Star Flower on Boogie Band Records (A/C); *Too Tough* (by Terrence Jones), recorded by En-Tux (pop); and *Got It Goin' On* (by Alan Walker), recorded by Executives, both on Mega-Star Records. Other artists include Wali Ali, A. Vis and Denise Parker.

BOUQUET RECORDS, Bouquet-Orchid Enterprises, P.O. Box 1335, Norcross GA 30091. (770)497-9086. President: Bill Bohannon. Record company, music publisher (Orchid Publishing/BMI), record producer (Bouquet-Orchid Enterprises) and management firm (Bouquet-Orchid Enterprises). Releases 3-4 singles and 2 LPs/year. Pays 5-8% royalty to artists on contract; pays statutory rate to publishers for each record sold.

- Bouquet Records' publishing company, Orchid Publishing, is listed in the Music Publishers section and Bouquet-Orchid Enterprises is in the Managers and Booking Agents section.

How to Contact: Submit demo tape by mail. Unsolicited submissions are OK. Prefers cassette with 3-5 songs and lyric sheet. SASE. Reports in 1 month.
Music: Mostly **religious** (contemporary or country-gospel, Amy Grant, etc.), **country** ("the type suitable for Clint Black, George Strait, Patty Loveless, etc.") and **Top 100** ("the type suitable for Billy Joel, Whitney Houston, R.E.M., etc."); also **rock** and **MOR**. Released *Blue As Your Eyes* (by Bill Bohannon), recorded by Adam Day (country); *Take Care of My World* (by Bob Freeman), recorded by Bandoleers (top 40); and *Making Plans* (by John Harris), recorded by Susan Spencer (country), all on Bouquet Records.
Tips: "Submit 3-5 songs on a cassette tape with lyric sheets. Include a short biography and perhaps a photo. Enclose SASE."

BRIARHILL RECORDS, 3484 Nicolette Dr., Crete IL 60417. (708)672-6457. A&R Director: Danny Mack. Record company, music publisher (Danny Mack Music, Syntony Publishing/BMI) and record producer (The Danny Mack Music Group). Estab. 1983. Releases 3-4 singles, 1 LP, 2 EPs and 1 CD/year. Pays negotiable royalty to artists on contract; statutory rate to publisher per song on record.

- Briarhill's publishing company, Danny Mack Music, is listed in the Music Publishers section.

How to Contact: Submit demo tape by mail. Unsolicited submissions are OK. Prefers cassette with 3 songs and lyric sheet. SASE. Reports in 4-5 weeks.
Music: Mostly **country, novelty** and **polka**; also **southern gospel** and **Christmas**. Released *Somewhere East of Eden* (by Ed Godleski), recorded by Helen Arbour; "The Ballad of Paul Bunyan" (by Joe Pickering Jr.), recorded by Danny Mack; and "Don't Call 911" (by Jerry Holsey), recorded by Steve Patrick, all on Briarhill Records.
Tips: "Be patient and don't expect others to invest financially to support your career goals. It's unrealistic."

BROKEN RECORDS INTERNATIONAL, 305 S. Westmore Ave., Lombard IL 60148. (630)916-6874. E-mail: 756630.0544@compuserve.com. International A&R: Roy Bocchieri. Record company. Estab. 1984. Payment negotiable.
How to Contact: Submit demo tape by mail. Unsolicited submissions are OK. Prefers cassette, CD or VHS videocassette with at least 2 songs and lyric sheet. Does not return material. Reports in 8 weeks.
Music: Mostly **rock, pop** and **dance**; also **acoustic** and **industrial**. Released *Electric*, written and recorded by LeRoy (pop); and *Hallowed Ground*, written and recorded by Day One (alternative), both on Broken Records.

BSW RECORDS, P.O. Box 2297, Universal City TX 78148. (210)599-0022. Fax: (210)653-3989. President: Frank Willson. Record company, music publisher (BSW Records/BMI), management firm (Universal Music Marketing) and record producer (Frank Willson). Estab. 1987. Releases 12 albums/year. Pays standard royalty to artists on contract; statutory rate to publisher per song on record.

- BSW's president, Frank Willson, is listed in the Record Producers section and their managment firm, Universal Music Marketing, is listed in the Managers and Booking Agents section.

How to Contact: Submit demo tape by mail. Unsolicited submissions are OK. Prefers cassette or ¾" videocassette with 3 songs and lyric sheet. SASE. Reports in 5 weeks.
Music: Mostly **country, rock** and **blues**. Released *If You Ever Leave Me*, written and recorded by Peter Caulton; *Horizontal Two-Step*, written and recorded by Davis Buescher; and *Love 101* (by Jerry Dougherty), recorded by Matters of Heart, all on BSW Records. Other artists include Candee Land, Patty David, Wes Wiginton, Shawn DeLorme, Maria Rose, Bob Jares and Celeste.

‡BUZZ FACTORY RECORDS, 61-36 160th St., Flushing NY 11365. (718)445-2302. E-mail: bzzfactory@aol.com. Co-Presidents: John Gallo/Linda La Porte. Distributed by Dutch East India and Dream Disc; labels include Psycho-Pop Records and Anti-Verve Music. Record company. Estab. 1993. Releases 1-3 singles and 1-3 CDs/year. Pays negotiable royalty to artists on contract; negotiable rate to publisher per song on record.

How to Contact: Submit demo tape by mail. Unsolicited submissions are OK. Prefers cassette with 3 songs. "Make sure there is a contact address! We can't stress this enough!!" Does not return material. Reports in 4-6 months.

Music: "We are looking for **HARD music**, whether it be Death, Hardcore, Thrash, Alternative, Industrial or Techno. We are receiving way too many submissions that fall far outside our scope. Please, if you do not fall within the scope mentioned above, please do not send your material." Released *Earthworm* (by Linda La Porte/Joe Heller), recorded by Killing June on Buzz Factory Records; and *Something Happened* (by Charles Caracciolo/John Gallo/Carol Caracciolo), recorded by Third Eye Butterfly on Psycho-Pop Records. Other artists include Gossamer, Deadlyne, Space Christ and Nail.

Tips: "We are really swamped with submissions. Please, if you do not fall within the scope mentioned above, please refrain from submitting your demos. We have gone through at least 400-500 submissions in 1996 and about a half a percent were within the label's scope. For those who do submit, a cassette of three songs is sufficient, whether it be 4-track or 48-track. We just want to get an idea about what your band is doing. We are a small independent label with a very small staff so we ask all those who submit music to us to be patient. We are still going through last year's submissions. We have a compilation project in the works so send those demos!"

C.E.G. RECORDS, INC., 102 E. Pikes Peak Ave. #200, Colorado Springs CO 80903. (719)632-0227. Fax: (719)634-2274. President: Robert A. Case. Record company and music publisher (New Pants Publishing/ASCAP, Old Pants Publishing/BMI). Estab. 1989. Releases 3-4 LPs and 3-4 CDs/year. Pays negotiable royalty to artists on contract.

How to Contact: Submit demo tape by mail. Unsolicited submissions are OK. Prefers cassette with 3-5 songs and lyric sheet. "Include a brief history of songwriter's career. Songs submitted must be copywritten or pending with copyright office." Does not return material. Reports in 3-4 months.

Music: Mostly **pop**, **rock** and **country**. Released *Sound of the Rain* and *Silence*, written and recorded by Silence; *Like No One Else*, written and recorded by Lisa Bigwood; and *Cross Roads*, written and recorded by C. Lee Clark, all on C.E.G. Records.

Tips: "Think of the music business as a job interview. You must be able to sell yourself and the music is your baby. You have to be strong and not deal with rejection as a personal thing. It is not a rejection of you, it's a rejection of the music. Most songwriters don't know how to communicate with labels. The best way is to start a friendship with people at the label."

CAMBRIA RECORDS & PUBLISHING, P.O. Box 374, Lomita CA 90717. (310)831-1322. Fax: (310)833-7442. Director of Recording Operations: Lance Bowling. Labels include Charade Records. Record company and music publisher. Estab. 1979. Pays 5-8% royalty to artists on contract; statutory rate to publisher for each record sold.

How to Contact: Write first and obtain permission to submit. Prefers cassette. SASE. Reports in 2 months.

Music: Mostly **classical**. Released *Songs of Elinor Remick Warren* on Cambria Records. Other artists include Marie Gibson (soprano), Mischa Leftkowitz (violin), Leigh Kaplan (piano), North Wind Quintet and Sierra Wind Quintet.

‡CANTILENA RECORDS, 972 4th Ave., Sacramento CA 95818. (916)441-6421. Website: http://members.aol.com/ufonia/zucker.html. A&R: Laurel Zucker. Record company. Estab. 1993. Releases 5 CDs/year. Pays negotiable royalty to artists on contract; statutory rate to publishers per song on record.

How to Contact: Write first and obtain permission to submit or to arrange personal interview. Prefers cassette. Does not return material.

Music: Mostly **classical**. Released *Poetic Justice* (by Davis Lynn), recorded by Poetic Justice (rock); *Laurel Zucker, Virtuoso Flutist* (by various), recorded by Laurel Zucker and Robin Sutherland (classical); and *Laurel Zucker, An American Flute Recital* (by various), recorded by Laurel Zucker and Marc Shapiro (classical), all on Cantilena Records. Other artists include Tim Gorman, Prairie Prince, Dave Margen, Israel Philharmonic, Erkel Chamber Orchestra, Samuel Magill and Renee Siebert.

CANYON RECORDS AND INDIAN ARTS, 4143 N. 16th St., Suite 1, Phoenix AZ 85016. (602)266-4823. Owner: Bob Nuss. Labels include Indian House and Indian Sounds. Record company and distributor of American Indian recordings. Estab. 1984. Releases 50 cassettes and 20 CDs/year. Royalty varies with project.

- Note that Canyon Records is a very specialized label, and only wants to receive submissions by Native American artists.

How to Contact: Write or call first and obtain permission to submit. Prefers cassette or VHS videocas-

sette. SASE. Reports in 2 months.
Music: Music by American Indians—any style (must be enrolled tribal members). Released *Islands of Bows*, written and recorded by R. Carlos Nakai (Native flute); *Southern Scratch Vol. 3*, written and recorded by Ron Joaquim and Southern Scratch (polkas), both on Canyon Records; and *Tewa Indian Women's Choir of San Juan Pueblo* (traditional), on Indian House Records. Other artists include Black Lodge Singers, John Rainer, Tree Cody and Joanne Shenandoah.
Tips: "We deal only with American Indian performers. We do not accept material from others. Please include tribal affiliation. *No* New Age 'Indian style' material."

CAPITOL RECORDS, 1750 N. Vine St., Hollywood CA 90028-5274. (213)462-6252. New York office: 1290 Avenue of the Americas, New York NY 10104. (212)492-5300. Website: http://www.hollywoodandvine.com. Distributed by EMD; labels include Blue Note Records, Grand Royal Records, Pangaea Records, Matador Records, The Right Stuff Records and Capitol Nashville Records. Record company.
How to Contact: Capitol Records does not accept unsolicited submissions.
Music: Released *Romeo & Juliet*, recorded by various artists (soundtrack); *Trainspotting*, recorded by various artists (soundtrack); and *Losing Streak*, recorded by Less Than Jake, all on Capitol Records. Other artists include Dave Koz and Richard Marx.

‡CAPRICORN RECORDS, 2205 State St., Nashville TN 37203. (615)320-8470. Fax: (615)320-8476. Atlanta office: 450 14th St. NW, Atlanta GA 30318. (404)873-3918. Fax: (404)874-2204. Website: http://www.capri.corn.com. Vice President of A&R: Harvey Schwartz. Distributed by Mercury Records. Record company.
How to Contact: Capricorn Records does not accept unsolicited submissions.
Music: Released *Fashion Nugget*, recorded by Cake; *311*, recorded by 311; and *Bombs & Butterflies*, recorded by Widespread Panic, all on Capricorn Records. Other artists include Box Set, Vigilantes of Love, Fiji Mariners, Ugly Americans, Fool's Progress, Syd Straw, Freddy Jones Band, Speaker, Jimmy Hall and Sonia Dada.

CAPSTAN RECORD PRODUCTION, P.O. Box 211, East Prairie MO 63845. (314)649-2211. Contact: Joe Silver or Tommy Loomas. Labels include Octagon and Capstan Records. Record company, music publisher (Lineage Publishing Co.), management firm (Staircase Promotion) and record producer (Silver-Loomas Productions). Pays 3-5% royalty to artists on contract.

- Capstan's publishing affiliate, Lineage Publishing Co., can be found in the Music Publishers section and Staircase Promotion can be found in the Managers and Booking Agents section.

How to Contact: Write first to obtain permission to submit. Prefers cassette or VHS videocassette with 2-4 songs and lyric sheet. "Send photo and bio." SASE. Reports in 1 month.
Music: Country, **easy listening**, **MOR**, **country rock** and **top 40/pop**. Released "Country Boy" (by Alden Lambert); "Yesterday's Teardrops" and "Round & Round," written and recorded by The Burchetts. Other artists include Bobby Lee Morgan, Skidrow Joe, Vicarie Arcole and Fleming.

CARLYLE RECORDS, INC., 1217 16th Ave. S., Nashville TN 37212. (615)327-8129. President: Laura Fraser. Record company. Estab. 1986. Releases 3 12″ singles, 6 LPs, 4 EPs and 6 CDs/year. Pays compulsory rate to publisher per song on record.

- See the listing for Carlyle Management in the Managers and Booking Agents section.

How to Contact: Submit demo tape by mail. Unsolicited submissions are OK. Prefers cassette or VHS videocassette. Does not return material. Reports in 1 month.
Music: Mostly **rock**. Released "Orange Room" (by Michael Ake), recorded by the Grinning Plowmen; *All Because of You*, written and recorded by Dorcha; and *Sun* (by John Elliot), recorded by Dessau, all on Carlyle Records.

‡CARMEL RECORDS, 2331 Carmel Dr., Palo Alto CA 94303. (415)856-3650. Contact: Jeanette Avenida. Labels includes Edgetone, Accoustic Moods, Rainin' Records Fountain, RMA, Canyon, Nightengale Music and Navarre Jazz. Record company and record producer. Estab. 1987. Releases 4 singles and 4 LPs/year. Pays standard royalty.
How to Contact: Submit demo tape by mail. Unsolicited submissions are OK. Prefers cassette or VHS videocassette and lyric sheet. Does not return material. Reports in 6 months.
Music: Mostly **A/C**, **folk/rock** and **classical**; also **instrumental**, **jazz**, **children's** and **light rock**. Released *A Thousand Ways to Love*, written and recorded by Larry Reed; *Primal Rage* (soundtrack to video game); and *2 Days Away*, written and recorded by Euphoria, all on Carmel Records.
Tips: "Send a complete demo with lyric sheet. Call to follow up. Be very nice—do something to make your submission different."

CAROLINE RECORDS, INC., 104 W. 29th St., 4th Floor, New York NY 10001. (212)886-7500. Website: http://www.caroline.com. A&R Director: Clay Sparks. Exclusive manufacturing and distribution of EG, Astralwerks (electronic), Real World (world music), Vernon Yard (alternative rock), Instant Mayhem (alternative rock), Scamp (retrocool), Mercator (world) and Gyroscope (eclectic). Record company and independent record distributor. Estab. 1979. Releases 10-12 12″ singles and 100 CDs/year. Pays varying royalty to artists on contract; statutory rate to publisher per song.
How to Contact: Submit demo tape by mail. Unsolicited submissions are OK. Prefers cassette with lead sheets and press clippings. SASE. Reports in 3 months.
Music: Mostly **alternative/indie/electronic**. Released *Three Sheets to the Wind*, written and recorded by Idaho on Caroline Records; *Ben Folds Five*, written and recorded by Ben Folds Five on Passenger/Caroline Records; and *Transmission*, written and recorded by Low on Vernon Yard/Caroline Records. Other artists include Acetone, Adrian Belew and Chemical Brothers.
Tips: "We are open to artists of unique quality and enjoy developing artists from the ground up. We listen to all types of 'alternative' rock, metal, funk and rap but do not sign mainstream hard rock or dance. We send out rejection letters so do not call to find out what's happening with your demo."

CASARO RECORDS, 932 Nord Ave., Chico CA 95926. (916)345-3027. Contact: Hugh Santos. Record company and record producer (RSA Productions). Estab. 1988. Releases 5-8 LPs/year. Pays variable royalty to artists on contract; statutory rate to publisher per song on record.
How to Contact: Write or call first and obtain permission to submit. Prefers cassette with full project demo and lyric sheet. Does not return material. Reports in 3 months.
Music: **Jazz** and **country**; also **R&B** and **pop**. Released *Potpourri* (by various), recorded by Liz Graffell (jazz); and *The War of '96* (by Hamm/Santos), recorded by Steve Hamm (blues rock), both on Casaro Records. Other artists include Lesley McDaniel, King Cotton Jazz Band, Jeff Dixon, Lory Dobbs and Charlie Robinson.
Tips: "Produce your song well (in tune—good singer). It doesn't need to be highly produced—just clear vocals. Include lyric sheet."

CAT'S VOICE PRODUCTIONS, P.O. Box 1361, Sanford ME 04073. (207)499-2170. Owner: Tom Reeves. Distributed by Northeast. Record company, music publisher (Rahsaan Publishing/ASCAP), record producer and recording studio. Estab. 1982. Releases 2 singles, 4 12″ singles and 4 CDs/year. Pays 15-20% royalty to artists on contract; statutory royalty to publishers per song on record.
How to Contact: Submit demo tape by mail. Unsolicited submissions are OK. Prefers cassette, CD or VHS videocassette with 3 songs and lyric sheet. "Publishing requires laser copy sheet music." SASE. Reports in 2-4 weeks.
Music: **Rock**, **R&B** and **country**; also **New Age** and **alternative**. Released *Signature*, written and recorded by Paul Wilcox; *Mangled Duckings* (by Dick D. Lux), recorded by Mangled Duckings; and *One Grove At A Time*, written and recorded by Cleanshot, all on Cat's Voice Records.

CEDAR CREEK RECORDS™, 44 Music Square East, Suite 503, Nashville TN 37203. (615)252-6916. Fax: (615)327-4204. President: Larry Duncan. Distributed by Interstate Records. Record company, music publisher (Cedar Creek Music/BMI and Cedar Cove Music/ASCAP), management firm and record producer (Cedar Creek Productions). Estab. 1992. Releases 20 singles, 5 LPs and 5 CDs/year. Pays 10% royalty to artists on contract; statutory rate to publisher per song on record.

- You can find listings for Cedar Creek Productions in the Record Producers and Managers and Booking Agents sections.

How to Contact: Submit demo tape by mail. Unsolicited submissions are OK. Prefers cassette or VHS videocassette. Does not return material. Reports in 2 months.
Music: Mostly **country**, **country/pop**, **country/R&B**, **Southern gospel** and **Christian contemporary**; also **pop**, **R&B**, **Christian country**, **contemporary jazz** and **light rock**. Released "When The Sun Goes Down Over Dixie" (by Brian McArdle/Gary Georgette); "A Mile In His Shoes" (by Deke Little/Lynn Guyo); and "Eleven Roses" (by Lamar Moriss/Darrel McCall), all recorded by Lynn Guyo on Interstate Records.
Tips: "Submit your best songs on a good fully produced demo or master using a great singer."

CELLAR RECORDS, 116 N. Peoria, Dixon IL 61021. (815)288-2900. E-mail: tjoos@aol.com. Owners: Todd Joos or Bob Brady. Distributed by Perris Records and Saraya Distribution; some projects through Cargo Distribution. Record company, music publisher (Sound Cellar Music/BMI) and record producer (Todd Joos). Estab. 1987. Releases 4-6 singles, 12 cassettes, 6 EPs and 6-8 CDs/year. Pays 100% royalty to artists on contract; statutory rate to publisher per song on record. Charges in advance "if you use our studio to record."

● Cellar Records' publishing affiliate, Sound Cellar Music, can be found in the Music Publishers section.
How to Contact: Submit demo tape by mail. Unsolicited submissions are OK. Prefers cassette or VHS videocassette with 3-4 songs and lyric sheet. Does not return material. "If we like it we will call you."
Music: Mostly **metal**, **country** and **rock**; also **pop**, **rap** and **blues**. Released *Salute*, written and recorded by Hot Stove Jimmy on Cargo Records (ska); *The Muse*, written and recorded by Eric Topper (alternative rock); and *Modify*, written and recorded by Haruspex (groove metal), both on Cellar Records. Other artists include John Stinson, Impetus, Snap Judgment, Justice 4, Pull and Cajun Anger.
Tips: "Make sure that you understand that your band is business and you must be willing to self invest time, effort and money just like any other new business. We can help you but you must also be willing to help yourself."

CENTIUM ENTERTAINMENT, INC., 499 N. Canon Dr., Beverly Hills CA 90210. (310)887-7006. Fax: (310)854-3966. President: Arthur Braun. Labels include Centium Records. Record company and music publisher. Estab. 1994. Releases 6 singles, 2 LPs, 10 EPs and 6 CDs/year. Pays negotiable royalty to artists on contract; statutory rate to publisher per song on record.
● See the interview with President Arthur Braun in the 1997 *Songwriter's Market*.
How to Contact: Submit demo tape by mail. Unsolicited submissions are OK. Prefers cassette with lyric sheet. SASE. Reports in 4-6 weeks.
Music: Mostly **R&B**, **rock** and **dance**; also **country**. Released "I Live For Your Love" (by Werfel/Reswick/Rich), recorded by Natalie Cole on Manhattan Records; "Never Give Up on a Good Thing," written and recorded by Monie Love on London Records; and "I Don't Give My Love to Just Anybody," written and recorded by Laura Enea on Next Plateau Records.

CEREBRAL RECORDS, 1236 Laguna Dr., Carlsbad CA 92008. (619)434-2497. Publicist: Lincoln Kroll. Record company, music publisher (Cerebral Records/BMI) and record producer (Cerebral Records). Estab. 1991. Releases 1-3 LPs and 1-3 CDs/year. Pays negotiable royalty.
How to Contact: Write first and obtain permission to submit. SASE. Reports in 2 months.
Music: Mostly **progressive rock**. Released *Broken Hands*, *I Am Myself* and *On With the Show*, all written and recorded by State of Mind on Cerebral Records.

CHA CHA RECORDS, P.O. Box 321, Port Washington WI 53074. (414)284-9777. Fax: (414)284-5242. President: Joseph C. De Lucia. Labels include Cap and Debby. Record company, record producer, and music publisher (Don Del Music/BMI). Estab. 1955. Pays negotiable royalty to artists on contract; negotiable rate to publishers per song on record.
● Cha Cha's publishing affiliate, Don Del Music, is listed in the Music Publishers section.
How to Contact: Write first and obtain permission to submit. Prefers cassette with 4-6 songs and lyric sheet. Does not return material. Reports in 3 months.
Music: **Acoustic** and **folk**.

CHATTAHOOCHEE RECORDS, 15230 Weddington St., Van Nuys CA 91411. (818)788-6863. Contact: Chris Yardum. Record company and music publisher (Etnoc/Conte). Member NARAS. Releases 4 singles/year. Pays negotiable royalty to artists on contract.
How to Contact: Submit demo tape by mail. Unsolicited submissions are OK. Prefers cassette with 2-6 songs and lyric sheet. Does not return material. "We contact songwriters if we're interested."
Music: **Rock**.

CHERRY STREET RECORDS, P.O. Box 52681, Tulsa OK 74152. (918)742-8087. President: Rodney Young. Record company and music publisher. Estab. 1990. Releases 2 CD/year. Pays 5-15% royalty to artists on contract; statutory rate to publisher per song on record.
How to Contact: Write first and obtain permission to submit. Prefers cassette or videocassette with 4 songs and lyric sheet. SASE. Reports in 6-8 weeks.
Music: **Rock**, **country** and **R&B**; also **jazz**. Released *Blue Dancer* (by Chris Blevins) and *Hardtimes* (by Brad Absher), both on CSR Records (country rock); and *She Can't Do Anything Wrong* (by Davis/Richmond), recorded by Bob Seger on Capitol Records.
Tips: "We are a songwriter label—the song is more important to us than the artist. Send only your best four songs."

CHRISTIAN MEDIA ENTERPRISES, 4041 W. Wheatland, Suite 156-372, Dallas TX 75237. Phone/fax: (214)283-2780. Owner: Craig R. Miles. Labels include Break Through Records, CME Records. Record company, music publisher (CME Publishing Co./ASCAP) and record producer (Craig R. Miles). Estab.

1988. Pays negotiable royalty to artists on contract; statutory rate to publisher per song on record.
How to Contact: Write first to arrange personal interview or submit demo tape by mail. Unsolicited submissions are OK. Prefers cassette, DAT or VHS videocassette with 3 songs and lyric and lead sheet. Does not return material. Reports in 2-3 months.
Music: Mostly **contemporary Christian**, **contemporary gospel**, **urban contemporary Christian** and **jazz gospel**. Released "I've Found Joy" (by Craig Miles), recorded by Onyx on CME Records (CCM). Other artists include Paul T. and Jason Watson.

CIMIRRON/RAINBIRD RECORDS, 607 Piney Point Rd., Yorktown VA 23692. (757)898-8155. E-mail: lpuckett@ix.netcom.com. President: Lana Puckett. Vice President: Kim Person. Distributed by Peaches and Plan 9. Record company and music publisher (Cimirron Music). Releases 3-6 CDs and cassettes/year. Pays variable royalty to artists on contract; negotiable rate to publisher per song on record.

- See the listing for Cimirron Music in the Music Publishers section.

How to Contact: Write or call first and obtain permission to submit. Prefers cassette or CD and lyric sheet. Does not return material. Reports in 3 months.
Music: Mostly **country/acoustic**, **bluegrass** and **singer/songwriter**. Released *Windows of Life*, recorded by Kim Person and Lana Puckett; *Nutcracker Suite for Guitar Orchestra*, recorded by Stephen Bennett; and *This Box I'm Looking Through*, recorded by Ron Fetner, all on Cimirron/Rainbird Records.

CLEOPATRA RECORDS, 8726 S. Sepulveda Blvd., Suite D-82, Los Angeles CA 90045. (310)305-0172. Fax: (310)821-4702. Contact: A&R. Labels include Zoth Ommog, Hypnotic, Hard Records Europe and Cherry Red. Record company. Estab. 1991. Releases 5 singles, 10 LPs, 5 EPs and 100 CDs/year. Pays 10-14% royalty to artists on contract; negotiable rate to publisher per song on record.
How to Contact: Submit demo tape by mail. Unsolicited submissions are OK. Prefers cassette or VHS videocassette with 5 songs and lyric sheet. Does not return material. Reports in 1 month.
Music: Mostly **industrial**, **gothic** and **ambient**; also **trance**, **space rock** and **electronic**. Released *Thoth*, written and recorded by Nik Turner (electronic/space rock); *Lost Minds* (by Rozz Williams/Evao), recorded by Christian Death (gothic); and *Lucy is Red*, written and recorded by Nosferato (gothic), all on Cleopatra Records. Other artists include Controlled Bleeding, Helios Creed, Rosetta Stone and Psychic TV.

‡COLLECTOR RECORDS, Box 2296, Rotterdam 3000 CG **Holland**. Phone: (1862)4266. Fax: (1862)4366. Research: Cees Klop. Labels include All Rock, Downsouth, Unknown, Pro Forma and White Label Records. Record company, music publisher (All Rock Music Publishing) and record producer (Cees Klop). Estab. 1967. Releases 10 singles and 30 LPs/year. Pays standard royalty to artist on contract.

- See the listings for All Rock Music in the Music Publishers section and Collector Records in the Record Producers section.

How to Contact: Submit demo tape by mail. Unsolicited submissions are OK. Prefers cassette. SAE and IRC. Reports in 1 month.
Music: Mostly **'50s rock**, **rockabilly**, **hillbilly boogie** and **country/rock**; also **piano boogie woogie**. Released *Roll Over Boogie*, written and recorded by A. Valkering; *Grand Hotel* (by Laurentis), recorded Rockin' Vincent, both on Down South Records; and *Henpecked Daddy*, written and recorded by Ralph Johnson on Collector Records.

COLUMBIA RECORDS, 550 Madison Ave., New York NY 10022. (212)833-8000. Fax: (212)883-7416. Santa Monica office: 2100 Colorado Ave., Santa Monica CA 90404. (310)449-2100. Fax: (310)449-2899. E-mail: sonymusiconline@sonymusic.com. Website: http://www.music.sony.com/Music/Columbia. Distributed by Sony; labels include So So Def Records and Ruffhouse Records. Record company.
How to Contact: Columbia Records does not accept demo tapes.
Music: Released *Nine Lives*, recorded by Aerosmith; *Ixnay On The Hombre*, recorded by The Offspring; and *Maxwell's Urban Hang Suite*, recorded by Maxwell, all on Columbia Records. Other artists include Journey, Tony Bennett, Bruce Springsteen, Shawn Colvin, Grover Washington Jr., Mariah Carey, Mary Chapin Carpenter, Sponge, Rick Trevino, Julio Iglesias and Kula Shaker.

REFER TO THE GEOGRAPHIC INDEX (at the back of this book) to find listings of companies by state, as well as foreign listings.

COM-FOUR, 7 Dunham Place, Brooklyn NY 11211. (718)599-2205. Distribution Manager: Albert Garzon. Distribution company. Estab. 1985. Distributes over 100,000 different titles including imports. Distributes 10-20 labels (INDI).
How to Contact: "We are an independent distributor looking for independent artists with market-ready product (no cassettes please)." Submit product by mail. Unsolicited submissions are OK. Does not return material. "We only respond if we like material."
Music: **All genres**.
Tips: "Be original and have some talent. Be willing and ready to work hard touring, promoting, etc."

COMMA RECORDS & TAPES, Postbox 2148, 63243 Neu-Isenburg, **Germany**. Phone: (6102)52696. Fax: (6102)52696. General Manager: Roland Bauer. Labels include Big Sound, Comma International and Max-Banana-Tunes. Record company and music publisher (R.D. Clèvere Musikverlag). Estab. 1969. Releases 50-70 singles and 20 LPs/year. Pays 7-10% royalty to artists on contract.
- Comma Records' publishing company, R.D. Clevère Musikverlag, is listed in the Music Publishers section.

How to Contact: Submit demo tape by mail. Unsolicited submissions are OK. Prefers cassette and lyric sheet. Does not return material. Reports in 3 weeks.
Music: Mostly **pop**, **disco**, **rock**, **R&B** and **country**; also **musicals** and **classical**.

COMSTOCK RECORDS LTD., 10603 N. Hayden Rd., Suite 114, Scottsdale AZ 85260. (602)951-3115. Fax: (602)951-3074. E-mail: songs@comstock-records.com. Website: http://comstock-records.com. Production Manager/Producer: Patty Parker. President: Frank Fara. Record company, music publisher (White Cat Music/ASCAP, Rocky Bell Music/BMI, How the West Was Sung Music/BMI), record producer (Patty Parker) and radio promotion. Member CMA, BBB, CCMA, BCCMA, British CMA and AF of M. "Comstock Records, Ltd. has three primary divisions: Production, Promotion and Publishing. We distribute and promote both our own Nashville productions, as well as already completed country or pop/rock CDs. We also offer CD design and mastering for products we promote. We can master from a copy of your DAT master or CD." Releases 24-30 CD singles and 6-8 CDs or 2 albums/year. Pays 10% royalty to artists on contract; statutory rate to publishers for each record sold. "Artists pay distribution and promotion fee to press and release their masters."
- Comstock Records' publishing company, White Cat Music, is listed in the Music Publishers section and Patty Parker can be found in the Record Producers section.

How to Contact: Submit demo tape by mail. Unsolicited submissions are OK. Prefers CD, DAT, cassette or VHS videocassette. SASE. "Enclose stamped return envelope if demo is to be returned." Reports in 2 weeks.
Music: Released "The Grind of Your Heel" (by Ria Anne Margret), recorded by Atlantic Freeway (pop/rock); *Darlin' Rita*, written and recorded by Ty Tomes (country); and *Somebody Else's Baby* (by Per Fredrik Kjolner), recorded by Bente Boe (country), all on Comstock Records. Other artists include Michael Grandé, Jae Gee, Kikki Danielsson, Southern Pacific Line, Karin Setter, Deb Hamilton and Don Emerson.

‡CONSPIRACY RECORDS, P.O. Box 332, Carbondale PA 18407-0332. (717)282-0863. Fax: (717)282-0362. E-mail: cmsmgmt@aol.com. Director of A&R: Diane Bassett. Distributed by ADA and Indie Net. Record company. Estab. 1993. Releases 4 CDs/year. Pays 10-12% royalty to artists on contract; statutory rate to publisher per song on record.
How to Contact: Submit demo tape by mail. Unsolicited submissions are OK. Prefers cassette or VHS videocassette with 3-5 songs and lyric sheet. Does not return material. Reports in 6 weeks.
Music: Mostly **alternative** and **rock**. Released *Graphic Violence*, written and recorded by Graphic Violence (metal); *Tribute*, written and recorded by Rhett Forester (rock), both on Conspiracy Records; and *Mystical Moments*, written and recorded by Mystical Moments on NIRC Records (New Age). Other artists include Museum of Fear.

CONTINENTAL RECORDS, 744 Joppa Farm Rd., Joppatowne MD 21085. (410)679-2262. CEO: Ernest W. Cash. Distributed by Laurie, Inc. Record company, management firm (Cash Productions) and music publisher (Ernie Cash Music/BMI). Estab. 1986. Pays 10% royalty to artists on contract; statutory rate to publisher per song on record.
- See the listings for Cash Productions Inc. in the Music Publishers and Managers and Booking Agents sections.

How to Contact: Call first and obtain permission to submit. Prefers cassette or VHS videocassette with 3 songs and lyric sheet. SASE. Reports in 2 weeks.
Music: Mostly **country** and **gospel**. Artists include Cindy Ashlin, Paul Gage, Carl Cooper and Eunice Morris.

‡COOKING VINYL AMERICA, P.O. Box 311, Port Washington NY 11050. (516)484-2863. Fax: (516)484-6179. E-mail: 104330.1030@compuserve.com. Head of A&R: Neil Armstrong. Record company. Estab. 1995. Releases 2 EPs and 30 CDs/year. Pays negotiable royalty to artists on contract; 75% rate to publisher per song on record.

How to Contact: Call first and obtain permission to submit. Prefers cassette or CD. Does not return material. Reports in 1 month.

Music: Mostly **singer/songwriter**, **rock** and **Celtic**. Released *Trawler*, recorded by Oysterband; *Wedding Present* (by Dave Geple), recorded by Wedding Present (rock); and *Singing the Storm*, recorded by June Tabor/Savourna Stevenson/Danny Thompson, all on Cooking Vinyl. Other artists include Bert Jansch, Jackie Leven and Andy White.

‡COUNTDOWN RECORDS, 207 Ashland Ave., Santa Monica CA 90405. (310)581-2700. Fax: (310)581-2727. E-mail: unitlab1@aol.com. Director of A&R: Chris Maggiore. Record company. Estab. 1993.

How to Contact: Submit demo tape by mail. Unsolicited submissions are OK. Prefers cassette. SASE. Reports in 3 weeks.

Music: Mostly **alternative rock**, **NAC** and **AAA**. Artists include Keiko Matsui (jazz keyboardist), Valerie Carter (adult alternative artist) and The Almighty Ultrasound (alternative rock).

COUNTRY BREEZE RECORDS, 1715 Marty, Kansas City KS 66103. (913)384-1316. President: Ed Morgan, Jr. Distributed by KAW Valley Distributors; labels include Angel Star Records and Crusader Records. Record company and music publisher (Country Breeze Music/BMI and Walkin' Hat Music/ASCAP). Releases 15 7" singles, 20 cassettes and 15-20 CDs/year. Pays 30% royalty to artists on contract; statutory rate to publisher per song on record.

- Country Breeze's publishing company, Country Breeze Music, is listed in the Music Publishers section.

How to Contact: Submit demo tape by mail. Unsolicited submissions are OK. Prefers studio-produced demo with 3 songs and lyric sheet. SASE. Reports in 2-3 weeks.

Music: All types of **country**. Released "God's My Right Hand" (by B. Bennett), recorded by Judy Reynolds on Crusader Records (gospel); "Always" (by E. Livermore/E. Morgan), recorded by Chris Anderson (country); and "Eldorado" (by E.A. Poe), recorded by Kyle London, both on Country Breeze Records. Other artists include David Dickenson, Faith Healers, Holy Kingdom and Country Roundup Band.

Tips: "Do not submit material and call me three days later wanting to know if it's recorded yet. It takes time."

COUNTRY STAR INTERNATIONAL, 439 Wiley Ave., Franklin PA 16323. (814)432-4633. President: Norman Kelly. Labels include CSI, Country Star, Process and Mersey Records. Record company, music publisher (Country Star Music/ASCAP, Process and Kelly/BMI), management firm (Country Star Attractions) and record producer (Country Star Productions). Member AFM and AFTRA. Estab. 1970. Releases 5-10 singles and 5-10 LPs/year. Pays 8% royalty to artists on contract; statutory rate to publisher per song on record.

- See the listings for Country Star Music in the Music Publishers section and Country Star Attractions in the Managers and Booking Agents section.

How to Contact: Submit demo tape by mail. Unsolicited submissions are OK. Prefers cassette with 2-4 songs and typed lyric or lead sheet. SASE. "No SASE no return." Reports in 1-9 weeks.

Music: Mostly **C&W** and **bluegrass**. Released "Holiday Waltz" (by F. Seltzer), recorded by Debbie Sue on Country Star Records. Other artists include Junie Lou and Bob Stamper.

COUNTRY STYLE RECORDS, P.O. Box 732, Hominy OK 74035. (918)885-2337. Fax: (918)885-6498. E-mail: gwicsfi@aol.com. President: Geri WyNell. Record company, music publisher (Country Style Country Music Inc.) and record producer (Ken Peade). Estab. 1995. Pays negotiable royalty to artists on contract; negotiable rate to publisher per song on record.

How to Contact: Submit demo tape by mail. Unsolicited submissions are OK. Prefers cassette or VHS videocassette. Does not return material. Reports in 3-4 weeks.

Music: Mostly **country**, **bluegrass** and **gospel**; also **easy listening**. Released *Country Style Forever* and "Talk to Me Oh Lonesome Heart," written and recorded by Geri Wynell; and "Cry Baby Heart," written and recorded by John Kurtz, all on Country Style Records. Other artists include Bill Fanning, Richard Vines and Barbara Jean Smith.

COWGIRL RECORDS, P.O. Box 6085, Burbank CA 91510. Contact: Vice President. Record company, record producer (Kingsport Creek Music) and music publisher (Kingsport Creek). Estab. 1980. Pays statutory rate to publishers for each record sold.

• See the listing for Kingsport Creek Music in the Record Producers section and Kingsport Creek Music Publishers in the Music Publishers section.

How to Contact: Submit demo tape by mail. Unsolicited submissions OK. Prefers cassette or VHS videocassette with any number of songs and lyric sheet or lead sheet. "Include a photo and bio if possible." Does not return material.

Music: Mostly **country**, **R&B**, **MOR** and **gospel**. Released "Leading Me On," "Pick Up Your Feet" and "With Me Still," all written and recorded by Melvena Kaye on Cowgirl Records.

‡CRANK! A RECORD COMPANY, 1223 Wilshire Blvd. #173, Santa Monica CA 90403. (310)917-9162. Fax: (310)917-9166. E-mail: crank@earthlink.net. Website: http://home.earthlink.net/~crank. Contact: Jeff Matlow. Distributed by RED, Cargo, Dutch East, Lumberjack, Revolver and Surefire. Record company and mail order/distribution company. Estab. 1994. Releases 6 singles, 5 LPs, 2 EPs and 5 CDs/year. Pays negotiable royalty to artists on contract.

How to Contact: Submit demo tape by mail. Unsolicited submissions are OK. Prefers cassette or CD with 3 songs. "Send whatever best represents your abilities." Does not return material. Reports in 2-3 weeks.

Music: Mostly **indie/alternative rock** and **pop**. Released *The Power of Failing*, written and recorded by Mineral (rock); *Boys Life*, written and recorded by Boys Life (rock); and *Vitreous Humor*, written and recorded by Vitreous Humor (rock), all on Crank! Records.

‡CREATIVE IMPROVISED MUSIC PROJECTS (CIMP) RECORDS, Cadence Building, Redwood NY 13679. (315)287-2852. Fax: (315)287-2860. Producer: Bob Rucsh. Distributed by North Country Distributors; labels include Cadence Jazz Records. Record company and record producer (Robert D. Rusch). Estab. 1983. Releases 25-30 CDs/year. Pays negotiable royalty to artists on contract.

How to Contact: Submit demo tape by mail. Unsolicited submissions are OK. Prefers cassette, CD or DAT. "We are not looking for songwriters but recording artists." SASE. Reports in 1 week.

Music: Mostly **jazz** and **creative improvised music**. Released *Essence*, recorded by Lee Shaw Trio; *Collective Voices*, recorded by Odean Pope Trio; and *Quick Wits*, recorded by Lou Grassi Saxtet, all on CIMP Records. Other artists include Kevin Norton Trio, John McPhee & David Prentice and Mark Whitecage Quartet.

Tips: "CIMP Records are produced to provide music to reward repeated and in-depth listenings. They are recorded live to two-track which captures the full dynamic range one would experience in a live concert. There is no compression, homogenization, eq-ing, post-recording splicing, mixing, or electronic fiddling with the performance. Digital recording allows for a vanishingly low noise floor and tremendous dynamic range. This compression of the dynamic range is what limits the 'air' and life of many recordings. Our recordings capture the dynamic intended by the musicians. In this regard these recordings are demanding. Treat the recording as your private concert. Give it your undivided attention and it will reward you. CIMP Records are not intended to be background music. This method is demanding not only on the listener but on the performer as well. Musicians must be able to play together in real time. They must understand the dynamics of their instrument and how it relates to the others around them. There is no fix-it-in-the-mix safety; either it works or it doesn't. What you hear is exactly what was played. Our main concern is music not marketing."

‡CREEK RECORDS, P.O. Box 1946, Cave Creek AZ 85331. (602)488-8132. Vice President: Jeff Lober. Labels include Tempe. Record company, music publisher (Creeker Music Publishing) and record producer (Jeff Lober). Estab. 1995. Releases 4-5 CDs/year. Pays negotiable royalty to artists on contract; statutory rate to publisher per song on record.

How to Contact: Submit demo tape by mail. Unsolicited submissions are OK. Prefers cassette, DAT or VHS videocassette with 4-6 songs. SASE. Reports in 1-2 months.

Music: Mostly **rock**, **country**, and **jazz**; also **classical**, **alternative** and **New Age**. Released *Pablo*, written and recorded by Pablo; *Belly Dance*, written and recorded by various artists; and *Strawman*, written and recorded by Strawman, all on Creek Records.

‡CRESCENT RECORDING CORPORATION (CRC), P.O. Box 520195, Bronx NY 10452. (212)462-9202. Fax: (718)716-2963. Commanding Officer: Quincy A. Allen. Record company and music publisher (Full Moon Music, Inc.). Estab. 1995. Releases 2-4 singles, 1-2 LPs, 1-2 EPs and 1-2 CDs/year. Pays negotiable royalty to artists on contract; statutory rate to publisher per song on record.

• See the listing for Full Moon Music, Inc. in the Music Publishers section.

How to Contact: Submit demo tape by mail. Unsolicited submissions are OK. Prefers cassette or CD with 2-5 songs and lyric sheet. "Please include bio/résumé, cover letter, and/or any other material to strengthen your submission." Does not return material. Reports in 2-3 months.

Music: Mostly **soul/R&B**, **rock/pop** and **rap**; also **dance/club**, **country** and **jazz**. Released "Crazytown," written and recorded by Dodging Reality (rock); "Something On My Mind," written and recorded by Camille Watson (R&B); and "The Sweeter He Is" (by Isaac Haynes/David Porter), recorded by Sav'vy (R&B), all on Crescent Records.

CRITIQUE RECORDS, INC., 50 Cross St., Winchester MA 01890. (617)729-8137. Fax: (617)729-2320. Director of A&R: Ian-John. Labels include Popular Records, Inc. Record company and record producer (Ian-John). Releases 8 LPs and 24 CDs/year. Pays negotiable royalty to artists on contract; statutory rate to publisher per song on record.
How to Contact: Call first and obtain permission to submit. Prefers cassette with 3 songs and lyric and/or lead sheet. SASE. Reports in 3 weeks.
Music: Mostly **dance-pop**, **R&B**, **hip-hop**, **rock** and **alternative**; also **country**, **house-techno** and **trance-HiNRG**. Released "Total Eclipse of the Heart," recorded by Nikki French; "Get Ready for This," recorded by 2 Unlimited; and "Stayin' Alive," recorded by N-trance, all on Critique Records (dance). Other artists include David Hasselhoff, X-Press, Digital Underground, Marty Haggard, McPotts and Ian-John.

‡CROSSPOINT INTERNATIONAL, INC., 30 Monument Square, Concord MA 02134. (508)371-2300. Fax: (508)287-5325. Product Development: Noah Tier. Record company and music publisher. Estab. 1995. Releases 4 LPs/year. Pays negotiable royalty to artists on contract; negotiable rate to publisher per song on record.

- See Crosspoint International's listing in the Music Publishers section.

How to Contact: Submit demo tape by mail. Unsolicited submissions are OK. Prefers cassette or VHS videocassette. Does not return material. Reports in 4 months.
Music: **Children's**. Released *Silly Song*, *ABC's* and *I've Got the Moos*, all written by John Sara.
Tips: "Self-esteem building products are our niche."

‡CUCA RECORD CO. (Division of American Music Co.), 3830 Hwy. 78, Mt. Horeb WI 53572. (608)695-1794. President: Jim Kirchstein. Labels include Night Owl, Top Gun, Jolly Dutchman, Sound Odessy, Age of Aquarius, Sara and Make Mine Old Time. Record company and music publisher. Estab. 1959. Releases 12 LPs and 2 CDs/year. Pays 8-12% royalty to artists on contract; statutory rate to publisher per song on record.
How to Contact: Submit demo tape by mail. Unsolicited submissions are OK. Prefers cassette. SASE. Reports in 1 month.
Music: Mostly **Chicago style blues** and **old time**. Released "Mule Skinner Blues" (by Rogers), recorded by Fendermen; *Genius of Earl Hooker*, written and recorded by Earl Hooker; and *Birdlegs* (by Banks), recorded by Birdlegs Pauline, all on Cuca Records. Other artists include Seven Sounds, Jimmy Dawkins, Billy Duncans, Harvey Scales, H.C. Reed and Comic Books, Jan Bradley and Pee Wee King.

‡CURB RECORDS, 47 Music Square E., Nashville TN 37203. (615)321-5050. Fax: (615)255-3370. Burbank office: 3907 W. Alameda Ave., Suite 102, Burbank CA 91505. (818)843-0378. Fax: (818)843-0601. Website: http://www.curb.com. Distributed by UNI. Record company.
How to Contact: Curb Records does not accept unsolicited submissions; accepts previously published material only. Do not submit without permission.
Music: Released *Unchained Melody/The Early Years* and *Blue*, both recorded by LeAnn Rimes; and *Goodnight Sweetheart*, recorded by David Kersh, all on Curb Records. Other artists include Mary Black, Bananarama, Junior Brown, Merle Haggard, Kal Ketchum, Kool & the Gang, Lyle Lovett, Tim McGraw, Wynonna and Sawyer Brown.

DAGENE/CABLETOWN RECORDS, P.O. Box 410851, San Francisco CA 94141. (415)822-1530. President: David Alston. Record company, music publisher (Dagene Music), management firm (Golden City International) and record producer (David-Classic Disc Productions). Estab. 1993. Pays standard royalty to artists on contract; statutory rate to publisher per song on record.

- See the listing for Dagene Music in the Music Publishers section.

How to Contact: Write or call first and obtain permission to submit. Prefers cassette or VHS videocassette with 2 songs and lyric sheet. SASE. Reports in 1 month.
Music: Mostly **R&B/rap**, **dance** and **pop**; also **gospel**. Released "Maxin" (by Marcus Justice/Bernard Henderson), recorded by 2 Dominatorz on Dagene Records; "Love Don't Love Nobody" (by David Alston), recorded by Rare Essence on Cabletown Records; and "Why Can't I Be Myself" (by David Alston), recorded by David Alston on E-lect-ric Recordings. Other artists include Chapter 1.

ALAN DALE PRODUCTIONS, 1630 Judith Lane, Indianapolis IN 46227. (317)786-1630. President: Alan D. Heshelman. Labels include ALTO Records. Record company. Estab. 1990. Pays 10% royalty to artists on contract.

How to Contact: Write or call first and obtain permission to submit or to arrange personal interview. Prefers cassette with 3 songs. Does not return material. Reports in 6 months.
Music: Mostly **A/C**, **country**, **jazz**, **gospel** and **New Age**. Released "Sweetest Humility," written and recorded by DeVen Scott; "He Made Me Who I Am" (by Alan Dale/Robert Vander), recorded by Robert Vander; and "Nothin' Better 'n' You," written and recorded by Alan Dale, all on A.D.P. Records. Other artists include Julianne, Cheryl Lynn and Judy G.

DANCER PUBLISHING CO., 166 Folkstone, Brampton, Ontario L6T 3M5 **Canada**. (905)791-1835. President: David Dancer. Labels include Cougar Records. Record company and music publisher. Estab. 1991. Releases 6 singles and 4 CDs/year. Pays 10% royalty to artists on contract; statutory rate to publisher per song on record.
How to Contact: Submit demo tape by mail. Unsolicited submissions are OK. Prefers cassette with 4 songs and lyric sheet. Does not return material. Reports in 1 month.
Music: Mostly **country**, **bluegrass** and **light rock**. Released "Old Habits Die Hard," (by Don Mittan) and "It's a Hello Goodbye World" (by Leonard H. Kohls), both on Cougar Records.

‡DAPMOR RECORDS, 3031 Acron St., Kenner LA 70003. (504)468-9820. Fax: (504)466-2896. President: Kelly Jones. Record company and music publisher (Dapmor Music). Estab. 1996.
- See the listing for Dapmor Music in the Music Publishers section.

How to Contact: Write first and obtain permission to submit. Prefers cassette, CD, DAT or videocassette with 10 songs and lyric sheet. Accepts old recordings that were not hits. Send finished product only. SASE. Reports in 6 weeks.
Music: Mostly **R&B**, **jazz** and **country**; also **blues**, **rap**, **reggae** and **rock**.

DEADEYE RECORDS, P.O. Box 5022-347, Lake Forest CA 92630. (714)768-0644. E-mail: deadeye@deadeye.com. Website: http://www.deadeye.com. Manager: Frank Jenkins. Record company. Estab. 1992. Releases 3 CDs/year. Pays varying royalty to artists on contract; statutory rate to publisher per song on record.
How to Contact: Write or e-mail first and obtain permission to submit. Prefers cassette or videocassette with 3 songs and lyric sheet. Does not return material. Reports in 2 months.
Music: Mostly **country**, **rock** and **blues**; also **R&B**. Released *Ragin' Wind* (by Frank Jenkins), recorded by Diamondback on Deadeye Records (country); and *Flemington*, recorded by Danny Federici (of the E Street Band).

‡dedicated records, 580 Broadway, Suite 1002, New York NY 10012. (212)334-5959. Fax: (212)334-5963. A&R Department: Jennie Davis. Record company. Estab. 1994. Releases 4 singles, 6 LPs, 6 EPs and 8 CDs/year. Pays negotiable royalty to artists on contract.
How to Contact: Write first and obtain permission to submit. Prefers cassette. "Keep it simple with a tape or CD, bio and your best press." SASE. Reports in 1 month.
Music: Mostly **alternative rock**, **top 40/pop** and **singer/songwriter**; also **hippie/granola**, **jam bands** and **progressive**. Released *Chandelier Musings* (by Jim Stone), recorded by Comet (psychedelic pop rock); *Arguments For Drinking* (by Sean Thompson), recorded by Long River Train (singer/songwriter); and *Lazer Guided Melodies* (by Jason Pierce), recorded by Spiritualized, all on dedicated records. Other artists include Muler, 30 Ampfuse, Silkscreen, Mulu, Cranes, Global Communication and DBH.
Tips: "Send only the songs/music you really like—don't send it and say, 'this isn't really representative/good.' Have a great live performance, and build a local following."

DEF BEAT RECORDS, 38 Cassis Dr., Etobicoke M9V 4Z6 **Canada**. (416)746-6205. Fax: (416)586-0853. Website: http://defbeat.com. President: Dalbert Myrie. A&R: Junior Smith. Labels include Worrel Productions, Myrie Associates Labels and DBR Records. Record company, music publisher (De La Musique Publishing, M.A.L. Music Publishing), record producer (Dalbert Myrie, D. Fresh) and management company (DBR Management). Estab. 1986. Releases 12 singles, 4 LPs, 3 EPs and 10 CDs/year. Pays negotiable royalty to artists on contract; ¾ statutory rate to publisher per song on record.
How to Contact: Write or call first and obtain permission to submit. Prefers cassette or VHS videocassette. SASE. Reports in 6 weeks.
Music: Mostly **soul**, **R&B**, **hip-hop** and **dance**; also **reggae**, **Euro** and **house**. Released *Ill Vision*, written and recorded by Godd Bodies (rap); *It's Only God Can* (by Worrel Edwards), recorded by Mercia Bunting (gospel), both on Def Beat Records; and *When It Rains in New York*, written and recorded by Daryl West on Defunkera Records (R&B/soul). Other artists include Gentlemen X, Jackie Bell, Norman and Karen David, Afterlife, MiC'N Gz Crew, D. Fresh, D'S Girls, Black Chrome, JC and Raynaldo Casino.
Tips: "Make sure your contact lists are updated on a regular basis. Make sure when you are submitting a

tape (songs), it is the best representation of your work."

‡DEF JAM RECORDS, 8981 Sunset Blvd., Suite 309, Los Angeles CA 90069. (310)724-7233. Fax: (310)246-9779. New York office: 160 Varick St., 12th Floor, New York NY 10013. (212)229-5200. Fax: (212)352-1951. Distributed by PGD; labels include Oakland Hills Records.

How to Contact: Def Jam Records does not accept unsolicited submissions.

Music: Released *Muddy Waters*, recorded by Redman; *All World*, recorded by L.L. Cool J; and *More . . .*, recorded by Montell Jordan, all on Def Jam Records. Other artists include Richie Rich.

‡DEL-FI RECORDS, INC., P.O. Box 69188, Los Angeles CA 90069. (800)993-3534. Fax: (213)876-7098. E-mail: del-fi@primenet.com. Website: http://www.del-fi.com. Owner and President: Bob Keane. Distributed by the Mutual Group: Twinbrook, Paul Starr, Rock Bottom, City Hall, Smash, Cargo and others; labels include Donna, Mustang, Bronco and others. Record company. Estab. 1957. Releases 5-10 LPs and 10-15 CDs/year. Pays negotiable royalty to artists on contract; statutory rate to publisher per song on record.

How to Contact: Submit demo tape by mail. Unsolicited submissions are OK. Prefers cassette or CD. "Please enclose bio information and photo if possible." Does not return material "unless specified. Allow several weeks." Reports in 1 month.

Music: Mostly **rock**, **R&B** and **alternative country**; also **surf/drag** and **exotica**. Released *Shakedown!* (by various artists), recorded by Bobby Fuller on Del-Fi Records (rock); *Shots in the Dark* and *Pulp Surfin'*, written and recorded by various artists on Donna Records. Other artists include Jenny Morris.

Tips: "Be sure you are making/writing music that specifically meets your own artistic/creative demands, and not someone else's. Write/play music from the heart and soul and you will always succeed on a personal rewarding level first. We are *the* surf label . . . home of the 'Delphonic' sound. We've also released many of the music world's best known artists, including Ritchie Valens and the Bobby Fuller Four."

DEMI MONDE RECORDS AND PUBLISHING, LTD., Foel Studio, Llanfair Caereinion, Powys, Wales, **United Kingdom**. Phone/fax: (01938)810758. Managing Director: Dave Anderson. Distributed by RTR/Disc, Magnum and Direct. Record company, music publisher (Demi Monde Records & Publishing, Ltd.) and record producer (Dave Anderson). Estab. 1983. Releases 5 12" singles, 10 LPs and 6 CDs/year. Pays 10% royalty to artists on contract; statutory rate to publisher per song on record.

- See their listings in the Music Publishers and Record Producers sections.

How to Contact: Submit demo tape by mail. Unsolicited submissions are OK. Prefers cassette with 3-4 songs. Does not return material. Reports in 6 weeks.

Music: Rock, **R&B** and **pop**. Released *Hawkwind*, *Amon Duul II & Gong* and *Groundhogs* (by T.S. McPhee), all on Demi Monde Records.

‡DISCOVERY RECORDS, 2034 Broadway, Santa Monica CA 90404. (310)828-1033. Fax: (310)828-1584. Website: http://www.discoveryrec.com. A&R: Gregg Bell. Distributed by WEA. Record company.

How to Contact: Submit demo tape by mail. Unsolicited submissions are OK. Prefers CD with picture, bio and cover letter.

Music: Released *Nowhere to Here*, recorded by Blue Rodeo; *Finn Brothers*, recorded by the Finn Brothers; and *Baptist Hospital*, recorded by Boo Hewerdine, all on Discovery Records. Other artists include The Egg, Sara Hickman, Warren Hill, Mars Needs Women, Morcheeba, Screaming Headless Torsos, Voice of the Beehive, Toni Price and William Orbit.

‡DISC-TINCT MUSIC, INC., P.O. Box 5837, Englewood NJ 07631. (201)568-7066. President: Jeffrey Collins. Labels include Music Station, Echo USA, Dancefloor, Soul Creation and Soul Vibes. Record company, music publisher (Distinct Music, Inc./BMI, Distinct Echo Music/ASCAP) and record producer (Echo USA Productions). Estab. 1985. Releases 50 12″ singles, 10 LPs, 4 EPs and 15 CDs/year. Pays 5-8% royalty to artists on contract; ⅔ statutory rate to publisher per song on record.

How to Contact: Submit demo tape by mail. Unsolicited submissions are OK. Prefers cassette or VHS videocassette with up to 5 songs. SASE. Reports in 1 month.

Music: Mostly **hip-hop**, **R&B**, **dance** and **house/techno**. Released *Your Attitude* (by Jimmie Fox), recorded by Kim Cummings on Music Station Records; and "As Quiet As It's Kept" (by Elis Pacheco), recorded by Colonel Abrams on Soul Creation Records. Other artists include Debbie Blackwell/Cook, Eleanor Grant, Black Rebels, Ready for the World, Llake, George Kerr and Quincy Patrick.

Tips: "Cue your cassettes, which should be labeled clearly."

DMT RECORDS, 11714-113th Ave., Edmonton Alberta T5G 0J8 **Canada**. (403)454-6848. Fax: (403)454-9291. E-mail: dmt@ccinet.ab.ca. A&R: Gerry Dere. President: Danny Makarus. Record com-

pany, music publisher (La Nash Publishing/Danny Makarus Music) and record producer (Gerry Derre). Estab. 1986. Releases 4 singles, 3-6 LPs, 1 EP and 3-6 CDs/year. Pays negotiable royalty to artists on contract; negotiated rate to publishers per song on record.
How to Contact: Submit demo tape by mail. Unsolicited submissions are OK. Prefers cassette with 4 songs and lyric sheet. Does not return material. Reports in 1 month (if interested).
Music: Mostly **country**, **pop-soft rock** and **MOR**. Released "Darlin When I'm Gone" (by D. Larabie), recorded by 5 Wheel Drive (country); "Gotta Get Back" (by K. Repkow), recorded by High Park (rock); and *North American Breed* (by B. Cree/D. Cree), recorded by Rising Cree (ethnic), all on DMT Records.
Tips: "Our mainstay is today's country music—we are interested in mainstream country music."

DON'T RECORDS, P.O. Box 11513, Milwaukee WI 53211. (414)224-9023. Fax: (414)224-8021. E-mail: dont@execpc.com. VP of A&R: Joe Vent. Record company. Estab. 1991. Releases 6 LPs/year. Pays negotiable royalty to artists on contract; statutory rate to publisher per song on record.
How to Contact: Submit demo tape by mail. Unsolicited submissions are OK. Prefers cassette. "Send studio quality material." Does not return material. Reports in 2 months.
Music: Mostly **pop/rock** and **alternative**. Released *Upstroke for Downfolk*, written and recorded by Paul Cebar & The Milwaukeeans (pop); *Star of Desire* (by Scott & Brian Wooldridge), recorded by Wooldridge Brothers (pop); and *Gag Me with Spoon*, written and recorded by various (pop), all on Don't Records. Other artists include Pet Engine and Yell Leaders.
Tips: "Play a lot and be selling your own release when you send us material."

‡DREAMWORKS, 9130 Sunset Blvd., Los Angeles CA 90069. (310)285-7300. Fax: (310)278-4617. Distributed by UNI. Record company.
How to Contact: Material must be submitted through an agent or attorney. Does not accept unsolicited submissions.
Music: Released *Older*, recorded by George Michael; and *Come In And Burn*, recorded by Henry Rollins, both on DreamWorks Records.

DRIVE ENTERTAINMENT, 10351 Santa Monica Blvd., Los Angeles CA 90025. (310)553-3490. Fax: (310)553-3373. E-mail: drive@earthlink.net. President: Don Grierson. Distributed by Navarre; labels include Drive Archive. Record company and music publisher (Drive Music, Donunda Music). Estab. 1992. Releases 50 LPs and 50 CDs/year. Pays negotiable royalty to artists on contract; statutory rate to publisher per song on record.

- See the listing for Drive Music in the Music Publishers section.

How to Contact: Submit demo tape by mail. Unsolicited submissions are OK. Prefers cassette or DAT with 3 songs and lyric sheet. SASE. Reports in 6 weeks.
Music: Mostly **pop**, **rock** and **Triple A**; also **dance**. Released *Swing Alive*, written and recorded by various artists (big band); *Singin' The Blues*, written and recorded by various artists (blues); and *Drop Till You Dance*, written and recorded by various artists, all on Drive Entertainment.

‡E.S.R. RECORDS, 40 Camperdown Terrace, Exmouth, Devon EX8 1EQ **United Kingdom**. Phone: (01392)57880. M.D: John Greenslade. Record company (P.R.S.) and record producer (E.S.R. Productions). Estab. 1965. Releases 4 singles and 10 LPs/year. Pays 50% royalty; statutory rate to publisher per song on record.
How to Contact: Submit demo tape by mail. Unsolicited submissions are OK. Prefers cassette with 4 songs and lyric sheet. SAE and IRC. Reports in 1 month.
Music: Mostly **country** and **MOR**. Released *And I'll Wait* (by J. Greenslade); *Gone Fishing* (by June Greenslade), both recorded by Johnny Solo (AOR); and *What's Your Tiple* (by Terry Whitehouse) (MOR), all on E.S.R. Records. Other artists include Kar Barron, Barracuda, Gary Kane, Gerry Ellen and Storm Rivers.

EARTHTONE/SONIC IMAGES, P.O. Box 691626, W. Hollywood CA 90069. (213)650-1000. Fax: (213)650-1016. E-mail: brad@sonicimages.com. Director of A&R: Brad Pressman. Record company. Es-

REFER TO THE CATEGORY INDEX (at the end of this section) to find exactly which companies are interested in the type of music you write.

tab. 1991. Releases 3 singles and 11 CDs/year. Pays negotiable royalty to artists on contract; statutory rate to publisher per song on record.
How to Contact: Submit demo tape by mail. Unsolicited submissions are OK. Prefers DAT or CD (for finished product deals) with 5 songs. Does not return material. Reports in 3 weeks.
Music: Mostly **New Age**, **world**, **electronic**, **jazz** and **techno**. Artists include Christopher Franke, Shadowfax, Mercs, Mark Shreve and Solar System.

EASTERN FRONT RECORDS, INC., 7 Curve St., Medfield MA 02052. (508)359-8003. Fax: (508)359-8090. E-mail: info@easternfront.com. Website: http://www.easternfront.com. Vice President: Robert Swalley. Distributed by Koch International (US and Canada) and Intersound (Italy). Record company and music publisher (Eastern Front Publishing). Estab. 1991. Releases 4-6 CDs/year. Pays negotiable royalty to artists on contract; statutory rate to publisher per song on record.
How to Contact: Call first and obtain permission to submit. Prefers cassette or DAT with 3 songs and lyric sheet. "Lyrics matter. If we accept the submission, we expect the artist/management to provide press kit and photo. Artist should feel free to call us to follow up—we are e-mail friendly!" Does not return material. Reports in 2 months.
Music: Mostly **rock/pop**, **contemporary folk** and **acoustic singer/songwriters**. Released *Black Sheep*, written and recorded by Martin Sexton (folk); *Singing For the Landlord*, written and recorded by Greg Greenway; and *Little Town*, written and recorded by Kevin Connolly, all on Eastern Front Records. Others artists include Peter Mulvey.
Tips: "Be prepared to put in hard work including touring. Lyrics matter—not expecting full production demo but we expect a well recorded vocal and a well thought-out representation of the material. Distinctive vocals a major plus!"

ELEKTRA ENTERTAINMENT GROUP, 345 N. Maple Dr., Beverly Hills CA 90210. (310)288-3814. Fax: (310)274-9491. New York office: 75 Rockefeller Plaza, New York NY 10019. (212)275-4000. Fax: (212)974-9314. Website: http://www.elektra.com. Director of A&R: Lara Hill. Distributed by WEA; labels include Elektra Records, Eastwest Records, Sire Records and Asylum Records. Record company.
How to Contact: Submit demo tape by mail. Unsolicited submisssions are OK. Prefers cassette or DAT with 3 songs. Does not return material. Reports in 3 months.
Music: Mostly **alternative/modern rock**. Released *Tigerlily*, recorded by Natalie Merchant; *New Beginning*, recorded by Tracy Chapman; and *Black Love*, recorded by Afghan Whigs, all on Elektra Entertainment. Other artists include Metallica, Keith Sweat, Bryan White, Phish, Björk, Spacehog, Pantera, The Cure, Silk and Natalie Cole.

‡ELEVEN RECORDS/MCGHEE ENTERTAINMENT, 8730 Sunset Blvd. #175, Los Angeles CA 90069. (310)358-9200. Fax: (310)358-9299. E-mail: mcgheela@aol.com. West Coast Director of A&R: Charrie Foglio. Record company and management company. Estab. 1994.
How to Contact: Submit demo tape by mail. Unsolicited submissions are OK. Prefers cassette or CD with 3 songs. SASE. Reports in 2-3 weeks.
Music: Mostly **rock**, **alternative** and **country**; also **folk**. Current artists include KISS, Skid Row, Green Jellÿ, Tracy Bohnam, CIV, Orange 9mm and Caroline's Spine.

EMA MUSIC INC., P.O. Box 91683, Washington DC 20090-1683. (202)319-1688. Fax: (202)575-1774. President: Jeremiah N. Murphy. Record company. Estab. 1993. Releases 2 LPs and 2 CDs/year. Pays statutory rate to publisher per song on record.
How to Contact: Write first and obtain permission to submit. "Do not call." SASE. Reports in 3 months.
Music: Mostly **gospel** and **contemporary Christian**. Released *Just Jesus* (by M. Brown); *I Must* (by J. Murphy); and *Blessed Assurance* (by P. Crosby), all recorded by J. Murphy on EMA Records (gospel).

EMERALD CITY RECORDS, Auburn Tower, 2426 Auburn Ave., Dayton OH 45046. Phone/fax: (937)275-4221. E-mail: chris.tanner@worldnet.att.net. Website: http://www.infochase.com/ent/dme/index.html. President: Jack Froschauer. Creative Director: Chris Tanner. Distributed by Rotation Record Distributors, Dream Machine Entertainment and GEM. Record company and publishing company (Barren Wood Publishing). Estab. 1992. Pays negotiable royalty to artists on contract; statutory rate to publisher per song on record.

- Emerald City's publishing company, Barren Wood Publishing, is listed in the Music Publishers section.

How to Contact: Submit demo tape by mail. Unsolicited submissions are OK. Prefers cassette or DAT with 1-4 songs and lyric or lead sheet. "If sending cassette, studio quality please." SASE. Reports in 4-6 weeks.

Music: Mostly **A/C**, **country** and **contemporary Christian**. Released "I've Got the Lord In Me" (by David Schafer), recorded by David Schafer with Stephen Seifert (gospel); "The Sergio Song" and "Goochee Goochee" (by Jack Froschauer), recorded by Cadillac Jack & the Reel-Time All-Stars, all on Emerald City Records. Other artists include Kent Pritchard & God's Will and Dale Walton.

EMF PRODUCTIONS, 1000 E. Prien Lake Rd., Suite D, Lake Charles LA 70601. Phone/fax: (318)474-0435. Owner: Ed Fruge. Record company, music publisher and record producer. Estab. 1977. Releases 3 singles, 3 LPs and 3 CDs/year. Pays 10-14% royalty to artists on contract; statutory rate to publisher per song on record.

- See their listing in the Music Publishers section.

How to Contact: Submit demo tape by mail. Unsolicited submissions are OK. Prefers cassette and lyric sheet. Does not return material. Reports in 6 weeks.
Music: Mostly **pop**, **R&B** and **country**.

‡EMF RECORDS & AFFILIATES, 633 Post. St. #145, San Francisco CA 94109. (415)263-5727. Fax: (415)752-2442. Director of Operations: Steven Lassiter. Distributed by GTI Marketing and Songs Publishing International; labels include Richland Communications, Sky Bent and Urbana Sounds. Record company. Estab. 1994. Releases 5 LPs and 5 CDs/year. Pays negotiable royalty to artists on contract; statutory rate to publisher per song on record.
How to Contact: Submit demo tape by mail. Unsolicited submissions are OK. Prefers cassette, CD or DAT with 3 songs and lyric and lead sheets. SASE. Reports in 2 months.
Music: Mostly **urban/pop/rock**, **jazz/Latin** and **New Age/classical (crossover)**; also **country**, **world beat** and **ethnic (world)**. Released *Like the Mist That Lingers*, written and recorded by Joe Tsongo on EMF Records (New Age/urban); *Hot on the Groove*, written and recorded by Slam Jam on Sky Beat Records (dance); and *Love Desire*, recorded by Flame on Richland Communications (soft jazz). Other artists include Orchestra deSarbor (salsa) and Urbana Sounds.

‡EMI RECORDS. As a result of the restructuring of EMI Music, EMI Records has been closed down. Many artists who were signed to EMI Records are being picked up by other EMD-distributed labels such as Virgin and Capitol.

‡THE ENCLAVE, 936 Broadway, New York NY 10010. (212)253-4900. Fax: (212)253-4999. Website: http://www.the-enclave.com. Contact: A&R. Distributed by EMD; labels include Spongebath Records. Record company.
How to Contact: At press time, The Enclave was being restructured as a result of the closing of EMI Records. Call or write the label for information on The Enclave's current submission policy.
Music: Artists include Fluffy, Vaselyn, September 67, Sweetwater and Sloan.

‡ENTOURAGE MUSIC GROUP, 11115 Magnolia Blvd., N. Hollywood CA 91601. (818)505-0001. (818)761-7956. E-mail: contact@entouragerecords.com. Website: http://www.entouragerecords.com/label. President: Guy Paonessa. Distributed by Touchwood Distribution. Record company and recording studio. Estab. 1995. Releases 4 cassettes and 4 CDs/year. Pays negotiable royalty to artists on contract; statutory rate to publisher per song on record.
How to Contact: Submit demo tape by mail. Unsolicited submissions are OK. Prefers cassette, CD, DAT or ½″ videocassette with 3-10 songs. "No phone calls please." SASE. Reports in 3 months.
Music: Mostly **rock**, **alternative** and **contemporary jazz**; also **alternative country**. Released *The Mustard Seeds*, written and recorded by The Mustard Seeds (alternative rock); and *P.O.L. Sprockett*, recorded by P.O.L. (rock), both on Entourage Records.

EPIC RECORDS, 550 Madison Ave., New York NY 10022. (212)833-8000. Fax: (212)833-4054. Santa Monica office: 2100 Colorado Ave., Santa Monica CA 90404. (310)449-2100. Fax: (310)449-2879. E-mail: sonymusiconline@sonymusic.com. Website: http://www.sony.dreammedia.com/EpicCenter/docs/index.qry. Distributed by Sony; labels include Epic Soundtrax, LV Records, Immortal Records, Word Records, Work Records and 550 Music. Record company.

How to Contact: Epic Records does not accept demo tapes.

Music: Released *The Day*, recorded by Babyface; *Freak Show*, recorded by Silverchair; and *Evil Empire*, recorded by Rage Against the Machine, all on Epic Records. Other artists include Gloria Estefan, Sweetback, Stephanie Bentley, Ty Herndon, Collin Raye, Amanda Marshall, Ottmar Leibert & Luna Negra, Joe Diffie and Patty Loveless.

‡¡EPIPHANY!, 910 S. Hohokam #101, Tempe AZ 85281. (602)804-0992. (602)929-0843. E-mail: epiprecord@aol.com. President: Brad Singer. Distributed by Caroline and Impact. Record company. Estab. 1994. Releases 5-7 CDs/year. Pays negotiable royalty to artists on contract; statutory rate to publisher per song on record.

How to Contact: Submit demo tape by mail. Unsolicited submissions are OK. Prefers cassette or CD (self produced) if available with no minimum of songs, lyric and lead sheet if available. "Submit biographical and press materials, photo, mission statement and contact information." SASE. Reports in 3-4 weeks.

Music: Mostly **rock**, **pop** and **alternative/garage**; also **punk**, **hip-hop** and **neo-country**. Released *Official Bootleg Volume I*, written and recorded by Giant Sand (alternative rock); *Unhappy Hour*, written and recorded by the Beat Angels (pop); and *Humbucker*, written and recorded by The Piersons (garage pop), all on ¡Epiphany! Records. Other artists include Dog & Pony Show, Fuzz, Yoko Love and Naked Prey.

Tips: "Our main objective here at ¡Epiphany! is to shove Arizona's finest music down the throat of the rest of the nation. We are a small independent label with very close relationships to our artists. Known for our rockin' garage pop and neo-country, we are looking to expand the palate of our roster into a tasty variety of music. Yummy!"

ETHEREAN MUSIC/VARIENA PUBLISHING, 9200 W. Cross Ave. #510, Littleton CO 80123. (303)973-8291. Fax: (303)973-8499. E-mail: ar@etherean.com. Contact: A&R Department. Labels include Elation Artists, Native Spirit, EM Pop. Record company and music publisher. Estab. 1979. Releases 4-10 CDs/year. Royalty negotiable.

- Note that Etherean Music does not accept tape submissions; they will only accept CDs or CD-Rs.

How to Contact: Submit demo CD by mail. Unsolicited submissions are OK. "Must include on package, 'unsolicited materials enclosed'." SASE. Reports in 2 months.

Music: Mostly **New Age/ethnic**, **jazz/contemporary** and **instrumental/world**; also **pop**. Released *Cat Food* (by various), recorded by Bryan Savage on Elation Artists Records; *Sons of Somerlied*, written and recorded by Steve McDonald; and *In the Presence of Angels*, written and recorded by Dik Darrell, both on Etherean Records. Other artists include Denean, Kenny Passarelli and Laura Theodore.

FAME AND FORTUNE ENTERPRISES, P.O. Box 121679, Nashville TN 37212. (615)244-4898. Producers: Jim Cartwright and Scott Turner. Labels include Legacy Records. Record company, music publisher (Pitchin' Hits Music/BMI), management firm and record producer. Estab. 1976. Releases 6 singles, 6 LPs and 6 CDs/year. Pays statutory rate to publisher per song on record.

How to Contact: Submit demo tape by mail. Unsolicited submissions are OK. Prefers cassette or VHS videocassette with 4 songs and lyric sheet. SASE. Reports in 6-10 weeks.

Music: Mostly **country**, **MOR**, **medium rock**, **contemporary Christian**, **gospel** and **pop**. Released "Tired of Standin' Here" (by Grady Schuman/Larry Williams/Terry Vonderhide), recorded by Bonnie Lou Bishop on Fame & Fortune Records (country). Other artists include Angel Connell, Chuck Lohmann, Arden Gatlin, Julie Carter, Angie Shaw, Dawn White, Slim Somerville, Dale LePiarz, Blake Scott, Anthony Cirillo and Marty James.

Tips: "Potential artists *must have* financial backers in place."

FAT CITY ARTISTS, 1906 Chet Atkins Place, Suite 502, Nashville TN 37212. (615)320-7678. Fax: (615)321-5382. President: Rusty Michael. Record company, music publisher, record producer and booking agency. Estab. 1972. Releases 4-6 singles, 4-6 LPs, 4-6 EPs and 4-6 CDs/year. Pays 12-15% royalty to artist on contract for demo work; statutory rate to publisher per song on record.

- See their listing in the Managers and Booking Agents section, as well as the listing for Fat City Publishing in the Music Publishers section.

How to Contact: Submit demo tape by mail. Unsolicited submissions are OK. Prefers cassette or VHS videocassette with 4-6 songs and lyric sheet. SASE (with at least 2 stamps). Reports in 2 months.

Music: Mostly **rock**, **country** and **blues**; also **alternative**, **rockabilly** and **jazz**.

Tips: "Provide us with as much information as you can with regard to your material and act and we will provide you with an evaluation as soon as possible. Our advertising/promotion division specializes in developing effective artist promotional packages, including demos, videos, video press kits, photography and copy. We will evaluate your present promotional material at no cost."

FICTION SONGS, 1540 Broadway, 27th Floor, New York NY 10036. (212)930-4910. Fax: (212)930-4295. E-mail: jdloveless@aol.com. Website: http://www.thecure.com. Director A&R: Jonathan Daniel. Distributed by Elektra, Sony and PolyGram. Record company and music publisher. Estab. 1977. Pays varying royalty to artists on contract.

How to Contact: Submit demo tape by mail. Unsolicited submissions are OK. Prefers cassette. Does not return material. "If we like it, we will respond immediately; if not, with SASE, we'll respond within 2 weeks."

Music: Mostly **alternative** and **rock**. Released *Rocket* (by Chris O'Connor), recorded by Primitive Radio Gods on Columbia/Sony Records (alternative rock); *Wild Mood Swings* (by Robert Smith), recorded by The Cure on Fiction/Elektra Records (alternative rock); and *Rather Be In New Orleans*, written and recorded by Flying Neutrinos on Fiction Records (swing). Other artists include Wilson, Die Warzau and God Machine.

FIREANT, 2009 Ashland Ave., Charlotte NC 28205. Phone/fax: (704)335-1400. E-mail: fireants@aol.com. Website: http://www.futuris.net/mabels/fireant.html. Owner: Lew Herman. Distributed by Dutch East, Twinbrook, Cityhall, North Country, Cargo, Get Hip and Redeye. Record company, music publisher (Fireant Music) and record producer (Lew Herman). Estab. 1990. Releases 3 CDs/year. Pays negotiable royalty to artists on contract; statutory royalty to publisher per song on record.

How to Contact: Submit demo tape by mail. Unsolicited submissions are OK. Prefers cassette, DAT or videocassette. Does not return material.

Music: "Anything except New Age and MOR. No disco, either." Mostly **progressive**, **traditional** and **musical hybrids**. Released *Jesse Helms Busted With Pornography* and *Pachuco Cadaver*, written and recorded by Eugene Chadbourne (country/rock/jazz); and *Bubbahey Mud Truck*, written and recorded by various artists (insurgent country), all on Fireant. Other artists include Mr. Peters' Belizian Boom and Chime Band.

FIRST TIME RECORDS, Sovereign House, 12 Trewartha Rd., Praa Sands, Penzance, Cornwall TR20 9ST **England**. (01736)762826. Fax: (01736)763328. E-mail: panamus@aol.com. Managing Director A&R: Roderick G. Jones. Labels include Pure Gold Records, Rainy Day Records and Mohock Records. Registered members of Phonographic Performance Ltd. (PPL). Record company, music publisher (First Time Music Publishing U.K./MCPS/PRS), management firm and record producer (First Time Management & Production Co.). Estab. 1986. Royalty to artists on contract varies; pays statutory rate to publisher per song on record subject to deal.

- See the listings for First Time Music Publishing in the Music Publishers section and First Time Management in the Managers and Booking Agents section.

How to Contact: Prefers cassette with unlimited number of songs and lyric or lead sheets, but not necessary. SAE and IRC. Reports in 1-3 months.

Music: Mostly **country/folk**, **pop/soul/top 20** and **country with an Irish/Scottish crossover**; also **gospel/Christian** and **HI NRG/dance**. Released *Songwriters and Artistes Compilation Volume III*, on Rainy Day Records; "The Drums of Childhood Dreams," written and recorded by Pete Arnold on Mohock Records (folk); and *The Light and Shade of Eddie Blackstone*, written and recorded by Eddie Blackstone on T.W. Records (country).

‡550 MUSIC, 550 Madison Ave., 21st Floor, New York NY 10022. (212)833-8000. Santa Monica office: 2100 Colorado Ave., Santa Monica CA 90404. (310)449-2100. Fax: (310)449-2932. Distributed by Sony. Record company.

How to Contact: 550 Music does not accept demo tapes.

Music: Released *Falling Into You*, recorded by Celine Dion; *Ginuwine . . . The Bachelor*, recorded by Ginuwine; and *White Light White Heat White Trash*, recorded by Social Distortion, all on 550 Music.

FLIP RECORDS, 8733 Sunset Blvd., Suite 205, W. Hollywood CA 90069. (310)360-8556. Fax: (310)360-8565. Website: http://www.flip-records.com. Record company. Estab. 1994.

How to Contact: Submit demo tape by mail. Unsolicited submissions are OK. Prefers cassette. Does not return material.

Music: Mostly **alternative**. Artists include Big Hate, Jane Jensen, Marcy, The Hotheads, Limp Bizkit, Grundig and D.J. Lethal.

Tips: "Have a hard, unique, fat sound."

FLYING HEART RECORDS, Dept. SM, 4026 NE 12th Ave., Portland OR 97212. (503)287-8045. E-mail: flyheart@teleport.com. Website: http://www.teleport.com/~flyheart. Owner: Jan Celt. Distributed by City Hall Records and Twin Brook Music. Record company and record producer (Jan Celt). Estab. 1982. Releases 2 LPs and 1 EP/year. Pays variable royalty to artists on contract; negotiable rate to publisher per song on record.

• See the listing for Jan Celt in the Record Producers section.

How to Contact: Submit a demo tape by mail. Unsolicited submissions are OK. Prefers cassette with 1-10 songs and lyric sheets. Does not return material. "SASE required for *any* response." Reports in 3 months.

Music: Mostly **R&B**, **blues** and **jazz**; also **rock**. Released *Vexatious Progr.*, written and recorded by Eddie Harris (jazz); *Juke Music*, written and recorded by Thara Memory (jazz); and *Lookie Tookie*, written and recorded by Jan Celt (blues), all on Flying Heart Records. Other artists include Janice Scroggins, Tom McFarland, Obo Addy, Snow Bud and The Flower People.

FOUNTAIN RECORDS, P.O. Box 35005 AMC, Greensboro NC 27425. (910))882-9990. President: Doris W. Lindsay. Record company, music publisher (Better Times Publishing/BMI, Doris Lindsay Publishing/ASCAP) and record producer. Estab. 1979. Releases 3 singles and 1 LP/year. Pays 5% royalty to artists on contract; statutory rate to publisher per song on record.

• See the listing for Doris Lindsay Publishing in the Music Publishers section.

How to Contact: Submit demo tape by mail. Unsolicited submissions are OK. Prefers cassette with 2 songs and lyric sheets. SASE. Reports in 2 months.

Music: Mostly **country**, **pop** and **gospel**. Released *Two Lane Life* (by D. Lindsay), recorded by Mitch Snow; "Grandma Bought A Harley" (by S. Rosario), recorded by Glenn Mayo; *Service Station Cowboy* (by Hoss Ryder), recorded by David Johnson, all on Fountain Records.

Tips: "Have a professional demo and include phone and address on cassette."

FRESH ENTERTAINMENT, 1315 Simpson Rd. NW, Suite 5, Atlanta GA 30314. (404)642-2645. Vice President, Marketing/A&R: Willie Hunter. Distributed by Ichiban Records, Warlock Records, Music Network and Hottrax Music. Record company and music publisher (Hserf Music/ASCAP, Blair Vizzion Music/BMI). Releases 5 singles and 2 LPs/year. Pays 7-10% royalty to artists on contract; statutory rate to publisher per song on record.

• See their listing in the Music Publishers section.

How to Contact: Submit demo tape by mail. Unsolicited submissions are OK. Prefers cassette or VHS videocassette with at least 3 songs and lyric sheet. SASE. Reports in 3 weeks.

Music: Mostly **R&B**, **rock** and **pop**; also **jazz**, **gospel** and **rap**. Released "Nasty Dancer," recorded by Kilo on Ichiban Records; "Good Thang" (by Cirocco/Mr. G.), recorded by Diamond on Warlock Records (R&B); and "That's Right" (by Taz/Raheem), recorded by DJ Taz on Ichiban Records (rap). Other artists include Chris Gantt, Jimmy Calhoun, Charles Pettaway, Cirocco, McIntosh and Vivian Memefee.

‡FRONT ROW RECORDS, Ridgewood Park Estates, 222 Tulane St., Garland TX 75043. Contact: Gene or Dea Summers. Public Relations/Artist and Fan Club Coordinator: Steve Summers. A&R: Shawn Summers. Labels include Juan Records. Record company and music publisher (Silicon Music/BMI). Estab. 1968. Releases 5-6 singles and 2-3 LPs/year. Pays negotiable royalty to artists on contract; standard royalty to songwriters on contract.

• See the listing for Front Row's publishing affiliate, Silicon Music, in the Music Publishers section.

How to Contact: Submit demo tape by mail. Unsolicited submissions are OK. Prefers cassette or VHS videocassette with 1-3 songs. Does not return material. Reports ASAP.

Music: Mostly **'50s rock/rockabilly**; also **country**, **bluegrass**, **old-time blues** and **R&B**. Released "Domino," recorded by Gene Summers on Pollytone Records (rockabilly); "Goodbye Priscilla" and "Cool Baby," both recorded by Gene Summers on Collectables Records.

Tips: "If you own masters of 1950s rock and rockabilly, contact us first! We will work with you on a percentage basis for overseas release. We have active releases in Holland, Switzerland, Belgium, Australia, England, France, Sweden, Norway and the US at the present. We need original masters. You must be able to prove ownership of tapes before we can accept a deal. We're looking for little-known, obscure recordings. We have the market if you have the tapes! Sample records available. Send SASE for catalogue. We are also interested in C&W and rockabilly *artists* who have not recorded for awhile but still have the voice and appeal to sell overseas. *We request a photo and bio with material submission.*"

‡FUNDAMENTAL RECORDING COMPANY, P.O. Box 118, Pass Christian MS 39571. Phone/fax: (601)864-1360. President: Richard Jordan. Distributed by Cargo, Datcha and Rough Trade (in Europe). Record company. Estab. 1984. Releases 6 CDs/year. Pays negotiable royalty to artists on contract; statutory rate to publisher per song on record.

How to Contact: Submit demo tape by mail. Unsolicited submissions are OK. Prefers cassette. Does not return material. Reports in 1 month.
Music: Mostly **roots** and **Americana**, **alternative** and **blues/Cajun**. Released *Six String Drag*, recorded by Six String Drag; *Eugene Chadbourne/Jimmy Carl Black*, recorded by Eugene Chadbourne and Jimmy Carl Black; and *Watertower*, recorded by Michael Hurley, all on Fundamental Recording Co. Other artists include The Johnsons, Used Carlotta, Drovers Old Time Medicine Show, Dirtball, Tim Lee, One Riot One Ranger and Lilybandits.

GEFFEN/DGC RECORDS, 9130 Sunset Blvd., Los Angeles CA 90069-6197. (310)278-9010. Fax: (310)271-4563. New York office: 1755 Broadway, New York NY 10019. (212)841-8600. Fax: (212)247-8852. Website: http://www.geffen.com. Distributed by UNI; labels include Almo Sounds, Minty Fresh Records, Republic Records and Outpost Recordings. Record company.
How to Contact: Geffen/DGC does not accept unsolicited material.
Music: Released *Recovering the Satellites*, recorded by Counting Crows; *Odelay*, recorded by Beck, both on DGC Records; and *Beavis and Butt-head Do America*, recorded by various artists (soundtrack) on Geffen Records. Other artists include Veruca Salt, Bloodhound Gang, Lisa Loeb, Hole, Cowboy Junkies, Elastica, Peter Gabriel, The Roots, White Zombie and the Pat Metheny Group.

GENERIC RECORDS, INC., 433 Limestone Rd., Ridgefield CT 06877. (203)438-9811. President: Gary Lefkowith. Labels include Outback, GLYN. Record company, music publisher (Sotto Music/BMI) and record producer. Estab. 1976. Releases 6 singles and 2 CDs/year. Pays 5% royalty to artists on contract; statutory rate to publisher per song on record.
How to Contact: Call and obtain permission to submit. Prefers cassette with 2-3 songs. SASE. Reports in 1 month.
Music: Mostly **alternative rock**, **rock** and **pop**; also **country** and **rap**. Released *Disconnected* and *Hi fi*, both recorded by Hi fi.

GLOBAL PACIFIC RECORDS/BLACKHORSE ENTERTAINMENT, 1275 E. MacArthur St., Sonoma CA 95476. (707)996-2748. Fax: (707)996-2658. E-mail: transvsn@community.net. Website: http://www.ninegates.com/global.html. A&R Director: Howard Sapper. Distributed by Navarre, Music Design, White Swann and Nature Company. Record company and music publisher (Global Pacific Publishing). Releases 10 singles, 12 LPs and 12 CDs/year.
How to Contact: Write or call first and obtain permission to submit. Prefers cassette with 3 songs. "Note style of music on envelope." Does not return material. Reports in 1-2 months.
Music: Mostly **New Age**, **pop**, **jazz**, **alternative rock** and "**pop/quiet storm**;" also **classical**. Released *Fringe of Blue* (by Bruce Burger), recorded by Rebbe Soul (world); *Ever Free Never Bound* (by Bob Kindler), recorded by Babaji Bob Kindler (world); and *Reunion* (by Joseph Rojo), recorded by Rojo (classical), all on Global Pacific Records. Other artists include David Friesen, Georgia Kelly, Ben Tavera King, Paul Greaver, Morgan Fisher, Steve Kindler and Charles Michael Brotman.

‡GLOW IN THE DARK, 3405 Ridgeway Rd., Orange CA 92867. (714)282-8386. Fax: (714)282-9086. President: Tad Banzuelo. Labels include Daisy Chain Indy Record Co. and CTRL + ALT + DEL Compact Disks. Record company and record producer (Glow in the Dark Studio). Estab. 1990. Releases 4 singles, 4 LPs and 2 CDs/year. Pays negotiable royalty to artists on contract; negotiable rate to publisher per song on record.
How to Contact: Call first to arrange personal interview. Prefers cassette, DAT or CD. "We are looking for a great Orange County band to form a deal (partnership) with. Your demo can sound like crap. Looking for talent!" Does not return material. Reports in 1 week.
Music: Mostly **alternative**, **rock** and **guitar bands**; also **female vocalists**, **dance music** and **hip-hop**. Released *Out About Somewhere Round*, written and recorded by The Roundabouts (rock); *Bedlam Inside*, written and recorded by Noise Within (punk), both on Daisy Chain Records; and *Crack Core*, written and recorded by Dail 7 on 7 Records (funk/rock). Other artists include The Bleak Composers, Masseed Productions and Spontaneous Combustion.

‡ **THE DOUBLE DAGGER** before a listing indicates that the listing is new in this edition.

‡**GODDESS RECORDS**, 15243 LaCruz Dr. #502, Pacific Palisades CA 90272. (310)287-1934. E-mail: mem@monitor.net. Website: http://www.goddessrecords.com. Head of A&R: Spanky Lankton. Record company, music publisher, record producer and management firm (Rock Goddess Music Management). Estab. 1990. Releases 6 singles, 2 LPs and 2 CDs/year. Pays negotiable royalty to artists on contract; statutory rate to publisher per song on record.

How to Contact: Submit demo tape by mail. Unsolicited submissions are OK. Prefers cassette and lyric sheet. Include SASE for response. Does not return material. Reports in 1 month.

Music: Mostly **pop songs, AAAcoustic** and **techno rock.**

GOLD CITY RECORDS, INC., 10 Deepwell Farms Rd., S. Salem NY 10590. (914)533-5096. Fax: (914)533-5097. E-mail: gcrecords@aol.com. Website: http://members.aol.com/GCRecords. President: Chris Jasper. Vice President/General Counsel: Margie Jasper. Labels include Gold City Label. Record company. Estab. 1986. Releases 5-10 singles, 5-10 12″ singles, 3-5 LPs and 3-5 CDs/year. Pays statutory rate to publisher per song on record.

How to Contact: Submit demo tape by mail. Unsolicited submissions are OK. Prefers cassette with 3 songs and lyric sheets. SASE. Reports in 4-6 weeks.

Music: Mostly **R&B/gospel**. Released *Deep Inside*, written and recorded by Chris Jasper; *Outfront*, written and recorded by Outfront; and "Forever" (by Chris Jasper), recorded by Brothaz By Choice, all on Gold City Records.

GOLDEN TRIANGLE RECORDS, 1051 Saxonburg Blvd., Glenshaw PA 15116. E-mail: marcels@earthlink.net. Website: http://www.geocities.com/Sunset Strip/6929/index.html. Producer: Sunny James. Labels include Rockin Robin and Shell-B. Music publisher (Golden Triangle/BMI) and record producer (Sunny James). Estab. 1987. Releases 8 singles, 6 12″ singles, 10 LPs and 19 CDs/year. Pays standard royalty to artists on contract; statutory rate to publishers per song on record.

- See the listing for Sunny James in the Record Producers section.

How to Contact: Submit demo tape by mail. Unsolicited submissions are OK. Prefers cassette, 15 IPS reel-to-reel or ½″ VHS videocassette with 3 songs and lyric or lead sheets. Does not return material. Reports in 1 month.

Music: Mostly **progressive R&B**, **rock** and **A/C**; also **jazz** and **country**. Released "Hot Dog Heaven," written and recorded by Peter Bittner; "You Don't Have to Cry Anymore," written and recorded by C. Harp; and "Tow Truck Blues," written and recorded by J. Sweeny, all on GTP Records. Other artists include the Marcels.

‡**GONZO! RECORDS INC.**, P.O. Box 3688, San Dimas CA 91773. Phone/fax: (909)598-9031. E-mail: gonzorcrds@aol.com. Website: http://www.jps.net/gonzo. President: Jeffrey Gonzalez. Record company. Estab. 1993. Releases 3 singles and 1-6 CDs/year. Pays negotiable royalty to artists on contract; statutory rate to publisher per song on record.

How to Contact: Submit demo tape by mail. Unsolicited submissions are OK. Prefers cassette or CD. "When submitting, please specify that you got the listing from *Songwriter's Market*." Does not return material. Reports in 4-6 weeks.

Music: Mostly **commercial industrial**, **dance** and **techno**; also **commercial alternative** and **synth pop**. Released *Hate Breeds Hate*, written and recorded by BOL (hard industrial); *Momentum*, written and recorded by Full Frequency (commerical industrial); and *Ruth in Alien Corn*, written and recorded by Pinch Point (alternative pop), all on Gonzo! Records. Other artists include Turning Keys.

Tips: "Gonzo! Records owner Jeffrey Gonzalez is 100% dedicated to his bands. He's got a label tour van and trailer to prove it. Further, the tour support includes a New York booking agency and a publicist to promote his groups."

‡**GOTHAM RECORDS**, 1841 Broadway, Suite 1012, New York NY 10023. (212)265-3820. Fax: (212)265-3145. E-mail: gothamrec@aol.com. Contact: A&R Dept. Distributed by Ichiban Records. Record company. Estab. 1994. Releases 4 LPs and 4 CDs/year. Pays negotiable royalty to artists on contract; statutory rate to publisher per song on record.

How to Contact: Submit demo tape by mail. Unsolicited submissions are OK. Prefers cassette, CD or VHS videocassette and bios, pictures and touring information. Does not return material. Reports in 6-8 weeks.

Music: Mostly **rock** and **AAA**. Released *Semi-Gloss*, recorded by Love Huskies; and *Head Shaking . . .*, recorded by John Monopoly, both on Gotham Records (alternative).

Tips: "Don't waste your money on jazzy packaging—spend it on good production. Any good A&R scout should care most about songs and production, not colored mailers and leather-bound bios!"

GRASS ROOTS RECORD & TAPE/LMI RECORDS, P.O. Box 532, Malibu CA 90265. (213)463-5998. President: Lee Magid. Record company, record producer (Lee Magid), music publisher (Alexis/ASCAP, Marvelle/BMI, Lou-Lee/BMI) and management firm (Lee Magid Management Co.). Member AIMP, NARAS. Estab. 1967. Releases 4 LPs and 4 CDs/year. Pays 50% royalty per record sold to artists on contract; statutory rate to publishers per song on record.

- Grass Roots Record's publishing company, Alexis, is listed in the Music Publishers section, and President Lee Magid is listed in the Record Producers section.

How to Contact: Submit demo tape by mail. Unsolicited submissions are OK. Prefers cassette with 3 songs and lyric sheet. "Please, no 45s." Does not return material. Reports in 2 months.
Music: Mostly **pop/rock**, **R&B**, **country**, **gospel**, **jazz/rock** and **blues**; also **bluegrass**, **children's** and **Latin**. Released "Mighty Hand" (by C. Rhone), recorded by Cajun Hart on LMI Records (R&B); *Don't You Know* (by B. Worth), recorded by Della Reese on RCA Records (pop); and *Blues For The Weepers* (by L. Magid/M. Rich), recorded by Lou Rawls on Capitol Records (R&B). Other artists include John Michael Hides, Julie Miller, Tramaine Hawkins and ZAD.

GREEN BEAR RECORDS, Rockin' Chair Center Suite 103, 1033 W. State Highway 76, Branson MO 65616. (417)334-2383. Fax: (417)334-2306. President: George J. Skupien. Labels include Green One Records and Bear Tracks Records. Record company, music publisher (Green One Music/BMI) and record producer (George Skupien). Estab. 1992. Releases 3-4 singles, 1-10 LPs and 2-6 CDs/year. Pays negotiable royalty to artists on contract; statutory rate to publisher per song on record.

- Green Bear's publishing company, Green One Music, is listed in the Music Publishers section.

How to Contact: Submit demo tape by mail. Unsolicited submissions are OK. Prefers cassette or DAT with 4-6 songs and lyric or lead sheet. Does not return material. Reports in 6-8 weeks.
Music: Mostly **polkas**, **waltzes** and **country**; also **Southern gospel**, **MOR** and **light rock**. Released "Oh My Aching Back" and "Lotto Polka," written and recorded by George Skupien (country); and "Keep On Keepin' On," written and recorded by Matt Row'd (country), all on Green Bear Records. Other artists include D. Mack, B. Jackson, Ted Thomas, Rudy Negron and The Mystics.
Tips: "Submit a well-produced, studio quality demo of your material on cassette or DAT with a clean vocal up front. If possible, submit your demo with and without lead vocal for presentation to recording artists."

‡GRP RECORDS, 555 W. 57th St., 10th Floor, New York NY 10019. (212)424-1000. Fax: (212)424-1007. Website: http://www.grp.com. Distributed by UNI; labels include Impulse! Records and Blue Thumb Records. Record company.
How to Contact: GRP Records does not accept unsolicited submissions.
Music: Released *Blues for Schuur*, recorded by Diane Schuur on GRP Records; *All For You (A Dedication to the Nat King Cole Trio)*, recorded by Diana Krall; and *Tales From the Hudson*, recorded by Michael Brecker, both on Impulse! Records. Other artists include George Benson, Danilo Perez, Groove Collective, Eric Reed, Keith Jarrett, Richard Page, The Crusaders, Candy Butchers, Nuyorcian Soul and Acoustic Alchemy.

GUESTSTAR RECORDS, 17321 Ritchie Ave. NE, Sand Lake MI 49343-9475. President: Raymond G. Dietz, Sr. Record company, management firm (Gueststar Entertainment Agency), record producer and music publisher (Sandlake Music/BMI). Estab. 1967. Releases 8 singles, 2 LPs and 2 CDs/year. Royalty varies to artist on contract, "depending on number of selections on product; 2 ½¢/per record sold; statutory rate to publisher per song on record."

- See the listing for Gueststar Entertainment Agency in the Managers and Booking Agents section.

How to Contact: Submit demo tape by mail. Unsolicited submissions are OK. Prefers cassette or VHS videocassette with lyric and lead sheet. "Send a SASE with submissions." Does not return material. Reports in 1 week.
Music: Mostly **country rock** and **country**; also **religious/country** and **mountain songs**. Released *Best of Mountain Man* (by Mike Gillette/Raymond Dietz); "Proud to be Your Boy" and "Back on the Job" (by

TO HELP YOU UNDERSTAND and use the information in these listings, see "How to Use *Songwriter's Market* to Get Your Songs Heard," on page 3.

Raymond Dietz), all recorded by Mountain Man on Gueststar Records (country). Other artists include Jamie "K" and Sweetgrass Band.
Tips: "Songwriters: send songs like you hear on the radio. Keep updating your music to keep up with the latest trends. Artists: send VHS video and press kit."

HALLWAY INTERNATIONAL RECORDS/1ST COAST POSSE MIXES, 8017 International Village Dr., Jacksonville FL 32211. (904)765-8276. Distributed by Endo-Toshiko, Inc. Record company, music publisher (Aljoni Music Co./BMI, Hallmarque Musical Works, Ltd./ASCAP), record producer (Hallways to Fame Productions) and video makers (Cosmic Eye). Estab. 1971. Releases 4-6 singles, 8 12″ singles and 6 LPs/year. Royalty negotiated per contract.
How to Contact: Submit demo tape by mail. Unsolicited submissions are OK. Prefers cassette or VHS videocassette with 2-3 songs and lyric or lead sheet. Does not return material. Reports in 2-3 months (when solicited).
Music: Mostly **rap**, **R&B**, **hop-hop** and **jazz**; also **world** (others will be considered). Released *Nomads* (by Al Hall Jr.), recorded by Cosmos Dwellers Arkestra on Hallway International Records (jazz-world); "Godz," written and recorded by Ghetto Prophets (new hip-hop); and "Hood Muzik" (by Al Money), recorded by Tha H.O.O.D. (new hip-hop), both on 1st Coast Family Records. Other artists include O.R.E.N./Elementz, Ron "Cos" Hall and Maya.

HAPPY MAN RECORDS, 4696 Kahlua Lane, Bonita Springs FL 34134. (941)947-6978. Executive Producer: Dick O'Bitts. Distributed by V&R; labels include Condor and Con Air. Record company, music publisher (Rocker Music/BMI, Happy Man Music/ASCAP) and record producer (Rainbow Collection Ltd.). Estab. 1972. Releases 4-6 singles, 4-6 12″ singles, 4-6 LPs and 4 EPs/year. Pays negotiable royalty to artists on contract; statutory rate to publisher per song on record.

- Happy Man's publishing company, Rocker Music/Happy Man Music, can be found in the Music Publishers section.

How to Contact: Submit demo tape by mail. Unsolicited submissions are OK. Prefers cassette or VHS videocassette with 3-4 songs and lyric sheet. SASE. Reports in 4 weeks.
Music: All types. Released *She Likes to Dance* (by Wallace/Skinner), recorded by Challengers (country) on Happy Man Records; *Alright, Already—The Lacys* (by various), recorded by Robin & Joan Lacy on Vrew Records (cajun); and *Meet the Bengtons* (by various), recorded by Bengton Sisters on Happy Man Records. Other artists include Ray Pack, Crosswinds, Overdue and Colt Gipson.

‡HI-BIAS RECORDS INC., 49 Beckett Ave., Toronto, Ontario MGL 2B3 **Canada**. (416)614-1581. Fax: (416)249-2799. E-mail: nick@hibias.ca. Website: http://www.hibias.ca/~hibias. Director: Nick Fiorucci. Distributed by Polygram; labels include Toronto Underground, Love From San Francisco, Mephisto Records, Crash and Club Culture. Record company, music publisher (Bend 60 Music/SOCAN) and record producer (Nick Fiorucci). Estab. 1990. Releases 30-40 singles, 4-8 LPs, 10 EPs and 5-10 CDs/year. Pays negotiable royalty to artists on contract; statutory rate to publisher per song on record.
How to Contact: Submit demo tape by mail. Unsolicited submissions are OK. Prefers cassette or DAT with 3 songs and lyric sheet. Does not return material. Reports in 4-6 weeks.
Music: Mostly **dance, pop** and **R&B**; also **acid jazz** and **house**. Released *Club Culture*, *Groove Construction* and *Rhythm Formula*, both written and recorded by various artists on BMG Records (dance). Other artists include Oval Emotion, DJ's Rule, Temperance and Ear Candy.

‡HOLLYWOOD RECORDS, 500 S. Buena Vista St., Burbank CA 91521. (818)560-5670. Fax: (818)841-5140. New York office: 170 Fifth Ave., Penthouse, New York NY 10010. Website: http://www.hollywoodrec.com. Distributed by PGD; labels include Acid Jazz Records, Mountain Division Records and Bar/None Records. Record company.
How to Contact: Hollywood Records does not accept unsolicited submissions. Queries accepted only from a manager or lawyer.
Music: Released *Destruction by Definition*, recorded by The Suicide Machines; and *Greatest Hits*, recorded by Queen. Other artists include Alice Cooper, Van Gogh's Daughter, Brian May, Super 8, Caroline's Spine, Seaweed, Coolbone, Roger McGuinn, Danzig and Pistoleros.

HOT WINGS ENTERTAINMENT, 429 Richmond Ave., Buffalo NY 14222. (716)884-0248. E-mail: dahotwings@aol.com. Manager, A&R: Dale Anderson. Distributed by Horizon/Goldenrod (in Canada) and Festival Distribution. Record company and music publisher (Buffalo Wings Music/BMI). Estab. 1994. Releases 2 LPs and 2 CDs/year. Pays 15-20% to artists on contract; statutory rate to publisher per song on record.
How to Contact: Call first and obtain permission to submit. Prefers cassette with 3 or more songs. Does

not return material. Reports in 6-8 weeks.
Music: Mostly **folk/acoustic**, **alternative rock** and **jazz**. (Preference to artists from Upstate New York.) Released *Down to Money*, written and recorded by Alison Pipitone (folk-rock); *Flavor* (by Geoffrey Fitzhugh Perry), recorded by Fitzhugh and the Fanatics (blues-rock); and *Demo* (by Hanna Grol), recorded by Is June (folk-rock), all on Hot Wings Records.

‡HOTTRAX RECORDS, 1957 Kilburn Dr., Atlanta GA 30324. (404)662-6661. Vice President, A&R: Oliver Cooper. Distributed by Southern Music Distribution and Action; labels include Dance-A-Thon and Hardkor. Record company, record producer (Alexander Janoulis Productions) and music publisher (Starfox Publishing). Releases 12 singles and 3-4 CDs/year. Pays 5-15% royalty to artists on contract.

- See the listing for Alexander Janoulis Productions in the Record Producers section.

How to Contact: Write first and obtain permission to submit. Prefers cassette with 3 songs and lyric sheet. SASE. "We will not return tapes without adequate postage." Reports in 3-6 months. "When submissions get extremely heavy, we do not have the time to respond/return material we pass on. We do notify those sending the most promising work we review, however."
Music: Mostly **top 40/pop**, **rock** and **country**; also **hardcore punk** and **jazz-fusion**. Released *Blues In Dixieland*, written and recorded by Bob Page (blues/jazz); *Live From the Eye of the Storm* (by R. Wilson/A. Janoulis), recorded by Roger Hurricane Wilson (blues/rock); and *Stuck In Bluesville*, written and recorded by Sammy Blue (blues), all on Hottrax Records. Other artists include Burl Compton (country), Sheffield-Webb (contemporary male-female duo), Michael Rozakis & Yorgos (pop), Starfoxx (rock), The Night Shadows (rock), The Bop (new wave) and Secret Lover.

‡HOUSE OF BLUES RECORDS, 8439 Sunset Blvd., Suite 102, W. Hollywood CA 90069. (213)848-4801. Fax: (213)650-1602. Contact: Bill Gilbert. Distributed by BMG.
How to Contact: Submit demo tape by mail. Unsolicited submissions are OK. Prefers CD with description of artist, press kit, bio and photo.

HOWDY RECORDS, 1810 S. Pea Ridge Rd., Temple TX 76502. (817)773-8001 or (817)939-8000. Owner: Andy Anderson. Distributed by Western Merchandising and Heart O' Country Distribution; labels include Border Serenade and Up Yonder. Record company, music publisher (Heart O' Country) and record producer (Lonnie Wright). Estab. 1960. Releases 18 singles, 6 EPs and 12 CDs/year. Pays 2.5% royalty to artists on contract; 2.5% rate to publisher per song on record.
How to Contact: Submit demo tape by mail. Unsolicited submissions are OK. Prefers cassette with 10 songs and lyric sheet. Does not return material. Reports in 6-8 weeks.
Music: Mostly **country**, **religious** and **Tex-Mex**. Released "Ball of Fire" (by J. Anderson), recorded by Cindy Anderson; "Lonely Heart" (by Joe Harris), recorded by Billie Royal; and "Boys Nite Out" (by Bobbie Jean), recorded by Lon Wright, all on Howdy Records. Other artists include Paul Aquilar, Joe Bailey, Paul White, Buzz Martin and Betty Rae.

hypnotic recordings usa, P.O. Box 7347, Fullerton CA 92834-7347. (213)312-4343. A&R Rep: Armando Vega. Distributed by Perris Records, Azra International, Rok Postage, Dream Discs, Sinbad Productions and Marquee (in Asia). Record company. Estab. 1995. Releases 2 singles, 4 LPs, 4 EPs and 4 CDs/year. Pays negotiable royalty to artists on contract; statutory rate to publisher per song on record.
How to Contact: Submit demo tape by mail. Unsolicited submissions are OK. Prefers cassette or VHS videotape with 3 songs. SASE. Reports in 2 months.
Music: Mostly **heavy metal**, **loud rock** and **hard rock**. Released *Wicked From the Womb* and "Erroresistable," both written and recorded by Hyperchild. Other artists include In Search Of, Da Meat Cleavers and Rated R.

IKON RECORDS, (formerly Rage-N-Records), 212 N. 12th St., Suite #3, Philadelphia PA 19107. (215)977-7779. E-mail: rage@netaxs.com. Website: http://www.ikonman.com. President: David Ivory. Labels include Rage-N-Records. Record company, music publisher (RNR Publishing/ASCAP) and record producer (Ivory Productions). Estab. 1986. Pays various royalty to artists on contract; statutory rate to publisher per song on record.
How to Contact: Call or write first and obtain permission to submit. Prefers cassette, DAT or VHS videocassette with 3-5 songs and lyric sheet. SASE. Reports in 4-6 weeks.
Music: Mostly **rock**, **pop** and **blues**; also **R&B**. Released *Focus*, written and recorded by Slideways; "Shelter," written and recorded by Billy Freeze; and *Insight, Outtasight*, written and recorded by Stevie LaRocca, all on Ikon Records.

IMI RECORDS, 541 N. Fairbanks Court, Chicago IL 60611. (312)245-9334. Fax: (312)245-9327. Contact: Head of A&R (specify style: rock, jazz, urban). Record company and music publisher (Vertical City

Music Inc./BMI; 2 Beep Music Inc./ASCAP). Estab. 1993. Releases 8 singles, 5-7 LPs, 2-3 EPs and 4-8 CDs/year. Pays negotiable royalty to artists on contract; negotiable rate to publishers per song on record.

- IMI is an independent label with international distribution. However, some releases are released through individual affiliations with Atlantic, Sony, MCA, TVT and other major labels, depending on the project.

How to Contact: Submit demo tape by mail. Unsolicited submissions are OK. Prefers cassette, DAT or ½" VHS videocassette with pictures, bios and press (if any). "Be very specific on what you're looking for in a label. Artist/songwriter, band, producer looking for a deal with specific artist, label looking for promotion and/or distribution. Above all, please be professional!" Does not return material. Reports in 4 weeks.
Music: Mostly **alternative/modern rock, urban R&B** and **jazz (traditional and progressive)**; also **artists (individual and bands)**, **producers** and **small label affiliations**. Released "Mindblowing," written and recorded by David Josias on IMI/Lava/Atlantic (R&B); *The Falling Wallendas* (by Scott Bennett/Allen Keller), recorded by The Falling Wallendas (rock/pop); and *Jazz Wagon* (by Jon Weber/various), recorded by Jon Weber (jazz), both on IMI Records.
Tips: "Research a label's work, as not all labels are appropriate for all artists. Be open to creative criticism as it is a team-oriented endeavor with regards to artists' careers and directions. Remember, the intention is to sell records. Great records don't come easy, so prepare to be flexible and grow."

INFERNO RECORDS, P.O. Box 28743, Kansas City MO 64118. (816)454-7638. E-mail: murtha@kcmetro.cc.mo.us. Director: Mark Murtha. Distributed by BPM Records and Infinity Records. Record company. Estab. 1989. Releases 6 LPs, 4 EPs and 4 CDs/year. Pays standard royalty to artists on contract; statutory rate to publisher per song on record.
How to Contact: Write first and obtain permission to submit. Prefers cassette with 4 songs. Does not return material. Reports in 1 month.
Music: Mostly **rock**, **alternative** and **country**. Released *Awake*, recorded by London Drive (rock); *We're Pretty Good—If You Turn Your Head*, recorded by Bad Hair Day (rock); and *Mass Spewage*, recorded by Phantasmagoria (alternative), all on Inferno Records. Other artists include CIZI and Eastern Sky.
Tips: "We're primarily looking for talented self-starters who have professional recordings ready for release. We release an annual compilation of unsigned artists."

‡INSIDE SOUNDS, 1122 Longreen, Memphis TN 38120, (901)682-2063. Fax: (901)682-0013. Website: http://www.amusic.com. Owner: Eddie Dattel. Labels include Inside Memphis, Memphis Archives, Inside Sounds Classic and Psychorock. Record company, music publisher (Inside Sounds Publishing) and record producer (Eddie Dattel). Estab. 1992. Releases 10 LPs and 12 CDs/year. Pays negotiable royalty to artists on contract; statutory rate to publisher per song on record.

- Inside Sounds and its affiliated labels are noted for releasing blues recordings from Memphis-area artists.

How to Contact: Submit demo tape by mail. Unsolicited submissions are OK. Prefers cassette. Does not return material. Reports in 3 weeks.
Music: Mostly **blues**, **folk** and **jazz**; also **pop**, **alternative rock** and **comedy**. Released *Diamond In The Bluff* (by Joe Sanders), recorded by Memphis Sheiks (blues); *At The Same Place Twice In Life* (by Klaudia Ploderer), recorded by Klaudia & Rico (alternative); and *Reed Between The Lines*, written and recorded by Carl Wolfe (jazz), all on Inside Memphis. Other artists include Wally Ford and The Lizzard Kings.

‡INTERSCOPE RECORDS, 10900 Wilshire Blvd., Suite 1230, Los Angeles CA 90024. (310)208-6547. Fax: (310)208-7343. Contact: A&R. New York office: 540 Madison Ave., 27th Floor, New York NY 10022. (212)508-5900. Fax: (212)980-7042. Website: http://www.interscoperecords.com. Distributed by UNI; labels include Death Row Records, Nothing Records, Aftermath Records and Trauma Records. Record company.
How to Contact: Submit demo tape by mail. Unsolicited submissions are OK. Any format is OK. Can take up to 6 months for a response.
Music: Released *Bringing Down the Horse*, recorded by The Wallflowers; *Another Level*, recorded by Blackstreet; and *Me Against the World*, recorded by 2 Pac, all on Interscope Records. Other artists include Jane Jensen, Helmet, Dr. Dre, Shaquille O'Neal, Red Five, Bush, No Doubt, Claw Hammer and Puzzlegut.

INTERSOUND INC., P.O. Box 1724, Roswell GA 30077. (770)664-9262. Fax: (404)664-7316. A&R Rep (gospel): Rev. Suffewel; (rap): J.W. Sewell and Ron Patterson. Labels include Branson and So-Lo Jam. Record company, music publisher and distributor. Estab. 1982. Releases 6-10 singles and 150 CDs/year. Pays negotiable royalty to artists on contract; negotiable rate to publisher per song on record.
How to Contact: Write or call first and obtain permission to submit. Prefers cassette with 3 songs. "We will contact the songwriter when we are interested in the material." Does not return material. Reports in 2 months.

Music: Mostly **rock, gospel** and **country**; also **rap, swing** and **classical**. Released *Back to the Innocence*, written and recorded by Jonathan Cain (rock); *Ronnie James and the Jez Hot Swing Club*, written and recorded by Ronnie James (swing); and *Hold On* (by Michael Scott), recorded by Michael Scott and the Outreach Choir (gospel), all on Intersound Inc. Other artists include Way 2 Real (rap), Jennifer Holliday (gospel), The Gatlin Brothers (country) and The Bellamy Brothers (country).
Tips: "Intersound is only interested in non-signed, non-published writers."

INTERSTATE 40 RECORDS, 9208 Spruce Mountain Way, Las Vegas NV 89134. (702)363-8506. President: Eddie Lee Carr. Labels include Tracker Records. Record company and music publisher (Watchesgro Music/BMI and Watch Us Climb/ASCAP). Estab. 1979. Releases 12 singles, 1 LP and 2 CDs/year. Pays 50% royalty to artists on contract; statutory rate to publisher per song on record.

- Interstate 40's publishing company, Watchesgro Music, can be found in the Music Publishers section.

How to Contact: Submit demo tape by mail. Unsolicited submissions are OK. Prefers cassette with 3 songs. SASE. Reports in 2 weeks.
Music: Mostly **country**. Movie and TV credits include "Mars Attacks," "Con Air," "Top of the World," "Fierce Creatures" and "McHale's Navy."

‡**INTREPID RECORDS**, 808 Travis, Suite 1409, Houston TX 77002. Director of Operations: Rick Eyk. Record company and record producer (Rick Eyk). Pays 50% royalty to artists on contract; statutory rate to publisher per song on record.
How to Contact: Submit demo tape by mail. Unsolicited submissions are OK. Prefers CDs ready for distribution. Does not return material. Reports in 1 month; include #10 SASE for response.
Music: Blues, jazz, classical, standards, country, New Age and **eclectic/folk**.

‡**ISLAND RECORDS**, 825 Eighth Ave., New York NY 10019. (212)333-8000. Fax: (212)233-8495. Los Angeles office: 8920 Sunset Blvd., Los Angeles CA 90069. (310)276-4500. Fax: (310)278-5862. Distributed by PGD; labels include T-Neck Records and Tuff Gong Records. Record company.
How to Contact: Island Records does not accept unsolicited submissions. "No phone calls, please."
Music: Released *Pop*, recorded by U2; *Dru Hill*, recorded by Dru Hill; and *To the Faithful Departed*, recorded by the Cranberries, all on Island Records. Other artists include Local H, Mona Lisa and Tricky.

JALYN RECORDING CO., 306 Millwood Dr., Nashville TN 37217. (615)366-9999. President: Jack Lynch. Labels include Nashville Bluegrass and Nashville Country Recording Company. Record company, music publisher (Jaclyn Music/BMI, JLMG Music/ASCAP), record producer, film company (Nashville Country Productions) and distributor (Nashville Music Sales). Estab. 1963. Releases 1-12 LPs/year. Pays statutory royalty to artists on contract; statutory rate to publisher per song on record.

- See the listings for Jaclyn Music in the Music Publishers section and Nashville Country Productions in the Record Producers section.

How to Contact: Submit demo tape by mail. Unsolicited submissions are OK. Prefers cassette with 1-4 songs and lyric sheet. SASE. Reports in 1 month.
Music: Country, bluegrass, gospel and **MOR**. Released *Time Will Tell* (by T.E. Morris), recorded by Odie Gal on NCP-19961 Records; *There'll Never Be Another* (by J.D. Lynch), recorded by Jack Lynch on NBC-19941 Records; and *I'm Wanted* (by Barbara Jackson), recorded by Don Hendrix on NCP-19964 Records.
Tips: "Send good performance on cassette, bio, picture and SASE."

JAMAKA RECORD CO., 3621 Heath Lane, Mesquite TX 75150. (214)279-5858. Contact: Jimmy Fields. Labels include Felco and Kick Records. Record company, record producer and music publisher (Cherie Music/BMI). Estab. 1955. Releases 2 singles/year. Pays .05% royalty to artists on contract; statutory rate to publisher for each record sold.

- Jamaka Record Co.'s publishing company, Cherie Music, is listed in the Music Publishers section.

How to Contact: Submit demo tape by mail. Unsolicited submissions are OK. Prefers cassette with lyric sheet. "A new singer should send a good tape with at least 4 strong songs, presumably recorded in a professional studio." SASE.
Music: Country and **progressive country**. Released "Cajun Baby Blues" and "If You Call This Loving," recorded by Steve Pride.

J&J MUSICAL ENTERPRISES LTD., P.O. Box 575, Kings Park NY 11754. Contact: Frances Cavezza. Labels include JAJ Records. Record company and record producer. Estab. 1983. Releases 1-2 CDs/year. Pays variable royalty.

INSIDER REPORT

Internet offers new opportunities for artists to promote themselves

Jay Barbieri

On the road to success in the music business, the greatest hurdle a band faces is getting heard—both by A&R execs and by the listening (and buying) public. After close to a decade of working in the music industry (including stints at both Angel and Polygram), Jay Barbieri, well aware of this problem, may have created a solution: He launched the record industry into cyberspace by creating J-Bird Records, the first Internet-only record label (http://www.j-birdrecords.com).

Traditionally bands have been marketed through MTV, radio and retail. Barbieri sees the Web as a logical outlet for artists to market their work. "I think this is one of the best developmental vehicles that bands can use," he says. "It's a way to get more exposure for more artists to a broader audience." With J-Bird, Barbieri's goal is to provide a global marketplace for musicians, giving tens of millions of Internet users access to their music. "We work from the bottom up—grass roots like record companies used to," Barbieri says. "We want to grow up with the college student. They have the greatest access to the Internet, and when they get out of school, they have less time to explore record stores. We want them to consider J-Bird their place to buy music and listen to music." Worldwide, the 15- to 24-year-old demographic annually spends $4 billion on music. Through his website Barbieri hopes to tap into that market.

In addition to reaching consumers, Barbieri sees the Web as a great place for bands to attract the attention of major record labels. "We're the farm team for the major leagues," he says. "Should a major label have to make a decision as to which up-and-coming band to focus on, [being on the J-Bird roster] gives them a better history and a proven track record." And thanks to an aggressive PR campaign, Barbieri is sure that all the major labels know about J-Bird Records. "Some have actually referred artists to us that they'd like to see get track records before they make judgments about whether to sign them."

Such judgments aren't made by J-Bird's A&R team, however. Any band can sign with J-Bird as long as they provide a quality master with 30-70 minutes of original music, and artwork for their CD. Each band pays a $600 production fee, which is refundable when they sell 500 CDs through J-Bird's website (CDs by J-Bird artists are sold only through the website, and are not available through traditional retail outlets). Bands can acquire their own CDs at a discounted rate for promotion and sales. "Most bands spend more to record a demo that sits on an executive's desk and gets played for 30 seconds," Barbieri says. "The fact is, more than 95% of all bands will never get a traditional record company deal or have their music exposed to the masses. My philosophy has always been that all bands have a potential fan base that never gets completely realized."

INSIDER REPORT, *Barbieri*

Artists who sign with J-Bird Records receive a 12 percent royalty, along with the bonus of being marketed by J-Bird. Each artist has three individual web pages on the site which include bios, photos, cover art and tour schedules. Being on the Web gives visitors the advantage of being able to listen to 90-second RealAudio and Shockwave sound samples of the bands they're interested in from ten categories—alternative, classical, country, gospel, jazz, pop, rap, rock, urban and world. "This is a discovery site where music lovers can find new and up-and-coming artists they'd never have the opportunity to hear otherwise," Barbieri says. "People don't tune in to MTV to see a particular video. They tune in to see new stuff, cool stuff. I want J-Bird to be the same way."

In addition to short soundbites, the site includes J-Bird Radio, the label's online radio station, playing all the J-Bird artists in rotation 24 hours a day, seven days a week. J-Bird also receives support from WLIR, a radio station on Long Island. "We have our own deejay and engineers that run 'The J-Bird Music Hour' from 11 to midnight. We play only our artists and have them come in and play and talk." Listeners are encouraged to visit the website.

Barbieri sees the Internet as the wave of the future for new bands trying to get music heard in the increasingly competitive music industry. "We must keep in mind that as the retail industry shrinks, record stores close, and as managing time becomes more of a priority for record buyers, the World Wide Web will become the easiest means of purchasing a product."

—Alice P. Buening

At right is a sample artist page from the J-Bird Records website. Once a user finds an artist he is interested in, he can read a bio of the band, listen to soundclips and even purchase the record, all with the click of a mouse.

How to Contact: Write first and obtain permission to submit. Prefers cassette with 4 songs and lyric sheet. SASE. Reports in 2 months. "Typed letters preferred."
Music: Mostly **progressive** and **jazz**.
Tips: "Letters should be neat, short and provide some kind of reply card."

‡J-BIRD RECORDS, http://www.j-birdrecords.com. President: Jay Barbieri. Record company.
- See the interview with President Jay Barbieri in this section.

How to Contact: Visit the website for information on J-Bird, the first Internet-only record label.

JIVE RECORDS, 137-139 W. 25th St., New York NY 10001. (212)620-8739. Fax: (212)337-0990. Senior Director of A&R: David McPherson. Hollywood office: 9000 Sunset Blvd., Suite 300, W. Hollywood CA 90069. (213)247-8300. Fax: (213)247-8366. Distributed by BMG. Record company. Estab. 1982. Releases 23 singles and 23 CDs/year.

- For more information, see the interview with Jive's Senior Director of A&R David McPherson in the 1997 *Songwriter's Market*.

How to Contact: Submit demo tape by mail. Unsolicited submissions are OK. Prefers cassette. Does not return material. Reports in 3 weeks.
Music: Mostly **R&B**, **pop** and **rap**. Released *R. Kelly*, recorded by R. Kelly; *Age Ain't Nothin' But A Number*, recorded by Aaliyah; and *Midnight Marauders*, recorded by A Tribe Called Quest, all on Jive Records. Other artists include Backstreet Boys, Joe, KRS-One and Too Short.

JOEY BOY RECORDS INC., 3081 NW 24th St., Miami FL 33142. (305)635-5588. Contact: Dorita Rodriguez. Labels include J.R. Records, American Faith Records. Record company. Estab. 1985. Releases 50 singles, 50 12″ singles, 15-20 LPs and 15-20 CDs/year. Pays 6% royalty to artists on contract; statutory rate to publisher per song on record.

- See the listing for Joey Boy Publishing in the Music Publishers section.

How to Contact: Submit demo tape by mail. Unsolicited submissions are OK. Prefers cassette with 3 songs and lyric sheet. SASE. Reports in 6-8 weeks.
Music: Mostly **bass**, **rap** and **dance**; also **jazz** and **comedy**. Released *Bass Rave* (by Bass Master Ace), recorded by David Suggs; *Trunk-A-Funk* (by Bass Patrol), recorded by Brian Graham/Robert Lewis; and "Get It Boy" (by Fresh Celeste), recorded by Celeste Mills, all on Joey Boy Records. Other artists include The Dogs, M-4-Sers and DF Fury.
Tips: "Be respectful and polite to people at all times when calling a place of business, even if they are not telling you what you want to hear."

JUSTIN TIME RECORDS INC., 5455 Pare, Suite 101, Montreal Quebec H4P 1P7 **Canada**. (514)738-9533. A&R Directors: Jean-Pierre Leduc and Denis Barnabé. Labels include Just a Memory Records. Record company, music publisher (Justin Time Publishing and Janijam Music/SOCAN) and record producer (Jim West). Estab. 1982. Releases 12 LPs and 12 CDs/year. Pays statutory rate to publisher per song on record.
How to Contact: Submit demo tape by mail. Unsolicited submissions are OK. Prefers cassette or VHS videocassette with at least 5 songs and lyric sheet. Does not return material. Reports in 3 months.
Music: Mostly **jazz**, **blues** and **gospel**; also **French pop**, **comedy** and **cajun**. Released *A Timeless Place* (by Jimmy Rowles/Johnny Mercer), recorded by Jeri Brown/Jimmy Rowles (jazz); *Jubilation VI*, written and recorded by Montreal Jubilation Gospel Choir (gospel); and "Heat Seeking Missile," written and recorded by Bryan Lee (blues), all on Justin Time Records.
Tips: "Offer a project that is unlike everything else. So many records are pleasant, but don't offer an angle that can help spread awareness about them."

K-ARK RECORDS, 400 Montego Cove, Hermitage TN 37076. (615)391-3450 or (615)391-5270. Contact: Office Staff. Distributed by Apollo. Record company, music publisher and record producer (Nolan Capps). Estab. 1955. Releases 12 singles, 12 LPs and 12 CDs/year. Pays 50% royalty to artists on contract; statutory rate to publisher per song on record.
How to Contact: Submit demo tape by mail. Unsolicited submissions are OK. Prefers cassette with 10 songs and lyric sheet. Does not return material. Reports in 2-4 weeks.
Music: Mostly **country**; also **gospel**. Released *Mickey De* (by Mike Hall), recorded by Mickey De; "L&P," written and recorded by Larry Patterson, both on Apollo Records (country); and *Terry Tavern* (by Terry Aires), recorded by Terry & Trisha on Artifax Records (jazz).

KAUPP RECORDS, Box 5474, Stockton CA 95205. (209)948-8186. E-mail: robnan7777@aol.com. President: Nancy L. Merrihew. Distributed by Merri-Webb Productions and Cal-Centron Distributing Co. Record company, music publisher (Kaupps and Robert Publishing Co./BMI), management firm (Merri-

Webb Productions) and record producer (Merri-Webb Productions). Estab. 1990. Releases 1 single and 4 LPs/year. Pays standard royalty to artists on contract; statutory rate to publisher per song on record.

- Kaupp Records' publishing company, Kaupps and Robert Publishing, can be found in the Music Publishers section, and their management firm, Merri-Webb Productions, is listed in the Managers and Booking Agents section.

How to Contact: Write first and obtain permission to submit or to arrange personal interview. Prefers cassette or VHS videocassette with 3 songs. SASE. Reports in 3 months

Music: Mostly **country**, **R&B** and **A/C rock**; also **pop**, **rock** and **gospel**. Released "Down In Dodge City" and "Familiar Strangers" (by N. Merrihew/B. Bolin), recorded by Nanci Lynn; and "Ms. Fire" (by N. Merrihew/B. Bolin), recorded by Bruce Bolin, all on Kaupp Records.

KEEPING IT SIMPLE AND SAFE, INC., 622 State St., Room 36, Springfield MA 01109. (413)747-4604. E-mail: tscottkiss@aol.com. President: Timothy Scott. Labels include Night Owl Records, Grand Jury Records, Second Time Around Records and Southend-Essex Records. Record company and music publisher (Tim Scott Music Group). Estab. 1993. Releases 3 singles, 2 LPs and 2 CDs/year. Pays 12-20% royalty to artists on contract; statutory rate to publisher per song on record.

- See the listing for Tim Scott Music Group in the Music Publishers section.

How to Contact: Submit demo tape by mail. Unsolicited submissions are OK. Prefers cassette, CD or VHS videocassette with 3-5 songs and lyric sheet. SASE. Reports in 2 months.

Music: Mostly **pop**, **R&B**, and **rap**; also **country**, **rock** and **gospel**. Released "Just In Time," written and recorded by Willie Gray; "Everything You" (by Tim Scott), recorded by Loveworld; and "Sweet Music," written and recorded by Mike Johnson, all on Night Owl Records. Other artists include S.E.D., Sweet Tooth and DJ Smoothe.

‡KICK-O-NAMIC RECORDS, 13561 Valerio, Van Nuys CA 91405. E-mail: kick@cyberverse.com. Director of Promotions: Michael Dane. Record company. Estab. 1990. Releases 5-10 CDs/year. Pays negotiable royalty to artists on contract; negotiable rate to publisher per song on record.

How to Contact: Write first and obtain permission to submit. Prefers cassette with lyric sheet. Does not return material. Reports in 4-6 weeks.

Music: Mostly **dance**, **pop** and **A/C**; also **house**. Released "You Treat Me Bad" and *Master of Jam II*, both written and recorded by Julian Vilante (pop); and "Cyco" (by D. Shannon), recorded by Cyco (industrial), all on Kick-O-Namic Records.

‡KILL ROCK STARS, 120 N.E. State #418, Olympia WA 98501. (360)357-9732. (360)357-6408. E-mail: slim@killrockstars.com. Website: http://www.killrockstars.com. Owner: Slim Moon. Distributed by Mordam Records, Caroline, Revolver, Cargo and Dutch East. Record company. Estab. 1991. Releases 6-8 singles, 6-8 LPs, 2-3 EPs and 6-8 CDs/year. Pays 50% of net profit to artists on contract; negotiated rate to publisher per song on record.

How to Contact: Submit demo tape by mail. Unsolicited submissions are OK. Prefers CD. Does not return material. Reports in 2 months.

Music: Mostly **punk rock**, **neo-folk** or **anti-folk** and **spoken word**. Released *Reject All American*, written and recorded by Bikini Kill (punk); "Martin Saints" (by Nick Soloman), recorded by Mary Lou Lord (guitar pop); and *Either/Or*, written and recorded by Elliott Smith (folk), all on Kill Rock Stars. Other artists include Unwound, Thrones, The Peechees, Great Unraveling, Emily's Sassy Lime, Sleater-Kinney, Long Hind Legs, Cold Cold Hearts, Witchypoo, Juliana Luecking and Free Kitten.

Tips: "Send a self-released CD. Prefer working with touring acts, so let us know if you are playing Olympia, Seattle or Portland. Particularly interested in young artists with indie-rock background."

KINGSTON RECORDS, 15 Exeter Rd., Kingston NH 03848. (603)642-8493. Coordinator: Harry Mann. Record company, record producer and music publisher (Strawberry Soda Publishing/ASCAP). Estab. 1988. Releases 3-4 singles, 2-3 12″ singles, 3 LPs and 2 CDs/year. Pays 3-5% royalty to artists on contract; statutory rate to publisher per song.

- See their listing in the Record Producers section.

How to Contact: Write first and obtain permission to submit. Prefers cassette, 15 ips reel-to-reel or videocassette with 3 songs and lyric sheet. Does not return material. Reports in 2 months.

Music: Mostly **rock**, **country** and **pop**; "no heavy metal." Released *Out of the Rain* and *Four On the Floor*, written and recorded by Doug Mitchell Band on Kingston Records (country/rock).

Tips: "Working only with N.E. and local talent."

KOTTAGE RECORDS, P.O. Box 121626, Nashville TN 37212. (615)726-3556. President: Neal James. Distributed by Emerald Worldsong Distributors. Record company, music publisher (Cottage Blue Music/

BMI) and record producer (Neal James). Estab. 1979. Releases 4 singles, 2 LPs and 3 CDs/year. Pays standard royalty to artists on contract; statutory rate to publisher per song on record.

• Kottage Records' publishing company, Cottage Blue Music, is listed in the Music Publishers section, and President Neal James is listed in the Record Producers section.

How to Contact: Submit demo tape by mail. Unsolicited submissions are OK. Prefers cassette with 2 songs and lyric sheet. SASE. Reports in 1 month.

Music: Mostly **country**, **rock/pop** and **gospel**; also **R&B** and **alternative**. Released "Lady Angel," written and recorded by Scott Dawson on Crosswind Records (country); "Hold Me Again," written and recorded by Jay S. Kay on Alternative Records (alternative); and "Tell Me" (by Neal James), recorded by Terry Barbay on Kottage Records (contemporary).

KSM RECORDS, 2305 Vista Court, Coquitlam British Columbia V3J 6W2 **Canada**. (604)202-3644. Fax: (604)469-9359. E-mail: ksmrecords@infomatch.com. Website: http://www.infomatch.com/~ksmrecords/. A&R Rep: David London. Distributed by Broken Seal (Germany), Factoria (Canada), Cri Du Chat (Brazil) and Dion Fortune (Germany). Record company, music publisher (Kwaz Song Music) and record producer (David London). Estab. 1991. Releases 2-5 singles and 2-5 CDs/year. Pays negotiable rate to artists on contract; statutory rate to publisher per song on record.

• KSM Records' publishing company, Kwaz Song Music, is listed in the Music Publishers section.

How to Contact: Submit demo tape by mail. Unsolicited submissions are OK. Prefers cassette or VHS videocassette and press material. Does not return material. Reports in 1 month.

Music: Mostly **industrial**, **Gothic**, **techno**, **heavy/extreme**, **electronic** and **experimental**. Released *Oracle Pool*, written and recorded by various artists (industrial); *Jagd Wild* (by Bryan Kortness), recorded by Come Join the Hunt (industrial); and "KSM Split Single" (by David London), recorded by Violet Black Orchid (electro), all on KSM Records. Other artists include Daed21, Idiot Stare, Fourthman, Bytet, Colour Clique, Naked Wavelength, 162 and Multiplex.

L.A. RECORDS, P.O. Box 1096, Hudson, Quebec J0P 1H0 **Canada**. (514)869-3236. Fax: (514)458-2819. E-mail: larecord@total.net. A&R: Mike Lengies. Record company, management firm (M.B.H. Music Management), music publisher (G-String Publishing) and record producer (M. Lengies). Estab. 1991. Releases 20-40 singles and 5-8 CDs/year. Pays negotiable royalty to artists on contract; statutory rate to publishers per song on record.

• L.A. Records' publishing company, G-String Publishing, is listed in the Music Publishers section and their management firm, M.B.H. Music Management, is listed in the Managers and Booking Agents section.

How to Contact: Submit demo tape by mail. Unsolicited submissions are OK. Prefers cassette or DAT with 3 songs and lyric sheet. SASE. Reports in 4 months.

Music: Mostly **commercial rock**, **alternative** and **A/C**; also **country** and **dance**. Released "Our Hearts Have Always Known" (by various), recorded by Maurice Pierre; *Li'l Crack In My Mirror* (by various), recorded by Jessica Ehrenworth; and "Love Machine" (by various), recorded by Steamer, all on L.A. Records. Other artists include Sharon Costello, On The Edge, Andy Jameson, Cheryl MacEachern and Matalis.

L.A. RECORDS, 26257 Regency Club Dr., Suite 6, Warren MI 48089. Music Director: Jack Timmons. Labels include Stark Records, R.C. Records and Fearless. Record company, record producer and music publisher (Abalone Publishing). Estab. 1984. Releases 20-30 singles, 1-10 12″ singles, 20-30 LPs, 1-5 EPs and 2-15 CDs/year. Pays 10% royalty to artists on contract; statutory rate to publisher per song on record.

• L.A. Records' publishing company, Abalone Publishing, is listed in the Music Publishers section.

How to Contact: Submit demo tape by mail. Unsolicited submissions are OK. Prefers cassette with 1-10 songs and lyric sheet. "It is very important to include a cover letter describing your objective goals." Reports in 1 month. "Due to fluctuation of postal rates include $1 to cover postage overage above 32¢. All others SASE is acceptable. Packages with 32¢ SASE are not acceptable."

Music: Mostly **rock/hard rock**, **heavy metal** and **pop/rock**; also **country/gospel**, **MOR/ballads**, **R&B**, **jazz**, **New Age**, **dance** and **easy listening**. Released *Tripper* (by J. Scott), recorded by The Pistol Kids (rock); "Renegade" (by Kate Smahl), recorded by Licks (dance); and *Love's Tough* (by Sam Steel), recorded by The Stars (pop/rock), all on L.A. Records. Other artists include The Simmones, Kevin Stark, The Comets and Fearless.

L. P. S. RECORDS, INC., 2140 St. Clair St., Bellingham WA 98226-4016. (360)733-3807. Website: http://www.silverlink.net/lps/index.htm. President: Mrs. Renie Peterson. Record company, music publisher (Heartstone/BMI; Cherrystone/ASCAP; Fourth Corner/SESAC) and record producer (Renie Peterson). Estab. 1970. Releases 1 CD/year. Pays standard royalty to artists on contract.

How to Contact: Write or call first and obtain permission to submit. Prefers cassette ("studio demos

only") with 3 songs and typed lyric sheet. "Do not include lengthy letters about the songs; we're only interested in unpublished songs. Looking for songs by established songwriters (country primarily). Only accredited BMI, ASCAP or SESAC songwriters should apply." SASE. Reports in 2 weeks.
Music: Country. Released *Out On Her Own* (by Renie Peterson/Gene Rabbai), recorded by Donna Vallance on LPS Records (country). Other artists include Neil Vosburgh, Claudette Dykstra, Marty Bowen, Tina Allen and Jimmy Murphy.
Tips: "Study what's airing on Top 40 country radio, learn your craft, send neat submissions. Teamwork is important; as is having the ability to get out on the road, meet people and sell records. Charisma and talent are prime as well as personal appearance."

‡LAFACE RECORDS, 8750 Wilhsire Blvd., 2nd Floor W., Beverly Hills CA 90211. (310)358-4980. Fax: (310)358-4981. Distributed by BMG. Record company.
How to Contact: Call first and obtain permission to submit. Prefers cassette with no more than 3 songs, photo and bio.
Music: Released *Secrets*, recorded by Toni Braxton; *Words*, recorded by The Tony Rich Project; and *Atliens*, recorded by Outkast, all on LaFace Records. Other artists include Az Yet and Donell Jones.

LAMON RECORDS, P.O. Box 25371, Charlotte NC 28229. (704)882-6134. Fax: (704)882-2063. E-mail: dmoody@lamonrecords.com. Website: http://www.lamonrecords.com. A&R: David Moody. Labels include Pan Handle. Record company and music publisher (Laymond Publishing Inc.). Estab. 1962. Releases 10 singles, 10 LPs, 5 EPs and 5 CDs/year. Pays negotiable royalty to artists on contract; statutory rate to publisher per song on record.
How to Contact: Submit demo tape by mail. Unsolicited submissions are OK. Prefers cassette with 3 songs and lyric sheet. SASE. Reports in 2 months.
Music: Mostly **rock**, **country** and **gospel**; also **R&B** and **soul**.

LANDMARK COMMUNICATIONS GROUP, P.O. Box 1444, Hendersonville TN 37077. Producer: Bill Anderson, Jr. Labels include Jana and Landmark Records. Record company, record producer, music publisher (Newcreature Music/BMI and Mary Megan Music/ASCAP) and management firm (Landmark Entertainment). Releases 10 singles, 8 LPs and 8 CDs/year. Pays 5-7% royalty to artists on contract; statutory rate to publisher for each record sold.

- See Landmark Communication Group's listing in the Record Producers section, as well as a listing for Newcreature Music in the Music Publishers section.

How to Contact: Prefers 7½ ips reel-to-reel or cassette with 4-10 songs and lyric sheet. SASE. Reports in 1 month.
Music: Country/crossover, **gospel**, **jazz**, **R&B**, **rock** and **top 40/pop**. Released *Joanne Cash Yates Live . . . w/Johnny Cash* on Jana Records (gospel); "You Were Made For Me," recorded by Skeeter Davis and Teddy Nelson on Elli Records/Norway; and "The Tradition Continues" (by Vernon Oxford) on Landmark Records (country).

LANDSLIDE RECORDS, 1800 Peachtree St., Suite 333, Atlanta GA 30309. (404)355-5580. E-mail: mrland@mindspring.com. President: Michael Rothschild. Distributed by Rock Bottom, City Hall, Action, Paul Starr and Twin Brook. Record company, music publisher (Frozen Inca Music/BMI) and record producer. Estab. 1981. Releases 4 LPs and 4 CDs/year. Pays negotiable royalty to artists on contract; negotiable rate to publisher per song on record.

- See the listing for Landslide's publishing company, Frozen Inca Music, in the Music Publishers section.

How to Contact: Submit demo tape by mail. Unsolicited submissions are OK. Prefers cassette with 6-12 songs and lyric sheet. SASE. Reports in 2 months.
Music: Mostly **blues** and **roots music**; also **jazz**. Released *Cigar Store Indians*, written and recorded by Cigar Store Indians; *Freak Doggin'* (by Gerald Jackson/various), recorded by various artists (hip hop); and *Navigator*, written and recorded by Paul McCandless (jazz), all on Landslide Records.

LANOR RECORDS, P.O. Box 233, 329 N. Main St., Church Point LA 70525. (318)684-2176. Contact: Lee Lavergne. Record company and music publisher (Jon Music/BMI). Releases 8-10 cassettes a year. Pays 3-5% royalty to artists on contract; statutory rate to writers for each record sold.

- Lanor Records' publishing company, Jon Music, is listed in the Music Publishers section.

How to Contact: Prefers cassette with 2-6 songs. SASE. Reports in 2 weeks.
Music: Mostly **country**; also **rock**, **soul**, **zydeco**, **cajun** and **blues**. Released *Cajun Pickin'*, recorded by L.A. Band (cajun); *Rockin' with Roy*, recorded by Roy Currier; and *Zydeco All Night*, recorded by Joe Walker (zydeco), all on Lanor Records.

Tips: Submit "good material with potential in today's market. Use good quality cassettes—I don't listen to poor quality demos that I can't understand."

LARI-JON RECORDS, 325 W. Walnut, Rising City NE 68658. (402)542-2336. Owner: Larry Good. Record company, management firm (Lari-Jon Promotions), music publisher (Lari-Jon Publishing/BMI) and record producer (Lari-Jon Productions). Estab. 1967. Releases 15 singles and 5 LPs/year. Pays varying royalty to artists on contract.

- Lari-Jon Publishing, Lari-Jon Productions and Lari-Jon Promotions are listed in the Music Publishers, Record Producers and Managers and Booking Agents sections, respectively.

How to Contact: Submit demo tape by mail. Unsolicited submissions are OK. Prefers cassette with 5 songs and lyric sheet. SASE. Reports in 2 months.
Music: Mostly **country**, **gospel-Southern** and **'50s rock**. Released "Glory Bound Train," written and recorded by Tom Campbell; *As Good As It Gets*, written and recorded by Larry Good (country); and *Her Favorite Songs*, written and recorded by Johnny Nace (country), all on Lari-Jon Records. Other artists include Kent Thompson and Brenda Allen.

LARK RECORD PRODUCTIONS, INC., P.O. Box 35726, Tulsa OK 74153. (918)786-8896. E-mail: janajae@aol.com. Website: http://members.aol.com/janajae/home.htm. Vice-President: Kathleen Pixley. Record company, music publisher (Jana Jae Music/BMI), management firm (Jana Jae Enterprises) and record producer (Lark Talent and Advertising). Estab. 1980. Pays negotiable royalty to artists on contract; statutory rate to publisher per song on record.

- See the listings for Jana Jae Music in the Music Publishers section, Lark Talent and Advertising in the Record Producers section and Jana Jae Enterprises in the Managers and Booking Agents section.

How to Contact: Submit demo tape by mail. Unsolicited submissions are OK. Prefers cassette or VHS videocassette with 3 songs and lead sheets. Does not return material.
Music: Mostly **country**, **bluegrass** and **classical**; also **instrumentals**. Released "Fiddlestix" (by Jana Jae); "Mayonnaise" (by Steve Upfold); and "Flyin' South" (by Cindy Walker), all recorded by Jana Jae on Lark Records (country). Other artists include Syndi, Hotwire and Matt Greif.

‡LAZY BONES RECORDINGS/PRODUCTIONS, INC., 9594 First Ave. NE, Suite 230, Seattle WA 98115. (206)820-6632. Fax: (206)821-5720. E-mail: lbri@aol.com. President: Scott Schorr. Distributed by ILS, Burnside and others. Record company, music publisher (Dorkus Publishing/ASCAP, Lazy Bones Music/BMI), record producer (Scott Schorr) and management firm. Estab. 1992. Releases 3-4 CDs/year. Pays negotiable royalty to artists on contract; statutory rate to publisher per song on record.

- See Lazy Bones' listing in the Managers and Booking Agents section.

How to Contact: Submit demo tape by mail. Unsolicited submissions are OK. Prefers cassette or CD with 5 songs. Include bio, photo and any press. Does not return material. Reports in 3 weeks.
Music: Mostly **rock** and **alternative**. Released *Headland* (by David Hadland), recorded by Headland on Lazy Bones Recordings (pop); *Togetherly*, written and recorded by Neros Rome on Mercury Records (rock); and *Turntable Bay* (by Ratboy/Da Blasta), recorded by Turntable Bay on Lazy Bones Recordings (hip-hop). Other artists include Blackhead.

LBI RECORDS, P.O. Box 328, Jericho VT 05465. (802)899-3787. Fax: (802)899-3805. President: Bobby Hackney. Record company and record producer. Estab. 1986. Releases 12 singles, 2 LPs and 2 CDs/year. Pays negotiable royalty to artists on contract; statutory rate to publisher per song on record.
How to Contact: Submit demo tape by mail. Unsolicited submissions are OK. Prefers cassette with 3 songs and lyric sheet. SASE. Reports in 4-5 weeks.
Music: Mostly **reggae**, **R&B** and **jazz**; also **poetry** and **hip hop/funk/rap**. Released *You're A Big Girl Now* and *Reggae Mood* (by B. Hackney), both recorded by Lambsbread (reggae); and "African Princess," written and recorded by Mikey Dread (reggae), all on LBI Records. Other artists include Trini.

LBJ PRODUCTIONS, 8608 W. College St., French Lick IN 47432. (812)936-7318. E-mail: lbjprod@intersource.com. Website: http://intersource.com/~lbjprod. Director A&R: Janet S. Jones. Owner/Producer: Larry Jones. Labels include Stone Country Records, SCR Gospel, SCR Rock. Record company, music publisher (Plain Country Publishing/ASCAP, Riff-Line Publishing/BMI), record producer (LBJ Productions) and producer of radio-spot ads and jingles. Estab. 1989. Releases 2-4 singles, 3-6 LPs, 2-3 EPs and 1-2 CDs/year. Pays 10-15% royalty to artists on contract; statutory rate to publisher per song on record.
How to Contact: Write first and obtain permission to submit. Prefers cassette or VHS videocassette with 4-6 songs and lyric sheet. SASE. Reports in 6-8 weeks.
Music: Mostly **country**, **gospel** and **rock**; also **R&B**, **MOR** and **pop**. Released "Angel" (by Bruce Taylor),

recorded by Borrowed Time on SCR Rock Records; "Smooth Operator" (by Wagner/Troutman), recorded by Heart & Soul on Riff Line Records (R&B); and *This Bud Ain't For You* (by Easterday/Fred), recorded by Bobby Easterday on SCR Records. Other artists include Rita White, Gordon Ray, C.L. Jones and Terry Tiallon.
Tips: "Make a good first impression. Put the song on your demo tape that you think is strongest first. If you catch our ear we'll listen to more music. We are not looking for someone that does imitations, we need new and exciting people with styles that cry out for attention. But remember, make your submissions to the point and professional—we'll decide if you've got what we want."

LE MATT MUSIC LTD., White House Farm, Stropshire TF9 4HA **England**. Phone: (01630)647374. Fax: (01630)647612. Contact: Ron or Cathrine Lee. Labels include Swoop, Zarg Records, Genouille, Pogo and Check Records. Record company, record producer and music publisher (Le Matt Music, Ltd., Lee Music, Ltd., R.T.F.M. and Pogo Records, Ltd.). Member MPA, PPL, PRS, MCPS. Estab. 1972. Releases 30 12″ singles, 20 LPs and 20 CDs/year. Pays negotiable royalty to artists on contract; negotiable rate to publisher for each record sold. Royalties paid to US songwriters and artists through US publishing or recording affiliate.

- Le Matt Music's publishing company, R.T.L. Music, is listed in the Music Publishers section.

How to Contact: Submit demo tape by mail. Unsolicited submissions are OK. Prefers CD, cassette, DAT or VHS 625 PAL standard videocassette with 1-3 songs and lyric sheet. Include bio and still photos. SAE and IRC. Reports in 6 weeks.
Music: Mostly **pop/top 40**; also **bluegrass, blues, country, dance-oriented, easy listening, MOR, progressive, R&B, '50s rock, disco, new wave, rock** and **soul**. Released *Down To Earth* (by M.J. Lawson), recorded by Emmitt Till; *Now And Then*, written and recorded by Daniel Boone; and *It's A Very Nice* (by Ron Lee), recorded by Groucho, all on Swoop Records. Other artists include Nightmare, Orphan, The Chromatics, Mike Sherede and the Nightriders, Johnny Moon and Dead Fish.

LOCONTO PRODUCTIONS/SUNRISE STUDIO, 10244 NW 47 St., Sunrise FL 33351. (954)741-7766. President: Frank X. Loconto. Labels include FXL Records. Record company, music publisher (Otto Music Publishing/ASCAP) and recording studio. Estab. 1978. Releases 10 singles, 10 cassettes/albums and 5 CDs/year. Pays negotiable royalty to artists on contract; statutory rate to publisher per song on record.

- Loconto Productions is also listed in the Record Producers section, and their publishing affiliate, Otto Publishing, is listed in the Music Publishers section.

How to Contact: Submit demo tape by mail. Unsolicited submissions are OK. Prefers cassette with lyric sheet or lead sheet. SASE. Reports in 2-3 months.
Music: Released *Love Is In The Air* (by various), recorded by Michael Moog (disco); *Totally Me*, written and recorded by Bob Orange (pop/gospel); and *New Life In Christ* (by various), recorded by Scott Dewey (gospel), all on FXL Records. Other artists include Michael Moog, Roger Bryant, Bill Dillon and Bob Orange.
Tips: "Be sure to prepare a professional demo of your work and don't hesitate to seek 'professional' advice."

‡LONDON RECORDS, 825 Eighth Ave., 2nd Floor, New York NY 10019. (212)333-8000. Fax: (212)333-8030. Distributed by PGD; labels include Mo Wax Records and FFRR Records. Record company.
How to Contact: London Records does not accept unsolicited submissions.
Music: Released *Chant D'Amour*, recorded by Cecilia Bartoli; *Pavarotti and Friends for War Child*, recorded by various artists; and *Berlin Cabaret Songs*, recorded by Ute Lemper, all on London Records.

LONESOME WIND CORPORATION, 111 E. Canton St., Broken Arrow OK 74012-7140. (800)210-4416. President: Marty R. Garrett. Labels include Lonesome Wind Records. Record company, record producer, music publisher and entertainment consultant. Estab. 1988. Releases 3-4 EPs and 1 CD/year. Pays 7-10% royalty to artists on contract; statutory rate to publisher per song on record.
How to Contact: Write or call first and obtain permission to submit. Prefers cassette with 4-5 songs and lyric or lead sheet with chord progressions listed. Does not return material. Reports in 3 weeks.
Music: Straight-up honky tonk, country or **scripturally-based gospel**. Released *Too Free Too Long* (by

REMEMBER: Don't "shotgun" your demo tapes. Submit only to companies interested in the type of music you write. For more submission hints, refer to Getting Started on page 6.

Cliff Voss), recorded by Mark Cypert on Stormy Heart Records; and *Carry Me Over*, written and recorded by The Cripple Jimmi Band on Kid Mega Records.
Tips: "We concentrate strictly on securing funding for artists who intend to record and release CD quality products to the public for sale. Artists must seriously intend to build a track record of sales and airplay used to secure a contract with a major record label. We do not require professional demos to submit, but make sure vocals are distinct, upfront and up-to-date. I personally listen and respond to each submission I receive, so call to see if we are currently reviewing for an upcoming project."

LONNY TUNES, P.O. Box 460086, Garland TX 75046. (214)497-1616. President: Lonny Schonfeld. Record company, record producer and music publisher (Lonny Tunes/BMI). Estab. 1988. Releases 8-10 singles, 8-10 LPs and 2 CDs/year. Pays 20% (of wholesale) to artists on contract; statutory rate to publisher per song on record.
How to Contact: Submit demo tape by mail. Unsolicited submissions are OK. Prefers cassette or VHS videocassette with 3-5 songs and lyric sheet. "Professional quality only." Does not return material. Reports in 6-8 weeks.
Music: Mostly **country**, **children's** and **rock**; also **jazz** and **comedy**. Released "Baby, With You" (by L. Schonfeld/R. Stout), recorded by Randy Stout (pop); *James Blonde 006.95* (by Marty Brill), recorded by various artists; and "One Word Question" (by L. Schonfeld), recorded by David Wilson, all on Lonny Tunes Records.

LRJ, Box 3, Belen NM 87002. (505)864-7441. Manager: Tony Palmer. Labels include Little Richie and Chuckie. Record company. Estab. 1959. Releases 5 singles and 2 LPs/year.

- See the listings for Little Richie Johnson Music in the Music Publishers section, and Little Richie Johnson in the Record Producers and Managers and Booking Agents sections.

How to Contact: Submit demo tape by mail. Unsolicited submissions are OK. Prefers cassette. Does not return material. Reports in 1 month.
Music: Mostly **country**. Released "Moonlight Roses and Wine," written and recorded by Gabe Nito; "Auction of My Life," written and recorded by Joe King; and "Helpless," recorded by Alan Godge, all on LRJ Records. Other artists include Reta Lee.

LUCIFER RECORDS, INC., P.O. Box 263, Brigantine NJ 08203-0263. (609)266-2623. President: Ron Luciano. Labels include TVA Records. Record company, music publisher (Ciano Publishing and Legz Music), record producer (Pete Fragale and Tony Vallo), management firm and booking agency (Ron Luciano Music Co. and TVA Productions). "Lucifer Records has offices in South Jersey; Palm Beach, Florida; and Las Vegas, Nevada."
How to Contact: Call or write to arrange personal interview. Prefers cassette with 4-8 songs. SASE. Reports in 3 weeks.
Music: Dance, **easy listening**, **MOR**, **rock**, **soul** and **top 40/pop**. Released "I Who Have Nothing," by Spit-N-Image (rock); "Lucky," by Legz (rock); and "Love's a Crazy Game," by Voyage (disco/ballad). Other artists include Bobby Fisher, Jerry Denton, FM, Zeke's Choice, Al Caz, Joe Vee and Dana Nicole.

LYRA HOUSE, LTD., 4750 N. Central, Suite 7N, Phoenix AZ 85012. (602)234-1809. Fax: (602)230-1991. E-mail: naaf@aol.com. Managing Director: Marc Parella. Record company and arts foundation. Estab. 1989. Releases 5 CDs/year.
How to Contact: "Lyra House does not work with songwriters. We are a classical/concert music label. Accepts demos by invitation only."
Music: Mostly **classical**, **contemporary concert music** and **orchestral**; also **ecletic new music** and **serious film scores**. Released *A Feast of Beethoven* and *A Festival of Chopin*, both recorded by Dickran Atamial; and *Bolet in Memorium*; recorded by Jorge Bolet, all on Lyra House Records. Other artists include Donald Keats, Luis Gonzales and Marc Parella.
Tips: "We do not work with popular songwriters. Persons interested in recording with Lyra House must first submit a proposal to our parent organization, North American Artists Foundation, at the above address."

M.E.G. RECORDS CO., 2069 Zumbehl Rd. #27, St. Charles MO 63303. Phone/fax: (314)447-1652. President: Brian Gleason. Record company, music publisher (Cow Jumping Over the Moon Music/BMI) and record producer (Brian Gleason), Estab. 1995. Pays negotiable royalty to artists on contract; statutory rate to publisher per song.
How to Contact: Write first and obtain permission to submit. Prefers cassette or VHS videocassette with 3-4 songs, pictures, bio, work history (résumé), day and nighttime phone numbers and lyric sheet. "Prefer writer and artist to be the same, but will accept material from either." SASE. Reports in 3-6 months.
Music: Mostly **country**, **country rock** and **easy listening**. Released *This Old House*, written and recorded

by Brian Winslow on M.E.G. Records (country).
Tips: "Submit original material only, clean vocal and guitar is adequate. Prefer singer/songwriter submissions."

‡MADDOG RECORDS II, P.O. Box 15207, Fremont CA 94539. Phone/fax: (510)353-1630. E-mail: dogtown1@aol.com. A&R Director: Kip Ernst. Labels include Crazy Cat Recordings. Record company. Estab. 1994. Releases 5-8 singles, 2-4 LPs, 2-4 EPs and 4-6 CDs/year. Pays 20% of gross sales to artists on contract; pays variable rate to publisher per song on record.
How to Contact: Submit demo tape by mail. Unsolicited submissions are OK. Prefers cassette, CD, DAT or videocassette. Does not return material. Reports in 4-5 weeks.
Music: Mostly **alternative rock**, **pop** and **punk**; also **top 40**, **R&B** and **Spanish**. Released "B-Mack" (by B. Edwards), recorded by B-Mack (rap); and *Off the Floor* (by Ted Welty/Don Scott/Eric Rogers), recorded by Iguana Jive (alternative), both on Maddog Records II. Other artists include Retromotive.

‡MAGIC KEY PRODUCTIONS INC., 405 S. Mesa Hills Dr., Cedar City UT 84720. Phone/fax: (801)586-1307. President: Art Kaufman. Record company, music publisher (Magic Key Publishing) and record producer. Estab. 1984. Releases 4 CDs/year. Pays negotiable royalty to artists on contract; statutory rate to publisher per song on record.
How to Contact: Submit demo tape by mail. Unsolicited submissions are OK. Prefers cassette, CD or DAT with 3 songs, lyric and lead sheet. Does not return material. Reports in 1 month.
Music: Mostly **country**, **pop** and **New Age**; also **western**, **folk** and **religious**. Released *Yellow Moon* (by Arthur Johnson), recorded by David Fox (country); *Touch My Heart* (by Carolyn Hartnett), recorded by Karen Whittemore (pop); and *Your Song & Mine* (by Denise Jankas), recorded by Curt Harpel (pop), all on Magic Key Records.

MAGNUM MUSIC CORP. LTD., 8607 128th Ave., Edmonton, Alberta T5E 0G3 **Canada**. (403)476-8230. Fax: (403)472-2584. General Manager: Bill Maxim. Record company and management firm. Estab. 1982. Pays standard royalty.
Affiliate(s): High River Music Publishing (ASCAP), Ramblin' Man Music Publishing (BMI).
- See their listing in the Managers and Booking Agents section.

How to Contact: Write or call first and obtain permission to submit. Prefers cassette or VHS videocassette with 3 songs and lyric sheet. Does not return material. Reports in 2 months.
Music: Mostly **country, gospel** and **contemporary**; also **pop, ballads** and **rock**. Published *Pray for the Family* and *Emotional Girl*, both written and recorded by C. Greenly (country); and *Don't Worry 'Bout It*, written and recorded by T. Anderson (country), all on Magnum Records.

MAKESHIFT MUSIC, P.O. Box 557, Blacktown, NSW 2148 **Australia**. Phone: (612)626-8991. Manager: Peter Bales. Record company and music publisher (Aria and Apra). Estab. 1980. "Makeshift Music is an administration and production company specializing within the recording and publishing fields of the music industry. Product and material is now leased out to third party companies such as BMG, Sony, Mushroom, etc." Pays statutory rate to publisher per song on record.
How to Contact: Submit demo tape by mail. Unsolicited submissions are OK. Prefers cassette or PAL/VHS videocassette with 2-3 songs and lyric sheet. Does not return material. Reports if interested.
Music: Mostly **rock/pop**. Released *Do You Believe*, recorded by Fantasm; and *Classic Classics*, recorded by various artists, both on Makeshift Records. Other artists include The Generator, Frank Seckold, Chimps and The Sessions.

MALACO RECORDS, 3023 W. Northside Dr., Jackson MS 39213. (601)982-4522. Executive Director: Jerry Mannery. Record company. Estab. 1986. Releases 20 projects/year. Pays 8% royalty to artists on contract; statutory rate to publisher per song.
How to Contact: Submit demo tape by mail. Unsolicited submissions are OK. Prefers cassette or VHS videocassette. Does not return material.
Music: Mostly **traditional** and **contemporary gospel**. Artists include Mississippi Mass Choir, Willie Neal Johnson & the Gospel Keynotes, Rev. James Moore, Mississippi Children's Choir, Bryan Wilson, The Pilgrim Jubilees, Lillian Lilly, Ruby Terry, Jackson Southernaires and Dorothy Norwood.

THE MAN ON PAGE 602, 708 W. Euclid, Pittsburg KS 66762. (316)231-6443. Labels include Antique, Catfish, Cisum and Big Brutus. Record company, music publisher and record producer. Estab. 1975. Pays statutory royalty to publisher per song on record.
- See the listing for Cisum in the Music Publishers section.

How to Contact: Write or call first and obtain permission to submit. Prefers cassette with 2 songs and

lyric sheet. Does not return material. Reports in 3 weeks.
Music: Mostly **country, gospel** and **R&B**; also **easy rock**. Released "Shade Tree Mechanic" (by Gene Strassey); "Tennessee River Blues" (by Jack Barlow); and "Lookin' At Our Hero" (by Mister X), all on Antique Records.

JOHN MARKS RECORDS, 19 Wright Ave., Wakefield RI 02879. (401)782-6298. Fax: (401)792-8375. E-mail: jmrcds@brainiac.com. Owner: John Marks. Distributed by Allegro. Record company. Estab. 1991. Releases 4 CDs/year. Royalty varies.
How to Contact: Write first and obtain permission to submit. Prefers cassette (analog or DAT) or CD. "Primarily interested in master tapes suitable for licensing." SASE. Reports in 1 month.
Music: Mostly **classical music for strings** and some **jazz**. Released *Reverie*, written and recorded by Nathaniel Rosen; *Sonatas of Brahms & Bach*, written and recorded by Artino Delmoni; and *Ysaje-Kreisler-Bach*, all on John Marks Records.
Tips: "Read Diane Rappaport's *How to Make and Sell Your Own Recording*."

MASTER-TRAK ENTERPRISES, Dept. SM, 413 N. Parkerson, Crowley LA 70526. (318)788-0773. General Manager and Chief Engineer: Mark Miller. Labels include Master-Trak, Showtime, Kajun, Blues Unlimited, Par T and MTE Records. Record company and recording studio. Releases 20 singles and 6-8 LPs/year. Pays 7% artist royalty.

- See the listing for Whitewing Music in the Music Publishers section.

How to Contact: Submit demo tape by mail. Unsolicited submissions are OK. Prefers cassette and lead sheet. Does not return material.
Music: Mostly **country**, **rock**, **R&B**, **Cajun**, **blues** and **zydeco**. Released "That's When I Miss You" (by J. Runyo), recorded by Sammy Kershaw; "Please Explain," written and recorded by Wade Richards, both on MTE Records; and "My Heart Is Hurting," written and recorded by Becky Richard on Kajun Records. Other artists include Al Ferrier, Fernest & The Thunders, River Road Band, Clement Bros., Lee Benoit and Kenné Wayne.

MAUI ARTS & MUSIC ASSOCIATION, Suite 208, P.O. Box 356, Paia, Maui HI 96779. (808)573-3100. Fax: (808)572-8099. E-mail: dream@maui.net. Website: http://www.maui.net/~dream. A&R Public Submissions: Jason Q. Publik. Labels include Survivor, Maui No Ka Oi, Revelation and Maui Country. Record company, record producer, music publisher and environmental association. Estab. 1974. Releases 1-12 singles, 1-12 LPs and 1-12 CDs/year. Pays 5-15% royalty to artists on contract; statutory royalty to publisher per song on record.
How to Contact: Submit demo tape by mail. Unsolicited submissions are OK. Prefers cassette or videocassette with 3 songs and lyric or lead sheet. SASE. Reports in 2-4 weeks.
Music: Mostly **pop**, **rock** and **blues**; also **country**, **jazz** and **instrumental**. Released "Unlock The Hope" (by Lono), recorded by Jason on Maui Country Records (pop) and *Seven Sacred Pools*, by Lono.

THE MAVERICK GROUP, 1122 Colorado St., Suite 1702, Austin TX 78751. (512)472-7137. Fax: (512)476-1257. E-mail: charlytex@aol.com. Managing Director: Charly Mann. Record company. Estab. 1989. Releases 5 LPs and 6 CDs/year. Pays negotiable royalty to artists on contract; statutory rate to publisher per song on record.
How to Contact: Write or call first and obtain permission to submit a demo. Prefers cassette or ½" or ¾" videocassette with 3 songs and lyric sheet. Does not return material. Reports in 2 weeks.
Music: Mostly **adult alternative**, **progressive country** and **progressive rock**; also **acoustic singer/songwriter**. Released *Camel Rock*, written and recorded by Chuck Pyle (progressive country); *Nights at the Chez*, written and recorded by David Roth (acoustic); and *Tales From the Erogenous Zone* (by Dan HR), recorded by HR (progressive rock), all on Maverick Records. Other artists include Kurt Kempter and the Southern Lights.

‡MAVERICK RECORDS, 8000 Beverly Blvd., Los Angeles CA 90048. (213)852-1177. Fax: (818)852-1505. Website: http://www.wbr.com. Distributed by WEA. Record company.
How to Contact: Maverick Records does not accept unsolicited submissions.
Music: Released *Jagged Little Pill*, recorded by Alanis Morissette; and *Something to Remember*, recorded by Madonna. Other artists include Candlebox, Deftones, Love Spit Love, Me'shell Ndegeocello, Neurotic Outsiders, The Rentals, Rule 62 and Summercamp.

MCA RECORDS, 1755 Broadway, 8th Floor, New York NY 10019. (212)841-8000. Contact: A&R Director. Universal City office: 70 Universal City Plaza, Universal City CA 91608. (818)777-4000. Fax: (818)866-1598. Nashville office: 60 Music Square E., Nashville TN 37203. (615)244-8944. Fax: (615)880-

7410. Website: http://www.mcarecords.com. Distributed by UNI. Record company and music publisher (MCA Music).

- See the listing for MCA Music Publishing in the Music Publishers section.

How to Contact: Call first and obtain permission to submit.

Music: Released *What If It's You*, recorded by Reba McEntire; *Love Songs*, recorded by Elton John; and *Home Again*, recorded by New Edition, all on MCA Records. Other artists include Tracy Byrd, George Strait, Vince Gill, The Mavericks and Trisha Yearwood.

MEGAFORCE WORLDWIDE ENTERTAINMENT, P.O. Box 779, New Hope PA 18938. (215)862-5411. Fax: (215)862-9470. Website: http://www.web.com/crazedworld. Director of Publicity/A&R: Maria Ferrero. Labels include Megaforce Records Inc. Record company. Estab. 1983. Releases 5 LPs, 2 EPs and 5 CDs/year. Pays various royalties to artists on contract; ¾ statutory rate to publisher per song on record.

How to Contact: Submit demo tape by mail. Unsolicited submissions are OK. Prefers cassette or ¾" videocassette with 4 songs. SASE. Reports ASAP.

Music: Mostly **rock**. Released *I Am Dog*, written and recorded by by Love in Reverse on Reprise Records (eclectic/ambient); *Filth Pig*, written and recorded by Ministry on Warner Bros. Records (heavy); and *Bif Naked*, written and recorded by Bif Naked on Her Royal Majesty's Records (pop). "We also manage Ministry, Testament, and Goudsthumb."

MEGATONE RECORDS INC., 7095 Hollywood Blvd. #349, Los Angeles CA 90028. (213)850-5400. Fax: (213)850-5302. E-mail: megatone@pacbell.net or megadisco@aol.com. Website: http://www.megatone.com. A&R: Thomas White. Distributed by INDI (America), EMI (England) and BMG (Germany); labels include Megatech, Megahouse and Airwave. Record company. Estab. 1981. Releases 24 singles, 6 LPs and 6 CDs/year. Pays 7-12% royalty to artists on contract; 75% of statutory rate to publisher per song on record.

How to Contact: Write first and obtain permission to submit or to arrange personal interview. Prefers cassette with 3 songs and lyric sheet. "Looking for strong songs with great lyrical hooks and memorable melodies." SASE. Reports in 1-2 months.

Music: Mostly **dance/house/disco, alternative/new rock** and **electronic music**; also **power pop, punk** and **groove oriented music**. Released "Nightlove" (by T. Mace), recorded by KK (dance); and "Live In Hollywood" (by various), recorded by Eartha Kitt (pop), both on Megatone Records. Other artists include Ernest Kohl, Linda Imperial, Shades of Grey, Decode 3, Sylvester, Blue Van Gogh and Darwin Zoo.

‡MEKKATONE RECORDS, 322 Eighth Ave., 2nd Floor, New York NY 10001. (212)294-7030. Fax: (212)294-1769. E-mail: mekkatone@aol.com. President: Dave Weschler. Record company. Estab. 1995. Releases 2 CDs/year. Pays negotiable royalty to artists on contract; negotiable rate to publisher per song on record.

How to Contact: Submit demo tape by mail. Unsolicited submissions are OK. Prefers any format; when sending cassettes, "leave the tabs in." Does not return material. Reports in 3 weeks.

Music: Mostly **personality**, **sense of humor** and **creativity**; also **the arcane**, **the absurd** and **polka**. Released *Pinataland*, written and recorded by Pinataland (polkabilly); *Varicose Days*, written and recorded by Jessica Kane (nursery rhymes for the criminally insane); and *Action Street*, written and recorded by the Adults (punk/pop/swing), all on Mekkatone Records.

Tips: "We're looking for highly personal, idiosyncratic material by songwriters who approach their songwriting the same way Canadian mounties go after fugitives. Fearlessly!"

‡MERCURY RECORDS, 825 Eighth Ave., New York NY 10019. (212)333-8000. Fax: (212)333-8245. Los Angeles office: 11150 Santa Monica Blvd., 10th Floor, Los Angeles CA 90025. (310)996-7200. Fax: (310)477-5023. Website: http://www.mercuryrecords.com/Mercury. Contact: A&R. Distributed by PGD; labels include Def Jam Records, Mouth Almighty Records, Pure Records, Scratchie Records, Tim/Kerr Records, Triloka Records, Capricorn Records and Mercury Nashville Records. Record company.

How to Contact: Mercury Records does not accept unsolicited submissions. Do not send material unless requested.

Music: Released *House of Music*, recorded by Tony Toni Tone; *Mr. Happy Go Lucky*, recorded by John Mellencamp; and *Vault—Greatest Hits 1980-1995*, recorded by Def Leppard, all on Mercury Records. Other artists include Gina Thompson, Crystal Waters, Cardigans, James, Redd Kross and downset.

METAL BLADE RECORDS, 2828 Cochran St., Suite 302, Simi Valley CA 93065. (805)522-9111. Fax: (805)522-9380. E-mail: mtlbldrcds@aol.com. Website: http://www.iuma.com/Metal_Blade. Contact: A&R. Record company. Estab. 1982. Releases 20 LPs, 2 EPs and 20 CDs/year. Pays negotiable royalty to artists on contract.

How to Contact: Submit demo tape by mail. Unsolicited submissions are OK. Prefers cassette with 3 songs. Does not return material. Reports in 1-3 months.
Music: Mostly **heavy metal**, **industrial** and **punk**; also **hardcore**, **gothic** and **noise**. Released *Rag Na Roc*, recorded by Gwar (metal/punk); *Solar Lovers*, recorded by Cellestia Season (gothic/metal); and *Haunted*, recorded by Six Feet Under (heavy metal), all on Metal Blade Records. Other artists include Grip Inc., Decoryah, Galactic Cowboys, Masquerade, Cannibal Corpse, Sacred Reich, King Diamond and Fates Warning.
Tips: "Metal Blade is known throughout the underground for quality metal-oriented acts."

MIGHTY RECORDS, 150 West End, Suite 6-D, New York NY 10023. (212)873-5968. Manager: Danny Darrow. Labels include Mighty Sounds & Filmworks. Record company, music publisher (Rockford Music Co.) and record producer (Danny Darrow). Estab. 1958. Releases 1-2 singles, 1-2 12″ singles and 1-2 LPs/year. Pays standard royalty to artists on contract; statutory rate to publisher per song on record.

- Manager Danny Darrow also has a listing in the Record Producers section and the Rockford Music Co. can be found in the Music Publishers section.

How to Contact: Submit demo tape by mail. Unsolicited submissions are OK. "No phone calls." Prefers cassette with 3 songs and lyric sheet. SASE. Reports in 1-2 weeks.
Music: Mostly **pop**, **country** and **dance**; also **jazz**. Released *Impulse* (by D. Darrow); *Corporate Lady* (by Michael Green); and *Falling In Love* (by Brian Dowen), all recorded by Danny Darrow on Mighty Records.

‡MINDSPORE RECORDS, 20120 Rt. 19, Suite 105-209, Cranberry PA 16066. Phone/fax: (412)779-2085. E-mail: listen@mindspore.com. Contact: William Kish. Record company. Estab. 1995. Releases 4-6 CDs/year. Pays negotiable royalty to artists on contract; statutory rate to publisher per song on record.
How to Contact: Submit demo tape by mail. Unsolicited submissions are OK. Prefers cassette or DAT. Does not return material. Reports in 1 month.
Music: Mostly **ambient**, **groove** and **intelligent dance**; also **experimental**. Released *Distributed Shared Memory*, written and recorded by various artists on Mindspore Records (ambient groove).
Tips: "Make sure demos are as complete and polished as possible. We prefer to license finished works."

MISSILE RECORDS, Box 5537, Kreole Station, Moss Point MS 39563. (601)475-2098. "No collect calls." President/Owner: Joe F. Mitchell. Distributed by KY Imports/Exports, Curtis Wood, Dixie Rak, KC/Saddlestone, Kickin' Mule and Trend Records. Record company, music publisher (Bay Ridge Publishing/BMI) and record producer. Estab. 1974. Releases 28 singles and 10 LPs/year. Pays "8-15¢ per song to new artists, higher rate to established artists"; statutory rate to publisher for each record sold.

- See the listing for Bay Ridge Publishing in the Music Publishers section.

How to Contact: Write first and obtain permission to submit. Include #10 SASE. "You must include sufficient return postage." Prefers cassette with 3-6 songs and lyric sheet. Reports in 6-8 weeks.
Music: Mostly **country**, **alternative**, **gospel**, **rap**, **heavy metal**, **hardcore**, **folk**, **contemporary**, **jazz**, **bluegrass** and **R&B**; also **soul**, **MOR**, **blues**, **ballads**, **reggae**, **world**, **rock** and **pop**. Released "Somewhere Downtown" and "Sick of Paying Taxes," recorded by Jerry Piper; and "Has Anyone Seen My Baby?," written and recorded by Herbert Lacey (R&B), all on Missile Records.

‡MJJ MUSIC, 2100 Colorado Ave., Santa Monica CA 90404. (310)449-2963. Fax: (310)449-2959. Distributed by Sony.
How to Contact: MJJ Music does not accept unsolicited submissions.
Music: Released "Anything," recorded by 3T on MJJ Records.

MODAL MUSIC, INC.™, P.O. Box 6473, Evanston IL 60204-6473. (847)864-1022. Contact: President. Record company and agent. Estab. 1988. Releases 1-2 LPs/year. Pays negotiable royalty to artists on contract; negotiable rate to publisher per song on record.
How to Contact: Submit demo tape by mail. Unsolicited submissions are OK. Prefers cassette with bio, PR, brochures, any info about artist and music. Does not return material. Reports in 2 months.
Music: Mostly **ethnic**, **folk** and **world**. Released *Dance The Night Away* (by T. Doehrer), recorded by Balkan Rhythm Band; *Sid Beckerman's Rumanian* (by D. Jacobs), recorded by Jutta & The Hi-Dukes; and *Notes to Myself* (by S. Korelc), recorded by Balkan Rhythm Band, all on Modal Music Records. Other artists include Ensemble M'Chaiya, Nordland Band and Terran's Greek Band.
Tips: "We must hear what you've done, but recording quality (for demos *only*) is not as important as performance and writing quality. We don't expect too many writers, however, due to the ethnic focus of the label. Make sure your name, address, and phone number are on *every item* you submit."

MODERN VOICES ENTERTAINMENT, LTD., 22 Yerk Ave., Ronkonkoma NY 11779. (516)585-5380. E-mail: 103016.252@compuserve.com. President/Staff Producer: Chris Pati. Record company and studio/production company. Estab. 1991. Releases 7-10 CDs/year.
How to Contact: Does not accept unsolicited material. Prefers cassette with photo and bio. SASE. Reports in 2-3 months.
Music: Mostly **blues**, **gospel** and **Americana/AAA**; also **pop/rock** and **alternative**. Released *Blufire*, written and recorded by Chris Pati (alternative); *Wax Poetic*, written and recorded by Wax Poetic; and *Heavenbound*, written and recorded by The Original Loving Brothers (gospel), all on Modern Voices Records. Other artists include Deborah Ann, Tony Mascolo, John Taylor, Ron Smith and Jimmy Quinn.

MONS RECORDS, Taubenplatz 42, Trippstadt **Germany** 67705. (49)6306-993222. Fax: (49)6306-993223. President: Thilo Berg. Record company, music publisher and record producer. Estab. 1992. Releases 30 CDs/year. Pays negotiable royalty to artists on contract; statutory rate to publisher per song on record.
How to Contact: Submit demo tape by mail. Unsolicited submissions are OK. Prefers cassette. Does not return material. Reports in 1 month.
Music: Mostly **jazz** and **pop**. Released *It's a Wonderful World*, written and recorded by Allan Harris; and *Wish Me Love*, written and recorded by Dee Daniels, both on Mons Records (jazz).

‡**MOONSTONE RECORDS**, 303 Andrita St., Los Angeles CA 90065. Contact: A&R Dept. Distributed by INDI. Record company and music publisher (Tanna Productions Inc.). Estab. 1990. Releases 5 CDs/year. Pays negotiable royalty to artists on contract; negotiable rate to publisher per song on record.
How to Contact: Submit demo tape by mail. Unsolicited submissions are OK. Prefers cassette, CD or VHS videocassette with 3 songs. "Send SASE for reply." Does not return material. Reports in 2 months.
Music: Mostly **rock/alternative**, **score/orchestral** and **pop**; also **indigenous**. Released *Bad Channels*, recorded by Blue Oyster Cult, Sykotik Sinfoney, Fair Game, DMT and Joker (rock); *Doctor Mordrid/Demonic Toys*, recorded by Richard Band (soundtrack); and *Pain*, written and recorded by Rhino Bucket (hard rock), all on Moonstone Records. Other artists include Pino Donaggio, David Bryan, Edgar Winter, David Arkenstone, Danny Elfman, Aman Folk Orchestra and Quiet Riot.

MOR RECORDS, 17596 Corbel Court, San Diego CA 92128. (619)485-1550. Fax: (619)485-1883. President: Stuart L. Glassman. Labels include MOR Jazztime. Record company and record producer. Estab. 1980. Releases 3 singles/year. Pays 4% royalty to artists on contract; negotiable rate to publisher per song on record.
How to Contact: Submit demo tape by mail. Unsolicited submissions are OK. Prefers cassette or VHS videocassette. SASE. Reports in 2-3 weeks.
Music: Mostly **pop instrumental/vocal MOR**; also **novelty**. Released *Let Loose*, written and recorded by Legends on MOR Records (MOR); *In The Deep Heart's Core* (poetry of W.B. Yeats), recorded by Joseph Sobol and Kiltartan Road Ensemble (ethnic); and *A Kiltartan Road Christmas*, written and recorded by Kiltartan Road Ensemble, both on MOR Classic Digital Records. Other artists include Frank Sinatra Jr., Dave Racan, Dave Austin, Wally Flaherty and Mr. Piano.

‡**MOTION CITY RECORDS**, 1847 Centinela, Santa Monica CA 90404. (310)264-4870. Fax: (310)264-4871. E-mail: kcaetans@motioncity.com. Website: http://motioncity.com. A&R Director: Kevin Caetans. Distributed by CRD and BMG. Record company. Estab. 1994. Releases 7 LPs and 7 CDs/year. Pays negotiable royalty to artists on contract; statutory rate to publisher per song on record.
How to Contact: Submit demo tape by mail. Unsolicited submissions are OK. Prefers cassette, CD or DAT with 3 songs. Does not return material. Reports in 1 month.
Music: Mostly **alternative**, **rock/metal** and **techno**. Released *Velvet*, recorded by Velvet (alternative); and *Mowed*, recorded by Voodoo (metal), both on Motion City Records. Other artists include Ten Pound Tray and UFO Band.

‡**MOTOWN RECORDS**, 825 Eighth Ave., New York NY 10019. (212)445-3353. Director of A&R: Kenny Burns. Los Angeles office: 5750 Wilshire Blvd., 3rd Floor, Los Angeles CA 90036. (213)634-3500. Distributed by PGD; labels include BIV Records, Illtown Records and MoJazz Records. Record company.
How to Contact: Motown Records does not accept unsolicited submissions.
Music: Released *Let's Get the Mood Right*, recorded by Johnny Gill on Motown Records; *No Doubt*, recorded by 702 on BIV Records; and *Better Days Ahead*, recorded by Norman Brown on MoJazz Records.

MOUNTAIN RECORDS, P.O. Box 1253, Easton PA 18044. (610)253-5744. Fax: (800)500-1339. E-mail: stewartbrodian@hotmail.com. President: Stewart Brodian. Distributed by Performance. Record com-

pany. Estab. 1983. Releases 1 single, 1 LP and 1 CD/year. Pays negotiable royalty to artists on contract; statutory rate to publisher per song on record.
How to Contact: Submit demo tape by mail. Unsolicited submissions are OK. Prefers cassette with any number of songs. SASE. Reports in 3 weeks.
Music: Mostly **pop, rock** and **alternative**; also **folk, industrial** and **heavy metal**. Released *Troubled Troubadour*, written and recorded by G.G. Allin (alternative); *Misplaced Messiah* and *Never Had to Unplug*, written and recorded by Stewart Brodian, all on Mountain Records. Other artists include the Zeros.
Tips: "Use wholesome lyrics—you can get your point across without swearing."

MSM RECORDS, P.O. Box 101, Sutton MA 01590. Publisher/Owner: John Scott. Labels include Hālo Records and Bronco Records. Record company and music publisher (Mount Scott Music/BMI and Pick The Hits Music/ASCAP). Estab. 1979. Releases 3-4 LPs/year. Pays standard royalty to artists on contract; statutory rate to publisher per song on record.
How to Contact: Write first and obtain permission to submit. Prefers cassette with 2 songs and lyric sheet. SASE. Reports in 1 month.
Music: Mostly **folk, traditional country, contemporary country**, and **theater/musical works**. Released *Backyard Strut*, written and recorded by Backyard Strut; *Same Old School*, written and recorded by Cactus (country); and *Fog* (by Jon Scott), recorded by various artists, all on MSM Records.
Tips: "Follow submission guidelines. Pro demos preferred. Lead sheets best, but will accept typed lyric sheets. Will discuss acceptance of theater works for review/possible collaboration. Write and include synopsis (two page maximum) if submitting theater works."

MULE KICK RECORDS, 5341 Silverlode Dr., Placerville CA 95667. (916)626-4536. Owner: Doug McGinnis, Sr. Distributed by Tower Records. Record company and music publisher (Freewheeler Publishing/BMI). Estab. 1949. Pays 25% royalty to artists on contract; statutory rate to publisher.
How to Contact: Submit demo tape by mail. Unsolicited submissions are OK. Prefers cassette or CD with 6-10 songs and lyric and lead sheet. SASE. Reports in 1-6 months.
Music: Mostly **C&W** and **c-rock**; also **pop**. Released *Pretending*, written and reported by Diana Blair; *Tribute to Joaquin*, written and recorded by Joaquin Murphy; and *Wild Country*, written and recorded by Don McGinnis, all on Mule Kick Records.

‡MUSIC CITY SOUND RECORDS, P.O. Box 128132, Nashville TN 37212. (615)826-4146. (615)826-1414. Producer: Marcus Alan. Distributed by Independent Distributors of Nashville. Record company, music publisher (Marcus Alan Music) and record producer (Marcus Alan). Estab. 1995. Released 4 singles, 2 LPs and 2 CDs/year. Pays negotiable royalty to artists on contract; statutory rate to publisher per song on record.

- See the listing for Marcus Alan Music in the Music Publishers section.

How to Contact: Submit demo tape by mail. Unsolicited submissions are OK. Prefers cassette with 5 songs. "Send a basic guitar or piano vocal produced outside of Nashville." Does not return material. Reports in 4-6 weeks.
Music: Mostly **country, rock** and **R&B**; also **jazz, pop** and **gospel**.

‡MUSIC QUEST ENTERTAINMENT & TELEVISION, P.O. Box 822, Newark NJ 07102. Phone/fax: (201)374-4421. E-mail: mqtv@iquest.com. Senior Vice President: Selina Stormer. Record company, music publisher (Music Quest Publishing), record producer (Music Quest Productions) and distribution (Music Quest Distribution). Estab. 1994. Releases 20 singles, 10 LPs, 20 EPs and 10 CDs/year. Pays negotiable royalty to artists on contract; ¾ rate to publisher per song on record.
How to Contact: Submit demo tape (or finished product) by mail. Unsolicited submissions are OK. Prefers cassette, CD or VHS videocassette with picture, bio and letter. "Please include past experience, where you are and where you want to go. Include number of years of professional experience." Does not return material. Reports in 1-3 months.
Music: Mostly **pop (radio friendly), hip-hop/R&B** and **jazz/urban/pop rock**; also **instrumental, children's/special** and **gospel/reggae**. Released *A Very Special Christmas Gift*, written and recorded by Melba Moore; *Love Poems & Affirmations*, written and recorded Synthia Saint James, both on Music Quest; and *How To Succeed in the Music Business* (by Marianne Eggleston), recorded by Dunn Pearson on Exposure Records. Other artists include Willie Asbury (comedian), Hollywood, FSB, Majestic and Norman Bradley. "Dunn Pearson currently writes and produces for *New York Undercover* on FOX-TV."
Tips: "Know what the marketplace (consumers) wants because MQT is a very commercial-oriented label. MQT follows the trends and looks to break new and innovative ideas. MQT is looking for serious talent with the experience to become the next Babyface. Call or write today!"

MUSIC SERVICES & MARKETING, P.O. Box 7171, Duluth MN 55807. (218)628-3003. President: Frank Dell. Record company, music publisher (Frank Dell Music/BMI) and record producer (MSM). Estab. 1970. Releases 2 singles, 1 LP and 1 CD/year. Pays 50% royalty to artists on contract; statutory rate to publisher per song on record.

- Music Services & Marketing's publishing company, Frank Dell Music, is listed in the Music Publishers section.

How to Contact: Submit demo tape by mail. Unsolicited submissions are OK. Prefers cassette with 2 songs. Does not return material. Reports in 3 months.

Music: Mostly **country** and **gospel**. Released "Memories," written and recorded by Frank Dell on Country Legends Records. Other artists include Betty Lee, John Voit, Ted Hall and Terry Panyon.

‡MUSIC WISE INC., P.O. Box 931, Englewood Cliffs NJ 07632. (201)871-4555. (201)871-3430. CEO: John Henry. Record company, music publisher (Show-Class Music/BMI, Aisha Music/BMI) and artist management. Estab. 1990. Pays negotiable royalty to artists on contract; statutory rate to publisher per song on record.

How to Contact: Submit demo tape by mail. Unsolicited submissions are OK. Prefers cassette with 3-4 songs and lyric sheet. "When submitting material please include photos and biography." SASE. Reports in 1-2 weeks.

Music: Mostly **R&B**, **hip hop** and **pop/contemporary**; also **jazz**, **gospel** and **country**.

MUSIKUS PRODUCTIONS, INC., 715 North Ave., New Rochelle NY 10801. (914)633-2506. President: Hugh Berberich. Distributed by Empire. Record company. Estab. 1992. Releases 4 cassettes and 12 CDs/year. Pays 15% royalty to artists on contract; negotiable rate to publisher per song on record.

How to Contact: Submit demo tape by mail. Unsolicited submissions are OK. Prefers cassette or DAT. Does not return material. Reports in 3 weeks.

Music: Mostly **pop**, **rock** and **R&B**; also **classical**, **show (musical)** and **blues**. Released *Jon Nakamatsu*, written and recorded by Jon Nakamatsu on Musikus Productions, Inc. (classical). Other artists include Christine McCabe, Andrew Burns, Michael Svetlev and Brian Hunter.

NERVOUS RECORDS, 7-11 Minerva Rd., London NW10 6HJ, **England**. Phone: 44(181)963-0352. E-mail: 100316.3456@compuserve.com. Website: http://www.nervous.co.uk/. Managing Director: R. Williams. Record company (Rage Records), record producer and music publisher (Nervous Publishing and Zorch Music). Member MCPS, PRS, PPL, ASCAP, NCB. Releases 10 CDs/year. Pays 8-12% royalty to artists on contract; statutory rate to publisher per song on records. Royalties paid directly to US songwriters and artists or through US publishing or recording affiliate.

- Nervous Records' publishing company, Nervous Publishing, is listed in the Music Publishers section.

How to Contact: Submit demo tape by mail. Unsolicited submissions are OK. Prefers cassette with 4-15 songs and lyric sheet. SAE and IRC. Reports in 3 weeks.

Music: Psychobilly and **rockabilly**. "No heavy rock, AOR, stadium rock, disco, soul, pop—only wild rockabilly and psychobilly." Released *Slimline Daddy*, written and recorded by Bill McElroy; *Back to The Beat* (by Griffiths), recorded by The Backbeats; and *The Astonishing* (by Eckhardt), recorded by King Memphis, all on Nervous Records. Other artists include Restless Wild and Taggy Tones.

NEW EXPERIENCE RECORDS/GRAND SLAM RECORDS, P.O. Box 683, Lima OH 45802. Contact: James Milligan. Record company, music publisher (A New Rap Jam Publishing/ASCAP and Party House Publishing/BMI), management (Creative Star Management) and record producer (James Milligan). Estab. 1989. Releases 15-20 singles, 5 12″ singles, 3 LPs, 2 EPs and 2-5 CDs/year. Pays 8% royalty; statutory rate to publisher per song on record.

- See the listings for A New Rap Jam Publishing in the Music Publishers section and New Experience Records in the Record Producers section.

How to Contact: Submit demo tape by mail. Unsolicited submissions are OK. Prefers cassette or VHS videocassette with 3-5 songs and lyric sheet. SASE. Reports in 1 month.

Music: Mostly **R&B**, **pop** and **rock/rap**; also **country**, **contemporary gospel** and **soul/top 40**. Released

LISTINGS OF COMPANIES in countries other than the U.S. have the name of the country in boldface type.

"Pure Heart" (by Carl Milligan), recorded by T.M.C. on Pump It Up Records (gospel); and *He Will Never Leave You*, written and recorded by Warren Caldwell on Grand Slam Records (gospel). Other artists include Carl Milligan (gospel singer), Brooks, Melvin Brooks of the World Famous Impressions, Terria Hays, Pamela Shipe, Mr. Ice, James Junior and Barbara Joyce Lomas.

NIGHTMARE RECORDS, 7751 Greenwood Dr., St. Paul MN 55112. Phone/fax: (612)784-9654. E-mail: nightdiscs@aol.com. Contact: Lance King. Record company, distributor and management firm (Jupiter Productions). Estab. 1983.

- See the listing for Jupiter Productions in the Managers and Booking Agents section.

How to Contact: Submit demo tape by mail. Unsolicited submissions are OK. Prefers cassette or CD with 3 songs. Include brief bio, photo and press clippings (if available). SASE. Reports in 4-6 weeks.
Music: Mostly **hard rock-metal**, with a special interest in **progressive metal**. Current acts include The Kings Machine (progressive groove metal), Visionary (progressive metal) and Sonic Boom (industrial dance).

NOCTURNAL RECORDS, P.O. Box 399, Royal Oak MI 48068. (810)542-NITE. Fax: (810)542-4342. President: Chris Varady. Record company and record producer. Estab. 1988.
How to Contact: Submit demo tape by mail. Unsolicited submissions are OK. Prefers cassette or CD. Does not return material.
Music: Mostly **alternative rock** and **punk**. Released *Sissy*, written and recorded by Cathouse (alternative); "Tennessee Hustler," written and recorded by Mule (punk); and *Perfect Largeness*, recorded by 13 Engines (alternative rock), all on Nocturnal Records.

‡NOO TRYBE RECORDS, P.O. Box 15007, Beverly Hills CA 90210. (310)288-1486. Contact: Alex Mejia. Distributed by EMD; labels include Rap-A-Lot Records.
How to Contact: Submit demo tape by mail. Unsolicited submissions are OK. Prefers cassette with any number of songs, press kit, bio and photo.
Music: Released *Picture This*, recorded by Do or Die; *The Untouchable*, recorded by Scarface; and *Resurrection*, recorded by Geto Boys, all on Rap-A-Lot Records.

NORTH STAR MUSIC, 22 London St., E. Greenwich RI 02818. (401)886-8888. President: Richard Waterman. Record company. Estab. 1985. Releases 5-10 LPs/year. Pays 4-10% royalty to artists on contract; statutory rate to publisher per song on record.
How to Contact: Submit demo tape by mail. Unsolicited submissions are OK. Prefers cassette with 4-5 songs and lyric sheet. Does not return material. Reports in 2 months.
Music: Mostly **instrumental**, **traditional and contemporary jazz**, **New Age**, **traditional world** and **classical**. Released *In the Arms of the Wind*, written and recorded by Robin Spielberg; *Crossing the Waters*, recorded by Steve Schuch and the Night Heron Consort; and *Fire and Rain*, recorded by Commonground, all on North Star Records. Other artists include Judith Lynn Stillman, David Osborne, LunaMoon, Emilio Kauderer, Greg Joy, Gerry Beaudoin, Cheryl Wheeler and Nathaniel Rosen.

NOT LAME RECORDINGS, P.O. Box 9756, Denver CO 80209. (303)744-0888. E-mail: popmusic@notlame.com. Website: http://www.notlame.com. Contact: Bruce Brodeen. Distributed by Cargo UK, Feedback, 3-D, Surefire, Parasol and Get Hip. Record company and distributor of indie power pop bands and labels. Estab. 1994. Releases 6-7 CDs/year. Pays 30-50% royalty to artists on contract; negotiable rate to publisher per song on record.
How to Contact: Submit demo tape by mail. Unsolicited submissions are OK. Prefers cassette, VHS videocassette, CD or LP with 3 songs. Does not return material. Reports in 3 weeks.
Music: Mostly **power pop**, **pop/punk** and **music with hooks!** Released *A Wishing Well* (by Mike Mazarella), recorded by The Rooks; *Music For A World Without Limitations* (by Tony Perkins), recorded by Martin Luther Lennon; and *Adventures of Johnny Platonic*, recorded by Wönderband, all on Not Lame Records.
Tips: "Not Lame proudly embraces artists who are not ashamed of Beatle-esque hooks and harmonies in their craft."

‡nu.millennia/records, 10585 Santa Monica Blvd., Suite 140, Los Angeles CA 90025. (310)446-8544. Fax: (310)446-8548. Website: http://www.numill.com. A&R: Monti Olson. A&R: Declan Morrell. A&R/multimedia: Jason Bergman. Labels include nu.millennia/records Nashville. Record company and enhanced CD manufacturer. Estab. 1995. Releases 5 LPs and 5 CDs/year. Pays negotiable royalty to artists on contract.
How to Contact: Write or call first and obtain permission to submit. Prefers cassette or DAT. "No

unsolicited material. Must be represented by an attorney, management, or industry-related professional." SASE. Reports in 6-8 weeks.
Music: Mostly **alternative, rock** and **pop**; also **country**. Released *Mary*, written and recorded by Her Majesty the Baby (alternative); *Brand New Worries*, written and recorded by 3 Penny Needle (alternative), both on nu.millennia/records; and *Self Portrait*, written and recorded by Clay Walker on Giant Records (country). Other artists include Toe and Cory Sipper.

NUCLEUS RECORDS, P.O. Box 282, 885 Broadway, Bayonne NJ 07002. President: Robert Bowden. Record company, record producer (Robert Bowden) and music publisher (Roots Music/BMI). Member AFM (US and Canada). Estab. 1979. Releases 2 singles and 1 LP/year. Pays 5% royalty to artists on contract; statutory rate to publisher per song on record.

- Nucleus Records' publishing company, Roots Music, is listed in the Music Publishers section, and Robert Bowden is listed in the Record Producers section.

How to Contact: Submit demo tape by mail. Unsolicited submissions are OK. Prefers cassette or videocassette with any number songs and lyric sheet. Prefers studio produced demos. SASE. Reports in 1 month.
Music: Mostly **country** and **pop**; also **church/religious, classical, folk, MOR, progressive, rock (soft, mellow)** and **top 40**. Released "Henrey C," "Always" and "Selfish Heart" (by Bowden), recorded by Marco Sission, all on Nucleus Records.

OBLIVION ENTERTAINMENT, 1660 E. Herndon #135, Fresno CA 93720. (209)432-7329. Fax: (209)432-0147. E-mail: oblivion@cybergate.com. Contact: A&R. Record company. Estab. 1992. Pays negotiable royalty to artists on contract; negotiable rate to publisher per song on record.
How to Contact: Submit demo tape by mail. Unsolicited submissions are OK. Prefers cassette with 3 songs and lyric sheet. Include photo. SASE. Reports in 3 weeks.
Music: Mostly **alternative rock, alternative pop** and **electronica**. Released *Blisskreig*, recorded by Candy Planet (alternative); *Problems* (by Tommy Joy), recorded by Pusher (alternative); and *She's My Dream*, recorded by Vodka (alternative), all on Oblivion Records. Other artists include Braindead Soundmachine and Lance Carlos.

OCP PUBLICATIONS, 5536 NE Hassalo, Portland OR 97213. (503)281-1191. Fax: (503)282-3486. Administrative Assistant/Submissions: Linda Neuman. Labels include Candleflame and NALR. Record company, music publisher and record producer. Estab. 1977. Releases 20 LPs and 10 CDs/year. Pays 10% royalty to artists on contract; negotiable rate to publisher per song on record.
How to Contact: Submit demo tape by mail. Unsolicited submissions are OK. Requires lead sheets (with chords, melody line and text minimum) with *optional* demo tape. Prefers cassette with lead sheet. "Detailed submission information available upon request." SASE. Reports in 3 months.
Music: Mostly **liturgical, Christian/listening** and **children's Christian**; also **choral Christian anthems** and **youth Christian anthems**. Released *Find Us Ready*, recorded by Tom Booth; *The Coming*, recorded by Leon Roberts; and *Table of Plenty*, recorded by John Michael Talbot, all on OCP. "There are over 80 artists signed by OCP."
Tips: "Know the Catholic liturgy and the music needs therein."

OGLIO RECORDS, 507-A Pier Ave., Hermosa Beach CA 90254. (310)798-2252. Fax: (310)798-3728. Contact: Michael Byer. Record company. Estab. 1992. Releases 20 LPs and 20 CDs/year. Pays negotiable royalty to artist on contract.
How to Contact: Write first and obtain permission to submit. Does not accept unsolicited demos. All formats. Does not return material. Reports in 6 weeks.
Music: Mostly **alternative rock** and **adult rock**.

OLD SCHOOL RECORDS, 179 Prospect Ave., Wood Dale IL 60191-2727. E-mail: oldschrec@aol.com. Owner/President: Peter J. Gianakopoulos. Distributed by Dutch East, Universal One-Stop, Not Lame Recordings and Twin Cities. Record company, music publisher (Old School Records/Goosongs, ASCAP). Estab. 1992. Releases 1-2 singles, 1-2 LPs, 1-2 EPs and 1-2 CDs/year. Pays 10-16% to artists on contract; statutory rate to publisher per song on record.
How to Contact: Submit demo tape by mail. Unsolicited submissions are OK. Prefers cassette with 3-5 songs and lyric sheet. SASE. Reports in 3 weeks.
Music: Mostly **alternative rock, blues** and **pop**; also **funk, punk** and **tribute albums**. Released *Delusion of Grandeur*, written and recorded by The Now (rock); *Goo*, written and recorded by Goo (rock); and *Resurrection of the Warlock—A Tribute to Marc Bolan & T. Rex*, recorded by various artists, all on Old School Records. Other artists include Futuristic Dragon and Cosa Nostra.

OMNI 2000 INC., 413 Cooper St., Camden NJ 08102. (609)963-6400. Fax: (609)964-FAX-1. President/Executive Producer: Michael Nise. Record company, music publisher and record producer. Estab. 1995. Pays 50% royalty to artists on contract; statutory rate to publisher per song on record.
How to Contact: Write or call first and obtain permission to submit. Prefers cassette. SASE. Reports in 6 months.
Music: Mostly **R&B**, **gospel** and **pop**; also **children's**.

‡ONLY NEW AGE MUSIC, INC., 8033 Sunset Blvd. #472, Hollywood CA 90046. (213)851-3355. Fax: (213)851-7981. E-mail: onam@loop.com or info@newagemusic.com. Website: http://www.newagemusic.com. President: Suzanne Doucet. Record company and music publisher. Estab. 1987.
How to Contact: Call first and obtain permission to submit. Does not return material.
Music: Mostly **New Age**; also **world music**.
Tips: "You should have a marketing strategy and at least a small budget for marketing your product."

ORBIT RECORDS, P.O. Box 120675, Nashville TN 37212. (615)883-9161. Owner: Ray McGinnis. Record company and music publisher (Nautical Music Co.). Estab. 1965. Releases 6-10 singles, 6 12″ singles and 4 CDs/year. Pays 5.25% royalty to artists on contract; statutory rate to publisher per song on record.

- Orbit Records' publishing affiliate, Nautical Music Co., is listed in the Music Publishers section.

How to Contact: Submit demo tape by mail. Unsolicited submissions are OK. Prefers cassette with 4 songs and lead sheet. SASE. Reports in 4-6 weeks.
Music: Country (ballads), **country rock** and **R&B**. Released "Falling" (by Alan Warren), recorded by Bo Jest; "I'm Gonna Be Strong" (by Gene Pitney), recorded by Michael Storm; and "Southern Living" (by McGregory/Hughes), recorded by Sonny Martin, all on Orbit Records.

ORINDA RECORDS, P.O. Box 838, Orinda CA 94563. A&R Director: Harry Balk. Record company. Pays negotiable rate to publisher per song on record.
How to Contact: Submit demo tape by mail. Unsolicited submissions are OK. Prefers cassette and lead sheet. Does not return material. Reports in 3 months.
Music: Mostly **pop**, **rock** and **jazz**.

‡OVERTIME STATION, P.O. Box 402, Massapequa Park NY 11762. (516)795-2721. (516)795-2721 *51. President: Jackie Chazey. Record company. Estab. 1996. Releases 1-2 singles and 1-2 cassettes/year. Pays negotiable royalty to artists on contract.
How to Contact: Submit demo tape by mail. Unsolicited submissions are OK. Prefers cassette, CD, VHS videocassette or vinyl. "I would refer product to other labels, as I am not signing any new artists, personally, at this time." SASE. Reports in 1-2 months.
Music: Mostly **hard rock**, **metal** and **blues rock**; also **jazz rock**, **children's** and **space rock**. Released *Gator Strikes Again*, written and recorded by various artists (rock); and *Alligator Music and Tulip Dreams* (by various), recorded by Hope Fly (rock), both on Overtime Station Records. Other artists include Dragon Aerogator and Maxine Swann.

P. & N. RECORDS, 61 Euphrasia Dr., Toronto, Ontario M6B 3V8 **Canada**. (416)782-5768. Fax: (416)782-7170. Presidents: Panfilo Di Matteo and Nicola Di Matteo. Record company, record producer and music publisher (Lilly Music Publishing). Estab. 1993. Releases 10 singles, 20 12″ singles, 15 LPs, 20 EPs and 15 CDs/year. Pays 25-50% royalty to artists on contract; statutory rate to publisher per song on record.

- P. & N.'s publishing affiliate, Lilly Music Publishing, is listed in the Music Publishers section.

How to Contact: Submit demo tape by mail. Unsolicited submissions are OK. Prefers cassette or videocassette with 3 songs and lyric or lead sheet. "We only contact if we are interested in the material." SASE. Reports in 1 month if interested.
Music: Mostly **dance**, **ballads** and **rock**. Released *Don't Know* (by P. Dimatte); *Never Knew a Love Like This* (by Ken Wank); and *I Will Stand* (by Tod Stewart), all recorded by Angelica Castro on P.&N. Records (ballads/dance).

PAINT CHIP RECORDS, P.O. Box 12401, Albany NY 12212. (518)765-4027. President: Dominick Campana. Distributed by Dutch East India Trading. Record company. Estab. 1992. Releases 2 singles and 4 CDs/year. Pays negotiable royalty to artists on contract.
How to Contact: Submit demo tape by mail. Unsolicited submissions are OK. Prefers cassette with 4 songs. "No wank-off guitar solos, tough guy musicians, crappy production or lyrics with the word 'baby' in them. Our dream roster might include The Clash, The Jam, The Replacements and X. Current faves

include Radiohead and Superdrag." Does not return material. Reports only if interested.
Music: Mostly **"alternative" guitar rock** (bands). Released *Disaffected*, recorded by Queer for Astro Boy; *Big Block* (by Crist/Pauley/Hogan), recorded by Bloom (alternative rock); and *Hold My Life* (by Ferrandino/Weiss/Blaine/Bell), recorded by Lughead, all on Paint Chip Records. Other artists include Dryer.
Tips: "Being good isn't good enough for new artists to break. You must be fully committed to the music."

‡PARADIGM PRODUCTIONS, 4419 Linden Ave., Suite 4, Long Beach CA 90807. (310)984-7841. Fax: (310)984-8241. A&R: Jacob Young. Distributed by Shapiro Distributing. Record company, music publisher (Paradigm Publishing), record producer (Andre Shapiro) and artist management. Estab. 1993. Releases 10 singles, 10 LPs, 5 EPs and 10 CDs/year. Pays 50/50% split royalty to artists on contract; statutory rate to publisher per song on record.

- See the listing for Paradigm Publishers in the Music Publishers section.

How to Contact: Submit demo tape by mail. Unsolicited submissions are OK. Prefers cassette with no more than 5 songs and lyric sheet. "Include photo and bio if you have one." SASE. "We do not report unless we're interested."
Music: Mostly **folk-rock**, **alternative** and **rock**; also **Christian contemporary rock** and **New Age**. Released *New Wine* (by R. Rossi), recorded by Dylan Ross on J&R Records (rock); *Full Circle*, recorded by Full Circle on Maverick Records (alternative); and *From the Heart*, written and recorded by Jewel X on Shapiro Records (folk). Other artists include Pieces of 8, Outsider, Archangel, Clear Intention, Lyfeworks, MUDD, Epiphany and Jack McGowan.
Tips: "Write from the uncomfortable places of your life, your past, and your pain. Take off your clothes emotionally and bare your soul. Passion is more important than perfection. Play anywhere, anytime for anybody until you have a following."

PARAGOLD RECORDS & TAPES, P.O. Box 292101, Nashville TN 37229-2101. (615)865-1360. Director: Teresa Parks Bernard. Record company, music publisher (Rainbarrel Music Co./BMI) and record producer. Estab. 1972. Releases 3 singles and 3 LPs/year. Pays statutory rate to publisher per song on record.
How to Contact: Write first and obtain permission to submit. Prefers cassette or VHS videocassette with 2 songs and lyric or lead sheet. No response without SASE (#10 envelope not acceptable). Reports in 2 months.
Music: Country. Released "Rose & Bittercreek" and "Bottle of Happiness," written and recorded by Johnny Bernard; and "Daddy's Last Letter" (by J. Bernard), recorded by JLyne, all on Paragold Records (country). Other artists include Sunset Cowboys.

PATTY LEE RECORDS, 6034 Graciosa Dr., Hollywood CA 90068. (213)469-5431 and 1920 Audubon St., New Orleans LA 70118. (504)866-4480. Assistant to the President: Susan Neidhart. Distributed by Big Easy Distributing and Great Southern Music Distributing. Record company and record producer. Estab. 1985. Releases 1-2 singles, 1-2 EPs and 2-3 CDs/year. Pays negotiable royalty to artists on contract.
How to Contact: Send query postcard only. Does not return material. Reports back only if interested.
Music: Mostly **New Orleans rock**, **bebop jazz** and **cowboy poetry**; also **eclectic**, **folk** and **country**. Released *Alligator Ball, Be Your Own Parade* and *Must Be the Mardi Gras*, all written and recorded by Armand St. Martin on Patty Lee Records. Other artists include Too Tall Timm, James T. Daughtry, Jim Sharpe and Erica.
Tips: "Our label is small, which gives us the ability to develop our artists at their own rate of artistry. We are interested in quality *only,* regardless of the genre of music or style. Keep in mind that Patty Lee Records is not Warner Bros.! So patience and a good query letter are great starts."

J. PAUL RECORDS, 1387 Chambers Rd., Columbus OH 43212. Phone/fax: (614)487-1911. Owner: Jim Bruce. Distributed by J.H. Lennon Music Ltd. Record company, music publisher (James Paul Music), record producer (Jim Bruce) and artist management. Estab. 1994. Releases 1-3 singles, 1-3 LPs and 1-3 CDs/year. Pays 7-15% royalty to artists on contract; statutory rate to publisher per song on record.
How to Contact: Submit demo tape by mail. Unsolicited submissions are OK. Prefers cassette, DAT or VHS videotape with 1-3 songs. Does not return material. Reports in 4-6 weeks.
Music: Mostly **country**, **gospel** and **top 40/pop**; also **country rock**. Released *That's The Way* (by various), recorded by Debbie Collins on J. Paul Records. Other artists include Brandi Lynn Howard.
Tips: "Upbeat songs a must, ballads OK for songwriters. Artist must have professional package and band in place and working."

‡PAVEMENT MUSIC, INC., 2123 S. Priest #206, Tempe AZ 85282. (602)736-9315. Fax: (602)736-9316. E-mail: pvmnt@aol.com. Website: http://www.pavementmusic.com. President: Mark Nawara. Dis-

tributed by INDI; labels include PM Records. Record company, music publisher (NMG Music Publishing) and record producer (Mark Nawara). Estab. 1993. Releases 5 singles and 15 LPs/year. Pays negotiable royalty to artists on contract; 75% statutory rate to publisher per song on record.
How to Contact: Submit demo tape by mail. Unsolicited submissions are OK. Prefers cassette or CD with 3 songs. Does not return material. "We will call if we are interested. Otherwise no call back."
Music: Mostly **metal**, **alternative rock** and **rock**. Released *Broken Glass*, written and recorded by Crowbar (metal); *Green*, written and recorded by Forbidden (metal); and *Fallin' In* (by Cliff Johnson), recorded by Off Broadway (pop), all on Pavement Music. Other artists include Malevolent Creation, Internal Bleeding and Solitude Acturnus.

PBM RECORDS, P.O. Box 1312, Hendersonville TN 37077-1312. (615)865-1696 Fax: (615)865-6432. Owner: Michele Gauvin. Distributed by Arrow Distributing. Record company. "PBM also independently produces 2 television shows from Nashville." Estab. 1990. Releases 1-2 products/year. Pays statutory rate to publisher per song on record.
How to Contact: Write first and obtain permission to submit. "Permission to submit calls not accepted." Prefers cassette or VHS videocassette with lyric sheet, photo and bio. "Submissions must include SASE. Submissions (even though received with written permission) that do not include SASEs will not be responded to." Reports in 6-8 months.
Music: Mostly **country** and **rock**. Released "Don't Touch Me" (by Hank Cochran); "Half A Mind" (by Roger Miller); and "You're Not the Only Heart In Town" (by Lonnie Wilson), all recorded by Michele Gauvin on PBM Records (country). Other artists include Jim Woodrum.
Tips: "Please pull shrink wrap from CDs and cassettes submitted."

PC MUSIC, 711 Eighth Ave., San Diego CA 92101. (619)236-0187. Fax: (619)236-1768. E-mail: corbin@pcfreaks.com. Website: http://pcfreaks.com. Contact: Corbin Dooley. Record company, music publisher (PC Acid, PC Buddah) and record producer (Corbin Dooley). Estab. 1995. Releases 5 singles, 5 LPs and 5 CDs/year. Pays negotiable royalty to artists on contract.
How to Contact: Submit demo tape by mail. Unsolicited submissions are OK. Prefers cassette, DAT or videocassette. "It's always good to follow up repeatedly—then we know you are serious about your work." Does not return material.
Music: Mostly **rock**, **alternative** and **electronica**; also **lounge**, **folk** and **hip/hop**. Has released music from Another Society (metal), Jack Johnson (funk), NRSHA (breakbeat) and Magnet (indie rock).
Tips: "We prefer very challenging material."

PEACHTOWN RECORD CO. INC., 3625 Seilene Dr., College Park GA 30349. (404)761-8262. CEO/President: Bill Freeman. Record company, music publisher (Tasma Publishing) and record producer (Bill Fleetwood). Estab. 1965. Releases 4 singles, 3 LPs and 2 CDs/year.
How to Contact: Write first and obtain permission to submit, or to arrange personal interview. Prefers cassette. SASE. Reports in 3 months.
Music: Mostly **spiritual** and **gospel**. Released *Born Again* and *I'm Not Ashamed* (by Bill Fleetwood), recorded by Noel Fleetwood on Peachtown Record Co. (gospel).

‡PEAK RECORDS, 16601 Ventura Blvd., Encino CA 91436. (818)784-7325. Fax: (818)789-8298. Contact: Andi Howard. Distributed by UNI.
How to Contact: Submit demo tape by mail. Unsolicited submissions are OK. Any format accepted.

‡PENTACLE RECORDS, P.O. Box 5055, Laguna Beach CA 92652. (714)494-3572. Fax: (714)494-5372. E-mail: pentaclerx@aol.com. Contact: A&R. Record company. Estab. 1991.
How to Contact: Write first and obtain permission to submit. Prefers cassette or CD with lyric sheet. "We like photos and information (bio, etc.) about the artist. Have you performed live? Reviews?" Does not return material. Reports in 6 weeks.
Music: Mostly **AAA**, **modern rock** and **AOR**. Released *Get This* (by Waters/Cassard), recorded by Cassard (rock); *Roux* and "Trying Too Hard" (by Doug Rouhier), both recorded by Roux (rock/AAA), all on Pentacle Records. Other artists include Guillotine and Pyramid Scheme.
Tips: "We are small and very selective. We look for music that is melodic and interesting with lyrics that reflect a unique point of view. We are looking for artists who can sustain a career of innovative, creative work that changes the way listeners view themselves and their lives. Nothing typical please! If you think, 'My stuff sounds as good as the stuff on the radio,' don't bother with us. Move forward until your music is better, different. Push yourself until your music is a contribution to the world, not just more clutter."

PERIDOT RECORDS, P.O. Box 8846, Cranston RI 02920. (401)785-2677. Owner/President: Amy Parravano. Distributed by Caprice International. Record company, music publisher (Parravano Music) and record producer (Peridot Productions). Estab. 1992. Releases 2 singles, 1 LP and 1 CD/year. Pays 10% royalty to artists on contract; statutory rate to publisher per song on record.

- See the listings for Parravano Music in the Music Publishers section and Peridot Productions in the Record Producers section.

How to Contact: Submit demo tape by mail. Unsolicited submissions are OK. Prefers cassette or DAT with 6-10 songs and lyric sheet. SASE. Reports in 6 months.

Music: Mostly **country**, **country/rock** and **country/blues**; also **ballads**, **MOR** and **rockabilly**. Released *All Night Long* (by Mike DiSano), recorded by Joe Kemp on BJD Records (country); *One Last Try* (by Mike DiSano), recorded by Joe Kemp (country); and "Doctor of Romance" (by Amy Parravano), recorded by Amy Beth, both on Peridot Records.

‡PERMANENT PRESS RECORDINGS, 14431 Ventura Blvd. #311, Sherman Oaks CA 91423. (818)981-7760. Fax: (818)365-7328. President/Director of A&R: Ray Paul Klimek. Distributed by M.S. Distributing Co. Record company, music publisher (Permanent Pop Music/BMI) and record producer (Ray Paul). Releases 0-1 singles and 4-6 CDs/year. Pays negotiable royalty to artists on contract; negotiable rate to publisher per song on record.

- One of Permanent Press's releases, *Letters From the Desk of Count S. Van DeLecki*, by the Van DeLecki's, was named one of the top 10 Best Pure Pop Albums of 1996 by *Goldmine* magazine.

How to Contact: Submit demo tape by mail. Unsolicited submissions are OK. Prefers cassette or CD with 5 songs and lyric sheet. "Please send any press material or biographical information with your submission." Does not return material. Reports in 1 month.

Music: Mostly **pop/power pop**, **rock/pop reissues** and **alternative pop**; also **country**, **acid jazz** and **A/C pop**. Released "Moonlight" (by Jamie Hoover), recorded by The Van DeLecki's (pop); "Gotta Have Pop," written and recorded by Bob Segarini (pop reissue); and "December Dream" (by John Woloschuk/Terry Draper), recorded by KLAATU (rock), all on Permanent Press Records. Other artists include The Carpet Frogs and Walter Clevenger.

Tips: "If you're looking for a publishing deal, submit only the best five songs you have. Artists looking to either license a finished master recording to Permanent Press or record for Permanent Press should submit a finished album either on CD or cassette, along with pertinent bio and press material. Permanent Press is known for signing artists who are either well-known or have had a history of some recordings released. We have begun to sign some new artists on the strength of their great songwriting and recordings submitted. We are known to release high quality product with excellent packaging. Our albums are reviewed very favorably in most major music magazines. Permanent Press is a nationally distributed label, with close ties to retail, industry trades, and AAA radio. We service all AAA stations, music trade publications, most music magazines, and the majority of weeklies, dailies and specialty newspapers."

PHOENIX RECORDS, INC., Dept. SM, P.O. Box 121076, Nashville TN 37212-1076. (615)244-5357. President: Reggie M. Churchwell. Labels include Nashville International Records and Monarch Records. Record company and music publisher. Estab. 1971. Releases 5-6 CDs/year. Pays standard royalty to artists on contract; statutory rate to publisher per song on record.

How to Contact: Write first and obtain permission to submit. "You must have permission before submitting any material." Prefers cassette with lyric sheets. SASE. Reports in 1 month.

Music: Mostly **country** and **pop**; also **gospel**.

Tips: "We are looking for songs with strong hooks and strong words. We are not simply looking for songs, we are looking for hits."

PICKWICK/MECCA/INTERNATION RECORDS, P.O. Box 725, Daytona Beach FL 32115. (904)252-4849. President: Clarence Dunklin. Record company and music publisher (Pritchett Publications). Estab. 1980. Releases 20 singles, 30 LPs and 30 CDs/year. Pays 5-10% royalty to artists on contract; negotiable rate to publisher per song on record.

- See the listing for Pritchett Publications in the Music Publishers section.

How to Contact: Submit demo tape by mail. Unsolicited submissions are OK. Prefers cassette with 12 songs and lyric or lead sheet. Does not return material.

Music: Mostly **gospel**, **disco** and **rock/pop**; also **country**, **ballads** and **rap**. Released *Give It To Me Baby* (by Loris Doby), recorded by Gladys Nighte; *Baby I Love You*, written and recorded by Joe Simmon; and *I Love Sweetie* (by Doris Doby), recorded by Bobby Blane.

PIRATE RECORDS, 221 W. 57th St., 8th Floor, New York NY 10019. (212)489-1500. A&R Department: Matt "Half Pint" Davis. Record company and music publisher (Majestic Control/BMI). Estab. 1994.

- See the listing for Majestic Control in the Music Publishers section.

How to Contact: Submit demo tape by mail. Unsolicited submissions are OK. Prefers cassette with 3 songs. SASE. Reports in 8 weeks.

Music: Mostly **rap** and **R&B**. Released "Spread It Around" and "Bridge 95," both recorded by Kamakaze on Pirate Records.

PISSED OFF RECORDS, INC., 152 S. Peck Dr., Office Suite 101, Beverly Hills CA 90212. President: Brent Lee Kendell, CPA. Director of A&R: Lisa Williams. Record company and business management/representation. Estab. 1990. Releases 6 CDs/year. Pays negotiable royalty to artists on contract; statutory rate to publisher per song on record.
How to Contact: Submit demo tape by mail. Unsolicited submissions are OK. Prefers 3-song cassette or CD. "Send three songs; no blank tape; repeat first side on reverse; song contact number on cassette." SASE. Reports in 6-8 weeks.
Music: Pissed off punk metal rock. Released *Hell On Wheels* (by Paylor), recorded by Hell On Wheels; *Buzzz . . . Bikers . . . Babes . . . Beer . . .* (by Blatchley), recorded by Buzzz . . .; and *Putrid* (by Serge), recorded by Putrid, all on Pissed Off Records (punk metal). Other artists include Bogus Toms, Slamhouse, Trendlaser, Nuclear Waste, Dogs of Pleasure and Say Uncle.
Tips: "Find a record label that specializes in your particular style of music. As always, build a following and play the best clubs in town. Get airplay at local college radio stations. If you're good, you're an artist, and even if it takes years keep expressing your art through your music. Remember, every artist from the Beatles to Metallica has been rejected by record labels."

PLATEAU MUSIC, P.O. Box 947, White House TN 37188. Phone/fax: (615)654-8191. E-mail: nuille93@aol.com. Owner: Tony Mantore. Record company and record producer. Estab. 1990. Releases 4 singles and 2 CDs/year. Pays negotiable royalty to artists on contract; statutory rate to publisher per song on record.
How to Contact: Call first and obtain permission to submit or to arrange personal interview. Prefers cassette with 4 songs and lyric sheet. Does not return material. Reports in 1-3 weeks.
Music: Mostly **country, gospel** and **rock/pop**. Artists include Lula Davis and Mark Knight.

PLATINUM BOULEVARD RECORDS, 525 E. Moana Lane, Reno NV 89502. (702)827-4424. President: Lawrence Davis. Record company and music publisher. Estab. 1986. Releases 2 singles and 1 LP/year. Pays negotiable royalty to artists on contract; negotiable rate to publisher per song on record.

- See Platinum Boulevard's listing in the Music Publishers section.

How to Contact: Submit demo tape by mail. Unsolicited submissions are OK. Prefers cassette or VHS videocassette with lyric or lead sheets. Does not return material. "We report back only if interested."
Music: Mostly **rock, pop** and **R&B**; also **country, jazz** and **New Age**. Released *Hear My Heart*, written and recorded by Carl Driggs on Platinum Boulevard Records (pop).
Tips: "When presenting material indicate which artists you have in mind to record it. If you desire to be the recording artist please indicate."

PLATINUM PLUS RECORDS INTERNATIONAL, 1300 Division St., Nashville TN 37203. (615)242-4722. (800)767-4984. Fax: (615)242-1177. E-mail: platinumr@aol.com. Producer: Robert Metzgar. Record company, record producer, management firm and music publisher (Aim High Music/ASCAP, Bobby and Billy Music/BMI). Estab. 1971. Releases 16-17 singles, 25 LPs and 25 CDs/year. Pays statutory rate to publisher per song on record.

- See the listings for Aim High Music in the Music Publishers section, Capitol Ad, Management and Talent in the Record Producers section and Capitol Management in the Managers and Booking Agents section.

How to Contact: Submit demo tape by mail. Unsolicited submissions are OK. Prefers cassette or VHS videocassette with 5-10 songs and lyric sheet. Does not return material. Reports in 3-4 weeks.
Music: Mostly **country, traditional country** and **pop country**; also **gospel, southern gospel** and **contemporary Christian**. Released *There By Now* (by T. Tucker), recorded by J. Leclere; *Country Boogie Baby* (by T. Williams), recorded by Legal Limit, both on Capitol Records; and *So Hello, Handsome* (by A. Davis), recorded by L. Davis on Sony Records. Other artists include Tommy Cash/Mark Allen Cash (CBS-Sony), Carl Butler (CBS-Sony), Tommy Overstreet (CBS-Sony), Mickey Jones (Capitol), Glen Campbell Band and others.

REMEMBER: Don't "shotgun" your demo tapes. Submit only to companies interested in the type of music you write. For more submission hints, refer to Getting Started on page 6.

PLAYBACK RECORDS, P.O. Box 630755, Miami FL 33163. (305)935-4880. Fax: (305)933-4007. Producer: Jack Gale. Labels include Gallery II Records, Ridgewood Records. Record company, music publisher (Lovey Music/BMI and Cowabonga Music/ASCAP) and record producer. Estab. 1983. Releases 20 CDs/year. Pays negotiable royalty; statutory rate to publisher per song on record.

- Playback's publishing company, Lovey Music, is listed in the Music Publishers section, and Jack Gale is listed in the Record Producers section.

How to Contact: Submit demo tape by mail. Unsolicited submissions are OK. Prefers cassette or VHS videocassette with 2 songs and lyric sheet. Does not return material. Reports in 2 weeks if interested.

Music: Mostly **country**. Released *Are You Sincere* (by W. Walker), recorded by Melba Montgomery (country); *Just Beyond the Pain* (by A. Butler), recorded by Charlie Louvin and Crystal Gayle (country); and *My Love Belongs to You* (by R. Rogers), recorded by Del Reeves, all on Playback Records. Other artists include Tommy Cash, Jimmy C. Newman, Jeannie C. Riley, Sammi Smith, Johnny Paycheck and Cleve Francis.

PLAYBONES RECORDS, Winterhuder Weg 142, D-22085 Hamburg **Germany**. Phone: (040)22716552 + -53. Fax: (040)22716554. Producer: Arno van Vught. Labels include Rondo Records. Record company, music publisher (Mento Music Group) and record producer (Arteg Productions). Estab. 1975. Releases 30 CDs/year. Pays 8-16% royalty to artists on contract.

- See the listing for Mento Music Group in the Music Publishers section.

How to Contact: Submit demo tape by mail. Unsolicited submissions are OK. Prefers cassette with 3-4 songs. Put your strongest/best song first. "Put your name and address on the inside sleeve of the tape. If you have a fax number, inform us. Tell us in a typed cover letter what you want/what you are looking for." Does not return material. Reports in 2 weeks.

Music: Mostly **instrumentals**, **country** and **jazz**; also **background music**, **rock** and **gospel**. Released *Jazz* (by E. Stanbert), recorded by E. Kammler; *Loose One* (by Brun/Kuhles), recorded by Daniel & Claudia on Playbones Records; and *Born Again*, written and recorded by Reifegerste on DA Music. Other artists include H.J. Knipphals, Gaby Knies, Jack Hals, H. Hausmann, Crabmeat and M. Frommhold.

PMG RECORDS, P.O. Box 312897, Penobscot Station, Detroit MI 48231. President: Bruce Henderson. Record company, music publisher (Prejippie Music Group/BMI) and record producer (PMG Productions, Prejippie Music Group). Estab. 1990. Releases 6-12 12″ singles, 2 LPs and 2 EPs/year. Pays variable royalty to artists on contract; statutory rate to publisher per song on record.

- See the listings for Prejippie Music Group in the Music Publishers and Record Producers sections.

How to Contact: Submit demo tape by mail. Unsolicited submissions are OK. Prefers cassette, CD or VHS videocassette with 3-4 songs and lyric sheet. Include photo if possible. No calls please. SASE. Reports in 3 months.

Music: Mostly **funk/rock**, **alternative R&B**, **alternative rock**, **experimental** and **techno/dance**. Released *Black Bourgeoise*, written and recorded by Bourgeoise Paper Jam (alternative R&B); and *Webbslinger*, written and recorded by Tony Webb (jazz), both on PMG Records. Other artists include Jezebel and the Prejippies.

‡POINTBLANK RECORDS, 338 N. Foothill Rd., Beverly Hills CA 90210. (310)288-2900. Fax: (310)288-1494. Website: http://www.virginrecords.com. President: John Wooler. Distributed by EMD, Pointblank is owned by Virgin Records America. Record company. Estab. 1989. Releases 10 LPs and 20 CDs/year.

How to Contact: Submit demo tape by mail. Unsolicited submissions are OK. Prefers cassette or CD. "Do not call—we will get in touch with you when the demo has been listened to." Does not return material. Reports in 6-12 months.

Music: Mostly **blues**, **roots** and **soul**. Released *Best of Blues Guitar*, written and recorded by various artists; *Found True Love*, written and recorded by John Hammond; and *Duke's Blues*, written and recorded by Duke Robillard, all on Pointblank Records. Other artists include John Lee Hooker, Pops Staples, Roy Rogers, Solomon Burke, Terrell, Swamp Dogg, Hadda Brooks, Zakiya Hooker, Marva Wright, Bill Perry, Johnny Winter, The Boneshakers, Charlie Musselwhite and Percy Sledge.

‡POLYDOR RECORDS, 1416 N. LaBrea Ave., Hollywood CA 90028. (213)856-6600. Fax: (213)856-6610. Director of A&R: Tom Storms. New York office: 825 Eighth Ave., New York NY 10019. (212)603-3905. Fax: (212)603-3919. Website: http://www.polygram.com/polydor. Distributed by PGD; labels include Rocket Records. Record company.

How to Contact: Submit demo tape by mail. Unsolicited submissions are OK. Prefers CD.

Music: Released *The Healing Game*, recorded by Van Morrison; *Pure Disco*, recorded by various artists; and *Lemon Parade*, recorded by Tonic, all on Polydor Records. Other artists include Fig Dish, Cast, Moody Blues, Gene, The Badlees, Bee Gees, Big Back Forty, Goodfellaz, Vibrolux and Senser.

POP RECORD RESEARCH, 10 Glen Ave., Norwalk CT 06850. (203)847-3085. Director: Gary Theroux. Labels include Surf City, GTP and Rock's Greatest Hits. Record company, music publisher (Surf City Music/ASCAP), record producer and archive of entertainment-related research materials (files on hits and hitmakers since 1877). Estab. 1962. Pays statutory rate to publisher per song on record.

- See their listing in the Organizations section.

How to Contact: Submit demo tape by mail. Unsolicited submissions are OK. Prefers cassette or VHS videocassette. Does not return material.
Music: Mostly **pop**, **country** and **R&B**. Released "The Declaration" (by Theroux-Gilbert), recorded by An American; "Thoughts From a Summer Rain," written and recorded by Bob Gilbert, both on Bob Records; and "Tiger Paws," written and recorded by Bob Gilbert on BAL Records. Other artists include Gary and Joan, The Nightflight Singers and Ruth Zimmerman.
Tips: "Help us keep our biographical file on you and your career current by sending us updated bios/press kits, etc. They are most helpful to writers/researchers in search of accurate information on your success."

POWERHOUSE RECORDS, P.O. Box 2213, Falls Church VA 22042. (703)916-7835. Fax: (703)538-6285. Owner: Tom Principato. Distributed by Ichiban Worldwide. Record company. Estab. 1983. Releases 1-2 CDs/year. Pays negotiable royalty to artists on contract; statutory rate to publisher per song on record.
How to Contact: Submit demo tape by mail. Unsolicited submissions are OK. Prefers cassette with lyric sheet. Does not return material. "We don't guarantee we will report back on all submissions."
Music: Mostly **rock**, **blues** and **jazz**; also **instrumental guitar music**. Released *In The Clouds* and *Tip of The Iceberg*, both written and recorded by Tom Principato (blues/rock); and *Blazing Telecasters*, recorded by Tom Principato and Danny Gatton, all on Powerhouse Records. Other artists include Bob Margolin, John Mooney and Big Joe Maher.

PPI/PETER PAN INDUSTRIES, 88 St. Francis St., Newark NJ 07105. (201)344-4214. Director of A&R: Marianne Eggleston. Labels include Compose Records, Current Records, Parade Video, Iron Bound Publishing/Compose Memories. Record company, music publisher and record producer (Dunn Pearson, Jr.) Estab. 1928. Releases more than 200 cassettes and CDs and 75-80 videos/year. Pays royalty per contract. "All services are negotiable!"

- See PPI/Peter Pan's listing in the Music Publishers section.

How to Contact: Write to obtain permission to submit. Prefers cassette or VHS videocassette with 10 songs (full cassette) and lyric sheet. SASE. Reports in 3 months.
Music: **Pop** and **R&B**; also **jazz** and **New Age**. Released "Color Tapestry," written and recorded by Dunn Pearson, Jr. on Compose Records; "A Different Light," by David Friedman; and "The Trollies," by Dennis Scott, Grammy Award winner.
Tips: "Make sure all submissions are presented typed and professional. All recordings must be mastered."

PPL ENTERTAINMENT GROUP, (formerly MCI Entertainment Group), P.O. Box 8442, Universal City CA 91608. (818)506-8533. Fax: (818)506-8534. Vice President A&R: Jaeson Effantic. Labels include Bouvier and Credence. Record company, music publisher (Pollybyrd Publications) and management firm (Sa'mall Management). Estab. 1979. Releases 10-30 singles, 12 12″ singles, 6 LPs and 6 CDs/year. Pays 15% royalty to artists on contract; statutory rate to publisher per song on record.

- See the listings for Pollybyrd Publications in the Music Publishers section and Sa'mall Management in the Managers and Booking Agents section.

How to Contact: Write or call first and obtain permission to submit. Prefers cassette or videocassette with 2 songs. SASE. Reports in 6 weeks.
Music: Released *We The People People* (by J. Jarrett), recorded by The Band AKA (pop); *What Up With This* (by Scotti), recorded by Lejenz (pop); and *Phyne as I Can Be* (by Maxx Diamond), recorded by I.B. Phyne (pop); all on Sony/PPL Records. Other artists include Phuntain, Buddy Wright, Riki Hendrix, Condottiere and D.M. Groove.

PRAVDA RECORDS, 3823 N. Southport, Chicago IL 60613. (773)549-3776. E-mail: pravdausa@aol.com. Website: http://pravdamusic.com. Director of A&R: Mark Luecke. Distributed by Caroline, Cargo, Hepcat and Dutch East; labels include Bughouse. Record company. Estab. 1985. Releases 3-6 singles, 1 EP and 5-6 CDs/year. Pays 10-15% royalty to artists on contract; statutory rate to publisher per song on record.
How to Contact: Submit demo tape by mail. Unsolicited submissions are OK. Prefers cassette or CD with 3-4 songs. Does not return material. "Will contact only if interested."
Music: Mostly **rock**. Released *Guys & Dolls*, recorded by Rex Daisy; *Stop the Ride* (by G. Mercer), recorded by Wake Ooloo; and *In-A-Gadda-Da-Vegas*, recorded by New Duncan Imperials, all on Pravda Records. Other artists include Tiny Tim, Frantic Flattops, Gringo, Javelin Boot and cheer-accident.
Tips: "Be nice! Tour behind your release, don't take yourself too seriously."

‡**PREMIÉRE RECORDS**, P.O. Box 21323, St. Paul MN 55121-0323. (612)686-5094. President: Mitch Viegut. VP and General Manager: Mark Alan. Record company, music publisher (Big Snow Music) and management firm (Mark Alan Agency). Estab. 1988. Releases 6 singles, 2-3 LPs, 2-3 cassettes and 2-3 CDs/year. Pays standard royalty to artists on contract; statutory rate to publisher per song on record.

- See the listings for Big Snow Music in the Music Publishers section and Mark Alan Agency in the Managers and Booking Agents section.

How to Contact: Call first and obtain permission to submit. Prefers cassette or VHS videocassette with 3-4 songs. Does not return material. Reports in 3 months.
Music: Mostly **rock**, **alternative** and **pop**. Released "Cherry Lane" and *Crash Alley*, both recorded by Crash Alley; and *Airkraft III*, recorded by Mitch Viegut, David Saindon and Peter Phippen, all on Premiére Records.

PRESENCE RECORDS, 67 Candace Lane, Chatham NJ 07928-1115. (201)701-0707. President: Paul Payton. Distributed by Clifton Music. Record company, music publisher (Paytoons/BMI) and record producer (Presence Productions). Estab. 1985. Pays 1-2% royalty to artists on contract; statutory rate to publisher per song on record.
How to Contact: Submit demo tape by mail. Unsolicited submissions are OK. "No phone calls." Prefers cassette with 2-4 songs and lyric sheet. SASE. Reports in 2-4 weeks. "Tapes not returned without prepaid mailer."
Music: Mostly **doo-wop ('50s)**, **rock** and **new wave rock**. Released "Ding Dong Darling," "Bette Blue Moon" and "Davilee/Go On" (by Paul Payton/Peter Skolnik), recorded by Fabulous Dudes (doo-wop), all on Presence Records.

‡**PRIORITY RECORDS**, 6430 Sunset Blvd., Suite 900, Hollywood CA 90028. (213)467-0151. Fax: (213)856-8796. New York office: 32 W. 18th St., 18th Floor, New York NY 10011. (212)627-8000. Fax: (212)627-5555. Distributed by EMD; labels include No Limit Records, Lench Mob Records, Freeze Records, Roc-A-Fella Record, Duck Down Records and Buzz Tone Records. Record company.
How to Contact: Priority Records does not accept unsolicited submissions.
Music: Released *Tru 2 Da Game*, recorded by Tru; *Master P Presents . . . West Coast Bad Boyz II*, recorded by various artists, both on No Limit Records; and *Rhyme & Reason*, recorded by various artists on Buzz Tone Records (soundtrack). Other artists include Ice Cube, Christopher Franke, Mach 10, Tha Truth!, Homicide, Cutty Ranks, Organized Konfusion, Heltah Skeltah and Camp Lo.

QUARK RECORDS, P.O. Box 7320, FDR Station, New York NY 10150. Phone/fax: (212)838-6775. E-mail: quarkent@aol.com. President: Curtis Urbina. Labels include Outer Limits. Record company and music publisher (Quarkette Music/Freedurb Music). Estab. 1984. Releases 4 singles and 2 LPs/year. Pays negotiable royalty to artists on contract; ¾ statutory rate to publisher per song on record.
How to Contact: Write first and obtain permission to submit. Prefers cassette or DAT with 2 songs. SASE. Reports in 4-6 weeks.
Music: Mostly **instrumental/New Age**, **dance/pop** and **storytelling**. Released *Forgotten Times*, written and recorded by Mark P. Adler on Quark Records (New Age).

‡**QWEST RECORDS**, 3800 Barham Blvd., Suite 503, Los Angeles CA 90068. (213)874-7770. Fax: (213)874-5049. Contact: A&R (pop, gospel, etc.). Distributed by WEA. Record company.
How to Contact: Submit demo tape by mail. Unsolicited submissions are OK. SASE. Reports in 4-6 weeks.
Music: Released *Q's Jook Joint*, recorded by Quincy Jones; and "Could You Learn to Love Me," (by Babyface), recorded by Tevin Campbell, both on Qwest Records.

R.E.F. RECORDS, 404 Bluegrass Ave., Madison TN 37115. (615)865-6380. Contact: Bob Frick. Record company, management firm (Bob Scott Frick Enterprises), record producer (Bob Scott Frick) and music publisher (Frick Music Publishing Co./BMI). Releases 10 LPs/year. Pays statutory rate to publisher per song on record.

- See the listings for Frick Music Publishing in the Music Publishers section, as well as Bob Scott Frick in the Record Producers section and Bob Scott Frick Enterprises in the Managers and Booking Agents section.

How to Contact: Submit demo tape by mail. Unsolicited submissions are OK. Prefers 7½ ips reel-to-reel or cassette with 2 songs and lyric sheet. SASE. Reports in 1 month.
Music: Country, **gospel**, **rock** and **top 40/pop**. Released *The Right Track* (by Camp/Frick), recorded by Bob Scott Frick on R.E.F. Records.

RADICAL RECORDS, 77 Bleecker St., Suite C2-21, New York NY 10012. (212)475-1111. Fax: (212)475-5676. E-mail: radical@mail.idt.net. Website: http://www.geocites.com/SunsetStrip/6271/index.html. A&R: Eric Rosen. Distributed by Cargo, Rotz, Dutch East, MS, Action, City Hall, Universal, Victory and Revelation. Record company. "We also do independent radio and retail promotion." Estab. 1986. Releases 5 singles, 1 LP and 4 CDs/year.
How to Contact: Submit demo tape by mail. Unsolicited submissions are OK. Prefers cassette or CD. Does not return material. Reports in 1 month.
Music: Mostly **modern rock**, **pop** and **ska**; also **industrial** and **rock**. Released *O No No O Zone*, recorded by J.C.U. (punk); *Oi! Skampilation, Vol. I & II*, recorded by various artists (ska/oi!); and *Killer Blanks*, recorded by Blanks 77 (oi!/punk), all on Radical Records.
Tips: "Create the best possible demos you can and show a past of excellent self-promotion."

‡RADIOACTIVE RECORDS, 8570 Hedges Place, Los Angeles CA 90069. (310)659-6598. Fax: (310)659-1679. Contact: A&R. Distributed by UNI. Record company.
How to Contact: Submit demo tape by mail. Unsolicited submissions are OK.
Music: Released *Throwing Copper* and *Secret Samadhi*, both recorded by Live on Radioactive Records.

RAMMIT RECORDS, 414 Ontario St., Toronto ON M5A 2W1 **Canada**. (416)923-7611. Fax: (416)923-3352. A&R, New Projects: Trevor G. Shelton. Record company, music publisher (Rammit Noise) and record producer (Trevor G. Shelton). Estab. 1983. Releases 5-10 singles, 5-10 12″ singles, 5 LPs, 5 cassettes and 5 CDs/year. Pays statutory rate to publisher per song.
How to Contact: Submit demo tape by mail. Unsolicited submissions are OK. Prefers cassette with 4 songs. SAE and IRC. Reports in 3-4 weeks.
Music: Mostly **R&B**, **hip hop** and **dance**; also **alternative rock**. Released *2 Versatile* (by D. Myrie/R. Clarke), recorded by 2 Versatile (hip hop); and *Line Up In Paris* (by Lipwork Pub.), recorded by Line Up in Paris (rock), both on Rammit/A&M Records. Other artists include Martha and the Muffins, Machinations, Mystery Romance and Andy McLean.
Tips: "Realize you may be turned down, but work hard. Don't be discouraged by thank you—but no thanks form letters. Keep writing and if A&R departments suggest ideas of improving your material—listen to them, if you think comments are valid, use them."

RANDOM RECORDS, 22 Milverton Blvd., Toronto, Ontario M4J 1T6 **Canada**. (416)778-6563. President: Peter Randall. Record company, music publisher (Random Image Music) and record producer (Peter Randall). Estab. 1986. Releases 2 singles and 3 CDs/year. Pays 15% royalty to artists on contract; statutory rate to publisher per song on record.
How to Contact: Submit demo tape by mail. Unsolicited submissions are OK. Prefers cassette, DAT or NTSC videocassette with no more than 2 songs and lyric sheet. SAE and IRC. Reports in 3 months.
Music: Mostly **pop**, **rock** and **country**; also **folk**. Released *The Raindogs* (by Farrar/Randall), recorded by Raindogs (pop rock); *Glockenspeil* (by Kay/House), recorded by Glockenspeil (pop); and *Quadras*, recorded by Quadras (rock), all on Random Records. Other artists include Timeline and Vice Versa.
Tips: "Songwriters would be much better off to rewrite and re-work one song until it's killer, than to try and submit 18 passable songs. We have no time or reason to rewrite them for you."

RAREFACTION, P.O. Box 170023, San Francisco CA 94117. (415)333-7653. E-mail: rmac@rarefaction.com. Website: http://www.rarefaction.com. Sound Designer: Ron MacLeod. Producer of CD-ROM sound libraries. Estab. 1995. Releases 3 CDs/year. Pays negotiable royalty to artists on contract; statutory rate to publisher per song on record.
How to Contact: Write or call first and obtain permission to submit. SASE. Reports in 1 month.
Music: Sound samples. Released *A Poke in the Ear With a Sharp Stick Vol. I-III*.

RAVE RECORDS, INC., 13400 W. Seven Mile Rd., Detroit MI 48235. (248)540-RAVE. Fax: (248)338-0739. E-mail: derrick@raverecords.com. Website: http://www.raverecords.com. Production Dept.: Derrick. Distributed by Action Music Sales. Record company and music publisher (Magic Brain Music/ASCAP). Estab. 1992. Releases 2-4 singles and 2 CDs/year. Pays various royalty to artists on contract; statutory rate to publisher per song on record.
How to Contact: Submit demo tape by mail. Unsolicited submissions are OK. Prefers cassette with lyric or lead sheet. "Be sure to include all press/promotional information currently used." Does not return material. Reports in 2-4 months.
Music: Mostly **alternative rock** and **dance**. Released "Strength" (by D. Hakim), recorded by Nicole; "Gothem" and "Chillin' With My Baby X-Mas Eve" (by S. Sholtes), recorded by Bukimi3, all on Rave Records. Other artists include Cyber Cryst and Dorothy.

Tips: "We are interested in artists who are new to the market place, but please include at least four songs on your demo. Also, if we have information regarding your demo, we will call you. Please do not call us about your submission."

RBW, INC., P.O. Box 14187, Parkville MO 64152. (816)587-5358. President: Russ Wojtkiewicz. Labels include RBW Record Co. and Blue City Records. Record company and production/recording broker. Estab. 1990. Releases 3-5 CDs/year. Pays varying royalty to artists on contract; statutory rate to publisher per song on record.
How to Contact: Submit demo tape by mail. Unsolicited submissions are OK. Prefers cassette or CD and lyric or lead sheet. "If no video, send recent b&w photo." Does not return material. Reports in 6-12 weeks.
Music: Mostly **blues**, **classical** and **jazz/big band**.
Tips: "Looking for artists with strong regional following, with or without recording track record. RBW/Blue City is looking for unique talent and sound. Will listen to all music submitted. Rejection letters will be sent. Do not call."

‡RCA RECORDS, 1540 Broadway, 36th Floor, New York NY 10036. (212)930-4000. Fax: (212)930-4546. Website: http://www.bmgmusic.com. Beverly Hills office: 8750 Wilshire Blvd., Beverly Hills CA 90211. (310)358-4000. Nashville office: One Music Circle N., Nashville TN 37203. (615)333-4300. Distributed by BMG; labels include Loud Records and Deconstruction Records. Record company.
How to Contact: RCA Records does not accept unsolicited submissions.
Music: Released *Crash*, recorded by Dave Matthews Band; *Villians*, recorded by The Verve Pipe; and *The Greatest Hits*, recorded by Clint Black, all on RCA Records. Other artists include SWV, Leah Andreone, Rome, Alabama, Aaron Tippin, Martina McBride and Wild Orchid.

REACT RECORDINGS, 9157 Sunset Blvd., Suite 210, W. Hollywood CA 90069. (310)550-0233. Fax: (310)550-0235. A&R Director: Sebastian Jones. Record company and music publisher (Startup Music/ASCAP). Estab. 1994. Releases 10 singles, 12 LPs and 12 CDs/year. Pays negotiable royalty to artists on contract; ¾ rate to publisher per song on record.
How to Contact: Submit demo tape by mail. Unsolicited submissions are OK. Prefers cassette with 3-5 songs and lyric sheet. Does not return material. Reports in 3-4 weeks.
Music: Mostly **hip hop jazz**, **blues**, **dance** and **R&B**. Released "Back 2 Tha' Funk," written and recorded by Rodney O & Joe Cooley (rap); "Da' Nayborhoodz," written and recorded by Da' Nayborhoodz (rap); and "No Brain Cells," written and recorded by Insane Poetry (rap), all on React Records.

‡RED ANT ENTERTAINMENT, 9720 Wilshire Blvd., 4th Floor, Beverly Hills CA 90212. (310)247-1133. Fax: (310)247-2233. New York office: 352 Park Ave., New York NY 10101. (212)685-6303. Fax: (212)685-7459. Record company.
How to Contact: Red Ant does not accept unsolicited submissions.
Music: Released *Cheap Trick*, recorded by Cheap Trick on Red Ant.

RED DOT/PUZZLE RECORDS, 1121 Market, Galveston TX 77550. (409)762-4590. President: A.W. Marullo, Sr. Record company, record producer and music publisher (A.W. Marullo Music/BMI). Estab. 1952. "We also lease masters from artists." Releases 14 12″ singles/year. Pays 8-10% royalty to artists on contract; statutory rate to publisher for each record sold.
How to Contact: Prefers cassette with 4-7 songs and lyric sheet. "Cassettes will not be returned. Contact will be made by mail or phone." Reports in 2 months.
Music: **Rock/top 40 dance songs**. Released "Do You Feel Sexy" (by T. Pindrock), recorded by Flash Point (top 40/rock); "You Put the Merry in My Christmas," (by E. Dunn), recorded by Mary Craig (rock/pop country); and "Love Machine" (by T. Pindrock), recorded by Susan Moninger, all on Puzzle/Red Dot Records. Other artists include Joe Diamond, Billy Wayde, Jerry Hurtado and Tricia Matula.
Tips: "All songs and masters must have good *sound* and be studio produced."

RED SKY RECORDS, P.O. Box 27, Stroud, Glos. GL6 0YQ **United Kingdom**. Phone: 01453-836877. Producer: Johnny Coppin. Distributed by Direct, ADA and CM. Record company and record producer. Estab. 1985. Releases 2 albums per year. Pays 8-10% to artists on contract; statutory rate to publisher per song on record.

- See the listing for Johnny Coppin/Red Sky Records in the Record Producers section.

How to Contact: Write first and obtain permission to submit. Does not return material. Reports in 6 months.
Music: Mostly **rock/singer-songwriters**, **modern folk** and **roots music**. Released *Dead Lively!*, written

and recorded by Paul Burgess; *Keep the Flame* and *A Country Christmas*, written and recorded by Johnny Coppin, all on Red Sky Records. Other artists include David Goodland.

REDEMPTION RECORDS, P.O. Box 3244, Omaha NE 68103-0244. (712)328-2771. Fax: (712)328-9732. E-mail: rediscs@aol.com. A&R: Ryan D. Kuper. Labels include Fahrenheit, Full Flavor and Mayhem. Record company. Estab. 1990. Releases 6-10 singles, 2 LPs, 2 EPs and 6 CDs/year. Pays negotiable royalty to artists on contract; statutory rate to publisher per song on record.
How to Contact: Submit demo tape by mail. Unsolicited submissions are OK. Prefers cassette with 4 songs and lyric and/or lead sheet. "Include band's or artist's goals." Does not return material. Reports in 2-4 weeks.
Music: Mostly **progressive rock**, **power pop** and **post hardcore**; also **hip hop**, **hardcore** and **punk**. Released *The Healing*, recorded by Martin's Dam (rock); *Goodbye To Alice*, recorded by Easter (rock); and *Suck Fumes*, recorded by Rosegarden Funeral (hard rock), all on Redemption Records. Other artists include Let's Rodeo, Downer, Anton Barbeau and Material Issue.
Tips: "Be prepared to tour to support the release. Make sure the current line-up is secure."

RED-EYE RECORDS, Wern Fawr Farm, Pencoed, Mid-Glam CF35 6NB **United Kingdom**. Phone: (0656)86 00 41. Managing Director: M.R. Blanche. Record company and music publisher (Ever-Open-Eye Music/PRS). Estab. 1979. Releases 4 singles and 2-3 LPs/year.

- Red-Eye Records' publishing company, Ever-Open-Eye Music, is listed in the Music Publishers section.

How to Contact: Submit demo tape by mail. Unsolicited submissions are OK. Prefers cassette, VHS videocassette or 7½ or 15 ips reel-to-reel with 4 songs. SAE and IRC. Does not return material.
Music: Mostly **R&B**, **rock** and **gospel**; also **swing**. Released "River River" (by D. John), recorded by The Boys; "Billy" (by G. Williams), recorded by The Cadillacs; and "Cadillac Walk" (by Moon Martin), recorded by the Cadillacs, all on Red-Eye Records. Other artists include Cartoon and Tiger Bay.

REITER RECORDS LTD., 308 Penn Estates, East Stroudsburg PA 18301. (717)424-9599. Fax: (717)424-0452. Vice President of A&R: Greg Macmillan. Record company. Estab. 1990. Releases 5 singles, 5-10 LPs and 5-10 CDs/year. Pays negotiable royalty to artists on contract; 75% of statutory rate to publisher per song on record.
How to Contact: Submit demo tape by mail. Unsolicited submissions are OK. Does not return material.
Music: Mostly **pop**, **jazz** and **rock**. Released *Black Rose '95*, written and recorded by various artists on Reiter Records. Other artists include Jim Cherry and Danger Zone.

REJOICE RECORDS OF NASHVILLE, 116 Roberta Dr., Hendersonville TN 37075. (615)264-1373. Owner: Gregg Hutchins. Record company and music publisher (Gregg Hutchins Music). Estab. 1993. Releases 3 CDs/year. Pays statutory rate to publisher per song on record.

- See the listing for Gregg Hutchins Music in the Music Publishers section.

How to Contact: Write first and obtain permission to submit. Prefers cassette with up to 3 songs and lyric sheet. Does not return material. "We don't report back unless we're interested."
Music: Mostly **southern gospel**, **country gospel** and **Christian country**; also **bluegrass gospel**. Released *Adam's Side* (by Jesse Wilson), recorded by Billy Walker (gospel); *Grand Ole Christmas*, recorded by Bobby Bare, Jeannie C. Riley, Tommy Cash, Charlie Louvin and Stu Phillips; and "The Last Time I Fall" (by Jim Watters), recorded by Charlie Louvin.

‡RELATIVITY RECORDS, 79 Fifth Ave., 16th Floor, New York NY 10003. (212)337-5300. Santa Monica office: 3420 Ocean Park Blvd., Suite 3050, Santa Monica CA 90405. (310)581-8200. Fax: (310)581-8205. Distributed by Sony; labels include Suave House Records, Ruthless Records, Mo Thugs Records and Violator Records. Record company.
How to Contact: Submit demo tape by mail. Unsolicited submissions are OK.

REPRISE RECORDS, 3300 Warner Blvd., Burbank CA 91505. (818)846-9090. Fax: (818)953-3712. E-mail: repriseear@aol.com. New York office: 75 Rockefeller Plaza, New York NY 10019. (212)275-4500. Fax: (212)275-4595. Website: http://www.repriserec.com. Distributed by WEA. Record company.
How to Contact: Reprise Records will accept inquiries via e-mail. Write to repriseear@aol.com for further instruction.
Music: Released *Phenomenon*, recorded by various artists (soundtrack); *The Boatman's Call*, recorded by Nick Cave & the Bad Seeds; and *The Memory of Trees*, recorded by Enya, all on Reprise Records. Other artists include Wilco, Paul Brandt, Eric Clapton, Chaka Khan, Brady Seals, Arkarna, Dinosaur Jr., Depeche Mode, Faith No More and Green Day.

‡RESTLESS RECORDS, 1616 Vista Del Mar, Hollywood CA 90028. (213)957-4357, ext. 223. Fax: (213)957-4355. Website: http://www.restless.com. A&R: Liz Garo. Distributed by BMG; labels include Medium Cool Records, Twin/Tone Records, Clean Records and On-U-Sound Records. Record company.
How to Contact: Submit demo tape by mail. Unsolicited submissions are OK. Prefers cassette, DAT or CD with press kit.
Music: Released *Murk Time Cruiser*, recorded by aMiniature; *Times Like This*, recorded by Slim Dunlap; and *Blue Moods of Spain*, recorded by Spain, all on Restless Records. Other artists include Perfect, Penny Dreadfuls, Suncatchers, Radar Bros., Polara, Golden Palominos, Gem, Lori Carson, Hang Ups and Jack Logan.

REVELATION RECORDS, P.O. Box 5232, Huntington Beach CA 92615. (714)375-4264. E-mail: info@revhq.com. Owner: Jordan Cooper. Labels include Crisis. Record company. Estab. 1987. Releases 2 singles, 2 12″ singles, 6 LPs, 4 EPs and 10 CDs/year. Royalty varies. Pays various amounts to publisher per song on record.
How to Contact: Submit demo tape by mail. Unsolicited submissions are OK. Send demos to the attention of Fred Knot. Prefers DAT or VHS videocassette with 3 songs and lyric sheet. "Send photos and bio/press sheet if you have one." Does not return material. Reports in 2 months.
Music: Mostly **rock**, **hardcore/punk** and **thrash**; also **country**, **rap** and **disco**. Released "Do You Know Who You Are?," recorded by Texas Is The Reason; *Sights* (by Mike Ferraro), recorded by Mike Judge & Old Smoke (country-folk-blues); and "Looking Back," written and recorded by Bold, all on Revelation Records. Other artists include Farside, Into Another, Sense Field, Iceburn, ORANGE 9mm, Function, Shades Apart, Civ, Gorilla Biscuits, Quicksand, Sick of it All, Youth of Today, State of the Nation, Ignite, Kiss it Goodbye, Sparkmarker and Enginekid.
Tips: "Don't be inhibited when sending songs, we listen to everything. Don't be discouraged, our taste is not anything more than opinion. E-mail us for a quicker response."

‡REVOLUTION RECORDS, 8900 Wilshire Blvd., Beverly Hills CA 90211. (310)289-5500. Fax: (310)289-5501. Director of A&R: Jeff Aldrich. Website: http://www.revolution-online.com. Distributed by WEA. Record company.
How to Contact: Submit demo tape by mail. Unsolicited submissions are OK. No song limit, any format.
Music: Released *Beautiful World*, recorded by Big Head Todd and the Monsters; *Michael*, recorded by various artists (soundtrack); and "Through Your Hands," recorded by Don Henley, all on Revolution Records. Other artists include Lotion, Kenny Wayne Shepherd, Letters to Cleo, Color Me Badd, Super Deluxe, Steve Forbert, Wakeland, Man Will Surrender, Sparkler and Agnes Gooch.

‡RHIANNON RECORDS, 20 Montague Rd., London, E8 2HW **United Kingdom**. Phone: (0171)275-8292. Fax: (0171)503-8034. E-mail: rhiannonrec@compuserve.com. Website: http://ourworld.compuserve.com/homepages/rhiannonrec. Owner: Colin Jones. Distributed by Direct and Vital. Record company, music publisher (Rhiannon Music) and record producer (Colin Jones). Estab. 1993. Releases 4-6 CDs/year. Pays negotiable royalty to artists on contract; pays according to agreement rate to publisher per song on record.
How to Contact: Submit demo tape by mail. Unsolicited submissions OK. "We only publish writers we also record. No separate publishing deals!" Prefers cassette or DAT with press writings, bio and photo. "Please ensure material submitted meets label requirements." SAE and IRC. Reports in 1 month.
Music: Mostly **acoustic**, **ethnic-based folk**, **folk rock**, **singer/songwriter**, **folk/country** and **contemporary**. Released *Wings of the Sphinx*, recorded by Barry Dransfield (British folk); *Sin É*, recorded by Sin É (contemporary Irish folk); and *By Heart*, by Maggie Holland (contemporary acoustic), all on Rhiannon Records. Other artists include Calico, Bob Pegg and Felicity Buirski.
Tips: "Don't imitate—originate! I'm not looking for imitation Chieftains or Nanci Griffith. I want to hear talented artists using their background and imagination to offer new ideas. One of my former artists said, 'Most singer/songwriters are putting down on record what they should be telling their therapist.' If this is you, please don't send me your material!"

‡RHINO RECORDS, 10635 Santa Monica Blvd., Los Angeles CA 90025. (310)474-4778. Fax: (310)441-6575. Website: http://www.rhino.com. Distributed by WEA; labels include Forward Records. Record company.

THE TYPES OF MUSIC each listing is interested in are printed in boldface.

How to Contact: Rhino is basically a reissue label, and is only interested in signing acts with long track records and who have an already-established audience.
Music: Released *The Very Best of Curtis Mayfield*, recorded by Curtis Mayfield; and *Foxy Lady*, recorded by RuPaul, both on Rhino Records.

RICHWAY RECORDS INTERNATIONAL, P.O. Box 110983, Nashville TN 37222. Phone/fax: (615)731-2935. President: Wayne G. Leinsz. Distributed by Quality Song Music. Record company, record producer and music publisher (Lion Hill Music). Estab. 1991. Releases 20 LPs and 4 CDs/year. Pays 25% royalty to artists on contract; statutory rate to publisher per song on record.

• Richway Records' publishing company, Lion Hill Music, is listed in the Music Publishers section.

How to Contact: Submit demo tape by mail. Unsolicited submissions are OK. Prefers cassette or VHS videocassette with 3 songs and lyric sheet. SASE. Reports in 1 month.
Music: Mostly **country**, **bluegrass** and **gospel**. Released "Gold Hill Gold," recorded by The Legendary Bobby Atkins (bluegrass); "Velvet & Stone," recorded by Jerry James (country); and "Date With A Memory," recorded by Linda Winner (country), all on Richway Records. Other artists include Walt Timmerman, Debbie Davis, Troy Madison, Jack Batey, Allen Maitland and The McArdle Bros. Band.

RISING STAR RECORDS, 52 Executive Park South, Suite 5203, Atlanta GA 30329. (404)636-2050. E-mail: info@ristar.com. Website: http://www.ristar.com. President: Barbara Taylor. Distributed by Passport, Music Design, New Leaf, Goldenrod, Silo, Ladyslipper, Lifedance, LeFon, Mill City and Rivertown. Record company and record distributor. Estab. 1987. Releases 5-6 CDs/year. Pays negotiated royalty to artists on contract; negotiated rate to publisher per song on record.
How to Contact: Write or call first and obtain permission to submit. SASE. Reports in 1-2 months.
Music: Mostly **contemporary instrumental**, **New Age**, **classical** and **comedy**. Released *Celestial Journey I & II*, written and recorded by various artists (space/ambient); *Classical Erotica I & II*, written and recorded by various artists (classical); and *Box Lunch*, written and recorded by Lea Delaria (comedy), all on Rising Star Records.

‡RML RECORDS, P.O. Box 4835, Petaluma CA 94955. (707)766-8338. Fax: (707)766-8440. E-mail: baldieray@aol.com. Vice President of A&R: Peter Finster or G.T. Albright. Distributed by Comlink Narrowcast Systems and The Peoples Network. Record company, record producer (G.T. Albright) and merchandiser (RML Merchandise). Estab. 1991. Releases 1-4 singles, 1 LP, 1 EP and 1 CD/year. Pays negotiable royalty to artists on contract; statutory rate to publisher per song on record.
How to Contact: Submit demo tape by mail. Unsolicited submissions are OK. Prefers cassette, CD, DAT or VHS videocassette with 1-15 songs and lyric sheet. "Voice and one instrument OK, produced demos preferred." Does not return material. Reports in 4-6 weeks.
Music: Mostly **pop**, **rock** and **R&B**; also **jazz/fusion**, **swing/big band** and **alternative rock**. Released *Postitive Points of View*, written and recorded by G.T. Albright (pop); *Traveler*, written and recorded by Audric Jankauskas (fusion); and *The Follenian Underground* (by Sherer/Albright), recorded by the Follenian Underground (blues/rock), all on RML Records.
Tips: "We are a small independent label with two very noteworthy producers in tow. James Fischer, associate producer on Grammy-nominated R&B LP *New World Order* by Curtis Mayfield and Steven Hart, internationally-acclaimed NAIRD Indie Award-winning producer on Alasdair Fraser's '95/'96 release *Dawn Dance*, are both producing for RML Records. We produce a first-class product. We serve the music!"

‡ROBBINS ENTERTAINMENT LLC, 30 W. 21st St., 11th Floor, New York NY 10010. (212)675-4321. Fax: (212)675-4441. E-mail: info@robbinsent.com. Associate Director A&R: Jonathan P. Fine. A&R Manager: Meredith Fisher. Distributed by BMG. Record company and music publisher (Rocks, No Salt). Estab. 1996. Releases 20 singles, 12-14 LPs and 12-14 CDs/year. Pays negotiable royalty to artists on contract.
How to Contact: Submit demo tape by mail. Unsolicited submissions are OK. Prefers cassette (high bias preferred) and videocassette (NTSC) with up to 5 songs and lyric sheet. "Please include photo, if possible." Does not return material. "Will call if interested."
Music: **Rap**, **dance**, **alternative rock** and **R&B**. Released "I Fell In Love" (by Ewart A. Wilson, Jr.), recorded by Rockell (dance); "Passion" (by KJ), recorded by K5 (dance/pop); and "Jellyhead" (by DeMatos/Male/Smith), recorded by Crush (pop), all on Robbins Entertainment Records. Other artists include Shanel and Meg Hentges.
Tips: "We are looking for original, but accessible music, with real crossover potential."

ROCK DOG RECORDS, P.O. Box 3687, Hollywood CA 90028. (213)661-0259. E-mail: patt2@netcom.com. or rockdogrec@aol.com. Website: http://members.aol.com/empathcd/web/index.htm. A&R Director:

Gerry North. C.E.O.: Patt Connolly. East Coast Division: Rock Dog Records, P.O. Box 884, Syosset NY 11791-0899. A&R Director: Maria Cuccia. In house distribution through Saturn Studios. Record company, record producer. Estab. 1987. Releases 3 singles, 1-3 12″ singles, 3-5 LPs, 1-3 EPs and 3 CDs/year. Pays negotiable royalty to artists on contract; statutory royalty to publisher per song on record.
How to Contact: Write first and obtain permission to submit. Prefers CD or VHS videocassette with 3-5 songs and lyric sheet. SASE. Reports in 3 weeks.
Music: Mostly **contemporary instrumental**, **jazz** and **ambiage (ambient/New Age)**. Released *Abduction* (by Maria Cuccia/Gerry Cannizzaro), recorded by Empath; *Chill* and *Saturn Studios Sampler 1*, both written and recorded by various (ambient), all on Rock Dog Records. Other artists include Stratos Dimantis, Michael Halaas, The Daughters of Mary, Mark Round and Chasm.

ROLL ON RECORDS®, 112 Widmar Pl., Clayton CA 94517. (510)672-8201. Owner: Edgar J. Brincat. Record company and music publisher (California Country Music). Estab. 1985. Releases 2-3 LPs/cassettes/year. Pays 10% royalty to artists on contract; statutory rate to publisher per song on record.

- See the listing for California Country Music in the Music Publishers section.

How to Contact: Submit demo tape by mail. Unsolicited submissions are OK. Do not call. Prefers cassette with 3 songs and lyric sheet. SASE. Reports in 4-6 weeks.
Music: Mostly **contemporary/country**, **MOR** and **R&B**; also **pop**, **light rock** and **modern gospel**. Released "Broken Record" (by Horace Linsley/Dianne Baumgartner), recorded by Edee Gordon on Roll On Records; *Maddy* and *For Realities Sake* (both by F.L. Pittman/Madonna Weeks), recorded by Ron Banks/L.J. Reynolds on Life Records/Bellmark Records.

‡THE ROSEBOWL, Reutter Str. 73, Munich **Germany** 80689. Phone: (+4989)562713. Fax: (+4989)5466371. A&R Manager/Director: Ken Rose. Distributed by EMI Music. Record company, music publisher and record producer (Ken Rose). Estab. 1995. Releases 10-15 singles, 10-15 LPs and 10-15 CDs/year. Pays negotiable royalty to artists on contract; statutory rate to publisher per song on record.
How to Contact: Submit demo tape by mail. Unsolicited submissions are OK. Prefers cassette, CD or DAT with 2 songs and lyric sheet. "Songs should be well crafted with meaningful lyrics and concise arrangements. Please, no sound-alike hits." Does not return material. Reports between 1-4 weeks.
Music: Mostly **college rock**, **alternative pop/rock** and **accoustic pop/folk**; also anything of artistic merit. Released *Mantra For the American Jungle* (by Glover/Rosenkrantz), recorded by Bright Blue Gorilla (AAA); *One Take*, written and recorded by Rick Keller (jazz); and *Clearly Clear*, written and recorded by Ken Rose (rock), all on The Rosebowl. Other artists include Levi Jones, Mario Knapp, On the Beach, Wolfgang Külzer, Little Sister, Luca & the Groovy Band, Susi, Dead Panman, Klaus K. and Philip Says.
Tips: "Send only original work that differs from stock 'writer for hire' material. Sound quality of submissions isn't as important as content, a good song works in all formats."

ROSEBUD RECORDS, P.O. Box 26044, Fraser MI 48026. (810)831-1380. Record company and publisher (Rose Music/BMI). Estab. 1990. Releases 12 singles and 12 CDs/year. Pays 45% royalty to artists on contract; statutory rate to publisher per song on record.
How to Contact: Submit demo tape by mail. Unsolicited submissions are OK. Prefers cassette with 3 songs and lyric sheet. Must be coded: Songwriter AD-25. "Please make sure that your recording is of good quality and that all songs are copyrighted. Any information relating to the artist's past accomplishments is appreciated." Does not return material. Reports in 4-6 weeks.
Music: Mostly **country**, **pop/country**, **rock**, **contemporary Christian** and also **R&B/jazz**. Released "And The Wind Will Sing to You" (by T. Senecal), recorded by D. Vecchine (folk); "One Plus One" (by T. Senecal), recorded by D. Manley (rock); and "Lord of My Life" (by T. Senecal), recorded by S. Hayes, all on Rosebud Records. Other artists include Elaine Serling, Russell Harns and Doris Reese.

ROTTEN RECORDS, P.O. Box 2157, Montclair CA 91763. (909)624-2332. Fax: (909)624-2392. E-mail: rotten@rottenrecords.com. Website: http://www.rottenrecords.com. President: Ron Peterson. Promotions/Radio/Video: Richard Shytlemeyer. Distributed by Caroline, Shock (Australia), Sonic Rendezvous (Europe), Smash and Cargo (Canada). Record company. Estab. 1985. Releases 3 LPs, 3 EPs and 3 CDs/year.
How to Contact: Submit demo tape by mail. Unsolicited submissions are OK. Prefers cassette. Does not return material.
Music: Mostly **rock**, **alternative** and **commercial**; also **punk** and **heavy metal**. Released *Paegan Terrorism . . .*, written and recorded by Acid Bath; *Kiss the Clown* (by K. Donivon), recorded by Kiss the Clown; and *Full Speed Ahead* (by Cassidy/Brecht), recorded by D.R.T., all on Rotten Records.
Tips: "Don't call and keep bugging us to listen to your demo—very annoying!"

ROUND FLAT RECORDS, P.O. Box 1676, Amherst NY 14226. E-mail: roundflt@pce.net. Website: http://www.rockfetish.com/roundflat/. President: Curt Ippolito. Record company and distributor. Estab. 1989. Releases 10 singles and 6 CDs/year. Pays varying royalty to artists on contract; varying rate to publisher per song on record.
How to Contact: Submit demo tape by mail. Unsolicited submissions are OK. Prefers cassette or VHS videocassette with 5 songs and lyric sheet. Does not return material. Reports in 4-6 weeks.
Music: Mostly **alternative**, **hardcore** and **ska**; also **industrial**. Artists include Against All Hope, Cropdogs and Powertrip.

‡**ROYAL RECORDS**, P.O. Box 5368, Buena Park CA 90622. (714)522-2383. A&R Director: Jerry Smith. Record company, music publisher (Royal King Music, Melodeer Music) and management firm (Five-Star Entertainment). Estab. 1959. Pays negotiable royalty to artists on contract; statutory rate to publisher per song on record.

- See the listings for Royal Records in the Advertising, AV and Commercial Music Firms section, Royal King Music in the Music Publishers section and Five-Star Management and Entertainment in the Managers and Booking Agents section.

How to Contact: Write first and obtain permission to submit. Enclose SASE for rapid reply. Prefers cassette, CD or VHS videocassette. "Submissions with any potential at all are filed and catalogued for further consideration. No submission is ever thrown out, but is either returned or catalogued." Reports in 1-3 weeks.
Music: **All styles**. Interested in songwriters, as well as performing artists and bands.

ROYALTY RECORDS, 176 Madison Ave. 4th Floor, New York NY 10016. (212)779-0101. Fax: (212)779-3255. A&R: Dave R. Record company. Estab. 1994. Releases 5 singles and 5 CDs/year. Pays negotiable royalty to artists on contract; ¾ statutory rate to publisher per song on record.
How to Contact: Submit demo tape by mail. Unsolicited submissions are OK. Prefers cassette or videocassette. Does not return material. Reports in 2 months.
Music: Mostly **heavy/alternative**. Released *Smothered*, written and recorded by Whorgasm; *Deviation*, written and recorded by Jayne County; and *Lemonade*, written and recorded by Fuzzbubble, all on Royalty Records.

‡**RUDE RECORDS**, 20121 Diehl St., Walnut CA 91789. Phone/fax: (909)595-7071. President: Rudy Chavarria. Record company. Estab. 1993. Releases 5 singles and 5 LPs/year. Pays negotiable royalty to artists on contract; statutory rate to publisher per song on record.
How to Contact: Call first and obtain permission to submit. Prefers cassette with 3 songs, photo, bio and lyric sheet. SASE. Reports in 3 weeks.
Music: Mostly **rock**, **alternative** and **rap**; also **folk**, **instrumental** and **children's**.

RUFFCUT PRODUCTIONS, 6472 Seven Mile, South Lyon MI 48178. Phone/fax: (810)486-0505. Producer: J.D. Dudick. Record company, record producer (J.D. Dudick) and music publisher (Al-Ky Music/BMI). Estab. 1991. Releases 4 singles and 4 CDs/year. Pays 10-14% royalty to artists on contract; statutory rate to publisher per song on record.

- See the listing for Al-Ky Music in the Music Publishers section and J.D. Dudick in the Record Producers section.

How to Contact: Submit demo tape by mail. Unsolicited submissions are OK. Prefers cassette with 2 songs and lyric sheet. Does not return material. Reports in 2 months.
Music: Mostly **rock**, **pop** and **country**; also **alternative**. Released *Something For Everyone* (by Bil Tol), recorded by Cidyzoo on Vehicle Garage; *Minddust* (by Chris Pierce), recorded by "Q"; and *Am I Different* (by Laya Phelps), recorded by Laya, both on Ruffcut Records. Other artists include Hubcaps, Jim Dean and Moon Toonsie.

RUSTRON MUSIC PRODUCTIONS, 1156 Park Lane, West Palm Beach FL 33417-5957. (561)686-1354. Executive Director: Rusty Gordon. A&R Director: Ron Caruso. Labels include Rustron Records and Whimsong Records. "Rustron administers 22 independent labels for publishing and marketing." Record company, record producer, management firm and music publisher (Whimsong/ASCAP and Rustron Music/BMI). Estab. 1970. Releases 5-10 CDs/year. Pays variable royalty to artists on contract. "Artists with history of product sales get higher % than those with no sales track record." Pays statutory rate to publisher.

- See the listings for Rustron Music in the Music Publishers section and Rustron Music Productions in the Record Producers and Managers and Booking Agents sections.

How to Contact: Submit demo tape by mail. Unsolicited submissions are OK. Prefers cassette with 3 songs and lyric sheet. "If singer/songwriter has independent product (cassette or CD) produced and sold

at gigs—send this product." SASE required for all correspondence, no exceptions. Reports in 4 months.
Music: Mostly **mainstream** and **women's music**, **A/C**, **electric acoustic**, **pop (cabaret, blues)** and **blues (R&B, country and folk)**; also **New Age fusions** (instrumentals), **modern folk fusions**, **environmental** and **socio-political**. Released "I'm Still Leaving You Today," written and recorded by Cilla Smith; "When I Look Into Your Eyes" (by Jayne Margo-Reby/Vic Bersok), recorded by Jayne Margo-Reby; and "Pass A Smile," written and recorded by Star Smiley, all on Rustron Records. Other artists include Whig Party, Deb Criss, Lori Surrency, Flash Silvermoon, Kathi Gibson and Chris Limardo, Boomsland Swampsinger and Dana Adams.
Tips: "Find your own unique style; write well-crafted songs with unpredictable concepts, strong hooks and definitive melody. New Age composers: evolve your themes and add multi-cultural diversity with instruments. Don't be predictable. Don't over-produce your demos and don't drown vocals."

SABRE PRODUCTIONS, P.O. Box 10147, San Antonio TX 78210. (210)533-6910. Producer: E.J. Henke. Labels include Fanfare, Satin and Legacy. Record company and record producer. Estab. 1965. Releases 48 singles, 5 LPs and 4 CDs/year. Pays 10% royalty to artists on contract; statutory rate to publisher per song on record.
How to Contact: Submit demo tape by mail. Unsolicited submissions are OK. Prefers cassette with 4 songs and lyric sheet. SASE. Reports in 1 month.
Music: Mostly **country** (all styles), **gospel** and **rock/R&B**. Released *Take A Number* (by Staggs/Norton/Wharton), recorded by Robert Beckom on Sabre Records (country); *Borderline Crazy* (by Betty Kay Miller), recorded by Darnell Miller on Fanfare Records (country); and "Hypnotized," (by Ted Snyder), recorded by Ace Diamond on Legacy Records (rockabilly). Other artists include Joe Terry, Suzie Rowles, Howard Alexander and Sunglows.

SABTECA RECORD CO., P.O. Box 10286, Oakland CA 94610. (510)465-2805. President: Duane Herring. Creative Manager: Sean Herring. Record company and music publisher (Sabteca Music Co./ASCAP, Toyiabe Music Co./BMI). Estab. 1980. Releases 3 singles and 1 12″ single/year. Pays 10% royalty to artists on contract; statutory rate to publisher per song on record.
Affiliate(s): Andre Romare Records.
- Sabteca's publishing company, Sabteca Music Co., can be found in the Music Publishers section.

How to Contact: Write first and obtain permission to submit. Prefers cassette with lyric sheet. SASE. Reports in 2 months.
Music: Mostly **R&B**, **pop** and **country**. Released "Sacrifice," "One Hundred Pounds of Love" and "One Day Man" (by Duane Herring/Tom Roller), recorded by Johnny B on André Romare Records (country). Other artists include Walt Coleman, Lil Brown and Lois Shayne.

‡SAFIRE RECORDS, 5617 W. Melvin, Milwaukee WI 53216. (414)444-3385. President: Darnell Ellis. Record company, music publisher (Ellis Enterprise Publishing), record producer (Darnell Ellis) and management firm (The Ellis International Talent Agency). Estab. 1997. Releases 3 singles, 3 LPs, 1 EP and 3 CDs/year. Pays negotiable royalty to artists on contract; statutory rate to publisher per song on record.
- See the listing for The Ellis International Talent Agency in the Managers and Booking Agents section.

How to Contact: Submit demo tape by mail. Unsolicited submissions are OK. Prefers cassette with 3-4 songs. Does not return material. Reports in 1-2 months. "We will respond only if we are interested."
Music: Mostly **top 40/commercial hits**, **country** and **rock**; also **alternative**, **industrial** and **jazz**.
Tips: "Because this company is just getting off the ground, we are very open minded. If we sign an artist or pick up a song, we are going to push it 100%. The artist has to have the same attitude. We would love to hear from acts in Canada and the United Kingdom."

SAHARA RECORDS AND FILMWORKS ENTERTAINMENT, 4475 Allisonville Rd., 8th Floor, Indianapolis IN 46205. (317)546-2912. President: Edward De Miles. Record company, music publisher (EDM Music/BMI, Edward De Miles Music Company) and record producer (Edward De Miles). Estab. 1981. Releases 15-20 CD singles and 5-10 CDs/year. Pays 9½-11% royalty to artists on contract; statutory rate to publishers per song on record.
- See the listings for Edward De Miles Music Company in the Music Publishers section, and Edward De Miles in the Record Producers section.

How to Contact: Write first and obtain permission to submit. Prefers cassette with 3-5 songs and lyric sheet. Does not return material. Reports in 1 month.
Music: Mostly **R&B/dance**, **top 40 pop/rock** and **contemporary jazz**; also **TV-film themes**, **musical scores** and **jingles**. Released "Hooked on U," "Dance Wit Me" and "Moments," written and recorded by Steve Lynn (R&B) on Sahara Records. Other artists include Lost in Wonder, D́von Edwards and Multiple Choice.

Tips: "We're looking for strong mainstream material. Lyrics and melodies with good hooks that grab people's attention."

SALEXO MUSIC, P.O. Box 18093, Charlotte NC 28218-0093. (704)536-0600. President: Samuel OBie. Record company. Estab. 1992. Releases 2 LPs and 2 CDs/year. Pays 2.5% royalty to artists on contract; variable rate to publisher per song on record.
How to Contact: Submit demo tape by mail. Unsolicited submissions are OK. Prefers cassette with 3 songs and lyric sheet. SASE. Reports in 3 months.
Music: Mostly **contemporary gospel**, **jazz** and **R&B**. Released *Vision & Message*, *Communion* and *He's My All & All* (by Samuel A. Obie), recorded by Fellowship Community Choir) on Salexo Records.

SATIN RECORDS, P.O. Box 632, Snohomish WA 98291-0632. (206)546-3038. Partner: John W. Iverson. Distributed by City Hall Records and Twinbrook Records; labels include Seafair-Bolo Records. Record company and music publisher (Bolmin Publishing/BMI). Estab. 1982. Releases 2 singles, 4 LPs, 1 EP and 4 CDs/year. Pays negotiable royalty to artists on contract; statutory rate to publisher per song on record.
How to Contact: Write first and obtain permission to submit. Prefers cassette, DAT or CD with lyric sheet. SASE. Reports in 2 months.
Music: Mostly **R&B**, **jazz** and **rock**. Released *Private Jungle* (by various), recorded by The Slamhound Hunters (blues/rock); *Sweet Harmony* (by various), recorded by The Main Attraction (R&B), both on Satin Records; and *The Transparent Two* (by various), recorded by UNT Two O'Clock Band on Bolo Records (jazz).

‡SCAT RECORDS, 6226 Southwood, St Louis MO 63105-3232. (314)862-3488. Fax: (314)862-0565. A&R Director: Cubby Watson. Distributed by Revolver, Surefire, Caroline, Ajax, Valley, Bayside, F.A.B., Cargo, Scratch, Matador, N.A.I.L. and more. Record company. Estab. 1989. Releases 0-4 singles, 4-8 LPs, 0-3 EPs and 4-8 CDs/year. Pays negotiable royalty to artists on contract; profit split rate to publisher per song on record.
How to Contact: Write first and obtain permission to submit. Prefers cassette, CD or vinyl record with 1-4 songs. "Do not submit unless you are familiar with releases on the label and think your material is appropriate for us." Does not return material. Reports in 2-8 weeks (only positive responses are sent).
Music: Mostly **non-commercial rock**; also **experimental** and **psychedelic**. Released *The Opponents* (by Damon Che), recorded by Thee Sspeaking Canariess (experimental rock); *Ten Cool Ones* (by various artists), recorded by Mono Men (rock); and *Cold Before Morning* (by Brian DiPlacido), recorded by A Bullet for Fidel (country folk), all on Scat Records. Other artists include Nothing Painted Blue, Prisonshake and Specula.
Tips: "99% of you do not belong here. We are an underground, independent label and have no interest in mainstream music of any kind."

SCRATCHED RECORDS, 1611 Arvada Dr., Richardson TX 75081. (214)680-1830. President: Gerard LeBlanc. Labels include Spectre. Record company. Estab. 1990. Releases 6 singles and 3 CDs/year. Pays 50% royalty to artists on contract; statutory rate to publisher per song on record. "We split all expenses 50/50."
How to Contact: Submit demo tape by mail. Unsolicited submissions are OK. Prefers cassette. "Will respond if interested." Does not return material. Reports in 2 weeks.
Music: Mostly **alternative**, **punk** and **hardcore**; also **girl bands**. Released *A Reason to Care*, written and recorded by Humungus (punk); *Phurly*, written and recorded by Third Leg (hard core); and *We're From Texas Vols. I, II and III*, written and recorded by 21 different bands (alternative), all on Scratched Records.

SHANG RECORDS, 404 Washington Ave., Suite 680, Miami Beach FL 33139. (305)531-7755. Fax: (305)672-8952. President: Luther McKenzie. Record company. Releases 30 singles, 6 LPs and 36 CDs/year.
How to Contact: Call first and obtain permission to submit a demo. Prefers cassette, photos and bio. Does not return material. Reports in 1 month.
Music: Mostly **reggae**, **rap** and **R&B**; also **hip hop**. Released *Milkman*, written and recorded by Mad Cobra on EMI/Capitol Records; "Let's Get It On," recorded by Shabba Ranks on Sony/Epic Records; and "Scent of Attraction," recorded by Patra/Aaron Hall on Shang/550 Records.

SHAOLIN FILM & RECORDS, P.O. Box 58547, Salt Lake City UT 84158. (801)595-1123. President: Richard O'Connor. A&R: Don DelaVega. Labels include Shaolin Communications. Record company, music publisher (Shaolin Music/ASCAP) and record producer (T.S. Coyote). Estab. 1984. Releases 4 singles, 2 LPs, 2 CDs and 2 EPs/year.

• See the listing for Shaolin Music in the Music Publishers section.
How to Contact: Submit demo tape by mail. Unsolicited submissions are OK. Prefers cassette with 3-4 songs and lyric sheet. Include bio and press kit. Does not return material. Reports in 6 weeks.
Music: Mostly **rock**, **hard rock** and **pop**; also **soundtracks**. Released *American Zen: Level 1* and *Tai Chi Magic*, both written and recorded by Coyote on Shaolin Film and Records.

SHEFFIELD LAB RECORDING, 408 Bryant Circle, Suite C, Ojai CA 93023. (805)640-2900 or (800)576-4745. Fax: (800)576-5640. Website: http://www.sheffieldlab.com. A&R: Gwen DeSevren Jacquet. Labels include Audiophile. Record company. Estab. 1968. Releases 10-20 CDs/year. Pays negotiable royalty to artists on contract.
How to Contact: Write or call first and obtain permission to submit a demo. Prefers cassette, CD or DAT with 3-4 songs and lyric sheet. Does not return material. Reports in 8-10 weeks.
Music: Mostly **classical**, **jazz** and **pop**; also **world music**. Released *Acoustic Storm*, written and recorded by Robert Stanton; *Matter of Time*, recorded by Michael Allen Harrison; and *River of My Own*, recorded by Mark Terry, all on Sheffield Lab Recordings.
Tips: "Sheffield Music has been started as a sister label and will be recording 1-2 projects a month—rock, jazz, country, classical. We are also looking for high quality *completed* masters."

‡SHEHESHE RECORDS, Rt. 1 Box 145A, Salem MO 65500-9721. (573)674-3299. President: Angel Davis. Record company, music publisher (Davis & Davis Music/BMI) and record producer. Estab. 1997. Releases 4-8 singles, 1-3 LPs and 1-3 CDs/year. Pays negotiable royalty to artists on contract; statutory rate to publisher per song on record.
• See the listing for Davis & Davis Music in the Music Publishers section.
How to Contact: Submit demo tape by mail. Unsolicited submissions are OK. Prefers cassette, DAT or videocassette with 3-4 songs, bio and photo. Does not return material.
Music: Mostly **country**, **blues** and **R&B**; also **Christian**, **contemporary Christian** and **gospel**. Released "Stranger on the Street" and "Silence of Yours," written and recorded by Cody Blake on Sheheshe Records.
Tips: "Be prepared to work with and for your label. Live gigs are essential, a 'fan base' is needed to succeed."

‡SIGNATURE SOUNDS RECORDINGS, P.O. Box 106, Whatley MA 01093. (413)665-4036. Fax: (413)665-9036. E-mail: info@signature-sounds.com. Website: http://www.signature-sounds.com. Contact: Jim Olsen. Distributed by Koch International. Record company and record producer. Estab. 1994. Releases 5-6 CDs/year. Pays negotiable royalty to artists on contract.
How to Contact: Submit demo tape by mail. Unsolicited submissions are OK. Prefers CD. Include press kit and tour itinerary. Does not return material.
Music: Mostly **folk**, **Americana** and **roots**; also **bluegrass**. Released *Bring Some Changes*, written and recorded by Brooks Williams/Jim Henry (folk); *More*, written and recorded by Deb Pasternak (singer/songwriter); and *The Harvest*, written and recorded by Erica Wheeler (folk), all on Signature Sounds Recordings. Other artists include Salamander Crossing, Louise Taylor, Pete Nelson and Maria Sangiolo.

‡SILAS RECORDS, 70 Universal City Plaza, Universal City CA 91608. (818)777-4026. Fax: (818)777-8915. Distributed by UNI.
How to Contact: Silas Records does not accept unsolicited submissions.

SILENT RECORDS, 340 Bryant St., 3rd Floor East, San Francisco CA 94107. (415)957-1320. Fax: (415)957-0779. E-mail: silent@sirius.com. Website: http://www.silent.org. President: Raul Lopez-Guerra III. A&R: Sang Hwang. Record company and record producer (Kim Cascone). Estab. 1986. Releases 20 CDs/year. Accepts LPs and CDs for consideration and distribution. Pays 15% of wholesale as royalty to artists on contract; negotiable rate to publishers per song on record.
How to Contact: Write first and obtain permission to submit. Prefers cassette or VHS videocassette with press kit (press clips, bio, etc.). Does not return material. Reports in 6 months.
Music: Mostly **ambient**. Released *Anechoic* (by Kim Cascone), recorded by The Heavenly Music Corpora-

REFER TO THE CATEGORY INDEX (at the end of this section) to find exactly which companies are interested in the type of music you write.

tion; *Sonic Acupuncture*, recorded by ATOI; and *Born of Earth and Torments* (by T. Hendricks/B. Matys/R. Robinson), recorded by 23 Degrees, all on Silent Records. Other artists include 303 Terrorists, Deeper Than Space and Michael Mantra.

SILVER WAVE RECORDS, P.O. Box 7943, Boulder CO 80306. (303)443-5617. Fax: (303)443-0877. E-mail: info@silverwave.com. Website: http://www.silverwave.com. Contact: Robert Newman. Labels include Silver Planet Productions. Record company. Estab. 1986. Releases 6-8 LPs, and 6-8 CDs/year. Pays varying royalty to artists on contract and to publisher per song on record.
How to Contact: Write first and obtain permission to submit. Prefers CD. SASE. Reports in 1 month.
Music: Mostly **world**, **New Age** and **contemporary instrumental**.
Tips: "Realize we are primarily an instrumental music label, though we are always interested in good music. Songwriters in the genres of world, New Age and contemporary instrumental are welcome to submit demos. Please include radio and press info, along with bio."

‡SILVERTONE RECORDS, 137-139 W. 25th St., New York NY 10001. (212)727-0016. Fax: (212)645-3783. Label Director: Michael Tedesco. Hollywood office: 9000 Sunset Blvd., Suite 300, W. Hollywood CA 90069. Fax: (213)247-8366. Distributed by BMG; labels include Essential Records. Record company.
How to Contact: Submit demo tape by mail. Unsolicited submissions are OK. Any format acceptable, with lyric and lead sheets.
Music: Released *Jars of Clay*, recorded by Jars of Clay on Essential Records. Other artists include Chris Duarte, Buddy Guy, Hed, Livingstone, John Mayall, Metal Molly and Solar Race.

‡JERRY SIMS RECORDS, P.O. Box 648, Woodacre CA 94973. (415)789-7322. Fax: (415)456-9197. Owner: Jerry Sims. Distributed by New Leaf, LeFon, DeVorss and Top (Hong Kong). Record company. Estab. 1984. Releases 6-7 CDs/year. Pays negotiable royalty to artists on contract; statutory rate to publisher per song on record.
How to Contact: Submit demo tape by mail. Unsolicited submissions are OK. Prefers cassette or CD. Does not return material. Reports in 1 month.
Music: Mostly **instrumental**, **Celtic** and **pop**. Released *Viaggio* and *December Days*, both written and recorded by Coral (Celtic); and *King of California*, written and recorded by Chuck Vincent (rock), all on Jerry Sims Records. Other artists include Disfunctional Family, Kim Y. Han and Mike Lovelace.

‡SIN KLUB ENTERTAINMENT, INC., P.O. Box 2507, Toledo OH 43606. (419)475-1189. President/A&R: Edward Shimborske III. Distributed by NRM; labels include Sin-Ka-Bob Records. Record company, music publisher (Morris St. James Publishing) and record producer (ES3). Estab. 1990. Releases 1 single, 1 LP and 5 CDs/year. Pays negotiable royalty to artists on contract; statutory rate to publisher per song on record.
How to Contact: Submit demo tape by mail. Unsolicited submissions are OK. Prefers cassette or CD with 3 songs and lyric sheet. "Send a good press kit (photos, bio, articles, etc.)." Does not return material. Reports in 1 month.
Music: Mostly **harder-edged alternative**, **punk** and **metal/industrial**; also **rap**, **alternative** and **experimental**. Released *The Other White Meat*, recorded by Chicken Dog (punk); *Game Face On*, recorded by False Face Society (metal); and *Blues For Henry*, recorded by Five Horse Johnson (blues/rock), all on Sin Klub Records. Other artists include The Thessalonian Dope Gods, Crashdog, Porn Flakes, Bunjie Jambo, Moby Jane, Irwin and Section 315.

SIRR RODD RECORD & PUBLISHING CO., P.O. Box 19052, Philadelphia PA 19138. President: Rodney J. Keitt. Record company, music publisher, record producer and management and booking firm. Releases 5 singles, 5 12″ singles and 2 LPs/year. Pays 5-10% royalty to artists on contract; statutory rate to publisher for each record sold.
How to Contact: Prefers cassette or videocassette with 3-5 songs and lyric sheet. SASE. Reports in 1 month.
Music: **Top 40**, **pop**, **gospel**, **jazz**, **dance** and **rap**. Released "All I Want For Christmas," recorded by The Ecstacies; "Guess Who I Saw Today," recorded by Starlene; and "Happy Birthday Baby," recorded by Rodney Jerome Keitt.

SMITHSONIAN FOLKWAYS RECORDINGS, 955 L'Enfant Plaza, Suite 2600, Smithsonian Institution, Washington DC 20560. (202)287-3251. Fax: (202)287-3699. E-mail: cfpcs.folkways@ic.si.edu. Website: http://www.si.edu/folkways. Curator/director: Anthony Seeger. Distributed by Koch Int'l; labels include Smithsonian Folkways, Dyer-Bennet, Cook and Paredon. Record company and music publisher. Estab. 1948. Releases 25 CDs/year. Pays negotiable royalty to artists on contract and to publisher per song on record.

How to Contact: Write first and obtain permission to submit or to arrange personal interview. Prefers cassette or DAT. Does not return material. Reports in 3 months.
Music: Mostly **traditional U.S. folk music, world music** and **children's music**. "We only are interested in music publishing associated with recordings we are releasing. Do not send demos of songwriting only."
Tips "If you are a touring artist and singer/songwriter, consider carefully the advantages of a non-museum label for your work. We specialize in ethnographic and field recordings of people around the world."

‡SMOKY MOUNTAIN RECORDING COMPANY, INC., 203 Hicks Dr., Sevienville TN 37862. (423)429-9088. Fax: (423)453-2842. E-mail: desrecords@aol.com. Publisher: Tammie Alexander. Distributed by Spring Arbor, Riverside and Appalachian; labels include Reformation Records. Record company, music publisher (Generation Sound/SESAC, 2nd Generation/BMI, 12th Generation/ASCAP) and record producer (Greg Alexander). Estab. 1997. Releases 14 singles, 7 LPs and 7 CDs/year. Pays 7-15% royalty to artists on contract; statutory rate to publisher per song on record.
How to Contact: Submit demo tape by mail. Unsolicited submissions are OK. Prefers cassette with 4 songs maximum and lyric sheet. Does not return material.
Music: Mostly **gospel** and **country**; also **bluegrass**. Artists include Faith Harmony Boys, Mighty River, JD Sumner & the Stamps, Sammy Hall, HIS and The Perkins Family.

‡SONIC IMAGES RECORDS, P.O. Box 691626, Hollywood CA 90067. (213)650-1000. Fax: (213)650-1016. E-mail: sonicimages@sonicimages.com. Website: http://sonicimages.com. Director of A&R: Brad Pressman. Distributed by INDI, New Leaf, Music Design, White Swan, Nature Co. and Natural Wonders; labels include Earthtone Records. Record company. Estab. 1991. Releases 15 cassettes, 1 EP and 20 CDs/year. Pays negotiable royalty to artists on contract; 75% of statutory rate to publisher per song on record.
How to Contact: Submit demo tape by mail. Unsolicited submissions are OK. Prefers CD or DAT with 12 songs. Does not return material. Reports in 6 weeks.
Music: Mostly **Celtic, female vocals** and **flamenco guitar**; also **trip hop, ambient/world** and **dreamhouse**. Released *Seven Seas*, written and recorded by Marcome (vocals); *Enchanting Nature*, written and recorded by Christopher Franke (New Age); and *Bonampak* (by Arturo Orozco), recorded by Ah-Kin (New Age), all on Earthtone Records. Other artists include Stephen DeRuby, Nocy, Stonecoat and Echoes of Incas.
Tips: "Send us a finished album which is available for the world and follow-up if you feel you must after eight weeks by e-mail to: cynthia@sonicimages.com."

‡SONIC RECORDS, INC., 220 W. Third St., Ayden NC 28513. (919)746-3021. Fax: (919)746-9300. President: Doug Thurston. Record company and music publisher (Sonrec Music Publisher/BMI). Estab. 1964.
How to Contact: Submit demo tape by mail. Unsolicited submissions are OK. Prefers cassette, CD, DAT or VHS videocassette with 1 song and lyric or lead sheet. Does not return material. Reports in 2-3 days.
Music: Mostly **country, alternative** and **rock**. Artists include CrossCreek, Lionel Ward and the New World Band and Paul Ryan.

‡sonic unyon records canada, P.O. Box 57347, Jackson Station, Hamilton, Ontario L8P 4X2 **Canada**. (905)777-1223. Fax: (905)777-1161. E-mail: jerks@sonicunyon/www.sonicunyon.com. Website: http://www.sonicunyon.com. Co-owners: Tim Potocic/Mark Milne/Andy McIntosh. Distributed by Caroline, Cargo, Revolver and Smash. Record company. Estab. 1992. Releases 2 singles, 2 EPs and 6 CDs/year. Pays negotiable royalty to artists on contract; statutory rate to publisher per song on record.
How to Contact: Call first and obtain permission to submit. Prefers cassette or CD. "Research our company before you send your demo. We are small; don't waste my time and your money." Does not return material. Reports in 3-4 months.
Music: Mostly **rock, heavy rock** and **pop rock**. Released *Doberman*, written and recorded by Kittens (heavy rock); *What A Life*, written and recorded by Smoother; and *New Grand*, written and recorded by New Grand on sonic unyon records (pop/rock). Other artists include Siansphere, gorp, Hayden and Poledo.
Tips: "Know what we are about. Research us. Know we are a small company. Know signing to us doesn't mean that everything will fall into your lap. We are only the beginning of an artist's career."

SPIRITUAL WALK RECORDS, P.O. Box 1674, Temple Hills MD 20757. (301)894-5467. Marketing Director: Yolanda Weir. Labels include Obadiah Records and J-Nozz Records. Record company, concert promoter and marketing company. Estab. 1993. Releases 4-5 singles, 5 LPs and 5 CDs/year. Pays 5% royalty to artists on contract; statutory rate to publisher per song on record.
How to Contact: Submit demo tape by mail. Unsolicited submissions are OK. Prefers cassette or VHS

videocassette with 3 songs and lyric sheet. SASE. Reports in 6-8 weeks.
Music: Strictly **gospel** (all styles). Released "The Power of Jesus Name" and "Get Right With God," written and recorded by Jamaal Ingram (spoken word/house/hip hop); and "What A Friend We Have In Jesus" (public domain), recorded by Kimberly Thomas, all on Spiritual Walk Records.
Tips: "Put your best and strongest song first. This determines whether or not we listen to the other songs on the tape. Strong vocals are a big plus."

STARCREST PRODUCTIONS, INC., 1602 Dellwood Court., Grand Forks ND 58201. (701)772-0518. President: George J. Hastings. Labels include Meadowlark and Minn-Dak Records. Record company, management firm and booking agency. Estab. 1970. Releases 2-6 singles and 1-2 LPs/year. Pays negotiable royalty to artists on contract; statutory rate to publisher for each record sold.
How to Contact: Submit demo tape by mail. Unsolicited submissions are OK. Prefers cassette with 1-6 songs and lead sheet. Does not return material. Reports in 2 months.
Music: Country and **top 40/pop**. Released "You and North Dakota Nights" (by Stewart & Hastings), recorded by Mary Joyce on Meadowlark Records (country).

STARDUST, 341 Billy Goat Hill Rd., Winchester TN 37398. (615)649-2577. Fax: (615)649-2732. President: Barbara Doss. Labels include Stardust, Wizard, Doss, Kimbolon, Flaming Star. Record company, music publisher (Buster Doss Music/BMI), management firm (Buster Doss Presents) and record producer (Colonel Buster Doss). Estab. 1959. Releases 50 singles and 25 CDs/year. Pays 8-10% royalty to artists on contract; statutory rate to publisher per song on record.

- Buster Doss's publishing company, Buster Doss Music, is listed in the Music Publishers section, and he is also listed in the Record Producers and Managers and Booking Agents sections.

How to Contact: Write first and obtain permission to submit. Prefers cassette with 2 songs and lyric sheet. SASE. Reports "on same day received."
Music: Mostly **country**; also **rock**. Released "Come On In," recorded by Duane Hall on Stardust Records; and "Rescue Me," recorded by Tommy D on Doss Records. Other artists include Linda Wunder, Rooster Quantrell, Don Sky, James Bryan, "Red" Reider, Holmes Bros., Donna Darlene, Jerri Arnold, "Bronco" Buck Cody and Dwain Gamel.

STARGARD RECORDS, P.O. Box 138, Boston MA 02101. (617)696-7474. E-mail: chizzg@aol.com. Artist Relations: Janice Tritto. Labels include Oak Groove Records. Record company, music publisher (Zatco Music/ASCAP and Stargard Publishing/BMI) and record producer. Estab. 1985. Releases 9 singles and 1 LP/year. Pays 6-8% royalty to artists on contract; statutory rate to publisher per song on record.
How to Contact: Submit demo tape by mail. Unsolicited submissions are OK. Prefers cassette and lyric sheet. SASE. Reports in 2-3 months. "Sending bio along with picture or glossies is appreciated but not necessary."
Music: Mostly **R&B** and **dance/hip hop**. Released "What About Me" (by Floyd Wilcox), recorded by U-Nek Aproach (R&B/hip hop); "Tell My Love," written and recorded by Joe Lanner (R&B); and "Don't Clown Me" (by Floyd Wilcox), recorded by Nasty Luv (R&B/funk), all on Stargard Records. Other artists include Tee Rex.

STARTRAK RECORDS, INC., P.O. Box 468, Baltimore MD 21085. (410)225-7600. Fax:(410)557-0883. Vice President, A&R: Jimmie McNeal. Labels include Moe Records, D&L Records and JLM Records. Record company. Estab. 1989. Releases 3-4 singles, 3-4 12" singles, 4 LPs, 3 EPs and 6 CDs/year. Pays varying royalty.
How to Contact: Write or call to arrange personal interview, or submit demo tape by mail. Unsolicited submissions are OK. Prefers cassette or VHS videocassette. SASE. Reports in 2 weeks.
Music: Mostly **R&B, rap** and **jazz**; also **gospel, rock/pop** and **country**. Released *Love Goddess* and *Magic Lady*, both recorded by Lonnie L. Smith on Startrak Records (jazz); and *Club Jazz*, recorded by Pieces of a Dream on Startrak/Capitol Records (jazz). Other artists include Terry Burrus, Dee D. McNeal and Tony Guy.

STRUGGLEBABY RECORDING CO., 2612 Erie Ave., P.O. Box 8385, Cincinnati OH 45208. (513)871-1500. Fax: (513)871-1510. A&R/Professional Manager: Pepper Bonar. Record company, music publisher (Hal Bernard Enterprises), record producer (Hal Bernard Enterprises) and management firm (Umbrella Artists Management). Estab. 1983. Releases 3-4 CDs/year. Pays negotiable royalty to artists on contract; statutory (per contract) rate to publisher per song on record.

- See the listings for Strugglebaby's affiliated company, Hal Bernard Enterprises, in the Music Publishers and Record Producers sections, and Umbrella Artists Management in the Managers and Booking Agents section.

How to Contact: Submit demo tape by mail. Unsolicited submissions are OK. Prefers cassette with 3 songs and lyric sheet. SASE. Reports in 3-4 weeks.
Music: Mostly **modern rock**, **rock** and **R&B**. Released *Awkwardsville*, written and recorded by psychodots (modern rock); *When the World Was Young*, recorded by Mary Ellen Tanner; and *Brian Lovely & the Secret*, written and recorded by Brian Lovely & the Secret (rock), all on Strugglebaby Recording Co.
Tips: "Keep it simple, honest, with a personal touch. Show some evidence of market interest and attraction and value as well as the ability to tour."

‡SUISONIC RECORDS, P.O. Box 16635, Phoenix AZ 85011. Phone/fax: (602)491-3642. E-mail: suisonic@primenet.com. A&R Director: Tony Lee. Labels include Tremble Rose. Record company. Estab. 1996. Releases 2 singles, 4 LPs, 4 EPs and 4 CDs/year. Pays negotiable royalty to artists on contract; statutory rate to publisher per song on record.
How to Contact: Submit demo tape by mail. Unsolicited submissions are OK. Prefers cassette, CD or DAT with 3 songs and lyric sheet. Does not return material. Reports in 2 weeks, "immediately if we like it a lot."
Music: Mostly **industrial**, **goth/dance** and **techno/cyber/punk**; also **pop punk**, **goth experimental** and **industrial/rap**. "No glam metal or gangsta please!" Released *Grace Overthrone*, written and recorded by Grace Overthrone (industrial); *Visual Purple*, written and recorded by Visual Purple (pop/punk), both on Suisonic Records; and *Raylene Baker*, written and recorded by Raylene Baker on Tremble Rose Records (goth rock).

SUNCOUNTRY RECORDS, 2709 W. Pine Lodge, Roswell NM 88201. (505)622-0244. E-mail: roswell@pvtnetworks.net. Website: http://www.pvtnetworks.net/willmon. President: Ray Willmon. Record company and music publisher (Pecos Valley Music). Estab. 1989. Releases 1-2 singles, 1 CD/year. Pays 2-10% royalty to artists on contract; statutory rate to publisher per song on record.

- SunCountry's publishing company, Pecos Valley Music, can be found in the Music Publishers section.

How to Contact: Submit demo tape by mail. Unsolicited submissions are OK. "No phone calls please—we will accept by mail." Prefers cassette, CD or VHS videocassette with 2 songs maximum and lyric sheet. Does not return material.
Music: Mostly **C&W** and **gospel (country)**. Released "Wrong Man" and "Wrong Woman" (by Ray Willmon), recorded by Jimmy Maples on SunCountry Records. Other artists include Jessie Wayne and Will Anderson.

SUNSET RECORDS, 12028 SW 75th St., Miami FL 33183. (305)273-0575. President: Rudy Ibarra. Record company, music publisher (Ridi Music) and record producer (Rudy Ibarra). Estab. 1995. Releases 1 CD/year. Pays negotiable royalty to artists on contract; statutory rate to publisher per song on record.
How to Contact: Submit demo tape by mail. Unsolicited submissions are OK. Prefers cassette, CD or DAT with 4 songs. "When submitting, please be specific about your goals. Include additional information if necessary." SASE. Reports in 2 weeks.
Music: Mostly **instrumental**, **Latin** and **pop**; also **children's**, **rock** and **techno**. Released *Pirata Del Amor*, written and recorded by Ray Guiu on Sunset Records (Latin).

THE SUNSHINE GROUP, 275 Selkirk Ave., Winnipeg Manitoba R2W 2L5 **Canada**. (204)586-8057. Fax: (204)582-8397. A&R: Ness Michaels. Labels include Jamco International, Baba's Records, Cherish Records and Sunshine Records. Record company, music publisher (Rig Publishing) and record producer (Brandon Friesen/Danny Schur.). Estab. 1974. Releases 85 LPs and 20 CDs/year. Pays negotiable royalty to artists on contract; negotiable rate to publishers per song on record.
How to Contact: Submit demo tape by mail. Unsolicited submissions are OK. Prefers cassette or VHS videocassette with 3 songs and lyric sheet. "Send bios and pictures along with any press information." Does not return material. Reports in 1-2 months.
Music: Mostly **country**, **MOR** and **ethnic**; also **aboriginal**, **fiddle** and **old tyme**. Released "Peyote" (by Marty-Porte), recorded by Rain Dance; "I've Got the Blues," written and recorded by Billy-Joe Green, both on Sunshine Records; and "Reservation Dog," recorded by Peacemaker on Jamco Records. Other artists include Whitefish Bay Singers, Eyabay, Wigwam, Mishi Donovan, Charlie Goertzen, Rick Burt and Billy Simard.
Tips: "Must have original materials, management and a burning desire to succeed. Professional appearance and stage presence a must. Have professional promo kits. Video is important."

SURESHOT RECORDS, P.O. Box 9117, Truckee CA 96162. (916)587-0111. E-mail: alanred@telis.org. Owner: Alan Redstone. Record company, record producer and music publisher. Estab. 1979. Releases 1 LP/year. Pays statutory rate to publisher per song on record.

How to Contact: Write or call first and obtain permission to submit. SASE. Reports in 2 weeks.
Music: Mostly **country**, **comedy**, **novelty** and **blues**. Released "Love & Life," "Emily" and "Family History," all written and recorded by Alan Redstone on Sureshot Records (country).

‡SURFACE RECORDS, 8377 Westview, Houston TX 77055. (713)464-4653. Fax: (713)464-2622. A&R: Jeff Wells or Richard Cagle. Distributed by Earth Records. Record company, music publisher (Earthscream Music Publishing Co./BMI) and record producer (Jeff Wells). Estab. 1996. Releases 4 CDs/year. Pays negotiable royalty to artists on contract; statutory rate to publisher per song on record.

- See the listing for Earthscream Music Publishing in the Music Publishers section.

How to Contact: Submit demo tape by mail. Unsolicited submissions are OK. Prefers cassette with 4 songs and lyric sheet. Does not return material. Reports in 6 weeks.
Music: Mostly **country**, **blues** and **pop/rock**. Released *Everest*, recorded by The Jinkies; *Joe "King" Carrasco*, recorded by Joe "King" Carrasco; and *Perfect Strangers*, recorded by Perfect Strangers, all on Surface Records (pop). Other artists include Rosebud.

SURPRIZE RECORDS, INC., 7231 Mansfield Ave., Philadelphia PA 19138-1620. (215)276-8861. President: W. Lloyd Lucas. Director of A&R: Darryl L. Lucas. Labels include SRI. Record company, music publisher (Delev Music Company) and record producer. Estab. 1981. Releases 4-6 singles, 1-3 12" singles and 2 LPs/year. Pays 8-10 royalty to artists on contract; statutory rate to publisher per song on record.

- See the listing for Delev Music Company in the Music Publishers section.

How to Contact: Submit demo tape by mail. Unsolicited submissions are OK. Prefers cassette or VHS videocassette with 3 songs and lyric or lead sheet. Does not return material. Reports in 4-6 weeks. "We will *not* accept certified mail!"
Music: Mostly **R&B ballads**, **R&B dance oriented** and **crossover country**. Released *Pleasure* (by Jerry Dean) and *Say It Again* (by R. Hamersma/G. Magallan), both recorded by Jerry Dean (R&B); and "Fat Girls" (by B. Heston/L. Walker/E. Webb/J. Hudson), recorded by Keewee, all on Surprize Records. Other artists include Lamar (R&B).

‡SWEET 'N SMOOTH PRODUCTIONS, P.O. Box 1065, Joshua Tree CA 92252. (760)366-9539. President: Dewey Dobson. Record company and music publisher. Estab. 1997. Releases 2 singles, 2 LPs and 2 CDs/year. Pays negotiable royalty to artists on contract; statutory rate to publisher per song on record.
How to Contact: Submit demo tape by mail. Unsolicited submissions are OK. Prefers cassette or CD with 3 songs and lyric sheet. Does not return material. Reports in 1 month.
Music: Mostly **jazz** and **ballads**. Released *For Dancin'*, written and recorded by various artists (jazz); *If I Knew Then* and *Just A Matter of Time* (by Dewey), recorded by Angie Scott (jazz), all on Sugarfoot Records.
Tips: "Write with the feeling of Cole Porter, Richard Arlen, Johnny Mercer, Mitchell Parish and Jerome Kern with Sinatra, Nat Cole and Ella Fitzgerald singing."

TANDEM RECORDS, 842 Stanton Rd., Burlingame CA 94010. (415)692-2866. Fax: (415)692-8800. E-Mail: trcdist@trcdist.com. Website: http://www.trcdist.com. A&R Representative: Dave Christian. Labels include Speed Records. Record company and music publisher (Atherton Music/ASCAP, Atherton Road Music/BMI). Estab. 1985. Pays statutory rate to publisher per song on record.
How to Contact: Submit demo tape by mail. Unsolicited submissions are OK. Prefers cassette and lyric sheet. Does not return material. Reports in 1 month.
Music: Mostly **rap**, **R&B** and **gospel**; also **modern** and **dance**. Released *Pilot Me* (by Steven Roberts/D. Christian), recorded by Rev. Fleetwood Irving on Tandem Records (gospel); *Faith* (by Dave Sears), recorded by 7 Red 7; and *In Love Again*, written and recorded by Aria on Speed Records (dance). Other artists include Funklab All Stars, Van Damme, Rated X and Tenda Tee, What The Hell, Tabb Doe and Aria.

‡TANGENT RECORDS, 1888 Century Park E., Suite 1900, Los Angeles CA 90067. (310)204-0388. Fax: (310)204-0995. E-mail: tangent@ix.netcom.com. President: Andrew Batchelor. Record company and music publisher (ArcTangent Music/BMI). Estab. 1988. Releases 10-12 CDs/year. Pays negotiable royalty to artists on contract; statutory rate to publisher per song on record.
How to Contact: Submit demo tape by mail. Unsolicited submissions are OK. Prefers cassette, CD, DAT or VHS videocassette with minimum of 3 songs and lyric or lead sheet if available. "Please include a brief biography/history of artist(s) and/or band, including musical training/education, performance experience, recording studio experience, discography and photos (if available)." Does not return material. Reports in 2-3 months.
Music: Mostly **alternative rock**, **artrock** and **contemporary instrumental/rock instrumental**; also **con-**

temporary classical, **world music**, **adult urban contemporary**, **smooth jazz**, **acid jazz**, **jazz/rock**, **ambient**, **electronic**, and **New Age**. Released *Moments Edge*, written and recorded by Andrew Batchelor on Tangent Records (jazz/rock, New Age electronic).
Tips: "Take the time to pull together a quality cassette or CD demo with package/portfolio, including such relevant information as experience (on stage and in studio, etc.), education/training, biography, career goals, discography, photos, etc. Should be typed. We are *not* interested in generic sounding or 'straight ahead' music. We are seeking music that is innovative, pioneering and eclectic with a fresh, unique sound."

TARGET RECORDS, P.O. Box 163, West Redding CT 06896. President: Paul Hotchkiss. Labels include Kastle Records. Record company, music publisher (Blue Hill Music/Tutch Music) and record producer (Red Kastle Productions). Estab. 1975. Releases 6 singles and 4 compilation CDs/year. Pays statutory rate to publisher per song on record.
• See the listing for Red Kastle Productions in the Record Producers section.
How to Contact: Write first and obtain permission to submit. Prefers cassette with 2 songs and lyric sheet. SASE. Reports in 2 weeks.
Music: Country and **crossover**. Released "Rock & Roll Heart" (by P. Hotchkiss), recorded by M. Terry; and "Don't Say A Word," written and recorded by Jett Edson, both on Roto-Noto Records. Other artists include Beverly's Hillbilly Band, Bigger Bros., Malone & Hutch and Rodeo.

‡TBS RECORDS, 611 N. Main St., Sweetwater TN 37874. Phone/fax: (423)337-SONG. Owner: Thomas B. Santelli. Record company and record producer. Estab. 1995. Releases 4 singles, 4 LPs and 4 CDs/year. Pays 8% royalty (negotiable) to artists on contract; statutory rate to publisher per song on record.
How to Contact: Submit demo tape by mail. Unsolicited submissions are OK. Prefers cassette or DAT with 3 songs and lyric sheet. Does not return material. Reports in 2-3 months.
Music: Mostly **ballads**, **blues** and **rock**. Released *Written in the Stars*, written and recorded by Tommy Santelli; *My Life*, written and recorded by Marc Santelli; and *Fantasy* (by Paul Gross), recorded by FA, all on TBS Records.

TEETER-TOT RECORDS, Rt. 1, Box 1658-1, Couch MO 65690. (417)938-4259. President/A&R Directors: Chad Sigafus/Terri Sigafus. Record company, record producer and music publisher. Estab. 1988. Releases 4 LPs/year. Pays negotiable royalty to artists on contract; statutory rate to publisher per song on record.
How to Contact: Submit demo tape by mail. Unsolicited submissions are OK. Prefers cassette with 4 songs. Does not return material. Reports in 1 month.
Music: Mostly **children's**, **all styles** and **Christian/children's**. Released *Water Color Ponies*, *Orange Tea & Molasses* and *Little Lamb, Little Lamb*, all written and recorded by Chad and Terri Sigafus on Teeter-Tot Records.
Tips: "In children's music, you must be sincere. It's not an easy market. It requires just as much in terms of quality and effort as any other music category. Your heart must be in it."

THICK RECORDS, 916 N. Damen, Chicago IL 60647. (773)252-5522. Fax: (773)252-5554. E-mail: thlck@aol.com. Contact: Zachary Einstein. Affiliated with Symbiotic (Buzz, Delmore, Anti Gravity, Fine Corinthian, Espresso). Record company. Estab. 1994. Releases 7-10 singles and 3-5 CDs/year.
How to Contact: Submit demo tape by mail. Unsolicited submissions are OK. Prefers cassette, CD or 7". "Put address directly on tape or CD booklet." Does not return material. Reports ASAP.
Music: Mostly **pop**, **punk** and **garage**; also **hardcore**, **slowcore** and **noize**. Released *I'm A Big Girl Now*, written and recorded by Judge Nothing (pop-punk); *Calliope*, written and recorded by Calliope (slowcore); and *Pill*, written and recorded by Orange (heavy garage), all on Thick Records. Other artists include Back of Dave, Dick Justice, The Laurels, Geezer Lake, Speed Duster, Not Rebecca and Liquor Bike.
Tips: "Be ready to work your own record, tour, tour, work, tour. Don't expect to be huge rock stars. Pay your dues and be independent. Become developed and exposed."

THIRD WAVE PRODUCTIONS LTD. P.O. Box 563, Gander Newfoundland A1V 2E1 **Canada**. (709)256-8009. Fax: (709)256-7411. Manager: Wayne Pittman. President: Arch Bonnell. Labels include Street Legal Records. Record company, music publisher, distributor and agent. Estab. 1986. Releases 2 singles, 2 LPs and 2 CDs/year. Pays negotiable royalty to artists on contract; statutory rate to publisher per song on record.
• See Third Wave's listing in the Music Publishers section.
How to Contact: Submit demo tape by mail. Unsolicited submissions are OK. Prefers cassette, DAT and lyric sheet. SASE. Reports in 2 months.
Music: Mostly **folk/traditional**, **bluegrass** and **country**; also **pop**, **Irish** and **Christmas**. Published *Salt*

Beef Junkie, written and recorded by Buddy Wasisname and Other Fellers (folk/traditional); *Newfoundland Bluegrass*, written and recorded by Crooked Stovepipe (bluegrass); and *Nobody Never Told Me*, written and recorded by The Psychobilly Cadillacs (rockabilly/country), all on Third Wave Productions. Other artists include Lee Vaughn.
Tips: "We are not really looking for songs but are always open to take on new artists who are interested in recording/producing an album. We market and distribute as well as produce albums. Not much need for 'songs' per se, except maybe country and rock/pop."

‡THROWING STONES RECORDS, P.O. Box 602, Columbus IN 47202. (812)375-9362. Fax: (812)372-3985. E-mail: suzrock@hsonline.net. Website: http://gemm.com/s.cgi/TSR. Contact: A&R Dept. Record company, music publisher, record producer (Glass House Productions) and management. Estab. 1995. Releases 10-12 singles, 5-10 LPs, 1-5 EPs and 5-10 CDs/year. Pays negotiable royalty to artists on contract; "negotiable rate on our publishing, statutory to outside publishers."
• See the listing for Glass House Productions in the Record Producers section.
How to Contact: Write first and obtain permission to submit. Prefers cassette with picture, bio, play dates list, 3 songs and lyric sheet. "Please send stamped self-addressed postcard when writing for permission. Include goals, time commitment, etc. Tell us how much you are gigging." Does not return material. Reports in 1 month (varies with submission load).
Music: Mostly **alternative**, **acoustic (singer/songwriter)**, **folk**, **acoustic rock (all types)** and **rock (mainstream, hard, metal, Christian, pop)**; also **blues/blues-rock**, **women artists** and **chorale/big band**. No country. Released "Place in My Heart" and *Fallen Empire*, written and recorded by Fallen Empire (rock); and *Guilty By Association*, written and recorded by Suzanne Glass (acoustic rock/pop), all on Throwing Stones Records. Other artists include Sacred Project, Dale Sechrest and Planet Caravan.
Tips: "Be professional, i.e., on time, easy to contact, business-like when required, etc. Don't let your ego get in the way, as criticism is always meant to be constructive for both artist and company. Understand that even an artist-friendly label like ours has to sell records to stay in business. Package yourself and your submissions creatively. We are looking for artists or bands in our region of the country with great songs, steady gigs, and a desire to learn and grow with our label. We offer extremely artist-friendly contracts."

‡TOMMY BOY RECORDS, 902 Broadway, New York NY 10010. (212)388-8300. Fax: (212)388-8400. Distributed by WEA. Record company.
How to Contact: Call to obtain current demo submission policy.
Music: Released *Jock Jams Vol. 2*, recorded by various artists; *Gangsta's Paradise*, recorded by Coolio; and *MTV Pary to Go Vol. 8*, recorded by various artists, all on Tommy Boy Records. Other artists include Amber.

TOP RECORDS, Gall. del Corso, 4 Milano 20122 **Italy**. Phone: (02)76021141. Fax: (0039)276021141. Website: http://www.staffre.interbusiness.it/md. Manager/Director: Guido Palma. Distributed by CGD/WEA, ERGA S.R.L.; labels include United Colors Productions, Dingo Music, Kiwi Record and Smoking Record and Tapes. Estab. 1979. Record company and music publisher (Dingo Music). Releases 20 12″ singles, 30 LPs, 15 EPs and 40 CDs/year. Pays standard royalty to artists on contract; statutory rate to publisher per song on record.
How to Contact: Submit demo tape by mail. Unsolicited submissions are OK. Prefers cassette or videocassette with 5 songs and lyric sheet. SAE and IRC. Reports in 1 month.
Music: Mostly **pop** and **dance**; also **soundtracks**. Released *Insight* (by J.A. Roussel/Vangelis), recorded by Demis Roussers; *Stammi Vincino* (by L. Albertelli), recorded by Rosanna Fratello; and *Now & Then*, written and recorded by Paul Mauriat, all on TOP Records.

TOP TEN HITS RECORDS INC., 6832 Hanging Moss Rd., Orlando FL 32807. (407)672-0101. Fax: (407)672-5742. President: Hector L. Torres. Labels include T.R., New Generation, Rana and CEG. Record company, music publisher and independent record distributor. Estab. 1979. Releases 20 singles, 15 LPs and 15-20 CDs/year. Pays varying royalty to artists on contract; statutory royalty to publisher per song on record.
How to Contact: Submit demo tape by mail. Unsolicited submissions are OK. Prefers cassette with lead

• **A BULLET** introduces comments by the editor of *Songwriter's Market* indicating special information about the listing.

sheet. SASE. Reports in 1 month.
Music: Mostly **Spanish: tropical/pop**, **salsa**, and **merengue**; also **Latin-jazz** and **cumbia.** Released *15 to Aniversario* (by Ringo Martinez), recorded by Datrullal 15 (merengue); *Now is the Time* (by Martin Arroyo), recorded by MAQ (jazz); and *Grupomania* (by various), recorded by Grupomania (merengue), all on Top Ten Hits Records. Other artists include Zona Roja, Bronx Horns, Bobby Valenin, Gran Daneses, Alfa 8 and Magnificos.
Tips: "We are an independent Latin record company specializing mostly in tropical rhythms and Latin jazz."

‡TOUCHÉ RECORDS, P.O. Box 96, El Cerrito CA 94530. Executive Vice President: James Bronson, Jr. Record company, record producer (Mom and Pop Productions, Inc.) and music publisher (Toulouse Music Co./BMI). Member AIMP. Releases 2 LPs/year. Pays statutory rate to publishers per song on record.

- See the listings for Toulouse Music in the Music Publishers section and Mom and Pop Productions in the Record Producers section.

How to Contact: Prefers cassette with 2-4 songs and lyric sheet. SASE. Reports in 1 month.
Music: Mostly **jazz**; also **bluegrass**, **gospel**, **R&B** and **soul**. Released *Bronson Blues* (by James Bronson), *Nigger Music* and *Touché Smiles* (by Smiley Winters), all recorded by Les Oublies du Jazz Ensemble on Touché Records. Other artists include Hi Tide Harris.

‡TOUCHWOOD RECORDS, LLC, 1650 Broadway, 12th Floor, New York NY 10019. (212)977-7800. Fax: (212)977-7963. Website: http://www.touchwood.com. Director of A&R: Chris Finch. Distributed by Touchwood Distribution; labels include After 9, Touchwood Classics and Before Dawn. Record company and music publisher (Touchwood Publishing). Estab. 1995. Releases 10 singles, 15 LPs, 5 EPs and 20 CDs/year.
How to Contact: Call first and obtain permission to submit. Prefers cassette or CD. Does not return material. Reports in 6 weeks.
Music: Mostly **rock**, **popular** and **jazz**; also **R&B**, **cabaret** and **classical**. Released *Billy's Not Bitter*, written and recorded by Bill White Acre on Touchwood Records (rock); *To Ella With Love* (by J. Kern/C. Porter/I. Gershwin/G. Gershwin), recorded by Ann Hampton Callaway on After 9 Records (jazz); and "Ruff Ride" (by Sam Johnson), recorded by Fraze on Before Dawn Records. Other artists include Brian Howe, the Divers, Neotone, Barbara Carroll, Julie Budd, Billy Stritch, Frankie Laine and Kinfusion.
Tips: "Limit demos to three songs. Send fully developed compositions with complete arrangements if possible. Include lyrics, if any."

TRAC RECORD CO., 170 N. Maple, Fresno CA 93702. (209)255-1717. Owner: Stan Anderson. Record company, record producer and music publisher (Sellwood Publishing/BMI). Estab. 1972. Releases 5 singles, 5 LPs and 2 CDs/year. Pays 13% royalty to artists on contract; statutory rate to publisher per song on record.

- See their listing in the Record Producers section, as well as a listing for Sellwood Publishing in the Music Publishers section.

How to Contact: Submit clear studio demo tape by mail. Unsolicited submissions are OK. Prefers cassette or VHS videocassette with 2-3 songs and lyric sheet. SASE. Reports in 3 weeks.
Music: Country, all styles. Released *Long Texas Highway* (by Jessica James/Debbie D) and *Grandpa's Old Piano* (by Ray Richmond), recorded by Jessica James; and *Kick Me When I'm Down*, written and recorded by Jimmy Walker, all on TRAC Records. Other artists include Double Trouble and Country Connection.

TREASURE COAST RECORDS (a division of Judy Welden Enterprises), 692 S.E. Port St. Lucie Blvd., Port St. Lucie FL 34984. Fax: (561)878-5755. E-mail: jwelden@flinet.com. Website: http://www.flinet.com/~jwelden. Distributed by Arabon Music, Independent Music Assoc. and Trend; labels include Heartfelt Records (Christian music only). President: Judy Welden. Record company, music publisher (Songrite Creations Productions/BMI, Sine Qua Non Music/ASCAP) and record producer. Estab. 1992. Releases 75-100 singles and 6-8 CDs/year. Pays 10-15% royalty to artists on contract; statutory rate to publisher per song on record.
How to Contact: Submit demo tape by mail. Unsolicited submissions are OK. "Send only your best unpublished songs (1 or 2 max), bio, press, number of songs written, releases, awards, etc." Prefers cassette with 1 or 2 songs and lyric sheet. SASE. Reports in 3 weeks.
Music: Mostly **contemporary country**, **crossover country/pop** and most types of **Christian** music (from contemporary to country gospel). Released "Men Like You" (by Lew Brodsky/Lori Kline/Paul Brand), recorded by Lori Kline; and "Shelter In The Rain" (by Judy Welden/Tom Littleby), recorded by Mitch Chanler and Judy Welden (duet), both on Treasure Coast Records (country).

TREND RECORDS, P.O. Box 201, Smyrna GA 30081. (770)432-2454. President: Tom Hodges. Labels include Trendsetter, Atlanta's Best, Trend Star, Trend Song, British Overseas Airways Music, Trendex, and Stepping Stone Records. Record company, music publisher (Mimic Music/BMI, Skipjack Music/BMI and British Overseas Airways Music/ASCAP), record producer and management firm. Estab. 1965. Releases 4 singles, 14 LPs and 10 CDs/year. Pays 15% royalty to artists on contract; standard royalty to songwriters on contract; statutory rate to publisher per song on records.

- Trend Records' publishing company, BOAM, can be found in the Music Publishers section.

How to Contact: Submit demo tape by mail. Unsolicited submissions are OK. Prefers cassette or VHS videocassette with 8-10 songs, lyric and lead sheet. SASE. Reports in 3 weeks.

Music: Mostly **R&B**, **country** and **MOR**; also **gospel**, **light rock** and **jazz**. Released *Nashville Sessions*, recorded by Jim Single; *Sweet Jesus*, recorded by Keith Bradford; and *A Big Smokin' Gun*, recorded by Hilda Gonzalez, all on Trend Records. Other artists include The Caps, "Little" Jimmy Dempsey, Candy Chase, Joe Terry, Charlie & Nancy Cole and Marion Frizzell.

‡TRILOKA, 306 Catron, Santa Fe NM 87501. (505)820-2833. Fax: (505)820-2834. Contact: A&R. Record company. Estab. 1990. Releases 10 LPs and 10 CDs/year. Pays negotiable royalty to artists on contract.

How to Contact: Write first and obtain permission to submit. Prefers cassette, CD or DAT. Does not return material.

Music: Mostly **world beat**, **new instrumental** and **jazz**. Released *Trance Planet Vol. 1-3*, written and recorded by various artists (world); *Beggars & Saints*, written and recorded by Jai Uttal (world); and *Garden of Dreams*, written and recorded by Ali Akbar Khan (world), all on Triloka.

TRIPLE X RECORDS, P.O. Box 862529, Los Angeles CA 90086-2529. (213)221-2204. Fax: (213)221-2778. A&R: Bruce Duff. Record company. Estab. 1986. Releases 5 singles, 10 LPs, 4 EPs and 25 CDs/year. Royalties not disclosed.

How to Contact: Call first and obtain permission to submit. "No unsolicited tapes, please." Prefers cassette. "Photo and bio are helpful." Does not return material. Reports in 1-2 months.

Music: Mostly **rock**, **industrial/goth** and **rap**; also **blues**, **roots** and **noise**. Released *Idjit Savant* (by Graves/Phillips/Lee), recorded by The Dickies (rock); *The Anti-Naturalists* (by Pfahler/Somoa), recorded by the Voluptuous Horror of Karen Black (rock); and *Bliss*, written and recorded by Jeff Dahl (rock), all on Triple X Records. Other artists include Rozz Williams, Bo Diddley, Angry Samoans, Vandals, Die Haut, Lydia Lunch and Miracle Workers.

Tips: "Looking for self-contained units that generate their own material and are willing and able to tour."

TRUMPETER RECORDS INC., 5660 E. Virginia Beach Blvd., Norfolk VA 23502. (804)455-8454. Fax: (804)461-4669. E-mail: trumprec@aol.com. Website: http://trumpeter.com. A&R: Tres Swann and Mike Lee. Distributed by Alliance One Stop Group, Dean's One Stop and LMS; labels include Peacetime Records. Record company, music publisher (Pen Cob Publishing) and management firm (Sirocco Productions). Estab. 1991. Releases 2 singles, 2 EPs and 10 CDs/year. Pays varying royalty to artists on contract; statutory rate to publisher per song on record.

- See the listing for Pen Cob Publishing in the Music Publishers section and Sirocco Productions in the Managers and Booking Agents section.

How to Contact: Write or call first and obtain permission to submit. Prefers CD or VHS videocassette. SASE. Reports in 3-4 weeks.

Music: Mostly **alternative/progressive** and **rock**. Released *Drowning in the Promised Land*, recorded by Egypt (alternative/progressive); and *Everything*, recorded by Everything, both on Trumpeter Records. Other artists include Big Stoner Creek, Doxy's Kitchen and The Mundahs.

TRUSTY RECORDS, 8771 Rose Creek Rd., Nebo KY 42441. (502)249-3194. E-mail: trusty@wko.com. Website: http://www.wko.com/business/trusty/trusty.htm. President: Elsie Childers. Record company and music publisher (Trusty Publications/BMI). Member CMAA, CMA. Estab. 1960. Releases 2 CDs/year. Pays various standard to artists on contract; statutory rate to publisher for each record sold.

- See the listing for Trusty Publications in the Music Publishers section.

How to Contact: Submit demo tape by mail. Unsolicited submissions are OK. Prefers cassette with 2-4 songs and lead sheet. Does not return material. Reports in 6 weeks (if SASE enclosed).

Music: Country, **blues**, **contemporary Christian**, **country Christian**, **easy listening**, **gospel**, **MOR**, **soul** and **top 40/pop**. Released *We Can*, written and recorded by Just Cause on E.T.C. Records; and *Still Water* (by Steve Holland/Ken Dall), recorded by Still Water on Still Water Records. Other artists include Noah Williams, Barry Russell and Barry Howard.

‡TUG BOAT RECORDS, 10 Luanita Lane, Newport News VA 23606. (804)930-1814. A&R: Judith Guthro. Record company, music publisher (Doc Publishing/BMI, Dream Machine/SESAC) and record producer (Doc Holiday Productions). Estab. 1967. Releases 12 singles, 15 12″ singles, 15 LPs, 15 EPs and 10 CDs/year. Pays varying royalty to artists on contract; statutory rate to publisher per song on record.

- Tug Boat's publishing company, Doc Publishing, is listed in the Music Publishers section and their management firm, Doc Holiday Productions, is in the Managers and Booking Agents section.

How to Contact: Submit demo tape by mail. Unsolicited submissions are OK. Prefers cassette with 1 song and lyric sheet. Does not return material. Reports in 2 weeks.

Music: Mostly **country**, **top 40** and **rock**. Released *Big Al* (by various), recorded by Big Al Downing; *Hot Digety Doug*, written and recorded by Doug Kershaw; and *Original Sensation* (by various), recorded by Wyndi Renee, all on Tug Boat Records (country). Other artists include Doc Holiday, Narvel Felts, Jon Washington and The Fortunes, Cory Sparks, Tim Bishop, Jerry Lee Scott and Pam Parco.

TVT RECORDS, 23 E. Fourth St., New York NY 10003. (212)979-6410. Fax: (212)979-6489. Website: http://www.tvtrecords.com. Vice President of A&R: Tom Sarig. Labels include Tee Vee Toons, Wax Trax! Records, 1001 Sundays, Blunt Recordings and Fuel Records. Record company and music publisher (TVT Music). Estab. 1986. Releases 25 singles, 20 12″ singles, 40 LPs, 5 EPs and 40 CDs/year. Pays varying royalty to artists on contract; statutory rate to publisher per song on record.

How to Contact: Submit demo tape by mail. Unsolicited submissions are OK. Prefers cassette or VHS videocassette. Does not return material. Reports in 6 weeks.

Music: Mostly **alternative rock**, **rap** and **techno**; also **jazz/R&B**. Released *Pretty Hate Machine* (by Trent Reznor), recorded by Nine Inch Nails (industrial rock); *Ring* (by Mike Connell), recorded by The Connells (alternative rock); and *Spirits*, written and recorded by Gil Scott-Heron (jazz/soul/rap), all on TVT Records. Other artists include Catherine, Mic Geronimo, Kinsui, DNote, Cords, KMFDM, Psykosonik, Rise Robots Rise, Gravity Kills, Underworld, Jester, Chris Connelly, AFX, Autechre, EBN, Spooky-Ruben, Fledgling and Birdbrain.

Tips: "We look for seminal, ground breaking, genre-defining artists of all types with compelling live presentation. Our quest is not for hit singles but for enduring important artists."

28 RECORDS, 19700 NW 86 Court, Miami FL 33015-6917. Phone/fax: (305)829-8142. E-mail: rec28@aol.com. President/CEO: Eric Diaz. Record company. Estab. 1994. Releases 2 LPs and 4 CDs/year. Pays negotiable royalty to artists on contract; statutory rate to publisher per song on record.

How to Contact: Submit demo tape by mail. Unsolicited submissions are OK. Prefers cassette, VHS videocassette or CD (if already released on own label for possible distribution or licensing deals). If possible send promo pack and photo. "Please put Attn: A&R on packages." Does not return material. Reports in 1 month.

Music: Mostly **hard rock/modern rock**, **metal** and **alternative**; also **punk** and **death metal**. Released *Julian Day*, recorded by Helltown's Infamous Vandal (modern/hard rock); and *Mantra*, recorded by Derek Cintron (modern rock), both on 28 Records.

Tips: "Be patient and ready for the long haul. We strongly believe in nurturing you, the artist/songwriter. If you're willing to do what it takes and have what it takes, we will do whatever it takes to get you to the next level. We are looking for artists to develop. We are a very small label but we are giving the attention that is a must for a new band as well as developed and established acts. Give us a call."

TWIN SISTERS PRODUCTIONS, INC., 1340 Home Ave., Suite D, Akron OH 44310. (800)248-TWIN. E-mail: twinsisters@twinsisters.com. Website: http://www.twinsisters.com. President: Kim Thompson. Record company. Estab. 1986. Releases 4-6 LPs/year. Pays negotiable royalty to artists on contract; statutory rate to publisher per song on record.

How to Contact: Write or call first and obtain permission to submit. Prefers cassette or VHS videocassette. SASE. Reports in 2 months.

Music: **Children's** only (video and audio). Released *I'd Like to Be An Astronaut*, *I'd Like to Be A Marine Biologist* and *I'd Like to Be A Zoologist* (by Kim Thompson/Karen Hilderbrand), recorded by various artists on Twin Sisters Productions.

Tips: "We are mainly interested in children's educational and entertaining audio. Artists wishing to become children's performers and songwriters skilled in children's audio are asked to call first before submitting. A demo will be required."

‡UNDERCOVER, INC., P.O. Box 14561, Portland OR 97293. (503)230-7728. Fax: (503)239-6558. E-mail: mnkyshine@aol.com. Contact: A&R. Distributed by Caroline, Cargo, Bayside, Choke, Parasol and Valley; labels include Slo-Mo. Record company. Estab. 1995. Releases 2 singles/year. Pays varying royalty to artists on contract.

How to Contact: Submit demo tape by mail. Unsolicited submissions are OK. Prefers cassette or CD. "Please, keep first contact concise." SASE. Reports in 2 months.

Music: Mostly **pop**. Released *Crash Course for the Ravers: Tribute to David Bowie* (by David Bowie), recorded by various artists (pop); *Used to Be Blues from the Pacific Delta for Bill Monroe*, written and recorded by various artists (new bluegrass); and *M Class: East & West Letters to Aliens*, written and recorded by various artists (space), all on Undercover Records. "We do not 'sign' artists. We are a project label."

Tips: "Keep in touch! We do different things all the time. If you don't make this one, maybe the next one. But, believe us when we say you're not right for us. Just be yourself, and don't be afraid to send anything. We are always looking for new bands and ideas. If you think you're interested in what we're about, get in touch!"

‡UNIVERSAL RECORDS, 1755 Broadway, New York NY 10019. (212)373-0662. Fax: (212)373-0000. Universal City office: 70 Universal City Plaza, Universal City CA 91608. Distributed by UNI; labels include Kedar Records, Uptown Records, Mojo Records, Bystorm Records and Gut Reaction Records. Record company.

How to Contact: Universal Records does not accept unsolicited submissions.

Music: Released *Baduizm*, recorded by Erykah Badu on Kedar Records; *Legal Drug Money*, recorded by Lost Boyz on Universal Records; and *Spiders*, recorded by Space on Gut Reaction Records. Other artists include Merrill Bainbridge.

UNIVERSAL-ATHENA RECORDS (UAR Records), Box 1264, Peoria IL 61654-1264. (309)673-5755. E-mail: uarltd@unitedcyber.co. Website: http://www.unitedcyber.com/~uarltd. A&R Director: Jerry Hanlon. Record company and music publisher (Jerjoy Music/BMI). Estab. 1978. Releases 1-2 singles and 1 LP/year. Pays standard royalty to artists on contract; statutory rate to publisher for each record sold.

- UAR's publishing affiliate, Jerjoy Music, is listed in the Music Publishers section.

How to Contact: Submit demo tape by mail. Unsolicited submissions are OK. Prefers cassette with 4-8 songs and lyric sheet. SASE. Reports in 2 weeks.

Music: Country. Released *When Autumn Leaves*, written and recorded by Clint Miller; *Livin' On Dreams* (by Eddie Grew); and *Shadows on the Wall* (by Matt Dorman), both recorded by Jerry Hanlon, all on UAR Records (country). Other artists include Steve Axley.

VAI DISTRIBUTION, 109 Wheeler Ave., Pleasantville NY 10570. (914)769-3691. Fax: (914)769-5407. Record company, video label and distributor. Estab. 1983. Pays negotiable royalty to artists on contract; other amount to publisher per song on record.

How to Contact: Write or call first and obtain permission to submit a demo. Prefers cassette, DAT or NTSC videocassette. Does not return material. Reports in 2-3 weeks.

Music: Mostly **opera (classical vocal)**, **classical (orchestral)** and **classical instrumental/piano**; also **jazz**. Released *Susannah* (by Carlisle Floyd), recorded by New Orleans Opera Orchestra and Chorus; *Caliph's Magician* (by Gabriel Von Wayditch), recorded by Orchestra and Chorus of Budapest National Opera, all on VAI Audio. Other artists include Jon Vickers, Evelyn Lear and Thomas Stewart.

VALTEC PRODUCTIONS, P.O. Box 2642, Santa Maria CA 93457. (805)934-8400. Owner/Producers: J. Anderson and J. Valenta. Record company and record producer (Joe Valenta). Estab. 1986. Releases 20 singles, 15 LPs and 10 CDs/year. Pays negotiable royalty to artists on contract; statutory rate to publisher per song on record.

How to Contact: Submit demo tape by mail. Unsolicited submissions are OK. Prefers DAT with 4 songs and lyric sheet. Does not return material. Reports in 1-2 months.

Music: Mostly **country**, **top 40** and **A/C**; also **rock**. Released *Just Me* (by Joe Valenta) and *Hold On* (by Joe Valenta/J. Anderson), both recorded by Joe Valenta (top 40); and *Time Out (For Love)* (by Joe Valenta), recorded by Marty K. (country), all on Valtec Records.

‡VANDER-MOON ENTERTAINMENT, P.O. Box 291951, Nashville TN 37229. (615)256-0895. Fax: (615)353-9975. E-mail: vandermoon@aol.com. Contact: A&R Dept. Record company and booking agency. Estab. 1995. Releases 1 CD/year. Pays negotiable royalty to artists on contract; statutory rate to publisher per song on record.

How to Contact: Submit demo tape by mail. Unsolicited submissions are OK. Prefers cassette, DAT or CD with any number of songs, lyric sheet and press kit. Does not return material. Reports in 6-8 weeks.

Music: Mostly **rock**, **alternative** and **pop**; also **rap** and **new country**. Released *Texas Vampires*, written and recorded by Texas Vampires on Vander-Moon Entertainment (alternative).

‡THE VERVE GROUP, Worldwide Plaza, 825 Eighth Ave., 26th Floor, New York NY 10019. (212)333-8000. Fax: (212)333-8194. Los Angeles office: 11150 Santa Monica Blvd., 11th Floor, Los Angeles CA 90025. (310)996-7905. Fax: (310)478-8328. Distributed by PGD; labels include Talkin' Loud Records and Verve Forecast Records. Record company.

How to Contact: Verve does not accept unsolicited submissions.
Music: Released *Beyond the Missouri Sky*, recorded by Charlie Hayden and Pat Metheny; *Loving You*, recorded by Shirley Horn; and *Forever Love*, recorded by Mark Whitfield, all on Verve Records. Other artists include Herbie Hancock and Antonio Carlos Jobim.

‡VIRGIN RECORDS, 338 N. Foothill Rd., Beverly Hills CA 90210. (310)278-1181. Fax: (310)278-6231. New York office: 1790 Broadway, New York NY 10019. (212)586-7700. Fax: (212)765-0989. Website: http://www.virginrecords.com. Distributed by EMD; labels include Rap-A-Lot Records, Charisma Records, Pointblank Records, Clean Up Records and Noo Trybe Records. Record company.
How to Contact: Virgin Records does not accept recorded material or lyrics unless submitted by a reputable industry source. "If your act has received positive press or airplay on prior independent releases, we welcome your written query. Send a letter of introduction accompanied by all pertinent artist information. Do not send a tape until requested." All unsolicited materials will be returned unopened.
Music: Released *Spice*, recorded by The Spice Girls; *Mellon Collie and the Infinite Sadness*, recorded by The Smashing Pumpkins; and *Earthling*, recorded by David Bowie, all on Virgin Records. Other artists include Tina Turner, Blur, John Lee Hooker, Enigma, DC Talk and Sacred Spirits.

VOKES MUSIC RECORD CO., P.O. Box 12, New Kensington PA 15068. (412)335-2775. President: Howard Vokes. Labels include Country Boy Records. Record company, booking agency (Vokes Booking Agency) and music publisher (Vokes Music Publishing). Releases 8 singles and 5 LPs/year. Pays 2½-4½% song royalty to artists and songwriters on contract.

- Vokes Music's publishing company, Vokes Music Publishing, is listed in the Music Publishers section and their booking agency, Vokes Booking Agency, is listed in the Managers and Booking Agents section.

How to Contact: Submit cassette only and lead sheet. SASE. Reports in 2 weeks.
Music: **Country**, **bluegrass** and **gospel-old time**. Released "Cherokee Trail Of Tears" and "City Of Strangers," recorded by Johnny Eagle Feather; and "Portrait Of An Angel," recorded by Lenny Gee, all on Vokes Records.

VOLCANO RECORDINGS, (formerly Zoo Entertainment), 8750 Wilshire Blvd., Beverly Hills CA 90211. A&R: David Maricich. Record company. Estab. 1971. Releases 5-10 singles and 15-20 LPs/year.
How to Contact: Submit demo tape by mail. Unsolicited submissions are OK. "3 to 4 song cassette or independent CD is best." Does not return material. "All submissions will be listened to within one month. We will contact the artist only if we are interested."
Music: Mostly **alternative minded rock/pop** (i.e., not necessarily the current flavor of the month. . . but that's OK too). Released *Replicants*, written and recorded by Replicants; *100% Fun*, written and recorded by Matthew Sweet; and *Subliminal Plastic Motives*, written and recorded by Self, all on Zoo Entertainment. Other artists include Tool.
Tips: "Make sure your songs have focus both structurally and stylistically."

WALL STREET MUSIC, 1189 E. 14 Mile Rd., Birmingham MI 48009. (810)646-2054. Fax: (810)646-1957. E-mail: wallstmus@aol.com. A&R Director: Joe Sanders. Record company and music publisher (Burgundy Bros.). Estab. 1985. Releases 6 singles, 4 12" singles, 4 LPs, 4 EPs and 8 CDs/year. Pays 8-14% royalty to artists on contract; statutory rate to publisher per song on record.

- See Wall Street's listing in the Record Producers section.

How to Contact: Call first and obtain permission to submit. Prefers cassette or VHS videocassette with 2 songs and photo. "Label all items completely." Does not return material. Reports in 6 weeks.
Music: Mostly **rap**, **hip hop** and **house**; also **rave**, **trance** and **R&B**. Released "Taste the Flava" (by Mike Buckholtz), recorded by Soulism; "Ooh LaLa" (by Lester Marlin), and *Nasty Sexual Thangs* (by Darell Campbell), both recorded by Simply Black, all on Wall Street Music. Other artists include Drueada and ANG.

THE WANSTAR GROUP, P.O. Box 6283, Charleston SC 29405. (803)853-5294. Fax: (803)853-7224. President/Executive Producer: Samuel W. Colston III. Labels include Tye Records and Chela Records. Record company, music publisher (Out On A Limb Publishing/BMI) and record producer (S. Colston III). Estab. 1990. Releases 3 singles, 2 LPs and 2 CDs/year. Pays 4% royalty to artists on contract; negotiable amount to publisher per song on record.
How to Contact: Submit demo tape by mail. Unsolicited submissions are OK. Prefers cassette or VHS videocassette with 3 songs and lyric sheet. Does not return material. Reports in 3-4 weeks.
Music: Mostly **R&B** and **hip hop**; also **contemporary gospel**. Released "When You Gonna Stop," "I've Got All the Honey" and "Treat Me Right" (by S. Colston III), recorded by Toscha M on Chela Records (R&B). Other artists include CZAR Justice of DA 3rd Generation.

‡WAREHOUSE CREEK RECORDING CORP., P.O. Box 102, Franktown VA 23354. (757)442-6883. Fax: (757)442-3662. E-mail: warehouse@esva.net. Website: http://www.esva.net/~warehouse/. President: Billy Sturgis. Distributed by Twinbrook Music, City Hall Records, Rock Bottom Inc. and Paulstarr Distribution. Record company, music publisher (Bayford Dock Music) and record producer (Billy Sturgis). Estab. 1993. Releases 11 singles and 1 CD/year. Pays negotiable royalty to artists on contract; statutory rate to publisher per song on record.
How to Contact: Submit demo tape by mail. Unsolicited submissions are OK. Prefers cassette, CD, DAT or VHS videocassette with lyric sheet. SASE. Reports in 1 month.
Music: Mostly **R&B**, **blues** and **gospel**. Released *If You Think That Jive Will Do* (by Wheeler/Wayne); *The Things I Used to Do* (by Eddie Johns); and *Leave My Girl Alone* (by Buddy Guy), all recorded by Guitar Slim Jr. on Warehouse Creek Records (blues).

WARNER BROS. RECORDS, 3300 Warner Blvd., Burbank CA 91505-4694. (818)846-9090. Fax: (818)846-8474. New York office: 75 Rockefeller Plaza, New York NY 10019. (212)275-4500. Fax: (212)275-4595. Atlanta office: 5440 Fulton Industrial Bldg., Atlanta GA 30336. (404)344-4933. Fax: (404)349-0553. Nashville office: 20 Music Square E., Nashville TN 37203. (615)748-8000. Fax: (615)214-1472. Website: http://www.wbr.com. Distributed by WEA; labels include American Recordings, Eternal Records, Reprise Records, Revolution Records, Imago Records, Mute Records, Giant Records, Malpaso Records, Slash Records and Maverick Records. Record company.
How to Contact: Warner Bros. Records does not accept unsolicited material. All unsolicited material will be returned unopened. Those interested in having their tapes heard should establish a relationship with a manager, publisher or attorney that has an ongoing relationship with Warner Bros. Records.
Music: Released *Howard Stern Private Parts: The Album*, recorded by various artists (soundtrack); *Evita*, recorded by various artists (soundtrack); and *Best of Volume I*, recorded by Van Halen, all on Warner Bros. Records. Other artists include Faith Hill, Tom Petty & the Heartbreakers, Jeff Foxworthy, Rod Stewart, Porno For Pyros, Travis Tritt, Yellowjackets, Bela Fleck and the Flecktones, Al Jarreau, Joshua Redmond, Little Texas and Curtis Mayfield.

WATUSI PRODUCTIONS, 516 Storrs, Rockwall TX 75087. Phone/fax: (972)771-3797. Website: www.rockwalltexas.com/tropikal. Producer: Jimi Watusi. Labels include World Beatnik Records. Record company and record producer (Jimi Towry). Estab. 1983. Releases 4 singles, 3 LPs, 4 EPs and 3 CDs/year. Pays negotiable royalty to artists on contract; statutory rate to publisher per song on record.
How to Contact: Submit demo tape by mail. Unsolicited submissions are OK. Prefers cassette, DAT or VHS videocassette with 3 songs and lyric sheet. SASE. Reports in 3 weeks.
Music: Mostly **world beat, reggae** and **ethnic**; also **jazz, hip hop/dance** and **pop**. Released *The Island* and *Cool Runner* (by J. Towry), recorded by Watusi; and *For The People*, written and recorded by Na Mele Rasta, all on World Beatnik Records. Other artists include Jimi Towry, Wisdom Ogbor (Nigeria), Joe Latch (Ghana), Dee Dee Cooper, Ras Lyrix (St. Croix), Ras Kumba (St. Kitts), Lee Mitchell, Gary Mon, Wave, Darbo (Gambia) and Ricki Malik (Jamaica).

‡WAY COOL MUSIC, P.O. Box 100, Sunset Beach CA 90742. (310)592-6157. E-mail: waycoolmus@aol.com. Contact: A&R. Distributed by UNI.
How to Contact: Submit demo tape by mail. Unsolicited submissions are OK. Prefers cassette or CD with any number of songs. Include press kit and bio.
Music: Alternative. Artists include The Why Store, fluf, Blink 182, The Clarks, Mr. Mirainga, The Vents and Blessed Ethel.

WENCE SENSE MUSIC/BILL WENCE PROMOTIONS, P.O. Box 110829, Nashville TN 37222. Contact: Kathy Wence. Labels include Six-One-Five Records and Skyway Records. Record company, music publisher (Wence Sense Music/ASCAP), record producer (Bill Wence). Estab. 1984. Releases 4-8 singles, 4 CDs/year. Pays statutory rate to publisher per song on record.
How to Contact: Submit demo tape by mail. Unsolicited submissions are OK. Prefers cassette with 1 song. SASE. Reports in 2 weeks.
Music: Prefers **country**. Released "Plastic Money" (by Glenn Warren/Emmanuel Ellis); "Rockin to the Radio" (by Bubba James Hudson/Randy Huston); and *The "L" Word* (by Chapin Hartford/Bubba James Hudson/Randy Huston), all recorded by Duke Michaels on 615 Records (country).

WHITE CAR RECORDS, 10611 Cal Rd., Baton Rouge LA 70809. (504)755-1400. Owner: Nelson Blanchard. Labels include Techno Sound Records. Record company, music publisher (White Car Music/BMI, Char Blanche/ASCAP) and independent record producer. Estab. 1980. Releases 6 singles, 4 12″ singles, 6 LPs, 1 EP and 2 CDs/year. Pays 7½-20% royalty to artists on contract; statutory rate to publisher per song on record.

How to Contact: Submit demo tape by mail. Unsolicited submissions are OK. Prefers cassette with 4 songs. Does not return material. Reports in 2 weeks.
Music: Mostly **country**, **rock** and **pop**; also **R&B**. Released "Time, You're No Friend of Mine," written and recorded by Howard Austin; "Closer to Heaven," written and recorded by Joey Dupuy, both on Techno Sound Records; and "I Read Between the Lines (by Stan Willis), recorded by Nelson Blanchard on White Car Records. Other artists include John Steve, B.J. Morgan and Bayon Country Band.

WHITEHOUSE RECORDS, P.O. Box 18439, Chicago IL 60618. (773)583-7499. Fax: (312)583-2526. E-mail: jaywhouse@aol.com. Website: http://www.housedog.com. Label Manager: Rob Gillis. Distributed by Big Daddy Music; labels include Waterdog Records. Record company. Estab. 1994. Releases 1 EP and 6 CDs/year. Pays negotiable royalty to artists on contract; statutory rate to publisher per song on record.
How to Contact: Submit demo tape by mail. Unsolicited submissions are OK. Prefers cassette or CD. Include cover letter, brief bio, itinerary and picture. SASE. Reports in 3 weeks.
Music: Mostly **rock**, **pop** and **folk**. Released *Bees* (by Tommy O'Donnell), recorded by Spelunkers; *Come In Threes* (by Jason Naroucy), recorded by Verbow; and *Visionary Traitorman* (by Al Rose), recorded by Al Rose and The Transcendos, all on Whitehouse Records. Other artists include Soulvitamins, Lava Sutra, MysteryDriver, the Bad Examples, Joel Frankel, Bucky Halker and Dean Goldstein.
Tips: "While we are primarily interested in artists who write their own material and perform live regularly, we are open to the artist with just a great song or two interested in having it included on a compilation."

WINCHESTER RECORDS, % McCoy, Route 2, Box 114, Berkeley Springs WV 25411. (304)258-9381. Labels include Master Records and Real McCoy Records. Record company, music publisher (Jim McCoy Music, Clear Music, New Edition Music/BMI), record producer (Jim McCoy Productions) and recording studio. Releases 20 singles and 10 LPs/year. Pays standard royalty to artists; statutory rate to publisher for each record sold.

- See the listings for Jim McCoy Music in the Music Publishers section and Jim McCoy Productions in the Record Producers section.

How to Contact: Write first and obtain permission to submit. Prefers 7½ ips reel-to-reel or cassette with 5-10 songs and lead sheet. SASE. Reports in 1 month.
Music: **Bluegrass**, **church/religious**, **country**, **folk**, **gospel**, **progressive** and **rock**. Released *Touch Your Heart*, written and recorded by Jim McCoy; "Leavin'," written and recorded by Red Steed, both on Winchester Records; and "The Taking Kind" (by Tommy Hill), recorded by J.B. Miller on Hilton Records. Other artists include Carroll County Ramblers, Bud Arnel, Nitelifers, Jubilee Travelers and Middleburg Harmonizers.

‡**WINDHAM HILL RECORDS**, 8750 Wilshire Blvd., 3rd Floor, Beverly Hills CA 90211. (310)358-4800. Website: http://www.windham.com. New York office: 1540 Broadway, New York NY 10036. (212)930-4748. Fax: (212)930-4827. Distributed by BMG; labels include Private Music, High Street Records and Dancing Cat Records. Record company.
How to Contact: Windham Hill Records does not accept unsolicited submissions.
Music: Released *Picture This*, recorded by Jim Brickman; *Sanctuary: 20 Years of Windham Hill*, recorded by various artists, both on Windham Hill Records; and *Linus & Lucy—The Music of Vince Guaraldi*, recorded by George Winston on Dancing Cat Records. Other artists include David Arkenstone, Patrick Cassidy, John Gorka, Michael Hedges, Patty Larkin, Liz Story, Keola Beamer, The Nylons, Nightnoise and Yanni.

‡**WINDY CITY RECORDS**, 1550 Amherst Ave., Suite 101, Los Angeles CA 90025. (310)207-6438. Fax: (310)207-8269. President: Robert Anderson. Distributed by MS Distribution. Record company. Estab. 1995. Releases 4 singles and 2 CDs/year. Pays negotiable royalty to artists on contract; per contract rate to publisher per song on record.
How to Contact: Submit demo tape by mail. Unsolicited submissions are OK. Prefers cassette, CD, DAT or VHS videocassette with 5 songs. "Prefer CD or DAT." Does not return material. Reports in 4-6 weeks.
Music: Mostly **rock**, **pop** and **A/C**; also **R&B** and **AAA**. Released *Moment of Truth*, written and recorded

REFER TO THE GEOGRAPHIC INDEX (at the back of this book) to find listings of companies by state, as well as foreign listings.

by Jack James on Windy City Records (rock/pop).

WIZMAK PRODUCTIONS, P.O. Box 477, Wingdale NY 12594. (914)877-3943. E-mail: wizmak@aol.com. Website: http://www.scoutserv.com/indie/wizmak. Manager: Geri White. Distributed by MS Distributing, Silo Music, Old Fogey, Gourd Music, PMSC and Folkcraft. Record company and recording studio. Estab. 1986. Releases 6-8 cassettes and CDs/year. Pays 12% royalty to artists on contract; statutory rate to publisher per song on record.

How to Contact: Call first and obtain permission to submit. Prefers cassette with 3 songs and lyric sheet. "Also include news article or review of a recent performance." SASE. Reports in 4-6 weeks.

Music: Mostly **dulcimer/folk, traditional (American & Irish)**; also **contemporary, acoustic** and **singer/songwriter with traditional sound**. Released *Autumn*, written and recorded by Mark Nelson; *The Pleasures of Hope*, written and recorded by Mike Casey; and *A Wizmak Sampler*, written and recorded by various artists, all on Wizmak Records. Artists include The Woods Tea Co. and Lorrianne & Bennett Hammond.

Tips: "We are a record label, please do not send songs that you want others to record or publish."

WOLFTRAX RECORDS, P.O. Box 40007, Houston TX 77240-0007. Website: http://www.microserve.net/vradio. President: Paul Domsalla. Distributed by Austin Record Distributors, Locator Distribution and Valley Distributors. Record company, music publisher (Puro Cielo Music) and record producer (Paul Domsalla, Puro Cielo Productions). Estab. 1993. Releases 1 CD/year. Pays negotiable royalty to artists on contract; statutory rate to publisher per song on record.

How to Contact: Submit demo tape by mail. Unsolicited submissions are OK. Prefers cassette with 5 songs and lyric sheet. SASE. Reports in 2 months.

Music: Mostly **blues, rock** and **country rock**. Released *Texas Thunder*, recorded by The Benny Valerio Band; and *American Standard* (by Mike Manning/Lucky Strike), recorded by Chiggers, all on Wolftrax Records (blues). Other artists include Abe Rose.

WONDERLAND RECORDS, 374 Treadwell St., Hamden CT 06514. (203)248-2170. Fax: (203)248-1460. E-mail: athena@wlr.com. Website: http://www.connix.com/~wlr. Contact: Athena. Record company. Estab. 1993. Releases 1-3 singles, 3-8 cassettes, 1-3 EPs and 3-8 CDs/year. Pays negotiable royalty to artist on contract; variable rate to publisher per song on record.

How to Contact: Submit demo tape by mail. Unsolicited submissions are OK. Only accepts submissions from performing artists—not non-performing songwriters. Prefers cassette, DAT, VHS videocassette or CD with 3 songs. "All of these formats are fine—we listen to *at least* 3 songs! Please include full contact info—name, address, phone, etc. Cover letters are fine—any press or similar artist promotion materials are helpful." Does not return material. Reports in 2 months.

Music: Mostly **original alternative music, creative expressive music** and **rock/pop**; also **acoustic artists** and **solo performers**. Released *Black River Falls*, written and recorded by Mighty Purple (alternative); *Dead Air*, written and recorded by Dead Air (alternative); and *Firenza*, written and recorded by Flood No. 9 (alternative), all on Wonderland Records. Other artists include Sylph and Gravityhead.

Tips: "Submissions must include full contact information. The enclosure of materials which may help paint a fuller picture of the artist is a good thing. Quality over quantity, and be ready to answer questions if we dig you."

WOODRICH RECORDS, P.O. Box 38, Lexington AL 35648. (205)247-3983. President: Woody Richardson. Record company, music publisher (Woodrich Publishing Co./BMI, Mernee Music/ASCAP and Tennessee Valley Music/SESAC) and record producer (Woody Richardson). Estab. 1959. Releases 12 singles and 12 LPs/year. Pays 10% royalty to artists on contract; statutory rate to publisher per song on record.

- Woodrich's publishing affiliate, Woodrich Publishing, is listed in the Music Publishers section.

How to Contact: Submit demo tape by mail. Unsolicited submissions are OK. Prefers cassette with 4 songs and lyric sheet. "Be sure to send a SASE (not a card) with sufficient return postage." Reports in 2 weeks. "We prefer a good studio demo."

Music: Mostly **country**; also **gospel, comedy, bluegrass, rock** and **jazz**. Released *Marty's Horn Song*, written and recorded by Marty Whiddon (comedy); *Let's Make a Deal* (by Gladys Mitchell), recorded by Rusty Stratton (gospel); and *Jesus Did An Inside Job on Me*, written and recorded by J.R. Thompson (gospel), all on Woodrich Records.

Tips: "Use a good studio with professional musicians. Don't send a huge package. A business envelope will do. It's better to send a cassette *not in a box*."

‡WORD RECORDS & MUSIC, 3319 West End Ave., Suite 200, Nashville TN 37203. (615)385-9673. Fax: (615)385-9696. Distributed by Sony. Record company.

How to Contact: Word Records does not accept unsolicited submissions.
Music: Released *Petra Praise 2 We Need Jesus*, recorded by Petra; and *Heavenly Place*, recorded by Jaci Velasquez, both on Word Records.

‡WORK GROUP, 2100 Colorado Ave., Santa Monica CA 90404. (310)449-2666. Fax: (310)449-2095. New York office: 550 Madison Ave., 24th Floor, New York NY 10022. (212)833-8236. Fax: (212)833-4389. Website: http://www.music.sony.com/Music/WORK. Distributed by Sony; labels include Clean Slate Records. Record company.
How to Contact: Work Group does not accept unsolicited submissions.
Music: Released *Tidal*, recorded by Fiona Apple on Clean Slate Records; *Traveling Without Moving*, recorded by Jamiroquai; and "All Over Your Face" (by J. Dupri/C.S. Lowe), recorded by Puff Johnson, both on Work Records. Other artists include Elephant Ride, ruby, Imperial Drag, Sabelle, Dan Bern, Midnight Oil, Chris Whitley, Protein, Pond and Maypole.

WORSHIP & PRAISE RECORDS INC., P.O. Box 593 Times Square Station, New York NY 10108. Phone/fax: (703)330-9604. Executive Producer/CEO: Minister Maharold L. Peoples, Jr.. Record company and music publisher (Worship & Praise Publishing). Estab. 1994. Releases 2 LPs and 2 CDs/year. Pays negotiable royalty to artists on contract; statutory rate to publisher per song on record.
How to Contact: Submit demo tape by mail. Unsolicited submissions are OK. Prefers cassette with 2 songs and lyric sheet. "Please submit bios, press releases or any other pertinent information on writer/artist." Does not return material. Reports in 3-4 weeks.
Music: Mostly **contemporary Christian**, **traditional Christian** and **black gospel**. Released *Take Off the Mask* recorded by Kanita Washington; *We're in This World* (by Min. Maharold Peoples), recorded by NY Convention Mass Choir; and *I Don't Want to Miss Heaven* (by Min. Maharold Peoples), recorded by The Worship & Praise Mass Choir, all on Worship & Praise Records (gospel).
Tips: "Your arrangements should be original, not rearrangements. Lyrics should be in line with the Bible."

XEMU RECORDS, 34 W. 17th St., 5th Floor, New York NY 10011. (212)957-2985. Fax: (212)957-2986. E-mail: xemu@xemu.com. Website: http://www.xemu.com. A&R: Dr. Claw. Distributed by Touchwood Records. Record company. Estab. 1992. Releases 4 CDs/year. Pays negotiable royalty to artists on contract; statutory rate to publisher per song on record.
How to Contact: Submit demo tape by mail. Unsolicited submissions are OK. Prefers cassette with 3 songs. Does not return material. Reports in 4-6 weeks.
Music: Mostly **alternative**. Released *My March*, recorded by Poets & Slaves; *What Is It?*, recorded by Baby Alive; and *Is That Your Beer*, recorded by Scary Chicken, all on Xemu Records (alternative rock). Other artists include Neanderthal Spongecake, Death Sandwich, The Latherhorns and Burhina Faso.

‡x:treme records, 800 E. Broward Blvd., Suite 700, Ft. Lauderdale FL 33301. (954)522-3900. (954)522-0280. Label Manager: John E. Vecchione. Distributed by Navarre Corporation; labels include Tigerbreath Inc. and x:press. Record company. Estab. 1991. Releases 26 CDs/year. Pays negotiable royalty to artists on contract; 75% of statutory rate to publisher per song on record.
How to Contact: Write or call first and obtain permission to submit. Prefers cassette or CD. Does not return material. Reports in 4-6 weeks.
Music: Mostly **dance/club**; also **New Age** and **rap**. Released *Absolute Dance Mix Vol. 1, Jungle USA* and *Club Classics*, all written and recorded by various artists on x:treme records.
Tips: "Please send CDs or cassettes that are of master quality and have various mixes available for each song. Up-tempo dance songs with vocals that are mainstream, but good for the clubs as well. Our main focus is releasing compilation albums. We are always looking for good tracks that are no more than seven minutes in length."

‡YAB YUM RECORDS, 8255 Beverly Blvd., Los Angeles CA 90048. (213)655-6400. Fax: (213)655-5101. Contact: A&R. Distributed by Sony.
How to Contact: Submit demo tape by mail. Unsolicited submissions are OK. Any format accepted.

YELLOW JACKET RECORDS, 10303 Hickory Valley, Ft. Wayne IN 46835. E-mail: alstraten@aol.com. President: Allan Straten. Record company and music publisher (Hickory Valley Music). Estab. 1985. Releases 8-10 singles, 1 LP and 1 CD/year. Pays 7-10% royalty to artists on contract; statutory rate to publisher per song on record.

- See the listing for Hickory Valley Music in the Music Publishers section.

How to Contact: Submit demo tape by mail. Unsolicited submissions are OK. Prefers cassette with 3-4 songs and typed lyric sheet. Does not return material. Reports in 3-4 weeks.

Music: Country and **MOR**. Released "She's My X and I Know Y" (by D. Crisman/S. Grogg/A. Straten), "Kisa Marie" (by S. Grogg/A. Straten) and "She's My Number One Fan" (by R. Hartman/S. Grogg/A. Straten), all recorded by Tom Woodard on Pharoah Records. Other artists include Roy Allan, Mike Vernaglia, Rick Hartman and Darin Crisman.
Tips: "Be professional. Be prepared to rewrite. When sending material use 6×9 envelope—no staples."

YOUNG COUNTRY RECORDS/PLAIN COUNTRY RECORDS, P.O. Box 5412, Buena Park CA 90620. (619)245-2920. Owner: Leo J. Eiffert, Jr. Labels include Eiffert Records and Napoleon Country Records. Record company, music publisher (Young Country Music Publishing Co./BMI, Eb-Tide Music/BMI) and record producer (Leo J. Eiffert, Jr). Releases 10 singles and 5 LPs/year. Pays negotiable royalty to artists on contract; negotiable rate to publishers per song on record.
How to Contact: Submit demo tape by mail. Unsolicited submissions are OK. "Please make sure your song or songs are copyrighted." Prefers cassette with 2 songs and lyric sheet. Does not return material. Reports in 3-4 weeks.
Music: Mostly **country**, **easy rock** and **gospel music**. Released *Like A Fool*, written and recorded by Pam Bellows; *Something About Your Love* (by Leo J. Eiffert, Jr.), recorded by Chance Waite Young (country); and *Cajunland*, written and recorded by Leo J. Eiffert, Jr., all on Plain Country Records. Other artists include Brandi Holland, Homemade, Crawfish Band and Larry Settle.

YOUNG STAR PRODUCTIONS, INC., 5501 N. Broadway, Chicago IL 60640. (312)989-4140. President: Starling Young, Jr. Distributed by Bassin, Unique and Big State; labels include Gold Karat Records. Record company, music publisher (Gold Karat Records/ASCAP) and record producer. Estab. 1991. Releases 7-8 singles, 7 LPs, 10 EPs and 9 CDs/year. Pays 6-10% royalty to artists on contract; statutory rate to publisher per song on record or ½ of statutory if we do not own publisher.
How to Contact: Submit demo tape by mail. Unsolicited submissions are OK. Prefers cassette or VHS videocassette with 4 songs and lyric or lead sheet. "Insert photo and bio." SASE. Reports in 1 month.
Music: Mostly **urban**, **dance**, **blues/jazz** and **gospel**; also **pop/rock**, **country** and **alternative**. Released "Whatcha Gonna Do" (by Michael Hearn), recorded by Linda Clifford; *Emerald City*, written and recorded by Abstract; and "Land of Lost and Found," written and recorded by Mr. Kofé, all on Gold Karat Records. Other artists include Internal Sanctuary, Dog Freddie, Madd Core, Anjee and Darrell Spenser.

ZERO HOUR RECORDS, 1600 Broadway, New York NY 10019. (212)957-1277. Fax: (212)957-1447. E-mail: ray@zerohour.com. Website: http://www.zerohour.com. President: Ray McKenzie. Distributed by Cargo, Koch Int'l. and UNI. Record company and music publisher. Estab. 1990. Releases 12 singles, 6-12 LPs, 3 EPs and 6-12 CDs/year. Pays 11-13% royalty to artists on contract; statutory rate to publisher per song on record.
How to Contact: Submit demo tape by mail. Unsolicited submissions are OK. Prefers cassette. SASE. Reports in 1 month.
Music: Mostly **rock**, **hip hop** and **spoken word**; also **acid jazz**, **ambient** and **techno**. Released *The Moray Eels Eat the Space Needle*, written and recorded by Space Needle; *Varnaline* (by Anders Parker), recorded by Varnaline; and *12*, written and recorded by Notwist, all on Zero Hour Records. Other artists include Shallow, Reservoir and Steve Wynn.
Tips: "Send us music that is very unique and unusual."

Category Index

The Category Index is a good place to begin searching for a market for your songs. Below is an alphabetical list of 20 general music categories. If you write rock music and are looking for a record company to submit your songs to, check the Rock section in this index. There you will find a list of record companies interested in hearing rock songs. Once you locate the listings for those record companies, read the music subheading *carefully* to determine which companies are most interested in the type of rock music you write. Some of the markets in this section do not appear in the Category Index because they have not indicated a specific preference. Most of these said they are interested in "all types" of music. Listings that were very specific, or whose description of the music they're interested in doesn't quite fit into these categories, also do not appear here.

Adult Contemporary

Allegheny Music Works; American Music Network, Inc.; Amiron Music/Aztec Productions; ‡Avenue Communications; Bolivia Records; Boogie Band Records; Capstan Record Production; Carmel Records; ‡Countdown Records; Country Style Records; Cowgirl Records; Dale Productions, Alan; DMT Records; ‡E.S.R. Records; Emerald City Records; Fame and Fortune Enterprises; Golden Triangle Records; Green Bear Records; Jalyn Recording Co.; Kaupp Records; ‡Kick-O-Namic Records; L.A. Records (MI); L.A. Records (Canada); LBJ Productions; Le Matt Music Ltd.; Lucifer Records, Inc.; M.E.G. Records Co.; Missile Records; MOR Records; Nucleus Records; Peridot Records; ‡Permanent Press Recordings; Roll On Records®; Rustron Music Productions; Sunshine Group, The; ‡Tangent Records; Trend Records®; Trusty Records; Valtec Productions; ‡Windy City Records; Yellow Jacket Records

Alternative

A&R Records; Aladdin Recordings; ‡Aquarius Records; ‡Artistic Noise; Avalanche Records; Baby Faze Records & Tapes; babysue; Basset Hound Productions; ‡Blue Duck!! Records; ‡Blue Eyed Kitty Productions; ‡Buzz Factory Records; Caroline Records, Inc.; Cat's Voice Productions; Cleopatra Records; ‡Conspiracy Records; ‡Countdown Records; ‡Crank! A Record Company; ‡Creek Records; Critique Records, Inc.; ‡dedicated records; Don't Records; Elektra Entertainment Group; ‡Eleven Records/McGhee Entertainment; ‡Entourage Music Group; ‡¡Epiphany!; Fat City Artists; Fiction Songs; Flip Records; ‡Fundamental Recording Company; Generic Records, Inc.; Global Pacific Records/Blackhorse Entertainment; ‡Glow in the Dark; ‡Gonzo! Records Inc.; ‡Gotham Records; Hot Wings Entertainment; IMI Records; Inferno Records; ‡Inside Sounds; Kottage Records; KSM Records; L.A. Records (MI); ‡Lazy Bones Recordings/Productions, Inc.; ‡Maddog Records II; Maverick Group, The; Megatone Records Inc.; Modern Voices Entertainment, Ltd.; ‡Moonstone Records; ‡Motion City Records; Mountain Records; Nocturnal Records; ‡nu.millennia/records; Oblivion Entertainment; Oglio Records; Old School Records; Paint Chip Records; ‡Paradigm Productions; ‡Pavement Music, Inc.; PC Music; Pentacle Records; PMG Records; Premiére Records; Radical Records; Rammit Records; Rave Records, Inc.; Revelation Records; ‡RML Records; ‡Robbins Entertainment LLC; ‡Rosebowl, The; Rotten Records; Round Flat Records; Royalty Records; ‡Rude Records; Ruffcut Productions; ‡Safire Records; Scratched Records; ‡Sin Klub Entertainment, Inc.; ‡Sonic Records, Inc.; Strugglebaby Recording Co.; Tandem Records; ‡Tangent Records; Thick Records; ‡Throwing Stones Records; Trumpeter Records Inc.; TVT Records; 28 Records; ‡Vander-Moon Entertainment; Volcano Recordings; ‡Way Cool Music; Wonderland Records; Xemu Records; Young Star Productions, Inc.

Blues

Aladdin Recordings; Albatross Records; ‡American Artist Records; Ancy Records; Big Bear Records; Black Diamond Records Inc.; Blue Wave; BSW Records; Cellar Records; ‡Cuca Re-

cord Co.; ‡Dapmor Records; Deadeye Records; Flying Heart Records; ‡Front Row Records; ‡Fundamental Recording Company; Grass Roots Record & Tape/LMI Records; Ikon Records; ‡Inside Sounds; ‡Intrepid Records; Justin Time Records Inc.; Landslide Records; Lanor Records; Le Matt Music Ltd.; Maui Arts & Music Association; Musikus Productions, Inc.; Old School Records; Peridot Records; ‡Pointblank Records; Powerhouse Records; RBW, Inc.; React Recordings; Rustron Music Productions; ‡Sheheshe Records; Sureshot Records; ‡Surface Records; ‡TBS Records; ‡Throwing Stones Records; Triple X Records; Trusty Records; ‡Warehouse Creek Recording Corp.; Wolftrax Records; Young Star Productions, Inc.

Children's

A&R Records; Berandol Music; Bodarc Productions; Carmel Records; ‡Crosspoint International, Inc.; Grass Roots Record & Tape/LMI Records; Lonny Tunes; ‡Music Quest Entertainment & Television; Omni 2000 Inc.; ‡Overtime Station; ‡Rude Records; Smithsonian Folkways Recordings; Sunset Records; Teeter-Tot Records; Twin Sisters Productions, Inc.

Classical

‡Ascencion Recordings, Inc.; babysue; Cambria Records & Publishing; Cantilena Records; Carmel Records; Comma Records & Tapes; ‡Creek Records; ‡EMF Records & Affiliates; Global Pacific Records/Blackhorse Entertainment; Intersound Inc.; ‡Intrepid Records; Lark Record Productions, Inc.; Lyra House, Ltd.; Marks Records, John; Musikus Productions, Inc.; North Star Music; Nucleus Records; RBW, Inc.; Rising Star Records; Sheffield Lab Recording; ‡Tangent Records; ‡Touchwood Records LLC; VAI Distribution

Country

A&R Records; Aladdin Recordings; Albatross Records; Allegheny Music Works; Alpha Recording Co.; Alyssa Records; ‡American Artist Records; American Music Network, Inc.; Americatone Records International USA; Ancy Records; Arial Records; Bagatelle Record Company; Bandit Records; ‡Big Whig Productions; Black Diamond Records Inc.; Blue Gem Records; Blue Wave; BMX Entertainment; BNA Records; Bold 1 Records; Bolivia Records; Bouquet Records; Briarhill Records; BSW Records; C.E.G. Records, Inc.; Capstan Record Production; Casaro Records; Cat's Voice Productions; Cedar Creek Records™; Cellar Records; Centium Entertainment, Inc.; Cherry Street Records; Cimirron/Rainbird Records; Collector Records; Comma Records & Tapes; Continental Records; Country Breeze Records; Country Star International; Country Style Records; Cowgirl Records; ‡Creek Records; ‡Crescent Recording Corporation; Critique Records, Inc.; Dale Productions, Alan; Dancer Publishing Co.; ‡Dapmor Records; Deadeye Records; ‡Del-Fi Records, Inc.; DMT Records; ‡E.S.R. Records; ‡Eleven Records/McGhee Entertainment; Emerald City Records; EMF Productions; ‡EMF Records & Affiliates; ‡Entourage Music Group; ‡¡Epiphany!; Fame and Fortune Enterprises; Fat City Artists; First Time Records; Fountain Records; ‡Front Row Records; Generic Records, Inc.; Golden Triangle Records; Grass Roots Record & Tape/LMI Records; Green Bear Records; Gueststar Records; ‡Hottrax Records; Howdy Records; Inferno Records; Intersound Inc.; Interstate 40 Records; ‡Intrepid Records; Jalyn Recording Co.; Jamaka Record Co.; K-ark Records; Kaupp Records; Keeping It Simple and Safe, Inc.; Kingston Records; Kottage Records; L.A. Records (MI); L.A. Records (Canada); L. P. S. Records, Inc.; Lamon Records; Landmark Communications Group; Lanor Records; Lari-Jon Records; Lark Record Productions, Inc.; LBJ Productions; Le Matt Music Ltd.; Lonesome Wind Corporation; Lonny Tunes; LRJ; M.E.G. Records Co.; ‡Magic Key Productions Inc.; Magnum Music Corp. Ltd.; Man on Page 602, The; Master-Trak Enterprises; Maui Arts & Music Association; Maverick Group, The; Mighty Records; Missile Records; MSM Records; Mule Kick Records; ‡Music City Sound Records; Music Services & Marketing; ‡Music Wise Inc.; New Experience Records/Grand Slam Records; ‡nu.millennia/records; Nucleus Records; Orbit Records; Paragold Records & Tapes; Patty Lee Records; Paul Records, J.; PBM Records; Peridot Records; ‡Permanent Press Recordings; Phoenix Records, Inc.; Pickwick/Mecca/Internation Records; Plateau Music; Platinum Boulevard Records; Platinum Plus Records International; Playback Records; Playbones Records; Pop Record Research; R.E.F. Records; Random Records; Rejoice Records of Nashville; Revelation Records; ‡Rhiannon Records; Richway Records International; Roll On Records®; Rosebud Records; Ruffcut Productions; Rustron Music Productions; Sabre Productions; Sabteca Record Co.; Safire Records; ‡Sheheshe Records; ‡Signature Sounds Recordings; ‡Smoky Mountain Recording Company, Inc.; ‡Sonic Records, Inc.; Starcrest Productions, Inc.; Stardust; Startrak Records, Inc.; SunCountry Records; Sunshine Group, The; Sureshot Records; ‡Surface Records; Surprize Records, Inc.; Target Records; Third Wave Productions Ltd.; Touché Records; Trac Record Co.; Treasure Coast Records; Trend Records®; Trusty Records; ‡Tug Boat Records; Universal-Athena Records; Valtec Productions; ‡Vander-Moon Entertainment; Vokes Music Record Co.; Wence Sense Music/Bill Wence Promotions; White Car Records; Winchester Records; Wolftrax Records; Woodrich Records; Yellow Jacket Records; Young Country Records/Plain Country Records; Young Star Productions, Inc.

Dance

All American Music Group; Alpha-Beat; Amiron Music/Aztec Productions; ‡Artistic Noise; Associated Artists Music International; ‡Atlan-Dec/Grooveline Records; Avalanche Records; Basset Hound Productions; ‡Bionic Records, Inc.; Bodarc Productions; Boogie Band Records; Broken Records International; Centium Entertainment, Inc.; Comma Records & Tapes; ‡Crescent Recording Corporation; Critique Records, Inc.; Dagene/Cabletown Records; Def Beat Records; ‡Disc-tinct Music, Inc.; Drive Entertainment; First Time Records; ‡Glow in the Dark; ‡Goddess Records; ‡Gonzo! Records Inc.; ‡Hi-Bias Records Inc.; Joey Boy Records Inc.; ‡Kick-O-Namic Records; L.A. Records (MI); L.A. Records (Canada); Le Matt Music Ltd.; Lucifer Records, Inc.; Megatone Records Inc.; Mighty Records; ‡Mindspore Records; Modern Voices Entertainment, Ltd.; P. & N. Records; Pickwick/Mecca/Internation Records; PMG Records; Quark Records; Rammit Records; Rave Records, Inc.; React Recordings; Red Dot/Puzzle Records; Revelation Records; ‡Robbins Entertainment LLC; Rosebud Records; Sahara Records and Filmworks Entertainment; Sirr Rodd Record & Publishing Co.; Stargard Records; ‡Suisonic Records; Sunset Records; Tandem Records; Top Records; Wall Street Music; Watusi Productions; ‡x:treme records; Young Star Productions, Inc.

Folk

A&R Records; ‡American Artist Records; Amiron Music/Aztec Productions; ‡Aquarius Records; Ariana Records; ‡Big Whig Productions; Carmel Records; Cha Cha Records; ‡Cooking Vinyl America; Eastern Front Records, Inc.; ‡Eleven Records/McGhee Entertainment; First Time Records; Hot Wings Entertainment; ‡Inside Sounds; ‡Intrepid Records; ‡Kill Rock Stars; ‡Magic Key Productions Inc.; Missile Records; Modal Music, Inc.™; Mountain Records; MSM Records; Nucleus Records; ‡Paradigm Productions; Patty Lee Records; PC Music; Random Records; Red Sky Records; ‡Rhiannon Records; ‡Rosebowl, The; ‡Rude Records; Rustron Music Productions; ‡Signature Sounds Recordings; Smithsonian Folkways Recordings; Third Wave Productions Ltd.; ‡Throwing Stones Records; Whitehouse Records; Winchester Records; Wizmak Productions

Instrumental

A&R Records; Berandol Music; Carmel Records; Lark Record Productions, Inc.; Maui Arts & Music Association; ‡Music Quest Entertainment & Television; North Star Music; Playbones Records; Powerhouse Records; Quark Records; Rock Dog Records; ‡Rude Records; Silver Wave Records; ‡Sims Records, Jerry; Sunset Records; ‡Tangent Records; ‡Triloka

Jazz

A&M Records; Albatross Records; All American Music Group; Americatone Records International USA; Amiron Music/Aztec Productions; Ariana Records; Arkadia Entertainment Corp.; ‡Ascencion Recordings, Inc.; ‡Atlan-Dec/Grooveline Records; audiofile Tapes; Big Bear Records; Black Diamond Records Inc.; BMX Entertainment; Bodarc Productions; Carmel Records; Casaro Records; Cedar Creek Records™; Cherry Street Records; ‡Creative Improvised Music Projects (CIMP) Records; ‡Creek Records; ‡Crescent Recording Corporation; Dale Productions, Alan; ‡Dapmor Records; Earthtone/Sonic Images; ‡EMF Records & Affiliates; ‡Entourage Music Group; Etherean Music/Variena Publishing; Fat City Artists; Flying Heart Records; Fresh Entertainment; Global Pacific Records/Blackhorse Entertainment; Golden Triangle Records; Grass Roots Record & Tape/LMI Records; Hallway International Records/1st Coast Posse

Mixes; ‡Hi-Bias Records Inc.; Hot Wings Entertainment; ‡Hottrax Records; IMI Records; ‡Inside Sounds; ‡Intrepid Records; J&J Musical Enterprises Ltd.; Joey Boy Records Inc.; Justin Time Records Inc.; L.A. Records (Canada); Landmark Communications Group; Landslide Records; LBI Records; Lonny Tunes; Marks Records, John; Maui Arts & Music Association; Mighty Records; Missile Records; Mons Records; ‡Music City Sound Records; ‡Music Quest Entertainment & Television; ‡Music Wise Inc.; North Star Music; Orinda Records; Patty Lee Records; ‡Permanent Press Recordings; Platinum Boulevard Records; Playbones Records; Powerhouse Records; PPI/Peter Pan Industries; RBW, Inc.; React Recordings; Reiter Records Ltd.; ‡RML Records; Rock Dog Records; Rosebud Records; ‡Safire Records; Sahara Records and Filmworks Entertainment; Salexo Music; Satin Records; Sheffield Lab Recording; Sirr Rodd Record & Publishing Co.; Startrak Records, Inc.; ‡Sweet 'N Smooth Productions; ‡Tangent Records; Touché Records; ‡Touchwood Records LLC; Trend Records®; ‡Triloka; TVT Records; VAI Distribution; Watusi Productions; Woodrich Records; Young Star Productions, Inc.; Zero Hour Records

Latin

African Diaspora Project, The; Albatross Records; Americatone Records International USA; BMX Entertainment; ‡EMF Records & Affiliates; Grass Roots Record & Tape/LMI Records; Howdy Records; ‡Maddog Records II; Sunset Records; Top Ten Hits Records Inc.

Metal

Azra International; babysue; ‡Buzz Factory Records; Cellar Records; ‡Goddess Records; hypnotic recordings usa; L.A. Records (Canada); Metal Blade Records; Missile Records; ‡Motion City Records; Mountain Records; ‡Nightmare Records; ‡Overtime Station; ‡Pavement Music, Inc.; Pissed Off Records, Inc.; Rotten Records; ‡Sin Klub Entertainment, Inc.; ‡Throwing Stones Records; 28 Records

New Age

Ariana Records; Azra International; Cat's Voice Productions; ‡Creek Records; Dale Productions, Alan; Earthtone/Sonic Images; ‡EMF Records & Affiliates; Etherean Music/Variena Publishing; Global Pacific Records/Blackhorse Entertainment; ‡Intrepid Records; L.A. Records (Canada); ‡Magic Key Productions Inc.; North Star Music; ‡Only New Age Music, Inc.; ‡Paradigm Productions; Platinum Boulevard Records; PPI/Peter Pan Industries; Quark Records; Rising Star Records; Rock Dog Records; Rustron Music Productions; Silver Wave Records; ‡Tangent Records; ‡x:treme records

Novelty

Azra International; Briarhill Records; ‡Inside Sounds; Joey Boy Records Inc.; Justin Time Records Inc.; Lonny Tunes; MOR Records; Rising Star Records; Sureshot Records; Woodrich Records

Pop

A&M Records; All American Music Group; Allegheny Music Works; Alpha-Beat; Alyssa Records; Amiron Music/Aztec Productions; Ancy Records; Arial Records; Arkadia Entertainment Corp.; ‡Artistic Noise; Associated Artists Music International; ‡Avenue Communications; Baby Faze Records & Tapes; babysue; ‡Beluga Records; Berandol Music; Big Rock Pty. Ltd.; ‡Big Whig Productions; ‡Blue Duck!! Records; Blue Gem Records; BMX Entertainment; Bolivia Records; Boogie Band Records; Broken Records; C.E.G. Records, Inc.; Capstan Record Production; Casaro Records; Cedar Creek Records™; Cellar Records; Comma Records & Tapes; ‡Crank! A Record Company; ‡Crescent Recording Corporation; Critique Records, Inc.; Dagene/Cabletown Records; ‡dedicated records; Demi Monde Records and Publishing, Ltd.; DMT Records; Don't Records; Drive Entertainment; Eastern Front Records, Inc.; EMF Productions; ‡EMF Records & Affiliates; ‡¡Epiphany!; Etherean Music/Variena Publishing; Fame and Fortune Enterprises; First Time Records; Fountain Records; Fresh Entertainment; Generic Records, Inc.; Global Pacific Records/Blackhorse Entertainment; ‡Goddess Records; ‡Gonzo! Records Inc.; Grass Roots Record & Tape/LMI Records; ‡Hi-Bias Records Inc.; ‡Hottrax Records; Ikon

Records; ‡Inside Sounds; Jive Records; Justin Time Records Inc.; Kaupp Records; Keeping It Simple and Safe, Inc.; ‡Kick-O-Namic Records; Kingston Records; Kottage Records; L.A. Records (Canada); Landmark Communications Group; LBJ Productions; Le Matt Music Ltd.; Lucifer Records, Inc.; ‡Maddog Records II; ‡Magic Key Productions Inc.; Magnum Music Corp. Ltd.; Makeshift Music; Maui Arts & Music Association; Megatone Records Inc.; Mighty Records; Missile Records; Modern Voices Entertainment, Ltd.; Mons Records; ‡Moonstone Records; MOR Records; Mountain Records; Mule Kick Records; ‡Music City Sound Records; ‡Music Quest Entertainment & Television; ‡Music Wise Inc.; Musikus Productions, Inc.; New Experience Records/Grand Slam Records; Not Lame Recordings; ‡nu.millennia/records; Nucleus Records; Oblivion Entertainment; Old School Records; Omni 2000 Inc.; Orinda Records; Paul Records, J.; ‡Permanent Press Recordings; Phoenix Records, Inc.; Pickwick/Mecca/Internation Records; Plateau Music; Platinum Boulevard Records; Pop Record Research; PPI/Peter Pan Industries; Premiére Records; Quark Records; R.E.F. Records; Random Records; Red Dot/Puzzle Records; Redemption Records; Reiter Records Ltd.; ‡RML Records; Roll On Records®; ‡Rosebowl, The; Ruffcut Productions; Rustron Music Productions; Sabteca Record Co.; ‡Safire Records; Sahara Records and Filmworks Entertainment; Shaolin Film & Records; Sheffield Lab Recording; ‡Sims Records, Jerry; Sirr Rodd Record & Publishing Co.; ‡sonic unyon records canada; Starcrest Productions, Inc.; Startrak Records, Inc.; ‡Suisonic Records; Sunset Records; ‡Surface Records; Thick Records; Third Wave Productions Ltd.; ‡Throwing Stones Records; Top Records; ‡Touchwood Records LLC; Treasure Coast Records; Trusty Records; ‡Tug Boat Records; ‡Undercover, Inc.; Valtec Productions; ‡Vander-Moon Entertainment; Watusi Productions; White Car Records; Whitehouse Records; ‡Windy City Records; Wonderland Records; Young Star Productions, Inc.

R&B

A&M Records; Aladdin Recordings; Albatross Records; All American Music Group; Allegheny Music Works; Alpha-Beat; Alyssa Records; ‡Aquarius Records; Arkadia Entertainment Corp.; ‡Artistic Noise; ‡Atlan-Dec/Grooveline Records; ‡Avenue Communications; Baby Faze Records & Tapes; Big Rock Pty. Ltd.; Black Diamond Records Inc.; Blue Gem Records; Blue Wave; BMX Entertainment; Bolivia Records; Boogie Band Records; Casaro Records; Cat's Voice Productions; Cedar Creek Records™; Cellar Records; Centium Entertainment, Inc.; Cherry Street Records; Comma Records & Tapes; Cowgirl Records; ‡Crescent Recording Corporation; Critique Records, Inc.; Dagene/Cabletown Records; ‡Dapmor Records; Deadeye Records; Def Beat Records; ‡Del-Fi Records, Inc.; Demi Monde Records and Publishing, Ltd.; ‡Disc-tinct Music, Inc.; EMF Productions; ‡EMF Records & Affiliates; First Time Records; Flying Heart Records; Fresh Entertainment; ‡Front Row Records; Gold City Records, Inc.; Golden Triangle Records; Grass Roots Record & Tape/LMI Records; Hallway International Records/1st Coast Posse Mixes; ‡Hi-Bias Records Inc.; Ikon Records; IMI Records; Jive Records; Kaupp Records; Keeping It Simple and Safe, Inc.; Kottage Records; L.A. Records (Canada); Lamon Records; Landmark Communications Group; Lanor Records; LBI Records; LBJ Productions; Le Matt Music Ltd.; Lucifer Records, Inc.; ‡Maddog Records II; Man on Page 602, The; Master-Trak Enterprises; Missile Records; ‡Music City Sound Records; ‡Music Quest Entertainment & Television; ‡Music Wise Inc.; Musikus Productions, Inc.; New Experience Records/Grand Slam Records; Omni 2000 Inc.; Orbit Records; Pirate Records; Platinum Boulevard Records; PMG Records; ‡Pointblank Records; Pop Record Research; PPI/Peter Pan Industries; Rammit Records; React Recordings; Red-Eye Records; ‡RML Records; ‡Robbins Entertainment LLC; Roll On Records®; Rosebud Records; Rustron Music Productions; Sabre Productions; Sabteca Record Co.; Sahara Records and Filmworks Entertainment; Salexo Music; Satin Records; Shang Records; ‡Sheheshe Records; Stargard Records; Startrak Records, Inc.; Strugglebaby Recording Co.; Surprize Records, Inc.; Tandem Records; Touché Records; ‡Touchwood Records LLC; Trend Records®; TVT Records; Wall Street Music; Wanstar Group, The; Warehouse Creek Recording Corp.; White Car Records; ‡Windy City Records; Young Star Productions, Inc.

Rap

A&M Records; Albatross Records; All American Music Group; Alpha-Beat; Ancy Records; Associated Artists Music International; ‡Atlan-Dec/Grooveline Records; Baby Faze Records & Tapes; Black Diamond Records Inc.; BMX Entertainment; Boogie Band Records; Cellar Records; ‡Crescent Recording Corporation; Critique Records, Inc.; Dagene/Cabletown Records;

‡Dapmor Records; Def Beat Records; ‡Disc-tinct Music, Inc.; ‡¡Epiphany!; Fresh Entertainment; Generic Records, Inc.; ‡Glow in the Dark; Hallway International Records/1st Coast Posse Mixes; Intersound Inc.; Jive Records; Joey Boy Records Inc.; Keeping It Simple and Safe, Inc.; LBI Records; Missile Records; ‡Music Quest Entertainment & Television; New Experience Records/Grand Slam Records; PC Music; Pickwick/Mecca/Internation Records; Pirate Records; Radical Records; Rammit Records; Redemption Records; Revelation Records; ‡Robbins Entertainment LLC; ‡Rude Records; Shang Records; ‡Sin Klub Entertainment, Inc.; Sirr Rodd Record & Publishing Co.; Stargard Records; Startrak Records, Inc.; Tandem Records; Triple X Records; TVT Records; ‡Vander-Moon Entertainment; Wall Street Music; Wanstar Group, The; Watusi Productions; x:treme records; Zero Hour Records

Religious

A&M Records; A&R Records; Aladdin Recordings; Allegheny Music Works; Alpha Recording Co.; American Music Network, Inc.; Ancy Records; ‡Atlan-Dec/Grooveline Records; babysue; Bagatelle Record Company; Bandit Records; ‡Big Whig Productions; Bouquet Records; Briarhill Records; Cedar Creek Records™; Christian Media Enterprises; Continental Records; Country Style Records; Cowgirl Records; Dagene/Cabletown Records; Dale Productions, Alan; EMA Music Inc.; Emerald City Records; Fame and Fortune Enterprises; First Time Records; Fountain Records; Fresh Entertainment; Gold City Records, Inc.; Grass Roots Record & Tape/LMI Records; Green Bear Records; Gueststar Records; Howdy Records; Intersound Inc.; Jalyn Recording Co.; Justin Time Records Inc.; K-ark Records; Kaupp Records; Keeping It Simple and Safe, Inc.; Kottage Records; L.A. Records (Canada); Lamon Records; Landmark Communications Group; Lari-Jon Records; LBJ Productions; Lonesome Wind Corporation; ‡Magic Key Productions Inc.; Magnum Music Corp. Ltd.; Malaco Records; Man on Page 602, The; Missile Records; Modern Voices Entertainment, Ltd.; ‡Music City Sound Records; ‡Music Quest Entertainment & Television; Music Services & Marketing; ‡Music Wise Inc.; New Experience Records/Grand Slam Records; Nucleus Records; OCP Publications; Omni 2000 Inc.; ‡Paradigm Productions; Paul Records, J.; Peachtown Record Co. Inc.; Phoenix Records, Inc.; Pickwick/Mecca/Internation Records; Plateau Music; Platinum Plus Records International; Playbones Records; R.E.F. Records; Red-Eye Records; Rejoice Records of Nashville; Richway Records International; Roll On Records®; Rosebud Records; Sabre Productions; Salexo Music; ‡Sheheshe Records; Sirr Rodd Record & Publishing Co.; ‡Smoky Mountain Recording Company, Inc.; Spiritual Walk Records; Startrak Records, Inc.; SunCountry Records; Tandem Records; Teeter-Tot Records; ‡Throwing Stones Records; Touché Records; Treasure Coast Records; Trend Records®; Trusty Records; Vokes Music Record Co.; Wanstar Group, The; ‡Warehouse Creek Recording Corp.; Winchester Records; Woodrich Records; Worship & Praise Records Inc.; Young Country Records/Plain Country Records; Young Star Productions, Inc.

Rock

Aladdin Recordings; American Music Network, Inc.; Americatone Records International USA; Amiron Music/Aztec Productions; Ancy Records; ‡Aquarius Records; Ariana Records; Arion Records/Sound Resources; Arkadia Entertainment Corp.; ‡Arula Records; Associated Artists Music International; ‡Atlan-Dec/Grooveline Records; audiofile Tapes; Avalanche Records; ‡Avenue Communications; Azra International; Baby Faze Records & Tapes; babysue; Basset Hound Productions; ‡Beluga Records; Big Rock Pty. Ltd.; ‡Big Whig Productions; Black Diamond Records Inc.; ‡Blue Duck!! Records; ‡Blue Eyed Kitty Productions; Blue Gem Records; Blue Wave; BMX Entertainment; Boogie Band Records; Bouquet Records; Broken Records International; BSW Records; C.E.G. Records, Inc.; Capstan Record Production; Carlyle Records, Inc.; Carmel Records; Cat's Voice Productions; Cedar Creek Records™; Cellar Records; Centium Entertainment, Inc.; Cerebral Records; Chattahoochee Records; Cherry Street Records; ‡Collector Records; Comma Records & Tapes; ‡Conspiracy Records; ‡Cooking Vinyl America; ‡Creek Records; ‡Crescent Recording Corporation; Critique Records, Inc.; Dancer Publishing Co.; ‡Dapmor Records; Deadeye Records; ‡Del-Fi Records, Inc.; Demi Monde Records and Publishing, Ltd.; Don't Records; Drive Entertainment; Eastern Front Records, Inc.; ‡Eleven Records/McGhee Entertainment; ‡EMF Records & Affiliates; ‡Entourage Music Group; ‡¡Epiphany!;

Fame and Fortune Enterprises; Fat City Artists; Fiction Songs; Flying Heart Records; Fresh Entertainment; Front Row Records; Generic Records, Inc.; ‡Glow in the Dark; ‡Goddess Records; Golden Triangle Records; ‡Gotham Records; Grass Roots Record & Tape/LMI Records; Green Bear Records; Guestar Records; ‡Hottrax Records; hypnotic recordings usa; Ikon Records; Inferno Records; Intersound Inc.; Kaupp Records; Keeping It Simple and Safe, Inc.; ‡Kill Rock Stars; Kingston Records; L.A. Records (MI); L.A. Records (Canada); Lamon Records; Landmark Communications Group; Lanor Records; Lari-Jon Records; ‡Lazy Bones Recordings/Productions, Inc.; LBJ Productions; Le Matt Music Ltd.; Lonny Tunes; Lucifer Records, Inc.; M.E.G. Records Co.; Magnum Music Corp. Ltd.; Makeshift Music; Man on Page 602, The; Master-Trak Enterprises; Maui Arts & Music Association; Maverick Group, The; Megaforce Worldwide Entertainment; Missile Records; Modern Voices Entertainment, Ltd.; ‡Moonstone Records; ‡Motion City Records; Mountain Records; ‡Music City Sound Records; ‡Music Quest Entertainment & Television; Musikus Productions, Inc.; New Experience Records/Grand Slam Records; ‡nu.millennia/records; Nucleus Records; Oglio Records; Orbit Records; Orinda Records; ‡Overtime Station; P. & N. Records; ‡Paradigm Productions; Patty Lee Records; Paul Records, J.; ‡Pavement Music, Inc.; PBM Records; PC Music; ‡Pentacle Records; Peridot Records; ‡Permanent Press Recordings; Pickwick/Mecca/Internation Records; Pissed Off Records, Inc.; Plateau Music; Platinum Boulevard Records; Playbones Records; PMG Records; Powerhouse Records; Pravda Records; Premiére Records; Presence Records; R.E.F. Records; Radical Records; Random Records; Red Dot/Puzzle Records; Red Sky Records; Redemption Records; Red-Eye Records; Reiter Records Ltd.; Revelation Records; ‡RML Records; Roll On Records®; ‡Rosebowl, The; Rosebud Records; Rotten Records; ‡Rude Records; Ruffcut Productions; Sabre Productions; ‡Safire Records; Satin Records; ‡Scat Records; Shaolin Film & Records; ‡Sonic Records, Inc.; ‡sonic unyon records canada; Stardust; Startrak Records, Inc.; Strugglebaby Recording Co.; Sunset Records; ‡Surface Records; ‡Tangent Records; ‡TBS Records; ‡Touchwood Records LLC; Trend Records®; Triple X Records; Trumpeter Records Inc.; ‡Tug Boat Records; 28 Records; Valtec Productions; ‡Vander-Moon Entertainment; White Car Records; Whitehouse Records; Winchester Records; ‡Windy City Records; Wolftrax Records; Wonderland Records; Woodrich Records; Young Country Records/Plain Country Records; Young Star Productions, Inc.; Zero Hour Records

World Music

African Diaspora Project, The; Arkadia Entertainment Corp.; audiofile Tapes; Avalanche Records; ‡Avenue Communications; ‡Blue Duck!! Records; ‡Dapmor Records; Def Beat Records; Earthtone/Sonic Images; ‡EMF Records & Affiliates; Etherean Music/Variena Publishing; Hallway International Records/1st Coast Posse Mixes; LBI Records; Missile Records; Modal Music, Inc.™; ‡Music Quest Entertainment & Television; North Star Music; ‡Only New Age Music, Inc.; Shang Records; Sheffield Lab Recording; Silver Wave Records; Smithsonian Folkways Recordings; ‡Sonic Images Records; Sunshine Group, The; ‡Tangent Records; ‡Triloka; Watusi Productions

‡ **THE DOUBLE DAGGER** before a listing indicates that the listing is new in this edition.

Record Producers

The independent producer can best be described as a creative coordinator. He's usually the one with the most creative control over a recording project and is ultimately responsible for the finished product. Although some larger record companies have their own in-house producers who work exclusively with artists signed to a particular label, it's common for a record company today to contract out-of-house, independent producers for recording projects.

Producers play a large role in deciding what songs will be recorded for a particular project, and are always on the lookout for new songs for their clients. They can be valuable contacts for songwriters because they work so closely with the artists whose records they produce. They usually have a lot more freedom than others in executive positions, and are known for having a good ear for hit song potential. Many producers are songwriters, musicians and artists themselves. Since they have a big influence on a particular project, a good song in the hands of the right producer at the right time stands a good chance of being cut. And even if a producer is not working on a specific project, he is well-acquainted with record company executives and artists, and can often get material through doors not open to you.

Even so, it can be difficult to get your tapes to the right producer at the right time. Many producers write their own songs and even if they don't write, they may be involved in their own publishing companies so they have instant access to all the songs in their catalogs. It's important to understand the intricacies of the producer/publisher situation. If you pitch your song directly to a producer first, before another publishing company publishes the song, the producer may ask you for the publishing rights (or a percentage thereof) to your song. You must decide whether the producer is really an active publisher who will try to get the song recorded again and again, or whether he merely wants the publishing because it means extra income for him from the current recording project. You may be able to work out a co-publishing deal, where you and the producer split the publishing of the song. That means he will still receive his percentage of the publishing income, even if you secure a cover recording of the song by other artists in the future. Even though you would be giving up a little bit initially, you may benefit in the future.

The listings that follow outline which aspects of the music industry each producer is involved in, what type of music he is looking for, and what records and artists he's recently produced. Study the listings carefully, noting the artists each producer works with, and consider if any of your songs might fit a particular artist's or producer's style.

Consult the Category Index at the end of this section to find producers who work with the type of music you write, and the Geographic Index at the back of the book to locate producers in your area.

"A" MAJOR SOUND CORPORATION, 80 Corley Ave., Toronto, Ontario M4E 1V2 **Canada**. Phone/fax: (416)690-9552. Producer: Paul C. Milner. Record producer and music publisher. Estab. 1989. Produces 12 LPs, 2 EPs and 12 CDs/year. Fee derived from sales royalty when song or artist is recorded, or outright fee from recording artist or record company.

How to Contact: Submit demo tape by mail. Unsolicited submissions are OK. Prefers cassette, DAT or VHS videocassette with 5 songs and lyric sheet (lead sheet if available). Reports in 2-6 months.

Music: Mostly **rock**, **A/C**, **alternative**, **pop** and **metal**; also **Christian** and **R&B**. Produced *Strange Hearts*, written and recorded by Gloria Blizzard on Amatish Records (acid jazz); *Cantos From A Small Room* (by Dario Decicio), recorded by I Am (rock); and "Thirst" (by Mark Zinkew), recorded by Zinq (alternative/dance). Other artists include Hokus Pick Manouver (Word/MCA) and Tribal Stomp.

‡ABERDEEN PRODUCTIONS, 524 Doral Country Dr., Nashville TN 37221. (615)646-9750. President: Scott Turner. Record producer and music publisher (Buried Treasure Music/ASCAP, Captain Kidd/

BMI). Estab. 1971. Produces 10 singles, 15-20 12″ singles, 8 LPs and 8 CDs/year. Fee derived from sales royalty when song or artist is recorded.

- Aberdeen Productions' publishing company, Buried Treasure Music, is listed in the Music Publishers section.

How to Contact: Submit demo tape by mail. Unsolicited submissions are OK. Prefers cassette with maximum 4 songs and lead sheet. SASE. Reports in 2 weeks. No "lyrics only."
Music: Mostly **country**, **MOR** and **rock**; also **top 40/pop**. Produced *One Heart* (by Scott Turner/Doc Pomus) and *Your Star's Still Shining* (by Scott Turner/Brett McNaul), both recorded by Dennis Marsh on BMG Records; and *Oh Caroline* (by S. Turner/J. Marascalco), recorded by Harry Nilsson on MCP Records (pop). Other artists include Del Reeves, Jerry Wallace, Rosemary Clooney, Vicki Carr and Waylon Jennings.

ACR PRODUCTIONS, P.O. Box 739, Hendersonville TN 37077-0739. (615)826-9233. Owner: Dwaine Thomas. Record producer, music publisher (Joranda Music/BMI) and record company (ACR Records). Estab. 1986. Produces 120 singles, 8-15 12″ singles, 25 LPs, 25 EPs and 25 CDs/year. Fee derived from sales royalty when song or artist is recorded. "We charge for in-house recording only. Remainder is derived from royalties."
How to Contact: Submit demo tape by mail. Unsolicited submissions are OK. Prefers cassette or VHS videocassette with 5 songs and lyric sheet. Does not return material. Reports in 6 weeks if interested.
Music: Mostly **country swing**, **pop** and **rock**; also **R&B** and **gospel**. Produced "It's Never Easy," "Dreams," and "Forever Yours" (by Aaron Miller), recorded by Off Limitz on ACR Records (pop).
Tips: "Be professional. No living room tapes!"

AIRWAVE PRODUCTION GROUP INC., 1916 28th Ave. S., Birmingham AL 35209. (205)870-3239. Producer: Marc Phillips. Record producer, music publisher and artist development company. Estab. 1985. Produces 5 singles, 2 12″ singles, 4 LPs, 5 EPs and 10 CDs/year. Fee derived from sales royalty when song or artist is recorded.
How to Contact: Submit demo tape by mail. Unsolicited submissions are OK. Prefers cassette with 3 songs and lyric sheet. SASE. Reports in 6-10 weeks.
Music: Mostly **rock**, **R&B** and **pop**; also **jazz**, **country** and **contemporary Christian**. Produced "Another Wheel" and "Take A Step," written and recorded by Kelly Garrett on Sony Records (country); and *House of Love* (by A.J. Vallejo), recorded by Vallejo (rock). Other artists include Parousia, 4 AM and Elvis' Grave.

AKO PRODUCTIONS, Dept. SM, 20531 Plummer, Chatsworth CA 91311. (818)998-0443. President: A. Sullivan. Record producer and music publisher (Amiron Music). Produces 2-6 singles and 2-3 LPs/year. Fee derived from sales royalty when song or artist is recorded.

- AKO Productions' publishing company, Amiron Music, is listed in the Music Publishers section.

How to Contact: Write first and obtain permission to submit. Prefers cassette or videocassette and lyric sheet. SASE. Reports in 1 month.
Music: **Pop/rock** and **modern country**. Produced *Ladies in Charge*, written and recorded by C. Ratliff on AKO Records.

ALADDIN PRODUCTIONS, P.O. Box 121738, Nashville TN 37212. (615)726-3556. Contact: A&R Dept. Record producer. Estab. 1996. Produces 6 singles, 3 LPs and 3 CDs/year. Fee derived from sales royalty when song or artist is recorded or outright fee from recording artist or record company.
How to Contact: Submit demo tape by mail. Unsolicited submissions are OK. Prefers cassette with 2 songs and lyric sheet. "Send any pertinent information for review." SASE. Reports in 1 month.
Music: Mostly **country**, **alternative** and **rock**; also **gospel**, **blues** and **contemporary**. Produced "Love Don't Lie" (by James & Lee), recorded by Deuces Wild on Aladdin Records (country); *Balladeer* (by Jim Hughes/Will Graveman), recorded by John Madrid on Crosswind Records (contemporary); and *Hold Me Again*, written and recorded by Jay S. Kay on Alternative Records (alternative).
Tips: "Quality is the only thing selling. Screen your material very carefully and only submit your best. We are looking for songs and artists with something different. We need artists and songs to possibly place not only with major record companies, but also for possible placement in movies, soundtracks, commercials and television programs."

STUART J. ALLYN, Skylight Run, Irvington NY 10533. (212)486-0856. Associate: Jack Walker. Record producer. Estab. 1972. Produces 6 singles and 3-6 CDs/year. Fee derived from sales royalty and outright fee from recording artist and record company.
How to Contact: Write first and obtain permission to submit. Prefers DAT, CD, cassette, 15 ips reel-to-reel or VHS videocassette with 3 songs and lyric or lead sheet. Does not return material. Reports in 12 months.

Music: Mostly **pop**, **rock**, **jazz** and **theatrical**; also **R&B** and **country**. Produced Dizzy Gillespie's "Winter in Lisbon" on Milan Records; *Mel Lewis & Jazz Orchestra* on Atlantic Records (jazz); and *Me & Him*, on Columbia Records (film score). Other artists include Billy Joel, Aerosmith, Carole Demas, Harry Stone, Bob Stewart, The Dixie Peppers, Nora York, Buddy Barnes and various video and film scores.

ANGEL FILMS COMPANY, 967 Hwy. 40, New Franklin MO 65247-9778. (573)698-3900. E-mail: angelfilm@aol.com. Vice President Production: Matthew Eastman. Record producer, motion picture company and record company (Angel One). Estab. 1980. Produces 5 LPs, 5 EPs and 5 CDs/year. Fee derived from sales royalty when song or artist is recorded.

• See Angel Films Company's listing in the Advertising, AV and Commercial Music Firms section.

How to Contact: Submit demo tape by mail. Unsolicited submissions are OK. Prefers cassette or VHS videocassette with 3 songs. "Send only original material, not previously recorded, and include a bio sheet on artist." SASE. Reports in 6 weeks.

Music: Mostly **pop**, **rock** and **rockabilly**; also **jazz** and **R&B**. Produced *Here in Time*, written and recorded by B.D.K.; *Euttland*, written and recorded by Euttland (rock); and *Teddies*, written and recorded by Marie Connors, all on Angel One Records. Other artists include Julian James, Patrick Donovon and Bill Hoehne.

APOPHIS MUSIC, 7135 Hollywood, Los Angeles CA 90046. (213)851-8552. Fax: (213)850-1467. Record Producer: Jimmy Stewart. Record producer. Estab. 1968. Produces 3 LPs and 3 CDs/year. Fee derived from sales royalty when song or artist is recorded or outright fee from recording artist or record company.

How to Contact: Write or call first and obtain permission to submit. Prefers cassette with 3 songs and lyric or lead sheet. Does not return material. Reports in 1-3 months.

Music: Mostly **jazz**, **alternative** and **rock**; also **R&B** and **classical**. Produced *Memorabilia*, written and recorded by Jimmy Stewart on J. Bird Records (jazz). Other artists include Gary Crosby.

‡JONATHAN APPELL, 333 E. 23rd St. #9C, New York NY 10010. (212)725-5613. E-mail: jonapple@aol.com. Producer/Engineer: Jonathan Appell. Record producer and audio engineer. Estab. 1992. Produces 2 singles and 5 LPs/year. Fee derived from sales royalty when song or artist is recorded, or outright fee from recording artist or record company.

How to Contact: Write first to arrange personal interview. Prefers cassette. Does not return material.

Music: Mostly **rock**, **pop** and **R&B**; also **jazz** and **reggae**. Produced *Deception In Your Eyes*, written and recorded by the Robert Charles Blues Band on Bahoomba Records (blues). Other artists include The Piranha Brothers, Rosanne Drucker, YNot and Eric Fleischman.

‡ARTISTIC NOISE, P.O. Box 230914, Grand Rapids MI 49523-0914. (616)281-0617. Contact: Darryl Shanon Holt. Record producer, record company and music publisher (Artistic Noise Publishing/BMI). Estab. 1996. Produces 2 singles and 1 CD/year. Fee derived from outright fee from recording artist or record company.

• See the listings for Artistic Noise in the Music Publishers and Record Companies sections.

How to Contact: Submit demo tape by mail. Unsolicited submissions are OK. Prefers cassette with 3-10 songs and lyric sheet. Does not return material. Reports in 2 months.

Music: Mostly **pop**, **dance** and **R&B**; also **alternative**, **ballads** and **techno**. Produced "This Is Love," "My Car" and "Why," written and recorded by Darryl Shanon Holt on Artistic Noise (pop/alternative).

AURORA PRODUCTIONS, 7415 Herrington, Belmont MI 49306. Producer: Jack Conners. Record producer, engineer/technician and record company (New World Records). Estab. 1984. Produces 1 CD/year. Fee derived from outright fee from recording artist.

How to Contact: Write first and obtain permission to submit. Prefers cassette with 1 or 2 songs. SASE. Reports in 6 weeks.

Music: Mostly **classical**, **folk** and **jazz**. Produced *Acousma* and *Akulka*, written and recorded by S.R. Turner on North Cedar Records; and "Peace on Earth" (by John and Danny Murphy), recorded by Murphy Brothers on Ocean Records. Other artists include The Burdons.

BAL RECORDS, P.O. Box 369, LaCanada CA 91012-0369. (818)548-1116. President: Adrian Bal. Record producer and music publisher (Bal & Bal Music). Estab. 1965. Produces 1-3 CDs/year. Fee derived from sales royalty when song or artist is recorded.

• Bal Records' publishing company, Bal & Bal Music, is listed in the Music Publishers section.

How to Contact: Submit demo tape by mail. Unsolicited submissions are OK. Prefers cassette with 3 songs and lyric sheet. SASE. Reports in 3 months.

Music: Mostly **MOR**, **country**, **jazz**, **R&B**, **rock** and **top 40/pop**; also **blues**, **church/religious**, **easy**

listening and **soul**. Produced *Special Day, What's The Matter With Me* and *Lord You Been So Good to Me*, written and recorded by Rhonda Johnson on BAL Records.

BELOTES FERRY MUSIC, (formerly Sharpe Sound Productions), 3129 Belotes Ferry Rd., Lebanon TN 37087. (615)449-7256. E-mail: edsharpe@aol.com. Producer/Engineer: Ed Sharpe. Record producer. Estab. 1990. Fee derived from sales royalty when song or artist is recorded or outright fee from recording artist or record company.
How to Contact: Submit demo tape by mail. Unsolicited submissions are OK. Prefers cassette or VHS videocassette with 4 songs and lyric sheet. Does not return material. Reports in 1 month.
Music: Acoustic, spoken word and **Native American/spiritual**. Produced *Johnny B!*, written and recorded by John Bellar on Belotes Ferry Records (country/jazz); and *Cherokee Legends*, written and recorded by Ed Sharpe on Cherokee Publications (spoken word). Other artists include Stacey Adkins, The Relatives and Dan Gunn.

HAL BERNARD ENTERPRISES, INC., P.O. Box 8385, Cincinnati OH 45208. (513)871-1500. Fax: (513)871-1510. President: Stan Hertzman. Record producer, record company (Strugglebaby Recording Co.), management firm (Umbrella Artists Management) and music publisher (Sunnyslope Music Inc. and Bumpershoot Music Inc.). Produces 5 singles and 3-4 LPs/year. Fee derived from sales royalty.

- See Hal Bernard's listing in the Music Publishers section, as well as listings for Strugglebaby Recording Co. in the Record Companies section and Umbrella Artists Management in the Managers and Booking Agents section.

How to Contact: Prefers cassette with 1-3 songs and lyric sheet. SASE. Reports in 1 month.
Music: Produced *Inner Revolution*, recorded by Adrian Belew on Atlantic Records; *Awkwardsville*, recorded by psychodots; and *When the World Was Young*, recorded by Mary Ellen Tanner, both on Strugglebaby Records.

‡BEWILDERING MUSIC, INC., 3-1 Park Plaza #162, Old Brookville NY 11545. (516)759-5560. E-mail: bminc@aol.com. President: Douglas W. Craig. Record producer. Estab. 1992. Produces 1 or 2 EPs and 3-5 CDs/year. Fee derived from sales royalty when song or artist is recorded.
How to Contact: Prefers cassette, CD or VHS videocassette with photo. "No metal, gangsta rap, jazz or country. It is essential that you make it possible for us to see your live show. We only record performing songwriters. A VHS cassette is strongly recommended for those who do not perform frequently in New York City." Does not return material (all submissions are kept on file).
Music: Mostly **alternative rock**; also **anything strange**, **unusual** or **eclectic**. Produced *World of Change*, written and recorded by Stevie Raye on Rediscovery Records (pop); and *Sit and Spin*, written and recorded by Chrome Omen on De Facto Records (industrial). Other artists include Charles Demar, Heliotrope, Hoover's G-String and Pie Grande.

BIG BEAR, Box 944, Birmingham, B16 8UT, **United Kingdom**. Phone: 44-21-454-7020. Managing Director: Jim Simpson. Record producer, music publisher (Bearsongs) and record company (Big Bear Records). Produces 10 LPs/year. Fee derived from sales royalty.

- See the listings for Bearsongs in the Music Publishers section and Big Bear Records in the Record Companies section.

How to Contact: Write first about your interest, then submit demo tape and lyric sheet. Does not return material. Reports in 2 weeks.
Music: Blues and **jazz**.

BIG SKY AUDIO PRODUCTIONS, 1035 E. Woodland Ave. #2, Springfield PA 19064. (610)328-4709. Fax: (610)328-7728. Producer: Drew Raison. Record producer. Estab. 1990. Produces 5-7 EPs and 10-12 CDs/year. Fee derived from sales royalty when song or artist is recorded or outright fee from recording artist or record company.
How to Contact: Submit demo tape by mail. Unsolicited submissions are OK. Prefers cassette or VHS videocassette with 3 songs and lyric sheet. "Don't send it to us if it isn't copyrighted!" Does not return material. Reports in 4-6 weeks.
Music: Rock, R&B and **New Age**; also **anything with strong vocals**. Produced *Speak On It* (by Syracuse/Gilham), recorded by Blue Noise; *Get It Right*, written and recorded by Johnny DeFrancesco, both on VAM Records; and *I Have Forgotten*, written and recorded by David E. Williamson on Ospedale Records. Other artists include Trash Planet, John Swiegart, Theodozia, Daniel Pry, Robert Hazzard, Joey DeFrancesco and Dreamlovers.

BLAZE PRODUCTIONS, 103 Pleasant Ave., Upper Saddle River NJ 07458. (201)825-1060. Record producer, music publisher (Botown Music), multimedia company, web designer and management firm.

Estab. 1978. Fee derived from sales royalty or outright fee from recording artist or record company.

- See Blaze Productions' listing in the Managers and Booking Agents section.

How to Contact: Submit demo tape by mail. Unsolicited submissions are OK. Prefers cassette or VHS videocassette with 1 or more songs and lyric sheet. Does not return material. Reports in 3 weeks.

Music: **Pop**, **rock** and **dance**. Produced *Anything Can Happen*, by Voices on Botown Records; and "Up On Blocks," recorded by Gearhead on Wild Boar Records.

‡BLUES ALLEY RECORDS, Rt. 1, Box 288, Clarksburg WV 26301. Producer: Joshua Swiger. Record producer, record company and music publisher (Blues Alley Publishing/BMI). Produces 2 singles, 1-2 LPs and 2 EPs/year. Fee derived from sales royalty when song or artist is recorded or outright fee from recording artist.

How to Contact: Submit demo tape by mail. Unsolicited submissions are OK. Prefers cassette with 4 songs and lyric and lead sheets. SASE.

Music: Mostly **rock**, **country** and **Christian rock**; also **alternative**, **pop** and **R&B**. Produced *Renaissance Project*, written and recorded by Davin Seamon & Joshua Swiger; and *Ricochet*, written and recorded by Matt Hanshaw, both on Blues Alley Records.

ROBERT BOWDEN, P.O. Box 282, 885 Broadway, Bayonne NJ 07002. President: Robert Bowden. Record producer, music publisher (Roots Music/BMI) and record company (Nucleus Records). Estab. 1979. Produces 3 singles and 1 LP/year. Fees derived from sales royalty when song or artist is recorded.

- Robert Bowden's publishing company, Roots Music, is listed in the Music Publishers section, and his record label, Nucleus Records, is listed in the Record Companies section.

How to Contact: Submit demo tape by mail. Unsolicited submissions are OK. Prefers cassette or VHS videocassette with 3 songs and lyric sheet. SASE. Reports in 1 month.

Music: Mostly **country**; also **pop**. Produced "Henrey C," "Always" and "Selfish Heart" (by Bowden), all recorded by Marco Sisison on Nucleus Records.

‡CACOPHONY PRODUCTIONS, 52-A Carmine St., Suite 544, New York NY 10014. (212)777-8763. Producer: Steven Miller. Record producer and music publisher (In Your Face Music). Estab. 1981. Fee derived from sales royalty when song or artist is recorded, or outright fee from recording artist or record company.

How to Contact: Call first and obtain permission to submit. Prefers cassette with 3 songs and lyric sheet. "Send a cover letter of no more than three paragraphs giving some background on yourself and the music. Also explain specifically what you are looking for Cacophony Productions to do." Does not return material. Reports in 3 months.

Music: Mostly **progressive pop/rock**, **singer/songwriter** and **progressive country**. Produced *Mortal City*, recorded by Dar Williams on Razor & Tie Records. Other artists include Suzanne Vega, John Gorka, Michael Hedges, Juliana Hatfield and Medeski-Martin & Wood.

CAPITOL AD, MANAGEMENT & TALENT GROUP, 1300 Division St., Suite 200, Nashville TN 37203. (615)242-4722, (615)244-2440, (800)767-4984. Fax: (615)242-1177. E-mail: www.platinumr@aol.com. Senior Producer: Robert Metzgar. Record producer, record company (Aim High Records, Hot News Records, Platinum Plus Records, SHR Records), management firm and music publisher (Aim High Music Co./ASCAP, Bobby & Billy Music Co./BMI). Estab. 1971. Produces 35 singles, 12-15 12″ singles, 20 LPs, 15 EPs and 35 CDs/year. Fee derived from sales royalty when song or artist is recorded or outright fee from recording artist or record company.

- Capitol's publishing company, Aim High Music, is listed in the Music Publishers section; Capitol Management and Talent is listed in the Managers and Booking Agents section; and their record company, Platinum Plus, is listed in the Record Companies section.

How to Contact: Submit demo tape by mail. Unsolicited submissions are OK. Prefers cassette or videocassette with 3-5 songs and lyric sheet. "We are interested in hearing only from *serious* artist/songwriters." Does not return material. Reports in 3-4 weeks.

Music: Mostly **country**, **gospel**, **pop** and **R&B**; also **jazz**, **contemporary Christian**, **rock** and **pop-rock**. Produced *Sounds of Music*, written and recorded by B. Enriquez on Sony Records (Latin); *Keep On Dancin'* (by H. Smiley), recorded by Satin (dance); and *Livin For The Dream* (M. Johnson), recorded by John Michael Montgomery (country), both on CBS Records. Other artists include Carl Butler (CBS/Sony), Tommy Cash (Columbia), Mickey Jones (Capitol), Tommy Overstreet (MCA Records), Warner Mack (MCA Records) and others.

CARLOCK PRODUCTIONS, 85 Sixth Ave., Apt. B, Brooklyn NY 11217. Producer: Dave Carlock. Record producer. Estab. 1990. Produces 6 LPs and 5 EPs/year. Fee derived from sales royalty when song

or artist is recorded or outright fee from recording artist or record company.
How to Contact: Write first and obtain permission to submit. Prefers cassette or VHS videocassette with 3-5 songs and lyric sheet. Does not return material. Reports in 2 weeks.
Music: Mostly **pop/rock**, **A/C** and **rock (alternative)**; also **contemporary Christian** and **gospel**. Produced *Long Way Down*, recorded by Greg Shafritz (pop/rock); *Daisy's Red Gravy Train*, recorded by Daisy's Red Gravy Train (pop/rock); and *There's A Space* (by Christopher Beerman).
Tips: "If contacting me from outside of NY metro area (NY, NJ, CT), be prepared to travel to New York for my services. In this instance, please be serious if you submit!"

CEDAR CREEK PRODUCTIONS, 44 Music Square E., Suite 503, Nashville TN 37203. (615)252-6916. Fax: (615)327-4204. President: Larry Duncan. Record producer, record company (Cedar Creek Records™), music publisher (Cedar Creek Music/BMI and Cedar Cove Music/ASCAP) and artist management. Estab. 1981. Produces 20 singles, 5 LPs and 5 CDs/year. Fee derived from sales royalty when song or artist is recorded.

- See Cedar Creek's listing in the Managers and Booking Agents section; Cedar Creek Records is listed in the Record Companies section.

How to Contact: Submit demo tape by mail. Unsolicited submissions are OK. Prefers cassette or VHS videocassette with 4-6 songs and lyric sheet (typed). "Put return address and name on envelope. Put telephone number in packet." Does not return material. Reports in 2 months.
Music: Mostly **country**, **country/pop** and **country/R&B**; also **pop**, **R&B**, **southern/gospel/Christian contemporary**, **Christian country**, **contemporary jazz** and **light rock**. Produced "Eleven Roses" (by Lamar Morris/Darrell McCall); "When The Sun Goes Down Over Dixie" (by Brian McArdle/Gary Georgett); and "A Mile In His Shoes" (by Lynn Guyo/Deke Little), all recorded by Lynn Guyo on Interstate Records (country).
Tips: "Submit your best songs on a good fully produced demo or master."

JAN CELT MUSICAL SERVICES, 4026 NE 12th Ave., Portland OR 97212. (503)287-8045. E-mail: flyheart@teleport.com. Website: http://www.teleport.com/~flyheart. Owner: Jan Celt. Record producer, music publisher (Wiosna Nasza Music/BMI) and record company (Flying Heart Records). Estab. 1982. Produces 3-5 CDs/year.

- See the listing for Flying Heart Records in the Record Companies section.

How to Contact: Submit demo tape by mail. Unsolicited submissions are OK. Prefers high-quality cassette with 1-10 songs and lyric sheet. SASE. Reports in 4 months. "If calling, please check time zone."
Music: Mostly **R&B**, **rock** and **blues**; also **jazz**. Produced "Vexatious Progressions," written and recorded by Eddie Harris (jazz); "Bong Hit" (by Chris Newman), recorded by Snow Bud & the Flower People (rock); and "She Moved Away" (by Chris Newman), recorded by Napalm Beach, all on Flying Heart Records. Other artists include The Esquires and Janice Scroggins.

‡CHAINSAW RECORDS, 13446 Poway Rd. #147, Poway CA 92064. (619)679-5881. E-mail: ncchainsaw@aol.com. Owner: Norwood C. Barber II. Record producer, record company and music publisher (Hell Of A Note/ASCAP). Estab. 1985. Releases 20 CDs/year. Fee derived from sales royalty when song or artist is recorded or outright fee from record company.
How to Contact: Write or call first and obtain permission to submit. Prefers cassette with 4 songs and lyric sheet. Does not return material. Reports in 3 weeks.
Music: Mostly **metal (all styles)**, **rock** and **alternative**; also **R&B**, **jazz** and **country**. Produced *Bleeding*, recorded by Psychotic Waltz on IRS Records (progressive metal); *Bridging the Gap*, recorded by Full Circle on Hometown Records (rock); and *Can't Take the Strain*, recorded by Epitaph on Chainsaw Records (metal). Other artists include Bordercrossing, The End, U.T.I., Sandjacket, Squeaky Fromme and Sanskara.

‡CHICAGO KID PRODUCTIONS, 1840 N. Kenmore #304, Los Angeles CA 90027. (213)660-6817. Fax: (213)660-4756. President: John Ryan. Record producer, music publisher and management firm. Estab. 1972. Produces 3-10 LPs/year. Fee is negotiable.
How to Contact: Submit demo tape by mail. Unsolicited submissions are OK. Prefers cassette with 3

‡ **THE DOUBLE DAGGER** before a listing indicates that the listing is new in this edition.

songs. Does not return material. Reporting time varies.
Music: Mostly **rock**, **pop** and **R&B**. Produced "Love Is Still Enough," written and recorded by Sovory on the *Jason's Lyric* soundtrack on Mercury Records; *Sovory*, written and recorded by Sovory on Polydor Records; and "Did You Mean What You Said," written and recorded by Sovory on *The Fan* soundtrack on TVT Records. Other artists include Baha Men, Styx, Vince Gill & Pure Prairie League and Santana.

CHUCKER MUSIC, INC., 345 E. 80th St., 15H, New York NY 10021. (212)744-2312. President: Chuck Dembrak. Record producer and music publisher (Cool One Music/ASCAP). Estab. 1978. Produces 3-6 12" singles and 1-2 LPs/year. Fees derived from outright fee from record company.
How to Contact: Submit demo tape by mail. Unsolicited submissions are OK. Prefers cassette or VHS videocassette with 3-4 songs and lyric sheet. Does not return material. Reports in 4 weeks.
Music: Mostly **R&B**, **pop** and **rock**. Produced *Ed Polcer Band* (by R. Hegel), recorded by Ed Polcer on Avion Records (jazz); *Gemini* (by various), recorded by Gemini on Viking Records (pop); and *Necessity* (by C. Frycki), recorded by Killing Words on Midnite Fantasy Records (rock). Other artists include Geri Mingori and Leslie Fradkin.

COFFEE AND CREAM PRODUCTIONS, 1138 E. Price St., Philadelphia PA 19138. Producer: Bolden Abrams, Jr.. Record producer, music publisher (Coffee and Cream Publishing Company/ASCAP) and record company (Coffee and Cream Records). Produces 12 singles, 12 12" singles and 6 LPs/year. Fee derived from sales royalty or outright fee from recording artist or record company.
How to Contact: Submit demo tape by mail. Unsolicited submissions are OK. Prefers cassette with 1-4 songs and lyric sheet. SASE. Reports in 2 weeks.
Music: Mostly **R&B**, **pop** and **country**; also **gospel** and **dance**. Produced "I Had A Talk With My Man" (by Leonard Caston/Billy Davis), recorded by Novella Sweetbriar on Stackhouse Records; "Sly Like A Fox" (by Regine Urbach), recorded by Joy Harvey; and "Drifting Away" (by Maurice Mertoli/Phil Nelson), recorded by Heather Murphy, all on Coffee and Cream Records. Other artists include Michal Beckham, Robert Benjamin, Darrall Campbell, Elektra, Christopher Shirk, Ron Hevener, Tony Gilmore, Janine Whetstone, Kissie Darnell and Debra Spice.

COLLECTOR RECORDS, Box 2296, Rotterdam Holland 3000 CG **The Netherlands**. Phone: 186-604266. Fax: 186-604366. Research: Cees Klop. Record producer and music publisher (All Rock Music). Produces 2 singles and 30 CDs/year. Fee derived from outright fee from recording artist.
- See the listing for All Rock Music in the Music Publishers section.

How to Contact: Submit demo tape by mail. Unsolicited submissions are OK. Prefers cassette. SAE and IRC. Reports in 1-2 months.
Music: Mostly **'50s rock**, **rockabilly** and **country rock**; also **piano boogie woogie**. Produced *Boogie Woogie Bill*, written and recorded by Teddy Redell on Collector Records (rock); *Grand Hotel* (by Laurentis), recorded by Rockin' Vincent (rock); and *Coco Boogie*, written and recorded by Andre Valkering, both on Down South Records.

JOHNNY COPPIN/RED SKY RECORDS, P.O. Box 27, Stroud, Glos. GL6 0YQ **UK**. Phone: 01453-836877. Record producer, music publisher (PRS) and record company (Red Sky Records). Estab. 1985. Produces 2 albums/year. Fee derived from sales royalty when song or artist is recorded.
- Red Sky Records is also listed in the Record Companies section.

How to Contact: Write first and obtain permission to submit. Does not return material. Reports in 6 months.
Music: Mostly **rock**, **modern folk** and **roots music**. Produced "A Country Christmas" and "Keep the Flame" written and recorded by Johnny Coppin; and "Dead Lively!," written and recorded by Paul Burgess, all on Red Sky Records. Other artists include David Goodland.

DANO CORWIN, 5839 Silvercreek Rd., Azle TX 76020. (817)530-7942. Record producer, music video and sound production company. Estab. 1986. Produces 6 singles, 3 12" singles, 5 EPs and 2 CDs/year. Fee derived from sales royalty when song or artist is recorded.
How to Contact: Submit demo tape by mail. Unsolicited submissions are OK. Prefers cassette or VHS videocassette with 3 songs and lyric sheet. "Keep songs under 5 minutes. Only copyrighted material will be reviewed. Please do not send material without copyright notices." Does not return material. Reports in 4-6 weeks.
Music: Mostly **rock**; also **pop** and **dance**. Produced *Dimensions*, written and recorded by Silent Shame on MLM Records (rock); "Hello" (by W.J. Ross), recorded by RTIC; and "Early Dawn" (by T. Darren), recorded by Zeph, both on WW Records (rock). Other artists include Complete, Sir Gray Wolf and Drune.

COUNTRY STAR PRODUCTIONS, P.O. Box 569, Franklin PA 16323. (814)432-4633. President: Norman Kelly. Record producer, music publisher (Country Star Music/ASCAP, Kelly Music/BMI and Process Music/BMI) and record company (Country Star, Process, Mersey and CSI Records). Estab. 1970. Produces 5-8 singles and 5-8 LPs/year. Fee derived from sales royalty when song or artist is recorded.
How to Contact: Submit demo tape by mail. Unsolicited submissions are OK. Prefers cassette with 2-4 songs and typed lyric or lead sheet. SASE. Reports in 1-2 weeks.
Music: Mostly **country** (80%); also **rock** (5%), **MOR** (5%), **gospel** (5%) and **R&B** (5%). Produced "The Holiday Waltz" (by Wrightman/Stelzer), recorded by Debbie Soe; "Red Heifer" (by J. Barbaria), recorded by Bob Stamper, both on Country Star Records; and "Climbing Mountains" (by D. Delamar), recorded by Sugar Belle on Mersey Records. Other artists include Gary King, Junie Loo, Larry Pieper and Jeffrey Alan Connors.

CREATIVE MUSIC SERVICES, 953 Rainbow Trail, Orange CT 06477. Owner: Craig Calistro. Record producer. Estab. 1989. Produces 50 singles, 20 12" singles, 15 LPs and 15 CDs/year. Fee derived from sales royalty when song or artist is recorded or outright fee from recording artist or record company.
How to Contact: Submit demo tape by mail. Unsolicited submissions are OK. Prefers cassette or VHS videocassette and 1-3 songs and lyric and lead sheets. "Send photo if available." Does not return material. Reports in 3 weeks.
Music: Mostly **pop/top 40** and **dance**; also **jazz**. Produced "If I Had You," written and recorded by Brenda Z (pop); *Just Enough*, written and recorded by Raymond Smith (jazz); and "Losing You" (by Craig Calistro), recorded by Mary Willis (pop), all on Ace Records.

D.S.M. PRODUCERS, INC., 161 W. 54th St., New York NY 10019. (212)245-0006. Contact: Associate Producer. Record producer, music publisher and music library. Estab. 1979. Fee derived from sales royalty when song or artist is recorded.

- See D.S.M.'s listings in the Music Publishing and Advertising, AV and Commercial Music Firms sections.

How to Contact: Write first and obtain permission to submit. Prefers cassette or VHS videocassette with 2 songs and lyric or lead sheet. SASE. Reports in 1-3 months. "Must include an SASE for submission."
Music: All styles. Produced *DSM Tunes Vol. 2*, *Dance America Vol. 2* and *Rock America Vol. 2*, written and recorded by various artists on AACL Records.
Tips: "It's getting more difficult for an artist who cannot present a master demo to a label. You're going to need financing for your demos/masters, but it's worth having a professional studio produce your first demos as they do it for a living. They can help you become an established artist/songwriter. Invest in yourself, and when you have the right product, you will be heard and you're on your way to success. Be sure to title and label your submissions."

S. KWAKU DADDY, P.O. Box 424794, San Francisco CA 94142-4794. (707)769-9479. E-mail: skwaku@isc.web.com. President: S. Kwaku Daddy. Record producer and record company (African Heritage Records Co.). Produces 6 LPs/year. Fee derived from outright fee from record company.
How to Contact: Call first and obtain permission to submit. Prefers cassette. SASE. Reports in 3 weeks.
Music: Mostly **African pop**, **R&B** and **gospel**. Produced *Times of Change*, *Life's Rhythms* and *The Circle*, all written and recorded by S. Kwaku Daddy on African Heritage Records.
Tips: "Place emphasis on rhythm."

‡DALIVEN MUSIC, P.O. Box 398, Nolensville TN 37135. (615)776-5686. E-mail: daliven1@aol.com. Owner Operator: R. Steve Cochran. Record producer, music publisher. Produces 4 singles, 2 LPs and 2 CDs/year. Fee derived from sales royalty when song or artist is recorded, or outright fee from recording artist or record company.
How to Contact: Submit demo tape by mail. Unsolicited submissions are OK. Prefers cassette or videocassette with 3 songs and lyric or lead sheet. "Can also send standard MIDI files of songs." Does not return material. Reports in 2 months.
Music: Mostly **A/C**, **R&B** and **rock**; also **jazz**, **dance** and **country**. Produced *Not Rocket Science*, written and recorded by Tommy Hannum on Ciam Records (rock); *Dalia Mercedes*, written and recorded by Dalia Mercedes on Bravo Records (pop); and *Darn Blu's*, written and recorded by Darin Favorite on Amber Records (blues). Other artists include Rex Sigmon and Tim Veazey.

DANNY DARROW, 150 West End Ave., Suite 6-D, New York NY 10023. (212)873-5968. Manager: Danny Darrow. Record producer, music publisher (Rockford Music Co.) and record company (Mighty Records). Estab. 1958. Produces 1-2 singles, 1-2 12" singles and 1-2 LPs/year. Fee derived from sales royalty when song or artist is recorded.

- Danny Darrow's record company, Mighty Records, is listed in the Record Companies section, and the Rockford Music Co. is listed in the Music Publishers section.

How to Contact: Submit demo tape by mail. Unsolicited submissions are OK. "No phone calls." Prefers cassette with 3 songs and lyric sheet. SASE. Reports in 1-2 weeks.
Music: Mostly **pop**, **country** and **dance**; also **jazz**. Produced *Wonderland of Dreams* (by Danny Darrow); *Look to the Wind* (by Peggy Stewart/Danny Darrow); and *Corporate Lady* (by Michael Barry Greer), all recorded by Danny Darrow on Mighty Records.
Tips: "At present, looking for songs like 'How Am I Supposed to Live Without You.' This type only!"

DAVINCI'S NOTEBOOK RECORDS, (formerly Musicom Music Productions), 12-111 Fourth Ave., Suite 182, Ridley Square, St. Catharines Ontario L2S 3P5 **Canada**. (905)682-5161. E-mail: krh1616@vaxxine.com. Website: http://www.vaxxine.com/davincis. Owners: Kevin Hotte and Andy Smith. Record producer, record company, music publisher and MIDI recording facility. Estab. 1992. Produces 1 cassette and 1 CD/year. Fee derived from commission on sales.
How to Contact: Submit demo tape by mail. Unsolicited submissions are OK. Prefers cassette or CD with 4-6 songs and lyric or lead sheet. Does not return material. Reports in 4-6 weeks.
Music: Mostly **rock**, **New Age** and **progressive-alternative**; also **R&B**, **pop** and **jazz**. Produced *Windows* (by Kevin Hotte/Andy Smith), recorded by Musicom on DaVinci's Notebook Records (power New Age).
Tips: "Be honest, be professional, be specific. Dare to be different. Don't expect to be able to quit your day job. We offer limited exposure to a target audience in Canada (mainly Ontario). You might not make a fortune but you will get some exposure. We are new, independent, open minded and above all we are just like you. If you're contacting us as a result of seeing our listing in *Songwriter's Market*, we would like to know."

EDWARD DE MILES, 4475 Allisonville Rd., 8th Floor, Indianapolis IN 46205. (317)546-2912. President: Edward De Miles. Record producer, music publisher (Edward De Miles Music Co./BMI) and record company (Sahara Records). Estab. 1981. Produces 15-20 singles, 15-20 12″ singles, 5-10 LPs and 5-10 CDs/year. Fee derived from sales royalty when song or artist is recorded.

- See the listing for the Edward De Miles Music Co. in the Music Publishers section, as well as Sahara Records and Filmworks Entertainment in the Record Companies section.

How to Contact: Write first and obtain permission to submit. Prefers cassette or VHS or Beta ½″ videocassette with 1-3 songs and lyric sheet. Does not return material. Reports in 1 month.
Music: Mostly **R&B/dance**, **top 40 pop/rock** and **contemporary jazz**; also **country**, **TV and film themes—songs and jingles**. Produced "Hooked on U," "Dance Wit Me" and "Moments," (by S. Page), recorded by Steve Lynn (R&B) on Sahara Records. Other artists include D'von Edwards and Multiple Choice.
Tips: "Copyright all material before submitting. Equipment and showmanship a must."

DEEP SPACE RECORDS, 7560 Meadowlark Dr., Sebastopol CA 95472. (707)824-8145. E-mail: kf@dspacer.com. Owner/Producer: Kenn Fink. Record producer. Estab. 1985. Produces 3 singles and 1 LP/year. Fee derived from sales royalty when song or artist is recorded.
How to Contact: Write first and obtain permission to submit. Prefers cassette with 3-5 songs and lyric sheet. Does not return material. Reports in 2 months.
Music: Mostly **hard rock**, **electronic** (not necessarily New Age) and **blends of the two**. Produced *Lifesigns* and *Locked In The Basement* (by Kenn Fink), recorded by The Outcast on Deep Space Records (electronic/rock).

AL DELORY AND MUSIC MAKERS, 3000 Hillsboro Rd. #11, Nashville TN 37215. (615)292-2140. President: Al DeLory. Record producer and career consultant (DeLory Music/ASCAP). Estab. 1987. Fee derived from outright fee from recording artist or record company and career consultant fees.
How to Contact: Write or call first and obtain permission to arrange personal interview. Prefers cassette or VHS videocassette. Does not return material.
Music: Mostly **pop**, **country** and **Latin**. Produced "Gentle On My Mind," "By the Time I Get to Phoenix" and "Wichita Lineman," all recorded by Glen Campbell.

DEMI MONDE RECORDS & PUBLISHING LTD., Foel Studio, Llanfair Caereinion, Powys, SY21 ODS **Wales**. Phone/fax: 01938-810758. Managing Director: Dave Anderson. Record producer, music publisher (PRS & MCPS) and record company (Demi Monde Records). Estab. 1982. Produces 5 singles, 15 12″ singles, 15 LPs and 10 CDs/year. Fee derived from sales royalty or outright fee from record company.

- See Demi Monde's listings in the Music Publishers and Record Companies sections.

How to Contact: Submit demo tape by mail. Unsolicited submissions are OK. Prefers cassette with 3

or 4 songs and lyric sheet. Does not return material. Reports in 6 weeks.
Music: Mostly **rock**, **pop** and **blues**. Produced *Average Man*, recorded by Mother Gong (rock); *Frozen Ones*, recorded by Tangle Edge (rock); and *Blue Boar Blues* (by T.S. McPhee), recorded by Groundhogs (rock), all on Demi Monde Records. Other artists include Gong and Hawkwind.

COL. BUSTER DOSS PRESENTS, 341 Billy Goat Hill Rd., Winchester TN 37398. Producer: Col. Buster Doss. Fax: (615)649-2732. Record producer, record company (Stardust, Wizard), management firm and music publisher (Buster Doss Music/BMI). Estab. 1959. Produces 100 singles, 10 12″ singles, 20 LPs and 20 CDs/year. Fee derived from sales royalty when song or artist is recorded.

- Buster Doss's publishing company, Buster Doss Music, is listed in the Music Publishers section, his management firm, Col. Buster Doss Presents, is in the Managers and Booking Agents section, and his record label, Stardust, is listed under Record Companies.

How to Contact: Write or call first and obtain permission to submit. Prefers cassette with 2 songs and lyric sheet. SASE. Reports in 1 day if interested.
Music: Pop, **country** and **gospel**. Produced *The Man I Love* (by Buster Doss), recorded by Jerri Arnold; "Let's Go Dancing" (by Buster Doss), recorded by Mike "Doc" Holliday; and "You Can't Take Texas Out of Me" (by Barbara Doss), recorded by "Bronco" Buck Cody, all on Stardust Records. Other artists include R.B. Stone, Cliff Archer, Linda Wunder, Honey James, Don Sky, Shelly Streeter, Rooster Quantrell, Dwain Gamel, Donna Darlene and Jersey Outlaw.

DUANE MUSIC, INC., 382 Clarence Ave., Sunnyvale CA 94086. (408)739-6133. President: Garrie Thompson. Record producer and music publisher. Fee derived from sales royalty.

- See Duane Music's listing in the Music Publishers section.

How to Contact: Prefers cassette with 1-2 songs. SASE. Reports in 1 month.
Music: Blues, **country**, **rock**, **soul** and **top 40/pop**. Produced "Wichita" on Hush Records (country); and "Syndicate of Sound" on Buddah Records (rock).

J.D. DUDICK, 6472 Seven Mile, South Lyon MI 48178. Phone/fax: (810)486-0505. Producer: J.D. Dudick. Record producer, music publisher (Al-Ky Music) and record company (Ruffcut Productions). Estab. 1990. Produces 10 singles and 3 CDs/year. Fee derived from sales royalty when song or artist is recorded or outright fee from recording artist or record company.

- J.D. Dudick's publishing company, Al-Ky Music, is listed in the Music Publishers section, and his record label, Ruffcut Productions, is in the Record Companies section.

How to Contact: Submit demo tape by mail. Unsolicited submissions are OK. Prefers cassette or VHS videocassette with 3 songs and lyric sheet. Does not return material. Reports in 2 months.
Music: Mostly **modern rock**, **country rock** and **alternative**; also **funk/pop** and **country**. Produced *Something For Everyone* (by Bil Tol), recorded by Cidyzoo on Vehicle Garage Records (rock); *Mind Dust* (by Chris Pierce), recorded by "Q" (modern rock); and *Am I Different Enuf* (by Laya Phelps), recorded by Laya, both on Ruffcut Records.

‡DAVID DURR PRODUCTIONS, P.O. Box 644, Cameron SC 29030. Phone/fax: (803)823-2225. Owner: David Durr. Record producer, record company and music publisher (Co-Creations Music Publishing/BMI). Estab. 1993. Produces 2 LPs and 2 CDs/year. Fee is derived from sales royalty when song or artist is recorded, outright fee from recording artist, or consultations.
How to Contact: Write first and obtain permission to submit. Prefers cassette with 3 songs and lyric sheet. "Submissions for lyrics and songs need not be studio quality, but New Age music should be near the final product." Does not return material. Reports in 2 weeks.
Music: Mostly **New Age**, **jazz** and **spiritual/Christian**; also **traditional reggae**, **R&B/pop/rock** and **ballads/folk/country**. Produced *Calvin & Friends* (by various), recorded by Calvin Hunter (reggae); *I Wonder As I Wander* (by various), recorded by Benjamin Smoak (Christian), both on CRS Records; and *The Heart of Nature*, written and recorded by David Durr on CCMP Records (New Age). Other artists include Cyndy McKeowen (Christian) and Sajata Griddle (R&B).

TO HELP YOU UNDERSTAND and use the information in these listings, see "How to Use *Songwriter's Market* to Get Your Songs Heard," on page 3.

EARMARK AUDIO, P.O. Box 196, Vashon WA 98070. (206)463-1980. Owner: Jerry Hill. Record producer. Estab. 1991. Produces 3 cassettes and 3 CDs/year. Fee derived from outright fee from recording artist.

How to Contact: Submit demo tape by mail. Unsolicited submissions are OK. Prefers cassette or VHS videocassette with 1 song and lead sheet. Does not return material.

Music: Mostly **rock**, **polka**, **contemporary** and **country**. Produced *Across the Plains Polka* (by Vern Meisner), recorded by Lyle and Lynn Schaefer (polka); *Troubled Hero*, written and recorded by Peter Morrow (modern) on Vestige Records; and *True Vine* (by True Vine), recorded by Jay Munger (Christian rock). Other artists include Randy Greco, Julie Hanson, Sylvia Storaasli and Smelter/Neves.

LEO J. EIFFERT, JR., P.O. Box 5412, Buena Park CA 90620. (619)245-2920. Owner: Leo J. Eiffert, Jr. Record producer, music publisher (Eb-Tide Music/BMI, Young Country Music/BMI), management firm (Crawfish Productions) and record company (Plain Country). Estab. 1967. Produces 15-20 singles and 5 LPs/year. Fee derived from sales royalty when song or artist is recorded.

- Leo J. Eiffert, Jr.'s management firm, Crawfish Productions, is listed in the Managers and Booking Agents section.

How to Contact: Submit demo tape by mail. Unsolicited submissions are OK. Prefers cassette with 2-3 songs, lyric and lead sheet. SASE. Reports in 3-4 weeks.

Music: Mostly **country** and **gospel**. Produced "Daddy I Know," written and recorded by Pam Bellows on Plain Country Records; "Little Miss," written and recorded by Johnny Horton; and "My Friend," written and recorded by Leo J. Eiffert Jr., both on Young Country Records. Other artists include Homemade, Crawfish Band, Brandi Holland, Mary T. Eiffert and David Busson.

Tips: "Just keep it real country."

EIGHT BALL MIDI & VOCAL RECORDING, 1250 NE 33rd Court, Pompano Beach FL 33064. (305)785-5248. Studio/Production Manager: Peter Brown. Record producer, record company (8 Ball), engineer and demo facility. Estab. 1990. Produced 10-20 singles/year. Fee derived from sales royalty when song or artist is recorded or outright fee from recording artist or record company.

How to Contact: Write or call first to arrange personal interview. Prefers cassette or DAT with 3-5 songs and lyric sheet. "We're a small business and welcome phone calls from prospective clients. Let's talk before you submit material." Does not return material. Reports in 3-5 weeks.

Music: Mostly **R&B jazz crossover**, **global big band** and **ethnic/Latino/Middle Eastern**; also **pop/rock/fusion contemporary ballads**, **elemental/New Age** and **world music**. Produced "Another Sunny Day" (by Peter Brown), recorded by Eddie Ananias (pop); "Child of the '90s" (by Peter Brown) and "Familiar One" (by Daniel Micucci/Peter Brown), both recorded by Donna Peterson on 8 Ball Records. Other artists include Omar Mesa and Larry Prestage.

‡EJECT PRODUCTIONS, 13968 Toepfer, Warren MI 48089. Chief Producer: Eric Kilgore. Record producer. Produces 6 EPs and 2-4 CDs/year. Fee is derived from individual arrangements with artist.

How to Contact: Write first and obtain permission to submit. Prefers cassette with 1-3 songs and legibly printed lyric sheet. SASE. Reports in 6-8 weeks.

Music: Mostly **folk/rock**, **folk** and **acoustic rock**; also **novelty** and **hard to define style combinations**. Produced *Rantings Of A Fool* (by E. Kilgore), recorded by Jah Man Bob on Ejector Seat Records (ballads); *Unclassified Ads*, written and recorded by various artists; and *Acronymic*, written and recorded by Reductive Synthesis (industrial), both on Schizophrenic Records. Other artists include Pantheon June.

ESQUIRE INTERNATIONAL, P.O. Box 6032, Station B, Miami FL 33101-6032. (305)547-1424. President: Jeb Stuart. Record producer, music publisher (Jeb Stuart Music) and management firm. Produces 6 singles and 2 LPs/year. Fee derived from sales royalty or independent leasing of masters and placing songs.

- Esquire International's publishing company, Jeb Stuart Music, has a listing in the Music Publishers section.

How to Contact: Submit demo tape by mail. Unsolicited submissions are OK. Prefers cassette or CD with 2-4 songs and lead sheet. SASE. Reports in 1 month.

Music: **Blues**, **church/religious**, **country**, **dance**, **gospel**, **jazz**, **rock**, **soul** and **top 40/pop**. Produced "Go to Sleep, Little Baby" (by Jeb Stuart), recorded by Cafidia and Jeb Stuart; "Guns Guns (No More Guns)" and "No One Should Be Alone on Christmas," both written and recorded by Jeb Stuart, all on Esquire Int'l Records. Other artists include Moments Notice and Night Live.

THE ETERNAL SONG AGENCY, 6326 E. Livingston Ave., Suite 153, Reynoldsburg OH 43068. (614)834-1272. Executive Producer: Leopold Xavier Crawford. Record producer, record company and

music publisher (Fragrance Records, Song of Solomon Records, Emerald Records, Lilly Records Ancient of Days Music, Anastacia Music). Estab. 1986. Produces 7-15 singles and 5 CDs/year. Fee derived from sales royalty when song or artist is recorded or outright fee from recording artist or record company.
How to Contact: Write first and obtain permission to submit. Prefers cassette or videocassette with 3 songs and lyric or lead sheet. "Send complete biography, pictures, tape. Type all printed material. Professionalism of presentation will get you an ear with us." SASE. Reports in 4-6 weeks.
Music: Mostly **pop music/top 40**, **country** and **instrumental**; also **contemporary Christian**, **Christian inspirational** and **southern gospel music**. Produced "Walking Out," written and recorded by Leopold Crawford; "Saul," written and recorded by Michael Higgins; and "Drink" (by Leopold Crawford), recorded by Streets of Gold, all on Fragrance Records. Other artists include Bloodbought, Yolanda Stewart, Greg Whightsell, Lynn Holloway and Seventh Dynasty.

‡FRANK D. FAGNANO, 413 Park Ave., Fairview NJ 07022-1116. (201)941-8528. Fax: (201)941-4856. E-mail: frankdf@aol.com. Contact: Frank D. Fagnano. Record producer and engineer. Produces 5 CDs/year. Fee is negotiated based on size of project.
How to Contact: Submit demo tape by mail. Unsolicited submissions are OK. Prefers cassette, DAT, VHS videocassette or CD with 1-4 songs and lyric sheet (preferred but not mandatory). "Send small cover letter indicating intentions (i.e., record deal, immediate/long term requirements, market targeting). Do you require engineering, production, co-writing or arranging assistance, lyric assistance?" Does not return material. Reports in 2-4 weeks.
Music: Mostly **rock** and **acoustic** or **electric jazz**; also **electronic/experimental**, **ethnic/world music** and **spoken word**. Produced *IDK*, recorded by IDK on Bush League Records (rock); *Closing of the Year*, recorded by Bill McKinley on Sunday's Child Records (jazz vocal); and *3/3*, recorded by Truthcircle on Airquake Records (rock). Other artists include Surrey Lane, Jennifer Hexney, Ralph Brande, Charles Cermele, Repeat After Me, Mr. Foote, Delforno, Hans und Rolf Sturm and Mary's Magnet.

DANNY FEDERICI'S SHARK RIVER MUSIC, 421 N. Rodeo Dr., Suite 15-5, Beverly Hills CA 90210. Phone/fax: (714)821-1810. E-mail: danny@deadeye.com. President: Danny Federici. Record producer, music publisher and new artist development/management. Estab. 1994. Fee derived from sales royalty when song or artist is recorded.
How to Contact: Write first and obtain permission to submit. Prefers cassette, DAT or VHS videocassette with 3 songs, lyric sheet and performer(s) bio. "Include address and phone of contact person and SASE. Please copyright material." Does not return material. Reports in 3-4 weeks.
Music: Mostly **rock, country** and **R&B/soul**; also **alternative** and **New Age**.
Tips: "You must have a strong desire to succeed in this business and be willing to use the constructive criticism of others to achieve that success. As founding member of the E Street Band, Danny Federici's years of recording and touring with Bruce Springsteen and others have given him experience, expertise and insight into all facets of the music business."

VITO FERA PRODUCTIONS, 345 Sprucewood Rd., Lake Mary FL 32746-5917. (407)321-3702. Fax: (407)321-2361. Website: http://spotnet.com/spin. President, A&R: Vito Fera. Office Manager: Rhonda Fera. Record producer, music publisher (NSP Publishing/ASCAP, Fera Music Publishing/BMI). Estab. 1980. Produces 5 singles, 1 LP and 4 EPs/year. Fee derived from sales royalty when song or artist is recorded.

- Vito Fera's publishing company, NSP Publishing, can be found in the Music Publishers section.

How to Contact: Submit demo tape by mail. Unsolicited submissions are OK. Prefers cassette or VHS videocassette with 3 songs maximum and lyric sheet. "Package song material carefully. To avoid damage to your tape, stamp or write *Please Hand Cancel* on the package. Always label (name, address and phone) both cassette and lyric sheets. Bio and photo helpful." SASE. Reports in 4-8 weeks.
Music: Mostly **jazz**, **R&B** and **rock/light**; also **children's**, **Christian** and **soundtracks**. Produced "The Magic is Hot" (by Vito Fera), recorded by The Neighbors (rock); "Two Can Play Your Game" (by M.L. Wolfgang/V. Fera), recorded by Judy Soto (country); and "Summer Dream" (by Jim Ivins) recorded by Zaughn Ivins (ballad), all on Spin Records. Other artists include Steve Clarke, Kari Regragui, Keith Hilley and Jerry Dean.
Tips: "Have songs that tell stories with simple hook lines and memorable melodies."

FINAL MIX MUSIC, 2219 W. Olive Ave., Suite 102, Burbank CA 91506. (818)840-9000. Contact: Rob Chiarelli. Record producer/remixer/mix engineer, record company (Metro Beat Records) and music publisher (Roachi World Music). Estab. 1989. Releases 12 singles, 3-5 LPs and 3-5 CDs/year. Fee derived from sales royalty when song or artist is recorded or outright fee from record company.

- See the interview with producer Rob Chiarelli in this section.

How to Contact: Submit demo tape by mail. Unsolicited submissions are OK. Prefers cassette with 3

INSIDER REPORT

It's all in the melody, says producer Rob Chiarelli

Rob Chiarelli

"A good song has all the elements—good lyrics, melody and harmonic structure," says producer Rob Chiarelli of Final Mix Music. "A lot of music today is rhythmic-based. The rhythm is important, of course, but it always comes down to the melody for me. A truly great song is one you can sit down at a piano and sing."

Chiarelli may be best known in the industry for his mixing and remixing skills. He's worked with a broad range of talents including R&B, pop, jazz and rap artists such as Coolio, Heavy D., Jodeci, Bobby Brown and Monifah. He works closely with the artists and producers to enhance songs and flavor them to fit different styles, crossing over from pop to urban and vice versa. Background elements can be changed, he says, but the melody usually remains intact. "Most successful producers and artists have great song ears," Chiarelli explains. "You can change the rhythmic undercurrent of a song, but great melodies always stay the same." Lyrics are vital, too. "You can always fix the beat, but trite lyrics will kill a song. When you get good lyrics and melody together, that's a defining moment."

Chiarelli warns that one mistake inexperienced songwriters make is sending their songs to labels or artists without first doing research. "Know who you are sending your work to. When I work with an artist, I try to know the artist's past so I know where the artist is coming from. It helps me to see where we might want to go."

This is very important for songwriters, he says. "It's so basic—if you are going to send a song to someone, make sure it's really for them. I've gotten demos that are way off the mark and this really hurts the songwriter's credibility.

"Songwriters also need to be students of the art. You have to be aware of more than just the piece [you are working on at the time]. An artist doesn't just grab a paint brush and paint a picture, he gets to know his subject first. You need to have a passion for the art, for the craft of writing songs.

"A lot of people are about 80 percent there, but they haven't really scrutinized their work. You need to ask yourself, 'Is this the best way I could say this? Is this the best melody?' A song has to take you somewhere and to get there, you must go back and refine, analyze every line. Those people whose songs I see on the charts over and over again are those who put in that extra 10 percent."

Another mistake songwriters make, says Chiarelli, is trying to sell more than the song. Some try to sell the artist singing on the demo as well. "If someone's trying to sell a song, that's what they should be doing. You've got to get the essence of the song on tape. Some people use singers who sound like the artist for whom the song is meant; this is not a bad idea but I'd say it's rarely necessary. I happen to like demos from songwriters singing

INSIDER REPORT, *Chiarelli*

their own songs. Even if they're out of tune a little, they know where the song is coming from. I love to get tapes from people who just say, 'Do you like this song?' or 'Would this be a good song for one of your artists?' "

Some songwriters tend to go overboard with production, he adds. "A lot of songs are hurt by overproduction. That's a big mistake. With all the crazy production in some tapes, it's hard to hear through it. Everyone has access to keyboards and other equipment these days, but the technology should help the art, not overwhelm it."

Songwriters, he says, should also be open to advice. "I do believe songwriting is an art and you shouldn't make changes in your art if it makes you feel uncomfortable. But, if the artist really likes the song, but asks for a couple of changes, as long as they are reasonable you should consider it. Don't be over-sensitive. After all, it's the artist's record—the cover has the artist's name on it, the artist's face, the rest of us are the support team."

When it comes to publishing rights, Chiarelli warns songwriters to be wary. He has a small publishing operation, but says he does not make a living from shopping other people's songs. "I may make a connection for someone and sometimes I publish or offer a co-publishing arrangement, but not often. I have agreements with my artists so I can afford to help promote a song, but I consider it a necessary evil. In this business there are some people who will try to grab everything. For writers, remember publishing is yours to give, not theirs to take. On the other hand, it doesn't mean you should be foolhardy about it and pass up a good deal. It depends on your situation."

One piece of advice Chiarelli says he wishes he had heeded a lot earlier in his career is "you have to be where it is. It's very hard not being in L.A. or New York where you'd be in the studio meeting others doing the same thing, collaborating, hearing about other opportunities. I hate to say this but that's hard to do in Flint, Michigan."

On the other hand, he says, "I'd never want to tell someone to move if they are not prepared for it. But, no matter where you are, when you get into a room with other creative people, whether they are artists, writers, vocalists or musicians, it adds a whole new factor, a new element comes into play. Other great talents can push you. There are so many great collaborations between artists and producers or lyricists and those who write melodies. Musically speaking, any creative environment can help you grow."

The industry overall is changing, he says. "Finally, melodies are coming back. I'm seeing less sampling of songs. That seems to have tapered off a bit. Now I'm hearing great melodies, real instruments and real people playing them. I predict we're going to be hearing a lot more great melodies instead of clever little sound bites. It used to be who's got the cool sounds, now it's who's got the cool songs. And I think this will keep going. There are going to be many more great songs coming along and I can't wait to hear them!"

—Robin Gee

songs. "No lyric sheets, no pictures or bios. Just the cassette. Have titles, artist and contact info printed on cassette."

Music: Dance, R&B and **rap**. Discography includes K-Ci and Jo Jo (of Zhané), Will Smith, Bobby Brown, Janet Jackson, Ice Cube, Queen Latifah, En Vogue, Naughty By Nature, Too Short, Boyz II Men, Dana Dane and Spice 1.

BOB SCOTT FRICK, 404 Bluegrass Ave., Madison TN 37115. (615)865-6380. Contact: Bob Scott Frick. Record producer, management firm, record company (R.E.F. Records) and music publisher (Frick

Music Publishing). Estab. 1958. Produces 12 singles, 30 12″ singles and 30 LPs. Fee derived from sales royalty when song or artist is recorded.

• Frick Music Publishing can be found in the Music Publishers section, Bob Scott Frick Enterprises is in the Managers and Booking Agents section and R.E.F. Records can be found in the Record Companies section.

How to Contact: Submit demo tape by mail. Unsolicited submissions are OK. Does not return material. Reports in 2 weeks.

Music: Produced "I Found Jesus in Nashville," recorded by Bob Scott Frick; "Love Divine," recorded by Backwoods; and "A Tribute," recorded by Visionheirs on R.E.F. (gospel). Other artists include Larry Ahlborn, Bob Myers Family, David Barton, The Mattingleys, Partners In Praise and Jim Pommert.

JACK GALE, P.O. Box 630755, Miami FL 33163. (305)935-4880. Fax: (305)933-4007. Contact: Jack Gale. Record producer, music publisher (Cowabonga Music/ASCAP, Lovey Music) and record company (Playback Records). Estab. 1983. Produces 48 singles and 20 CDs/year. Fee derived from sales royalty when song or artist is recorded.

• Jack Gale's publishing company, Lovey Music, can be found in the Music Publishers section, and his record label, Playback, is listed in the Record Companies section.

How to Contact: Submit demo tape by mail. Unsolicited submissions are OK. Prefers cassette or VHS videocassette with 2 songs maximum and lyric sheet. Does not return material. Reports in 2 weeks if interested.

Music: Mostly **contemporary country** and **country crossover**. Produced "Take This Job and Shove It" (by David Allen Coe), recorded by Johnny Paycheck (country); *Makin' Music* (by J. Barnes), recorded by Willie Nelson/Charlie Louvin/Waylon Jennings (country); and "Guess Things Happen That Way" (by Jack Clements), recorded by Johnny Cash/Tommy Cash (country), all on Playback Records. Other artists include Jeannine C. Riley, Melba Montgomery, Cleve Francis, Ernie Ashworth, Riley Coyle, David Frizzell, Margo Smith, Sammi Smith and Del Reeves.

‡GALLWAY BAY MUSIC, 690 Greenwich St. #2A, New York NY 10014. (212)255-9710. E-mail: gallbay@aol.com. Contact: Peter Gallway. Record producer and production company. Estab. 1983. Produces 4-5 CDs/year. Fee derived from sales royalty when song or artist is recorded or outright fee from recording artist or record company.

How to Contact: Write first and obtain permission to submit. Prefers cassette or DAT with 4 songs. Does not return material. Reports in 1 month.

Music: Great songwriters of all kinds specializing in **contemporary folk** and **alternative pop**. Produced *Mona Lisa Cafe*, written and recorded by Cliff Eberhardt on Shanachie Records (folk/pop); *Industrial Twilight*, written and recorded by Devon Square on DEV Records (folk/pop); *Titanic*, recorded by Jim Infantino on Gadfly Records (alternative/folk); and *Time and Love (the music of Laura Nyro)*, featuring Suzanne Vega, Rosanne Cash, Jane Siberry, Jonatha Brooke and 10 other contemporary women artists, on Astor Place Records.

‡GLASS HOUSE PRODUCTIONS, P.O. Box 602, Columbus IN 47202. (812)375-9362. Fax: (812)372-3985. E-mail: suzrock@hsonline.net. Executive Producer: Suzanne Glass. Producer, engineer: Paul Bultman. Producer, arranger: Patrick Ruffner. Record producer, record company (Throwing Stones Records), music publisher and management firm. Estab. 1989. Produces 20 singles, 10 LPs, 10 EPs and 10 CDs/year. Fee is negotiable.

• Glass House's record label, Throwing Stones Records, has a listing in the Record Companies section.

How to Contact: Write first and obtain permission to submit. Prefers cassette and promo materials with 3 songs and lyric sheet. "Include SAS query card when writing for permission and short cover letter." Does not return material. Reports in 1 month (depends on work load).

Music: Mostly **alternative**, **rock (all types)**, **pop** and **acoustic**; also **blues**, **women's** and **all types**. Produced *Fallen Empire*, written and recorded by Fallen Empire (rock); *Guilty By Association*, written and recorded by Suzanne Glass (acoustic rock), both on Throwing Stones Records; and *No Flowers* (by M. Askern), recorded by No Flowers (alternative). Other artists include Jr. Lewis, Sacred Project, File 13, Dale Sechrest, Lonesome & Blue, Giggin' Fer God, Planet Caravan, Leigacy, Torment and Here & Gone.

Tips: "Be professional, timely, courteous and act with integrity. Work with us, not against. Don't have a closed mind on arrangements, listen to suggestions. Gig alot, learn the business well enough to communicate, and focus on your art. If you've got talent and desire, contact us; we can help you succeed. Mostly interested in artists/bands from our region of the country."

‡GUERILLA AUDIO, 1307 Corona Dr., Austin TX 78723. Phone/fax: (512)302-4724. E-mail: imix4u@pemail.com. Owner/engineer: Mike Cohn. Record producer and recording studio. Estab. 1993. Fee derived from outright fee from recording artist or record company.
How to Contact: Submit demo tape by mail. Unsolicited submissions are OK. Prefers cassette, DAT or CD. SASE. Reports in 2 weeks.
Music: Mostly **rock**, **country** and **alternative**. Produced *Hunk Papa* (by Ted Richardson), recorded by Hunk Papa on Milk Boy Records (alternative).

HAILING FREQUENCY MUSIC PRODUCTIONS, 7438 Shoshone Ave., Van Nuys CA 91406. (818)881-9888. Fax: (818)881-0555. E-mail: blowin@jukejoint.com. President: Lawrence Weisberg. Record producer, record company (Blowin' Smoke Records), management firm (Blowin' Smoke Productions) and music publisher (Hailing Frequency Publishing). Estab. 1992. Produces 3 LPs and 3 CDs/year. Fee derived from sales royalty when song or artist is recorded or outright fee from artist.
● See the listing for Blowin' Smoke Productions in the Managers and Booking Agents section.
How to Contact: Write or call first and obtain permission to submit. Prefers cassette or VHS ½" videocassette. "Write or print legibly with complete contact instructions." SASE. Reports in 3-4 weeks.
Music: Mostly **contemporary R&B**, **blues** and **blues-rock**; also **songs for film**, **jingles for commercials** and **gospel (contemporary)**. Produced *Get the Urge!* (by Mark Will/Larry Knight), recorded by The Urge (alternative); *Bayou Blues* (by various), recorded by Carolyn Basley (blues/R&B); and *Too Hot!* (by Larry Knight/Aina Olsen), recorded by Larry Knight (R&B), all on Blowin' Smoke Records. Other artists include Christina Vierra and the Fabulous Smokettes.

HARLOW SOUND, 31 Harlow Crescent, Rexdale, Ontario M9V 2Y6 **Canada**. (416)741-5007. Owner/Engineer: Gregory English. Record producer and recording studio. Estab. 1984. Produces 15-25 CDs/year. Fees derived from outright fee from recording artist.
How to Contact: Write or call first to arrange personal interview. Prefers cassette or DAT with 3-5 songs. SAE and IRC. Reports in 1-3 weeks.
Music: Produced *Sing or Die*, written and recorded by Courage of Lassie; *Beyond 7*, written and recorded by Gordon Deppe; and *Random Order*, written and recorded by Random Order. Other artists include Viciousphere, Andy Curren and Universal Honey.
Tips: "Be prepared for changes. Example: have three or four different choruses for any given song and be willing to try different things in the studio."

‡HARMONY ALLEY AUDIO CO., 2025 Tyler St., Hollywood FL 33020. (954)922-4770. (954)921-9894. E-mail: songcoach@aol.com. Vice President of A&R: Jules Lynn. Record producer and music publisher (Reel Harmony Music Publishing Co./BMI). Estab. 1986. Produces 6 singles, 4 LPs and 10 CDs/year. Fee derived from sales royalty when song or artist is recorded, or outright fee from recording artist or record company.
How to Contact: Call first and obtain permission to submit. Prefers cassette, DAT or VHS videocassette. SASE. Reports in 3 weeks.
Music: Mostly **rock** and **country**; also **contemporary pop**. Produced *Katie P. Jones* (by various), recorded by Katie P. Jones (country); "Looking for Pancho Villa," written and recorded by Benji Brumberg (rock); and *One-You*, written and recorded by Robert Whagneux (rock). Other artists include Michael Stanley, Joe Walsh, the Eagles, Bob Seger and the Bee Gees.

HEART CONSORT MUSIC, 410 First St. W., Mt. Vernon IA 52314. (319)895-8557. Manager: Catherine Lawson. Record producer, record company and music publisher. Estab. 1980. Produces 2-3 CDs/year. Fee derived from sales royalty when song or artist is recorded.
How to Contact: Submit demo tape by mail. Unsolicited submissions are OK. Prefers cassette or VHS videocassette with 3 songs and 3 lyric sheets. SASE. Reports in 3 months.
Music: Mostly **jazz**, **New Age** and **contemporary**. Produced *Elena*, *Pachyderm* and *Time Will Tell*, all written and recorded by James Kennedy on Heart Consort Music (world/jazz).
Tips: "We are interested in jazz/New Age artists with quality demos and original ideas. We aim for an international market."

‡BRAD HECK, P.O. Box 355, Ogden IA 50212. (515)275-2885. Producer: Brad Heck. Estab. 1993. Produces 20 CDs/year. Fee derived from outright fee from recording artist or record company.
How to Contact: Write first and obtain permission to submit. Prefers cassette with 3 songs and lyric sheet. Does not return material. Reports in 2 weeks.
Music: Mostly **country**, **rock** and **alternative**; also **instrumental**, **techno** and **jazz**. Produced *Hiway*, written and recorded by Jason Reed (country); *Cars Don't Rust*, written and recorded by Junior's Army

(techno), both on Junior's Motel Records; and *Meerkats*, written and recorded by Meerkats on Oar Fin Records (alternative). Other artists include 6240, Radio Caroline, Charles Cort, Flipp, Curbfeelers, Dare Force, Hookers Farm and Larry Myer.

HICKORY LANE PUBLISHING AND RECORDING, P.O. Box 2275, Vancouver, British Columbia V6B 3W5 **Canada**. (604)987-3756. Fax: (604)987-0616. E-mail: curban4048@gnn.com. President: Chris Michaels. A&R Manager: David Rogers. Record producer, record company and music publisher. Estab. 1988. Fee derived from sales royalty when song or artist is recorded.

- See Hickory Lane's listing in the Music Publishers section.

How to Contact: Submit demo tape by mail. Unsolicited submissions are OK. Prefers cassette or VHS videocassette with 1-5 songs and lyric or lead sheet if available. SAE and IRC. Reports in 4-6 weeks.
Music: Country. Produced "Country Drives Me Wild," recorded by Chris Michaels on Hickory Lane Records; and "Until Now," recorded by Chris Michaels.
Tips: "Send only original material, send your best. Keep vocals up front and make a professional presentation. Be patient."

HORRIGAN PRODUCTIONS, 26591 Briarwood Lane, San Juan Capistrano CA 92675. (714)347-8316. E-mail: thisbox@tia.net. President/Owner: Tim Horrigan. Record producer and music publisher (Buck Young Music/BMI). Estab. 1982. Produces 5-10 singles, 3-5 LPs, 3-5 EPs and 3-5 CDs/year. Fee derived from outright fee from recording artist or record company. "We do some work on spec but the majority of the time we work on a work-for-hire basis."
How to Contact: Submit demo tape by mail. Unsolicited submissions are OK. Prefers cassette or VHS videocassette with 1-3 songs and lyric sheets. SASE. "Please do not call first; just let your music do the talking. Will reply in 4-8 weeks if interested."
Music: Mostly **pop**, **rock** and **country**. Produced *Silly Willy Moves Through the ABCs*, recorded by Brenda Colgate (children's); "Let it Shine" and *Too Much Fun!*, written and recorded by Jim Rule (children's). Other artists include Michael Silversher, Patti Shannon and Johnny Legend (rockabilly).

‡HOT SOUND PRODUCTIONS, 130 W. 25th St., New York NY 10001. (212)243-0098. Fax: (212)929-2193. Producer Representative: Bob Brophy. Record producer and commercial recording studio. Estab. 1990. Produces 8-10 singles and 5-6 cassettes/year. Fee is derived from outright fee from recording artist.
How to Contact: Submit demo tape by mail. Unsolicited submissions are OK. Prefers cassette with 3-5 songs and lyric sheet. Does not return material. Reports in 3 weeks.
Music: Mostly **rock**, **pop** and **jazz**; also **country**.

HOUSE OF RHYTHM, 12403 Ventura Court, Suite G, Studio City CA 91604. (818)980-8887. Fax: (818)980-9111. President: Stuart Wiener. Producer: Mike Jett. Record producer and production company. Estab. 1991. Produces 3-5 singles, 3-5 12″ singles, 2 LPs, 2 EPs and 2 CDs/year. Fee derived from sales royalty when song or artist is recorded.
How to Contact: Submit demo tape by mail. Unsolicited submissions are OK. Prefers cassette with 3 songs and lyric sheet. "Do not call to follow up; if we like it we will call you." SASE. Reports in 1 month.
Music: Mostly **dance**, **pop**, **R&B** and **rock**; also **new artists** and **new producers**. Produced "The Truth" (by Mike Nally), recorded by SYSTM X on Innerkore Records (dance); "Nasty Groove" and "Lift Em" (by Mike Jett), both recorded by Cold Automatic Eyes on Crap Records (dance). Other artists include Natasha, Richard Grieco and L'Simone.

‡INTEGRATED ENTERTAINMENT, 2300 Walnut St. #321, Philadelphia PA 19103. (215)977-9339. E-mail: gelboni@aol.com. President: Lawrence Gelburd. Record producer. Estab. 1991. Produces 6 EPs and 6 CDs/year. Fee derived from sales royalty when song or artist is recorded, outright fee from recording artist or record company.
How to Contact: Submit demo tape by mail. Unsolicited submissions are OK. Prefers cassette or CD with 3 songs. "Draw a guitar on the outside of envelope so we'll know it's from a songwriter." SASE. Reports in 2 months.
Music: Mostly **rock** and **AAA**. Produced *Gold Record*, written and recorded by Dash Rip Rock on Ichiban Records (rock); *Virus*, written and recorded by Margin of Error on Treehouse Records (modern rock); and *I Divide*, written and recorded by Amy Carr on Evil Twin Records (AAA). Other artists include Land of the Blind, Grimace, Harpoon, Sprawl, Lockdown and Tripe.

INTRIGUE PRODUCTION, 6245 Bristol Pkwy., Suite 206, Culver CA 90230. (213)417-3084, ext. 206. Producer: Larry McGee. Record producer, music publisher (Operation Perfection), management firm

(LMP Management Firm) and record company (Boogie Band Records). Estab. 1986. Produces 6 singles, 3 12″ singles, 1 LP, 4 EPs and 2 CDs/year. Fee derived from sales royalty when song or artist is recorded.

• See the listings for Operation Perfection in the Music Publishers section, Boogie Band Records in the Record Companies section and LMP Management Firm in the Managers and Booking Agents section.

How to Contact: Submit demo tape by mail. Unsolicited submissions are OK. Prefers cassette, reel-to-reel or VHS videocassette with 1-4 songs and lyric sheets. "Please put your strongest performance upfront. Select material based on other person's opinions." SASE. Reports in 2 months.

Music: Mostly **R&B**, **pop**, **rap** and **rock**; also **dance** and **A/C**. Produced "Starflower" (by Joe Cacamisse), recorded by Starflower (A/C); "Too Tough" (by Terrence Jones), recorded by En-Tux (pop); and "Got It Going On" (by Alan Walker), recorded by Executives (R&B), all on Cross-Over Records. Other artists include Wali Ali, A. Vis and Denise Parker.

IVORY PRODUCTIONS, INC., 212 N. 12th St., Suite #3, Philadelphia PA 19107. (215)977-9777. Fax: (215)569-4939. E-mail: ivory@phat.com. Website: http://ikonman.com. Contact: David Ivory. Record producer, record company and music publisher. Estab. 1986. Produces 10 CDs/year. Fee derived from "varying proportions of outright fee and royalties."

• See the listing for Ikon Records in the Record Companies section and RNR Publishing in the Music Publishers section.

How to Contact: Call or write first and obtain permission to submit. Prefers cassette with 3 songs. SASE. Reports in 6-8 weeks.

Music: Mostly **rock** and **pop**. Produced *Excess In Moderation*, written and recorded by Pat Godwin on Blood Records (rock); *Tony White*, written and recorded by Tony White on D.A. Music (jazz); and "Do You Want More?," written and recorded by The Roots on Geffen Records. Other artists include Steve LaRocca & Billy Freeze, Jimmy Bruno, The Spelvins, Crossbone Pie, Don Himlin, Iota, Do Or Die, Slide, The Peaks, O.M.S.F., Load, Love Revolution and Black Harvest.

NEAL JAMES PRODUCTIONS, P.O. Box 121626, Nashville TN 37212. (615)726-3556. President: Neal James. Record producer, music publisher (Cottage Blue Music/BMI, Neal James Music/BMI), management firm (James Gang Management) and record company (Kottage Records). Estab. 1971. Produces 16 singles and 4 CDs and LPs/year. Fee derived from sales royalty when song or artist is recorded or outright fee from recording artist or record company.

• Neal James' publishing company, Cottage Blue Music, is listed in the Music Publishers section, his record label, Kottage Records, is listed in the Record Companies section and his management firm, James Gang Management, is listed in the Managers and Booking Agents section.

How to Contact: Submit demo tape by mail. Unsolicited submissions are OK. Prefers cassette or VHS videocassette with 2 songs and lyric sheet. SASE. Reports in 1 month.

Music: Mostly **country**, **pop/rock** and **R&B**; also **gospel**, **alternative** and **blues**. Produced *A Woman's Place* (by Jim Weatherly/Jeff Tweel), recorded by Terry Barbay on Kottage Records (country); *Do You Want Paradise*, written and recorded by Allusion on Crosswind Records (alternative rock); and "Searching For Home," written and recorded by Davis James on Alternative Records (rock). Other artists include Allen Hayes, Alan Height, Taylor Reed Band, Allusion Band, Artica and Bill Fraser.

SUNNY JAMES, 1051 Saxonburg Blvd., Glenshaw PA 15116. (412)487-6565. E-mail: marcels@earthlink.net. Producer: Sunny James. Record producer, music publisher and record company (Golden Triangle). Estab. 1987. Produces 2 singles, 8 12″ singles and 9 CDs/year. Fee derived from sales royalty when song or artist is recorded.

• See the listing for Golden Triangle Records in the Record Companies section.

How to Contact: Submit demo tape by mail. Unsolicited submissions are OK. Prefers cassette, 15 ips reel-to-reel or ½″ VHS videocassette with 3 songs and lyric or lead sheet. SASE. Reports in 1 month.

Music: Mostly **R&B**, **country** and **rock**; also **A/C** and **jazz**. Produced *Over the Rainbow* and "You Don't Have to Cry Anymore," by The Marcels on Golden Triangle Records; and "Slippery Rocks," written and recorded by Robin Cvetnick on Rockin' Robin Records. Other artists include Bobby Wayne (Atlantic Records), Steve Grice (The Boxtops), Bingo Mundy, Cornelius Harp, Fred Johnson, Richard Knauss, Brian (Badfinger) McClain and City Heat.

ALEXANDER JANOULIS PRODUCTIONS/BIG AL JANO PRODUCTIONS, 1957 Kilburn Dr., Atlanta GA 30324. (404)662-6661. CEO: Alex Janoulis. Record producer and record company (Hottrax Records). Produces 6 singles and 2 CDs/year. Fee derived from sales royalty or outright fee from recording artist or record company.

• See the listing for Hottrax Records in the Record Companies section.

How to Contact: Write first and obtain permission to submit. "Letters should be short, requesting

submission permission." Prefers cassette with 1-3 songs. Does not return material. Reports in 6-12 weeks.
Music: Mostly **top 40**, **rock** and **pop**; also **black** and **disco**. Produced *Real Time* (by Bill Sheffield/Liane Webb), recorded by Sheffield-Webb (roots rock); *Stuck in Bluesville*, written and recorded by Sammy Blue (blues); and *Vol. 2: The Little Phil Era* (by various), recorded by The Night Shadows (top 40 rock), all on Hottrax Records. Other artists include Diamond Lil, The Bop, Butch Trivette and Danny Deese.

JANUS MANAGEMENT, 54A Brookmount Rd., Toronto Ontario M4L 3N2 **Canada**. Phone/fax: (416)698-6581. E-mail: janus@passport.ca. Producer/Engineer: Nick Blagona. Record producer. Estab. 1991. Produces 8 cassettes, 2 EPs, 6 CDs/year. Fee derived from outright fee from recording artist or record company.
How to Contact: Submit demo tape by mail. Unsolicited submissions are OK. Prefers cassette, DAT or VHS videocassette, promotional materials and lyric/lead sheet (if applicable). "Please include all applicable lyrics (typed)." SAE and IRC. Reports in 4-6 weeks.
Music: Mostly **rock**, **jazz** and **folk**; also **classical** and **filmscoring**. Produced *Toronto Tabla Ensemble* (by Ritesh Das), recorded by Toronto Tabla Ensemble on Festival Records (world); *Paint*, written and recorded by Phinger; and *Singing Naked*, written and recorded by G. Koller/J. Michels (jazz). Other artists include Deep Purple, Kim Mitchell, April Wine, Streetheart and Boys Brigade.

JAY JAY PUBLISHING & RECORD CO., 35 NE 62nd St., Miami FL 33138. (305)758-0000. Owner: Walter Jagiello. Record producer, music publisher (BMI) and record company (Jay Jay Record, Tape and Video Co.). Estab. 1951. Produces 12 singles, 12 LPs and 12 CDs/year. Fee derived from sales royalty when song or artist is recorded.
How to Contact: Submit demo tape by mail. Unsolicited submissions are OK. Prefers cassette or VHS videocassette with 6 songs and lyric and lead sheet. "Quality cassette or reel-to-reel, sheet music and lyrics." SASE. Reports in 3 months.
Music: Mostly **ballads, love songs**, **country music** and **comedy**; also **polkas** and **waltzes**. Produced "Feel Good," *18 Beautiful Polish Songs*, and "Happy Times" (by W.E. Jagiello), recorded by Li'L Wally, all on Jay Jay Records. Other artists include Mil-Eu Duo, Eddie Kuta and Orchestra.

JAZMIN PRODUCTIONS, P.O. Box 92913, Long Beach CA 90809. E-mail: jazminpro@aol.com. Owner/Producer: Gregory D. Dendy. Record producer. Estab. 1991. Produces 2-4 LPs/year. Fee derived from sales royalty when song or artist is recorded or outright fee from recording artist or record company.
How to Contact: Submit demo tape by mail. Unsolicited submissions are OK. Prefers cassette with lyric sheet. Does not return material. Reports in 5 weeks.
Music: Mostly **gospel**. Produced *Broderick Rice Alive*, written and recorded by Broderick Rice on Born Again Records (gospel); and and *Make Us One* (by William Charles/Kevin Davis), recorded by Make Us One (contemporary gospel). Other artists include Enlightment, Kim & Dave, Rejoyce, Pentecostal Community Choir and Mary Floyd.

JGM RECORDING STUDIO, 4121 N. Laramie, Chicago IL 60641. Producer: Lito Manlucu. Record producer. Estab. 1991. Produces 1 single, 1 LP and 1 CD/year. Fee derived from sales royalty when song or artist is recorded.
How to Contact: Submit demo tape by mail. Unsolicited submissions OK. Prefers cassette with 3 songs and lyric sheet. Does not return material. Reports in 1 month.
Music: Mostly **pop**, **R&B** and **rock**; also **foreign music** and **dance**. Produced "Blue Jean" (by Lito Manlucu), recorded by Jane Park on Independent Records (dance/pop).

JK JAM PRODUCTIONS, Aviation Mall, Aviation Rd., Queens Ferry NY 12804. (518)793-2330. Director of A&R: Jamie Keats. Record producer and music publisher (JK Jam Music). Estab. 1990. Fee derived from sales royalty when song or artist is recorded, or outright fee from recording artist.
How to Contact: Call first and obtain permission to submit. "Mastered quality recordings only." Does not return material. Reports in 1-4 months.
Music: Mostly **alternative**, **R&B/dance** and **rock**; also **pop/country**. Produced *Paul Traudt*, written and recorded by Paul Traudt (alternative); *Doug Lawler*, written and recorded by Doug Lawler (pop/country); and *Tommy Higgins*, written and recorded by Tommy Higgins (rock), all on JK Jam Productions.

‡DAVID JOHN PRODUCTIONS, 26 Amidon Dr., Ashford CT 06278. (860)487-3613. Fax: (860)487-3614. E-mail: primus@nai.net. Producer: David John. Record producer and record company (Rock-It Records). Estab. 1983. Produces 2 singles, 8-12 LPs, 4 EPs and 10 CDs/year. Fee derived from outright fee from recording artist or record company.
How to Contact: Submit demo tape by mail. Unsolicited submissions are OK. Prefers cassette with 4

songs. Does not return material. Reports in 3-4 weeks.
Music: Mostly **original rock**, **alternative** and **computer-generated**; also **anything good**! Produced *25 Hours* (by Tom Bailey), recorded by Silicon Safari on Incas Records (dance); *Metal Storm*, written and recorded by various artists on Metal Storm Records (metal); and "Heart of Gold" (by David Foster), recorded by Shaboo Allstars on Rock-It Records (rock). Other artists include New Johnny 5, Keith Ammo, Type-O and Harvey Brooks.

LITTLE RICHIE JOHNSON, P.O. Box 3, Belen NM 87002. (505)864-7441. Contact: Tony Palmer. Record producer, management firm, music publisher and record company (LRJ). Estab. 1959. Produces 6 singles, 3 12″ singles, 6 CDs and 6 LPs/year. Fee derived from sales royalty when song or artist is recorded.

- Little Richie Johnson's publishing company, Little Richie Johnson Music, is listed in the Music Publishers section; his management firm, Little Richie Johnson Agency, is listed in the Managers and Booking Agents section; and his record label, LRJ, is listed in the Record Companies section.

How to Contact: Write first and obtain permission to submit. Prefers cassette with 4 songs. SASE. Reports in 6 weeks.
Music: Mostly **country**. Produced *Moonlight, Roses and the Wine* (by Jerry Jaramillo), recorded Gabe Neito; *Ship of Fools*, recorded by Reta Lee; and *Honky Tonk Cinderella*, written and recorded by Jerry Jaramillo, all on LRJ Records. Other artists include Alan Godage.

‡**JUMP PRODUCTIONS**, 71 Langemunt, 9420 Aaigem **Belgium**. Phone: (053)62-73-77. General Manager: Eddy Van Mouffaert. Record producer and music publisher (Jump Music). Estab. 1976. Produces 25 singles and 2 CDs/year. Fee derived from sales royalty when song or artist is recorded.

- See the listing for Jump Music in the Music Publishers section.

How to Contact: Write first and obtain permission to submit. Prefers cassette. Does not return material. Reports in 2 weeks.
Music: Mostly **ballads**, **up-tempo**, **easy listening**, **disco** and **light pop**; also **instrumentals**. Produced *Evelien* (by Eddy Govert), recorded by Evelien on Quartz Records (Flemish); *Liefde Komt En Liefde Gaat* (by Les Reed), recorded by Lina on Scorpion Records; and "Father Damiaan" (by Jan De Vuyst), recorded by Eigentijdse Jeugd on Youth Sound Records.

KAREN KANE PRODUCER/ENGINEER, 9 Wheatfield Rd., Etobicoke, Ontario M8V 2P5 **Canada**. (416)259-9177. Fax: (416)252-0464. E-mail: mixmama@astral.magic.ca. Website: www.magic.ca/~mixmama. Contact: Karen Kane. Record producer and recording engineer. Estab. 1978. Produces 5-10 singles and 5-10 CDs/year. Fee derived from outright fee from recording artist or record company, or sales royalty when song or artist is recorded.
How to Contact: Write first and obtain permission to submit. Unsolicited submissions are *not* OK. Does not return material. Reports in 2 weeks.
Music: Mostly **pop**, **alternative**, **R&B/reggae** and **acoustic**. Produced *Jumpin Jack*, written and recorded by Jack Grunsky on BMG Music (world/children's); *Walk Me Inside* (by various), recorded by Fulign (rock); and *Another Live Show*, written and recorded by Marcia Beck (folk/rock). Other artists include Wishing Chair, Kyn and David Abramsky.
Tips: "Get proper funding to do your projects right."

MATTHEW KATZ PRODUCTIONS, 29903 Harvester Rd., Malibu CA 90265. (310)457-4844. President: Matthew Katz. Record producer, music publisher (After You Publishing/BMI) and record company (San Francisco Sound, Malibu Records). Produces 6 singles, 6 12″ singles and 2 CDs/year. Fee derived from sales royalty when song or artist is recorded, or outright fee from record company.
How to Contact: Submit demo tape by mail. Unsolicited submissions are OK. Prefers cassette (or 8mm videocassette) and lead sheet. Does not return material.
Music: Mostly **San Francisco rock** and **jazz**. Produced Jefferson Airplane, Moby Grape, It's A Beautiful Day, Indian Puddin' & Pipe, Fraternity of Man and Tim Hardin.
Tips: "We're interested in original New Age material for Malibu Records and message songs. Not interested in 'Why is she making it with some other guy, not me?' "

GENE KENNEDY ENTERPRISES, INC., 3950 N. Mt. Juliet Rd., Mt. Juliet TN 37122. (615)754-0417. President: Gene Kennedy. Vice President: Karen Jeglum Kennedy. Record producer, independent distribution/promotion firm and music publisher (Chip 'N' Dale Music Publishers, Inc./ASCAP, Door Knob Music Publishing, Inc./BMI and Lodestar Music/SESAC). Estab. 1975. Produces 5-10 CDs/year. Fee derived from sales royalty when song or artist is recorded or outright fee from recording artist or record company.
How to Contact: Submit demo tape by mail. Unsolicited submissions are OK. Prefers cassette with up to 3 songs and lyric sheet. "Do not send in a way that has to be signed for." SASE (appropriate size for tapes). Reports in 2-3 weeks.
Music: Country and **gospel**. Produced "Santa's Gonna Boogie" (by Vince Guzetta), recorded by Vince Anthony on Midnight Gold Records (Christmas country); *He Thought She Always Knew* (by Larry Smith/Frank Gallagher), recorded by Scott Hoff; and *It's Hard Not Knowin' You Mama* (by Mary Helen Mares), recorded by Christina Dawn, both on Door Knob Records. Other artists include Floyd Mitchell and Rhonda Rock.

KINGSPORT CREEK MUSIC, P.O. Box 6085, Burbank CA 91510. Contact: Vice President. Record producer, record company (Cowgirl Records) and music publisher.

- Kingsport Creek Music's record label, Cowgirl Records, is listed in the Record Companies section and Kingsport Creek Music Publishing is listed in the Music Publishers section.

How to Contact: Submit demo tape by mail. Unsolicited submissions are OK. Prefers cassette or VHS videocassette. Does not return material. "Include photo and bio if possible."
Music: Mostly **country**, **MOR**, **R&B**, **pop** and **gospel**. Produced "Leading Me On," "Pick Up Your Feet" and "With Me Still," all written and recorded by Melvena Kaye on Cowgirl Records.

KINGSTON RECORDS AND TALENT, 15 Exeter Rd., Kingston NH 03848. (603)642-8493. Coordinator: Harry Mann. Record producer, music publisher (Strawberry Soda Publishing/ASCAP) and record company (Kingston Records). Estab. 1988. Produces 3-4 singles, 2-3 12″ singles, 2-3 LPs and 1-2 CDs/year. Fee derived from sales royalty when song or artist is recorded. Deals primarily with NE and local artists.

- See Kingston Records' listing in the Record Companies section.

How to Contact: Write or call first and obtain permission to submit. Prefers cassette with 1-2 songs and lyric sheet. Does not return material. Reports in 2 months.
Music: Mostly **rock**, **country** and **pop**; "no heavy metal." Produced *Out of the Rain*, written and recorded by Doug Mitchell; and *Songs Piped from the Moon*, written and recorded by S. Pappas, both on Kingston Records. Other artists include Bob Moore, Candy Striper Death Orgy, Pocket Band, Jeff Walker, J. Evans, NTM, Miss Bliss and Four On The Floor.

KMA, 1650 Broadway, Suite 900, New York NY 10019-6833. (212)265-1570. A&R Director: Morris Levy. Record producer and music publisher (Block Party Music/ASCAP). Estab. 1987. Produces 2 12″ singles, 3 LPs and 3 CDs/year. Fee derived from sales royalty or outright fee from recording artist or record company.
How to Contact: Submit demo tape by mail. Prefers cassette. SASE. Reports in 3 months.
Music: Mostly **R&B**, **dance** and **rap**; also **movie** and **ethnic**. Produced "I Found It," recorded by Daphne on Maxi Records; "Through the Day," recorded by Millenium on 143/Atlantic Records; and "I Want You for Me," recorded by Raw Stilo on dv8/A&M Records.
Tips: "*Original* lyrics a huge plus."

KNOWN ARTIST PRODUCTIONS, 1219 Kerlin Ave., Brewton AL 36426. (334)867-2228. President: Roy Edwards. Record producer, music publisher (Cheavoria Music Co./BMI, Baitstring Music/ASCAP) and record company (Bolivia Records, Known Artist Records). Estab. 1972. Produces 10 singles and 3 LPs/year. Fee derived from sales royalty when song or artist is recorded.

- Known Artist's publishing company, Cheavoria Music, is listed in the Music Publishers section, and their record label, Bolivia Records, is in the Record Companies section.

How to Contact: Write first and obtain permission to submit. Prefers cassette with 3 songs and lyric sheet. Reports in 1 month. "All tapes will be kept on file."
Music: Mostly **R&B**, **pop** and **country**; also **easy listening**, **MOR** and **soul**. Produced "Got To Let You Know," "You Are My Sunshine" and "You Make My Life So Wonderful," all written and recorded by Roy Edwards on Bolivia Records (R&B). Other artists include Jim Portwood, Bobbie Roberson and Brad Smiley.

ROBERT R. KOVACH, P.O. Box 7018, Warner Robins GA 31095-7018. (912)953-2800. Producer: Robert R. Kovach. Record producer. Estab. 1976. Produces 6 singles, 2 cassettes and 1 CD/year. Fee derived from sales royalty when song or artist is recorded.
How to Contact: Submit demo tape by mail. Unsolicited submissions are OK. Prefers cassette with 4 songs and lyric sheet. SASE. Reports in 4 months.
Music: Mostly **country** and **pop**; also **easy listening**, **R&B**, **rock** and **gospel**.

L.A. ENTERTAINMENT, 6367 Selma Ave., Hollywood CA 90028. (213)467-1411. Fax: (213)462-8562. E-mail: gduncan@newenterprises.com. Vice President/A&R: Glen D. Duncan. Record producer, record company (Warrior Records) and music publisher (Songbroker Publishing/ASCAP). Estab. 1988. Fee derived from sales royalty when song or artist is recorded.
How to Contact: Submit demo tape by mail. Unsolicited submissions are OK. Prefers cassette or videocassette with 3 songs, lyric and lead sheet if available. "All written submitted materials (i.e. lyric sheets, letter, etc.) should be typed." SASE. Reports in 4-6 weeks.
Music: Mostly **alternative** and **R&B**.

LANDMARK COMMUNICATIONS GROUP, P.O. Box 1444, Hendersonville TN 37077. Producer: Bill Anderson Jr. Record producer, record company, music publisher (Newcreature Music/BMI) and TV/radio syndication. Produces 12 singles and 12 LPs/year. Fee derived from sales royalty.

- See Landmark Communication Group's listing in the Record Companies section, as well as a listing for Newcreature Music in the Music Publishers section.

How to Contact: Write first and obtain permission to submit. Prefers 7½ ips reel-to-reel, cassette or videocassette with 4-10 songs and lyric sheet. SASE. Reports in 1 month.
Music: Mostly **country crossover**; also **blues**, **country**, **gospel**, **jazz**, **rock** and **top 40/pop**. Produced "Good Love," written and recorded by Gail Score (R&B); "A Hero Never Dies," written and recorded by Joanne Cash Yates on Jana Records (gospel); and "Nothin' Else Feels Quite Like It" (by B. Nash/K. Nash/B. Anderson), recorded on TV Theme Records (country). Other artists include Skeeter Davis and Vernon Oxford.

LARI-JON PRODUCTIONS, 325 W. Walnut, Rising City NE 68658. (402)542-2336. Owner: Larry Good. Record producer, music publisher (Lari-Jon Publishing/BMI), management firm (Lari-Jon Promotions) and record company (Lari-Jon Records). Estab. 1967. Produces 10 singles and 5 LPs/year. Fee derived from sales royalty when song or artist is recorded.

- See the listings for Lari-Jon Publishing in the Music Publishers section, Lari-Jon Records in the Record Companies section and Lari-Jon Promotions in the Managers and Booking Agents section.

How to Contact: Submit demo tape by mail. Unsolicited submissions are OK. "Must be a professional demo." SASE. Reports in 2 months.
Music: **Country**, **gospel-Southern** and **'50s rock**. Produced *Does The Oldies* (by various), recorded by Kent Thompson; *Her Favorite Song*, written and recorded by Johnny Nace; and *As Good As It Gets*, written and recorded by Larry Good, all on Lari-Jon Records. Other artists include Brenda Allen, Tom Campbell and Tom Johnson.

LARK TALENT & ADVERTISING, P.O. Box 35726, Tulsa OK 74153. (918)786-8896. E-mail: janajae@aol.com. Owner: Jana Jae. Record producer, music publisher (Jana Jae Music/BMI) and record company (Lark Record Productions, Inc.). Estab. 1980. Fee derived from sales royalty when song or artist is recorded.

- Jana Jae's publishing company, Jana Jae Music, can be found in the Music Publishers section, and her record label, Lark Records, can be found in the Record Companies section.

How to Contact: Submit demo tape by mail. Unsolicited submissions are OK. Prefers cassette or VHS videocassette with 3 songs and lead sheet. Does not return material.
Music: Mostly **country**, **bluegrass** and **classical**; also **instrumentals**. Produced "Fiddlestix" (by Jana Jae); "Mayonnaise" (by Steve Upfold); and "Flyin' South" (by Cindy Walker), all recorded by Jana Jae on Lark Records. Other artists include Sydni, Hotwire and Matt Greif.

LEEWAY ENTERTAINMENT GROUP, 100 Wilshire Blvd., 20th Floor, Santa Monica CA 90401. (310)260-6900. Fax: (310)260-6901. Branch: Leeway London, 177 High Street, Harelsden, London NW10 4TE **England**. Producer: Daniel Leeway. Record producer, music publisher, recording studios (The Leeway Studios, 32 Track Digital). Estab. 1991. Fee derived from sales royalty when song or artist is recorded, or outright fee from recording artist, unless other arrangements have been made.
How to Contact: Write or call first to arrange personal interview, or submit demo tape/CD by mail. Unsolicited submissions are OK. Prefers cassette, DAT or CD with 2 songs and lyric sheet. SASE. Reports in 1 month minimum.

Music: Mostly **dance**, **pop** and **New Age**.
Tips: "Send all submissions as though you were submitting a business proposal to an investor. We are not going to invest in you or your material if you are not willing to invest in yourself. Be well prepared, patient, and confident about your talents. We will contact you if we are interested. No phone calls please."

LINEAR CYCLE PRODUCTIONS, P.O. Box 2608, Sepulveda CA 91393-2608. Producer: R. Borowy. Record producer. Estab. 1980. Produces 15-25 singles, 6-10 12″ singles, 15-20 LPs and 10 CDs/year. Fee derived from sales royalty when song or artist is recorded.
How to Contact: Submit demo tape by mail. Unsolicited submissions are OK. Prefers cassette, 7⅞ ips reel-to-reel or ½″ VHS or ¾″ videocassette. SASE. Reports in 6 weeks to 6 months.
Music: Mostly **rock/pop**, **R&B/blues** and **country**; also **gospel** and **comedy**. Produced "Mess 'O Film" (by B. Beat), recorded by Olif Splash on Old-Art Records (alternative); "My Woodpooker And Mee" (by M. Pandancski), recorded by Ggrfaf on No Sound Records (alternative); and "She's Cryin' For My Beer" (by Dumb), recorded by Bill mcBill IV on Kuntry Records (country).
Tips: "If you can provide a demo reel on CD or high quality cassette, the more likely we'll audition it. No cheap tapes, or records!"

MICK LLOYD PRODUCTIONS, 1018 17th Ave. S., Nashville TN 37212. (615)329-9093. Fax: (615)329-9094. President: Mick Lloyd. Record producer and music publisher. Estab. 1982. Produces 20 singles and 7 LPs/year. Fee derived from sales royalty when song or artist is recorded.
How to Contact: Write first and obtain permission to submit. Prefers cassette with 2 songs and lyric sheets. Does not return material. Responds if interested.
Music: Mostly **country**, **rock** and **dance**. Produced *The Best of Johnny Lee* (by various), recorded by Johnny Lee on Quality Records (country); *Precious Memories* (by various), recorded by Slim Whitman on K-Tel Records (gospel); and *Country Colors* (by various), recorded by Mick Lloyd Music Machine on Metacom Records (MOR). Other artists include Malissa Martin, Lesia Turner, David Grey and Corinda Carford.

LOCONTO PRODUCTIONS, P.O. Box 16540, Plantation FL 33318. (305)741-7766. President: Frank X. Loconto. Record producer, record company and music publisher. Estab. 1978. Produces 10 cassettes/albums and 10 CDs/year. Fee derived from sales royalty or outright fee from songwriter/artist and/or record company.

- Loconto Productions is also listed in the Record Companies section, and its publishing company, Otto Publishing Co., is listed in the Music Publishers section.

How to Contact: Submit demo tape by mail. Unsolicited submissions are OK. Prefers cassette. SASE. Reports in 2-3 months.
Music: Produced *Aurore* (by various), recorded by Aurore (gospel); *Vodec* (by various), recorded by Vodec (gospel); and *Total Package*, written and recorded by Jos. E. Ford, all on FXL Records. Other artists include Roger B. Bryant, Mark Goldman and Chris Risi.

LONDON BRIJJ PRODUCTIONS, 817 E. Locust Ave., Philadelphia PA 19138. (215)438-9882. Producer/engineer: Jae London. Record producer, music publisher (Amaj Int'l Music/BMI) and production company. Estab. 1984. Produces 7 singles, 3 12" singles, 3 LPs and 2 CDs/year. Fee derived from outright fee from record company.
How to Contact: Submit demo tape by mail. Unsolicited submissions are OK. Prefers cassette or VHS videocassette with 3 songs and lyric sheet. SASE. Reports in 1-2 months.
Music: Mostly **R&B**, **hip hop** and **ballads**; also **reggae** and **club/house**. Produced *All Nite* (by A. Arthurs), recorded by Seenya (reggae); *Da Void* (by D. Robinson), recorded by Da Void (R&B/hip hop); and "Smooth Sailing" (by J. London), recorded by various (jazz), all on Amaj Records. Other artists include Poppa Bassie and Keith Huggins.

HAROLD LUICK & ASSOCIATES, Box B, Carlisle IA 50047. (515)989-3748. Record producer, music industry consultant, music print publisher and music publisher. Produces 20 singles and 6 LPs/year. Fee derived from sales royalty, outright fee from artist/songwriter or record company, and from consulting fees for information or services.

- See their listing in the Music Print Publishers section.

How to Contact: Call or write first and obtain permission to submit. Prefers cassette with 3-5 songs and lyric sheet. SASE. Reports in 3 weeks.
Music: Traditional country, **gospel**, **contemporary country** and **MOR**. Produced *Everhart*, written and recorded by Bob Everhart; and *Ballads of Deadwood S.D.*, written and recorded by Don McLaughlin. "Over a 12-year period, Harold Luick has produced and recorded 412 singles and 478 albums, 7 of which

charted and some of which have enjoyed independent sales in excess of 30,000 units."

‡MAC-ATTACK PRODUCTIONS, 20603 N.E. Seventh Court, Miami FL 33179. (305)949-1422. Engineer/Producer: Michael McNamee. Record producer and music publisher (Mac-Attack Publishing/ASCAP). Estab. 1986. Fee derived from outright fee from recording artist or record company.
How to Contact: Submit demo tape by mail. Unsolicited submissions are OK. Prefers cassette or VHS videocassette with 3-5 songs, lyric sheet and bio. Does not return material. Reports in 1-4 weeks.
Music: Mostly **pop**, **alternative rock** and **dance**.

JIM McCOY PRODUCTIONS, Rt. 2, Box 114, Berkeley Springs WV 25411. President: Jim McCoy. Record producer, record company (Winchester Records) and music publisher (Jim McCoy Music/BMI). Estab. 1964. Produces 12-15 singles and 6 LPs/year. Fee derived from sales royalty.

- Jim McCoy's publishing company, Jim McCoy Music, can be found in the Music Publishers section, and his record label, Winchester Records, can be found in the Record Companies section.

How to Contact: Submit demo tape by mail. Unsolicited submissions are OK. Prefers cassette, 7½ or 15 ips reel-to-reel or Beta or VHS videocassette with 6 songs and lyric or lead sheets. Does not return material. Reports in 1 month.
Music: Mostly **country**, **rock** and **gospel**; also **country/rock** and **bluegrass**. Produced "Dyin' Rain" and "I'm Gettin Nowhere," both written and recorded by J.B. Miller on Hilton Records (country). Other artists include Mel McQuain, Red Steed, R. Lee Gray, John Aikens and Jim McCoy.

LEE MAGID PRODUCTIONS, P.O. Box 532, Malibu CA 90265. (213)463-5998. President: Lee Magid. Record producer, music publisher (Alexis Music, Inc./ASCAP, Marvelle Music Co./BMI, Gabal Music Co./SESAC), record company (Grass Roots Records, LMI Records) and management firm (Lee Magid Management). Estab. 1950. Produces 4 singles, 4 12" singles, 8 LPs and 8 CDs/year. Fee derived from sales royalty when song or artist is recorded.

- See the listings for Alexis Music in the Music Publishers section and Grass Roots Record & Tape/LMI Records in the Record Companies section.

How to Contact: Submit demo tape by mail. Unsolicited submissions are OK. "Send cassette giving address and phone number." Prefers cassette or VHS videocassette with 3-6 songs and lyric sheet. "Please only one cassette, and photos if you are an artist/writer." Does not return material. Reports in 6 weeks only if accepted.
Music: Mostly **R&B**, **rock**, **jazz** and **gospel**; also **pop**, **bluegrass**, **church/religious**, **easy listening**, **folk**, **blues**, **MOR**, **progressive**, **soul**, **instrumental** and **Top 40**. Produced *I'll Be Seeing You Around* (by Lorna McGough/John Scott/Mark Newbar), recorded by 2AD on LMI Records (R&B); *It's Only Money* (by John M. Hides), recorded by J. Michael Hides on Grass Roots Records (pop); and *Blues For the Weepers* (by Lee Magid/Max Rich), recorded by Bob Stewart on VWC Records (jazz). Other artists include Tramaine Hawkins, Della Reese, Rod Piazza, "Big Joe" Turner, Tom Vaughn and Laura Lee.

‡MAGNETIC OBLIVION MUSIC CO., P.O. Box 1446, Eureka CA 95502. Phone/fax: (707)445-2698. E-mail: magob@aol.com. President: Matthew Knight. Record producer, record company (Magnetic Oblivion Records) and music publisher. Estab. 1984. Produces 3 singles, 1 EP and 6-10 CDs/year. Fee derived from sales royalty when song or artist is recorded or percentage of sales.
How to Contact: Submit demo tape by mail. Unsolicited submissions are OK. Prefers cassette, DAT or videocassette. "All material must be copyrighted. Non-copyrighted material will be trashed without review." Does not return material. Reports in 2-3 months.
Music: Mostly **experimental**, **early music** and **alternative**; also **Celtic**, **novelty** and **acid jazz**. Produced *Absence* (by Xeff Scolari), recorded by Chowderhead (alternative); *Moss Clad Stone* (by Tama Roberts), recorded by Tamarian (Celtic); and *Let Us Servire Cantico* (by various), recorded by Country Matters (Christmas), all on MOR Records. Other artists include Goofus & Gallant, Trinity, Small Fish, Dipthongs, Steve Faught and Matty Dread & the Troubled Loners.
Tips: "Magnetic Oblivion is a home for unusual acts."

‡COOKIE MARENCO, P.O. Box 874, Belmont CA 94002. Record producer/engineer. Estab. 1981. Produces 10 CDs/year. Fee derived from sales royalty and outright fee from recording artist or record company.
How to Contact: Write first and obtain permission to submit. Do not send cassettes. Does not return material.
Music: Mostly **alternative modern rock**, **country**, **folk**, **rap**, **ethnic** and **avante-garde**; also **classical**, **pop** and **jazz**. Produced *Winter Solstice II*, written and recorded by various artists; *Heresay* (by Paul McCandless); and *Deep At Night* (by Alex DeGrassi), all on Windham Hill Records (instrumental). Other

artists include Ladysmith Black Mambazo, Steve Owen, Oregon, Brain & Buckethead, Roy Hargrove, Monterey Jazz Festival, J.A. Deane, Mark Isham and Diamanda Galas.

PETE MARTIN/VAAM MUSIC PRODUCTIONS, P.O. Box 29550, Hollywood CA 90029-0688. (213)664-7765. President: Pete Martin. Record producer, music publisher (Vaam Music/BMI, Pete Martin Music/ASCAP) and record company (Blue Gem Records). Estab. 1982. Produces 12 singles and 5 LPs/year. Fee derived from sales royalty when song or artist is recorded.

- See the listings for Vaam Music Group in the Music Publishers section and Blue Gem Records in the Record Companies section.

How to Contact: Prefers cassette with 2 songs and lyric sheet. Send small packages only. SASE. Reports in 1 month.

Music: Mostly **top 40/pop**, **country** and **R&B**. Produced Sherry Weston, Vero, Frank Loren, Brian Smith & The Renegades, Victoria Limon, Brandy Rose and Cory Canyon.

Tips: "Study the market in the style that you write. Songs must be capable of reaching Top 5 on charts."

DAVID MATHES PRODUCTIONS, P.O. Box 22653, Nashville TN 37202. (615)252-6912. President: David W. Mathes. AF of M licensed. Record producer and music publisher (Mathes Company). Estab. 1962. Produces 6-10 singles, 4-16 12″ singles and 4-6 LPs/year. Fee derived from outright fee from recording artist.

- See the listing for the Mathes Company in the Music Publishers section.

How to Contact: Submit demo tape by mail. Unsolicited submissions are OK. "No certified mail accepted." Prefers 7½ or 15 ips reel-to-reel, cassette or videocassette with 2-4 songs and lyric sheet. "Enclose correctly stamped envelope for demo return." Reports in 1 month.

Music: Mostly **country** and **gospel**; also **bluegrass**, **R&B** and **instrumental**. Produced "(I Want A) One Life Stand" (by Dorothy Hampton), recorded by Johnny Newman (country); and "Rag Doll For Christmas" (by Merle Baasch), recorded by DeAnna, both on Star Image Records.

SCOTT MATHEWS, D/B/A HIT OR MYTH PRODUCTIONS, 36 Lisbon St., San Rafael CA 94901. Fax: (415)389-9682. E-mail: hitormyth@aol.com. President: Scott Mathews. Record producer and music publisher (Hang On to Your Publishing/BMI). Estab. 1975. Produces 6-9 CDs/year. Fee derived from recording artist or record company (with royalty points).

- Scott Mathews has several gold and platinum awards for sales of over 12 million records.

How to Contact: Submit demo tape by mail. Unsolicited submissions are OK. Prefers DAT (cassette and CD accepted). SASE. Reports in 2-4 months. "Absolutely no phone calls, please."

Music: Mostly **rock/pop** and **alternative**. Produced *Vibrolux*, written and recorded by Vibrolux on Polydor Records (alternative); *The Tail Wagging the Dog*, written and recorded by Scott Mathews/Huey Lewis/Mark Knopfler (movie theme); and "The Warmth of the Sun" (by Brian Wilson), recorded by Scott Mathews/Phil Aaberg on Windham Hill Records. Has produced Roy Orbison, Rosanne Cash, John Hiatt and many more. Has recorded with everyone from Barbra Streisand to Sammy Hagar, including The Beach Boys, Keith Richards, John Lee Hooker, Van Morrison, Elvis Costello, Huey Lewis, Bonnie Raitt and Eric Clapton to name but a few.

Tips: "I am primarily working with artists currently signed to labels. I do however always keep my eyes and ears open for new, undeniably great talent. Once or twice a year I find time to schedule an unsigned act and produce a finished record that can get them signed to the right label. When you're ready, let me know."

‡MEGA TRUTH RECORDS, P.O. Box 4988, Culver City CA 90231. E-mail: jonbare@aol.com. CEO: Jon Bare. Record producer and record company. Estab. 1994. Produces 2 LPs and 2 CDs/year. Fee negotiable.

How to Contact: Submit demo tape by mail. Unsolicited submissions are OK. Prefers cassette with 4 songs. "We specialize in recording world-class virtuoso musicians and bands with top players." Does not return material. Reports in 2 weeks only if interested.

Music: Mostly **rock**, **blues** and **country rock**; also **swing**, **dance** and **instrumental**. Produced *Party Platter*, recorded by Hula Monsters (swing); *Killer Whales* (by Jon Bare) (rock); and *Illegal Characters*, recorded by Techno Dudes (rock), all on Mega Truth Records. Other artists include The Torpedos, Rich Harper and The Buzzyrds.

Tips: "Create a unique sound that blends great vocals and virtuoso musicianship with a beat that makes us want to get up and dance."

MR. WONDERFUL PRODUCTIONS, INC., 149 Alden Ave. N.W., J-1, Atlanta GA 30309. President: Ronald C. Lewis. Record producer, music publisher (Ron "Mister Wonderful" Music/BMI and 1730

Music/ASCAP) and record company (Wonderful Records and Ham Sem Records). Estab. 1984. Produces 2 singles and 3 12″ singles/year. Fee is derived from sales royalty when song or artist is recorded.
How to Contact: Submit demo tape by mail. Unsolicited submissions are OK. Prefers cassette with 4 songs and lyric sheet. SASE. Reports in 3 weeks.
Music: Mostly **R&B**, **black gospel** and **rap**. Produced *Spraggie Bad Boys*, written and recorded by Spraggie (reggae); *Do That to Me*, written and recorded by Jerry Green (rock); and *Tell Them*, recorded by Sylvester Gough, all on Wonderful Records.

GARY MOFFET, P.O. Box 941 N.D.G., Montreal, Quebec H4A 3S3 **Canada**. (514)487-8953. Contact: Gary Moffet. Record producer and music publisher (Sci-Fi Music). Estab. 1985. Produces 3 LPs, 4 EPs and 3 CDs/year. Fee derived from sales royalty when song or artist is recorded.
- Gary Moffet's publishing company, Sci-Fi Music, is listed in the Music Publishers section.

How to Contact: Submit demo tape by mail. Unsolicited submissions are OK. Prefers cassette with 6 songs and lyric sheet. SAE and IRC.
Music: Mostly **rock, pop** and **acoustic**. Produced *Back to Reality* (by T. Mitchell), recorded by Mindstorm on Aquarius Records (heavy rock); *See Spot Run* (by C. Broadbeck), recorded by See Spot Run on Primer Records (rock); and *The Storm*, written and recorded by Ray Lyell on Spy Records (rock). Other artists include Marie Carmen, Marjo and Manon Brunet.

‡MOM AND POP PRODUCTIONS, INC., P.O. Box 96, El Cerrito CA 94530. Executive Vice President: James Bronson, Jr. Record producer, record company (Touche Records) and music publisher (Toulouse Music/BMI).
- Mom and Pop's publishing company, Toulouse Music, can be found in the Music Publishers section, and their record label, Touche Records, can be found in the Record Companies section.

How to Contact: Prefers cassette with 2-4 songs and lyric sheet. SASE. Reports in 1 month.
Music: Bluegrass, **gospel**, **jazz**, **R&B** and **soul**. Artists include Les Oublies du Jazz Ensemble.

MUSICLAND PRODUCTIONS, INC., 911 NE 17th Ave., Ocala FL 34470. (352)622-5529. Owner: Bobby Land. Record producer. Estab. 1986. Produces 2 singles and 2 CDs/year. Fee derived from financial backers.
How to Contact: Call first and obtain permission to submit. Prefers cassette with 4 songs and lyric sheet. "Professional demos only." Does not return material. Reports in 1-2 weeks.
Music: Mostly **country** and **gospel**. Produced "Cowboy Lady," written and recorded by Curt Powers on MPR Records; and *Right Back Where We Ended*, recorded by Charles Allen on Pleasentville Records. Other artists include David Mathis.

MUST ROCK PRODUCTIONZ WORLDWIDE, 167 W. 81st St., Suite 5C, New York NY 10024-7200. (212)799-9268. President: Ivan "DJ/DOC" Rodriguez. Record producer and recording engineer. Estab. 1980. Produces 5 singles, engineers 2 LPs, 3 EPs and 2 CDs/year. Fee derived from sales royalty when song or artist is recorded. "We do not shop deals."
How to Contact: Call first and obtain permission to submit. Prefers cassette or VHS videocassette and lyric sheet. Does not return material. Reports in 3-5 weeks.
Music: Mostly **hip-hop**, **R&B** and **pop**; also **soul**, **ballads** and **soundtracks**. Produced "Poor Georgie" (by MC Lyte/DJ DOC), recorded by MC Lyte on Atlantic Records (rap). Other artists include Caron Wheeler, The Hit Squad, The Awesome II, Black Steel Music, Underated Productions, EPMD, Redman, Dr. Dre & Ed-Lover, Das-EFX, Biz Markie, BDP, Eric B & Rakim, The Fugees, The Bushwackass, Shai and Pudgee.
Tips: "Services provided include production (pre/post/co), tracking, mixing, remixing, live show tapes, jingles, etc. Additional info available upon request."

NASHVILLE COUNTRY PRODUCTIONS, 306 Millwood Dr., Nashville TN 37217. (615)366-9999. President/Producer: Colonel Jack Lynch. Record producer, music publisher (Jaclyn Music/BMI), record companies (Jalyn and Nashville Country Productions) and distributor (Nashville Music Sales). Estab. 1987.

REMEMBER: Don't "shotgun" your demo tapes. Submit only to companies interested in the type of music you write. For more submission hints, refer to Getting Started on page 6.

Produces 1-12 LPs/year. Fee derived from sales royalty or outright fee from recording artist or record company. "We do both contract and custom recording."

- Jack Lynch's publishing company, Jaclyn Music, can be found in the Music Publishers section, and his record label, Jalyn Recording Co., is in the Record Companies section.

How to Contact: Submit demo tape by mail. Unsolicited submissions are OK. Prefers cassette with 1-2 songs and lyric or lead sheet. SASE. Reports in 1 month.

Music: Mostly **country**, **bluegrass**, **MOR** and **gospel**; also **comedy**. Produced *There'll Never Be Another*, written and recorded by Jack Lynch on NBC-19962 Records; *Time Will Tell* (by T.E. Morris), recorded by Odie Gal on NCP-19961 Records; and *Love Takes Time* (by Franklin Kincaid), recorded by Don Hendrix on NCP-19964 Records.

Tips: "Prepare a good quality cassette demo, send to us along with a neat lyric sheet for each song and a bio, picture and SASE."

NEBO RECORD COMPANY, P.O. Box 194 or 457, New Hope AL 35760. Manager: Jim Lewis. Record producer, music publisher (Nebo Ridge Publishing/ASCAP) and record company. Estab. 1985. Fee derived from sales royalty when song or artist is recorded.

How to Contact: Submit demo tape by mail. Unsolicited submissions are OK. Prefers cassette with 1 song and lyric sheet. "It is OK to send a videocassette, but not a must. Songwriters must send a SASE. Send a neat professional package. Send only 1 song." Does not return material. Reports "as soon as possible."

Music: Mostly **modern country**, **traditional country** and **gospel**; also **rock**, **R&B** and **pop**. Produced "I Want You" (by Linda Best), recorded by Diane Hart; *On Top Again* (by Pat West), recorded by Donna Rose; and *Don't Stop Now* (by Kathy Jones), recorded by Mary Rivers, all on Nebo Records. Other artists include Jean Baty, John Hunt, Bradley Hill, Cindy Clark, Nancy Dudley, Sandy Sands, Darlene Dandy, Linda Stanley, Brandy Moses and Sharon Tandy.

Tips: "We need several female singers for our Nebo Record label. Female singers should send a personal bio, some full-length photos, and a demo cassette tape of their songs for a review. Also, SASE should be included."

BILL NELSON, 45 Perham St., W. Roxbury MA 02132. Contact: Bill Nelson. Record producer and music publisher (Henly Music/ASCAP). Estab. 1987. Produces 6 singles and 6 LPs/year. Fee derived from outright fee from recording artist.

- See the listing for Henly Music Associates in the Music Publishers section.

How to Contact: Submit demo tape by mail. Unsolicited submissions are OK. Prefers cassette with 3-4 songs and lyric sheet. Does not return material. Reports in 3-4 weeks.

Music: Mostly **country**, **pop** and **gospel**. Produced "Do You Believe in Miracles" (by B. Nelson), recorded by Part-Time Singers; "Big Bad Bruce" (by J. Dean) and "Don't Hurry With Love" (by B. Bergeron), both recorded by B.N.O., all on Woodpecker Records.

‡NEO SYNC LABS, 45 Kirkwood Ave., Binghamton NY 13901. (607)771-1060. E-mail: neosync@hancock.net. Owner: Bob Damiano. Record producer and recording studio. Estab. 1987. Produces 2-3 LPs, 2-3 EPs and 1 CD/year. Fee derived from outright fee from recording artist.

How to Contact: Submit demo tape by mail. Unsolicited submissions are OK. Prefers DAT or cassette with 1-10 songs. Include SASE for response. Does not return unsolicited material. Reports in 1 month.

Music: Mostly **progressive rock**, **hard rock** and **country**; also **jazz** and **dance**. Produced *The Journey*, written and recorded by Joe Rose on Up Front Music (light rock); *Expect Love*, written and recorded by P.C. Mantree on Pure Water Records (light rock); and *The Big If*, written and recorded by Bob Damiano on E.O.M. Records (rock). Other artists include Phil Guidici, AKA, Simple Simon and Angela Carnegie.

Tips: "Be original. Don't just jump on the 'grunge wagon.' Let us bring out strengths and downplay weaknesses."

NEU ELECTRO PRODUCTIONS, P.O. Box 1582, Bridgeview IL 60455. (630)257-6289. Owner: Bob Neumann. Record producer, record company. Estab. 1984. Produces 16 singles, 16 12" singles, 20 LPs and 4 CDs/year. Fee derived from outright fee from recording artist or record company.

How to Contact: Submit demo tape by mail. Unsolicited submissions are OK. Prefers cassette or VHS videocassette with 3 songs and lyric sheet or lead sheet. "Accurate contact phone numbers and addresses, promo packages and photos." SASE. Reports in 2 weeks.

Music: Mostly **dance**, **house**, **techno**, **rap** and **rock**; also **experimental**, **New Age** and **top 40**. Produced "Juicy," written and recorded by Juicy Black on Dark Planet International Records (house); "Make Me Smile," written and recorded by Roz Baker (house); and *Reactovate-6* (by Bob Neumann), recorded by Beatbox-D on N.E.P. Records (dance).

NEW EXPERIENCE RECORDS, P.O. Box 683, Lima OH 45802. Music Publisher: James L. Milligan Jr. Record producer, music publisher (A New Rap Jam Publishing), management firm (Creative Star Management) and record company (New Experience Records, Grand-Slam Records, Pump It Up Records). Estab. 1989. Produces 15-20 12″ singles, 2 LPs, 3 EPs and 2-5 CDs/year. Fee derived from sales royalty when song or artist is recorded or outright fee from record company, "depending on services required."

• See the listings for A New Rap Jam Publishing in the Music Publishers section and New Experience/Grand Slam Records in the Record Companies section.

How to Contact: Submit demo tape by mail. Unsolicited submissions are OK. Address material toA&R Dept. or Talent Coordinator (Carl Milligan). Prefers cassette with a minimum of 3 songs and lyric or lead sheet (if available). "If tapes are to be returned, proper postage should be enclosed and all tapes and letters should have SASE for faster reply." Reports in 1 month.

Music: Mostly **pop**, **R&B** and **rap**; also **gospel**, **contemporary gospel** and **rock**. Produced *Habit*, written and recorded by Pamela Shipe on N.E.R. Records; *Freak Me*, written and recorded by Mr. Ice on Pump It Up Records; and *I'm A Winner*, recorded by W. Caldwell and the Glory Gospel Choir on Grand Slam Records. Other artists include The Ellis Sisters and Melquan Khalijah.

NEW HORIZON RECORDS, 3398 Nahatan Way, Las Vegas NV 89109. (702)732-2576. President: Mike Corda. Record producer. Fee derived from sales royalty when song or artist is recorded.

How to Contact: Submit demo tape by mail. Unsolicited submissions are OK. Prefers cassette with 1-3 songs and lyric sheet. SASE. Reports in 3 weeks.

Music: Blues, **easy listening**, **jazz** and **MOR**. Produced "Lover of the Simple Things," "Offa the Sauce" (by Corda & Wilson) and "Go Ahead and Laugh," all recorded by Mickey Rooney on Prestige Records (London). Artists include Bob Anderson, Jan Rooney, Joe Williams, Robert Goulet and Bill Haley and the Comets.

Tips: "Send good musical structures, melodic lines, and powerful lyrics or quality singing if you're a singer."

‡THE NEW VIZION STUDIOS, 27 Olcott St., Suite A, Manchester CT 06040. (860)645-7030. Talent Coordinators: Amy Miller and Annette Berry. Record producer. Estab. 1990. Produces 2-3 singles, 3-5 LPs and 3-5 CDs/year. Fee derived from outright fee from recording artist or producer/artist development contract.

How to Contact: Submit demo tape by mail. Unsolicited submissions are OK. Prefers cassette or CD with 2-9 songs and lyric sheet. "We are an artist development company. Do not send photocopies or black and white promos. Originals and color promos only. Unlike most of the clichés in our industry, we are interested in the color of your eyes! Just because most people copy each other does not mean we all do. We set trends and break new ground." SASE. Reports in 1-2 weeks.

Music: Mostly **pop**, **A/C**, **pop/rock** and **crossover styles**; also **rock**, **R&B** and **New Age**. Produced "Embrace Of My Heart" (by Steve Sossin), recorded by Bonnie G. (country); "I Can't Find the Words" and "That's Why I Ran" (by Steve Sossin), both recorded by Dianne Glynn on Vizion Records (A/C). Other artists include Kristine Kozuch.

Tips: "We are a 'rarity' in the recording industry. We are highly specialized as an artist development company and seek to work with emerging artists."

NIGHTWORK RECORDS, 355 W. Potter Dr., Anchorage AK 99518. (907)562-3754. Contact: Kurt Riemann. Record producer and music licensor (electronic). Produces 2 singles, 8 LPs and 2 CDs/year. Fees derived from sales royalty.

How to Contact: Submit demo tape by mail. Unsolicited submissions are OK. Prefers cassette or 15 ips reel-to-reel with 2-3 songs "produced as fully as possible. Send jingles and songs on separate reels." Does not return material. Reports in 1-2 months.

Music: Mostly **electronic**, **electronic jingles** and **Alaska-type music**. Produced *Alaska*, written and recorded by Kurt Riemann; *Aracus*, written and recorded by Jennifer Stone, both on Nightworks Records (New Age); and *Into the Night*, written and recorded by Jeanene Walker on Windsong Records (country).

OMNI 2000 INC., 413 Cooper St., Camden NJ 08102. (609)963-6400. Contact: Director A&R. Record producer, music publisher and record company. Estab. 1995. Produces 1-5 singles and 1-5 LPs/year. Fee derived from sales royalty when song or artist is recorded.

• See Omni 2000's listing in the Music Publishers section.

How to Contact: Write first and obtain permission to submit. Prefers cassette with 3 songs and lyric sheet. SASE. Reports in 1-3 months.

JOHN "BUCK" ORMSBY/ETIQUETTE PRODUCTIONS, 2442 NW Market, Suite 273, Seattle WA 98107. (206)524-1020. Fax: (206)524-1102. Publishing Director: John Ormsby. Record producer and music publisher (Valet Publishing). Estab. 1980. Produces 1-2 singles, 3-5 LPs and 3-5 CDs/year. Fee varies.

• See the listing for Valet Publishing in the Music Publishers section.

How to Contact: Submit demo tape by mail—"always looking for new material but please call first." Prefers cassette or VHS videocassette with lyric or lead sheet. SASE. Reports in 6-8 weeks.

Music: R&B, **rock**, **pop** and **country**.

Tips: "Tape production must be top quality; lead or lyric sheet professional."

PANIO BROTHERS LABEL, P.O. Box 99, Montmartre, Saskatchewan S0G 3M0 **Canada**. Executive Director: John Panio, Jr. Record producer. Estab. 1977. Produces 1 single and 1 LP/year. Fee derived from sales royalty or outright fee from artist/songwriter or record company.

How to Contact: Submit demo tape by mail. Unsolicited submissions are OK. Prefers cassette with any number of songs and lyric sheet. SAE and IRC. Reports in 1 month.

Music: Country, **dance**, **easy listening** and **Ukrainian**. Produced *Ukranian Country*, written and recorded by Vlad Panio on PB Records.

PATTY PARKER, 10603 N. Hayden Rd., Suite 114, Scottsdale AZ 85260. (602)951-3115. Fax: (602)951-3074. E-mail: parker@comstock-records.com. Producer: Patty Parker. Record producer, music publisher (White Cat Music) and record company (Comstock Records). Estab. 1978. Produces 18 CD singles and 4-5 albums/year. Fee derived from outright fee from recording artist or recording company.

• See the listing for Comstock Records in the Record Companies section and White Cat Music in the Music Publishers section.

How to Contact: Submit demo tape by mail. Unsolicited submissions are OK. Prefers CD, cassette or VHS videocassette with 2-4 songs and lyric sheet. Voice up front on demos. SASE. Reports in 2 weeks.

Music: Mostly **country—traditional** to **crossover**, **western** and some **pop/rock**. Produced "She's Bad News" (by Roy G. Ownbey/Alexandria Sheraton), recorded by Danielle St. Pierre (country); "Maybe I Lie," written and recorded by Deb Hamilton (country); and "Don't You Ever Call Me Darlin' " (by Ken Wesley), recorded by R.J. McClintock (country), all on Comstock Records. Other artists include Sharon Lee Beavers, Colin Clark, Brigitte Burke, Phil West, Patty Mayo and Pam Farens.

Tips: "With today's international scope of music I need good medium to up-tempo songs for European country singers whom I produce in Nashville. The U.S. artists I produce are also in need of good up-tempo songs to catch the ears of radio programmers worldwide."

PERENNIAL PRODUCTIONS, P.O. Box 1102, 73 Hill Rd., Redding CT 06875. (203)938-9392. E-mail: seanmcn@aol.com. Owner: Sean McNamara. Record producer. Estab. 1992. Fee derived from outright fee from recording artist.

How to Contact: Submit demo tape by mail. Unsolicited submissions are OK. Prefers cassette or VHS videocassette with 4-8 songs and lyric or lead sheet. "Include a promo pack." Does not return material. Reports in 1 month.

Music: Mostly **alternative rock**, **contemporary jazz** and **folk**. Produced *Feel the Heat*, written and recorded by Flashpoint on Flight Path Records (fusion jazz); *Gary Wofsey Introduces the Contemporary Philharmonic Orchestra*, written and recorded by Gary Wofsey; and "Dischord," written and recorded by John Nutscher on Caffeine Disk Records (alternative).

Tips: "Send a bio about yourself and explain your intentions for the music submitted."

PERIDOT PRODUCTIONS, 17 Woodbine St., Cranston RI 02910. (401)785-2677. President: Amy Parravano. Record producer, record company (Peridot Records) and music publisher (Parravano Music). Estab. 1992. Produces 2 singles, 2 12" singles and 1 LP/year. Fee derived from outright fee from recording artist.

• See the listing for Parravano Music in the Music Publishers section and Peridot Records in the Record Companies section.

How to Contact: Submit demo tape by mail. Unsolicited submissions are OK. Prefers cassette with 3-4 songs and lyric sheet. SASE. Reports in 6 months.

Music: Mostly **country**, **gospel** and **folk**; also **MOR**, **children's**, **country blues**, **blues** and **novelty**.

LISTINGS OF COMPANIES in countries other than the U.S. have the name of the country in boldface type.

Produced *One Number Away* (by Dave Cooper/Amy Parravano), recorded by Amy Beth on Caprice Records (country); *The Love That We Share* (by Amy Parravano), recorded by Lulu Roman on IMX Records (country); and *Santa Won't You Find My Daddy* (by Bill Ruby/Amy Parravano), recorded by Joe Kempf on BJ's Records (country). Other artists include Joe Antonelli and Ron Myers.

PHILLY BREAKDOWN, 216 W. Hortter St., Philadelphia PA 19119. (215)848-6725. President: Matthew Childs. Record producer, music publisher (Philly Breakdown/BMI) and record company. Estab. 1974. Produces 3 singles and 2 LPs/year. Fee derived from sales royalty when song or artist is recorded.
How to Contact: Call first and obtain permission to submit. Prefers cassette with 4 songs and lead sheet. Does not return material. Reports in 8-10 weeks.
Music: Mostly **R&B**, **hip hop** and **pop**; also **jazz**, **gospel** and **ballads**. Produced *The Magic of Clyde Terrell* (by various), recorded by Clyde Terrell (jazz); *This is Jazz* (by Clarence Patterson), recorded by Nina Bundy (jazz); and "To Those In Love" (by Jim Tompson), recorded by Gloria Clark (pop), all on Philly Breakdown Records. Other artists include Leroy Christy, Charlie Nesbitt, Kenny Gates, Jerry Walker and Emmit King.

JIM PIERCE, 101 Hurt Rd., Hendersonville TN 37075. (615)824-5900. Fax: (615)824-8800. President: Jim Pierce. Record producer, music publisher (Strawboss Music/BMI, Pier-Jac Music/ASCAP) and record company (Round Robin Records). Estab. 1974. Fee derived from sales royalty or outright fee from recording artist. "Some artists pay me in advance for my services." Has had over 200 chart records to date.
How to Contact: Write first and obtain permission to submit or to arrange personal interview. Prefers cassette with any number of songs and lyric sheet. Does not return material. Reports in 2-3 months.
Music: Mostly **country**, **contemporary**, **country/pop** and **traditional country**. Produced "Don't Call Us, We'll Call You," written and recorded by Harlen Helgeson; "You Can't Keep a Good Love Down" (by Jerry Fuller), recorded by Lenny Valenson; and "If I Live To Be A Hundred" (by Mae Borden Axton), recorded by Arne Benoni, all on Round Robin Records (country). Other artists include Jimmy C. Newman, Margo Smith, Bobby Helms, Sammi Smith, Tim Gillis, Roy Drusky, Charlie Lowin, Melba Montgomery and Harlan Craig.

PLANET DALLAS, P.O. Box 191447, Dallas TX 75219. (214)521-2216. Fax: (214)528-1299. President: Rick Rooney. Record producer and music publisher (Stoli Music/ASCAP and Planet Mothership/BMI). Estab. 1984. Produces 8-12 LPs, 5-12 EPs and 8-12 CDs/year. Fee derived from sales royalty when song or artist is recorded.

- Planet Dallas also has a listing in the Music Publishers section.

How to Contact: Call first and obtain permission to submit a demo. Prefers cassette or DAT. Does not return material. Reports in 2-4 weeks.
Music: Mostly **pop/rock**, **R&B** and **country**; also **soul** and **instrumental**. Produced albums by Gone By Dawn on Burn Records (rock) and Tripping Daisy on Island Records (rock). Other artists include Fu Schnickens and MC 900 Ft. Jesus.
Tips: "There is no luck in this business, only the result of hard work, inspiration and determination."

POKU PRODUCTIONS, 176-B Woodridge Crescent, Nepran Ontario K2B 759 **Canada**. (613)820-5715. President: Jon E. Shakka. Record producer. Estab. 1988. Produces 1 single and 1 12" single/year. Fee derived from sales royalty when song or artist is recorded.
How to Contact: Write or call first and obtain permission to submit. Prefers cassette or VHS videocassette with 4 songs and lyric sheet. SAE and IRC. Reports in 3 months.
Music: Mostly **funk**, **rap** and **house music**; also **pop**, **ballads** and **funk-rock**. Produced "Good Man/Woman," "Dear O" and "Any Abuse Is Wrong" (by Poku), recorded by Jon E. Shakka on Poku Records. Other artists include James T. Flash.

‡POMGAR PRODUCTIONS, P.O. Box 707, Nashville TN 37076-0707. Manager: Don Pomgar. Record producer and music publisher (One Time Music/BMI, Two Time Music/ASCAP). Estab. 1989. Produces 1 12" single, 1 EP and 4 CDs/year. Fee derived from sales royalty when song or artist is recorded.
How to Contact: Submit demo tape by mail. Unsolicited submissions are OK. Prefers cassette with 1-10 songs and lyric sheet. "If you're an artist send a picture and your best vocal songs. If you're a writer don't send a picture—just your best songs." SASE. Reports in 6 weeks.
Music: Mostly **country**, **pop** and **rock**. Produced "God Bless This Honky Tonk" and "I'm On A Roll," both written by Tony Kinkade and recorded by Tim Murphy on NV Records (country); and "Back Home in Texas" (by Tony Kinkade), recorded by Terry Bullard on NV Records (country). Other artists include Jimmy Sampson (country) and Chris Myers.
Tips: "Here's what we're about. We try to find great songs to use with the artists we produce. Our artists

are released on independent labels with the goal of shopping them to a major label for re-release or distribution. We also pitch songs regularly to major artists through our publishing company. We're growing fast—we need songs."

PREJIPPIE MUSIC GROUP, P.O. Box 312897, Penobscot Station, Detroit MI 48231. President: Bruce Henderson. Record producer, music publisher (Prejippie Music Group/BMI) and record company (PMG Records). Estab. 1990. Produces 5 12″ singles, 2 LPs and 2 EPs/year. Fee derived from outright fee from record company.

- See their listing in the Music Publishers section, as well as PMG Records in the Record Companies section.

How to Contact: Submit demo tape by mail. Unsolicited submissions are OK. No phone calls please. Prefers cassette with 3-4 songs and lyric sheet. SASE. Reports in 3 months.

Music: Mostly **alternative R&B**, **experimental**, **alternative rock** and **techno/house**. Produced *Black Bourgeoisie*, written and recorded by Bourgeoisie Paper Jam; and *Webbslinger*, written and recorded by Tony Webb, all on PMG Records.

THE PRESCRIPTION CO., P.O. Box 222249, Great Neck NY 11021. (516)482-7697. President: David F. Gasman. Vice President A&R: Kirk Nordstrom. Branch: 525 Ashbury St., San Francisco CA 94117. (415)553-8540. VP Sales: Bruce Brennan. Record producer and music publisher (Prescription Co./BMI). Fee derived from sales royalty when artist or song is recorded or outright fee from record company.

- See Prescription Co.'s listing in the Music Publishers section.

How to Contact: Write or call first about your interest then submit demo. Prefers cassette with any number of songs and lyric sheet. Does not return material. Reports in 1 month.

Music: Mostly **bluegrass**, **blues**, **children's**, **country**, **dance**, **easy listening**, **jazz**, **MOR**, **progressive**, **R&B**, **rock**, **soul** and **top 40/pop**. Produced "You Came In," "Rock 'n' Roll Blues" and *Just What the Doctor Ordered*, all recorded by Medicine Mike.

RAINBOW RECORDING, 113 Shamrock Dr., Mankato MN 56001. Phone/fax: (507)625-4027. E-mail: mtotman@prairie.lakes.com. Contact: Michael Totman. Record producer and recording studio. Estab. 1986. Produces 4 singles and 4 CDs/year. Fee derived from outright fee from recording artist or record company.

How to Contact: Submit demo tape by mail. Unsolicited submissions are OK. Prefers cassette, DAT or CD with 4 songs and lyric sheet or lead sheet. Does not return material. Reports in 4-6 weeks.

Music: Mostly **rock**, **country** and **top 40**; also **old time**, **alternative** and **R&B**. Produced *Hosanna Praise Group Songs*, recorded by Hosanna Praise Group (contemporary Christian); *Structure Lake Two*, recorded by Structure/Jody Miller (rock); and *Untitled*, recorded by Morning Star/John Weber (rock opera).

REAL ENTERTAINMENT, (formerly Sandbox Productions), 11684 Ventura Blvd., Suite 134, Studio City CA 91604. (818)386-9135. Fax: (818)386-2862. Producer/Engineer: Mark Wolfson. Record producer, engineer/music supervisor. Estab. 1972. Produces 2 CDs and supervises 4 film projects a year. Fee derived from sales royalty when song or artist is recorded or outright fee from record company or management.

- See the listing for The Sandbox in the Advertising, AV and Commercial Music Firms section.

How to Contact: Submit demo tape by mail. Unsolicited submissions are OK. "No calls please." SASE. Reports in 6 weeks.

Music: Produced *That Thing You Do!* soundtrack for Epic Records; "Marie Down the Street," recorded by Stone Temple Pilots on Savage Records; and "Don't Want to Fall in Love," recorded by Jane Child on Warner Bros. Records.

REALWORLD ENTERTAINMENT CORP., 23330 Commerce Park Rd., Cleveland OH 44122. (216)292-6566. Fax: (216)292-1765. Producers/music publishers: Howard Perl and Lee Mars. Record producer and music publisher. Estab. 1994. Produces 3 acts/year. Fee derived from sales royalty when song or artist is recorded.

How to Contact: Submit demo tape by mail. Unsolicited submissions are OK. Prefers DAT, cassette or videocassette with 1-4 songs. "Label every part of submission with phone number and name." SASE. Reports in 5 weeks.

Music: Mostly **R&B/urban**, **rap** and **pop**; also **alternative**. Produced "Groove With You" (by H. Paul/Lee Mars), recorded by Carey Kelly; *Black America* (by Jazzmarc), recorded by VHB (rap), both on RNR Records; and "Get Ya Moan On" (by H. Paul/Lee Mars), recorded by Myron Davis on Island Records (R&B).

RED KASTLE PRODUCTIONS, P.O. Box 163, West Redding CT 06896. President: Paul Hotchkiss. Record producer, music publisher (Blue Hill Music) and record company (Target Records). Produces 10 singles, 2 EPs, 2 LPs and 2 CDs/year. Fee derived from sales royalty.

- Red Kastle's record label, Target Records, is listed in the Record Companies section.

How to Contact: Prefers cassette with 2 songs and lyric sheet. Include bio. SASE. Reports in 3 weeks.
Music: Mostly **country** and **country/pop**. Produced "Honky Tonk Darlin" and "Thinking About You," (by P. Hotchkiss), recorded by Susan Rose Manning on Target Records (country); and "Destination You," written and recorded by Michael Terry on Roto Noto Records (country). Other artists include Big John Hartman, Beverly's Hill-Billy Band, Susan Rose, Jett and Road Dawgs.

REEL ADVENTURES, 9 Peggy Lane, Salem NH 03079. (603)898-7097. Chief Engineer/Producer: Rick Asmega. Record producer. Estab. 1972. Produces 45 singles, 1 12" single, 23 LPs, 2 EPs and 6 CDs/year. Fee derived from sales royalty when song or artist is recorded, or outright fee from recording artist or record company.
How to Contact: Submit demo tape by mail. Unsolicited submissions are OK. Prefers cassette or CD and lyric sheet. Include photos and résumé. SASE. Reports in 4-6 weeks.
Music: Mostly **pop**, **funk** and **country**; also **blues**, **reggae** and **rock**. Produced *Cry Sin* (by Peter Sin), recorded by Cry Sin (pop); *Reunion* (by Anne Saltmarsh), recorded by New Hampshire Notibles (easy listening), both on Indi Records; and *Lazy Smoke*, written and recorded by John Pollano on Onyx Records (easy rock). Other artists include Larry Sterling, Broken Men, Melvin Crockett, Fred Vigeant, Monster Mash, Carl Armand, Cool Blue Sky, Ransome, Backtrax, Push, Too Cool for Humans and Burn Alley.

ROAMALONE MUSIC, 522 44th St., Suite 3F, Brooklyn NY 11220. Owner: Chris Irish. Record producer/engineer. Fee derived from outright fee from record company.
How to Contact: Submit demo tape by mail. Unsolicited submissions are OK. Does not return material. Reports in 4-6 weeks.
Music: Mostly **rap** and **R&B**. Engineered *Semi-Automatic*, written and recorded by Wu-Tang Clan on Big Beat Records (rap); *Very Necessary*, recorded by Salt-N-Pepa on London Records (rap); and *Tight Team*, recorded by Shamus on Raw Track Records (rap). Other artists include Zhané, Chubb Rock, Redman, Los Pericos, Jodeci, Mary J. Blige and SWV.

ROCKSTAR PRODUCTIONS, P.O. Box 131, Southeastern PA 19399. Executive Vice President: Jeffrey Sacks. Director of Marketing: Roni Sacks. Record producer. Estab. 1988. Produces 5 singles/year. Fee derived from sales royalty when song or artist is recorded.
How to Contact: Submit demo tape by mail. Unsolicited submissions are OK. Prefers cassette with 2 songs and lyric sheet. Does not return material. Reports in 3 months.
Music: Mostly **rock** and **pop**. Produced "I'm Not You" (by S. Sax), recorded by Wanderlust; "You First" and "Alive" (by S. Sax), recorded by The Speddles (pop/rock), all on RKS Records (rock). Other artists include Nancy Falkow and Lola.
Tips: "Musical tastes should include The Beatles, The Kinks, Queen, The Cars. Be original with classic rock roots."

MIKE ROSENMAN, 45-14 215 Place, Bayside NY 11361. (718)229-4864. E-mail: mkrosenman@aol.com. Producer: Mike Rosenman. Record producer and arranger. Estab. 1984. Produces 4-8 singles/year. Fee derived from sales royalty when song or artist is recorded or outright fee from recording artist or record company.
How to Contact: Write first and obtain permission to submit. Prefers cassette or VHS videocassette with 2-4 songs and lyric sheet. Include address and phone number. Put name and phone number on cassette. Will not return any tapes without SASE. Reports in 2-3 months.
Music: Pop, **R&B**, **dance** and **rock**. Remixed "Sleepy Maggie," recorded by Ashley MacIssac (dance); "Feel What You Want," recorded by Kristine W. (dance); and produced "Watercolors," recorded by Richard Robinson (New Age).

RUSTRON MUSIC PRODUCTIONS, 1156 Park Lane, West Palm Beach FL 33417-5957. (561)686-1354. A&R Directors: Rusty Gordon, Ron Caruso and Kevin Reeves. Record producer, record company, manager and music publisher (Rustron Music Publishers/BMI, Whimsong Publishing/ASCAP). Estab. 1970. Produces 6-10 LP/cassettes and 6 CDs/year. Fee derived from outright fee from record company. "This branch office reviews all material submitted for the home office in Ridgefield, CT."

- See Rustron Music's listings in the Record Companies and Managers and Booking Agents sections, as well as Rustron Music Publishers in the Music Publishers section.

How to Contact: Submit demo tape by mail. Unsolicited submissions are OK. Prefers cassette with 1-

3 songs and lyric or lead sheet. "Songs should be 3½ minutes long or less and must be commercially viable for today's market. Exception: New Age fusion compositions 3-10 minutes each, ½ hour maximum. Singer/songwriters and collaborators are preferred." SASE required for all correspondence. Reports in 2-4 months.

Music: Mostly **progressive country**, **pop** (ballads, blues, theatrical, cabaret), **folk/rock**, and **A/C electric acoustic**; also **R&B**, **New Age folk fusion**, **women's music** and **New Age instrumentals**. Produced "Survivalist Librarian," written and recorded by Boomslang Swampsinger on PRMC Records; and "When I Look Into Your Eyes" (by Jayne Margo-Reby/Vic Bersok), recorded by Jayne Margo-Reby on Rustron Records. Other artists include Ellen Hines, Deb Criss, Robin Plitt, Lori Surrency, Gary Jess and Terry Andrews.

RAY SANDERS COMPANY, P.O. Box 384252, Waikoloa HI 96738. (808)883-9383. Owner: Ray Sanders. Record producer and music publisher (Pacific Coast Music/BMI). Estab. 1954. Produces 24 singles and 4-5 CDs/year.

How to Contact: Submit lyrics *only*—must be typed! No cassettes. "If I want to hear a cassette, I'll request it." SASE. Reports in 1 week.

Music: **Country**. Produced "My Buddy Red" (by Hal Johnson), recorded by Ray Sanders on Stardust Records; *Cowboy Hat* (by Ted Vassos), recorded by Ray Sanders on Jackson Hole Records; and "Meet Me In Laredo" (by Mabel Cordle/Marty Robbins), recorded by Ray Sanders on Stardust Records. Other artists include Denny Hemingson, Raising Cane and Dennis O'Niel.

Tips: "You are always better off to work with a co-writer, publisher/record company with a *track record* of success. We have an open door policy to any good writer. Typed lyrics only—no cassettes!"

SAS CORPORATION/SPECIAL AUDIO SERVICES, 503 Broadway, Suite 520, New York NY 10012. (212)226-6271. Fax: (212)226-6357. E-mail: specaudio@aol.com. Owner: Paul Special. Record producer. Estab. 1988. Produces 3 singles, 1 12″ single, 5 LPs, 1 EP and 5 CDs/year. Fee derived from sales royalty when song or artist is recorded or outright fee from recording artist or record company.

How to Contact: Submit demo tape by mail. Unsolicited submissions are OK. Prefers cassette with 1-10 songs and lyric sheet. SASE. Reports in 6-8 weeks.

Music: **Hard rock**, **funk**, **rock**, **metal**, **alternative** and **industrial**. Produced "Color Of Darkness," written and recorded by Maria Excommunikata on Megaforce Records (alternative); "Love U/Duke," written and recorded by Heads Up! on Emergo Records (funk rock); and "Hope/Emelda" (by Van Orden/Hoffman), recorded by The Ordinaires on Bar None Records (alternative). Other artists include Central Europe, Band Of Weeds, Peter Moffit, Kablama Chunk, The Brain Surgeons, Cherry Twister and 12th Planet.

‡STEVE SATKOWSKI PRODUCTIONS, P.O. Box 3403, Stuart FL 34995. (561)781-4657. Fax: (561)283-2374. Engineer/producer: Steven Satkowski. Record producer and recording engineer. Estab. 1987. Produces 25 LPs and 10 CDs/year. Fee derived from outright fee from recording artist or record company.

How to Contact Submit demo tape by mail. Unsolicited submissions are OK. Prefers cassette. Does not return material. Reports in 2 weeks.

Music: Mostly **classical**, **jazz** and **big band**; also **ethnic**, **folk** and **Latin**. Produced recordings by the Miami Symphony, Southwest Florida Symphony and Atlantic Classical Orchestra. Engineered recordings for Steve Howe, Patrick Moraz, Kenny G and Michael Bolton.

SEGAL'S PRODUCTIONS, 16 Grace Rd., Newton MA 02159. (617)969-6196. Contact: Charles Segal. Record producer, music publisher (Segal's Publications/BMI, Samro South Africa) and record company (Spin Records). Produces 6 singles and 6 LPs/year. Fee derived from sales royalty when song or artist is recorded.

- See the listing for Segal's Publications in the Music Publishers section.

How to Contact: Submit demo tape by mail. Unsolicited submissions are OK. Prefers cassette or videocassette with 3 songs and lyric sheet or lead sheet of melody, words, chords. "Please record keyboard/voice or guitar/voice if you can't get a group." Does not return material. Reports in 3 months (only if interested).

Music: Mostly **rock**, **pop** and **country**; also **R&B** and **comedy**. Produced "What Is This Love" (by Paul/Motou), recorded by Julia Manin (rock); "Lovely Is This Memory" (by Segal/Paul), recorded by Nick Chosn on AU.S. (ballad); and *There'll Come A Time* (by Charles Segal), recorded by Rosemary Wills on Spin Records (ballad). Other artists include Art Heatley, Dan Hill and Melanie.

Tips: "Make a good and clear production on cassette even if it is only piano rhythm and voice. Also do a lead sheet of music, words and chords."

‡SEPTEMBER MUSIC PRODUCTIONS, P.O. Box 1181, St. Louis MO 63031. (314)837-4095. Fax: (314)830-3985. E-mail: kirkland@primary.net. Creative Director: Russ Kirkland. Record producer and music publisher (Solid Jammin' Music). Estab. 1979. Produces 3 CDs/year. Fee derived from sales royalty when song or artist is recorded or standard record label/producer deal.
How to Contact: Write first and obtain permission to submit. Prefers cassette with 3 songs and lyric sheet. "Provide name and address for return response, along with a phone number where you can be reached." Does not return material. Reports in 3 weeks.
Music: Mostly **rock/pop**, **alternative** and **instrumental**. Produced *Other Side of Heaven*, written and recorded by Dale Tiemann; *Witness of Love*, written and recorded by Kirkland, both on Ocean/Word Records (pop); and *Tim Darton*, written and recorded by Tim Darton on In House Records (instrumental).

SHU'BABY MONTEZ MUSIC, P.O. Box 28816, Philadelphia PA 19151. (215)473-5527. General Manager: Leroy Schuler. Record producer. Estab. 1986. Produces 6 singles, 25 12″ singles and 3 LPs/year. Fee derived from sales royalty when song or artist is recorded.
How to Contact: Call first and obtain permission to submit. Prefers cassette with 4 songs and lyric sheet. SASE. Reports in 1 month.
Music: Mostly **R&B**, **hip-hop** and **funk**. Produced "Secret Love Affair" (by Clint Washington/Shu'Baby), recorded by P.K. Lyle (pop); "Voodoo Girl," written and recorded by Savanna Gold featuring King (R&B); and "Heaven's Door," written and recorded by Charles Mintz (gospel), all on Urban Logic Records. Other artists include James Lewis, Tow White, the Dead Pigeons, Reggie Height and Ken Chaney.

SILVER BOW PRODUCTIONS, 6260 130 St., Surrey, British Columbia V3X 1R6 **Canada**. (604)572-4232. Fax: (604)572-4252. A&R: Candice James. Record producer. Estab. 1986. Produces 16 singles, 4 LPs and 6 CDs/year. Fee derived from outright fee from recording artist.
How to Contact: Call first and obtain permission to submit. Prefers cassette with 2 songs and lyric sheet. Does not return material. Reports in 6 weeks.
Music: Mostly **country**, **pop**, and **rock**; also **gospel**, **blues** and **jazz**. Produced *Fragile-Handle With Care*, written and recorded by Razzy Bailey on SOA Records (country); *Sugar* (erotic mix) (by Martin Richmond), recorded by Martini (rock); and *Somewhere Downtown* (by Marsh Gardner), recorded by Clancy Wright on Saddlestone Records (country). Other artists include Rex Howard, Gerry King, Joe Lonsdale, Barb Farrell, Dorrie Alexander, Peter James, Matt Audette and Cordel James.

SILVER THUNDER MUSIC GROUP, P.O. Box 41335, Nashville TN 37204. (615)391-5035. Fax: (615)902-0200. President: Rusty Budde. Record producer, record company (Silver Thunder Records), music publisher (Silver Thunder Publishing) and management firm. Estab. 1982. Produces 20 singles, 5-7 LPs and 5-7 CDs/year. Fee derived from sales royalty when song or artist is recorded or outright fee from recording artist or record company.
How to Contact: Write first and obtain permission to submit or to arrange personal interview. Prefers cassette. "Artists should submit 8×10 photo along with demo tape." Does not return material. Reports in 6-16 weeks.
Music: Mostly **country**, **rock** and **R&B**; also **gospel** and **pop**. Produced *What's Not To Love* (by D.J. Music), recorded by Heather Hartsfield (country); and *Radio Active* (by G. McCorkel), recorded by J.D. Treece (country), both on STR Records. Other artists include Rod Woodson, Jeff Samules, Jodi Collins and Hank Thompson.

MIKE SISKIND PRODUCTIONS, 285 Chestnut St., West Hempstead NY 11552. (516)489-0738. Fax: (516)565-9425. E-mail: platear1@aol.com. Producer: Mike Siskind. Record producer. Estab. 1993. Produces 1-2 singles, 1-2 LPs and 1-2 CDs/year. Fee derived from sales royalty when song or artist is recorded.
How to Contact: Write first and obtain permission to submit. Prefers cassette with 3 songs and lyric sheet. "Serious acts only." SASE. Reports in 2-3 months.
Music: Mostly **rock**, **folk** and **country** (work best with women singers); also **pop** and **A/C**. Produced *Generations*, written and recorded by Georgi Smith on Red Hand Records (rock); and *Slice of Life*, written and recorded by Michael Ellis on Storehouse Records (rock). Other artists include Off The Wall.
Tips: "Be willing to let me produce. Every project I've done has been cited for its production."

SLAVESONG CORPORATION, INC., P.O. Box 41684, Dallas TX 75241-0233. (972)225-8428. Chief Executive Officer: Keith Hill. Record producer and music publisher. Estab. 1991. Produces 2 singles, 2 12″ singles, 1 LP, 1 EP and 1 CD/year. Fee derived from sales royalty when song or artist is recorded or outright fee from record company.
How to Contact: Submit demo tape by mail. Unsolicited submissions are OK. Prefers cassette or VHS

videocassette with 3-5 songs and lyric sheet. Send photo. Does not return material. Reports in 1 month.
Music: Mostly **R&B/dance**, **reggae** and **jazz**; also **world beat**. Produced "Oil Spill" and "Hi In My Hello" (by S.W./G.C.), recorded by George Clinton on Warner Bros. Records (R&B); and "Why?" (by S.W./K.H./2 Pos.), recorded by Two Positive M.C. on Slavesong Records (rap). Other artists include X-Slave.

SMASH THE RADIO PRODUCTIONS, 13659 Victory #456, Van Nuys CA 91401. (818)365-4425. Fax: (818)904-0512. Producer: Steven T. Easter. Record producer, record company (Smash the Radio/Mushi-Mushi) and music publisher (Easter Eyes Music/BMI). Estab. 1987. Produces 2 singles, 2 EPs and 2 CDs/year. Fee derived from sales royalty when song or artist is recorded or outright fee from recording artist or record company.
How to Contact: Submit demo tape by mail. Unsolicited submissions are OK. Prefers cassette or CD. SASE. Reports in 3 weeks.
Music: Mostly **techno/house**, **pop** and **reggae**; also **alternative**, **R&B** and **rap**. Produced "Skating on Thin Ice," recorded by The Wailing Wall. Other artists include Mushi-Mushi, Scooter Bradley, Lorena Bello, Sweet Cheeks, Neil Kramer and The Dooley Boys.

S'N'M RECORDING/HIT RECORDS NETWORK, 403 Halkirk, Santa Barbara CA 93110. (805)964-3035. Producers: Cory Orosco, Greg Lewalt and Ernie Orosco. Record producer, record company (Night City Records, Warrior Records, Tell International Records), radio and TV promotion and music publisher. Estab. 1984. Produces 4 singles, 2 12″ singles, 4 LPs, 2 EPs and 2-4 CDs/year. Fee derived from sales royalty when song or artist is recorded.
How to Contact: Call or write first and obtain permission to submit. Prefers VHS videocassette with 4 songs and lyric sheet. Does not return material. Reports in 1 month.
Music: Mostly **pop-rock**, **country** and **top 40**; also **top 40 funk**, **top 40 rock** and **top 40 country**. Produced *Ride for the Brand*, written and recorded by Art Green (country); *Socrates' Notes* (by Patrick Lopez), recorded by Non-Sequiter (alternative); and *40 oz.* (by Ed Diamond), recorded by 40 oz. Band (rap/funk), all on Hit Records. Other artists include New Vision, Jade, Ernie and the Emperors, Hollywood Heros, Cornelius Bumpus (Doobie Brothers), Tim Bogert (Vanilla Fudge, Jeff Beck), Floyd Sneed (3 Dog Night), Peter Lewis, Jim Calire (America) and Mike Kowalski.
Tips: "Keep searching for the infectious chorus hook and don't give up."

‡JOE SOLO PRODUCTIONS, 1825 S. Beverly Glen #204, Los Angeles CA 90025-6900. (310)319-6721. Fax: (310)210-0436. E-mail: oloseoj@aol.com. Assistant: Angela Bennett. Record producer. Estab. 1984. Produces 5 singles, 3 EPs and 3 CDs/year. Fee derived from sales royalty when song or artist is recorded or outright fee from recording artist or record company.
How to Contact: Submit demo tape by mail. Unsolicited submissions are OK. Prefers cassette, DAT or videocassette. "No phone calls please." Does not return material. Reports in 1 month.
Music: Mostly **rock**, **New Age** and **hip hop**; also **country**, **jazz** and **R&B**. Produced *Thing of Beauty* (by Joe Solo), recorded by Macy Gray on Atlantic Records (rock); *Joe Solo*, written and recorded by Joe Solo on Greatmark Records (rock); and *Hope & Dream Explosion* (by Mike Long), recorded by Drill Team on Warner Records (rock). Other artists include Pamela & Richard Williams and Larry Glenn Jones.

‡SOUND ARTS RECORDING STUDIO, 8377 Westview Dr., Houston TX 77055. (713)464-GOLD. President: Jeff Wells. Record producer and music publisher (Earthscream Music). Estab. 1974. Produces 12 singles and 3 LPs/year. Fee derived from outright fee from recording artist.

- See the listing for Earthscream Music Publishing in the Music Publishers section.

How to Contact: Submit demo tape by mail. Unsolicited submissions are OK. Prefers cassette with 2-5 songs and lyric sheet. SASE. Reports in 6 weeks.
Music: Mostly **pop/rock**, **country** and **blues**. Produced Tim Nichols, Perfect Strangers, B.B. Watson, Jinkies, Joe "King" Carasco (on Surface Records), Mark May (on Icehouse Records), The Barbara Pennington Band (on Earth Records), Tempest Under the Sun and Atticus Finch.

SOUND CELL, 601 Meridian St., Huntsville AL 35801. (205)539-1868. Fax: (205)533-1622. Contact: Doug Smith. Record producer, record company and music publisher. Estab. 1981.
How to Contact: Write first and obtain permission to submit a demo. Prefers cassette. Does not return material. Reports in 1 month.
Music: Mostly **country**, **folk** and **bluegrass**; also **R&B** and **pop**. Produced Brian McKnight, Pierce Pettis, Claire Lynch, Take 6 and Vova Nova.

SOUND CONTROL PRODUCTIONS, 2814 Azalea Place, Nashville TN 37204. (615)269-5638. Producer: Mark. Record producer and record company (Mosrite Records). Estab. 1982. Produces 30 singles,

8 LPs and 2 CDs/year. Fee derived from sales royalty or outright fee from recording artist or record company—"sometimes all or a combination of these." Charges 50% in advance for services.
How to Contact: Submit demo tape by mail. Unsolicited submissions are OK. Prefers cassette with 3 songs and lyric sheet. "Don't submit anything in which you need to explain what the song or you are trying to say—let the performance do that." Does not return material. Reports in 2 months.
Music: Mostly **country**, **gospel** and **bluegrass**; also **Christmas**. Produced *Paddy Kelly* (by various), recorded by Paddy Kelly (country); *The Thorntons* (by various), recorded by Thorntons on Bridge Records (gospel); and *The Lewis Family* (by various), recorded by The Lewistown on Benson Records (gospel bluegrass).

SOUND SOUND/SAVAGE FRUITARIAN, P.O. Box 22999, Seattle WA 98122-0999. (206)322-6866. Fax: (206)720-0075. Owner: Tom Fallat. Record producer and recording studio. Estab. 1991. Produces 8 LPs and 5 CDs/year. Fee derived from outright fee from recording artist or record company.
How to Contact: Write or call first and obtain permission to submit a demo. Prefers cassette with 1 song and lyric or lead sheet. SASE. Reports in 2 months.
Music: Mostly **pop/rock/alternative**, **jazz** and **New Age**; also **anything unusual**. Produced *Victim of the Gat* (by Zone & Mac Tenshun), recorded by Lethal Crew (rap); *Led Jaxson* (by Doug Caulkins/Mark Malloy), recorded by Led Jaxson (blues); and *The Ocean Shows the Sky*, written and recorded by Joe Panzetta (folk/pop). Other artists include Robin Wes, Mecca Normal and Mojo Skill.
Tips: "Be unique, authentic and creative. We're more interested in honest expression than quick money making music."

‡SOUND SOUND WEST, 52 Julian Ave., San Francisco CA 94103. (415)281-3301. (415)522-6618. E-mail: 100662.1506@compuserve.com. Owner: 'Dan Dan' Fitzgerald. Record producer. Estab. 1980. Produces 4 CDs/year. Fee derived from outright fee from recording artist or record company.
How to Contact: Write or call first and obtain permission to submit. Prefers cassette with 3 songs and lyric sheet. Does not return material. Reports in 1 month.
Music: Mostly **acoustic**, **rock** and **folk/traditional**; also **songwriters**. Produced *A Different Shore*, written and recorded by Nightnoise on Windham Hill Records (acoustic instrumental); *Good People All*, recorded by The Voice Squad on Shanachie Records (folk); and *Interference*, written and recorded by Interference on Whelan's Records (rock). Other artists include Mary Black.

‡SOUND WORKS ENTERTAINMENT PRODUCTIONS INC., P.O. Box 26691, Las Vegas NV 89126-0691. (702)787-1870. Fax: (702)878-2284. E-mail: soundworks@msn.com. President: Michael E. Jones. Record producer, record company (Sound Works Records) and music publisher (Sound Works). Estab. 1989. Produces 16 singles, 2 LPs and 20 CDs/year. Fee derived from sales royalty when song or artist is recorded or outright fee from recording artist.
How to Contact: Submit demo tape by mail. Unsolicited submissions are OK. Prefers cassette with 3-6 songs and lyric sheet. "Please include short bio and statement of goals and objectives." Does not return material. Reports in 6 weeks.
Music: Mostly **country**, **folk** and **pop**; also **rock**. Produced "Pasadena Playwright" (by Michael Jones) and "Alabama Slammer" (by Wake Eastman), both recorded by Wake Eastman (country); and *The Highway*, written and recorded by Michael Jones (folk), all on Sound Works Records. Other artists include Matt Dorman, Steve Gilmore and J.C. Clark.

SOUNDBOARD STUDIOS, 2600 Kennedy Blvd., Jersey City NJ 07306. (201)451-6140. Producer: Paul Harlyn. Record producer. Estab. 1984. Produces 5 singles, 2 EPs and 4 CDs/year. Fee derived from outright fee from record company.
How to Contact: Submit demo tape by mail. Unsolicited submissions are OK. Prefers cassette with 3 songs. SASE. Reports in 1 month.
Music: Mostly **trance dance**, **pop dance** and **alternative rock/dance**; also **alternative rock**. Produced *Poppyseed (Blue Daze)* (by Paul Harlyn/Scott Slachter), recorded by Poppyseed on CNS Records; "Guantanamera" (by Jose Marti/H. Angulo/P. Seeger), recorded by J.M. Dorathan on Polygram Records; and

REFER TO THE CATEGORY INDEX (at the end of this section) to find exactly which companies are interested in the type of music you write.

Indian Spirets (by Paul Harlyn), recorded by Harlyn on Radikal/BMG Records. Other artists include Great Barrier.

‡SOUTH FLORIDA RECORDING STUDIO, 1885 N.E. 149th St., Miami FL 33181. (305)945-0170. E-mail: wexo@icanect.net. President: John Thomas. Record producer, record company (Radar Records) and music publisher (Zillionaire Music). Estab. 1990. Produces 20 singles, 5 LPs and 10 CDs/year. Fee derived from sales royalty when song or artist is recorded or outright fee from recording artist or record company.

How to Contact: Submit demo tape by mail. Unsolicited submissions are OK. Prefers cassette, DAT or videocassette with 3-4 songs and lyric sheet. "Label very carefully and explain in detail the nature of the work (demo, idea, rough mix, full production finished product)." SASE. Reports in 3 weeks.

Music: Mostly **rock**, **pop** and **dance**; also **R&B**, **rap** and **techno**. Produced "I Like It Like That," written and recorded by Kali Aleman on Hot Records (dance); "Father MC," written and recorded by Father MC on Intersound Records (rap); and *K.C. Live* (by Harry Casey), recorded by K.C. and the Sunshine Band (disco). Other artists include Gioia (from Exposé), Lourdes Rosado and Lis Labarta; has done promos for Howard Stern.

SPHERE PRODUCTIONS, P.O. Box 991, Far Hills NJ 07931-0991. (908)781-1650. Fax: (908)781-1693. President: Tony Zarrella. Talent Manager: Louisa Pazienza. Record producer, artist development and management firm. Produces 5-6 singles and 3 CDs/year. Estab. 1986.

How to Contact: Submit demo tape by mail. Unsolicited submissions are OK. Prefers cassette, CD or VHS videocassette with 3-5 songs and lyric sheets. "Must include: photos, press, résumé, goals and specifics of project submitted, etc." SASE. Reports in 10-12 weeks.

Music: Specializes in **pop/rock (mainstream)**, **progressive/rock**, **New Age** and **crossover country/pop**; also **film soundtracks**. Produced *Take This Heart*, *It's Our Love* and *You and I (Are Dreamers)* (by T. Zarrella), recorded by 4 of Hearts (pop/rock) on Sphere Records. Other artists include Oona Falcon, Traveller, Forever More and Elexus Quinn & Ziggy True (the "Nothing is Meaningless Project").

Tips: "Be able to take direction and have trust and faith in yourself, your producer and manager. Currently seeking artists/groups incorporating various styles into a focused mainstream product."

STUART AUDIO SERVICES, 11 Ridgeway Ave., Gorham ME 04038. (207)839-3569. E-mail: jstuart105@aol.com. Producer/Owner: John A. Stuart. Record producer and music publisher. Estab. 1979. Produces 1-2 singles, 3 LPs and 3 CDs/year. Fee derived from sales royalty when song or artist is recorded, outright fee from recording artist or record company, or demo and consulting fees.

How to Contact: Write or call first and obtain permission to submit or to arrange a personal interview. Prefers cassette with 4 songs and lyric sheet. SASE. Reports in 1-2 months.

Music: Mostly **alternative folk-rock**, **rock** and **country**; also **contemporary Christian**, **children's** and **unusual**. Produced *Big Mouth Soul*, written and recorded by Charlie Schmidt; *Flowerchildren Blues*, written and recorded by Don Campbell, both on Outer Green Records; and *Refuge*, written and recorded by Nate Schrodt on Hoholone Records.

STUDIO D RECORDING, 425 Coloma, Sausalito CA 94965. (415)332-6289. Fax: (415)332-0249. Manager/Co-owner: Joel Jaffe. Record producer and engineer. Estab. 1983. Produces 6-8 LPs and 6-8 CDs/year. Fee derived from sales royalty when song or artist is recorded or outright fee from artist or record company.

How to Contact: Write first and obtain permission to submit demo. Prefers cassette with 3-4 songs and lyric sheet. Does not return material. Reports in 1-2 months. "No response means not accepting material."

Music: Mostly **rock**, **alternative** and **pop**; also **country** and **R&B**. Engineered and co-produced *Greatest Hits*, written and recorded by Huey Lewis and the News on Elektra Records (rock); *Watcha Lookin' For*, written and recorded by Kirk Franklin & the Family on Gospocentric Records; and *Jimmy Dylan & the Gypsies*, written and recorded by Jimmy Dylan & the Gypsies (European release). Other artists include Michael Been and Lenny Williams.

‡STUDIO SEVEN, 417 N. Virginia, Oklahoma City OK 73106. (405)236-0643. Fax: (405)236-0686. E-mail: copesetic@thor.net. Website: http://www.thor.net/~copesetic/. Director of Production: Dave Copenhaver. Record producer, record company (Lunacy Records) and music publisher (DavenRon Music, Bo Kope Music). Estab. 1990. Produces 10 LPs and CDs/year. Fee is derived from sales royalty when song or artist is recorded or outright fee from recording artist or record company.

How to Contact: Submit demo tape by mail. Unsolicited submissions are OK. Prefers cassette with lyric sheet. SASE. Reports in 6 weeks.

Music: Mostly **rock**, **jazz-blues** and **world-Native American**; also **country** and **blues**. Produced *Solitaire*, recorded by Pinetop Perkins (blues); *Los Locos*, recorded by Benny Garcia (jazz); and *Thon-gya*, recorded by Thon-gya (native jazz), all on Lunacy Records. Other artists include Pay Payne, Otis Watkins and Greg Mainus.

SYNDICATE SOUND, INC., 475 Fifth St., Struthers OH 44471. (330)755-1331. President: Jeff Wormley. Producer: Billy Moyer. Record producer, audio and video production company and record and song production company. Estab. 1981. Produces 6-10 singles and 15-20 CDs/year. Fee derived from sales royalty when song or artist is recorded or outright fee from recording artist.
How to Contact: Submit demo tape by mail. Unsolicited submissions are OK. "Please send a promo package or biography (with pictures) of artist, stating past and present concerts and records." Does not return material. Reports in 4-6 weeks.
Music: Mostly **rock**, **pop** and **Christian rock**; also **country**, **R&B** and **alternative**. Produced *Change in My Life* (by Bob Noble), recorded by the Lost Then Found on Syndicate Sound Records (contemporary Christian); *The Universe* (by Paul Rader), recorded by the Paul Rader Band on PR Universe Records (rock); and *Pour* (by Billy Moyer), recorded by Killing Jonas on Yenshee Records (rock). Other artists include Glass House, Blinkk, the Earth Quakers, the Ascensions, No Poultry, Jas the Ace, Potion and Falling Down.

‡ROGER VINCENT TARI, P.O. Box 576, Piscataway NJ 08855. (908)253-9318 or (201)263-9888. Fax: (201)263-9880. E-mail: rvt@worldvista.com. President/Producer: Roger Vincent Tari. Record producer, record company (Nu-Vibe Records) and music publisher (Vintari Music/ASCAP). Estab. 1979. Produces 10-15 singles/year. Fee derived from sales royalty when song or artist is recorded or outright fee from recording artist.
How to Contact: Submit demo tape by mail. Unsolicited submissions are OK. Prefers cassette or VHS videocassette with 3 songs and lyric sheet (videocassette is optional). "The artist should send any relevant literature and a simple black and white picture along with the 3-song cassette and lyric sheet." SASE. Reports in 3-4 weeks.
Music: Mostly **creative pop**, **electronic exotica** and **avant-jazz**; also **world music**, **no-wave** and **indie rock**. Produced "Garden of Life" (by Roger Vincent Tari), recorded by Jee Young Lee (avant pop); "Shih-Ah-Ijah-Seh" (by Roger Vincent Tari), recorded by Mind Dope (free jazz), both on Nu-Vibe Records; and "Sister Asia" (by Roger Vincent Tari), recorded by Joseph Tsai (synth/pop). Other artists include Ling Ling and David Huziu.

TEXAS FANTASY MUSIC, 2932 Dyer St., Dallas TX 75205. (214)691-5318. Fax: (214)692-1392. E-mail: dashley@airmail.net. Creative Director: Barbara McMillen. Record producer and music publisher (Showcat Music, Flying Red Horse Publishing). Estab. 1982. Produces 35 singles/year. Fee derived from sales royalty when song or artist is recorded.

- See the listing for Flying Red Horse Publishing in the Music Publishers section.

How to Contact: Write or call first and obtain permission to submit. Prefers cassette with 2 songs and lyric sheet (if applicable). SASE. Reports in 3 months.
Music: Mostly **instrumental for film** and **all styles**. Produced *Theme for Billy Bob Country Countdown* (by Barbara McMillen/Don Ashley) syndicated TV show; *Theme for Impact* (by Don Ashley) syndicated TV; and *When I Was A Dinosaur Musical* (by Beverly Houston/Barbara McMillen/Richard Theisen), recorded by various artists on Remarkable Records (children's).

‡TIME-OUT PRODUCTIONS/BRAMLA MUSIC, 69 Piccadilly Downs, Lynbrook NY 11563. (516)599-5025. Owner/Producer: Brian Albano. Record producer and music publisher (Bramla Music). Estab. 1989. Fee derived from sales royalty when song or artist is recorded, outright fee from record company or co-production with artist or label.
How to Contact: Submit demo tape by mail. Unsolicited submissions are OK. Prefers cassette. SASE. Reports within 1 month.
Music: All types. Produced *Carl Thomas* (by various artists), recorded by Carl Thomas; *Time-Out Sampler*, written and recorded by various artists; and *Christine Lepera* (by various artists), recorded by Christine Lepera, all on Time-Out Productions. Other artists include Rocket 88, Sheer Magic, Joseph Dedominicis, Roger Calleo, David Bridges and Cheryl Padula.

TMC PRODUCTIONS, P.O. Box 12353, San Antonio TX 78212. (210)829-1909. Producer: Joe Scates. Record producer, music publisher (Axbar Productions/BMI, Scates & Blanton/BMI and Axe Handle Music/ASCAP), record company (Axbar, Trophy, Jato, Prince and Charro Records) and record distribution and promotion. Produces 3-4 LPs and 4-6 CDs/year. Fee derived from sales royalty.
How to Contact: Write or call first and obtain permission to submit. Prefers cassette with 1-5 songs and

lyric sheet. Does not return material. Reports "as soon as possible, but don't rush us."
Music: Mostly **traditional country**; also **blues**, **comedy** and **rock (soft)**. Produced "Chicken Dance" (traditional), recorded by George Chambers and "Hobo Heart," written and recorded by Juni Moon, both on Axbar Records. Other artists include Rick Will, Wayne Carter, Kathi Timm, Leon Taylor and Kenny Dale.

TRAC RECORD CO., 170 N. Maple, Fresno CA 93702. (209)255-1717. Owner: Stan Anderson. Record producer, music publisher (Sellwood Publishing/BMI) and record company (TRAC Records). Estab. 1972. Produces 5 12″ singles, 5 LPs and 5 CDs/year. Fee derived from outright fee from recording artist or outside investor.

- TRAC Records is also listed in the Record Companies section, and Sellwood Publishing is listed in the Music Publishers section.

How to Contact: Submit demo tape by mail. Unsolicited submissions are OK. Prefers cassette with 3 songs and lyric sheet. "Send clear studio demos." SASE. Reports in 3 weeks.
Music: Mostly **country, all styles**. Produced *Long Texas Highway* (by Jessica James/Debbie D.), recorded by Jessica James; *Grandpa's Old Piano* (by Ray Richmond), recorded by Jessica James; and "Outlaw for Your Love," written and recorded by Jimmy Walker; all on TRAC Records (country). Other artists include Double Trouble and The Country Connection.

‡TRACK ONE STUDIOS, 185 Marie St., Williston SC 29853. (803)266-3410. Fax: (803)266-4257. E-mail: track1@sc.tds.net. Owner: Barry Keel. Record producer and recording studio. Estab. 1989. Fee derived from outright fee from recording artist or record company.
How to Contact: Write or call first and obtain permission to submit. Prefers cassette or DAT. SASE. Reports in 2-3 weeks.
Music: Mostly **rock**, **country** and **pop**; also **alternative**. Produced *Why Can't It Be You* (by J. DeVine), recorded by Firecreek (country); and *Where Do I Go* (by D. Bentley), recorded by Wax Bean (pop). Other artists include Upton Trio.

THE TRINITY STUDIO, P.O. Box 1417, Corpus Christi TX 78403. (512)854-4658. E-mail: trinitystudio@juno.com. Owner: Jim Wilken. Record producer and recording studio. Estab. 1988. Fee derived from outright fee from recording artist or record company.
How to Contact: Submit demo tape by mail. Unsolicited submissions are OK. Prefers cassette or VHS videocassette. Does not return material. Reports in 1 month.
Music: Mostly **Christian-country**. Produced *Miracle Man*, written and recorded by Merrill Lane; and *Jesus Is Crying*, written and recorded by Lofton Kline (country), both on TC Records. Other artists include Kerry Patton, Lucy McGuffin, Leah, Jimmy Louis and Charlotte McGee.

TRIPLITT PRODUCTION, (formerly Triplane Production), 120 Cloud Crest Dr., Henderson NV 89015. (702)564-3794. Producer: Vales Crossley. Record producer and music publisher. Estab. 1978. Produces 6 singles, 2 12″ singles, 3 LPs, 3 EPs and 2 CDs/year. Fee derived from sales royalty when song or artist is recorded.
How to Contact: Write or call first and obtain permission to submit. Prefers cassette or videocassette with 3-6 songs and lyric sheet. Does not return material. Reports in 4-6 weeks.
Music: Mostly **top 40**, **R&B**, **soul** and **rap**; also **New Age** and **rock**. Produced "Lapp Dog" (by S. Spann), recorded by Sweet Luie on Cryptic Records; "Hittin' Fo" (by R. Nullems), recorded by Baby Jon on Thump Records; and "Same Heart" (by V. Crossley/C. Burton), recorded by Twin Force on Dynasty Records. Other artists include Platters, Chrissie Zastrow and The Henleys.

TWIST TUNES, 757 Nanoose Ave., Parksville, British Columbia V9P 1E8 **Canada**. (250)752-9291. Producer/Owner: Michael Donegani. Record producer. Estab. 1977. Produces 3 singles, 4 LPs, 1 EP and 2 CDs/year. Fee derived from outright fee from recording artist.
How to Contact: Submit demo tape by mail. Unsolicited submissions are OK. Prefers cassette with 3 songs and lyric sheet. SASE. Reports in 1 month.
Music: Mostly **personal**, **different** and **clear**; also **rock**, **pop** and **country**. Produced *Filth*, written and recorded by Filth (heavy metal); and "Michael Twist," written and recorded by Michael Twist (top 40), both on Private Records. Other artists include John Lynsley, 2:AM, Chris Otcasek, Hassel & Twist, Lendahand, Mean Streets, Danny Click and Jerry Jeff Walker.

‡TWO CHORD MUSIC, 532 LaGuardia Place #277, New York NY 10012-1428. (212)228-7358. Fax: (212)529-1541. E-mail: tmas1@aol.com. President: Tony Maserati. Record producer. Estab. 1992. Produces 2 singles and 3 LPs/year. Fee derived from outright fee from record company.

How to Contact: Write or call first and obtain permission to submit. Prefers cassette with lyric sheet. "Make sure all material is copywritten before submission." Does not return material. Reports in 2 months.
Music: Mostly **pop, R&B** and **alternative rock**. Produced "Miracle Goodnight," written and recorded by David Bowie on Arista Records (pop); and "Love Enough," written and recorded by Soul II Soul on Virgin Records (pop).

UP FRONT MANAGEMENT, 1906 Seward Dr., Pittsburg CA 94565. Phone/fax: (510)427-7210. CEO/ President: Charles Coke. Record producer, management firm, record company (Man Network/Heavyweight Productions) and music publisher (Brother Frog Music). Estab. 1980. Produces 10 singles, 10 LPs, 4 EPs and 10 CDs/year. Fee derived from sales royalty when song or artist is recorded or outright fee from record company or recording artist..

- See Up Front's listing in the Managers and Booking Agents section.

How to Contact: Submit demo tape by mail. Unsolicited submissions are OK. Prefers cassette or CD with lyric sheet. Does not return material. Reports in 2 weeks.
Music: Mostly **rock, country** and **R&B**; also **jazz, alternative** and **blues**. Produced *John Payne*, written and recorded by John Payne (R&B); *Under the Covers*, written and recorded by Bedroom Cowboys (country), both on Mad Network Records; and *Crush*, written and recorded by Crush on 911 Records (rock). Other artists include Simon Stinger.

‡**VALTEC PRODUCTIONS**, P.O. Box 2642, Santa Maria CA 93457. (805)934-8400. Producer: Joe Valenta. Record producer. Estab. 1986. Produces 20 singles and 10 CDs/year. Fee derived from sales royalty when song or artist is recorded.
How to Contact: Submit demo tape by mail. Unsolicited submissions are OK. Prefers cassette, DAT or 8mm videocassette with 3 songs and lyric or lead sheet. Send photo. Does not return material (kept on file for 2 years). Reports in 3-6 weeks.
Music: Mostly **country**, **pop/AC** and **rock**. Produced *Lisa Sanchez*, written and recorded by Lisa Sanchez (country); *John Jacobson*, written and recorded by John Jacobson on Valtone Records (pop); and *Taxi*, written and recorded by Groupe Taxi on Tesoro Records (Spanish/pop).

‡**GARY M. VANDY MUSIC PRODUCTION/ENGINEERING**, 1847 Englewood Rd. #351, Englewood FL 34223. (841)475-6125. E-mail: gvandy@prodigy.com. Contact: Gary Vandy. Record producer. Estab. 1985. Produces 1-2 singles, 1-2 LPs and 1-2 CDs/year. Fee is derived from sales royalty when song or artist is recorded or outright fee from recording artist or record company.
How to Contact: Write first and obtain permission to submit. Prefers cassette, DAT or VHS videocassette with 5-10 songs and lyric and lead sheets. "Include pictures, budget and goals of songwriter." SASE. Reports in 3-6 months.
Music: Mostly **acoustic**, **rock** and **jazz**; also **folk**, **classical** and **reggae**. Recorded and mixed "Do You Wanna Get Funky," written and recorded by Peter Brown (dance); "Get Off," written and recorded by Foxy (dance), both on TK Records; and "Jammin'," written and recorded by Memory of Justice on Platinum Express Records (reggae). Other artists include the Nasty Boys.

CHARLES VICKERS MUSIC ASSOCIATION, P.O. Box 725, Daytona Beach FL 32015-0725. (904)252-4849. President/Producer: Dr. Charles H. Vickers D.M. Record producer, music publisher (Pritchett Publication/BMI, Alison Music/ASCAP) and record company (King of Kings Records, L.A. International Records and Bell Records International). Produces 3 singles and 6 LPs/year. Fee derived from sales royalty when song or artist is recorded.
How to Contact: Submit demo tape by mail. Unsolicited submissions are OK. Prefers 7½ ips reel-to-reel or cassette with 1-6 songs. Does not return material. Reports in 1 week.
Music: Mostly **church/religious**, **gospel** and **hymns**; also **bluegrass**, **blues**, **classical**, **country**, **easy listening**, **jazz**, **MOR**, **progressive**, **reggae (pop)**, **R&B**, **rock**, **soul** and **top 40/pop**. Produced *Have You Heard of That Holy City*, *Every Feeling I Have Comes From God* and *Christ Is Mine*, all written and recorded by Charles Vickers on King of King Records. Other artists include James Franklin, Gladys Nighton and Charles Gardy.

‡**W.C.E. AUDIO INC. AND SRA STUDIOS**, P.O. Box 786, Scotch Plains NJ 07076. (908)322-1869 or (908)753-2378. Fax: (908)228-2585. Studio engineers: Wayne Errickson and Seth Alexander. Record producer, recording engineer and vocal trainer. Produces 15 singles and 15 LPs/year. Fee derived from outright fee from recording artist.
How to Contact: Write or call first and obtain permission to submit. Prefers cassette with 3 songs and lyric sheet. SASE. Reports in 2-3 weeks.
Music: Mostly **R&B**, **hip hop** and **rap**; also **rock**, **country** and **jazz**.

‡WALBASH RIVER AND BROKEN ARROW PRODUCTIONS, P.O. Box 1613, Brunswick GA 31520. (912)264-9837. Executive Producer: Sammie Lee Marler. Record producer, record company, music publisher and distributor. Estab. 1989. Produces 15 singles, 6 LPs, 2 EPs and 10 CDs/year. Fee derived from outright fee from recording artist.
How to Contact: Submit demo tape by mail. Unsolicited submissions are OK. Prefers cassette with 3 songs and lyric sheet. "Send cover letter with goals and history of your music career." SASE. Reports in 2-3 weeks.
Music: Mostly **country**, **gospel** and **traditional country**; also **Native American**, **cowboy** and **pop**. Produced *I Know the Lord is Real* (by Emanuel Skipper), recorded by New Creations (gospel); *A Love Like You* (by Marler/Smyley), recorded by Sammie Lee Marler (country); and *We Shall Reign on High*, written and recorded by Elsa Richards (gospel), all on Five Roses Records. Other artists include Mary Vincent, Regina Price and From the Heart.

WALL STREET PRODUCTIONS, 1189 E. 14 Mile, Birmingham MI 48009. (810)646-2054. Fax: (810)646-1957. Executive Producers: Tim Rochon and Joe Sanders. Record producer, record company, music publisher. Estab. 1985. Produces 6 singles, 4 12″ singles, 3 LPs and 6 CDs/year. Fee derived from sales royalty when song or artist is recorded.
- See Wall Street's listing in the Record Companies section.

How to Contact: Call first and obtain permission to submit. Prefers cassette (or videocassette if available) with 2 songs and lyric sheet. "Label all materials completely." Does not return material. Reports in 6 weeks.
Music: Mostly **rap**, **hip hop** and **dance**; also **R&B** and **jazz**. Produced "Taste the Flava" (by Mike Buckholtz), recorded by Soulism; "Ooh La La" (by Lester Marlin) and *Nasty Sexual Thangs* (by Darrell Campbell), both recorded by Simply Black, all on WSM Records. Other artists include Drueada and ANG.

WALTON RECORD PRODUCTIONS, P.O. Box 218146, Nashville TN 37221-8146. (615)646-0506. Website: http://www.geocities.com/sunsetstrip/palms/3915. Executive Producer: Jimmy Walton. Project Director: S. Hardesty. Record producer, record company and music publisher (JW One Music Publishing/BMI, Jimmy Walton Music Publishing/ASCAP). Estab. 1963. Produces 6-20 CDs/year. Fee derived from sales royalty when song or artist is recorded or outright fee from record company.
- See the listing for JW One Music Publishing in the Music Publishers section.

How to Contact: Submit demo tape by mail. Unsolicited submissions are OK. Prefers cassette with 1-4 songs and lyric sheet. "Lyric sheets must be clearly printed. Submit proof of copyright ownership. Artist and performing groups send bio and photo." SASE. Reports in 1-8 weeks.
Music: Mostly **country ballads**, **new country/uptempo**, **pop/MOR** and **comedy**; also **R&B**, **lite rock** and **modern gospel**. Produced *One Too Many Times* (by Bob Bates/Paula St. Gelais), recorded by Bob Bates; *Long Way To Denver* (by James Phillips), recorded by Ray Barnette; and *How Many Heartaches* (by Herman House/Jimmy Walton), recorded by Sally Evans, all on Walton Record Productions.

‡WATERBURY PRODUCTIONS, 6833 Murietta Ave., Van Nuys CA 91405. Owner: Dave W. Record producer and music publisher (Dave Shavu Publishing). Estab. 1987. Produces 10 singles, 10 LPs, 4 EPs and 4-6 CDs/year. Fee derived from sales royalty when song or artist is recorded or outright fee from recording artist or record company.
How to Contact: Submit demo tape by mail. Unsolicited submissions are OK. Prefers cassette with 3-4 songs and lyric sheet. SASE. Reports in 2-8 weeks.
Music: Mostly **lyricists**, **modern rock** and **danceable music**; also **New Age/lite jazz**, **any cutting edge rock** and **lyricists and poets**. Produced *L.A.s Finest*, written and recorded by various artists on Vantage Records; *Exotika*, written and recorded by The XOT-X on Ultimate Records (alternative); and *Look Into The Future*, written and recorded by various artists on U.O.C. Records (modern rock). Other artists include Guitar Jack, Onion, Frank Gilman, Preacha Man, P-Belly, the Elements and the Ultra-Matix.

THE WEISMAN PRODUCTION GROUP, 449 N. Vista St., Los Angeles CA 90036. (213)653-0693. Contact: Ben Weisman. Record producer and music publisher (Audio Music Publishers). Estab. 1965. Produces 10 singles/year. Fee derived from sales royalty when song or artist is recorded.
- The Weisman Production Group's publishing company, Audio Music Publishers, is listed in the Music Publishers section.

How to Contact: Submit demo tape by mail. Unsolicited submissions are OK. Prefers cassette with 3-10 songs and lyric sheet. SASE. "Mention *Songwriter's Market*. Please make return envelope the same size as the envelopes you send material in, otherwise we cannot send everything back. Just send tape." Reports in 4-8 weeks.
Music: Mostly **R&B**, **soul**, **dance**, **rap** and **top 40/pop**; also **all types of rock**.

WESTWIRES DIGITAL USA, 1042 Club Ave., Allentown PA 18103. (610) 435-1924. Contacts: Wayne Becker and Larry Dix. Record producer and production company. Fee derived from sales royalty when song or artist is recorded or outright fee from artist or record company.
How to Contact: Submit demo tape by mail. Unsolicited submissions are OK. Prefers cassette or VHS videocassette with 3 songs and lyric sheet. SASE. Reports in 1 month.
Music: R&B, **dance**, **alternative**, **folk** and **improvisation**. Produced *The Light of Day*, written and recorded by Steve Gillette/Cindy Mangsen on Compass Rose Records; and *A Survivor's Smile*, written and recorded by Gary Hassay on Dbops Records (jazz). Other artists include William Parkse, Nikki Hill and Traveler.
Tips: "We are interested in singer/songwriters and alternative artists living in the mid-Atlantic area. Performance experience is paramount."

‡WICH AUDIO SERVICES, P.O. Box 66100, Los Angeles CA 90066. (213)896-1922. Producer/Engineer: John Karpowich. Record producer. Estab. 1991. Produces 5 singles, 3 LPs, 5 EPs and 3 CDs/year. Fee derived from outright fee from record company.
How to Contact: Submit demo tape by mail. Unsolicited submissions are OK. Prefers DAT with 3 songs and lyric or lead sheet. Does not return material. Reports in 3 weeks.
Music: Mostly **Latin rock**, **American rock** and **pop**; also **flamenco**, **blues** and **alternative**. Produced *Dame Tu Sueños*, recorded by Sistema on Sony Records Mexico (rock); *Dance of The Hangman*, recorded by Kevin Bening (gothic); and *Jah Bandis*, recorded by Wadi Gad (reggae), both on W.A.S. Records.

‡WILBUR PRODUCTIONS, 159 W. Fourth St. #10, New York NY 10014. (212)255-5544. E-mail: pilot@interport.net. Website: http://www.interport.net/~pilot. President: Will Schillinger. Record producer and recording engineer/studio owner. Estab. 1989. Produces 50 singles, 20 LPs and 20 CDs/year. Fee derived from sales royalty when song or artist is recorded or outright fee from record company.
How to Contact: Submit demo tape by mail. Unsolicited submissions are OK. Prefers cassette with 3-5 songs. Does not return material. Reports in 2 weeks.
Music: Mostly **rock** and **jazz**. Produced *My Truck is My Home*, written and recorded by Marshall Crenshaw on Razor & Tie Records (rock); *Masters of Suspense*, written and recorded by Jack Walrath & Band on Kokopelli Records (jazz); and *Groovalaya*, written and recorded by In The Groove on Wally Records (funk).
Tips: "Don't worry about your demo quality. Send good songs. Very interested in new bands as well."

FRANK WILLSON, P.O. Box 2297, Universal City TX 78148. (210)659-2557. E-mail: bswr18@txdiret.net. Producer: Frank Willson. Record producer, management firm (Universal Music Marketing) and record company (BSW Records/Universal Music Records). Estab. 1987. Produces 20-25 albums/year. Fee derived from sales royalty when song or artist is recorded.

- Frank Willson's record company, BSW Records, can be found in the Record Companies section and his management firm, Universal Music Marketing, is in the Managers and Booking Agents section.

How to Contact: Submit demo tape by mail. Unsolicited submissions are OK. Prefers cassette with 3-4 songs and lyric sheets. SASE. Reports in 4-5 weeks.
Music: Mostly **country**, **blues**, **jazz** and **soft rock**. Produced *Cowboy* (by Jennifer Pierce/Ron Twist), recorded by Shawn DeLorme (country); *Who Drove the Mystery Train* (by Kenny Joe Blake), recorded by Peter Caulton, both on BSW Records; and *Listen to Voices*, written and recorded by Celeste on Universal Records (dance). Other artists include Candee Land, Wes Washington, Harold Dean and David Buescher.

‡WIR (WORLD INTERNATIONAL RECORDS), A-1090 Vienna, Servitengasse 24, **Austria**. Phone: 707-37-10. Fax: 707-84-22. Contact: Peter Jordan. Record producer, music publisher (Aquarius Publishing) and record company (WIR). Estab. 1986. Produces 5-10 singles and 5-8 LPs/year. Fee derived from outright fee from recording artist or record company.

- World International's publishing company, Aquarius Publishing, is listed in the Music Publishers section.

How to Contact: Write or call first and obtain permission to submit. Prefers cassette. SASE. Reports in 2-4 weeks.
Music: Produced *Another Night* (by Ballard), recorded by Jackie (ballad); *Heartbreak Hill* (by Laufenberg), recorded by Dave Johnson (C&W); and *Take Me to the River* (by Whitley), recorded by Tee Williams (C&W), all on WIR Records. Other artists include C.W. Smith, Joe Cannon, Richard Oates, Clemens Hoffman, Keith Gibson, Don McGinnis, Carroll Baker and Lightmare.

WIZARDS & CECIL B, 1111 Second St., San Rafael CA 94901. (415)453-0335. Producer: Pete Slauson. Record producer and music publisher. Estab. 1978. Produces 10 singles, 10 12" singles, 15 LPs and 15 CDs/year. Fee derived from sales royalty when song or artist is recorded.
How to Contact: Submit demo tape by mail. Unsolicited submissions are OK. Prefers cassette with several songs. Does not return material. Reports in 1-2 months.
Music: All kinds. Produced *San Francisco Maritime Hall Live* series recordings; *New Riders of Purple Sage*, recorded on MU Records; and *Reggae on the River* for Warner Brothers Records. Other artists include George Clinton & P-Funk, Jimmy Cliff, Gilberto Gil, Zero, Moby Grape, The Geezers, Caribbean All Stars with Carlos Santana, Shana Morrison and Caledonia.

WLM MUSIC/RECORDING, 2808 Cammie St., Durham NC 27705-2020. (919)471-3086. E-mail: wlmmusrec@juno.com. Owner: Watts Lee Mangum. Record producer. Estab. 1980. Fee derived from outright fee from recording artist. "In some cases, an advance payment requested for demo production."
How to Contact: Submit demo tape by mail. Unsolicited submissions are OK. Prefers cassette with 2-4 songs and lyric or lead sheet (if possible). SASE. Reports in 4-6 months.
Music: Mostly **country**, **country/rock** and **blues/rock**; also **pop**, **rock**, **blues**, **gospel** and **bluegrass**.

STEVE WYTAS PRODUCTIONS, Dept. SM, 11 Custer St., West Hartford CT 06110. (860)953-2834. Contact: Steven J. Wytas. Record producer. Estab. 1984. Produces 4-8 singles, 3 LPs, 3 EPs and 4 CDs/year. Fee derived from outright fee from recording artist or record company.
How to Contact: Submit demo tape by mail. Unsolicited submissions are OK. Prefers cassette or VHS ¾" videocassette with several songs and lyric or lead sheet. "Include live material if possible." Does not return material. Reports in 3 months.
Music: Mostly **rock**, **pop**, **top 40** and **country/acoustic**. Produced *Already Home*, recorded by Hannah Cranna on Big Deal Records (rock); *Under the Rose*, recorded by Under the Rose on Utter Records (rock); and *Sickness & Health*, recorded by Legs Akimbo on Joyful Noise Records (rock). Other artists include King Hop!, The Shells, The Gravel Pit, G'nu Fuz and Toxic Field Mice.

‡Y-N-A/C.D.T. PRODUCTIONS, 170 Rosedale Rd., Yonkers NY 10710. (914)961-1051. Fax: (914)961-5906. E-mail: niftrik@aol.com. Producer: Rikk Angelori. Record producer. Estab. 1984. Produces 30 singles, 5 LPs, 5 EPs and 5 CDs/year. Fee derived from outright fee from recording artist or record company.
How to Contact: Write or call first and obtain permission to submit. Prefers DAT or VHS videocassette with 3 songs, photo and lyric or lead sheet. SASE.
Music: Mostly **R&B/dance**, **soul** and **house**; also **underground** and **rock**. Produced *All Becuz of U* (by Y-N-A), recorded by Sonda of Seduction (dance); *Beautiful* (by Kara D./Y-N-A), recorded by Kara D. (smooth R&B); and *Love Me Like U Do*, written and recorded by Y-N-A, all on T.O. Records. Other artists include Rikk Angel, Frank Jay, Tanya's Dream, Go For It, U & Me, Ray Tabano (formerly of Aerosmith), Tom Low and Creative You.

Category Index

The Category Index is a good place to begin searching for a market for your songs. Below is an alphabetical list of 20 general music categories. If you write dance music and are looking for a record producer to submit your songs to, check the Dance section in this index. There you will find a list of record producers who work with dance music. Once you locate the listings for those producers, read the music subheading *carefully* to determine which companies are most interested in the type of dance music you write. Some of the markets in this section do not appear in the Category Index because they have not indicated a specific preference. Most of these said they are interested in "all types" of music. Listings that were very specific, or whose description of the music they're interested in doesn't quite fit into these categories, also do not appear here.

Adult Contemporary

"A" Major Sound Corporation; ‡Aberdeen Productions; Bal Records; Carlock Productions; Country Star Productions; ‡Daliven Music; Intrigue Production; James, Sunny; ‡Jump Productions; Kingsport Creek Music; Known Artist Productions; Kovach, Robert R.; Luick & Associates, Harold; Magid Productions, Lee; Nashville Country Productions; New Horizon Records; ‡New Vizion Studios, The; Panio Brothers Label; Peridot Productions; Planet Dallas; Prescription Co., The; Rustron Music Productions; Siskind Productions, Mike; ‡Valtec Productions; Vickers Music Association, Charles; Walton Record Productions

Alternative

"A" Major Sound Corporation; Aladdin Productions; Apophis Music; ‡Artistic Noise; Bewildering Music, Inc.; ‡Blues Alley Records; Carlock Productions; ‡Chainsaw Records; DaVinci's Notebook Records; Dudick, J.D.; Federici's Shark River Music, Danny; ‡Glass House Productions; ‡Guerilla Audio; ‡Heck, Brad; James Productions, Neal; JK Jam Productions; ‡John Productions, David; Kane Producer/Engineer, Karen; L.A. Entertainment; ‡Mac-Attack Productions; ‡Magnetic Oblivion Music Co.; ‡Marenco, Cookie; Mathews, Scott, d/b/a Hit or Myth Productions; Perennial Productions; Prejippie Music Group; Rainbow Recording; Realworld Entertainment Corp.; SAS Corporation/Special Audio Services; ‡September Music Productions; Smash the Radio Productions; Sound Sound/Savage Fruitarian; Soundboard Studios; Stuart Audio Services; Studio D Recording; Syndicate Sound, Inc.; ‡Tari, Roger Vincent; ‡Track One Studios; ‡Two Chord Music; Up Front Management; ‡Waterbury Productions; Westwires Digital USA; ‡Wich Audio Services

Blues

Aladdin Productions; Bal Records; Big Bear; Celt Musical Services, Jan; Demi Monde Records & Publishing Ltd.; Duane Music, Inc.; Esquire International; ‡Glass House Productions; Hailing Frequency Music Productions; James Productions, Neal; Landmark Communications Group; Linear Cycle Productions; Magid Productions, Lee; Mega Truth Records; New Horizon Records; Peridot Productions; Prescription Co., The; Reel Adventures; Silver Bow Productions; ‡Sound Arts Recording Studio; ‡Studio Seven; TMC Productions; Up Front Management; Vickers Music Association, Charles; ‡Wich Audio Services; Willson, Frank; WLM Music/Recording

Children's

Fera Productions, Vito; Peridot Productions; Prescription Co., The; Stuart Audio Services

Classical

Apophis Music; Aurora Productions; Janus Management; Lark Talent & Advertising; ‡Marenco, Cookie; ‡Satkowski Productions, Steve; ‡Vandy Music Production/Engineering, Gary M.; Vickers Music Association, Charles

Country

‡Aberdeen Productions; ACR Productions; Airwave Production Group Inc.; AKO Productions; Aladdin Productions; Allyn, Stuart J.; Bal Records; ‡Blues Alley Records; Bowden, Robert; ‡Cacophony Productions; Capitol Ad, Management & Talent Group; Cedar Creek Productions; ‡Chainsaw Records; Coffee and Cream Productions; Country Star Productions; ‡Daliven Music; Darrow, Danny; De Miles, Edward; DeLory and Music Makers, Al; Doss Presents, Col. Buster; Duane Music, Inc.; Dudick, J.D.; ‡Durr Productions, David; Earmark Audio; Eiffert, Jr., Leo J.; Esquire International; Eternal Song Agency, The; Federici's Shark River Music, Danny; Gale, Jack; ‡Guerilla Audio; ‡Harmony Alley Audio Co.; ‡Heck, Brad; Hickory Lane Publishing and Recording; Horrigan Productions; ‡Hot Sound Productions; James Productions, Neal; James, Sunny; Jay Jay Publishing & Record Co.; JK Jam Productions; Johnson, Little Richie; Kennedy Enterprises, Inc., Gene; Kingsport Creek Music; Kingston Records and Talent; Known Artist Productions; Kovach, Robert R.; Landmark Communications Group; Lari-Jon Productions; Lark Talent & Advertising; Linear Cycle Productions; Lloyd Productions, Mick; Luick & Associates, Harold; McCoy Productions, Jim; Magid Productions, Lee; ‡Marenco, Cookie; Martin, Pete/Vaam Music Productions; Mathes Productions, David; Mega Truth Records; ‡Mom and Pop Productions, Inc.; Musicland Productions, Inc.; Nashville Country Productions; Nebo Record Company; Nelson, Bill; ‡Neo Sync Labs; Ormsby, John "Buck"/Etiquette Productions; Panio Brothers Label; Parker, Patty; Peridot Productions; Pierce, Jim; Planet Dallas; ‡Pomgar Productions; Prescription Co., The; Rainbow Recording; Red Kastle Productions; Reel Adventures; Rustron Music Productions; Sanders Company, Ray; Segal's Productions; Silver Bow Productions; Silver Thunder Music Group; Siskind Productions, Mike; S'N'M Recording/Hit Records Network; ‡Solo Productions, Joe; ‡Sound Arts Recording Studio; Sound Cell; Sound Control Productions; ‡Sound Works Entertainment Productions Inc.; Sphere Productions; Stuart Audio Services; Studio D Recording; ‡Studio Seven; Syndicate Sound, Inc.; TMC Productions; Trac Record Co.; ‡Track One Studios; Trinity Studio, The; Twist Tunes; Up Front Management; ‡Valtec Productions; Vickers Music Association, Charles; ‡W.C.E. Audio Inc. and SRA Studios; ‡Walbash River and Broken Arrow Productions; Walton Record Productions; Willson, Frank; WLM Music/Recording; Wytas Productions, Steve

Dance

‡Artistic Noise; Blaze Productions; Coffee and Cream Productions; Corwin, Dano; Creative Music Services; ‡Daliven Music; Darrow, Danny; De Miles, Edward; Esquire International; Final Mix Music; House of Rhythm; Intrigue Production; Janoulis Productions, Alexander/Big Al Jano Productions; JGM Recording Studio; JK Jam Productions; ‡Jump Productions; KMA; Leeway Entertainment Group; Lloyd Productions, Mick; London Brijj; ‡Mac-Attack Productions; Mega Truth Records; ‡Neo Sync Labs; Neu Electro Productions; Panio Brothers Label; Poku Productions; Prejippie Music Group; Prescription Co., The; Rosenman, Mike; Slavesong Corporation, Inc.; Smash the Radio Productions; Soundboard Studios; ‡South Florida Recording Studio; Wall Street Productions; ‡Waterbury Productions; Weisman Production Group, The; Westwires Digital USA; Y-N-A/C.D.T. Productions

Folk

Aurora Productions; Coppin, Johnny/Red Sky Records; ‡Durr Productions, David; ‡Eject Productions; ‡Gallway Bay Music; ‡Glass House Productions; Janus Management; Magid Productions, Lee; ‡Marenco, Cookie; Perennial Productions; Peridot Productions; Rustron Music Productions; ‡Satkowski Productions, Steve; Siskind Productions, Mike; Sound Cell; ‡Sound Sound West; ‡Sound Works Entertainment Productions Inc.; ‡Vandy Music Production/Engineering, Gary M.; Westwires Digital USA

Instrumental

Eternal Song Agency, The; ‡Heck, Brad; ‡Jump Productions; Lark Talent & Advertising; Magid Productions, Lee; Mathes Productions, David; ‡September Music Productions

Jazz

Airwave Production Group Inc.; Allyn, Stuart J.; Angel Films Company; Apophis Music; ‡Appell, Jonathan; Aurora Productions; Bal Records; Big Bear; Capitol Ad, Management & Talent

Group; Cedar Creek Productions; Celt Musical Services, Jan; ‡Chainsaw Records; Creative Music Services; ‡Daliven Music; Darrow, Danny; DaVinci's Notebook Records; De Miles, Edward; ‡Durr Productions, David; Eight Ball MIDI & Vocal Recording; Esquire International; ‡Fagnano, Frank D.; Fera Productions, Vito; Heart Consort Music; ‡Heck, Brad; ‡Hot Sound Productions; James, Sunny; Janus Management; Katz Productions, Matthew; Landmark Communications Group; Magid Productions, Lee; ‡Magnetic Oblivion Music Co.; ‡Marenco, Cookie; ‡Mom and Pop Productions, Inc.; ‡Neo Sync Labs; New Horizon Records; Perennial Productions; Philly Breakdown; Prescription Co., The; ‡Satkowski Productions, Steve; Silver Bow Productions; Slavesong Corporation, Inc.; ‡Solo Productions, Joe; Sound Sound/Savage Fruitarian; ‡Studio Seven; ‡Tari, Roger Vincent; Up Front Management; ‡Vandy Music Production/Engineering, Gary M.; Vickers Music Association, Charles; ‡W.C.E. Audio Inc. and SRA Studios; Wall Street Productions; ‡Waterbury Productions; ‡Wilbur Productions; Willson, Frank

Latin

DeLory and Music Makers, Al; Eight Ball MIDI & Vocal Recording; ‡Satkowski Productions, Steve; ‡Wich Audio Services

Metal

"A" Major Sound Corporation; ‡Chainsaw Records; SAS Corporation/Special Audio Services

New Age

Big Sky Audio Productions; DaVinci's Notebook Records; ‡Durr Productions, David; Eight Ball MIDI & Vocal Recording; Federici's Shark River Music, Danny; Heart Consort Music; Leeway Entertainment Group; Neu Electro Productions; ‡New Vizion Studios, The; Rustron Music Productions; ‡Solo Productions, Joe; Sound Sound/Savage Fruitarian; Sphere Productions; Triplitt Production; ‡Waterbury Productions

Novelty

‡Eject Productions; Jay Jay Publishing & Record Co.; Linear Cycle Productions; ‡Magnetic Oblivion Music Co.; Nashville Country Productions; Peridot Productions; Segal's Productions; TMC Productions

Pop

"A" Major Sound Corporation; ‡Aberdeen Productions; ACR Productions; Airwave Production Group Inc.; AKO Productions; Allyn, Stuart J.; Angel Films Company; ‡Appell, Jonathan; ‡Artistic Noise; Bal Records; Blaze Productions; ‡Blues Alley Records; Bowden, Robert; ‡Cacophony Productions; Capitol Ad, Management & Talent Group; Carlock Productions; Cedar Creek Productions; ‡Chicago Kid Productions; Chucker Music, Inc.; Coffee and Cream Productions; Corwin, Dano; Creative Music Services; Darrow, Danny; DaVinci's Notebook Records; De Miles, Edward; DeLory and Music Makers, Al; Demi Monde Records & Publishing Ltd.; Doss Presents, Col. Buster; Duane Music, Inc.; Dudick, J.D.; Durr Productions, David; Eight Ball MIDI & Vocal Recording; Esquire International; Eternal Song Agency, The; ‡Gallway Bay Music; ‡Harmony Alley Audio Co.; Horrigan Productions; ‡Hot Sound Productions; House of Rhythm; Intrigue Production; Ivory Productions, Inc.; James Productions, Neal; Janoulis Productions, Alexander/Big Al Jano Productions; JGM Recording Studio; JK Jam Productions; ‡Jump Productions; Kane Producer/Engineer, Karen; Kingsport Creek Music; Kingston Records and Talent; Known Artist Productions; Kovach, Robert R.; Landmark Communications Group; Leeway Entertainment Group; Linear Cycle Productions; ‡Mac-Attack Productions; Magid Productions, Lee; ‡Marenco, Cookie; Martin, Pete/Vaam Music Productions; Mathews, Scott, d/b/a Hit or Myth Productions; Moffet, Gary; Must Rock Productionz Worldwide; Nebo Record Company; Nelson, Bill; Neu Electro Productions; New Experience Records; ‡New Vizion Studios, The; Ormsby, John "Buck"/Etiquette Productions; Parker, Patty; Philly Breakdown; Planet Dallas; Poku Productions; ‡Pomgar Productions; Prescription Co., The; Rainbow Recording; Realworld Entertainment Corp.; Red Kastle Productions; Reel Adventures; Rockstar Productions; Rosenman, Mike; Rustron Music Productions; Segal's Productions; ‡September Music Productions; Silver Bow Productions; Silver Thunder Music Group; Siskind Productions, Mike;

Smash the Radio Productions; S'N'M Recording/Hit Records Network; ‡Sound Arts Recording Studio; Sound Cell; Sound Sound/Savage Fruitarian; ‡Sound Works Entertainment Productions Inc.; ‡South Florida Recording Studio; Sphere Productions; Studio D Recording; Syndicate Sound, Inc.; ‡Tari, Roger Vincent; ‡Track One Studios; Triplitt Production; Twist Tunes; ‡Two Chord Music; ‡Valtec Productions; Vickers Music Association, Charles; ‡Walbash River and Broken Arrow Productions; Walton Record Productions; Weisman Production Group, The; ‡Wich Audio Services; WLM Music/Recording; Wytas Productions, Steve

R&B

"A" Major Sound Corporation; ACR Productions; Airwave Production Group Inc.; Allyn, Stuart J.; Angel Films Company; Apophis Music; ‡Appell, Jonathan; ‡Artistic Noise; Bal Records; Big Sky Audio Productions; ‡Blues Alley Records; Capitol Ad, Management & Talent Group; Cedar Creek Productions; Celt Musical Services, Jan; ‡Chainsaw Records; ‡Chicago Kid Productions; Chucker Music, Inc.; Coffee and Cream Productions; Country Star Productions; Daddy, S. Kwaku; ‡Daliven Music; DaVinci's Notebook Records; De Miles, Edward; Duane Music, Inc.; ‡Durr Productions, David; Eight Ball MIDI & Vocal Recording; Esquire International; Federici's Shark River Music, Danny; Fera Productions, Vito; Final Mix Music; Hailing Frequency Music Productions; House of Rhythm; Intrigue Production; James Productions, Neal; James, Sunny; Janoulis Productions, Alexander/Big Al Jano Productions; JGM Recording Studio; JK Jam Productions; Kane Producer/Engineer, Karen; Kingsport Creek Music; KMA; Known Artist Productions; Kovach, Robert R.; L.A. Entertainment; Linear Cycle Productions; London Brijj; Magid Productions, Lee; Martin, Pete/Vaam Music Productions; Mathes Productions, David; Mr. Wonderful Productions, Inc.; ‡Mom and Pop Productions, Inc.; Must Rock Productionz Worldwide; Nebo Record Company; New Experience Records; ‡New Vizion Studios, The; Ormsby, John "Buck"/Etiquette Productions; Planet Dallas; Prescription Co., The; Rainbow Recording; Realworld Entertainment Corp.; ‡RoamAlone Music; Rosenman, Mike; Rustron Music Productions; Segal's Productions; Shu'Baby Montez Music; Silver Thunder Music Group; Slavesong Corporation, Inc.; Smash the Radio Productions; ‡Solo Productions, Joe; Sound Cell; ‡South Florida Recording Studio; Studio D Recording; Syndicate Sound, Inc.; Triplitt Production; ‡Two Chord Music; Up Front Management; Vickers Music Association, Charles; ‡W.C.E. Audio Inc. and SRA Studios; Wall Street Productions; Walton Record Productions; Weisman Production Group, The; Westwires Digital USA; ‡Y-N-A/C.D.T. Productions

Rap

Final Mix Music; Intrigue Production; KMA; London Brijj; ‡Marenco, Cookie; Mr. Wonderful Productions, Inc.; Must Rock Productionz Worldwide; Neu Electro Productions; New Experience Records; Philly Breakdown; Poku Productions; Realworld Entertainment Corp.; ‡RoamAlone Music; Shu'Baby Montez Music; Smash the Radio Productions; ‡Solo Productions, Joe; South Florida Recording Studio; Triplitt Production; ‡W.C.E. Audio Inc. and SRA Studios; Wall Street Productions; Weisman Production Group, The

Religious

"A" Major Sound Corporation; ACR Productions; Airwave Production Group Inc.; Aladdin Productions; Bal Records; ‡Blues Alley Records; Capitol Ad, Management & Talent Group; Carlock Productions; Cedar Creek Productions; Coffee and Cream Productions; Country Star Productions; Daddy, S. Kwaku; Doss Presents, Col. Buster; ‡Durr Productions, David; Eiffert, Jr., Leo J.; Esquire International; Eternal Song Agency, The; Fera Productions, Vito; Hailing Frequency Music Productions; James Productions, Neal; Jazmin Productions; Kennedy Enterprises, Inc., Gene; Kingsport Creek Music; Kovach, Robert R.; Landmark Communications Group; Lari-Jon Productions; Linear Cycle Productions; Luick & Associates, Harold; McCoy Productions, Jim; Magid Productions, Lee; Mathes Productions, David; Mr. Wonderful Productions, Inc.; ‡Mom and Pop Productions, Inc.; Musicland Productions, Inc.; Nashville Country Productions; Nebo Record Company; Nelson, Bill; New Experience Records; Peridot Productions; Philly Breakdown; Silver Bow Productions; Silver Thunder Music Group; Sound Control Productions; Stuart Audio Services; Syndicate Sound, Inc.; Trinity Studio, The; Vickers Music Association, Charles; ‡Walbash River and Broken Arrow Productions; Walton Record Productions; WLM Music/Recording

Rock

"A" Major Sound Corporation; ‡Aberdeen Productions; ACR Productions; Airwave Production Group Inc.; AKO Productions; Aladdin Productions; Allyn, Stuart J.; Angel Films Company; Apophis Music; ‡Appell, Jonathan; Bal Records; Big Sky Audio Productions; Blaze Productions; ‡Blues Alley Records; ‡Cacophony Productions; Capitol Ad, Management & Talent Group; Carlock Productions; Cedar Creek Productions; Celt Musical Services, Jan; ‡Chainsaw Records; ‡Chicago Kid Productions; Chucker Music, Inc.; Collector Records; Coppin, Johnny/Red Sky Records; Corwin, Dano; Country Star Productions; ‡Daliven Music; DaVinci's Notebook Records; Deep Space Records; Demi Monde Records & Publishing Ltd.; Duane Music, Inc.; Dudick, J.D.; ‡Durr Productions, David; Earmark Audio; Eight Ball MIDI & Vocal Recording; ‡Eject Productions; Esquire International; ‡Fagnano, Frank D.; Federici's Shark River Music, Danny; Fera Productions, Vito; ‡Glass House Productions; ‡Guerilla Audio; Hailing Frequency Music Productions; ‡Harmony Alley Audio Co.; ‡Heck, Brad; Horrigan Productions; ‡Hot Sound Productions; House of Rhythm; ‡Integrated Entertainment; Intrigue Production; Ivory Productions, Inc.; James Productions, Neal; James, Sunny; Janoulis Productions, Alexander/Big Al Jano Productions; Janus Management; JGM Recording Studio; JK Jam Productions; ‡John Productions, David; Katz Productions, Matthew; Kingston Records and Talent; Kovach, Robert R.; Landmark Communications Group; Lari-Jon Productions; Linear Cycle Productions; Lloyd Productions, Mick; McCoy Productions, Jim; Magid Productions, Lee; Mathews, Scott, d/b/a Hit or Myth Productions; Mega Truth Records; Moffet, Gary; Nebo Record Company; ‡Neo Sync Labs; Neu Electro Productions; New Experience Records; ‡New Vizion Studios, The; Ormsby, John "Buck"/Etiquette Productions; Parker, Patty; Planet Dallas; Poku Productions; ‡Pomgar Productions; Prejippie Music Group; Prescription Co., The; Rainbow Recording; Reel Adventures; Rockstar Productions; Rosenman, Mike; Rustron Music Productions; SAS Corporation/Special Audio Services; Segal's Productions; ‡September Music Productions; Silver Bow Productions; Silver Thunder Music Group; Siskind Productions, Mike; S'N'M Recording/Hit Records Network; ‡Solo Productions, Joe; ‡Sound Arts Recording Studio; Sound Sound/Savage Fruitarian; ‡Sound Sound West; ‡Sound Works Entertainment Productions Inc.; ‡South Florida Recording Studio; Sphere Productions; Stuart Audio Services; Studio D Recording; ‡Studio Seven; Syndicate Sound, Inc.; TMC Productions; ‡Track One Studios; Triplitt Production; Twist Tunes; Up Front Management; ‡Valtec Productions; ‡Vandy Music Production/Engineering, Gary M.; Vickers Music Association, Charles; ‡W.C.E. Audio Inc. and SRA Studios; Walton Record Productions; ‡Waterbury Productions; Weisman Production Group, The; ‡Wich Audio Services; Wilbur Productions; Willson, Frank; WLM Music/Recording; Wytas Productions, Steve; ‡Y-N-A/C.D.T. Productions

World Music

‡Appell, Jonathan; Daddy, S. Kwaku; ‡Durr Productions, David; Eight Ball MIDI & Vocal Recording; ‡Fagnano, Frank D.; Kane Producer/Engineer, Karen; KMA; London Brijj; Reel Adventures; Slavesong Corporation, Inc.; Smash the Radio Productions; ‡Studio Seven; ‡Tari, Roger Vincent; ‡Vandy Music Production/Engineering, Gary M.; Vickers Music Association, Charles

‡ **THE DOUBLE DAGGER** before a listing indicates that the listing is new in this edition.

Managers and Booking Agents

Of all the music industry players surrounding successful artists, managers are usually the people closest to the artists themselves. The artist manager can be a valuable contact, both for the songwriter trying to get songs to a particular artist and for the songwriter/performer. Getting songs to an artist's manager is yet another way of attempting to get your songs recorded, since the manager may play a large part in deciding what material his client uses. For the performer seeking management, a successful manager should be thought of as the foundation for a successful career. Therefore, it pays to be extremely careful when seeking management to represent you.

Choosing a manager can be one of the most important decisions you can make as a songwriter or performer. The relationship between a manager and his client relies on mutual trust. A manager works as the liaison between you and the rest of the music industry, and he must know exactly what you want out of your career in order to help you achieve your goals. His handling of publicity, promotion and finances, as well as the contacts he has within the industry, can make or break your career. You should never be afraid to ask questions about any aspect of the relationship between you and a prospective manager. Always remember that a manager works *for the artist*. A good manager is able to communicate his opinions to you without reservation, and should be willing to explain any confusing terminology or discuss plans with you before taking action. A manager needs to be able to communicate successfully with all segments of the music industry in order to get his client the best deals possible. He needs to be able to work with booking agents, publishers, lawyers and record companies. Keep in mind that you are both working together toward a common goal: success for you and your songs. Talent, originality, professionalism and a drive to succeed are qualities that will attract a manager to an artist—and a songwriter.

The function of the booking agent is to find performance venues for their clients. They usually represent many more acts than a manager does, and have less contact with their acts. A booking agent charges a commission for his services, as does a manager. Managers usually ask for a 15-50% commission on an act's earnings; booking agents usually charge around 10%.

Before submitting to a manager or booking agent, be sure you know exactly what you need. If you're looking for someone to help you with performance opportunities, the booking agency is the one to contact. They can help you book shows either in your local area or throughout the country. If you're looking for someone to help guide your career, you need to contact a management firm. Some management firms may also handle booking; however, it may be in your best interest to look for a separate booking agency. A manager should be your manager—not your agent, publisher, lawyer or accountant. It pays to have a team of people working to get your songs heard, adding to the network of professionals guiding your career and making valuable contacts in the industry.

The firms listed in this section have provided information about the types of music they work with and the types of acts they represent. You'll want to refer to the Category Index at the end of this section to find out which companies deal with the type of music you write, and the Geographic Index at the back of the book to help you locate companies near where you live. Each listing also contains submission requirements and information about what items to include in a press kit, and will also specify whether the company is a management firm or a booking agency. Remember that your submission represents you as an artist, and should be as organized and professional as possible.

ABBA-TUDE ENTERTAINMENT, 1875 Century Park East, 7th Floor, Los Angeles CA 90067. (310)788-2666. Fax: (818)735-0543. Attorney At Law: Mark "Abba" Abbattista. Management firm, music publisher (Abba-Cadaver), attorney. Estab. 1991. Represents individual artists, groups, songwriters, producers, artists from anywhere; currently handles 4 acts. Reviews material for acts.
How to Contact: Submit demo tape by mail. Unsolicited submissions are OK. Prefers cassette or CD with 3-4 songs and lead sheet. If seeking management, press kit should include bio, CD, tape, photo. "Be sure to put name and phone number on inside of tape." SASE. Reports in 2-4 weeks.
Music: Mostly **quality**; also **established acts**. Works primarily with bands, solo artists, singers, guitarists. Current acts include Souls at Zero (metal band) and Skeletones (ska).

AFTERSCHOOL PUBLISHING COMPANY, P.O. Box 14157, Detroit MI 48214. (313)894-8855. President: Herman Kelly. Management firm, booking agency, record company (Afterschool Co.) and music publisher (Afterschool Pub. Co.). Estab. 1978. Represents individual artists, songwriters, producers, arrangers and musicians. Currently handles 2 acts. Reviews material for acts.
How to Contact: Submit demo tape by mail. Unsolicited submissions are OK. Prefers cassette with 3 songs and lyric or lead sheet. If seeking management, include résumé, photo with demo tape and bio in press kit. SASE. Reports in 1 week.
Music: Mostly **pop**, **jazz**, **rap**, **country** and **folk**. Works primarily with small bands and solo artists. Current acts include Black Prince and Musiranma Comedy play.

AKO PRODUCTIONS, 20531 Plummer, Chatsworth CA 91311. (818)998-0443. President: A.E. Sullivan. Management firm, booking agency, music publisher and record company (AKO Records, Dorn Records, Aztec Records). Estab. 1980. Represents local and international artists, groups and songwriters; currently handles 5 acts. Receives 5-25% commission. Reviews material for acts.
- AKO's record label, Amiron Music/Aztec Productions, is listed in the Record Companies section.

How to Contact: Write or call first and obtain permission to submit. Prefers cassette with maximum of 5 songs and lyric sheet. If seeking management, include cassette, videotape if available, picture and history in press kit. SASE. Reports in 2-8 weeks.
Music: Mostly **pop**, **rock** and **top 40**. No heavy metal. Works primarily with vocalists, dance bands and original groups. Current acts include Big Bang (pop), Everyday People (pop) and CoCo Ratcliff (R&B).

MARK ALAN AGENCY, P.O. Box 21323, St. Paul MN 55121. President: Mark Alan. Management firm, publishing company (Big Snow Music) and booking agency. Represents individual artists and groups; currently handles 9 acts. Receives 15-20% commission. Reviews material for acts.
- Mark Alan's publishing company, Big Snow Music, is listed in the Music Publishers section.

How to Contact: Write or call first and obtain permission to submit. If seeking management, press kit should include demo tape, photos, biography and reviews. Prefers cassette or VHS videocassette with 3 songs. Does not return material. Reports in 1 month.
Music: Rock, **alternative**, **New Age** and **black contemporary**. Works primarily with groups and solo artists. Current acts include Airkraft (rock band), Zwarté (rock band), Every Mother's Nightmare (rock band), Jon Doe (rock) and 7 Day Weekend (rock).

ALERT MUSIC INC., 41 Britain St., Suite 305, Toronto Ontario M5A 1R7 **Canada**. (416)364-4200. Fax: (416)364-8632. E-mail: alert@inforamp.net. President: W. Tom Berry. Management firm and record company. Represents local and regional individual artists and groups; currently handles 6 acts. Reviews material for acts.
How to Contact: Write first and obtain permission to submit. Prefers cassette or CD. If seeking management, press kit should include finished CD or 3-4 song cassette, photo and bio. SASE.
Music: Mostly **rock** and **pop**. Works primarily with bands and singer/songwriters. Current acts include Holly Cole (pop vocalist), Kim Mitchell (rock singer/songwriter), The Breits (rock group), Universal Honey (pop/rock) and Piltch & Davis (instrumental).

ALEXAS MUSIC PRODUCTIONS, 1935 S. Main St., Suite 407, Salt Lake City UT 84115. (801)467-2104. President: Patrick Melfi. Management firm, booking agency, record company (Alexas Records/ASCAP) and concert promoter. Estab. 1976. Represents local, regional or international individual artists, groups and songwriters; currently handles 100 acts. Receives 15% commission. Reviews material for acts.
How to Contact: Write or call first and obtain permission to submit. Submit VHS videocassette only with 1-3 songs and lyric sheets. If seeking management, include bio, video, demo and press kit. SASE. Reports in 10 weeks.
Music: Mostly **country** and **pop**; also **New Age** and **gospel**. Represents well-established bands and vocalists. Current acts include A.J. Masters (singer/songwriter), Randy Meisner (Eagles, Poco), Juice Newton and Fats Johnson.

Tips: "Be strong, be straight and be persistent/no drugs."

ALL MUSICMATTERS, P.O. Box 6156, San Antonio TX 78209. (210)651-5858. President: Jean Estes. Management firm. Represents artists from anywhere; currently handles 2 acts.
How to Contact: Call first and obtain permission to submit. Prefers cassette. Does not return material. Reports in 2 weeks.
Music: Mostly **jazz**. Current acts include True Diversity (jazz group) and Joe Gannon (country).

ALL STAR MANAGEMENT, 1229 S. Prospect St., Marion OH 43302-7267. (614)382-5939. President: John Simpson. Management firm and booking agency. Estab. 1990. Represents individual artists, groups and songwriters artists from anywhere; currently handles 9 acts. Receives 15-20% commission. Reviews material for acts.
How to Contact: Submit demo tape by mail. Unsolicited submissions are OK. Prefers cassette or videocassette with 3 songs and lyric or lead sheet. If seeking management, press kit should include audio with 3 songs, bio, 8×10 photo or any information or articles written on yourself or group, video if you have one. SASE. Reports in 2 months.
Music: Mostly **country** and **Christian country**; also **gospel**. Works primarily with bands and singers/songwriters. Current acts include Leon Seiter (country singer/songwriter), Debbie Robinson (country) and Austin Rangers (country).

ALL STAR TALENT AGENCY, P.O. Box 717, White House TN 37188. (615)643-4208. Agent: Joyce Kirby. Booking agency. Estab. 1966. Represents professional individuals, groups and songwriters; currently handles 6 acts. Receives 10% commission. Reviews material for acts.
How to Contact: Submit demo tape by mail. Unsolicited submissions are OK. Prefers cassette or VHS videocassette with 4 songs (can be cover songs) and lead sheet. If seeking management, press kit should include bios and photos. Does not return material. Reports in 1 month.
Music: Mostly **country**; also **bluegrass, gospel, MOR, rock (country)** and **top 40/pop**. Works primarily with dance, show and bar bands, vocalists, club acts and concerts. Current acts include Alex Houston (MOR), Chris Hartley (country), Jesse Chavez (country/gospel) and Jack Greene (country).

MICHAEL ALLEN ENTERTAINMENT DEVELOPMENT, P.O. Box 111510, Nashville TN 37222. (615)754-0059. Contact: Michael Allen. Management firm and public relations. Represents individual artists, groups and songwriters; currently handles 3 acts. Receives 15-25% commission. Reviews material for acts.
How to Contact: Submit demo tape by mail. Unsolicited submissions are OK. Prefers cassette or VHS videocassette with 3 songs and lyric or lead sheets. If seeking management, press kit should include photo, bio, press clippings, letter and tape. SASE. Reports in 3 months.
Music: Mostly **country**, **pop** and **R&B**; also **rock** and **gospel**. Works primarily with vocalists and bands. Currently doing public relations for Shotgun Red, Ricky Lynn Gregg and Easy Street.

‡**AMERICAN BANDS MANAGEMENT**, P.O. Box 840607, Houston TX 77284. (713)783-1406. Fax: (713)789-7331. President: John Blomstrom. Management firm and booking agent. Estab. 1973. Represents groups from anywhere; currently handles 6 acts. Receives 15% commission. Reviews material for acts.
How to Contact: Submit demo tape by mail. Unsolicited submissions are OK. Prefers cassette or VHS videocassette. Does not return material. Reports in 2-4 weeks.
Music: Mostly **rock (all forms)** and **modern country**. Works primarily with bands. Current acts include Neal Zaza (guitarist), Haji's Kitchen (grunge meets Pantera) and Noize Boyz (glam rock).

AMOK INC., Box 12, Fergus Ontario N1M 2W7 **Canada**. (519)787-1100. Fax: (519)787-0084. E-mail: amok@inforamp.net. Website: http://www.netbistro.com/amok2/index.html. Contact: Hugo Ranpen. Management firm and booking agent. Estab. 1985. Represents groups from anywhere. Currently handles 14 acts. Receives 15-20% commission.
How to Contact: Submit demo tape by mail. Unsolicited submissions are OK. Prefers cassette, VHS

‡ **THE DOUBLE DAGGER** before a listing indicates that the listing is new in this edition.

videocassette or CD if available, with lyric sheet. If seeking management, press kit should include bio, past performances, photo, cassette, CD or video. "Due to the large amount of submissions we receive we can only respond to successful applicants." Does not return material.
Music: Mostly **world beat**, **new roots** and **folk**. Works primarily with bands in the world music and new roots field; no mainstream rock/pop. Current acts include Courage of Lassie (new roots, Beggars Banquet/PolyGram), Ashkaru (world beat, Triloka/Worldly Music) and Tarig Abubakar & The Afro Nubians (pan African, Stern's Africa).

ANDERSON ASSOCIATES COMMUNICATIONS GROUP, 9748 NW 14th St., Suite 31, Coral Spring FL 33071. (954)753-5440. Fax: (954)753-9715. E-mail: rjppny@aol.com. CEO: Richard Papaleo. Management firm. Estab. 1992. Represents individual artists and groups from anywhere; currently handles 2 acts. Receives 15-20% commission. Reviews material for acts.
How to Contact: Submit demo tape by mail. Unsolicited submissions are OK. Prefers cassette, bio and/or picture with 3 songs and lead sheet. If seeking management, press kit should include cassette with 3 songs (video OK), bio and picture. Does not return material. Reports in 1 month.
Music: Mostly **R&B**, **pop/dance** and **pop/rock**; also **A/C**, **pop/mainstream** and **mainstream rock**. Current acts include Neutron Cafe (modern rock) and R.M. Dest (R&B/dance).

AQUILA ENTERTAINMENT, 10979 Bluffside Dr., Suite 3217, Studio City CA 91604. (818)623-9573. Music Producer/Publisher: Rick Mata. Management firm, music publisher (Rick Mata) and record producer (Rick Mata). Estab. 1990. Represents individual artists, groups and songwriters from anywhere; currently handles 7 acts. Receives 15-25% commission. Reviews material for acts.
How to Contact: Submit demo tape by mail. Unsolicited submissions are OK. Prefers cassette with 2 songs and lyric sheet. If seeking management, press kit should include tape with 3 songs, bio, reviews and photos. "Best (uptempo) song first!" SASE. Reports in 6 weeks.
Music: Mostly **alternative**, **New Age** and **progressive rock**; also **contemporary**, **Latin** and **classical guitar compositions**. Works primarily with bands, songwriters/musicians and composers. Current acts include Agony (band), Diablo (band) and Kane (New Age).

ARDENNE INT'L INC., 1800 Argyle St., Suite 444, Halifax, N.S. B3J 3N8 **Canada**. (902)492-8000. Fax: (902)423-2143. E-mail: ardenne@fox.nstn.ca. Website: http://emporium.turnpike.net/A/AAllen/events.ardenne.html. President: Michael Ardenne. Management firm. Estab. 1988. Represents local, individual artists and songwriters from anywhere; currently handles 2 acts. Receives 20% commission. Reviews material for acts.
How to Contact: Call first and obtain permission to submit. Prefers cassette with lyric sheet. "Put name, address, phone number and song list on the tape. Send maximum 3 songs." If seeking management, include b&w photo, bio, chart placings. Does not return material. Reports in 2-6 weeks.
Music: Mostly **country**, **pop** and **soft rock**. Works primarily with vocalists/songwriters. Current acts include Annick Gagnon (pop/soft rock) and Trina (country).

ARTIST REPRESENTATION AND MANAGEMENT, 1257 Arcade St., St. Paul MN 55106. (612)483-8754. Fax: (612)776-6338. Office Manager: Roger Anderson. Management firm, booking agency. Estab. 1983. Represents artists from anywhere; currently handles 15 acts. Receives 15% commission. Reviews material for acts.
How to Contact: Submit demo tape by mail. Unsolicited submissions are OK. Prefers cassette or videocassette with 3 songs and lyric sheet. If seeking management, press kit should include demo tape or videotape, preface, bio, etc. "Priority is placed on original artists with product who are willing to tour." Does not return material. Reports in 2 weeks.
Music: Mostly **rock**, **heavy metal** and **R&B**; also **southern rock** and **pop**. Works primarily with bands. Current acts include Crow (R&B, rock), Austin Healy (southern rock), Strawberry Jam & Hifi Horns (R&B), Nick St Nicholas & the Lone Wolf (rock), Fergie Frederikson (former lead vocalist for Toto) and Knight Crawler (contemporary hard rock).

ATCH RECORDS AND PRODUCTIONS, Fondren, Suite 380, Houston TX 77096-4502. (713)981-6540. Chairman/CEO: Charles Atchison. Management firm and record company. Estab. 1989. Represents local, regional and international individual artists, groups and songwriters; currently handles 4 acts. Receives 20% commission. Reviews material for acts.
How to Contact: Submit demo tape by mail. Unsolicited submissions are OK. Prefers cassette with 2 songs and lyric sheet. If seeking management, include bio, photo, demo and lyrics. Does not return material. Reports in 3 weeks.
Music: Mostly **R&B**, **country** and **gospel**; also **pop**, **rap** and **rock**. Works primarily with vocalists and

groups. Current acts include B.O.U. (rap), Blakkk Media (rap), Gotham Kidz (hip hop) and Slamm (R&B).
Tips: "Send a good detailed demo with good lyrics. Looking for wonderful love stories, also songs for children."

ATI MUSIC, 75 Parkway Ave., Markham, Ontario L3P 2H1 **Canada**. (905)294-5538. President: Scoot Irwin. Management firm, music publisher and record company. Estab. 1983. Represents individual artists and groups from anywhere. Currently handles 8 acts. Receives 15% commission. Reviews material for acts.
How to Contact: Submit demo tape by mail. Unsolicited submissions are OK. Prefers cassette or VHS videocassette with 2-3 songs and lyric sheet. If seeking management, press kit should include photo (2 different), video (if available), bio and background. "Don't load with press clippings." Does not return material. Reports in 2-3 weeks.
Music: Mostly **country** and **gospel**. Current acts include Dick Damron (country/country gospel), Allana Myrol (contemporary country) and Jamie Watling (country).

ATLANTIC ENTERTAINMENT GROUP, 1125 Atlantic Ave., 7th Floor, Atlantic City NJ 08401-4806. (609)823-6400. Fax: (609)823-4846. E-mail: aegprods@aol.com. Director of Artist Services: Scott Sherman. Management firm and booking agency. Represents individual artists and groups from anywhere; currently handles over 50 acts. Receives 10-20% commission. Reviews material for acts.
How to Contact: Submit demo tape by mail. Unsolicited submissions are OK. Prefers cassette, CD or VHS videocassette with 3 songs and lyric or lead sheet. If seeking management, press kit should include bio, demo and reviews. SASE. Reports in 2-4 weeks.
Music: Mostly **dance**, **R&B** and **contemporary**; also **house** and **specialty**. Current acts include Candace Jourdan (singer/writer), Candy J (singer/songwriter), C&C Music Factory, Deborah Cooper, Ernest Kohl, Candy Girls, Tory Beatty and Lonnie Gordon.

babysue, P.O. Box 8989, Atlanta GA 30306. (404)875-8951. E-mail: babysue@babysue.com. Website: http://www.babysue.com. President: Don W. Seven. Management firm, booking agency and record company (babysue). "We also publish a magazine which reviews music." Estab. 1983. Represents local, regional or international individual artists, groups and songwriters; currently handles 5 acts. Receives 5-25% commission. Reviews material for acts.

- babysue's record label is listed in the Record Companies section.

How to Contact: Submit demo tape by mail. Unsolicited submissions are OK. Prefers cassette or VHS videocassette if available with 4 songs and lyric sheets. Does not return material. Reports in 2 months.
Music: Mostly **rock**, **pop** and **alternative**; also **country** and **religious**. Works primarily with multi-talented artists (those who play more than one instrument). Current acts include LMNOP (rock), Mushcakes (folk) and the Mommy (heavy metal).

‡BACKSTAGE ENTERTAINMENT/LOGGINS PROMOTION, 26239 Senator Ave., Harbor City CA 90710. (310)325-2800. Fax: (310)325-2560. E-mail: logprod@aol.com. Personal Manager: Paul Loggins. Management firm, record producer (Paul Loggins) and radio promotion. Represents individual artists, groups and songwriters from anywhere; currently handles 8 acts. Receives 15-25% commission. Reviews material for acts.
How to Contact: Call first and obtain permission to submit. If seeking management, press kit should include picture, short bio, audio cassette or CD (preferred). "Mark on cassette or CD which cut you as the artist feel is the strongest." SASE. Reports in 2 weeks.
Music: Mostly **adult**, **top 40** and **AAA**; also **jazz** and **Americana**. Works primarily with bands and solo artists. Current acts include Andi Harrison (A/C, top 40 crossover solo musician), Reda (A/C, AAA crossover solo artist), Tim Ryan (A/C artist) and Kenny Loggins (currently signed to Columbia Records).

‡BARBARY COAST PRODUCTIONS, INC., P.O. Box 94, Camp Hill PA 17001-0094. (717)737-9831. President: Barby Holder. Management firm, record company and record producer. Estab. 1990. Represents local individual artists; currently handles 2 acts. Receives 15% commission.
How to Contact: Write first and obtain permission to submit. Prefers cassette with lyric and lead sheet. Does not return material. Reports in 3 months.
Music: Mostly **Celtic**, **country** and **folk**; also **blues**, **fingerstyle** and **hammered dulcimer**. Current acts include Barby Holder (traditional folk, country) and Christopher McCune (traditional/original).

BARNARD MANAGEMENT SERVICES (BMS), 1443 Sixth St., Santa Monica CA 90401. (310)587-0771. Agent: Russell Barnard. Management firm. Estab. 1979. Represents artists, groups and songwriters; currently handles 3 acts. Receives 10-20% commission. Reviews material for acts.

How to Contact: Write first and obtain permission to submit. Prefers cassette with 3-10 songs and lead sheet. Artists may submit VHS videocassette (15-30 minutes) by permission only. Does not return material. Reports in 2 months.
Music: Mostly **country crossover**; also **blues**, **country**, **R&B**, **rock** and **soul**. Works primarily with country crossover singers/songwriters and show bands. Current acts include Helen Hudson (singer/songwriter), Mark Shipper (songwriter/author) and Mel Trotter (singer/songwriter).
Tips: "Semi-produced demos are of little value. Either save the time and money by submitting material 'in the raw,' or do a finished production version."

BASSLINE ENTERTAINMENT, INC., P.O. Box 2394, New York NY 10185. (212)769-6956. Executive Director: Sharon Williams. Management firm. Estab. 1993. Represents local and regional individual artists, groups and songwriters; currently handles 2 acts. Receives 20% commission. Reviews material for acts.
How to Contact: Submit demo tape by mail. Unsolicited submissions are OK. Prefers cassette, DAT or VHS videocassette. If seeking management, press kit should include bio (include physical description), demo (cassette, DAT or VHS video), picture and accurate contact telephone number. SASE. Reports in 2-3 weeks.
Music: Mostly **pop**, **R&B**, **club/dance** and **hip hop/rap**; also **Latin** and **rock**. Works primarily with singer/songwriters, rappers and bands. Current acts include Michael Anthony (pop/R&B vocalist) and Baller (rap artist).

DICK BAXTER MANAGEMENT, P.O. Box 1385, Canyon Country CA 91386. (805)268-1659. Owner: Dick Baxter. Management firm and music publisher. Estab. 1963. Represents individual artists and groups from anywhere; currently handles 3-5 acts. Receives 15-20% commission. Reviews material for acts.
How to Contact: Write first and obtain permission to submit. Prefers cassette or VHS videocassette with 3 or more songs and lyric sheet. If seeking management, press kit should include photos, bio, press clips, audio and video if available. Does not return material. Reports in 2 weeks.
Music: Mostly **country**, **gospel** and **pop**. Current acts include Dean Dobbins (country singer/songwriter) and Ted & Ruth Reinhart (cowboy/western).

BIG BEAT PRODUCTIONS, INC., 1515 University Dr., Suite 108A, Coral Springs FL 33071. (954)755-7759. Fax: (954)755-8733. President: Richard Lloyd. Management firm and booking agency. Estab. 1986. Represents individual artists, groups, songwriters from anywhere; currently handles 350 acts. Receives 15-20% commission. Reviews material for acts.
How to Contact: Submit demo tape by mail. Unsolicited submissions are OK. Prefers cassette or VHS videocassette with 5 songs and lyric and lead sheets. If seeking management, press kit should include video, audiocassette, bio, press release info, and 8×10 photo. Does not return material. Reports in 1 month.
Music: Mostly **pop/rock**, **country/variety** and **jazz/contemporary**. Current acts include Jonny Loew (singer/songwriter), Barry St. Ives (singer) and Carlos Manuel Santana (singer).

BIG HAND, 67-2001 Bonnymede Dr., Mississauga Ontario L5J 4H8 **Canada**. (905) 855-3277. Fax: (905)855-2882. E-mail: puddin@interlog.com. President: Rick Gratton. Management firm, booking agency and music publisher (Maureen B. Close Publishing.) Estab. 1993. Represents local and Southern Ontario individual artists, groups and songwriters; currently handles 2 acts. Receives 15% commission. Reviews material for acts.
How to Contact: Submit demo tape by mail. Unsolicited submissions are OK. Prefers cassette or VHS videocassette with lyric and/or lead sheet. If seeking management, press kit should include bio, tape or CD, video, press clippings and photo. SAE and IRC. Reports in 2 months only if interested.
Music: Mostly **R&B/soul**, **blues** and **funk**; also **jazz**, **rock/pop** and **fusion**. Works primarily with drummers, bands, songwriters and instrumentalists. Current acts include The Maureen Brown Band (blues/R&B/jazz) and Big Hand (funk/R&B/blues big band).

BIG J PRODUCTIONS, 2516 S. Sugar Ridge, Laplace LA 70068. (504)652-2645. Agent: Frankie Jay. Booking agency. Estab. 1968. Represents individual artists, groups and songwriters; currently handles over 50 acts. Receives 15-25% commission. Reviews material for acts.
How to Contact: Call first and obtain permission to submit. Prefers cassette or VHS videocassette with 3-6 songs and lyric or lead sheet. "It would be best for an artist to lip-sync to a prerecorded track. The object is for someone to see how an artist would perform more than simply assessing song content." Artists seeking management should include pictures, biography, tape or CD and video. Does not return material. Reports in 2 weeks.
Music: Mostly **rock**, **pop** and **R&B**. Works primarily with groups with self-contained songwriters. Current

acts include Zebra (original rock group), Crowbar (heavy metal) and Kyper (original dance).

J. BIRD ENTERTAINMENT AGENCY, 4905 S. Atlantic, Daytona Beach FL 32127. (904)767-1919. Fax: (904)767-1019. President: John Bird II. Management firm, booking agency, record company. Estab. 1963. Represents individual artists, groups and songwriters from anywhere; currently handles 55 acts. Receives 15-20% commission. Reviews material for acts.
How to Contact: Submit demo tape by mail. Unsolicited submissions are OK. Prefers cassette or VHS videocassette and photo with 3 songs and lyric sheet. Does not return material. Reports in 2 weeks.
Music: Mostly **rock**, **top 40** and **country**. Current acts include Kansas, Little River Band and ELO.

BISCUIT PRODUCTIONS INC., 3315 E. Russell Rd., H-117, Las Vegas NV 89120. (702)451-1796. President: Steve Walker. Management firm. Estab. 1989. Represents individual artists and groups from anywhere; currently handles 3 acts. Receives 20% commission. Reviews material for acts.
How to Contact: Submit demo tape by mail. Prefers cassette or VHS videocassette. Does not return material. Reports in 2 months.
Music: Mostly **rap**, **R&B** and **dance**; also **pop** and **alternative**. Current acts include Mr. Freeze, Biscuit and Brand X.

BLACK STALLION COUNTRY, INC., P.O. Box 368, Tujunga CA 91043. (818)352-8142. E-mail: kennking@aol.com. President: Kenn E. Kingsbury, Jr.. Management firm, production company and music publisher (Black Stallion Country Publishing/BMI). Estab. 1979. Represents individual artists from anywhere; currently handles 20 acts. Receives 15-20% commission. Reviews material for acts.

- Black Stallion's publishing company, Black Stallion Country Publishing, can be found in the Music Publishers section.

How to Contact: Submit demo tape by mail. Unsolicited submissions are OK. Prefers cassette with 3 songs and lyric sheet. If seeking management, press kit should include picture/résumé and audio and/or video tape. "I would also like a one-page statement of goals and why you would be an asset to my company or me." SASE. Reports in 1-2 months.
Music: Mostly **country**, **R&B** and **A/C**. Works primarily with country acts, variety acts and film/TV pictures/actresses. Current acts include Lane Brody (singer country), Thom Bresh (musician) and Barbara Nickell (film/television actress).

BLACKGROUND, 15250 Ventura Blvd., Sherman Oaks CA 91403. (818)995-4683. Fax: (818)995-4398. A&R: Al Carter. Management firm and record company. Estab. 1993. Represents individual artists, groups, songwriters and producers from anywhere; currently handles 4 acts. Reviews material for acts.
How to Contact: Call first and obtain permission to submit. Prefers cassette or DAT with 3 or 4 songs. If seeking management or record deal, press kit should include picture, bio, 3 or 4 songs, name and contact number on cassette or DAT. Does not return material. Reports in 2-3 weeks.
Music: Mostly **R&B**, **hip hop** and **gospel**. Works primarily with songwriters/producers, musicians. Current acts include R. Kelly (R&B singer, producer and songwriter), Aaliyah (R&B singer) and The Winans (gospel singers, producers and songwriters).
Tips: "Submit complete songs with original music. Emphasis should be on strong hooks with commercial R&B appeal."

BLANK & BLANK, 1530 Chestnut St., Suite 308, Philadelphia PA 19102. (215)568-4310. Treasurer, Manager: E. Robert Blank. Management firm. Represents individual artists and groups. Reviews material for acts.
How to Contact: Submit demo tape by mail. Unsolicited submissions are OK. Prefers videocassette. Does not return material.

BLAZE PRODUCTIONS, 103 Pleasant Ave., Upper Saddle River NJ 07458. (201)825-1060. Fax: (201)825-4949. E-mail: blazepro@ix.netcom.com. Office Manager: Toni Lynn. Management firm, music publisher (Botown Music), production company, record company (Wild Boar Records). Represents local, individual artists, groups and songwriters from anywhere; currently handles 6 acts. Receives 15-20% commission. Reviews material for acts.

- See their listing in the Record Producers section.

How to Contact: Submit demo tape by mail. Unsolicited submissions are OK. Prefers cassette or VHS videocassette with 3-5 songs and lyric sheet. If seeking management, press kit should include tape, lyrics, picture, bio and "something that gets across the band's vibe." Does not return material. Reports in 1 month.
Music: Mostly **modern rock** and **all music**; also **tribute acts**. "If you're the *best* we want to represent you. The best band, kazoo orchestra, tribute act, etc. Any type of music or act." Works primarily with

bands and solo artists. Current acts include Dog Voices (regional touring act), Danny V's 52nd St. (tribute to Billy Joel), Hot Legs (tribute to Rod Stewart) and Waxface (Wild Boar Records/modern rock).
Tips: "Be persistent, yet polite, and be as creative as possible with your materials. A press kit should contain the band's vibe, not just a bio."

BLOWIN' SMOKE PRODUCTIONS, 7438 Shoshone Ave., Van Nuys CA 91406-2340. (818)881-9888. Fax: (818)881-0555. E-mail: blowin@jukejoint.com. Website: http://www.jukejoint.com/bands/blowin.htm. President: Larry Knight. Management firm and record producer. Estab. 1990. Represents local and West Coast individual artists and groups. Currently handles 5 acts. Receives 15-20% commission. Reviews material for acts.

- See the listing for Hailing Frequency Music in the Record Producers section.

How to Contact: Call first and obtain permission to submit. Prefers cassette. If seeking management, press kit should include résumé, photo, bios, contact telephone numbers and any info on legal commitments already in place. Does not return material. Reports in 3-4 weeks.
Music: Mostly **R&B**, **blues** and **blues-rock**. Works primarily with single and group vocalists and a few R&B/blues bands. Current acts include Carolyn Basley (formerly with Ike & Tina Turner), Baby Butter Blues Band, Larry "Fuzzy" Knight (blues singer/songwriter), The Smokettes (female vocal trio) and The Blowin' Smoke Rhythm & Blues Band.

THE BLUE CAT AGENCY/EL GATO AZUL AGENCY, P.O. Box 399, Novato CA 94948. Phone/fax: (415)883-1011. E-mail: klkindig@ecst.csuchico.edu. Owner/agent: Karen Kindig. Management firm and booking agency. Estab. 1989. Represents individual artists and/or groups from anywhere; currently handles 4 acts. Receives 10-15% commission. Reviews material for acts.
How to Contact: Write or call first and obtain permission to submit. Prefers cassette or CD. If seeking management, press kit should include demo tape, bio and press clippings (photo optional). SASE. Reports in 6 weeks.
Music: Mostly **Latin jazz**, **rock/pop "en español"** and any other style "en español." Works primarily with singer/songwriters, instrumentalists and bands. Current acts include Ylonda Nickell (alto saxophonist), Alejandro Santos (flutist/composer), "El Eco" and Ania Paz (pianist/composer).

‡BLUE WAVE PRODUCTIONS, 3221 Perryville Rd., Baldwinsville NY 13027. (315)638-4286. Fax: (315)635-4757. Owner/president: Greg Spencer. Management firm, music publisher (G.W. Spencer Music/ASCAP), record company (Blue Wave Records) and record producer (Blue Wave Productions). Estab. 1985. Represents individual artists and/or groups, songwriters from anywhere; currently handles 3 acts. Receives 20% commission. Reviews material for acts.
How to Contact: Submit demo tape by mail. Unsolicited submissions are OK. Prefers cassette or VHS videocassette with 3-6 songs. "Just the music first, reviews and articles are OK. No photos or lyrics until later." SASE. Reports in 1 month.
Music: Mostly **blues**, **blues/rock** and **roots rock**. Current acts include Kim Lembo (female blues vocalist), Kim Simmonds (blues guitarist and singer/songwriter) and Built For Comfort (blues band).
Tips: "I'm looking for great singers with soul. Not interested in pop/rock commercial material."

BOHEMIA ENTERTAINMENT GROUP, 8159 Santa Monica, #202, Los Angeles CA 90046. (213)848-7966. Fax: (213)848-9069. Contact: Susan Ferris. Management firm. Estab. 1992. Represents individual artists and groups from anywhere; currently handles 3 acts. Receives 15% commission. Reviews material for acts.
How to Contact: Submit demo tape by mail. Prefers cassette. If seeking management, press kit should include a tape (cassette) with a little blurb written about the band. Does not return material. Reports in 3 weeks.
Music: Mostly **alternative** and **adult alternative**. Works primarily with punk and alternative bands.

BOJO PRODUCTIONS INC., 3935 Cliftondale Place, College Park GA 30349. (404)969-1913. Management firm and record company (Bojo Records). Estab. 1982. Represents local, regional or international

TO HELP YOU UNDERSTAND and use the information in these listings, see "How to Use *Songwriter's Market* to Get Your Songs Heard," on page 3.

individual artists, groups and songwriters; currently handles 5 acts. Receives 20% commission. Reviews material for acts.
How to Contact: Submit demo tape by mail. Unsolicited submissions are OK. Prefers cassette or videocassette with 3 songs and lyric or lead sheets. If seeking management, press kit should include résumé, tape or video. SASE. Reports in 3 weeks.
Music: Mostly **R&B**, **gospel** and **country**; also **MOR**. Works primarily with vocalists and dance bands. Current acts include Rita Graham (jazz), George Smith (jazz singer) and Tommy Gill (piano).
Tips: "Send clean recording tape with lead sheets."

BOUQUET-ORCHID ENTERPRISES, P.O. Box 1335, Norcross GA 30091. (770)497-9086. President: Bill Bohannon. Management firm, booking agency, music publisher (Orchid Publishing/BMI) and record company (Bouquet Records). Represents individuals and groups; currently handles 4 acts. Receives 10-15% commission. Reviews material for acts.

- See the listings for Orchid Publishing in the Music Publishers section and Bouquet Records in the Record Companies section.

How to Contact: Submit demo tape by mail. Unsolicited submissions are OK. Prefers cassette or videocassette with 3-5 songs, song list and lyric sheet. Include brief résumé. If seeking management, press kit should include current photograph, 2-3 media clippings, description of act, and background information on act. SASE. Reports in 1 month.
Music: Mostly **country**, **rock** and **top 40/pop**; also **gospel** and **R&B**. Works primarily with vocalists and groups. Current acts include Susan Spencer, Jamey Wells, Adam Day and the Bandoleers.

‡BREAKTHROUGH MANAGEMENT, 1695 E. University, Auburn AL 36830. President: Mike Hooks. Management firm. Estab. 1990. Represents individual artists and groups from anywhere; currently handles 3 acts. Receives 20% commission. Reviews material for acts.
How to Contact: Submit demo tape by mail. Unsolicited submissions are OK. Prefers any recorded format. If seeking management, press kit should include as much history as possible on the artist. Does not return material. Reports in 2 weeks.
Music: Mostly **alternative** and **country**. Current acts include Josh Joplin Band, Law of Nature and Tara Vandevender.

‡BULLET MANAGEMENT, 7919 Fairfax Court, Niwot CO 80503. (303)652-3489. Fax: (303)530-4488. CEO: Stephen Bond Garvan. Management firm. Estab. 1976. Represents individual artists, groups and songwriters from anywhere; currently handles 4 acts. Receives 20% commission. Reviews material for acts.
How to Contact: Write first and obtain permission to submit. Prefers cassette with lyric sheet. Does not return material. Reports in 1 month.
Music: Mostly **contemporary country**, **singer/songwriter** and **rock**; also **pop**, **folk** and **Celtic**. Current acts include Dianne Canon, Michael Killen and Shauna Strecker.

CAPITOL MANAGEMENT & TALENT, 1300 Division St., Suite 200, Nashville TN 37203. (800)767-4984; (615)244-2440; (615)244-3377. Fax: (615)242-1177. Producer: Robert Metzgar. Management firm, booking agency, music publisher (Aim High Music Co., Bobby & Billy Music) and record company (Stop Hunger Records International, Aim High Records, Hot News Records, Platinum Plus Records, SHR Records). Estab. 1971. Represents local, regional or international individual artists, groups and songwriters; currently handles 24 acts. Receives 15% commission. Reviews material for acts.

- Capitol Management's publishing company, Aim High Music, is listed in the Music Publishers section, Capitol Management is listed in the Record Producers section, and their record label, Stop Hunger Records, is listed in the Record Companies section.

How to Contact: Submit demo tape by mail. Unsolicited submissions are OK. Prefers cassette or videocassette of live performance, if available. If seeking management, include photo, bio, résumé and demo tape. Does not return material. Reports in 2 weeks.
Music: Mostly **traditional country**, **contemporary country** and **southern gospel**; also **pop rock**, **rockabilly** and **R&B**. Works primarily with major label acts and new acts shopping for major labels. Current acts include Tommy Cash (CBS Records), Tommy Overstreet (CBS Records), Mark Allen Cash, Mickey Jones, The Glen Campbell Band (Warner Bros.) and Billy Walker (MCA Records).
Tips: "Call us on our toll-free line for advice before you sign with anyone else."

CARLYLE MANAGEMENT, 1217 16th Ave. S., Nashville TN 37212. (615)327-8129. Fax: (615)321-0928. President: Laura Fraser. Management firm. Estab. 1990. Represents individual artists and groups from anywhere. Currently handles 4 acts.

• See the listing for Carlyle Records in the Record Companies section.

How to Contact: Call first and obtain permission to submit. Prefers cassette with 3 songs. If seeking management, press kit should include tape, photo, bio and press. Does not return material. Reports in 2 months.

Music: Mostly **rock** and **country**. Current acts include Aven Kepler (folk), The Vegas Cocks (rock) and The Grinning Plowmen (rock).

CASH PRODUCTIONS, INC., 744 Joppa Farm Rd., Joppa Towne MD 21085. Phone/fax: (410)679-2262. President: Ernest W. Cash. Management firm, music publisher (Ernie Cash Music/BMI) and record company (Continental Records). Estab. 1988. Represents local, regional or international individual artists, groups and songwriters; currently represents 4 acts. Receives 20% commission. Reviews material for acts.

• See Cash Productions' listing in the Music Publishers section, as well as a listing for Continental Records in the Record Companies section.

How to Contact: Call first and obtain permission to submit. Prefers cassette or VHS videocassette with 3 songs and lyric and lead sheet. SASE. Reports in 2 weeks.

Music: Mostly **country**, **pop** and **gospel**; also **contemporary**, **light rock** and **blues**. Works primarily with individual country artists and groups. Current acts include Cindy Ashlin, Paul Gage, Carl Cooper and Eunice Morris.

Tips: "Above all be honest with me and I will work with you. Please give me time to review your material and give it a justifiable chance with our music group."

CAVALRY PRODUCTIONS, P.O. Box 70, Brackettville TX 78832. (210)563-2759. Contact: Rocco Fortunato. Management firm and record company. Estab. 1979. Represents regional (Southwest) individual artists and groups; currently handles 2 acts. Receives 10-30% comission. Reviews material for acts.

How to Contact: Submit demo tape by mail. Unsolicited submissions are OK. Prefers cassette with 3 songs and lyric sheet. "We look for material useable for our artist library." If seeking management, press kit should include picture, cassette, goals and experience. Does not return material. Reports in 1-2 months.

Music: Mostly **country** and **Hispanic**; also **gospel** and **novelty**. Works primarily with single vocalists and various vocal groups with with 2 to 4 voices. Current acts include Darryl Earwood (country) and Josie Lujan (Tejano).

Tips: "Material 'in the raw' is OK if you are willing to work with us to develop it. Make songs available to our artists for review from our library of possibilities. Songs not used immediately may be useable in the future. We will promote artist/writer collaborations where styles warrant. We are looking for artist/writer chemistry. Co-operation in working or developing submitted material is a big plus."

CEDAR CREEK PRODUCTIONS AND MANAGEMENT, 44 Music Square E., Suite 503, Nashville TN 37203. (615)252-6916. Fax: (615)327-4204. President: Larry Duncan. Management firm, music publisher (Cedar Creek Music/BMI, Cedar Cove Music/ASCAP), record company (Cedar Creek Records) and record producer. Estab. 1992. Represents individual artists, groups and songwriters from anywhere; currently represents 1 act. Receives 20% of gross. Reviews material for acts.

• See Cedar Creek's listing in the Record Producers section; Cedar Creek Records can be found in the Record Companies section.

How to Contact: Submit demo tape by mail. Unsolicited submissions are OK. Prefers cassette or VHS videocassette with 4-6 songs and lyric sheet. If seeking management, press kit should include 8×12 color or b&w picture, bio, 4 songs on cassette tape and VHS video if available. Does not return material. Reports in 2 months.

Music: Mostly **country**, **country/pop** and **country/R&B**; also **pop**, **southern gospel/Christian contemporary**, **R&B**, **Christian country**, **contemporary jazz** and **light rock**. Works primarily with vocalists, singer/songwriters and groups. Current acts include Lynn Guyo.

Tips: "Submit your best songs and a good full demo with vocal upfront with five instruments on tracks backing the singer."

‡CHUCKER MUSIC INC., 345 E. 80th St., 15H, New York NY 10021. Fax: (212)879-9621. President: Chuck Dembrak. Management firm, music publisher (Cool 1) and record producer (Chuck Dembrak). Estab. 1984. Represents individual artists, groups and songwriters from anywhere; currently handles 3 acts. Receives 20% commission. Reviews material for acts.

How to Contact: Submit demo tape by mail. Unsolicited submissions are OK. Prefers cassette, VHS videocassette or CD. If seeking management, press kit should include photos. Does not return material. Reports in 1 month.

Music: Mostly **R&B**, **top 40** and **dance**; also **jazz**, **rock** and **A/C**. Works primarily with singer/songwriters. Current acts include Kim Waters (smooth jazz), Killing Words (rock) and Rob Hegel (pop/rock).

CIRCUIT RIDER TALENT & MANAGEMENT CO., 123 Walton Ferry Rd., Hendersonville TN 37075. (615)824-1947. Fax: (615)264-0462. President: Linda S. Dotson. U.K. office: 8 The Lindens, Mascot Rd., Watford Herts WD1 3RE **UK**. Phone: 011-44-1923-819415. Management firm, booking agency and music publisher (Channel Music, Cordial Music). Represents individual artists, songwriters and actors. Currently handles 9 acts (for management) but works with a large number of recording artists, songwriters, actors, producers. (Includes multi Grammy-winning producer/writer Skip Scarborough). Receives 10-15% commission. Reviews material for acts.
How to Contact: Write or call first and obtain permission to submit. Prefers cassette or videocassette with 3 songs and lyric sheet. If seeking management, press kit should include bio, photo and tape with 3 songs. Videocassettes required of artist's submissions. SASE. Reports in 6-8 weeks.
Music: Mostly **pop**, **country** and **gospel**; also **R&B** and **comedy**. Works primarily with vocalists, special concerts, movies and TV. Current acts include Sian Michael Townley (pop), Cam-Keyz (R&B), Willie John Ellison (blues), Frank White (blues), Alton McClain (gospel), Brad Martin (country), Hammond Brothers (country) and Doug Swander (country).
Tips: "Artists, have your act together. Have a full press kit, videos and be professional. Attitudes are a big factor in my agreeing to work with you (no egotists). This is a business and your career we will be building."

CLASS ACT PRODUCTIONS/MANAGEMENT, P.O. Box 55252, Sherman Oaks CA 91413. (818)980-1039. E-mail: p.kimmel@worldnet.att.net. President: Peter Kimmel. Management firm, music publisher and production company. Estab. 1985. Currently handles 3 acts. Receives 20% commission. Reviews material for acts.
How to Contact: Submit demo tape by mail. Unsolicited submissions are OK. Include cover letter, pictures, bio, lyric sheets (essential) and cassette tape or CD in press kit. SASE. Reports in 1 month.
Music: All styles. Current acts include Terpsichore (cyber dance/pop), Don Cameron (country/western beat) and Alfredo Caravelli (pop/Sinatra).

CLOCKWORK ENTERTAINMENT MANAGEMENT AGENCY, 227 Concord St., Haverhill MA 01830. (508)373-5677. President: Bill Macek. Management firm. Represents groups and songwriters throughout New England; currently handles 2 acts. Receives 15% commission. Reviews material for acts.
How to Contact: Submit demo tape by mail. Unsolicited submissions are OK. Prefers cassette or CD with 3-12 songs. "Also submit promotion and cover letter with interesting facts about yourself." If seeking management, press kit should include tape or CD, photo, bio and press. SASE. Reports in 1 month.
Music: Rock (all types) and **top 40/pop**. Works primarily with bar bands and original acts. Current acts include Herland (band) and Savage (female vocalist).

CLOUSHER PRODUCTIONS, P.O. Box 1191, Mechanicsburg PA 17055. (717)766-7644. Fax: (717)766-1490. Owner: Fred Clousher. Booking agency and production company. Estab. 1972. Represents groups from anywhere; currently handles over 100 acts.
How to Contact: Submit demo tape by mail. Unsolicited submissions are OK. Prefers VHS videocassette. If seeking bookings, press kit should include glossies, video demo tape plus references and bio. Does not return material. "Performer should check back with us!"
Music: Mostly **country**, **old rock** and **ethnic** (German, Italian, etc.); also **dance bands** (regional) and **classical quartets**. "We work mostly with country, old time R&R, regional variety dance bands, tribute acts, and all types of variety acts." Current acts include Robin Right (country vocalist), Johnny Counterfit, "The Singing Impressionist" and Tribute To The Beatles.
Tips: "The songwriters we work with are entertainers themselves, which is the aspect we deal with. They usually have bands or do some sort of show, either with tracks or live music. We engage them for stage shows, dances, strolling, etc. We do not publish music or submit performers to recording companies for contracts. We strictly set up live performances for them."

CODY ENTERTAINMENT GROUP, P.O. Box 456, Winchester VA 22604. Phone/fax: (540)722-4625. President: Phil Smallwood. Management firm and booking agency. Estab. 1975. Represents individual artists and groups from anywhere; currently handles 32 acts. Receives 10-20% commission.
How to Contact: Submit demo tape by mail. Unsolicited submissions are OK. Prefers cassette, DAT or

videocassette with 3 songs and lead sheet. Does not return material. Reports in 2 weeks.
Music: Mostly **show acts** and **writers of love songs**. Current acts include Tyler (country recording act), Phil Zuckerman (writer) and Arlo Haines (writer/performer).

CONCEPT 2000 INC., P.O. Box 2950, Columbus OH 43216-2950. (614)276-2000. Fax: (614)275-0163. E-mail: c2info@concept.2000.com. Website: Website: http://www.concept-2000.com. President: Brian Wallace. Management firm and booking agency. Estab. 1981. Represents international individual artists, groups and songwriters; currently handles 7 acts. Receives 20% commission. Reviews material for acts.
How to Contact: Submit demo tape by mail. Unsolicited submissions are OK. Prefers cassette with 4 songs. If seeking management, include demo tape, press clips, photo and bio. Does not return material. Reports in 2 weeks.
Music: Mostly **country**, **gospel** and **pop**; also **jazz**, **R&B** and **soul**. Current acts include Bryan Hitch (contemporary gospel), The Breeze (country), The Andrew Jackson Piano Forte, Shades of Grey (R&B/soul), Jenny Morris (country), Ras Matunji and Earth Force (reggae) and Gene Walker (jazz).
Tips: "Send quality songs with lyric sheets. Production quality is not necessary."

CONSCIENCE MUSIC, P.O. Box 740, Oak Park IL 60303. Phone/fax: (312)226-8115. Owner/Manager: Karen M. Smith. Management firm and record company (TOW Records). Estab. 1985. Represents individual artists, groups and songwriters from anywhere; currently handles 4 acts. Receives 15% commission. Reviews material for acts.
How to Contact: Write first and obtain permission to submit. Prefers cassette or current release with 2-3 songs and lyric sheet. If seeking management, press kit should include current reviews, bio or letter with band or artist objectives. "Cannot overemphasize the importance of having objectives you are ready to discuss with us." SASE. Reports in 2 months.
Music: Mostly **rock** and **pop**; also **visual artists**, **writers** and **models**. Works primarily with indie bands in the States and Great Britain. Currently represents Wait For Light (folk rock band), Keith Kessinger (scattered pop songwriter) and PO! (U.K. pop band).

COOKMAN INTERNATIONAL, 5625 Willowcrest Ave., North Hollywood CA 91601. Fax: (818)763-1398. Management firm and music publisher (El Leon Music). Estab. 1989. Represents individual artists, groups and songwriters from anywhere; currently handles 3 acts. Receives 20% commission. Reviews material for acts.
How to Contact: Submit demo tape by mail. Unsolicited submissions are OK. Prefers cassette with 3 songs and lyric sheet. Include a bio and photo. SASE. Reports in 2 weeks.
Music: Mostly **Latin music**. Works primarily with bands and singer/songwriters. Current acts include Fabulosos Cadillacs (platinum-selling Latin rock band), King Chango (Luaka Bop/Warner Bros.) and MC Skeey (Warner International).

COOL RECORDS, 12121 Wilshire Blvd., Suite 1201, Los Angeles CA 90025. (310)826-2410. Fax: (310)846-5450. General Manager: Tracey O'Brien. Entertainment law firm. Estab. 1978. Represents individual artists and/or groups from anywhere; currently handles 2 acts. Receives 10% commission.
How to Contact: Call first and obtain permission to submit. Prefers cassette or CD. If seeking management, press kit should include picture, bio, press clippings. SASE. Reports in 2 weeks.
Music: Mostly **alternative rock**, **singer/songwriter** and **alternative country**; open to suggestion. Currently represents (as an attorney) Patrick Moraz (keyboard), Bug Music, Academy of Country Music.
Tips: "We are part of a team and it's a lot of hard work. Be diplomatic at all times."

CORVALAN-CONDLIFFE MANAGEMENT, 563 Westminster Ave., Venice CA 90291. (310)399-8625. Manager: Brian Condliffe. Management firm. Estab. 1982. Represents local and international individual artists, groups and songwriters; currently handles 3 acts. Receives 15% commission.
How to Contact: Call first and obtain permission to submit. Prefers cassette with 4-6 songs. If seeking management, include bio, professional photo and demo. SASE. Reports in 2 months.
Music: Mostly **pop** and **rock**; also **Latin**. Works primarily with alternative rock and pop/rock/world beat bands. Current acts include Ramiro Medina, Eleanor Academia and Adam Rudolph.
Tips: "Be professional in all aspects of your kit and presentation. Check your grammar and spelling in your correspondence/written material. Know your music and your targeted market (rock, R&B, etc.)."

COUNTDOWN ENTERTAINMENT, 109 Earle Ave., Lynbrook NY 11563. (516)599-4157. President: James Citkovic. Management firm and consultants. Estab. 1983. Represents local, regional and international individual artists, groups, songwriters and producers; currently handles 2 acts. Receives 10-30% commission.

How to Contact: Submit demo tape by mail. Unsolicited submissions are OK. "Please, no phone calls." Prefers cassette or VHS (SP speed) videocassette with lyric sheet. If seeking management, include cassette tape of best songs, 8×10 pictures, VHS video, lyrics, press and radio playlists in press kit. SASE. Reports in 1 month.
Music: Mostly **pop/rock**, **modern music** and **alternative/dance**; also **R&B**, **pop/dance**, **industrial/techno** and **hard rock**. Deals with all styles of artists/songwriters/producers. Current acts include World Bang (alternative rock), Needulhed (rock), and Ken Kushner and Drew Miles (producers).

COUNTRY STAR ATTRACTIONS, 439 Wiley Ave., Franklin PA 16323. (814)432-4633. Contact: Norman Kelly. Management firm, booking agency, music publisher (Country Star Music/ASCAP), record producer (Country Star Productions) and record company (Country Star, Process, Mersey and CSI Records). Estab. 1970. Represents artists and musical groups; currently handles 6-10 acts. Receives 10-15% commission. Reviews material for acts.

- See the listings for Country Star Music in the Music Publishers section, Country Star International in the Record Companies section and Country Star Productions in the Record Producers section.

How to Contact: Submit demo tape by mail. Unsolicited submissions are OK. Prefers cassette with 2-4 songs and typed lyric or lead sheet; include photo. If seeking management, press kit should include cassette or CD, lyric sheet, brief bio and photo. SASE. Reports in 2 weeks.
Music: Mostly **country** (85%), **rock** (5%), **gospel** (5%) and **R&B** (5%). Works primarily with vocalists. Current acts include Junie Lou, Debbie Sue and Larry Pieper (country singers).

COURTRIGHT MANAGEMENT INC., 201 E. 87th St., New York NY 10128. (212)410-9055. Contacts: Hernando or Doreen Courtright. Management firm. Estab. 1984. Represents local, regional and international individual artists, groups, songwriters and producers. Currently handles 2 acts. Receives 20% commission.
How to Contact: Call first and obtain permission to submit. Prefers cassette or VHS videocassette with 3 or 4 songs and lyric sheet. If seeking management, include photos, bio, video, tape and press in press kit. Does not return material. Reports in 1 month.
Music: Mostly **rock**, **alternative** and **metal**; also **pop** and **blues**. Current acts include Deena Miller (alternative), Noo Voo Doo (world pop) and various producers, such as Neil Kernon, Mark Dodson, Eddie Kramer and many others.

CRANIUM MANAGEMENT, P.O. Box 240, Annadale NSW 2038 **Australia**. E-mail: cranium@enternet.com.au. Manager: Peter "Skip" Beaumont-Edmonds. Management firm. Estab. 1992. Represents individual artists, groups and songwriters from anywhere; currently handles 5 acts. Receives 17-20% commission. Reviews material for acts.
How to Contact: Write first and obtain permission to submit. Prefers cassette. "The minimum—don't waste money on being elaborate. Talent will show through. Be sensible—if it doesn't suit us don't send it." If seeking management, include demo tape, press release/bio and cover letter in press kit. Does not return material. Reports in 1 month.
Music: Mostly **alternative** and **pop**; also **country**. Works primarily with pop/rock, alternative bands and singer/songwriters. Current acts include Mental As Anything, Dog Trumpet, Louis Tillett and David Mason-Cox.

CRAWFISH PRODUCTIONS, P.O. Box 5412, Buena Park CA 90620. (619)245-2920. Producer: Leo J. Eiffert, Jr. Management firm, music publisher (Young Country/BMI), record producer (Leo J. Eiffert) and record company (Plain Country Records). Estab. 1968. Represents local and international individual artists and songwriters; currently handles 4 acts. Commission received is open. Reviews material for acts.

- See the listing for Leo J. Eiffert, Jr. in the Record Producers section.

How to Contact: Submit demo tape by mail. Unsolicited submissions are OK. Prefers cassette with 2-3 songs and lyric sheet. SASE. Reports in 3 weeks.
Music: Mostly **country** and **gospel**. Works primarily with vocalists. Current acts include Brandi Holland, Teeci Clarke, Joe Eiffert (country/gospel), Mary T. Vertiz (songwriter), Crawfish Band (country) and Homemade.

CREATIVE STAR MANAGEMENT, 615 E. Second St., Lima OH 45804. Department of Creative Services: James Milligan. Address country material to: Robin Lynnell, P.O. Box 5678, Lima OH 45802. Management firm, booking agency, music publisher (Party House Publishing/BMI, A New Rap Jam Publishing), record company (New Experience Records/Grand Slam Records). Estab. 1989. Represents individual artists, groups and songwriters from anywhere; currently handles 15-20 acts. Receives 15-20% commission. Reviews material for acts.

● Creative Star Management's publishing company, A New Rap Jam Publishing, is listed in the Music Publishers section, and their record label, New Experience Records/Grand Slam Records, is listed in the Record Companies section.

How to Contact: Submit demo tape by mail. Unsolicited submissions are OK. Prefers cassette or VHS videocassette with 3-5 songs and lyric sheet. If seeking management, press kit should include press clippings, bios, résumé, 8×10 glossy photo, any information that will support material and artist. SASE. Reports in 1 month.

Music: Mostly **R&B**, **pop** and **country**; also **rap**, **contemporary gospel** and **soul/funk**. Current acts include T.M.C. (R&B/group), James Junior, The Impressions, Vanesta Compton (soul) and Barbara Lomas.

‡CRICKET INC., 3226 S. 90th Ave., Tulsa OK 74145. (918)663-9181. Manager: Michael Lanter. Management firm, booking agency, record producer and club owner. Estab. 1997. Represents individual artists and groups from anywhere. Reviews material for acts.

How to Contact: Submit demo tape by mail. Unsolicited submissions are OK. Prefers cassette or VHS videocassette with lyric or lead sheet. If seeking management, press kit should include photo, set list, bio and contact sheet. SASE. Reports in 2-4 weeks.

Music: Mostly **rock**, **alternative** and **new wave**; also **punk**, **pop** and **new wave dance**. Works primarily with bands and alternative acts. Current acts include Cricket (alternative modern rock), Crave (punk pop rock) and Black Wednesday (rock).

CROWE ENTERTAINMENT INC., 1009 17th Ave. S., Nashville TN 37212-2202. (615)327-0411. Fax: (615)329-4289. President: J. Crowe. Management firm and music publisher (Midnight Crow/ASCAP, Cro Jo/BMI). Estab. 1986. Represents individual artists and/or groups and songwriters from anywhere; currently handles 4 acts. Receives 20% commission. Reviews material for acts.

How to Contact: Write or call first and obtain permission to submit. Prefers DAT, CD or cassette with no more than 3 songs and lyric sheet. If seeking management, press kit should include press clips, bio, picture, tape, CD or DAT. SASE. Reports in 2 weeks.

Music: Mostly **country**. Current acts include Darryl and Don Ellis (Sony/Epic recording artists), Six-Gun (country band), Hollie Dukes (female country act), Just Passing Thru (contemporary positive Christian act) and John Primm (Christian country).

CYCLE OF FIFTHS MANAGEMENT, INC., 331 Dante Ct., Suite H, Holbrook NY 11741-3800. (516)467-1837. Fax: (516)467-1645. E-mail: fifths@aol.com. Vice President/Business Affairs: James Reilly. Management firm. Represents individual artists and/or groups from anywhere. Receives 20% commission. Reviews material for acts.

How to Contact: Send demo tape by mail. Unsolicited submissions are OK. Prefers cassette. Does not return material. Reports in 6-8 weeks, via e-mail only.

Music: Mostly **rock** and **alternative**. Works primarily with established groups.

‡FRANKIE DALE MANAGEMENT, 2733 Riley Oaks Court, Las Vegas NV 89108. (702)645-7383. Fax: (702)645-7385. Owner: Frankie Dale. Management firm. Estab. 1989. Represents individual artists and groups from anywhere; currently handles 5 acts. Receives 20% commission. Reviews material for acts.

How to Contact: Submit demo tape by mail. Unsolicited submissions are OK. Prefers cassette or CD with 4 songs. If seeking management, press kit should include standard CD and/or cassette with 3-4 tracks, short bio and picture. Does not return material. Reports in 2 weeks.

Music: Mostly **alternative**, **college radio** and **metal**. Works primarily with national acts along with opening acts. Current acts include Skillethead (alternative), Stranger (metal) and Sloth (rock).

D&D TALENT ASSOCIATES, P.O. Box 254, Burkeville VA 23922. (804)767-4223. Owner: J.W. Dooley, Jr. Booking agency. Estab. 1976. Currently handles 2 acts. Receives 15% commission. "Reviews songs for individuals in the jazz and '40s-'50s field only."

How to Contact: Write first and obtain permission to submit. Prefers cassette or videocassette with 1-6 songs and lead sheet. SASE. Reports in 2-3 weeks.

Music: Mostly **jazz** and **'40s-'50s music**. Works primarily with vocalists and comics. Current acts include Johnny Pursley (humorist) and David Allyn (vocalist).

Tips: "Just send demos of Tin Pan Alley (great American popular song) type of music. No rock, no country."

DAS COMMUNICATIONS, LTD., 83 Riverside Dr., New York NY 10024. (212)877-0400. Management firm. Estab. 1975. Represents individual artists, groups and producers from anywhere; currently handles 14 acts. Receives 20% commission.

How to Contact: Call first and obtain permission to submit. Reports in 1 month. Prefers demo with 3 songs, lyric sheet and photo. Does not return material. Reports in 1 month.
Music: Mostly **rock**, **pop**, **R&B** and **alternative**. Current acts include Spin Doctors (rock), Jimmy Cliff (reggae), Jim Steinman (producer/songwriter), Diana King (R&B/reggae), Joan Osborne (rock), Vibrolush (alternative), Fugees (hip hop), Spacehog (modern rock) and Keith Thomas (producer/songwriter).

DCA PRODUCTIONS, 437 W. 44th St., New York NY 10036. (212)245-2063. Fax: (212)245-2367. E-mail: dcaplus@panix.com. Contact: Kate Magill. Booking agency. Estab. 1975. Represents individual artists, groups and songwriters from anywhere; currently handles 26 acts. Reviews material for acts.
How to Contact: Call first and obtain permission to submit. Prefers cassette or VHS videocassette with 2 songs. "All materials are reviewed and kept on file for future consideration. No material is returned. We do not report back, only if interested."
Music: Mostly **acoustic**, **rock** and **mainstream**; also **cabaret** and **theme**. Works primarily with acoustic singer/songwriters, top 40 or rock bands. Current acts include Roger Gillen (singer/songwriter), groovelily (melodic rock) and Fourth Avenue (a cappella).
Tips: "Please do not call for a review of material."

THE EDWARD DE MILES COMPANY, Vantage Point Towers, 4475 N. Allisonville Rd., 8th Floor, Indianapolis, IN 46205. (317)546-2912. President & CEO: Edward De Miles. Management firm, booking agency, entertainment/sports promoter and TV/radio broadcast producer. Estab. 1984. Represents film, television, radio and musical artists; currently handles 15 acts. Receives 10-20% commission. Reviews material for acts. Regional operations in Chicago, Dallas, Houston and Nashville through marketing representatives. Licensed A.F. of M. booking agent.

- See Edward De Miles's listing in the Record Producers section.

How to Contact: Write first and obtain permission to submit or to arrange personal interview. Prefers cassette with 3-5 songs, 8x10 b&w photo, bio and lyric sheet. "Copyright all material before submitting." If seeking management, include demo cassette with 3-5 songs, 8×10 b&w photo and lyric sheet in press kit. SASE. Reports in 1 month.
Music: Mostly **country**, **dance**, **R&B/soul**, **rock**, **top 40/pop** and **urban contemporary**; also looking for material for television, radio and film productions. Works primarily with dance bands and vocalists. Current acts include Lost in Wonder (progressive rock), Steve Lynn (R&B/dance), Multiple Choice (rap) and D'vou Edwards (jazz).
Tips: "Performers need to be well prepared with their presentations (equipment, showmanship a must)."

DEBUTANTE MANAGEMENT/CATALYST ENTERTAINMENT, 3603 Corp. Kennedy St., Bayside NY 11361. Phone/fax: (718)357-4867. E-mail: debmgmt@aol.com. President: J. Miller. Management, publicity and promotional firm. Estab. 1989. Represents individual artists from anywhere; currently handles 3 acts. Receives 10-25% commission.
How to Contact: Submit demo tape by mail. Unsolicited submissions are OK. Prefers CD, cassette or VHS videocassette. "Make sure there's a contact phone number." SASE. Reports in 2 months.
Music: Mostly **rock**, **punk** and **alternative**; also **great songs** and **great music**. Works primarily with bands and solo performers. Current acts include Tommy Floyd (blues based, 3-chord rock) and OCD (Obsessive Compulsive Disorder) (thrash "new" metal).

DEPTH OF FIELD MANAGEMENT, 1501 Broadway, Suite 1304, New York NY 10019. (212)302-9200. Fax: (212)382-1639. Contact: Peter McCallum. Management firm. Represents individual artists and groups from anywhere; currently handles 6 acts. Receives variable commission.
How to Contact: Call to obtain permission to submit. Prefers cassette with 3 or more songs. If seeking management, press kit should include bio and cassette. "Don't submit 'rough' mixes/recordings." Does not return material.
Music: Mostly **rock** and **alternative**. Current acts include Andreas Vollenweider (Swiss harpist), Michael Brecker (jazz saxophonist) and Randy Brecker (jazz trumpeter).

‡BILL DERN MANAGEMENT, 8455 Fountain Ave., Suite 530, Los Angeles CA 90069. (213)650-5369. Fax: (213)656-5188. Contact: Bill Dern. Management firm. Estab. 1986. Represents individual artists, groups, songwriters and producers from anywhere; currently handles 4 acts. Receives 20% commission. Reviews material for acts.
How to Contact: Submit demo tape by mail. Unsolicited submissions are OK. Prefers cassette and lyric sheet. If seeking management, press kit should include b&w photo, bio, clippings and tape/CD. "Be patient. We do listen to all material, although at times we may not get back to you in a timely fashion." SASE. Reports in 1 month.

Music: All types. Works primarily with bands, producers and songwriters. Current acts include Impromp2 (jazz/R&B group, Mojazz Records), Funkdoobiest (hip-hop group, Immortal Records), Ebony Tay (rock singer, Murphy Dog Records) and Ray Roll (producer of Nice & Smooth, Funkdoobiest, Naughty By Nature and Queen Latifah).

‡BILL DETKO MANAGEMENT, 127 Shamrock Dr., Ventura CA 93003. (805)644-0447. (805)644-0469. President: Bill Detko. Management firm. Estab. 1984. Represents individual artists, groups and songwriters from anywhere; currently handles 3 acts. Receives 20% commission. Reviews material for acts.
How to Contact: Submit demo tape by mail. Unsolicited submissions are OK. "Artist must follow up by phone." Prefers cassette, VHS videocassette (if available) or CD with 3-6 songs and lyric sheet. If seeking management, press kit should include bio plus above and any press or radio action. Does not return material. Reports in 1-2 weeks.
Music: Mostly **alternative**, **jazz** and **world**. Current acts include Paul Ventimiglia (jazz), Yulduz Usmanova (world) and EMOK (alternative).

DETOUR ENTERTAINMENT INC., (formerly Classic Rock Entertainment Agency), 12700 Park Central Dr. #1413, Dallas TX 75251. (972)239-2503. Fax: (972)239-2509. E-mail: detourinc@aol.com. Website: http://www.unsignedartists.com. Owner: Traci L. Parsons. Booking agency. Estab. 1992. Represents individual artists and groups from anywhere. Currently handles 300 acts. Receives 10-20% commission. Reviews material for acts.
How to Contact: Call first and obtain permission to submit a demo. Prefers cassette with 4 songs and lyric or lead sheet. If seeking management, press kit should include picture, biography of members, demo cassette, experience with music (references). "Please allow management company to have 6-8 weeks to review original material and consult with publishers." Does not return material. Reports in 2-6 weeks.
Music: Classic rock/dance, **jazz/blues** and **funk/alternative**; also **folk** and **rap/contemporary R&B**. Works primarily with bands, solos, duets and trios. Current acts include Random Axis (band), Passing Strangers (original), Hard Night's Day (Beatles tribute) and Emerald City (cover music band/dance).

LIESA DILEO MANAGEMENT, P.O. Box 414731, Miami Beach FL 33141. President: Liesa DiLeo. Management firm, booking agency and music publisher. Estab. 1984. Represents individual artists, groups, songwriters, and actors from anywhere; currently handles 4 acts. Receives 20-30% commission. Reviews material for acts.
How to Contact: Submit demo tape by mail. Unsolicited submissions are OK. Prefers cassette with 2 songs and lyric sheet. If seeking management, press kit should include photo, bio, press clippings and videocassette. SASE. Reports in 1 month.
Music: Rock, **pop**, **Latin**, **salsa** and **R&B**.

ANDREW DINWOODIE MANAGEMENT, P.O. Box 5052, Victoria Point QLD 4165 **Australia**. Phone: (07)32070502. Manager: Andrew Dinwoodie. Management firm and booking agency. Estab. 1983. Represents regional (Australian) individual artists, groups and songwriters; currently handles 3 acts. Receives 10-20% commission. Reviews material for acts.
How to Contact: Submit demo tape by mail. Unsolicited submissions are OK. Prefers cassette or VHS PAL videocassette with lyric sheet. If seeking management, press kit should include bio, photo, goals, audio or videotape and CD if available. SAE and IRC. Reports in 6 weeks.
Music: Mostly **country**, **R&B** and **rock/pop**; also **bluegrass**, **swing** and **folk**. Current acts include Bullamakanka (good time Australian music), Donna Heke (blues/soul) and Bluey the Bastard.

DIRECT MANAGEMENT, 645 Quail Ridge Rd., Aledo TX 76008-2835. Owner: Danny Wilkerson. Management firm and booking agency. Estab. 1986. Represents individual artists and/or groups from anywhere; currently handles 5 acts. Receives 10-20% commission. Reviews material for acts.
How to Contact: Submit demo tape by mail. Unsolicited submissions are OK. Prefers CD, cassette or VHS videocassette with 3 songs. If seeking management, press kit should include bio, cassette or CD, photo and reviews. Does not return material. Reports in 1 month.
Music: Mostly **college rock**, **Christian** and **children's**. Current acts include Waltons (pop/rock), Generation Rumble (alternative), The EPs (rock) and Emily Rogers (country).

DME MANAGEMENT, 1020 Pico Blvd., Suite A, Santa Monica CA 90405. (310)396-5008. Fax: (310)396-1966. E-mail: laserdme@aol.com. President: David Ehrlich. Management firm, record company (Laser Records) and music publisher (Dukare Music). Estab. 1992. Represents individual artists, groups, songwriters, producers and engineers from anywhere; currently handles 5 acts. Receives 15-20% commission. Reviews material for acts.

How to Contact: Submit demo tape by mail. Unsolicited submissions are OK. Prefers cassette. Does not return material. Reports in 1 month.
Music: Mostly **urban/rap, R&B** and **rock—made in England**. Current acts include Gravediggaz (rap, Gee Street/V2 Records) and Holly McNarland (rock, Universal/MCA Records).

DMR AGENCY, Galleries of Syracuse, Suite 250, Syracuse NY 13202-2416. (315)475-2500. E-mail: dmr@ican.net. Contact: David M. Rezak. Booking agency. Represents individuals and groups; currently handles 50 acts. Receives 15% commission.
How to Contact: Submit demo tape by mail. Unsolicited submissions are OK. Submit cassette or videocassette with 1-4 songs and press kit. Does not return material.
Music: Mostly **rock (all styles)**, **pop** and **blues**. Works primarily with cover bands. Current acts include Joe Whiting (R&B), Little Georgie and the Shufflin' Hungarians (blues), Ghost Monkeys (modern rock), Tryx (rock) and Windsong (pop).
Tips: "You might want to contact us if you have a cover act in our region. Many songwriters in our area have a cover group in order to make money."

JAMES R. DORAN, P.C., 1722 S. Glenstone, UU, Springfield MO 65804. (417)881-4174. Fax: (417)886-3846. Owner: James R. Doran. Management firm and booking agency. Estab. 1975. Represents individual artists, groups and songwriters from anywhere; currently handles 5 acts. Receives variable commission. Reviews material for acts.
How to Contact: Submit demo tape by mail. Unsolicited submissions are OK. Prefers cassette. If seeking management, press kit should include bio and cassette. Does not return material. Reports in 2 weeks.
Music: Mostly **country**; also **rock**. Current acts include Ray Price (country artist).

COL. BUSTER DOSS PRESENTS, 341 Billy Goat Hill Rd., Winchester TN 37398. (615)649-2577. Fax: (615)649-2732. Producer: Col. Buster Doss. Management firm, booking agency, record company (Stardust Records), record producer and music publisher (Buster Doss Music/BMI). Estab. 1959. Represents individual artists, groups, songwriters and shows; currently handles 14 acts. Receives 15% commission. Reviews material for acts.

- Buster Doss's publishing company, Buster Doss Music, is listed in the Music Publishers section, and his record label, Stardust, is in the Record Companies section. Buster Doss is also listed under Record Producers.

How to Contact: Write first and obtain permission to submit. Prefers cassette with 2-4 songs and lyric sheet. If seeking management, press kit should include demo, photos, video if available and bio. SASE. Reports back on day received.
Music: Country, **gospel** and **progressive**. Works primarily with show and dance bands, single acts and package shows. Current acts include Mike "Doc" Holliday, "Rooster" Quantrell, Dee Dee Tompkins, Linda Wunder, The Border Raiders, "Bronco" Buck Cody and Jerri Arnold.

DRASTIC MEASURES, INC., 4511 Balmoral Rd., Kennesaw GA 30144. (770)425-6543. President: Nancy Camp. Management firm. Estab. 1991. Represents local and regional (United States and Canada) groups; currently handles 2 acts. Receives 20% commission.
How to Contact: Submit demo tape by mail. Unsolicited submissions are OK. Prefers cassette or VHS videocassette with minimum of 3 songs and lyric sheet. If seeking management, press kit should include photo, bio, cassette (minimum 3 songs), video (if available), tearsheets, cover letter stating objective, tour history and current itinerary. Does not return material. Reports in 4-6 weeks.
Music: Mostly **hard rock** and **heavy alternative rock**; also **pop metal** and **punk**. Works primarily with bands. Current acts include Stuck Mojo (Century Media Records, hard rock band) and 3 Lost Souls (Bonfire Records, heavy pop).
Tips: "Don't attempt to write a hit, or what you think the industry wants to hear. Write what you feel, and write what you know about."

DUCKWORTH/ATLANTICA, 198 Duckworth St., St. John's Newfoundland A1C 1G5 **Canada**. (709)753-9292. President: Fred Brokenshire. Management firm, record company (Duckworth/Atlantica)

REMEMBER: Don't "shotgun" your demo tapes. Submit only to companies interested in the type of music you write. For more submission hints, refer to Getting Started on page 6.

and distributor. Estab. 1990. Represents local and Atlantic Canadian individual artists and groups. Currently handles 42 acts. Reviews material for acts.
How to Contact: Submit demo tape by mail. Unsolicited submissions are OK. Prefers cassette and press/bio kit. "3 songs max per tape, properly labelled." Does not return material. Reports in 1-2 months.
Music: Mostly **Celtic traditional**, **Celtic rock** and **singer/writer ballads**. Works primarily with folk, folk-rock bands, singer-songwriters. Current acts include Irish Descendants (Celtic folk band), Damhnait Doyle (female singer/writer) and Sandbox (pop band).
Tips: "Know the artists we are working with; send us quality demos, and don't forget your name and number."

‡E.M.E. RECORDS, LTD., 7127 E. Becker Lane, Suite 105, Scottsdale AZ 85254. (602)569-9390. President: Rick Brock. Vice President: Gerry Mottley. Management firm, music publisher (E.M.E., Ltd.), record company, record producer (Entertainment Music Enterprises, Ltd.) and recording studio. Estab. 1989. Represents local individual artists, groups and songwriters; currently handles 2 acts. Receives 20% commission. Reviews material for acts.
How to Contact: Call first and obtain permission to submit a demo. Prefers cassette, DAT, VHS videocassette or full length CDs *sometimes* with 3 songs and lyric sheet. Does not return material. Reports in 2 months.
Music: Mostly **medium, hard rock**, **techno dance music** and **R&B**; also **acoustic rock**, **pop** and **unusual rap**. Works primarily with rock bands and singer/songwriters. Current acts include Poet's Moon (pop/AC), Venus Butterfly (solo singer/dance), and Buddha Stick (alternative funk).
Tips: "We are a small independent label that works closely with developing our talent, recording them, releasing their product, promoting them, producing albums and videos for them. We work with only three or four at a time so as to give each our undivided attention. Because of this we are most selective. Our artists do not get lost in the shuffle and get personal attention in all areas of their careers. However, we expect as much in return. They must be totally committed to long hours and hard work and adhere to all the requirements our company demands. If they give 150% . . . then so do we. It is a win-win situation."

EARTH TRACKS ARTISTS AGENCY, 4809 Ave. N., Suite 286, Brooklyn NY 11234. E-mail: enigpublus@aol.com. Managing Director-Artist Relations: David Krinsky. Management firm. Estab. 1990. Represents individual artists, groups and songwriters from anywhere. Receives 15-20% commission. Reviews material for acts.
How to Contact: Submit demo tape by mail. Unsolicited submissions are OK. Prefers cassette with 3-6 songs and lyric sheet. If seeking management, include 1 group photo, all lyrics with songs, a cassette/CD of original songs and the ages of the artists. Does not return material. Reports in 1 month. "We will contact artist if interested."
Music: Mostly **commercial rock** (all kinds), **pop** and **alternative**. No rap or metal. Works primarily with commercial, original, solo artists and groups, songwriters in the rock, pop, areas (no country, thrash or punk).
Tips: "Currently reviewing folk/blues and acoustic 'Delta'-style blues and acoustic alternative for upcoming film project. Seeking a female singer/songwriter with a 'Jewel'-type image as well. A composer who can write music to pre-existing lyrics sought as well."

EBI INC., 928 Broadway, Suite 405, New York NY 10010. (212)228-8300. Fax: (212)228-8495. E-mail: inpress@aol.com. Contact: Ellen Bello. Management firm and public relations firm. Estab. 1991. Represents individual artists, groups and songwriters. Receives 20% commission or weekly fee. Reviews material for acts.
How to Contact: Write or call first and obtain permission to submit. Prefers cassette or VHS videocassette with lyric sheet. Does not return material. Reports in 4-6 weeks.
Music: Native American, **alternative rock** and **mainstream**; also **country**. Works primarily with singer/songwriters and bands. Current acts include Joan Armatrading, Cirque de Soleil soundtrack, Burning Sky and Robert Mirabal.

‡EDEN RECORDS, 11908 Ventura Blvd., Suite 201, Studio City CA 91604. (818)762-5648. Fax: (818)762-8224. Manager: Frank Volpe. Management firm and record company. Estab. 1996. Represents individual artists and groups from anywhere; currently handles 8 acts. Receives 15% commission. Reviews material for acts.

How to Contact: Submit demo tape by mail. Unsolicited submissions are OK. Prefers cassette with 4-6 songs. If seeking management, press kit should include photos, press and names of clubs played. Does not return material. Reports in 2 months.
Music: Mostly **alternative** and **triple A**. Current acts include Ass Ponys (modern rock) and Jane Jensen (alternative/industrial).

‡THE ELLIS INTERNATIONAL TALENT AGENCY, 5617 W. Melvina, Milwaukee WI 53216. (414)444-3385. Artist Representative: Darrien Kingston. Management firm, booking agency, music publisher (Ellis Enterprise Publishing), record company (Safire Records) and record producer (Darnell Ellis). Estab. 1997. Represents individual artists, groups and songwriters from anywhere. Receives 15-20% commission. Reviews material for acts.

- See the listing for Safire Records in the Record Companies section.

How to Contact: Submit demo tape by mail. Unsolicited submissions are OK. Prefers cassette or videocassette with 4-6 songs and press kit. If seeking management, press kit should include cassette tape (demo), 8x10 photo, video tape and reviews. Does not return material. Reports in 4-6 weeks. "We will respond only if we are interested."
Music: Mostly **top 40/pop hits**, **country** and **alternative**; also **dance** and **jazz**. Works primarily with singers, singer/songwriters, songwriters and bands.

GINO EMPRY ENTERTAINMENT, 120 Carlton St., Suite 315, Toronto MSA 4K2 **Canada**. (410)928-1044. Fax: (416)928-1415. E-mail: gempry@direct.com. President: Gino Empry. Management firm, booking agency and public relations. Estab. 1970. Represents individual artists, groups, songwriters and actors from anywhere; currently handles 10 acts. Receives 10-15% commission. Reviews material for acts.
How to Contact: Submit demo tape by mail. Unsolicited submissions are OK. Prefers cassette or VHS videocassette with lyric sheet. If seeking management, press kit should include list of performances, CD or cassette, photo, background, résumé and newspaper reprints. Does not return material. Reports in 2 months.
Music: Mostly **pop**, **country** and **jazz/blues**; also **theatrical**. Works primarily with singer/songwriters, actors, dancers and soloists. Current acts include Roch Voisine (singer/composer), Andre Gagnon (composer), Philippe Leduc (composer), Steve Barracat (composer), Patrick Norman (singer/composer) and Richard Samuels (singer/composer).

ENTERCOM, 372 Richmond St. W. Suite 205, Ontario, Quebec M5V 1X6 **Canada**. (416)598-3330. Fax: (416)598-5428. Manager: James MacLean. Management firm. Estab. 1989. Represents groups from anywhere; currently handles 4 acts. Receives 20% commission. Reviews material for acts.
How to Contact: Submit demo tape by mail. Unsolicited submissions are OK. Prefers cassette. Does not return material. Reports in 6 weeks.
Music: Mostly **alternative, pop, rock** and **metal**. Works primarily with original cutting edge bands. Current acts include Doughboys (power punk pop, A&M Records), Voivod (cybermetal/punk, Hypnotic/A&M Records), Mrs. Torrance (MMG Records), Made (MCA Records) and Scratching Post (Enclave Records).
Tips: "Send to recommended people or companies. Random solicitation is useless. Research and educate yourself. If you come across as professional and down to earth you'll get a lot further. Forget what's popular at the moment. All music is current again or recycled, so write from the experience of your life, not anyone else's. Be true to yourself. Don't follow a trend, lead music into a new dimension. Create your own!"

THE ENTERTAINMENT GROUP, 9112 Fireside Dr., Indianapolis IN 46250. President: Bob McCutcheon. Management firm. Estab. 1987. Represents local, regional and international individual artists and groups; currently handles 3 acts. Receives 20% commission. Reviews material for acts.
How to Contact: Write first and obtain permission to submit. Prefers cassette with 3 songs. If seeking management include photo and tape. Does not return material. Reports in 1 month.
Music: Mostly **hard rock** and **R&B**. Current acts include The Remainders (college radio), The Common (college radio) and Jon Huffman Project (alternative).

LISTINGS OF COMPANIES in countries other than the U.S. have the name of the country in boldface type.

ENTERTAINMENT INTERNATIONAL USA, P.O. Box 7189, Canton OH 44705-0189. (330)455-1488. A&R: Diane Bennafield. Management firm, booking agency and music publisher. Estab. 1969. Represents individual artists and/or groups, songwriters from anywhere; currently handles 15 acts. Receives 20% commission. Reviews material for acts.
How to Contact: Submit demo tape by mail. Unsolicited submissions are OK. Prefers cassette or VHS/Beta videocassette with 4 songs and lyric sheet. If seeking management, press kit should include bio, demo and photos. SASE. Reports in 3 weeks.
Music: All types. Current acts include Sirene (R&B), Mary White (country) and Chico (rap).
Tips: "Put your package together carefully in a professional manner."

ENTERTAINMENT SERVICES INTERNATIONAL, 6400 Pleasant Park Dr., Chanhassen MN 55317. (612)470-9000. Fax: (612)474-4449. Owner: Randy Erwin. Booking agency. Estab. 1988. Represents groups from anywhere; currently handles 20 acts. Receives 10-20% commission. Reviews material for acts.
How to Contact: Submit demo tape by mail. Unsolicited submissions are OK. Prefers CD or VHS videocassette. If seeking management, press kit should include photos, biography, instrumentation, references, list of places performed, reviews, video, cassette or CD. SASE. Reports in 1-2 weeks.
Music: Mostly **rock, R&B, alternative rock** and **country**. Works primarily with bands.

ENTERTAINMENT WORKS, 2400 Poplar Dr., Baltimore MD 21207. Phone/fax: (410)594-9486. E-mail: nanlewis@erols.com. President: Nancy Lewis. Management firm, booking agency and public relations/publicity firm. Estab. 1989. Represents regional and international groups; currently handles 3 acts. Receives 10-15% commission. Reviews material for acts.
How to Contact: Write or call first and obtain permission to submit. Prefers cassette or CD "plus biography/publicity clips/photo." If seeking management, include group biography, individual biographies, 8×10 b&w glossy, all press clips/articles, PA requirements list and stage plot in press kit. Does not return material. Reports in 2 months.
Music: Reggae. Works primarily with vocalists/dance bands. Current acts include Winston Grennan Ska Rocks Band, the Original Jamaican All Stars and Jah Levi & the Higher Reasoning (all reggae).
Tips: "Start with a phone call to introduce yourself, followed by a well-recorded 3-song demo or CD, band member biographies, photo and all publicity clips. This agency works only with reggae artists."

ETERNAL RECORDS/SQUIGMONSTER MANAGEMENT, 1598 E. Shore Dr., St. Paul MN 55106-1121. (612)771-0107. President/Owner: Robert (Squiggy) Yezek. Management firm and record company (PMS Records). Estab. 1983. Represents groups from anywhere; currently handles 30 acts. Receives 5-20% commission. Reviews material for acts.
How to Contact: Submit demo tape by mail. Unsolicited submissions are OK. Prefers CD (if available) with songs (no limit) and lead sheet. If seeking management, press kit should include CD or tape, bio, promo package and any press. Mail to attention: A&R Dept. Does not return material. Reports in 1 month.
Music: Mostly **alternative rock**, **heavy metal** and **hard rock**; also **comedy**, **R&B**, **rap** and **new pop**. Current acts include No Man's Land (alternative metal), Bad Boyz (R&B), MC Sly (rap), Deth Squad IV (thrash), Power Play and Zombie.

SCOTT EVANS PRODUCTIONS, 4747 Hollywood Blvd. #274, Hollywood FL 33021-6503. (954)963-4449. Artistic Director: Scott Evans. Management firm and booking agency. Estab. 1979. Represents local, regional or international individual artists, groups, songwriters, comedians, novelty acts, dancers and theaters; currently handles 200 acts. Receives 25% commission. Reviews material for acts.
How to Contact: Submit demo tape by mail. Unsolicited submissions are OK. Prefers cassette or ½" videocassette with 3 songs. If seeking management, include picture, résumé, flyers, cassette or video tape. Does not return material.
Music: Mostly **pop**, **R&B** and **Broadway**. Deals with "all types of entertainers; no limitations." Current acts include Scott Evans and Company (variety song and dance), Dori Zinger (female vocalist), Jeff Geist, Actors Repertory Theatre, Entertainment Express, Perfect Parties and Joy Deco (dance act).
Tips: "Submit a neat, well put together, organized press kit."

EXCLESISA BOOKING AGENCY, 716 Windward Rd., Jackson MS 39206. Phone/fax: (601)366-0220. Booking Managers/Owners: Roy and Esther Wooten. Booking agency. Estab. 1989. Represents groups from anywhere; currently handles 9 acts. Receives 15% commission. Reviews material for acts.
How to Contact: Submit demo tape by mail. Unsolicited submissions are OK. Prefers cassette or videocassette. If seeking management, press kit should include CD or cassette, videocassette, pictures, address and telephone contact and bio. Does not return material. Reports in 2 months.

Music: Gospel only. Current acts include The Jackson Southernaires, Slim & The Supreme Angels and The Mississippi Seminar Choir.
Tips: "Make sure your demo is clear with a good sound so the agent can make a good judgement."

JAMES FAITH ENTERTAINMENT, P.O. Box 346, Port Jefferson NY 11777. (516)331-0808. Fax: (516)331-0994. President: James Faith. Management firm and booking agency. Estab. 1989. Represents individual artists, groups and songwriters from anywhere; currently handles 5 acts. Receives 10-15% commission. Reviews material for acts.
How to Contact: Call first and obtain permission to submit. Prefers cassette or VHS videocassette with 6 songs and lyric and/or lead sheet. If seeking management, press kit should include audio—cassette, CD, etc., explain how and who recorded it; print—bio, references, photos; video—if available; and personal letter—explain what you are looking for in management. List desires, expectations, personal beliefs and goals. Does not return material. Reports in 2 months.
Music: Mostly **jazz**, **rock**, **folk**, **blues** and **funk**; also **classical**, **world** and **big band**. Works primarily with soloists, bands and singer/songwriters. Current acts include Peter Duchin (big band and society music), Big Picnic (13 piece funk band) and Subject to Change (jazz trio).
Tips: "Have all info presented clearly and professionally."

FAME INTERNATIONAL, 939 Kimball St., Philadelphia PA 19147. (215)629-0709. Exec. V.P. Productions: Albert R. Bauman. Management firm and music publisher (Jazz Lady Publishing/ASCAP). Estab. 1986. Represents individual artists, groups, songwriters and specialty acts from anywhere; currently handles 12 acts. Receives 10-25% commission. Reviews material for acts.
How to Contact: Submit demo tape by mail. Unsolicited submissions are OK. Prefers cassette or VHS videocassette with 3 songs. If seeking management, press kit should include as much relevant material as possible—head shot, bio, reviews, list of previous year's engagements, contracted future dates and commitments. Does not return material. Reports in 2 weeks.
Music: Mostly **jazz** and **country**; also **specialty acts for casinos and cruises**. Works primarily with vocalists, singer/songwriters, big bands and comedy acts. Current acts include Nancy Kelly (jazz singer), Jim Craine, the Bob Crosby Orchestra and The Guy Lombardo Orchestra.
Tips: "On cover letter, be as specific as possible in describing your career goals and what has prevented you from attaining them thus far. Be honest."

FAST LANE INTERNATIONALS, P.O. Box 4856, Haydood #200, Virginia Beach VA 23455. (757)481-9662. Fax: (804)481-9227. E-mail: fastlan@exis.net. Agent: George Michailow. Booking agency and consultant for overseas artists seeking US licensing/distribution. Represents individual artists and groups from anywhere; currently handles 40 acts. Receives 15% commission. Reviews material for acts.
How to Contact: Submit demo tape by mail. Unsolicited submissions are OK. Prefers cassette, ½" NTSC or CD (preferred). If seeking management, press kit should include bio, press, tour history—min. 1 year (including: date, venue and capacity, headliner or opener, fee and attendance info), tech rider (including: stage plan, mic assignment list), backline required and personnel list for all traveling (including each person's function, if not sure, list function as TBA). "Submit only relevant materials (listed above), no playbills, copies of ads or posters, etc." Does not return material. Reports in 2 weeks.
Music: Mostly **world beat**, **reggae** and **African pop**; also **Latin**, **New Age** and **ska**. Works primarily with music acts capable of touring. Current acts include Inner Circle (reggae), Lucky Dube (pop reggae/South African) and Culture (roots reggae/Jamaican).
Tips: "Have a record company willing to provide adequate promotional and tour support."

FASTBACK MANAGEMENT, 1321 Sixth Ave., San Francisco CA 94122. (415)564-7404. Fax: (415)564-2927. E-mail: spydog@well.com. Contact: Cathy Cohn. Management firm. Estab. 1992. Represents individual artists and groups; currently handles 3 acts.
How to Contact: Submit demo tape by mail. Unsolicited submissions are OK. Prefers cassette or VHS videocassette. If seeking management, press kit should include artist history (bio), press and tape. SASE.
Music: All types. Current acts include Meat Beat Manifesto, The Grassy Knoll and Freaky Chakra.

FAT CITY ARTISTS, 1906 Chet Atkins Place, Suite 502, Nashville TN 37212. (615)320-7678. Fax: (615)321-5382. President: Rusty Michael. Management firm, booking agency, lecture bureau and event management consultants. Estab. 1972. Represents international individual artists, groups, songwriters and authors; currently handles over 100 acts. Receives 20% commission. Reviews material for acts.

- See their listing in the Record Companies section, and the listing for Fat City Publishing in the Music Publishers section.

How to Contact: Submit demo tape and any other promotional material by mail. Unsolicited submissions

are OK. Prefers cassette, CD or video with 4-6 songs. Does not return material. Reports in 1 month.
Music: Mostly **rock**, **top 40**, **country** and **blues**; also **rockabilly**, **alternative** and **jazz**. "To date our company has agreements with 140 artists that represent every genre of music." Current acts include Duane Eddy (rock), The Belmont Playboys (rockabilly), James Brown, Amazing Rhythm Aces, Shaver, Wet Willie (blues), Nina Simone and Stanley Turrentine (jazz).
Tips: "Send all available information including audio, video, photo and print. Creative Communications Workshop, our advertising/promotion division, specializes in developing effective artist promotional packages, including demos, videos, photography and copy. We will evaluate your present promotional material at no cost."

S.L. FELDMAN & ASSOCIATES, 1505 W. Second Ave. #200, Vancouver, British Columbia V6H 3Y4 **Canada**. (604)734-5945. Fax: (604)732-0922. E-mail: feldman@slfa.com. Website: http://www.slfa.com. Contact: Janet York. Management firm and booking agency. Estab. 1970. Represents individual artists and groups from anywhere; currently handles over 100 acts.
How to Contact: Submit demo tape by mail. Unsolicited submissions are OK. Prefers cassette and lyric sheet. If seeking management, include photo, bio, cassette and video (if available) in press kit. SAE and IRC. Reports in 6-8 weeks.
Music: Current acts include Bryan Adams, The Chieftains, Joni Mitchell, Anne Muuray, Odds, Sarah McLachlan and Spirit of the West.

FRED T. FENCHEL ENTERTAINMENT AGENCY, 2104 S. Jefferson Avenue, Mason City IA 50401. (515)423-4177. Fax: (515)423-8662. General Manager: Fred T. Fenchel. Booking agency. Estab. 1964. Represents local and international individual artists and groups; currently handles up to 10 acts. Receives 20% commission. Reviews material for acts.
How to Contact: Submit demo tape by mail (videocassette if available). Unsolicited submissions are OK. Does not return material. Reports in 3 weeks.
Music: Mostly **country**, **pop** and some **gospel**. Works primarily with dance bands and show groups; "artists we can use on club dates, fairs, etc." Current acts include The Memories, "Hot" Rod Chevy, The Sherwin Linton Show and Convertibles. "We deal primarily with established name acts with recording contracts, or those with a label and starting into popularity."
Tips: "Be honest. Don't submit unless your act is exceptional rather than just starting out, amateurish and with lyrics that are written under the pretense they are qualified writers."

B.C. FIEDLER MANAGEMENT, PH#6-40 Alexander St., Toronto Ontario M4Y 1B5 **Canada**. (416)967-1421. Fax: (416)967-1991. E-mail: bcf@the-wire.com. Partners: B.C. Fiedler/Elisa Amsterdam. Management firm, music publisher (B.C. Fiedler Publishing) and record company (Sleeping Giant Music). Estab. 1964. Represents individual artists, groups and songwriters from anywhere; currently handles 6 acts. Receives 20-25% or consultant fees. Reviews material for acts.
How to Contact: Call first and obtain permission to submit. Prefers cassette or VHS videocassette with 3 songs and lyric sheet. If seeking management, press kit should include bio, list of concerts performed in past two years including name of venue, repertoire, reviews and photos. Does not return material. Reports in 2 months.
Music: Mostly **classical/crossover**, **voice** and **pop**; also **country**. Works primarily with classical/crossover ensembles, instrumental soloists, operatic voice and pop singer/songwriters. Current acts include Liona Boyd (classical guitar).
Tips: "Invest in demo production using best quality voice and instrumentalists. If you write songs, hire the talent to best represent your work. Submit tape and lyrics. Artists should follow up 6-8 weeks after submission."

FIRESTAR PROMOTIONS INC., P.O. Box 165, 1896 W. Broadway, Vancouver, B.C. V6J 1Y9 **Canada**. Phone/fax: (604)732-4012. President: Frances Wennes. Management firm and record producer. Estab. 1991. Works with individual artists and songwriters from anywhere; currently handles 3 acts. Receives 25% commission. Reviews material for acts.
How to Contact: Submit demo tape by mail. Unsolicited submissions are OK. Prefers cassette or VHS videocassette with letter and picture. If seeking management, press kit should include one page biography, references, picture, cassette, introduction letter, contact person, address and telephone number. Does not return material. Reports in 3 months.
Music: Mostly **New Age** and **instrumental**. Current acts include Firestar (angelic folk harpist), Orca Tribe (Jeffrey Bloom, composer/performer) and Jerry Wennes & the Happy Wanderers (European polka band).
Tips: "Have your personal finances in control. Do not ask for financial support."

FIRST TIME MANAGEMENT, Sovereign House, 12 Trewartha Rd., Praa Sands-Penzance, Cornwall TR20 9ST **England**. Phone: (01736)762826. Fax: (01736)763328. E-mail: panamus@aol.com. Managing Director: Roderick G. Jones. Management firm, record company (First Time Records) and music publisher (First Time Music). Estab. 1986. Represents local, regional and international individual aritsts, groups and songwriters. Receives 20% commission. Reviews material for acts.

- See the listings for First Time Records in the Record Companies section and First Time Music in the Music Publishers section.

How to Contact: Submit demo tape by mail. Unsolicited submissions are OK. Prefers cassette, 15 ips reel-to-reel or VHS videocassette with 3 songs and lyric sheets. SAE and IRC. Reports in 4-8 weeks.
Music: Mostly **dance**, **top 40**, **rap**, **country**, **gospel** and **pop**; also **all styles**. Works primarily with songwriters, composers, vocalists, groups and choirs. Current acts include Pete Arnold (folk) and Willow.
Tips: "Become a member of the Guild of International Songwriters and Composers. Keep everything as professional as possible. Be patient and dedicated to your aims and objectives."

FIVE STAR ENTERTAINMENT, 10188 Winter View Dr., Naples FL 34109. (941)566-7701. Fax: (941)566-7702. E-mail: tk5star@aol.com. Co-owners: Sid Kleiner and Trudy Kleiner. Booking agency and audiovisual firm (Sid Kleiner Music Enterprises). Estab. 1976. Represents local and regional individual artists and groups; currently handles 400 acts. Receives 15-25% commission. Reviews material for acts.
How to Contact: Submit demo tape by mail. Unsolicited submissions are OK. Prefers cassette or VHS videocassette with 4 songs and lyric or lead sheet. If seeking management, press kit should include song list, demo, equipment list, available dates, rates and references. Does not return material. Reports in 1 month.
Music: Mostly **MOR**, **country** and **folk**. Current acts include Dave Kleiner (alternative), Sid Kleiner (guitarist) and Diamond & Steed (magic).

5 STAR MUSIC GROUP/MIKE WADDELL & ASSOCIATES, 4301 S. Carothers Rd., Franklin TN 37064. (615)790-7452. Fax: (615)790-9958. E-mail: fivestar01@aol.com. President: Mike Waddell. Management firm, music publisher and record producer (James Hudson). Estab. 1977. Represents regional individual artists and songwriters; currently handles 2 acts. Receives variable commission. Reviews material for acts.
How to Contact: Submit demo tape by mail. Unsolicited submissions are OK. Prefers cassette, DAT or ½" VHS videocassette with 3 songs and lyric sheet. If seeking management, press kit should include tape, bio, picture and press information. "Should we be interested in any material received, we will contact the writer or artist by telephone or mail. All material should be copyrighted prior to submission." Does not return material. Reports in 3 weeks.
Music: Mostly **country**, **rock** and **Christian**. Current acts include Nathan Whitt (alternative), Gerd Rube (Germany) and Johnathon Bloom (alternative).
Tips: "Research the song market and be confident that your songs will hold up. Do not waste the valuable time of publishers and labels with anything less than professional songs. In past years we have signed songs from submissions via the mail. One of those, Reece Wilson, was named BMI writer of the year in 1995."

‡FIVE-STAR MANAGEMENT & ENTERTAINMENT INTERNATIONAL, P.O. Box 5368, Buena Park CA 90622. (714)522-2383. Executive Director: Jerry Smith. Management firm, booking agency, music publisher (Royal King Music, Melodeer Music), record company (Royal Records), record producer (Royal Recording Co.), audiovisual firm (Royal Records), recording facility and graphics and multimedia studio. Estab. 1959. Represents individual artists, groups and songwriters from anywhere. Commission varies 15-25% depending on services provided. Reviews material for acts.

- See the listing for Royal Records in the Record Companies section.

How to Contact: Write first and obtain permission to submit. Enclose SASE for rapid reply. Prefers cassette, VHS videocassette or CD with any number of songs. "The more we hear the better we're able to judge your abilities." For bookings, live performance videos are best; however, if none is available, a regular demo tape will do for initial review. Include press kit with list of past performances. Content of press kit is more important than how fancy it looks. Also do you perform original material only, or cover tunes as well." Reports in 1-3 weeks.
Music: All styles.

FLINTER MUSIC, PB15, Antwerp 17, B-2018, Antwerp **Belgium**. Phone: +(0)32480376. Fax: +(0)32483186. E-mail: flinterm@www.dma.be. Website: http://www.dma.be/p/bewoner/FlinterM/index.htm. President: Luc Nuitten. Management firm and booking agency. Estab. 1991. Represents artists from anywhere; currently handles 6 acts. Receives 15% commission. Reviews material for acts.
How to Contact: Write first and obtain permission to submit. Prefers CD or VHS videocassette (PAL)

with 3 songs. If seeking management, press kit should include VHS video, CD, references, photos, bio, press book financial dossier. "Always looking for new talent—please present a complete neat and self-explanatory promo kit." Does not return material. Reports once a year (August).
Music: Mostly **jazz** and **world music**. Works primarily with concert tour bands, festival bands and European touring acts. Current acts include the Brussels Jazz Orchestra (big band).

FOGGY DAY MUSIC, P.O. Box 99, Newtonville MA 02160. (617)969-0810. Fax: (617)969-6761. Owner: Paul Kahn. Management firm, booking agency and music publisher (Foggy Day Music). Represents individual artists, groups and songwriters from anywhere; currently handles 5 acts. Commission varies. Reviews material for acts.
How to Contact: Submit demo tape by mail. Unsolicited submissions are OK. Prefers cassette with lyric sheet. "No management submissions." Does not return material.
Music: Folk, **country** and **rock**; also **world music** and **blues**. Current acts include Luther Johnson (blues singer), Paul Bernard (folk singer/songwriter) and J.B. Hulto (blues singer).
Tips: "Simple recorded demo is OK, with lyrics."

FOLEY ENTERTAINMENT, P.O. Box 642, Carteret NJ 07008. (908)888-4646. Fax: (908)888-2973. President: Eugene Foley, J.D., Ph.D. Management firm. Estab. 1989. Represents individual artists and/or groups and songwriters from anywhere; currently handles 12 acts. Receives 20% commission. Reviews material for acts.
How to Contact: Submit demo tape by mail. Unsolicited submissions are OK. Copyright all material before submitting. Reports in 1 month if SASE is enclosed. Does not return material.
Music: Mostly **rock**, **alternative**, **pop**, **country** and **R&B**. Currently represents Steve Parry (rock guitarist/songwriter), grace (alternative) and Joyride (dance/R&B).
Tips: "Our client base is worldwide and quite diverse in scope. Our songwriter clients have had songs cut by recording artists such as Vanessa Williams, Joan Jett and Lita Ford. We have contacts at all of the major record companies."

PETER FREEDMAN ENTERTAINMENT, 1790 Broadway, Suite 1316, New York NY 10019. (212)265-1776. Fax: (212)265-3678. E-mail: pfent@aol.com. President: Peter Freedman. Director: Steve Smith. Management firm. Estab. 1986. Represents individual artists, groups and songwriters from anywhere; currently handles 5 acts. Receives 15-20% commission. Reviews material for acts.
How to Contact: Write or call first and obtain permission to submit. Prefers cassette or VHS videocassette with 1-2 songs. If seeking management, press kit should include 3-4 song demo, short bio and picture. Does not return material. Reports in 3-4 weeks.
Music: Mostly **alternative/pop/rock**. Works primarily with bands. Current acts include Live (modern rock), Muse (modern rock), The Ocean Blue (modern rock), Local H (alternative rock) and Portion (alternative rock).

BOB SCOTT FRICK ENTERPRISES, 404 Bluegrass Ave., Madison TN 37115. (615)865-6380. President: Bob Frick. Booking agency, music publisher (Frick Music Publishing Co./BMI and Sugarbaker Music Publishing/ASCAP), record producer and record company (R.E.F. Recording Co). Represents individual artists and songwriters; currently handles 5 acts. Reviews material for acts.

- Bob Scott Frick's publishing company, Frick Music Publishing, is listed in the Music Publishers section; his record label, R.E.F. Records, is in the Record Companies section; and he is listed in the Record Producers section.

How to Contact: Submit demo tape by mail, or write or call first to arrange personal interview. Prefers cassette with 3 songs and lyric sheet. SASE. Reports in 1 month.
Music: Mostly **gospel**, **country** and **R&B**. Works primarily with vocalists. Current acts include Larry Ahlborn (singer), Bob Myers (singer), Teresa Ford, Eddie Isaacs, Scott Frick, Jim and Ruby Mattingly, David Barton and Partners in Praise.

FRITZ/BYERS MANAGEMENT, (formerly Ken Fritz Management), 648 N. Robertson Blvd., Los Angeles CA 90069. (310)854-6488. Fax: (310)854-1015. E-mail: fritzed1@aol.com. President: Ken Fritz.

REFER TO THE GEOGRAPHIC INDEX (at the back of this book) to find listings of companies by state, as well as foreign listings.

Vice-President: Pam Byers-Carter. Management firm. Represents individual artists and groups from anywhere; currently handles 1 act. Receives 15% commission. Reviews material for acts.
How to Contact: Write or call first and obtain permission to submit. Prefers cassette or VHS videocassette with 2-3 songs and lyric sheet. "Submissions should be short and to the point." SASE. Reports in 1-2 months.
Music: Mostly **alternative**, **rock** and **pop**; also **jazz** and **kids**. Current acts include Rebekah Del Rio (country singer/songwriter).

FUTURE STAR ENTERTAINMENT, 315 S. Beverly Dr., Beverly Hills CA 90212. (310)553-0990. President: Paul Shenker. Management firm. Estab. 1982. Represents individual artists and groups from anywhere; currently handles 2 acts. Receives 20% commission. Reviews material for acts.
How to Contact: Call first and obtain permission to submit. Prefers cassette or VHS videocassette with 3-5 songs and lyric sheet. If seeking management, press kit should include photo, bio, tape or CD and press material. Does not return material. Reports in 6 weeks.
Music: Mostly **rock**, **pop** and **R&B**. Works primarily with rock bands. Current acts include Rachel Paschall (acoustic solo artist) and Tom Batoy (solo pop artist).

GALLUP ENTERTAINMENT, 93-40 Queens Blvd., Rego Park NY 11374. (718)897-6428. Fax: (718)997-7531. President: A. Gallup. Management firm. Estab. 1986. Represents individual artists and/or groups from anywhere; currently handles 5 acts. Receives 15% commission. Reviews material for acts.
How to Contact: Submit demo tape by mail. Unsolicited submissions are OK. Prefers cassette and lyric or lead sheet. If seeking management, press kit should include demo tape, bio, photo and clippings. Does not return material. Reports in 3-4 months.
Music: Mostly **rock** and **country**. Current acts include Tommy Sands (singer), Excellents (doo-wop) and Cathy Jean and the Roomates (doo-wop).

‡GANGLAND ARTISTS, P.O. Box 191, 101-1001 W. Broadway, Vancouver, British Columbia V6H 4E4 **Canada**. (604)685-5317. Fax: (604)682-8572. E-mail: natashad@gangland.com. Contact: Allen Moy. Management firm, production house and music publisher. Estab. 1985. Represents artists and songwriters; currently handles 2 acts. Reviews material for acts.
How to Contact: Write first and obtain permission to submit. Prefers cassette or VHS videocassette and lyric sheet. "Videos are not entirely necessary for our company. It is certainly a nice touch. If you feel your audio cassette is strong—send the video upon later request. Something wildly creative and individual will grab our attention." Does not return material. Reports in 2 months.
Music: Rock, **pop** and **R&B**. Works primarily with "original rock/left of center" show bands. Current acts include 54-40 (rock/pop) and Copyright (rock/pop).

GLAD PRODUCTIONS, P.O. Box 418, Purcellville VA 20134-0418. (540)338-2017. Fax: (540)338-7319. E-mail: glad@mediasoft.net. Website: http://www.glad-pro.com. Vice President: Don Nalle. Management firm, booking agency, music publisher (Champion of Love Music/ASCAP, Aux Send Music/BMI) and record producer (Ed Nalle). Estab. 1976. Represents individual artists, groups and songwriters from anywhere; currently handles 1 act. Receives 20% commission. Reviews material for acts.
How to Contact: Submit demo tape by mail. Unsolicited submissions are OK. Prefers cassette with 3 songs and lyric sheet. If seeking management, press kit should include photo, bio, references and demo. Does not return material. "No response guaranteed." Reports in 6 weeks.
Music: Mostly **Christian** (any style). Current acts include Glad (vocal group).

GLO GEM PRODUCTIONS, INC., 2640 Huckleberry, Port Huron MI 48060. (810)984-4471. Producer/Director: James David. Management firm and booking agency. Estab. 1976. Represents individual artists, groups and songwriters from anywhere; currently handles 15 acts. Receives 20% commission. Reviews material for acts.
How to Contact: Submit demo tape by mail. Unsolicited submissions are OK. Prefers cassette or ½″ VHS videocassette. If seeking management, press kit should include bio, recent press, photo or video. Does not return material. Reports in 2 months.
Music: Mostly **pop**, **country** and **jazz**; also **MOR**. Works primarily with bands, singer/songwriters and variety acts. Current acts include Cliff Erickson (singer/songwriter), B.A.S.I.C. (Boys Always Singing in Class) (pop quartet) and Pixee Wales (variety performer).
Tips: "Any sentence you ever say is the first line to your song."

‡THE GLOTZER MANAGEMENT CO., 1547 Sunset Plaza Dr., Los Angeles CA 90069. (310)659-8831. Fax: (310)855-8061. E-mail: msg@wavenet.com. Partner: Michael Glotzer. Management firm. Estab.

1967. Represents individual artists, groups and songwriters from anywhere; currently handles 2 acts. Receives 15-20% commission. Reviews material for acts.
How to Contact: Submit demo tape by mail. Unsolicited submissions are OK. Prefers cassette or CD. If seeking management, press kit should include CD or cassette, picture, bio (optional) and contact information. SASE. Reports in 2 weeks.
Music: All types, with an emphasis on **alternative**, **rock** and **roots rock**. "We are currently working with singer/songwriters and would be interested in managing a band, new or already established." Current acts include Alana Swidler (folk/rock) and The Hookers (rock, MCA Records).
Tips: "Past managed artists include Frank Zappa, Nina Hagen, Gang of Four, Janis Joplin, Bob Dylan, The Band, Sea Train, Gordon Lightfoot, Tom Rush, Orleans and many more. Practiced law for ten years prior to managing bands."

GMI ENTERTAINMENT INC., 666 Fifth Ave. #302, New York NY 10103. (212)541-7400. Fax: (212)541-7547. Vice President: Karen Gibson Lampiasi. Management firm and music publisher (Hats Off Music/ASCAP, Hats On Music/BMI). Estab. 1987. Represents individual artists and songwriters from anywhere; currently handles 1 act. Receives 20% commission. Reviews material for acts.
How to Contact: Write first and obtain permission to submit. Prefers cassette with 3 songs and lyric sheet. If seeking management, press kit should include photo, bio, cassette, press (if any) and lyrics. Does not return material. Reports in 3 months.
Music: Mostly **country**, **pop** and **R&B**. Works primarily with vocalists and singer/songwriters. Current acts include Deborah Gibson.
Tips: "Make sure the demos are clear and well-done. Spending a lot of money on production doesn't make the song any better. However, be sure the demos accurately reflect the feel and direction of the song. Use a professional singer if possible to avoid the listener being distracted by the vocal performance."

GOLDEN BULL PRODUCTIONS, P.O. Box 15142, Minneapolis MN 55415. (612)649-4631. Manager: Jesse Dearing. Management firm. Estab. 1984. Represents local and regional (Midwest) individual artists, groups and songwriters; currently handles 4 acts. Receives 12-15% commission. Reviews material for acts.
How to Contact: Submit demo tape by mail. Unsolicited submissions are OK. Prefers cassette or VHS videocassette with 4-5 songs and lyric or lead sheet. If seeking management, include demo tape, bio and 8×10 black and white photo in press kit. Does not return material. Reports in 6-8 weeks.
Music: Mostly **R&B**, **pop** and **rock**; also **gospel**, **jazz** and **blues**. Works primarily with vocalists and bands. Current acts include Lost and Found (R&B band), Keith Steward (songwriter), A. Lock (singer) and Black Crome (rap).

GOLDEN GURU ENTERTAINMENT, 10 Reed St., Philadelphia PA 19147. (215)755-8668. Fax: (215)440-7367. Owners: Eric J. Cohen, Esq. and Larry Goldfarb. Management firm, music publisher and record company. Estab. 1988. Represents individual artists, groups and songwriters from anywhere; currently handles 5 acts. Reviews material for acts.
How to Contact: Submit demo tape by mail. Unsolicited submissions are OK. Prefers cassette or VHS videocassette with 3-6 songs. If seeking management, press kit should include tape, press, photo, etc. SASE. Reports in 3-4 weeks.
Music: Mostly **rock**, **singer/songwriters**, **urban** and **pop**; "anything that is excellent!" Current acts include Jeffrey Gaines, Ben Arnold and Susan Werner (all 3 are major label recording artists).
Tips: "Be patient for a response. Our firm also renders legal and business affairs services. We also do bookings for the Tin Angel, the premier acoustic venue (200 capacity) in Philadelphia."

GOODKNIGHT PRODUCTIONS, 2854 Fountainhead Blvd., Melbourne FL 32935. (407)259-1855. E-mail: gknight@iu.net. Contact: Robert John or Greg Vadimsky. Management firm and record producer. Estab. 1992. Currently hands 4 acts.
How to Contact: Submit demo tape by mail. Unsolicited submissions are OK. Prefers cassette with 3 songs and lyric sheet. SASE. Reports in 2 weeks.
Music: Alternative and **pop**. Artists include Brian Arnold, Tango Palace and Garrett Louis Vadimsky.
Tips: "We are always looking for artists who have potential but need an experienced, patient management and production team."

GREAT LAKES COUNTRY TALENT AGENCY, 167 Sherman, Rochester NY 14606. (716)647-1617. President: Donald Redanz. Management firm, booking agency, music publisher, record company and record producer. Estab. 1988. Represents individual artists and/or groups, songwriters from anywhere; currently handles 10 acts. Receives 15% commission. Reviews material for acts.

How to Contact: Submit demo tape by mail. Unsolicited submissions are OK. Prefers cassette with 4 songs. If seeking management, press kit should include picture, places played and tape. SASE. Reports in 2-3 weeks.
Music: Mostly **country**, **gospel**, and **top 40**; also **bluegrass**. Works primarily with vocalists, singer/songwriters and bands. Current acts include Donnie Lee Baker (country), Tony Starr (songwriter) and James C (top 40).
Tips: "Write heart-touching songs."

CHRIS GREELEY ENTERTAINMENT, P.O. Box 593, Bangor ME 04402-0593. (207)827-4382. General Manager: Christian D. Greeley. Management firm, shopping/contact service and consultation. Estab. 1986. Represents local, regional and international individual artists, groups and songwriters; currently handles 3 acts. Receives variable commission. Reviews material for acts.
How to Contact: Submit demo tape by mail. Unsolicited submissions are OK. "Please don't call!" Prefers cassette or VHS videocassette with 1-4 songs. If seeking management, press kit should include business card and demo tape with return postage. SASE. Reports in 1 month.
Music: Mostly **rock**, **country** and **pop**. "I'm open to anything marketable." Wide range of musical styles. Current acts include Hey Mister (acoustic duo), Missy Tasker (vocalist) and G.T. Sound (regional DJs).
Tips: "Treat your music interests as a business venture. Don't be afraid to work hard and spend money to get where you want to go."

TIM GREENE ENTERTAINMENT, 6312 Hollywood Blvd., Suite 165, Hollywood CA 90028. (213)368-8100. President: Tim Greene. Management firm, record company (Greene Group Records) and record producer. Estab. 1983. Represents individual artists and groups from anywhere; currently handles 2 acts. Receives 10-20% commission. Reviews material for acts.
How to Contact: Submit demo tape by mail. Unsolicited submissions are OK. Prefers cassette or VHS videocassette. If seeking management, press kit should include bio, photo, video and cassette tape with best 2 songs. SASE. Reports in 3 weeks.
Music: Mostly **R&B, hip hop** and **rap**. Current acts include Rappin Granny (has appeared on Regis & Kathie Lee, CNN News, Today Show) and Fat Daddy (rapper/producer).

GREIF-GARRIS MANAGEMENT, 2112 Casitas Way, Palm Springs CA 92264. (619)322-8655. Fax: (619)322-7793. Vice President: Sid Garris. Management firm. Estab. 1961. Represents individual artists and/or groups, songwriters from anywhere; currently handles 2 acts. Receives 10% commission. Reviews material for acts.
How to Contact: Submit demo tape by mail. Unsolicited submissions are OK. Prefers cassette. If seeking management, press kit should include demo and complete brochure. SASE. Reports in 1 month.
Music: All types. Current acts include The New Christy Minstrels (folk) and Soulfolk (funky folk).

GSI, INC., P.O. Box 56757, New Orleans LA 70156. (504)948-4848. Fax: (504)943-3381. C.E.O.: John Shoup. Management firm, music publisher, record company, record producer and television producer (network). Estab. 1990. Represents groups and songwriters from anywhere; currently handles 1 act. Reviews material for act.
How to Contact: Write first and obtain permission to submit a demo. Prefers cassette with 1 song and lyric and lead sheet. Does not return material.
Music: Mostly **jazz**. Current acts include Bobby Short, Manhattan Transfer, Bela Fleck, Charlie Byrd, Bill Monroe, Silver Sage and Dukes of Dixieland.

GUESTSTAR ENTERTAINMENT AGENCY, 17321 Ritchie Ave. NE, Sand Lake MI 49343-9475. (616)636-5068. President: Raymond G. Dietz, Sr. Management firm, booking agency, music publisher (Sandlake Music/BMI), record company (Gueststar Records, Inc.), record producer and record distributor (Gueststar Music Distributors). Represents individual artists, groups, songwriters and bands from anywhere; currently handles 3 acts. Receives 20% commission. Reviews material for acts.

- Gueststar Entertainment's record company, Gueststar Records, is listed in the Record Companies section.

How to Contact: Submit demo tape by mail. Unsolicited submissions are OK. Prefers cassette or VHS videocassette with unlimited songs, but send your best with lyric or lead sheet. If seeking management, press kit should include photo, demo tape, bio, music résumé and VHS videocassette (live on stage) if possible. Does not return material. Reports in 1 week.
Music: Mostly **contemporary country**, **hit country** and **traditional country**; also **contemporary Christian**, **MOR** and **mountain songs**. Current acts include Mountain Man (singer), Jamie "K" (singer) and Sweetgrass (band).

BILL HALL ENTERTAINMENT & EVENTS, 138 Frog Hollow Rd., Churchville PA 18966-1031. (215)357-5189. Fax: (215)357-0320. Contact: William B. Hall III. Booking agency and production company. Represents individuals and groups; currently handles 20-25 acts. Receives 15% commission. Reviews material for acts.

How to Contact: Submit demo tape by mail. Unsolicited submissions are OK. Prefers cassette or videocassette of performance with 2-3 songs "and photos, promo material and record or tape. We need quality material, preferably before a 'live' audience." Does not return material. Reports in 2-4 months.

Music: Marching band, circus and **novelty**. Works primarily with "unusual or novelty attractions in musical line, preferably those that appeal to family groups." Current acts include Fralinger and Polish-American Philadelphia Championship Mummers String Bands (marching and concert group), Erwin Chandler Orchestra (show band), "Mr. Polynesian" Show Band and Hawaiian Revue (ethnic group), the "Phillies Whiz Kids Band" of Philadelphia Phillies Baseball team, Paul Richardson (Phillies' organist/entertainer), Mummermania Musical Quartet, Paul Cirilis Band, Philadelphia German Brass Band (concert band) and Vogelgesang Circus Calliope.

Tips: "Please send whatever helps me to most effectively market the attraction and/or artist. Provide me with something that gives you a clear edge over others in your field!"

M. HARRELL & ASSOCIATES, 5444 Carolina, Merrillville IN 46410. (219)887-8814. Owner: Mary Harrell. Management firm and booking agency. Estab. 1984. Represents individual artists, groups, songwriters, all talents—fashion, dancers, etc.; currently handles 40-60 acts. Receives 10-15% commission. Reviews material for acts.

How to Contact: Write first and obtain permission to submit. Prefers cassette or videocassette with 2-3 songs. If seeking management, press kit should include résumé, bio, picture and videocassette. "Keep it brief and current." Does not return material. Reports in 2-3 weeks.

Music: Mostly **country** and **R&B**. Current acts include Bill Shelton and 11th Ave. ('50s music) and Kim Porter (country singer).

HAWKEYE ATTRACTIONS, 102 Geiger St., Huntingburg IN 47542. (812)683-3657. President: David Mounts. Booking agency. Estab. 1982. Represents individual artists and groups; currently handles 1 act. Receives 10% commission. Reviews material for acts.

How to Contact: Submit demo tape by mail. Unsolicited submissions are OK. Prefers cassette with 4 songs and lyric sheet. SASE. If seeking management, press kit should include bio, press clippings, 8×10 b&w glossy and cassette. Reports in 9 weeks.

Music: Mostly **country** and **western swing**. Works primarily with show bands, Grand Ole Opry style form of artist and music. Current acts include Bill Mounts (country singer) and Midwest Cowboys (country/western swing).

HEADLINE MANAGEMENT, 125 E. 88th St., Suite 2A, New York NY 10028. Phone/fax: (212)410-6722. Vice President: Max Rosen. Management firm. Estab. 1991. Represents individual artists and groups from anywhere; currently handles 3 acts. Receives 20% commission. Reviews material for acts.

How to Contact: Submit demo tape by mail. Unsolicited submissions are OK. Prefers cassette or VHS videocassette with 3 songs. If seeking management, press kit should include 3 song demo, photo and strong press. Does not return material. Reports in 3 weeks.

Music: Mostly **modern rock** and **pop**. Works with alternative bands and pop singer/songwriters.

DOC HOLIDAY PRODUCTIONS, 10 Luanita Lane, Newport News VA 23606. (804)930-1814. President: Doc Holiday. Management firm, booking agency, music publisher (Doc Holiday Productions and Publishing/ASCAP, Doc Publishing/BMI and Dream Machine Publishing/SESAC), record producer and record company (Tug Boat International). Estab. 1985. Represents international individual artists, groups and songwriters; currently handles 46 acts. Receives 10-15% commission. Reviews material for acts.

- See the listing for Doc Publishing in the Music Publishers section.

How to Contact: Submit demo tape by mail. Unsolicited submissions are OK. Prefers cassette or VHS videocassette with 1 song and lyric sheet. If seeking management, include 8×10 photo, press clippings, bio, VHS, performance history, press experiments and demo tape in press kit. Does not return material. Reports in 2 weeks.

Music: Mostly **country**, **pop** and **R&B**; also **gospel** and **rap**. Works primarily with vocalist dance bands. Current acts include Wyndi Renee (country), Doc Holiday (rock), the Fortunes (top 40), the Johnson Family (gospel), Doug "The Ragin Cajun" Kenshaw (cajun), Big Al Downing (country) and Drew Kleeber (rock).

HOOKER ENTERPRISES, 5958 Busch Dr., Malibu CA 90265. (310)589-3240. Fax: (310)589-3242. E-mail: hook1325@aol.com. President: Jake Hooker. Management firm, music publisher, record company

and record producer. Estab. 1976. Represents individual artists, groups and songwriters from anywhere; currently handles 3 acts. Receives 20% commission. Reviews material for acts.
How to Contact: Write first and obtain permission to submit. Prefers cassette or DAT. If seeking management, press kit should include bio, picture and cassette (or CD). Does not return material. Reports in 1 month.
Music: Works primarily with solo artists (but groups OK). Current acts include Edgar Winter (rock artist), Larry Blank (composer) and Streak (rock group).

HORIZON MANAGEMENT INC., P.O. Box 8538, Endwell NY 13762. (607)785-9670. Contact: New Talent Department. Management firm, booking agency and concert promotion. Estab. 1967. Represents regional, national and international artists, groups and songwriters; currently handles 1,500 acts. Receives 20% commission. Reviews material for acts.
How to Contact: Write or call first and obtain permission to submit. Prefers cassette or VHS videocassette with 1-4 songs and 1 lyric or lead sheet. Send photo, bio, song list, equipment list, audio and/or video, press clippings, reviews, etc. Does not return material. Reports in 1 week.
Music: All styles, originals or covers. Current acts include the cast of Beatlemania (Broadway show), The Boxtops (oldies), Blue Norther (jazz) and Broderick Rice (gospel).

‡JOE HUPP ENTERPRISES, Rt. 2, Box 1687, Jennings OK 74038. (918)865-7026. Fax: (918)865-7403. E-mail: huppent@aol.com. Presidents: Joe Hupp or Patti Llovet Hughes. Management firm, booking agency and music publisher (Ol' Hippie Music). Estab. 1984. Represents individual artists, groups and songwriters from anywhere; currently handles 8 acts. Receives 10-20% commission. Reviews material for acts.
How to Contact: Call first to arrange personal interview or submit demo tape by mail. Prefers cassette or VHS videocassette with 1-4 songs. If seeking management, press kit should include photo, bio/fact sheet, cassette or CD and videocassette (if available). Does not return material. Reports in 1 month.
Music: Mostly **country**, **rock**, **alternative**; also **folk**, **R&B** and **pop**. Works primarily with bands singer/songwriters. Current acts include Carl Perkins (Mr. "Blue Suede Shoes," King of Rockabilly), Leon Russell (rock legend) and David Allan Coe (the original "Rhinestone Cowboy").

IMAGE PROMOTIONS INC., 1581 General Booth Blvd., Suite #107, Virginia Beach VA 23454. Phone/fax: (757)491-6632. E-mail: imagepromotions@cyberg.com. Website: http://www.namusic.com/ipm. President: Kim I. Plyler. Management firm and public relations. Estab. 1992. Represents individual artists, groups and songwriters from anywhere; currently handles 5 acts. Receives 20% commission. Reviews material for acts.
How to Contact: Call first and obtain permission to submit. Prefers cassette, CD or VHS videocassette with 3 songs and lyric sheet. If seeking management, press kit should include video, audio cassette, photo (b&w 8×10), biography and any press items. Does not return material. Reports in 1 month.
Music: Mostly **acoustic rock**, **folk** and **progressive**; also **country** and **R&B**. Works primarily with singer/songwriters. "We will accept material from progressive and country bands. We work a lot with the college market." Current acts include Tammy Gardner (folk singer/songwriter), Bitterlily (progressive), The Mann Sisters (country duo/band) and Lewis McGehee (acoustic rock/songwriter).

IMANI ENTERTAINMENT INC., P.O. Box 150-139, Brooklyn NY 11215. (718)622-2132. E-mail: imanigrp@aol.com. Directors: Guy Anglade and Alfred Johnston. Management firm and music publisher (Imani Hits/BMI). Estab. 1991. Represents individual artists, groups, songwriters, producers and remixers from anywhere; currently handles 1 act. Receives 15-20% commission. Reviews material for acts.
How to Contact: Submit demo tape by mail. Unsolicited submissions are OK. Prefers cassette or VHS videocassette with 3 songs. If seeking management, press kit should include a bio, photograph and 3-song demo tape. SASE. Reports in 4-6 weeks.
Music: Mostly **R&B** and **hip-hop**. Works primarily with vocalists, singer/songwriters. Current acts include Infinite (rap artist).

IMMIGRANT MUSIC INC., 3575 Blvd. St. Laurent #409, Montreal Quebec H2X 2T7 **Canada**. Phone/fax: (514)849-5052. E-mail: deckmktg@generation.net. President: Dan Behrman. Management firm, book-

THE TYPES OF MUSIC each listing is interested in are printed in boldface.

ing agency and music publisher (Balenjo Music). Estab. 1979. Represents individual artists, groups and songwriters from anywhere; currently handles 7 acts. Receives 20% commission. Reviews material for acts.
How to Contact: Call first and obtain permission to submit or to arrange personal interview. Prefers cassette, VHS videocassette, CD or vinyl with 4 songs. If seeking management, press kit should include bio, press clippings, photo, references, recordings, technical and personal rider and requirements if known. Does not return material. Reports in 2 weeks.
Music: Mostly **world music**, **original ethnic** and **new acoustic music**; also **singer/songwriters**, **folk** and **ethnic/ambient**. Current acts include Stefka Iordanova (Sony Music, lead singer of Deep Forest), Ray Bonneville (Audiogram Records, Delta swampfolk blues singer/songwriter) and Simbi (Xenophile Records, vodou-roots band).

‡IMPERIAL ARTIST MANAGEMENT, P.O. Box 4185, Huntington Beach CA 92605. (714)445-9193. President: James R. Wehmer, Jr. Management firm. Estab. 1995. Represents local individual artists and groups; currently handles 3 acts. Receives 15% commission. Reviews material for acts.
How to Contact: Submit demo tape by mail. Unsolicited submissions are OK. Prefers cassette, DAT or CD with 4 songs and lyric sheet. If seeking management, press kit should include band photo, brief history of band and lyric sheet. Does not return material. Reports within 1 week.
Music: Mostly **alternative rock**, **heavy metal** and **acoustics**. Works primarily with bands, and a few individual artists. Current acts include Malachi Sunday, Downer-cap (heavy groovy rock) and Troy Combs (lead guitarist).

‡INCENTIVE PRODUCTIONS, 1711 Fourth St. S.W., Suite 433, Calgary Alberta T2S 1V8 **Canada**. (403)541-0003. Fax: (403)228-1889. Executive Producer: Kenneth Cappos. Management firm, music publisher (Thickwood Music), record company (Thickwood Music and Entertainment) and record producer. Estab. 1987. Represents individual artists from anywhere; currently handles 3 acts. Receives 10-20% commission. Reviews material for acts.
How to Contact: Submit demo tape by mail. Prefers cassette or VHS videocassette with lyric sheet. "Please send cassette with as many songs as possible, one-page (can be handwritten) summary of career goals and interests as well as past accomplishments. Photo helpful. Follow up with phone call in 4-6 weeks." Does not return material. Reports in 2 months.
Music: Mostly **country**; also **modern rock-pop**. "We are looking for artists who are also composers and are writing constantly." Current acts include Jazlyn Richard, The Hakabillies and Tammy Jackson (country artists).
Tips: "We are interested in original material for new country and country-rock artists. Please do not send traditional country songs."

INTERMOUNTAIN TALENT, P.O. Box 942, Rapid City SD 57709. (605)348-7777. Owner: Ron Kohn. Management firm, booking agency and music publisher (Big BL Music). Estab. 1978. Represents individual artists, groups and songwriters; currently handles 30 acts. Receives 15% commission. Reviews material for acts.
How to Contact: Submit demo tape by mail. Unsolicited submissions are OK. Prefers cassette with 3 songs and lyric sheet. Artist may submit videocassette. If seeking management, include tape, video and photo in press kit. SASE. Reports in 1 month.
Music: Mostly **rock**; also **country/rock**. Current acts include Moon Dogs (band), Sierra (band) and Sandy Peratte (songwriter).

INTERNATIONAL ENTERTAINMENT BUREAU, 3612 N. Washington Blvd., Indianapolis IN 46205-3592. (317)926-7566. E-mail: intleb@prodigy.com. Contact: David Leonards. Booking agency. Estab. 1972. Represents individual artists and groups from anywhere; currently handles 131 acts. Receives 20% commission.
How to Contact: Submit demo tape by mail. Unsolicited submissions are OK. Prefers VHS videocassette. If seeking management, press kit should include picture, testamonials, sample song list and press clippings. "Do not call us, please." Does not return material. Reports in 6 months.
Music: Mostly **rock**, **country** and **A/C**; also **jazz**, **nostalgia** and **ethnic**. Works primarily with bands, comedians and speakers. Current acts include Five Easy Pieces (A/C), Doug Lawson (country) and Wray Brothers (gospel).

ITS HAPPENING PRESENT ENTERTAINMENT, P.O. Box 222, Pittsburg CA 94565. (510)980-0893. Fax: (510)432-4342. President: Bobellii Johnson. Management firm, booking agency and record company (Black Diamond Records, Flash Point Records, Triple Beam Records, Stay Down Records,

Hitting Hard Records and D. City Records). Estab. 1989. Represents local, regional or international individual artists and songwriters; currently handles 12 acts. Receives 5-15% commission. Reviews material for acts.

- See the listing for one of Its Happening Present's record companies, Black Diamond Records, in the Record Companies section.

How to Contact: Write first and obtain permission to submit. Prefers cassette with 2 songs and lyric sheet. If seeking management, press kit should include 8×10 photo, bio, video, 2-song demo, demo voice tape and lyric sheet. Does not return material. Reports in 2-6 months.

Music: Mostly **pop**, **R&B** and **jazz**; also **rap** and **country**. Works primarily with vocalist songwriters, rap groups, bands and instrumentalists. Current acts include Deanna Dixon (R&B), Profile 'J' (rap), Format (R&B vocal group), Marty "G." (rapper), Flikk (R&B), Dangerous Dane (rap), Family Unit (R&B), Special Request (R&B) and Lyn Durné.

Tips: "Please, copyright all your material as soon as possible. Don't let anyone else hear it until that's done first."

J & V MANAGEMENT, 143 W. Elmwood, Caro MI 48723. (517)673-2889. Management: John Timko. Management firm, booking agency and music publisher. Represents local, regional or international individual artists, groups and songwriters; currently handles 3 acts. Receives 10% commission. Reviews material for acts.

How to Contact: Call first and obtain permission to submit. Prefers cassette with 3 songs maximum and lyric sheet. If seeking management, include cassette tape, photo and short reference bio in press kit. SASE. Reports in 2 months.

Music: Mostly **country**. Works primarily with vocalists and dance bands. Current acts include John Patrick (country), Alexander Depue (fiddle) and Most Wanted (country).

JACKSON ARTISTS CORP., (Publishing Central), Suite 200, 7251 Lowell Dr., Shawnee Mission KS 66204. (913)384-6688. CEO: Dave Jackson. Booking agency (Drake/Jackson Productions), music publisher (All Told Music/BMI, Zang/Jac Publishing/ASCAP and Very Cherry/ASCAP). Represents artists, groups and songwriters; currently handles 12 acts. Receives 15-20% commission. Reviews material for acts.

How to Contact: Submit demo tape by mail. Unsolicited submissions are OK. Prefers cassette or VHS videocassette of performance with 2-4 songs and lead sheet. "List names of tunes on cassettes. May send up to 4 tapes. Although it's not necessary, we prefer lead sheets with the tapes—send 2 or 3 that you are proud of. Also note what 'name' artist you'd like to see do the song. We do most of our business by phone. We prefer good enough quality to judge a performance, however, we do not require that the video or cassettes be of professional nature." Will return material if requested with SASE.

Music: Mostly **gospel**, **country** and **rock**; also **bluegrass**, **blues**, **easy listening**, **disco**, **MOR**, **progressive**, **soul** and **top 40/pop**. Works with acts that work grandstand shows for fairs as well as bar bands that want to record original material. Current acts include Dixie Cadillacs (country/rock), Britt Hammond (country), The Booher Family (bluegrass/pop/country), Paul & Paula, Bill Haley's Comets, Max Groove (jazz) and The Dutton Family (classical to pop).

Tips: "Be able to work on the road, either as a player or as a group. Invest your earnings from these efforts in demos of your originals that have been tried out on an audience. And keep submitting to the industry."

JACOBS MANAGEMENT, 382-C Union, Campbell CA 95008. (408)559-1669. Fax: (408)559-6664. E-mail: midnitemgt@aol.com. Owner: Mitchell Jacobs. Management firm. Estab. 1988. Represents individual artists and groups from anywhere; currently handles 2 acts. Receives 20% commission. Reviews material for acts.

How to Contact: Write or call first and obtain permission to submit. Prefers cassette with 3 songs and lyric sheet. SASE. Reports in 1 month.

Music: Mostly **rock**, **R&B** and **roots**. Works primarily with singer/songwriters, bands. Current acts include Loved Ones and Katharine Chase.

JANA JAE ENTERPRISES, P.O. Box 35726, Tulsa OK 74153. (918)786-8896. Vice President: Kathleen Pixley. Booking agency, music publisher (Jana Jae Publishing/BMI) and record company (Lark Record Productions, Inc.). Estab. 1979. Represents individual artists and songwriters; currently handles 12 acts. Receives 15% commission. Reviews material for acts.

- Jana Jae's publishing company, Jana Jae Publishing, is listed in the Music Publishers section, and its record label, Lark Records, is listed in the Record Companies section.

How to Contact: Submit demo tape by mail. Prefers cassette or videocassette of performance if available. SASE.

Music: Mostly **country**, **classical** and **jazz instrumentals**; also **pop**. Works with vocalists, show and concert bands, solo instrumentalists. Represents Jana Jae (country singer/fiddle player), Matt Greif (classical guitarist), Sydni (solo singer) and Hotwire (country show band).

JAMES GANG MANAGEMENT, P.O. Box 121626, Nashville TN 37212. (615)726-3556. Contact: Neal James. Management firm, music publisher (Cottage Blue Music), record company (Kottage Records) and record producer. Estab. 1991. Represents individual artists and/or groups, songwriters from anywhere; currently handles 3 acts. Receives standard commission. Reviews material for acts.

- James Gang's publishing affiliate, Cottage Blue Music, is listed in the Music Publishers section, and their record label, Kottage Records, is listed in the Record Companies section; Neal James Productions is listed in the Record Producers section.

How to Contact: Submit demo tape by mail. Unsolicited submissions are OK. Prefers cassette and lyric sheet. If seeking management, press kit should include full bio, photo, cassette, references, objectives, list of clubs played. SASE. Reports in 1 month.
Music: Mostly **country**, **pop** and **gospel**; also **R&B**, **beach**, **blues** and **alternative rock**. Works primarily with vocalists, singer/songwriters, bands. Current acts include Tangle James (contemporary), Terry BarBay (contemporary) and Jay S. Kay (alternative rock).

ROGER JAMES MANAGEMENT, 10A Margaret Rd., Barnet, Herts EN4 9NP **England**. Phone: (0181)440-9788. Professional Manager: Laura Skuce. Management firm and music publisher (R.J. Music/PRS). Estab. 1977. Represents songwriters. Receives 50% commission (negotiable). Reviews material for acts.

- See the listing for R.J. Music in the Music Publishers section.

How to Contact: Submit demo tape by mail. Unsolicited submissions are OK. Prefers cassette with 3 songs and lyric sheet. Does not return material.
Music: Mostly **pop**, **country** and "any good song."

‡JAMPOP LTD., 27 Parkington Plaza, Kingston 10 W.I. **Jamaica**. Phone: (809)968-9235. Fax: (809)968-2199. President: Ken Nelson. Management firm and booking agency. Estab. 1990. Represents local, regional and international individual artists, groups and songwriters; currently handles 30 acts. Receives 10% commission. Reviews material for acts.
How to Contact: Submit demo tape by mail. Unsolicited submissions are OK. Prefers cassette with lyric sheet. Does not return material. Reports in 4 weeks.
Music: Mostly **R&B** and **pop**; also **gospel**. Works primarily with vocalists. Current artists include Chalice, Charles Hyatt and Fab 5.

JAS MANAGEMENT, 2141 W. Governor's Circle, Suite H, Houston TX 77092. (713)683-0806. Manager: Tony Randle. Management firm, booking agency. Estab. 1988. Represents individual artists and/or groups and songwriters from anywhere; currently handles 20 acts. Receives 10-20% commission. Reviews material for acts.
How to Contact: Submit demo tape by mail. Unsolicited submissions are OK. Prefers cassette with 4 songs. If seeking management, press kit should include cassette, bio, pictures and press (if any). SASE. Reports in 2 months.
Music: Mostly **rap**, **R&B** and **gospel**. Works primarily with rapper/songwriters. Current acts include Scarface, Geto Boys and DMG.

JERIFKA PRODUCTIONS, INC., 1020 E. Desert Inn Rd. #603, Las Vegas NV 89109-2823. (702)593-3602. Fax: (702)732-0847. E-mail: jerifka@robvale.com. Website: http://www.robvale.com. A&R: Robert Vale. Management firm, booking agency, music publisher (Ritvale Music Corp./ASCAP, Robvale Music/BMI) and record company (The Robert Vale Record Company). Estab. 1969. Represents individual artists, groups and songwriters from anywhere; currently handles 7 acts. Receives 10% commission. Reviews material for acts.
How to Contact: Submit demo tape by mail. Unsolicited submissions are OK. Prefers cassette, DAT or VHS videocassette with 1 song, lyric and lead sheet. If seeking management, press kit should include press, bio and picture. SASE. Reports in 2 weeks.
Music: Mostly **rock**, **alternative** and **New Age**. Current acts include Jerry Vale, James Moyer Blues Experience and Question Mark.

LITTLE RICHIE JOHNSON AGENCY, P.O. Box 3, Belen NM 87002. (505)864-7441. Fax: (505)864-7442. Manager: Tony Palmer. Management firm, music publisher (Little Richie Johnson Music), record producer and record company (LRJ Records). Estab. 1958. Represents individual artists from anywhere; currently handles 4-6 acts. Reviews material for acts.

● Listings for Little Richie Johnson Music can be found in the Music Publishers section; Little Richie Johnson in the Record Producers section; and one for LRJ Records can be found in the Record Companies section.

How to Contact: Write first and obtain permission to submit. Prefers cassette. If seeking management, press kit should include tape, bio and any other important information. SASE. Reports in 6 weeks.

Music: Mostly **country**; also **Spanish**. Works primarily with vocalists and singers. Current acts include Alan Godage, Faron Young, Kim Frazee, Reta Lee and Gabe Neito.

C. JUNQUERA PRODUCTIONS, P.O. Box 393, Lomita CA 90717. (213)325-2881. Co-owner: C. Junquera. Management consulting firm and record company (NH Records). Estab. 1987. Represents local, regional and international individual artists and songwriters; currently handles 3 acts. Receives a flat fee for consulting, percentage for business management. Reviews material for acts.

How to Contact: Submit demo tape by mail. Unsolicited submissions are OK. Prefers cassette with 1-3 songs and lyric sheet. If seeking management, include recent 8×10 photo, bio, photocopies of news articles, cover letter stating goals and sample of product. SASE. Reports in 1-2 months.

Music: Mostly **traditional country** and **country pop**; also **easy listening**. Works primarily with songwriters and vocalists. Current recording acts include Nikki Hornsby (singer/songwriter), N. Kelel (songwriter) and Eric Oswald (songwriter).

Tips: "Be specific on goals you wish to obtain as artist or songwriter—submit a sample of your product and don't give up! Obtain outside financial support for production of your product—invest your talent, not your own money."

JUPITER PRODUCTIONS, 7751 Greenwood Dr., St. Paul MN 55112. (612)784-9654. E-mail: nightdiscs@aol.com. C.E.O.: Lance King. Management firm, booking agency and record company (Nightmare). Estab. 1983. Represents individual artists, groups, songwriters from anywhere; currently handles 20 acts. Receives negotiable commission. Reviews material for acts.

● See the listing for Nightmare Records in the Record Companies section.

How to Contact: Submit demo tape by mail. Unsolicited submissions are OK. Prefers cassette or CD with 3 songs and lyric sheet. If seeking management, press kit should include 8×10 photo, poster (if available), song list, if self contained production or not and press clippings. "Send only important information." Does not return material. Reports in 4-6 weeks.

Music: Mostly **cutting edge rock**, **melodic metal** and **grunge**; also **rap metal** and **progressive rock**. Works primarily with vocalists, singer/songwriters and bands. Current acts include Visionary (metal), The King's Machine (melodic groove with attitude) and Sonic Boom (dance industrial metal).

SHELDON KAGAN PRODUCTIONS, 35 McConnell, Dorval, Quebec H9S 5L9 **Canada**. (514)631-2160. Fax: (514)631-4430. President: Sheldon Kagan. Booking agency. Estab. 1965. Represents local individual artists and groups; currently handles 4 acts. Receives 10-20% commission. Reviews materials for acts.

How to Contact: Submit demo tape by mail. Unsolicited submissions are OK. Prefers cassette or VHS videocassette with 6 songs. SASE. Reports in 3 weeks.

Music: Mostly **top 40**. Works primarily with vocalists and bands.

KKR ENTERTAINMENT GROUP, 1300 Clay St., 6th Floor, Oakland CA 94612. (510)464-8024. Fax: (510)769-8024 or 763-9004. Administrator: Keith Washington. Management firm. Estab. 1989. Represents individual artists, groups and producers from anywhere. Reviews material for acts.

How to Contact: Call first and obtain permission to submit. Prefers cassette. If seeking management, press kit should include tape and photo (if available). "We do not accept unsolicited material." SASE. Reports in 2 weeks.

Music: Mostly **R&B**, **rap** and **rock**. Current acts include E-A-Ski & CMT (producer/artist, Relativity Records/Sony Music), Spice One (Jive recording artist) and Christion (R&B group, Def Jam Records).

Tips: "Always learn who you are working with and stay involved in everything."

‡JOANNE KLEIN, 130 W. 28 St., New York NY 10001. Phone/fax: (212)741-3949. Contact: Joanne Klein. Management firm and music publisher. Estab. 1982. Represents individual artists and songwriters

REFER TO THE CATEGORY INDEX (at the end of this section) to find exactly which companies are interested in the type of music you write.

from anywhere; currently handles 4 acts. Receives 15-20% commission. Reviews material for acts.
How to Contact: Write first and obtain permission to submit. Prefers cassette or CD. If seeking management, press kit should include bio, photos, press/reviews, discography, information on compositions. Does not return material. Reports in 1 month.
Music: Mostly **jazz**. Works primarily with instrumentalist/composers. Current acts include Kenny Barron (jazz), Victor Lewis (jazz) and Terell Stafford (jazz).

BOB KNIGHT AGENCY, 185 Clinton Ave., Staten Island NY 10301. (718)448-8420. President: Bob Knight. Management firm, booking agency, music publisher and royalty collection firm. Estab. 1971. Represents artists, groups and songwriters; currently handles 6 acts. Receives 10-15% commission. Reviews material for acts and for submission to record companies and producers.
How to Contact: Submit demo tape by mail. Unsolicited submissions are OK. Prefers cassette or videocassette with 5 songs and lead sheet "with bio and references." If seeking management, include bio, videocassette and audio cassette in press kit. SASE. Reports in 6 weeks.
Music: Mostly **top 40/pop**; also **easy listening**, **MOR**, **R&B**, **soul**, **rock (nostalgia '50s and '60s)**, **alternative**, **jazz**, **blues** and **folk**. Works primarily with recording and name groups and artists—'50s, '60s and '70s acts, high energy dance and show groups. Current acts include Delfonics (R&B nostalgia), B.T. Express, Brass Construction, Main Ingredient and Big Smoothies (nostalgia).
Tips: "We're seeking artists and groups with completed albums/demos."

KRC RECORDS & PRODUCTIONS, HC 73, Box 5060, Harold KY 41635. (606)478-2169. President: Keith R. Carter. Management firm, booking agency, music publisher and record company. Estab. 1987. Represents local and regional individual artists; currently handles 1 act. Receives 15% commission. Reviews material for acts.
How to Contact: Submit demo tape by mail. Unsolicited submissions are OK. Prefers cassette or videocassette with 1-10 songs and lyric sheet. "Feel free to send any material." Does not return material.
Music: Mostly **country**; also **gospel** and **bluegrass**. Current acts include Kimberly Carter (singer).

KRIETE, KINCAID & FAITH, 1574-61st St., Brooklyn NY 11219. (718)259-1402. Fax: (718)259-0634. E-mail: kkfmgmt@aol.com. Website: http://members.aol.com/brtagency/bayridge.html. Contact: Ken Kriete. Management firm. Estab. 1990. Represents individual artists and groups from anywhere; currently handles 6 acts. Receives variable commission. Reviews material for acts.
How to Contact: Submit demo tape by mail. Unsolicited submissions are OK. Prefers cassette or VHS-NTSC videocassette with 3-4 songs. If seeking management, press kit should include CD or cassette, photo, bio, VHS if possible and small amount of relevant press. Does not return material. Reports in 1 month.
Music: Mostly **hard alternative**. Works primarily with bands, singer/songwriters and producers. Current acts include Type O Negative, Lordz of Brooklyn and The Misfits.

KUPER PERSONAL MANAGEMENT, P.O. Box 66274, Houston TX 77266. (713)520-5791. Fax: (713)523-1048. E-mail: kuper_i@hccs.cc.tx.us. Owner: Ivan Kuper. Management firm and music publisher (Kuper-Lam Music/BMI and Uvula Music/BMI). Estab. 1979. Represents individual artists, groups and songwriters from Texas; currently handles 1 act. Receives 20% commission. Reviews material for acts.
How to Contact: Submit demo tape by mail. Unsolicited submissions are OK. Prefers cassette. If seeking management, press kit should include photo, bio (one sheet) tearsheets (reviews, etc.) and cassette. Does not return material. Reports in 2 months.
Music: Mostly **singer/songwriters**, **urban contemporary** and **alternative college rock**. Works primarily with self-contained and self-produced artists. Current acts include Philip Rodriguez (singer/songwriter).
Tips: "Create a market value for yourself, produce your own master tapes, create a cost-effective situation."

L.D.F. PRODUCTIONS, P.O. Box 406, Old Chelsea Station, New York NY 10011. (212)925-8925. President: Mr. Dowell. Management firm and booking agency. Estab. 1982. Represents artists and choirs in the New York area. Currently handles 3 acts. Receives 20-25% commission. Reviews material for acts.
How to Contact: Write first and obtain permission to submit or to arrange personal interview. Prefers cassette (or videocassette of performance—well-lighted, maximum 10 minutes) with 2-8 songs and lyric sheet. If seeking management, press kit should include résumé and photo, audio cassette and videocassette. SASE. Reports in 1 month. "Do not phone expecting a return call unless requested by L.D.F. Productions. Videos should be imaginatively presented with clear sound and bright colors."
Music: Mostly **gospel**, **pop**, **rock** and **jazz**. Works primarily with inspirational and contemporary pop artists. Current acts include L.D. Frazier (gospel artist/lecturer), Peter Matthews (bassist) and Bernard Rosat (bassist).

‡LAKES ENTERTAINMENT GROUP, P.O. Box 34412, Los Angeles CA 90034. (213)969-2578. Fax: (310)643-4499. President and CEO: Jeffery Lakes. Management firm. Estab. 1990. Represents individual artists, groups and songwriters from anywhere; currently handles 1 act. Receives 15% commission. Reviews material for acts.
How to Contact: Call first and obtain permission to submit. Prefers cassette. If seeking management, press kit should include bio and photo. Does not return material.
Music: Mostly **R&B/sound**, **rap** and **hip hop**; also **jazz**, **gospel**, **A/C** and **top 40**. Works primarily with singer/vocalist/songwriters. "The ability to (at least) co-produce own material is important."

LARI-JON PROMOTIONS, 325 W. Walnut, P.O. Box 216, Rising City NE 68658. (402)542-2336. Owner: Larry Good. Management firm, music publisher (Lari-Jon Publishing Co./BMI) and record company (Lari-Jon Records). Represents individual artists, groups and songwriters; currently handles 5 acts. Receives 15% commission. Reviews material for acts.

- Lari-Jon Publishing is listed in the Music Publishers section, and Lari-Jon Records is listed in the Record Companies section.

How to Contact: Submit demo tape by mail. Unsolicited submissions are OK. Prefers cassette with 5 songs and lyric sheet. If seeking management, include 8×10 photos, cassette, videocassette and bio sheet in press kit. SASE. Reports in 2 months.
Music: Mostly **country**, **gospel** and **'50s rock**. Works primarily with dance and show bands. Represents Kent Thompson (singer), Nebraskaland 'Opry (family type country show) and Brenda Allen (singer/comedienne).

LAZY BONES RECORDINGS/PRODUCTIONS, INC., 9594 First Ave. NE, Suite 230, Seattle WA 98115-2012. (206)820-6632. Fax: (206)821-5720. President: Scott Schorr. Management firm, publisher and record company (Lazy Bones Recordings). Estab. 1992. Represents individual artists and groups from anywhere; currently handles 3 acts. Receives 18-20% commission. Reviews material for acts.
How to Contact: Submit demo tape by mail. Unsolicited submissions are OK. Prefers cassette, VHS videocassette or CD with 4 songs (minimum). If seeking management, press kit should include demo tape, picture, contact number with address, video (if available) and any press. Does not return material. Reports in 1 month.
Music: Mostly **alternative rock**, **singer/songwriters** and **hip-hop**; also **any other music**—*except* country. Works primarily with bands or singer/songwriters. Current acts include Neros Rome (psychedelic alternative rock), Turntable Bay (hip-hop/dance hall) and Headland (pop rock).

LENTHALL & ASSOCIATES, Falcon Ave., Suite 2-2447, Ottawa, Ontario K1V 8C8 **Canada**. (613)738-2373. Fax: (613)523-7941. President, General Manager: Helen Lenthall. Management firm and record production. Represents individual artists, groups and songwriters from all territories. Reviews material for acts.
How to Contact: Submit demo tape by mail. Unsolicited submissions are OK. Prefers cassette or VHS videocassette with 3-8 songs maximum and lyric sheet or lead sheet. If seeking management, press kit should include bio, media package, photos, reviews, tracking if available. SAE and IRC. Reports back on "acts that we consider."
Music: Mostly **soul**, **pop/rock** and **country**; also **hip hop**, **rap** and **gospel**. Primarily works with bands and vocalists.

LEVINSON ENTERTAINMENT VENTURES INTERNATIONAL, INC., 1440 Veteran Ave., Suite 650, Los Angeles CA 90024. (213)460-4545. E-mail: leviinc@aol.com. President: Bob Levinson. Management firm. Estab. 1978. Represents national individual artists, groups and songwriters; currently handles 3 acts. Receives 15-25% commission. Reviews material for acts.
How to Contact: Write first and obtain permission to submit. Prefers cassette or VHS videocassette with 6 songs and lead sheet. Does not return material. Reports in 2-4 weeks.
Music: **Rock**, **MOR**, **R&B** and **country**. Works primarily with rock bands and vocalists.
Tips: "Should be a working band, self-contained and, preferably, performing original material."

RICK LEVY MANAGEMENT, 1881 S. Kirkman Rd. #715, Orlando FL 32811. (407)521-6135. Fax: (407)521-6153. President: Rick Levy. Office manager: Leiza Levy. Management firm, music publisher (Flying Governor Music/BMI) and record company (Luxury Records). Estab. 1985. Represents local, regional or international individual artists and groups; currently handles 6 acts. Receives 15-20% commission. Reviews material for acts.

- See the interview with President Rick Levy in this section.

How to Contact: Submit demo tape by mail. Unsolicited submissions are OK. Prefers cassette or VHS videocassette with 3 songs and lyric sheet. If seeking management, include tape, VHS video, photo and press. SASE. Reports in 1 month.
Music: Mostly **R&B** (no rap), **pop**, **country** and **oldies**. Current acts include Jay & the Techniques ('60s hit group), Rock Roots (variety-classic rock, rockabilly), Robert "Boz" Boswell (country artist), The Original Box Tops ('60s), St. John's Alliance and Steel Dog (rock).

‡DORIS LINDSAY PRODUCTIONS/SUCCESSFUL PRODUCTIONS, P.O. Box 35005 AMC, Greensboro NC 27425. (910)882-9990. President: Doris Lindsay. Management firm and music publisher (Doris Lindsay Publishing/ASCAP, Better Times/BMI). Estab. 1979. Represents individual artists and/or songwriters from anywhere; currently handles 2 acts. Receives 15% commission. Reviews material for acts.

- Doris Lindsay Publishing is listed in the Music Publishers section.

How to Contact: Submit demo tape by mail. Unsolicited submissions are OK. Prefers cassette or VHS videocassette with 2-3 songs and lyric sheet. If seeking management, press kit should include photo, cassette and bio. SASE. Reports in 4 months.
Music: Mostly **country**, **contemporary Christian** and **pop**; also **children's**. Primarily works with singers, songwriters. Current acts include Mitch Snow (country).
Tips: "Have a professional studio type demo. Don't send too many songs at one time. Be patient."

LITTLE BIG MAN BOOKING, 39A Gramercy Park N., New York NY 10010. (212)598-0003. Fax: (212)598-0249. President: Marty Diamond. Booking agency. Estab. 1994. Represents national acts with recording deals *only*; currently handles 35 acts. Receivew 10% commission. Reviews material for acts.
How to Contact: Submit demo tape by mail. Unsolicited submissions are OK. Prefers cassette or CD with 4 songs. "Don't be a pest!" Does not return material. Reports in 1 month.
Music: Mostly **alternative music**. Current acts include Sarah McLachlan, Michelle Shocked, Letters to Cleo, Chieftains, The Auteurs, Tricky and Whale.
Tips: "Develop a base in your hometown. Create a database of contacts."

LIVE-WIRE MANAGEMENT, P.O. Box 653, Morgan Hill, CA 95038. (408)778-3526. Fax: (408)453-3836. E-mail: bruce@L-WM.com. Website: http://www.L-WM.com. President: Bruce Hollibaugh. Management firm. Estab. 1990. Represents individual artists and groups from anywhere; currently handles 2 acts. Receives 15-25% commission. Reviews material for acts.
How to Contact: Submit demo tape by mail. Unsolicited submissions are OK. Prefers DAT with 3-6 songs and lyric sheet. If seeking management, press kit should include what region you are currently performing in; how often you are doing live shows; any reviews; photos. Does not return material. Reports in 1 month.
Music: Mostly **pop**, **acoustic pop** and **New Age**; also **jazz**, **R&B** and **country**. Works primarily with bands and singer/songwriters. Current acts include Tommy Elskes (singer/songwriter) and The Bartron Tyler Group (acoustic jazz).

LIVING EYE PRODUCTIONS LTD., P.O. Box 12956, Rochester NY 14612. (716)544-3500. Fax: (716)544-8860. E-mail: c.kings@worldnet.att.net. Managing Director: Carl Labate. Management firm, music publisher (Pussy Galore Publishing/BMI) and record producers (Andy Babiuk and Greg Prevost). Estab. 1982. Represents individual artists, groups and songwriters from anywhere; currently handles 4 acts. Receives 20% commission. Reviews material for acts.
How to Contact: Submit demo tape by mail. Unsolicited submissions are OK. Prefers cassette and "what the artist feels necessary." Does not return material. Reports in 2 weeks.
Music: Mostly **'60s rock**, **'50s rock** and **blues**; also **folk rock** and **surf**. Works primarily with bands that can tour to promote record releases. Current acts include The Chesterfield Kings (rock), The Mean Red Spiders (rock) and The Frantic Flattops ('50s rock).
Tips: "We don't like trendy new stuff. Don't follow fads, create your own music by having good rock-n-roll influences."

LMP MANAGEMENT FIRM, 6245 Bristol Pkwy., Suite 206, Culver City CA 90230. Contact: Larry McGee. Management firm, music publisher (Operation Perfection, Inc.), record producer (Intrigue Productions) and record company (Boogie Band Records Corp.). Represents individual artists, groups and songwriters; currently handles 4 acts. Receives 10-15% commission. Reviews material for acts.

- LMP's publishing company, Operation Perfection Inc., is listed in the Music Publishers section; Intrigue Production is in the Record Producers section; and their record label, Boogie Band Records, is listed in the Record Companies section.

INSIDER REPORT

Self-promotion is key to finding a good manager

Rick Levy

Rick Levy, president of Rick Levy Management in Orlando, Florida, believes that the more an artist does to promote himself, the more appealing he is to a manager. One of the bands on Levy's roster, Steel Dog, caught his attention by doing all they could to further their career *without* a manager. "I was attracted to them because of their total package," says Levy, "and what they've done as artists as well as young business people. They put a finished package together of competent, really good progressive rock. They marketed it themselves, and by the time they came to me they were getting airplay in Sweden, Belgium, Germany and France. They were already starting their second album all on their own. I look for that in the artists I sign."

Such self-promotion is something Levy knows about first-hand. He learned the business of management by acting as manager for his own rock band, The Limits. "I handled everything," he says. "Promotion, marketing, licensing, publishing . . . I started doing these things because no one else was there to do them. I had somewhat of a business background, having worked in the clothing business, and I found I had a flair for business. I enjoyed the business end of music as well as the creative end." From there, Levy started managing a group from the '60s, Jay and the Techniques, with whom he also played guitar. "I kind of took on managing the group, and again, by osmosis, learned what needed to be done." This eventually led Levy, along with his wife Leiza, to start managing bands full-time, as well as start a small record label, Luxury Records, and a publishing company, Flying Governor Music. Other acts on Levy's management roster include '60s stalwarts The Box Tops (featuring all the original members), country artist Boz Boswell and pop/rock band St. John's Alliance.

Sometimes a gut reaction is all Levy needs to work with an act; such was the case with Boz Boswell. "It was his ability to entertain that blew me away," he explains. With another of his acts, St. John's Alliance, it was purely the music that Levy loved. "They have very strong roots in '60s rock, and I just love their songs." Levy also looks at the people behind the music when looking for new acts. "I ask myself, what kind of people are these, and do they have integrity in what they're doing? In this day and age, obviously, I don't want to be involved with people who have personal habits that are going to mess them up and reflect on me. Because you really are your word in this business, and your reputation."

Levy is always interested in hearing from new artists. "I will listen to anything," he says, "although I understand why some companies don't accept unsolicited submissions." The sheer volume of them, he says, can be overwhelming. Because of this volume, many record labels will only accept material from an established manager, agent or publisher—basically, an industry professional. "So as a manager it became incumbent on me to

INSIDER REPORT, *Levy*

become an industry professional," Levy says, "whether it was for me as a writer, or for any of the acts I'm involved with."

Finding such an 'industry professional' can be difficult, but Levy offers some advice. "What I've learned over the years in business is never to burn bridges," he says. "If someone says no to you, it doesn't mean they're always going to say no to you. I also recommend learning about the business side of the industry. No one really taught me, it was just watching and learning and making a lot of mistakes along the way."

Levy recommends using sourcebooks to start your search for a manager. "Sourcebooks can tell you if such and such a person will accept a unsolicited package. Books like *Songwriter's Market* and Billboard's *This Business of Music* are good . . . you need to get familiar with these things. I don't think there's anything wrong in finding out who manages acts you admire, and tracking them down. Same with publishers. Through constant effort, and keeping that smile on your face while you're doing it, those doors will open."

Be sure you have material ready to send if you find someone who is willing to listen. "Have a package that's ready to go," Levy says. "If a manager says, 'yes, let me hear what you have,' have a package that's professionally done. I'm a great believer that you don't have to spend thousands and thousands of dollars, but a good tape, good photos, and a video are necessary these days."

When searching for a prospective manager, Levy recommends you ask yourself certain questions. "Ask yourself, can they get my stuff heard? Who are they working with, and what are those acts doing? Does this management company handle acts similar to yours? If you're in an original band and it's a management company that's handling generic weekend talent, maybe you shouldn't be going to them because that's just not their niche. For instance, I would tell an act that wanted to work conventions in Orlando not to come to me. Because there are great guys in this town that know that area well, and they should go to them."

Once you find a manager you can work with, it's important to remember that finding a manager isn't a guarantee of success. "A manager can't make an artist good," says Levy. "And he shouldn't try to change an artist's basic direction." A manager is there to "be very involved in getting material for an artist, creating an image, creating some media hype, creating a profile for the artist, and making sure the artist becomes as well-known as he can." It also involves putting demo packages together, helping select and package the material, and making contact with record companies, producers and publishers.

A good manager should not only promote artists' work but educate them as well. "Part of the manager's role is to educate the client about the industry and the realities of the business," Levy says. "An artist has to understand the mechanics and the politics of it." Artists need to know how many people are out there trying to do the same thing, and that it isn't going to be easy. "Sometimes it's incredibly frustrating," Levy adds, "and a lot of artists think the manager doesn't feel the same frustrations they do. But sometimes we feel it more acutely because part of our job is to shield our acts from a lot of the rejection. That's one thing I don't think a lot of acts realize, that we're the ones getting said no to 99 times out of a hundred."

Through the years of working with his artists, Levy has found himself in a unique position of being well-known and respected in the industry. "I'm very proud of the relationships I've been able to cultivate," he says. "Whether I've been accepted or rejected at a certain level or a certain company, I know if it's done professionally that any door I open doesn't close. And that's real important."

—*Cindy Laufenberg*

How to Contact: Submit demo tape by mail. Unsolicited submissions are OK. Prefers cassette or videocassette of performance with 1-4 songs and lead sheet. "Try to perform one or more of your songs on a local TV show. Then obtain a copy of your performance. Please only send professional quality material. Keep it simple and basic." If seeking management, include audio cassette, videocassette, photo and any additional promotional materials in press kit. SASE. Reports in 2 months.
Music: Mostly **pop-oriented R&B**; also **rock** and **MOR/adult contemporary**. Works primarily with professionally choreographed show bands. Current acts include Wali Ali, A. Vis and Denise Parker.

LONG ARM TALENT, 1655 Angelus Ave., Los Angeles CA 90026. (213)663-2553. Fax: (213)663-0851. E-mail: longarm@earthlink.net. Contact: Chris Lamson. Management firm. Estab. 1986. Represents individual artists and groups from anywhere; currently handles 3 acts. Receives 15-20% commission.
How to Contact: Write first and obtain permission to submit. Prefers cassette with 3 songs and lyric sheet. If seeking management, press kit should include photo, press and touring experience. Does not return material. Reports in 1 month.
Music: Mostly **alternative**, **rock** and **AAA (adult)**. Current acts include Stan Ridgway (alternative rock), Billy Katz (alternative rock) and Ultraviolet (alternative rock).

LOWELL AGENCY, 4043 Brookside Court, Norton OH 44203. (330)825-7813. Contact: Leon Seiter. Booking agency. Estab. 1985. Represents regional (Midwest and Southeast) individual artists; currently handles 3 acts. Receives 10% commission. Reviews material for acts.
How to Contact: Submit demo tape by mail. Unsolicited submissions are OK. Prefers cassette with 4 songs and lyric sheet. If seeking management, include demo cassette tape and SASE in press kit. Does not return material. Reports in 2 months.
Music: Mostly **country**. Works primarily with country vocalists. Current acts include Leon Seiter (country singer/entertainer/songwriter), Ford Nix (bluegrass singer and 5 string banjo picker) and Tom Durden (country singer, co-writer of "Heartbreak Hotel").

RICHARD LUTZ ENTERTAINMENT AGENCY, 5625 O St., Lincoln NE 68510. (402)483-2241. E-mail: r/94521@navix.net. General Manager: Cherie Worley. Management firm and booking agency. Estab. 1964. Represents individuals and groups; currently handles 50 acts. Receives 20% commission.
How to Contact: Submit demo tape by mail. Unsolicited submissions are OK. Prefers cassette or videocassette with 5-10 songs "to show style and versatility" and lead sheet. "Send photo, résumé, tape, partial song list and include references. Add comedy, conversation, etc., to your videocassette. Do not play songs in full—short versions preferred." If seeking management, include audio cassette and photo in press kit. SASE. Reports in 2 weeks.
Music: Mostly **top 40** and **country**; also **dance-oriented** and **MOR**. Works primarily with bar and dance bands for lounge circuit. "Acts must be uniformed." Current acts include Sherwin Linton (country), Sweet 'N' Sassy (variety) and Endless Summer (nostalgia).

M. &. G. ENTERTAINMENT CONSORTIUMS, INC., Executive Plaza East, 130 Spearman St., Lumberton NC 28358. (910)738-3793. Fax: (910)618-1760. Management firm, booking agency (Headline Booking Agency), music publisher (AZ Music), record company and record producer. Estab. 1972. Represents individual artists, groups and songwriters from anywhere; currently handles 30 acts. Receives 15% commission. Reviews material for acts.
How to Contact: Submit demo tape by mail. Unsolicited submissions are OK. Prefers cassette, DAT or VHS videocassette with lyric and/or lead sheet. If seeking management, press kit should include history, photos, CDs, tapes, videos, objectives and contractual commitments. "Cover letter mandatory." SASE. Reports in 1 week.
Music: Mostly **contemporary**, **rock** and **rap**; also **gospel**, **jazz** and **country**. Works primarily with singers and performing artists. Current acts include Psalmist (contemporary gospel), The Rickochet Mob featuring Big Cee, Scientific (rapper) and Allah's Annointed Gospel Singers.

M.B.H. MUSIC MANAGEMENT, P.O. Box 1096, Hudson, Quebec J0P 1H0 **Canada**. (613)780-1163. Fax: (514)458-2819. E-mail: larecord@total.net. Manager: Tanya Hart. Management firm, publishing company (G-String Publishing) and record company (L.A. Records). Estab. 1982. Works with local and regional individual artists and groups; currently handles 4 acts. Receives 20-30% commission. Reviews material for acts.

- M.B.H.'s publishing company, G-String Publishing, can be found in the Music Publishers section, and their record label, L.A. Records, is in the Record Companies section.

How to Contact: Submit demo tape by mail. Unsolicited submissions are OK. Prefers cassette or DAT with 3 songs and lyric sheet. If seeking management, press kit should include demo, 8×10 glossy, bio/résumé and song list. SASE. Reports in 4 months.

Music: Mostly **commercial rock**, **alternative** and **A/C**; also **country** and **dance**. Works primarily with singer/songwriters and solo artists. Current acts include Jessica Ehrenworth (dream pop singer), Cheryl MacEachern (heavy alternative) and Matulis (alternative).

‡M.E.G. MANAGEMENT, 6255 Sunset Blvd. #1006, Hollywood CA 90028. (213)860-3430. Fax: (213)860-3435. E-mail: tysupancic@aol.com. Vice President Artist Development: Ty Ronald Supancic. Management firm. Estab. 1996. Represents individual artists, groups and songwriters from anywhere; currently handles 3 acts. Receives 20% commission.
How to Contact: Write first and obtain permission to submit. Prefers cassette or VHS videocassette and lyric sheet. If seeking management, press kit should include press, photos, bio. "We believe in first impressions. Make it professional." SASE. Reports in 1 month.
Music: Mostly **alternative rock**. Current acts include ON (alternative/dance, signed to Warner Bros.), Nick Frost (folk/alternative) and Ant Sue (fungle/junk, on Cosmos Records).

‡KEVIN MABRY MINISTRIES, 8 E. State, Box 385, Milford Center OH 43045. Phone/fax: (937)349-2971. Owner: Kevin Mabry. Booking agency. Estab. 1970. Represents individual artists, groups and songwriters from anywhere; currently handles 1 act. Receives 15-20% commission. Reviews material for acts.
How to Contact: Submit demo tape by mail. Unsolicited submissions are OK. Prefers cassette with 1-3 songs and lyric sheet. "Picture and bio is helpful." Does not return material. Reports in 4-5 weeks.
Music: Mostly **gospel songs (no rock)** and **positive country songs**. Works primarily with gospel and country artists, solo and groups. Current acts include Kevin Mabry (gospel artist).

THE McDONNELL GROUP, 27 Pickwick Lane, Newtown Square PA 19073. (610)353-8554. E-mail: fmcdonn@concentric.net. Contact: Frank McDonnell. Management firm. Estab. 1985. Represents local, regional or international individual artists, groups and songwriters; currently handles 5 acts. Receives 20-25% commission. Reviews material for acts.
How to Contact: Write first and obtain permission to submit. Prefers cassette or VHS videocassette with 4 songs and lyric sheet. If seeking management, include press, tape or video, recent photos and bio. SASE. Reports in 1 month.
Music: Mostly **rock**, **pop** and **R&B**; also **country** and **jazz**. Current acts include Johnny Bronco (rock group), Mike Forte (producer/songwriter) and Pat Martino (jazz guitarist).

MADSTORM PRODUCTION COMPANY, 68 Wrentham St., Dorchester, MA 02124. (617)288-8991. Director: Edgiton Farquharson. Management firm and record producer. Estab. 1992. Represents regional individual artists and songwriters; currently handles 5 acts. Receives 20% commission. Reviews material for acts.
How to Contact: Submit demo tape by mail. Unsolicited submissions are OK. Prefers cassette, DAT or videocassette. If seeking management, press kit should include bio, picture and music type. SASE. Reports in 3 weeks.
Music: Mostly **reggae**, **rap** and **urban contemporary**; also **rappers**, **reggae singers** and **DJ's**. Current acts include Fitzroy Francis (reggae singer), Karen Brown (singer) and Kenroy Scott (DJ/rapper).

MAGNUM MUSIC CORPORATION LTD., 8607-128 Avenue, Edmonton Alberta **Canada** T5E 0G3. (403)476-8230. Fax: (403)472-2584 Manager: Bill Maxim. Booking agency, music publisher (Ramblin' Man Music Publishing/PRO, High River Music Publishing/ASCAP) and record company (Magnum Records). Estab. 1984. Represents international individual artists, groups and songwriters; currently handles 4 acts. Receives 15% commission. Reviews material for acts.

- See their listing in the Record Companies section.

How to Contact: Write or call first and obtain permission to submit. Prefers cassette with 3-4 songs. If seeking management, include tape or CD, photo, press clippings and bio in press kit. SAE and IRC. Reports in 6-8 weeks.
Music: Mostly **country** and **gospel**. Works primarily with "artists or groups who are also songwriters." Current acts include Catheryne Greenly (country), Thea Anderson (country) and Gordon Cormier (country).
Tips: "Prefers finished demos."

‡MALLA ENTERTAINMENT, 310 N. Fonda, LaHabra CA 90631. (213)549-9424. Fax: (213)549-9440. E-mail: mallaent@aol.com. President: Jay Malla. Management firm. Estab. 1985. Represents individual artists and groups from anywhere; currently handles 3 acts. Receives 20% commission. Reviews material for acts.
How to Contact: Write or call first and obtain permission to submit. Prefers cassette or VHS videocassette with 3 songs and lyric sheet. SASE. Reports in 2 weeks.

Music: Mostly **rock** and **pop**. Current acts include Jetland, Quimby Bros. and April.

MANAGEMENT PLUS, P.O. Box 65089, San Antonio TX 78265. (210)650-0609. Fax: (210)650-5968. Manager/Agent: Bill Angelini. Management firm and booking agency. Estab. 1980. Represents individual artists and groups from anywhere; currently handles 5 acts. Receives 10-20% commission. Reviews material for acts.
How to Contact: Submit demo tape by mail. Unsolicited submissions are OK. Prefers cassette, VHS videocassette and biography. If seeking management, press kit should include pictures, bios and discography. Does not return material. Reports in 1 week.
Music: Mostly **Latin American**, **tejano** and **international**; also **norteño** and **country**. Current acts include Los Padrez (tejano), Anna Roman (tejano) and Jorge Alejandro (tejano).

MANAPRO ENTERTAINMENT, 82 Sherman St., Passaic NJ 07055. (201)777-6109. Fax: (201)458-0303. E-mail: manapro@aol.com. President: Tomasito Bobadilla. Management firm, record company, music publisher and record producer. Estab. 1988. Represents individual artists and/or groups from anywhere; currently handles 4 acts. Receives 20% commission. Reviews material for acts.
How to Contact: Submit demo tape by mail. Unsolicited submissions are OK. Prefers cassette or VHS videocassette with 3 songs and lyric sheet. If seeking management, press kit should include bio, 8×10 photo, lyric sheet, 3-song demo and fact sheet. SASE. Reports in 2 months.
Music: Mostly **dance**, **pop** and **contemporary**; also **R&B** and **alternative**. Works primarily with vocalists and bands. Current acts include Blas (Latin pop), Cuepo 4 Alma (merengue) and Sassie Valenzuela (Latin pop).

MARSUPIAL LTD., Roundhill Cottage, The Ridge, Cold Ash, Newbury, Berks RG18 9HZ **United Kingdom**. Phone: 01635 862200. Fax: 01635 866449. Record Producer, Artist Manager: John Brand. Management firm, music publisher and record producer. Estab. 1990. Represents individual artists and/or groups, songwriters, producers and remixers from anywhere; currently handles 4 acts. Receives 20% commission. Reviews material for acts.
How to Contact: Submit demo tape by mail. Unsolicited submissions are OK. Prefers cassette or PAL videocassette with 4 songs and lyric sheet. If seeking management, press kit should include tape, photos, video (if possible) and any press. SAE and IRC. Reports in 1 month.
Music: **All types**. Current acts include Pooka (Island Records), Stereophonics (V2 Records), Kyra (Virgin Records, blues/house) and Sally Anne Marsh (Love This Records/pop).

RICK MARTIN PRODUCTIONS, 125 Fieldpoint Road, Greenwich CT 06830. (203)661-1615. E-mail: easywayric@aol.com. President: Rick Martin. Personal manager and independent producer. Holds the Office of Secretary of the National Conference of Personal Managers. Represents actresses and vocalists; currently handles 2 acts. Receives 15-25% commission. "Occasionally, we are hired as consultants, production assistants or producers of recording projects."
How to Contact: Write first and obtain permission to submit. SASE.
Music: **Top 40**, **dance** and **easy listening**. No rock or folk music. Produces vocal groups and female vocalists. Current acts include Marisa Mercedes (vocalist/pianist/songwriter) and Rob and Steve (songwriters/vocalists).
Tips: "The tape does not have to be professionally produced—it's really not important what you've done—it's what you can do now that counts."

PHIL MAYO & COMPANY, P.O. Box 304, Bomoseen VT 05732. (802)468-5011. President: Phil Mayo. Management firm and record company (AMG Records). Estab. 1981. Represents international individual artists, groups and songwriters; currently handles 4 acts. Receives 20% commission. Reviews material for acts.
How to Contact: Submit demo tape by mail. Unsolicited submissions are OK. Prefers cassette and/or CD with 3 songs and lyric or lead sheet. If seeking management, include bio, photo and lyric sheet in press kit. Does not return material. Reports in 1-2 months.
Music: Mostly **rock**, **pop** and **country**; also **blues** and **Christian pop**. Works primarily with dance bands, vocalists and rock acts. Current acts include The Drive (R&B), Athena and Blind Date.

MAZUR PUBLIC RELATIONS, (formerly Amazing Maze Productions), P.O. Box 360, E. Windsor NJ 08520. E-mail: mazurpr@aol.com. Contact: Michael Mazur. Management and PR firm. Estab. 1987. Represents groups from anywhere; currently handles 12 acts. Commission varies.
How to Contact: Submit demo tape by mail. Unsolicited submissions are OK. Prefers cassette or VHS videocassette with 2 songs. If seeking management, press kit should include CD/cassette, photo, bio and video. Does not return material.

Music: Current acts include Angra, Black Tape for A Blue Girl, Cold Meat Industry, Ace Frehley, Klank, Grither and Lycia.

MC PROMOTIONS & PUBLIC RELATIONS, 8504 Willis Ave. #6, Panorama City CA 91402. (818)892-1741. Management firm. Currently handles 1 act. Receives 10% commission. Reviews material for acts.
How to Contact: Write first and obtain permission to submit. Prefers cassette or videocassette. SASE. Reports in 2 weeks.
Music: Mostly **country**. Works primarily with vocalists. Current acts include Sierra Highway.

MERRI-WEBB PRODUCTIONS, P.O. Box 5474, Stockton CA 95205. (209)948-8186. E-mail: robnan7777@aol.com. President: Nancy L. Merrihew. Management firm, music publisher (Kaupp's & Robert Publishing Co./BMI) and record company (Kaupp Records). Represents regional (California) individual artists, groups and songwriters; currently handles 7 acts. Receives 10-15% commission.
- See the listings for Kaupp's and Robert Publishing in the Music Publishers section and Kaupp Records in the Record Companies section.

How to Contact: Write first and obtain permission to submit or to arrange personal interview. Prefers cassette or VHS videocassette with 3 songs maximum and lyric sheet. SASE. Reports in 3 months.
Music: Mostly **country**, **A/C rock** and **R&B**; also **pop**, **rock** and **gospel**. Works primarily with vocalists, bands and songwriters. Current acts include Bruce Bolin (singer/songwriter), Nanci Lynn (singer/songwriter) and Rapture (gospel songwriters).

‡MIDCOAST, INC., 1002 Jones Rd., Hendersonville TN 37075. (615)264-3896. Managing Director: Bruce Andrew Bossert. Management firm and music publisher (MidCoast, Inc./BMI). Estab. 1984. Represents individual artists, groups and songwriters; currently handles 2 acts. Reviews material for acts.
How to Contact: Submit demo tape by mail. Unsolicited submissions are OK. Prefers cassette, VHS videocassette or DAT with 2-4 songs and lyric sheet. If seeking management, include "short" bio, tape, video, photo and announcements of any performances in Nashville area in press kit. Does not return material. Reports in 6 weeks if interested.
Music: Mostly **rock, pop** and **country**. Works primarily with original rock and country bands and artists. Current acts include Room 101 (alternative rock).

MID-EAST ENTERTAINMENT INC., P.O. Box 25027, Lexington KY 40524. (606)885-5507. Agent: Robert Moser. Management firm. Represents artists and groups; currently handles 200 acts. Receives 15-20% commission. Reviews material for acts.
How to Contact: Submit demo tape by mail. Unsolicited submissions are OK. Prefers cassette with 3-6 songs, photo and songlist. Songs should have 1 verse, 1 bridge and 1 chorus. If seeking management, include tape, photo and playlist in press kit. SASE. Reports in 6 months.
Music: Mostly **top 40** and **R&B**; also **country**, **dance**, **easy listening**, **jazz**, **rock**, **soul** and **pop**. Works primarily with dance bands. Current acts include The Sensations (top 40/classics), The Marvells (top 40/oldies), Retroactive (Top 40/rock) and Nervous Melvin (college rock).

MIDNIGHT MUSIC MANAGEMENT, 8165 Robertson Blvd., Los Angeles CA 90035. (310)659-1784. Fax: (310)659-9347. Agents: Bob Diamond, Stuart Wax, Adam Katz and Jon Boyer. Management firm. Estab. 1989. Represents individual artists, groups, songwriters and producers from anywhere; currently handles 10 acts. Receives 18% commission. Reviews material for acts.
How to Contact: Write first and obtain permission to submit a demo. Prefers cassette with 4 songs, lyric sheet, bios and press. If seeking management, press kit should include bio, press, tape and video (if available). Does not return material. Reports in 1 month.
Music: All kinds. Works primarily with R&B/pop songwriters and producers, punk/alternative bands and acoustic rock bands. Current acts include Irene Cara (pop/R&B), Evon and Jarron Band (alternative folk pop/Island), Brutal Juice (hard alternative rock/Interscope Records), Denise Rich (pop/R&B songwriter), Andy Statman (clarinetist, Shanachie Records), Nancy Bryan (alternative folk/Acoustic Sounds Records), Reggie Magloire (R&B), Francesca Capasso (rock/blues), Lauran G. (alternative pop), Michael Garvin, Alan Roy Scott, Gloria Sklerov, Mary Unobsky and Dorothy Sea Gazeley.

MIDNIGHT SPECIAL PRODUCTIONS, INC., P.O. Box 916, Hendersonville TN 37077. (615)822-6713. Fax: (615)824-3830. E-mail: marty.martel@nashville.com. Website: http://www.infinet.com/webheads/msp. President: Marty Martel. Management firm, booking agency, music publisher (Brittkrisderon), record company (BAM) and record producer (Marty Martel). Estab. 1971. Represents Nashville individual artists and songwriters; currently handles 6 acts. Receives 10-20% commission. Reviews material for acts.

How to Contact: Submit demo tape by mail. Unsolicited submissions are OK. Prefers cassette with 3 songs and lyric sheet. If seeking management, press kit should include photo, tape or CD and bio. SASE. Reports in several weeks.
Music: Mostly **country**. Works primarily with singers. Current acts include Johnny Paycheck (country), Geneva Keene (contemporary country) and Ray Price (country).

MILAM MUSIC GROUP, (formerly The Nashville Connection), P.O. Box 710188, Dallas TX 75371. (214)828-2700. Fax: (214)823-9976. E-mail: mmg7373@connect.net. Contact: John Milam. Management firm, booking agency and music publisher. Estab. 1973. Represents individual artists and/or groups, songwriters from anywhere; currently handles 3 acts. Receives 15% commission. Reviews material for acts.
How to Contact: Submit demo tape by mail. Unsolicited submissions are OK. Prefers cassette or videocassette with 5 songs maximum and lyric sheet. If seeking management, press kit should include photo, tape, bio and work references. Does not return material. Reports in 2 weeks if interested.
Music: Country only. Works primarily with groups that have potential of being national acts—no one that doesn't currently work. Current acts include Dallas, Chuck Koble and Diamondback, and Savannah Rose. National artists who have previously worked through agency include Clay Walker, Doug Supernaw, Ty Herndon, Lonestar, Ricochette and Toby Keith.

MILESTONE MEDIA, P.O. Box 869, Venice CA 90291. (310)396-1234. Co-President: Mr. Sverdlin. Management firm. Estab. 1985. Represents individual artists, groups and songwriters from anywhere; currently handles 12 acts. Receives 20% commission.
How to Contact: Submit demo tape by mail. Unsolicited submissions are OK. Prefers cassette or videocassette with 3 songs. If seeking management, press kit should include credits and photo. Does not return material. Reports in 2 weeks.
Music: Mostly **rap**, **rock** and **dance**; also **country**, **house** and **movie**. Works primarily with singers, producers and composers. Current acts include Ray Goldman, Lori Lane and Feed.

THOMAS J. MILLER & COMPANY, 1802 Laurel Canyon Blvd., Los Angeles CA 90046. (213)656-7212. Fax: (213)656-7757. Artist Relations: Karen Deming. Management firm, music publisher and record company (Wilshire Park Records). Estab. 1975. Represents individual artists, groups and songwriters from anywhere; currently handles 12 acts. Reviews material for acts.
How to Contact: Submit demo tape by mail. Unsolicited submissions are OK. Prefers cassette or NTSC videocassette and lyric sheet. If seeking management, press kit should include photos, bio and video. Does not return material. Reports in 2-3 weeks.
Music: Mostly **rock**, **pop** and **jazz**; also **stage** and **country**. Current acts include Manowar, Fury in the Slaughterhouse and Champaign.

MIRKIN MANAGEMENT, 906½ Congress Ave., Austin TX 78701. (512)472-1818. Fax: (512)472-6915. Administrative Assistant: Erica Stall. Management firm. Estab. 1986. Represents individual artists, groups and songwriters from anywhere; currently handles 2 acts. Reviews material for acts.
How to Contact: Write or call first and obtain permission to submit a demo. Prefers cassette with 4 songs. If seeking management, press kit should include photo, press clippings and tape. SASE.
Music: All types. Current acts include Ian Moore Band (blues/rock).

MONOPOLY MANAGEMENT, 162 N. Milford, Highland MI 48357. Vice President: Bob Zilli. Management firm. Estab. 1984. Represents songwriters from anywhere; currently handles 1 act. Receives 15% commission. Reviews material for acts.
How to Contact: Submit demo tape by mail. Unsolicited submissions are OK. Prefers cassette or VHS videocassette with 4 songs and lyric sheet. If seeking management, press kit should include tape, photo, bio and résumé of live performances. SASE. Reports in 1 month.
Music: Mostly **country**, **alternative** and **top 40**. Works primarily with singer/songwriters. Current acts include Robbie Richmond (songwriter).

● **A BULLET** introduces comments by the editor of *Songwriter's Market* indicating special information about the listing.

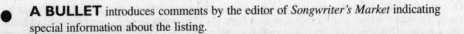

MONTEREY ARTISTS, INC., 901 18th Ave. S., Nashville TN 37212. (615)321-4444. Fax: (615)321-2446. Booking agency. Represents individual artists, groups from anywhere; currently handles 37 acts. Receives 10% commission. Reviews material for acts.
How to Contact: Write or call first to arrange personal interview.
Music: Mostly **country**. Current acts include John Michael Montgomery, Lyle Lovett, The Mavericks, Hal Ketchum, Ricky Skaggs, Sawyer Brown and Junior Brown.

GARY F. MONTGOMERY MANAGEMENT, P.O. Box 5106, Macon GA 31208. (912)749-7259. Fax: (912)757-0002. President: Gary F. Montgomery. Management firm, music publisher (g.f.m. Music/ASCAP, 12/31/49 Music/BMI) and production company. Estab. 1981. Represents individual artists, groups, songwriters, record producers and engineers; currently handles 6 acts. Receives 10-25% commission (it varies depending on the act). Reviews material for acts.
How to Contact: Write or call first and obtain permission to submit a demo. Prefers cassette with 3-5 songs and lyric sheet. "Call first to see if we are accepting new clients." Does not return material. Reports in 2 months.
Music: All types. Works primarily with singer/songwriters. Current acts include Otis Redding III (singer/songwriter), Jan Krist (singer/songwriter folk, alterntive), Jerome "Bigfoot" Brailey (drummer/songwriter, funk) and Davis Causey (guitarist/songwriter, New Age).

MOORE ENTERTAINMENT GROUP, 11 Possum Trail, Saddle River NJ 07458. (201)327-3698. President: Barbara Moore. Estab. 1984. Represents individual artists and groups; currently handles 3 acts. Receives 10% commission. Reviews material for acts.
How to Contact: Submit demo tape by mail. Unsolicited submissions are OK. Prefers cassette or videocassette and lyric sheet. "Include photo and bio." If seeking management, include tape, photo and bio in press kit. Does not return material. Reports in 6 weeks.
Music: Mostly **dance**, **rock**, **R&B** and **pop**. Works primarily with vocalists. Current acts include Rene Rollins (country/pop), Kitani (R&B) and 4 Play (R&B).

‡MORNINGSIDE MANAGEMENT, P.O. Box 676, Concord MA 01742. (617)259-8759. Contact: Robin Right. Management firm. Estab. 1981. Represents local and regional (New England) individual artists and groups; currently handles 6 acts. Receives 15% commission. Reviews material for acts.
How to Contact: Submit demo tape by mail. Unsolicited submissions are OK. Prefers cassette with 1-12 songs and lyric sheet. "We are only looking for 'hot new country' songs with catchy hook lines and country novelty songs. Uptempo mostly." SASE. Reports in 2-3 weeks.
Music: Mostly **country**. Current acts include Robin Right (country), One People (reggae) and Sabor Latino (Latin).

MUSIC MATTERS, P.O. Box 3773, San Rafael CA 94912-3773. (415)457-0700. Management firm. Estab. 1990. Represents local, regional or international individual artists, groups and songwriters; currently handles 6 acts. Receives 15% commission. Reviews material for acts.
How to Contact: Submit demo tape by mail. Unsolicited submissions are OK. Prefers cassette or VHS videocassette with lyric sheet. If seeking management, include lyric sheets, demo tape, photo and bio. Does not return material.
Music: Mostly **rock**, **blues** and **pop**; also **jazz** and **R&B**. Works primarily with songwriting performers/bands (rock). Current acts include Olivia Rosestone (singer/songwriter), Sam Andrew (singer/songwriter from Big Brother and The Holding Company), Zakiya Hooker, Walter Trout, Mud Hut and New Riders.
Tips: "Write great *radio-friendly* songs."

‡MUSIC STAR AGENCY, INC., P.O. Box 8538, Endwell NY 13762. (607)785-9120. Fax: (607)785-4516. Contact: New Talent Dept. Management firm and booking agency. Estab. 1967. Represents individual artists, groups and songwriters from anywhere; currently handles 100 acts. Receives 20% commission. Reviews material for acts.
How to Contact: Call first and obtain permission to submit. Prefers cassette or videocassette with 2-4 songs and lead sheet (if possible). If seeking management, press kit should include photo, bio, audio or video. Does not return material. Reports in 1 week.
Music: Any type. Current acts include Jay Hewlin (contemporary Christian), The Cast of Beatlemania (Broadway show), Kool Bubba Ice (comedy) and Jeff Hackworth (contemporary jazz).

MUSICA MODERNA MANAGEMENT, 5626 Brock St., Houston TX 77023. (713)926-4436. Fax: (713)926-2253. President: Max Silva. Management firm and booking agency. Represents individual artists and/or groups from anywhere; currently handles 6 acts. Receives 20% commission. Reviews material for acts.

How to Contact: Call first to arrange personal interview or submit demo tape by mail. Unsolicited submissions are OK. Prefers cassette or VHS videocassette with 3 songs and lyric sheet. If seeking management, press kit should include bio, photo and demo tape. Does not return material. Reports in 4-5 weeks.
Music: Mostly **tejano**. Works primarily with bands. Current acts include The Hometown Boys, Los Pekadorez and Annette y Axxion.

‡NASH-ONE MANAGEMENT, INC., 118 16th Ave. S. #209, Nashville TN 37203. (615)254-6999. Fax: (615)254-6968. President: Bill Quisenberry. Management firm and booking agency (Talent Group International, Inc.). Estab. 1990. Represents local individual artists and groups; currently handles 2 acts. Reviews material for acts.
How to Contact: Write first and obtain permission to submit. Prefers cassette. SASE. Reports in 1 month.
Music: Mostly **country** and **some rock**. Current acts include Pete Andrew (singer/songwriter) and Sean O'Brien (country singer).

BRIAN NELSON ENTERTAINMENT INC., P.O. Box 3008, Long Branch NJ 07740. (908)870-6911. Fax: (908)870-9664. President: Brian Nelson. Management firm. Estab. 1991. Represents individual artists, groups and songwriters from anywhere (specializes in local artists); currently handles 1 act. Receives 15-25% commission. Reviews material for acts.
How to Contact: Submit demo tape by mail. Unsolicited submissions are OK. Prefers CD, tape or VHS videocassette with 3 or less songs and lyric sheet. If seeking management, press kit should include cassette or CD, bio, photo, letter stating what artist is looking for in management company, contact name and number. Artist will only be contacted if accepted. Does not return material. Reports in 1-2 months only if interested.
Music: Mostly **rock**, **alternative** and **A/C**. Works primarily with bands. Current acts include Mars Needs Women (Discovery/Warner Bros., alternative pop).

‡NETWORK ENTERTAINMENT, 1280 Winchester Pkwy., Suite 245, Smyrna GA 30080. (770)319-8822. Fax: (770)319-6738. President: Mike Hooks. Vice President: Dan Jason. Management firm and booking agency. Estab. 1987. Represents individual artists and groups from anywhere; currently handles 11 acts. Receives 20% commission. Reviews material for acts.
How to Contact: Submit demo tape by mail. Unsolicited submissions are OK. Prefers whatever is available. "The more information and material we have, the better analysis we can make." Does not return material. Reports in 1 month.
Music: Mostly **commercial alternative** and **country**. Works primarily with alternative rock bands. Current acts include Law of Nature (alternative rock), Tara Vandevender (alternative rock) and Hobex (alternative rock).

J.P. NEWBY MANAGEMENT, P.O. Box 120725, Nashville TN 37212. (615)383-0889. Fax: (615)320-0889. President: Judith Newby. Management firm and public relations. Estab. 1975. Represents individual artists and groups from anywhere; currently handles 4 acts. Commission is individually negotiated. Reviews material for acts.
How to Contact: Submit demo tape by mail. Unsolicited submissions are OK. Prefers cassette with lyric sheet. If seeking management, press kit should include photo, bio and tape. Does not return material. Reports in 2 weeks.
Music: Mostly **country** and **rock**. Current acts include Everly Bros. (rock), RhymShot (country), Laura Sheridan (country) and Joe Dalton (country).

NIC OF TYME PRODUCTIONS, INC., P.O. Box 2114, Valparaiso IN 46384. Phone/fax: (219)477-4075. President: Tony Nicoletto. Management firm, record promoter, music publisher (Twin Spin Publishing/BMI) and record company (KNG Records). Estab. 1990. Represents individual artists, groups and songwriters from anywhere; currently represents 12 acts. Receives 15-20% commission. Reviews material for acts.

- Nic Of Tyme's publishing affiliate, Twin Spin Publishing, is listed in the Music Publishers section.

How to Contact: Write or call first and obtain permission to submit. Prefers cassette or videocassette with 3 songs and lyric sheet. If seeking management, press kit should include picture, demo tape, lyrics and autobiography of the artist. "Must be original and copyrighted material." Does not return material. Reports in 1-3 months.
Music: Mostly **country**, **R&B** and **pop**; also **rock**, **jazz**, **contemporary** and **gospel**. Works primarily with singers, bands and songwriters. Current acts include Bobby Lewis (R&B singer/songwriter), John Kontol (pop singer/songwriter), Neotone (adult alternative), Alison's Mailbox (alternative), Rising Jes (rock group) and Jokers Death & Taxes (rock group).

Tips: "Review your material for clean-cut vocals. We work primarily as a record promoter for the artist in mind. We pre-solicit labels that are interested in your style of music."

NIK ENTERTAINMENT COMPANY, 274 N. Goodman St., Rochester NY 14607. (716)244-0331. Fax: (716)244-0356. E-mail: niknicegu y@aol.com. Owner/President: Gary Webb. Management firm and booking agency. Estab. 1988. Represents groups from anywhere; currently handles 5 acts. Receives 10-20% commission. Reviews material for acts.
How to Contact: Submit demo tape by mail. Unsolicited submissions are OK. Prefers cassette or VHS videocassette with lyric or lead sheet. Does not return material. Reports in 3 weeks.
Music: Mostly **mainstream rock**, **pop** and **country**. Works primarily with bands. Current acts include Nik and the Nice Guys, Otis Rama & the Shama Lama Ding Dongs, Nik Fever-the Wrath of Polyester, Wild Nik West and The Blues Family.

CHRISTINA NILSSON PRODUCTION, Skeppargatan 45, 11458 Stockholm **Sweden**. Phone: (08)663-0831. Managing Director: Christina Nilsson. Management firm and booking agency. Estab. 1972. Represents individual artists, groups and songwriters; currently handles 3 acts. Receives 15% commission. Reviews material for acts.
How to Contact: Submit demo tape by mail. Unsolicited submissions are OK. Prefers cassette or VHS videocassette with 4-6 songs and lyric or lead sheet. If seeking management, include photo, bio and cassette tape. Does not return material. Reports in 1 month.
Music: Mostly **R&B**, **rock** and **gospel**; also "texts for stand-up comedians." Works primarily with concert bands. Current acts include Jan Schaffer (lead guitar, songwriter), Ted Astrom (singer, actor) and Malou Berg (gospel singer).

NORTHSTAR ARTIST MANAGEMENT, P.O. Box 2627, Dearborn MI 48123. (313)274-7000. E-mail: angelg911@aol.com. President: Angel Gomez. Management firm. Estab. 1979. Represents local and international individual artists, groups and songwriters; currently handles 24 acts. Receives 15-20% commission. Reviews material for acts.
How to Contact: Write first and obtain permission to submit. Prefers cassette or videocassette of performance with 3-5 songs. If seeking management, include photo, tape/CD, bio and itinerary of dates. Does not return material. Reports in 6-8 weeks.
Music: Mostly **rock**, **pop** and **top 40**; also **metal**. Works primarily with individual artists, groups (bar bands) and songwriters. Current artists include RH Factor (rock), The Rev. Right Time and the First Cuzins of Funk ('90s funk) and Greg Isles (alternative rock).

‡NOTEWORTHY ENTERPRISES, 3741 Sunny Isles Blvd., N. Miami Beach FL 33160. (305)949-9192. Fax: (305)949-9492. E-mail: 73754.1221@compuserve.com. President: Sheila Siegel. Booking agency, music publisher (On the Water Publications/BMI) and talent buyer. Estab. 1987. Represents individual artists, groups and songwriters from anywhere. Reviews material for acts.
How to Contact: Write first and obtain permission to submit. If seeking management, press kit should include photos, press clippings and bio. Does not return material.
Music: Mostly **big band**. Works primarily with jazz artists. Current acts include Noteworthy Orchestra (big band), Southlanders Traditional Jazz Band, David Siegel and Jack Siegel.

NOTEWORTHY PRODUCTIONS, 124½ Archwood Ave., Annapolis MD 21401. (410)268-8232. Fax: (410)268-2167. E-mail: mcshane@erols.com. President: McShane Glover. Management firm and booking agency. Estab. 1985. Represents individual artists, groups and songwriters from everywhere; currently handles 13 acts. Receives 15-20% commission. Reviews material for acts.
How to Contact: Write first and obtain permission to submit. Prefers cassette with lyric sheet. If seeking management, press kit should include cassette or CD, photo, bio, venues played and press clippings (preferably reviews). "Follow up with a phone call 3-5 weeks after submission." Does not return material. Reports in 3 weeks.
Music: Mostly **country**, **folk**, and **bluegrass**; also **pop**. Works primarily with performing singer/songwriters. Current acts include Five Chinese Brothers (new country), Debi Smith (Celtic country) and Fred Koller (singer/songwriter).

NOVA PRODUCTIONS & MANAGEMENT, P.O. Box 7892, Tampa FL 33605. (813)273-8796. CEO/A&R: A. Howard. Management firm, booking agency, record company (Quantum Records) and record producer. Estab. 1957. Represents individual artists, groups and songwriters from anywhere; currently handles 12 acts. Receives 18% commission. Reviews material for acts.
How to Contact: Submit demo tape by mail. Unsolicited submissions are OK. Prefers cassette with lyric

or lead sheet. If seeking management, press kit should include demo, photo, musical goals and bio. Does not return material. Reports in 2 months.
Music: Mostly **jazz**, **blues** and **new country**. Works primarily with vocalists, singer/songwriters and bands. Current acts include Gypsy Eden (singer), Fred Shatwell (keyboard/singer) and Max Troll (singer).
Tips: "Send a professional looking promo kit with a professionally recorded demo. I want to take you seriously."

OB-1 ENTERTAINMENT, P.O. Box 22552, Nashville TN 37202. (615)672-0307. E-mail: jimpepe@aol.com. Website: http://members.aol.com/jimpepe/OB-1.html. Partners: Jim O'Baid and Karen Hillebrand. Management firm, music publisher and songplugger. Estab. 1990. Represents local, regional and international individual artists, groups and songwriters. Receives 20% commission. Reviews material for acts.
How to Contact: Submit demo tape by mail. Unsolicited submissions are OK. Prefers cassette or DAT with 3 songs. If seeking management, include 8×10 photo, tape, bio and videocassette (if possible) in press kit. Does not return material. Reports in 6 weeks.
Music: Primarily **country**, but also **pop** and **rock**.
Tips: "Don't spend a lot of money on demos until you really know the song is good enough to warrant the expense."

ODOM-MEADERS MANAGEMENT, 449½ Moreland Ave., Atlanta GA 30307. (404)521-9747. Fax: (404)521-0990. E-mail: odommeader@aol.com. Co-President: Kevin Meaders. Management firm. Estab. 1994. Represents groups from the Southeast mainly; currently handles 4 acts. Reviews material for acts.
How to Contact: Submit demo tape by mail. Unsolicited submissions are OK. Prefers cassette or CD. If seeking management, press kit should include bio, any available press, and audible CD or tape. SASE. Reports in 4-6 weeks.
Music: Mostly **rock**, **jazz** and **blues**. Works primarily with national and regional acts with a variety of styles and influences. Current acts include The Derek Trucks Band (nationally recognized guitar player),The Urban Shakedancers (straight ahead rock), Fiji Mariners (featuring Col. Bruce Hampton, eclectic mix of rock, blues, jazz and everything else/Capricorn Records) and Grapes (hippie jam band).

ON STAGE MANAGEMENT, P.O. Box 679, Bronx NY 10469. (718)798-6980. E-mail: onstagemgt@aol.com. President: Paul M. Carigliano. Management firm and record producer. Estab. 1988. Represents individual artists and/or groups and songwriters from anywhere; currently handles 10 acts. Receives 15-25% commission. Reviews material for acts.
How to Contact: Submit demo tape by mail. Unsolicited submissions are OK. Prefers cassette or VHS videocassette with at least 2 songs, "the more the better." If seeking management, press kit should include cassette or VHS video tape, picture and bio. Does not return material. Reports in 2 weeks.
Music: Mostly **dance music**, **rock**, and **pop**; also **R&B**. Current acts include Lil' Suzy (dance artist), Eclipz and Strings of Time (rock group).
Tips: "Our artists sing songs with positive messages. We don't want songs that glorify violence or are too risqué."

‡ON THE LEVEL MUSIC!, 622 E. Main St., Jenks OK 74037. (918)298-8881. Fax: (918)298-8882. CEO/President: Fred Gage. Management firm, booking agency and music publisher (On The Level Music! Publishing). Estab. 1970. Represents individual artists, groups and songwriters from anywhere; currently handles 12 acts. Receives 15% commission. Reviews material for acts.
How to Contact: Submit demo tape by mail. Unsolicited submissions are OK. Prefers cassette, DAT or VHS videocassette with 4 songs and lyric or lead sheet. If seeking management, press kit should include 8×10 and bio. Does not return material. Reports in 1 month.
Music: Mostly **rock**, **alternative** and **jazz**. Current acts include Jane & Joy (alternative) and Chase (rock).

OPERATION MUSIC ENTERPRISES, 1400 E. Court St., Ottumwa IA 52501. (515)682-8283. President: Nada C. Jones. Management firm and booking agency. Represents artists, groups and songwriters; currently handles 4 acts. Receives 15% commission. Reviews material for acts.
How to Contact: Submit demo tape by mail. Unsolicited submissions are OK. Prefers cassette or VHS videocassette and lyric sheet. "Keep material simple. Groups—use *only group* members—don't add extras. Artists should include references." Does not return material. Reports in 6-8 weeks.
Music: Mostly **country**; also **blues**. Works primarily with vocalists and show and dance groups. Current acts include Reesa Kay Jones (country vocalist and recording artist), Chaparell Show and White River Country (country/bluegrass).

‡DEE O'REILLY MANAGEMENT, LTD., 112 Gunnersbury Ave., London W54HB **England**. Phone: (0181)993-7441. Management firm and music publisher (Orestes Music Publishing, Ltd.). Represents indi-

vidual artists, groups and songwriters; currently handles 10 acts. Receives variable commission.
How to Contact: Write first and obtain permission to submit. "We're not really in the market for new acts or material right now as we are very busy." SAE and IRC.
Music: Mostly **pop** and **rock**; also "special music projects for recording and/or television." Works primarily with pop vocalists and bands. Current acts include Lovatux, Bobby Pearce and Hannah Jones.

THE OTHER ROAD, 1337 Forest Glen, Cuyahoga Falls OH 44221. Phone/fax: (330)945-4923. E-mail: otherroad@aol.com. Director: Gary Davis. Management firm and record producer. Estab. 1992. Represents individual artists from anywhere; currently handles 5 acts. Receives 15% commission. Reviews material for acts.
How to Contact: Call first and obtain permission to submit a demo. Prefers cassette or DAT, VHS videocassette or CD with 4 or more songs and lyric and/or lead sheet. If seeking management, press kit should include recording (CD preferable, but other formats accepted), photo(s), bio, reviews, etc. "Remember, you're selling yourself." SASE. Reports in 1 month.
Music: Mostly **progressive**, **New Age** and **jazz**; also **classical** and **avante garde**. Works primarily with individual artists who are virtuosos at their instrument. Current acts include Peter Banks (progressive guitarist formerly of Yes and Flash), Rhonda Larson (classical, folk, jazz flutist from Paul Winter Consort) and Richard Johnson (acoustic guitarist combining many styles).

TOMMY OVERSTREET MUSIC COMPANIES, 3555 S. Mentor Ave., Springfield MO 65804. (417)889-8080. Fax: (417)889-8090. Owner: Tommy Overstreet. Management firm, booking agency (On Stage Productions), recording studio, music publisher (Tommy Overstreet Music/BMI) and record company (De Ja Vu Records and Ram Records). Estab. 1969. Represents individual artists, groups and songwriters from anywhere; currently handles 3 acts. Receives 15% commission. Reviews material for acts.
How to Contact: Submit demo tape by mail. Unsolicited submissions are OK. Prefers cassette with 3 songs and lyric sheet. If seeking management, press kit should include pictures (8×10 or 5×7), short biography and tape (no more than 5 songs). SASE. Reports "as soon as it's reasonably possible."
Music: Mostly **country** and **gospel**; also **light rock**. Current acts include Tommy Overstreet (country singer), Ken Fowler (country) and Rick Thompson (country).

PAQUIN ENTERTAINMENT GROUP, 1067 Sherwin Rd., Winnipeg, Manitoba R3H 0T8 **Canada**. (204)694-3104. E-mail: paquin@magic.mb.ca. Contact: Artist Relations. Management firm, music publisher (Branch Music Group) and booking agency. Estab. 1984. Represents local, regional and international individual artists; currently handles 5 acts. Receives 10-20% commission. Reviews material for acts.

- See the listing for Branch Group Music in the Music Publishers section.

How to Contact: Call first and obtain permission to submit or to arrange personal interview. Prefers cassette or VHS videocassette with 3 songs and lyric sheet. Does not return material. Reports in 4-6 months.
Music: Mostly **children's**, **folk** and **comedy**; also **New Age** and **classical**. Works primarily with family performers. Current acts include Fred Penner (family entertainer/songwriter), Marc Jordan (singer/songwriter), Al Simmons (family entertainer/songwriter), Amy Sky (singer/songwriter) and Norman Foote (family entertainer/songwriter).

JACKIE PAUL ENTERTAINMENT GROUP, INC., 559 Wanamaker Rd., Jenkintown PA 19046. (215)884-3308. Fax: (215)884-1083. President: Jackie Paul. Management and promotion firm (East-2-West Marketing, Promotion and Publicity). Estab. 1985. Represents local and national artists, groups, producers and musicians; currently handles 1 act. Commission varies. Reviews material for acts.
How to Contact: Call first and obtain permission to submit. "Do not write—calls only." Prefers CD, cassette or VHS videocassette with 1-3 songs and lyric or lead sheets. "It's not mandatory but if possible, I would prefer a videocassette. A video simply helps get the song across visually. Do the best to help portray the image you represent, with whatever resources possible." If seeking management, include no more than 3 copyrighted songs, photo, bio (short and to the point), video (if possible), contact name, telephone number and address in press kit. SASE. Reports in 4-12 weeks.
Music: **All types**. Works primarily with vocalists (all original acts). Current acts include Blue Eagle (mainstream).

PERFORMERS OF THE WORLD INC. (P.O.W.), 8901 Melrose Ave., 2nd Floor, Los Angeles CA 90069-5605. President: Terry Rindal. Agents: Nita Scott, Bruce Eisenberg, Bob Ringe. Booking agency. Estab. 1987. Represents national and international individual artists and groups; currently handles 60-75 acts. Receives 10-15% commission.
How to Contact: Write or call first and obtain permission to submit. Prefers cassette or VHS videocassette with several songs and lyric sheet. If seeking management, include photo, bio, press clippings and recorded

material in press kit. Does not return material. Reports in 1 month (depends on quality). "Send SASE for reply."

Music: Mostly **rock**, **world music**, **alternative**, **jazz**, **R&B**, **folk** and **pop**. Current acts include Herbie Hancock (jazz legend), Joe Sample (jazz legend), Karla Bonoff (singer/songwriter), John Cale, David Wilcox, Bryndle and Lydia Lunch.

Tips: "Don't harrass us after you submit. We are looking for artistry and quality—if you're not really prepared please don't waste your time (or ours)."

PEROM INTERNATIONAL, 2461 Santa Monica Blvd. #C331, Santa Monica CA 90404. (310)450-3677. President: Stephanie Perom. Management firm and music publisher (Pretty Shayna Music/BMI). Estab. 1992. Represents individual artists and songwriters from anywhere; currently handles 2 acts. Receives 15% commission.

- Perom International's publishing company, Pretty Shayna Music, is listed in the Music Publishers section.

How to Contact: Write first and obtain permission to submit, only if you are already generating income from your music. Prefers cassette with 1-2 songs and lyric sheet. If seeking management, press kit should include photo, bio, any recent press clips and 2 song demo. SASE. Reports in 2-3 months.

Music: Mostly **pop**, **dance** and **R&B**; also **pop/rock**. Works primarily with singers, singer/songwriters and songwriter/producers. Current acts include Tim Tobias (jazz pop pianist-producer) and Susan Barth (songwriter/pop rock).

PHIL'S ENTERTAINMENT AGENCY LIMITED, 889 Smyth Rd., Ottawa Ontario K1G 1P4 **Canada**. (613)731-8983. President: Phyllis Woodstock. Booking agency. Estab. 1979. Represents artists and groups; currently handles 50 acts. Receives 10% commission.

How to Contact: Submit demo tape by mail. Unsolicited submissions are OK. Prefers cassette or videocassette with 4-7 songs. "Be sure the name of artist and date of completion are on the video." Does not return material. Reports in 2-3 weeks.

Music: Mostly **country**; also **country/rock**, **MOR jazz**, **Dixieland** and **old rock 'n' roll**. "We work with show bands, male and female vocalists, bar bands and dance bands on a regular basis." Current acts include Elvis Aaron Presley Jr., The Valley Legends (country) and Eddy & The Stingrays ('50s and '60s dance band).

Tips: "Be professional and business-like. Keep agency supplied with up-to-date promo material and develop entertainment ability. Videotape your live performance, then give yourself an honest review."

PILLAR RECORDS, P.O. Box 858, Carlisle PA 17013-0858. Phone/fax: (717)249-2536. E-mail: webmaster@pillarworld.com. Website: http://www.pillarworld.com/records. Contact: A&R Department. Management firm, music publisher and record company. Estab. 1994. Represents individual artists, groups and songwriters from anywhere; currently handles 2 acts. Receives 20% commission. Reviews material for acts.

How to Contact: Submit demo tape by mail. Unsolicited submissions are OK. Prefers cassette or CD with 3 songs and lyric sheet. If seeking management, press kit should include bio, photo, reviews, mailing list, tape or CD. "Please be neat and as professional as possible." Does not return material. Reports in 6 weeks.

Music: Mostly **pop/rock**, **rock** and **alternative rock**; also **country**, **blues** and **instrumental**. Works primarily with solo artists and bands. Current acts include the Craig Kelley Band (mainstream rock).

PLATINUM EARS PERSONAL MANAGEMENT, 285 Chestnut St., West Hempstead NY 11552. (516)489-0738. Fax: (516)565-9425. E-mail: platear1@aol.com. Website: http://members.aol.com/PlatEar1/index.html. President: Mike Siskind. Management firm and music publisher (Siskatune Music Publishing Co./BMI). Estab. 1988. Represents national and international individual artists, groups and songwriters; currently handles 2 acts. Receives 20% commission.

- Platinum Ears' publishing company, Siskatune Music Publishing, is listed in the Music Publishers section.

How to Contact: Write first and obtain permission to submit. "No calls!" Prefers cassette with 1-3

REFER TO THE GEOGRAPHIC INDEX (at the back of this book) to find listings of companies by state, as well as foreign listings.

songs and lyric sheet. If seeking management, include photo, press, who you've opened for and radio airplay in press kit. SASE. Reports in 2-3 months.

Music: **Rock** and **pop**. Current acts include Off The Wall (rock) and Michael Ellis (songwriter).

Tips: "Send us your stuff only if it is *realistically* ready to submit to major label. Otherwise, we'll pass."

PLATINUM TRACKS PRODUCTIONS, P.O. Box 5551, Wilmington DE 19808-0551. (302)456-3331. Fax: (302)456-3556. E-mail: producer@bdsnet.com. Website: http://www.banksnet.com/platinum. Producer: Dean A. Banks. Management firm, music publisher (Pisces-Leo Music/BMI) and record producer. Estab. 1979. Represents individual artists, groups and songwriters from anywhere; currently handles 3 acts. Receives 20% commission. Reviews material for acts.

How to Contact: Write first and obtain permission to submit. Prefers cassette, DAT, VHS videocassette or CD with 3 songs and lyric sheet. If seeking management, press kit should include cover letter, newsletter, bio, picture and press clippings. "Send query letters with bounce-back postcards." Does not return material. Reports in 2 months.

Music: Mostly **pop**, **rock** and **blues**; also **soundtracks**, **country** and **zydeco**. Works primarily with singer/songwriters, solo acts, bands and songwriters. Current acts include Joe Grant (blues-rock guitarist/singer/songwriter), Suzanne Oliver (pop-rock/vocalist/songwriter) and Vic Sadot (cajun/zydeco singer/songwriter).

Tips: "Don't reinvent the wheel, or argue with what works. Send material that is thought provoking and well produced. What's most important to me is the quality of the song, not lavish production. Please keep song length under four minutes."

‡POWER PLAY PROMOTIONS, P.O. Box 2198, Whitney TX 76692. (817)694-4047. Fax: (817)694-2522. President: Allen Newton. Management firm, music publisher (Four Newton Publishing/BMI, Stephash Publishing/ASCAP) and record company (Narciscus/New Essex/Pristine/Pleasure). Estab. 1981. Represents individual artists and groups from anywhere; currently handles 12-14 acts. Receives 10-15% commission. Reviews material for acts.

How to Contact: Submit demo tape by mail. Unsolicited submissions are OK. Prefers cassette with 3 songs and lyric sheet. If seeking management, press kit should include cassette, bio, photo and booking schedule. SASE. Reports in 1 month.

Music: Mostly **rock**, **R&B** and **pop**; also **country**, **Latin** and **punk**. Works primarily with bands and singer/songwriters. Current acts include Dave (rock band), BT&T (pop band) and Black Saddle (country band).

PRAIRIE FIRE MUSIC COMPANY, P.O. Box 9411, Mission KS 66201. (913)362-3084. President: Chris Stout. Management firm, booking agency, music publisher (Wild Prairie Publishing/BMI), record company (Prairie Fire Records) and record producer (Chris Stout). Estab. 1991. Represents midwest and southwest individual artists, groups and songwriters; currently handles 10-20 acts. Receives 15% commission. Reviews material for acts.

How to Contact: Submit demo tape by mail. Unsolicited submissions are OK. Prefers cassette with 3-15 songs and lyric and/or lead sheet. If seeking management, press kit should include bio, press releases, promotional materials, photograph and cassette/CD. "If SASE enclosed material will be returned if we have no interest." Reports in 4-6 weeks.

Music: Mostly **country**, **alternative** and **rock**; also **folk**, **New Age** and **crossover**. Works primarily with singer/songwriters and bands. Current acts include Cosmic Cactus (roots/alternative/country band), Matt Pollock (original folk/country/blues singer/songwriter) and Duane Woner (original folk/rock singer/songwriter, bass guitarist).

Tips: "We consider all materials submitted. Don't be afraid to submit a low quality demo. Let us decide."

PRECISION MANAGEMENT, 825 N. King St. #A-1, Hampton VA 23669-2814. (804)728-0046. Fax: (804)728-9144. Representative: Cappriccieo Scates. Management firm and music publisher (Mytrell/BMI). Estab. 1990. Represents individual artists and/or groups and songwriters from anywhere; currently handles 2 acts. Receives 20% commission. Reviews material for acts.

How to Contact: Write first and obtain permission to submit. Prefers cassette or VHS videocassette with 3-4 songs and lyric sheet. If seeking management, press kit should include photo, bio and all relevant press information. SASE. Reports in 4-6 weeks.

Music: Mostly **R&B**, **rap** and **gospel**; also **all types**. Current acts include Mi-L (R&B vocal act) and Different Flavor (R&B vocal act).

‡PRESTIGE MANAGEMENT, 8600 Wilbur Ave., Northridge CA 91324. (818)993-3030. Fax: (818)993-4151. E-mail: prestige@gte.net. Vice President: Waddell Solomon. Management firm. Estab.

1987. Represents individual artists, groups and songwriters from anywhere; currently handles 2 acts. Receives 15% commission. Reviews material for acts.
How to Contact: Submit demo tape by mail. Unsolicited submissions are OK. Prefers cassette with 3 songs, photo/bio and lyric sheet. If seeking management, press kit should include photos, bio, recent show dates and recent show reviews. Does not return material. Reports in 1 month.
Music: Mostly **pop rock**, **hard rock**, **alternative rock**; also **R&B** and **AAA**. Works primarily with pop/rock bands with strong songs and live shows; also songwriters for film/TV projects. Current acts include Neve (modern pop rock) and Michael Raphael (singer/songwriter).

PRO STAR TALENT AGENCY, P.O. Box 290 186, Nashville TN 37229. (615)754-2950. President: Ralph Johnson. Booking agency. Estab. 1960. Represents individual artists and/or groups; currently handles 15 acts. Receives 15% commission. Reviews material for acts.
How to Contact: Submit demo tape by mail. Unsolicited submissions are OK. If seeking management, press kit should include photo, demo and bio. SASE. Reports in 2 weeks.
Music: **All types**. Works primarily with vocalists and bands. Current acts include Dave Martin, Carrie Osborne and Chatli Nicole (country artists).

PRO TALENT CONSULTANTS, P.O. Box 1192, Clearlake Oak CA 95423. (707)998-3587. Coordinator: John Eckert. Management firm and booking agency. Estab. 1979. Represents individual artists and groups; currently handles 11 acts. Receives 9-13% commission. Reviews material for acts.
How to Contact: Submit demo tape by mail. Unsolicited submissions are OK. Prefers cassette or VHS videocassette with at least 4 songs and lyric sheet. "We prefer audio cassette (4 songs). Submit videocassette with live performance only." If seeking management, include an 8×10 photo, a cassette or CD of at least 4-6 songs, a bio on group/artist, references and business card or a phone number with address to contact in press kit. Does not return material. Reports in 3-4 weeks.
Music: Mostly **country**, **country/pop** and **rock**. Works primarily with vocalists, show bands, dance bands and bar bands. Current acts include Jon Richard (country singer), The Classics IV featuring Dennis Yost (pop group) and the Beau Brummels (pop group).

PRODUCTIONS UNLIMITED, 6107 Elmendorf Dr., Suitland MD 20746. (301)568-1100. Fax: (301)736-6290. Manager: Frank Disalvo. Management firm and booking agency. Represents individual artists, groups and songwriters from anywhere. Receives 15% commission. Reviews material for acts.
How to Contact: Call first and obtain permission to submit a demo. Prefers cassette or CD. If seeking management, press kit should include tape or CD, picture, promo songlist and list of recent performances. Does not return material. Reports in 6 weeks.
Music: Mostly **rock (alternative, college)**, **blues/R&B** and **country**; also **jazz** and **dance companies**. Works primarily with bands, soloists and singer/songwriters. Current acts include Genghis Angus (alternative rock band), Bobby Rush (blues/R&B), A La Carte Brass & Percussion (jazz) and Tommy Lepson & The Lazyboys (R&B).

PROFESSIONAL ARTIST MANAGEMENT, LTD., P.O. Box 755, Shelburne VT 05482. (800)610-7625. Fax: (802)985-9023. E-mail: artistmgmt@aol.com. General Manager: Tom Hughes. Management firm. Estab. 1994. Represents northeast and New York individual artists and groups; currently handles 14 acts. Receives 10-20% commission. Reviews material for acts.
How to Contact: Submit demo tape by mail. Unsolicited submissions are OK. Prefers cassette, DAT, VHS videocassette or CD with 4 or more songs. If seeking management, press kit should include any commercial releases, reviews and airplay, artist's background—other bands/acts, credits etc. SASE. Reports in 2 weeks.
Music: Mostly **alternative metal** and **acoustic blues/folk**.

RADIOACTIVE, 130 Shore Rd., Suite 300, Port Washington NY 11050. (516)428-0207 or (212)592-4085. E-mail: ambrosia74@aol.com. Agent: Kenjamin Franklin. Booking and talent agency. Estab. 1983. Represents individual artists, groups and broadcasters from anywhere; currently handles 10 acts. Receives 10% commission. Reviews material for acts.
How to Contact: Submit demo tape by mail. Unsolicited submissions are OK. "Please do not phone." Prefers cassette or video with 3 songs and lyric sheet. If seeking management, press kit should include bio, press clippings, photo and 3 radio-friendly original songs. "Label all cassettes with phone number." Does not return material. Reports in 3 weeks. "We only call upon further interest."
Music: Mostly **modern rock**, **ballads** and **AAA**; also **A/C** and **pop/CHR**. Current acts include Ambrosia and Orleans.

RAINBOW COLLECTION LTD., 4696 Kahlua Lane, Bonita Springs FL 34134. (941)947-6978. Executive Producer: Richard (Dick) O'Bitts. Management firm, record company (Happy Man Records) and music publisher (Rocker Music, Happy Man Music). Represents individual artists, groups, songwriters and producers; currently handles 8 acts. Receives 10-20% commission. Reviews material for acts.

- Rainbow Collection's publishing affiliate, Rocker Music/Happy Man Music, is listed in the Music Publishers section, and their record label, Happy Man Records, is listed in the Record Companies section.

How to Contact: Submit demo tape by mail. Unsolicited submissions are OK. Prefers cassette or VHS videocassette of live performance with 4 songs and lyric sheet. If seeking management, include photos, bio and tapes in press kit. SASE. Reports in 1 month.
Music: Mostly **country**, **pop** and **rock**. Works primarily with writer/artists and groups of all kinds. Current acts include Holly Ronick, Colt Gipson (traditional country), Overdue (rock), Flo Carter and the Bengter Sisters (gospel), The Challengers (country pop), Carl Hausman (instrumental) and Crosswinds (rock).

RAZ MANAGEMENT CO., 254 W. 54th St., 14th Floor, New York NY 10019. (212)757-1289. Fax: (212)586-5175. E-mail: zeevon@aol.com. President: Ron Zeelens. Management firm. Estab. 1983. Represents individual artists and/or groups from anywhere; currently handles 4 acts. Receives 20% commission. Reviews material for acts.
How to Contact: Submit demo tape by mail. Unsolicited submissions are OK. Prefers cassette. If seeking management, press kit should include demo, photo, bio, press. SASE. Reports in 1-2 months.
Music: Mostly **rock**, **pop** and **metal**. Works primarily with bands and singer/songwriters. Current acts include Tom Lavin (blues singer/songwriter), Kim Masters (pop singer/songwriter), Mike Hickey (metal songwriter) and Andrew McIntosh (pop singer/songwriter).

RDR MUSIC GROUP, 299 Lesmill Rd., Toronto, Ontario M3B 2V1 **Canada**. Phone/fax: (416)445-3077. E-mail: rdrmusic@interlog.com. Contact: Joe Wood. Management firm and record company (Rosedale Records). Represents local and regional individual artists; currently handles 1 act.
How to Contact: Write or call first and obtain permission to submit a demo. Does not return material.
Music: Mostly **alternative** and **country**. Current acts include Rena Gaile (country).

RENAISSANCE ENTERTAINMENT GROUP, P.O. Box 1222, Mountainside NJ 07092-1222. Director: Kevin A. Joy. Management firm, booking agency, record company (Suburan Records) and record producer (Onyx Music, Bo^{2}Legg Productions). Estab. 1992. Represents local and regional individual artists, groups and songwriters; currently handles 20 acts. Receives 20% commission. Reviews material for acts.
How to Contact: Write first and obtain permission to submit. Prefers cassette with 3 songs and lyric or lead sheet. If seeking management, press kit should include pictures and bio. Does not return material. Reports in 5 weeks.
Music: Mostly **R&B**, **rap** and **rock**. Works primarily with R&B groups, rap and vocalists. Current acts include The Roots (rap), SWV (R&B) and A Mother's Child (rock).

RGK ENTERTAINMENT GROUP, P.O. Box 243, Station C, Toronto Ontario M6J 3P4 **Canada**. (416)516-8267. Fax: (416)516-3557. E-mail: rgkent@netcom.ca. Contact: Ron Kitchener. Management firm. Estab. 1988. Represents individual artists, groups and songwriters from anywhere; currently handles 2 acts. Receives 15-20% commission. Reviews material for acts.
How to Contact: Submit demo tape by mail. Unsolicited submissions are OK. Prefers cassette or VHS videocassette with 2-4 songs and lyric sheet. If seeking management, press kit should include cassette of recent material, photos, recent press and bio. Does not return material. Reports in 1 month.
Music: Mostly **country**, **rock** and **folk**; also **roots**. Works primarily with singer/songwriters. Current acts include Jason McCoy (country singer/songwriters).
Tips: "Submit a cross section of tempos within your style of music."

RHYME SYNDICATE MANAGEMENT, 451 N. Reese Place, Burbank CA 91506. (818)563-1030. Fax: (818)563-2826. Contact: Paul Filippone. Management firm. Represents individual artists, groups and

‡ **THE DOUBLE DAGGER** before a listing indicates that the listing is new in this edition.

songwriters from anywhere; currently handles 7 acts. Receives 15-20% commission.
How to Contact: Submit demo tape by mail. Unsolicited submissions are OK. Prefers cassette, DAT or VHS videocassette with 4 songs. If seeking management, press kit should include photo, bio and press, "although none of this is very important compared to the tape." Does not return material. Reports in 1-2 months (artist should call).
Music: Mostly **alternative rock**, **rock** and **folk/acoustic**; also **all types**. Works primarily with bands. Current acts include Ice-T (rapper, Rhyme Syndicate Records), Body Count (hard rock band, Virgin Records), Silver Jet (rock/pop band, Virgin Records), Jimmy Eat World (band, Capitol Records), Agnes Gooch (band, Revolution Records), Spain (band, Restless Records) and Jacob Marley's Ghost (band, Capitol Records).

‡RHYTHMIC TEMPLE ENTERTAINMENT INC., 3315 E. Russell Rd., Suite H-117, Las Vegas NV 89120. (800)243-2189. Fax: (702)451-4809. Vice President: Steve Buckley. Management firm and record producer. Estab. 1993. Represents individual artists and groups from anywhere; currently handles 3 acts. Receives 10-20% commission. Reviews material for acts.
How to Contact: Submit demo tape by mail. Unsolicited submissions are OK. Prefers cassette or VHS videocassette. If seeking management, press kit should include cassette or CD, bio and pictures. Does not return material. Reports in 1-2 months.
Music: Mostly **R&B**, **pop** and **gospel**; also **rap** and **contemporary Christian**. Current acts include Biscuit and Mr. Freeze.

JOEY RICCA, JR.'S ENTERTAINMENT AGENCY, 408 S. Main St., Milltown NJ 08850. (201)287-1230. Owner/President: Joseph Frank Ricca, Jr. Management firm and booking agency. Estab. 1985. Represents individual artists, groups and songwriters; currently handles 80 acts. Receives 10-15% commission. Reviews material for acts.
How to Contact: Write for permission to submit. "We prefer that all material be copyrighted and that a letter be sent right before submitting material, but neither of these is essential." Prefers cassette or videocassette with 3-4 songs and lyric or lead sheets. If seeking management, press kit should include tape (cassette, CD or video) 8×10 promo photo, bios, lead and lyric sheets and photocopy news clippings of performances. SASE. Reports in 6-8 weeks.
Music: Mostly **love songs/ballads**, **songs for big band vocalists**, and **soft jazz/Latin**; also **good commercial material**. Works with show bands, dance bands and bar bands. Current acts include Stewart Ward, Donny "Z" and Angela Murcurri.
Tips: "Good lyrics and strong musical arrangements are essential if our vocalists are to select a song they would like to sing. I look for good love songs, ballads and Broadway play type compositions. No metal."

‡RICH & FAMOUS MANAGEMENT, INC., 267 Park Place, Brooklyn NY 11238. (718)638-6950. Fax: (718)638-2879. Directors of A&R: Richard Levine and Mary Logswell. Management firm. Estab. 1983. Represents individual artists and groups from anywhere; currently handles 3 acts. Receives 15% commission.
How to Contact: Submit demo tape by mail. Unsolicited submissions are OK. Prefers cassette, VHS videocassette, CD and lyric sheet. "Send anything you feel is appropriate." Does not return material. Reports in 4-5 weeks.
Music: Mostly **alternative rock**, **folk rock** and **country**. Current acts include Jolene (roots rock), John Crooke (singer/songwriter) and Hard Soul Poets (alternative rock).

DIANE RICHARDS WORLD MANAGEMENT, INC., 530 Manhattan Ave., New York NY 10027. Phone/fax: (212)663-6730. E-mail: drworldmgm@aol.com. President: Diane Richards. Management firm. Estab. 1994. Represents individual artists, groups, songwriters and producers from anywhere; currently handles 3 acts. Receives 20-25% commission. Reviews material for acts.
How to Contact: Write first and obtain permission to submit. If seeking management, press kit should include photograph, biography, cassette tape, telephone number and address. Does not return material. Reports only if there is an interest in signing artist to company.
Music: Mostly **dance**, **pop** and **rap**; also **New Age**, **A/C** and **jazz**. Works primarily with pop and dance acts, and songwriters who also are recording artists. Current acts include Sappho (songwriter/artist), Menace (songwriter/producer/artist) and Big L (rap artist on Columbia Records).

RIOHCAT MUSIC, P.O. Box 764, Hendersonville TN 37077-0764. (615)824-9313. E-mail: tachoir@cris.com. Website: http://www.cris.com/~tachoir. Contact: Robert Kayne. Management firm, booking agency, record company (Avita Records) and music publisher. Estab. 1975. Represents individual artists and groups; currently handles 4 acts. Receives 20% commission. Reviews material for acts.

How to Contact: Submit demo tape by mail. Unsolicited submissions are OK. Prefers cassette and lead sheet. Does not return material. Reports in 1 month.
Music: Mostly **contemporary jazz** and **fusion**. Works primarily with jazz ensembles. Current acts include Group Tachoir (jazz), Tachoir Duo (jazz) and Jerry Tachoir (jazz).

ROCK OF AGES PRODUCTIONS, 517 Northlake Blvd. #4, N. Palm Beach FL 33408. (561)848-1500. Fax: (561)848-2400. President/Agency Director: Joe Larson. Booking agent. Estab. 1980. Represents individual artists and groups from anywhere. Currently handles 500 acts. Receives 15-25% commission. Reviews material for acts.
How to Contact: Submit demo tape by mail. Unsolicited submissions are OK. Prefers cassette or VHS videocassette with 3 or more songs and lead sheet. If seeking management, press kit should include videocassette and/or audio cassette, relevant press and bio, including recent photo. SASE. Reports in 3 months.
Music: Mostly **top 40**, **country/western** and **rock**; also **gospel** and **opera**. Works primarily with bands, singers, singer/songwriters. Current acts include Andrew Epps (ballad singer/songwriter), John Michael Ferrari (singer/songwriter) and Paola Semprini (opera star).

CHARLES R. ROTHSCHILD PRODUCTIONS INC., 330 E. 48th St., New York NY 10017. (212)421-0592. President: Charles R. Rothschild. Booking agency. Estab. 1971. Represents local, regional and international individual artists, groups and songwriters; currently handles 22 acts. Receives 25% commission. Reviews material for acts.
How to Contact: Call first and obtain permission to submit. Prefers cassette, CD or VHS videocassette with 1 song and lyric and lead sheet. If seeking management, include cassette, photo, bio and reviews. SASE. Reports in 4-6 weeks.
Music: Mostly **rock**, **pop** and **folk**; also **country** and **jazz**. Current acts include Judy Collins (pop singer/songwriter), Leo Kottke (guitarist/composer), Emmylou Harris (country songwriter), David Grover (kid's performer and folksinger) and John Forster (satirist).

RUSTRON MUSIC PRODUCTIONS, Send all artist song submissions to: 1156 Park Lane, West Palm Beach FL 33417-5957. (516)686-1354. Main Office: 42 Barrack Hill Rd., Ridgefield CT 06877. ("Main office does not review new material—only South Florida Branch office does.") Artist Consultants: Rusty Gordon and Davilyn Whims. Composition Management: Ron Caruso. Management firm, booking agency, music publisher (Rustron Music Publishers/BMI and Whimsong Publishing/ASCAP), record company and record producer. Estab. 1970. Represents individuals, groups and songwriters; currently handles 25 acts. Receives 10-25% commission. Reviews material for acts.

- See Rustron's listings in the Music Publishers, Record Companies and Record Producers sections.

How to Contact: Submit demo tape by mail. Unsolicited submissions are OK. Send cassette with 3-6 songs (CD/cassette produced for sale preferred). Provide lyric or lead sheet for every song in the submission. "SASE required for all correspondence." Reports in 4 months.
Music: Blues (country folk/urban, Southern), **country (rock, blues, progressive)**, **easy listening**, **soft rock (ballads)**, **women's music**, **R&B**, **folk/rock**, **New Age instrumentals** and **New Age folk fusion**. Current acts include Gary Jess (New Age fusion), Jayne Margo-Reby (adult contemporary fusion), Boom Slang Swampsinger (country/folk, road house music), Star Smiley (country) and Cilla Smith (pop).
Tips: "Send cover letter, typed lyric sheets for all songs. Carefully mix demo, don't drown the vocals, 3-6 songs in a submission. Prefer independent CD/cassette (store-ready product). Send photo if artist is seeking marketing and/or production assistance. Very strong hooks, definitive melody, evolved concepts, unique and unpredictable themes. Flesh out a performing sound unique to the artist."

S.T.A.R.S. PRODUCTIONS, 1 Professional Quadrangle, 2nd Floor, Sparta NJ 07871. (201)729-7242. Fax: (201)729-2979. President: Steve Tarkanish. Booking agency. Estab. 1983. Represents individual artists, groups, songwriters from anywhere; currently handles 35-40 acts. Receives 15-20% commission. Reviews material for acts.
How to Contact: Submit demo tape by mail. Unsolicited submissions are OK. Prefers cassette with lyric or lead sheet. If seeking management, press kit should include biography, photo, cassette, video, calendar and song list. Does not return material. Reports in 2 months.
Music: Mostly **rock**, **alternative** and **country**; also **singles/duos** and **folk**. Primarily works with bands. Current acts include The Nerds (classic/party rock), Yasgurs Farm (Woodstock-era rock), Dog Voices (classic/alternative rock) and Soft Parade (Doors tribute).

SAFFYRE MANAGEMENT, 1200 Riverside Dr., Suite 371, Burbank CA 91506. (818)842-4368. Fax: (310)453-4478. President: Esta G. Bernstein. Management firm. Estab. 1990. Represents individual artists, groups and songwriters from anywhere; currently handles 3 acts. Receives 10% commission. Reviews material for acts.

How to Contact: Submit demo tape by mail. Unsolicited submissions are OK. Prefers cassette, bio and photos with 3 songs and lyric sheet. Does not return material. Reports in 2 weeks (only if interested).
Music: Mostly **rock**, **top 40** and **jazz**; also **new wave** and **metal**. "We work only with bands and solo artists who write their own material; our main objective is to obtain recording deals and contracts, while advising our artists on their careers and business relationships." Current artists include JÖW (top 40 funk/rock), Art Ashes (jazz instrumentalist) and Scott Moss (top 40 singer/songwriter).

‡ST. JOHN ARTISTS, P.O. Box 619, Neenah WI 54957-0619. (920)722-2222. Fax: (920)725-2405. Website: http://www.St.John-Artists.com/. Owner: Jon St. John. Booking agency. Estab. 1977. Represents local and regional individual artists and groups; currently handles 15-20 acts. Receives 15-20% commission. Reviews material for acts.
How to Contact: Write first and obtain permission to submit. Prefers cassette or VHS videocassette. If seeking management, press kit should include picures, song lists, audio and audio visual and bio. Does not return material.
Music: Mostly **rock** and **MOR**. Current acts include Vic Ferrari Band (variety rock) and Torpedoes (show and variety rock).

SA'MALL MANAGEMENT, P.O. Box 8442, Universal City CA 91608. (818)506-8533. Fax: (818)506-8534. Manager: Nikki Ray. Management firm, music publisher (Pollybyrd Publications) and record company (PPL Entertainment Group). Estab. 1990. Represents local, regional and international individual artists, groups and songwriters; currently handles 5 acts. Receives 25% commission. Reviews material for acts.

- See the listings for Pollybyrd Publications in the Music Publishers section and PPL Entertainment Group in the Record Companies section.

How to Contact: Write or call first and obtain permission to submit. Prefers cassette with 2 songs and lyric and lead sheet. If seeking management, press kit should include picture, bio and tape. SASE. Reports in 2 months.
Music: **All types**. Current acts include I.B. Phyne, Suzette Cuseo, The Band Aka and LeJenz.

CRAIG SCOTT ENTERTAINMENT, P.O. Box 1722, Paramus NJ 07653-1722. (201)587-1066. Fax: (201)587-0481. E-mail: csent@mail.idt.net. Management firm. Estab. 1985. Represents individual artists and/or groups from anywhere; currently handles 3 acts. Commission varies. Reviews material for acts.
How to Contact: Submit demo tape by mail. Unsolicited submissions are OK. Prefers cassette. If seeking management, press kit should include tape/CD, bio, picture, relevant press. Does not return material. Reports in 3-4 weeks.
Music: Current acts include The Apples In Stereo (alternative), The Lilys (alternative) and Tom Gioia (songwriter/artist).

‡SEA CRUISE PRODUCTIONS, INC., P.O. Box 1875, Gretna LA 70054-1875. (504)392-4615. Fax: (504)392-4512. President/General Manager: Ken Keene. Management firm, booking agency, music publisher (Sea Cruise Music/BMI), record company (Briarmeade Records) and record producer (Sea Cruise Productions, Inc.). Estab. 1970. Represents individual artists, groups and songwriters from anywhere; currently handles 12 acts. Receives 15% commission. Reviews material for acts.
How to Contact: Submit demo tape by mail. Unsolicited submissions are OK. Prefers cassette or VHS videocassette with 5-6 songs and lyric or lead sheet. If seeking management, press kit should include cassette, videocassette, publicity photos, bio and press clipping copies. Does not return material. "No phone calls." Reports in 2-4 weeks "if we are interested in the act."
Music: Mostly **nostalgia '50s/'60s**, **country rock** and **R&B**; also **ballads**, **double entendre** and **novelty songs**. "Most of our acts are '50s, '60s and '70s artists, all of whom have had million selling records, and who are still very active on the concert/night club circuit." Current acts include Frankie Ford (legendary rock 'n' roll singer/pianist), Troy Shondell (singer/songwriter) and Jean Knight (Grammy nominated R&B singer).

SECRET AGENT ENTERTAINMENT GROUP, LTD., 6351 W. Montrose, Suite 333, Chicago IL 60634. (312)458-9888. Fax: (312)697-6380. E-mail: agent@ripro.com. Contact: Agent. Management firm. Estab. 1994. Represents individual artists, groups and songwriters from anywhere. Currently handles 5 acts. Receives 20% commission.
How to Contact: Submit demo tape by mail. Unsolicited submissions are OK. Prefers cassette or DAT with 2 songs and lyric sheet. If seeking management, press kit should include history of act. Does not return material. Reports in 1 month.
Music: **All types**. Current acts include Pete Special (pop/R&B) and Batteries Not Included (pop).

WILLIAM SEIP MANAGEMENT, INC., 1615 Highland Rd., W. Kitchener, Ontario N2N 3K5 **Canada**. (519)741-1252. Fax: (519)742-3398. Manager: William Seip. Management firm. Estab. 1978. Represents individual artists, groups, songwriters from anywhere; currently handles 3 acts. Receives 15-20% commission. Reviews material for acts.
How to Contact: Submit demo tape by mail. Unsolicited submissions are OK. Prefers cassette or videocassette and lyric sheet. If seeking management, press kit should include tape, lyric sheet, bio and photo. Does not return material. Reports in 2 months.
Music: Mostly **rock** and **country**. Current acts include Helix, Ray Lyell and The Result.

‡SENDYK, LEONARD & CO. INC., 8439 Sunset Blvd. #405, W. Hollywood CA 90069. (213)656-9484. Fax: (213)656-8143. Partner: Gerri Leonard. Business management. Represents individual artists, groups and songwriters from anywhere. Receives 5% commission.
How to Contact: "We do not solicit any songwriters for works to be submitted to artists, but are certainly interested in representing songwriters with respect to their financial affairs. We can also monitor their royalties; we have an extensive royalty administration department."
Music: Current acts include Marilyn Manson, Stevie Nicks and Perry Farrell/Porno for Pyros.

SEPETYS ENTERTAINMENT GROUP, 1223 Wilshire Blvd., Suite 804, Santa Monica CA 90403. Fax: (310)581-9353. E-mail: sepetys@aol.com. President: Ruta E. Sepetys. Management firm. Estab. 1994. Represents individual artists, groups and songwriters from anywhere; currently handles 4 acts. Receives 15% commission. Reviews material for acts.
How to Contact: Write first and obtain permission to submit or to arrange personal interview. Prefers cassette with lyric sheet. If seeking management, press kit should include press clips, tape, lyrics, bio and photo. "No phone calls please." Does not return material. Reports in 1 month.
Music: All types. Works primarily with bands, singer/songwriters and individual artists. Current acts include Steve Vai (guitarist on Epic Records), Lit (band on Malicious Vinyl/Red Ant Records), Danny Peck (singer/songwriter) and Hair of the Dog (rock band).

SERGE ENTERTAINMENT GROUP, P.O. Box 672216, Marietta GA 30006-0037. (770)850-9560. Fax: (770)850-9646. E-mail: musmorsels@aol.com. President: Sandy Serge. Management firm and shopping firm/songplugger. Estab. 1987. Represents individual artists, groups, songwriters from anywhere; currently handles 20 acts. Receives 15-25% commission.
How to Contact: Submit demo tape or CD by mail. Unsolicited submissions are OK. Prefers cassette, CD or VHS videocassette (press kit optional) with 4 songs and lyric sheet. If seeking management, press kit should include 8×10 photo, bio, max of 4 press clips, VHS videocassette, performance schedule and demo tape. "All information submitted must include name, address and phone number on each item." Does not return material. Reports in 4-6 weeks.
Music: Mostly **rock**, **pop** and **country**; also **R&B** and **New Age**. Works primarily with singer/songwriters and bands. Current acts include The Steve Grimm Band (rock), Masino (hard rock band), Andrew Elt (rock), Jesse Graham (R&B) and Kelly Jo Keaton (country).
Tips: "We have acquired numerous publishing deals for all clients. Member of NARAS, Atlanta Songwriters Association, Songwriters of Wisconsin. We have professional relationships with over 300 publishers and have connections at all the major labels."

THE SEWITT GROUP, 17 Ash Court, Highland Mills NY 10930. (914)928-8481. Fax: (914)928-8463. President: George Sewitt. Management and consulting firm. Estab. 1983. Represents individual artists, groups and songwriters from anywhere; currently handles 2 acts. Receives 20-25% commission. Reviews material for acts.
How to Contact: Write or call first and obtain permission to submit demo. Prefers cassette or VHS videocassette with 3 songs and lyric sheet, and photo. "Quality of material is far more important than production values." Does not return material. Reports in 6 weeks.
Music: Mostly **rock**, **pop** and **country**; also **soul/R&B**, **rap** and **heavy metal**. Works primarily with solo artists, bands and singer/songwriters. Current acts include Ace Frehley (singer/guitarist) and Peter Criss (singer/drummer).

SHANKMAN DEBLASIO MELINA, INC./SUNSET BLVD. ENTERTAINMENT, 740 N. La Brea Ave., 1st Floor, Los Angeles CA 90038. (213)933-9977. Fax: (213)933-0633. E-mail: sbe740@earthlink.net. Contact: A&R Manager. Management firm, music publisher and record company. Estab. 1979. Represents individual artists, groups, songwriters from anywhere. Reviews material for acts.
How to Contact: Write first and obtain permission to submit. Prefers cassette with lyric sheet. Does not return material. Reports in 3 months.

SHAPIRO & COMPANY, C.P.A. (A Professional Corporation), 9229 Sunset Blvd., Suite 607, Los Angeles CA 90069. (310)278-2303. Certified Public Accountant: Charles H. Shapiro. Business management firm. Estab. 1979. Represents individual recording artists, groups and songwriters. Fee varies.
How to Contact: Write or call first to arrange personal interview.
Music: Mostly **rock** and **pop**. Works primarily with recording artists as business manager.
Tips: "We assist songwriters with administration of publishing."

PHILL SHUTE MANAGEMENT PTY. LTD., Box 273, Dulwich Hill NSW 2203 **Australia**. Phone: (02)5692152. Managing Director: Phill Shute. Management firm, booking agency and record company (Big Rock Records). Estab. 1979. Represents local individual artists and groups; currently handles 8 acts. Receives 10% commission. Reviews material for acts.

- See the listing for Big Rock Pty. Ltd. in the Record Companies section.

How to Contact: Write first and obtain permission to submit. Prefers cassette with 4 songs and lyric sheet. SASE. Reports in 2 months.
Music: Mostly **rock**, **pop** and **R&B**; also **country rock**. Works primarily with rock bands, pop vocalists and blues acts (band and vocalists). Current acts include The Lips (show band), Collage (pop/rock band) and Adam Carl Stephens (guitarist).
Tips: "Make all submissions well organized (e.g. bio, photo and experience of the act). List areas in which the act would like to work, complete details for contact."

SIDDONS & ASSOCIATES, 584 N. Larchmont Blvd., Hollywood CA 90004. (213)462-6156. Fax: (213)462-2076. President: Bill Siddons. Management firm. Estab. 1972. Represents individual artists and groups from anywhere; currently handles 4 acts. Reviews material for acts.
How to Contact: Write first and obtain permission to submit a demo. Prefers cassette or VHS videocassette with 3 songs and lyric sheet. If seeking management, press kit should include cassette of 3 songs, lyric sheet, VHS videocassette if available, biography, past credits and discography. Does not return material. Reports in 2 months.
Music: **All styles**. Current acts include Jonathan Butler and Elayne Boosler.

SIEGEL ENTERTAINMENT LTD., 101-1648 W. Seventh Ave., Vancouver British Columbia V6J 1S5 **Canada**. (604)736-3896. Fax: (604)736-3464. E-mail: jdudley@direct.ca. President: Robert Siegel. Management firm and booking agency. Estab. 1975. Represents individual artists, groups and songwriters from anywhere; currently handles 100 acts (for bookings). Receives 15-20% commission. Reviews material for acts.
How to Contact: Submit demo tape by mail. Unsolicited submissions are OK. Prefers cassette or VHS videocassette with 3 songs and lyric sheet. If seeking management, press kit should include 8×10 and cassette and/or video. Does not return material. Reports in 1 month.
Music: Mostly **rock**, **pop** and **country**; also **children's**. Current acts include Falcon Scream (rock group), Michael Behm (rock/pop) and Tim Brecht (pop/children's).

SILVER BOW MANAGEMENT, 6260 130 St., Surrey, British Columbia V3X 1R6 **Canada**. (604)572-4232. Fax: (604)572-4252. E-mail: 75321.3576@compuserve.com. or saddles@uniserve.com. Website: http://home.xl.ca/aadesign/ssi.htm. CEO: Candice James. Management firm, music publisher (Saddlestone Publishing, Silver Bow Publishing), record company (Saddlestone Records) and record producer (Silver Bow Productions, Krazy Cat Productions). Estab. 1988. Represents individual artists, groups, songwriters from anywhere; currently handles 8 acts. Receives 10-20% commission. Reviews material for acts.

- See the listings for Saddlestone Publishing in the Music Publishers section and Silver Bow Productions in the Record Producers section.

How to Contact: Submit demo tape by mail. Unsolicited submissions are OK. Prefers cassette with 3 songs and lyric sheet. If seeking management, press kit should include 8×10 photo, bio, demo tape or CD with lyric sheets and current itinerary. "Visuals are everything—submit accordingly." SASE. Reports in 2 months.
Music: Mostly **country**, **pop** and **rock**; also **R&B**, **Christian** and **alternative**. Works primarily with bands, vocalists and singer/songwriters. Current acts include Aaron Roland, 400, Shade of Earth and Darrell Meyers, Gerry King and Stan Giles.

‡SIMCO AND ASSOCIATES, 2165 Ridgemont Dr., Los Angeles CA 90046-1839. (213)656-4771. Fax: (213)656-0414. A&R Scout: Mark Banks. Management firm. Estab. 1995. Represents local and regional (Western region including Southwest) individual artists, groups and songwriters; currently handles 8 acts. Receives 15-20% commission. Reviews material for acts.
How to Contact: Write first and obtain permission to submit. Prefers cassette or VHS videocassette with

3 songs. If seeking management, press kit should include head shot or group shot photo, bio, reviews, videocassette of permformance, cassette (demo) and 11×14 SASE. Reports in 4-6 weeks.
Music: All types. Works primarily with single artists. Current acts include Lisa Lauren (A/C), Daniella (acid jazz), Julia Hunter (country/pop) and Ellen Anderson (rock).

SIMMONS MANAGEMENT GROUP, P.O. Box 18711, Raleigh NC 27619. (919)832-2090. Fax: (919)832-0690. President: Harry Simmons. Management firm and music publisher. Represents producers, artists, groups and songwriters; currently handles 7 acts. Receives 15-20% commission. Reviews material for acts.
How to Contact: Write or call first and obtain permission to submit. Prefers cassette, DAT or VHS videocassette of performance with 3-6 songs and lyric sheet; also submit promotional material, photos and clippings. "Videocassette does not have to be professional. Any information helps." If seeking management, include 3-song demo (tape or DAT) and photos in press kit. Does not return material. Reports in 6 weeks.
Music: Mostly **modern pop**; also **modern rock**, **rock**, **metal**, **R&B**, **industrial** and **top 40/pop**. Works primarily with "original music recording acts or those that aspire to be." Current acts include Don Dixon (producer, songwriter and recording artist), Marti Jones (recording artist), Jim Brock (recording artist), Terry Anderson (songwriter, recording artist), Mark Williams (producer), Jim Wann (songwriter, recording artist) and The Veldt (recording artists).

SINGERMANAGEMENT, INC., 161 W. 54th St., Suite 1403, New York NY 10019. (212)757-1217. President: Robert Singerman. Management consulting firm. Estab. 1982. Represents local, regional or international individual artists and groups; currently handles 10-15 acts. Receives 5% commission. Reviews material for acts.
How to Contact: Submit demo tape by mail. Unsolicited submissions are OK. Prefers cassette or VHS videocassette. If seeking management consultation, include tape, lyric sheet, video (if available) and bio in press kit. Does not return material. Reports in 3 weeks.
Music: Current acts include Lach ("anti-folk" songwriter), Gary Lucas (guitar/vocals) and The Young Gods (industrial).

SIRIUS ENTERTAINMENT, 13531 Clairmont Way #8, Oregon City OR 97045-8450. (503)657-1813. E-mail: danblair@teleport.com. Website: http://www.teleport.com/~luckylg. Owners: Dan Blair, Rhonda Ellis. Management firm and booking agency. Estab. 1991. Represents individual artists and/or groups and songwriters from anywhere; currently handles 22 acts. Receives 10-15% commission. Reviews material for acts.
How to Contact: Submit demo tape by mail. Unsolicited submissions are OK. Prefers cassette with 3 songs and lyric sheet. If seeking management, press kit should include 8×10 photo, résumé, CD or cassette, video if available, copies of press releases, a list of past performances and credits. "Résumé should include total career progress from beginning with all schooling listed." SASE. Reports in 2-3 weeks.
Music: Mostly **R&B** and **rock**; also **jazz**, **blues** and **classical**. Current acts include Dorothy Moore (R&B/blues), Doro and Morre (Americana) and Mac Charles (A/C rock).
Tips: "If you can't afford the services of a good studio and good studio musicians to play your material, then use one acoustic instrument (guitar or piano). Send lyric sheet with original material."

SIROCCO PRODUCTIONS, INC., 5660 E. Virgina Beach Blvd., #104, Norfolk VA 23502. (757)461-8987. Fax: (757)461-4669. Contact: Leonard A. Swann, Jr.. Management firm. Estab. 1991. Represents groups from anywhere; currently handles 4 acts. Commission varies. Reviews material for acts.

- See the listings for Pen Cob Publishing in the Music Publishers section and Trumpeter Records in the Record Companies section.

How to Contact: Write first to obtain permission to submit and arrange personal interview. Prefers VHS videocassette. If seeking management, press kit should include video, audio cassette, bio, songlist, publicity material, photos and reviews. SASE.
Music: Mostly **alternative**. Current acts include On Beyond Zee, Sea of Souls, The Mundahs and Egypt.

TO HELP YOU UNDERSTAND and use the information in these listings, see "How to Use *Songwriter's Market* to Get Your Songs Heard," on page 3.

T. SKORMAN PRODUCTIONS, INC., 3660 Maguire Blvd., Suite 250, Orlando FL 32803. (407)895-3000. Fax: (407)895-1422. E-mail: ted@talentagency.com. Website: http://www.talentagency.com. President: Ted Skorman. Management firm and booking agency. Estab. 1983. Represents groups; currently handles 40 acts. Receives 10-25% commission. Reviews material for acts.
How to Contact: Call first for permission to send tape. Prefers cassette with 3 songs, or videocassette of no more than 15 minutes. "Live performance—no trick shots or editing tricks. We want to be able to view act as if we were there for a live show." SASE. Reports in 6 weeks.
Music: **Top 40**, **techno**, **dance**, **MOR** and **pop**. Works primarily with high-energy dance acts, recording acts, and top 40 bands. Current acts include Rusty Rose (R&B/pop), Ravyn Dixon (country), Michelle Lynn (country), Dana Kamide (rock) and Big Daddy (R&B).
Tips: "We have many pop recording acts, and are looking for commercial material for their next albums."

‡SLATUS MANAGEMENT, 208 E. 51st St., Suite 151, New York NY 10022. (212)866-5371. E-mail: cpwrecds@aol.com. Manager: Teddy Slatus. Management firm and record company (CPW Records). Estab. 1981. Represents individual artists and groups from anywhere; currently handles 2 acts. Reviews material for acts.
How to Contact: Submit demo tape by mail. Unsolicited submissions are OK. Prefers cassette. If seeking management, press kit should include picture of artist, cassette and discography if available. "If Slatus Management does not contact you within 60 days we have passed!" Does not return material. Reports in 2 months.
Music: Mostly **rock** and **blues**. Current acts include Johnny Winter.

GARY SMELTZER PRODUCTIONS, 603 W. 13th #2A, Austin TX 78701. (512)478-6020. Fax: (512)472-3850. Contacts: Gary Smeltzer/James Cruz/Don Torosian. Management firm and booking agency. Estab. 1967. Represents individual artists and groups from anywhere. "We book about 100 different bands each year—none are exclusive." Receives 20% commission. Reviews material for acts.
How to Contact: Submit demo tape by mail. Unsolicited submissions are OK. Prefers cassette, videocassette or CD. If seeking management, press kit should include cassette or CD, bio, picture. Does not return material. Reports in 2 weeks.
Music: Mostly **alternative**, **R&B** and **country**. Current acts include Ro Tel & the Hot Tomatoes (nostalgic '60s showband), Apollo Soul (nostalgic '60s-'90s showband) and Lunar Sue (alternative).
Tips: "We prefer performing songwriters that can gig their music as a solo or group."

SOUND AND SERENITY MANAGEMENT, P.O. Box 22105, Nashville TN 37202. (615)731-3100. Fax: (615)731-3005. E-mail: jyoke@edge.net. Management firm. Represents individual artists from anywhere; currently handles 3 acts. Receives standard commission.
How to Contact: Call first and obtain permission to submit a demo. Prefers cassette with lyric sheet. If seeking management, press kit should include photo, bio, press clippings and cassette. Does not return material; will reply with SASE. Reports in 3 months.
Music: Mostly **country**, **Americana**. Works primarily with individual artists. Current acts include Ken Mellons (traditional country singer/songwriter), Kevin Sharp (contemporary country singer/songwriter), Gene Watson (country singer/songwriter) and Jo'el Sonnier.

SOUND '86 TALENT MANAGEMENT, P.O. Box 222, Black Hawk SD 57718. Management firm. Estab. 1974. Represents 10 artists and groups. Receives 20% commission. Reviews material for acts.
How to Contact: Submit demo tape by mail. Unsolicited submissions are OK. Prefers cassette or professional VHS videocassette with 3-8 songs and lyric sheet. If seeking management, press kit should include tape, publicity, picture and any other promo information. SASE. Reports in 1 month.
Music: **Rock** (all types); also **bluegrass**, **country**, **dance**, **easy listening** and **top 40/pop**. Works primarily with single artists. Current artists include Bold Lightning (roadhouse blues band) and Hot Rod Dee Luxx.

‡SOUND MANAGEMENT, 328 Flatbush Ave., Suite 252, Brooklyn NY 11238. E-mail: 104726.3603@compuserve.com. Owner/Manager: Tiffany Barsotti. Management firm. Estab. 1989. Represents individual artists, groups and songwriters from anywhere; currently handles 2 acts. Receives 15% commission. Reviews material for acts.
How to Contact: Call first and obtain permission to submit. Prefers cassette, bio or discography with lyric or lead sheet. If seeking management, press kit should include bio, photo, demo cassette or CD, video tape wherever possible. "Everything should be of the best quality. A cover letter giving some background on your musical development, capabilities, influences would be good." SASE. Reports in 6 months "depending on artist."
Music: Mostly **jazz**, **A/C** and **pop**; also **rock**, **country** and **spoken word-poetry**. Works primarily with

vocalists, musicians, producers, songwriters and bands. Current acts include Dianne Reeves (jazz singer) and Jacky Terrasson (jazz pianist).

‡SOUTHEASTERN ATTRACTIONS, 120 Vulcan Rd., Birmingham AL 35209. (205)942-6600. Fax: (205)942-7700. Contact: Agent. Booking agency. Estab. 1967. Represents groups from anywhere; currently handles 200 acts. Receives 20% commission.
How to Contact: Submit demo tape by mail. Unsolicited submissions are OK. Prefers cassette or VHS videocassette. Does not return material. Reports in 2 weeks.
Music: Mostly **rock**, **alternative** and **oldies**; also **country**. Works primarily with bands. Current acts include Second Hand Jive (contemporary rock), Telluride (Southern rock) and Undergrounders (variety to contemporary).

‡SOUTHERN NIGHTS ENTERTAINMENT, 2707 N. Andrews Ave., Ft. Lauderdale FL 33311. (954)563-4000. Fax: (954)563-4763. President: Dick Barten. Management firm and booking agency. Estab. 1976. Represents local and regional groups from South Florida; currently handles 30 acts. Receives 15-20% commission. Reviews material for acts.
How to Contact: Write first and obtain permission to submit or to arrange personal interview. Prefers cassette or videocassette with 10 songs, songs list and pictures. If seeking management, press kit should include background bio, audio tape and pictures. "Make sure what you submit represents what you do best. You will not get a second chance too often!" Does not return material. Reports in 2 weeks.
Music: Mostly **top 40**, **rock** and **A/C**; also **alternative**. Works primarily with bands, current dance top 40, classic rock and some alternative. Current acts include In Flyght (dance top 40), Baja Live (dance, rock) and Mad Hatter (classic rock).

SP TALENT ASSOCIATES, P.O. Box 475184, Garland TX 75047. Talent Coordinator: Richard Park. Management firm and booking agency. Represents individual artists and groups; currently handles 7 acts. Receives 15% commission. Reviews material for acts.
How to Contact: Submit demo tape by mail. Unsolicited submissions are OK. Prefers VHS videocassette with several songs. Send photo and bio. Does not return material. Reports back as soon as possible.
Music: Mostly **rock**, **nostalgia rock** and **country**; also **specialty acts** and **folk/blues**. Works primarily with vocalists and self-contained groups. Current acts include Joe Hardin Brown (country), Rock It! (nostalgia), Renewal (rock group) and Juan Madera & the Supple Grain Seeds.

‡SPLENDOR PRODUCTIONS, INC., P.O. Box 521776, Longwood FL 32752. Fax: (407)339-3826. E-mail: spicmi@aol.com. Contact: Submission Department. Management firm, booking agency and music publisher (Great Sweetwater). Represents individual artists and groups from anywhere; currently handles 4 acts. Receives variable commission. Reviews material for acts.
How to Contact: Write first and obtain permission to submit. Prefers cassette or VHS videocassette with 3 or less songs. If seeking management, press kit should include "absolutely everything you have that's great. This is a sell job . . . so sell us!" Does not return material. Reports in 2-4 weeks.
Music: Mostly **gospel/Christian**, **contemporary** and **inspirational**. Current acts include Larnelle Harris (gospel music male vocalist), The Spurrlows (Christian contemporary group) and Dan Oxley (trumpeter).

SQUAD 16, P.O. Box 65, Wilbraham MA 01095. (413)599-1456. E-mail: thesquad16@aol.com. President: Tom Najemy. Booking agency. Estab. 1990. Represents individual artists, groups and songwriters; currently handles 16 acts. Specializes in the college marketplace. Receives 20% commission. Reviews material for acts.
How to Contact: Submit demo tape by mail. Unsolicited submissions are OK. Prefers CD. SASE. Reports in 6 weeks.
Music: Mostly **contemporary**, **funk/hiphop**, **rock**, **reggae**, **world beat** and **jazz & blues**; also **contemporary rock**, **funk**, or **dance bands** and **acoustic performers**. Current acts include Chuck (funk/hip hop/rap), Letters to Cleo (alternative), 22 Brides (rock), The Mighty Charge (reggae), Waiting Rates (rock), Conehead Buddha (ska), The Allstonians (ska) and Orbit (rock).

STAIRCASE PROMOTION, P.O. Box 211, East Prairie MO 63845. (573)649-2211. President: Tommy Loomas. Vice President: Joe Silver. Management firm, music publisher (Lineage Publishing) and record company (Capstan Record Production). Estab. 1975. Represents individual artists and groups from anywhere; currently handles 6 acts. Receives 25% commission. Reviews material for acts.

- See the listings for Lineage Publishing in the Music Publishers section and Capstan Record Production in the Record Companies section.

How to Contact: Submit demo tape by mail. Unsolicited submissions are OK. Prefers cassette with 3

songs and lyric sheet. If seeking management, press kit should include bio, photo, audio cassette and/or video and press reviews, if any. "Be as professional as you can." SASE. Reports in 2 months.
Music: Mostly **country**, **pop** and **easy listening**; also **rock**, **gospel** and **alternative**. Current acts include Skidrow Joe (country comedian, on Capstan Records), Vicarie Arcoleo (pop singer, on Treasure Coast Records) and Bobby Lee Morgan (rock singer, on Capstan Records).

STANDER ENTERTAINMENT, 6309 Ben Ave., N. Hollywood CA 91606. Phone/fax: (818)769-6365. E-mail: stander@earthlink.net. Manager: Jacqueline Stander. Management firm, music publisher (DocRon Publishing), record company (Soaring Records) and consulting firm. Estab. 1970. Represents local individual artists, groups and songwriters; currently handles 6 acts. Receives 15-20% commission. Reviews material for acts.
How to Contact: Call first and obtain permission to submit. Prefers cassette or VHS videocassette with 3-5 songs and lyric sheet. If seeking management, press kit should include photo, bio, press publicity, CD or cassette. Does not return material. Reports in 3 weeks.
Music: Mostly **jazz**, **pop** and **R&B** (no rap); also **world music** and **Broadway**. Works primarily with national recording artists, film composers and singer/songwriters. Current acts include Bill Cunliffe (jazz pianist/producer), Jazz at the Movies Band (jazz group), Freddie Ravel (contemporary Latin jazz keyboardist), Gregg Karukas (NAC jazz keyboardist/producer), Lauren Wood (vocalist/songwriter) and Ruby (blues singer).
Tips: "Always looking for long term professionals who have worked to establish themselves in their market, yet want to go to the next level. For those who have something to offer and are just starting out, I am available for consulting by phone or in person. Please call for submission request."

STAR ARTIST MANAGEMENT INC., P.O. Box 114, Fraser MI 48026. Phone/fax: (810)979-5115. E-mail: gtaxman@aol.com. Director of Canadian Operations: Brian Courtis. Director of West Coast Operations: Lindsey Feldman. Director of East Coast Operations: Nat Weiss. Management firm (business and personal). Estab. 1972. Represents solo acts and groups; currently handles 6 acts. Receives 5% (business management), 15-25% (personal management) commission. Reviews material for acts.
How to Contact: Submit demo tape by mail. Unsolicited submissions are OK. Prefers cassette, CD or videocassette with 2-3 songs. If seeking management, press kit should include photo, video (if available) and press clippings. Does not return material. Reports in 1 month.
Music: Rock, **pop** and **alternative (pop, metal, college)**. Current acts include Elvis Hitler (Needle Time Records), Frank Turner (Track Records), His Name Is Alive (4AD/Warner Bros. Records), Insane Clown Posse (Hollywood Records), Jimmy Marinos (EMI Music Publishing) and The Suicide Machines (Hollywood Records).

‡STARKRAVIN' MANAGEMENT, 18075 Ventura Blvd., Encino CA 91316. (818)345-0311. Fax: (818)345-0340. E-mail: bcmclane@aol.com. Contact: B.C. McLane, Esq. Management and law firm. Estab. 1994. Represents individual artists, groups and songwriters from anywhere; currently handles 5 acts. Receives 20% commission (management); $125/hour as attorney. Reviews material for acts.
How to Contact: Submit demo tape by mail. Unsolicited submissions are OK. Prefers cassette. If seeking management, press kit should include picture, bio and press. Does not return material. Reports in 2-4 weeks.
Music: Mostly **rock**, **pop** and **R&B**. Works primarily with bands. Current acts include Majority Dog, End, Jennys, Hummingfish and Sky Cappelletti.

‡STAY GOLD PRODUCTIONS, 1611 S. Utica, Suite 144, Tulsa OK 74104-4909. (918)742-4141. Fax: (918)742-4554. E-mail: STAGOLD@aol.com. President: Joey Baker. Management firm, booking agency and promoter. Estab. 1989. Represents individual artists, groups and songwriters from anywhere; currently handles 10 acts. Receives 15-20% commission. Reviews material for acts.
How to Contact: Write or call first and obtain permission to submit. Prefers cassette with 3 songs. If seeking management, press kit should include tape, bio, photo, press and references if available. Does not return material. Reports in 1-2 months.
Music: Mostly **jazz**, **rock** and **R&B**; also **funk**, **blues** and **alternative**. Works primarily with solo artists, bands and songwriters. Current acts include Terry Holmes (jazz guitarist), Choclate Hippies (rock) and Dennis Mitcheltree (jazz saxophonist).
Tips: "Make sure your submissions are neat and complete. Realize that most agents and managers receive many submissions weekly and are inclined to ignore those that arrive as a re-used demo tape with a hand-scrawled letter on notebook paper in a #10 envelope. Take yourself seriously and so will those you approach."

‡JIM STEPHANY MANAGEMENT, 1021 Preston Dr., Nashville TN 37206. (615)228-5638. President: Jim Stephany. Management firm. Estab. 1987. Represents individual artists and groups; currently handles 2 acts. Reviews material for acts.
How to Contact: Submit demo tape by mail. Unsolicited submissions are OK. Prefers cassette or VHS videocassette with 3 songs. SASE. Reports in 1 month.
Music: Mostly **country**. Works primarily with single artists and bands. Current acts include Bobby Goldsboro (singer) and The Nichols Brothers (band).

HARRIET STERNBERG MANAGEMENT, 4268 Hazeltine Ave., Sherman Oaks CA 91423. (818)906-9600. Fax: (818)906-1723. President: Harriet Sternberg. Management firm. Estab. 1987.
How to Contact: Write first and obtain permission to submit. Prefers cassette or VHS videocassette with 3 songs and lyric sheet. If seeking management, press kit should include detailed history of the artist and professional experience. "Industry referrals are crucial." SASE. Reports in 1 month.
Music: Works primarily with signed acts. Current acts include Delbert McClinton and Spinal Tap.
Tips: "Be knowledgeable about my artists and/or roster."

STEVE STEWART MANAGEMENT, 8225 Santa Monica Blvd., Los Angeles CA 90046. (213)650-9700. Fax: (213)650-2690. President: Steve Stewart. Management firm. Estab. 1993. Represents individual artists and/or groups from anywhere; currently handles 3 acts. Receives 20% commission.
How to Contact: Submit demo tape by mail. Unsolicited submissions are OK. Prefers cassette. If seeking management, press kit should include tape, photo, bio and video if available. "Mail first, call 4-6 weeks later. Cannot return any material." Reports in 2 months.
Music: Mostly **alternative** and **rock**. Works primarily with bands. Current acts include Stone Temple Pilots, Orbit, 10 Speed, Gordon and Eleven.

STORMIN' NORMAN PRODUCTIONS, 27 Broad St., Red Bank NJ 07701. (908)741-8733. (908)747-3516. Owner: Norman Seldin. Management firm, booking agency, music publisher (Noisy Joy Music/BMI) and record company (Ivory Records). Estab. 1967. Represents individual artists, groups and songwriters from anywhere; currently handles 10 acts. Receives 15% commission. Reviews material for acts.
How to Contact: Submit demo tape by mail. Unsolicited submissions are OK. Prefers cassette with 2-4 songs and lyric sheet. If seeking management, press kit should include demo cassette with cover and original songs, photo, song list, appearance credits, home base area, phone and address. SASE. Reports in 3-5 weeks.
Music: Mostly **country, rock** and **reggae**; also **soft rock, dynamic blues** and **folk**. Current acts include Stormin' Norman Band, Ronnie Dove and Darrell Norman.

STRICTLEY BIZINESS MUSIC MANAGEMENT, 691½ N. 13th St., Philadelphia PA 19123. (215)265-9418. CEO: Justus. President: Corey Hicks. Management and consulting firm. Estab. 1989. Represents local, regional and international individual artists, groups, songwriters and producers; currently handles 15 acts. Receives 20% commission. Reviews material for acts.
How to Contact: Submit demo tape by mail. Unsolicited submissions are OK. Prefers cassette or VHS videocassette with 3-5 songs, lyric sheet, information on the artist and photo. Does not return material. Reports in 1 month.
Music: Mostly **R&B**, **pop**, **rock** and **rap**; also **gospel**. Current acts include Phoenix (rapper), Rich Tucker (producer/writer) and AZIZ (rap group).

STRICTLY FORBIDDEN ARTISTS, 595 St. Clair West, Suite 1, Toronto M6C 1A3 **Canada**. (416)656-0085. Fax: (416)654-9436. A&R Director: Brad Black. Management firm, booking agency and record company. Estab. 1986. Represents individual artists and groups from anywhere; currently handles 5 acts. Receives 20-35% commission. Reviews material for acts.
How to Contact: Submit demo tape by mail. Unsolicited submissions are OK. Prefers cassette with 3-6 songs and lyric sheet. If seeking management, press kit should include biography, press clippings, 8×10 and promo materials. "Once you've sent material, don't call us, we'll call you." Does not return material. Reports in 4-6 weeks.
Music: Mostly **alternative rock, art rock** and **grindcore**; also **electronic, hip hop** and **experimental**. Works primarily with performing bands, studio acts and performance artists. Current acts include Squidhead (alternative rock/metal), Black-Book (hooky pop), Rigid Wonzer (low-fi noise rock) and Andy Warhead (driving art-punk).
Tips: "As long as you have faith in your music, we'll have faith in promoting you and your career."

SUNSHADOW PRODUCTIONS, P.O. Box 1239, Wickenburg AZ 85358. (520)684-3075. Fax: (520)684-7010. Talent Manager: Travis Cole. Management firm, booking agency, music publisher (Sunshadow Music Publishers), record company (Silver Saddle Records) and record producer. Estab. 1991. Represents individual artists, groups and songwriters from anywhere; currently handles 12 acts. Receives 10-15% commission. Reviews material for acts.
How to Contact: Write or call first and obtain permission to submit. Prefers cassette or VHS videocassette with 1-3 songs and lyric and/or lead sheet. If seeking management, press kit should include photos, demo, résumé and recent bookings. "No B.S.—say what you mean and mean what you say. No long rambling life stories!" SASE. Reports in 2-3 weeks.
Music: Mostly **western** (cowboy). Works primarily with western singers, songwriters, bands, variety artists, animals acts and comedians. Current acts include Tex Hill (singing cowboy/songwriter), Jack Alan (singing cowboy/songwriter) and Janet Stone (gospel singer).

SURFACE MANAGEMENT INC., 2935 Church St. Station, New York NY 10008. Phone/fax: (212)468-2828. E-mail: patb@surfacemgmt.com. President: Patti Beninati. Management firm. Estab. 1990. Represents local individual artists and groups; currently handles 3 acts. Receives 20% commission. Reviews material for acts.
How to Contact: Call first and obtain permission to submit. Prefers cassette with 5 songs and lyric sheet. Does not return material. Reports in 6 weeks.
Music: Mostly **alternative** and **heavy rock**. Current acts include Eye Wish Eye and Big Stupid Guitars.

T.J. BOOKER LTD., P.O. Box 969, Rossland, B.C. V0G 1Y0 **Canada**. (604)362-7795. Contact: Tom Jones. Management firm, booking agency and music publisher. Estab. 1976. Represents local, regional or international individual artists, groups and songwriters; currently handles 12 acts. Receives 15% commission. Reviews material for acts.
How to Contact: Submit demo tape by mail. Unsolicited submissions are OK. Prefers cassette or videocassette with 3 songs. If seeking management, include demo tape or CD, picture and bio in press kit. Does not return material.
Music: Mostly **MOR**, **crossover**, **rock**, **pop** and **country**. Works primarily with vocalists, show bands, dance bands and bar bands. Current acts include Kirk Orr (comedian), Tommy and T Birds ('50s show band), Zunzee (top 40/pop) and Mike Hamilton and Eclipse.

T.L.C. BOOKING AGENCY, 37311 N. Valley Rd., Chattaroy WA 99003. (509)292-2201. Fax: (509)292-2205. Agent/Owners: Tom or Carrie Lapsansky. Booking agency. Estab. 1970. Represents individual artists and groups from anywhere; currently handles 17 acts. Receives 10-15% commission. Reviews material for acts.
How to Contact: Submit demo tape by mail. Unsolicited submissions are OK. Prefers cassette with 3-4 songs. Does not return material. Reports in 2-3 weeks.
Music: Mostly **rock**, **country** and **variety**; also **comedians** and **magicians**. Works primarily with bands, singles and duos. Current acts include Nobody Famous (variety/rock/country), Rope Trick (country) and Stronghold (rock).

T.S.J. PRODUCTIONS, 422 Pierce St. NE, Minneapolis MN 55413-2514. (612)331-8580. President/Artist Manager: Katherine J. Lange. Management firm and booking agency. Estab. 1974. Represents artists, groups and songwriters; currently handles 1 act. Receives 20% commission. Reviews material for acts.
How to Contact: Submit demo tape by mail. Unsolicited submissions are OK. Prefers "cassette tapes only for music audio with 4-6 songs and lyric sheets." SASE. Reports in 1 month.
Music: Mostly **country rock**, **symphonic rock**, **easy listening** and **MOR**; also **blues**, **country**, **folk**, **jazz**, **progressive**, **R&B** and **top 40/pop**. Currently represents Thomas St. James (songwriter/vocalist).
Tips: "We will view anyone that fits into our areas of music. However, keep in mind we work only with national and international markets. We handle those starting out as well as professionals, but all must be marketed on a professional level, if we work with you."

‡TAKE OUT MANAGEMENT, 5605 Woodman Ave. #206, Van Nuys CA 91401. (818)901-1122. Fax: (818)901-6513. Contact: Steven Clark. Management firm. Estab. 1985. Represents individual artists, groups and songwriters from anywhere; currently handles 4 acts. Receives 20% commission. Reviews material for acts.
How to Contact: Submit demo tape by mail. Unsolicited submissions are OK. Prefers cassette or CD with any number of songs and lyric sheet. If seeking management, press kit should include tape or CD, picture and bio. Does not return material. Reports in 1 week.
Music: Mostly **pop**, **A/C** and **rock**; also **R&B** and **dance**. Works primarily with singer/songwriters, writer/

arrangers and bands. Current acts include Dan Hill (A/C artist), Rodney Sheldon (R&B songwriter) and Jana (R&B).

TALENT ASSOCIATES OF WISCONSIN, INC., P.O. Box 588, Brookfield WI 53008. (414)786-8500. President: John A. Mangold. Booking agency. Estab. 1971. Represents local groups; currently handles 25 acts. Receives 15-20% commission. Reviews material for acts.
How to Contact: Submit demo tape by mail. Unsolicited submissions are OK. Prefers cassette or VHS videocassette with 3 songs. If seeking management, press kit should include video, songlist, bio and picture poster. Does not return material. Reports in 1 month.
Music: Mostly **variety shows**, **rock/pop** and **dance**; also **R&B** and **jazz**. Works primarily with variety, rock and dance bands. Current acts include Temperament (R&B '90s style), Booze Bros. (take-off of Blues Bros.) and Brian McLaughlin Band (top dance hits from '80s-'90s).
Tips: "We're always looking for bands with high energy and a good stage presence, who enjoy what they're doing and radiate that through the audience, leaving all parties involved with a good feeling."

THE TANGLEWOOD GROUP INC., 2 Sheppard Ave. E., #900, Willowdale Ontario M2N 5Y7 **Canada**. (416)787-8687. Fax: (416)787-8647. President: Bruce Davidson. Management firm, music publisher (William James Music Publishing Co.) and record company (Tanglewood Records). Estab. 1975. Represents individual artists, groups and songwriters from anywhere; currently handles 5 acts. Receives 20% commission. Reviews material for acts.

- One of Tanglewood's clients, Eric Nagler, has won two Juno Awards (the Canadian equivalent of the Grammy Awards).

How to Contact: Write or call first and obtain permission to submit a demo or write to arrange personal interview. Prefers cassette. Does not return material.
Music: Mostly **family**, **children's** and **country**. Works primarily with family/children's entertainers. Current acts include Eric Nagler, Glenn Bennett and Carmen Campagne.
Tips: "Remember to *never* talk/write down to children!"

TANNER ENTERTAINMENT, 463 Summit Ave. 2 Southwest, Park Ridge IL 60068. (312)320-1940. E-mail: m.a.glover@worldnet.att.net. Website: www.mcs.net/~rainking. President: Margaret Glover. Management firm and booking agency. Estab. 1992. Represents groups from anywhere; currently handles 1 act. Receives 20% commission. Reviews material for acts.
How to Contact: Call first and obtain permission to submit or to arrange personal interview. Prefers cassette or vinyl/CD with 3 songs. If seeking management, press kit should include picture, bio, press releases, upcoming shows and tape/CD/vinyl. "Tell me what you are looking for in a manager/label/booker." Does not return material. Reports in 1 month.
Music: Mostly **college alternative**, **garage rock** and **punk**; also **country alternative** and **pop**. Current acts include The Rainkings (pop rock).

TAS MUSIC CO./DAVE TASSE ENTERTAINMENT, N2467 Knollwood Dr., Lake Geneva WI 53147-9731. Contact: David Tasse. Booking agency, record company and music publisher. Represents artists, groups and songwriters; currently handles 21 acts. Receives 10-20% commission. Reviews material for acts.
How to Contact: Submit demo tape by mail. Unsolicited submissions are OK. Prefers cassette with 2-4 songs and lyric sheet. Include performance videocassette if available. If seeking management, include tape, bio and photo. Does not return material. Reports in 3 weeks.
Music: Mostly **pop** and **jazz**; also **dance**, **MOR**, **rock**, **soul** and **top 40**. Works primarily with show and dance bands. Current acts include Dave Hulburt (blues), David Tasse (jazz) and Major Hamberlin (jazz).

‡**TEN NINETY NINE PROMOTIONS**, P.O. Box 21422, Washington DC 20009. (301)949-8517. Fax: (301)365-0803. Producer: Rob Verheij. Management firm, booking agency and record company (Agari Records, Rotterdam). Estab. 1982. Represents individual artists and groups from anywhere. Receives 28% commission. Reviews material for acts.
How to Contact: Submit demo tape by mail. Unsolicited submissions are OK. Prefers CD if available, cassette, DAT or VHS videocassette. If seeking management, press kit should include reviews, bio, photo and promotional material. Does not return material.
Music: **All types**. Current acts include Rise (alternative rock band), Wailers (reggae) and Ambient.

WILLIAM TENN ARTIST MANAGEMENT, #431-67 Mowat Ave., Toronto, Ontario M6K 3E3 **Canada**. (416)534-7763. Fax: (416)534-9726. E-mail: pmwtm@io.org. Management Assistant: Anna Marie. Management firm. Estab. 1981. Represents individual artists and groups in Canada, but not limited to that;

currently handles 3 acts. Receives variable commission. Reviews material for acts.
How to Contact: Submit demo tape or CD by mail. Unsolicited submissions are OK. Prefers cassette or CD with at least 3 songs, lyric sheet optional. If seeking management, press kit should include cassette with minimum 3 songs; recent press, reviews (live and/or album); photo (either b&w, color copied—to your discretion); contact info and return address. "Please do not call for at least two weeks to check on your submission. You will receive a response in the mail." SASE. Reports in 2 months.
Music: Mostly **rock/pop** and **alternative rock**. "We work with what we like. You don't need to be a certain type of artist." Current acts include Waltons (Sire/Elektra/Warner, pop), Barstool Prophets (Mercury/Polygram, rock) and Hayden (Hardwood/Outpost recordings, alternative rock).

THEATER ARTS NETWORK/STEPHEN PRODUCTIONS, 15 Pleasant Dr., Lancaster PA 17602. (717)394-0970. Fax: (717)394-2783. Promotions: Stephanie Lynn Brubaker. Management firm and booking agency. Estab. 1977. Represents East Coast artists and groups; currently handles 3 acts. Receives 10-20% commission. Reviews material for acts.
How to Contact: Submit demo tape by mail. Unsolicited submissions are OK. Prefers cassette or VHS videocassette. If seeking management, press kit should include 8×10 photo, tape, video and tour schedule. Does not return material. Reports in 2 weeks if interested.
Music: Mostly **comedy/music**, **Christian contemporary** and **rock**. Current acts include Stephen and Other Dummies (comedy/music/ventriloquism), John Westford (magic) and Pete Geist (comedy).
Tips: "We book live acts only."

‡THIRD STAGE PRODUCTIONS, 208 W. Dewey, Flint MI 48505-6607. (810)789-3339. Fax: (810)744-2017. President: Willie Jenkins. Management firm, booking agency, music publisher, record company and record producer. Estab. 1989. Represents individual artists and groups from anywhere; currently handles 25 acts. Receives 35% commission. Reviews material for acts.
How to Contact: Submit demo tape by mail. Unsolicited submissions are OK. Prefers cassette, DAT or videocassette with 2 songs and lyric sheets. If seeking management, press kit should include résumé, demo, 2-minute cassette or videocassette and promo photo. SASE. Reports in 10 weeks.
Music: Mostly **gospel**, **R&B** and **rock**; also **country** and **rap**. Current acts include Gospel Songbirds, Magic Streak and Zepbutar.

315 BEALE STUDIOS/TALIESYN ENTERTAINMENT, 2087 Monroe St., Memphis TN 38104. (901)276-0056. Fax: (901)753-2375. President: Eddie Scruggs. Management firm and music publisher. Estab. 1972. Represents individual artists and/or groups and songwriters from anywhere; currently handles 6 acts. Receives 20% commission. Reviews material for acts.
How to Contact: Submit demo tape by mail. Unsolicited submissions are OK. Prefers cassette. If seeking management, press kit should include bio, picture, tape and clippings. Does not return material. Reports in 3 weeks.
Music: Mostly **rock**, **urban** and **country**.

THREE GUYS FROM VERONA, INC., (formerly Grass Management), 144 S. Beverly Dr., Beverly Hills CA 90212. (310)247-9975. Fax: (310)247-9976. Owner: Clancy Grass. Management firm. Estab. 1976. Represents individual artists, groups and songwriters from anywhere; currently handles 6 acts. Receives 15% commission. Reviews material for acts.
How to Contact: Call first and obtain permission to submit. Prefers cassette, CD or VHS videocassette with 1-6 songs and lyric sheet. If seeking management, press kit should include CD or tape (audio and video if possible), photo and résumé. Does not return material. Reports in 2 weeks.
Music: Mostly **country**, **rock** and **R&B**; also **pop/rock**. Works primarily with singer/songwriters, bands and writers. Current acts include Darryl Phinnessee (R&B/soul), Sugar Bones (R&R) and Dan Crow (children's).

TIGER'S EYE ENTERTAINMENT MANAGEMENT & CONSULTING, 1876 Memorial Drive, Green Bay WI 54303. (414)494-1588. Manager/CEO: Thomas C. Berndt. Management firm and record producer. Estab. 1992. Represents individual artists, groups and songwriters from anywhere; currently handles 5 acts. Receives 20% commission. Reviews material for acts.
How to Contact: Submit demo tape by mail. Unsolicited submissions are OK. Prefers cassette or VHS videocassette with 3-4 songs and lyric sheet. If seeking management, press kit should include tape, lyric sheet, photo, relevant press and bio. "Artist should follow up with a call after 2 weeks." Does not return material. Reports in 2 weeks.
Music: Mostly **alternative**, **hard rock** and **folk-blues**; also **classical**, **funk** and **jazz**. Works primarily with vocalists, singer/songwriters and fresh alternative grunge. Current acts include B.B. Shine (variety

act), Spastic Mime (hard rock), Ugly Stick (alternative/hard rock), Dusk (ambient doom) and Rezn (alternative/hard rock).

TERRI TILTON MANAGEMENT, 7135 Hollywood, Suite 601, Los Angeles CA 90046. (213)851-8552. Fax: (213)850-1467. Personal Manager: Terri Tilton Stewart. Management firm. Estab. 1984. Represents individual artists and groups from anywhere; currently handles 6 acts. Receives 20% commission. Reviews material for acts.
How to Contact: Write or call first and obtain permission to submit. Prefers cassette. Does not return material. If seeking management, include bio, letter, CD or tape, photo and résumé. Reports in 2 months.
Music: Mostly **jazz**, **pop**, **blues** and **R&B**. Current acts include Jimmy Stewart (guitarist/producer/composer), Laurie Bono (blues/jazz), Brian Tarquin (acid jazz guitarist), Kal David (blues guitarist/singer/songwriter) and Toni Lee Scott (singer).

TOPNOTCH® MUSIC & RECORDS, P.O. Box 1515, Sanibel Island FL 33957-1515. (941)982-1515. Fax: (941)472-5033. President/CEO/Producer: Vincent M. Wolanin. Management firm, merchandising company, music publisher (TopNotch® Publishing), record company and record producer (Vincent M. Wolanin). Estab. 1990. Represents individual artists, groups and songwriters from anywhere; currently handles 3 acts. Receives 20% commission. Reviews material for acts.
How to Contact: Submit demo tape by mail. Unsolicited submissions are OK. Prefers cassette, DAT, MD, CD or VHS videocassette with 3 songs and lyric and/or lead sheet. If seeking management, press kit should include picture, news clippings (if any), list of gigs played, résumé of education and touring (if applicable). Does not return material. Reports in 2 months.
Music: Mostly **alternative rock**, **pop-dance** and **modern rock**; also **blues-rock**. "Prefer groups that are cutting edge where all members are accomplished musicians, are sober, hard working and original in their musical and lyrical tastes." Current acts include Lyndal's Burning (alternative rock), Natalia (pop/dance), Katzenjammer (industrial rock), Tamara (opera) and Brian Fox (modern rock).
Tips: "It has got to be a slammin' tune in all respects. If it has a great melody, memorable lyrics and music, with at least one major hook (but preferably two) with potential for crossover to Top 40 as well as rock, TopNotch® is interested."

A TOTAL ACTING EXPERIENCE, Dept. Rhymes-1, 20501 Ventura Blvd., Suite 399, Woodland Hills CA 91364. Agent: Dan A. Bellacicco. Talent agency. Estab. 1984. Represents vocalists, lyricists, composers and groups; currently handles 30 acts. Receives 10% commission. Reviews material for acts. Agency License: TA-0698.
How to Contact: Submit demo tape by mail. Unsolicited submissions are OK. Prefers cassette or VHS videocassette with 3-5 songs and lyric or lead sheets. Please include a revealing "self talk" at the end of your tape. "Singers or groups who write their own material must submit a VHS videocassette with photo and résumé." If seeking management, include VHS videotape, 5 8×10 photos, cover letter, professional typeset résumé and business card in press kit. Does not return material. Reports in 3 months only if interested. "Please include your e-mail address."
Music: Mostly **top 40/pop**, **jazz**, **blues**, **country**, **R&B**, **dance** and **MOR**; also "theme songs for new films, TV shows and special projects."
Tips: "No calls please. We will respond via your SASE. Your business skills must be strong. Please use a new tape and keep vocals up front. We welcome young, sincere talent who can give total commitment, and most important, *loyalty*, for a long-term relationship. We are seeking female vocalists (a la Streisand or Whitney Houston) who can write their own material, for a major label recording contract. Your song's story line must be as refreshing as the words you skillfully employ in preparing to build your well-balanced, orchestrated, climactic last note! Try to eliminate old, worn-out, dull, trite rhymes. A new way to write/compose or sing an old song/tune will qualify your originality and professional standing."

‡TRANSATLANTIC MANAGEMENT, P.O. Box 2831, Tucson AZ 85702. (520)881-5880. Fax: (520)881-8001. Website: http://euphoria.org/home/transmgt. Owner: English Cathy. Management firm. Estab. 1979. Represents individual artists, groups and songwriters from anywhere; currently handles 15 acts.

Receives 20% commission. "Transatlantic Management primarily showcase their artists through the use of compilation CDs presented at music conferences worldwide and also through their website." Reviews material for acts.
How to Contact: Submit demo tape by mail. Unsolicited submissions are OK. If seeking management, press kit should include tape/CD/bio/photo. SASE. Reports in 4-6 weeks.
Music: Mostly **all types** from **New Age to country to hard rock**. Current acts include Kathi McDonald (rock blues singer), Morgann Price (jazz singer) and L.J. Porter (gospel blues singer).

TRIANGLE TALENT, INC., 10424 Watterson, Louisville KY 40299. (502)267-5466. Fax: (502)267-8244. President: David H. Snowden. Booking agency. Represents artists and groups; currently handles 85 acts. Receives 10-20% commission. Reviews material for acts.
How to Contact: Submit demo tape by mail. Unsolicited submissions are OK. Prefers cassette or VHS videocassette with 2-4 songs and lyric sheet. If seeking management, include photo, audio cassette of at least 3 songs, and video if possible in press kit. Does not return material. Reports in 3-4 weeks.
Music: Rock/top 40 and **country**. Current acts include Lee Bradley (contemporary country), Karen Kraft (country) and Four Kinsmen (Australian group).

TUTTA FORZA MUSIC, 34 Haviland St. #310, Norwalk CT 06854. Phone/fax: (203)855-0095. Proprietor: Andrew Anello. Management firm, booking agency, music publisher (Tutta Forza Publishing/ASCAP) and record company. Estab. 1990. Represents New York Metro Area artists; currently handles 6 acts. Receives 10% commission. Reviews material for acts.
How to Contact: Submit demo tape by mail. Unsolicited submissions are OK. Prefers cassette, VHS videocassette or CD with 3 songs. If seeking management, press kit should include recent press releases, music reviews, biography and cover letter. SASE. Reports in 1 week.
Music: Mostly **jazz fusion**, **classical** and **modal combat jazz**; also **instrumentalists**, **composers** and **improvisors**. Works primarily with single artists, composers, improvisors and instrumentalists. Current acts include Andrew Anello (clarinetist/composer) and The Jazz X-Centrix.
Tips: "Looking for self-sufficient individualists; musicians who bring their own unique artistic qualities to work with. Genre of music not nearly as important as quality and taste in their style!"

UMBRELLA ARTISTS MANAGEMENT, INC., 2612 Erie Ave., P.O. Box 8385, Cincinnati OH 45208. (513)871-1500. Fax: (513)871-1510. President: Stan Hertzman. Management firm, record producer (Hal Bernard Enterprises), music publisher (Hal Bernard Enterprises) and record company (Strugglebaby Recording Co.). Represents artists, groups and songwriters; currently handles 4 acts.

- See the listings for Hal Bernard Enterprises in the Record Producers and Music Publishers sections, and for Strugglebaby Recording Co. in the Record Companies section.

How to Contact: Submit demo tape by mail. Unsolicited submissions are OK. Prefers cassette with 3 songs and lyric sheet. SASE. If seeking management, press kit should include a short bio, reviews, photo and cassette. Reports in 2 months.
Music: Progressive, **rock** and **top 40/pop**. Works with contemporary/progressive pop/rock artists and writers. Current acts include The Blue Birds (R&B/rock band), America Smith (rock), The Spanic Boys (modern band), Adrian Belew, Ric Hordinski and Rob Fetters.

UMPIRE ENTERTAINMENT ENTERPRIZES, 1507 Scenic Dr., Longview TX 75604. (903)759-0300. Owner/President: Jerry Haymes. Management firm, music publisher (Golden Guitar, Umpire Music) and record company (Enterprize Records). Estab. 1974. Represents individual artists, groups, songwriters and rodeo performers from anywhere; currently handles 6 acts. Receives 15% commission. Reviews material for acts.
How to Contact: Write first and obtain permission to submit. Prefers cassette with lyric and lead sheets. If seeking management, press kit should include bio, picture and any recordings. Does not return material. "Submissions become part of files for two years, then disposed of." Reports in 1 month.
Music: Mostly **country, pop** and **gospel**. Artists include Kelly Grant (country-pop artist), Tommy Cash (Nashville artist) and Santa Rosa Palamino Riding Club (international rodeo special act).

UNIVERSAL MUSIC MARKETING, P.O. Box 2297, Universal City TX 78148. (210)599-0022. E-mail: bswrl8@txdirect.net. Contact: Frank Willson. Management firm, record company (BSW Records), booking agency, music publisher and record producer (Frank Willson). Estab. 1987. Represents individual artists and groups from anywhere; currently handles 16 acts. Receives 15% commission. Reviews material for acts.

- See the listings for BSW Records in the Record Companies section and Frank Willson in the Record Producers section.

How to Contact: Submit demo tape by mail. Unsolicited submissions are OK. Prefers cassette or ¾" videocassette with 3 songs and lyric sheet. If seeking management, include tape/CD, bio, photo and current activities. SASE. Reports in 3-5 weeks.
Music: Mostly **country** and **light rock**; also **blues** and **jazz**. Works primarily with vocalists, singer/songwriters and bands. Current acts include Patty David, Maria Rose, Candee Land, Bob Jares, Wes Wiginton, Peter Caulton, Shawn DeLorme, Celeste, Davis Buescher, Matters of the Heart and Rusty Doherty.

UP FRONT MANAGEMENT, 1906 Seward Dr., Pittsburg CA 94565. Phone and fax: (510)427-7210. CEO/President: Charles Coke. Management firm, record company (Man Network) and record producer (Heavyweight Productions). Estab. 1977. Represents individual artists, groups, songwriters and producers from anywhere. Currently handles 3 acts. Receives 10-15% commission. Reviews material for acts.
- See their listing in the Record Producers section.

How to Contact: Submit demo tape by mail. Unsolicited submissions are OK. Prefers cassette, videocassette or CD's with 3-5 songs and lyric sheet. If seeking management, press kit should include bio, CD or cassette and picture. Does not return material. Reports in 1-3 weeks.
Music: Mostly **rock, country** and **R&B**. Works primarily with bands and singers. Current acts include John Payne, Psycho Betty (rock), Uncle Yazz (pop) and Van Zen (rock).

VALIANT RECORDS & MANAGEMENT, P.O. Box 180099, Dallas TX 75218. (214)327-5477. Fax: (214)327-4888. E-mail: valiant@master.net. Website: http://www.master.net/valiant/. President: Andy Stone. Booking agency, music publisher (Brightstone Publishing Co.), record company and record producer (Ed Loftus). Estab. 1971. Represents individual artists, groups and songwriters from anywhere; currently handles 4 acts. Receives 10-20% commission. Reviews material for acts.
How to Contact: Submit demo tape by mail. Unsolicited submissions are OK. Prefers cassette or VHS videocassette with 4 songs, lyric and/or lead sheet, if possible, and bio. "No more than four songs at a time, recorded clearly and professionally, with lyric sheets. I must be able to hear the words and melody. No arty mixes." SASE (no guarantees). Reports in 2-6 weeks.
Music: Mostly **top 40** and **top 40 country**; also **children's songs** and **novelty**. Works primarily with show groups for booking/managing, songwriters for placing songs and artists for release of new product. Current acts include Vince Vance & The Valiants (pop/pop country), Edward C. Loftus (A/C singer/songwriter), Copralingus (alternative) and Mike Boyd (country/pop singer).

HANS VAN POL MANAGEMENT, P.O. Box 9010, Amsterdam HOL 1006AA **Netherlands**. Phone: (31)20610-8281. Fax: (31)20610-6941. Managing Director: Hans Van Pol. Management firm, booking agency, consultant (Hans Van Pol Music Consultancy), record company (J.E.A.H.! Records) and music publisher (Blue & White Music). Estab. 1984. Represents regional (Holland/Belgium) individual artists and groups; currently handles 14 acts. Receives 15-25% commission. Reviews material for acts.
How to Contact: Submit demo tape by mail. Unsolicited submissions are OK. Prefers cassette or VHS videocassette with 3 songs and lyric sheets. If seeking management, include demo, possible video (VHS/PAL), bio, photo and release information. Does not return material. Reports in 1 month.
Music: Mostly **dance**: **rap/swing beat/hip house/R&B/soul/c.a.r.** Current acts include Tony Scott (rap), Erica (house/pop), Roxanna (R&B female singer), King Bee (rap/hard-core), Fixx-itt (rapper/dancer), OK 4 Now (R&B/rock), All Star Fresh (producer/D.J.), Stereo Explosion and Anoir (Euro/house).

RICHARD VARRASSO MANAGEMENT, P.O. Box 387, Fremont CA 94537. (510)792-8910. Fax: (510)792-0891. E-mail: rvarrasso@aol.com. President: Richard Varrasso. A&R: Saul Vigil. Management firm. Estab. 1976. Represents individual artists, groups and songwriters from anywhere; currently handles 3 acts. Receives 20% commission. Reviews material for acts.
How to Contact: Submit demo tape by mail. Unsolicited submissions are OK. Prefers cassette. If seeking management, press kit should include photos, bios, cover letter, cassette and contact numbers. Does not return material. Reports in 3 months.
Music: Mostly **rock** and **young country**. Works primarily with concert headliners and singers. Current acts include Uncle Richie, Art Najera Band and Radio Flyer.

VICTORY ARTISTS, 1321 Commerce St., Suite P, Petaluma CA 94954. (707)769-1210. Contact: Shelly Trumbo. Management firm, music publisher (ASCAP) and record company (Victory Label/Bay City). Estab. 1985. Represents individual artists and groups; currently handles 2 acts. Receives 10-25% commission. Reviews material for acts.
How to Contact: Write first and obtain permission to submit. Prefers cassette or VHS videocassette with 3 songs and lyric sheets. If seeking management, include photo, 3-song tape (video preferred), press

clippings, bio, cover letter and short paragraph on "what the band wants to do and what they want us to do." Does not return material. Reports in 1 month.
Music: Mostly **alternative**, **rock**, **pop** and **country**. Current acts include Freudian Slip (alternative), Este (rock) and Mark Allan (songwriter).

VOKES BOOKING AGENCY, P.O. Box 12, New Kensington PA 15068-0012. (412)335-2775. President: Howard Vokes. Booking agency, music publisher (Vokes Music Publishing) and record company (Vokes Record Co.). Represents individual traditional country and bluegrass artists. Books name acts in on special occasions. For special occasions books nationally known acts from Grand Ole Op'ry, Jamboree U.S.A., Appalachian Jubliee, etc. Receives 10-20% commission.

- See the listings for Vokes Music Publishing in the Music Publishers section and Vokes Record Co. in the Record Companies section.

How to Contact: New artists send 45 rpm record, cassette, LP or CD. Reports back within a week.
Music: Traditional **country**, **bluegrass**, **old time** and **gospel**; definitely no rock or country rock. Current acts include Howard Vokes & His Country Boys (country) and Mel Anderson.
Tips: "We work mostly with traditional country bands and bluegrass groups that play various bars, hotels, clubs, high schools, malls, fairs, lounges, or fundraising projects. We work at times with other booking agencies in bringing acts in for special occasions. Also we work directly with well-known and newer country, bluegrass and country gospel acts not only to possibly get them bookings in our area, but in other states as well. We also help 'certain artists' get bookings in the overseas marketplace."

VTC ENTERTAINMENT MANAGEMENT, 20186-1395 Lawrence Ave. W., Toronto, Ontario M6L IA7 **Canada**. (416)536-9250. Fax: (416)248-2682. E-mail: vtcent@idirect.com. Website: http://www.geocites.com/SunsetStrip/Alley/4025/index.html. Owner: Vickie Theofanous. Management firm. Estab. 1994. Represents local groups; currently handles 1 act. Receives 20% commission.
How to Contact: Submit demo tape by mail. Unsolicited submissions are OK. Prefers cassette or CD with 4 songs and lyric sheet. If seeking management, press kit should include bio, photo, tearsheets, reviews, fact sheets and cassette/CD. "Be sure to include contact numbers/names and a return address." Does not return material. Reports in 1-2 months.
Music: Mostly **modern rock**, **alternative** and **pop**. Works primarily with bands in the modern rock genre who are visually and musically interesting. Current acts include Q (modern rock 4 piece).

‡WILLIAM F. WAGNER AGENCY, 14343 Addison St. #221, Sherman Oaks CA 91423. (818)905-1033. Owner: Bill Wagner. Management firm and record producer (Bill Wagner). Estab. 1957. Represents individual artists and groups from anywhere; currently handles 3 acts. Receives 15% commission. Reviews materials for acts.
How to Contact: Submit demo tape by mail. Unsolicited submissions are OK. Prefers cassette or CD with 5 songs and lead sheet. If seeking management, press kit should include current bio, picture, tape or CD with 5 songs. "If SASE and/or return postage are included, I will reply in 30 days. I will not reply by telephone or fax." SASE. Reports in 1 month.
Music: Mostly **jazz**, **contemporary pop** and **contemporary country**; also **classical**, **MOR** and **film and TV background**. Works primarily with singers, with or without band, big bands and smaller instrumental groups. Current acts include Page Cavanaugh (jazz trio), Faunda Hinton (pop female singer and actress) and Sandy Graham (female jazz singer).
Tips: "Indicate in first submission what artists you are writing for, by name if possible. Don't send material blindly. Be sure all material is properly copyrighted. Be sure package shows 'all material herein copyrighted' on outside."

‡CHERYL K. WARNER PRODUCTIONS, P.O. Box 1721, Midland MI 48641-1721. Phone/fax: (517)839-5846. E-mail: davidsan@cris.com. Owners: Cheryl K. Warner and David M. Warner. Management firm, booking agency, music publisher (Cheryl K. Warner Music), record company (CKW Records) and record producer (Cheryl K. Warner). Estab. 1988. Currently handles 2 acts. Receives 20% commission. Reviews material for acts.
How to Contact: Submit demo tape by mail. Unsolicited submissions are OK. Prefers cassette or VHS videocassette with 3 best songs, lyric or lead sheet, bio and picture. If seeking management, press kit should include CD or cassette with up-to-date bio and picture, videocassette if available. Does not return material. Reports in 4-6 weeks. "Please contact our office by mail, e-mail or phone within 4-6 weeks if we have not contacted you."
Music: Mostly **country/traditional and contemporary**, **Christian/gospel** and **A/C/pop**. Works primarily with singer/songwriters and bands with original and versatile style. Current acts include Cheryl K. Warner (Nashville recording artist/entertainer) and Dixie Crossroad Band (country/country crossover band).

WESTWOOD ENTERTAINMENT GROUP, 1115 Inman Ave., Suite 330, Edison NJ 08820. (908)548-6700. Fax: (908)548-6748. President: Victor Kaply. A&R Coordinator: Steve Willoughby. Management agency and music publisher (Westunes Music). Estab. 1985. Represents regional artists and groups; currently handles 5 acts. Receives 15% commission. Reviews material for acts.

• Westwood Entertainment's publishing affiliate, Westunes Music, is listed in the Music Publishers section.

How to Contact: Write first and obtain permission to submit. Prefers cassette with 3 songs, lyric sheet, bio, press clippings, and photo. SASE. Reports in 2 months.

Music: Mostly **rock**; also **pop**. Works primarily with singer/songwriters, show bands and rock groups. Current acts include Punching Judy, Renee Grace, Tradia, B.B. & The Stingers and Tradia (rock).

Tips: "Present a professional promotional/press package with three song limit."

SHANE WILDER ARTISTS' MANAGEMENT, P.O. Box 3503, Hollywood CA 90078. (805)251-7526. President: Shane Wilder. Management firm, music publisher (Shane Wilder Music/BMI) and record producer (Shane Wilder Productions). Represents artists and groups; currently handles 3 acts. Receives 15% commission. Reviews material for acts.

• See the listing for Shane Wilder Music in the Music Publishers section.

How to Contact: Submit demo tape by mail. Unsolicited submissions are OK. Prefers cassette or videocassette of performance with 4-10 songs and lyric sheet. If seeking management, send cassette with 4-10 songs, photos of individuals or groups, video if possible and any press releases. "Submissions should be highly commercial." SASE. Reports in 2 weeks.

Music: Country. Works primarily with single artists and groups. Current acts include Inez Polizzi, Billy O'Hara, Melanie Ray and Kimber Cunningham.

YVONNE WILLIAMS MANAGEMENT, 6433 Topanga Blvd. #142, Canoga Park CA 91303. (818)831-3426. Fax: (818)831-3427. President: Yvonne Williams. Management firm, music publisher (Jerry Williams Music), record company (S.D.E.G.) and record producer (Jerry Williams). Estab. 1978. Represents individual artists and songwriters from anywhere; currently handles 5 acts. Receives 10-20% commission. Reviews material for acts.

How to Contact: Write first and obtain permission to submit a demo. Prefers cassette or DAT with any number of songs and lyric sheet. Include SASE, name, phone and any background in songs placed. Reports in 1-2 weeks.

Music: Mostly **R&B**, **rock** and **country**; also **gospel**. Works primarily with singer/songwriters and singers. Current acts include Swamp Dogg (rock), Ndesecent Xposure (X-rated rap) and Ruby Andrews (blues).

Tips: "Make a good clean dub, with a simple pilot vocal that is understandable."

WILLIS ENTERTAINMENT, INC., 314 Stations Ave., Woodstock GA 30189. (770)592-0043. Fax: (770)517-9525. E-mail: mwillis@random.com. Vice President/Management-Promotions: Mark Willis. Management firm. Estab. 1987. Represents international groups; currently handles 2 acts. Receives 20% commission. Reviews material for acts.

How to Contact: Submit demo tape by mail. Unsolicited submissions are OK. Prefers cassette or CD. If seeking management, press kit should include picture, bio, 3 song tape or CD, a list of upcoming performance dates. Does not return material. Reports in 2 months.

Music: Mostly **rock** and **alternative rock**. Works primarily with rock bands, all original, able to tour. Current acts include Stuck Mojo (metal), Jaye Swift & Co. and Redrum (industrial).

RICHARD WOOD ARTIST MANAGEMENT, 69 North Randall Ave., Staten Island NY 10301. (718)981-0641. Contact: Richard Wood. Management firm. Estab. 1974. Represents musical groups; currently handles 3 acts. Receives 20% commission. Reviews material for acts.

How to Contact: Submit demo tape by mail. Unsolicited submissions are OK. Prefers cassette and lead sheet. If seeking management, press kit should include demo tape, photo and bio. SASE. Reports in 3-4 weeks.

Music: Mostly **dance**, **R&B** and **top 40/pop**; also **MOR**. Works primarily with "high energy" show bands, bar bands and dance bands. Current acts include F.O.N. (rap), Salsa Gang (Latin) and Romero (dance).

WORLD BEYOND TALENT & PUBLICITY NETWORK, 73A Crawford St., Eatontown NJ 07724. (908)935-7218. Fax: (908)219-9548. Director/Management Consultant: Christopher Barry. Management firm, booking agency and publicity/public relations. Estab. 1986. Represents Jersey Shore/Northeast individual artists, songwriters and spoken word artists; currently handles 10 acts. Receives variable commission. Reviews material for acts.

How to Contact: Submit demo tape by mail. Unsolicited submissions are OK. Prefers cassette or VHS videocassette. If seeking management, press kit should include photographs and any pertinent news or magazine clippings. SASE. Reports in 6 weeks.
Music: Mostly **alternative**, **folk/'new folk'** and **experimental performance art**. Works primarily with singer/songwriters and spoken word artists. Current acts include R.W. Kingbird (singer/songwriter), The Lone Paranoid (spoken word artist), The Jersey Jerkoff (stand-up), The Sullen Savior (female singer/songwriter) and Not For Nothing (grunge/pop alternative band).

WORLD WIDE MANAGEMENT, P.O. Box 536, Bronxville NY 10708. (914)337-5131. Fax: (914)337-5309. Director: Steve Rosenfeld. Management firm and music publisher (Neighborhood Music/ASCAP). Estab. 1971. Represents artists, groups, songwriters and actors; currently handles 5 acts. Receives 20-25% commission. Reviews material for acts.
How to Contact: Write first and obtain permission to submit. Prefers CD, cassette or videocassete of performance with 3-4 songs. If seeking management, press kit should include bio, reviews, CD or cassette with lyrics and photo. Does not return material. Reports in 1-2 months.
Music: Mostly **contemporary pop**, **folk**, **folk/rock** and **New Age**; also **A/C**, **rock**, **jazz**, **bluegrass**, **blues**, **country** and **R&B**. Works primarily with self-contained bands and vocalists. Current acts include Small Things Big, Anya Block, Slō Leak, The Wiggins Sisters and Spinning Images.

‡WRIGHT PRODUCTIONS, 11718 Hwy. 64 E., Tyler TX 75707. Phone/fax: (903)566-5653. Owner: Lonnie Wright. Management firm, music publisher (Fer-De-Lance/BMI, Juke Box Music/ASCAP), record producer and studio owner. Estab. 1970. Represents individual artists and songwriters from anywhere; currently handles 4 acts. Receives variable commission. Reviews material for acts.
How to Contact: Submit demo tape by mail. Unsolicited submissions are OK. Prefers cassette with 4 songs and lyric sheet. If seeking management, press kit should include picture, bio and tape. SASE. Reports in 6 weeks.
Music: Mostly **country**, **gospel** and **blues**. Works primarily with artist/writer combinations. Current acts include Hyde Brothers (country duet), Floyd Mitchell (singer/country) and Craig Robbins (singer/songwriter, Polygram Music).

Y-NOT PRODUCTIONS, P.O. Box 902, Mill Valley CA 94942. (415)561-9760. Administrative Asst.: Anthony Washington. Management firm and music publisher (Lindy Lane Music/BMI, LaPorte Ave. Music/BMI). Estab. 1989. Represents West Coast-USA individual artists, groups and songwriters; currently handles 5 acts. Receives 20% commission. Reviews material for acts.
How to Contact: Submit demo tape by mail. Unsolicited submissions are OK. Prefers cassette or VHS videocassette with 3 songs. Send tapes to the attention of Anthony Washington. If seeking management, press kit should include photo, video or DAT or cassette. SASE. Reports in 2 months.
Music: Mostly **contemporary jazz**, **pop** and **R&B/rock**. Works primarily with instrumental groups/vocalists. Current acts include Tony Saunders (bassist/songwriter), Paradize (R&B), Phyliss Scott (R&B), Rankin Screw & Ginger (reggae), Renee Rice (R&B/pop) and Collen Bell.

Category Index

The Category Index is a good place to begin searching for a market for your songs. Below is an alphabetical list of 20 general music categories. If you write pop songs and are looking for a manager or booking agent to submit your songs to, check the Pop section in this index. There you will find a list of managers and booking agents who work with pop performers. Once you locate the listings for those publishers, read the music subheading *carefully* to determine which companies are most interested in the type of pop music you write. Some of the markets in this section do not appear in the Category Index because they have not indicated a specific preference. Most of these said they are interested in "all types" of music. Listings that were very specific, or whose description of the music they're interested in doesn't quite fit into these categories, also do not appear here.

Adult Contemporary

All Star Talent Agency; Anderson Associates Communications Group; ‡Backstage Entertainment/Loggins Promotion; Black Stallion Country, Inc.; Bojo Productions Inc.; ‡Chucker Music Inc.; Five Star Entertainment; Glo Gem Productions, Inc.; Guestar Entertainment Agency; International Entertainment Bureau; Jackson Artists Corp.; Junquera Productions, C.; Knight Agency, Bob; Lakes Entertainment Group; Levinson Entertainment Ventures International, Inc.; LMP Management Firm; Long Arm Talent; Lutz Entertainment Agency, Richard; M.B.H. Music Management; Martin Productions, Rick; Merri-Webb Productions; Mid-East Entertainment Inc.; Nelson Entertainment Inc., Brian; Phil's Entertainment Agency Limited; ‡Prestige Management; RadioActive; Richards World Management, Inc., Diane; Rustron Music Productions; ‡St. John Artists; Skorman Productions, Inc., T.; Sound '86 Talent Management; Sound Management; ‡Southern Nights Entertainment; Staircase Promotion; T.J. Booker Ltd.; T.S.J. Productions; ‡Take Out Management; Tas Music Co./Dave Tasse Entertainment; Total Acting Experience, A; ‡Wagner Agency, William F.; ‡Warner Productions, Cheryl K.; World Wide Management

Alternative

Alan Agency, Mark; Aquila Entertainment; babysue; Biscuit Productions Inc.; Bohemia Entertainment Group; ‡Breakthrough Management; Countdown Entertainment; Courtright Management Inc.; Cranium Management; ‡Cricket Inc.; Cycle of Fifths Management, Inc.; ‡Dale Management, Frankie; DAS Communications, Ltd.; Debutante Management/Catalyst Entertainment; Depth of Field Management; Detko Management, Bill; Detour Entertainment Inc.; Direct Management; Drastic Measures, Inc.; Earth Tracks Artists Agency; EBI Inc.; ‡Eden Records; ‡Ellis International Talent Agency, The; Entercom; Entertainment Services International; Eternal Records/Squigmonster Management; Fat City Artists; Foley Entertainment; Freedman Entertainment, Peter; Fritz/Byers Management; ‡Glotzer Management Co., The; GoodKnight Productions; Headline Management; ‡Hupp Enterprises, Joe; ‡Imperial Artist Management; James Gang Management; Jerifka Productions, Inc.; Knight Agency, Bob; Kriete, Kincaid & Faith; Kuper Personal Management; Lazy Bones Recordings/Productions, Inc.; Little Big Man Booking; Long Arm Talent; M.B.H. Music Management; ‡M.E.G Management; Manapro Entertainment; Midnight Music Management; Monopoly Management; Nelson Entertainment Inc., Brian; ‡On The Level Music!; Performers of the World Inc.; Pillar Records; Prairie Fire Music Company; ‡Prestige Management; Productions Unlimited; RadioActive; RDR Music Group; Rhyme Syndicate Management; ‡Rich & Famous Management, Inc.; S.T.A.R.S. Productions; Silver Bow Management; Simmons Management Group; Sirocco Productions, Inc.; Smeltzer Productions, Gary; ‡Southeastern Attractions; ‡Southern Nights Entertainment; Staircase Promotion; Star Artist Management Inc.; ‡Stay Gold Productions; Stewart Management, Steve; Strictly Forbidden Artists; Surface Management Inc.; Tanner Entertainment; Tenn Artist Management, William; Tiger's Eye Entertainment Management & Consulting; Topnotch® Music & Records; Victory Artists; VTC Entertainment Management; Willis Entertainment, Inc.; World Beyond Talent & Publicity Network

Blues

‡Barbary Coast Productions, Inc.; ‡Barnard Management Services; Big Hand; Blowin' Smoke Productions; ‡Blue Wave Productions; Cash Productions, Inc; Courtright Management Inc.; Detour Entertainment Inc.; DMR Agency; Empry Entertainment, Gino; Faith Entertainment, James; Fat City Artists; Foggy Day Music; Golden Bull Productions; James Gang Management; Knight Agency, Bob; Living Eye Productions Ltd.; Mayo & Company, Phil; Midnight Music Management; Music Matters; Nova Productions & Management; Odom-Meaders Management; Operation Music Enterprises; Pillar Records; Platinum Tracks Productions; Productions Unlimited; Professional Artist Management, Ltd.; Rustron Music Productions; Sirius Entertainment; ‡Slatus Management; SP Talent Associates; Squad 16; ‡Stay Gold Productions; Stormin' Norman Productions; T.S.J. Productions; Tiger's Eye Entertainment Management & Consulting; Tilton Management, Terri; Topnotch® Music & Records; Total Acting Experience, A; Universal Music Marketing; ‡Wright Productions

Children's

Direct Management; Fritz/Byers Management; ‡Lindsay Productions, Doris/Successful Productions; Paquin Entertainment Group; Siegel Entertainment Ltd.; Tanglewood Group Inc., The; Valiant Records & Management

Classical

Aquila Entertainment; Clousher Productions; Faith Entertainment, James; Fiedler Management, B.C.; Jae Enterprises, Jana; Other Road, The; Paquin Entertainment Group; Rock of Ages Productions; Sirius Entertainment; Tiger's Eye Entertainment Management & Consulting; Tutta Forza Music; ‡Wagner Agency, William F.

Country

Afterschool Publishing Company; Alexas Music Productions; All Star Management; All Star Talent Agency; Allen Entertainment Development, Michael; ‡American Bands Management; Ardenne Int'l Inc.; Atch Records and Productions; ATI Music; babysue; ‡Barbary Coast Productions, Inc.; Barnard Management Services; Baxter Management, Dick; Big Beat Productions, Inc.; Bird Entertainment Agency, J.; Black Stallion Country, Inc.; Bojo Productions Inc.; Bouquet-Orchid Enterprises; ‡Breakthrough Management; ‡Bullet Mangement; Capitol Management & Talent; Carlyle Management; Cash Productions, Inc; Cavalry Productions; Cedar Creek Productions and Management; Circuit Rider Talent & Management Co.; Clousher Productions; Concept 2000 Inc.; Cool Records; Country Star Attractions; Cranium Management; Crawfish Productions; Creative Star Management; Crowe Entertainment Inc.; De Miles Company, The Edward; Dinwoodie Management, Andrew; Doran, P.C., James R.; Doss Presents, Col. Buster; EBI Inc.; ‡Ellis International Talent Agency, The; Empry Entertainment, Gino; Entertainment Services International; Fame International; Fat City Artists; Fenchel Entertainment Agency, Fred T.; Fiedler Management, B.C.; First Time Management; Five Star Entertainment; 5 Star Music Group/Mike Waddell & Associates; Foggy Day Music; Foley Entertainment; Frick Enterprises, Bob Scott; Gallup Entertainment; Glo Gem Productions, Inc.; GMI Entertainment Inc.; Great Lakes Country Talent Agency; Greeley Entertainment, Chris; Gueststar Entertainment Agency; M. Harrell & Associates; Hawkeye Attractions; Holiday Productions, Doc; ‡Hupp Enterprises, Joe; Image Promotions Inc.; ‡Incentive Productions; Intermountain Talent; International Entertainment Bureau; Its Happening Present Entertainment; J & V Management; Jackson Artists Corp.; James Gang Management; James Management, Roger; Jae Enterprises, Jana; Johnson Agency, Little Richie; Junquera Productions, C.; KRC Records & Productions; Lari-Jon Promotions; Lenthall & Associates; Levinson Entertainment Ventures International, Inc.; Levy Management, Rick; ‡Lindsay Productions, Doris/Successful Productions; Live-Wire Management; Lowell Agency; Lutz Entertainment Agency, Richard; M. & G. Entertainment Consortiums, Inc.; M.B.H. Music Management; ‡Mabry Ministries, Kevin; McDonnell Group, The; Magnum Music Corporation Ltd.; Management Plus; Mayo & Company, Phil; MC Promotions & Public Relations; Merri-Webb Productions; ‡Midcoast, Inc.; Mid-East Entertainment Inc.; Midnight Music Management; Midnight Special Productions, Inc.; Milam Music Group; Milestone Media; Miller & Company, Thomas J.; Monopoly Management; Monterey Artists, Inc.; ‡Morningside

Management; ‡Nash-One Management Inc.; ‡Network Entertainment; Newby Management, J.P.; NIC of Tyme Productions, Inc.; Nik Entertainment Company; Noteworthy Productions; Nova Productions & Management; OB-1 Entertainment; Operation Music Enterprises; Overstreet Music Companies, Tommy; Phil's Entertainment Agency Limited; Pillar Records; Platinum Tracks Productions; ‡Power Play Promotions; Prairie Fire Music Company; Pro Talent Consultants; Productions Unlimited; Rainbow Collection Ltd.; RDR Music Group; RGK Entertainment Group; ‡Rich & Famous Management, Inc.; Rock of Ages Productions; Rothschild Productions Inc., Charles R.; Rustron Music Productions; S.T.A.R.S. Productions; Seip Management, Inc., William; Serge Entertainment Group; Sewitt Group, The; Siegel Entertainment Ltd.; Silver Bow Management; Smeltzer Productions, Gary; Sound and Serenity Management; Sound '86 Talent Management; ‡Sound Management; ‡Southeastern Attractions; SP Talent Associates; Staircase Promotion; ‡Stephany Management, Jim; Stormin' Norman Productions; Sunshadow Productions; T.J. Booker Ltd.; T.L.C. Booking Agency; T.S.J. Productions; Tanglewood Group Inc., The; Tanner Entertainment; ‡Third Stage Productions; Three Guys From Verona, Inc.; 315 Beale Studios/Taliesyn Entertainment; Total Acting Experience, A; Triangle Talent, Inc.; Umpire Entertainment Enterprizes; Universal Music Marketing; Up Front Management; Valiant Records & Management; Victory Artists; Vokes Booking Agency; ‡Wagner Agency, William F.; ‡Warner Productions, Cheryl K.; Wilder Artists' Management, Shane; Williams Management, Yvonne; World Wide Management; ‡Wright Productions

Dance

Anderson Associates Communications Group; Atlantic Entertainment Group; Bassline Entertainment, Inc.; Biscuit Productions Inc.; ‡Chucker Music Inc.; Clousher Productions; Countdown Entertainment; ‡Cricket Inc.; De Miles Company, The Edward; Detour Entertainment Inc.; ‡E.M.E. Records, Ltd.; ‡Ellis International Talent Agency, The; First Time Management; Jackson Artists Corp.; Lutz Entertainment Agency, Richard; M.B.H. Music Management; Manapro Entertainment; Martin Productions, Rick; Mid-East Entertainment Inc.; Milestone Media; Moore Entertainment Group; On Stage Management; Perom International; Productions Unlimited; Richards World Management, Inc., Diane; Skorman Productions, Inc., T.; Sound '86 Talent Management; Squad 16; ‡Take Out Management; Talent Associates of Wisconsin, Inc.; Tas Music Co./Dave Tasse Entertainment; Topnotch® Music & Records; Total Acting Experience, A; Van Pol Management, Hans; Wood Artist Management, Richard

Folk

Afterschool Publishing Company; Amok Inc.; ‡Barbary Coast Productions, Inc.; ‡Bullet Mangement; Detour Entertainment Inc.; Dinwoodie Management, Andrew; Duckworth/Atlantica; Faith Entertainment, James; Five Star Entertainment; Foggy Day Music; ‡Hupp Enterprises, Joe; Image Promotions Inc.; Immigrant Music Inc.; Knight Agency, Bob; Living Eye Productions Ltd.; Noteworthy Productions; Paquin Entertainment Group; Performers of the World Inc.; Prairie Fire Music Company; Professional Artist Management, Ltd.; RGK Entertainment Group; Rhyme Syndicate Management; ‡Rich & Famous Management, Inc.; Rothschild Productions Inc., Charles R.; Rustron Music Productions; S.T.A.R.S. Productions; SP Talent Associates; Stormin' Norman Productions; T.S.J. Productions; Tiger's Eye Entertainment Management & Consulting; World Beyond Talent & Publicity Network; World Wide Management

Instrumental

Pillar Records; Tutta Forza Music; ‡Wagner Agency, William F.

Jazz

Afterschool Publishing Company; All Musicmatters; ‡Backstage Entertainment/Loggins Promotion; Big Beat Productions, Inc.; Big Hand; Blue Cat Agency/El Gato Azul Agency, The; Cedar Creek Productions and Management; ‡Chucker Music Inc.; Concept 2000 Inc.; D&D Talent Associates; ‡Detko Management, Bill; Detour Entertainment Inc.; ‡Ellis International Talent Agency, The; Empry Entertainment, Gino; Faith Entertainment, James; Fame International; Fat City Artists; Flinter Music; Fritz/Byers Management; Glo Gem Productions, Inc.; Golden Bull Productions; GSI Inc.; International Entertainment Bureau; Its Happening Present Entertainment;

Jae Enterprises, Jana; ‡Klein, Joanne; Knight Agency, Bob; L.D.F. Productions; ‡Lakes Entertainment Group; Live-Wire Management; M. & G. Entertainment Consortiums, Inc.; McDonnell Group, The; Mid-East Entertainment Inc.; Miller & Company, Thomas J.; Music Matters; NIC of Tyme Productions, Inc.; ‡Noteworthy Enterprises; Nova Productions & Management; Odom-Meaders Management; ‡On The Level Music!; Other Road, The; Performers of the World Inc.; Phil's Entertainment Agency Limited; Productions Unlimited; Ricca, Jr.'s Entertainment Agency, Joey; Richards World Management, Inc., Diane; Riohcat Music; Rothschild Productions Inc., Charles R.; Saffyre Management; Sirius Entertainment; ‡Sound Management; Squad 16; Stander Entertainment; ‡Stay Gold Productions; T.S.J. Productions; Talent Associates of Wisconsin, Inc.; Tas Music Co./Dave Tasse Entertainment; Tiger's Eye Entertainment Management & Consulting; Tilton Management, Terri; Total Acting Experience, A; Tutta Forza Music; Universal Music Marketing; ‡Wagner Agency, William F.; World Wide Management; Y-Not Productions

Latin

Aquila Entertainment; Bassline Entertainment, Inc.; Blue Cat Agency/El Gato Azul Agency, The; Cavalry Productions; Cookman International; Corvalan-Condliffe Management; DiLeo Management, Liesa; Fast Lane Internationals; Johnson Agency, Little Richie; Management Plus; Musica Moderna Management; ‡Power Play Promotions; Ricca, Jr.'s Entertainment Agency, Joey

Metal

Artist Representation and Management; Courtright Management Inc.; ‡Dale Management, Frankie; Drastic Measures, Inc.; Entercom; Eternal Records/Squigmonster Management; ‡Imperial Artist Management; Jupiter Productions; Northstar Artist Management; Professional Artist Management, Ltd.; Raz Management Co.; Saffyre Management; Sewitt Group, The; Simmons Management Group

New Age

Alan Agency, Mark; Alexas Music Productions; Aquila Entertainment; Fast Lane Internationals; Firestar Promotions Inc.; Jerifka Productions, Inc.; Live-Wire Management; Other Road, The; Paquin Entertainment Group; Prairie Fire Music Company; Richards World Management, Inc., Diane; Rustron Music Productions; Serge Entertainment Group; World Wide Management

Novelty

Cavalry Productions; Circuit Rider Talent & Management Co.; Eternal Records/Squigmonster Management; Hall Entertainment & Events, Bill; Paquin Entertainment Group; ‡Sea Cruise Productions, Inc.; Valiant Records & Management

Pop

Afterschool Publishing Company; AKO Productions; Alert Music, Inc.; Alexas Music Productions; All Star Talent Agency; Allen Entertainment Development, Michael; Anderson Associates Communications Group; Ardenne Int'l Inc.; Artist Representation and Management; Atch Records and Productions; babysue; ‡Backstage Entertainment/Loggins Promotion; Bassline Entertainment, Inc.; Baxter Management, Dick; Big Beat Productions, Inc.; Big Hand; Big J Productions; Bird Entertainment Agency, J.; Biscuit Productions Inc.; Blue Cat Agency/El Gato Azul Agency, The; Bouquet-Orchid Enterprises; ‡Bullet Mangement; Capitol Management & Talent; Cash Productions, Inc; Cedar Creek Productions and Management; ‡Chucker Music Inc.; Circuit Rider Talent & Management Co.; Clockwork Entertainment Management Agency; Concept 2000 Inc.; Conscience Music; Corvalan-Condliffe Management; Countdown Entertainment; Courtright Management Inc.; Cranium Management; Creative Star Management; ‡Cricket Inc.; DAS Communications, Ltd.; De Miles Company, The Edward; DiLeo Management, Liesa; Dinwoodie Management, Andrew; DMR Agency; ‡E.M.E. Records, Ltd.; Earth Tracks Artists Agency; ‡Ellis International Talent Agency, The; Empry Entertainment, Gino; Entercom; Eternal Records/Squigmonster Management; Evans Productions, Scott; Fat City Artists; Fenchel Entertainment Agency, Fred T.; Fiedler Management, B.C.; First Time Management; Foley Entertainment; Freedman Entertainment, Peter; Fritz/Byers Management; Future Star Entertainment; ‡Gangland

Artists; Glo Gem Productions, Inc.; GMI Entertainment Inc.; Golden Bull Productions; Golden Guru Entertainment; GoodKnight Productions; Great Lakes Country Talent Agency; Greeley Entertainment, Chris; Headline Management; Holiday Productions, Doc; ‡Hupp Enterprises, Joe; ‡Incentive Productions; Its Happening Present Entertainment; Jackson Artists Corp.; James Gang Management; James Management, Roger; ‡Jampop Ltd.; Jae Enterprises, Jana; Junquera Productions, C.; Kagan Productions, Sheldon; Knight Agency, Bob; L.D.F. Productions; ‡Lakes Entertainment Group; Lenthall & Associates; Levy Management, Rick; ‡Lindsay Productions, Doris/Successful Productions; Live-Wire Management; Long Arm Talent; Lutz Entertainment Agency, Richard; McDonnell Group, The; ‡Malla Entertainment; Manapro Entertainment; Martin Productions, Rick; Mayo & Company, Phil; Merri-Webb Productions; ‡Midcoast, Inc.; Mid-East Entertainment Inc.; Miller & Company, Thomas J.; Monopoly Management; Moore Entertainment Group; Music Matters; NIC of Tyme Productions, Inc.; Nik Entertainment Company; Northstar Artist Management; ‡Noteworthy Productions; OB-1 Entertainment; On Stage Management; ‡O'Reilly Management, Ltd., Dee; Performers of the World Inc.; Perom International; Pillar Records; Platinum Ears Personal Management; Platinum Tracks Productions; ‡Power Play Promotions; ‡Prestige Management; Pro Talent Consultants; RadioActive; Rainbow Collection Ltd.; Raz Management Co.; ‡Rhythmic Temple Entertainment Inc.; Richards World Management, Inc., Diane; Rock of Ages Productions; Rothschild Productions Inc., Charles R.; Saffyre Management; Serge Entertainment Group; Sewitt Group, The; Shapiro & Company, C.P.A.; Shute Management Pty. Ltd., Phill; Siegel Entertainment Ltd.; Silver Bow Management; Simmons Management Group; Skorman Productions, Inc., T.; Sound '86 Talent Management; ‡Sound Management; ‡Southern Nights Entertainment; Staircase Promotion; Stander Entertainment; Star Artist Management Inc.; ‡Starkravin' Management; Strictley Biziness Music Management; T.J. Booker Ltd.; T.S.J. Productions; ‡Take Out Management; Talent Associates of Wisconsin, Inc.; Tanner Entertainment; Tas Music Co./Dave Tasse Entertainment; Tenn Artist Management, William; Three Guys From Verona, Inc.; Tilton Management, Terri; Topnotch® Music & Records; Total Acting Experience, A; Triangle Talent, Inc.; Umbrella Artists Management, Inc.; Umpire Entertainment Enterprizes; Valiant Records & Management; Victory Artists; VTC Entertainment Management; ‡Wagner Agency, William F.; ‡Warner Productions, Cheryl K.; Westwood Entertainment Group; Wood Artist Management, Richard; World Wide Management; Y-Not Productions

R&B

Alan Agency, Mark; Allen Entertainment Development, Michael; Anderson Associates Communications Group; Artist Representation and Management; Atch Records and Productions; Atlantic Entertainment Group; Barnard Management Services; Bassline Entertainment, Inc.; Big Hand; Big J Productions; Biscuit Productions Inc.; Black Stallion Country, Inc.; Blackground; Blowin' Smoke Productions; Bojo Productions Inc.; Bouquet-Orchid Enterprises; Capitol Management & Talent; Cedar Creek Productions and Management; ‡Chucker Music Inc.; Circuit Rider Talent & Management Co.; Concept 2000 Inc.; Countdown Entertainment; Country Star Attractions; Creative Star Management; DAS Communications, Ltd.; De Miles Company, The Edward; Detour Entertainment Inc.; DiLeo Management, Liesa; Dinwoodie Management, Andrew; ‡E.M.E. Records, Ltd.; Entertainment Group, The; Entertainment Services International; Eternal Records/Squigmonster Management; Evans Productions, Scott; Foley Entertainment; Frick Enterprises, Bob Scott; Future Star Entertainment; ‡Gangland Artists; GMI Entertainment Inc.; Golden Bull Productions; Greene Entertainment, Tim; M. Harrell & Associates; Holiday Productions, Doc; ‡Hupp Enterprises, Joe; Image Promotions Inc.; Imani Entertainment Inc.; Its Happening Present Entertainment; Jackson Artists Corp.; Jacobs Management; James Gang Management; ‡Jampop Ltd.; JAS Management; KKR Entertainment Group; Knight Agency, Bob; ‡Lakes Entertainment Group; Lenthall & Associates; Levinson Entertainment Ventures International, Inc.; Levy Management, Rick; Live-Wire Management; LMP Management Firm; McDonnell Group, The; Madstorm Production Company; Manapro Entertainment; Merri-Webb Productions; Mid-East Entertainment Inc.; Midnight Music Management; Moore Entertainment Group; Music Matters; NIC of Tyme Productions, Inc.; Nilsson Production, Christina; On Stage Management; Performers of the World Inc.; Perom International; ‡Power Play Promotions; Precision Management; ‡Prestige Management; Productions Unlimited; Renaissance Entertainment Group; ‡Rhythmic Temple Entertainment Inc.; Rustron Music Productions; ‡Sea Cruise Productions, Inc.; Serge Entertainment Group; Sewitt Group, The; Shute Management Pty. Ltd.,

Phill; Silver Bow Management; Simmons Management Group; Sirius Entertainment; Smeltzer Productions, Gary; Stander Entertainment; ‡Starkravin' Management; ‡Stay Gold Productions; Strictley Biziness Music Management; T.S.J. Productions; ‡Take Out Management; Talent Associates of Wisconsin, Inc.; Tas Music Co./Dave Tasse Entertainment; ‡Third Stage Productions; Three Guys From Verona, Inc.; 315 Beale Studios/Taliesyn Entertainment; Tilton Management, Terri; Total Acting Experience, A; Up Front Management; Van Pol Management, Hans; Williams Management, Yvonne; Wood Artist Management, Richard; World Wide Management; Y-Not Productions

Rap

Afterschool Publishing Company; Atch Records and Productions; Bassline Entertainment, Inc.; Biscuit Productions Inc.; Blackground; Creative Star Management; Detour Entertainment Inc.; DME Management; ‡E.M.E. Records, Ltd.; Eternal Records/Squigmonster Management; First Time Management; Greene Entertainment, Tim; Holiday Productions, Doc; Imani Entertainment Inc.; Its Happening Present Entertainment; JAS Management; Jupiter Productions; KKR Entertainment Group; ‡Lakes Entertainment Group; Lazy Bones Recordings/Productions, Inc.; Lenthall & Associates; M. & G. Entertainment Consortiums, Inc.; Madstorm Production Company; Milestone Media; Precision Management; Renaissance Entertainment Group; ‡Rhythmic Temple Entertainment Inc.; Richards World Management, Inc., Diane; Sewitt Group, The; Squad 16; Strictley Biziness Music Management; Strictly Forbidden Artists; ‡Third Stage Productions; Van Pol Management, Hans

Religious

Alexas Music Productions; All Star Management; All Star Talent Agency; Allen Entertainment Development, Michael; Atch Records and Productions; ATI Music; babysue; Baxter Management, Dick; Blackground; Bojo Productions Inc.; Bouquet-Orchid Enterprises; Capitol Management & Talent; Cash Productions, Inc; Cavalry Productions; Cedar Creek Productions and Management; Circuit Rider Talent & Management Co.; Concept 2000 Inc.; Country Star Attractions; Crawfish Productions; Creative Star Management; Direct Management; Doss Presents, Col. Buster; Exclesisa Booking Agency; Fenchel Entertainment Agency, Fred T.; First Time Management; 5 Star Music Group/Mike Waddell & Associates; Frick Enterprises, Bob Scott; Glad Productions; Golden Bull Productions; Great Lakes Country Talent Agency; Gueststar Entertainment Agency; Holiday Productions, Doc; Jackson Artists Corp.; James Gang Management; ‡Jampop Ltd.; JAS Management; KRC Records & Productions; L.D.F. Productions; ‡Lakes Entertainment Group; Lari-Jon Promotions; Lenthall & Associates; ‡Lindsay Productions, Doris/Successful Productions; M. & G. Entertainment Consortiums, Inc.; ‡Mabry Ministries, Kevin; Magnum Music Corporation Ltd.; Mayo & Company, Phil; Merri-Webb Productions; NIC of Tyme Productions, Inc.; Nilsson Production, Christina; Overstreet Music Companies, Tommy; Precision Management; ‡Rhythmic Temple Entertainment Inc.; Rock of Ages Productions; Silver Bow Management; ‡Splendor Productions, Inc.; Staircase Promotion; Strictley Biziness Music Management; Theater Arts Network/Stephen Productions; ‡Third Stage Productions; Umpire Entertainment Enterprizes; Vokes Booking Agency; ‡Warner Productions, Cheryl K.; Williams Management, Yvonne; ‡Wright Productions

Rock

AKO Productions; Alan Agency, Mark; Alert Music, Inc.; All Star Talent Agency; Allen Entertainment Development, Michael; ‡American Bands Management; Anderson Associates Communications Group; Aquila Entertainment; Ardenne Int'l Inc.; Artist Representation and Management; Atch Records and Productions; babysue; Barnard Management Services; Bassline Entertainment, Inc.; Big Beat Productions, Inc.; Big Hand; Big J Productions; Bird Entertainment Agency, J.; Blaze Productions; Blowin' Smoke Productions; Blue Cat Agency/El Gato Azul Agency, The; ‡Blue Wave Productions; Bouquet-Orchid Enterprises; ‡Bullet Mangement; Capitol Management & Talent; Carlyle Management; Cash Productions, Inc; Cedar Creek Productions and Management; ‡Chucker Music Inc.; Clockwork Entertainment Management Agency; Clousher Productions; Conscience Music; Corvalan-Condliffe Management; Countdown Entertainment; Country Star Attractions; Courtright Management Inc.; ‡Cricket Inc.; Cycle of Fifths Management, Inc.; DAS Communications, Ltd.; DCA Productions; De Miles Company, The

Edward; Debutante Management/Catalyst Entertainment; Depth Of Field Management; Detour Entertainment Inc.; DiLeo Management, Liesa; Dinwoodie Management, Andrew; DME Management; DMR Agency; Doran, P.C., James R.; ‡E.M.E. Records, Ltd.; Earth Tracks Artists Agency; Entercom; Entertainment Group, The; Entertainment Services International; Eternal Records/Squigmonster Management; Faith Entertainment, James; Fat City Artists; 5 Star Music Group/Mike Waddell & Associates; Foggy Day Music; Foley Entertainment; Freedman Entertainment, Peter; Fritz/Byers Management; Future Star Entertainment; Gallup Entertainment; ‡Gangland Artists; ‡Glotzer Management Co., The; Golden Bull Productions; Golden Guru Entertainment; Greeley Entertainment, Chris; ‡Hupp Enterprises, Joe; Image Promotions Inc.; ‡Incentive Productions; Intermountain Talent; International Entertainment Bureau; Jackson Artists Corp.; Jacobs Management; Jerifka Productions, Inc.; Jupiter Productions; KKR Entertainment Group; Knight Agency, Bob; L.D.F. Productions; Lari-Jon Promotions; Lenthall & Associates; Levinson Entertainment Ventures International, Inc.; Living Eye Productions Ltd.; LMP Management Firm; Long Arm Talent; M. & G. Entertainment Consortiums, Inc.; M.B.H. Music Management; McDonnell Group, The; ‡Malla Entertainment; Mayo & Company, Phil; Merri-Webb Productions; ‡Midcoast, Inc.; Mid-East Entertainment Inc.; Milestone Media; Miller & Company, Thomas J.; Moore Entertainment Group; Music Matters; ‡Nash-One Management Inc.; Nelson Entertainment Inc., Brian; Newby Management, J.P.; NIC of Tyme Productions, Inc.; Nik Entertainment Company; Nilsson Production, Christina; Northstar Artist Management; OB-1 Entertainment; Odom-Meaders Management; On Stage Management; ‡On The Level Music!; ‡O'Reilly Management, Ltd., Dee; Overstreet Music Companies, Tommy; Performers of the World Inc.; Perom International; Phil's Entertainment Agency Limited; Pillar Records; Platinum Ears Personal Management; Platinum Tracks Productions; ‡Power Play Promotions; Prairie Fire Music Company; ‡Prestige Management; Pro Talent Consultants; Productions Unlimited; RadioActive; Rainbow Collection Ltd.; Raz Management Co.; Renaissance Entertainment Group; RGK Entertainment Group; Rhyme Syndicate Management; Rock of Ages Productions; Rothschild Productions Inc., Charles R.; Rustron Music Productions; S.T.A.R.S. Productions; Saffyre Management; ‡St. John Artists; ‡Sea Cruise Productions, Inc.; Seip Management, Inc., William; Serge Entertainment Group; Sewitt Group, The; Shapiro & Company, C.P.A.; Shute Management Pty. Ltd., Phill; Siegel Entertainment Ltd.; Silver Bow Management; Simmons Management Group; Sirius Entertainment; ‡Slatus Management; Sound '86 Talent Management; ‡Sound Management; ‡Southeastern Attractions; ‡Southern Nights Entertainment; SP Talent Associates; Squad 16; Staircase Promotion; Star Artist Management Inc.; ‡Starkravin' Management; ‡Stay Gold Productions; Stewart Management, Steve; Stormin' Norman Productions; Strictley Biziness Music Management; Strictly Forbidden Artists; Surface Management Inc.; T.J. Booker Ltd.; T.L.C. Booking Agency; T.S.J. Productions; ‡Take Out Management; Talent Associates of Wisconsin, Inc.; Tanner Entertainment; Tas Music Co./Dave Tasse Entertainment; Tenn Artist Management, William; Theater Arts Network/Stephen Productions; ‡Third Stage Productions; Three Guys From Verona, Inc.; 315 Beale Studios/Taliesyn Entertainment; Tiger's Eye Entertainment Management & Consulting; Topnotch® Music & Records; Triangle Talent, Inc.; Umbrella Artists Management, Inc.; Universal Music Marketing; Up Front Management; Varrasso Management, Richard; Victory Artists; Westwood Entertainment Group; Williams Management, Yvonne; Willis Entertainment, Inc.; World Wide Management; Y-Not Productions

World Music

Amok Inc.; ‡Detko Management, Bill; Entertainment Works; Faith Entertainment, James; Fast Lane Internationals; Flinter Music; Foggy Day Music; Immigrant Music Inc.; Madstorm Production Company; Management Plus; Midnight Music Management; Performers of the World Inc.; Squad 16; Stander Entertainment; Stormin' Norman Productions

‡ **THE DOUBLE DAGGER** before a listing indicates that the listing is new in this edition.

Advertising, Audiovisual and Commercial Music Firms

It's happened a million times—you hear a jingle on the radio or television and you can't get it out of your head. That's the work of a successful jingle writer, writing songs that catch your attention and make you aware of the product being advertised. But the field of commercial music consists of more than just memorable jingles. It also includes background music that many companies use in videos for corporate and educational presentations, as well as films and TV shows.

More than any other market listed in this book, the commercial music market expects composers to have made an investment in the recording of their material before submitting. A sparse, piano/vocal demo won't work here; when dealing with commercial music firms, especially audiovisual firms and music libraries, high quality production is important. Your demo may be kept on file at one of these companies until a need for it arises, and it may be used or sold as you sent it. Therefore, your demo tape or reel must be as fully produced as possible.

The presentation package that goes along with your demo must be just as professional. A list of your credits should be a part of your submission, to give the company an idea of your experience in this field. If you have no experience, look to local television and radio stations to get your start. Don't expect to be paid for many of your first jobs in the commercial music field; it's more important to get the credits and exposure that can lead to higher-paying jobs.

Commercial music and jingle writing can be a lucrative field for the composer/songwriter with a gift for writing catchy melodies and the ability to write in many different music styles. It's a very competitive field, so it pays to have a professional presentation package that makes your work stand out.

Three different segments of the commercial music world are listed here: advertising agencies, audiovisual firms and commercial music houses/music libraries. Each looks for a different type of music, so read these descriptions carefully to see where the music you write fits in.

ADVERTISING AGENCIES

Ad agencies work on assignment as their clients' needs arise. Through consultation and input from the creative staff, ad agencies seek jingles and music to stimulate the consumer to identify with a product or service.

When contacting ad agencies, keep in mind they are searching for music that can capture and then hold an audience's attention. Most jingles are short, with a strong, memorable hook. When an ad agency listens to a demo, it is not necessarily looking for a finished product so much as for an indication of creativity and diversity. Many composers put together a reel of excerpts of work from previous projects, or short pieces of music which show they can write in a variety of styles.

AUDIOVISUAL FIRMS

Audiovisual firms create a variety of products, from film and video shows for sales meetings, corporate gatherings and educational markets, to motion pictures and TV shows. With the increase of home video use, how-to videos are a big market for audiovisual firms, as are spoken word educational videos. All of these products need music to accompany them.

Like ad agencies, audiovisual firms look for versatile, well-rounded songwriters. When submitting demos to these firms, you need to demonstrate your versatility in writing specialized background music and themes. Listings for companies will tell what facet(s) of the audiovisual field they are involved in and what types of clients they serve. Your demo tape should also be as professional and fully produced as possible; audiovisual firms often seek demo tapes that can be put on file for future use when the need arises.

COMMERCIAL MUSIC HOUSES AND MUSIC LIBRARIES

Commercial music houses are companies which are contracted (either by an ad agency or the advertiser) to compose custom jingles. Since they are neither an ad agency nor an audiovisual firm, their main concern is music. They use a lot of it, too—some composed by inhouse songwriters and some contributed by outside, freelance writers.

Music libraries are different in that their music is not custom composed for a specific client. Their job is to provide a collection of instrumental music in many different styles that, for an annual fee or on a per-use basis, the customer can use however he chooses.

In the following listings, commercial music houses and music libraries, which are usually the most open to works by new composers, are identified as such by **bold** typeface.

The commercial music market is similar to most other businesses in one aspect: experience is important. Until you develop a list of credits, pay for your work may not be high. Don't pass up opportunities if a job is non- or low-paying. These assignments will add to your list of credits, make you contacts in the field, and improve your marketability.

Many of the companies listed in this section pay by the job, but there may be some situations where the company asks you to sign a contract that will specify royalty payments. If this happens, research the contract thoroughly, and know exactly what is expected of you and how much you'll be paid.

Depending on the particular job and the company, you may be asked to sell one-time rights or all rights. One-time rights involve using your material for one presentation only. All rights means the buyer can use your work any way he chooses, as many times as he likes. Be sure you know exactly what you're giving up, and how the company may use your music in the future.

For additional names and addresses of ad agencies that may use jingles and/or commercial music, refer to the *Standard Directory of Advertising Agencies* (National Register Publishing). For a list of audiovisual firms, check out the latest edition of *AV Marketplace* (R.R. Bowker). Both these books may be found at your local library. To contact companies in your area, see the Geographic Index at the back of this book.

THE AD AGENCY, P.O. Box 470572, San Francisco CA 94147. Creative Director: Michael Carden. Advertising agency and **jingle/commercial music production house**. Clients include business, industry and retail. Estab. 1971. Uses the services of music houses, independent songwriter/composers and lyricists for scoring of commercials, background music for video production, and jingles for commercials. Commissions 20 composers and 15 lyricists/year. Pays by the job or by the hour. Buys all or one-time rights.
How to Contact: Submit demo tape of previous work. Prefers cassette with 5-8 songs and lyric sheet. SASE. Reports in 2 weeks.
Music: Uses variety of musical styles for commercials, promotion, TV, video presentations.
Tips: "Our clients and our needs change frequently."

‡ADVERTEL, INC., P.O. Box 18053, Pittsburgh PA 15236-0053. (412)469-0307. Fax: (412)469-8244. President/CEO: Paul Beran. Telephonic/Internet production company. Clients include small and multinational companies. Estab. 1983. Uses the services of music houses and independent songwriters/composers for scoring of instrumentals (all varieties) and telephonic production. Commissions 3-4 composers/year. Pay varies. Buys all rights and phone exclusive rights.

How to Contact: Submit demo tape of previous work. Prefers cassette. "Most compositions are 2 minutes strung together in 6, 12, 18-minute length productions." Does not return material; prefers to keep on file. Reports "right away if submission fills an immediate need."
Music: Uses all varieties, including unusual; mostly subdued music beds. Radio-type production used exclusively in telephone and Internet applications.
Tips: "Go for volume. We have continuous need for all varieties of music in 2-minute lengths."

AGA COMMUNICATIONS, 2557C N. Terrace Ave., Milwaukee WI 53211-3822. (414)962-9810. Fax: (414)456-0886. CEO: Arthur Greinke. Advertising agency, public relations/music artist management and media relations. Clients include small business, original music groups and special events. Estab. 1984. Uses the services of music houses, independent songwriters/composers and lyricists for scoring of motion picture and video productions; background music for special events; jingles for TV and radio. Commissions 4-6 composers and 4-6 lyricists/year. Pays on a per job basis.
How to Contact: Submit demo tape of previous work. Prefers CD, cassette, DAT or VHS videocassette with any number of songs and lyric sheet. "We will contact only when job is open, but will keep submissions on file." Does not return material. Reports in 4-6 weeks.
Music: Uses original rock, pop and heavy rock for recording groups, commercials and video projects.
Tips: "Try to give as complete a work as possible without allowing us to fill in the holes. High energy, unusual arrangements, be creative, different and use strong hooks!"

ALLEGRO MUSIC, 3990 Sunsetridge, Suite 203, Moorpark CA 93021-3757. E-mail: dannymuse@aol.com. Owner: Daniel O'Brien. Scoring service, **jingle/commercial music production house**. Clients include film-makers, advertisers, network promotions and aerobics. Estab. 1991. Uses the services of independent songwriters/composers and lyricists for scoring of films, jingles for ad agencies and promotions, and commercials for radio and TV. Commissions 3 composers and 1 lyricist/year. Pays $500-2,000/job. Buys all rights.
How to Contact: Query with résumé of credits or submit demo tape of previous work. Prefers cassette and lyric sheet. Does not return material. Reports in 4-6 weeks (if interested).
Music: Varied: Contemporary to orchestral.

ANDERSON COMMUNICATIONS, Dept. SM, 2245 Godby Rd., Atlanta GA 30349. (404)766-8000. President: Al Anderson. Producer: Vanessa Vaughn. Advertising agency and syndication operation. Estab. 1971. Clients include major corporations, institutions and media. Uses the services of music houses, independent songwriters/composers and lyricists for background music for commercials and jingles for syndicated radio programs. Commissions 5-6 songwriters or composers and 6-7 lyricists/year. Pays by the job. Buys all rights.
How to Contact: Write first to arrange personal interview or submit demo tape of previous work. Prefers cassette. Does not return material. Reports in 2 weeks or "when we have projects requiring your services."
Music: Uses a variety of music for music beds for commercials and jingles for nationally syndicated radio programs and commercials targeted at the black consumer market.
Tips: "Be sure the composition plays well in a 60-second format."

ANGEL FILMS COMPANY, 967 Hwy. 40, New Franklin MO 65274-9778. Phone/fax: (573)698-3900. E-mail: angelfilm@aol.com. President: Arlene Hulse. Motion picture and record production company (Angel One Records). Estab. 1980. Uses the services of music houses, independent songwriters/composers and lyricists for scoring of feature films, animation, TV programs and commercials, background music for TV and radio commercials and jingles. Commissions 12-20 composers and 12-20 lyricists/year. Payment depends upon budget; each project has a different pay scale. Buys all rights.

- See the listing for Angel Films Company in the Record Producers section.

How to Contact: Submit demo tape of previous work or query with résumé of credits. Prefers cassette or VHS videocassette with 3 pieces and lyric and lead sheet. "Do not send originals." SASE, but prefers to keep material on file. Reports in 6 weeks.
Music: Uses basically MOR, but will use anything (except C&W and religious) for record production, film, television and cartoon scores.

LISTINGS OF COMPANIES within this section which are either commercial music production houses or music libraries will have that information printed in boldface type.

Tips: "Don't copy others, just do the best that you can. We freelance all our work for our film and television production company, plus we are always looking for that one break-through artist for Angel One Records."

BEVERLY HILLS VIDEO GROUP, 2046 Armacost, W. Los Angeles CA 90025. (310)207-3319. Fax: (310)207-2798. E-mail: orsi2@ix.netcom.com. Website: http://www.BHVG.com. Senior VP: Thomas W. Orsi. Motion picture production company, **music sound effect library** and 10 bay production studio. Clients include Fox, UPN, Warner, A&E, Discovery. Estab. 1990. Uses the services of music houses and independent songwriters/composers for scoring of TV movies, background music for commercials and infomercials and commercials for TV. Commissions 6 composers/year. Pay varies. Rights purchased varies per job.
How to Contact: Submit demo tape of previous work. Prefers cassette, DAT or videocassette. SASE, but prefers to keep submitted material on file. "We will contact when client match is established."
Music: Uses all types for all assignments.
Tips: "Create a demo that has the most variety—no one type need be more than 90 seconds. Use only the 'best' sections of the material you have at hand, and be prepared—by being concise and to-the-point—for a phone call from us inquiring of your modus operandi. References are a must and will be contacted."

BLATTNER/BRUNNER INC., 1 Oxford Center, 6th Floor, Pittsburgh PA 15219. (412)263-2979. Broadcast Production Coordinator: Karen Smith. Clients include retail/consumer, service, high-tech/industrial/medical. Estab. 1975. Uses the services of music houses and independent songwriters/composers for background music for TV and radio spots and jingles for TV and radio spots. Commissions 2-3 composers/year. Pays by the job. Buys all rights or one-time rights, depending on the job.
How to Contact: Submit demo tape of previous work demonstrating background music or jingle skills. Prefers clearly labeled cassette or VHS or ¾" videocassette with 3-5 songs. Does not return material. Reports in 1-2 months.
Music: Uses upbeat, "unique-sounding music that stands out" for commercials and industrial videos.
Tips: "Send relevant work in conjunction to the advertising business—i.e., jingles."

‡BLUMENTHAL CADY & ASSOCIATES, INC., 10040 Regency Circle, Omaha NE 68114. (402)397-2077. Fax: (402)397-1958. E-mail: bcadver@earthlink.net. Executive Vice President/Creative Director: Bob Blumenthal. Advertising agency. Clients include financial, bank, health services, computer software design, retail, legal, other business to business. Estab. 1989. Uses the services of music houses, independent songwriters/composers and lyricists for background music for AV and shows (infomercials), jingles for commercials and commercials for radio and TV. Commissions 3-5 composers and 3-5 lyricists/year. Pays by the job. Buys all rights.
How to Contact: Submit demo tape of previous work. Prefers cassette or VHS videocassette. Prefers to keep submitted material on file. Reports back "if work matches our proposals to clients."
Music: Uses up-tempo, jazz, New Age for jingles, commercials and videos.

DAVID BOWMAN PRODUCTIONS, 28 Park Lane, Feasterville PA 19053. (215)942-9059 or (215)322-8078. Fax: (215)396-8693. President/Artistic Director: W. David Bowman. Scoring service, **jingle/commercial music production house**, music library producers/music production house and music publisher. Clients include television, radio, video production houses, computer/video game manufacturers, music production houses and multimedia developers. Estab. 1989. Uses the services of independent songwriters/composers and own team of music staff writers for scoring of films, documentaries and video productions, background music for television, radio, video productions and all multimedia applications, commercials for radio and TV, and background instrumental works for use in their music library. Commissions 5-10 composers/year. Pays by the job. Buys all rights or one-time rights.

- See their listing in the Music Publishers section.

How to Contact: Submit demo tape of previous work. Prefers cassette with 3-5 songs. "We are looking for instrumental pieces of any length not exceeding three minutes for use in our music library." Does not return material. Reports in 1-2 months.
Music: Uses all styles for television and radio commercials, video productions, various multimedia applications.
Tips: "Network. Get your name and your work out there. Let everyone know what you are all about and what you are doing. Be patient, persistent and professional. What are you waiting for? Do it!"

BOZELL KAMSTRA, (formerly Kamstra Communications, Inc.), 5914 W. Courtyard, Suite 320, Austin TX 78730. (512)343-8484. Fax: (512)343-6010. Contact: Beth Weersing, production manager. Advertising agency. Estab. 1963. Uses the services of music houses for jingles for radio and TV. Pays by the job. Buys all rights and one-time rights.

How to Contact: Submit demo tape of previous work. Prefers cassette. Does not return material.

BRg MUSIC WORKS, (formerly Philadelphia Music Works, Inc.), P.O. Box 202, Bryn Mawr PA 19010. (610)825-5656. E-mail: jandron@erols.com. Vice President Production: Jim Andron. **Jingle producers/ music library producers**. Uses independent composers and music houses for background music for AV/ broadcast and jingles for local and regional clients. Commissions 20 songwriters/year. Pays per job. Buys all rights.
How to Contact: Submit demo tape of previous work. Prefers cassette. "We are looking for quality jingle tracks already produced, as well as instrumental pieces between 2 and 3 minutes in length for use in AV music library." Does not return material; prefers to keep on file. Reports in 4 weeks.
Music: All types.
Tips: "Send your best and put your strongest work at the front of your demo tape."

‡BRYAN/DONALD INC. ADVERTISING, 2345 Grand, Suite 1625, Kansas City MO 64108. (816)471-4866. Fax: (816)421-7218. Creative Director: Don Funk. Advertising agency. Clients include food, franchise, business to business. Estab. 1966. Uses the services of independent songwriters/composers and lyricists for background music, jingles and commercials for radio. Commissions 1-2 composers and 1 lyricist/year. Pays negotiable. Buys all rights.
How to Contact: Submit demo tape of previous work. Prefers cassette. Prefers to keep material on file.

CALDWELL VANRIPER, 1314 N. Meridian, Indianapolis IN 46202. (317)632-6501. Vice President/ Executive Producer: Sherry Boyle. Advertising agency and public relations firm. Clients include industrial, financial and consumer/trade firms. Uses the services of music houses for scoring of radio, TV and A/V projects, jingles and commercials for radio and TV.
How to Contact: Submit demo tape of previously aired work. Prefers standard audio cassette. Does not return material. Prefers to keep materials on file. "Sender can follow up on submission. Periodic inquiry or reel update is fine."
Tips: "We do not work directly with composers, we work with music production companies. There are companies we work with locally in our market, and when we do use outside market companies, they are usually established production companies. I would suggest that composers contact the production companies directly."

CANARY PRODUCTIONS, P.O. Box 202, Bryn Mawr PA 19010. (215)825-1254. GM: Jan Manser. **Music library.** Estab. 1984. Uses the services of music houses and independent songwriters for background music for library and jingles for retailers. Commissions 10 composers/year. Pays $150-500 per job. Buys all rights.
How to Contact: Query with résumé of credits. Prefers cassette with 5-10 pieces. Does not return material. Reports in 1 month.
Music: All styles, but concentrates on industrial. "We pay cash for produced tracks of all styles and lengths. Production value is imperative. No scratch tracks accepted."

CANTRAX RECORDERS, Dept. SM, 2119 Fidler Ave., Long Beach CA 90815. (562)498-6492. Owner: Richard Cannata. Recording studio. Clients include anyone needing recording services (i.e. industrial, radio, commercial). Estab. 1980. Uses the services of independent songwriters/composers for scoring of and background music for commercials for radio and TV. Commissions 10 composers/year. Pays by the job.
How to Contact: Query with résumé of credits or submit demo tape of previous work. Prefers cassette, 7½/15 ips reel-to-reel or DAT with lyric sheets. "Indicate noise reduction if used." SASE, but prefers to keep material on file. Reports in 3 weeks.
Music: Uses jazz, New Age, rock, easy listening and classical for slide shows, jingles and soundtracks.
Tips: "Send a 7½ or 15 ips reel, cassette or DAT tape for us to audition; you must have a serious, professional attitude."

CASANOVA-PENDRILL PUBLICIDAD, 3333 Michelson, Suite 300, Irvine CA 92715. (714)474-5001. Production: Anna Jiminez. Advertising agency. Clients include consumer and corporate advertising—Hispanic markets. Estab. 1985. Uses the services of music houses, independent songwriters/composers and lyricists for radio, TV and promotions. Pays by the job or per hour. Buys all rights or one-time rights.
How to Contact: Submit demo tape of previous work, tape demonstrating composition skills and manuscript showing music scoring skills. Prefers cassette (or ¾ videocassette). "Include a log indicating spot(s) titles." Does not return material; prefers to keep on file.
Music: All types of Hispanic music (e.g., salsa, merengue, flamenco, etc.) for TV/radio advertising.

CINÉPOST FILM & VIDEO, 1937 Ontario Ave., Saskatoon, Saskatchewan S7K 1T5 **Canada**. (306)244-7788. Fax: (306)244-7799. President: Bill Stampe. Motion picture production company. Clients include broadcasting, corporate and retail. Estab. 1983. Uses the services of music houses, independent songwriter/composers and lyricists for scoring of corporate video/documentaries, background music for corporate videos and jingles for retail accounts. Commissions 6-10 composers and 3-4 lyricists/year. Pays negotiable fee per job. Buys all rights.
How to Contact: Query with résumé of credits, or submit demo tape of previous work. Prefers cassette or VHS/¾″/Beta with 3 songs. SASE. Reports in 3 weeks.
Music: Uses modern contemporary, dramatic and uptempo for corporate, video, drama and educational films.
Tips: "Show me a creative style that doesn't sound like canned music and is up to speed with today's music."

CINEVUE, P.O. Box 428, Bostwick FL 32007. (904)325-9356. Director/Producer: Steve Postal. Motion picture production company. Estab. 1955. Serves all types of film distributors. Uses the services of music houses, independent songwriters, composers and lyricists for scoring and background music for films. Commissions 10 composers and 5 lyricists/year. Pays by the job. Buys all rights.
How to Contact: Query with résumé of credits or submit demo tape of previous work ("good tape only!"). Submit manuscript showing music scoring skills. Prefers cassette with 10 pieces and lyric or lead sheet. Does not return material. "Send good audio-cassette, then call me in a week." Reports in 2 weeks.
Music: Uses all styles of music for features (educational films and slide presentations). "Need horror film music on traditional instruments—no electronic music."
Tips: "Be flexible, fast—do first job free to ingratiate yourself and demonstrate your style. Follow up with two phone calls."

COMMUNICATIONS FOR LEARNING, 395 Massachusetts Ave., Arlington MA 02174. (617)641-2350. E-mail: comlearn@thecia.net. Executive Producer/Director: Jonathan L. Barkan. Audiovisual and design firm. Clients include multi-nationals, industry, government, institutions, local, national and international nonprofits. Uses services of music houses and independent songwriters/composers for background music for videos and multimedia. Commissions 1-2 composers/year. Pays $2,000-3,000/job and one-time fees. Rights purchased varies.
How to Contact: Submit demo tape of previous work. Prefers cassette, CD or 7½ or 15 ips reel-to-reel (or ½″ or ¾″ videocassette). Does not return material; prefers to keep on file. "For each job we consider our entire collection." Reports in 2-3 months.
Music: Uses all styles of music for all sorts of assignments.
Tips: "Please don't call. Just send good material and when we're interested, we'll be in touch. Make certain name and phone number are on all submitted work itself, not only cover letter."

‡COMPRO PRODUCTIONS, 2080 Peachtree Ind. Court, Atlanta GA 30341-2281. (770)455-1943. Fax: (770)455-3356. E-mail: compro@compro-atl.com. Director: Nels Anderson. Film and video production company. Clients include corporations. Estab. 1977. Uses the services of independent songwriters/composers for scoring and background music for corporate communications, jingles for commercials and commercials for TV. Commissions 5-10 composers/year. Pays by the job. Buys all rights.
How to Contact: Query with résumé of credits, call first to arrange personal interview or submit demo tape of previous work. Prefers cassette, DAT or videocassette. SASE.
Music: Uses complete variety of assignments for numerous applications.

CREATIVE ASSOCIATES, Dept. SM, 44 Park Ave., Madison NJ 07940. (201)377-4440. Production Coordinator: Susan Graham. Audiovisual/multimedia firm. Clients include commercial, industrial firms. Estab. 1975. Uses the services of music houses and independent songwriters/composers for scoring of video programs, background music for press tours and jingles for new products. Pays $300-5,000/job. Buys all or one-time rights.
How to Contact: Submit demo tape of previous work demonstrating composition skills or query with résumé of credits. Prefers cassette or ½″ or ¾″ VHS videocassette. Prefers to keep material on file.
Music: Uses all styles for many different assignments.

CREATIVE SUPPORT SERVICES, 1950 Riverside Dr., Los Angeles CA 90039. (213)666-7968. Contact: Michael M. Fuller. **Music/sound effects library**. Clients include audiovisual production houses. Estab. 1978. Uses the services of independent songwriters and musicians for production library. Commissions 3-5 songwriters and 1-2 lyricists/year. Buys all rights.
How to Contact: Submit demo tape of previous work. Prefers cassette ("chrome or metal only") or 7½

ips reel-to-reel with 3 or more pieces. Does not return material; prefers to keep on file. "Will call if interested."
Music: Uses "industrial music predominantly, but all other kinds or types to a lesser degree."
Tips: "Don't assume the reviewer can extrapolate beyond what is actually on the demo."

D.S.M. PRODUCERS INC., 161 W. 54th St., Suite 803, New York NY 10019. (212)245-0006. President, CEO: Suzan Bader. CFO, CPA: Kenneth R. Wiseman. Submit to: Jannell McBride, Director A&R. Vice President, National Sales Director: Doris Kaufman. Scoring service, **jingle/commercial music production house** and original stock library called "All American Composers Library (administered world wide except USA by Warner/Chappell Music, Inc.)" Clients include networks, corporate, advertising firms, film and video, book publishers (music only). Estab. 1979. Uses the services of independent songwriters/composers for scoring of TV and feature films, background music for feature films and TV, jingles for major products and commercials for radio and TV. Pays 50% royalty. Buys all rights.

• See their listings in the Music Publishers and Record Producers sections.

How to Contact: Write first and enclose SASE for return permission. Prefers cassette or VHS videocassette with 2 songs and lyric or lead sheet. "Use a large enough return envelope to put in a standard business reply letter." Reports in 3 months.
Music: Uses dance, New Age, country and rock for adventure films and sports programs.
Tips: "Carefully label your submissions. Include a short bio/résumé of your works. Lyric sheets are very helpful to A&R. Only send your best tapes and tunes. Invest in your profession and get a local professional to help you produce your works. A master quality tape is the standard today. This is your competition so if you really want to be a songwriter, act like the ones who are successful—get a good tape of your tune. This makes it easier to sell overall."

dbF A MEDIA COMPANY, P.O. Box 2458, Waldorf MD 20604. (301)843-7110. President: Randy Runyon. Advertising agency, audiovisual and media firm and audio and video production company. Clients include business and industry. Estab. 1981. Uses the services of music houses, independent songwriters/composers and lyricists for background music for industrial videos, jingles and commercials for radio and TV. Commissions 5-12 composers and 5-12 lyricists/year. Pays by the job. Buys all rights.
How to Contact: Submit demo tape of previous work. Prefers cassette or 7½ ips reel-to-reel or VHS videocassette with 5-8 songs and lead sheet. SASE, but prefers to keep material on file. Reports in 1 month.
Music: Uses up-tempo contemporary for industrial videos, slide presentations and commercials.
Tips: "We're looking for commercial music, primarily A/C."

DISK PRODUCTIONS, 1100 Perkins Rd., Baton Rouge LA 70802. (504)343-5438. Director: Joey Decker. **Jingle/production house.** Clients include advertising agencies, slide production houses and film companies. Estab. 1982. Uses the services of music houses, independent songwriters/composers and lyricists for scoring of TV spots and films and jingles for radio and TV. Commissions 7 songwriters/composers and 7 lyricists/year. Pays by the job. Buys all rights.
How to Contact: Submit demo tape of previous work. Prefers cassette, DAT or ½" videocassette and lead sheet. Does not return material. Reports in 2 weeks.
Music: Needs all types of music for jingles, music beds or background music for TV and radio, etc.
Tips: "Advertising techniques change with time. Don't be locked in a certain style of writing. Give me music that I can't get from pay needle-drop."

ENSEMBLE PRODUCTIONS, P.O. Box 2332, Auburn AL 36831. (334)703-5963. E-mail: mcconbj@mail.auburn.edu. Owner: Barry J. McConatha. Interactive multimedia and video production/post production. Clients include corporate, governmental and educational. Estab. 1984. Uses services of music houses and independent songwriters/composers for background music for corporate public relations, educational and training videos. Commissions 0-5 composers/year. Pays $25-250/job depending upon project. Buys all or one-time rights.
How to Contact: Submit demo tape of previous work demonstrating composition skills. "Needs are sporadic, write first if submission to be returned." Prefers cassette or VHS videocassette with 3-5 songs. "Most needs are upbeat industrial sound but occasional mood setting music also. Inquire for details." Does not return material; prefers to keep on file. Reports in 3 months if interested.
Music: Uses upbeat, industrial, New Age, and mood for training, PR, education and multi-media.
Tips: "Make sure your printed material is as precise as your music."

ENTERTAINMENT PRODUCTIONS, INC., 2118 Wilshire Blvd. #744, Santa Monica CA 90403. (310)456-3143. Fax: (310)456-8950. President/Producer: Edward Coe. Motion picture and television production company. Clients include motion picture and TV distributors. Estab. 1972. Uses the services of

music houses and songwriters for scores, production numbers, background and theme music for films and TV and jingles for promotion of films. Commissions/year vary. Pays by the job or by royalty. Buys motion picture and video rights.
How to Contact: Query with résumé of credits. Demo should show flexibility of composition skills. "Demo records/tapes sent at own risk—returned if SASE included." Reports by letter in 1 month, "but only if SASE is included."
Tips: "Have résumé on file. Develop self-contained capability."

ESTILO COMMUNICATIONS, 1000 E. Cesar Chavez St., Austin TX 78702-4208. (512)499-0580. Fax: (512)499-0907. E-mail: estilo@eden.com. Website: http://www.eden.com/~estilo. President: Marion Sanchez-Lozano. Advertising agency. Clients include Hispanic and general. Estab. 1989. Uses the services of independent songwriter/composers for jingles for radio and commercials for radio and TV. Commissions 1 composer and 2 lyricists/year. Pays by the job. Buys all rights.
How to Contact: Query with résumé of credits. Submit demo tape of previous work. Prefers cassette. SASE. Reports in 2-3 weeks.
Tips: "Keep calling and sending new materials."

FILM CLASSIC EXCHANGE, 143 Hickory Hill Circle, Osterville MA 02655-1322. (508)428-7198. Vice President: Elsie Aikman. Motion picture production company. Clients include motion picture industry/ TV networks and affiliates. Estab. 1916. Uses the services of music houses, independent songwriters/ composers and lyricists for scoring and background music for motion pictures, TV and video projects. Commissions 10-20 composers and 10-20 lyricists/year. Pays by the job. Buys all rights.
How to Contact: Submit demo tape of previous work. Prefers cassette or VHS videocassette. SASE, but prefers to keep material on file. Reports in 3 weeks to 2 months.
Music: Uses pop and up-tempo for theatrical films/TV movies.
Tips: "Be persistent."

FINE ART PRODUCTIONS MULTIMEDIA, INTERACTIVE, 67 Maple St., Newburgh NY 12550-4034. Phone/fax: (914)561-5866. E-mail: rs7.fap@mhx.net or richie.suraci@bbs.mhv.net. Website: http://ww2.audionet.com/pub/books/fineart/fineart.htm. Producer/Researcher: Richard Suraci. Advertising agency, audiovisual firm, scoring service, **jingle/commercial music production house**, motion picture production company (Richie Suraci Pictures) and **music sound effect library**. Clients include corporate, industrial, motion picture and broadcast firms. Estab. 1987. Uses services of music houses, lyricists and independent songwriters/composers for scoring, background music and jingles for various projects and commercials for radio and TV. Commissions 1-10 songwriters or composers and 1-10 lyricists/year. Pays by the job. Buys all or one-time rights.
How to Contact: Submit demo tape of previous work or tape demonstrating composition skills or query with résumé of credits. Prefers cassette (or ½", ¾", or 1" videocassette) with as many songs as possible and lyric or lead sheets. SASE, but prefers to keep material on file. Reports in 3-9 months.
Music: Uses all types of music for all types of assignments.

FITZMUSIC, 208 W. 30th St., Suite 1006, New York NY 10001. (212)695-1992. Producer: Gary Fitzgerald. Scoring service, **commercial music production house and music/sound effects library**. "We service the advertising, film and television community." Estab. 1987. Uses the services of independent songwriters and lyricists for scoring of TV, radio and industrials, background music for movies and jingles and commercials for radio and TV. Commissions 4-5 composers and 2 lyricists/year. "*New York talent only.*" Pays per project. Buys all rights.
How to Contact: Call first to obtain permission to submit demo tape of previous work. Will not open unsolicited submissions. Prefers cassette. SASE, but prefers to keep on file. "A follow-up call must follow submission."
Music: Uses all styles of music.
Tips: "Complete knowledge of how the advertising business works is essential. Currently looking for all types of vocalists."

THE FRANKLYN AGENCY, 1010 Hammond St. #312, Los Angeles CA 90069. (213)272-6080. President: Audrey Franklyn. Advertising agency, public relations, audiovisual firm and cable production company. Clients include "everything from holistic health companies to singers." Estab. 1960. Uses the services of independent songwriters/composers and music houses for background music for cable and TV commercials. Commissions 4 composers and 2 lyricists/year. Pays flat fee per job. Buys all rights.
How to Contact: Query with résumé of credits. Prefers cassette or videocassette. Does not return material. Reports in 3 months.

Music: Uses all types for cable background, live performance.

FREDRICK, LEE & LLOYD, 235 Elizabeth St., Landisville PA 17538. (717)898-6092. Vice President: Dusty Rees. **Jingle/commercial music production house**. Clients include advertising agencies. Estab. 1976. Uses the services of independent songwriters/composers and staff writers for jingles. Commissions 2 composers/year. Pays $650/job. Buys all rights.
How to Contact: Submit tape demonstrating composition skills. Prefers cassette or 7½ ips reel-to-reel with 5 jingles. "Submissions may be samples of published work or original material." SASE. Reports in 3 weeks.
Music: Uses pop, rock, country and MOR.
Tips: "The more completely orchestrated the demos are, the better."

GK & A ADVERTISING, INC., 8200 Brookriver Dr., Suite 510, Dallas TX 75247. (214)634-9486. E-mail: rlmgka@aol.com. Advertising agency. Clients include retail. Estab. 1982. Uses the services of music houses, independent songwriters/composers and lyricists for background music, jingles and commercials for radio and TV. Commissions 1 composer and 1 lyricist/year. Buys all rights.
How to Contact: Submit demo tape of previous work. Prefers cassette. Does not return material; prefers to keep on file. Reports in 1 month.
Music: Uses all types for commercials.

‡GOLD & ASSOCIATES, INC., 100 Executive Way, Ponte Vedra Beach FL 32082. (904)285-5669. Fax: (904)285-8186. Creative Director: Keith Gold. Marketing, design and advertising firm. Clients include Time-Warner, Disney, Mercury Records, Time-Life Music. Estab. 1988. Uses the services primarily of music houses, but also composers. Agency develops its own lyrics for scoring of films—mostly corporate, background music for TV and radio commercials and videos. Commissions 5-10 music projects/year. "We pay 2-3 firms $500-1,000 for demos. For the final production, we pay between $5,000 and $35,000. We normally buy all rights. However, sometimes just for a year or specific markets."

- Gold & Associates, Inc. has won over 650 regional, national and international awards, including Clio Awards, American Music Awards and London International Awards.

How to Contact: Submit demo tape of previous work. Prefers audio cassette, videocassette or CD. Will keep submitted material on file. "We contact writers and music houses when we are ready to have music developed."
Music: Uses any and every style.
Tips: "Keep sending demos—at least two a year. Most of the time, we select three companies to take our lyrics, and produce a rough demo. We select companies or individuals that have the 'sound' we are looking for. We then choose one for final production."

GUIGUI MUSIC, (formerly Big Ears Music/Ducktape Studio), 435 Dorset #51, South Burlington VT 05403. (802)864-9871. Fax: (802)864-9869. Producer: Martin Guigui. **Commercial music production house** and publisher/album production. Clients include record labels, film and television. Estab. 1992. Uses the services of music houses, independent songwriters/composers and lyricists for scoring of film and TV, background music for industrials, commercials for radio and TV, and album production. Commissions 2 composers and 2 lyricists/year. Pay varies depending on projects and clients. Buys between 0-50% of rights.
How to Contact: Submit demo tape of current work. Prefers cassette. "No more than 3 songs per tape. Make sure they are your best songs." Does not return material. Reports in 4-6 weeks.
Music: Uses all styles but mostly a concentration on pop and R&B for film and TV (mostly children's).

HEYWOOD FORMATICS & SYNDICATION, 1103 Colonial Blvd., Canton OH 44714. (216)456-2592. Owner: Max Heywood. Advertising agency and consultant. Clients include radio, TV, restaurants/lounges. Uses the services of music houses for commercials for radio and TV. Payment varies per project. Buys all rights.
How to Contact: Submit demo tape of previous work. Prefers cassette or 7½ or 15 ips reel-to-reel or VHS/Beta videocassette. Does not return material.
Music: Uses pop, easy listening and CHR for educational films, slide presentations and commercials.

HILLMANN & CARR INC., 2121 Wisconsin Ave. NW, Washington DC 20007. (202)342-0001. E-mail: hcbulk@aol.com. President: Alfred Hillmann. Vice President/Treasurer: Ms. Michal Carr. Audiovisual firm and motion picture production company. Estab. 1975. Clients include corporate, government, associations and museums. Uses the services of independent songwriters/composers for scoring of film and video documentaries (mostly informational) and PSAs for TV. Commissions 2-3 composers/year. Payment negotiable. Buys all rights.

How to Contact: Submit demo tape of previous work. Prefers cassette or ¾" VHS or Beta videocassette with 5-10 pieces. Does not return material; prefers to keep on file. Reports only when interested.
Music: Uses contemporary, classical, up-tempo and thematic music for documentary film and video productions, multi-media exposition productions, public service announcements.
Tips: "Demonstrate comprehensive musicianship and ability to produce scoring for pictures cost-effectively. Don't include weak work, no matter what client or style."

THE HITCHINS COMPANY, 22756 Hartland St., Canoga Park CA 91307. (818)715-0510. E-mail: whitchins@aol.com. President: W.E. Hitchins. Advertising agency. Estab. 1985. Uses the services independent songwriters/composers for jingles and commercials for radio and TV. Commissions 1-2 composers and 1-2 lyricists/year. Will negotiate pay.
How to Contact: Query with résumé of credits. Prefers cassette or VHS videocassette. "Check first to see if we have a job." Does not return material; prefers to keep on file.
Music: Uses variety of musical styles for commercials.

HODGES ASSOCIATES, INC., P.O. Box 53805, 912 Hay St., Fayetteville NC 28305. (910)483-8489. President/Production Manager: Chuck Smith. Advertising agency. Clients include industrial, retail and consumer ("We handle a full array of clientele"). Estab. 1974. Uses the services of music houses and independent songwriters/composers for background music for industrial films and slide presentations, and commercials for radio and TV. Commissions 1-2 composers/year. Pays by the job. Buys all rights.
How to Contact: Submit demo tape of previous work. Prefers cassette. Does not return material; prefers to keep on file. Reports in 2-3 months.
Music: Uses all styles for industrial videos, slide presentations and TV commercials.

HOME, INC., 731 Harrison Ave., Boston MA 02118. (617)266-1386. Director: Alan Michel. Audiovisual firm and video production company. Clients include cable television, nonprofit organizations, pilot programs, entertainment companies and industrial. Uses the services of music houses and independent songwriters/composers for scoring of music videos, background music and commercials for TV. Commissions 2-5 songwriters/year. Pays up to $200-600/job. Buys all rights and one-time rights.
How to Contact: Submit demo tape of previous work. Prefers cassette with 6 pieces. Does not return material; prefers to keep on file. Reports as projects require.
Music: Mostly synthesizer. Uses all styles of music for educational videos.
Tips: "Have a variety of products available and be willing to match your skills to the project and the budget."

IZEN ENTERPRISES, INC., 2809 Bentree Court, Las Vegas NV 89134. (702)233-4473. President: Ray Izen. Video services. Estab. 1980. Uses the services of music houses and independent songwriters/composers. Commissions 2 composers and 2 lyricists/year. Pays by the job. Buys all rights.
How to Contact: Submit demo tape of previous work. Prefers cassette or VHS videocassette. Does not return material; prefers to keep on file.

K&R'S RECORDING STUDIOS, 28533 Greenfield, Southfield MI 48076. (248)557-8276. Contact: Ken Glaza. Scoring service and **jingle/commercial music production house**. Clients include commercial, industrial firms. Services include sound for pictures (music, dialogue). Uses the services of independent songwriters/composers and lyricists for scoring of film and video, jingles and commercials for radio and TV. Commissions 1 composer/month. Pays by the job. Buys all rights.
How to Contact: Submit demo tape of previous work. Prefers cassette or ¾" VHS videocassette with 5-7 pieces minimum. "Show me what you can do in 5 to 7 minutes." Does not return material.

KATSIN/LOEB ADVERTISING INC., 825 Battery St., San Francisco CA 94111. (415)399-9960. Fax: (415)399-9264. Head of Production: Pamela Zellers. Advertising agency. Clients include travel, health care, entertainment and retail. Estab. 1989. Uses the services of music houses and independent songwriters/composers for commercials for radio and TV. Commissions 3-6 composers/year. Pays by the job. Buys all rights.
How to Contact: Submit demo tape of previous work. Does not return material; prefers cassette or ¾" videocassette. Prefers to keep submitted material on file.
Music: Uses all kinds for commercials.
Tips: "We look for great musical ideas that work in harmony with the commercials we produce. If you've got a reel filled with same, we may be able to do business."

KEATING MAGEE ADVERTISING, 2223 Magazine, New Orleans LA 70130. (504)523-2121. President: Merrimac Dillon. Advertising agency. Clients include retail, consumer products and services, busi-

INSIDER REPORT

Commercial music writers should look to music houses to get their start

Brian Olesky

When 30 seconds of commercial music can cost $30,000, creative directors expect songs to do more than just fill the background. They have to sing. They also have to evoke a positive emotion that will rub off on the advertised product, says Brian Olesky, senior vice president/creative director for the Houston-based advertising agency McCann-Erickson Worldwide. Olesky has worked in the commercial music business for 25 years. He knows an emotion-packed song when he hears it.

"You hear Bob Seger singing 'Like A Rock,' and you see these great all-American shots of trucks working hard, and it says something about the truck. The song is a great hook. It's very memorable and you feel good about that. You feel maybe Chevy trucks are like a rock. Maybe Chevy trucks are unbreakable, sturdy, tough. That's a great marriage of a very good song with a product. You put them together and you've got a great advertising campaign."

The same thing can be said of other commercials that utilize well-established music like Nike and the Beatles' "Revolution" or Windows 95 and the Rolling Stones' "Start Me Up." "People feel that with really well-established music they can take a shortcut to making their point," Olesky says. "There are certain songs in our society that make people feel a certain way." Those feelings can be worth a lot of money if they translate into sales. But it's not always wise to spend a fortune on a few notes. That's where beginners have the best shot at breaking in.

Although Olesky says he nearly always works with established commercial music houses, companies that compose custom music for commercials, television and movies, if money is an object he'll look elsewhere. "If somebody shows me something for Nike [on their demo reel] I know he's established, he's probably big budget, and he's probably pretty good. If somebody shows me stuff that he did on his own then I know this person's just getting started and if I have a low budget I might be more likely to go with him. I might think, 'Well, I don't have any money and this guy's done some interesting stuff, so I can probably get him at a low price, and if he's fresh and new he might be able to think in ways the established guys don't. He might give me something really interesting.' "

The hardest thing for these "new guys" is getting Olesky to hear their music. With three or four demo reels coming in a week, he doesn't usually have time to just sit down and listen. Instead, "when I get a few spare minutes I'll throw one in the machine and listen for a bit or if it's someone I've heard of I might be curious about his music. If I'm looking for music for a particular commercial I might play a few of these and see if anything turns me on or whether I should just go back to the people I usually work with."

INSIDER REPORT, *Olesky*

Olesky might also try someone new if he's working in a different city. "Sometimes you may shoot a commercial in Chicago and you just don't want to go through the hassle of doing all the work in Chicago and then running off to New York for the music. So you just might look around for a good Chicago music company. I've done some music like that in the past couple of years."

Olesky relies on music houses because they provide a reputation that is invaluable to busy creative directors. "These are very talented people. Some of them have spent years in the music business. A lot of them have composed music for top singers and top groups. A lot of these people are musicians who have toured with top groups and for one reason or another they get out of the touring life or the pop music business and they start doing commercials because they can be very lucrative."

He also knows each house's specialty and whether he can rely on them in a crunch. "If you have a crisis and you need something over the weekend, and you're a steady customer, they'll go out of their way to give you what you need. Also, after a while you've done so many pieces with a company they sort of read your mind. They know what you're looking for. It's like when your wife or girlfriend says, 'I'm making spaghetti tonight,' and you have a pretty good idea what spaghetti's going to taste like. When some total stranger says, 'I'm making spaghetti tonight,' well, you don't know what's in store."

Olesky believes music houses provide the best route for young songwriters to get into the commercial music business. Music houses can help writers get the exposure they need to catch the attention of ad agencies. To find both local and national music houses, Olesky recommends *Shoot*, an industry publication that lists the current, hot music houses. Songwriters can also call advertising agencies and ask for the production department to find out which music houses they work with. Even if they live in small towns with no ad agencies, songwriters can call local companies and ask who does their advertising.

Olesky says songwriters should call music houses and ask for guidelines before submitting their demos. Different music houses will have different expectations. The most important part of the demo, however, is the quality. Writers should have their music professionally produced if its quality will not come through on home equipment. It's important to make a good impression because "once you make a first contact, it grows from there." Some music houses may even offer advice about more appropriate places for songwriters to send their work. "Eventually some of their (music) will get picked up, they'll start doing well and eventually break out on their own."

Success, consistency and an understanding of a creative director's needs are what bring repeat business to commercial musicians. "If you work with somebody over and over it's sort of like money in the bank," Olesky says. Knowing where to turn for a specific kind of music makes his job a little easier. And because he wants his commercials to stand out, he's always looking for a fresh sound.

This search for a stand-out song is what makes it tough for musicians to follow trends in commercial music. Once something becomes a trend and everyone has jumped on the bandwagon, commercials start to sound the same and everyone jumps off, says Olesky. "The whole thing you're trying to do is get a unique sound. It's so important when you're doing a commercial. So many commercials look alike and sound alike. You'll spend a lot of money and you'll spend a lot of time, so when you put your commercial on the air the music helps it stand out." And, with luck, good commercial music will help make consumers hum a product jingle all the way to the store.

—Megan Lane

ness-to-business. Estab. 1981. Uses the services of music houses and independent songwriters/composers and lyricists for scoring of, background music and jingles for radio and TV commercials. Commissions 4 composers/year. Pays by the job. Buys all or one time rights.
How to Contact: Submit demo tape of previous work. Prefers cassette or VHS videocassette. Does not return material; prefers to keep on file. Reports in 2 weeks.
Music: Uses all types for commercials, presentations.
Tips: "Send reel of actual work and references."

KEN-DEL PRODUCTIONS INC., First State Production Center, 1500 First State Blvd., Wilmington DE 19804-3596. (302)999-1164. Estab. 1950. A&R Director: Shirl Lotz. General Manager: Edwin Kennedy. Clients include publishers, industrial firms and advertising agencies, how-to's and radio/TV. Uses services of songwriters for radio/TV commercials, jingles and multimedia. Pays by the job. Buys all rights.
How to Contact: "Submit all inquiries and demos in any format to general manager." Does not return material. Will keep on file for three years. Generally reports in 1 month.

‡KJD ADVERTISING & TELEPRODUCTIONS, INC., 30 Whyte Dr., Voorhees NJ 08043. (609)751-3500. Fax: (609)751-7729. E-mail: mactoday@earthlink.net. President/Executive Producer: Larry Scott. Audio-video production and media buyers. Clients are varied. Estab. 1989. Uses the services of music houses, independent songwriters/composers or lyricists for background music for commercials, industrials, TV programming themes and jingles; also commercials for radio and TV. Commissions 1-2 composers and 1-2 lyricists/year. Pay varies. Buys all rights.
How to Contact: Query with résumé of credits or submit demo tape of previous work. Prefers cassette, DAT, IPS reel-to-reel or ½″ or ¾″ Beta SP videocassette. SASE; but prefers to keep material on file. Reports in 6 weeks.

LAPRIORE VIDEOGRAPHY, 86 Allston Ave., Worcester MA 01604. (508)755-9010. Owner: Peter Lapriore. Video production company. Clients include corporations, retail stores, educational and sports. Estab. 1985. Uses the services of music houses, independent songwriters/composers for background music for marketing, training and educational films. "We also own several music libraries." Commissions 2 composers/year. Pays $150-1,000/job. Buys all rights.
How to Contact: Submit demo tape of previous work. Prefers cassette or VHS videocassette with 5 songs and lyric sheet. Does not return material; prefers to keep on file. Reports in 3 weeks.
Music: Uses slow, medium, up-tempo, jazz and classical for marketing, educational films and commercials.
Tips: "Be very creative and willing to work on all size budgets."

McCANN-ERICKSON WORLDWIDE, Dept. SM, 1360 Post Oak Blvd., Suite 1900, Houston TX 77056. (713)965-0303. Creative Director: Glen Bently. Advertising agency. Serves all types of clients. Uses services of music houses and independent songwriters for background music for television, jingles for radio, commercials for radio and TV, and videos. Commissions 10 songwriters/year. Pays production cost and registrated creative fee. Arrangement fee and creative fee depend on size of client and size of market. "If song is for a big market, a big fee is paid; if for a small market, a small fee is paid." Buys all rights.

- See the interview with McCann-Erickson's Senior Vice President/Creative Director Brian Olesky in this section.

How to Contact: Submit demo tape of previously aired work. Prefers 7½ ips reel-to-reel. "There is no minimum or maximum length for tapes. Tapes may be of a variety of work or a specialization. We are very open on tape content; agency does own lyrics." Does not return material. Responds by phone when need arises.
Music: All types.

MALLOF, ABRUZINO & NASH MARKETING, 477 E. Butterfield Rd., Lombard IL 60148. (708)964-7722. President: Ed Mallof. Advertising agency. Works primarily with auto dealer jingles. Estab. 1980. Uses music houses for jingles for retail clients and auto dealers, and commercials for radio and TV. Commissions 5-6 songwriters/year. Pays $600-2,000/job. Buys all rights.
How to Contact: Submit demo tape of previous work. Prefers cassette with 4-12 songs. SASE. Reports

LISTINGS OF COMPANIES within this section which are either commercial music production houses or music libraries will have that information printed in boldface type.

in 1 month.
Tips: "Send us produced jingles we could re-lyric for our customers' needs."

MARK CUSTOM RECORDING SERVICE, INC., 10815 Bodine Rd., Clarence NY 14031-0406. (716)759-2600. Vice President: Mark J. Morette. **Jingle/commercial music production house**. Clients include ad agencies. Estab. 1962. Uses the services of independent songwriters/composers for commercials for radio and TV.
How to Contact: Write first and obtain permission to submit. Prefers cassette with 3 songs. Does not return material; prefers to keep on file.
Music: Uses pop and jazz for radio commercials.

MEDIA CONSULTANTS, INC., P.O. Box 130, Sikeston MO 63801. (573)472-1116. E-mail: media@ldd.net. Owner: Richard Wrather. Advertising agency. Clients are varied. Estab. 1979. Uses the services of music houses, independent songwriters/composers and lyricists for jingles. Commissions 10-15 composers and 10-15 lyricists/year. Pays varying amount/job. Buys all rights.
How to Contact: Submit a demo tape or CD of previous work demonstrating composition skills. Prefers cassette or ½" or ¾" videocassette. Does not return material; prefers to keep on file. "Send samples and prices."
Music: Uses all styles of music for varied assignments.

PATRICK MOORE COMPOSITIONS, 91 Cambermere Dr., North York, Ontario M3A 2W4 **Canada**. (416)446-2974. Owner/President: Patrick Moore. Scoring service and **jingle/commercial music production house**. Clients include producers of documentaries/films (educational). Estab. 1988. Uses the services of orchestrators for scoring of orchestral scores. Commissions 1 composer/year. Pays by royalty. Buys synchronization rights.
How to Contact: Write first to arrange personal interview. Prefers cassette. Does not return material. Prefers to keep submitted material on file. Reports in 4 weeks.
Music: "I specialize in combining ethnic music with current music for educational films/documentaries."
Tips: "My needs are very specific and must meet the requirements of the producer and music editor on each project. It is not unusual for me to work with film producers and music writers from all over the world. I do a great deal of work by mailing video tapes and cassette tapes of rough drafts to producers and other professionals involved in a film production."

MOTIVATION MEDIA, INC., 1245 Milwaukee Ave., Glenview IL 60025. (708)297-4740. Production Manager: Glen Peterson. Audiovisual firm, video, multi-media production company and business meeting planner. Clients include business and industry. Estab. 1969. Uses the services of independent songwriters/composers for scoring of soundtracks/AV, modules; background music for business meeting videos, multi-image production and motivational pieces. Commissions 3-5 composers/year. Payment varies. Buys one-time rights.
How to Contact: Submit demo tape of previous work. Prefers cassette with 5-7 songs. Does not return material. Responds in 1 month.
Music: Uses "upbeat contemporary music that motivates an audience of sales people."

MULTI IMAGE PRODUCTIONS, Dept. SM, 8849 Complex Dr., San Diego CA 92123. (619)560-8383. Website: http://www.multiimage.com. Contact: Mark Maisonneuve. Audiovisual firm and motion picture production company. Serves business, corporate, industrial, commercial, military and cultural clients. Uses the services of independent songwriters/composers and lyricists for scoring of video and motion pictures, background music for videos, jingles and commercials for radio and TV, as well as corporate videos. Commissions 2-10 composers and 2-5 lyricists/year.
How to Contact: Submit demo tape of previous work. Prefers DAT with 2-5 pieces. SASE. Reports in 2-3 weeks.
Music: Uses "contemporary, pop, specialty, regional, ethnic, national and international" styles of music for "background scores written against script describing locales, action, etc. We try to stay clear of stereotypical 'canned' music and prefer a more commercial and dramatic (film-like) approach."
Tips: "We have established an ongoing relationship with a local music production/scoring house with whom songwriters would be in competition for every project; but an ability to score clean, full, broad, contemporary commercial and often 'film score' type music, in a variety of styles, would be a benefit."

NEW & UNIQUE VIDEOS, 2336 Sumac Dr., San Diego CA 92105. (619)282-6126. E-mail: videos@concentric.net. Website: http://www.concentric.net/~videos. Contact: Candace Love. Production of videotapes. Estab. 1981. Occasionally uses the services of independent songwriters for background music in

corporate, business and industrial videos. Commissions 2-3 composers/year. Pays by the job. Buys all rights.
How to Contact: Query with résumé of credits or submit demo tape of previous work. Prefers cassette. SASE. Keeps demos on file. Will contact songwriter if music is apropos to current upcoming projects.
Music: Uses up-tempo, easy listening and jazz.

NORTON RUBBLE & MERTZ, INC. ADVERTISING, 150 N. Wacker St., Suite 2900, Chicago IL 60606. (312)422-9500. Fax: (312)422-9501. President: Sue Gehrke. Advertising agency. Clients include consumer products, retail, business to business. Estab. 1987. Uses the services of music houses and independent songwriters/composers for jingles and background music for radio/TV commercials. Commissions 2 composers/year. Pays by the job.
How to Contact: Submit tape of previous work; query with résumé of credits. Prefers cassette. Does not return materials; prefers to keep on file.
Music: Uses up-tempo and pop for commercials.

ON-Q PRODUCTIONS, INC., 618 Gutierrez St., Santa Barbara CA 93103. (805)963-1331. President: Vincent Quaranta. Audiovisual firm. Clients include corporate accounts/sales conventions. Uses the services of music houses, independent songwriters/composers and lyricists for scoring, background music and jingles for AV shows. Commissions 1-5 composers and 1-5 lyricists/year. Buys all or one-time rights.
How to Contact: Query with résumé of credits. Prefers cassette or 15 ips reel-to-reel or VHS videocassette. Prefers to keep material on file.
Music: Uses up-tempo music for slide, video and interactive presentations.

PHOTO COMMUNICATION SERVICES, INC., 6055 Robert Dr., Traverse City MI 49684. (616)943-8800. President: M'Lynn Hartwell. Audiovisual firm and motion picture production company. Serves commercial, industrial and nonprofit clients. Uses services of music houses, independent songwriters, and lyricists for jingles and scoring of and background music for multi-image, film and video. Negotiates pay. Buys all or one-time rights.
How to Contact: Submit demo tape of previous work, tape demonstrating composition skills or query with résumé of credits. Prefers cassette. Does not return material; prefers to keep on file. Reports in 6 weeks.
Music: Uses mostly industrial/commercial themes.

PRICE WEBER MARKETING COMMUNICATIONS, INC., Dept. SM, P.O. Box 99337, Louisville KY 40223. (502)499-9220. E-mail: cfrank@priceweber.com. Producer/Director: Charles Frank. Advertising agency and audiovisual firm. Estab. 1968. Clients include Fortune 500, consumer durables, light/heavy industrials and package goods. Uses services of music houses and independent songwriters/composers for background music for videos and shows. Commissions 6-8 composers/year. Pays by the job ($500-2,000). Buys all or one-time rights.
How to Contact: Submit demo tape of previous work demonstrating composition skills. Prefers cassette with 10 pieces. "Enclose data sheet on budgets per selection on demo tape." Does not return material; prefers to keep on file. "We report back only if we use it."
Music: Uses easy listening, up-tempo, pop, jazz, rock and classical for corporate image industrials and commercials.
Tips: "We want fresh music. Composer must be able to work with tight budgets, $500-$2,000. Your music must enhance our message."

QUALLY & COMPANY INC., 2238 Central St. #3, Evanston IL 60201-1457. (847)864-6316. Creative Director: Robert Qually. Advertising agency. Uses the services of music houses, independent songwriters/composers and lyricists for scoring, background music and jingles for radio and TV commercials. Commissions 2-4 composers and 2-4 lyricists/year. Pays by the job. Buys various rights depending on deal.
How to Contact: Submit demo tape of previous work or query with résumé of credits. Prefers cassette or ¾" Beta videocassette. SASE, but prefers to keep material on file. Reports in 2 weeks.
Music: Uses all kinds of music for commercials.

‡ROYAL RECORDS OF AMERICA, P.O. Box 5368, Buena Park CA 90622. (714)522-2383. Executive Director: Jerry Smith. Audiovisual firm, scoring service, **music sound effect library, jingle/commercial music production house**, recording facility, record company, music publisher (Royal King Music), management firm (Five-Star Management & Entertainment) and graphics/multimedia studio. Clients include motion picture, television, ad agencies, AV companies. Estab. 1959. Uses the services of music houses, independent songwriters/composers, lyricists, composers, musicians and producers for scoring of TV and film, background music for TV, film and environmental background, jingles and commercials for radio and TV. Pays by the job, or job plus royalty.

- See their listing in the Record Companies section, as well as listings for Royal King Music in the Music Publishers section and Five-Star Management & Entertainment in the Managers and Booking Agents section.

How to Contact: Write first and obtain permission to submit. Enclose SASE for rapid reply. Prefers cassette, DAT, VHS videocassette or CD with any number of songs. "Submissions with any potential are filed and catalogued for further consideration." Reports in 1-3 weeks.
Music: Uses all styles. "We work with Hollywood film producers, TV producers, radio, ad agencies and multimedia companies and acquire the services of singers, songwriters, bands, musicians, orchestras, electronic musicians, composers, arrangers, choreographers, Hollywood actors and entertainers."

RS MUSIC PRODUCTIONS, 378 Brooke Ave., Toronto, Ontario M5M 2L6 **Canada**. (416)787-1510. President: Richard Samuels. Scoring service, **jingle/commercial music production house**. Clients include songwriters (private sector), ad agencies, direct retailers, communications companies. Estab. 1989. Uses the services of music houses and independent songwriters/composers and lyricists for background music for film and commercials for radio and TV. Commissions 2-3 composers and 4-6 lyricists/year. Buys all or one-time rights.
How to Contact: Submit demo tape of previous work. Prefers cassette or VHS videocassette with 4 songs and lyric sheet. Does not return material; prefers to keep on file. Reports in 2 months.
Music: Uses up-tempo and pop for jingles, corporate video underscore.
Tips: "Be exact in what you want to accomplish by contacting our company, i.e., what area of composition your forté is."

THE SANDBOX, 11684 Ventura Blvd., Suite 134, Studio City CA 91604. (818)386-9135. Fax: (818)386-2862. Producer/writer: Mark Wolfson. Scoring service and record production. Clients include film and record companies. Estab. 1984. Uses the services of independent songwriters/composers for scoring of films. Commissions 1 composer and 10 lyricists/year. Pays by royalty; each project is different. Buys assorted rights.

- See the listing for Real Entertainment in the Record Producers section.

How to Contact: Submit demo tape of previous work. Prefers cassette with 4 songs and lyric sheet. SASE. Reports in 2 weeks.
Music: Uses pop, R&B, new country, alternative for records, films, new artist packaging.
Tips: "Send your best work or a work in progress. No more than four songs (ever)."

SOLOMON FRIEDMAN ADVERTISING, Dept. SM, 2000 N. Woodward, Suite 300, Bloomfield Hills MI 48304. (810)540-0660. Creative Director: Chato Hill. Advertising agency. Clients include package goods, food service accounts, convenience stores, retail accounts and small service businesses. Uses independent songwriters, lyricists and music houses for jingles and special presentations. Commissions 1-10 songwriters and 1-10 lyricists/year. Pays by the job. Buys all rights.
How to Contact: Submit demo tape of previously aired work. Prefers cassette or 7½ ips reel-to-reel with 1-5 pieces and lyric or lead sheets. "Submissions must be up-to-date and up to industry standards." Does not return material; prefers to keep on file.
Music: MOR, pop or rock jingles describing specific products or services.
Tips: "Please make sure all information presented is CURRENT!"

‡SORIN PRODUCTIONS INC., 919 Highway 33, Suite 46, Freehold NJ 07728. (908)462-1785. Fax: (908)462-8411. E-mail: sorinvideo@aol.com. President: David Sorin. Audiovisual firm. Clients include corporations. Estab. 1982. Uses the services of music houses and independent songwriters/composers for background music for industrials and commercials for radio and TV. Commissions 2-3 composers/year. Pays negotiable amount/job. Buys all rights.
How to Contact: Query with résumé of credits or send e-mail. Does not return material.
Music: Uses contemporary, upbeat, corporate for video, educational and local spots.

SOTER ASSOCIATES INC., 209 N. 400 W., Provo UT 84601. (801)375-6200. President: N. Gregory Soter. Advertising agency. Clients include financial, health care, municipal, computer hardware and software. Estab. 1970. Uses services of music houses, independent songwriters/composers and lyricists for background music for audiovisual presentations and jingles for radio and TV commercials. Commissions 1 composer, 1 lyricist/year. Pays by the job. Buys all rights.
How to Contact: Submit tape demonstrating previous work and composition skills. Prefers cassette or VHS videocassette. Does not return submissions; prefers to keep materials on file.

NATE STEWART ADVERTISING, 401 S. Main St., Cleburne TX 76031. (817)641-4389. Fax: (817)641-7446. Owner: Nate Stewart. Advertising agency and recording studio. Clients include "top musicians for work on the projects we are involved in and songwriters." Estab. 1983. Uses the services of music houses and independent songwriters/composers for background music for videos, "music for release on CD and tapes for specific purposes such as spiritual, political, educational and romantic." Commissions 4 composers and 2 lyricists/year. Pays by the job or the hour.
How to Contact: Query with résumé of credits. "If the résumé of credits fits the needs of the project, then current material may be requested." Prefers cassette with 3 songs and lyric sheet. "Please send an introductory letter if no résumé is available. Please send both introductory letter and résumé if possible." Prefers to keep submitted material on file. Reports in 4-6 weeks.
Music: Top 40 crossover.

SULLIVAN & FINDSEN ADVERTISING, Dept. SM, 2165 Gilbert Ave., Cincinnati OH 45206. (513)281-2700. Fax: (513)281-2729. Director of Broadcast Production: Kirby Sullivan. Advertising agency. Clients include consumer and business-to-business firms. Uses the services of music houses and independent songwriters/composers for jingles and commercials for radio and TV. Commissions 3 composers and 3 lyricists/year. Pays by the job. Buys all rights.
How to Contact: Submit demo tape of previous work. Prefers cassette. Does not return material; prefers to keep on file. "We report back when we need some work."
Music: Uses all styles for commercials.
Tips: "Don't call!"

TIERNEY & PARTNERS, Dept. SM, 200 S. Broad St., Philadelphia PA 19102. (215)790-4100. Broadcast Business Manager: Gloria Anderson. Advertising agency. Serves industrial and consumer clients. Uses music houses for jingles and background music in commercials. Pays creative fee asked by music houses.
How to Contact: Submit demo tape of previously aired work, all types of music. "You must send in previously published work. We do not use original material." Prefers cassette. Will return with SASE if requested, but prefers to keep on file.

TRF PRODUCTION MUSIC LIBRARIES, Dept. SM, 747 Chestnut Ridge Rd., Chestnut Ridge NY 10977. (914)356-0800. President: Michael Nurko. **Music/sound effect libraries.** Estab. 1931. Uses the services of independent composers for jingles, background and theme music for all media including films, slide presentations, radio and TV commercials. Pays 50% royalty.
How to Contact: Submit demo tape of new compositions. Prefers cassette with 3-7 pieces.
Music: Primarily interested in instrumental music for assignments in all media.

27TH DIMENSION INC., P.O. Box 992, Newnan GA 30264. (800)634-0091. E-mail: 70711.103@compuserve.com. President: John St. John. Scoring service, **jingle/commercial music production house** and **music sound effect library**. Clients include audiovisual producers, video houses, recording studios and radio and TV stations. Estab. 1986. Uses the services of independent songwriters/composers for background music for commercials, industrials and A/V and for scoring of library material. Commissions 10 composers/year. Pays $100-1,000/job. "We buy the right to use in our library exclusively." Buys all rights except writer's publishing. Writer gets all performance fees (ASCAP or BMI).
How to Contact: Submit demo tape of previous work. Prefers CDR or DAT. "Call before sending." SASE, but prefers to keep on file. Reports in 1 month.
Music: Uses industrial, pop jazz, sports, contemporary and New Age for music library.

VIDEO I-D, INC., Dept. SM, 105 Muller Rd., Washington IL 61571. (309)444-4323. E-mail: videoid@videoid.com. Website: http://www.VideoID.com. Manager, Marketing Services: Gwen Wagner. Post production/teleproductions. Clients include industrial and business. Estab. 1977. Uses the services of music houses and independent songwriters/composers for background music for video productions. Pays per job. Buys one-time rights.
How to Contact: Submit demo tape of previous work. Prefers cassette or VHS videocassette with 5 songs and lyric sheet. Does not return material. Reports in 3-4 weeks.

WARD AND AMES, 7500 San Felipe, #350, Houston TX 77063. Phone/fax: (713)266-9696. Danny Ward and Nancy Ames. Composing and scoring service, **jingle/commercial music production house**, event design and consultancy. Clients include corporations, ad agencies, political entities, TV markets, film studios and production houses. Estab. 1982. Composes and produces custom music packages in-house recording studios for scoring of background music, jingles and commercials for all media; also industrials.

How to Contact: Submit project RFP and budget or call to discuss availability. Reports in 3 weeks.
Music: Uses all types for custom productions, jingles, industrials, product launches, ad campaigns and film.

‡WEISS/STAFFORD PRODUCTIONS, P.O. Box 101107, San Antonio TX 78201. Phone/fax: (210)733-7170. E-mail: faweiss@txdirect.net. Producer: Fred Weiss. Television production company. Clients include advertising and TV stations. Estab. 1996. Uses the services of independent songwriters/composers and lyricists for TV programs and music videos. Commissions 100 composers and 100 lyricists/year. Pays statutory royalty. Buys all rights.
How to Contact: Submit demo of the work to be considered. Prefers cassette with 3-4 songs and lyric sheet. "Prefer commercial cuts for young adult male and female artists and bands." Does not return material. Reports in 6 weeks.
Music: Uses Latin, Tejano, international pop and R&B (also Christmas) for talent-search weekly TV show (22 shows/year).

EVANS WYATT ADVERTISING, 346 Mediterranean Dr., Suite 220, Corpus Christi TX 78418. (512)939-7200. Fax: (512)939-7999. Owner: E. Wyatt. Advertising agency. Clients are general/all types. Estab. 1975. Uses the services of music houses and independent songwriters/composers for background music for soundtracks, jingles for advertising and commercials for radio and TV. Commissions 10-12 composers/year. Pays by the job. Buys all rights.
How to Contact: Submit demo tape of previous work demonstrating composition skills, query with résumé of credits or write first to arrange personal interview. Prefers cassette. SASE, but prefers to keep material on file. Reports in 2 months.
Music: Uses all types for commercials and videos.

GREG YOUNGMAN MUSIC, P.O. Box 381, Santa Ynez CA 93460. (805)688-1136. Advertising agency/audio production. Serves all types of clients. Local, regional and national levels. Uses the services of music houses and independent composers/lyricists for commercials, jingles and audiovisual projects. Commissions 12-20 composers/year. Pays $500-10,000/project. Buys all or one-time rights.
How to Contact: Submit demo tape of previously aired work. Prefers cassette, R-DAT or reel-to-reel. Does not return material; prefers to keep on file. Reports in 1 month.
Music: Uses all types for radio commercials, film cues.
Tips: "Keep demos to ten minutes."

Play Producers and Publishers

Getting a play produced is one of the the biggest challenges a playwright faces, and finding a theater company willing to invest large amounts of time and money into producing a play by an unknown playwright can be frustrating. But opportunities do exist, and the companies listed in this section are interested in hearing new works.

This section covers two segments of the industry: theater companies, producers and dinner theaters come under the heading of Play Producers, and the publishers of musical theater works are listed under the Play Publishers heading. All these markets are actively seeking new works of all types for their stages or publications.

When preparing to submit your work to any of the companies listed within these pages, keep in mind that many of the listings in the Play Producers section are small theaters run on a nonprofit basis. Research each company carefully and learn about their past performances, the type of musicals they present, and the kinds of material they're looking for. When you find theaters you think may be interested in your work, attend as many performances as possible, so you know exactly what type of material each theater presents. Volunteer to work at a theater, whether it be moving sets or selling tickets. This will give you valuable insight into the day-to-day workings of a theater and the creation of a new show. Look into professional internships at theaters and attend theater workshops in your area (see the Workshops and Conferences section for more information). The more knowledgeable you are about the workings of a particular company or theater, the easier it will be to tailor your work to fit its style and the more responsive they will be to you and your work. As a composer for the stage, you need to know as much as possible about a theater and how it works, its history and the different roles played by the people involved in it. Flexibility is the key to successful productions, and having a knowledge of how a theater works will only help you in cooperating and collaborating with the director, producer, technical people and actors.

If you're a playwright looking to have his play published in book form or in theater publications, see the listings under the Play Publishers section. To find play producers and publishers in your area, consult the Geographic Index at the back of this book.

A.D. PLAYERS, 2710 W. Alabama, Houston TX 77098. (713)526-2721. Contact: Literary Manager. Play producer. Estab. 1967. Produces 5 full-length, 5 children's and approximately 20 1 acts in repertory and 1-2 musicals/year. Audience tends to be conservative; main stage shows, children/families; repertory shows, churches, schools, business. Payment varies.

How to Contact: Query with synopsis, character breakdown and set description. SASE. Reports in 6-12 months.

Musical Theater: "We prefer musicals for family and/or children, comedy or drama, full-length, original or classic adaptations with stories that reflect God's relevence and importance in our lives. Any style. Maximum 10 actors. No fly space required. Minimum wing space required. No New Age; anything contradictory to a Christian perspective; operatic; avant garde cabaret. Music should be simple, easy to learn and perform, we utilize a broad range of musical ability; will consider musical revue to musical comedy, plays with music."

Productions: *Narnia*, by Jules Tasca (children, family, fantasy, musical); *Smoke on the Mountain*, by Connie Ray and Alan Bailey (family gospel, hymn heritage); and *Myrtle: A Melodrama*, by Jeannette Clift George (old-fashioned melodrama based on story of Esther).

Tips: "Learn the craft, structure and format of scriptwriting before submitting. Then be flexible and open to learning from any producing theatre which takes an interest in your work."

THE ACTING COMPANY, Dept. SM, P.O. Box 898, Times Square Station, New York NY 10108. (212)564-3510. Play producer. Estab. 1972. Produces 2-3 plays/year. "Have done musicals in the past. We

are a national touring company playing universities and booking houses." Pays by royalty or negotiated fee/commission.
How to Contact: Submit through agent only.
Musical Theater: "We would consider a wide variety of styles—although we remain a young, classical ensemble. Most of our classical plays make use of a lot of incidental music. Our company consists of 13 actors. All productions must be able to tour easily. We have no resident musicians. Taped sound is essential. Actors tend to remain active touring members for 2-3 seasons. Turnover is considerable. Musical ability of the company tends to vary widely from season to season. We would avoid shows which require sophisticated musical abilities and/or training."

‡AMAS MUSICAL THEATRE, INC., 450 W. 42nd St., Suite 2J, New York NY 10036. (212)563-2565. Fax: (212)268-5501. Producing Director: Donna Trinkoff. Play producer. Estab. 1968. Produces 2 musicals/year and musical development series (AMAS Six O'Clock Musical Theatre Lab) produces 5-6 concert versions of new musicals. "Our emphasis is on multicultural audiences." Performance space is on Off-off Broadway theater with 76-99 seats. Payment is negotiable.
How to Contact: Submit complete manuscript and tape of songs. SASE. Reports in 3-6 months.
Musical Theater: Seeks "innovative, well-written, good music. We seek musicals that lend themselves to multiracial casting."
Productions: *Time and the Wind*, lyrics by Norman Matlock, music by Galt McDermott; *Bobos*, lyrics by Ed Shockley, music by James McBride (urban street opera); and *The Princess & the Black-Eyed Pea*, book and lyrics by Karole Foreman, music and additional lyrics by Andy Chukerman (fairy-tale retold).

AMERICAN LIVING, History Theater, Box 752, Greybull WY 82426. (307)765-9449. President and Artistic Director: Dorene Ludwig. Play producer. Estab. 1975. Produces 1-2 plays/year. Performs all over U.S.—conventions, schools, museums, universities, libraries, etc. Pays by royalty.
How to Contact: Query first. SASE. Reports in 6-12 months.
Musical Theater: "We use only primary source, historically accurate material: in music—*Songs of the Civil War* or *Songs of the Labor Movement*, etc.—presented as a program rather than play would be the only use I could foresee. We need music historians more than composers."
Tips: "Do not send fictionalized historical material. We use primary source material only."

AMERICAN MUSIC THEATER FESTIVAL, 123 S. Broad St., Suite 1820, Philadelphia PA 19109. (215)893-1570. Fax: (215)893-1233. Artistic Director: Ben Levit. Play producer. Estab. 1984. Produces 4 new musicals/year. Plays performed at "Plays and Players theater, an old turn-of-the-century vaudeville house. 320 seats in Center City, Philadelphia." Pays royalties.
How to Contact: Query with synopsis and character breakdown. SASE. Reports in 6 months.
Music: "We seek musicals ranging from the traditional to very experimental. We encourage multimedia and technological applications. Topics can range. We are interested in music theater/opera that comments on current life. Musical styles can vary from folk through opera. Orchestra generally limited to a maximum of 7 pieces; cast size maximum of 10-12."
Musical Theater: *Floyd Collins*, by Adam Guettel/Tina Landau; *Black Water*, by John Duffy/Joyce Carol Oates; and *Another Midsummer Night*, by Jeff Lunden/Art Pearlman.
Tips: "We look for pieces that are music/lyric driven, not merely plays with music."

‡AMERICAN MUSICAL THEATRE OF SAN JOSE, 1717 Technology Dr., San Jose CA 95110-1305. (408)453-7100. Fax: (408)453-7123. E-mail: amtsj@amtsj.org. Associate Artistic Director: Marc Jacobs. Play producer. Estab. 1935. Produces 4 mainstage musicals and 1 musical in concert/year (just starting New Works program). "Our season subscribers are generally upper-middle class families. However, we plan to open a second stage where we can do works which would appeal to a more eclectic audience. Our main season is in the 2,500-seat San Jose Center for the Performing Arts. This is a state-of-the-art theatre. We are currently looking for a flexible 200-800 seat space to be a second stage which would be partially dedicated to producing new works." Pays variable royalty.
How to Contact: Submit complete manuscript, score and tape of songs. SASE. Reports in 3 months.
Musical Theater: "We are not looking for children's musicals, Christmas shows or puppet shows. We are looking for high quality (professional caliber) musicals to develop for either our 2,500 seat main stage theatre or a proposed smaller second stage, a national tour or possible Broadway production. Submissions from composers and writers with some previous track record only, please. We are especially interested in works which are presented in non-traditional (non-linear) styles. The first thing we look for is quality and originality in the music and lyrics. Next we look for librettos that offer exciting staging possibilities. If writing original music to a pre-existing play please be sure all rights have been cleared."
Productions: *The Who's Tommy*, by The Who (pinball wizard); *Anything Goes*, by Cole Porter ('20s madcap); and *Will Rogers Follies*.

Tips: "We are a company with a $6 million per season operating budget and one of the largest subscription audiences in the country. We are looking for shows we can develop for possible main stage or Broadway productions. Therefore it is advisable that any composers or writers have some professional production history before submitting to us."

AMERICAN STAGE FESTIVAL, P.O. Box 225, Milford NH 03055. (603)889-2330. Producing Director: Matthew Parent. Play producer. Estab. 1975. Produces 5 mainstage plays, 10 children's and 2-3 musicals/year. Plays are produced in 496 seat proscenium stage for a general audience. Pays 5-12% royalty.
How to Contact: Query with synopsis, character breakdown and set description. SASE. Reports in 3 months.
Musical Theater: "We seek stories about interesting people in compelling situations. Besides our adult audience we have an active children's theater. We will not do a large chorus musical if cast size is over 18. We use original music in plays on a regular basis, as incidental music, pre-show and between acts, or as moments in and of themselves."
Productions: *1776*, by Edwards/Stone (history); *Alice Revisited*, by Julianne Boyd and Joan Micklin Silver (women's issues); and *Forever Plaid*, by Stuart Ross (revue of 1950s songs).
Tips: "We need musicals with a strong, intelligent book. Send tape of music along with initial query. Our decisions regarding musicals are based heavily upon the quality of the score."

ARDEN THEATRE COMPANY, 40 N. Second St., Philadelphia PA 19106. (215)922-8900. Website: http://www.libertynet.org/~arden. Producing Artistic Director: Terrence J. Nolen. Play producer. Estab. 1988. Produces 3-4 plays and 1-2 musicals/year. Adult audience—diverse. Mainstage: 299+ seats, flexible. Studio: 175 seats, flexible. Pays 5% royalty.
How to Contact: Submit letter of interest, synopsis and tape of songs. SASE. Reports in 6 months.
Musical Theater: Full length plays and musicals. Intimate theater space, maximum cast approximately 15, minimum can be smaller. Not interested in children's music. Will consider original music for use in developing or pre-existing play. Composers should send samples of music on cassette.
Productions: *Tiny Island*, by Michael Hollinger (new play); *Hedda Gabler*, by Ibsen (classic drama); and *Merrily We Roll Along*, by Sondheim/Furth (musical comedy).

ARIZONA THEATRE COMPANY, P.O. Box 1631, Tucson AZ 85702. (520)884-8210. Artistic Director: David Goldstein. Professional regional theater company. Members are professionals. Performs 6 productions/year, including 1 new work. Audience is middle and upper-middle class, well-educated, aged 35-64. "We are a two-city operation based in Tucson, where we perform in a 603-seat newly renovated, historic building, which also has a 100-seat flexible seating cabaret space. Our facility in Phoenix, the Herberger Theater Center, is a 712-seat, proscenium stage." Pays 4-10% royalty.
How to Contact: Query first. Reports in 5 months.
Musical Theater: Musicals or musical theater pieces. 15-16 performers maximum including chorus. Instrumental scores should not involve full orchestra. No classical or operatic.
Productions: *Quilters*, by Barbara Damashek (musical theater piece); *Candide*, by Sondheim/Bernstein (musical); and *Dreamers of the Day*, by Anita Ruth (musical theater piece).
Tips: "As a regional theater, we cannot afford to produce extravagant works. Plot line and suitability of music to further the plot are essential considerations."

ARKANSAS REPERTORY THEATRE, 601 Main, P.O. Box 110, Little Rock AR 72203. (501)378-0445. Contact: Brad Mooy. Play producer. Estab. 1976. Produces 8 plays and 4 musicals (1 new musical)/year. "We perform in a 354-seat house and also have a 99 seat blackbox." Pays 5-10% royalty or $75-150 per performance.
How to Contact: Query with synopsis, character breakdown and set description. SASE. Reports in 6 months.
Musical Theater: "Small casts are preferred, comedy or drama and prefer shows to run 1:45 to 2 hours maximum. Simple is better; small is better, but we do produce complex shows. We aren't interested in children's pieces, puppet shows or mime. We always like to receive a tape of the music with the book."
Productions: *Sing, Baby Sing*, by Don Jones/Jack Heifner (original swing musical); and *Always . . . Patsy Cline*, by Ted Swindley (bio-musical).
Tips: "Include a *good* cassette of your music, *sung well*, with the script."

ASOLO THEATRE COMPANY, Dept. SM, 5555 N. Tamiami Trail, Sarasota FL 34243. (941)351-9010. Literary Manager: Bruce E. Rodgers. Play producer. Produces 7-8 plays (1 musical)/year. Plays are performed at the Asolo Mainstage (500-seat proscenium house). Pays 5% minimum royalty.
How to Contact: Query with synopsis, character breakdown, set description and one page of dialogue.

SASE. Reports in 3 months.
Musical Theater: "We want small to mid-size non-chorus musicals only. They should be full-length, any subject. There are no restrictions on production demands; however, musicals with excessive scenic requirements or very large casts may be difficult to consider."
Productions: *Sweet and Hot*, by Julie Boyd; *Svengali*, by Boyd, Wildhorn and Bettis; and *Das Barbecü*, by Warrender and Luis.

BAILIWICK REPERTORY, Bailiwick Arts Center, 1229 W. Belmont, Chicago IL 60657. (773)883-1091. Executive Director: David Zak. Artistic Director: Cecilie D. Keenan. Play producer. Estab. 1982. Produces 5 mainstage, 5 one-act plays and 1-2 new musicals/year. "We do Chicago productions of new works on adaptations that are politically or thematically intriguing and relevant. We also do an annual director's festival which produces 50-75 new short works each year." Pays 5-8% royalty.
How to Contact: "Send SASE (business size) first to receive manuscript submission guidelines. Material returned if appropriate SASE attached." Reports in 6 months.
Musical Theater: "We want innovative, dangerous, exciting material."
Productions: *The Christmas Schooner*, by John Reeger and Julie Shannon (holiday musical); *Pope Joan*, by Christopher Moore (dark ages); and *In The Deep Heart's Core*, by Joseph Sobel (Yeats).
Tips: "Be creative. Be patient. Be persistent. Make me believe in your dream."

BARTER THEATRE, P.O. Box 867, Abingdon VA 24212. (540)628-2281. Fax: (540)628-4551. Artistic Director: Richard Rose. Play producer. Estab. 1933. Produces 12 plays and 2-3 musicals (1 new musical)/year. Audience "varies; middle American, middle age, tourist and local mix." 500 seat proscenium stage, 150 seat thrust stage. Pays by $2,500 fee or 5% royalty.
How to Contact: Query with synopsis, character breakdown and set description. SASE. Reports in 1 year.
Musical Theater: "We investigate all types. We are not looking for any particular standard. Prefer sellable titles with unique use of music. Prefer small cast musicals, although have done large scale projects with marketable titles or subject matter. We use original music in almost all of our plays." Does not wish to see "political or very urban material, or material with very strong language."
Productions: *Doctor! Doctor!* and *Girl of My Dreams*, by Peter Ekstrom and David DeBoy; and *WMKS*, by Frank Higgins (old time folk and country music).
Tips: "Be patient. Be talented. Don't be obnoxious. Be original."

BIRMINGHAM CHILDREN'S THEATRE, P.O. Box 1362, Birmingham AL 5201. (205)458-8181. (205)458-8895. E-mail: bctadmin@aol.com. Website: http://www.bham.net/bct. Executive Director: Charlotte Lane Dominick. Play producer. Estab. 1947. Produces 9 plays and 1-4 new musicals/year; "typically, original adaptations of classic children's stories for pre-school through grade 1, K-6, and junior and senior high school." "Wee Folks" Series: preschool through grade 1; Children's Series: K-6; Young Adult Series: junior and senior high. Performs in 1,072-seat flexible thrust mainstage, 250 seat black box (touring venues vary). Pay is negotiable.
How to Contact: Query with synopsis, character breakdown and set description. SASE. Reports in 3 months.
Musical Theater: " 'Wee Folks' productions should be 40-45 minutes; Children's Series 55-60 minutes; Young Adult Series 85-95 minutes. 'Wee Folks' shows should be interactive; all others presentational. Most productions tour, so sets must be lightweight, simple and portable. 'Wee Folks' shows prefer cast of four. Touring Children's Series shows prefer cast of six. All others prefer cast of 12 or less. BCT traditionally ultilizes a great deal of music for underscoring, transitions, etc. We welcome submissions from prospective sound designers."
Productions: *Teddy Roosevelt and the Star Spangled Christmas Tree*, by Elliot Street; *Heidi*, by Ann Pugh; and *Three Billy Goats Gruff*, by Jean Pierce.

THE BLOWING ROCK STAGE COMPANY, P.O. Box 2170, Blowing Rock NC 28605. (704)295-9168. Fax: (704)295-9104. E-mail: theatre@blowingrock.com. Producing Director: Mark Wilson. Play producer. Estab. 1986. Produces 2 plays, 2 musicals and 1 new musical/year. Performances take place in a 240 seat proscenium summer theater in the Blue Ridge Mountains. Pays 5-10% royalty.
How to Contact: Query with synopsis, character breakdown and set description. SASE. Reports in 6 months.
Musical Theater: "Casts of 10 or less are preferred, with ideal show running time of 2 hours, intermission included. Limit set changes to three or less; or unit concept. Some comic relief, please. Not producing children's theater or stark adult themes."
Productions: *The IT Girl*, by McNicholl/Small/McKibbins; *The Melody Lingers On*, by Irving Berlin/Baker/Barrett; and *Last Of the Red Hot Mamas*, by Parise/Baker (the Sophie Tucker "revusical").

Tips: "We're looking for inspiration. We enjoy supporting projects which are soulful and uplifting. Not saccharine, though. There's a difference."

BRISTOL RIVERSIDE THEATRE, Dept. SM, P.O. Box 1250, Bristol PA 19007. (215)785-6664. Artistic Director: Susan D. Atkinson. Business Manager: Jo Lalli. Play producer. Estab. 1986. Produces 5 plays and 2 musicals/year (1 new musical every 2 years) and summer concert series. "302-seat proscenium Equity theater with audience of all ages from small towns and metropolitan area." Pays 6-8% royalty.
How to Contact: Submit complete manuscript, score and tape of songs. SASE. Reports in 6 months.
Musical Theater: "No strictly children's musicals. All other types with small to medium casts and within reasonable artistic tastes. Prefer one-set; limited funds restrict. Do not wish to see anything catering to prurient interests."
Productions: *Sally Blane, World's Greatest Girl Detective*, by David Levy/Leslie Eberhard (spoof of teen detective genre); *Moby Dick*, by Mark St. Germain, music by Doug Katsarous; and *Alive and Well*, by Larry Gatlin.
Tips: "You should be willing to work with small staff, open to artistic suggestion, and aware of the limitations of newly developing theaters."

WILLIAM CAREY COLLEGE DINNER THEATRE, William Carey College, Hattiesburg MS 39401-5499. (601)582-6218. Managing Director: O.L. Quave. Play producer. Produces 2 plays and 2 musicals/year. "Our dinner theater operates only in summer and plays to family audiences." Payment negotiable.
How to Contact: Query with synopsis, character breakdown and set description. Does not return material. Reports in 1 month.
Musical Theater: "Plays should be simply-staged, have small casts (8-10 maximum), and be suitable for family viewing; two hours maximum length. Score should require piano only, or piano, synthesizer."
Productions: *Smoke on the Mountain*; *Taffetas*; and *Pump Boys and Dinettes*.

CENTENARY COLLEGE, THEATRE DEPARTMENT, Shreveport LA 71134-1188. (318)869-5011. Fax: (318)869-5760. Chairman: Robert R. Buseick. Play producer. Produces 6 plays (1-2 new musicals)/year. Plays are presented in a 350-seat playhouse to college and community audiences.
How to Contact: Submit manuscript and score. SASE. Reports in 1 month.
Productions: *Into the Woods*; *Little Shop of Horrors*; and *Jerry's Girls*, by Todd Sweeney.

CIRCA' 21 DINNER PLAYHOUSE, Dept. SM, P.O. Box 3784, Rock Island IL 61204-3784. (309)786-2667. Producer: Dennis Hitchcock. Play producer. Estab. 1977. Produces 1-2 plays and 4-5 musicals (1 new musical)/year. Plays produced for a general audience. Three children's works/year, concurrent with major productions. Payment is negotiable.
How to Contact: Query with synopsis, character breakdown and set description or submit complete manuscript, score and tape of songs. SASE. Reports in 8 weeks.
Musical Theater: "We produce both full length and one act children's musicals. Folk or fairy tale themes. Works that do not condescend to a young audience yet are appropriate for entire family. We're also seeking full-length, small cast musicals suitable for a broad audience." Would also consider original music for use in a play being developed.
Productions: *A Closer Walk with Patsy Cline*, by Dean Regan; *Sleeping Beauty*, by Jim Eiler; and *Wild About the West (Buffalo Gals)*, by Will Osborne and Nick Plakias.
Tips: "Small, upbeat, tourable musicals (like *Pump Boys*) and bright musically-sharp children's productions (like those produced by Prince Street Players) work best. Keep an open mind. Stretch to encompass a musical variety—different keys, rhythms, musical ideas and textures."

CIRCLE IN THE SQUARE THEATRE, Dept. SM, 1633 Broadway, New York NY 10019. (212)307-2700. Contact: Literary Advisor. Play producer. Estab. 1951. Produces 3 plays/year; occasionally produces a musical. Pays by royalty.
How to Contact: Submit through agent only. Does not return material. Reports in 6 months.
Musical Theater: "We are looking for original material with small cast and orchestra requirements. We're not interested in traditional musical comedies."
Productions: *Pal Joey*, *Sweeney Todd* and *Anna Karenina*.
Tips: "The material has to be 'do-able' in our unique arena space."

COCKPIT IN COURT SUMMER THEATRE, 7201 Rossville Blvd., Baltimore MD 21237. (410)780-6534. Managing Director: F. Scott Black. Play producer. Estab. 1973. Produces 6-8 plays and 5-7 musicals/year. "Plays are produced at four locations: Mainstage (proscenium theater), Courtyard (outdoor theater), Cabaret (theater-in-the-round) and Lecture Hall (children's theater)."

How to Contact: Query with synopsis, character breakdown and set description. SASE. Reports in 1 month.
Musical Theater: "Seeking musical comedy and children's shows. We have the capacity to produce large musicals with up to 50 cast members."
Productions: *42nd Street*, *Kismet* and *Robin Hood*.
Tips: "We look for material that appeals to a community theater audience."

THE COTERIE, 2450 Grand Ave., Kansas City MO 64108. (816)474-6785. Artistic Director: Jeff Church. Play producer. Estab. 1979. Produces 7-8 plays/year. Plays produced at Hallmark's Crown Center in downtown Kansas City in The Coterie's resident theater (capacity 240). Musicals are produced for adventurous families and schools K-12. A typical performance run is one month in length. "We retain some rights on commissioned plays. Writers are paid a royalty for their work per performance or flat fee."
How to Contact: Query with synopsis and character breakdown. Submit complete manuscript and score "if established writer in theater for young audiences. We will consider musicals with smaller orchestration needs (3-5 pieces), or a taped score." SASE. Reports in 10 months.
Musical Theater: "Types of plays we produce: pieces which are universal in appeal; plays for all ages. They may be original or adaptations of classic or contemporary literature. Limitations: typically not more than 12 in a cast—prefer 5-9 in size. No fly space or wing space. No couch plays. Prefer plays by seasoned writers who have established reputations. Groundbreaking and exciting scripts from the youth theater field welcome. It's perfectly fine if your musical is a little off center."
Productions: *I Can't Eat Goat Head*, by Sylvia Gonzales S. (Latino journey); *The Little Prince*, by Jeff Church (adaptation of classic literature); and *A Woman Called Truth*, by Sandra Asher (life of Sojourner Truth).
Tips: "Make certain your submitted musical is very theatrical and not cinematic. Writers need to see how far the field of youth and family theater has come—the interesting new areas we're going—before sending us your query or manuscript. We like young protagonists in our plays, but make sure they're not romanticized or stereotyped good-and-bad like the children's theater playwrights of yesterday would have them."

CREATIVE PRODUCTIONS, INC., 2 Beaver Place, Aberdeen NJ 07747. (908)566-6985. Director: Walter L. Born. Play producer. Estab. 1970. Produces 2 musicals (1-2 new musicals)/year. "Our audience is unsophisticated, middle class, elderly, disabled and baby boomers. We use local public school theater facilities." Pays negotiable fee.
How to Contact: Query first. SASE. Reports in 1 month.
Musical Theater: "We want family type material (i.e. *Brigadoon*, *Charlie Brown*) with light rock to classical music and a maximum running time of two hours. We have no flying capability in facility; cast size is a maximum 10-12; the sets are mostly on small wagons, the orchestra is chamber size with standard instruments. We don't want pornographic material or children's shows. We want nothing trite and condescending in either the material or the treatment. We like the unusual treatment well-structured and thought out, with minimal sets and changes. We can't handle unusual vocal requirements. We prefer an integrated piece with music a structural part from the beginning."
Productions: *The Last Leaf*, by John Lallis/Mario Lombardo (aspiring artists in NYC); *For Love Or Money*, by M. Lombardo/J. Lallis (based on O. Henry); and *Champion Kid's Foods*, by Don Tenenblatt (abandoned kids).
Tips: "Prepare/send representative script and music based on above criteria and follow up with phone call after our response."

CREEDE REPERTORY THEATRE, P.O. Box 269, Creede CO 81130. (719)658-2541. Producing/Artistic Director: Richard Baxter. Play producer. Estab. 1966. Produces 6 plays and 1 musical/year. Performs in 243-seat proscenium theatre; audience is ½ local support and ½ tourist base from Texas, Oklahoma, New Mexico and Colorado. Pays 7% royalty.
How to Contact: Query first. SASE. Reports in 1 year.
Musical Theater: "We prefer historical Western material with cast no larger than 11. Staging must be flexible as space is limited."
Productions: *Baby Doe Tabor*, by Kenton Kersting (Colorado history); *A Frog in His Throat*, by Feydeau, adapted by Eric Conger (French farce); and *Tommyknockers*, by Eric Engdahl, Mark Houston and Chris Thompson (mining).
Tips: "Songwriter must have the ability to accept criticism and must be flexible."

STEVE DOBBINS PRODUCTIONS, 650 Geary St., San Francisco CA 94102. Administrative Director: Alan Ramos. Play producer. Estab. 1978. Produces 4 plays and 1 new musical/year. Plays performed for San Francisco Bay Area avante garde, racially mixed audiences. Pays by royalty.

INSIDER REPORT

Make musical plays intimate and immediate

Musicals are hot, comedy is lacking and New York is no longer "the center of the universe" in the theatrical world, according to D. Lynn Meyers, producing artistic director at Cincinnati's Ensemble Theatre. Before reaching the 202-seat house in her hometown, she spent 12 years as associate artistic director at the Cincinnati Playhouse and seven years writing, producing and directing plays in theaters across the United States and Canada. She has also written scripts for television. Meyers's candid and enthusiastic perspective of the market and the challenges faced by aspiring playwrights yields hope for those who are skilled writers and wise promoters.

Most notable in today's market is what Meyers calls "the revitalization of the Broadway musical." Hits such as *Cats* and her personal favorite, the classic *Follies*, are testimony to what theatergoers are seeking. "The country looks to the arts to embody something they can't do themselves. As a society we're looking for hope. The musical embodies this." In contrast, "a few years ago, everything was Sam Shepard, you know, dark . . . this decade looks to revitalization."

Also changing is the venue for plays and musical debuts. Citing Los Angeles, Denver and Chicago as ripe locations for up-and-coming works, Meyers sees opportunity in Cincinnati as well. "It's a growing town," she says of the city. The Ensemble Theatre produces an average of two musicals a year, and the city's new arts center, with a steady stream of touring plays and Broadway hits, consistently draws crowds. In addition, "the music coming out of this area is really exciting," Meyers says. Whether you're in New Orleans or Omaha, "breaking in is not easy, but some hit it the first time out," Meyers says. You can increase your chances if your work has a comical bent. "There seems to be a great lack of humor" in scripts submitted to producers. "Eight out of ten are dramas," Meyers says of the works she reviews. "It's easier to find a heavy, sad script than a lighthearted one, yet audiences crave levity and wit." Meyers has also noticed a lack of pieces that combine music with dance and a strong, well-crafted script.

A novice writer is just as capable of achieving this harmony as a seasoned musical playwright with a dozen credits, so Meyers doesn't look at a writer's résumé when choosing musical plays. "Ensemble Theatre is dedicated to producing new works," she says. She has produced musicals crafted by those with extensive theatrical training and those with absolutely none. Last year's production of *Cars, Dogs, Money and the Moon*, written by local songwriter David Kisor, quickly received several inquiries for the script and tape.

Although she credits her study of English, accompanied by theatrical training at Kentucky's Thomas More College, for forcing her "to read and experience different writing," all aspiring musical playwrights can gain similar exposure through ambitious use of the local library, neighborhood theaters, and through networking with other playwrights and songwriters. So read as much as possible and see what your local theater has to offer.

INSIDER REPORT, *Meyers*

Then concentrate on writing. Above all else, Meyers seeks honest, compelling writing and memorable songs, and advises writers to make the most of their own style and genre. "Write from your heart," she advises. And as you conquer the blank page, "make it immediate," she says emphatically. At Ensemble Theatre, "the most important thing is what's on the page. The emphasis is on the script, not the set."

When writing for the stage, remember that "the action takes place in a limited space and a limited time." She wants to see action that's "intimate," happening right before you, whether it's sung or spoken. So skip the tedious background information. "A lot of writers overwrite. Their scripts are more like novels." Of the plays she reads, "many are 90 percent monologue. It doesn't work," she says.

How to avoid the drastically overwritten script? First, "read it out loud," says Meyers. Although a script may look good on paper, this exercise brings home the fact that "a play is meant to be heard and seen." Second, read it with other playwrights. Meet regularly with a writer's group and allow skilled musicians to put your score to the test. Share your work with them and listen to their suggestions before you start submitting your musical.

In addition to professional expertise, writers can benefit from the camaraderie of those doing similar work. "I recommend that all writers work with other writers, and that some work with songwriter's groups," Meyers says. "Writing can be the loneliest profession in the world."

Once you've worked out the kinks and you're ready to submit your work, follow the guidelines of the theater you're interested in submitting to. And know your market. Keep in mind that your music may not work in all theaters. "Because we're in a small space, I need something that's not orchestral," Meyers says of the needs of the Ensemble Theatre. "And I detest music done on tapes or click tracks. I find no joy in taped productions. I want to see the players." Meyers recommends you skip the synopsis of the musical as well. Just submit the full script accompanied by a quality tape of a few good songs. "You don't need to submit the full musical score."

Sending your carefully-crafted musical script and tape out into the world can be daunting, but if you've researched your market and perfected your writing, you'll increase your chance of success in this competitive arena. A great cheerleader of novice playwrights/composers, Meyers affords one final word of advice. "Just start . . . the worst you can do is not do it at all."

—*Jennifer Hogan-Redmond*

How to Contact: Query with synopsis, character breakdown and set description. SASE. Reports in 4 months.
Musical Theater: "We seek all types of material as long as the ideas are new. No formula scripts." Would consider original music for use in a play being developed.
Productions: *Fab*, by Heather Brothers; *Doo Wop*, by David Glover ('50s black musical); and *A Slice of Saturday Night*, by Heather Brothers ('60s teen musical).
Tips: "Write to us explaining your idea."

GEOF ENGLISH, PRODUCER, SADDLEBACK CIVIC LIGHT OPERA, Saddleback College, 28000 Marguerite Pkwy., Mission Viejo CA 92692. (714)582-4763. E-mail: english_g@sccd.cc.ca.us. Performing Arts Director: Geofrey English. Play producer for musical theater. Produces 4 musicals/year. Community audience of mostly senior citizens. Pays by royalty and performance.
How to Contact: Submit complete manuscript, score and tape of songs. Does not return material. Reports in 2-3 months.
Musical Theater: "Looking for mainly family musicals. No limitations, open to options. It is important

that music must be sent along with scripts. Best not to call. Just send materials."
Productions: More than 50 musicals produced since company formed in 1978.
Tips: "Submit materials in a timely manner—usually at least one year in advance."

‡ENSEMBLE THEATRE, 1127 Vine St., Cincinnati OH 45210. (513)421-3555. Fax: (513)421-8002. Website: http://www.Cincinnati.com/etc./etc.html. Producing Artistic Director: D. Lynn Meyers. Play producer. Estab. 1986. Produces 14 plays, 1 musical and 1 new musical/year. Audience is multi-generational and multi-cultural. 202 seats, ¾ stage. Pays negotiated royalty (between 5 and 8 percent).

- See the interview with the Ensemble Theatre's Producing Artistic Director, D. Lynn Meyers, in this section.

How to Contact: Query with synopsis, character breakdown and set description. SASE. Reports in 6 months.
Musical Theater: "All types of musicals are acceptable. Cast not over 10; minimum set, please."
Productions: *Cars, Dogs, Money and the Moon*, by David Kisor (musical about growing up in West Virginia); *Hi Hat Hattie*, by Larry Parr; and *Robin Hood*, by David Richmond (adventure).
Tips: Looking for "creative, inventive, contemporary subjects or classic tales. Send materials as complete as possible."

FOOLS COMPANY, INC., 356 W. 44th St., New York NY 10036. (212)307-6000. Website: http://www.foolsco.com. Artistic Director: Martin Russell. Play producer. Estab. 1970. Produces 4-6 plays/year; produces 1-2 new musicals/year. "Audience is comprised of hip, younger New Yorkers. Plays are performed at our own mid-Manhattan theater." Pay is negotiable.
How to Contact: Submit complete manuscript, score and tape of songs. SASE. Reports in 1 month.
Musical Theater: "We seek new and unusual, contemporary and experimental material. We would like small, easy-to-tour productions. Nothing classical, folkloric or previously produced." Would also consider original music for use in a play being developed.
Productions: *Zen Puppies Unleashed* (company collective); *No Dust*, by Fools Co. Collaborators (humanity); and *Relief*, by I. P. Daly (youth growth).
Tips: "Save your pennies and showcase in NYC."

THE FOOTHILL THEATRE COMPANY, P.O. Box 1812, Nevada City CA 95959. (916)265-9320. Artistic Director: Philip Charles Sneed. Play producer. Estab. 1977. Produces 6-10 plays and 1-2 musicals/year. Rural audience, with some urban visitors to the area. 250-seat historic proscenium house; built in 1865 (oldest in CA). "We haven't yet produced a new play, but will seriously consider it within the next 2 years; payment will be decided later." Payment negotiated.
How to Contact: Query with synopsis, character breakdown and set description. SASE. Reports in 6 months.
Musical Theater: "We're particularly interested in works which deal with the region's history or with issues relevant to the area today. We are also interested in one-act musicals and children's musicals. We have limited space backstage, especially in the wings. We also have very limited fly space. We're interested in original ideas, nothing derivative (except in an adaptation, of course). A good rock musical would be nice. Will consider original music for use in a play being developed, or for use in a pre-existing play. The use will depend upon the play: could be preshow, or underscoring, or scene change, or any combination."
Productions: *Quilters*, by Damaschek and Newman (pioneer story with music); *Jacques Brel*, by Herbert Blau (cabaret musical); and *Man of La Mancha*, by Dale Wasserman, Mitch Leigh and Joe Darion.
Tips: "Know something about our region and its history."

‡FOUNTAIN THEATRE, 5060 Fountain Ave., Los Angeles CA 90029. (213)663-2235. Fax: (213)663-1629. Producing Director/Dramaturg: Simon Levy. Play producer. Estab. 1990. Produces 6 plays, 1 musical and 1 new musical/year. General multicultural Los Angeles audience. Performances take place in a small (30×18) professional theater with 78 seats. Pays 6% royalty.
How to Contact: Query with synopsis, character breakdown and set description. SASE. Reports in 4-6 months.
Musical Theater: "Musical theater pieces of all sorts. We demand quality melodic and lyric material. Strong characters and through line. No big set or large casts (up to 10 or 11 only). Cast max—10-11, unit/concept staging, low (9′) ceiling."
Productions: *Dottie!*, by Jay Alan Quantrill (Dorothy Parker); *Women of Guernica*, by Deborah Lawlor (Spanish Civil War); and *Viva Yo!*, by Jay Alan Quantrill (18th century Spanish actors).

THE WILL GEER THEATRICUM BOTANICUM, P.O. Box 1222, Topanga CA 90290. (310)455-2322. Artistic Director: Ellen Geer. Play producer. Produces 4 plays, 1 new musical/year. Plays are performed in "large outdoor amphitheater with 60′x 25′ wooden stage. Rustic setting." Pays negotiable royalty.

How to Contact: Query with synopsis, tape, character breakdown, example and tape. SASE. Submit scripts in September for prompt reply.

Musical Theater: Seeking social or biographical works, children's works, full length musicals with cast of up to 10 equity actors (the rest non-equity). Requires "low budget set and costumes. We emphasize paying performers." Would also consider original music for use in a play being developed. Does not wish to see "anything promoting avarice, greed, violence or apathy."

Productions: *Dory, A Musical Portrait*, adaptation (Dory Previn); and *Three Penny Opera*, by Brecht.

GREAT AMERICAN HISTORY THEATRE, 30 E. Tenth St., St. Paul MN 55101. (612)292-4323. Artistic Director: Ron Peluso. Play producer. Estab. 1978. Produces 5-6 plays, 1 or 2 new musicals/year. Pays 5-10% royalty or by commission.

How to Contact: Query first with synopsis, character breakdown and set description. SASE. Reports in 6 months.

Musical Theater: "Plays based on people, events, ideas in history. Preferably Midwestern or American history. However, must be *real* plays, we *do not* teach history. *No* pageants. No larger than cast of 10. Technical considerations must be simple. We like nonrealism."

Productions: *Mesabi Red*, by Lance S. Belville (iron range musical); *Inner-City Opera*, by J.D. & Fred Steele (growing up in the inner-city); and *Small Town Triumphs & Cowboy Colors*, by Bart Sutter/Paul Zarzyski (poetry adapted to stage about small towns and cowboys).

GREAT AMERICAN MELODRAMA & VAUDEVILLE, P.O. Box 1026, Oceano CA 93445. (805)481-4880, ext. 32. Fax: (805)489-5539. Owner/producer: John Schlenker. Play producer. Estab. 1976. Produces 7 plays and 2-3 musicals/year. "Family entertainment—all ages." Performances held in a 260 seat theater, cabaret-style seating with bench seats surrounding theater. Payment by outright purchase or percentage of royalty.

How to Contact: Query with synopsis, character breakdown and set description. "All plays are selected for the year July through September." Does not return material. Reports in 5 weeks.

Musical Theater: "Everything from Gilbert & Sullivan, Cinderella to Western shoot-'em-up spoofs play extremely well here. Must be shows suitable for families. Victorian melodramas are our bread and butter, therefore, musical adaptations of period melodramas would be great! Cast size 10-12, usually 6 men and 4 women." Does not wish to see "realistic hardcore contemporary dramatic literature. People do not come to our theater looking for a slice of their daily lives. All plays and/or musicals must play in 75 minutes actual playing time, since they are followed with a 35 minute musical revue. High style action-packed shows work like gangbusters. A little adult humor is okay as long as it is done with taste and adults get it but children don't."

Productions: *Dames at Sea*; *Once Upon A Mattress*; and *The Madman's Daughter*, by Gene Casey (original melodrama).

Tips: "Call me regarding our theatrical style and playbill. We do a lot of original plays (melodramas, thrillers, high-style comedies and musicals). Everything is followed by a revue. We are a 22-year-old, well established full-time, year-round theater and we produce a *lot* of original work. I am always looking."

HARTFORD STAGE COMPANY, 50 Church St., Hartford CT 06103. (860)525-5601. Fax: (860)525-4420. Director of New Play Development: Shawn Renee Graham. Play producer. Estab. 1963. Produces 6 plays and 1-2 musicals/year. "Mainly white-collar, upper middle-class audience; plays performed on a thrust stage, seats 489 people." Pays royalty.

How to Contact: Query with synopsis, character breakdown and set description, 10-page dialogue sample and tape if possible, or submit through agent. SASE. Reports in 3-6 months.

Musical Theater: Looking for "any kind of musicals except for children's theater. Musicals are preferred to be 2-2½ hours in length, but longer ones accepted also. We are mainly interested in small to medium-sized casts, up to 12 actors, although larger ones are also accepted." Does not wish to see "anything in the vein of the typical Broadway musical—*Phantom of the Opera*, *Miss Saigon*, etc."

Productions: *Herringbone*, by Tom Cone (one-man show); *Martin Gtuerre*, by Laura Harrington (adapta-

REFER TO THE GEOGRAPHIC INDEX (at the back of this book) to find listings of companies by state, as well as foreign listings.

tion of French film); and *March of the Falsettos and Falsettolands*, by William Finn (gay man's journey among friend's family).

HIP POCKET THEATRE, 7344 Love Circle, Ft. Worth TX 76135. (817)237-5977. Artistic Director: Johnny Simons. Play producer. Produces 7 plays/year (including new musicals). Estab. 1977. "Our audience is an eclectic mix of Ft. Worth/Dallas area residents with varying levels of incomes and backgrounds. Payment varies according to type of script, reputation of playwright, etc."
How to Contact: Query with synopsis, character breakdown and set description "with script portion and selected songs on tape." SASE. Reports in 5 weeks.
Musical Theater: "We are not interested in cabaret revues, but rather in full-length pieces that can be for adults and/or children. We tend to produce more fanciful, whimsical musicals (something not likely to be found anywhere else), but would also consider political pieces and other subjects. Basically, we're open for anything fresh and well-written. We prefer no more than 15 in a cast, and a staging adapted to an outdoor environmental thrust stage to be considered for summer season."
Productions: *Dada Cabaret*, by Pete Gooch and Little Jack Melody (dada art movement); *Riders of the Purple Sage*, by Zane Grey, adapted by Johnny Simons (the Old West); and *A Bowl of Red*, by Johnny Simons and Douglas Balentine (the history of chili—the kind you eat).
Tips: "Think creative, complex thoughts and musical visions that can be transformed into reality by creative, visionary musicians in theaters that rarely have the huge Broadway dollar."

HORIZON THEATRE CO., P.O. Box 5376, Station E, Atlanta GA 30307. (404)523-1477. E-mail: horizonco@mindspring.com. Website: http://www.mindspring.com/~horizonco/. Artistic Directors: Lisa and Jeff Adler. Play producer. Estab. 1983. Produces 4 plays and 1 musical/year. "Our audience is comprised mostly of young professionals looking for contemporary comedy with some social commentary. Our theater features a 185-seat facility with flexible stage." Pays 6-8% royalty.
How to Contact: Query with synopsis, character breakdown and set description. SASE. Reports in 3 months (to query).
Musical Theater: "We prefer musicals that have a significant book and a lot of wit (particularly satire). Our casts are restricted to 10 actors. We prefer plays with equal number of male and female roles, or more female than male roles. We have a limited number of musicians available. No musical revues and no dinner theater fluff. One type of play we are currently seeking is a country musical with women's themes. We generally contract with a musician or sound designer to provide sound for each play we produce. If interested send résumé, synopsis, references, tape with music or sound design samples."
Productions: *Angry Housewives*, by A.M. Collins/Chad Henry; *A. . . . My Name Is Still Alice*, conceived by Julianne Boyd/Joan Micklin Silver; and *The Good Times Are Killing Me*, by Lynda Barry.
Tips: "Have patience and use subtle persistence. Work with other theater artists to get a good grasp of the form."

JEWISH REPERTORY THEATRE, 1395 Lexington Ave., New York NY 10128. (212)415-5550. Director: Ran Avni. Play producer. Estab. 1974. Produces 4 musicals and plays/year. Pays royalty.
How to Contact: Submit complete manuscript and tape of songs. SASE. Reports in 6-12 weeks.
Musical Theater: Seeking "musicals and plays in English relating to the Jewish experience. No more than 8 characters."
Productions: *That's Life!* (musical revue); *Theda Bara and the Frontier Rabbi* (musical comedy); and *The Shop on Main Street* (musical drama).

‡LAGUNA PLAYHOUSE, 606 Laguna Canyon Rd., Laguna Beach CA 92651. (714)497-5900, ext. 206. Artistic Director: Andrew Barnicle. Play producer. Estab. 1920. Produces 7-10 plays/year; produces 2-3 musicals/year. Audience is "middle to upper class suburban, 9,000 subscribers in resort town. Plays performed in 420 seat luxury theater." Payment is negotiable.
How to Contact: Submit complete manuscript, score and tape of songs. SASE. Reports in 6 or more months.
Musical Theater: "Seek children's plays ('we have an acclaimed youth theater'), adult, aesthetic non-'dance' shows with small orchestra ('Tintypes', *1940's Radio Hour*), limited dance budget. Cast 15-20 maximum on large proscenium stage."
Productions: *Working*, by Terkel, Schwartz, et.al.; *Company*, by Stephen Sondheim, George Furth, et.al., and *Oliver!*, by Bart (Dickens' book).
Tips: "Be patient. We receive over 250 submissions each year and only occasionally do original work."

LOS ANGELES DESIGNERS' THEATRE, P.O. Box 1883, Studio City CA 91614-0883. (213)650-9600. Fax: (818)985-9200. Artistic Director: Richard Niederberg. Play producer. Estab. 1970. Produces

20-25 plays, 8-10 new musicals/year. Audience is predominantly Hollywood production executives in film, TV, records and multimedia. Plays are produced at several locations, primarily Studio City, California. Pay is negotiable.
How to Contact: Submit proposal for new work. Does not return material. Reports in 4 months.
Musical Theater: "We seek out controversial material. Street language OK, nudity is fine, religious themes, social themes, political themes are encouraged. Our audience is very 'jaded' as it consists of TV, motion picture and music publishing executives who have 'seen it all'." Does not wish to see bland, 'safe' material. "We like first productions. In the cover letter state in great detail the proposed involvement of the songwriter, other than as a writer (i.e. director, actor, singer, publicist, designer, etc.). Also, state if there are any liens on the material or if anything has been promised."
Productions: *St. Tim*, by Fred Grab (historical '60s musical); *Slipper and the Rose* (gang musical); and *1593* (historical musical).
Tips: "Make it very 'commercial' and inexpensive to produce. Allow for non-traditional casting. Be prepared with ideas as to how to transform your work to film or videotaped entertainment."

‡DON AND PAT MACPHERSON PRODUCTIONS, 461 Parkway, Gatlinburg TN 37738. (423)436-4039. Co-owners/producers: Don MacPherson and Pat MacPherson. Play producer. Estab. 1977. Produces 2 musicals/year. Plays are performed at Sweet Fanny Adams Theatre, Gatlinburg, Tennessee to tourist audience. Pays $25/per performance.
How to Contact: Query with synopsis, character breakdown and set description. SASE. Reports in 1 month.
Musical Theater: "Produce musicals that are funny, fast—in fact, silly; musical farces. Theater is 1890 style so shows should fit that period. Have done many westerns. Cast size limited to 7 or 8 with 2 musicians. Stage very small. Use old-time backdrops for sets. Shows should be no longer than 90 minutes." Does not wish to see "shows that would not fit 1890s style—unless it had a country theme."
Productions: *Phantom of the Opry*, by Don & Pat MacPherson/J. Lovensheimer (spoof of *Phantom of the Opera*); *Life & Times of Billy Kincaid*, by MacPherson/Lovensheimer (western); and *Not Quite Frankenstein*, by Don and Pat MacPherson.
Tips: "See a production at Sweet Fanny Adams."

MANHATTAN THEATRE CLUB, 453 W. 16th St., New York NY 10011. (212)645-5590. Director of Musical Theater Program: Clifford Lee Johnson III. Associate Artistic Director: Michael Bush. Play producer. Estab. 1971. Produces 8 plays and sometimes 1 musical/year. Plays are performed at the Manhattan Theatre Club before varied audiences. Pays negotiated fee.
How to Contact: Query first. SASE. Reports in 6 months.
Musical Theater: "Original work."
Productions: *Groundhog*, by Elizabeth Swados; *1-2-3-4-5*, by Maury Yeston and Larry Gelbart; and *Putting It Together*, by Stephen Sondheim.
Tips: "Make sure your script is tightly and securely bound."

MILL MOUNTAIN THEATRE, 1 Market Square, 2nd Floor, Roanoke VA 24011-1437. (540)342-5730. Fax: (540)342-5745. Literary Manager: Jo Weinstein. Play producer. Estab. 1964. Produces 11-14 plays and generally 3 established musicals (1-2 new musicals)/year. General theater audience on mainstage; a more open minded audience in Theatre B; also children's musicals. 400 seat proscenium mainstage; 125 seat alternate space. Pays variable royalty.
How to Contact: Query with synopsis, character breakdown and demo tape. SASE. Reports in 6 months.
Musical Theater: "We seek children's musicals (especially those adapted from recognizable children's works); we also accept contemporary musicals which explore new forms and themes, especially those which encourage diversity of life experiences. Smaller cast musicals with a minimum of technical requirements are encouraged. We have, in the past, used original music for existing plays (*Midsummer Night's Dream, To Kill A Mockingbird*), usually to set the production's mood and emphasize the action on stage."
Productions: *The Christmas Cup*, based on the book by Nancy Ruth Patterson, adapted by Jere Lee Hodgin (girl's coming of age); *Through The Picture Tube*, by Ed Sala, music by Michael Hirsch (TV's influence on one family); and *Everything I Need To Know I Learned in Kindergarten*, based on books by Robert Fulgum, adapted by Ernest Zulia (life and its everyday wonders).

MIXED BLOOD THEATRE CO., 1501 S. Fourth St., Minneapolis MN 55454. (612)338-0937. Script Czar: David Kunz. Play producer. Estab. 1976. Produces 4-5 plays a year and perhaps 1 new musical every 2 years. "We have a 200-seat theater in a converted firehouse. The audience spans the socio-economic spectrum." Pays royalty or per performance.

- See the listing for the Mixed Blood Versus America Playwriting Contest in the Contests and Awards section.

How to Contact: Query first. SASE. Reports in 2-6 weeks.
Musical Theater: "We want full-length, non-children's works with a message. Always query first. Never send unsolicited script or tape."
Productions: *Black Belts II*, musical revue (black female vocalists and their music); and *A . . . My Name Is Still Alice*.
Tips: "Always query first. Be concise. Make it interesting. Contemporary comedies, politically-edged material and sports-oriented shows are usually of interest."

NEW YORK STATE THEATRE INSTITUTE, 155 River St., Troy NY 12180. (518)274-3200. Producing Artistic Director: Patricia Di Benedetto Snyder. Play producer. Produces 5 plays (1 new musical)/year. Plays performed for student audiences grades K-12, family audiences and adult audiences. Theater seats 900 with full stage. Pay negotiable.
How to Contact: Query with synopsis, character breakdown and set description or submit complete manuscript, score and tape of songs. SASE. Reports in 2-3 weeks for synopsis, 3-4 months for manuscript.
Musical Theater: Looking for "intelligent and well-written book with substance, a score that enhances and supplements the book and is musically well-crafted and theatrical." Length: up to 2 hours. Could be play with music, musical comedy, musical drama. Excellence and substance in material is essential. Cast could be up to 12; orchestra size up to 8.
Productions: *A Tale of Cinderella*, by W.A. Frankonis/Will Severin/George David Weiss (adaptation of fairy tale); *The Silver*, by Lanie Robertson/Byron Janis/George David Weiss (adaptation of book); and *Big River*, by William Hauptman/Roger Miller (adapted from Mark Twain).
Tips: "There is a great need for musicals that are well-written with intelligence and substance which are suitable for family audiences."

ODYSSEY THEATRE ENSEMBLE, Dept. SM, 2055 S. Sepulveda Blvd., Los Angeles CA 90025. (310)477-2055. Director of Literary Programs: Jan Lewis. Play producer. Estab. 1969. Produces 9 plays, 1 musical and 1-2 new musicals/year. "Our audience is predominantly over 35, upper middle-class audience interested in eclectic brand of theater which is challenging and experimental." Pays by royalty (percentage to be negotiated).
How to Contact: Query with synopsis, character breakdown, 8-10 pages of libretto, cassette of music and set description. Query should include résumé(s) of artist(s) and tape of music. SASE. "Unsolicited material is not read or screened at all." Reports on query in 1 month; manuscript in 6 months.
Musical Theater: "We want nontraditional forms and provocative, unusual, challenging subject matter. We are not looking for Broadway-style musicals. Comedies should be highly stylized or highly farcical. Works should be full-length only and not requiring a complete orchestra (small band preferred.) Political material and satire are great for us. We're seeking interesting musical concepts and approaches. The more traditional Broadway-style musicals will generally not be done by the Odyssey. If we have a work in development that needs music, original music will often be used. In such a case, the writer and composer would work together during the development phase. In the case of a pre-existing play, the concept would originate with the director who would select the composer."
Productions: *Frauleins In Underwear*, by various (Germany in the '30s); *Avenue X*, by John Jiler and Ray Leslee; and *Lucky Stiff*, by Lynn Ahrens/Stephen Flaherty.
Tips: "Stretch your work beyond the ordinary. Look for compelling themes or the enduring questions of human existence. If it's a comedy, go for broke, go all the way, be as inventive as you can be."

OMAHA MAGIC THEATRE, 325 S. 16th St., Omaha NE 68102. (402)346-1227. Artistic Director: Jo Ann Schmidman. Play producer. Estab. 1968. Produces 8 performance events with music/year. "Plays are produced in our Omaha facility and on tour throughout the nation. Our audience is a cross-section of the community." Pays standard royalty, outright purchase ($500-1,500) or per performance ($20-25).
How to Contact: Query with synopsis, character breakdown and set description. SASE. Reports in 6 months.
Musical Theater: "We want the most avant of the avant garde—plays that never get written, or if written are buried deep in a chest because the writer feels there are not production possibilities in this nation's theaters. Plays must push form and/or content to new dimensions. The clarity of the playwright's voice must be strong and fresh. We do not produce standard naturalistic or realistic musicals. At the Omaha Magic Theatre original music is considered as sound structure and for lyrics."
Productions: *Body Leaks* (self-censorship) and *Sound Fields*, by Megan Terry, Jo Ann Schmidman and Sora Kimberlain (a new multi-dimensional performance event about acute listening); and *Belches on Couches*, by Megan Terry, Jo Ann Schmidman and Sora Kimberlain.
Tips: "Looking for alternative music."

THE OPEN EYE THEATER, P.O. Box 959, Margaretville NY 12455. Artistic Director: Amie Brockway. Play producer. Estab. 1972. Produces approximately 3 full length or 3 new plays for multi-generational audiences. Pays on a fee basis.
How to Contact: Query first. "We deeply regret that we are forced to discontinue our policy of accepting unsolicited manuscripts. Until further notice, a manuscript will be accepted and read only if it is a play for multi-generational audiences and is: 1) Submitted by a recognized literary agent; 2) Requested or recommended by a staff or company member; or 3) Recommended by a professional colleague with whose work we are familiar. Playwrights may submit a one-page letter of inquiry including a very brief plot synopsis. Please enclose a self-addressed (but not stamped) envelope. We will reply only if we want you to submit the script."
Musical Theater: "The Open Eye Theater is a not-for-profit professional company working in a community context. Through the development, production and performance of plays for all ages, artists and audiences are challenged and given the opportunity to grow in the arts. In residence, on tour, and in the classroom, The Open Eye Theater strives to stimulate, educate, entertain, inspire and serve as a creative resource."
Productions: *Selkie*, by Laurie Brooks Gollobin, music by Elliot Sokolov.

PLAYHOUSE ON THE SQUARE, 51 S. Cooper, Memphis TN 38104. (901)725-0776. Executive Producer: Jackie Nichols. Play producer. Produces 12 plays (4 musicals)/year. Plays are produced in a 260-seat proscenium resident theater. Pays $500 for outright purchase.
How to Contact: Submit complete manuscript and score. Unsolicited submissions OK. SASE. Reports in 4 months.
Musical Theater: Seeking "any subject matter—adult and children's material. Small cast preferred. Stage is 26′ deep by 43′ wide with no fly system." Would also consider original music for use in a play being developed.
Productions: *Gypsy*, by Stein and Laurents; *The Spider Web*, by Agatha Christie; and *A Midsummer Night's Dream*, by William Shakespeare.

PLAYWRIGHTS HORIZONS, 416 W. 42nd St., New York NY 10036. (212)564-1235. Artistic Director: Tim Sanford. Play producer. Estab. 1971. Produces about 4 plays and 1 new musical/year. "A general New York City audience." Pays by fee/royalty.
How to Contact: Submit complete manuscript, score and tape of songs. Attn: Musical Theater Program. SASE. Reports in 4-5 months.
Musical Theater: American writers. "No revivals or children's shows; otherwise we're flexible. We generally develop work from scratch; we're open to proposals for shows, and scripts in early stages of development."
Productions: *Assasins*, by Stephen Sondheim/John Weidman; *Jack's Holiday*, by Randy Courts/Mark St. Germain; and *Floyd Collins*, by Adam Guettel/Tina Landau.

THE REPERTORY THEATRE OF ST. LOUIS, P.O. Box 191730, St. Louis MO 63119. (314)968-7340. Associate Artistic Director: Susan Gregg. Play producer. Estab. 1966. Produces 9 plays and 1 or 2 musicals/year. "Conservative regional theater audience. We produce all our work at the Loretto Hilton Theatre." Pays by royalty.
How to Contact: Query with synopsis, character breakdown and set description. Does not return material. Reports in 2 years.
Musical Theater: "We want plays with a small cast and simple setting. No children's shows or foul language. After a letter of inquiry we would prefer script and demo tape."
Productions: *Almost September* and *Esmeralda*, by David Schechter and Steve Lutvak; and *Jack*, by Barbara Field and Hiram Titus.

SECOND STAGE THEATRE, P.O. Box 1807, Ansonia Station, New York NY 10023. (212)787-8302. Dramaturg/Literary Manager: Christopher Burney. Play producer. Estab. 1979. Produces 4 plays and 1 musical (1 new musical)/year. Plays are performed in a small, 108-seat Off Broadway House. Pays per performance.
How to Contact: Query with synopsis, character breakdown and set description. No unsolicited manuscripts. Does not return material. Reports in 4-6 months.
Musical Theater: "We are looking for innovative, unconventional musicals that deal with sociopolitical themes."
Productions: *In a Pig's Valise*, by Eric Overmyer and Kid Creole (spoof on '40s film noir); *A . . . My Name Is Still Alice*, by various (song/sketch revue); and *The Good Times Are Killing Me*, by Lynda Barry (a play with music).
Tips: "Submit through agent; have strong references; show a sample of the best material."

SHENANDOAH INTERNATIONAL PLAYWRIGHTS RETREAT (A PROJECT OF SHENAN ARTS, INC.), Rt. 5, Box 167-F, Staunton VA 24401. (703)248-1868. Director of Playwriting and Screenwriting Programs: Robert Graham Small. Play producer. Estab. 1976. Develops 10-12 plays/year for family audience. Pays fellowships.
How to Contact: Query with synopsis, character breakdown tape of songs and set description. SASE. Reports in 4 months.
Productions: *Smoke On the Mountain, Joseph and the Amazing Technicolor Dreamcoat* and *Pump Boys and Dinettes.*
Tips: "Submit materials January-February 1. Submit synopsis and demo tape to Paul Hildebrand for touring and full production."

STAGE ONE, 5 Riverfront Plaza, Louisville KY 40202. (502)589-5946. E-mail: kystage@aol.com. Website: http://www.stageone.org. Producing Director: Moses Goldberg. Play producer. Estab. 1946. Produces 7-8 plays and 0-2 new musicals/year. "Audience is mainly young people ages 5-18, teachers and families." Pays 3-6% royalty, flat fee or $25-75 per performance.
How to Contact: Submit complete manuscript and tape of songs. SASE. Reports in 3-4 months.
Musical Theater: "We seek stageworthy and respectful dramatizations of the classic tales of childhood, both ancient and modern. Ideally, the plays are relevant to young people and their families, as well as related to school curriculum. Cast is rarely more than 12."
Productions: *The Great Gilly Hopkins*, by David Paterson/Steve Liebman (foster home); *Green Eggs and Ham*, by Robert Kapilon (Dr. Seuss); and *Puss N' Boots*, by Moses Goldberg/Steve Liebman (fairytale).
Tips: "Stage One accepts unsolicited manuscripts that meet our artistic objectives. Please do not send plot summaries or reviews. Include author's résumé, if desired. In the case of musicals, a cassette tape is preferred. Cast size is not a factor, although, in practice, Stage One rarely employs casts of over 12. Scripts will be returned in approximately 3-4 months, if SASE is included. No materials can be returned without the inclusion of a SASE. Due to the volume of plays received, it is not possible to provide written evaluations."

‡SYRACUSE STAGE, 820 E. Genesee St., Syracuse NY 13204. (315)443-4008. (315)443-9846. Contact: Artistic Director. Play producer. Estab. 1974. Produces 8 plays/year (including 1 children's production). Audience is "predominantly female, above the age of 35, married, well-educated (70% have graduate or undergraduate degrees); many are professionals, educators, or retired; predominantly middle to upper middle class or wealthy; 12-15% persons of color; approximately 70,000 over age 18; we also serve an audience of approximately 18,000 between grades K-12; we are in a university community and share a unique co-existence with Syracuse University's drama department." Main performance space: "Proscenium (apron size and width of pros. opening are somewhat flexible); 499-seat house." Pay negotiable.
How to Contact: Query with synopsis, character breakdown, résumé, and 10-page dialogue sample. SASE. Reports in 2 months for synopsis; 6-9 months for scripts.
Musical Theater: "No specified type, topic, length, etc. We could produce musicals for adult audiences or children. Some of the children's shows tour. Length of children's musical should not be much longer than an hour. We don't have any specified limitations but the larger the musical, in general—i.e., in terms of cost size, number of sets, number of musicians, size of set, etc.—the less likely it is that we will be able to produce it. We might use incidental music for a straight play, or we might produce a play with music or musical theater."
Productions: *All In The Timing*, by David Ives; *The Piano Lesson*, by August Wilson; and *Something Unspoken: Three One-Act Plays*, by Tennessee Williams.

TADA!, 120 W. 28th St., New York NY 10001. (212)627-1732. E-mail: tada@ziplink.net. Website: http://www.tadatheater.com. Artistic Director: Janine Nina Trevens. Play producer. Estab. 1984. Produces 4 staged readings and 2-4 new musicals/year. "TADA! is a company producing works performed by children ages 6-17 for family audiences in New York City. Performances run approximately 30-45 performances. Pays varying royalty.

- For more information, see the interview with Artistic Director Janine Nina Trevens in the 1997 *Songwriter's Market.*

How to Contact: Submit complete manuscript with synopsis, character breakdown, score and tape of songs. SASE. Reports in 6-12 months.
Musical Theater: "We do not produce plays as full productions. At this point, we do staged readings of plays. We produce original commissioned musicals written specifically for the company."
Productions: *Maggie and the Pirate*, book and lyrics by Winnie Holzman, music by David Evans; *The Little Moon Theater*, book by Michael Slade, lyrics and music by Joel Gelpe; and *Flies in The Soup*, book, music, and lyrics by Dan Feigelson and Jon Agee.
Tips: "Musical playwrights should concentrate on themes and plots meaningful to children and their

families as well as consider our young actors' abilities and talents as well. Vocal ranges of children 7-17 should be strongly considered when writing the score."

THE TEN-MINUTE MUSICALS PROJECT, P.O. Box 461194, West Hollywood CA 90046. (213)656-8751. Producer: Michael Koppy. Play producer. Estab. 1987. All pieces are new musicals. Pays equal share of 6-7% royalty.
How to Contact: Submit complete manuscript, score and tape of songs. SASE. Reports in 3 months.
Musical Theater: Seeks complete short stage musicals of between 8 and 15 minutes in length. Maximum cast: 9. "No parodies—original music only."
Productions: *The Furnished Room*, by Saragail Katzman (the O. Henry story); *An Open Window*, by Enid Futterman and Sara Ackerman (the Saki story); and *Pulp's Big Favor*, by David Spencer and Bruce Peyton (an original detective mystery).
Tips: "Start with a *solid* story—either an adaptation or an original idea—but with a solid beginning, middle and end (probably with a plot twist at the climax)."

THEATRE THREE, INC., 2800 Routh St., Dallas TX 75201. (214)871-2933. Fax: (214)871-3139. Musical Director: Terry Dobson. Play producer. Estab. 1961. Produces 10-12 plays and 3-4 musicals (1 or 2 new musicals)/year. "Subscription audience of 4,500 enjoys adventurous, sophisticated musicals." Performance space is an "arena stage (modified). Seats 250 per performance. Quite an intimate space." Pays varying royalty.
How to Contact: Query with synopsis, character breakdown and set description. SASE. Reports in 2-8 weeks.
Musical Theater: "Off the wall topics. We have, in the past, produced *Little Shop of Horrors*, *Angry Housewives*, *Sweeney Todd*, *Groucho*, *A Life in Revue*, *The Middle of Nowhere* (a Randy Newman revue) and *A . . . My Name Is Alice*. We prefer small cast shows, but have done shows with a cast as large as 15. Orchestrations can be problematic. We usually do keyboards and percussion or some variation. Some shows can be a design problem; we cannot do 'spectacle.' Our audiences generally like good, intelligent musical properties. Very contemporary language is about the only thing that sometimes causes 'angst' among our subscribers. We appreciate honesty and forthrightness . . . and good material done in an original and creative manner."
Productions: *Lucky Stiff*, by Flaherty/Ahrens (death and grand theft); *Pump Boys & Dinettes*, by Hardwick/Monk/Wann (C&W revue); and *The Cocoanuts*, by Haufman/Berlin (Marx Brothers in Florida).

THEATRE WEST VIRGINIA, P.O. Box 1205, Beckley WV 25802. (800)666-9142. Play producer. Estab. 1955. Produces 5 plays and 2 musicals/year. "Audience varies from mainstream summer stock to educational tours (ages K—high school)." Pays 5% royalty or $25/performance.
How to Contact: Query with synopsis, character breakdown and set description; should include cassette tape. SASE.
Musical Theater: "Theatre West Virginia is a year-round performing arts organization that presents a variety of productions including community performances and statewide educational programs on primary, elementary and secondary levels. This is in addition to our summer, outdoor dramas of *Hatfields & McCoys* and *Honey in the Rock*, now in their 37th year." Anything suitable for secondary school tours and/or dinner theater type shows. No more than 7 in cast. Play should be able to be accompanied by piano/synthesizer.
Productions: *Man In The Iron Mask*, adapted by Craig Johnson (literary); and *The Three Little Pigs* (for marionette company).

THEATREVIRGINIA, 2800 Grove Ave., Richmond VA 23221-2466. (804)353-6100. Artistic Director: George Black. Play producer. Estab. 1955. Produces 5-9 plays (2-5 musicals)/year. "Plays are performed in a 500-seat LORT-C house for the Richmond-area community." Payment negotiable.
How to Contact: Query first. "If material seems to be of interest to us, we will reply with a solicitation for a complete manuscript and cassette. Response time for synopses is 4 weeks; response time for scripts once solicited is 5 months." SASE.
Musical Theater: "We do not deal in one-acts or in children's material. We would like to see full length, adult musicals. There are no official limitations. We would be unlikely to use original music as incidental/underscoring for existing plays, but there is potential for adapting existing plays into musicals."
Productions: *Five Guys Named Moe*, by Clarke Peters (jazz); *A Closer Walk with Patsy Cline*, by Dean Regan (Patsy Cline); and *The Pirates of Penzance*, by Gilbert and Sullivan.
Tips: "Read plays. Study structure. Study character. Learn how to concisely articulate the nature of your work. A beginning musical playwright wishing to work for our company should begin by writing a wonderful, theatrically viable piece of musical theater. Then he should send us the material requested in our listing, and wait patiently."

THEATREWORKS/USA, 890 Broadway, New York NY 10003. (212)677-5959. Literary Manager: Barbara Pasternack. Play producer. Produces 10-13 plays, most are musicals (3-4 are new musicals)/year. Audience consists of children and families. Pays 6% royalty and aggregate of $1,500 commission-advance against future royalties.

How to Contact: Query with synopsis, character breakdown and sample scene and song. SASE. Reports in 6 months.

Musical Theater: "One hour long, 5-6 adult actors, highly portable, good musical theater structure; adaptations of children's literature, historical or biographical musicals, issues, fairy tales—all must have something to say. We demand a certain level of literary sophistication. No kiddy shows, no camp, no fractured fables, no shows written for school or camp groups to perform. Approach your material, not as a writer writing for kids, but as a writer addressing any universal audience. You have 1 hour to entertain, say something, make them care—don't preach, condescend. Don't forget an antagonist. Don't waste the audience's time. We always use original music—but most of the time a project team comes complete with a composer in tow."

Productions: *Freaky Friday*, music by Mary Rodgers, book and lyrics by John Forster; *Little Prince*, by Jeff Linden and Art Perlman; and *Where's Waldo*, book by Michael Slade, music by David Evans, lyrics by Faye Greenberg.

Tips: "Write a good show! Make sure the topic is something we can market! Come see our work to find out our style."

13TH STREET REPERTORY COMPANY, 50 W. 13th St., New York NY 10011. (212)675-6677. Dramaturg: Ken Terrell. Play producer. Estab. 1974. Produces 6 plays/year including 2 new musicals. Audience comes from New York City, New Jersey and surrounding area. Children's theater performs at 50 W. 13th in NYC. "We do not pay. We are an off-off Broadway company and provide a stepping stone for writers, directors, actors."

How to Contact: Query with synopsis, character breakdown and set description. Does not return material. Reports in 6 months.

Musical Theater: Children's musicals and original musical shows. Small cast with limited musicians. Stagings are struck after each performance. Would consider original music for "pre-show music or incidental music."

Productions: *Journeys*, a collaborative effort about actors' work in New York City; *New York, Paris, Everywhere*, by Ken Terrell; and *The Smart Set*, by Enrico Garzilli.

UNIVERSITY OF ALABAMA NEW PLAYWRIGHTS' PROGRAM, P.O. Box 870239, Tuscaloosa AL 35487-0239. (205)348-9032. Fax: (205)348-9048. E-mail: pcastagn@woodsquad.as.ua.edu. Director/Dramaturg: Dr. Paul Castagno. Play producer. Estab. 1982. Produces 8-10 plays and 1 musical/year; 1 new musical every other year. University audience. Pays by arrangement. Stipend is competitive. Also expenses and travel.

How to Contact: Submit complete manuscript, score and tape of songs. Submit only August-March. SASE. Reports in 4-6 months.

Musical Theater: Any style or subject (but no children's or puppet plays). No limitations—just solid lyrics and melodic line. Drama with music, musical theater workshops, and chamber musicals. "We love to produce a small-scale musical."

Productions: *Gospels According to Esther*, by John Erlanger.

Tips: "Take your demos seriously. We really want to do something small scale, for actors, often without the greatest singing ability. Use fresh sounds not derivative of the latest fare. While not ironclad by any means, musicals with Southern themes might stand a better chance."

WALNUT STREET THEATRE COMPANY, 825 Walnut St., Philadelphia PA 19107. (215)574-3550. Literary Manager: Beverly Elliott. Play producer. Estab. 1982. Produces 7 plays and 3 musicals/year. Plays produced on a mainstage with seating for 1,052 to a family audience; and in studio theaters with seating for 79-99 to adult audiences. Pays by royalty or outright purchase.

How to Contact: Does not accept unsolicited scripts from individuals.

Musical Theater: "We seek musicals with lyrical non-operatic scores and a solid book. We are looking

● **A BULLET** introduces comments by the editor of *Songwriter's Market* indicating special information about the listing.

for a small musical for springtime and one for a family audience at Christmas time. We remain open on structure and subject matter and would expect a tape with the script. Cast size: around 20 equity members (10 for smaller musical); preferably one set with variations." Would consider original music for incidental music and/or underscore. This would be at each director's discretion.
Productions: *Goodbye Girl*, *Crazy For You* and *Blood Brothers*.

WATERLOO COMMUNITY PLAYHOUSE, P.O. Box 433, Waterloo IA 50704. (319)235-0367. Managing Artistic Director: Charles Stilwill. Play producer. Estab. 1917. Produces 12 plays (1-2 musicals)/ year. "Our audience prefers solid, wholesome entertainment, nothing risqué or with strong language. We perform in Hope Martin Theatre, a 366-seat house." Pays $15-150/performance.
How to Contact: Submit complete manuscript, score and cassette tape of songs. SASE. Reports in 8-10 months.
Musical Theater: "Casts may vary from as few as 6 people to 54. We are producing children's theater as well. We're *especially* interested in new adaptations of classic children stories."
Productions: *Ramona Quimby* (children's); *It's A Wonderful Life* (holiday); and *Joseph and the Amazing Technicolor Dreamcoat* (traditional).
Tips: "The only 'new' musicals we are likely to produce are adaptations of name shows that would fit in our holiday slot or for our children's theater."

WEST COAST ENSEMBLE, P.O. Box 38728, Los Angeles CA 90038. (310)449-1447. Artistic Director: Les Hanson. Play producer. Estab. 1982. Produces 4-8 plays and 1 new musical/year. "Our audience is a wide variety of Southern Californians. Plays will be produced in our theater in Hollywood." Pays $35-50 per performance.

- See the listing for West Coast Ensemble Musical Stairs in the Contests and Awards section.

How to Contact: Submit complete manuscript, score and tape of songs. SASE. Reports in 6-8 months.
Musical Theater: "There are no limitations on subject matter or style. Cast size should be no more than 12 and sets should be simple. If music is required we would commission a composer, music would be used as a bridge between scenes or to underscore certain scenes in the play."
Productions: *The Human Comedy*, by Galt McDermott (adaptation of the Saroyan novel); *The Much Ado Musical*, by Tony Tanner (adaptation of Shakespeare); and *A Grand Night for Singing*.
Tips: "Submit work in good form and be patient. We look for musicals with a strong book and an engaging score with a variety of styles."

WEST END ARTISTS, 18034 Ventura Blvd. #291, Encino CA 91316. (818)501-0495. Artistic Director: Edmund Gaynes. Play producer. Estab. 1983. Produces 5 plays and 3 new musicals/year. Audience "covers a broad spectrum, from general public to heavy theater/film/TV industry crowds." Payment is negotiable.
How to Contact: Submit complete manuscript and score. SASE. Reports in 3 months.
Musical Theater: "Prefer small-cast musicals and revues. Full length preferred. Interested in children's shows also." Cast size: "Maximum 12; exceptional material with larger casts will be considered."
Productions: *The Taffetas*, by Rick Lewis ('50s nostalgia, received 3 Ovation Award nominations); *Songs the Girls Sang*, by Alan Palmer (songs written for women now sung by men, received one Ovation Award nomination); and *Broadway Sings Out!*, by Ray Malvani (Broadway songs of social significance).
Tips: "If you feel every word or note you have written is sacred and chiseled in stone, and are unwilling to work collaboratively with a professional director, don't bother to submit."

WESTBETH THEATRE CENTER, 151 Bank St., New York NY 10014. (212)691-2272. Literary Manager: Steven Bloom. Play producer. Estab. 1978. Produces 1-2 musicals/year. Audience consists of New York theater professionals and Village neighborhood. "We have 5 performance spaces, including a music hall and cafe theater." Uses usual New York showcase contract.
How to Contact: Query with synopsis, character breakdown and set description. Does not return material. Reports in 4 months. "Artists must be accessible to NYC."
Musical Theater: "Full length musicals, all Broadway styles. Small, ensemble casts the best." Does not wish to see "one character musicals, biographies and historical dramas. Musicals selected for development will undergo intense process. We look for strong collaborators."
Productions: *20th Century Man*, by Ray Davies (of the Kinks, his music biography); *The Hunchback of Notre Dame*, by Scully/Hackaday/Janis (adaptation); and *Bodyshop*, by Walter Marks (strippers).
Tips: "Be open to the collaborative effort. We are a professional theater company, competing in the competitive world of Broadway and off-Broadway, so the work we present must reach for the highest standard of excellence."

WILLOWS THEATRE COMPANY, 1975 Diamond Blvd., A-20, Concord CA 94520. (510)798-1300. E-mail: willowsth@aol.com. Artistic Director: Richard H. Elliott. Play producer. Estab. 1973. Produces 8

plays and 4 musicals (0-4 new musicals)/year. "The 203-seat Willows Theatre is a proscenium stage in Concord, located in suburban San Francisco." Pays 6% royalty.
How to Contact: Query with synopsis, character breakdown and set description. SASE. Reports in 6 months.
Musical Theater: "Full-length musicals addressing contemporary themes or issues, small to mid-size cast (maximum 15 characters) with maximum 15 instruments. Topics which appeal to an educated suburban and liberal urban audience are best. Maximum 10 cast members, 9 musicians, prefer unit set (we have no fly loft or wing space)."
Productions: *Smoke On The Mountain*, by Ray/Bailey (white southern gospel); *Jamboree*, by Goggin; and *A . . . My Name Is Still Alice* (contemporary musical revue).

Play Publishers

AMELIA MAGAZINE, 329 "E" St., Bakersfield CA 93304. (805)323-4064. Editor: Frederick A. Raborg, Jr. Play publisher. Estab. 1983. Publishes 1 play/year. General audience; one-act plays published in *Amelia Magazine*. The annual Frank McClure One-Act Play Award awards $150 plus publication. Deadline May 15 annually.
How to Contact: Submit complete manuscript and score. Reports in 6-8 weeks. "We would consider publishing musical scores if submitted in clean, camera-ready copy—also single songs. Best bet is with single songs complete with clear, camera-ready scoresheets, for regular submissions. We use only first North American serial rights. All performance and recording rights remain with songwriter. Payment same as for poetry—$35 plus copies for regular acceptance. Write for guidelines for McClure Award with SASE." Sample copy: $8.95 ppd.
Tips: "Be polished, professional, and submit clear, clean copy."

ART CRAFT PUBLISHING CO., P.O. Box 1058, Cedar Rapids IA 52406. (319)364-6311. E-mail: editor@hitplays.com. Editor: C. Emmett McMullen. Play publisher. Estab. 1928. Publishes 10-15 plays/year. "We publish plays and musicals for the amateur market including middle, junior and smaller senior high schools and church groups." Pays varying rate for outright purchase or varying royalty.
How to Contact: Query with synopsis, character breakdown and set description or submit complete manuscript and score. SASE. Reports in 2 months.
Musical Theater: "Seeking material for high school productions. All writing within the scope of high school groups. No works with X-rated material or questionable taboos. Simplified staging and props. Currently seeking material with larger casts, preferably with more female than male roles."
Publications: *Brave Buckaroo*, by Renee J. Clark; *Rest Assured*, by Donald Payton; and *Murder At Coppersmith Inn*, by Dan Neidermyer.
Tips: "We are primarily interested in full length musical comedies, farces, and mysteries with a large number of characters. Since the vast majority of people who perform our plays have little or no theatrical experience, simplicity and ease of production are chief factors in the acceptance of a play. As our primary markets are junior and senior high schools, we are unable to publish works that are offensive or controversial in nature."

BAKER'S PLAYS, 100 Chauncy St., Boston MA 02111. (617)482-1280. Fax: (617)482-7613. Associate Editor: Raymond Pape. Play publisher. Estab. 1845. Publishes 15-22 plays and 0-3 new musicals/year. Plays are used by children's theaters, junior and senior high schools, colleges and community theaters. Pays negotiated royalty.

- See the listing for Baker's Plays High School Playwriting Contest in the Contests and Awards section.

How to Contact: Submit complete manuscript, score and cassette tape of songs. SASE. Reports in 2-6 months.
Musical Theater: "Seeking musicals for teen production and children's theater production. We prefer large cast, contemporary musicals which are easy to stage and produce. Plot your shows strongly, keep your scenery and staging simple, your musical numbers and choreography easily explained and blocked out. We want innovative and tuneful shows but no X-rated material." Would consider original music for use in a play being developed or in a pre-existing play.
Tips: "As we publish musicals that can be produced by high school theater departments with high school talent, the writer should know if their play can be done on the high school stage. I recommend that the writer go to performances of original musicals whenever possible."

I.E. CLARK PUBLICATIONS, P.O. Box 246, Schulenburg TX 78956. General Manager: Donna Cozzaglio. Play publisher. Estab. 1956. Publishes 10-15 new plays and 2-4 new musicals/year. Pays negotiable royalty.

How to Contact: Query with synopsis, character breakdown and set description. SASE. Reports in 2-4 months.
Musical Theater: "Musicals for children's theater and for high school and community theater, adaptations of well-known stories and novels. We do not publish puppet shows. We seek plays that appeal to a wide spectrum of producers—professional, community, college, high school, junior high, elementary schools, children's theater, etc. The more of these groups a play will appeal to, the better the sales—and the better the chance that we will accept the play for publication." Does not wish to see plays with obscenities or blasphemous material. "We feel that the songs and musical numbers in a play should advance the plot and action, rather than interrupting the flow of the play for the sake of the music."
Publications: *Peter Pan in Neverland*, by R. Eugene Jackson/David Ellis (a "non-flying" adaptation); *The Age of Discretion*, by Sharon Ferranti/Jay Ferranti (a play about AIDS); and *The Ghost Sonata*, by August Strindberg, translated by Joe Martin with music by Anna Larson.
Tips: "We demand originality and high literary quality. Avoid clichés, both in plot and music."

CONTEMPORARY DRAMA SERVICE, 885 Elkton Dr., Colorado Springs CO 80907. (719)594-4422. Executive Editor: Arthur Zapel. Assistant Editor: Rhonda Wray. Play publisher. Estab. 1979. Publishes 40-50 plays and 4-6 new musicals/year. "We publish for young children and teens in mainstream Christian churches and for teens and college level in the secular market. Our musicals are performed in churches, schools and colleges." Pays 10% royalty (for music books), 50% royalty for performance and "sometimes we pay royalty up to buy-out fee for minor works."
How to Contact: Submit complete manuscript, score and tape of songs. SASE. Reports in 2 months.
Musical Theater: "For churches we publish musical programs for children and teens to perform at Easter, Christmas or some special occasion. Our school musicals are for teens to perform as class plays or special entertainments. Cast size may vary from 5-25 depending on use. We prefer more parts for girls than boys. Music must be written in the vocal range of teens. Staging should be relatively simple but may vary as needed. We are not interested in elementary school material. Elementary level is OK for church music but not public school elementary. Music must have full piano accompaniment and be professionally scored for camera-ready publication."
Publications: *No Ordinary Night*, by Eleanor Miller and Roland A. Caire (Christmas musical for children); *Three Wishes*, by Ted Sod/Suzanne Grant (musical about teenage pregnancy); and *Christmas Is Coming!*, by Jarl K. Iverson (Christmas musical for children).
Tips: "Familiarize yourself with the type of musicals we publish. Note general categories, then give us something that would fit, yet differs from what we've already published. Religious Christmas musicals for church performance and classics or issues-oriented musicals for high school performance are your best bets."

THE DRAMATIC PUBLISHING COMPANY, 311 Washington St., Woodstock IL 60098. (815)338-7170. E-mail: 75712.3621@compuserve.com. Website: http://dramaticpublishing.com. Music Editor: Dana Wolworth. Play publisher. Publishes 35 plays (3-5 musicals)/year. Estab. 1885. Plays used by community theaters, high schools, colleges, stock and professional theaters and churches. Pays negotiable royalty.
How to Contact: Submit complete manuscript, score and tape of songs. SASE. Reports in 10-12 weeks.
Musical Theater: Seeking "children's musicals not over 1¼ hours, and adult musicals with two-act format. No adaptations for which the rights to use the original work have not been cleared. If directed toward high school market, large casts with many female roles are preferred. For professional, stock and community theater small casts are better. Cost of producing a play is always a factor to consider in regard to costumes, scenery and special effects." Would also consider original music for use in a pre-existing play "if we or the composer hold the rights to the non-musical work."
Publications: *The Secret Garden*, by Sharon Burgett/Jim Crabtree; *Frankenstein Unbound*, by Sheldon Allman/Bobby Pickett; and *The Adventures of Beatrix Potter and Her Friends*, by Joe Robinette/Evelyn Swensson.
Tips: "A complete score, ready to go is highly recommended. Tuneful songs which stand on their own are a must. Good subject matter which has wide appeal is always best but not required."

‡EASTERN MUSICALS, P.O. Box 9052, Fall River MA 02720. (508)676-3312. President: Raymond Carreiro. Play publisher. Estab. 1996. Publishes 3 musicals/year. Pays standard royalty.
How to Contact: Submit complete manuscript and tape of songs. Does not return material. Reports in 3 weeks.
Musical Theater: Seeks rock musicals, classical musicals, contemporary and non-musical theater.
Publications: *Lizzie Borden—The Musical*, by Jay Brillient/Maria Esteves; *Through Orphans' Eyes*, by Raymond Carreiro/Richard Shore; and *Agent Orange Blues*, by Raymond Carreiro.

ELDRIDGE PUBLISHING CO., INC., P.O. Box 1595, Venice FL 34284. (800)HI-STAGE. E-mail: info@histage.com. Website: http://www.histage.com. Editor: Nancy S. Vorhis. Play publisher. Estab. 1906. Publishes 40 plays and 2-3 musicals/year. Seeking "large cast musicals which appeal to students. We like variety and originality in the music, easy staging and costuming. Also looking for children's theater musicals which have smaller casts and are easy to tour. We serve the school and church market, 6th grade through 12th; also Christmas and Easter musicals for churches." Would also consider original music for use in a play being developed; "music that could make an ordinary play extraordinary." Pays 50% royalty and 10% copy sales in school market.
How to Contact: Submit manuscript, score or lead sheets and tape of songs. SASE. Reports in 2 months.
Publications: *Mother Goose, Inc.*, by Stephen Murray (fairy tale MTV); *The World of Beauty and the Beast*, by Burch & Madsen (children's musical theater); and *Magnolia*, by Sodaro and Francoeur (a *Gone with the Wind* takeoff).
Tips: "We're always looking for talented composers but not through individual songs. We're only interested in complete school or church musicals. Lead sheets, cassette tape and script are best way to submit. Let us see your work!"

ENCORE PERFORMANCE PUBLISHING, P.O. Box 692, Orem UT 84059. (801)225-0605. E-mail: encoreplay@aol.com. Website: http://www.howlinwolf/com/Encoreplay. Editor: Michael C. Perry. Play publisher. Estab. 1979. Publishes 20-30 plays (including musicals)/year. "We are interested in plays which emphasize strong family values and play to all ages." Pays 50% royalty.
How to Contact: Query with synopsis, character breakdown and set description. SASE. Reports in 2 months.
Musical Theater: Musicals of all types for all audiences. Can be original or adapted. "We tend to favor shows with at least an equal male/female cast." Do not wish to see works that can be termed offensive or vulgar. However, experimental theater forms are also of interest.
Publications: *Boy Who Knew No Fear*, by Mark Levenson and Gary Mills (youth quest); *Right Around the Corner*, by Joe Bell, Hope Hommersand and Nate Herman (Twain adaptation); and *Carpenter's Son*, by Al Viola (Christian).
Tips: "Always write with an audience in mind."

THE FREELANCE PRESS, P.O. Box 548, Dover MA 02030. (508)785-8250. Managing Editor: Narcissa Campion. Play publisher. Estab. 1979. Publishes 3 new musicals/year. "Pieces are primarily to be acted by elementary to high school students; large casts (approximately 30); plays are produced by schools and children's theaters." Pays 10% of purchase price of script or score, 50% of collected royalty.
How to Contact: Query first. SASE. Reports in 6 months.
Musical Theater: "We publish previously produced musicals and plays to be acted by children in the primary grades through high school. Plays are for large casts (approximately 30 actors and speaking parts) and run between 45 minutes to 1 hour and 15 minutes. Subject matter should be contemporary issues (sibling rivalry, friendship, etc.) or adaptations of classic literature for children (*Alice in Wonderland*, *Treasure Island*, etc.). We do not accept any plays written for adults to perform for children."
Publications: *Tortoise vs. Hare*, by Stephen Murray (modern version of classic); *Tumbleweed*, by Sebastian Stuart (sleepy time western town turned upside down); and *Mything Links*, by Sam Abel (interweaving of Greek myths with a great pop score).
Tips: "We enjoy receiving material that does not condescend to children. They are capable of understanding many current issues, playing complex characters, handling unconventional material, and singing difficult music."

SAMUEL FRENCH, INC., 45 W. 25th St., New York NY 10010. (212)206-8990. President: Charles R. Van Nostrand. Play publisher. Estab. 1830. Publishes 40-50 plays and 2-4 new musicals/year. Amateur and professional theaters.
How to Contact: Query first. SASE. Reports in minimum 10 weeks.
Musical Theater: "We publish primarily successful musicals from the NYC, London and regional stage."
Publications: *Eating Raoul*, by Paul Bartel; *Hello Muddah Hello Faddah*, by Bernstein/Krause; and *Love and Shrimp*, by Judith Viorst.

HEUER PUBLISHING CO., P.O. Box 248, Cedar Rapids IA 52406. (319)364-6311. E-mail: hitplays@netins.net. Website: http://www.hitplays.com. Publisher: C. Emmett McMullen. Musical play publisher. Estab. 1928. Publishes plays and musicals for the amateur market including middle schools, junior and senior high schools and church groups. Pays by outright purchase or percentage royalty.
How to Contact: Query with synopsis, character breakdown and set description or submit complete manuscript and score. SASE. Reports in 2 months.
Musical Theater: "We prefer two or three act comedies or mystery-comedies with a large number of

characters."

Publications: *Brave Buckaroo*, by Renee J. Clark (musical melodrama).

Tips: "We sell almost exclusively to junior and smaller senior high schools. Thus flexible casting is extremely important. In middle school, girls' voices are generally stronger than boys', so if you are writing musicals, we stress more choral numbers and more solos for girls than boys."

PIONEER DRAMA SERVICE, P.O. Box 4267, Englewood CO 80155. (303)779-4035. E-mail: piodrama @aol.com. Website: http://websites.earthlink.net/~pioneerdrama/. Play publisher. Estab. 1963. "Plays are performed by junior high and high school drama departments, church youth groups, college and university theaters, semi-professional and professional children's theaters, parks and recreation departments." Playwrights paid 50% royalty (10% sales).

How to Contact: Query first. SASE. Reports in 2-4 months.

Musical Theater: "We seek full length children's musicals, high school musicals and one act children's musicals to be performed by children, secondary school students, and/or adults. As always, we are seeking musicals easy to perform, simple sets, many female roles and very few solos. Must be appropriate for educational market. Developing a new area, we are actively seeking musicals to be produced by elementary schools—20 to 30 minutes in length, with 2 to 3 songs and large choruses. We are not interested in profanity, themes with exclusively adult interest, sex, drinking, smoking, etc. Several of our full-length plays are being converted to musicals. We edit them, decide where to insert music and then contract with someone to write the music and lyrics."

Publications: *Shakespeare Comes to Calamity Creek*, book by Tim Kelly, music and lyrics by Bill Francoeur; *Little Princess*, book by Tim Kelly, music and lyrics by Bill Francoeur; and *Give My Regards to Broadway*, book by Steven Fendrick, music and lyrics by George M. Cohen.

Tips: "Research and learn about our company. Our website and catalog provide an incredible amount of information."

PLAYERS PRESS, INC., P.O. Box 1132, Studio City CA 91614. (818)789-4980. Associate Editor: Marjorie Clapper. Vice President: Robert W. Gordon. Play publisher. Estab. 1965. Publishes 20-70 plays and 1-3 new musicals/year. Plays are used primarily by general audience and children. Pays 10-50% royalty and 25-80% of performance.

How to Contact: Query first. SASE. Reports in 1 year (1 week on query).

Musical Theater: "We will consider all submitted works. Presently musicals for adults and high schools are in demand. When cast size can be flexible (describe how it can be done in your work) it sells better."

Publications: *Phantom of the Music Hall*, by Judith Prior (musical comedy); *Button Bush*, by James P. McMahon (young audience musical); and *Best of Times*, by Stephen Porter (musical-light opera).

Tips: "Have your work produced at least twice. Be present for rehearsals and work with competent people. Then submit material asked for in good clear copy with good audio tapes."

Classical Performing Arts

Composers of classical music are different from popular songwriters in that they are more interested in finding groups to perform their work rather than a publishing or recording deal. Once a composer has his work performed for an audience and establishes himself as a talented newcomer in the concert music community, it can lead to more performances and perhaps even commissions for new works.

Most classical music organizations are nonprofit groups, and don't have a large budget to spend on acquiring new works. The time and money it takes to put together a classical performance of a composer's work can be extensive, and therefore these groups are quite selective when choosing new works to perform. Don't be disappointed if the payment offered by these groups is small or even non-existent. What you're looking to gain is the chance to have your music performed for an appreciative audience.

All of the groups listed in this section are interested in hearing new works from contemporary classical composers. Pay close attention to the music needs of each group, and when you find one you feel might be interested in your music, follow submission guidelines carefully. Since many classical groups are understaffed, it may take longer than expected to hear back on your submission, so it pays to be patient. To locate classical performing arts groups in your area, consult the Geographic Index at the back of this book.

ACADIANA SYMPHONY ORCHESTRA, P.O. Box 53632, Lafayette LA 70505. (318)232-4277. Fax: (318)237-4712. Music Director: Xiao-lu Li. Symphony orchestra. Estab. 1984. Members are amateurs and professionals. Performs 20 concerts/year, including 1 new work. Commissions 1 new work/year. Performs in 2,230-seat hall with "wonderful acoustics." Pays "according to the type of composition."
How to Contact: Query first. Does not return material.
Music: Full orchestra—10 minutes at most. Reduced orchestra, educational pieces—short, not more than 5 minutes.
Performances: Quincy Hilliard's *Universal Covenant* (orchestral suite); James Hanna's *In Memoriam* (strings/elegy); and Gregory Danner's *A New Beginning* (full orchestra fanfare).

ADRIAN SYMPHONY ORCHESTRA, 110 S. Madison St., Adrian MI 49221. (517)264-3121. Music Director: David Katz. Symphony orchestra and chamber music ensemble. Estab. 1981. Members are professionals. Performs 25 concerts/year including 2-3 new works. Commissions 1 new composer or new work/year. 1,200 seat hall—"Rural city with remarkably active cultural life." $100-2,500 for outright purchase or commission.
How to Contact: Submit complete score and tapes of piece(s). SASE. Reports in 6 months.
Music: Chamber ensemble to full orchestra. "Limited rehearsal time dictates difficulty of pieces selected." Does not wish to see "rock music or country—not at this time."
Performances: Michael Pratt's *Dancing on the Wall* (orchestral—some aleatoric); Sir Peter Maxwell Davies' *Orkney Wedding* (orchestral); and Gwyneth Walker's *Fanfare, Interlude, Finale* (orchestral).

THE AKRON CITY FAMILY MASS CHOIR, 429 Homestead St., Akron OH 44306. (330)773-8529. President: Walter E.L. Scrutchings. Vocal ensemble. Estab. 1984. Members are professionals. Performs 5-7 concerts/year, including 30-35 new works. Commissions 10-15 composers or new works/year. Audience mostly interested in new original black gospel music. Performs in various venues. Composers paid 50% royalty.
How to Contact: Submit complete score and tapes of piece(s). Does not return material. Reports in 2 months.
Music: Seeks "traditional music for SATB black gospel; also light contemporary. No rap or non-spiritual themes."
Performances: R.W. Hinton's *I Can't Stop Praising God*; W. Scrutchings' *A Better Place*; and Rev. A. Wright's *Christ In Your Life*.

THE AMERICAN BOYCHOIR, 19 Lambert Dr., Princeton NJ 08540. (609)924-5858. Music Director: James H. Litton. Professional boychoir. Estab. 1937. Members are musically talented children. Performs 250 concerts/year, including 20 new works. Commissions 1 composer or new work/year. Performs community concerts, orchestral concerts, for local concert associations, church concert series and other bookings.

• See the interview with Music Director James H. Litton in the 1997 *Songwriter's Market*.

How to Contact: Query first. SASE. Reports in 1 year.

Music: Dramatic works for boys voices (age 10-14); 15 to 20 minutes short opera to be staged and performed throughout the US. Choral pieces, either in unison, SSA, SA or SSAA division; unaccompanied and with piano or organ; occasional chamber orchestra accompaniment. Pieces are usually sung by 26 to 50 boys. Composers must know boychoir sonority.

Performances: *Disney Medley* and *Gershwin Medley*, arranged by Bill Holcombe; and Lawrence Siegel's *Do They Just Sing All Day*?

AMERICAN JAZZ PHILHARMONIC, 10811 Washington Blvd., Suite 250, Culver City CA 90232. (310)845-1900. Fax: (310)845-1909. Music Director: Jack Elliott. Executive Director: Mitchell Glickman. Symphonic jazz orchestra (72 piece). Estab. 1979. Members are professionals. Performs 3-4 concerts/year, all new works. Commissions 1-2 composers or new works/year. Performs in major concert halls nationwide: Avery Fisher (New York), Karen & Richard Carpenter Performing Arts Center (Long Beach), Royce Hall (Los Angeles), Pick-Staiger (Chicago). Pays $2,500-5,000 for commission.

How to Contact: Query first then submit complete score and tape of piece(s) with résumé. SASE. "Newly commissioned composers are chosen each July. Submissions should be sent by June 15th, returned by August 15th."

Music: "The AJP commissions 1-2 new symphonic jazz works annually. Decisions to commission are based on composer's previous work in the symphonic jazz genre. The AJP is a 72-piece symphonic jazz ensemble that includes a rhythm section and woodwinds who double on saxophones, plus traditional symphonic orchestra."

Performances: John Clayton's *Three Shades of Blue* (solo tenor sax and orchestra); Lennie Niehaus' *Tribute to Bird* (solo alto sax and orchestra); and Eddie Karam's *Stay 'N See* (symphonic jazz overture).

Tips: "The AJP has been a recipient of a Reader's Digest/Meet the Composer grant and has received awards from ASCAP and the American Symphony Orchestra League for its programming. The ensemble has also received a Grammy Award nomination for its debut album on GRP Records featuring Ray Brown and Phil Woods. The AJP has recently established the Henry Mancini Institute—a four-week summer educational music program for talented young musicians and composer/arrangers chosen from auditions held nationally. Participants study and perform with the principal players of the AJP and guest artists and composers/conductors. Program includes private lessons, ensemble rehearsals, panel discussions/clinics, master classes, soloist opportunities and performances in orchestra, big band, chamber ensembles and combos."

‡AMERICAN OPERA MUSICAL THEATRE CO., 400 W. 43rd St. #19D, New York NY 10036. Phone/fax: (212)594-1839. Artistic Director: Diana Corto. Chamber music ensemble, chamber opera and musical theater producing/presenting organization. Estab. 1994. Members are professionals and amateurs. Performs 5 concerts/year; all are new works. Audience is sophisticated and knowledgeable about music and theater. "We rent different performance spaces." Pays negotiable royalty.

How to Contact: Submit tape and background materials first. No score. Does not return material.

Music: "Must be vocal (for opera or for music theater) with chamber groups. Cast should not exceed 10. Orchestration should not exceed 22, smaller chamber groups preferred. No rock 'n' roll, brassy pop or theater material."

Performances: Paul Griffiths's *The Jewel Box* (opera); *Shostakovich Concert* (premiere of song cycles); and *Haydn Opera* (New York premiere).

AMHERST SAXOPHONE QUARTET, 137 Eagle St., Williamsville NY 14221-5721. (716)632-2445. Director: Steve Rosenthal. Chamber music ensemble. Estab. 1978. Performs 80-100 concerts/year including 10-20 new works. Commissions 1-2 composers or new works/year. "We are a touring ensemble." Payment varies.

• See the interview with Director Steve Rosenthal in this section.

How to Contact: Query first. SASE. Reports in 1 month.

Music: "Music for soprano, alto, tenor and baritone (low A) saxophone. We are interested in great music of many styles. Level of difficulty is commensurate with full-time touring ensembles."

Performances: Lukas Foss's *Saxophone Quartet* (classical); David Stock's *Sax Appeal* (New Age); and Chan Ka Nin's *Saxophone Quartet* (jazz).

Tips: "Professionally copied parts help! Write what you truly want to write."

INSIDER REPORT

Non-traditional ensembles offer composers new outlets for their work

Stephen Rosenthal

When most inhabitants of twentieth century America think of classical music, two images generally arise: powdered wigs and hose straight out of *Amadeus* or tuxedo-clad symphonies with a Pavarotti-type figure belting out Italian into the rafters of a mammoth concert hall.

For those with only passing or no interest in classical music, it's difficult to spot trends in an art form that's dominated most of the millennium, particularly when it's been eclipsed in recent decades by other forms of music and entertainment. However, it doesn't take more than a glance at the classical section of a record store to see that one of the major movements in classical music lately has been the rise of the small ensemble.

Artists like the Kronos Quartet, Brodsky String Quartet and Canadian Brass have found success on the world's classical stages with more traditional ensemble instrumentation, i.e., strings or brass. Helping break new ground two decades ago was the Amherst Saxophone Quartet, taking what was "too strange an idea to be successful" and turning it into an inspiration for new groups to form all over the world.

The reason a classical saxophone quartet seemed like an idea from left field is grounded mainly in snobbery. The saxophone was a jazz instrument (and therefore inferior), and worse yet, rock and roll bands used saxophones. "The saxophone was invented after the death of Beethoven," says Stephen Rosenthal, director and tenor saxophonist of the Amherst Saxophone Quartet, "so it's a relatively new instrument. Therefore there wasn't a great body of music written for a saxophone quartet." The saxophone is not considered part of a "standard" symphony orchestra, and it is still occasionally derided in some circles as an exclusively contemporary instrument. All of this forces saxophone players to rely heavily on new pieces and arrangements.

"We want composers and audiences to regard the saxophone as a natural instrument for an ensemble," says Rosenthal, and his quartet has been fulfilling that goal. Entering their twentieth anniversary season, the Amherst Saxophone Quartet (Sal Andolina, soprano; Harry Fackelman, baritone; Rosenthal, tenor saxophone; and Russ Carere, alto saxophonist) is one of a handful of full-time touring saxophone quartets in the country. Several tours across America and Japan, as well as recordings for MCA Records, Mark Records and the Musical Heritage Society, have proven successful for the quartet.

Success in the studio and on stage has not only benefited the Quartet, but it's served their loftier goals as well: to ensure the saxophone quartet as an "accepted" classical ensemble and to expand the body of music written for saxophone quartets. "Pieces written exclusively for saxophone quartets were rare," says Rosenthal, "but we've received

INSIDER REPORT, *Rosenthal*

several hundred pieces that people have written specifically for us to play. Where before compositions for sax quartets were few and far between, now there are more than 1,000 pieces of all styles and difficulty levels.

"We've played nearly every style of music, from the great composers to jazz, to all styles of contemporary music from atonal and minimalist to popular and back again. There are many, many well-trained composers writing music, and we are very interested in finding them, so we are always looking for submissions. Even if it means that many submissions aren't up to the quality that we would like, it's worth it for the diamonds you may find."

Starting from square one in the creation of a new form of musical ensemble has allowed Rosenthal and company to explore and experiment any way they wanted. This versatility gives composers several new outlets for their creations in classical arrangements, new classical pieces, plus jazz and all forms of experimental and contemporary music. This increases the body of saxophone quartet music and helps the cause of boosting the saxophone's standing as a classical instrument, furthering the basic goals of the group.

An added, if overlooked, bonus to diversity is that it keeps audiences interested and returning to concert venues to hear flexible ensembles like the Amherst Saxophone Quartet. They perform 50 to 100 concerts every year, including a quarterly concert series in Buffalo, New York (of which Amherst is a suburb). "We've been playing the series for about 15 years, and we try not to repeat any music," Rosenthal says. "This causes a tremendous need for lots of new and different pieces."

Diverse influences lead to diverse performances and a constant hunt for new music and new composers. "In the long term, music is in jeopardy with severe cuts in federal funding for the arts and the demolition of music education by many schools. But for the moment, there are lots of presenters who have concert halls waiting to be filled and audiences to fill them." Add ensembles willing to perform and composers building a saxophone quartet's repertoire to the mix and the relationship benefits everybody.

Fresh outlets for a composer's energy and creativity and new approaches for not only saxophone players, but for all musicians are crucial to sustain and strengthen an art form already centuries old. Audiences come to listen, and by supporting a new classical ensemble they also assist their other local chamber groups, symphonies and opera companies. Given such a cycle, a small innovation such as a saxophone quartet playing Bach may not seem like a giant leap, but it's another vital step in the continuing history of classical music.

—*Andrew Lucyszyn*

ANDERSON SYMPHONY ORCHESTRA, P.O. Box 741, Anderson IN 46015. (317)644-2111. Conductor: Dr. Richard Sowers. Symphony orchestra. Estab. 1968. Members are professionals. Performs 7 concerts/year including 1 new work. Performs for typical mid-western audience in a 1,500-seat restored Paramount Theatre. Pay negotiable.
How to Contact: Query first. SASE. Reports in several months.
Music: "Shorter lengths better; concerti OK; difficulty level: mod high; limited by typically 3 full service rehearsals."
Performances: Garland Anderson's *Piano Conterto #2* and Michael Wooden's *Brother? Man?*

ATLANTA POPS ORCHESTRA, P.O. Box 723172, Atlanta GA 31139-0172. (770)435-1222. Musical Director/Conductor: Albert Coleman. Pops orchestra. Estab. 1945. Members are professionals. Performs

10-20 concerts/year. Concerts are performed for audiences of 5,000-10,000, primarily middle-aged. Composers are paid by outright purchase or per performance.
How to Contact: Submit complete score and tape of piece(s). SASE. Reports in 1 week.
Performances: Vincent Montana, Jr.'s *Magic Bird of Fire*; Louis Alter's *Manhattan Serenade*; and Nelson Riddle's *It's Alright With Me*.
Tips: "My concerts are pops concerts—no deep classics."

THE ATLANTA YOUNG SINGERS OF CALLANWOLDE, 980 Briarcliff Rd. N.E., Atlanta GA 30306. (404)873-3365. Fax: (404)973-0756. Music Director: Stephen J. Ortlip. Community children's chorus. Estab. 1975. Members are amateurs. Performs 25 concerts/year including a few new works. Audience consists of community churches, retirement homes, schools. Performs most often at churches. Pay is negotiable.
How to Contact: Submit complete score and tape of piece(s). SASE. Reports in accordance with request.
Music: "Subjects and styles appealing to grammar and junior high boys and girls. Contemporary concerns of the world of interest. Unusual sacred, folk, classic style. Internationally and ethnically bonding. Medium difficulty preferred, with keyboard accompaniment."
Performances: Bill Hofelot's *Chaconne* (intermediate level).
Tips: "Look for exposure, very little money! Our budget for commissions is $0."

AUREUS QUARTET, 22 Lois Ave., Demarest NJ 07627-2220. (201)767-8704. Artistic Director: James J. Seiler. Vocal ensemble (a cappella). Estab. 1979. Members are professionals. Performs 75 concerts/year, including 3 new works. Pays for outright purchase.
How to Contact: Query first. SASE. Reports in 2-3 weeks.
Music: "We perform anything from pop to classic—mixed repertoire so anything goes. Some pieces can be scored for orchestras as we do pops concerts. Up to now, we've only worked with a quartet. Could be expanded if the right piece came along. Level of difficulty—no piece has ever been too hard." Does not wish to see electronic or sacred pieces. "Electronic pieces would be hard to program. Sacred pieces not performed much. Classical/jazz arrangements of old standards are great!"
Tips: "We perform for a very diverse audience—luscious, four-part writing that can showcase well-trained voices is a must. Also, clever arrangements of old hits from '20s through '50s are sure bets. (Some pieces could take optional accompaniment.)"

BALTIMORE OPERA COMPANY, INC., 1202 Maryland Ave., Baltimore MD 21201. (410)625-1600. Artistic Administrator: James Harp. Opera company. Estab. 1950. Members are professionals. Performs 16 concerts/year. "The opera audience is becoming increasingly diverse. Our performances are given in the 3,000-seat Lyric Opera House." Pays by outright purchase.
How to Contact: Submit complete score and tapes of piece(s). SASE. Reports in 2 months.
Music: "Our General Director, Mr. Michael Harrison, is very much interested in presenting new works. These works would be anything from Grand Opera with a large cast to chamber works suitable for school and concert performances. We would be interested in perusing all music written for an operatic audience."
Performances: Weill's *Regina*; Ponchielli's *La Gioconda*; and Verdi's *Il Trovatore*.
Tips: "Opera is the most expensive art form to produce. Given the current economic outlook, opera companies cannot be too avant garde in their selection of repertoire. The modern operatic composer must give evidence of a fertile and illuminating imagination, while also keeping in mind that opera companies have to sell tickets."

BILLINGS SYMPHONY, 401 N. 31st St., Suite 530, Box 7055, Billings MT 59103. (406)252-3610. Fax: (406)252-3353. Music Director: Dr. Uri Barnea. Symphony orchestra, orchestra and chorale. Estab. 1950. Members are professionals and amateurs. Performs 15 concerts/year, including 6-7 new works. Traditional audience. Performs at Alberta Bair Theater (capacity 1,418). Pays by outright purchase (or rental).
How to Contact: Query first. SASE. Reports in 2-3 months.
Music: Any style. Traditional notation preferred.
Performances: Jerod S. Tate's *Winter Moons* (ballet suite); Alberto Ginastera's *Harp Concerto* (concerto); and Olga Victorova's *Compliments to American Audience* (orchestral piece).
Tips: "Write what you feel (be honest) and sharpen your compositional and craftsmanship skills."

BIRMINGHAM-BLOOMFIELD SYMPHONY ORCHESTRA, 1592 Buckingham, Birmingham MI 48009. (810)645-2276. Fax: (810)645-22760. Executive Director: Carla Lamphere. Symphony orchestra. Estab. 1975. Members are professionals. Performs 6 concerts including 1 new work/year. Performs for middle-to-upper class audience at Temple Beth El's Sanctuary. "Composers pay us to perform."

How to Contact: Query first. SASE. Reports in 1-2 months.
Music: "We are a symphony orchestra but also play pops. Usually 3 works on program (2 hrs.) Orchestra size 65-75. If pianist is involved, they must rent piano."
Performances: Shawn Wygant's *Piano Concerto No. 1* (classical).

BRAVO! L.A., 16823 Liggett St., North Hills CA 91343. (818)892-8737. Fax: (818)892-1227. Director: Dr. Janice Foy. An umbrella organization of recording/touring musicians, formed in 1994. Includes the following musical ensembles: Trio of the Americas (piano, clarinet, cello); the New American Quartet (string quartet); Festive Strings! (string trio); Moonlight Serenaders (harp, violin, cello or harp/cello duo); and the Sierra Chamber Players (piano with strings).
How to Contact: Submit complete score and tape of piece(s). SASE. Reports in 1-2 months.
Music: "Classical, Romantic, Baroque, Popular (including new arrangements done by Shelly Cohen, from the 'Tonight Show Band'), ethnic (including gypsy) and contemporary works (commissioned as well). The New American Quartet just finished a recording project which features music of Mozart, Eine Kleine Nachtmusik, Borodin Nocturne, Puccini Opera Suite (S. Cohen), Strauss Blue Danube Waltz, Trepak of Tschaikovsky, 'El Choclo' (Argentinian tango), Csardas! and arrangements of Cole Porter, Broadway show tunes and popular classics."
Performances: Alfred Carlson's *Angels' Flight* (piano trio); Mike Pavlocki's *Rhapsody* (cello and piano); and Jim Centorino's *Dreams* (cello and piano).
Tips: "Please be open to criticism/suggestions about your music and try to appeal to mixed audiences."

BUFFALO GUITAR QUARTET, 402 Bird Ave., Buffalo NY 14213. (716)883-8429. Fax: (716)883-8429. E-mail: piorkowski@fredonia.edu. Executive Director: James Piorkowski. Chamber music ensemble and classical guitar quartet. Estab. 1976. Members are professionals. Performs 40 concerts/year including 2 new works. Commissions 1 composer or new work every 2 years. Pays for outright purchase.
How to Contact: Submit complete score. SASE. Reports in 2 months.
Music: "Any style or length. 4 classical guitarists, high level of difficulty."
Performances: Loris O. Chobanian's *Dream Sequence* (programmatic); S. Funk-Pearson's *Mummychogs (LeMonde)* (experimental); and Edward Green's *Quartet For Guitars* (mainstream).
Tips: "Don't be afraid of trying new approaches, but know the instrument."

CALGARY BOYS CHOIR, 305-10 Ave. SE, Calgary T2G 0W9 **Canada**. (403)262-7742. Fax: (403)571-5049. Artistic Director: Gerald Wirth. Boys choir. Estab. 1973. Members are amateurs. Performs 70 concerts/year including 1-2 new works. Pay negotiable.
How to Contact: Query first. SASE. Reports in 1 month.
Music: "Style fitting for boys choir. Lengths depending on project. Orchestration preferable a cappella/ for piano/sometimes orchestra."
Performances: G. Wirth's *Sadhaka* and *Our Normoste*; and Shri Mataji Nirmala Devi's *Binati Suniye*.

‡**CANADIAN CHILDREN'S OPERA CHORUS**, 227 Front St. E. #215, Toronto, Ontario M5A 1E8 **Canada**. (416)366-0467. Manager: Ann Hartford Marshall. Children's vocal ensemble. Estab. 1968. Members are amateurs. Performs 40 operas and concerts/year. Commissions "usually 1 new composer every 2 years." Audience consists of schools, families and seniors. Performs choral winter concert, spring opera production often at Harbourfront, Toronto. Pays for outright purchase; "CCOC applies to Ontario Arts Council or the Canada Council for commission fees."
How to Contact: Query first. SAE and IRC. Reports in 2 months.
Music: "Operas of approximately 1 hour in length representing quality composers. In addition, the portability of a production is important; minimal sets and accompaniment. CCOC prefers to engage Canadian composers whose standards are known to be high. Being a nonprofit organization with funding difficulties, we prefer piano accompaniments or just a few instruments."
Performances: John Greer's *To Music, the Innocent Passion* (choral piece for children); Imant Raminsh's *Songs of the Lights* (choral piece for children); and Derek Holman's *Doctor Canon's Cure* (opera for children).

CANADIAN OPERA COMPANY, 227 Front St. E., Toronto, Ontario M5A 1E8 **Canada**. (416)363-6671. Associate Artistic Administrator: Sandra J. Gavinchuk. Opera company. Estab. 1950. Members are professionals. 50 performances, including a minimum of 1 new work/year. "New works are done in the DuMaurier Theatre, which seats approximately 250." Pays by contract.
How to Contact: Submit complete score and tapes of vocal and/or operatic works. "Vocal works please." SASE. Reports in 5 weeks.
Music: Vocal works, operatic in nature. 12 singers maximum, 1½ hour in duration and 18 orchestral

players. "Do not submit works which are not for voice. Ask for requirements for the Composers-In-Residence program."

Performances: Gary Kulesha's *Red Emma* (1995-96); Bartok's *Bluebeard's Castle* (1995); and Schöenberg's *Erwartung*.

Tips: "We have a Composers-In-Residence program which is open to Canadian composers or landed immigrants."

CARMEL SYMPHONY ORCHESTRA, P.O. Box 761, Carmel IN 46032. (317)844-9717. Website: http://www.mcp.com/people/erika/cso.html. Music Director/Conductor: David Pickett. Symphony orchestra. Estab. 1976. Members are professionals and amateurs. Performs 15 concerts/year, including 1-2 new works. Audience is "40% senior citizens, 85% white." Performs in a 1,500 seat high school performing arts center. Pay is negotiable.

How to Contact: Query first. SASE. Reports in 3 months.

Music: "Full orchestra works, 10-20 minutes in length. Can be geared toward 'children's' or 'Masterworks' programs. 65-70 piece orchestra, medium difficulty."

Performances: Malcolm Arnold's *Four Cornish Dances* (full orchestra); Percy Grainger's *Molly on the Shore* (full orchestra); and Frank Glover's *Impressions of New England* (full orchestra and jazz quartet).

CARSON CITY CHAMBER ORCHESTRA, P.O. Box 2001, Carson City NV 89702-2001 or 191 Heidi Circle, Carson City NV 89701-6532. (702)883-4154. Fax: (702)883-4371. E-mail: dcbugli@aol.com. Music Director/Conductor: David C. Bugli. Amateur community orchestra. Estab. 1984. Members are amateurs. Performs 5 concerts, including 1 new work/year. "Most concerts are performed in the Carson City Community Center Auditorium, which seats 840. We pay composers on rare occasions."

How to Contact: Query first. Does not return material. Reports in 2 months.

Music: "We want classical, pop orchestrations, orchestrations of early music for modern orchestras, concertos for violin or piano, holiday music for chorus and orchestra (children's choirs and handbell ensemble available), music by women, music for brass choir. Most performers are amateurs, but there are a few professionals who perform with us. Available winds and percussion: 2 flutes and flute/piccolo, 2 oboes (E.H. double), 2 clarinets, 1 bass clarinet, 2 bassoons, 3 or 4 horns, 3 trumpets, 3 trombones, 1 tuba, timpani, and some percussion. Harp and piano. Strings: 8-10-5-5-2. Avoid rhythmic complexity (except in pops) and music that lacks melodic appeal. Composers should contact us first. Each concert has a different emphasis. Note: Associated choral group, Carson Chamber Singers, performs several times a year with the orchestra and independently."

Performances: David Ott's *Festive Christmas Overture*; Gwyneth Walker's *A Concerto of Hymns and Spirituals for Trumpet and Orchestra*; and Ronald R. Williams' *Noah: Suite After Andre Obey*.

Tips: "It is better to write several short movements well than to write long, unimaginative pieces, especially when starting out. Be willing to revise after submitting the work, even if it was premiered elsewhere."

‡CASCADE SYMPHONY ORCHESTRA, P.O. Box 550, Edmonds WA 89020. (206)778-4688. Musical Director: Gregory Sullivan Isaacs. Symphony orchestra. Estab. 1960. Members are professionals and amateurs. Performs 12 concerts/year including many new works. Commissions 1 composer or new work/year. Performs in 900-seat theater. Pays rental and royalty.

How to Contact: Submit complete score and tape of piece(s). SASE. Reports in 3 months.

Music: Full orchestra. No choral works.

Performances: Samuel Jones's *Overture for a City; Gang Situ's Concerto for Ehru*; and Paul Cresion's *Dance Overture*.

Tips: "Don't send a large oversized score."

CHASPEN SYMPHONY ORCHESTRA, 27819 NE 49th St., Redmond WA 98053. Phone/fax: (206)880-6035. E-mail: chaspen@aol.com. Executive Director: Penny Orloff. Symphony orchestra, chamber music ensemble and opera/music theater ensemble. Estab. 1991. Members are professionals. Performs 6-10 concerts/year including 2 new works. Audience is generally upper-middle class families and seniors. Performs in space with 250-600 seats, depending upon space requirements. Pay negotiable.

How to Contact: Query first. SASE. Reports in 2 months.

Music: "Thematic revues for 6-8 singers, pianist, auxiliary keyboard; accessible symphonic pieces for voice and 40-50 piece symphony orchestra on contemporary themes; small chamber works for narrator/voice(s), and mixed chamber ensemble. 12-tone or serial pieces are NOT considered, nor are symphonic works using more players than a standard Mozart symphony orchestration. We do not wish to see any work which may not be performed for a family audience. Keep it clean!"

Performances: P. Orloff's *Lone Star Ladies* (revue); and C. Fraley's *Little Red Riding Hood* (opera for young audiences).

Tips: "Flexibility, imagination, economy: If you are difficult to work with, and your piece requires a lot of extras, we won't be producing it. Have a heart. Have a sense of humor."

CHEYENNE SYMPHONY ORCHESTRA, P.O. Box 851, Cheyenne WY 82003. (307)778-8561. CSO Music Director: Mark Russell Smith. Symphony orchestra. Estab. 1955. Members are professionals. Performs 6 concerts/year including 1-3 new works. "Orchestra performs for a conservative, mid-to-upper income audience of 1,200 season members." Pay varies.
How to Contact: Query first. Does not return material. Reports in 3-8 weeks.
Performances: Bill Hill's *Seven Abstract Miniatures* (orchestral).

CIMARRON CIRCUIT OPERA COMPANY, P.O. Box 1085, Norman OK 73070. (405)364-8962. E-mail: ccoc@aol.com. Music Director: Kevin Smith. Opera company. Estab. 1975. Members are semi-professional. Performs 75 concerts/year including 1-2 new works. Commissions 1 or less new works/year. "CCOC performs for children across the state of Oklahoma and for a dedicated audience in central Oklahoma. We do not have a permanent location. As a touring company, we adapt to the performance space provided, ranging from a classroom to a full raised stage." Pay is negotiable.
How to Contact: Query first. Does not return material. Reports in 6 months.
Music: "We are seeking operas or operettas in English only. We would like to begin including new, American works in our repertoire. Children's operas should be no longer than 45 minutes and require no more than a synthesizer for accompaniment. Adult operas should be appropriate for families, and may require either full orchestration or synthesizer. CCOC is a professional company whose members have varying degrees of experience, so any difficulty level is appropriate. There should be a small to moderate number of principals. Children's work should have no more than four principals. Our slogan is 'Opera is a family thing to do.' If we cannot market a work to families, we do not want to see it."
Performances: Mozart's *Cosi Fan Tutte*; Barab's *Little Red Riding Hood*; and Gilbert & Sullivan's *The Mikado*.
Tips: "45-minute fairy tale-type children's operas with possibly a 'moral' work well for our market. Looking for works appealing to K-8 grade students. No more than four principles."

COLORADO CHILDREN'S CHORALE, 910 15th St., Suite 1020, Denver CO 80202. (303)892-5600. Artistic Director: Duain Wolfe. Vocal ensemble and highly trained children's chorus. Estab. 1974. Members are professionals and amateurs. Performs 150 concerts/year including 3-5 new works. Commissions 2-5 composers or new works/year. "Our audiences' ages range from 5-80. We give school performances and tour (national, international). We give subscription concerts and sing with orchestras (symphonic and chamber). Halls: schools to symphony halls to arenas to outdoor theaters." Pays $100-500 outright purchase (more for extended works).
How to Contact: Submit complete score and tapes of piece(s). Does not return material. Reports in 1-3 months. "No guarantee of report on unsolicited material."
Music: "We want short pieces (3-5 minutes): novelty, folk arrangement, serious; longer works 5-20: serious; staged operas/musicals 30-45 minutes: piano accompaniment or small ensemble; or possible full orchestration if work is suitable for symphony concert. We are most interested in SA, SSA, SSAA. We look for a variety of difficulty ranges and encourage very challenging music for SSA-SSAA choruses (32 singers, unchanged voices). We don't want rock, charts without written accompaniments or texts that are inappropriate for children. We are accessible to all audiences. We like some of our repertoire to reflect a sense of humor, others to have a message. We're very interested in well crafted music that has a special mark of distinction."
Performances: John Kuzma's *O, Excellence* (virtuosit encore); Normand Lockwood's *Thought of Him I Love* (15-minute series with chamber orchestra); and Samuel Lancaster's *Stocking Stuffer 1994* (8-minute comic number with full symphony orchestra).
Tips: "Submit score and tape with good cover letter, résumé and record of performance. Wait at least three weeks before a follow-up call or letter. Materials should be in excellent condition. We review a great quantity of material that goes through several channels. Please be patient. Sometimes excellent material simply doesn't fit our current needs and is put in a 'future consideration file.' "

COMMONWEALTH OPERA INC., P.O. Box 391, Northampton MA 01061-0391. (413)586-5026. Artistic Director: Richard R. Rescia. Opera company. Estab. 1977. Members are professionals and amateurs. Performs 4 concerts/year. "We perform at the Academy of Music at Northampton in an 800-seat opera house. Depending on opera, audience could be family oriented or adult."
How to Contact: Query first. Does not return material.
Music: "We are open to all styles of opera. We have the limitations of a regional opera company with local chorus. Principals come from a wide area. We look only at opera scores."
Performances: Leoncavallo's *I Pagliacci* (opera); Mozart's *Don Giovanni* (opera); and Puccini's *La Boheme*, as well as short traveling operas.

Tips: "We're looking for opera that is accessible to the general public and performable by a standard opera orchestra."

DESERT CHORALE, P.O. Box 2813, Santa Fe NM 87504-2813. (505)988-2282. Fax: (505)988-7522. Music Director: Lawrence Bandfield. Vocal ensemble. Members are professionals. Performs 35 concerts/year including 2 new works. Commissions 1 new composer or new work/year. "Highly sophisticated audiences who are eager for interesting musical experiences. We pay $5,000 to $2,000 for premieres, often as part of consortium."
How to Contact: Query first. Submit complete score and tape *after* query. Does not return material. Reports in 1-2 years.
Music: "Challenging chamber choir works 6 to 20 minutes in length. Accompanied works are sometimes limited by space—normally no more than 5 or 6 players. "We sing both a cappella and with chamber orchestra; size of choir varies accordingly (20-32). No short church anthem-type pieces."
Performances: Edwin London's *Jove's Nectar* (choral with 5 instruments); Lanham Deal's *Minituras de Sor Juana* (unaccompanied); and Steven Sametz's *Desert Voices* (choral with 4 instruments).
Tips: "Call me or see me and I'll be happy to tell you what I need and I will also put you in touch with other conductors in the growing professional choir movement."

DÚO CLÁSICO, 31-R Fayette St., Cambridge MA 02139-1111. (617)864-8524. Fax: (617)491-4696. E-mail: dwitten@wellesley.edu. Contact: David Witten. Chamber music ensemble. Estab. 1986. Members are professionals. Performs 15 concerts/year including 5 new works. Commissions 1 composer or new work/year. Performs in small recital halls. Pays 15% royalty.
How to Contact: Query first. SASE. Reports in 2 months.
Music: "We welcome scores for flute solo, piano solo or duo. Particular interest in Latin American composers."
Performances: Diego Luzuriaga's *La Múchica* (modern, with extended techniques); Robert Starer's *Yizkor & Anima Aeterna* (rhythmic); and Piazzolla's *Etudes Tanguistiques* (solo flute).
Tips: "Extended techniques, or with tape, are fine!"

EASTERN NEW MEXICO UNIVERSITY, Station 16, Portales NM 88130. (505)562-2374. E-mail: radmerr@enmu.edu. Director of Orchestral Activities: Robert Radmer. Symphony orchestra, small college-level orchestra with possible choral collaboration. Estab. 1934. Members are students (with some faculty). Performs 9-10 concerts/year including 1 new work. "Our audiences are members of a college community and small town. We perform in a beautiful, acoustically fine 240-seat hall with a pipe organ." Payment is negotiable.
How to Contact: Query first. SASE. Reports in 3 months.
Music: "Pieces should be 12-15 minutes; winds by 2, full brass. Work shouldn't be technically difficult. Organ, harpsicord, piano(s) are available. We are a small college orchestra; normal instrumentation is represented but technical level is uneven throughout orchestra. We have faculty available to do special solo work. We like to see choral-orchestral combinations and writing at different technical levels within each family, i.e., 1st clarinet might be significantly more difficult than 2nd clarinet."
Performances: Rhoade's *Three Mexican Dances* (popular dance); and Vaughn William's *Five Mystical Songs*.
Tips: "I'm looking for a 20-minute suite (four-five movements). Call us and discuss your work prior to submitting."

EUROPEAN UNION CHAMBER ORCHESTRA, Fermain House, Dolphin St., Colyton EX13 6LU **United Kingdom**. Phone: (44)1297 552272. Fax: (44)1297 553744. E-mail: 101461.330@compuserve.com. General Manager: Ambrose Miller. Chamber orchestra. Members are professionals. Performs 70 concerts/year, including 6 new works. Commissions 2 composers or new works/year. Performs regular tours of Europe, Americas and Asia, including major venues. Pays per performance or for outright purchase, depending on work.
How to Contact: Query first. Does not return material. Reports in 6 weeks.
Music: Seeking compositions for strings, 2 oboes and 2 horns with a duration of about 10 minutes.

REMEMBER: Don't "shotgun" your demo tapes. Submit only to companies interested in the type of music you write. For more submission hints, refer to Getting Started on page 6.

Performances: G. Sollima's *The Columbus Egg* (suite for strings); J. Woolrich's *Ulysses Awakes* (solo viola and solo strings); and M. Arnold's *Sinfonietta Op. 48* (oboes, horns and strings).
Tips: "Keep the work to less than 15 minutes in duration, it should be sufficiently 'modern' to be interesting but not too difficult as this could take up rehearsal time. It should be possible to perform without a conductor."

FLORIDA SPACE COAST PHILHARMONIC, INC., P.O. Box 3344, Cocoa FL 32924 or 2150 Lake Dr., Cocoa FL 32926. (407)632-7445. General Manager: Alyce Christ. Music Director and Conductor: Dr. Candler Schaffer. Philharmonic orchestra and chamber music ensemble. Estab. 1986. Members are professionals. Performs 6-10 concerts/year, including 2 or 3 new works. Concerts are performed for "average audience—they like familiar works and pops. Concert halls range from 600 to 2,000 seats." Pays $250/performance.
How to Contact: Query first. SASE. Reports "as soon as we can."
Music: Seeks "pops and serious music for full symphony orchestra, but not an overly large orchestra with unusual instrumentation. We use about 60 musicians because of hall limitations. Works should be medium difficulty—not too easy and not too difficult—and not more than 10 minutes long." Does not wish to see avant-garde music.
Performances: Dr. Elaine Stone's *Cello Concerto* (cello solo with orchestra).
Tips: "If we would commission a work it would be to feature the space theme in our area."

FONTANA CONCERT SOCIETY, 821 W. South St., Kalamazoo MI 49007. (616)382-0826. Artistic Director: Paul Nitsch. Chamber music ensemble presenter. Estab. 1980. Members are professionals. Performs 20 concerts/year including 1-3 new works. Commissions 1-2 composers or new works/year. Audience consists of "well-educated people who expect to be challenged but like the traditional as well." Summer—180 seat hall; Fall/winter—various venues, from churches to libraries to 500-seat theaters.
How to Contact: Submit complete score and tapes of piece(s). SASE. Reports in 1 month.
Music: "Good chamber music—any combination of strings, winds, piano." No "pop" music, new age type. "We like to see enough interest for the composer to come for a premiere and talk to the audience."
Performances: Ramon Zupko's *Folksody* (piano trio-premiere); Sebastian Currier's *Vocalissimus* (soprano, 4 percussion, strings, winds, piano); and Mark Schultz's *Work for Horn & Piano*.
Tips: "Provide a résumé and clearly marked tape of a piece played by live performers."

‡FORT WORTH CHILDREN'S OPERA, 3505 W. Lancaster, Fort Worth TX 76107. (817)731-0833. (817)731-0835. Director of Education: Rebecca Hildabrand. Opera company. Estab. 1946. Members are professionals and amateurs. Performs 2 concerts/year. Audience consists of elementary and middle school-age children; performs in school auditoriums, cafetoriums and gymnasiums. Pays $35/performance.
How to Contact: Submit complete score and tape of piece(s). SASE. Reports in 3 months.
Music: "Familiar fairy tales or stories adapted to music of opera composers. 35-45 minutes in length. Piano or keyboard accompaniment. Prefer operatic styles with some dialogue. Must include moral, safety or school issues. Can be multi-racial and speak to all ages from pre-K through middle school-age children. Prefer pieces with easy to learn, memorable melodies. Performed by young, trained professionals for children. No greater than five performers plus accompanist/narrator."
Performances: *Little Red's Most Unusual Day* (adapted story by John Davies, music of Rossini/Offenbach, children's opera); *Wolfgang and the Three Little Pigs* (adapted story by John Davies, music of Mozart, children's opera); and *Jack and the Beanstalk* (adapted story by John Davies, music of Gilbert and Sullivan, children's opera).
Tips: "Use characters easily identifiable to children in situations which relate to their world, school and society. Adapted stories to opera music by great composers is preferred."

GREAT FALLS SYMPHONY ASSOCIATION, P.O. Box 1078, Great Falls MT 59403. (406)453-4102. Music Director and Conductor: Gordon J. Johnson. Symphony orchestra. Estab. 1959. Members are professionals and amateurs. Performs 6 concerts (2 youth concerts)/year including 1-2 new works. Commissions 1-2 new works/year. "Our audience is conservative. Newer music is welcome; however, it might be more successful if it were programatic." Plays in Civic Center Auditorium seating 1,850. Pays per performance.
How to Contact: Query first. SASE. Reports in 2 months.
Music: "Compositions should be for full orchestra. Should be composed idiomatically for instruments avoiding extended techniques. Duration 10-20 minutes. Avoid diverse instruments such as alto flute, saxophones, etc. Our orchestra carries 65 members, most of whom are talented amateurs. We have a resident string quartet and woodwind quintet that serve as principals. Would enjoy seeing a piece for quartet or quintet solo and orchestra. Send letter with clean score and tape (optional). We will reply within a few weeks."

Peformances: Bernstein's *Chichester Psalms* (choral and orchestra); Hodkinson's *Boogie, Tango and Grand Tarantella* (bass solo); and Stokes' *Native Dancer.*
Tips: "Music for orchestra and chorus is welcome. Cross cues will be helpful in places. Work should not require an undue amount of rehearsal time (remember that a concerto and symphony are probably on the program as well)."

‡GREATER GRAND FORKS SYMPHONY ORCHESTRA, P.O. Box 7084, Grand Forks ND 58202-7084. (701)777-3359. Fax: (701)777-3395. Music Director: Timm Rolek. Symphony orchestra. Estab. 1908. Members are professionals and/or amateurs. Performs 6 concerts/year. "New works are presented in 5 of 6 of our programs." Audience is "a mix of ages and musical experience. In 1997-98 we move into a renovated, 450-seat theater. Various local venues until then." Pay negotiable, depending on licensing agreements.
How to Contact: Submit complete score. SASE. Reports in 6-12 months.
Music: "Style is open, instrumentation the limiting factor. Music can be scored for an ensemble up to but not exceeding: 3,3,3,2/4,3,3,1/3 perc./strings. Rehearsal time limited to 3 hours for new works."
Performances: Richard Corbett's *Reminiscences* (tone poem); Jerré Tanner's *Aukele* (tone poem); and J.J. Swift's *Festival of Carols* (chorus/orchestral/Christmas).

‡GREATER TWIN CITIES YOUTH SYMPHONIES, 430 Oak Grove #205, Minneapolis MN 55403. (612)870-7611. Fax: (612)870-7613. Music Director: William LaRue Jones. Youth orchestra. Estab. 1972. Members are amateurs. Performs 16 concerts/year including 4-5 new works. Commissions 10 composers or new works/year. Performs in Orchestra Hall, Ordway and O'Shaughnesy Auditorium (Minneapolis/St. Paul). Pays per performance.
How to Contact: Query first. SASE. Reports in 2-3 weeks.
Music: Full orchestra—5-17″ length; string orchestra—5-17″ length; programmatic works—stories or thematic (can use narrator, ballet, etc.) Traditional orchestrations (no "hand bell choirs", etc.)
Performances: Augusta Read Thomas's *Waltz in the Cave of Eros* (full orchestra); Carol Barnett's *We The Peoples* (full orchestra with chorus); and Jonathan Holland's *Festival Music* (string orchestra).

HASTINGS SYMPHONY ORCHESTRA, Fuhr Hall, Ninth & Ash, Hastings NE 68901. (402)463-2402. E-mail: jjohnson@hastings.edu. Conductor/Music Director: Dr. James Johnson. Symphony orchestra. Estab. 1926. Members are professionals and amateurs. Performs 6-7 concerts/year including 1 new work. "Audience consists of conservative residents of mid-Nebraska who haven't heard most of the classics." Concert Hall: Masonic Temple Auditorium (950). Pays percentage royalty or per performance.
How to Contact: Submit complete score and tapes of piece(s). SASE. Reports in 1-2 months.
Music: "We are looking for all types of music within the range of an accomplished community orchestra. Write first and follow with a phone call."
Performances: Richard Wilson's *Silhouette*; and James Oliverio's *Pilgrimage* (symphonic).
Tips: "Think about the size, ability and budgetary limits. Confer with our music director about audience taste. Think of music with special ties to locality."

‡HEARTLAND MEN'S CHORUS, P.O. Box 32374, Kansas City MO 64171-5374. (816)931-3338. Music Director: Reuben Reynolds III. Men's chorus. Estab. 1985. Members are professionals and amateurs. Performs 3 concerts/year; 75% are new works. Commissions 2 composers or new works/year. Performs for a gay male audience at the Folley Theater (1,200 seats). Pays per performance.
How to Contact: Query first. SASE. Reports in 2 months.
Music: "Interested in works for male chorus (ttbb). Must be suitable for performance by a gay male chorus. We will consider any orchestration, or a cappella."
Performances: Roger Bourland's *Hidden Leagues* (song cycle for chorus); Chris Anthony's *When We No Longer Touch* (requiem for chorus and orchestra); and Robert Seeley's *Naked Man* (cycle for chorus and orchestra).
Tips: "Find a text that relates to the contemporary gay experience, something that will touch peoples' lives."

‡HEARTLAND SYMPHONY ORCHESTRA, P.O. Box 241, Little Falls MN 56345. (800)826-1997. Music Director: Timm Rolek. Symphony orchestra. Estab. 1977. Members are amateurs. Performs 8 concerts/year; "new works presented in every program. The majority of our audience is families. Two primary venues: one holds 700, the other 900. Two of our concerts are run-outs." Pay negotiable, depending on licensing agreements.
How to Contact: Submit complete score, or score with tape of piece(s). SASE. Reports in 6 months.
Music: "Style is open, instrumentation the limiting factor. Music can be scored for an ensemble up to, but

not exceeding: 2,2,2,2/4,2,3,1/2 perc./strings. Rehearsal time limited to 3 hours for new works. Majority of players are amateurs."
Performances: Paul Karvonen's *Prelude to "Farewell"*; Ted Donohoo's *On Picnic*; and Timm Rolek's *Birthday Variations*.

HELENA SYMPHONY, P.O. Box 1073, Helena MT 59624. (406)442-1860. Symphony orchestra. Estab. 1955. Members are professionals and amateurs. Performs 10-12 concerts/year including 2 new works. Performance space is an 1,800 seat concert hall. Payment varies.
How to Contact: Query first. SASE. Reports in 3 months.
Music: "Imaginative, collaborative, not too atonal. We want to appeal to an audience of all ages. We don't have a huge string complement. Medium to difficult okay—at frontiers of professional ability we cannot do."
Performances: Eric Funk's *A Christmas Overture* (orchestra); Donald O. Johnston's *A Christmas Processional* (orchestra/chorale); and Elizabeth Sellers' *Prairie* (orchestra/short ballet piece).
Tips: "Try to balance tension and repose in your works. New instrument combinations are appealing."

HERMAN SONS GERMAN BAND, P.O. Box 162, Medina TX 78055. (210)589-2268. Music Director: Herbert Bilhartz. Community band with German instrumentation. Estab. 1990. Members are both professionals and amateurs. Performs 12 concerts/year including 6 new works. Commissions no new composers or new works/year. Performs for "mostly older people who like German polkas, waltzes, and marches. We normally play only published arrangements from Germany."
How to Contact: Query first; then submit full set of parts & score, condensed or full. SASE. Reports in 6 weeks.
Music: "We like European-style polkas or waltzes (Viennese or Missouri tempo), either original or arrangements of public domain tunes. Arrangements of traditional American folk tunes in this genre would be especially welcome. Also, polkas or waltzes featuring one or two solo instruments (from instrumentation below) would be great. OK for solo parts to be technically demanding. Although we have no funds to commission works, we will provide you with a cassette recording of our performance. Also, we would assist composers in submitting works to band music publishers in Germany for possible publication. Polkas and waltzes generally follow this format: Intro; 1st strain repeated; 2nd strain repeated; DS to 1 strain; Trio: Intro; 32 bar strain; 'break-up' strain; Trio DS. Much like military march form. Instrumentation: fl/picc, 3 clars in Bb, 2 fluegelhorns in Bb; 3 tpts in Bb, 2 or 4 hns in F or Eb, 2 baritones (melody/countermelody parts; 1 in Bb TC, 1 in BC), 2 baritones in Bb TC (rhythm parts), 3 trombones, 2 tubas (in octaves, mostly), drum set, timpani optional. No saxes. Parts should be medium to medium difficult. All parts should be considered one player to the part. No concert type pieces; no modern popular or rock styles. However, a 'theme and variations' form with contrasting jazz, rock, country, modern variations would be clever, and our fans might go for such a piece (as might a German publisher)."
Performances: Siegfried Rundel's *Sounds of Friendship* (march); Pavel Stanek's *Folk Music Polonaise* (Polonaise); and Freek Mestrini's *Bohemian Serenade* (polka).
Tips: "German town bands love to play American tunes. There are many thousands of these bands over there and competition among band music publishers in Germany is keen. Few Americans are aware of this potential market, so few American arrangers get published over there. Simple harmony is best for this style, but good counterpoint helps a lot. Make use of the dark quality of the fluegelhorns and the bright, fanfare quality of the trumpets. Give the two baritones (one in TC and one in BC) plenty of exposed melodic material. Keep them in harmony with each other (3rds and 6ths), unlike American band arrangements, which have only one baritone line. If you want to write a piece in this style, give me a call, and I will send you some sample scores to give you a better idea."

HERSHEY SYMPHONY ORCHESTRA, P.O. Box 93, Hershey PA 17033. (800)533-3088. Music Director. Dr. Sandra Dackow. Symphony orchestra. Estab. 1969. Members are professionals and amateurs. Performs 4-5 concerts/year, including 1-3 new works. Commissions "possibly 1-2" composers or new works/year. Performance space is a 1,900 seat grand old movie theater. Payment varies.
How to Contact: Submit complete score and tape of piece(s). SASE. Reports in 3 months.
Music: "Symphonic works of various lengths and types which can be performed by a non-professional orchestra. We are flexible but like to involve all our players."
Performances: Paul W. Whear's *Lyrical Dances* (suite) and *The Nativity* (Christmas, with narrator).
Tips: "Please lay out rehearsal numbers/letter and rests according to phrases and other logical musical divisions rather than in groups of ten measures, etc., which is very unmusical and wastes time and causes a surprising number of problems. Also, please do not send a score written in concert pitch; use the usual transpositions so that the conductor sees what the players see; rehearsal is much more effective this way. Cross cue all important solos; this helps in rehearsal where instruments may be missing."

‡HUDSON VALLEY PHILHARMONIC, P.O. Box 191, Poughkeepsie NY 12602. (914)454-1222. Fax: (914)454-1267. Director of Operations: Gail Schumacher. Symphony orchestra. Estab. 1969. Members are professionals. Performs 20 concerts/year including 1-5 new works. Commissions 1 composer or new work every other year. "Classical subscription concerts: older patrons primarily; Pops concerts: all ages; New Wave concerts: baby boomers. New Wave concerts are crossover projects with a rock 'n' roll artist performing with an orchestra. HVP performs in three main theatres which are concert auditoriums with stages and professional lighting and sound." Pay is negotiable.
How to Contact: Query first. SASE. Reports in 6-8 months.
Music: "HVP is open to serious classical music, pop music and rock 'n' roll crossover projects. Desired length of work between 10-20 minutes. Orchestrations can be varied but should always include strings. There is no limit to difficulty since our musicians are professional. The ideal number of musicians to write for would include up to a Brahms-size orchestra 2222, 4231, T, 2P, piano, harp, strings."
Performances: Joan Tower's *Island Rhythms* (serious classical work); Bill Vanaver's *P'nai El* (symphony work with dance); and Joseph Bertolozzi's *Serenade* (light classical, pop work).
Tips: "Don't get locked into doing very traditional orchestrations or styles. Our music director is interested in fresh, creative formats. He is an orchestrator as well and can offer good advice on what works well. Songwriters who are into crossover projects should definitely submit works. Over the past four years, HVP has done concerts featuring the works of Natalie Merchant, John Cale, Sterling Morrison and Richie Havens, all reorchestrated by our music director for small orchestra with the artist."

KENTUCKY OPERA, 101 S. Eighth St. at Main, Louisville KY 40202. (502)584-4500. Director of Music: Mr. Robin Stamper. Opera company. Estab. 1952. Members are professionals. Performs 16 times/year. Performs at Whitney Hall, The Kentucky Center for the Arts, seating is 2,400; Bomhard Theatre, The Kentucky Center for the Arts, 620; Macauley Theatre, 1,400. Pays by royalty, outright purchase or per performance.
How to Contact: Submit complete score. SASE. Reports in 6 months.
Music: Seeks opera—1 to 3 acts with orchestrations. No limitations.
Performances: *Cinderella*; *Side by Side by Sondheim*; and *Cavalleria Rusticana/I Pagliacci*.

KITCHENER-WATERLOO CHAMBER ORCHESTRA, Box 34015, Highland Hills P.O., Kitchener, Ontario N2N 3G2 **Canada**. (519)744-3828. Music Director: Graham Coles. Chamber Orchestra. Estab. 1985. Members are professionals and amateurs. Performs 5 concerts/year. "We perform mainly baroque and classical repertoire, so any contemporary works must not be too dissonant, long or far fetched." Pays per performance.
How to Contact: "It's best to query first so we can outline what not to send. Include: complete CV—list of works, performances, sample reviews." Does not return material. Reports in 2 months.
Music: "Musical style must be accessible to our audience and players (3 rehearsals). Length should be under 20 minutes. Maximum orchestration 2/2/2/2 2/2/0/0 Timp/or 1 Percussion String 5/5/3/4/2. We have limited rehearsal time, so keep technique close to that of Bach-Beethoven. We also play chamber ensemble works—octets, etc. We do not want choral or solo works."
Performances: Peter Jona Korn's *4 Pieces for Strings* (string orchestra); Graham Coles' *Variations on a Mozart Rondo* (string orchestra); and Alan Heard's *Sinfonietta* (orchestra).
Tips: "If you want a first-rate performance, keep the technical difficulties minimal."

KNOX-GALESBURG SYMPHONY, Box 31, Knox College, Galesburg IL 61401. (309)343-0112, ext. 208. Music Director: Bruce Polay. Symphony orchestra. Estab. 1951. Members are professionals and amateurs. Performs 7 concerts/year including 1-3 new works. High diverse audience; excellent, recently renovated historical theater. Pays is negotiable.
How to Contact: Submit complete score and tapes of piece(s). "Pops material also welcome." SASE. Reporting time varies.
Music: Moderate difficulty 3222/4331/T piano, harpsichord, celesta and full strings. No country.
Performances: Polay's *Bondi's Journey: An Orchestra Rhapsody on Jewish Themes* (orchestra); Finko's *Russia: A Symphony Poem*; and Wallace's *Introduction and Passacaglia*.
Tips: "Looking for moderately difficult, 8-10 minute pieces for standard orchestra."

LA STELLA FOUNDATION, 14323 64th Ave. W., Edmonds WA 98026. (206)743-5010. Managing Director: Thomas F. Chambers. Artistic Director: Sheila Wormer. Opera company. Estab. 1990. Members are professionals. Performs 10 concerts/year, including 2 new works. Produces operatic performances exclusively for recordings, video and television markets. Payment individually negotiated.
How to Contact: Submit complete score and tape of piece(s). SASE. Reports in 6 months.
Music: "Music must have strong melodic value (Puccini-ish) with good harmonic chord structures and regular solid rhythms. Smaller casts with no chorus parts and smaller orchestras will get first consideration.

Do not submit contemporary 'a-tonal,' non-harmonic, non-melodic, rhythmically weird garbage! Looking for pieces with romantic flavor like Puccini and dramatic movement like Verdi, written to showcase heavy lyric voices (i.e. soprano, tenor, baritone)."
Performances: Frank DeMiero's *Now You're Gone* and *I Want to Hold You In My Arms* (pop); and Hayden Wayne's *Dracula* (opera).
Tips: "Looking for hit tunes/melodies with good chord structures and strong rhythmic values."

LAKESIDE SUMMER SYMPHONY, 236 Walnut Ave., Lakeside OH 43440. (419)798-4461. Contact: G. Keith Addy. Conductor: Robert L. Cronquist. Symphony orchestra. Members are professionals. Performs 8 concerts/year. Performs "Chautauqua-type programs with an audience of all ages (2-102). Hoover Auditorium is a 3,000-seat auditorium."
How to Contact: Query first. SASE.
Music: Seeking "classical compositions for symphony composed of 50-55 musicians. The work needs to have substance and be a challenge to our symphony members. No modern jazz, popular music or hard rock."

LAMARCA SINGERS, 2655 W. 230th Place, Torrance CA 90505. (310)325-8708. Director: Priscilla LaMarca Kandel. Vocal ensemble. Estab. 1979. Members are professionals and amateurs. Performs 20 concerts/year including 5 new works. Performs at major hotels, conventions, community theaters, fund raising events, cable TV, community fairs and Disneyland.
How to Contact: Query first or submit score and tape. SASE. Reports in 2 weeks.
Music: "Seeks 3-10 or 15 minute medleys; a variety of musical styles from Broadway—pop styles to humorous specialty songs. Top 40 dance music, Linda Ronstadt-style to Whitney Houston. Light rock and patriotic themes. Also interested in music for children. No heavy metal or anything not suitable for family audiences."
Performances: Priscilla LaMarca's *Hip Hop Alphabet* (upbeat educational); Mariah Carey's *Hero* (inspirational); and *Colors of the Wind* (ballad).

LEHIGH VALLEY CHAMBER ORCHESTRA, Box 20641, Lehigh Valley PA 18002-0641. (610)266-8555. Music Director: Donald Spieth. Symphony orchestra. Estab. 1979. Performs 25 concerts/year including 2-3 new works. Members are professionals. Commissions 1-2 composers or new works/year. Typical orchestral audience, also youth concerts. Pays commission for first 2 performances, first right for recording.
How to Contact: Submit complete score and tape of piece(s). SASE. Reports in 4 months.
Music: "Classical orchestral; works for youth and pops concerts. Duration 10-15 minutes. Chamber orchestra 2222-2210 percussion, strings (76442). No limit on difficulty."
Performances: David Stock's *String Set* (4 dances for strings); and John Scully's *Letters from Birmingham Jail* (soprano and orchestra).
Tips: "Send a sample tape and score of a work(s) written for the requested medium."

LEXINGTON PHILHARMONIC SOCIETY, 161 N. Mill St., Arts Place, Lexington KY 40507. (606) 233-4226. Music Director: George Zack. Symphony orchestra. Estab. 1961. Performs 50-60 concerts/year including 12-15 new works. Members are professionals. Commissions 1-2 composers or new works/year. Series includes "8 serious, classical subscription concerts (hall seats 1,500); 3 concerts called Unplugged and Untied; 30 outdoor pops concerts (from 1,500 to 5,000 tickets sold); 3-5 run-out concerts (½ serious/½ pops); and 10 children's concerts, 2 family concerts, 2 rock/pops concerts (hall seats 1,500)." Pays via ASCAP and BMI, rental purchase and private arrangements.
How to Contact: Submit complete score and tape of piece(s). SASE.
Music: Seeking "good current pops material and good serious classical works. No specific restrictions, but overly large orchestra requirements, unusual instruments and extra rentals help limit our interest."
Performances: Zwillich's *Celebration* (overture); Crumb's *A Haunted Landscape* (tone poem); and Corigliano's *Promenade* (overture).
Tips: "When working on large-format arrangement, use cross-cues so orchestra can be cut back if required. Submit good quality copy, scores and parts. Tape is helpful."

LIMA SYMPHONY ORCHESTRA, 67 Town Square, P.O. Box 1651, Lima OH 45802. (419)222-5701. Fax: (419)222-6587. Director: Allen E. Beck, interim. Symphony orchestra. Estab. 1952. Members are professionals. Performs 17-18 concerts including at least 1 new work/year. Commissions at least 1 composer or new work/year. Middle to older audience; also Young People's Series. Mixture for stage and summer productions. Performs in Veterans' Memorial Civic & Convention Center, a beautiful hall seating 1,670; Locomotive Erecting Shop (Pops At The Loco); various temporary shells for summer outdoors events; churches; museums and libraries. Pays $2,500 for outright purchase (Anniversary commission) or grants $1,500-5,000.

How to Contact: Submit complete score if not performed; otherwise submit complete score and tape of piece(s). SASE. Reports in 3 months.
Music: "Good balance of incisive rhythm, lyricism, dynamic contrast and pacing. Chamber orchestra to full (85-member) symphony orchestra." Does not wish to see "excessive odd meter changes."
Performances: Frank Proto's *American Overture* (some original music and fantasy); Werner Tharichen's *Concerto for Timpani and Orchestra*; and James Oliverio's *Pilgrimage—Concerto for Brass* (interesting, dynamic writing for brass and the orchestra).
Tips: "Know your instruments, be willing to experiment with unconventional textures, be available for in depth analysis with conductor, be at more than one rehearsal. Be sure that individual parts are correctly matching the score and done in good, neat calligraphy."

LITHOPOLIS AREA FINE ARTS ASSOCIATION, 3825 Cedar Hill Rd., Canal Winchester OH 43110-9507. (614)837-8925. Series Director: Virginia E. Heffner. Performing Arts Series. Estab. 1973. Members are professionals and amateurs. Performs 6 concerts/year including 1 new work. "Our audience consists of couples and families 30-80 in age. Our hall is acoustically excellent and seats 400. It was designed as a lecture-recital hall in 1925." Composers "may apply for Ohio Arts Council Grant under the New Works category."
How to Contact: Query first. SASE. Reports in 1 month.
Music: "We prefer that a composer is also the performer and works in conjunction with another artist, so they could be one of the performers on our series. Piece should be musically pleasant and not too dissonant. It should be scored for small vocal or instrumental ensemble. Dance ensembles have difficulty with 15′ high 15′ deep and 27′ wide stage. We do not want avant-garde or obscene dance routines. No ballet (space problem). We're interested in something historical—national or Ohio emphasis would be nice. Small ensembles or solo format is fine."
Performances: John McCutcheon's *Stone by Stone*, *Happy Adoption Day* and *Cut the Cake* (folk-family).
Tips: "Call after September '97 for queries about our '97-'98 season. We do a varied program. We don't commission artists. Contemporary music is used by some of our artists or groups. By contacting these artists, you could offer your work for inclusion in their program."

MELROSE SYMPHONY ORCHESTRA, P.O. Box 175, Melrose MA 02176. (617)662-0641. President and CEO: Millie Rich. Symphony orchestra. Estab. 1918. Members are both professionals and amateurs. Performs 4 concerts/year. Audience covers all ages from children to senior citizens; performances take place in a 1,000 seat capacity auditorium. Pays through ASCAP.
How to Contact: Query first. SASE. "Reporting time varies depending on time of submission. We are all volunteers."
Music: Full orchestral pieces. 60 performers, all community level performers.

MILWAUKEE YOUTH SYMPHONY ORCHESTRA, 929 N. Water St., Milwaukee WI 53202. (414)272-8540. E-mail: frichman@aol.com. Executive Director: Frances Richman. Youth orchestra. "We also have a Junior Wind Ensemble." Estab. 1956. Members are students. Performs 12-15 concerts/year including 1-2 new works. "Our groups perform in Uihlein Hall at the Marcus Center for the Performing Arts in Milwaukee plus area sites. The audiences usually consist of parents, music teachers and other interested community members. We sometimes are reviewed in the *Milwaukee Journal Sentinel*. Payment varies."
How to Contact: Query first. SASE. Reports in 1 month.
Performances: John Downey's *Ode to Freedom* (wind/brass).
Tips: "Be sure you realize you are working with students (albeit many of the best in southeastern Wisconsin) and not professional musicians. The music needs to be on a technical level students can handle. Our students are 8-18 years of age, in five different large ensembles, plus two flute choirs, advanced chamber orchestra and 15-20 small chamber ensembles."

THE MIRECOURT TRIO, 3308 94th St., Lubbock TX 79423. (806)795-8201. Fax: (806)795-8402. Contact: Terry King. Chamber music ensemble; violin, cello, piano. Estab. 1973. Members are professionals. Performs 20 concerts/year including 4 new works. Commissions 1-2 composers or new works/year. Concerts are performed for university, concert series, schools, societies and "general chamber music audiences of 100-1,500." Pays for outright purchase, percentage royalty or per performance.
How to Contact: Query first. SASE. Reports in 6 months.
Music: Seeks "music of short to moderate duration (5-20 minutes) that entertains, yet is not derivative or clichéd. Orchestration should be basically piano, violin, cello, occasionally adding voice or instrument. We do not wish to see academic or experimental works."
Performances: Jeffrey Price's *Quartet No. 2* (string quartet); Otto Leuning's *Solo Sonata* (solo cello); and Lukas Foss's *Three American Pieces* (cello, piano premiere).

Tips: "Submit works that engage the audience or relate to them, that reward the players as well."

MOHAWK TRAIL CONCERTS, P.O. Box 75, Shelburne Falls MA 01370. (413)625-9511 or (888)MTC-MUSE. Program Consultant: Ruth Black. Artistic Director: Arnold Black. Chamber music presenter. Estab. 1970. Members are professionals. Performs 15 concerts/year including 3-5 new works. Conducts school performances. "Audience ranges from farmers to professors, children to elders. Concerts are performed in churches widely in western MA." Pays by variable rate.
How to Contact: Query first. (Attention: Arnold Black, Artistic Director). SASE. Reports in months.
Music: "We want chamber music, generally not longer than 30 minutes. We are open to a variety of styles and orchestrations for a maximum of 8 performers. We don't want pop, rock or theater music."
Performances: Michael Cohen's *Fantasia for Flute, Piano and Strings* (chamber); William Bolcom's *Nes Songs* (piano/voice duo); and Arnold Black's *Laments & Dances* (string quartet and guitar duo).
Tips: "We are looking for artistic excellence, a committment to quality performances of new music, and music that is accessible to a fairly conservative (musically) audience."

MONTREAL CHAMBER ORCHESTRA, 1200 McGill College Ave., Suite 1100, Montreal Quebec H3B 4G7 **Canada**. (514)871-1224. Fax: (514)393-9069. Conductor and Music Director: Wanda Kaluzny. Chamber orchestra. Estab. 1974. Members are professionals. Performs 6 concerts including 1-3 new works/year. Commissions various new works/year (Canadian composers only). Audience is mixed ages, mixed income levels. Orchestra performs in a church, seating 800. Pays "through the composer's performing arts organization."
How to Contact: Submit complete score. Does not return material. Reports "only if performing the work."
Music: Works with string orchestra (6 / 4 / 2 / 2 / 1), 8-12 min. duration. Strings (6 / 4 / 2 / 2 / 1).
Performances: Hope Lee's *Chan Chan* (string orchestra); David Eagle's *Waves Echo Upon Stone* (chamber orchestra); and John Plant's *Dreams in the Mirror* (chamber orchestra, world premiere).

MOZART FESTIVAL ORCHESTRA, INC., 33 Greenwich Ave., New York NY 10014. (212)675-9127. Conductor: Baird Hastings. Symphony orchestra. Estab. 1960. Members are professionals. Performs 1-4 concerts/year including 2 new works. Audience members are Greenwich Village professionals of all ages. Performances are held at the First Presbyterian Church, Fifth Ave. and 12th St., ("wonderful acoustics"). Pay varies.
How to Contact: Query first. SASE. Reports in 2 weeks.
Music: "We are an established chamber orchestra interested in *unusual* music of all periods, but not experimental. Orchestra size usually under 20 performers."
Performances: Gary Sunden's *Sganarelle* (overture); and Virgil Thomson's *Portrait*.

NATIONAL ASSOCIATION OF COMPOSERS/USA, P.O. Box 49256, Los Angeles CA 90049. (310)541-8213. President: Marshall Bialosky. Chamber music ensemble and composers' service organization. Estab. 1932. Members are professionals. Performs 3-4 concerts/year—all new works. Usually performed at universities in Los Angeles and at a mid-town church in New York City. Paid by ASCAP or BMI (NACUSA does not pay composers).
How to Contact: Query first. SASE.
Music: Chamber music for five or fewer players; usually in the 5 to 20 minute range. "Level of difficulty is not a problem; number of performers is solely for financial reasons. We deal in serious, contemporary concert hall music. No 'popular' music."
Performances: Bruce Taub's *Sonata for Solo Viola*; Tom Flaherty's *Quartet for Viola, Cello, and Digital Synthesizer*; and Maria Newman's *Sonata for Bass Trombone and Piano*.
Tips: "Send in modest-sized pieces—not symphonies and concertos."

NEW JERSEY SYMPHONY ORCHESTRA/GREATER NEWARK YOUTH ORCHESTRA, 2 Central Ave., Newark NJ 07102. (201)624-3713. Fax: (201)624-2115. Assistant Conductor: David Commanday. Symphony orchestra and youth orchestra. Estab. 1922. Members are professionals and students

for youth orchestra. Performs 2-10 new works/year. Commissions 1-3 composers or new works/year.
How to Contact: Query first or submit complete score and tape of piece(s). SASE. Reports in 1-2 months.
Music: Classical with jazz, pop influence, or the fusion of the above. Compositions for young people's concerts.

NEW WORLD YOUTH SYMPHONY ORCHESTRA, 10815 Brenda Court, Fortville IN 46040. (317)485-6022. Fax: (317)485-5247. Music Director: Susan Kitterman. Youth orchestra. Estab. 1982. Members are amateurs. Performs 6 concerts/year including 1 or 2 new works. Commissions 1 composer or new work every other year. "Typically 500-1,500 in attendance, broad spectrum of arts patrons and educators." Performs at Circle Theatre, downtown Indianapolis, home of Indianapolis Symphony; also at the Warren Performing Arts Center. Pay variable for outright purchase.
How to Contact: Query first. SASE. Reports in 2 months.
Music: "Innovative, creative works for full or string orchestra, brass or woodwind or percussion ensemble—may be with vocal or instrumental soloist. Any length."
Performances: David Baker's *Alabama Landscape* (orchestral with narration); Robert Ward's *Jubilation* (orchestral overture); and Paul Hindemith's *Symphonic Metamorphases* (orchestral).
Tips "Come hear and meet our ensemble. Make the creative process highly individualized and one all can participate in."

THE NEW YORK CONCERT SINGERS, 75 East End Ave., Suite 9L, New York NY 10028. (212)879-4412. Music Director/Conductor: Judith Clurman. Chorus. Estab. 1988. Performs 3-4 concerts/year including new works. Frequently commissions new composers. "Audience is mixture of young and old classical music 'lovers.' Chorus performs primarily at Merkin Concert Hall, Carnegie Hall and Lincoln Center, NYC." ASCAP, BMI fees paid. Records for New World and Delos Records.
How to Contact: Submit complete score with tape of piece(s). SASE. Reports in 2 months.
Music: Seeks music "for professional ensemble, with or without solo parts, a cappella or small instrumental ensemble. Looking for pieces ranging from 7-20 minutes."
Performances: Ellen Taaffe Zurlich's *Magnificat*; Stephen Paulus' *Meditation of Li Po*; and William Bokom's *The Mask*.
Tips: "When choosing a piece for a program I study both the text and music. Both are equally important."

NORFOLK CHAMBER MUSIC FESTIVAL/YALE SUMMER SCHOOL OF MUSIC, 96 Wall St., New Haven CT 06520-8246. (203)432-1966. Summer music festival. Estab. 1941. Members are international faculty/artists plus young professionals. Performs 20 concerts, 15 recitals/year, including 3-6 new works. Commissions 1 composer or new work/year. Pays a commission fee. Also offers a Composition Search and Residency biennially. The Norfolk Chamber Music Festival-Yale Summer School of Music seeks new chamber music works from American composers under the age of 35. The goal of this search is to identify promising young composers and to provide a visible and high quality venue for the premiere of their work. A maximum of two winning compositions are selected. Winners are invited to the Norfolk Chamber Music Festival for a week-long residency.

- The Norfolk Chamber Music Festival/Yale Summer School of Music has won an ASCAP/Chamber Music America award for adventurous programming.

How to Contact: Submit complete score and tapes of piece(s), SASE and completed application form (available by calling (203)432-1966). Reports in 6 months.
Music: "Chamber music of combinations, particularly for strings, woodwinds, brass and piano. There are 1-2 chamber orchestra concerts per season which include the students and feature the festival artists. Other than this, orchestra is not a featured medium, rather, chamber ensembles are the focus."
Performances: Betsy Jolas's *Music For Here* (trio); Scott Robbins' *Samba & Epilogue* (chamber ensemble); and Peter Schickele's *Bestiary* (Renaissance ensemble).

THE NORFOLK SINGERS' CHORUS AND ORCHESTRA, P.O. Box 955, Simcoe, Ontario N0E 1Y0 **Canada**. (519)428-3185. Fax: (519)426-1573. Director: Ronald Beckett. Semi-professional chorus and orchestra. Estab. 1983. Members are both professionals and amateurs. Performs 3 concerts/year including 1 new work. Commissions 1 composer or new work/year. Pay negotiable.
How to Contact: Submit complete score and tape of piece(s). SASE.
Music: "Compositions appropriate for ensemble accustomed to performance of chamber works, accompanied or unaccompanied, with independence of parts. Specialize in repetoire of 17th, 18th and 20th centuries. Number of singers does not exceed 45. Orchestra is limited to strings, supported by a professional quartet. No popular, commercial, or show music."
Performances: Benjamin Britten's *St. Nicholas Cantata* (cantata) and *Hymn to St. Cecilia* (SSATB unaccompanied); and Ronald A. Beckett's *Ruth* (drama).

Tips: "Write for conservative resources (i.e., small ensembles). Performance level must take into account the limited amount of time available for rehearsal. Small-scale is generally more effective than large-scale. Ensemble is very interested in and capable of performance of new music, and is very experienced with stage performance. It is willing to perform such works as part of its touring schedule."

NORTH ARKANSAS SYMPHONY ORCHESTRA, P.O. Box 1243, Fayetteville AR 72702. (501)521-4166. General Manager: Conley Cook. Symphony orchestra, chamber music ensemble, youth orchestra and community chorus. Estab. 1950. Members are professionals and amateurs. Performs 20 concerts/year including 4-5 new works. "General audiences—performs in Walton Arts Center (capacity 1,200)." Pays $500 for outright purchase.
How to Contact: Query first. Does not return material.
Music: Seeks "audience pleasers—rather short (10-15 minutes); and full orchestra pieces for subscription (classical) concerts. Orchestra is 80 members."
Performances: Kimo Williams' *Symphony for Sons of 'Nam* (orchestral); Michael Woods' *Brother Man* (orchestral and choral); and Corigliano's *Symphony No. 1* (orchestral).

OPERA MEMPHIS, Campus Box 526331, Memphis TN 38152. (901)678-2706. Fax: (901)678-3506. E-mail: mrbillow@juno.com. Website: http://gray.music.rhodes.edu/operahtmls/opera.html. Artistic Director: Michael Ching. Opera company. Estab. 1955. Members are professionals. Performs 8-12 concerts/year including 1 new work. Commissions 1 composer or new work/year. Audience consists of older, wealthier patrons, along with many students and young professionals. Pay is negotiable.
How to Contact: Query first. SASE. Reports in 1 year.
Music: Accessible practical pieces for educational or main stage programs. Educational pieces should not exceed 90 minutes or 4-6 performers. "We encourage songwriters to contact us with proposals or work samples for theatrical works. We are very interested in crossover work."
Performances: Mike Reid's *Different Fields* (one act opera); David Olney's *Light in August* (folk opera); and Sid Selvidge's *Riversongs* (one act opera).
Tips: "Spend many hours thinking about the synopsis (plot outline)."

OPERA ON THE GO, 184-61 Radnor Rd., Jamaica Estates NY 11432. (718)380-0665. Artistic Director: Jodi Rose. American opera chamber ensemble. Estab. 1985. Members are professionals. Performs about 60-80 operas/year including 1-2 new works. "We perform primarily in schools and community theaters. We perform only American contemporary opera. It must be lyrical in sound and quality as we perform for children as well as adults. We prefer pieces written for children based on fairy tales needing 2-4 singers." Pays $20-30 per performance. "We also help composers acquire a 'Meet the Composer' grant."
How to Contact: Query first, then submit complete score and tapes of piece(s). SASE. Reports in 2 months.
Music: Need works in all age groups including adults. For older ages the pieces can be up to 60 minutes. Rarely use orchestra. "Keep the music as short as possible since we do a prelude (spoken) and postlude involving the children's active participation and performance. If it is totally atonal it will never work in the schools we perform in."
Performances: Arne Christiansen's *Tumbleweeds* (performed by children); Mark Bucci's *Sweet Betsy From Pike* (opera for 6 grade-adult); and Seymour Barab's *Little Red Riding Hood* (children's opera).
Tips: "Be flexible. Through working with children we know what works best with different ages. If this means editing music to guarantee its performance, don't get offended or stubborn. All operas must have audience participatory sections."

OREGON SYMPHONY, 711 SW Alder, Portland OR 97205. (503)228-4294. Website: http://www.orsymphony.org. General Manager: Tony Beadle. Symphony orchestra. Estab. 1896. Members are professionals. Performs 125 concerts/year including 3 new works. Commissions varying number of new works. "Classical concerts are attended predominantly by 35-60 year olds. Hall seats 2,776—renovated vaudeville house." Pay is negotiable.
How to Contact: Submit complete score and tapes of piece(s). Does not return material. Reports in 2 months.
Music: "Classical 10-20 min.: 3333-5331 3 perc, 1 tmp, 1 harp, 1 keyboard, strings: 16-14-12-10-8; pops, jazz: same, except strings 12-10-8-6-4. No country. Send a list of other orchestras with whom you have performed."
Performances: John Adams' *Slonimsky's Earbox*; David Dzubuy's *Symphony #1*; and R. Murray Schaefer's *Statement in Blue*.

PICCOLO OPERA COMPANY, 24 Del Rio Blvd., Boca Raton FL 33432-4737. (800)282-3161. Executive Director: Marjorie Gordon. Opera company. Estab. 1962. Members are professionals. Performs 1-50

concerts/year including 1-2 new works. Commissions 1 composer or new work/year. Operas are performed for a mixed audience of children and adults. Pays by performance or outright purchase.
How to Contact: Query first and submit complete score and tape of piece(s). SASE.
Music: "Musical theater pieces, lasting about one hour, for adults to perform for adults and/or youngsters. Performers are mature singers with experience. The cast should have few performers (up to 10), no chorus or ballet, accompanied by piano or orchestra. Skeletal scenery. All in English."
Performances: Menotti's *The Telephone* and *The Old Maid and the Thief*.

PRINCETON CHAMBER SYMPHONY, P.O. Box 250, Princeton NJ 08542. (609)497-0020. (609)924-3935. E-mail: pcs7@ix.netcom.com. Music Director: Mark Laycock. Symphony orchestra. Estab. 1980. Members are professionals. Performs 6-10 concerts/year including some new works. Commissions 1 composer or new work/year. Performs in a "beautiful, intimate 800-seat hall with amazing sound." Pays by arrangement.
How to Contact: Submit through agent only. SASE. Reports in 6 months.
Music: "Orchestra usually numbers 40-60 individuals."

PRISM SAXOPHONE QUARTET, 257 Harvey St., Philadelphia PA 19144. (215)438-5282. President, New Sounds Music Inc. Prism Quartet: Matthew Levy. Chamber music ensemble. Estab. 1984. Members are professionals. Performs 80 concerts/year including 10-15 new works. Commissions 5 composers or new works/year. "Ours are primarily traditional chamber music audiences." Pays royalty per performance from BMI or ASCAP or commission range from $100 to $15,000.
How to Contact: Submit complete score (with parts) and tape of piece(s). Does not return material. Reports in 3 months.
Music: "Orchestration—sax quartet, SATB. Lengths—5-60 minutes. Styles—contemporary, classical, jazz, crossover, ethnic, gospel, avant-garde. No limitations on level of difficulty. No more than 4 performers (SATB sax quartet). No transcriptions. The Prism Quartet places special emphasis on crossover works which integrate a variety of musical styles."
Performances: Franch Amsallem's *The Farewell* (jazz); Bradford Ellis's *Tooka-Ood Zasch* (ethnic-world music); and William Albright's *Fantasy Etudes* (contemporary classical).

QUEENS OPERA, P.O. Box 140066, Brooklyn NY 11214. (908)390-9472. General Director: Joe Messina. Opera company. Estab. 1961. Members are professionals. Performs 9 concerts/year including 1 new work.
How to Contact: SASE. Reports in 1 month.
Music: "Operatic scores and songs, small orchestra."
Performances: Rossini's *Il Barbiere di Siviglia*; Verdi's *Il Trovatore*; and Owen's *Tom Sawyer*.

RENO CHAMBER ORCHESTRA, P.O. Box 547, Reno NV 89504. (702)348-9413. Fax: (702)348-0643. Music Director: Vahe Khochayan. Chamber orchestra. Estab. 1974. Members are professionals. Performs 6-7 concerts/year including 1 new work every other year. Students and retirees are largest segment of audience. Nightingale concert hall, 615 seats with fine acoustics. Payment to be negotiated—depends if composer is also guest soloist.
How to Contact: Query first. Does not return material. Reports in 3 months.
Music: "Pieces of 10-15 minutes in length—can be longer if very accessible—for string orchestra or strings plus solo instrument, strings and winds. Preferably 35 players or less. Our professional orchestra can handle most anything." Not interested in stridently atonal compositions, pops, jazz.
Performances: Armin Schibler's *Concerto For Strings* (concerto); James Winn's *Concerto in E-flat Minor* (piano concerto); and Efrem Zimbalist Sr.'s *Suite in the Olden Style*.
Tips: "Take advantage of our strong viola and cello sections."

RIDGEWOOD SYMPHONY ORCHESTRA, P.O. Box 176, Ridgewood NJ 07451. (201)612-0118. Fax: (201)445-2762. Music Director: Dr. Sandra Dackow. Symphony orchestra. Estab. 1939. Members are professionals and amateurs. Performs 4 concerts/year including 0-2 new works. Audience is "sophisticated." Performance space is 800-seat school auditorium. Payment varies.
How to Contact: Submit complete score and tape of piece(s). SASE. Reports in 3 months ("it depends on how busy we are").
Music: "Symphonic works of various lengths and types which can be performed by a nonprofessional orchestra. We are flexible but would like to involve all of our players; very restrictive instrumentations do not suit our needs."
Performances: Paul W. Whear's *Fanfare for the Century*; Richard Lane's *Kaleidoscope Overture*; and Wayne Barlow's *Winter's Passed* (oboe-strings).

Tips: "Please lay out rehearsal numbers/letters and rests according to phrases and other logical musical divisions rather than in groups of ten measures, etc., which is very unmusical, wastes time and causes a surprising number of problems. Also, please *do not* send a score written in concert pitch; use the usual transpositions so that the conductor sees what the players see. Rehearsal is much more effective this way. Cross cue all important solos; this helps in rehearsal where instruments may be missing."

‡SACRAMENTO MASTER SINGERS, P.O. Box 215501, Sacramento CA 95821. (916)965-7464. Conductor/Artistic Director: Ralph Hughes. Vocal ensemble. Estab. 1984. Members are professionals and amateurs. Performs 7-8 concerts/year. Audience is made up of mainly high school age and older patrons. Performs mostly in churches with 500-900 seating capacity. Composers are "paid to perform premiere of piece and have piece dedicated to group prior to publication."

- The Sacramento Master Singers' CD, *How Still He Rests*, a collection of holiday music, was named one of the Top Ten Holiday CDs by KXPR, a Sacramento classical radio station.

How to Contact: Query first. SASE. Reports in 2 months.
Music: "A cappella works; works with small orchestras or few instruments; works based on classical styles with a 'modern' twist; multi-cultural music; shorter works probably preferable, but this is not a requirement. We usually have 34-38 singers capable of a high level of difficulty, but find that often simple works are very pleasing."
Performances: Ralph Prime's *A Spotless Rose* and *Peace This Christmas* (holiday); and Linda Dawson's *Deck the Hall* and *Away in a Manger* (holiday).
Tips: "Keep in mind we are a chamber ensemble, not a 100-voice choir. We usually have approximately 34-38 singers."

ST. LOUIS CHAMBER CHORUS, P.O. Box 11558, Clayton MO 63105. (314)458-4343. Music Director: Philip Barnes. Vocal ensemble, chamber music ensemble. Estab. 1956. Members are professionals and amateurs. Performs 5-6 concerts/year including 5 new works. Commissions 1-3 new works/year. Performances take place at various auditoria noted for their excellent acoustics—churches, synagogues, schools and university halls. Pays by arrangement.
How to Contact: Submit complete score. SASE. "Panel of 'readers' submit report to Artistic Director. Reports in 3 months. 'General Advice' leaflet available on request."
Music: "Only *a cappella* writing; no contemporary 'popular' works; historical editions welcomed. No improvisatory works. Our programs are tailored for specific acoustics—composers should indicate their preference."
Performances: Stuart McIntosh's *The Ruling Moon* (secular partsong); Charles Collins' *Joulupuu Rakenettu* (Christmas carol); and Richard Rodney Bennett's *Missa Brevis* (Mass).
Tips: "We only consider a cappella works which can be produced in five rehearsals. Therefore pieces of great complexity or duration are discouraged."

‡THE SAINT THOMAS CHOIR OF MEN AND BOYS, One W. 53rd St., New York NY 10019. (212)757-7013. Organist/Director of Music: Dr. Gerre Hancock. Church choir. Estab. 1919. Members are professionals. Performs 4 concerts/year including 1 new work. Commissions 1 composer or new work every other year. Performs for a cosmopolitan New York audience in a Gothic Church. Pays by outright purchase or per performance.
How to Contact: Query first. SASE. Reports in 2 weeks.
Music: "Music for chorus appropriate to religious observances and Anglican liturgies: unaccompanied, organ accompaniment with or without chamber orchestra. The choir consists of 16-20 boy choristers/sopranos (unchanged voices), 4 adult male altos, 4 tenors, 4 basses. All adults are professional singers."
Performances: Gunther Schuller's *Magnificat and Nonc Dimittis* (chorus and organ); Randall Thompson's *Place of the Blest* (chorus and orchestra); and William Walton's *The Twelve* (chorus and orchestra).

SALT LAKE SYMPHONIC CHOIR, P.O. Box 45, Salt Lake City UT 84110. (801)466-8701. Manager: Richard M. Taggart. Professional touring choir. Estab. 1949. Members are professionals and amateurs. Performs 5-15 concerts/year, including 2 new works. Commissions 1-2 new works or composers/year. "We tour throughout U.S. and Canada for community concert series, colleges and universities." Pay is negotiable.
How to Contact: Query first. Does not return material. Reports in 3-6 months.
Music: Seeking "4-8 part choral pieces for a 100-voice choir—from Bach to rock."
Performances: Howard Hanson's *Song of Democracy.*

SAN ANTONIO OPERA COMPANY, 10-100 Reunion Place, Suite 745, San Antonio TX 78216. (210)524-9665. Fax: (210)340-8019. President: Wilford Lee Stapp. Opera company. Estab. 1991. Members

are professionals. Performs 6 events including 1 new work/year. High school and college level audiences. Performs at high school auditoriums and college stages. Pay is negotiable.
How to Contact: Query first. SASE. Reports in 5 weeks.
Music: "Currently our voices are tenor and soprano and string quartet (2 violins, viola and cello). Subject material should be appropriate for conservative high school. Can use one or both voices. Soprano range, tenor range (bass baritone range is also possible. Please write to consult)."
Performances: Alice Gomez's *Somewhere In Time* (wedding reception).

SAN FRANCISCO GIRLS CHORUS, P.O. Box 15397, San Francisco CA 94115-0397. (415)673-1511. Fax: (415)673-0639. Artistic Director: Dr. Sharon J. Paul. Vocal ensemble. Estab. 1978. Volunteer chorus with a core of paid professionals. Performs 8-10 concerts/year including 3-4 new works. Commissions 2-3 composers or new works/year. Concerts are performed for "choral/classical music lovers of all ages, plus family audiences; audiences interested in international repertoire. Season concerts are performed in a 900-seat church with excellent acoustics; one concert is performed in San Francisco's Davies Symphony Hall, a 2,800-seat state-of-the-art auditorium." Pay negotiable for outright purchase.

- The San Francisco Girls Chorus was a featured guest performer on the San Francisco Symphony's recording of Carl Orff's *Carmina Burana*, which won a 1993 Grammy Award for best choral recording.

How to Contact: Submit complete score. SASE. Reports in 6 months.
Music: "Music for treble voices (SSAA); a cappella, piano accompaniment, or small orchestration; 3-10 minutes in length. Wide variety of styles; 45 singers; challenging music is encouraged."
Performances: Einojuhani Rautavaara's *Suite de Lorca*; David MacIntyre's *Ave Maria*; and József Karai's *Rhythmus e Mariali* (all a cappella).
Tips: "Choose excellent texts and write challenging and beautiful music! The San Francisco Girls Chorus has pioneered in establishing girls choral music as an art form in the United States. The Girls Chorus is praised for its 'stunning artistic standard' (*San Francisco Chronicle*) in performances in the San Francisco Bay Area on tour. SFGC's annual concert season showcases the organization's concert/touring ensembles, Chorissima and Virtuose, in performances of choral masterworks from around the world, commissioned works by contemporary composers, and 18th-century music from the Venetian Ospedali which SFGC has brought out of the archives and onto the concert stage. Chorissima and Virtuose tour through California with partial support provided by the California Arts Council Touring Program and have represented the U.S. and the City of San Francisco nationally and abroad. The choruses provide ensemble and solo singers for performances and recordings with the San Francisco Symphony and San Francisco Opera, Women's Philharmonic, and many other music ensembles. SFGC's discography includes two 1996 CD recordings, *I Never Saw Another Butterfly* (20th Century music); and *A San Francisco Christmas* (Benjamin Britten's *A Ceremony of Carols* and other holiday music)."

SASKATOON SYMPHONY ORCHESTRA, P.O. Box 1361, Saskatoon, Saskatchewan S7K 3N9 **Canada**. (306)665-6414. Fax: (306)652-3364. Artistic Director: Earl Stafford. General Manager: Sigrid-Ann Thors. Symphony orchestra. Performs 20 full orchestra concerts/year including 4-8 new works. Commissions 1-2 composers or new works/year.
How to Contact: Query first. Does not return material. Reporting time "depends upon conductor."
Music: "We are a semi-professional orchestra with a full time core of ten artists-in-residence. Our season runs from September to May with classical concerts, chamber series and children's series."
Performances: Murray Adaskin's *Suite for Orchestra* (symphonic); Benjamin Britten's *St. Nicholas Cantata* (choir and orchestra); and Michael Horwood's *Amusement Park Suite* (symphonic).

SAULT STE. MARIE SYMPHONY ORCHESTRA, 3128 Lakeshore Dr., Sault Ste. Marie MI 49783. (906)635-2265. Music Director: Dr. John Wilkinson. Symphony orchestra. Estab. 1972. Members are professionals and amateurs. Performs 8 full orchestra concerts/year including 1-2 new works. "Our audience is conservative. Our performance hall seats 964."
How to Contact: Query first. SASE.
Music: "We have traditional orchestra size 2222/4231/2, plus strings. String 88552. We want pieces of length (5-15 minutes) in approachable styles. We have 45-50 performers. Pieces should be of moderate difficulty (or less!). Engage the listener; make it playable."
Performances: Ridout-Quesnel's *Colas et Colinette* (light overture); S. Glick's *Elegy* (elegy); and J. Weinzweig's *The Red Ear of Corn* (ballet suite).

SINGERS FORUM, 39 W. 19th St., New York NY 10011. (212)366-0541. Fax: (212)366-0546. Administrator: Denise Galon. Vocal school and presenting organization. Estab. 1978. Members are professionals and amateurs. Performs more than 50 concerts/year including 4 new works. Commissions 2 composers or new works/year. 75-seat performance space with varied audience. Pays through donations from patrons.

How to Contact: Query first. SASE. Reports in 2 months.
Music: "All popular music, art songs, full musicals and small operas with minimal orchestration. No rock. I'm always looking for works to fit our current voices, mainly new operas and musicals."
Performances: Bill Daniels' *Take Me Down With You* (new music); *I'm Just Going to Sing Some Songs to Make You Feel Good* (contemporary mixed cabaret); and *Red, White & the Blues* (collection of music composed and performed by women).
Tips: "Think of the voice."

SINGING BOYS OF PENNSYLVANIA, P.O. Box 206, Wind Gap PA 18091. (610)759-6002. Director: K. Bernard Schade, Ed. D. Vocal ensemble. Estab. 1970. Members are professional children. Performs 100 concerts/year including 3-10 new works. "We attract general audiences: family, senior citizens, churches, concert associations, university concert series and schools." Pays $300-3,000 for outright purchase.
How to Contact: Query first. SASE. Reports in 3 months.
Music: "We want music for commercials, voices in the SSA or SSAA ranges, sacred works or arrangements of American folk music with accompaniment. Our range of voices are from G below middle C to A (13th above middle C). Reading ability of choir is good but works which require a lot of work with little possibility of more than one performance are of little value. We sing very few popular songs except for special events. We perform music by composers who are well-known and works by living composers who are writing in traditional choral forms. Works which have a full orchestral score are of interest. The orchestration should be fairly light, so as not to cover the voices. Works for Christmas have more value than some other, since we perform with orchestras on an annual basis."
Performances: Don Locklair's *The Columbus Madrigals* (opera).
Tips: "It must be appropriate music and words for children. We do not deal in pop music. Folk music, classics and sacred are acceptable."

SOLI DEO GLORIA CANTORUM, 3402 Woolworth Ave., Omaha NE 68105. (402)341-9381. Music Director: Almeda Berkey. Professional choir. Estab. 1988. Members are professionals. Performs 5-7 concerts/year; several are new works. Commissions 1-2 new works/year. Performance space: "cathedral, symphony hall, smaller intimate recital halls as well." Payment is "dependent upon composition and composer."
How to Contact: Submit complete score and tape of piece(s). SASE. Reports in 1-2 months.
Music: "Generally a cappella compositions from very short to extended range (6-18 minutes) or multi-movements. Concerts are of a formal length (approx. 75 minutes) with 5 rehearsals. Difficulty must be balanced within program in order to adequately prepare in a limited rehearsal time. 28 singers. Not seeking orchestral pieces, due to limited budget."
Performances: Jackson Berkey's *Anniversary Carols*; John Rutter's *Hymn to the Creator of Light*; and Arvo Part's *Te Deum.*

STAR WITHIN ENTERPRISES, 170 W. 73rd St., New York NY 10023. (212)873-9531. E-mail: starwithin@juno.com. Artistic Director: David Leighton. Chamber music ensemble and chamber opera producers. Estab. 1994. Members are professionals. Performs 20 concerts including 5 new works/year. Commissions 2-3 new composers or new works/year. Diverse audience—classical music enthusiasts and avant-garde art scene. Spaces: 100-400 seat theaters, traditional and experimental. Pay is negotiable.
How to Contact: Submit complete score and tape of piece(s). SASE. Reports in 2-3 months.
Music: "Seeking innovative chamber opera and concert pieces for small-medium size groups, innovative use of synthesizers."
Performances: G. Holst's *Savitri* (opera); Menotti's *The Medium*; and Peter Maxwell Davis' *Martyrdom of St. Magnus* (chamber opera).

STAR-SCAPE, (formerly The New Star-Scape Singers), P.O. Box 793, Station F, Toronto Ontario M4Y 2N7 **Canada**. (905)470-8634 or (800)437-1454. Fax: (905)470-1632. Assistant to the Conductor: Ellen Mann. A cappella choir (10-12 voices). Estab. 1976. Members are professionals. Performs 15 concerts/year including over 170 original works. Audience is appreciative of extraordinary technical ability of the ensemble and recognize that "this music, this art opens up the soul." Performances take place in concert halls and churches. Does not pay composers.
How to Contact: Query first. SASE.
Performances: Kenneth G. Mills/Christopher Dedrick's *Hey There!* (a cappella); *He's Got The Whole World In His Hands* (spiritual); and Kenneth G. Mills/Jacek Sykulski's *Love Answers* (a cappella).

SUSQUEHANNA SYMPHONY ORCHESTRA, P.O. Box 485, Forest Hill MD 21050. (410)838-6465. E-mail: sbzbair@erols.com. Music Director: Sheldon Bair. Symphony orchestra. Estab. 1978. Mem-

bers are amateurs. Performs 6 concerts/year including 3-4 new works. "We perform in one hall, 600 seats with fine acoustics. Our audience encompasses all ages."
How to Contact: Query first. SASE. Reports in 3-6 or more months.
Music: "We desire works for large orchestra any length, in a 'conservative 20th century' style. Seek fine music for large orchestra. We are a community orchestra, so the music must be within our grasp. Violin I to 7th position by step only; Violin II—stay within 5th position; English horn and harp are OK. Full orchestra pieces preferred."
Performances: David Amram's *Celebration Suite* (multi-cultural); Kile Smith's *Three Dances* (dance); and Gwyneth Walker's *Match Point* (tennis).

TORONTO MENDELSSOHN CHOIR, 60 Simcoe St., Toronto, Ontario M5J 2H5 **Canada**. (416)598-0422. Manager: Donna White. Vocal ensemble. Members are professionals and amateurs. Performs 25 concerts/year including 1-3 new works. "Most performances take place in Roy Thomson Hall. The audience is reasonably sophisticated, musically knowledgeable but with moderately conservative tastes." Pays by commission and ASCAP/SOCAN.
How to Contact: Query first or submit complete score and tapes of pieces. SASE. Reports in 6 months.
Music: All works must suit a large choir (180 voices) and standard orchestral forces or with some other not-too-exotic accompaniment. Length should be restricted to no longer than ½ of a nocturnal concert. The choir sings at a very professional level and can sight-read almost anything. "Works should fit naturally with the repertoire of a large choir which performs the standard choral orchestral repertoire."
Performances: Holman's *Jezebel*; Orff's *Catulli Carmina*; and Lambert's *Rio Grande*.

‡VANCOUVER CHAMBER CHOIR, 1254 W. Seventh Ave., Vancouver, British Columbia V6H 1B6 **Canada**. E-mail: vcc@dowco.com. Website: http://www.sitegeist.com/vcc. Artistic Director: Jon Washburn. Vocal ensemble. Members are professionals. Performs 40 concerts/year including 5-8 new works. Commissions 3-4 composers or new works/year. Pays SOCAN royalty or negotiated fee for commissions.
How to Contact: Submit complete score and tapes of piece(s). Does not return material. Reports in 6 months.
Music: Seeks "choral works of all types for small chorus, with or without accompaniment and/or soloists. Concert music only. Choir made up of 20 singers. Large or unusual instrumental accompaniments are less likely to be appropriate. No pop music."
Performances: Alice Parker's *That Sturdy Vine* (cantata for chorus, soloists and orchestra); R. Murray Schafer's *Magic Songs* (SATB a cappella); and Jon Washburn's *A Stephen Foster Medley* (SSAATTBB/piano).
Tips: "We are looking for choral music that is performable yet innovative, and which has the potential to become 'standard repertoire.' Although we perform much new music, only a small portion of the many scores which are submitted can be utilized."

VENTUS MUSICUS, P.O. Box 141, Redlands CA 92373. (909)793-0513. Trumpet Player: Larry Johansen. Chamber music ensemble (organ/trumpet duo). Estab. 1978. Members are professionals. Performs 2-10 concerts/year including 1-4 new works (as available). Most performances done in churches. "Have paid $250/work."
How to Contact: Submit complete score. SASE. Reports in 4 months.
Music: "Most organ/trumpet material is church oriented (hymns, chants, stained glass, etc.); this is useful, but not mandatory—we play for college and A.G.O. Groups as well as church recital series. We are open to pretty much anything, except improvised jazz. We are interested in the composer's ideas, not ours. Go for it! And we'll try it."
Performances: O.D. Hall's *Crown Him*; Donald Grantham's *Ceremony*; and Daniel Pinknam's *Psalms*.
Tips: "Send a good piece and we'll try to perform it. We play in various situations—not all pieces work in all situations. Always looking for new stuff."

VIRGINIA OPERA, P.O. Box 2580, Norfolk VA 23501. (804)627-9545. Fax:(804)622-0058. E-mail: grimese@erols.com. Director or Education: Helen Stevenson. General Director: Peter Mark. Opera company. Estab. 1974. Members are professionals. Performs 625 concerts/year. Concerts are performed for school children throughout Virginia, grades K-5, 6-8 and 9-12 at the Harrison Opera House in Norfolk, and at public/private schools in Virginia. Pays on commission.
How to Contact: Submit complete score and tape of piece(s). SASE. Reports in 6 weeks.
Music: "Audience accessible style approximately 45 minutes in length. Limit cast list to three vocal artists of any combination. Accompanied by piano and/or keyboard. Works are performed before school children of all ages. Pieces must be age appropriate both aurally and dramatically. Musical styles are encouraged to be diverse, contemporary as well as traditional. Works are produced and presented with sets, costumes, etc." Limitations: "Three vocal performers (any combination). One keyboardist. Medium to difficult ac-

ceptable, but prefer easy to medium. Seeking only pieces which are suitable for presentation as part of an opera education program for Virginia Opera's education and outreach department. Subject matter must meet strict guidelines relative to Learning Objectives, etc. Musical idiom must be representative of current trends in opera, musical theater. Extreme dissonance, row systems not applicable to this environment."
Performances: Seymour Barab's *Snow White and the Seven Dwarfs*; John David Earnest's *The Legend of Sleepy Hollow*; and James Newton's *Songs of Freedom.*
Tips: "Theatricality is very important. New works should stimulate interest in musical theater as a legitimate art form for school children with no prior exposure to live theatrical entertainment. Composer should be willing to create a product which will find success within the educational system."

THE DALE WARLAND SINGERS, 119 N. Fourth St., Minneapolis MN 55401-1792. (612)339-9707. Fax: (612)339-9826. E-mail: dwsingers@aol.com. Website: http://www.winternet.com/~webpage/warland.html. Composer in Residence: Carol Barnett. Vocal ensemble. Estab. 1972. Members are professionals. Performs 20-25 concerts/year including 5-10 new works. Commissions 4-8 composers or new works/year. Audience is a typical classical music concert audience; also college and high school students and occasional "popular Christmas" audience. Performance spaces vary, including concert halls, high school/college auditoriums and churches. Pay varies, depending on published status, length, etc.
How to Contact: Submit complete score and tape of piece(s). SASE. Reports in 2-4 months.
Music: "A cappella or with small accompanying forces; texts primarily secular; works for concert choir or vocal jazz ensemble (a 'cabaret' subgroup); 5-15 minutes in length (semi-extended)." Does not wish to see "show choir material or gospel."
Performances: Brent Michael David's *Native American Suite*; Judith Lang Zaimont's *Miracle of Light—A Festival Piece*; and Jing Jing Luo's *An Huan—A Chinese Requiem.*
Tips: "Keep in mind that there will never be enough rehearsal time. Be clear and concise in notation, and write for the capabilities of the choral voice. We seek from our composers not only craft, but a certain 'magic' quality."

WESTMINSTER PRESBYTERIAN CHURCH, 724 Delaware Ave., Buffalo NY 14209-2294. (716)884-9437. Fax: (716)884-3450. E-mail: thomasswan@aol.com. Organist and Choirmaster: Thomas Swan. Vocal ensemble. Estab. 1976. Members are professionals and amateurs. Performs 4 concerts/year including 1 new work. Commissions 1 composer or new work/year. Performs in Kleinhans Music Hall (2,800) and church (1,000). Pays up to $1,500 for outright purchase.
How to Contact: Query first. SASE. Reports in 2 months.
Music: Choral/orchestral-SATB, with or without soloists. A cappella SATB—sacred or secular. Chamber orchestra/choral. "My semi-professional church choir numbers 45."
Performances: Libby Larsen's *Three Summer Scenes*; Fred Thayer's *Three Motets* (a cappella); and Mack Wilberg's *Tres Cantus Laudeni* (SATB/large brass and percussion).
Tips: "Composers writing for the church should carefully consider text and instrumentation. Music written for a cappella singing is especially useful."

WHEATON SYMPHONY ORCHESTRA, 344 Spring Ave., Glen Ellyn IL 60137. (708)790-1430. Manager: Donald C. Mattison. Symphony orchestra. Estab. 1959. Members are professionals and amateurs. Performs 3 summer concerts/year including 1 new work. Pays $500/per performance.
How to Contact: Query first. SASE. Reports in 1 month.
Music: "This is a *good* amateur orchestra that wants pieces in a traditional idiom. Large scale works for orchestra only. No avant garde, 12-tone or atonal material. Pieces should be 20 minutes or less and must be prepared in 3 rehearsals. Instrumentation is woodwinds in 3s, full brass 4-3-3-1, 4-5 percussion and strings—maximum instrumentation only."
Performances: Jerry Bilik's *Aspects of Man* (4-section suite); Walton's *Variations on a Theme of Hindeminth's*; and Augusta Read Thomas' *A Crystal Planet.*

Organizations

One of the first places a beginning songwriter should look to for guidance and support is a songwriting organization. Offering encouragement, instruction, contacts and feedback, these groups of professional and amateur songwriters can help provide a songwriter with the skills needed in order to compete in the ever-changing music industry.

Most of the organizations listed in this book are non-profit groups with membership open to specific groups of people—songwriters, musicians, classical composers, etc. They can be local groups with a membership of less than 100 people, or large national organizations with thousands of members from all over the country. Most of these organizations offer regular meetings of their membership and occasionally sponsor events such as seminars and workshops to which music industry people are invited to talk about the business and perhaps listen to and critique demo tapes. If you are unable to locate an organization within an easy distance of your home (check the following listings, bulletin boards at local music stores and your local newspaper), you may want to consider joining one of the national groups. These groups, based in New York, Los Angeles and Nashville, keep their members involved and informed through newsletters, regional workshops and large yearly conferences. They can help a writer who feels isolated in his hometown get his music heard by professionals in the major music centers.

The type of organization you choose to join depends on what you want to get out of it. Local groups can offer you a friendly, supportive environment where you can work on your songs and have them critiqued in a constructive way by other songwriters. They're also great places to meet collaborators, if you're looking for someone to write with. Larger, national organizations can give you access to music business professionals and other songwriters across the country.

In the following listings, organizations describe their purpose and activities, as well as how much it costs to join. Before joining any organization, consider what they have to offer and how becoming a member will benefit you. To locate organizations close to home, see the Geographic Index at the back of this book.

‡AARON ENTERPRISES SONGWRITERS GROUP, P.O. Box 2438, Petersburg VA 23842. (804)733-5908. Founder: Cham Laughlin. Estab. 1997. "Songwriters of all ages, all styles and all skill levels are welcome to join. Applicants must have an interest in songwriting—music writing, lyric writing or co-writing. The main purpose of this organization is to educate songwriters about the business of songwriting, the art and craft of songwriting, lyric writing and structure, musical composition, song structure or arranging and professional presentation of your songs." Offers newsletter, evaluation services, seminars, discounts on demos and leads to publishers. Applications accepted year-round. Membership fee: $25/year with discounts for multiple years.

Tips: "Networking is a very important part of this business. Members are offered a large amount of information and that information is explained to them through free seminars, the newsletter or one-on-one phone consultations to insure the best possible support network for their songwriting career."

ACADEMY OF COUNTRY MUSIC, 6255 Sunset Blvd., #923, Hollywood CA 90028. (213)462-2351. Executive Director: Fran Boyd. Estab. 1964. Serves producers, artists, songwriters, talent buyers and others involved with the country music industry. Eligibility for professional members is limited to those individuals who derive some portion of their income directly from country music. Each member is classified by one of the following categories: artist/entertainer, club operator/employee, musician/trend leader, DJ, manager/booking agent, composer, music publisher, promotion, publications, radio, TV/motion picture, record company or affiliated (general). The purpose of ACM is to promote and enhance the image of country music. The Academy is involved year-round in activities important to the country music community. Some of these activities include charity fund-raisers, participation in country music seminars, talent contests, artist showcases, assistance to producers in placing country music on television and in motion pictures and backing legislation that benefits the interests of the country music community. The ACM is governed by directors and run by officers elected annually. Applications are accepted throughout the year. Membership is $60/year.

AMERICAN COMPOSERS FORUM, 332 Minnesota St. #E145, St. Paul MN 55101. (612)228-1407. Fax: (612)291-7978. E-mail: compfrm@maroon.tc.umn.edu. Website: http://www.umn.edu/nlhome/m111/compfrm. Contact: Larry Fuchsberg. Estab. 1973. "The American Composers Forum links communities with composers and performers, encouraging the making, playing, and enjoyment of new music. Building two-way relationships between artists and publics, the Forum develops programs that educate today's and tomorrow's audiences, energize composers' careers, stimulate entrepreneurship and collaboration, promote musical creativity, and serve as models of effective support for the arts. The Forum's members, more than a thousand strong, live in 46 states and 16 countries; membership is open to all."

AMERICAN SOCIETY OF COMPOSERS, AUTHORS AND PUBLISHERS (ASCAP), One Lincoln Plaza, New York NY 10023. (212)621-6000 (administration); (212)621-6240 (membership). President and Chairman of the Board: Marilyn Bergman. CEO: John LoFrumento. Regional offices: 7920 Sunset Blvd., 3rd Floor, Los Angeles, CA 90046, (213)883-1000; 2 Music Square W., Nashville, TN 37203, (615)742-5000; 1608 W. Belmont Ave., Suite 200, Chicago IL 60657, (773)472-1157; 8 Cork St., London WIX IPB England, 011-44-171-439-0909; 1519 Ponce de Leon Ave., Suite 505, Santurce, Puerto Rico 00909, (787)725-1688. ASCAP is a membership association of over 75,000 composers, lyricists, songwriters, and music publishers, whose function is to protect the right of its members by licensing and collecting royalties for the nondramatic public performance of their copyrighted works. ASCAP licensees include radio, television, cable, live concert promoters, bars, restaurants, symphony orchestras, and other users of music. ASCAP is the leading performing rights society in the world, with 1996 revenues of more than $482 million. All revenues, less operating expenses, are distributed to members (over 84 cents of each dollar, almost $400 million, in 1996). Founded in 1914, ASCAP is the only society created and controlled by writers and publishers. The ASCAP Board of Directors consists of 12 writers and 12 publishers, elected by the membership. ASCAP offers a variety of tailor-made benefits to its members, including medical, dental and term insurance, instrument and equipment insurance, and credit union access. ASCAP hosts a wide array of showcases and workshops throughout the year, and offers grant and special award opportunities in a variety of genres.

AMERICAN SONGWRITERS NETWORK (ASN), Dept A95, Box 15312, Boston MA 02215. (617)576-8836. Fax: (617)388-3179. E-mail: asn@tiac.net. Website: http://www.tiac.net/users/asn/index.htm. Contact: Network Manager. Estab. 1995. Serves "professional level songwriters/composers with monthly tipsheet. The tipsheet includes the most current listing of producers, A&R managers, record labels, entertainment attorneys, agents and publishing companies that are looking for material. Any songwriter from any part of the country or world can be a member of this organization. The purpose of this organization is to foster a better professional songwriting community by helping members to place their songs." Applications accepted year-round. Membership fee: $140/year.
Tips: "Please send SASE or e-mail for application form."

ARKANSAS SONGWRITERS, 6817 Gingerbread, Little Rock AR 72204. (501)569-8889. President: Peggy Vining. Estab. 1979. Serves songwriters, musicians and lovers of music. Anyone interested may join. The purpose of this organization is to promote and encourage the art of songwriting. Offers competitions, instruction, lectures, newsletter, performance opportunities, social outings and workshops. Applications accepted year-round. Membership fee: $20/year.
Tips: "We also contribute time, money and our energies to promoting our craft in other functions. Meetings are held on the first Thursday of each month at Books-A-Million in Little Rock."

ASSOCIATED MALE CHORUSES OF AMERICA, RR1, Box 106, Dunsford, Ontario K0M 1L0 **Canada**. Website: http://www.tc.umn.edu/nlhome/M042/thoma075/scholar.html. Executive Secretary: William J. Bates. Estab. 1924. Serves musicians and male choruses of US and Canada. "Our members are people from all walks of life. Many of our directors and accompanists are professional musicians. Age ranges from high school students to members in their 70's and 80's. Potential members must be supportive of Male Chorus Singing. They do not have to belong to a chorus to join. We have both Associate and Affiliate memberships. Our purpose is to further the power of music, not only to entertain and instruct, but to uplift the spirit, arouse the finest instincts, and develop the soul of man. With so little male chorus music being written, we as a 1,500 member organization provide a vehicle for songwriters, so that the music can be performed." Offers competitions, instruction, lectures, library, newsletter, performance opportunities, social outings and workshops. Also sponsors annual Male Chorus Competition Contest. Applications accepted year-round. Membership fees are Regular Members: $5; Chorus Members: $7 (per singer); Affiliate (Individual or Organization) Members: $10; Student Members: $2; Life Members: $125 (one time fee).

‡ATLANTA SONGWRITERS ASSOCIATION, INC., 3121 Maple Dr., Suite 113, Atlanta GA 30305. (404)266-2666. President: Philip J. King. Estab. 1978. "Members are comprised of all ages from amateur to professionals in the music industry. Membership is open to all music industry personnel worldwide. The Atlanta Songwriters Association supports and educates songwriters, performers, music publishers, producers and other industry professionals on the business of music and the craft of songwriting." Offers competitions, newsletter, lectures, workshops, performance opportunities and educational panels. Applications accepted year-round. Membership fee: $45/year.

ATLANTIC CANADIAN COMPOSERS ASSOCIATION, 214 Jones St., Moncton, New Brunswick E1C 6K3 **Canada**. (506)388-4224. E-mail: lhoffman@is.dal.ca. Member at Large: Richard Gibson. Estab. 1980. "Our membership consists of people who write 'serious' (as opposed to commercial, pop, jazz, industrial) music. An applicant must be resident in one of the four Atlantic Canadian provinces and must be able to demonstrate a fluency with a variety of genres of notated music. An applicant must be prepared to submit five completed scores." Offers performance opportunities. Applications accepted year-round. Membership fee is 35 Canadian dollars.

AUSTIN SONGWRITERS GROUP, P.O. Box 2578, Austin TX 78768. (512)442-TUNE. Fax: (512)442-8863. President: Mary Bouc. Estab. 1986. Serves all ages and all levels, from just beginning to advanced. Prospective members should have an interest in the field of songwriting, whether it be for profit or hobby. The main purpose of this organization is "to educate members in the craft and business of songwriting; to provide resources for growth and advancement in the area of songwriting; and to provide opportunities for performance and contact with the music industry." The primary benefit of membership to a songwriter is "exposure to music industry professionals, which increases contacts and furthers the songwriter's education in both craft and business aspects." Offers competitions, instruction, lectures, library, newsletter, performance opportunities, evaluation services, workshops and "contact with music industry professionals through special guest speakers at meetings, plus our yearly 'Austin Songwriters Conference,' which includes instruction, song evaluations, and song pitching direct to those pros currently seeking material for their artists, publishing companies, etc." Applications accepted year-round. Membership fee: $40/year.

Tips: "Our newsletter is top-quality—packed with helpful information on all aspects of songwriting—craft, business, recording and producing tips, and industry networking opportunities. (Members also receive and are included in the ASG Directory, which aids networking among the membership.)"

BERMUDA SONGWRITERS ASSOCIATION, P.O. Box 2857, Hamilton HM LX **Bermuda**. (441)296-5774. Fax: (441)234-0943. E-mail: bsa@bermuda.com. Website: http://www.bermuda.com/Song. President: Richard T. Bassett. Estab. 1995. "Ages range from 20 to approximately 60 years. Interest ranges from hobbyists to persons seeking publishing and record deals. Skill levels range from amateur to professional musician/recording artists. BSA is open to all writers at all skill levels. BSA's objectives are to provide local and international songwriting networking and collaborative opportunities and to provide education that will help develop songwriting skills through seminars and workshops. It was formed for the advancement of creative songwriting and to provide talent discovery opportunities for Bermuda-based songwriters." Offers lectures, performance opportunities, instruction, newsletter and workshops. Applications accepted year-round. Membership fee: $75/full year.

THE BLACK ROCK COALITION, P.O. Box 1054, Cooper Station, New York NY 10276. (212)713-5097. E-mail: brcny@aol.com. Website: http://members.aol.com/brcny. Membership Manager: Joel Brockman. Estab. 1985. Serves musicians, songwriters—male and female ages 18-40 (average). Also engineers, entertainment attorneys and producers. Looking for members who are "mature and serious about music as an artist or activist willing to help fellow musicians. The BRC independently produces, promotes and distributes Black alternative music acts as a collective and supportive voice for such musicians within the music and record business. The main purpose of this organization is to produce, promote and distribute the full spectrum of black music along with educating the public on what black music is." Offers instruction, newsletter, lectures, free seminars and workshops, monthly membership meeting, quarterly magazine, performing opportunities, evaluation services, business advice, full roster of all members. Applications accepted year-round. Bands must submit a tape, bio with picture and a self-addressed, stamped envelope before sending their membership fee. Membership fee: $25 per individual/$100 per band.

THE BOSTON SONGWRITERS WORKSHOP, 14 Skelton Rd., Burlington MA 01803. (617)499-6932. E-mail: elliott_a._jacobowitz@bmugbos.org. Website: http://www.dcreators.com/bsw. Executive Director: Elliott Jacobowitz. Estab. 1989. "The Boston Songwriters Workshop is made up of a very diverse group of people, ranging in age from late teens to people in their forties, fifties, and sixties. The interest areas are also diverse, running the gamut from folk, pop and rock to musical theater, jazz, R&B, dance, rap and classical. Skill levels within the group range from relative newcomers to established veterans that have had cuts and/or songs published. By virtue of group consensus, there are no eligibility requirements other than a serious desire to pursue one's songwriting ventures, and availability and interest in volunteering for the various activities required to run the organization. The purpose of the BSW is to establish a community of songwriters and composers within the greater Boston area, so that its members may better help each other to make further gains in their respective musical careers." Offers performance opportunities, instruction, newsletter, workshops and bi-weekly critique sessions. Applications accepted year-round. Full membership: $35/year; flyer (newsletter) membership: $17.50/year; guest (nonmember) fees: $3/meeting.

BROADCAST MUSIC, INC. (BMI), 320 W. 57th St., New York NY 10019. (212)586-2000; 8730 Sunset Blvd., Los Angeles CA 90069, (310)659-9109; and 10 Music Square East, Nashville TN 37203, (615)291-6700. President and CEO: Frances W. Preston. Senior Vice President, Performing Rights: Del R. Bryant. Vice President, California: Rick Riccobono. Vice President, New York: Charlie Feldman. Vice President, Nashville: Roger Sovine. BMI is a performing rights organization representing over 160,000 songwriters, composers and music publishers in all genres of music, including pop, rock, country, R&B, rap, jazz, Latin, gospel and contemporary classical. "Applicants must have written a musical composition, alone or in collaboration with other writers, which is commercially published, recorded or otherwise likely to be performed." Purpose: BMI acts on behalf of its songwriters, composers and music publishers by insuring payment for performance of their works through the collection of licensing fees from radio stations, broadcast and cable TV stations, hotels, nightclubs, aerobics centers and other users of music. This income is distributed to the writers and publishers in the form of royalty payments, based on how the music is used. BMI also undertakes intensive lobbying efforts in Washington D.C. on behalf of its affiliates, seeking to protect their performing rights through the enactment of new legislation and enforcement of current copyright law. In addition, BMI helps aspiring songwriters develop their skills through various workshops, seminars and competitions it sponsors throughout the country. Applications accepted year-round. There is no membership fee for songwriters; a one-time fee of $100 is required to affiliate a publishing company.

BROADWAY ON SUNSET, 10800 Hesby, Suite 9, North Hollywood CA 91601. (818)508-9270. Fax: (818)508-1806. E-mail: broadwayonsunset@aol.com. Artistic Director: Allison Bergman. Estab. 1981. Sponsored by the National Academy of Songwriters. Members are musical theater writers (composers, lyricists, librettists) at all skill levels. All styles of music and musicals accepted. Participants need to have access to the Los Angeles area to attend our programs. "We provide writers of new musicals with a structured development program that gives them a full understanding of the principles and standards of Broadway-level craft, and provides them with opportunities to test their material in front of an audience." Offers lectures, production opportunities, evaluation and consultation services, workshops and instruction. Co-produces full productions of developed original musicals in various local theaters. Applications accepted year-round. No membership fee per se; writers pay nominal fees to participate in classes and workshops. Certain scholarships are available.

‡CALIFORNIA LAWYERS FOR THE ARTS, 1641 18th St., Santa Monica CA 90404. (310)998-5590. Fax: (310)998-5594. E-mail: ula@kspace.com. Website: http://kspace.com. or USATTORNEYS.com/california/lawyersfor the arts. Estab. 1974. "For artists of all disciplines, skill levels, and ages, supporting individuals and organizations, and arts organizations. Artists of all disciplines are welcome, whether professionals or amateurs. We also welcome groups and individuals who support the arts. We work most closely with the California Arts Community. We want to establish a bridge between the legal and arts communities so that artists and art groups may handle their creative activities with greater business and legal competence; the legal profession will be more aware of issues affecting the arts community; and the law will become more responsive to the arts community." Offers newsletter, lectures, library, workshops, mediation service, attorney referral service, housing referrals, publications and advocacy. Membership fee: Individuals: $15 for full time student; $20 for working artist; $35 for genreal individual; $50 for panel attorney; $100 to $1,000 patrons. Organizations: $40 for small organization (budget under $50,000), $75 for large organization (budget over $50,000), $100 to $1,000 for corporate sponsor.

CANADA COUNCIL FOR THE ARTS/CONSEIL DES ARTS DU CANADA, 350 Albert St., P.O. Box 1047, Ottawa, Ontario K1P 5V8 **Canada**. (613)566-4365 or (613)566-4366. Website: http://www.canadacouncil.ca. Information Officers: Michelle Chawla, Maria Martin and Lise Rochon. Estab. 1957. An independent agency that fosters and promotes the arts in Canada by providing grants and services to professional artists including songwriters and musicians. "Individual artists must be Canadian citizens or permanent residents of Canada, and must have completed basic training and/or have the recognition as professionals within their fields. The Canada Council offers grants to professional musicians to pursue their own personal and creative development. There are specific deadline dates for the various programs of assistance." Call or write for more details.

CANADIAN ACADEMY OF RECORDING ARTS & SCIENCES (CARAS), 124 Merton St., 3rd Floor, Toronto, Ontario M4S 2Z2 **Canada**. (416)485-3135. Fax: (416)485-4978. Executive Director: Daisy C. Falle. Membership is open to all employees (including support staff) in broadcasting and record companies, as well as producers, personal managers, recording artists, recording engineers, arrangers, composers, music publishers, album designers, promoters, talent and booking agents, record retailers, rack jobbers, distributors, recording studios and other music industry related professions (on approval). Applicants must be affliliated with the Canadian recording industry. Offers newsletter, Canadian artist record discount program, nomination and voting privileges for Juno Awards and discount tickets to Juno awards show. Also discount on trade magazines and complimentary Juno Awards CD. "CARAS strives to foster the development of the Canadian music and recording industries and to contribute toward higher artistic standards." Applications accepted year-round. Membership fee is $45/year. Applications accepted from individuals only, not from companies or organizations.

CANADIAN AMATEUR MUSICIANS/MUSICIENS AMATEURS DU CANADA (CAMMAC), 1751 Richardson, #2509, Montreal, Quebec H3K 1G6 **Canada**. (514)932-8755. Fax: (514)932-9811. E-mail: cammac@odyssee.net. Website: http://www.odyssee.net/~cammac. Executive Director: Danièle Rhéaume. Estab. 1953. Serves amateur musicians of all ages and skill levels. "CAMMAC is a nonprofit organization that provides opportunities for amateur musicians of all ages and levels to develop their skills in a supportive and non-competitive environment, and to enjoy making music together. We provide contact with musicians of varying levels and interests—the perfect testing ground for any number of styles and challenges. We also offer a variety of musical workshops, including singing, playing and improvisation at our summer camp at Lake McDonald in the Laurentians." Offers performance opportunities, library, instruction, newsletter, workshops and summer camp (families and individuals). Applications accepted year-round. Regular membership fee is Adult: $35, Family: $50, Student and Senior: $20, Group $50 plus $2/member for library borrowing privileges.

CANADIAN COUNTRY MUSIC ASSOCIATION (CCMA), 3800 Steeles Ave. W., Suite 127, Woodbridge, Ontario L4L 4G9 **Canada**. (905)850-1144. Fax: (905)856-1330. E-mail: ccma@sprynet.com. Executive Director: Sheila Hamilton. Estab. 1976. Members are songwriters, musicians, producers, radio station personnel, managers, booking agents and others. Offers newsletter, workshops, performance opportunities and annual awards. "Through our newsletters and conventions we offer a means of meeting and associating with artists and others in the industry. During our workshops or seminars (Country Music Week), we include a songwriters' seminar. The CCMA is a federally chartered, nonprofit organization, dedicated to the promotion and development of Canadian country music throughout Canada and the world and to providing a unity of purpose for the Canadian country music industry." Send for application.

‡CENTRAL CAROLINA SONGWRITERS ASSOCIATION (CCSA), 1144 Amber Acres Lane, Knightdale NC 27545. (919)266-5791. Founder: Shantel R. Davis. Estab. 1996. "CCSA welcomes all songwriters and musicians, regardless of age. Our members vary in musical interests, and we cover all types of music. From the beginning songwriter to the experienced professional, all songwriters and musicians can find benefit in joining CCSA. Our headquarters are located just outside of Raleigh, NC. We are open to all songwriters who could possibly make it to our meetings, or those who are too far away could use our Critique-By-Mail service. All members must be active participants in CCSA for the benefit of the group, as well as for their own benefit, dedicated songwriters/musicians. The main purpose of the CCSA is to provide each songwriter and musician a resourceful organization where members can grow musically by learning and sharing with one another. We want to reach every songwriter we can and attend to his/her musical needs." Offers instruction, newsletter, library, workshops, evaluation services and musicians/collaborators network. Applications accepted year-round.

‡CENTRAL MISSISSIPPI SONGWRITERS ASSOCIATION (CMSA), Rt. 1, Box 30-B, Ethel MS 39067. (601)674-9292 (call after 5 pm weekdays/afternoon weekends). President: Chuck Everhart. Estab. 1997. "Our members range from age 13 on up. Poets, singers, lyricists and musicians of any kind make up our association. Skills range from amateur to professional musicians, singers and songwriters. You must have a love for your music and be willing to learn to develop your skills. A good sense of humor will help. Ability to accept constructive criticism will help those from all over the world to unite as we build

a better organization. Our purpose is to promote talent into the music industry and develop the skills the industry needs, and to provide a way for songwriters to become acknowledged by the public." Offers instruction, newsletter, lectures, library, workshops, performance opportunities, evaluation services and music discounts. Applications accepted year-round. Membership fee: $60/year or $5/month.
Tips: "We offer members discounts on musical equipment 10-50% off with 100% credit, should you decide to trade up later. We are setting up a web page, newsletter and Saturday night Opry. We have meetings every Monday night, as well as tape sessions, reviews, in-house demo studio, songwriter review sessions and a library for members."

‡CHICAGO ALLIANCE FOR PLAYWRIGHTS, 1225 W. Belmont, Chicago IL 60657. (773)929-7367, ext. 60. Fax: (773)327-1404. President: Joanne Koch. Estab. 1990. "Organizational members include Chicago Dramatists Workshop, Writer Bloc, New Tuners, Women's Theatre Alliance, The Saints, Studio Z and API Theatre; there are over 150 individual members. Members must be Chicago-area residents (past or present); no pro status is required. CAP is a service organization that establishes a network for Chicago-area playwrights and others committed to the development of new work for the stage. The Alliance sponsors forums of interest to writers and publishes an annual directory of CAP members and their works." Offers instruction, newsletter, lectures, workshops and annual directory of CAP members. Applications accepted year-round. Membership fee: $25/year individual, $100/year organization.

CHICAGO MUSIC ALLIANCE, 410 S. Michigan Ave., Suite 819, Chicago IL 60647. (312)987-9296. Fax: (312)987-1127. Executive Director: Matthew Brockmeier. Estab. 1984. "Chicago Music Alliance is comprised of organizations and individuals involved in music of all styles at all levels of skill. Administrators, composers, students, performers, educators and others are members as well as groups from the smallest ensemble to full symphony orchestras. Ensembles should reside and perform in the Chicago area, as should individuals. Individuals across the country are CMA members, but they have a connection with Chicago in some way (want to stay in touch, are interested in moving to Chicago, their work is performed in Chicago, etc). Our mission is to celebrate and support all of the music produced in the Chicago area. As a service organization we are committed to meeting the needs of our members. We act as a center for the exchange of ideas and resources, maintain ties with the educational community, and develop programs to serve our members with their direct input. Our activities include workshops, radio broadcasts, events listings, music performance and merchandise discounts, and résumé/career counseling." Offers newsletter, lectures, workshops, performance opportunities, research and information finding services, information on auditions and competitions. Applications accepted year-round. Membership fee: $35/individuals. Fees for ensembles vary by budget size.

THE COLLEGE MUSIC SOCIETY, 202 W. Spruce St., Missoula MT 59802. (406)721-9616. Fax: (406)721-9419. E-mail: cms@music.org. Website: http://www.music.org. Estab. 1959. Serves college, university, and conservatory professors, as well as independent musicians. "It is dedicated to gathering, considering and disseminating ideas on the philosophy and practice of music as an integral part of higher education, and to developing and increasing communication among the various disciplines of music." Offers journal, newsletter, lectures, workshops, performance opportunities, job listing service, directory of music faculty, mailing lists of music faculty. Applications accepted year-round. Membership fee: $60 (regular dues).

COMPOSERS GUILD, 40 N. 100 West, Box 586, Farmington UT 84025. (801)451-2275. Resident: Ruth Gatrell. Estab. 1963. Serves all ages, including children. Musical skill varies from beginners to professionals. An interest in composing is the only requirement. The purpose of this organization is to "help composers in every way possible through classes, workshops and symposiums, concerts, composition contests and association with others of similar interests." Offers competitions, instruction, lectures, newsletter, performance opportunities, evaluation services and workshops. Applications accepted year-round. Membership fee is $25/year. Associate memberships for child, spouse, parent, grandchild or grandparent of member: $15. "Holds four concerts/year. January: Composer's Spectacular featuring contest winners; June: Farmington Composers Concert in the Park; July: Americana, Patriotic and American Scene compositions; and December: New Sounds for Christmas. Annual Composition Contest: Deadline August 31. Fees: Less than 7 minutes: $5/members, $15/non-dues-paying; 7 minutes or more, including multi-movement works: $10/members, $20/non-members. Comments from judges given on all compositions. Return of materials if mailers and postage furnished. Categories: Arrangements, Children's, Choral, Instrumental, Jazz/New Age, Keyboard, Orchestra/Band, Popular, Vocal Solo and Young Composer (18 or under on Aug. 31). Age groups: 16-18, 13-15, 10-12, 7-9, 6 or under. Awards in each category: First prize $100, 2nd prize $50, 3rd prize: $25. Best of Contest in lieu of 1st prize: $500. Honorable Mention and Best of Age Group awards also given."

CONNECTICUT SONGWRITERS ASSOCIATION, P.O. Box 1292, Glastonbury CT 06033. (860)659-8992. E-mail: ddcsa@aol.com. Website: http://www.rimact.com/csalunch. Executive Director: Don Donegan. "We are an educational, nonprofit organization dedicated to improving the art and craft of original music. Founded in 1979 by Don Donegan, CSA has grown to over 250 active members and has become one of the best known songwriter's associations in the country. Membership in the CSA admits you to 12-18 seminars/workshops/song critique sessions per year at 3 locations in Connecticut. Out of state members may mail in songs for free critique at our meetings. Noted professionals deal with all aspects of the craft and business of music including lyric writing, music theory, music technology, arrangement and production, legal and business aspects, performance techniques, song analysis and recording techniques. CSA offers 2-3 song screening sessions per year for members (songs which are voted on by the panel). Songs that 'pass' are then eligible for inclusion on the *Best of CSA* anthology cassette series. Five 16-song tapes have been released so far and are for sale at local retail outlets and are given to speakers and prospective buyers. CSA also offers showcases and concerts which are open to the public and designed to give artists a venue for performing their original material for an attentive, listening audience. CSA benefits help local soup kitchens, group homes, hospice, world hunger, libraries, nature centers, community centers and more. CSA shows encompass ballads to bluegrass and Bach to rock. Our monthly newsletter, *Connecticut Songsmith*, offers free classified advertising for members, and has been edited and published by Bill Pere since 1980. Annual dues: $40; senior citizen and full time students $30; organizations $80. Memberships are tax-deductible as business expenses or as charitable contributions to the extent allowed by law."

COUNTRY MUSIC SHOWCASE INTERNATIONAL, INC., P.O. Box 368, Carlisle IA 50047. (515)989-3748. President: Harold L. Luick. Vice President: Barbara A. Luick. "We are a nonprofit, educational performing arts organization for songwriters, recording artists and entertainers. The organization showcases songwriters at different seminars and workshops held at the request of its members in many different states across the nation. It also showcases recording artists/entertainer members at many Fair Association showcases held across the United States. When a person becomes a member they receive a membership card, newsletters, an educational information packet (about songwriting/entertainment business), a question and answer service by mail or phone, a song evaluation and critique service, info on who's looking for song material, songwriters who are willing to collaborate, and songwriting contests. Members can submit 1 song per month for a critique. We offer good constructive criticism and honest opinions. We maintain that a songwriter, recording artist or entertainer should associate himself with professional people and educators that know more about the business of music than they do; otherwise, they cannot reach their musical goals." Supporting Songwriter membership donation: $100 per year; Supporting Recording Artist/Entertainer membership donation: $100/year; Supporting Band, Group or music related business membership donation: $100/year. For free information, brochure or membership application send SASE to the above address.

DALLAS SONGWRITERS ASSOCIATION, 7139 Azalea, Dallas TX 75230. (214)750-0916. E-mail: richcrid@applink.net. President: Richard Crider. Estab. 1988. Serves songwriters and lyricists of Dallas/Ft. Worth metroplex. Members are adults ages 18-65, Dallas/Ft. Worth area songwriters/lyricists who aspire to be professionals. Purpose is to provide songwriters an opportunity to meet other songwriters, share information, find co-writers and support each other through group discussions at monthly meetings; to provide songwriters an opportunity to have their songs heard and critiqued by peers and professionals by playing cassettes and providing an open mike at monthly meetings and by offering contests judged by publishers; to provide songwriters opportunities to meet other music business professionals by inviting guest speakers to monthly meetings and the Dallas Songwriters Seminar; and to provide songwriters opportunities to learn more about the craft of songwriting and the business of music by presenting mini-workshops at each monthly meeting. "We offer a chance for the songwriter to learn from peers and industry professionals and an opportunity to belong to a supportive group environment to encourage the individual to continue his/her songwriting endeavors." Offers competitions, field trips, instruction, lectures, newsletter, performance opportunities, social outings, workshops and seminars. "Our members are eligible to join the Southwest Community Credit Union and for discounts at several local music stores and seminars." Applications accepted year round. Membership fee: $45. When inquiring by phone, please leave complete mailing address and phone number where you can be reached day and night.

THE DRAMATISTS GUILD, INC., 1501 Broadway, Suite 701, New York NY 10036. (212)398-9366. Executive Director: Richard Garmise. "For over three-quarters of a century, The Dramatists Guild has been the professional association of playwrights, composers and lyricists, with more than 6,000 members across the country. All theater writers, whether produced or not, are eligible for Associate membership ($75/year); those who are engaged in a drama-related field but are not a playwright are eligible for Subscribing membership ($50/year); students enrolled in writing degree programs at colleges or universities are eligible for Student membership ($35/year); writers who have been produced on Broadway, Off-Broadway or on the main stage of a resident theater are eligible for Active membership ($125/year). The Guild offers its members the following activities and services: use of the Guild's contracts (including the Approved Production Contract for Broadway, the Off-Broadway contract, the LORT contract, the collaboration agreements for both musicals and drama, the 99 Seat Theatre Plan contract, the Small Theatre contract, commissioning agreements, and the Underlying Rights Agreements contract; advice on all theatrical contracts including Broadway, Off-Broadway, regional, showcase, Equity-waiver, dinner theater and collaboration contracts); a nationwide toll-free number for all members with business or contract questions or problems; advice and information on a wide spectrum of issues affecting writers; free and/or discounted ticket service; symposia led by experienced professionals in major cities nationwide; access to two health insurance programs and a group term life insurance plan; a reference library; and a spacious and elegant meeting room which can accommodate up to 60 people for readings and auditions on a rental basis. The Guild's publications are: *The Dramatists Guild Quarterly*, a journal containing articles on all aspects of the theater, an annual marketing directory with up-to-date information on agents, grants, producers, playwriting contests, conferences and workshops; and *The Dramatists Guild Newsletter*, issued 8 times a year, with announcements of all Guild activities and current information of interest to dramatists."

‡THE FIELD, 161 Sixth Ave., New York NY 10013. (212)691-6969. (212)255-2053. E-mail: thefield@aol.com. Executive Director: Katherine Longstreth. Estab. 1986. "The Field's constituents consist of artists in the disciplines of dance, performance art, theater, writing, music and video. We have a commitment to serve all artists, from those making their first work, to those who are experienced, supported and recognized, as well as artists from diverse cultural backgrounds and aesthetic points of view. There are no eligibility requirements. The Field does not engage in any curatorial activity, maintaining an open, non-exclusive forum which any artist can join. The Field was created to help independent performing artists continue to make art. This mission has led us to offer programs based in three areas which cover the basic needs of independent artists. These include art-based programs, focusing on aesthetic development and refinement; career-based programs, which foster professional growth and opportunity; and exploration-based programs, centered on exploration of new options for artists during a time when the arts environment is undergoing significant change. The Field was established in 1986 by a group of artists who responded to working in isolation by creating a structure within which to share their work, ideas and resources with one another. These artists, who had common roots in contemporary dance, theater and music, began meeting on a regular basis and presenting their work to each other. Through an organic process of development, a two-part mission emerged. The first was a commitment to serve all artists, regardless of aesthetic, cultural background or level of development. The second was to remain responsive to the changing needs of the community of independent artists. These two tenets clearly served a prevailing need as The Field has developed into a thriving service organization, providing workshops, performances, management, regranting, publications and other services for more than 900 artists. Furthermore, The Field's programs have been replicated in satellite sites in Atlanta, Chicago, Dallas, Houston, Miami, Philadelphia, San Francisco, Seattle, Toronto and Washington, DC." Offers newsletter, workshops and performance opportunities. Applications accepted year-round. Membership fee: $75/year.

THE FOLK ALLIANCE, 1001 Connecticut Ave. NW, #501, Washington DC 20036. (202)835-3655. Fax: (202)835-3656. E-mail: fa@folk.org. Website: http://www.hidwater.com/folkalliance/. Contact: Phyliss Barney. Estab. 1989. Serves songwriters, musicians and folk music and dance organizations. Members are organizations and individuals involved in traditional and contemporary folk music and dance in the US and Canada. Members must be active in the field of folk music (singers/songwriters in any genre—blues, bluegrass, Celtic, Latino, old-time, etc.). The Folk Alliance serves members through education, advocacy, field development, professional development, networking and showcases. Offers newsletter, performance opportunities, workshops and "database of members, organizations, presenters, folk radio, etc." Applications accepted year round. Membership fee: $40/year for individual (voting); $100-400/year for organizational. "The Folk Alliance hosts its annual conference (which includes performance showcases) in late February at different locations in the US and Canada. 1998 site: Memphis, TN; 1999: Albuquerque, NM. We *do not* offer songwriting contests. We are *not* a publisher—no demo tapes, please."

FORT BEND SONGWRITERS ASSOCIATION, P.O. Box 1273, Richmond TX 77406. (713)665-4676. Info line: 713-CONCERT (Access Code FBSA). Fax: (713)665-5576. Contact: Membership Director. Estab. 1991. Serves "any person, amateur or professional, interested in songwriting or music. Our members write pop, rock, country, rockabilly, gospel, R&B, children's music and musical plays." Open to all, regardless of geographic location or professional status. The FBSA provides its membership with help to perfect their songwriting crafts. The FBSA provides instruction for beginning writers and publishing and artist tips for the more accomplished writer. Offers competitions, field trips, instruction, lectures, newsletter, performance opportunities, workshops, mail-in critiques and collaboration opportunities. Applications accepted year-round. Membership fees are: Regular: $35; Renewals; $25; Family or Band: $45; Associate:

$20; Business: $150; and Lifetime: $250. For more information send SASE.

GOSPEL MUSIC ASSOCIATION, 1205 Division St., Nashville TN 37203. (615)242-0303. E-mail: gmatoday@aol.com. Website: http://www.gospelmusic.org/. Membership Coordinator: Tim Marshall. Estab. 1964. Serves songwriters, musicians and anyone directly involved in or who supports gospel music. Professional members include advertising agencies, musicians, agents/managers, composers, retailers, music publishers, print and broadcast media, and other members of the recording industry. Associate members include supporters of gospel music and those whose involvement in the industry does not provide them with income. The primary purpose of the GMA is to promote the industry of gospel music, and provide professional development series for industry members. Offers library, newsletter, performance opportunities and workshops. Applications accepted year round. Membership fee: $75/year (professional) and $50/year (associate).

THE GUILD OF INTERNATIONAL SONGWRITERS & COMPOSERS, Sovereign House, 12 Trewartha Rd., Praa Sands, Penzance, Cornwall TR20 9ST **England**. Phone: (01736)762826. Fax: (01736)763328. E-mail: songmag@aol.com. Website: http://www.icn.co.uk/gisc.html. Secretary: C.A. Jones. Serves songwriters, musicians, record companies, music publishers, etc. "Our members are amateur and professional songwriters and composers, musicians, publishers, studio owners and producers. Membership is open to all persons throughout the world of any age and ability, from amateur to professional. The Guild gives advice and services relating to the music industry. A free magazine is available upon request with an SAE or 3 IRC's. We provide contact information for artists, record companies, music publishers, industry organizations; free copyright service; *Songwriting & Composing Magazine*; and many additional free services." Applications accepted year round. Annual dues: £35 in the U.K.; £40 in E.E.C. countries; £40 overseas. (Subscriptions in pounds sterling only).

‡HARBOR THEATRE LAB, % M&C Productions, 160 W. 71st. St. #20A, New York NY 10023. (212)787-1845. Artistic Director: Stuart Warmflash. Estab. 1994. "The Harbor Theatre, a company of playwrights, actors and directors, is seeking a limited number of additional Lab playwrights (including musical theatre writing teams). For the past three seasons, The Harbor Lab has been developing projects in weekly sessions through a process of in-house development followed by in-house readings. The Harbor Theatre has subsequently produced a series of public readings. Serious playwrights with a body of work, a commitment to rewrites and the ability to work with others in a supportive atmosphere are encouraged to apply. The Harbor Theatre is a non-profit organization. Playwrights share the cost of the expenses with a $350 annual fee. For further information, contact Artistic Director Stuart Warmflash."

‡HAWAI'I SONGWRITERS ASSOCIATION, P.O. Box 88129, Honolulu HI 96830. (808)923-1644. Fax: (808)923-0949. E-mail: hitman@lava.net. Secretary: Victor Rittenband. Estab. 1972. "We have two classes of membership: Professional (must have had at least one song commercially published and for sale to general public) and Regular (any one who wants to join and share in our activities). Both classes can vote equally, but only Professional members can hold office. Must be 18 years old to join. Our members include musicians, entertainers and record producers. Membership is world-wide and open to all varieties of music, not just ethnic Hawaiian." Offers competitions, instruction, newsletter, lectures, workshops, performance opportunities and evaluation services. Applications accepted year-round. Membership fee: $24.

IMC TRENDSETTER, P.O. Box 201, Smyrna GA 30081. (770)432-2454. President: Tom Hodges. Estab. 1965. "Our members range from young to old, from interested listener to accomplished songwriter/performer. The IMC is a network sales organization dedicated to selling and promoting independent music product. We have international distributor set-up. Music is promoted via a radio program of pre-recorded tapes of artists. Our members help to promote and sell member tapes and CDs to friends, family and associates. Our goal is to create a mid-level market for the independent artist/songwriter. Songwriters will have new chances at release, as our independent artists finally have a market to sell their product. Artists with studio masters also have the opportunity for release on our Stepping Stone Records label. We are creating a 'middle class' in the music industry. More releases will translate into more songwriters being paid. Call or write for free information." Offers performance opportunities, newsletter and product distribution. Applications accepted year-round. Membership fee: $12/1st year (with free CD or cassette/album); $12 renewal.

THE INDIANAPOLIS SONGWRITERS ASSOCIATION, INC., P.O. Box 44724, Indianapolis IN 46244-0724. (317)862-3366 or 862-4922. President: Nancy J. Seibert. Estab. 1983. Purpose is "to create an affiliation of serious-minded songwriters, promote the artistic value of the musical composition, the business of music and recognition for the songwriter and his craft." Sponsors quarterly newsletter, monthly meetings, periodic showcases and periodic seminars and workshops. "The monthly critiques are helpful for improving songwriting skills. The meetings offer opportunities to share information concerning publishing, demos, etc. Also offers discounts to recording studios and monthly tip sheets. In addition, it provides the opportunity for members to meet co-writers." Membership fee: $20/year.

INTERNATIONAL ALLIANCE FOR WOMEN IN MUSIC, George Washington University, Academic Center B144, Washington DC 20052. E-mail: reid@acuvax.acu.edu. Website: http://music.acu.edu/www/iawm/home.html. Estab. 1975. Serves women composers of serious concert music. "Created in January 1995 through the uniting of the International Congress on Women in Music (ICWM), the American Women Composers (AWC) and the International League of Women Composers (ILWC), the IAWM is dedicated to fulfilling the purposes of the three organizations it unites, creating and expanding opportunities for women composers of serious music and documenting the contributions of women musicians, past, present and future. A coalition of professional composers, conductors, performers, musicologists, educators, librarians and lovers of music, men as well as women, the IAWM encourages the dissemination of music through its various projects, including publication of the IAWM Journal, the student Search for New Music, recording grants, broadcast series and the International Congresses on Women in Music. An additional annual journal, *Women and Music: A Journal of Gender and Culture* began publication in 1997, and is included in regular membershhip. The IAWM has an electronic mailing list (send message "subscribe" to iawm-request@acuvax.acu.edu) and a website archive. Annual dues: $40 for individuals; $25 for students and seniors; $75 for affiliates (organizations with affiliate board status) and $50 for institutions (libraries)."

‡INTERNATIONAL ASSOCIATION FOR THE ARTS (IAA), P.O. Box 16555, Santa Fe NM 87506-6555. (505)474-7343. Fax: (505)474-7344. President: Susan Pond. "We are paralegals dedicated to providing self-help to songwriters and music companies. We specialize in tracking and collecting foreign royalties. We also provide a variety of self-help services relating to the music industry." Membership fee: $50/year (songwriters), $75/year (music companies).

INTERNATIONAL BLUEGRASS MUSIC ASSOCIATION (IBMA), 207 E. Second St., Owensboro KY 42303. (502)684-9025. E-mail: ibma@occ-uky.campus.mci.net. Executive Director: Dan Hays. Estab. 1985. Serves songwriters, musicians and professionals in bluegrass music. "IBMA is a trade association composed of people and organizations involved professionally and semi-professionally in the bluegrass music industry, including performers, agents, songwriters, music publishers, promoters, print and broadcast media, local associations, recording manufacturers and distributors. Voting members must be currently or formerly involved in the bluegrass industry as full or part-time professionals. A songwriter attempting to become professionally involved in our field would be eligible. We promote the bluegrass music industry and unity within it. IBMA publishes bimonthly *International Bluegrass*, holds an annual trade show/convention in the fall, represents our field outside the bluegrass music community, and compiles and disseminates databases of bluegrass related resources and organizations. The primary value in this organization for a songwriter is having current information about the bluegrass music field and contacts with other songwriters, publishers, musicians, and record companies." Offers social outings, workshops, liability insurance, rental car discounts, consultation and databases of record companies, radio stations, press, organizations and gigs. Applications accepted year-round. Membership fee: for a non-voting patron $25/year; for an individual voting professional $50/year; for an organizational voting professional $125/year.

INTERNATIONAL SONGWRITERS ASSOCIATION LTD., 37b New Cavendish St., London WI **England**. (0171)486-5353. Membership Department: Anna M. Sinden. Serves songwriters and music publishers. "The ISA headquarters is in Limerick City, Ireland, and from there it provides its members with assessment services, copyright services, legal and other advisory services and an investigations service, plus a magazine for one yearly fee. Our members are songwriters in more than 50 countries worldwide, of all ages. There are no qualifications, but applicants under 18 are not accepted. We provide information and assistance to professional or semi-professional songwriters. Our publication, *Songwriter*, which was founded in 1967, features detailed exclusive interviews with songwriters and music publishers, as well as directory information of value to writers." Offers competitions, instruction, library and newsletter. Applications accepted year-round. Membership fee for European writers is £19.95; for non-European writers, US $30.

‡IRISH MUSIC RIGHTS ORGANISATION, Copyright House, Pembroke Row, Dublin 2 **Ireland**. Phone: 6614844. Fax: 6763125. E-mail: paula.mcdermott@imro.ie. Manager Membership Services: Paula McDermott. Estab. 1988. "For songwriters, composers and publishers who must have one work which has been recorded and released for sale, or broadcast on radio or television in the past two years." The main purpose of this organization is "the collection and distribution of royalties for the public performance of copyrighted music." Offers newsletter and workshops. Applications accepted year-round.

KERRVILLE MUSIC FOUNDATION INC., P.O. Box 1466, Kerrville TX 78029-1466. (830)257-3600. E-mail: kfest@hilconet.com. Website: http://www.fmp.com/~KerrFest. Executive Director: Rod Kennedy. The Kerrville Music Foundation was "founded in 1975 for the recognition and promotion of original music and has awarded more than $27,000 to musicians over the last 24 years through open competitions designed to recognize and encourage excellence in songwriting. Annually, 32 new folk finalists are selected to sing their 2 songs entered and 6 new folk Award Winners receive $150 prize money each and are invited to share 20 minutes of their songs at the Kerrville Folk Festival with one or more selected to perform on the main stage the next year." Opportunities include: The New Folk Concerts for Emerging Songwriters at the Kerrville Folk Festival (do not send entries without requesting complete rules first.) Also offers booking and management seminar. A three-day intensive with four of the nation's outstanding managers and agents working in the folk music field, the seminar includes 12 hours of booking seminars and discussions; 12 hours of management seminars and discussions; 3 lunches; free camping at Quiet Valley Ranch during the Kerrville Folk Festival three weekdays in June. Call (830)257-3600 to receive information.

KNOXVILLE SONGWRITERS ASSOCIATION, P.O. Box 603, Knoxville TN 37901. Estab. 1982. Serves songwriters of all ages. "Some have been members since 1982, others are beginners. Members must be interested in learning the craft of songwriting. Not only a learning organization but a support group of songwriters who want to learn what to do with their song after it has been written. We open doors for aspiring writers. The primary benefit of membership is to supply information to the writer on how to write a song. Eight members have received major cuts." Offers video showcases, instruction, lectures, library, newsletter, performance opportunities, evaluation services and workshops. Applications accepted year-round. Membership fee: $30/year.

THE LAS VEGAS SONGWRITERS ASSOCIATION, P.O. Box 42683, Las Vegas NV 89116-0683. (702)223-7255. President: Betty Kay Miller. Estab. 1980. "We are an educational, nonprofit organization dedicated to improving the art and craft of the songwriter. We offer quarterly newsletters, monthly information meetings, workshops three times a month and quarterly seminars with professionals in the music business." Dues: $20/year. Members must be at least 18 years of age.

LOS ANGELES MUSIC NETWORK, P.O. Box 8934, Universal City CA 91618-8934. (818)769-6095. E-mail: lamnetwork@aol.com. Estab. 1988. "Ours is an association of record industry professionals, i.e., people who work at record companies, in publishing, management, entertainment law, etc. Members are ambitious and interested in advancing their careers. We prefer people who are employed full-time in some capacity in the record business, not so much singers and songwriters because there already exist so many organizations to meet and promote their needs. LAMN is an association created to promote career advancement, communication and continuing education among record industry professionals and top executives. LAMN sponsors industry events and educational panels held bi-monthly at venues in the Hollywood area." Offers instruction, newsletter, lectures, seminars, record industry job listings. See our website for current job listings and a calendar of upcoming events at http://www.iuma.com/LAMN. Applications accepted year-round. Membership fee is $75.

THE LOS ANGELES SONGWRITERS SHOWCASE (LASS), now part of the National Academy of Songwriters. See their listing in this section.

LOUISIANA SONGWRITERS ASSOCIATION, P.O. Box 80425, Baton Rouge LA 70898-0425. (504)924-0804. E-mail: pvida@intersurf.com. Website: http://www.tyrell.net/~pvida/lsa. Chairman: Pete Cicero. Vice President of Membership: Martha Boutwell. Serves songwriters. "LSA has been organized to educate songwriters in all areas of their trade, and promote the art of songwriting in Louisiana. We are of course honored to have a growing number of songwriters from other states join LSA and fellowship with us. LSA membership is open to people interested in songwriting, regardless of age, musical ability, musical preference, ethnic background, etc. One of our goals is to work together as a group to establish a line of communication with industry professionals in order to develop a music center in our area of the country. LSA offers competitions, lectures, library, newsletter, directory, marketing, performance opportunities, workshops, discounts on various music-related books and magazines, discounts on studio time, and we are developing a service manual that will contain information on music related topics, such as copyrighting, licensing, etc." Also offers regular showcases in Baton Rouge and New Orleans. General membership dues: $25/year.

MANITOBA AUDIO RECORDING INDUSTRY ASSOCIATION (MARIA), 221B-100 Arthur St., Winnipeg Manitoba R3B 1H3 **Canada**. (204)942-8650. Fax: (204)956-5780. Website: http://www.ivideo.mb.ca/maria. Executive Director: Gaylene Dempsey. Estab. 1987. Organization consists of "songwriters, producers, agents, musicians, managers, retailers, publicists, radio, talent buyers, media, record labels, etc. (no age limit, no skill level minimum). Must have interest in the future of Manitoba's sound recording industry." The main purpose of this organization is "to foster growth in all areas of Manitoba's sound recording industry." Offers newsletter, lectures, directory of Manitoba's music industry, workshops and performance opportunities; also presents demo critiquing sessions. MARIA also presents the All Indie Weekend conference and festival. Applications accepted year-round. Membership fee: $25 (Canadian funds).

MEET THE COMPOSER, 2112 Broadway, Suite 505, New York NY 10023. (212)787-3601. E-mail: mtc@panix.com. Estab. 1974. "Meet the Composer serves all American composers working in all styles of music, at every career stage, through a variety of grant programs and information resources. A nonprofit organization, Meet The Composer raises money from foundations, corporations, individual patrons and government sources and designs programs that support all genres of music—from folk, ethnic, jazz, electronic, symphonic, and chamber to choral, music theater, opera and dance. Meet The Composer awards grants for composer fees to non-profit organizations that perform, present, or commission original works. This is not a membership organization; all composers are eligible for support. Meet the Composer was founded in 1974 to foster the creation and performance of music by American composers and to broaden the audience for music of our time." Offers grant programs and information services. Deadlines vary for each grant program.

MEMPHIS SONGWRITERS' ASSOCIATION, 1494 Prescott St., Memphis TN 38111. (901)744-4121. Fax: (901)743-4987. President: David Edmaiston. Estab. 1973. "MSA is a nonprofit songwriters organization serving songwriters nationally. Our mission is to dedicate our services on a monthly basis to promote, advance, and help songwriters in the composition of music, lyrics and songs; to work for better conditions in our profession; and to secure and protect the rights of MSA songwriters. We offer a correspondence course for all members outside of Memphis. MSA provides a monthly Basic Lyric Writing Course for beginners with a focus on commercial songwriting. We also supply copyright forms, pitch sheets and a collaborator's guide. We offer critique sessions for advanced writers at our monthly meetings. We also have monthly jam sessions to encourage creativity, networking and co-writing. We host an annual songwriter's seminar and an annual songwriter's showcase, as well as a bi-monthly guest speaker series, which provide education, competition and entertainment for the songwriter. In addition, our members receive a monthly newsletter to keep them informed of MSA activities, demo services and opportunities in the songwriting field." Annual fee: $35.

MICHIGAN SONGWRITERS ASSOCIATION, 28935 Flanders Dr., Warren MI 48093. (810)831-1380. Estab. 1990. Serves songwriters, musicians, artists and beginners. "Members are from NY, IL, MI, OH, etc. with interests in country, pop, rock and R&B. The main purpose of this organization is to educate songwriters, artists and musicians in the business of music." MSA offers performance opportunities, evaluation services, instruction, quarterly newsletter and 4 workshops/year. Applications accepted year-round. Membership fee: $40/year. Newsletter subscription available for $15/year.

MIDWESTERN SONGWRITERS ASSOCIATION, 238 Eldon Ave., Columbus OH 43204. (614)279-1892. President: Dean Martin. Estab. 1978. Serves songwriters. All interested songwriters are eligible—either amateur or professional residing in the Midwestern region of US. Main purpose is the education of songwriters in the basics of their craft. Offers competitions, instruction, lectures, library, newsletter, monthly tip sheet, social outings and workshops. Applications accepted year-round. Membership fee is $20/year, pro-rated at $5 per calendar quarter (March, June, September, December).
Tips: "We do not refer songwriters to publishers or artists—we are strictly an educational organization."

MINNESOTA ASSOCIATION OF SONGWRITERS, P.O. Box 581816, Minneapolis MN 55458. (612)649-4636. Website: http://www.isc.net/mas. President: Joe Schreifels. "Includes a wide variety of members, ranging in age from 18 to 60; types of music are very diverse ranging from alternative rock to contemporary Christian; skill levels range from newcomers to songwriting to writers with published material and songs on CDs in various parts of the country. Main requirement is an interest in songwriting—although most members come from the Minneapolis-St. Paul area, others come in from surrounding cities and nearby Wisconsin. Some members are fulltime musicians, but most represent a wide variety of occupations. MAS is a nonprofit community of songwriters which informs, educates, inspires, and assists its members in the art and business of songwriting." Offers instruction, newsletter, lectures, library, workshops, performance opportunities, evalutation services, MAS compilation CDs and bimonthly meetings. Applications accepted year-round. Membership fee: $25.

Tips: "Through a monthly newsletter and announcements at bimonthly meetings, members are kept current on resources and opportunities. Original works are played at meetings and are critiqued by the group. Through this process, writers hone their skills and gain experience and confidence in submitting their works to others. Members vote to endorse the songs critiqued at meetings. The MAS assists writers of endorsed songs by selectively marketing the compositions and by providing access to an expanding pool of industry contacts."

‡MISSOURI SOCIETY OF SONGWRITERS AND MUSICIANS, HCR1 Box 157E, Eminence MO 65466. (573)226-5620. Co-Founders: Susan Brinkley and David Brinkley. Estab. 1995. "Members live all over Missouri and range in age from 15 to 77. They include amateur and professional songwriters and musicians as well as recording studio owners, music instructors, booking agents, managers, venue owners, video producers, music publishers, radio personnel and record producers. We have several members who have recently self-released CDs. Out-of-state members are welcome—anyone with an interest in the music industry is invited to join. Those unable to travel to monthly meetings will still benefit from joining: our monthly newsletter is full of insider tips, industry information, and interviews with today's singer/songwriters and industry professionals. Each issue also contains an in-depth recap of the previous meeting's guest speaker's presentation. We offer members a great opportunity to network and share knowledge with colleagues from all over the state in a friendly, creative atmosphere. Our monthly meetings in centrally located Rolla are held on the first Saturday of each month. Guest speakers have ranged from recording studio owners to voice instructors to singer/songwriters with gold records. Our Songwriter's Workshops allow members to play an original work (live or demo cassette) and receive constructive feedback and criticism from a supportive audience of their peers." Offers competitions, instruction, newsletter, lectures, library, workshops, performance opportunities, evaluation services, networking and discounts. Send $1 for a sample newsletter. Membership fee: $27/year; $20/year out-of-state.

Tips: "One of the goals of MSSM is to gain recognition and attract the attention of music industry professionals, including publishers and producers, from around the country. There is an incredible amount of talent in Missouri, and by coming together we can create a strong enough voice to be heard from L.A. to Nashville and beyond. MSSM also gives songwriters and musicians in rural areas a chance to meet one another."

MISSOURI SONGWRITERS ASSOCIATION, INC., 693 Green Forest Dr., Fenton MO 63026. (314)343-6661. President: John G. Nolan, Jr. Serves songwriters and musicians. No eligibility requirements. "The MSA (a non-profit organization founded in 1979) is a tremendously valuable resource for songwriting and music business information outside of the major music capitals. Only with the emphasis on education can the understanding of craft and the utilization of skill be fully realized and in turn become the foundation for the ultimate success of MSA members. Songwriters gain support from their fellow members when they join the MSA, and the organization provides 'strength in numbers' when approaching music industry professionals. As a means toward its goals the organization offers: (1) an extremely informative newsletter; (2) Annual Songwriting Contest; prizes include CD and/or cassette release of winners, publishing contract, free musical merchandise and equipment, free recording studio time, plaque or certificate; (3) Annual St. Louis Original Music Celebration featuring live performances, recognition, showcase, radio simulcast, videotape for later broadcast and awards presentation; (4) seminars on such diverse topics as creativity, copyright law, brainstorming, publishing, recording the demo, craft and technique, songwriting business, collaborating, etc.; (5) workshops including song evaluation, establishing a relationship with publishers, hit song evaluations, the writer versus the writer/artist, the marriage of collaborators, the business side of songwriting, lyric craft, etc; (6) services such as collaborators referral, publisher contacts, consultation, recording discounts, musicians referral, library, etc. The Missouri Songwriters Association belongs to its members and what a member puts into the organization is returned dynamically in terms of information, education, recognition, support, camaraderie, contacts, tips, confidence, career development, friendships and professional growth." Applications accepted year round. Tax deductible dues: $50/year.

MUSICIANS CONTACT SERVICE, P.O. Box 788, Woodland Hills CA 91365. (818)347-8888. E-mail: mcs@westworld.com. Website: http://www.musicianscontact.com. Estab. 1969. "A referral service for bands and musicians seeking each other. Job openings updated daily on 24-hour hotline. Bands and collaborators phone in to hear voice classified ads of available players, many with demo tapes."

NASHVILLE SONGWRITERS ASSOCIATION INTERNATIONAL (NSAI), 15 Music Square W., Nashville TN 37203. (615)256-3354. Purpose: a not-for-profit service organization for both aspiring and professional songwriters in all fields of music. Membership: Spans the United States and several foreign countries. Songwriters may apply in one of four annual categories: Active ($70—for songwriters who have at least one song contractually signed to a publisher affiliated with ASCAP, BMI or SESAC); Associate ($70—for songwriters who are not yet published or for anyone wishing to support songwriters); Student ($35—for full-time college students or for students of an accredited senior high school); Professional ($100—for songwriters who derive their primary source of income from songwriting or who are generally recognized as such by the professional songwriting community). Membership benefits: music industry information and advice, song evaluations by mail, quarterly newsletter, access to industry professionals through weekly Nashville workshop and several annual events, regional workshops, use of office facilities, discounts on books and blank audio cassettes, discounts on NSAI's three annual instructional/awards events. There are also "branch" workshops of NSAI. Workshops must meet certain standards and are accountable to NSAI. Interested coordinators may apply to NSAI.

• For more information, see the interview with NSAI workshop coordinator Jim Melko in the 1997 *Songwriter's Market*.

NATIONAL ACADEMY OF POPULAR MUSIC (NAPM), 30 W. 58th St., Suite 411, New York NY 10019-1827. (212)957-9230. Fax: (212)957-9227. E-mail: 73751.1142@compuserve.com. Website: http://www.popularsongs.org. Projects Director: Bob Leone. Estab. 1969. "The majority of our members are songwriters, but also on NAPM's rolls are music publishers, producers, record company executives, music attorneys, and lovers of popular music of all ages. Professional members are affiliated with ASCAP, BMI and/or SESAC; or are employed by music industry firms. Associate membership, however, merely requires a completed application and $25 dues. NAPM was formed to determine a variety of ways to celebrate the songwriter (e.g., induction into the Songwriters' Hall of Fame). We also provide educational and networking opportunities to our members through our workshop and showcase programs." Offers newsletter, workshops, performance opportunities and scholarships for excellence in songwriting. Applications accepted year-round. Membership fee: $25.

Tips: "Our priority at this time is to locate a site for the re-establishment of the Songwriters' Hall of Fame Museum in New York City."

NATIONAL ACADEMY OF SONGWRITERS (NAS), 6255 Sunset Blvd., Suite 1023, Hollywood CA 90028. (213)463-7178 or (800)826-7287. E-mail: nassong@aol.com. Executive Director: Lola Thomas-Butler. A nonprofit organization dedicated to the education and protection of songwriters. Estab. 1974. Offers group legal discount; toll free hotline; *Songwriters Musepaper* newspaper with songwriter interviews; collaborators network; song evaluation workshops; song screening sessions; open mics; and more. Also produces the highly acclaimed "Acoustic Underground" Showcase, "Writers In The Round," "Noches Calientes" (Latin music), "A Hip-Hop Kinda Thang" (R&B/hip hop), "Nashville on Fairfax" (country), the annual "Songwriter's Expo" (international songwriters event), annual Lifetime Achievement Awards dinner and the annual "Salute to the American Songwriter." "We offer services to all songwriter members from street-level to superstar: substantial discount on books and tapes, song evaluation through the mail, health and dental insurance program and mail-in publisher pitches for members. Our services provide education in the craft and opportunities to market songs." Membership fees: $95 general; $125 professional (written proof of monies earned from songwriting); $200 gold (RIAA certification gold record or single on a gold album).

NATIONAL ASSOCIATION OF CHRISTIAN ARTISTS AND SONGWRITERS (NACAS), 134 Linda, Houston TX 37069. (800)79-NACAS. E-mail: nacas2@aol.com. Website: http://www.nashville.net/~nacas. President/Founder: Chuck Sugar. Executive Director: Bethany Harrell. Estab. 1990. "All ages and skill levels are welcome." The main purpose of this organization is "to support Christian artists and songwriters by providing education, building relationships and offering exposure to the Christian music industry." Offers newsletters, lectures, workshops, evaluation services and Internet activity. Applications accepted throughout the year. Fee: $25/year (individual), $45/year (groups).

THE NATIONAL ASSOCIATION OF COMPOSERS/USA, P.O. Box 49256, Barrington Station, Los Angeles CA 90049. (310)541-8213. President: Marshall Bialosky. Estab. 1932. Serves songwriters, musicians and classical composers. "We are of most value to the concert hall composer. Members are serious music composers of all ages and from all parts of the country, who have a real interest in composing, performing, and listening to modern concert hall music. The main purpose of our organization is to perform, publish, broadcast and write news about composers of serious concert hall music—mostly chamber and solo pieces. Composers may achieve national notice of their work through our newsletter and concerts, and the fairly rare feeling of supporting a non-commercial music enterprise dedicated to raising the musical and social position of the serious composer." Offers competitions, lectures, performance opportunities, library and newsletter. Applications accepted year-round. Membership fee: $20; $40 for Los Angeles and New York chapter members.

Tips: "99% of the money earned in music is earned, or so it seems, by popular songwriters who might feel they owe the art of music something, and this is one way they might help support that art. It's a chance to foster fraternal solidarity with their less prosperous, but wonderfully interesting classical colleagues at a time when the very existence of serious art seems to be questioned by the general populace."

NEW JERSEY AND PENNSYLVANIA SONGWRITERS ASSOCIATION, 226 E. Lawnside Ave., Westmont NJ 08108. (609)858-3849. President and Founder: Bruce M. Weissberg. Estab. 1985. Serves songwriters and musicians. Members are ages 16-80, representing all types of music from Delaware, Philadelphia and North and South Jersey area. Must be serious about songwriting. Provides networking, information and promotional center for workshops and guest speakers. "Primary value is that it enables musicians to network with other songwriters in the area." Offers lectures, library, newsletter, performance opportunities and workshops. Applications accepted year-round. Membership fee: $30/year (single), $35/year (band). "Our group is always interested in new ideas, new interested guest speakers and a true professional type of atmosphere."

NORTH FLORIDA CHRISTIAN MUSIC WRITERS ASSOCIATION, P.O. Box 61113, Jacksonville FL 32236. (904)786-2372. President: Jackie Hand. Estab. 1974. "Members are people from all walks of life who promote Christian music—not just composers or performers, but anyone who wants to share today's message in song with the world. No age limit. Anyone interested in promoting Christian music is invited to join. If you are talented in several areas you might be asked to conduct a training session or workshop. Your expertise is wanted and needed by our group. The group's purpose is to serve God by using our God-given talents and abilities and to assist our fellow songwriters, getting their music in the best possible form to be ready for whatever door God chooses to open for them concerning their music. Members works are included in songbooks published by our organization—also biographies." Offers competitions, performance opportunities, field trips, instruction, newsletter, workshops and critiques. Applications accepted year-round. Membership fee: $15/year, $20 for husband/wife team. Make checks payable to Jackie Hand.
Tips: "If you are serious about your craft, you need fellowship with others who feel the same. A Christian songwriting organization is where you belong if you write Christian songs."

NORTHERN CALIFORNIA SONGWRITERS ASSOCIATION, 855 Oak Grove Ave., Suite 211, Menlo Park CA 94025. (415)327-8296. Fax: (415)327-0301, or (800)FORSONG (California and Nashville only). E-mail: ianncsa@aol.com. Executive Director: Ian Crombie. Serves songwriters and musicians. Estab. 1979. "Our 1,200 members are lyricists and composers from ages 16-80, from beginners to professional songwriters. No eligibility requirements. Our purpose is to provide the education and opportunities that will support our writers in creating and marketing outstanding songs. NCSA provides support and direction through local networking and input from Los Angeles and Nashville music industry leaders, as well as valuable marketing opportunities. Most songwriters need some form of collaboration, and by being a member they are exposed to other writers, ideas, critiquing, etc." Offers annual Northern California Songwriting Conference, "the largest event in northern California. This 2-day event held in September features 16 seminars, 50 screening sessions (over 1,200 songs listened to by industry profesionals) and a sunset concert with hit songwriters performing their songs." Also offers monthly visits from major publishers, songwriting classes, seminars conducted by hit songwriters ("we sell audio tapes of our seminars—list of tapes available on request"), mail-in song-screening service for members who cannot attend due to time or location, a monthly newsletter, monthly performance opportunities and workshops. Applications accepted year-round. Dues: $75/year; $30 extra for industry tipsheet (sent out on a quarterly basis).
Tips: "NCSA's functions draw local talent and nationally recognized names together. This is of a tremendous value to writers outside a major music center. We are developing a strong songwriting community in Northern California. We serve the San Jose, Monterey Bay, East Bay, San Francisco and Sacramento areas and we have the support of some outstanding writers and publishers from both Los Angeles and Nashville. They provide us with invaluable direction and inspiration."

OKLAHOMA SONGWRITERS & COMPOSERS ASSOCIATION, %Humanities Division, Rose State College, 6420 SE 15th St., Midwest City OK 73110. 24 hour info line: (405)949-2938. President: Ann Wilson. Estab. 1983. Serves songwriters, musicians, professional writers, amateur writers, college and university faculty, musicians, poets and others from labor force as well as retired individuals. "A nonprofit, all-volunteer organization sponsored by Rose State College and local music merchants. Providing educational and networking opportunities for songwriters, lyricists, composers and performing musicians. All styles of music. Each month we sponsor workshops, open-mic nights, demo critiques and the *OSCA News*. Throughout the year we sponsor workshops, contests and original music showcases." Applications accepted year-round. Membership fee: $25 for new members, $15 for renewal.

OPERA AMERICA, 1156 15th St., NW, Suite 810, Washington DC 20005-1704. (202)293-4466. E-mail: harris@operaam.org. Website: http://www.operaam.org. Estab. 1970. Members are composers, musicians and opera/music theater producers. "OPERA America maintains an extensive library of reference books and domestic and foreign music periodicals, and the most comprehensive operatic archive in the United States. OPERA America draws on these unique resources to supply information to its members." Offers conferences. Publishes directories of opera/music theater companies in the US and Canada. Publishes directory of opera and musical performances world-wide and US. Applications accepted year-round. Membership fee is on a sliding scale.

‡OUTMUSIC, P.O. Box 1575, New York NY 10013-1575. (212)330-9197. E-mail: outmusic@nycnet.com. Co-Chair-Membership: Frank Grimaldi. Estab. 1990. "OUTMUSIC is comprised of gay men and lesbians in their 20s, 30s and 40s. They represent all different musical styles from rock to classical. Many are writers of original material. We are open to all levels of accomplishment—professional, amateur, and interested industry people. The only requirement for membership is an interest in the growth and visibility of music and lyrics created by the gay and lesbian community. We supply our members with support and networking opportunities. In addition, we help to encourage artists to bring their work 'OUT' into the world." Offers newsletter, lectures, workshops, performance opportunities, networking, industry leads and monthly open mikes. Applications accepted year-round. Membership fee: $25/year.
Tips: "OUTMUSIC has spawned The Gay Music Guide, The Gay and Lesbian American Music Awards (GLAMA), several compilation albums and many independent recording projects."

PACIFIC MUSIC INDUSTRY ASSOCIATION, 400-177 W. Seventh Ave., Vancouver, British Columbia V5Y 1L8 **Canada**. (604)873-1914. Fax: (604)876-4104. E-mail: ellieo@pmia.org. Website: http://www.pmia.org. Executive Director: Ellie O'Day. Estab. 1990. Serves "mostly young adults and up from semi-pro to professional. Writers, composers, performers, publishers, engineers, producers, broadcasters, studios, retailers, manufacturers, managers, publicists, entertainment lawyers and accountants, etc. Must work in some area of music industry." The main purpose of this organization is "to promote B.C. music and music industry; stimulate activity in B.C industry; promote communication and address key issues." Offers competitions, newsletters, monthly managers forum, library and workshops. Applications accepted year-round. Membership fee: $50 Canadian (plus 7% sales tax).
Tips: "We also administer the Pacific Music/Fraser MacPherson Music Scholarship Fund for young B.C. instrumentalists (up to age 25). The fund awards $2,000 bursaries to further their music education."

PACIFIC NORTHWEST SONGWRITERS ASSOCIATION, P.O. Box 98564, Seattle WA 98198. (206)824-1568. "PNSA is a nonprofit organization, serving the songwriters of the Puget Sound area since 1977. Members have had songs recorded by national artists on singles, albums, videos and network television specials. Several have released their own albums and the group has done an album together. For only $35 per year, PNSA offers monthly workshops, a quarterly newsletter, free legal advice and direct contact with national artists, publishers, producers and record companies. New members are welcome and good times are guaranteed. And remember, the world always needs another great song!"

‡THE PHILADELPHIA SONGWRITERS FORUM, 332 Eastwood Ave., Feasterville PA 19053. Phone/fax: (215)953-0952. E-mail: a1foster@aol.com. Chairman: Allen Foster. Estab. 1986. Membership consists of all ages and levels; an interest in songwriting is the common bond. The main purpose of this organization is to provide support and instruction for songwriters. Offers instruction, newsletter, lectures, workshops and performance opportunities. Applications accepted year-round. Membership fee: $10/year.

PITTSBURGH SONGWRITERS ASSOCIATION, 408 Greenside Ave., Canonsburg PA 15317. Website: http://trfn.clpgh.org/psa. President: Deborah J. Berwyn. Estab. 1983. Serves songwriters. "Any age group is welcome. Current members are from mid-20s to mid-50s. All musical styles and interests are welcome. Country and pop predominate the current group; some folk, jazz, instrumental, dance, rock and R&B also. Our organization wants to serve as a source of quality material for publishers and other industry professionals. We assist members in developing their songs. Also, we provide a support group for area songwriters, showcases, collaboration opportunities, instruction, industry guests, library and social outings. Annual dues: $30. We have no initiation fee." Interested parties please call Van Stragand at (412)751-9584.

POP RECORD RESEARCH, 10 Glen Ave., Norwalk CT 06850. Director: Gary Theroux. Estab. 1962. Serves songwriters, musicians, writers, researchers and media. "We maintain archives of materials relating to music, TV and film, with special emphasis on recorded music (the hits and hitmakers 1877-present): bios, photos, reviews, interviews, discographies, chart data, clippings, films, videos, etc." Offers library and clearinghouse for accurate promotion/publicity to biographers, writers, reviewers, the media. Offers programming, annotation and photo source for reissues or retrospective album collections on any artist (singers, songwriters, musicians, etc.), also music consultation services for film or television projects. "There is no charge to include publicity, promotional or biographical materials in our archives. Artists, writers, composers, performers, producers, labels and publicists are always invited to add or keep us on their publicity/promotion mailing list with career data, updates, new releases and reissues of recorded performances, etc. Fees are assessed only for reference use by researchers, writers, biographers, reviewers, etc. Songwriters and composers (or their publicists) should keep or put us on their publicity mailing lists to ensure that the information we supply others on their careers, accomplishments, etc. is accurate and up-to-date."

PORTLAND SONGWRITERS ASSOCIATION, 1920 N. Vancouver, Portland OR 97227. (503)727-9072. E-mail: psa@teleport.com. Website: http://www.teleport.com/~psa/. Estab. 1991. President: Steve Cahill. "The PSA is a nonprofit organization providing education and opportunities that will assist writers in creating and marketing their songs. The PSA offers an annual National Songwriting Contest, monthly workshops, songwriter showcases, special performance venues, discounted legal services and seminars by music industry pros." Annual dues: $35. Associate memberships: $15 (no eligibility requirements).
Tips: "Although most of our members are from the Pacific Northwest, we offer services that can assist songwriters anywhere. Our goal is to provide information and contacts to help songwriters grow artistically and gain access to publishing, recording and related music markets. For more information, please call or write."

RHODE ISLAND SONGWRITERS' ASSOCIATION (RISA), P.O. Box 1149, Annex Station, Providence RI 02901-1149. (401)461-7245. E-mail: risa@chowda.com. Co-Chairs: Steve Valentine and Peter Hail. Founder: Mary Wheelan. Estab. 1993. "Membership consists of novice and professional songwriters. RISA provides opportunities to the aspiring writer or performer as well as the established regional artists who have recordings, are published and perform regularly. The only eligibility requirement is an interest in the group and the group's goals. Non-writers are welcome as well." The main purpose is to "encourage, foster and conduct the art and craft of original musical and/or lyrical composition through education, information, collaboration and performance." Offers instruction, newsletter, lectures, workshops, performance opportunities and evaluation services. Applications accepted year-round. Membership fee: $25/year. "The group holds twice monthly critique sessions; twice monthly performer showcases (one performer featured) at a local coffeehouse; songwriter showcases (usually 6-8 performers); weekly open mikes; and a yearly songwriter festival called 'Hear In Rhode Island,' featuring approximately 50 acts, over two days. Group is also a member group of The North American Folk Alliance."

‡ROCKY MOUNTAIN MUSIC ASSOCIATION, 10 South Broadway, Denver CO 80209-1506. (303)623-6910. Estab. 1987. "We are open to all ages. Members are original musical performers and songwriters who range in skills from amateur to professional. Membership is open to anyone interested in the music industry. The only requirement is submiting an application with appropriate membership dues. The main purpose of the Rocky Mountain Music Association is to encourage and support the development and performance of original music by providing educational programs, broadening public appreciation, facilitating national access and exposure to regional talent and acting as central database for the regional community. The primary benefit of membership is to help in exposing talent and honing skills." Offers competitions, lectures, performance opportunities, evaluation services, newsletter and workshops. Applications accepted year-round. Membership fee: $25 individual, $50 band, $100 business.

SAN DIEGO SONGWRITERS GUILD, 3368 Governor Dr., Suite F-326, San Diego CA 92122. (619)225-2131. Secretary: Randy Fischer. President: HC Markus. Membership/correspondence: Amy Villafranca. Estab. 1982. "Members range from their early 20s to senior citizens with a variety of skill levels. Several members perform and work full time in music. Many are published and have songs recorded. Some are getting major artist record cuts. Most members are from San Diego county. New writers are encouraged to participate and meet others. All musical styles are represented." The purpose of this organization is to "serve the needs of songwriters, especially helping them in the business and craft of songwriting through industry guest appearances." Offers competitions, newsletter, workshops, performance opportunities, in-person song pitches and evaluations by publishers, producers and A&R executives. Applications accepted year-round. Membership dues: $45.
Tips: "Members benefit most from participation in meetings and concerts. Generally, one major meeting held monthly on a Monday evening, at the Red Lion Hotel, Mission Valley, San Diego. Call for meeting details. Can join at meetings."

SAN FRANCISCO FOLK MUSIC CLUB, 885 Clayton, San Francisco CA 94117. (415)661-2217. Website: http://www.c2.org/harmony/Folknik.html. Serves songwriters, musicians and anyone who enjoys folk music. "Our members range from age 2 to 80. The only requirement is that members enjoy, appreciate and be interested in sharing folk music. As a focal point for the San Francisco Bay Area folk music community, the SFFMC provides opportunities for people to get together to share folk music, and the newsletter *The Folknik* disseminates information. We publish 2 songs by our members an issue (6 times a year) in our newsletter, our meetings provide an opportunity to share new songs, and at our camp-outs there are almost always songwriter workshops." Offers library, newsletter, informal performance opportunities, annual free folk festival, social outings and workshops. Applications accepted year-round. Membership fee: $7/year.

SESAC INC., 421 W. 54th St., New York NY 10019. (212)586-3450; 55 Music Square East, Nashville TN 37203. (615)320-0055. Website: http://sesac.com. President and Chief Operating Officer: Bill Velez. Serves writers and publishers in all types of music who have their works performed by radio, television, nightclubs, cable TV, etc. Purpose of organization is to collect and distribute performance royalties to all active affiliates. "Prospective affiliates are requested to present a demo tape of their works which is reviewed by our Screening Committee." For possible affiliation, call Nashville or New York for appointment.

SOCIETY OF COMPOSERS, AUTHORS AND MUSIC PUBLISHERS OF CANADA (SOCAN), Head Office: 41 Valleybrook Dr., Don Mills, Ontario M3B 2S6 **Canada**. (416)445-8700, (800)55 SOCAN. Fax: (416)445-7108. General Manager: Michael Rock. The purpose of the society is to collect music user license fees and distribute performance royalties to composers, lyricists, authors and music publishers. The SOCAN catalogue is licensed by ASCAP, BMI and SESAC in the US.

‡SOCIETY FOR THE PROMOTION OF NEW MUSIC (SPNM), Francis House, Francis St., London SW1P 1DE **United Kingdom**. Phone: (+44)1718289696. Fax: (+44)1719319928. Administrator: Peter Craik. Executive Director: Cathy Graham. Estab. 1943. "All ages and backgrounds are welcome, with a common interest in the innovative and unexplored. We enable new composers to hear their works performed by top-class professionals in quality venues." Offers newsletter, lectures, workshops, special offers and concerts. Annual selection procedure, deadline July 31. "SPNM administrates ISCM British section (International Society of Contemporary Music), whose World Music Days 1998 will be in Manchester, UK. It also manages the Chagrin Fund which supplies funds for mechanical reproduction and binding of scores, parts and types for first performances. Details on request." Other calls for specific events throughout year. Membership fee: Ordinary: £15 sterling, concessions: £5, friend: £25.
Tips: "Most calls for pieces are restricted to those living and/or studying in UK/Ireland, or to British composers living overseas."

SODRAC INC., 759 Square Victoria, Suite 420, 759, Montreal, Quebec H2Y 2J7 **Canada**. (514)845-3268. Fax: (514)845-3401. E-mail: sodrac@login.net. Membership Department: George Vuotto. Estab. 1985. "In Canada, SODRAC represents the musical repertoire of about forty countries." Serves those with an interest in songwriting and music publishing no matter what their age or skill level is. "Members must have written or published at least one musical work that has been reproduced on an audio (CD, cassettte, LP) or audio-visual support (TV, video). The main purpose of this organization is to administer the reproduction rights of its members: author/composers and publishers. The new member will benefit of a society working to secure his reproduction rights (mechanicals)." Applications accepted year-round. "There is no membership fee or annual dues. SODRAC retains a commission currently set at 10% for amounts collected in Canada and 5% for amounts collected abroad. SODRAC is the only Reproduction Rights Society in Canada where both songwriters and music publishers are represented, directly and equally."

THE SONGWRITERS ADVOCATE (TSA), 47 Maplehurst Rd., Rochester NY 14617. (716)266-0679. E-mail: jerrycme@aol.com. Director: Jerry Englerth. "TSA is a nonprofit educational organization that is striving to fulfill the needs of the songwriter. We offer opportunities for songwriters which include song evaluation workshops to help songwriters receive an objective critique of their craft. TSA evaluates tapes and lyric sheets via the mail. We do not measure success on a monetary scale, ever. It is the craft of songwriting that is the primary objective. If a songwriter can arm himself with knowledge about the craft and the business, it will increase his confidence and effectiveness in all his dealings. However, we feel that the songwriter should be willing to pay for professional help that will ultimately improve his craft and attitude." Membership dues: $10/year. Must be member to receive discounts or services provided.

SONGWRITERS & LYRICISTS CLUB, %Robert Makinson, P.O. Box 23304, Brooklyn NY 11202-0066. Director: Robert Makinson. Estab. 1984. Serves songwriters and lyricists. Gives information regard-

INSIDER REPORT

The Songwriters Guild of America: helping songwriters take care of business

George David Weiss

President for the past 15 years of The Songwriters Guild of America, the largest and oldest songwriters' organization in the U.S., George David Weiss has worked since the '70s to protect songwriters' rights and increase their earnings. The efforts of Weiss and others led to the passage of new copyright legislation in 1976 that guaranteed songwriters greater protection from infringement than ever before. And songwriters' royalties on sheet music and record sales have more than doubled since Weiss lobbied his first Washington legislator at a cocktail party in the '70s.

Today, Weiss travels worldwide, especially in Europe and the Far East, working for the business interests of songwriters everywhere. He also stays busy in Washington monitoring legislation that affects songwriters. "Sometimes I feel like I live in Washington more than in my New Jersey home," he says. "We're always involved in another potential problem for songwriters which we have to kill or a new situation in the world where business people are again trying to take advantage of songwriters. The Songwriters Guild has always been an independent association of what we call 'independent contractors.' We join together to fight for ourselves in our business of songwriting."

The Guild originally recruited Weiss as a songwriters' advocate because of his reputation as a respected, award-winning songwriter. Frank Sinatra, Bette Midler, Elvis Presley and Natalie Cole are just a few top artists who have recorded Weiss's songs. Weiss's long list of classic hits includes "Can't Help Falling in Love," Elvis Presley's closing theme song that also was named one of the Most Played Songs of the ASCAP Catalog in the '80s and one of the Ten Most Performed Songs of Movie Music for that same period. The song enjoys continued success in the '90s as a cut by U2's lead singer, Bono, as a worldwide hit for the band UB-40, and on the soundtrack of the movie *Honeymoon in Vegas*. "The Lion Sleeps Tonight," another Weiss-penned classic, has been featured in five films including *The Lion King*, and Weiss's often-recorded "What a Wonderful World" was the theme of *Good Morning Vietnam*.

Weiss's success did not happen without hard work and initiative. While attending the prestigious Julliard School of Music, Weiss's "personal course in songwriting" was to study every piece of sheet music that arrived in his father's New York City music shop. "I would grab sheet music from the racks and amaze myself at the talent of the writers. Studying those songs was like going to school—the themes, the harmonies, the rhymes inspired me and taught me." When Weiss wrote his first mini-composition, an eight-bar

INSIDER REPORT, *Weiss*

introduction to his arrangement of the old standard "Dinah," he says, "the music exploded in me. I knew I had to write songs. That's all I did day and night from then on."

Today, Weiss tells those who want to be songwriters to keep writing. "You don't conquer the world with one or two songs. You have to write 50, 100, 200, 300 songs. And you keep writing because while you are writing you keep getting better and better at your craft, whether you realize it or not."

Once you have a cache of songs, Weiss says, "get some money, make some demos, then go to a music center and stay there for as long as your money holds out. Go from office to office and, the more times they say, 'no, we can't listen to your demo,' the more you come back to those same offices with great professionalism—no nastiness, no demands. Finally, one of the people at an outer office desk may realize you are really serious and give your demo to a boss. This happens more often than you might think."

If your demo finally gets heard and rejected, "you dare not become discouraged. Take it as one person's opinion and continue to write. The point is, you don't give up. You keep saying to yourself, 'The reason I'm doing this is because God gave me talent, and in giving me talent, he gave me the responsibility to hone this craft, to work at it to be better than I am. I must keep trying.' There are enough success stories out there to know that it can happen to you if you only believe in yourself and keep working."

For getting through the tough times and celebrating the good times, Weiss says songwriters' organizations offer the important benefits of community and moral support. "Belonging to any songwriting organization is good because it is like an extension of your family. You need to be together. You need to cry on each other's shoulders. You need to tell each other your problems. And, especially, you need to meet each other creatively to find collaborators."

But, unlike most organizations, says Weiss, The Songwriters Guild of America provides songwriters with the services, activities and protection they need to succeed in the *business* of music. "At the Guild, if you cry on a shoulder and talk to us, we can help you with your problem because we're a business organization in addition to a music organization." Benefits offered by The Guild include: a contract that provides the ultimate protection for songwriters; audits of music publishers' books; a Royalty Collection Plan to assure prompt, accurate payments to writers; a Catalogue Administration Program for the self-publisher, a Copyright Renewal Service; a collaboration service; and numerous seminars, workshops and publications.

Remembering the time when very little was available for songwriters, Weiss says, "I think every songwriter in America should belong to The Songwriters Guild. The added strength of more members makes us even stronger when we go to Washington. By joining us, songwriters are looking at their futures. By giving us more votes in Washington, they help me continue helping them."

—Barbara Kuroff

ing songwriting: creation of songs, reality of market, collaboration, disc jockeys and other contacts. Only requirement is ability to write lyrics or melodies. Beginners are welcome. The primary benefits of membership for the songwriter are opportunities to collaborate and assistance with creative aspects and marketing of songs through publications and advice. Offers newsletter and assistance with lead sheets and demos. Songwriters & Lyricists Club Newsletter will be mailed semi-annually to members. Other publications, such as "Climbing the Songwriting Ladder" and "Roster of Songs by Members," are mailed to new members upon joining. Applications accepted year-round. Dues: $35/year, remit to Robert Makinson. Write with SASE for more information. "Plan and achieve realistic goals. If you have a great song, we'll make every effort to help promote it."

SONGWRITERS AND POETS CRITIQUE, 11599 Coontz Rd., Orient OH 43146. (614)877-1727. Founder/Publicity Director: Ellis Cordle. Estab. 1985. Serves songwriters, musicians, poets, lyricists and performers. Meets second and fourth Friday of every month to discuss club events and critique one another's work. Offers seminars and workshops with professionals in the music industry. Has established Nashville contacts. "We critique mail-in submissions from long-distance members. We have over 200 members from the local area, 16 states, and Canada. Our goal is to provide support, opportunity and community to anyone interested in creating songs or poetry." Applications are accepted year-round. Call or write (please include legal size SASE) for more information. Annual dues: $25.

SONGWRITERS ASSOCIATION OF WASHINGTON, 4200 Wisconsin Ave. NW, Suite 100-137, Washington DC 20016. (301)654-8434. Website: http://www.saw.org. President: Jordan Musen. Estab. 1979. "S.A.W. is a nonprofit organization committed to providing its members with the means to improve their songwriting skills, learn more about the music business and gain exposure in the industry. S.A.W. sponsors various events to achieve this goal, such as workshops, open mikes, song swaps, seminars, meetings, member directory with sound bites, showcases and the Mid-Atlantic song contest. S.A.W. publishes *S.A.W. Notes*, a bimonthly newsletter containing information on the music business, upcoming events around the country, tip sheets and provides free classifieds to its members. Joint membership is available with the Washington Area Music Association. For more information regarding membership write or call."

THE SONGWRITERS GUILD OF AMERICA, 1500 Harbor Blvd, Weehawken NJ 07087-6732. (201)867-7603. E-mail: songnews@aol.com. Website: http://www.songwriters.org. West Coast: Suite 317, 6430 Sunset Blvd., Hollywood CA 90028. (213)462-1108. Nashville: 1222 16th Ave. S., Nashville TN 37203. (615)329-1782. "The Songwriters Guild of America is the nation's largest, oldest, most respected and most experienced songwriters' association devoted exclusively to providing songwriters with the services, activities and protection they need to succeed in the business of music." President: George David Weiss. Executive Director: Lewis M. Bachman. National Projects Director: George Wurzbach. West Coast Regional Director: Aaron Meza. Nashville Regional Director: Debbie McClure. "A full member must be a published songwriter. An associate member is any unpublished songwriter with a desire to learn more about the business and craft of songwriting. The third class of membership comprises estates of deceased writers. The Guild contract is considered to be the best available in the industry, having the greatest number of built-in protections for the songwriter. The Guild's Royalty Collection Plan makes certain that prompt and accurate payments are made to writers. The ongoing Audit Program makes periodic checks of publishers' books. For the self-publisher, the Catalogue Administration Program (CAP) relieves a writer of the paperwork of publishing for a fee lower than the prevailing industry rates. The Copyright Renewal Service informs members a year in advance of a song's renewal date. Other services include workshops in New York and Los Angeles, free Ask-A-Pro sessions with industry pros, critique sessions, collaborator service and newsletters. In addition, the Guild reviews your songwriter contract on request (Guild or otherwise); fights to strengthen songwriters' rights and to increase writers' royalties by supporting legislation which directly affects copyright; offers a group medical and life insurance plan; issues news bulletins with essential information for songwriters; provides a songwriter collaboration service for younger writers; financially evaluates catalogues of copyrights in connection with possible sale and estate planning; operates an estates administration service; and maintains a nonprofit educational foundation (The Songwriters Guild Foundation)."

- See the interview with SGA President George David Weiss in this section.

SONGWRITERS OF OKLAHOMA, P.O. Box 4121, Edmond OK 73083-4121. (405)348-6534. President: Harvey Derrick. Offers information on the music industry: reviews publishing/artist contracts, where and how to get demo tapes produced, presentation of material to publishers or record companies, royalties and copyrights. Also offers information on the craft of songwriting: co-writers, local songwriting organizations, a written critique of lyrics, songs and compositions on tapes as long as a SASE is provided for return of critique. A phone service is available to answer any questions writers, composers or artists may have. All of these services are provided at no cost; there is no membership fee.

SONGWRITERS OF WISCONSIN INTERNATIONAL, P.O. Box 874, Neenah WI 54957-0874. (414)725-1609. E-mail: sowtoner@aol.com. President: Tony Ansems. Estab. 1983. Serves songwriters. "Membership is open to songwriters writing all styles of music. Residency in Wisconsin is recommended but not required. Members are encouraged to bring tapes and lyric sheets of their songs to the meetings,

but it is not required. We are striving to improve the craft of songwriting in Wisconsin. Living in Wisconsin, a songwriter would be close to any of the workshops and showcases offered each month at different towns. The primary value of membership for a songwriter is in sharing ideas with other songwriters, being critiqued and helping other songwriters." Offers competitions, field trips, instruction, lectures, newsletter, performance opportunities, social outings, workshops and critique sessions. Applications accepted year-round. Membership dues: $20/year.
Tips: "Songwriters of Wisconsin now offers three critique meetings each month. For information call: Fox Valley chapter, Dana Erlandson (414)435-9052; Milwaukee chapter, Joe Warren (414)475-0314; La Crosse chapter, Jeff Cozy (608)781-4391."

THE SONGWRITERS WORKSHOP, P.O. Box 238, Babylon NY 11702-0238. (516)969-0375. President: Sal Rainone. Estab. 1975. "Members are all ages (18 and up) with an interest in writing songs (music or lyrics) and production of demos and professional recordings." The main purpose of this organization is to help songwriters (and lyric writers) to perfect songs and introducing lyric writers to music writers to form collaborations. Assistance at no charge for copyright information, free evaluation of lyrics/music and lyrics and introduction to publishers. Offers newsletter, lectures, workshops, evaluation services and production of demo recordings. Applications accepted year-round. No dues required—only SASE for assistance.
Tips: "We have assisted many songwriters in perfecting and having songs accepted and recorded by publishers and record companies."

‡SOUTHERN SONGWRITERS GUILD, INC., P.O. Box 6817, Shreveport LA 71136-6817. (318)798-1122. Founders/Co-Executive Directors: Ray and Rita Horton. Estab. 1984. "The purpose of the Southern Songwriters Guild is to promite the art and craft of songwriting through all available educational and charitable means and to endeavor to uphold its objectives in harmony with society. SSG hosts an annual Awards Banquet that features winners of our 'Song of the Year' contest that provides cash prizes; and to induct new members into 'SSG Songwriters Hall of Fame,' who may have local or regional roots in either heritage or career development. SSG has monthly Board and General Membership meetings aimed toward education. Fundraiser benefits are occasionally conducted for specific needs. A small educational scholarship program is infrequently available for those who meet certain criteria for need and purpose. SSG offers an opportunity to network or collaborate with other songwriters and songwriter organizations and encourages dual or multi-memberships with other organizations whose purposes are consistent with those of SSG. A newsletter is distributed to the membership and to non-member related entities. Performance opportunities, open mike sessions, songwriting workshops, clinics, annual family picnic, Christmas party and song critiques are additional functions. Please send SASE for membership application or other information." Applications accepted year-round. Membership fee: $30/year, $25 for each additional family member, $100 for organization or institution.

SOUTHWEST VIRGINIA SONGWRITERS ASSOCIATION, P.O. Box 698, Salem VA 24153. (540)586-2696. President: Mike Pearrell. Estab. 1981. 80 members of all ages and skill all levels, mainly country, gospel and rock but other musical interests too. "Prospective members are subject to approval by SVSA Board of Directors. The purpose of SVSA is to increase, broaden and expand the knowledge of each member and to support, better and further the progress and success of each member in songwriting and related fields of endeavor." Offers performance opportunities, evaluation services, instruction, newsletter, workshops, monthly meetings and monthly newsletter. Application accepted year-round. Membership fee: $15 one time fee (initiation); $12/year, due in January.

THE TENNESSEE SONGWRITERS INTERNATIONAL, P.O. Box 2664, Hendersonville TN 37077-2664. TSA Hotline: (615)969-5967. (615)824-4555. Fax: (615)822-2048. Executive Director: Jim Sylvis. Serves songwriters. "Our membership is open to all ages and consists of both novice and experienced professional songwriters. The only requirement for membership is a serious interest in the craft and business of songwriting. Our main purpose and function is to educate and assist the songwriter, both in the art/craft of songwriting and in the business of songwriting. In addition to education, we also provide an opportunity for camaraderie, support and encouragement, as well a chance to meet co-writers. We also critique each others' material and offer suggestions for improvement, if needed. We offer the following to our members: Informative monthly newsletters; 'Pro-Rap'—once or twice a month a key person from the music industry addresses our membership on their field of specialty. They may be writers, publishers, producers and sometimes even the recording artists themselves; 'Pitch-A-Pro'—we schedule a publisher, producer or artist who is currently looking for material to come to our meeting and listen to songs pitched by our members; Annual Awards Dinner—honoring the most accomplished of our TSAI membership during the past year; Tips—letting our members know who is recording and how to get their songs to the right people. Other activities—a TSAI summer picnic, parties throughout the year, and opportunities to participate in music industry-related charitable events, such as the annual Christmas For Kids, which the TSAI proudly supports." Applications accepted year-round. Membership runs for one year from the date you join. Membership fee is $35/year.

‡TEXAS MUSIC OFFICE, P.O. Box 13246, Austin TX 78711. (512)463-6666. Fax: (512)463-4114. E-mail: music@governor.texas.gov. Director: Casey Monahan. Estab. 1990. "The main purpose of the Texas Music Office is to promote the Texas music industry and Texas music, and to assist music professionals around the world with information about the Texas market. The Texas Music Office serves as a clearinghouse for Texas music industry information using their seven databases: Texas Music Industry (5,800 Texas music businesses in 94 music business categories); Texas Music Events (700 Texas music events); Texas Talent Register (900 Texas recording artists); Texas Radio Stations (733 Texas stations); US Record Labels; Classical Texas (detailed information for all classical music organizations in Texas); and International (450 foreign businesses interested in Texas music). Provides referrals to Texas music businesses, talent and events in order to attract new business to Texas and/or to encourage Texas businesses and individuals to keep music business in-state. Serves as a liaison between music businesses and other government offices and agencies. Publicizes significant developments within the Texas music industry." Publishes the *Texas Music Industry Directory* (see the Publications of Interest section for more information).

TORONTO MUSICIANS' ASSOCIATION, 101 Thorncliffe Park Dr., Toronto Ontario M4H 1M2 **Canada**. (416)421-1020. Fax: (416)421-7011. Executive Assistant: Nancy. Estab. 1887. Serves musicians—*All* musical styles, background, areas of the industry. "Must provide two letters of recommendation from people within the music industry, and be a Canadian citizen (or show proof of immigrant status)." The purpose of this organization is "to unite musicians into one organization, in order that they may, individually and collectively, secure, maintain and profit from improved economic, working and artistic conditions." Offers newsletter. Applications accepted year-round. Membership fee: $235.

TREASURE COAST SONGWRITERS ASSN. (TCSA), P.O. Box 7066, Port St. Lucie FL 34985-7066. E-mail: jwelden@flinet.com. Director: George Boley. Founder/Advisor: Judy Welden. Estab. 1993. A service organization for and about songwriters. Age range of members, 20-85; varying levels of ability, from beginning writer to professional writers with substantial catalogs, publishing track records, radio airplay and releases. General Members—no requirement except desire to write and learn. Professional Members—at least 1 commercially released song, or a substantial marketable catalog, but no commercial releases. Gold Members—at least 1 song on RIAA-certified gold release. Offers competitions, lectures, performance opportunities, evaluation services, instruction, newsletter, workshops and local radio airplay through station-sponsored contests. Applications accepted year-round. Membership fee: $45 general, $60 professional, $100 gold. Those with financial hardship can work as volunteers to entitle them to membership (except for Gold status.)

TULSA SONGWRITERS ASSOCIATION, INC., P.O. Box 254, Tulsa OK 74101-0254. (918)665-3334. President: Don Blevins. Estab. 1983. Serves songwriters and musicians. Members are age 18 and older and have interests in all types of music. Main purpose of the organization is "to create a forum to educate, develop, improve, discover and encourage songwriting in the Tulsa area." Offers competitions, lectures, performance opportunities, field trips, social outings, instruction, newsletter and workshops. Applications accepted year-round. Dues: $30/year, students $15/year.
Tips: "We hold a monthly 'Writer's Night' open to the public for performance of original songs to expose the many talented writers in Tulsa."

UTAH SONGWRITERS ASSOCIATION (USA), P.O. Box 571325, Salt Lake City UT 84157. (801)596-3058. Secretary/Treasurer: Marie Vosgerau. Estab. 1984. "Anyone who is interested in songwriting may join. Primarily we want to promote the craft of songwriting. USA is a support group for songwriters. We distribute information; teach workshops on how to write better songs; showcase members and original material. Provides song analyses ($6 per song with SASE), contest opportunities, seminars with professional music business people. The newsletter, *The Melody Line*, gives valuable information on contests, publishers looking for material, tips, etc. Sponsors the Intermountain Songwriting Contest and Songwriting Seminar. "For a copy of our book of songwriting tips, *Tricks of The Trade*, send $8." Applications accepted year-round. Membership fee: $25 per member/year or $30 for a family membership/year. For contest rules and registration information, send SASE.
Tips: "The USA exchanges newsletters with many songwriting associations across the United States. We welcome any exchange of ideas with other songwriting associations."

VERMONT SONGWRITERS ASSOCIATION, RD 2 Box 277, Underhill VT 05489. (802)899-3787. President: Bobby Hackney. Estab. 1991. "Membership open to anyone desiring a career in songwriting,

or anyone who seeks a supportive group to encourage co-writing, meeting other songwriters, or to continue their songwriting endeavors." Purpose is to give songwriters an opportunity to meet industry professionals at monthly meetings and seminars, to have their works critiqued by peers and to help learn more about the craft and the complete business of songwriting. Offers competitions, instruction, lectures, library, newsletter, performance opportunities and workshops. Applications accepted year-round. Membership fee: $30/year.
Tips: "We are a nonprofit association dedicated to creating opportunities for songwriters. Even though our office address is Underhill, Vermont, our primary place of business is in Jericho, Vermont, where monthly meetings and seminars are held."

VICTORY MUSIC, P.O. Box 7515, Bonney Lake WA 98390. (206)863-6617. E-mail: victory@wolfenet.com. Estab. 1969. All-volunteer organization serves songwriters, audiences and local acoustic musicians of all music styles. Victory Music provides places to play, showcases, opportunities to read about the business and other songwriters, referrals and seminars. Produced 6 albums of NW songwriters. Offers library, magazine, newsletter, performance opportunities, business workshops and music business books. Applications accepted year-round. Membership fee: $20/year single; $50/year business; $28/year couple; $175 lifetime.

VOLUNTEER LAWYERS FOR THE ARTS, One E. 53rd St., 6th Floor, New York NY 10022. (212)319-2910 (Monday-Friday 9:30-4:30 EST). E-mail: vlany@bway.net. Estab. 1969. Serves songwriters, musicians and all performing, visual, literary and fine arts artists and groups. Offers legal assistance and representation to eligible individual artists and arts organizations who cannot afford private counsel. Also sells publications on arts-related issues. In addition, there are affiliates nationwide who assist local arts organizations and artists. Offers conferences, lectures, seminars and workshops. Call for information.
Tips: "VLA now offers a monthly copyright seminar, 'Copyright Basics,' for songwriters and musicians as well as artists in other creative fields."

‡WASHINGTON AREA MUSIC ASSOCIATION, 1690 36th St., NW, Washington DC 20007. (202)338-1134. Fax: (703)237-7923. E-mail: askmike@crosstownarts.com. Website: http://crosstownarts.com. President: Mike Schreibman. Estab. 1985. Serves songwriters, musicians and performers, managers, club owners and entertainment lawyers; "all those with an interest in the Washington music scene. The organization is designed to promote the Washington music scene and increase its visibility. Its primary value to members is its seminars and networking opportunities. Offers lectures, newsletter, performance opportunities and workshops. WAMA sponsors the annual Washington Music Awards (The Wammies) and The Crosstown Jam, our annual showcase of more than 300 artists at 60 venues in the DC area." Applications accepted year-round. Annual dues: $30.

‡WOMEN OF THE MUSIC BUSINESS MENTORING PROGRAM & AWARDS, 325 N. Maple Dr. #510, Beverly Hills CA 90209-5170. (213)464-4300. Fax: (213)467-8468. Contact: Director. Estab. 1996. Membership includes women over 21, music executives and artists. "Currently accepting those in and around the Los Angeles/Southern California area (looking to start programs around the country in the next year) and accepting music industry professionals who fill out applications and meet requirements. Women of the Music Business empowers young (and mature) women to fulfill their unique destiny through community, self-expression and the realization of dreams. Generating partnerships and opportunities between industry and youth, and the access to discovery and leadership." Offers competitions, instruction, newsletter, lectures and performance opportunities. Applications accepted year-round. Membership fee: $40/semi-annual. "Donations are accepted towards our mentoring program, scholarships for students, college tuition program, the enhancement of school music department program (we will purchase instruments and materials for school music departments) and executive field internship program."

Workshops and Conferences

For a songwriter just starting out, conferences and workshops can provide valuable learning opportunities. At conferences, songwriters can have their songs evaluated, hear suggestions for further improvement and receive feedback from music business experts. They are also excellent places to make valuable industry contacts. Workshops can help a songwriter improve his craft and learn more about the business of songwriting. They may involve classes on songwriting and the business, as well as lectures and seminars by industry professionals.

Hundreds of workshops and conferences take place all over the country, from small regional workshops held in someone's living room to large national conferences such as South by Southwest in Austin, Texas, which hosts more than 6,000 industry people, songwriters and performers each year. Many songwriting organizations, from national ones like the Songwriter's Guild of America to small hometown groups, host workshops that offer instruction on just about every songwriting topic imaginable, from lyric writing and marketing strategy to contract negotiation. Conferences provide songwriters the chance to meet one on one with publishing and record company professionals and give performers the chance to showcase their work for a live audience (usually consisting of industry people) during the conference.

There are conferences and workshops that address almost every type of music, offering programs for songwriters, performers, musical playwrights and much more. This section includes national and local workshops and conferences with a brief description of what they offer, when they are held and how much they cost to attend. Write or call any that interest you for further information. To find out what workshops or conferences take place in specific parts of the country, see the Geographic Index at the end of this book.

APPEL FARM ARTS AND MUSIC FESTIVAL, P.O. Box 888, Elmer NJ 08318. (609)358-2472. E-mail: appelarts@aol.com. Website: http://www.ROWAN.edu/~APPEL. Artistic Director: Sean Timmons. Estab. Festival: 1989; Series: 1970. "Our annual open air festival is the highlight of our year-round Performing Arts Series which was established to bring high quality arts programs to the people of South Jersey. Festival includes acoustic and folk music, blues, etc." Past performers have included Randy Newman, Nanci Griffith, Shawn Colvin, Arlo Guthrie, Patty Larkin and John Gorka. In 1996, Appel Farm added a Country Music Festival in September. Past headliners include Ricky Van Shelton, Doug Stone and Marge Calhoun. Programs for songwriters and musicians include performance opportunities as part of Festival and Performing Arts Series. Programs for musical playwrights also include performance opportunities as part of Performing Arts Series. Festival is a one-day event held in June, and Performing Arts Series is held year-round. Both are held at the Appel Farm Arts and Music Center, a 176-acre farm in Southern New Jersey. Up to 20 songwriters/musicians participate in each event. Participants are songwriters, individual vocalists, bands, ensembles, vocal groups, composers, individual instrumentalists and dance/mime/movement. Participants are selected by demo tape submissions. Applicants should send a press packet, demonstration tape and biographical information. Application materials accepted year round. Faculty opportunities are available as part of residential Summer Arts Program for children, July/August.

ARCADY MUSIC FESTIVAL, P.O. Box 780, Bar Harbor ME 04609. (207)288-3151. Executive Director: Dr. Melba Wilson. Estab. 1980. Promotes classical chamber music, chamber orchestra concerts, master classes and a youth competition in Maine. Offers programs for performers. Workshops take place year-round in several towns in Eastern Maine. 30-50 professional, individual instrumentalists participate each year. Performers selected by invitation. "Sometimes we premiere new music by songwriters but usually at request of visiting musician."

ASPEN MUSIC FESTIVAL AND SCHOOL, 2 Music School Rd., Aspen CO 81611. (970)925-3254. Fax: (970)925-5708. E-mail: festival@aspenmusic.org. Website: http://www.aspen.com/musicfestival. Estab. 1949. Promotes classical music by offering programs for composers, including an advanced master class in composition which meets weekly during the nine-week 1997 season. Offers several other music programs as well. School and Festival run June 19 to August 17 in Aspen CO. Participants are amateur and professional composers, individual instrumentalists and ensembles. Send for application. Charges $2,100 for full 9 weeks, $1,400 for one of two 4½ week sessions. Scholarship assistance is available.

BMI-LEHMAN ENGEL MUSICAL THEATRE WORKSHOP, 320 W. 57th St., New York NY 10019. (212)830-2515. Website: http://bmi.com. Director of Musical Theatre: Norma Grossman. Estab. 1961. "BMI is a music licensing company which collects royalties for affiliated writers. We have departments to help writers in jazz, concert, Latin, pop and musical theater writing." Offers programs "to musical theater composers and lyricists. The BMI-Lehman Engel Musical Theatre Workshops were formed in an effort to refresh and stimulate professional writers, as well as to encourage and develop new creative talent for the musical theater." Each workshop meets one afternoon a week for two hours at BMI, New York. Participants are professional songwriters, composers and playwrights. "BMI-Lehman Engel Musical Theatre Workshop Showcase presents the best of the workshop to producers, agents, record and publishing company execs, press and directors for possible option and production." Call for application. Tape and lyrics of 3 compositions required with application. "BMI nows sponsors a jazz composers workshop. For more information call Burt Korall at (212)586-2000."

BROADWAY TOMORROW PREVIEWS, % Broadway Tomorrow Musical Theatre, 191 Claremont Ave., Suite 53, New York NY 10027. Artistic Director: Elyse Curtis. Estab. 1983. Purpose is the enrichment of American theater by nurturing new musicals. Offers series in which composers living in New York City area present scores of their new musicals in concert. 2-3 composers/librettists/lyricists of same musical and 1 musical director/pianist participate. Participants are professional singers, composers and opera/musical theater writers. Submission by recommendation of past participants only. Submission is by audio cassette of music, script if completed, synopsis, cast breakdown, résumé, reviews, if any, acknowledgement postcard and SASE. Participants selected by screening of submissions. Programs are presented in fall and spring with possibility of full production of works presented in concert. No entry fee.

CANADIAN MUSIC WEEK, 5399 Eglinton Ave. W., Suite 301, Toronto Ontario M9C 5K6 **Canada**. (416)695-9236. Fax: (416)695-9239. President: Neill Dixon. Estab. 1985. Offers annual programs for songwriters, composers and performers. Event takes place mid-March in Toronto. 100,000 public, 400 bands and 1,200 delegates participate in each event. Participants are amateur and professional songwriters, vocalists, composers, bands and instrumentalists. Participants are selected by submitting demonstration tape. Send for application and more information. Concerts take place in 25 clubs and 5 concert halls, and 3 days of seminars and exhibits are provided. Fee: $375 (Canadian).

CANADIAN MUSICIAN SEMINARS, 23 Hannover Dr., #7, St. Catharines, Ontario L2W 1A3 **Canada**. (905)641-3471. Fax: (905)641-1648. E-mail: mail@nor.com. Contact: Sue Grierson, special events coordinator. Estab. 1980. Offers programs for songwriters, composers and performers. Offers programs year-round. Held in different locations across Canada and the US. 100-300 songwriters/musicians participate in each event. Participants are amateur and professional songwriters, composers, vocalists, bands and instrumentalists. Contact via phone, fax or e-mail. Fee varies. Offers workshops, roundtables, networking areas and demo critiques.

CHICAGO'S NEW MUSIC FESTIVAL, (formerly Independent Label Festival), 600 S. Michigan Ave., Chicago IL 60605. (312)341-9112. E-mail: indiefest@aol.com. Executive Director: Leopoldo Lastre. Estab. 1993. An annual conference promoting all types of independent music. Offers programs for songwriters, composers and performers, such as seminars, workshops and showcases. Offers showcases year-round. "Workshops take place in the summer, generally July in downtown Chicago (usually in or around Columbia College)." Participants are professional songwriters, bands, composers, individual vocalists and instrumentalists, managers, promoters and professionals in the music industry. Participants are selected by demo tape audition or invitation. Call for submission and registration information. Closing date for submissions is April 30 ($10 submission fee). Registration fee: $95 by March 17, $150 by May 16, $200 by July 18 and $250 walk-up. 10% discount for students and indie labels.

‡CMJ MUSIC MARATHON & MUSIC FEST, 11 Middleneck Rd., Suite 400, Great Neck NY 11021. (516)466-6000. Fax: (516)466-7161. E-mail: mminfo@cmjmusic.com. Website: http://www.cmjmusic.com/marathon/. Estab. 1981. Promotes alternative music of all genres to introduce new artists to the music business and to college radio programmers and music directors. Offers programs for songwriters and performers. Offers programs annually. Event takes place at Lincoln Center, NYC. 7,000 songwriters/musicians participate in each event. Participants are amateur and professional songwriters, vocalists, bands, music business professionals and college radio programmers. Offers daytime panel discussions and seminars. Participants are selected by submitting demonstration tape. Send for application.

CROSSROADS MUSIC EXPO, P.O. Box 41858, Memphis TN 38174-1858. (901)526-4280. Fax: (901)527-8326. Managing Director: Corey Robertson. Event Coordinator: Bob Camp. Estab. 1990. "Crossroads' main purpose is to showcase unsigned music (rock, pop, alternative, country, gospel, singer/songwriter, etc.) to a host of industry executives and reps. In addition to showcasing over 200 acts, Crossroads offers panels, clinics, workshops and networking opportunities. Offers programs for songwriters and performers. Event takes place annually in historic downtown Memphis, TN, in April. Call for dates. Approximately 200 bands are showcased. Participants are songwriters, vocalists, bands and instrumentalists. Participants are selected by demo tape audition. Send for application. Fee: $20.

CUTTING EDGE MUSIC BUSINESS CONFERENCE, 1524 N. Claiborne Ave., New Orleans LA 70119. (504)945-1800. Fax: (504)945-1873. E-mail: 74777.754@compuserve.com. Website: http://www.satchmo.com/cuttingedge/. Director: Eric L. Coger. Estab. 1993. "The conference is a five-day international conference which covers the business and educational aspects of the music industry. As part of the conference, the New Works showcase features over 200 bands and artists from around the country and Canada in showcases of original music. All music genres are represented." Offers programs for songwriters and performers. "Bands and artists should submit material for consideration of entry into the New Works showcase." Event takes place mid-September in New Orleans. 1,000 songwriters/musicians participate in each event. Participants are songwriters, vocalists and bands. Send for application. Deadline: June 1. Fee: $20. "The Music Business Institute offers a month-long series of free educational workshops for those involved in the music industry. The workshops take place each October."

PETER DAVIDSON'S WRITER'S SEMINAR, P.O. Box 497, Arnolds Park IA 51331. Seminar Presenter: Peter Davidson. Estab. 1985. "Peter Davidson's Writer's Seminar is for persons interested in writing all sorts of materials, including songs. Emphasis is placed on developing salable ideas, locating potential markets for your work, copyrighting, etc. The seminar is not specifically for writers of songs, but is very valuable to them, nevertheless." Offers programs year-round. One-day seminar, 9:00 a.m.-4:00 p.m. Event takes place on various college campuses. In even-numbered years offers seminars in Minnesota, Iowa, Nebraska, South Dakota, Kansas, Colorado and Wyoming. In odd-numbered years offers seminars in Minnesota, Iowa, South Dakota, Nebraska, Missouri, Illinois, Arkansas and Tennessee. Anyone can participate. Send SASE for schedule. Deadline: day of the seminar. Fee: $40-59. "All seminars are held on college campuses in college facilities—various colleges sponsor and promote the seminars."

FOLK ALLIANCE ANNUAL CONFERENCE, 1001 Connecticiut Ave. NW, #501, Washington DC 20036. (202)835-3655. Fax: (202)835-3656. E-mail: fa@folk.org. Website: http://www.hidwater.com/folkalliance/. Contact: Phyllis Barney. Estab. 1989. Conference/workshop topics change each year. Conference takes place mid-February and lasts 4 days at a different location each year. 1,000 amateur and professional musicians participate. Offers songwriter critique sessions. Artist showcase participants are songwriters, individual vocalists, bands, ensembles, vocal groups and individual instrumentalists. Participants are selected by demo tape submission. Applicants should write for application form. Closing date for application is May 31. Application fee $15 for members, $50 for non-members. Charges $75 on acceptance. Additional costs vary from year to year. For 1996 the cost was $165 in advance, which coverd 2 meals, a dance, workshops and showcase. Performers' housing is separate for the event, which is usually held in Convention hotel. 1998: Memphis, TN; 1999: Albuquerue, NM.

FOUNDATIONS FORUM/F MUSICFEST, 1133 Broadway #1220, New York NY 10010. (212)645-1360. Fax: (212)645-2607. Website: http://www.themusiczone.com. President: Bob Chiappardi. Vice President: Russ Gerroir. Estab. 1988. "Foundations Forum/The F Musicfest is the only major rock music festival to take place in the greater Los Angeles area, presenting a wide range of signed and unsigned bands encompassing alternative, metal, punk, Americana and pop. The festival brings together the music community from around the world, and we have plenty of opportunities for unsigned artists to get involved through our CD compilation, demo competition, directory, video channel and club showcases. There are also panels on A&R, management, and publishing." Event takes place annually in Hollywood, with over 4,000 songwriters/musicians participating. Registrants include amateur and professional bands, managers, booking agents, record company execs, publishers, equipment manufacturers, lifestyle companies, press and radio. Artists are selected for showcases by submitting demonstration tape. Call for information. Registration fee for 3 days: $195. No submission fee for unsigned band demos.

‡INDEPENDENT MUSIC FEST, 566 LaGuardia Pl., Loeb Room 103, New York NY 10012. (212)998-4987. Fax: (212)995-3163. E-mail: sir7333@is2.nyu.edu. Co-chairs of IMF: Stacy Rink and Molly Templeton. Estab. 1991. "The IMF is a 3-day music conference dedicated to promoting unsigned bands and bands on independent labels. All diferent types of music are encouraged." Offers programs for performers. Event takes place spring at NYU and Greenwich Village area clubs. 150+ bands and 1,000 registrants participate in each event. Participants are amateur and professional bands. Participants are selected by invitation and by submitting demonstration tape. Send for registration application or "send a sample of music and contact information to us by January 15. No submission fee." Deadline: January 15. Registration: early: $10 NYU student, $15 student; $30 general. Late: $30 student; $40 general. Offers panels, listening sessions, exhibition booths and daytime showcases.

JAZZTIMES CONVENTION, 8738 Colesvile Rd., 5th Floor, Silver Spring MD 20910. (301)588-4114. Fax: (301)588-5531. E-mail: jtimes@aol.com. Website: jazzcentralstation.com. Convention Director: Lee Mergner. Estab. 1979. "Brings together entire jazz industry in a series of workshops, panels and showcase performances." Offers programs for performers. Offers programs annually. Event takes place mid-November in the New York City area. 800-1,000 industry professionals participate in each event. Participants are professional vocalists, bands, instrumentalists and industry professionals. Showcase performers are selected by invitation.

KERRVILLE FOLK FESTIVAL, Kerrville Festivals, Inc., P.O. Box 1466, Kerrville TX 78029. (210)257-3600. E-mail: kfest@hilconet.com. Website: http://www.fmp.com/~kerrfest. Founder/President: Rod Kennedy. Estab. 1972. Hosts 3-day songwriters' school, a 3 day advanced songwriters school, a booking and management seminar and New Folk concert competition sponsored by the Kerrville Music Foundation. Programs held in late spring and late summer. Spring festival lasts 18 days and is held outdoors at Quiet Valley Ranch. Around 120 artists participate. Performers are professional songwriters and bands. "Now hosting an annual 'house concert' seminar to encourage the establishment and promotion of monthly house concerts for traveling singers/songwriters to provide additional dates and income for touring." Participants selected by submitting demo, by invitation only. Send cassette, or CD, promotional material and list of upcoming appearances. "Songwriter schools include lunch, experienced professional instructors, camping on ranch and concerts. Rustic facilities—no electrical hookups. Food available at reasonable cost. Audition materials accepted at above address. Kerrville as added an advanced songwriter's school for those who have attended previous Kerrville schools. Also added is a booking and management seminar to teach newcomers and bring additional insight to established agents and managers. These three-day seminars include noon meals, handouts and camping on the ranch. Usually held during Kerrville Folk Festival, first week in June. Write for contest rules, schools and seminars information, and festival schedules."

KLASSIK KOMM, Rottscheidter Str. 6, 42329 Wuppertal **Germany**. Phone: (0202)278310. Fax: (0202)789161. E-mail: klassikkomm@musikkomm.de. Head PR: Andrea Zech. Estab. 1994. Offers programs for songwriters, composers, musical playwrights and performers. Offers programs annually. Events take place in September in Hamburg, Germany. 1,600 songwriters/musicians participate in each event. Participants are amateur and professional songwriters, composers, musical playwrights, vocalists, bands and instrumentalists. Anyone can participate. Send or call for application. Charges fee.

‡MID-ATLANTIC SOUND, SURF & SKATE SYMPOSIUM, 6766G Wrightsville Ave., Suite 214, Wilmington NC 28403. Phone/fax: (910)256-1119 or (212)583-0496. E-mail: juicesss@aol.com. Director: Terri Craft. Estab. 1996. Showcases "all types of rock, punk, alternative country, rockabilly, singer/songwriter and surf music. Consists of three nights of showcasing in eight bars within walking distance in downtown Wilmington. Seminars and panels take place during the day, covering how to survive on your own as a musician, touring information, promoting yourself, getting a record contract, etc." Offers annual programs for performers. Event takes place in June in Wilmington, NC. 3,000-6,000 songwriters/musicians participate in the event. Participants are amateur and professional songwriters, vocalists, composers and bands. Participants are selected by submitting a demo tape. Send for application. Deadline: April. Fee: $10.

MUSIC BUSINESS SOLUTIONS/CAREER BUILDING WORKSHOPS, P.O. Box 230, Astor Station, Boston MA 02123-0266. (617)639-1971. E-mail: success@mbsolutions.com. Website: http://www.mbsolutions.com. Director: Peter Spellman. Estab. 1991. Workshop titles include "How to Succeed in Music Without Overpaying Your Dues," "How to Release an Independent Record" and "Promoting and Marketing Music Toward the Year 2000." Offers programs for music entrepreneurs, songwriters, musical playwrights, composers and performers. Offers programs year-round, annually and bi-annually. Event takes place at various colleges, recording studios, hotels, conferences. 10-100 songwriters/musicians participate in each event. Participants are both amateur and professional songwriters, vocalists, music business professionals, composers, bands, musical playwrights and instrumentalists. Anyone can participate. Call or write (regular or e-mail) for application. Fee: $50-125. "Music Business Solutions offers a number of other services and programs for both songwriters and musicians including: private music career counseling, business plan development and internet marketing; and publication of *Music Biz Insight: Power Reading for Busy Music Professionals*, a quarterly infoletter chock full of music management and marketing tips and resources."

MUSIC WEST, 306-21 Water St., Vancouver B.C. V6B 1A1 **Canada**. (604)684-9338. Fax: (604)684-9337. E-mail: festival@musicwest.com. Website: http://www.musicwest.com/. Producer: Maureen Jack. Estab. 1990. A four day music festival and conference held May each year in Vancouver, B.C. The conference offers songwriter intensive workshops; demo critique sessions with A&R and publishers; information on the business of publishing. The festival offers songwriters in the round and 250 original music showcases. Largest music industry event in the North Pacific Rim. Fee varies pending on conference/festival options preference.

MUSICAL THEATRE WORKS, INC., 440 Lafayette St., New York NY 10003. (212)677-0040. Executive Director: Jacqueline Anne Siegel. Estab. 1983. "We develop and present new works for the musical theater: informal readings, staged readings and workshops of new musicals." Functions year-round. Participants are emerging and established composers and songwriters and opera/musical theater writers. Participants are selected through a critique/evaluation of each musical by the Literary Manager and his staff. To contact, send letter of inquiry to the above address.

‡NATIONAL ACADEMY OF POPULAR MUSIC SONGWRITING WORKSHOP PROGRAM, 330 W. 58th St. #411, New York NY 10019. (212)957-9230. Fax: (212)957-9227. E-mail: 73751.1142@compuserve.com. Website: http://www.popularsongs.org. Projects Director: Bob Leone. Estab. 1969. "For all forms of pop music, from rock to R&B to dance." Offers programs for member lyricists and composers. "The Abe Olman Scholarship for excellence in songwriting is awarded ($1,200) to a student who has been in our program for at least 4 quarters." Offers programs 3 times/year: fall, winter and spring. Event takes place mid-September to December, mid-January to April, mid-April to July (10 2 hour weekly sessions) at New York Spaces, 131 W. 72nd St., New York City. 50 students involved in 4 different classes. Participants are amateur and professional lyricists and composers. Some participants are selected by submitting demonstration tape (pro-song class), and by invitation (master class). Send for application. Deadline: first week of classes. Fee: $160. Sponsors songwriter showcases in March, June, September and December.

‡NORTH BY NORTHEAST MUSIC FESTIVAL AND CONFERENCE (NXNE), 185A Danforth Ave., 2nd Floor, Toronto, Ontario M4K 1N2 **Canada**. (416)469-0986. Fax: (416)469-0576. E-mail: inquire@nxne.com. Website: http://www.nxne.com. Managing Director: Andy McLean. Operations Manager: Ann Kennedy. Estab. 1995. "Our festival takes place mid-June at 24 venues and 2 outdoor stages in downtown Toronto, drawing over 1,500 conference delegates, 350 bands and 20,000 music fans. Musical genres include everything from folk to funk, roots to rock, polka to punk and all points in between, bringing exceptional new talent, media front-runners, music business heavies and music fans from all over the world to Toronto. Participants include emerging and established songwriters, vocalists, composers, bands and instrumentalists. Festival performers are selected by submitting a demo tape and package. Send for an application form, or call, fax or e-mail. Submission deadline: February 3. Submission fee: $10. Our conference is held at world-class hotel facilities and the program includes mentor sessions—15-minute one-on-one opportunities for songwriters and composers to ask questions of industry experts—and our conference agenda includes a songwriting panel that explores the creative process with seasoned pros."

NORTHERN CALIFORNIA SONGWRITERS ASSOCIATION CONFERENCE, 855 Oak Grove Ave. #211, Menlo Park CA 94025. (415)327-8926 or (800)FOR-SONG. Fax: (415)327-0301. E-mail: ianncsa@aol.com. Executive Director: Ian Crombie. Estab. 1980. "Conference offers opportunity and education. 16 seminars, 50 song screening sessions (1,500 songs reviewed), performance showcases, one on one sessions and concerts." Offers programs for songwriters, composers and performers. "During the year we have competitive open mics. Winners go into the playoffs. Winners of the playoffs perform at the sunset concert at the conference." Event takes place second weekend in September at Foothill College, Los Altos Hills, CA. Over 500 songwriters/musicians participate in this event. Participants are songwriters, composers, musical playwrights, vocalists, bands, instrumentalists and those interested in a career in the music business. Send for application. Deadline: September 1. Fee: $90-175. "See our listing in the Organizations section."

‡NSAI SPRING SYMPOSIUM, 15 Music Square W., Nashville TN 37203. (615)256-3354. Fax: (615)256-0034. Administrative Assistant: Lesa Williams. Covers "all types of music. Participants take part in publisher and professional songwriter evaluations, as well as large group sessions with different guest speakers." Offers annual programs for songwriters. Event takes place in April at Loews Vanderbilt Plaza Hotel in Nashville. 350 amateur songwriters/musicians participate in each event. Send for application. Deadline: March. Fee: TBA.

ORFORD FESTIVAL, Orford Arts Centre, 3165 Chemim DuParc, Canton D'Orford Quebec J1X 3W3 **Canada**. (819)843-3981. E-mail: arts.orford@sympatico.ca. Website: http://www3.sympatico/arts.orford. Artistic Director: Yuli Turovsky. Estab. 1951. "Each year, the Centre d'Arts Orford produces up to 30 concerts in the context of its Music Festival. It receives artists from all over the world in classical and chamber music." Offers master classes for music students, young professional classical musicians and chamber music ensembles. New offerings include master classes for all instruments and voice, orchestral repertoire, workshop for brass instruments, and music competition for piano, violin and cello students. Master classes last 7-8 weeks and take place at Orford Arts Centre from June 30 to August 16. 350 students participate each year. Participants are selected by demo tape submissions. Send for application. Closing date for application is March 14. Scholarships for qualified students. Registration fees $45 (Canadian). Tuition fees $250 (Canadian)/week. Accommodations $250 (Canadian)/week.

PHILADELPHIA MUSIC CONFERENCE, P.O. Box 29363, Philadelphia PA 19125. (215)426-4109. Fax: (215)426-4138. E-mail: gopmc@aol.com. Website: http://www.gopmc.com. Showcase Director: Michael Kunze. Estab. 1992. "The purpose of the PMC is to bring together rock, hip hop and acoustic music for three days of panels and four nights of showcases. Offers programs for songwriters, composers and performers, including one-on-one sessions to meet with panelists and song evaluation sessions to have your music heard. "We present 45 panels on topics of all facets of the music industry; 350 showcases at clubs around the city. Also offer a DJ cutting contest." Held annually at the Doubletree Hotel in Philadelphia in October. 3,000 amateur and professional songwriters, composers, individual vocalists, bands, individual instrumentalists, attorneys, managers, agents, publishers, A&R, promotions, club owners, etc. participate each year. "As per showcase application, participants are selected by independent panel of press, radio and performing rights organizations." Send for application. Deadline: September 1. Fee: $15 showcase application fee. "The Philadelphia Music Conference is one of the fastest-growing and exciting events around. Our goal is not just to make the Philadelphia Music Conference one of the biggest in America, but to make it one of the best. 23 artists were signed to major label deals in the first four years of the conference. We will continue to build upon our ideas to keep this an event that is innovative, informative and fun."

POPKOMM, Rottscheidter Str. 6, 42329 Wuppertal **Germany**. Phone: (0202)278310. Fax: (0202)789161. E-mail: popkomm@musikkomm.de. Website: http://www.musikkomm.de/popkomm. Head PR: Andrea Zech. Estab. 1989. Offers programs for songwriters, composers, musical playwrights and performers. Offers programs annually. Events take place in August in Cologne, Germany. 14,000 amateur and professional songwriters, composers, musical playwrights, vocalists, bands, instrumentalists, record companies and media participate each year. Anyone can participate. Send for application or call + +49-202-278310. Charges fee.

‡RIVER'S EDGE SONGWRITER'S RETREAT WITH PAT PATTISON, hosted by REO Rafting Adventure Resort, 355-535 Thurlow St., Vancouver B.C. V6E 3L2 **Canada**. (604)684-4438 or (800)736-7238. Fax: (604)684-9536. E-mail: info@reorafting.com. President: Bryan Fogelman. Estab. 1996. "A two-day songwriter's workshop with Writer's Digest author Pat Pattison. Evening object writing and campfire sessions included. Relevant to all musical styles with lyrics." Event takes place July 20-22, 1998 and July 19-21, 1999 at Nahatlatch River Resort, a wilderness retreat 3 hours from Vancouver, B.C. Up to 25 songwriters can participate. Participants are amateur and professional songwriters, vocalists and composers. Send or call for application. Deadline: when full at 25 participants or 1 week prior. Fee: For 1998, $295 US or $245 US with early registration. "This two-day workshop with Pat Pattison is a wilderness retreat with a beautiful setting on a jade-green river. Includes 6 delicious meals; beverages; camping in own tent or upgrade to cabin tent or log cabin; scenic hot tub and sauna; private beach on river; hot showers, etc. Optional adventure activities such as rafting, hiking, horseback riding, etc. also available. Songwriting critiques and special services can be arranged with Pat Pattison by calling (615)463-2226."

‡ROUTE ONE SOUTH MUSIC CONFERENCE & FESTIVAL, P.O. Box 5563, Richmond VA 23220. (804)648-0364. (804)648-0366. E-mail: dano@i2020.net. Website: http://www.cvaweb.com/route1south. Managing Director: Dan-O. Event Coordinator: Brett Cassis. Estab. 1996. "The Route 1 South Music Conference and Festival is the Mid-Atlantic's fastest growing music industry seminar and talent showcase. This four-day, three-night music conference and showcase brings together music industry leaders, journalists, artists and fans for panel discussions, label representative sessions, industry workshops and electrifying performances. Three hundred of the country's best unsigned bands perform nightly in front of 250 industry experts and 20,000 fans in more than 25 venues throughout the Richmond area, including clubs, theaters, ballrooms, conference centers, outdoor venues and festival parks. The two-day seminar highlights 45 trade show exhibitors while 25 seminar and panel discussions encourage networking and growth through the Mid-Atlantic region."

SONGCRAFT SEMINARS, 441 E. 20th St., Suite 11B, New York NY 10010-7515. (212)674-1143. Estab. 1986. Year-round classes for composers and lyricists conducted by teacher/consultant Sheila Davis, author of *The Craft of Lyric Writing*, *Successful Lyric Writing* and *The Songwriter's Idea Book*. The teaching method, grounded in fundamental principles, incorporates whole-brain writing techniques. The objective: To express your unique voice. All courses emphasize craftsmanship and teach principles that apply to every musical idiom—pop, theater, or cabaret. For details on starting dates, fees and location of classes, write or call for current listing.
Successful Lyric Writing: A 3-Saturday course. Three 6-hour classes on the fundamental principles of writing words for and to music. Required text: *Successful Lyric Writing*. Held 3 times a year at The New School. Limited to 12.
Beyond the Basics: An 8-week workshop open to all "grads" of the *Successful Lyric Writing* Basics Course. It features weekly assignments and in-depth criticism to help writers turn first drafts into "music-ready" lyrics. Held four times a year at The Songwriters Guild of America (SGA).
The Figurative Language Master Class: An 8-week intensive course/workshop that expands your usual ways of thinking and expressing ideas through the practice of figurative language. You'll learn to identify, define and use with competence the four master figures of speech—metaphor, synecdoche, metonymy and irony—and their many subtypes. And you'll acquire new skills in structuring your thoughts to make your songs more memorable and thus, more marketable. Held twice a year at the Songwriters Guild.
Successful Lyric Writing Consultation Course: This course, an outgrowth of the instructor's book, covers the same theory and assignments as The Basics Course. Participants receive critiques of their work by the book's author via 1-hour phone sessions.

‡SONGWRITERS EXPO, 6255 Sunset Blvd. #1023, Hollywood CA 90046. (213)463-7178. Fax: (213)463-2146. E-mail: nassong@aol.com. Creative Director: Dan Kimpel. Estab. 1976. Offers programs for songwriters, composers and performers. Offers programs annually. Event takes place in October in Los Angeles, CA. Over 500 songwriters/musicians participate in each event. Participants are amateur and professional songwriters, vocalists, composers and bands. Anyone can participate. Send or call for application. Deadline: October. Fee: $200. Offers classes, panels, workshops, song-pitches/evaluations and showcases involving all aspects of the music business.

THE SONGWRITERS GUILD FOUNDATION, 6430 Sunset Blvd., Suite 1002, Hollywood CA 90028. (213)462-1108. West Coast Director: B. Aaron Meza.
Ask-A-Pro/Song Critique: SGA members are given the opportunity to present their songs and receive constructive feedback from industry professionals. A great chance to meet industry people, make contacts, ask questions and get your song heard! Free to SGA members. Reservations required. Call for schedule. Members outside regional area send tape with lyric and SASE for tape return.
Jack Segal's Songshop: This very successful 9-week workshop focuses on working a song through to perfection, including title, idea, rewrites and pitching your songs. Please call for more information regarding this very informative workshop. Dates to be announced. Fee.
Phil Swan Country Music Workshop: This six-week shop is perfect for those writers who want an inside look into the world of country music. Fee.
Special Seminars and Workshops: Held through the year. Past workshops included Sheila Davis on lyrics, tax workshops for songwriters, MIDI workshops, etc. Call for schedule.
Dr. George Gamez's Creativity Workshop: A four-week class designed to help songwriters discover their creative possibilities and give them the tools and techniques they need to increase their creative abilities. Fee.

SONGWRITERS PLAYGROUND®, 1085 Commonwealth Ave. #323, Boston MA 02215. (617)424-9490. E-mail: bljjms@tiac.net. Director: Barbara Jordan. Estab. 1990. "To help songwriters, performers and composers develop creative and business skills through the critically acclaimed programs *Songwriters Playground®*, *The 'Reel' Deal on Getting Songs Placed in Film and Television*, and the *Mind Your Own Business* Seminars. We offer programs year-round. Workshops last anywhere from 2-15 hours. Workshops are held at various venues throughout the United States. Prices vary according to the length of the workshop." Participants are amateur and professionals. Anyone can participate. Send or call for application.

- See the interview with Director Barbara Jordan in the 1997 *Songwriter's Market*.

SOUTH BY SOUTHWEST MUSIC AND MEDIA CONFERENCE, P.O. Box 4999, Austin TX 78765. (512)467-7979. Fax: (512)451-0754. E-mail: sxsw@sxsw.com. Website: http://sxsw.com/sxsw. Estab. 1987. "We have over 600 bands perform in over 40 venues over 5 nights featuring every genre of alternative-based music." Offers programs for songwriters and performers. Annual event takes place the third weekend in March at the Austin Convention Center, Austin, TX. Participants are songwriters, vocalists, bands and instrumentalists. Participants are selected by demo tape audition. Deadline: November 15. Fee: $10 early fee; $20 late fee. "We have a mentor program during the conference where participants can have a one-on-one with professionals in the music business."

THE SWANNANOA GATHERING—CONTEMPORARY FOLK WEEK, Warren Wilson College, P.O. Box 9000, Asheville NC 28815-9000. (704)298-3325, ext. 426. Fax: (704)299-3326. E-mail: gathering@warren-wilson.edu. Website: http://www.hidwater.com/gathering/. Director: Jim Magill. "For anyone who ever wanted to make music for an audience, we offer a comprehensive week in artist development, divided into four major subject areas: Songwriting, Performance, Sound & Recording and Vocal Coaching, along with daily panel discussions of other business matters such as promotion, agents and managers, logistics of touring, etc. 1997 staff includes Tom Paxton, Catie Curtis, David Massengill, Leslie Ritter, Scott Petito, Bridget Ball, Christopher Shaw, Paul Reisler, Rex Fowler, Bob Franke, Freyda Epstein and Eric Garrison. For a brochure or other info contact Jim Magill, Director, The Swannanoa Gathering, at the phone number/address above. Tuition: $290. Takes place last week in July. Housing (including all meals): $200. Annual program of The Swannanoa Gathering Folk Arts Workshops."

THE TEN-MINUTE MUSICALS PROJECT, P.O. Box 461194, West Hollywood CA 90046. (213)656-8751. Producer: Michael Koppy. Estab. 1986. Promotes short complete stage musicals. Offers programs for songwriters, composers and musical playwrights. "Works selected are generally included in full-length 'anthology musical'—11 of the first 16 selected works are now in the show *Stories*, for instance." Awards a $250 royalty advance for each work selected. Participants are amateur and professional songwriters, composers and musical playwrights. Participants are selected by demonstration tape, script, lead sheets. Send for application. Deadline: August 31st annually.

UNDERCURRENTS, P.O. Box 94040, Cleveland OH 44101-6040. (216)397-9921. Fax: (216)932-1143. E-mail: music@undercurrents.com. Website: http://www.undercurrents.com. Director: John Latimer. Estab. 1989. A yearly music industry expo featuring seminars, trade show, media center and showcases of rock, alternative, metal, folk, jazz and blues music. Offers programs for songwriters, composers, music industry professionals and performers. Dates for Undercurrents '98 are May 21-23. Deadline for showcase consideration is February 1, 1998. Participants are selected by demo tape, biography and 8×10 photo audition. Send for application. Fee: $10.

Contests and Awards

Participating in contests is another way to gain exposure for your music. Prizes vary from contest to contest, with cash prizes, musical merchandise, studio time and even publishing and recording deals being offered for a winning song. For musical theater and classical composers, the prize may be a performance of your work. Even if you don't win a prize, valuable contacts can be made through contests. Many times, contests are judged by music publishers and other industry professionals, so your music may find its way into the hands of key industry people who can help further your career.

It's important to remember when entering any contest to do proper research before signing anything or sending any money. We have confidence in the contests listed in *Songwriter's Market*, but it pays to be aware of several things. Be sure you understand the contest rules and stipulations once you receive the entry forms and guidelines. You need to weigh what you will gain against what they're asking you to give up. If a publishing or recording contract is the only prize a contest is offering, you may want to think twice before entering. Basically, the company that's sponsoring the contest is asking you to pay a fee for them to listen to your song under the guise of a contest, something a legitimate publisher or record company would not do. For those contests offering studio time, musical equipment or cash prizes, you need to decide if the entry fee you're paying is worth the chance to win such prizes.

Be wary of exorbitant entry fees, and if you have any doubts whatsoever as to the legitimacy of a contest, it's best to stay away. Songwriters need to approach a contest, award or grant in the same manner as they would a record or publishing company. Make sure your submission is as professional as possible; follow directions and submit material exactly as stated on the entry form.

Contests in this section encompass all types of music and levels of competition. Read each listing carefully and contact them if the contest interests you. Many contests now have websites that offer additional information and even entry forms you can print. Be sure to read the rules carefully and be sure you understand exactly what a contest is offering before entering.

‡AARON ENTERPRISES SUMMERTIME SONG FESTIVAL, P.O. Box 2438, Petersburg VA 23804. (804)733-5908. Song Contest Director: Cham Laughlin. Estab. 1997. For songwriters in the US and Canada. Annual award sponsored by the Aaron Enterprises Songwriters Group.

Requirements: "Entries are accepted from May 1st through the postal deadline of June 30th in each contest year. Categories available for entry are: new country, traditional country, folk, rock, pop and R&B, instrumental, humorous and song lyric." Deadline: June 30. Send SASE for application. Entry fee: $10 per song.

Awards: "Prizes include cash, t-shirts, certificates of merit, publishing contracts, memberships in our songwriter's group, newsletter subscriptions, songwriter's kits, and more." Entries judged by industry professionals.

AGO/ECS PUBLISHING AWARD IN CHORAL COMPOSITION, American Guild of Organists, 475 Riverside Dr., Suite 1260, New York NY 10115. (212)870-2310. Fax: (212)870-2163. E-mail ago@walrus.com. For composers. Biannual award.

Requirements: One work for SATB chorus and organ in which the organ plays a distinctive and significant role. Specifics vary from year to year. Work submitted must be unpublished. Competitors must be citizens of the United States, Canada or Mexico. There is no age restriction. Deadline: July 31 during even numbered years. Send for application.

Awards: $2,000; performances at Regional Convention and National Convention; publication of winning composition by ECS Publishing.

ALEA III INTERNATIONAL COMPOSITION PRIZE, 855 Commonwealth Ave., Boston MA 02215. (617)353-3340. Executive Administrator: Synneve Carlino. For composers. Annual award.

Purpose: To promote and encourage young composers in the composition of new music.

Requirements: Composers 40 years of age and younger may apply; one score per composer. Works may be for solo voice or instrument or for chamber ensemble up to 15 members lasting between 6 and 15 minutes. All works must be unpublished. Deadline: March 15. Send for application. Submitted work required with application. "Real name should not appear on score; a nome de plume should be signed instead. Sealed envelope with entry form should be attached to each score."

Awards: ALEA III International Composition Prize: $2,500. Awarded once annually. Between 8-10 finalists are chosen and their works are performed in a competition concert by the ALEA III contemporary music ensemble. One grand prize winner is selected by a panel of judges.

Tips: "Emphasis placed on works written in 20th century compositional idioms."

AMERICAN SONGWRITER LYRIC CONTEST, 121 17th Ave. S., Nashville TN 37203-2707. (615)244-6065. Fax: (615)742-1123. E-mail: asongmag@aol.com. Website: http://www.nol.com/asongmag.html. Editor: Vernell Hackett. Estab. 1984. For songwriters and performing artists. Award for each bimonthly issue of *American Songwriter* magazine, plus grand prize at year-end.

Purpose: To promote the art of songwriting and to allow readers the opportunity to be actively involved.

Requirements: Lyrics must be typed and check for $10 (per entry) must be enclosed. Deadlines: January 24, March 28, May 23, July 25, September 26, November 26. Samples are not required. Call for required official form. Lyrics only, no cassettes.

Awards: A guitar, with different sponsors each year. Lyrics judged by 5-6 industry people—songwriters, publishers, journalists.

Tips: "Pick your best lyric, don't just send them at random."

ARTISTS' FELLOWSHIPS, New York Foundation for the Arts, 155 Avenue of Americas, 14th Floor, New York NY 10013. To receive an application, or contact the fellowship's department, call: (212)366-6900, ext. 217. Fax: (212)366-1778. E-mail: nyfaafp@artswire.org. Website: http://www.tmn.com/Artswire/www/nyfa.html. Director, Artists' Programs and Services: Penelope Dannenberg. For songwriters, composers and musical playwrights. Annual award, but each category funded biennially. Estab. 1984.

Purpose: "Artists' Fellowships are $7,000 grants awarded by the New York Foundation for the Arts to individual originating artists living in New York State. The Foundation is committed to supporting artists from all over New York State at all stages of their professional careers. Fellows may use the grant according to their own needs; it should not be confused with project support."

Requirements: Must be 18 years of age or older; resident in New York State for 2 years prior to application; and cannot be enrolled in any graduate or undergraduate degree program. Applications will be available in July. Deadline: October. Samples of work are required with application. 1 or 2 original compositions on separate audiotapes and at least 2 copies of corresponding scores or fully harmonized lead sheets.

Awards: All Artists' Fellowships awards are for $7,000. Payment of $6,300 upon verification of NY State residency, and remainder upon completion of a mutually agreed upon public service activity. Nonrenewable. "Fellowships are awarded on the basis of the quality of work submitted and the evolving professional accomplishments of the applicant. Applications are reviewed by a panel of 5 composers representing the aesthetic, ethnic, sexual and geographic diversity within New York State. The panelists change each year and review all allowable material submitted."

Tips: "Please note that musical playwrights may submit only if they write the music for their plays—librettists must submit in our playwriting category."

ASCAP FOUNDATION MORTON GOULD GRANTS TO YOUNG COMPOSERS, ASCAP Bldg., 1 Lincoln Plaza, New York NY 10023. (212)621-6327. Fax: (212)721-9056. Contact: Frances Richard.

Purpose: To provide grants to young composers to encourage the development of talented young American composers.

Requirements: Applicants must be citizens or permanent residents of the United States of America who have not reached their 30th birthday by March 15. Original music of any style will be considered. However, works which have earned awards or prizes in any other national competition or grant giving program are ineligible. Arrangements are ineligible. Each applicant must submit a completed application form; one reproduction of a manuscript or score; biographical information listing prior music studies, background and experience; a list of compositions to date; and one professional recommendation to be mailed by the referee directly to ASCAP under separate cover. A cassette tape of the composition submitted for the competition may be included if it is marked with the composer's name, the title of the work and the names of the performers. Tapes of electronic music must also be accompanied by written information concerning source material and electronic equipment used. A composition that involves a text must be accompanied

by information about the source of the text with evidence that it is in the public domain or by written permission from the copyright proprietor. Deadline: All materials must be postmarked no later than March 15.
Awards: ASCAP Foundation awards total $20,000 and grants range from $500-2,500. Length: 1 year. Applications judged by screening-panel of composers.

BAKER'S PLAYS HIGH SCHOOL PLAYWRITING CONTEST, Baker's Plays 100 Chauncy St., Boston MA 02111. (617)482-1280. Fax: (617)482-7613. Associate Editor: Raymond Pape. Estab. 1990. For musical playwrights. Annual award.
Requirements: Plays should be about the "high school experience," but may also be about any subject and of any length, so long as the play can be reasonably produced on the high school stage. Plays must be accompanied by the signature of a sponsoring high school drama or English teacher, and it is recommended that the play receive a production or a public reading prior to the submission. Multiple submissions and co-authored scripts are welcome. Teachers may not submit a student's work. The ms must be firmly bound, typed and come with a SASE. Include enough postage to cover the return of the ms. Plays that do not come with an SASE will not be returned. Do not send originals; copies only. Deadline: January 31st. 1998 winners notified by May 31, 1998. Send for guidelines.
Awards: First Place: $500 and the play will be published by Baker's Plays; Second Place: $250 and an Honorable Mention; Third Place: $100 and an Honorable Mention.

BILLBOARD SONG CONTEST, P.O. Box 60628, Oklahoma City OK 73146-0628. (405)523-4814. Fax: (405)523-4815. Website: http://www.billboard.com. Director: Derrick Davis. Estab. 1988. For songwriters. Annual international contest.
Purpose: "To reward deserving songwriters and performers for their talent."
Awards: To be announced. For entry forms and additional information send SASE to the above address.

‡BLANK THEATRE COMPANY YOUNG PLAYWRIGHTS FESTIVAL, 1301 Lucile Ave., Los Angeles CA 90026. (213)662-7734. (213)661-3903. E-mail: btc@primenet.com. Producer: Ginnie Held. Estab. 1993. For musical playwrights. Annual award.
Purpose: "To give young playwrights an opportunity to learn more about playwriting and to give them a chance to have their work produced."
Requirements: Playwrights must be 19 years old or younger on April 14, 1998. Send legible, original plays of any length and on any subject (co-written plays are acceptable provided all co-writers meet eligibility requirements). Submissions must by postmarked by April 14, 1998 and must include a cover sheet with the playwright's name, date of birth, school (if any), home address and home phone number. Manuscripts will not be returned—please do not send originals. We will contact semi-finalists and winners in May 1998. Send for application. Samples of work are required with application.
Awards: Winning playwrights receive a workshop presentation of their work.

BUSH ARTIST FELLOWSHIPS, E-900 First National Bank Bldg., 332 Minnesota St., St. Paul MN 55101. (612)227-5222. Estab. 1976. For songwriters, composers, and musical playwrights. Applications in music composition are accepted in alternate years.
Purpose: "To provide artists with significant financial support that enables them to further their work and their contribution to their communities."
Requirements: Applicant must be a Minnesota, North Dakota, South Dakota or western Wisconsin resident for 12 of preceeding 36 months, 25 years or older, not a student. Deadline: late October. Send for application. Samples of work on cassette required with application. "Music composition applications will not be taken again until the fall of 1998. Applications will be taken in the fall of 1998 in the following areas: music composition, scriptworks (screenwriting and playwriting), literature (creative non-fiction, fiction, poetry) and film/video.
Awards: Fellowships: $36,000 stipend. Award is good for 12-18 months. "5 years after completion of preceeding fellowship, one may apply again." Applications are judged by peer review panels.

COLUMBIA ENTERTAINMENT COMPANY'S JACKIE WHITE MEMORIAL PLAYWRITING CONTEST, 309 Parkade Blvd., Columbia MO 65202. (314)874-5628. Director, CEC Contest: Betsy Phillips. For musical playwrights. Annual award.
Purpose: "We are looking for top-notch scripts for theater school use, to challenge and expand the talents of our students, ages 10-15. We want good plays with large casts (20-30 characters) suitable for use with our theater school students. Full production of the winning script will be done by the students. A portion of travel expenses, room and board offered to winner for production of show."
Requirements: "Must be large cast plays, original story lines and cannot have been previously published.

Because theatre school enrollment is typically composed of more girls than boys, scripts should have at least 50% of characters female. Please write for complete rules." Send SASE for application; then send scripts to address above. Full-length play, neatly typed. No name on title page, but name, address and name of play on a 3×5 index card. Cassette tape of musical numbers required. $10 entry fee. SASE for entry form."

Awards: $250 first prize and partial travel expenses to see play produced. Second place winner gets no prize money but receives production of the play by the theater school plus partial travel expenses. This is a one-time cash award, given after any revisions required are completed. "The judging committee is taken from members of Columbia Entertainment Company's Executive and Advisory boards, and from theatre school parents. At least eight members, with at least three readings of all entries, and winning entries being read by entire committee. We are looking for plays that will work with our theater school students."

Tips: "Remember the play we are looking for will be performed by 10-15 year old students with normal talents—difficult vocal ranges, a lot of expert dancing and so forth will eliminate the play. We especially like plays that deal with current day problems and concerns. However, if the play is good enough, any suitable subject matter is fine. It should be fun for the audience to watch."

COMPOSERS COMMISSIONING PROGRAM, ACF, 332 Minnesota St., #E-145, St. Paul MN 55101. (612)228-1407. Fax: (612)291-7978. E-mail: compfrm@maroon.tc.umn.edu. Website: http://www.umn.edu/nlhome/m111/compfrm. Program Director: Philip Blackburn. Estab. 1979. For songwriters, musical playwrights, composers and performers. Annual award.

Purpose: "CCP provides grants to support the commissioning of new works by emerging composers."

Requirements: Membership of American Composers Forum (not for students). Deadline: end of July. Send for application. Samples of work are required with application. Send score/tape.

Awards: 18-22 commissioning grants of $500-6,000; each grant good for 5 years. Applications are judged by peer review panel (anonymous).

Tips: "Composers pair up with performers: one party must be based in Minnesota or New York City."

‡COMPOSERS GUILD ANNUAL COMPOSITION CONTEST, P.O. Box 586, Farmington UT 84025. (801)451-2275. President: Ruth B. Gatrell. Estab. 1963. For songwriters, musical playwrights and composers. Annual award.

Purpose: "To stimulate musical composition and help composers through judge's comments on each composition submitted. Composers can broaden their creative skills by entering different categories. Categories: Arrangements (original in public domain or with composer's permission); music for children; choral; instrumental; jazz/New Age; keyboard; orchestra/band; popular (all types); vocal solo; young composer (18 or under on August 31)."

Requirements: Score and/or cassette. Entry fee: $20 for work 7 minutes or more in length (may include multimovements on compositions), $15 for work less than 7 minutes. Dues are $25/year. Member entry fees: $10 for work 7 minutes or more, $5 less than 7 minutes. Deadline: August 31. Send or call for application.

Awards: Award of Excellence $500; 1st prize in each category except Award of Excellence category $100; 2nd prize in each category $50; 3rd prize in each category $25; Honorable Mention certificate. Judge has a doctorate in music, plus compositions published and performing (usually has vast teaching experience). Same judge never used in successive years.

Tips: "Submit good clear copies of score. Have cassette cued up. Only one composition per cassette (each entry requires separate cassette). No composer names to appear on score or cassette. Enter as many categories and compositions as you wish. Separate entry for each. One check can cover all entries and dues."

CRS NATIONAL COMPOSERS COMPETITION, 724 Winchester Rd., Broomall PA 19008. (610)544-5920. Fax: (610)544-5921. Administrative Assistant: Caroline Hunt. For songwriters, composers and performing artists. Annual award.

Requirements: Write with SASE for application. Send a detailed résumé with application form. Samples of work required with application. Application fee $50.

Awards: 1st Prize: Commercial recording grant. Applications are judged by panel of judges determined each year.

CUNNINGHAM PRIZE FOR PLAYWRITING, The Theatre School, DePaul University, 2135 N. Kenmore Ave., Chicago IL 60614. (773)325-7938. Fax: (773)325-7920. E-mail: lgoetsch@wppost.depaul.edu. Public Relations Director: Lara Goetsch. Estab. 1990. For musical playwrights. Annual award.

Purpose: "The purpose of the prize is to recognize and encourage the writing of dramatic works which affirm the centrality of religion, broadly defined, and the human quest for meaning, truth and community. It is the intent of the endowment to consider submissions of new dramatic writing in all genres, including works for children and young people."

Requirements: "The focus for the awarding of the prize is metropolitan Chicago. The candidates for the award must be writers whose residence is in the Chicago area, defined as within 100 miles of the Loop." Deadline: December 1. Send for application with SASE.
Awards: $5,000. "Winners may submit other work for subsequent prize year. The Selection Committee is composed of distinguished citizens including members of DePaul University, representatives of the Cunningham Prize Advisory Committee, critics and others from the theater professions, and is chaired by John Ransford Watts, dean of The Theatre School."

‡KENNETH DAVENPORT NATIONAL COMPETITION FOR ORCHESTRAL WORKS, P.O. Box 1131, New York NY 12561-1131. (914)257-3860. Fax: (914)257-3861. Assistant to Dean: Eileen Channer. Estab. 1988. For composers. Annual award.
Requirements: Deadline: March 31. Send for application. Works requiring chorus, solo voice or electronic tape are not eligible.
Awards: Panel of judges reviews all scores submitted.
Tips: "Apply for prize by sending your score for orchestral works."

DELTA OMICRON INTERNATIONAL COMPOSITION COMPETITION, 12297 W. Tennessee Place, Lakewood CO 80228. (303)989-2871. Composition Competition Chairman: Judith L. Eidson. For composers. Triennial award.
Purpose: "To encourage composers worldwide to continually add to our wonderful heritage of musical creativity instrumentally and/or vocally."
Requirements: People from college age on (or someone younger who is enrolled in college). Work must be unpublished and unperformed in public. Deadline: mid-March of 2nd year of triennium. Send for application. Samples of work are required with application.
Awards: 1st place: $500 and world premiere at Delta Omicron Triennal Conference. Judged by 2-3 judges (performers and/or composers).

‡EUROPEAN INTERNATIONAL COMPETITION FOR COMPOSERS, 226 E. 2nd St., Suite 5D, New York NY 10009. (212)387-0111. Fax: (212)388-0102. Chairman: Dr. S. Moltisanti. Estab. 1995. For songwriters and composers. Annual award.
Purpose: "To promote the winners' career through exposure, publicity, recordings with Athena Records and nationwide distribution with the Empire Group."
Requirements: Deadline: March 15. Send for application. Samples of work are required with application.
Awards: $10,000 to sponsor the promotion of the winners.

FREE STAGED READING SERIES PLAYWRITING COMPETITION, 120 W. 28th St., New York NY 10001. (212)627-1732. Fax: (212)243-6736. E-mail: tuda@ziplink.net. Website: http://www.tadatheater.com. Assistant to the Artistic Director: Tara Bahna-James. Estab. 1984. For musical playwrights or anyone wanting to write a play.
Purpose: "The series, now entering its sixth year, was initiated to encourage playwrights, composers, and lyricists to write for family audiences and to involve children and their parents in the excitement of the play development process."
Requirements: "Script must be original, unproduced and unpublished. Any age may apply. One act musical or non-musical cast must be primarily youth ages 7-18; children do not play adults—adult actors can be hired. Script must be typed, include character breakdown, set and costume description. Playwrights should adhere to the topic given—teen topics—and take into consideration that they need to not only write for young audiences but young performers as well. Meaningful family topics are also appropriate for this particular staged reading contest with an emphasis on the children's relationship with parents rather than a spotlight on the parents." Deadline: February 1. Send for guidelines.
Tips: "Issues having to do with children and what they are going through in life and good teen issues are especially relevant."

FULBRIGHT SCHOLAR PROGRAM, COUNCIL FOR INTERNATIONAL EXCHANGE OF SCHOLARS, 3007 Tilden St. NW, Suite 5M, Box News, Washington DC 20008-3009. (202)686-7877. E-mail: cies1@ciesnet.cies.org. Website: http://www.cies.org. Estab. 1946. For composers and academics. Annual award.
Purpose: "Awards for university lecturing and advanced research abroad are offered annually in virtually all academic disciplines including musical composition."
Requirements: "U.S. citizenship at time of application; M.F.A., Ph.D. or equivalent professional qualifications; for lecturing awards, university teaching experience." Applications become available in March each year, for grants to be taken up 1½ years later. Application deadlines: August 1, all world areas. Write or call for application. Samples of work are required with application.

Awards: "Benefits vary by country, but generally include round-trip travel for the grantee and for most full academic-year awards, one dependent; stipend in U.S. dollars and/or local currency; in many countries, tuition allowance for school age children; and book and baggage allowance. Grant duration ranges from 2 months-1 academic year."

FUTURE CHARTERS, 332 Eastwood Ave., Feasterville PA 19053. (800)574-2986. Phone/fax: (215)953-0952. E-mail: a1foster@aol.com. Editor/Publisher: Allen Foster. Estab. 1993. For songwriters. Quarterly award.
Requirements: To enter, send a clean demo tape of one song with vocals up front, a photo, a bio, lyric sheet, contact information and a SASE (if you'd like your tape returned).
Awards: Winners will receive a writeup in an upcoming issue of *Songwriter's Monthly*, plus your song will be placed on the Songwriter's Telephone Showcase so interested parties will be able to call up and listen to your song.
Tips: "There is no application form or entry fee. Just send your best song. It doesn't have to be an expensive demo, but it does have to sound clean."

HARVEY GAUL COMPOSITION CONTEST, The Pittsburgh New Music Ensemble, Inc., School of Music, Duquesne University, Pittsburgh PA 15282. (412)261-0554. Fax: (412)396-5479. Conductor/Executive Director: David Stock/Eva Tumiel-Kozak. For composers. Biennial.
Purpose: Objective is to encourage composition of new music. Winning piece to be premiered by the PNME.
Requirements: "Must be citizen of the US. New works scored for 6 to 16 instruments drawn from the following: flute, oboe, 2 clarinets, bassoon, horn, trumpet, trombone, tuba, 2 violins, cello, bass, 2 percussion, piano, harp, electronic tape." Deadline: April 15. Send SASE for application. Samples of work are required with application. "Real name must not appear on score—must be signed with a 'nom de plume'." Entry fee: $15.
Awards: Harvey Gaul Composition Contest: $3,000.

HENRICO THEATRE COMPANY ONE-ACT PLAYWRITING COMPETITION, P.O. Box 27032, Richmond VA 23273. (804)672-5100. Cultural Arts Coordinator: J. Larkin Brown. For musical playwrights. Annual award.
Purpose: Original one-act musicals for a community theater organization.
Requirements: "Only one-act plays or musicals will be considered. The manuscript should be a one-act original (not an adaptation), unpublished, and unproduced, free of royalty and copyright restrictions. Scripts with smaller casts and simpler sets may be given preference. Controversial themes should be avoided. Standard play script form should be used. All plays will be judged anonymously, therefore, there should be two title pages; the first must contain the play's title and the author's complete address and telephone number. The second title page must contain only the play's title. The playwright must submit two excellent quality copies. Receipt of all scripts will be acknowledged by mail. Scripts will be returned if SASE is included. No scripts will be returned until after the winner is announced. The HTC does not assume responsibility for loss, damage or return of scripts. All reasonable care will be taken." Deadline: July 1st. Send for application first.
Awards: 1st prize $250; 2nd prize $125; 3rd prize $125.

HOLTKAMP-AGO AWARD IN ORGAN COMPOSITION, American Guild of Organists, 475 Riverside Dr., Suite 1260, New York NY 10115. E-mail: ago@walrus.com. Biannual award.
Requirements: Organ solo, no longer than eight minutes in duration. Specifics vary from year to year. Composer must be a citizen of the United States, Canada or Mexico. Deadline: June 1 (odd-numbered years). Send for application.
Award: $2,000 provided by the Holtkamp Organ Company; publication by Hinshaw Music Inc.; performance at the biennial National Convention of the American Guild of Organists.

INDIANA OPERA THEATRE/MACALLISTER AWARDS FOR OPERA SINGERS, 2825 E. 56th St., Indianapolis IN 46220. (317)253-1001. Fax: (317)253-2008. E-mail: ginny50@juno.com. Website: http://www.iquest.net/~opera/. Artister/General Director: E. Bookwalter. Estab. 1980. For college and professional opera singers.
Requirements: For professional and amateurs. New works for high school/college students. Send for application.

‡INNER CITY CULTURAL CENTER'S AUGUSTIN LARA COMPETITION FOR COMPOSERS & SONGWRITERS, P.O. Box 272, Los Angeles CA 90028. (213)627-7670. For songwriters, composers and musical playwrights. Annual award.

Purpose: "Named in honor of famed Mexican composer of 'Granada,' the primary purpose of the competition is to bring songwriters, composers and those who perform original music into contact with those in the music and entertainment industry who are in a position to hire them, and to bring to public prominence the role played by creators of original music."
Requirements: "One entry per participant, maximum length 7 minutes. Entry must be performed live, may not have been previously published. Deadline: June. Send for application. Samples are not required.
Awards: $1,000 (1st place), $500 (2nd place), $250 (3rd place). Additional prizes to be announced at time of competition. Criteria: 1. Originality 2. Overall presentation (performance) 3. Thematic development 4. Structural unity 5. Fullfillment of functional intent. Judges are recruited from the ranks of music industry professionals. Members of the audience cast ballots during a series of 3 elimination rounds to determine which entries proceed to the final round.
Tips: "Have a sponsor capable of providing the support necessary to gather resources needed to make an effective performance presentation (performers, transportation to competition site, rehearsal space, on-site accommodations, special equipment, etc.). This is done LIVE! Competition is open to all. There are NO categories or distinctions made based on genre (classical, jazz, country western, reggae, etc.). Lyrics or librettos may be in any language. There is no citizenship or U.S. residency requirement. Compositions designed to support other media (dance, film, etc.) must be presented in their original context. Keep in mind that the goal of the competition is to develop employment opportunities for gifted writers and to bring attention to the craft in all of its diversity. The competition is divided into two divisions: Adult (over 18) and youth (under 18). ICCC has successfully conducted competitions resulting in professional employment and production for actors over the past 13 years as well as for playwrights and performers."

INTERNATIONAL AWARD OF MUSICAL COMPOSITIONS CIUTAT DE TARRAGONA, Ajuntament de Tarragona, Placa de la Font 1, E43003 Tarragona **Spain**. E-mail: ajtargna@tinet.fut.es. Website: http://www.fut.es/~ajtargna. Contact: Registre General. For composers. Annual award.
Requirements: "Any symphonic composition may be submitted for this award, either with or without soloists and with or without electro-acoustics. The composition must be unpublished, never have been performed in public nor been awarded a prize." Deadline: November 15. Send for application.
Awards: First prize: 1.000.000 pesetas and performance of the composition; Second prize: 500.000 pesetas.

‡INTERNATIONAL CLARINET ASSOCIATION COMPOSITION COMPETITION, Dept. of Music, Miami University, Oxford OH 45056. Fax: (513)523-6720. E-mail: gingram@muohio.edu. Professor: Michèle Gingras. Estab. 1992. For composers. Annual award.
Purpose: To expand the clarinet repertoire.
Requirements: Unpublished work, no age limit, no length limit. Legit repertoire or legit neo-jazz OK. Submit a tape and score. Entries must be labeled with composer's name, address and phone number on the score and tape. Deadline: mid-April every year. Send score and tape.
Awards: One $1,000 prize and a performance at the annual clarinet congress run by ICA. Applications judged by international jury.
Tips: "Submit recent compositions which would enrich the present clarinet repertoire. For next year's competition, the address will change. For 1998, send to: Michele Gingras, Université Laval, Faculté de Musique, Quebec G1K 7P4, Canada. (418)656-2131, ext. 5898. Fax: (418)651-6056."

KATE NEAL KINLEY MEMORIAL FELLOWSHIP, 608 E. Lorado Taft Dr. #117, Champaign IL 61820. (217)333-1661. Secretary: Ruth Wilcoxon. Estab. 1931. For students of architecture, art or music. Annual award.
Purpose: The advancement of study in the Fine Arts.
Requirements: "The Fellowship will be awarded upon the basis of unusual promise in the Fine Arts." Deadline: February 15. Send for application or call. Samples of work are required with application.
Awards: "Two or three major Fellowships which yield the sum of $7,000 each which is to be used by the recipients toward defraying the expenses of advanced study of the Fine Arts in America or abroad." Good for 1 year. Grant is nonrenewable.

LEE KORF PLAYWRITING AWARD, Cerritos College, 11110 Alondra Blvd., Dept. of Theatre, Norwalk CA 90650. (310)860-2451, ext. 2638. Fax: (310)467-5005. Theatre Production: Gloria Manriquez. For musical playwrights and playwrights. Annual award.
Purpose: "We look for promising playwrights who have something exciting to say with a fresh innovative way of saying it."
Requirements: Submit two firmly bound manuscripts and entry fee of $5 with SASE for return. Deadline: September 1, 1998. Send for complete guidelines and application.
Awards: Prizes range from $250 for workshop to $750 for full scale production. Award is one time

only. Award is nonrenewable. "Submissions are read by faculty. Recommended scripts are discussed by directors."
Tips: "We are looking for previously unproduced works."

L.A. DESIGNERS' THEATRE MUSIC AWARDS, P.O. Box 1883, Studio City CA 91614-0883. (213)650-9600. (818)769-9000 (T.D.D.). Fax: (818)985-9200. Artistic Director: Richard Niederberg. For songwriters, composers, performing artists, musical playwrights and rights holders of music.
Purpose: To produce new musicals, operettas, opera-boufes and plays with music, as well as new dance pieces with new music scores.
Requirements: Submit nonreturnable cassette, tape, CD or other medium by first or 4th class mail. Acceptance: continuous. Submit nonreturnable materials with cover letter. No application form or fee is necessary.
Awards: Music is commissioned for a particular project. Amounts are negotiable. Applications judged by our artistic staff.
Tips: "Make the material 'classic, yet commercial' and easy to record/re-record/edit. Make sure rights are totally free of all 'strings,' 'understandings,' 'promises,' etc. ASCAP/BMI/SESAC registration is OK, as long as 'grand' or 'performing rights' are available."

‡THE JOHN LENNON SONGWRITING CONTEST, 83 Riverside Dr., New York NY 10024. E-mail: info@jlsc.com. Associate Director: Gregg Ross. Estab. 1996. For songwriters. Annual award.
Purpose: "The purpose of the John Lennon Songwriting Contest is to promote the art of songwriting by assisting in the discovery of new talent as well as providing more established songwriters with an opportunity to advance their careers."
Requirements: Each entry must consist of the following: completed and signed application; audio cassette containing 1 song only, 5 minutes or less in length; lyric sheet typed or printed legibly (English translation is required when applicable); $30 entry fee. Deadline: August 15, 1998. Applications can be found in various music-oriented magazines. Prospective entrants can send for an application or contact the Contest via e-mail at info@jlsc.com.
Awards: Entries are accepted in the following 12 categories: rock, country, jazz, pop, world, gospel/inspirational, R&B, hip-hop, Latin, dance, folk and a special category of children's music. 1997 prize packages were: 12 Grand Prize winners received $2,000 in cash, $5,000 in Yamaha project studio equipment, and a $5,000 advance from EMI Music Publishing. One Grand Prize winner received an additional $15,000 for the "Song of the Year" courtesy of Maxell. 36 Finalists received $1,000. 72 winners received portable CD players. The 12 category winning songs were recorded and released on a compilation album. Winners will be chosen by an Executive Committee comprised of noted songwriters, producers and recording artists. Songs will be judged based upon originality, lyrics (when applicable), melody and composition. The quality of performance and production will not be considered.

MCKNIGHT VISITING COMPOSER PROGRAM, ACF, 332 Minnesota St., #E-145, St. Paul MN 55101. (612)228-1407. Fax: (612)291-7978. E-mail: compfrm@maroon.tc.umn.edu. Website: http://www.umn.edu/nlhome/m111/compfrm. Program Director: Philip Blackburn. Estab. 1994. For songwriters, musical playwrights and composers. Annual award.
Purpose: "Up to 2 annual awards for non-Minnesota composers to come to Minnesota for a self-designed residency of at least 2 months."
Requirements: Not for Minnesota residents or students. American Composers Forum membership required. Deadline: March. Send for application. Samples of work are required with application. Send score/tape.
Awards: McKnight Visiting Composer $10,000 stipend. Each award good for 1 year. Applications are judged by peer review panel.
Tips: "Find committed partners in Minnesota with whom to work, and explore diverse communities."

McLAREN COMEDY PLAYWRITING COMPETITION, 2000 W. Wadley, Midland TX 79705. (915)682-2544. Fax: (915)682-6136. Coordinator: Mary Lou Cassidy. Estab. 1990. For musical playwrights. Annual award.
Purpose: "The purpose of The McLaren Competition is to develop new comedy scripts suitable for production by community theaters and other nonprofit theaters. The competition honors Mike McLaren, a writer, actor and radio personality, who often appeared in Midland Community Theatre productions."
Requirements: "We are seeking comedy scripts only. Plays submitted should be unproduced. We do not count previous 'readings' as productions; we will consider plays produced once in a nonprofit setting. Length, number of characters, setting is not limited. The playwright retains all rights to the work submitted." Deadline: January 31. Send for application. Scripts should be submitted between December 1 and January 31 with a $5 entry fee.

Awards: The four finalists will be presented in a staged reading at Midland Community Theatre in July or August of the year selected. The winning playwright will receive a $400 cash prize and accommodations in Midland during the rehearsal and production period of his or her play. The winning play will be included in the following membership season at MCT." Scripts are judged by a committee.

MAXIM MAZUMDAR NEW PLAY COMPETITION, One Curtain Up Alley, Buffalo NY 14202-1911. (716)852-2600. E-mail: alleywayth@aol.com. Website: http://www.alleyway.com. Dramaturg: Joyce Stilson. For musical playwrights. Annual award.
Purpose: Alleyway Theatre is dedicated to the development and production of new works. Winners of the competition will receive production and royalties.
Requirements: Unproduced full-length work not less than 90 minutes long with cast limit of 10 and unit or simple set, or unproduced one-act work less than 60 minutes long with cast limit of 6 and simple set; prefers work with unconventional setting that explores the boundaries of theatricality; limit of submission in each category; guidelines available, no entry form. $5 playwright entry fee. Script, résumé, SASE optional. Cassette preferred, but not mandatory. Deadline: July 1.
Awards: $400, production with royalty and travel and housing to attend rehearsals for full-length play or musical; $100 and production for one-act play or musical.
Tips: "Entries may be of any style, but preference will be given to those scripts which take place in unconventional settings and explore the boundaries of theatricality. No more than ten performers is a definite, unchangeable requirement."

MID-ATLANTIC SONG CONTEST, 4200 Wisconsin Ave., NW, Suite 100-137, Washington DC 20016. (301)654-8434. Website: http://www.saw.org. Contact: Director. Estab. 1982. Sponsored by BMI and the Songwriters of Washington. Annual award.
Purpose: "Contest is designed to afford rising songwriters the opportunity of receiving awards/exposure/feedback of critical nature in an environment of peer competition." Applicants must send for application to: Mid-Atlantic Song Contest, P.O. Box 10703, McClean, VA 22102. Rules and regulations explained—amateur status is most important requirement. Samples of work are required with application: cassette, entry form and 3 copies of lyrics.
Awards: "Awards usually include free recording time, merchandise and cash. Awards vary from year to year. Awards must be used within one calendar year. Winning songs will be placed on a winners CD, which will be distributed to major music publishers. Grand prize is $1,000. Winners can perform their songs at the Awards Night Gala. Last year's Awards Night Gala was held at the Hard Rock Cafe in Washington DC."
Requirements: Applications are judged by a panel of 3 judges per category, for 3 levels, to determine top winners in each category and to arrive at the Grand Prize winner. Grand Prize winner will be determined by a panel of representatives from music publishers and performing rights organizations specifically selected by BMI. Reduced entry fees are offered for SAW members. Membership also entitles one to a newsletter and reduced rates for special events/seminars.
Tips: "Keep intros short; avoid instrumental solos; get to the chorus quickly and; don't bury vocals."

MIXED BLOOD VERSUS AMERICA PLAYWRITING CONTEST, 1501 S. Fourth St., Minneapolis MN 55454. (612)338-0937. Script Czar: Dave Kunz. For musical playwrights. Annual award. Estab. 1983.
Purpose: To encourage emerging musical playwrights.
Requirements: "Send previously unproduced play (musical) and résumé." Deadline March 15. Send SASE for copy of contest guidelines. Samples are not required. No translations or adaptations.
Awards: The winning musical will receive a cash prize of $2,000 if Mixed Blood chooses to produce the musical and $1,000 if Mixed Blood decides not to produce the winning musical.
Tips: "Professionalism is always a plus. Surprise us. Political satires and shows involving sports (baseball, golf, etc.) always of interest."

MUSEUM IN THE COMMUNITY COMPOSER'S AWARD, P.O. Box 251, Scott Depot WV 25560. (304)562-0484. Fax: (304)562-5375. E-mail: mitc@newwave.net. Competition Administrator: Patricia Fisher. For composers. Biennial award.
Purpose: The Composer's Competition is to promote the writing of new works. "Specific type of competition changes. Past competitions have included string quartet, full orchestra and nonet."
Requirements: Work must not have won any previous awards nor have been published, publicly performed or used commercially. Requires 3 copies of the original score, clearly legible and bound. Title to appear at the top of each composition, but the composer's name must not appear. Entry forms must be filled out and a SASE of the proper size enclosed for return of entry. "If you happen to move while competition is underway please let us know." Enclose $25 entry fee (non-refundable). Send for application.

Awards: "Next competition will open in winter 1998. Contest format undecided at present. Winning composition announced January 1999 with concert in Spring 1999. Prize will be from $2,500 to $5,000 depending on type of competition." Jurors will be 3 nationally known musicologists. Winning composer will be awarded a cash prize and a premiere concert of the composition. Transportation to the premiere from anywhere in the continental United States will be provided by the Museum.
Tips: "Read *and* follow rules listed in Prospectus. Neatness still counts!"

NEW FOLK CONCERTS FOR EMERGING SONGWRITERS, P.O. Box 1466, Kerrville TX 78029. (210)257-3600. E-mail: kfest@hilconet.com. Website: http://www.fmp.com/~kerrfest. Attn: New Folk. For songwriters. Annual award.
Purpose: "Our objective is to provide an opportunity for unknown songwriters to be heard and rewarded for excellence."
Requirements: Songwriter enters 2 previously unrecorded songs on same side of cassette tape—$8 entry fee; no more than one tape may be entered; 6-8 minutes total for 2 songs. No written application necessary; no lyric sheets or press material needed. Deadline: April 1st. Call for detailed information.
Awards: New Folk Award Winner. 32 finalists invited to sing the 2 songs entered during The Kerrville Folk Festival. 6 writers are chosen as award winners. Each of the 6 receives a cash award of $150 and performs at a winner's concert during the Kerrville Folk Festival. Initial round of entries judged by the Festival Producer. 40 finalists judged by panel of 3 performer/songwriters.
Tips: "Make certain cassette is rewound and ready to play. Do not allow instrumental accompaniment to drown out lyric content. Don't enter without complete copy of the rules. Former winners include Lyle Lovett, Nanci Griffith, Hal Ketchum, John Gorka, David Wilcox, Lucinda Williams and Robert Earl Keen."

OMAHA SYMPHONY GUILD NEW MUSIC COMPETITION, 1605 Howard St., Omaha NE 68102-2705. (402)342-3836. Contact: Chairman, New Music Competition. For composers with an annual award. Estab. 1976.
Purpose: "The objective of the competition is to promote new music scored for chamber orchestra."
Requirements: Competition open to applicants 25 and up for entry fee of $25. "Follow competition guidelines including orchestration and length of composition." Deadline: usually May 15. Send for application or call (402)342-3836. Each fall new guidelines and application forms are printed.
Awards: "Monetary award is $2,500. Winner has an optional premiere performance by the Omaha Symphony Chamber Orchestra. Applications are screened by Omaha Symphony music director. Finalists are judged by a national panel of judges."
Tips: "This is an annual competition and each year has a new Symphony Guild chairman; all requests for extra information sent to the Omaha Symphony office will be forwarded. Also, 1,700-1,800 application information brochures are sent to colleges, universities and music publications each fall."

PLAYHOUSE ON THE SQUARE NEW PLAY COMPETITION, 51 S. Cooper, Memphis TN 38104. (901)725-0776. Executive Director: Jackie Nichols. For musical playwrights. Annual award. Estab. 1983.
Requirements: Send script, tape and SASE. "Playwrights from the South will be given preference." Open to full-length, unproduced plays. Musicals must be fully arranged for piano when received. Deadline: April 1.
Awards: Grants may be renewed. Applications judged by 3 readers.

‡PORTLAND SONGWRITERS ASSOCIATION ANNUAL SONGWRITING COMPETITION, 1920 N. Vancouver, Portland OR 97227. (503)727-9072. E-mail: psa@teleport.com. Website: http://www.teleport.com/~psa/. President: Steve Cahill. Estab. 1994. For songwriters. Annual award.
Purpose: "To support and acknowledge excellence in songwriting by offering cash awards, bonus prizes and industry exposure."
Requirements: For information, send SASE. All amateur songwriters may enter.
Awards: Multiple awards totaling $1,400 in prizes. All songs will be reviewed by at least three qualified judges, including industry pros. Finalists may have their songs reviewed by celebrity judges.

PULITZER PRIZE IN MUSIC, 702 Journalism, Columbia University, New York NY 10027. (212)854-3841. Website: http://www.pulitzer.org. Music Secretary: Elizabeth Mahaffey. For composers and musical playwrights. Annual award.
Requirements: "For distinguished musical composition by an American in any of the larger forms including chamber, orchestral, choral, opera, song, dance or other forms of musical theater. The piece must have its American premiere between March 2 and March 1 of the one-year period in which it is submitted for consideration." Deadline: March 1. Samples of work are required with application, biography and

photograph of composer, date and place of performance, score or manuscript and recording of the work, entry form and $50 entry fee.
Awards: "One award: $5,000. Applications are judged first by a nominating jury, then by the Pulitzer Prize Board."

RIVER POETS MUSIC SONG CONTEST, 9 Music Square S., Suite 382, Nashville TN 37203. (615)370-4331. E-mail: pstevens@wbrnash.com. Website: http://members.aol.com/tennhomes/rpm.htm. Co-Director of Operations: Kyle Stevenson. Estab. 1995. For songwriters and composers. Annual award.
Purpose: "Our objective is to provide an outlet for songs from writers all over the nation to be heard by the people who need to hear them. We provide the opportunity for the music to be analyzed by top industry professionals. The goals of the artists should never be forgotten."
Requirements: "No more than 3 copyrighted songs (any style), with lyric sheets, composer/writer names and addresses, contact phone, and $5 entry fee per song. Songs should be no more than 5 minutes in length." Deadline: December 31. Send or call for application.
Awards: 1st: $100, single song contract and certificate; 2nd: $50 and certificate; 3rd: $25 and certificate; 2 Honorable Mentions. Applications judged on lyrics, musicality, commercial and overall appeal.

RICHARD RODGERS AWARDS, American Academy of Arts and Letters, 633 W. 155th St., New York NY 10032. (212)368-5900. Estab. 1978. "The Richard Rodgers Awards subsidize full productions, studio productions, and staged readings by nonprofit theaters in New York City of works by composers and writers who are not already established in the field of musical theater. The awards are only for musicals—songs by themselves are not eligible. The authors must be citizens or permanent residents of the United States." Guidelines for this award may be obtained by sending a SASE to above address.

‡ROME PRIZE FELLOWSHIP IN MUSICAL COMPOSITION, American Academy in Rome, 7 E. 60th St., New York NY 10022-1001. (212)751-7200. Fax: (212)751-7220. Contact: Programs Department. For composers. Annual award.
Purpose: "Rome Prize winners pursue independent projects, which vary in content and scope."
Requirements: "Applicants for one-year fellowships must hold a bachelor's degree in music, musical composition or its equivalent." Deadline: November 15. Send or call for application. Samples of work are required with application; send CDs and/or tapes and scores.
Awards: Fellowship stipend is up to $12,000 for one year. "Juries convene from January through March to review all work submitted in the competition. In all cases, excellence is the primary criterion for selection, based on the quality of the materials submitted."

LOIS AND RICHARD ROSENTHAL NEW PLAY PRIZE, % Cincinnati Playhouse, P.O. Box 6537, Cincinnati OH 45206. (513)345-2242. E-mail: theater1@tso.cin.ix.net. Website: http://www.cincyplay.com Contact: Artistic Associate. For playwrights and musical playwrights. Annual award.
Purpose: The Lois and Richard Rosenthal New Play Prize was established in 1987 to encourage the development of new plays that are original, theatrical, strong in character and dialogue and that are a significant contribution to the literature of American theater. Lois Rosenthal is the author of books in the consumer information field and is the editor of *Story* magazine, the classic literary quarterly. Richard Rosenthal operates F&W Publications, a family company founded in 1910, which publishes books and magazines for writers and artists. Residents of Cincinnati, the Rosenthals are committed to supporting arts organizations and social agencies that are innovative and that foster social change.
Requirements: "The play must be full-length and can be of any style: comedy, drama, musical, etc. Individual one-acts are not acceptable. Collaborations are welcome, in which case the prize benefits are shared. The play must not have received a full-scale, professional production, and it must be unpublished prior to submission. A play that has had a workshop, reading or non-professional production is eligible. Playwrights with past production experience are especially encouraged to submit new work. Any play previously submitted for the Rosenthal Prize is ineligible. Only one submission per playwright. Submit a 2-page maximum abstract of the play including title, playwright, character breakdown, story synopsis, a short bio of the playwright and any other information you wish to provide. Also send up to five pages of sample dialogue. All abstracts will be read. From these, selected manuscripts will be solicited. Do not send a manuscript with or instead of the abstract. All unsolicited manuscripts will be returned unread. The Rosenthal Prize is open for submission from October 15th to February 1st."
Awards: The Rosenthal Prize play is produced at the Cincinnati Playhouse in the Park as part of the theater's annual season, and it is given regional and national promotion. The playwright receives a $10,000 prize plus travel expenses and residency in Cincinnati during production. In addition to the prize winning play, a number of plays are selected to be given a workshop at the Playhouse with a professional director and actors. Playwrights are provided travel expenses and residency in Cincinnati for these workshops. It

is possible for a play that has been given a workshop to be chosen as the Rosenthal Prize recipient for the following season with complete prize benefits.

SALOP/SLATES MEMORIAL COMPOSITION CONTEST, P.O. Box 6968, Radford VA 24142. E-mail: bmahin@runet.edu. Vice President-Southeastern Composers League: Bruce Mahin. For composers. Annual award.
Requirements: Undergraduate or graduate students in Maryland, Delaware, Washington D.C., Virginia, West Virginia, North and South Carolina, Tennessee, Kentucky, Georgia, Florida, Alabama, Louisiana, Mississippi and Arkansas are eligible. Deadline: October 31. Send for application. Samples of work are required with application. Send clean, legible score.
Awards: 1st Place $150; 2nd Place $100 (for both undergraduate and graduate competitions). Applications judged by officers of the Southeastern Composers League.

REVA SHINER FULL-LENGTH CONTEST, Bloomington Playwrights Project, 308 S. Washington St., Bloomington IN 47401. (812)334-1188. Contact: Literary Manager. For musical playwrights. Annual award.
Purpose: "The Bloomington Playwrights Project is a script-developing organization. Winning playwrights are expected to become part of the development process, working with the director in person or via long-distance. The Reva Shiner contest is intended to encourage production and development of new plays."
Requirements: "Plays must be unpublished and unproduced. Must be full-length (75-150 minutes). Submissions must include a cover letter, a SASE for the script to be returned, and a $5 reader's fee." Deadline: January 15. Send for application. Samples of work are required with application. Submit complete script with tape. "We are a small theatre and can produce only very simple musicals."
Awards: $500 and production of play in following season. Applications are judged by a committee of readers, including the Artistic Director and Literary Manager.

SONG SPREE SONGWRITER COMPETITION, 2417 Pinewood Rd. W., Dept. 97, Nunnelly TN 37137. E-mail: spree@earthlink.net. Website: http://www.earthlink.net/~spree/. President: Lynda Bostwick. Estab. 1995. For songwriters, lyricists and composers. Annual award.
Purpose: "Seeking best songs and/or lyrics in 4 categories: rock/pop, country, blues and R&B, and soft alternatives. (Note: gospel accepted in all categories.) Winners to be recorded and released on CD at our expense. Winners are also widely promoted to industry."
Requirements: Send lyric, separate cassette and entry blank (or 3×5 card) for each song along with entry fee ($20 first song, $15 each additional song). "Lyrics are entered in our Lyric Competition free." For complete rules and prize info send #10 SASE.
Awards: "Song Category winners receive trip to Nashville, get recorded or remastered on CD and earn royalties. Publishing contracts are offered, but signing with us is not mandatory. Lyric Category winners get to co-write and publish with established hit songwriters. Resulting songs will also be presented on our CD. We promote our winners in every way possible. All entrants receive a free CD of winning songs. Honorable Mention winners receive an additional CD from a prior contest year and their songs are also held for possible industry pitches."

MARVIN TAYLOR PLAYWRIGHTING AWARD, P.O. Box 3030, Sonora CA 95370. (209)532-3120. Fax: (209)532-7270. Producing Director: Dennis Jones. Estab. 1981. For all playwrights (comedy, drama, musical). Annual award.
Purpose: "To encourage new voices in American theater."
Requirements: "Any new plays and unpublished scripts with no more than 2 previous productions are eligible." Deadline: August 31. Send for application. Samples of work are required with application. Scripts should be typed.
Awards: $500. "Applications are read by our Dramaturg and the Producing Director."

THE TEN-MINUTE MUSICALS PROJECT, P.O. Box 461194, West Hollywood CA 90046. (213)656-8751. Producer: Michael Koppy. For songwriters, composers, musical playwrights. Annual award.
Purpose: "We are building a full-length stage musical comprised of complete short musicals, each of which play for between 8-14 minutes. Award is $250 for each work chosen for development towards inclusion in the project, plus a share of royalties when produced."
Requirements: Deadline: August 31, annually. For guidelines, write or phone. Final submission should include script, cassette and lead sheets.
Awards: $250 for each work selected. "Works should have complete stories, with a definite beginning, middle and end."

THEATER AT LIME KILN REGIONAL PLAYWRITING CONTEST, 14 S. Randolph St., Lexington VA 24450. (540)463-7088. Fax: (540)463-1082. E-mail: limekiln@cfw.com. Website: http://www.cfw.com/limekiln. Community Liaison/Dramaturg: Eleanor Connor. For musical playwrights. Annual award.
Purpose: "This contest was created to encourage writers to celebrate the culture, history and events of the Appalachian Region."
Requirements: Deadline: August 1-September 30. Send for guidelines. Samples of work are required only upon submission in contest.
Awards: 1st place: $1,000; 2nd place: $500, with possibility of staged readings. Applications are judged by a reading panel of professionals and lay people.
Tips: "Theater at Lime Kiln is an outdoor theater with a summer season. We prefer smaller cast shows and are always looking for new musicals or plays with music."

U.S.A. SONGWRITING COMPETITION, Dept A.W. 98, Box 15312, Boston MA 02215-5312. (617)576-9732. Fax: (617)738-7292. E-mail: bliss@tiac.net. Website: http://www.tiac.net/users/asn/songcontest.html. Contact: Contest Manager. Estab. 1994. For songwriters and composers. Annual award.
Purpose: "To honor good songwriters all over the world, especially the unknown ones."
Requirements: Contest runs from November 1 to February 28 each year. Open to professional and beginner songwriters. No limit on entries. Each entry must include an entry fee, a cassette tape of song(s) and lyric sheet(s). Winners will be announced on May 1st. Past judges have included record label representatives from MCA and EMI. Deadline: March 1. Send or e-mail for application. Samples of work are not required.
Awards: Prizes include cash and merchandise in 9 different categories: pop, rock, country, Latin, R&B, gospel, folk, jazz and instrumental.

U.S.-MEXICO FUND FOR CULTURE, Londres 16-PB, Col. Juarez Mexico City **Mexico** 06600. (525)592-5386. Fax: (525)208-8943. Website: http://www.laneta.apc.org/usmexcult/intro.html. Coordinator of Projects: Beatriz E. Nava. Estab. 1991. For songwriters, composers, choreographers, musical playwrights and performers. Annual award.
Purpose: "The U.S.-Mexico Fund for Culture, an independent body created through a joint initiative of the Bancomer Cultural Foundation, The Rockefeller Foundation and Mexico's National Fund for Culture and the Arts, provides financial support for the development of cultural binational projects in music, theater, dance, visual arts, cultural studies, literary and cultural publications, media arts and libraries."
Requirements: Deadline: March 31. Send for application with SASE (8½×11 envelope) or contact us at our website. Samples of work are required with application in duplicate.
Awards: Range from $2,500-25,000. Award is good for 1 year. Judged by binational panel of experts in each of the disciplines, one from Mexico and one from the USA.
Tips: "Proposals must be binational in character and have a close and active collaboration with artists from Mexico. The creation of new works is highly recommendable."

V.O.C.A.L. SONGWRITER'S CONTEST, P.O. Box 34606, Richmond VA 23234-0606. 24 hr. hotline: (804)342-0550. E-mail: vocal10@aol.com. Website: http://members.aol.com/vocal 10/. Contact: Contest Director. For songwriters, lyricists and composers. Annual award with up to 11 categories.
Purpose: "To recognize good songs and lyrics as well as the writers of same."
Requirements: "Original songs/lyrics/compositions only." Postal deadline: March 31 of the contest year. Send for entry forms and information. Song entries must be on cassette tape. Lyric entries should be typed or neatly printed on white paper." Contest entries and inquiries should be sent to the above address. Include SASE.
Awards: Prizes for first, second, third places awarded for best song overall, the lyric competition, and category competitions. Prizes include: Cash, merchandise, T-shirts, certificates and more.
Tips: "Be sure to use a fresh tape to record your entry. Listen to the entry to be sure it's not distorted or too low in volume. A clean sounding tape stands a much better chance. The judges can only grade based on what they hear. Don't over produce your entry. That will take away from the song itself. Fill out the entry form completely and follow all rules of the contest. The contest begins January 1 and entries must be postmarked no later than March 31 of that contest year. Mail your entry early."

WEST COAST ENSEMBLE–MUSICAL STAIRS, P.O. Box 38728, Los Angeles CA 90038. (310)449-1447. Artistic Director: Les Hanson. For musical playwrights. Annual award.
Purpose: To provide an arena and encouragement for the development of new musicals for the theater.
Requirements: Submit book and a cassette of the score to the above address.
Awards: The West Coast Ensemble Musical Stairs Competition Award includes a production of the selected musical and $500 prize. The selected musical will be part of the 1998 season. Panel of judges reads script and listen to cassette. Final selection is made by Artistic Director.

Tips: "Submit libretto in standard playscript format along with professional sounding cassette of songs."

WORDS BY, 332 Eastwood Ave,. Feasterville PA 19053. (800)574-2986. Phone/fax: (215)953-0952. E-mail: a1foster@aol.com. Editor/Publisher: Allen Foster. Estab. 1992. For lyricists. Monthly contest.
Requirements: To enter, send your best lyrics and contact information."
Awards: Winning lyrics will be published along with your address so interested parties may contact you directly. Also, the top lyric for each month receives a voucher for a free book compliments of Writer's Digest Books.
Tips: "There is no application form or entry fee. Just send your best lyrics."

‡THE WORLD WIDE SONGWRITING CONTEST™, P.O. Box 15338, Honolulu HI 96830-5338. (808)539-3346. Fax: (888)863-7664. E-mail: hitman@lava.net. Website: http://www.tvjobs.com/userpage/contest.htm. Director: Richard Reb'll. Estab. 1995. For songwriters and composers. Annual award.
Purpose: "Cash prizes of more than $15,000 will be awarded for the best songs, as well as possible publishing and/or recording contracts."
Requirements: Deadline: September 30. Send SASE, download from website, e-mail or fax your request. Samples of work are required with application. Send cassette and lyrics (if applicable).
Awards: Grand prize of $5,000 cash; 10 category prizes at $1,000 each; 100 honorable mentions. All entries are judged by music industry professionals for quality, craftsmanship and commercial potential.
Tips: "Record your song at home or in a studio. You can sing it yourself or have someone else sing it for you. Make sure the vocals are upfront."

YOUNG COMPOSERS AWARDS, % NGCSA, 40 North Van Brunt St., Suite 32, Box 8018, Englewood NJ 07631. (201)871-3337. Executive Director: Lolita Mayadas. For composers. Open to students age 13-18. Annual award.
Purpose: "To encourage young students to write music, so that the art of composition—with no restrictions as to the category of music in which the works are written—will once again occupy the place in the center of music education where it belongs. It takes tons of ore to extract one ounce of gold: by focusing on the inventiveness of many students, the Awards may lead to the discovery of genuine creative talents—that is the eventual goal."
Requirements: "Applicants must be enrolled in a public or private secondary school, in a recognized musical institution, or be engaged in the private study of music with an established teacher. No compositions will be considered without certification by the applicant's teacher. Each applicant may submit only one work. Deadline: May 1. Send for application. Samples of work are required with application. Four photocopies of the work must be submitted and, if available, a cassette recording. All manuscripts must be in legible form and may be submitted on usual score paper or reduced under a generally accepted process. The composer's name must not appear on the composition submitted. The composition must be marked with a pseudonym on the manuscript as well as on the optional accompanying cassette recording."
Awards: Herbert Zipper Prizes: First Prize, $1,000; Second Prize, $750; Third Prize, $500; Fourth Prize, $250. "Announcement of the Awards are made no later than May 1 each year. In the event that no entry is found to be worthy of the $1,000 Prize, the jury may award one or both of the other Prizes or none at all. NGCSA appoints an independent jury to review all entries submitted. The jury consists of not less than three qualified judges."
Tips: "Paramount would be neatness and legibility of the manuscript submitted. The application must be complete in all respects."

Publications of Interest

Knowledge about the music industry is essential for both creative and business success. Staying informed requires keeping up with constantly changing information. Updates on the changing trends in the music business are available to you in the form of music magazines, music trade papers and books. There is a publication aimed at almost every type of musician, songwriter and music fan, from the most technical knowledge of amplification systems to gossip about your favorite singer. These publications can enlighten and inspire you and provide information vital in helping you become a more well-rounded, educated, and, ultimately, successful musical artist.

This section lists all types of magazines and books you may find interesting. From home-grown fanzines and glossy music magazines to tip sheets and how-to books, there should be something listed here that you'll enjoy and benefit from.

PERIODICALS

THE ALBUM NETWORK, 120 N. Victory Blvd., Burbank CA 91502. (818)955-4000. *Weekly music industry trade magazine.*

ALERT ARTS & ENTERTAINMENT MAGAZINE, (formerly *Songwriter Alert*), 1719 West End Ave., Suite 214E, Nashville TN 37203. (615)327-9977. *Professional newsletter for songwriters.*

AMERICAN SONGWRITER MAGAZINE, 121 17th Ave. S., Nashville TN 37203. (615)244-6065. E-mail: asongmag@aol.com. Website: http://www.nol.com/asongmag.html. *Bimonthly publication for and about songwriters.*

AUDIO IMAGES 2000, P.O. Box 250806, Holly Hill FL 32125-0806. (904)238-3820. E-mail: bjsrecords@aol.com. *Bimonthly songwriters' newsletter.*

BILLBOARD, 1515 Broadway, New York NY 10036. (800)247-2160. Website: http://www.billboard.com. *Weekly industry trade magazine.*

CANADIAN MUSICIAN, 23 Hannover Dr., Suite 7, St. Catharines, Ontario L2W 1A3 Canada. (905)641-1512. Website: http://www.nor.com/cm. *Bimonthly publication for amateur and professional Canadian musicians.*

CMJ NEW MUSIC REPORT, 11 Middle Neck Rd., Suite 400, Great Neck NY 11021-2301. (800)CMJ-9997 or (516)466-6000. E-mail: cmj@cmjmusic.com. Website: http://www.cmjmusic.com. *Weekly college radio and alternative music tip sheet.*

DAILY VARIETY, 5700 Wilshire Blvd., Suite 120, Los Angeles CA 90036. (213)857-6600. *Daily entertainment trade newspaper.*

THE DRAMATISTS GUILD QUARTERLY, 1501 Broadway, Suite 701, New York NY 10036. (212)398-9366. *The quarterly journal of the Dramatists Guild, the professional association of playwrights, composers and lyricists.*

ENTERTAINMENT LAW & FINANCE, New York Law Publishing Co., 345 Park Ave. S., 8th Floor, New York NY 10010. (212)545-6220. E-mail: leader@ljextra.com. *Monthly newsletter covering music industry contracts, lawsuit filings, court rulings and legislation.*

FAST FORWARD, Disc Makers, 7905 N. Rt. 130, Pennsauken NJ 08110-1402. (800)468-9353. E-mail: discman@discmakers.com. Website: http://www.discmakers.com. *Quarterly newsletter featuring compa-*

nies and products for performing and recording artists in the independent music industry.

THE GAVIN REPORT, 140 Second St., San Francisco CA 94105. (415)495-1990. *Weekly listing of radio charts.*

HITS MAGAZINE, 14958 Ventura Blvd., Sherman Oaks CA 91403. (818)501-7900. Website: http://www.buzznetonline.com. *Weekly music industry trade publication.*

JAZZTIMES, 8737 Colesville Rd., 5th Floor, Silver Spring MD 20910-3921. (301)588-4114. E-mail: jtimes@aol.com. *10 issues/year magazine covering the American jazz scene.*

THE LEADS SHEET, Allegheny Music Works, 306 Cypress Ave., Johnstown PA 15902. (814)535-3373. *Monthly tip sheet.*

MIX BOOKSHELF, 100 Newfield Ave., Edison NJ 08837. (800)233-9604. E-mail: mall@gibson.com. *Catalog of information resources for music professionals.*

MUSIC BUSINESS INTERNATIONAL MAGAZINE, 460 Park Ave. S., 9th Floor, New York NY 10016. (212)378-0400. *Bimonthly magazine for senior executives in the music industry.*

MUSIC CONNECTION MAGAZINE, 4731 Laurel Canyon Blvd., N. Hollywood CA 91607. (818) 755-0101. E-mail: muscon@earthlink.net. Website: http://www.musicconnection.com. *Biweekly music industry trade publication.*

THE MUSIC PAPER, Sound Resources Ltd., P.O. Box 304, Manhasset NY 11030. (516)883-8898. *Monthly music magazine for musicians.*

MUSIC ROW MAGAZINE, Music Row Publications, Inc., 1231 17th Ave. S., Nashville TN 37212. (615)321-3617. E-mail: news@musicrow.com. Website: http://www.musicrow.com. *Biweekly Nashville industry publication.*

MUSICIAN MAGAZINE, Billboard Publications, 1515 Broadway, 11th Floor, New York NY 10036. (212)536-5208. E-mail: musicianmag@earthlink.net. *Monthly music magazine.*

NATIONAL SONGWRITER'S NETWORK, 3870 La Sierra #101, Riverside CA 92505. (909)359-1078. *National monthly news update for songwriters.*

OFFBEAT MAGAZINE, OffBeat, Inc., 333 St. Charles Ave. #614, New Orleans LA 70130. (504)522-5533. E-mail: offbeat@neosoft.com. Website: http://www.neosoft.com/~offbeat. *Monthly magazine covering Louisiana music and artists.*

THE PERFORMING SONGWRITER, 6620 McCall Dr., Longmont CO 80503. (800)883-7664 or (303)682-1442. E-mail: perfsong@aol.com. *Bimonthly songwriters' magazine.*

PROFESSIONAL SOUND, Norris-Whitney Communications Inc., 23 Hannover Dr., Suite 7, St. Catharine's, Ontario L2W 1A3 Canada. (905)641-3471. Website: http://nor.com/cm/mpb. *Bimonthly publication for professionals in the sound and light industry.*

PUBLIC DOMAIN REPORT, P.O. Box 3102, Margate NJ 08402. (609)822-9401. E-mail: pdrcpub@aol.com. *Monthly guide to significant titles entering the public domain.*

RADIO AND RECORDS, 10100 Santa Monica Blvd., 5th Floor, Los Angeles CA 90067. (310)553-4330. E-mail: mailroom@rronline.com. Website: http://www.rronline.com. *Weekly newspaper covering the radio and record industries.*

RADIR, BBH Software, Inc., 15072 E. Mississippi Ave. Suite 33, Aurora CO 80012. (303)592-3780. E-mail: info@bbhsoftware.com. Website: http://www.bbhsoftware.com. *Quarterly radio station database on disk.*

SING OUT!, P.O. Box 5253, Bethlehem PA 18015-0253. (610)865-5366. Website: http://www.libertynet.org/singout. *Quarterly folk music magazine.*

SONGLINK INTERNATIONAL, 23 Belsize Crescent, London NW3 5QY England. E-mail: david@songlink.demon.co.uk. Website: http://webcom.com/genoagrp/songlink. *10 issues/year newsletter including details of recording artists looking for songs; contact details for industry sources; also news and features on the music business.*

SONGWRITER PRODUCTS, IDEAS AND NECESSITIES, NSP Music Publishing, 345 Sprucewood Rd., Lake Mary FL 32746-5917. (407)321-3702. Fax: (407)321-2361. Website: http://www.spotnet.com/spin. *Free semi-annual catalog of songwriting tips, tools and accessories, including tapes, duplication products and music business career packages.*

SONGWRITER'S MONTHLY, The Stories Behind Today's Songs, 332 Eastwood Ave., Feasterville PA 19053. (215)953-0952. E-mail: a1foster@aol.com. *Monthly songwriters' magazine.*

VARIETY, 5700 Wilshire Blvd., Suite 120, Los Angeles CA 90036. (213)857-6600. *Weekly entertainment trade newspaper.*

WORDS AND MUSIC, 41 Valleybrook Dr., Don Mills, Ontario M3B 2S6 Canada. (416)445-8700. Website: http://www.socan.ca. *Monthly songwriters' magazine.*

BOOKS AND DIRECTORIES

THE A&R REGISTRY, by Ritch Esra, SRS Publishing, 7510 Sunset Blvd. #1041, Los Angeles CA 90046-3418. (800)377-7411 or (800)552-7411. Fax: (213)882-6813. E-mail: 76513.3543@compuserve.com or srspubl@aol.com.

ATTENTION: A&R, second edition, by Teri Muench and Susan Pomerantz, Alfred Publishing Co. Inc., Box 10003, Van Nuys CA 91410-0003. (800)292-6122.

BEGINNING SONGWRITER'S ANSWER BOOK, by Paul Zollo, Writer's Digest Books, 1507 Dana Ave., Cincinnati OH 45207. (800)289-0963.

CMJ DIRECTORY, 11 Middle Neck Rd., Suite 400, Great Neck NY 11021-2301. (516)466-6000.

THE CRAFT AND BUSINESS OF SONGWRITING, by John Braheny, Writer's Digest Books, 1507 Dana Ave., Cincinnati OH 45207. (800)289-0963.

DIRECTORY OF INDEPENDENT MUSIC DISTRIBUTORS, by Jason Ojalvo, Disc Makers, 7905 N. Rt. 130, Pennsauken NJ 08110. (800)468-9353. E-mail: discman@discmakers.com. Website: http://www.discmakers.com.

FILM/TV MUSIC GUIDE, by Ritch Esra, SRS Publishing, 7510 Sunset Blvd. #1041, Los Angeles CA 90046-3418. (800)377-7411 or (800)552-7411. Fax: (213)882-6813. E-mail: 76513.3543@compuserve.com or srspubl@aol.com.

FINDING FANS & SELLING CDs, by Veronique Berry and Jason Ojalvo, Disk Makers, 7905 N. Rt. 130, Pennsauken NJ 08110-1402. (800)468-9353. E-mail: discman@diskmakers.com. Website: http://www.discmakers.com.

GUIDE TO INDEPENDENT MUSIC PUBLICITY, by Veronique Berry, Disc Makers, 7905 N. Rt. 130, Pennsauken NJ 08110-1402. (800)468-9353. E-mail: discman@discmakers.com.

GUIDE TO MASTER TAPE PREPARATION, by Dave Moyssiadis, Disk Makers, 7905 N. Rt. 130, Pennsauken NJ 08110-1402. (800)468-9353. E-mail: discman@discmakers.com.

HOW YOU CAN BREAK INTO THE MUSIC BUSINESS, by Marty Garrett, Lonesome Wind Corporation, P.O. Box 2143, Broken Arrow OK 74013-2143. (800)210-4416.

THE INTERNATIONAL SONGWRITER, by Dennis R. Sinnott, Christel Music Ltd., Fleet House, 173 Haydons Rd., Wimbledon London SW19 8TB England. (0181)679-5010.

LOUISIANA MUSIC DIRECTORY, OffBeat, Inc., 333 St. Charles Ave., Suite 614, New Orleans LA 70130. (504)522-5533. E-mail: offbeat@neosoft.com. Website: http://www.offbeat.com.

MUSIC ATTORNEY LEGAL & BUSINESS AFFAIRS REGISTRY, by Ritch Esra and Steve Trumbull, SRS Publishing, 7510 Sunset Blvd. #1041, Los Angeles CA 90046-3418. (800)377-7411 or (800)552-7411. Fax: (213)882-6813. E-mail: 76513.3543@compuserve.com or srspubl@aol.com.

MUSIC DIRECTORY CANADA, sixth edition, Norris-Whitney Communications Inc., 23 Hannover Dr., Suite 7, St. Catherines, Ontario L2W 1A3 Canada. (905)641-3471.

MUSIC, MONEY AND SUCCESS: THE INSIDER'S GUIDE TO THE MUSIC INDUSTRY, by Jeffrey Brabec and Todd Brabec, Schirmer Books, 866 Third Ave., New York NY 10022. (800)223-2336.

MUSIC PUBLISHING: A SONGWRITER'S GUIDE, by Randy Poe, Writer's Digest Books, 1507 Dana Ave., Cincinnati OH 45207. (800)289-0963.

THE MUSIC PUBLISHER REGISTRY, by Ritch Esra, SRS Publishing, 7510 Sunset Blvd. #1041, Los Angeles CA 90046-3418. (800)377-7411 or (800)552-7411. Fax: (213)882-6813. E-mail: 76513.3543@compuserve.com or srspubl@aol.com.

MUSICIANS' PHONE BOOK, THE LOS ANGELES MUSIC INDUSTRY DIRECTORY, Get Yourself Some Publishing, 28336 Simsalido Ave., Canyon Country CA 91351. (805)299-2540.

NASHVILLE MUSIC BUSINESS DIRECTORY, by Mark Dreyer, NMBD Publishing, P.O. Box 120675, Nashville TN 37212. Phone/Fax: (615)826-4141. E-mail: nashvillemusicbusinessdirectory@juno.com.

NATIONAL DIRECTORY OF RECORD LABELS AND MUSIC PUBLISHERS, fifth edition, Rising Star Music Publishers, 52 Executive Park S., Suite 5203, Atlanta GA 30329. (800)247-3108. E-mail: ristar@mindspring.com.

THE OFFICIAL COUNTRY MUSIC DIRECTORY, P.O. Box 7000, Rancho Mirage CA 92270. (619)773-0995. Fax: (619)773-9812.

RECORDING INDUSTRY SOURCEBOOK, Cardinal Business Media, 100 Newfield Ave., Edison NJ 08837. (800)233-9604.

SONGWRITER'S MARKET GUIDE TO SONG & DEMO SUBMISSION FORMATS, Writer's Digest Books, 1507 Dana Ave., Cincinnati OH 45207. (800)289-0963.

SONGWRITER'S PLAYGROUND - INNOVATIVE EXERCISES IN CREATIVE SONGWRITING, by Barbara L. Jordan, Creative Music Marketing, 1085 Commonwealth Ave., Suite 323, Boston MA 02215. (617)424-9490.

SONGWRITING AND THE CREATIVE PROCESS, by Steve Gillette, Sing Out! Publications, P.O. Box 5253, Bethlehem PA 18015-0253. (800)4-WE-SING.

TIM SWEENEY'S GUIDE TO RELEASING INDEPENDENT RECORDS, by Tim Sweeney, TSA Books, 21213-B Hawthorne Blvd. #5255, Torrance CA 90503. (310)542-6430. E-mail: tsahq@aol.com.

TIM SWEENEY'S GUIDE TO SUCCEEDING AT MUSIC CONFERENCES, by Tim Sweeney, TSA Books, 21213-B Hawthorne Blvd. #5255, Torrance CA 90503. (310)542-6430. E-mail: tsahq@aol.com.

TEXAS MUSIC INDUSTRY DIRECTORY, Texas Music Office, Office of the Governor, P.O. Box 13246, Austin TX 78711. (512)463-6666. Website: http://www.governor.state.tx.us/music.

THE YELLOW PAGES OF ROCK, The Album Network, 120 N. Victory Blvd., Burbank CA 91502. (818)944-4000.

Websites of Interest

The Internet can provide a wealth of information for songwriters and performers, and the number of sites devoted to music grows each day. Below is a list of some websites that can offer you information, links to other music sites, contact with other songwriters and places to showcase your songs. Since the online world is changing and expanding at such a rapid pace, this is hardly a comprehensive list, and some of these addresses may be obsolete by the time this book goes to print. But it gives you a place to start on your journey through the Internet to search for opportunities to get your music heard.

AMERICAN MUSIC CENTER: http://www.amc.net/amc/index.html
Classical/jazz archives, includes a list of composer organizations and contacts.

ARTIST UNDERGROUND: http://www.aumusic.com
A place for artists to place songs and information on the Internet, along with the capability to sell their CDs and tapes online.

CHILDREN'S MUSIC WEB: http://www.childrensmusic.org
Website dedicated to music for kids.

CPCC: http://www.under.org/cpcc
Website for the Center for the Promotion of Contemporary Composers.

THE DELIVERY ROOM: http://www.metaverse.com/droom
A biweekly, hour-long radio show for unsigned bands.

FILM MUSIC: http://www.filmmusic.com
Website relating to film and TV music composition.

INDIE NET: http://www.indienet.com
Internet radio station for new artists.

INTERNET UNDERGROUND MUSIC ARCHIVE (IUMA): http://www.iuma.com
Features unsigned bands, news and 'zines, as well as record label sites, a record store and more.

JAZZ CENTRAL STATION: http://www.jazzcentralstation.com
Jazz-related information, including reviews, magazines, a listing of jazz record labels and contacts, managers and more.

KALEIDOSPACE: http://kspace.com.
Website for independent artists to place their material online, along with the capability to contact the artists and purchase their work.

L.A. MUSIC: http://www.lamusic.com
Links to music industry sites, bands, organizations, labels, etc.

LAW CYBERCENTER: http://www.hollywoodnetwork.com/Law/music/survival2.html
Tips on negotiating and dealing with songwriting contracts.

LI'L HANK'S GUIDE FOR SONGWRITERS IN L.A.: http://www.halsguide.com
Website for songwriters with information on clubs, publishers, books, etc. as well as links to other songwriting sites.

LOS ANGELES GOES UNDERGROUND: http://www.primenet.com/~matthew/lagu/lagu.html
Website dedicated to underground rock bands from Los Angeles and Hollywood.

LOS ANGELES MUSIC ACCESS (LAMA): http://com.primenet.com/home
Database of Los Angeles bands, clubs and resources sponsored by a group that promotes independent artists.

METAVERSE: http://www.metaverse.com
Provides a forum for unsigned bands to showcase their work.

MUSIC & AUDIO CONNECTION: http://www.vaxxine.com/music
Guide to Canadian artists, associations and other resources from Norris-Whitney Communications, Inc.

MUSIC INDUSTRY PAGES: http://www.musicindustry.com
Listings of labels, magazines, products, music schools, retailers, etc.

MUSIC POWER NETWORK: http://www.musicpowernetwork.com
Musicians' database of venues, services, classifieds and jobs, and a digital music magazine.

MUSIC PUBLISHERS ASSOCIATION: http://host.mpa.org
Provides a copyright resource center, directory of member publishers and information on the organization.

MUSIC YELLOW PAGES: http://www.musicyellowpages.com
Phone book listings of music-related businesses.

NASHVILLE PUBLISHERS NETWORK: http://www.songnet.com/npn
Website dedicated to networking in the Nashville music community.

NATIONAL MUSIC PUBLISHERS ASSOCIATION: http://www.nmpa.org/nmpa.html
The organization's online site with information about copyright, legislation and other concerns of the music publishing world.

THE NATIONAL ONLINE MUSIC ALLIANCE: http://songs.com/noma
Forum for indie artists and labels to showcase and sell their work online.

RHYTHM NET: http://www.rhythmnet.com
Information on artists, labels, entertainment establishments and more.

ROCKTROPOLIS: http://www.rocktropolis.com
Music-based virtual "city" featuring the work of established and new artists.

SONGSCAPE: http://www.genoagrp.com/genoagrp
Music database and music industry news service.

SONIC NET: http://www.sonicnet.com
Music news, chat and reviews.

TAXI: http://www.taxi.com
Independent A&R vehicle that shops tapes to A&R professionals.

UNFURLED: http://www.unfurled.com
Search engine for music-related sites.

UNITED STATES COPYRIGHT OFFICE: http://lcweb.loc.gov/copyright
The homepage for the U.S. copyright office, offering information on registering songs.

YAHOO!: http://www.yahoo.com/Entertainment/Music/
Use this search engine to retrieve over 20,000 music listings.

Glossary

A&R Director. Record company executive in charge of the Artists and Repertoire Department who is responsible for finding and developing new artists and matching songs with artists.

A/C. Adult contemporary music.

Advance. Money paid to the songwriter or recording artist before regular royalty payment begins. Sometimes called "up front" money, advances are deducted from royalties.

AFM. American Federation of Musicians. A union for musicians and arrangers.

AFTRA. American Federation of Television and Radio Artists. A union for performers.

AIMP. Association of Independent Music Publishers.

Airplay. The radio broadcast of a recording.

AOR. Album-Oriented Rock. A radio format which primarily plays selections from rock albums as opposed to hit singles.

Arrangement. An adaptation of a composition for a recording or performance, with consideration for the melody, harmony, instrumentation, tempo, style, etc.

ASCAP. American Society of Composers, Authors and Publishers. A performing rights society.

Assignment. Transfer of rights of a song from writer to publisher.

Audiovisual. Refers to presentations which use audio backup for visual material.

Bed. Prerecorded music used as background material in commercials.

BMI. Broadcast Music, Inc. A performing rights society.

Booking agent. Person who schedules performances for entertainers.

Business manager. Person who handles the financial aspects of artistic careers.

b/w. Backed with. Usually refers to the B-side of a single.

C&W. Country and western.

Catalog. The collected songs of one writer, or all songs handled by one publisher.

CD. Compact Disc (see below).

CD-ROM. Compact Disc-Read Only Memory. A computer information storage medium capable of holding enormous amounts of data. Information on a CD-ROM cannot be deleted. A computer user must have a CD-ROM drive to access a CD-ROM.

Chart. The written arrangement of a song.

Charts. The trade magazines' lists of the best-selling records.

CHR. Comtemporary Hit Radio. Top 40 pop music.

Compact disc. A small disc (about 4.7 inches in diameter) holding digitally encoded music that is read by a laser beam in a CD player.

Co-publish. Two or more parties own publishing rights to the same song.

Copyright. The exclusive legal right giving the creator of a work the power to control the publishing, reproduction and selling of the work.

Cover recording. A new version of a previously recorded song.

Crossover. A song that becomes popular in two or more musical categories (e.g., country and pop).

Cut. Any finished recording; a selection from a LP. Also to record.

DAT. Digital Audio Tape. A professional and consumer audio cassette format for recording and playing back digitally-encoded material. DAT cassettes are approximately one-third smaller than conventional audio cassettes.

DCC. Digital Compact Cassette. A consumer audio cassette format for recording and playing back digitally-encoded tape. DCC tapes are the same size as analog cassettes.

Demo. A recording of a song submitted as a demonstration of a writer's or artist's skills.

Distributor. Marketing agent responsible for getting records from manufacturers to retailers.

Donut. A jingle with singing at the beginning and end and instrumental background in the middle. Ad copy is recorded over the middle section.

E-mail. Electronic mail. Computer address where a company or individual can be reached via modem.

Engineer. A specially-trained individual who operates recording studio equipment.

Enhanced CD. General term for an audio CD that also contains multimedia computer information. It is playable in both standard CD players and CD-ROM drives.

EP. Extended play record or cassette containing more selections than a standard single, but fewer than a standard album.

Exploit. To seek legitimate uses of a song for income.

Folio. A softcover collection of printed music prepared for sale.

Harry Fox Agency. Organization that collects mechanical royalties.

Hip-hop. A dance oriented musical style derived from a combination of disco, rap and R&B.

Hit. A song or record that achieves top 40 status.

Hook. A memorable "catch" phrase or melody line which is repeated in a song.

House. Dance music created by remixing samples from other songs.

Hypertext. Words or groups of words in an electronic document that are linked to other text, such as a definition or a related document. Hypertext can also be linked to illustrations.

Indie. An independent record label, music publisher or producer.

Internet. A worldwide network of computers that offers access to a wide variety of electronic resources.

ips. Inches per second; a speed designation for tape recording.

IRC. International reply coupon, necessary for the return of materials sent out of the country. Available at most post offices.

Jingle. Usually a short verse set to music designed as a commercial message.

Lead sheet. Written version (melody, chord symbols and lyric) of a song.

Leader. Plastic (non-recordable) tape at the beginning and between songs for ease in selection.

LP. Designation for long-playing record played at 33⅓ rpm.

Lyric sheet. A typed or written copy of a song's lyrics.

Market. A potential song or music buyer; also a demographic division of the record-buying public.

Master. Edited and mixed tape used in the production of records; the best or original copy of a recording from which copies are made.

MD. MiniDisc. A 2.5 inch disk for recording and playing back digitally-encoded music.

Mechanical right. The right to profit from the physical reproduction of a song.

Mechanical royalty. Money earned from record, tape and CD sales.

MIDI. Musical instrument digital interface. Universal standard interface which allows musical instruments to communicate with each other and computers.

Mix. To blend a multi-track recording into the desired balance of sound.

Modem. MOdulator/DEModulator. A computer device used to send data from one computer to another via telephone line.

MOR. Middle of the road. Easy-listening popular music.

Ms. Manuscript.

Multimedia. Computers and software capable of integrating text, sound, photographic-quality images, animation and video.

Music jobber. A wholesale distributor of printed music.

Music publisher. A company that evaluates songs for commercial potential, finds artists to record them, finds other uses (such as TV or film) for the songs, collects income generated by the songs and protects copyrights from infringement.

NARAS. National Academy of Recording Arts and Sciences.

Needle-drop. Use of a prerecorded cut from a stock music house in an audiovisual soundtrack.

Network. A group of computers electronically linked to share information and resources.

NMPA. National Music Publishers Association.

One-off. A deal between songwriter and publisher which includes only one song or project at a time. No future involvement is implicated. Many times a single song contract accompanies a one-off deal.

One-stop. A wholesale distributor of records representing several manufacturers to record stores, retailers and jukebox operators.

Overdub. To record an additional part (vocal or instrumental) onto a basic multi-track recording.

Payola. Dishonest payment to broadcasters in exchange for airplay.

Performing rights. A specific right granted by U.S. copyright law that protects a composition from being publicly performed without the owner's permission.

Performing rights organization. An organization that collects income from the public performance of songs written by its members and then proportionally distributes this income to the individual copyright holder based on the number of performances of each song.

Personal manager. A person who represents artists to develop and enhance their careers. Personal managers may negotiate contracts, hire and dismiss other agencies and personnel relating to the artist's career, review material, help with artist promotions and perform many services.

Piracy. The unauthorized reproduction and selling of printed or recorded music.

Pitch. To attempt to solicit interest for a song by audition.

Playlist. List of songs that a radio station will play.

Points. A negotiable percentage paid to producers and artists for records sold.

Producer. Person who supervises every aspect of a recording project.

Production company. Company that specializes in producing jingle packages for advertising agencies. May also refer to companies that specialize in audiovisual programs.

Professional manager. Member of a music publisher's staff who screens submitted material and tries to get the company's catalog of songs recorded.

Public domain. Any composition with an expired, lapsed or invalid copyright.

Purchase license. Fee paid for music used from a stock music library.

Query. A letter of inquiry to an industry professional soliciting his interest.

R&B. Rhythm and blues.

Rate. The percentage of royalty as specified by contract.

Release. Any record issued by a record company.

Residuals. In advertising or television, payments to singers and musicians for use of a performance.

RIAA. Recording Industry Association of America.

Royalty. Percentage of money earned from the sale of records or use of a song.

RPM. Revolutions per minute. Refers to phonograph turntable speed.

SAE. Self-addressed envelope (with no postage attached).

SASE. Self-addressed stamped envelope.

Self-contained. A band or recording act that writes all their own material.

SESAC. A performing rights organization.

SFX. Sound effects.

Shop. To pitch songs to a number of companies or publishers.

Single. 45 rpm record with only one song per side. A 12″ single refers to a long version of one song on a 12″ disc, usually used for dance music.

SOCAN. Society of Composers, Authors and Music Publishers of Canada. A Canadian performing rights organization.

Solicited. Songs or materials that have been requested.

Song plugger. A songwriter representative whose main responsibility is promoting uncut songs to music publishers, record companies, artists and producers.

Song shark. Person who deals with songwriters deceptively for his own profit.

Soundtrack. The audio, including music and narration, of a film, videotape or audiovisual program.

Split publishing. To divide publishing rights between two or more publishers.

Statutory royalty rate. The maximum payment for mechanical rights guaranteed by law that a record company may pay the songwriter and his publisher for each record or tape sold.

Subpublishing. Certain rights granted by a U.S. publisher to a foreign publisher in exchange for promoting the U.S. catalog in his territory.

Synchronization. Technique of timing a musical soundtrack to action on film or video.

Take. Either an attempt to record a vocal or instrument part, or an acceptable recording of a performance.

Top 40. The first 40 songs on the pop music charts at any given time. Also refers to a style of music which emulates that heard on the current top 40.

Track. Divisions of a recording tape (e.g., 24-track tape) that can be individually recorded in the studio, then mixed into a finished master.

Trades. Publications that cover the music industry.

12″ Single. A 12-inch record containing one or more remixes of a song, originally intended for dance club play.

Unsolicited. Songs or materials that were not requested and are not expected.

VHS. ½″ videocassette format.

Website. An address on the World Wide Web that can be accessed by computer modem. It may contain text, graphics and sound.

World Wide Web (WWW). An Internet resource that utilizes hypertext to access information. It also supports formatted text, illustrations and sounds, depending on the user's computer capabilities.

Geographic Index

This Geographic Index will help you locate companies by state, as well as those in countries outside of the U.S. Once you find the names of companies in this index you are interested in, check the listings within each section for addresses, phone numbers, contact names and submission details.

The double dagger (‡) next to a listing denotes markets that are new to this edition.

Mercury Records
Metal Blade Records
‡MJJ Music
‡Moonstone Records
MOR Records
‡Motion City Records
‡Motown Records
Mule Kick Records
‡Noo Trybe Records
‡nu.millennia/records
Oblivion Entertainment
Oglio Records
‡Only New Age Music, Inc.
Orinda Records
‡Paradigm Productions
Patty Lee Records
PC Music
‡Peak Records
‡Pentacle Records
‡Permanent Press Recordings
Pissed Off Records, Inc.
‡Pointblank Records
‡Polydor Records
PPL Entertainment Group
‡Priority Records
‡Qwest Records
‡Radioactive Records
Rarefaction
‡RCA Records
React Recordings
‡Red Ant Entertainment
‡Relativity Records
Reprise Records
‡Restless Records
Revelation Records
‡Revolution Records
‡Rhino Records
‡RML Records
Rock Dog Records
Roll On Records®
Rotten Records
‡Royal Records
‡Rude Records
Sabteca Record Co.
Sheffield Lab Recording
‡Silas Records
Silent Records
‡Silvertone Records
‡Sims Records, Jerry
‡Sonic Images Records
Sureshot Records
‡Sweet 'N Smooth Productions
Tandem Records
‡Tangent Records
‡Touché Records
Trac Record Co.
Triple X Records
‡Universal Records
Valtec Productions
Verve Group, The
‡Virgin Records
Volcano Recordings
Warner Bros. Records
‡Way Cool Music
‡Windham Hill Records
‡Windy City Records
‡Work Group
‡Yab Yum Records
Young Country Records/Plain Country Records

Record Producers

AKO Productions
Apophis Music
Bal Records
‡Chainsaw Records
‡Chicago Kid Productions
Daddy, S. Kwaku
Deep Space Records
Duane Music, Inc.
Eiffert, Jr., Leo J.
Federici's Shark River Music, Danny
Final Mix Music
Hailing Frequency Music Productions
Horrigan Productions
House of Rhythm
Intrigue Production
Jazmin Productions
Katz Productions, Matthew
Kingsport Creek Music
L.A. Entertainment
Leeway Entertainment Group
Linear Cycle Productions
Magid Productions, Lee
‡Magnetic Oblivion Music Co.
‡Marenco, Cookie
Martin, Pete/Vaam Music Productions
Mathews, Scott, d/b/a Hit Or Myth Productions
‡Mega Truth Records
‡Mom and Pop Productions
Real Entertainment
Smash the Radio Productions
S'N'M Recording/Hit Records Network
‡Solo Productions, Joe
‡Sound Sound West
‡Studio D Recording
Trac Record Co.
Up Front Management
‡Valtec Productions
‡Waterbury Productions
Weisman Production Group
‡Wich Audio Services
Wizards & Cecil B

Managers and Booking Agents

Abba-Tude Entertainment
AKO Productions
Aquila Entertainment

Advertising, AV and Commercial Music Firms

Play Producers and Publishers

Classical Performing Arts

San Francisco Girls Chorus
Ventus Musicus

Organizations
Academy of Country Music
American Society of Composers, Authors and Publishers (ASCAP)
Broadcast Music, Inc. (BMI)
Broadway On Sunset
‡California Lawyers for the Arts
Los Angeles Music Network
Musicians Contact Service
National Academy of Songwriters (NAS)
National Association of Composers/USA, The
Northern California Songwriters Association
San Diego Songwriters Guild
San Francisco Folk Music Club
‡Women of the Music Business Mentoring Program & Awards

Workshops and Conferences
Northern California Songwriters Association Conference
‡Songwriters Expo
Songwriters Guild Foundation
Ten-Minute Musicals Project

COLORADO

Record Companies
C.E.G. Records, Inc.
Etherean Music/VarIena Publishing
Not Lame Recordings
Silver Wave Records

Managers and Booking Agents
‡Bullet Mangement

Play Producers and Publishers
Contemporary Drama Service
Creede Repertory Theatre
Pioneer Drama Service

Classical Performing Arts
Colorado Children's Chorale

Organizations
‡Rocky Mountain Music Association

Workshops and Conferences
Aspen Music Festival and School

CONNECTICUT

Music Publishers
Antelope Publishing Inc.
‡Pascarella Music Publishing
Ridge Music Corp.

Record Companies
BMX Entertainment
Generic Records, Inc.
Pop Record Research
Target Records
Wonderland Records

Record Producers
Creative Music Services
‡John Productions, David
‡New Vizion Studios, The
Perennial Productions
Red Kastle Productions
Wytas Productions, Steve

Managers and Booking Agents
Martin Productions, Rick
Tutta Forza Music

Play Producers and Publishers
Hartford Stage Company

Classical Performing Arts
Norfolk Chamber Music Festival/Yale Summer School of Music

Organizations
Connecticut Songwriters Association
Pop Record Research

DELAWARE

Managers and Booking Agents
Platinum Tracks Productions

Advertising, AV and Commercial Music Firms
Ken-Del Productions Inc.

DISTRICT OF COLUMBIA

Record Companies
EMA Music Inc.
Smithsonian Folkways Recordings

Managers and Booking Agents
‡Ten Ninety Nine Promotions

Advertising, AV and Commercial Music Firms
Hillmann & Carr Inc.

Organizations
Folk Alliance, The
International Alliance for Women in Music
Opera America
Songwriters Association of Washington
‡Washington Area Music Association

Workshops and Conferences
Folk Alliance Annual Conference

FLORIDA

Music Publishers
‡ARAS Music
Audio Images Two Thousand Music Publishing
‡Bare Minimum Music
Cowboy Junction Flea Market and Publishing Co.

Montgomery Management, Gary F.
‡Network Entertainment
Odom-Meaders Management
Serge Entertainment Group
Willis Entertainment, Inc.

Advertising, AV and Commercial Music Firms
Anderson Communications
‡Compro Productions
27th Dimension Inc.

Play Producers and Publishers
Horizon Theatre Co.

Classical Performing Arts
Atlanta Pops Orchestra
Atlanta Young Singers of Callanwolde, The

Organizations
‡Atlanta Songwriters Association, Inc.
IMC Trendsetter

HAWAII

Music Publishers
Samuel Three Productions

Record Companies
Alpha Recording Co.
Maui Arts & Music Association

Record Producers
Sanders Company, Ray

Organizations
‡Hawai'i Songwriters Association

IDAHO

Record Companies
Big Whig Productions

ILLINOIS

Music Publishers
Andyland Music
Jerjoy Music
Kidsource Publishing
Mack Music, Danny
Mighty Twinns Music
Music in the Right Keys Publishing Company
Sound Cellar Music
World Famous Music Co.

Music Print Publishers
Foster Music Company, Mark
Shelley Music

Record Companies
‡Beluga Records
Briarhill Records
Broken Records International
Cellar Records
IMI Records
Modal Music, Inc.™
Old School Records
Pravda Records
Thick Records
Universal-Athena Records
Whitehouse Records
Young Star Productions, Inc.

Record Producers
JGM Recording Studio
Neu Electro Productions

Managers and Booking Agents
Conscience Music
Secret Agent Entertainment Group, Ltd.
Tanner Entertainment

Advertising, AV and Commercial Music Firms
Mallof, Abruzino & Nash Marketing
Motivation Media, Inc.
Norton Rubble & Mertz, Inc. Advertising
Qually & Company Inc.
Video I-D, Inc.

Play Producers and Publishers
Bailiwick Repertory
Circa' 21 Dinner Playhouse
Dramatic Publishing Company, The

Classical Performing Arts
Knox-Galesburg Symphony
Wheaton Symphony Orchestra

Organizations
American Society of Composers, Authors and Publishers (ASCAP)
‡Chicago Alliance for Playwrights
Chicago Music Alliance

Workshops and Conferences
Chicago's New Music Festival

INDIANA

Music Publishers
De Miles Music Company, The Edward
Dream Seekers Publishing
Hammel Associates, Inc., R.L.
Hickory Valley Music
Interplanetary Music
Ontrax Companies
Twin Spin Publishing

Record Companies
Dale Productions, Alan
LBJ Productions
Sahara Records and Filmworks Entertainment
‡Throwing Stones Records
Yellow Jacket Records

Play Producers and Publishers
Centenary College, Theatre Department

Classical Performing Arts
Acadiana Symphony Orchestra

Organizations
Louisiana Songwriters Association
‡Southern Songwriters Guild

Workshops and Conferences
Cutting Edge Music Business Conference

MAINE

Record Companies
Cat's Voice Productions

Record Producers
Stuart Audio Services

Managers and Booking Agents
Greeley Entertainment, Chris

Workshops and Conferences
Arcady Music Festival

MARYLAND

Music Publishers
Cash Productions, Inc.
‡Cherasny Elijah Entertainment Production Company
Country Showcase America

Record Companies
Continental Records
Spiritual Walk Records
Startrak Records, Inc.

Managers and Booking Agents
Cash Productions, Inc
Entertainment Works
Noteworthy Productions
Productions Unlimited

Advertising, AV and Commercial Music Firms
dbF A Media Company

Play Producers and Publishers
Cockpit in Court Summer Theatre

Classical Performing Arts
Baltimore Opera Company
Susquehanna Symphony Orchestra

Workshops and Conferences
JazzTimes Convention

MASSACHUSETTS

Music Publishers
‡Crosspoint International, Inc.
‡East Coast Music Publishing
Halo International
Henly Music Associates
Scott Music Group, Tim
Segal's Publications
‡Sound and Fury Music Publishing

Music Print Publishers
Boston Music Co.
ECS Publishing
Warren Music Service, Frank E.

Record Companies
‡Arula Records
Critique Records, Inc.
‡Crosspoint International, Inc.
Eastern Front Records, Inc.
Keeping It Simple and Safe
MSM Records
‡Signature Sounds Recordings
Stargard Records

Record Producers
Nelson, Bill
Segal's Productions

Managers and Booking Agents
Clockwork Entertainment Management Agency
Foggy Day Music
Madstorm Production Company
‡Morningside Management
Squad 16

Advertising, AV and Commercial Music Firms
Communications for Learning
Film Classic Exchange
Home, Inc.
Lapriore Videography

Play Producers and Publishers
Baker's Plays
‡Eastern Musicals
Freelance Press, The

Classical Performing Arts
Commonwealth Opera, Inc.
Dúo Clásico
Melrose Symphony Orchestra
Mohawk Trail Concerts

Organizations
American Songwriters Network
Boston Songwriters Workshop, The

Workshops and Conferences
Music Business Solutions/Career Building Workshops
Songwriters Playground®

MICHIGAN

Music Publishers
Abalone Publishing
Al-Ky Music

Managers and Booking Agents
Doran, P.C., James R.
Overstreet Music Companies, Tommy
Staircase Promotion

Advertising, AV and Commercial Music Firms
Angel Films Company
‡Bryan/Donald Inc. Advertising
Media Consultants, Inc.

Play Producers and Publishers
Coterie, The
Repertory Theatre of St. Louis

Classical Performing Arts
‡Heartland Men's Chorus
St. Louis Chamber Chorus

Organizations
‡Missouri Society of Songwriters and Musicians
Missouri Songwriters Association, Inc.

MONTANA

Classical Performing Arts
Billings Symphony
Great Falls Symphony Association
Helena Symphony

Organizations
College Music Society

NEBRASKA

Music Publishers
Lari-Jon Publishing

Record Companies
Lari-Jon Records
Redemption Records

Record Producers
Lari-Jon Productions

Managers and Booking Agents
Lari-Jon Promotions
Lutz Entertainment Agency, Richard

Advertising, AV and Commercial Music Firms
‡Blumenthal Cady & Associates, Inc.

Play Producers and Publishers
Omaha Magic Theatre

Classical Performing Arts
Hastings Symphony Orchestra
Soli Deo Gloria Cantorum

NEVADA

Music Publishers
‡Americatone International
Flaming Star West Music
Platinum Boulevard Publishing
Watchesgro Music

Record Companies
Interstate 40 Records
Platinum Boulevard Records

Record Producers
New Horizon Records
‡Sound Works Entertainment Productions Inc.
Triplitt Production

Managers and Booking Agents
Biscuit Productions Inc.
‡Dale Management, Frankie
Jerifka Productions, Inc.
‡Rhythmic Temple Entertainment Inc.

Advertising, AV and Commercial Music Firms
Izen Enterprises, Inc.

Classical Performing Arts
Carson City Chamber Orchestra
Reno Chamber Orchestra

Organizations
Las Vegas Songwriters Association, The

NEW HAMPSHIRE

Record Companies
Kingston Records

Record Producers
Kingston Records and Talent
Reel Adventures

Play Producers and Publishers
American Stage Festival

NEW JERSEY

Music Publishers
Black Rose Productions
Gary Music, Alan
Genetic Music Publishing
Omni 2000, Inc.
PPI/Peter Pan Industries
Roots Music
T.C. Productions/Etude Publishing Co.
Westunes Music Group
Yorgo Music

Record Companies
‡Bionic Records, Inc.
‡Disc-tinct Music, Inc.
Lucifer Records, Inc.
‡Music Quest Entertainment & Television
‡Music Wise Inc.
Nucleus Records
Omni 2000 Inc.
‡PPI/Peter Pan Industries
Presence Records

Arkadia Entertainment Corp.
Atlantic Records
audiofile Tapes
Blue Wave
‡Buzz Factory Records
Capitol Records
Caroline Records, Inc.
Columbia Records
Com-Four
‡Cooking Vinyl America
‡Creative Improvised Music Projects (CIMP) Records
‡Crescent Recording Corporation
‡dedicated records
Elektra Entertainment Group
‡EMI Records
‡Enclave, The
Epic Records
Fiction Songs
‡550 Music
Geffen/DGC Records
Gold City Records, Inc.
‡Gotham Records
‡GRP Records
‡Hollywood Records
Hot Wings Entertainment
‡Interscope Records
‡Island Records
J&J Musical Enterprises Ltd.
Jive Records
‡London Records
MCA Records
‡Mekkatone Records
‡Mercury Records
Mighty Records
Modern Voices Entertainment
‡Motown Records
Musikus Productions, Inc.
‡Overtime Station
Paint Chip Records
Pirate Records
‡Polydor Records
Priority Records
Quark Records
Radical Records
‡RCA Records
‡Red Ant Entertainment
‡Relativity Records
Reprise Records
‡Robbins Entertainment LLC
Rock Dog Records
Round Flat Records
Royalty Records
‡Silvertone Records
‡Tommy Boy Records
‡Touchwood Records LLC
TVT Records
‡Universal Records
VAI Distribution
‡Verve Group, The
‡Virgin Records
Warner Bros. Records
‡Windham Hill Records
Wizmak Productions
‡Work Group
Worship & Praise Records Inc.
Xemu Records
Zero Hour Records

Record Producers

Allyn, Stuart J.
‡Appell, Jonathan
‡Bewildering Music, Inc.
‡Cacophony Productions
Carlock Productions
Chucker Music, Inc.
D.S.M. Producers, Inc.
Darrow, Danny
‡Gallway Bay Music
‡Hot Sound Productions
JK Jam Productions
KMA
Must Rock Productionz Worldwide
‡Neo Sync Labs
Prescription Co., The
‡RoamAlone Music
Rosenman, Mike
SAS Corporation/Special Audio Services
Siskind Productions, Mike
‡Time-Out Productions/Bramla Music
‡Two Chord Music
‡Wilbur Productions
‡Y-N-A/C.D.T. Productions

Managers and Booking Agents

Bassline Entertainment, Inc.
‡Blue Wave Productions
‡Chucker Music Inc.
Countdown Entertainment
Courtright Management Inc.
Cycle of Fifths Management
DAS Communications, Ltd.
DCA Productions
Debutante Management/Catalyst Entertainment
Depth of Field Management
DMR Agency
Earth Tracks Artists Agency
EBI Inc.
Faith Entertainment, James
Freedman Entertainment, Peter
Gallup Entertainment
GMI Entertainment Inc.
Great Lakes Country Talent Agency
Headline Management
Horizon Management Inc.
Imani Entertainment Inc.

NORTH CAROLINA

Advertising, AV and Commercial Music Firms
Hodges Associates, Inc.

Play Producers and Publishers
Blowing Rock Stage Company

Organizations
‡Central Carolina Songwriters Association (CCSA)

Workshops and Conferences
‡Mid-Atlantic Sound, Surf & Skate Symposium
Swannanoa Gathering—Contemporary Folk Week

NORTH DAKOTA

Record Companies
Starcrest Productions, Inc.

Classical Performing Arts
‡Greater Grand Forks Symphony Orchestra

OHIO

Music Publishers
Alexander Sr. Music
Barkin' Foe the Master's Bone
Barren Wood Publishing
Bernard Enterprises, Inc., Hal
Faiella Publishing, Doug
Harbor Gospel Music Production
Jacksong Music
New Rap Jam Publishing, A
Scrutchings Music
Without Papers Music Publishing Inc.

Music Print Publishers
Lorenz Corporation, The

Record Companies
Bold 1 Records
Emerald City Records
New Experience Records/Grand Slam Records
Paul Records, J.
‡Sin Klub Entertainment, Inc.
Strugglebaby Recording Co.
Twin Sisters Productions, Inc.

Record Producers
Bernard Enterprises, Inc., Hal
Eternal Song Agency, The
New Experience Records
Realworld Entertainment Corp.
Syndicate Sound, Inc.

Managers and Booking Agents
All Star Management
Concept 2000 Inc.
Creative Star Management
Entertainment International USA
Lowell Agency
‡Mabry Ministries, Kevin
Other Road, The
Umbrella Artists Management

Advertising, AV and Commercial Music Firms
Heywood Formatics & Syndication
Sullivan & Findsen Advertising

Play Producers and Publishers
‡Ensemble Theatre

Classical Performing Arts
Akron City Family Mass Choir
Lakeside Summer Symphony
Lima Symphony Orchestra
Lithopolis Area Fine Arts Association

Organizations
Midwestern Songwriters Association
Songwriters and Poets Critique

Workshops and Conferences
Undercurrents

OKLAHOMA

Music Publishers
Enid Oklahoma Music Publishing
Furrow Music
Jae Music, Jana
Old Slowpoke Music

Record Companies
Cherry Street Records
Country Style Records
Lark Record Productions, Inc.
Lonesome Wind Corporation

Record Producers
Lark Talent & Advertising
‡Studio Seven

Managers and Booking Agents
‡Cricket Inc.
‡Hupp Enterprises, Joe
Jae Enterprises, Jana
‡On the Level Music!
‡Stay Gold Productions

Classical Performing Arts
Cimarron Circuit Opera Company

Organizations
Oklahoma Songwriters & Composers Association
Songwriters of Oklahoma
Tulsa Songwriters Association

OREGON

Music Publishers
Earitating Music Publishing
High-Minded Moma Publishing & Productions

Record Producers
Peridot Productions

Organizations
Rhode Island Songwriters' Association

SOUTH CAROLINA

Music Publishers
Riverhawk Music

Record Companies
Wanstar Group, The

Record Producers
‡Durr Productions, David
‡Track One Studios

SOUTH DAKOTA

Managers and Booking Agents
Intermountain Talent
Sound '86 Talent Management

TENNESSEE

Music Publishers
Aim High Music Company
Aladdin Music Group
‡Alan Music, Marcus
AlliSongs Inc.
‡Ancy Music Group
Beaverwood Audio-Video
Best Buddies, Inc.
‡BMG Music Publishing
Buried Treasure Music
Calinoh Music Group
Castle Music Group
Copperfield Music Group
Cornelius Companies, The
Cottage Blue Music
Country Rainbow Music
Craig Music, Loman
Denny Music Group
Doss Music, Buster
ESI Music Group
Farr-Away Music
Fat City Publishing
‡Fretboard Publishing
Frick Music Publishing Co.
‡Fricon Music Company
‡Golden Harp Music
Goodland Music Group Inc.
Green Zebra Music
Hitsburgh Music Co.
Holton Music
Hutchins Music, Gregg
Iron Skillet Music
Jaclyn Music
Jolson Black & White Music, Al
JW One Music Publishing Co.
Lion Hill Music Publishing Co.
Mathes Company, The
Nautical Music Co.
‡New Clarion Music Group
Newcreature Music
Panchatantra Music Enterprises
Peters Music, Justin
Silver Thunder Music Group
Simply Grand Music, Inc.
Sizemore Music
Song Farm Music
Sun Star Songs
Surespin Songs
‡Twin Bears Publishing
Ultimate Peak Music

Music Print Publishers
Abingdon Press
Genevox Music Group

Record Companies
A&R Records
Aladdin Recordings
Ancy Records
Arion Records/Sound Resources
Arista Records
‡Asylum Records Nashville
Bandit Records
BNA Records
‡Capricorn Records
Carlyle Records, Inc.
Cedar Creek Records™
‡Curb Records
Fame and Fortune Enterprises
Fat City Artists
‡Inside Sounds
Jalyn Recording Co.
K-Ark Records
Kottage Records
Landmark Communications Group
M.E.G. Records Co.
MCA Records
‡Music City Sound Records
Orbit Records
Paragold Records & Tapes
PBM Records
Phoenix Records, Inc.
Plateau Music
Platinum Plus Records International
R.E.F. Records
RCA Records
Rejoice Records of Nashville
Richway Records International
‡Smoky Mountain Recording Company, Inc.
Stardust
‡TBS Records
‡Vander-Moon Entertainment
Warner Bros. Records
Wence Sense Music/Bill Wence Promotions
‡Word Records & Music

HOLLAND

Music Publishers
All Rock Music

Record Companies
‡Collector Records

Record Producers
Collector Records

Managers and Booking Agents
Van Pol Management, Hans

IRELAND

Organizations
Irish Music Rights Organisation

ITALY

Music Publishers
Dingo Music

Record Companies
Top Records

JAMAICA

Managers and Booking Agents
‡Jampop Ltd.

THE NETHERLANDS

Record Companies
Associated Artists Music International

NEW ZEALAND

Music Publishers
Pegasus Music

PUERTO RICO

Organizations
American Society of Composers, Authors and Publishers (ASCAP)

SCOTLAND

Music Publishers
Brewster Songs, Kitty
Jammy Music Publishers Ltd.

SWEDEN

Managers and Booking Agents
Nilsson Productions, Christina

UNITED STATES VIRGIN ISLANDS

Music Publishers
‡Island Culture Music Publishers

WALES

Music Publishers
Demi Monde Records and Publishing Ltd.

Record Companies
Demi Monde Records and Publishing Ltd.

Record Producers
Demi Monde Records and Publishing Ltd.

General Index

You'll notice as you flip through this index that more than 400 double daggers (‡) appear. This symbol denotes markets that are new to this edition. Also, we list companies that appeared in the 1997 edition of *Songwriter's Market*, but do not appear this year. Instead of page numbers beside these markets you will find two-letter codes in parenthesis that explain why these markets no longer appear. The codes are: **(ED)**—Editorial Decision, **(NS)**—Not Accepting Submissions, **(NR)**—No (or late) Response to Listing Request, **(UC)**—Unable to Contact.

A

B

Companies that appeared in the 1997 edition of *Songwriter's Market*, but do not appear this year, are listed in this General Index with the following codes explaining why these markets were omitted: (ED)—Editorial Decision, (NS)—Not Accepting Submissions, (NR)—No (or late) Response to Listing Request, (OB)—Out of Business, (RR)—Removed by Market's Request, (UC)—Unable to Contact.

C

D

E

F

G

Companies that appeared in the 1997 edition of *Songwriter's Market*, but do not appear this year, are listed in this General Index with the following codes explaining why these markets were omitted: (ED)—Editorial Decision, (NS)—Not Accepting Submissions, (NR)—No (or late) Response to Listing Request, (OB)—Out of Business, (RR)—Removed by Market's Request, (UC)—Unable to Contact.

H

M

Companies that appeared in the 1997 edition of *Songwriter's Market*, but do not appear this year, are listed in this General Index with the following codes explaining why these markets were omitted: (ED)—Editorial Decision, (NS)—Not Accepting Submissions, (NR)—No (or late) Response to Listing Request, (OB)—Out of Business, (RR)—Removed by Market's Request, (UC)—Unable to Contact.

N

O

P

Companies that appeared in the 1997 edition of *Songwriter's Market*, but do not appear this year, are listed in this General Index with the following codes explaining why these markets were omitted: (ED)—Editorial Decision, (NS)—Not Accepting Submissions, (NR)—No (or late) Response to Listing Request, (OB)—Out of Business, (RR)—Removed by Market's Request, (UC)—Unable to Contact.

Q

R

S

Companies that appeared in the 1997 edition of *Songwriter's Market*, but do not appear this year, are listed in this General Index with the following codes explaining why these markets were omitted: (ED)—Editorial Decision, (NS)—Not Accepting Submissions, (NR)—No (or late) Response to Listing Request, (OB)—Out of Business, (RR)—Removed by Market's Request, (UC)—Unable to Contact.

T

U

V

W

More Books for Great Songwriting!

The Musician's Guide to Making & Selling Your Own CDs & Cassettes—Now you can gain the freedom that comes with producing your own albums! This essential guide explains the wisdom of making and marketing your own CDs and cassettes—and shows you how to get the biggest sound for your buck. *#10522/$18.99/160 pages/paperback*

Music Publishing: A Songwriter's Guide, Revised Edition—Take the mystery out of music publishing as you learn how to get the best for yourself and your songs! From the range of royalty choices, to publishing options, this classic gives you all the facts you need to make the right decisions while getting your work into print. *#10505/$18.99/144 pages/paperback*

Writing Better Lyrics—Make every song sizzle using this unique, in-depth approach to lyric writing. You'll examine 17 extraordinary songs to discover what makes them so effective. Plus, you'll work through more than 30 language exercises as you learn to find snappy themes, avoid clichés and create meaningful metaphors and similes. *#10453/$19.99/192 pages*

The Craft of Lyric Writing—You'll get a complete guide on writing words for and to music, choosing song formats and creating lyrics with universal appeal from bestselling author and songwriter, Sheila Davis. *#01148/$23.99/350 pages*

The Craft and Business of Songwriting—From generating a song idea to signing a record deal, you'll discover how to create and market artistically and commercially successful songs in today's tough market. *#10429/$21.99/322 pages/paperback*

Making Money Making Music (No Matter Where You Live)—Cash-in on scores of ways to make a profitable living with your musical talent—no matter where you live. This guide covers performing as a soloist or in a group, writing music for the radio, jingles and more! *#10174/$18.95/180 pages/paperback*

Hot Tips for the Home Recording Studio—Discover the tricks to recording a tight, polished, professional demo! Musicians acquainted with recording technology will learn how to lay down basic tracks, add vocals and mix to get exactly the sound they want. *#10415/$18.99/160 pages*

The Songwriter's Market Guide to Song & Demo Submission Formats—Get your foot in the door with knock-out query letters, slick demo presentations and the best advice for dealing with every player in the industry. *#10401/$19.99/160 pages*

Making Money Teaching Music—Discover how to find lucrative teaching opportunities. This guide shows you how to market yourself as a professional, recruit students of all ages, manage time and work schedules and much more! *#10428/$18.99/240 pages/44 b&w illus./paperback*

Who Wrote That Song?—If you're a music buff, you'll love the 12,000 songs listed here! Find everything from mid-nineteenth century ballads to today's Top Forty hits, with an emphasis on the last forty years. Each listing includes the title, composer, lyricist and publication year. Where appropriate, listings also reveal who made the song popular, others who recorded it and who sang it on Broadway or in the movies. *#10403/$19.99/448 pages/paperback*

Networking in the Music Business—Who you know can either make—or break—your music career. Discover how to make and capitalize on the contacts you need to succeed. *#10365/$17.99/128 pages/paperback*